# WATER POLLUTION AND
# WATER QUALITY LAW

# WATER POLLUTION
## and
# WATER QUALITY LAW

*by*

**William Howarth**

*and*

**Donald McGillivray**

**Shaw & Sons**

*Published by*
Shaw & Sons Limited
Shaway House
21 Bourne Park
Bourne Road
Crayford
Kent DA1 4BZ

www.shaws.co.uk


© Shaw & Sons Limited 2001

Published December 2001



ISBN 0 7219 1102 1



A CIP catalogue record for this book is available from the
British Library

*Printed and bound in Great Britain by*
MPG Books Limited, Bodmin

# SUMMARY OF CONTENTS

# CONTENTS

**Chapter 1    WATER POLLUTION AND WATER QUALITY:
                         ISSUES AND THEMES**

1.1    **Introduction**

1.2    **Water**

1.3    **Water 'Pollution'**
         1.3.1    Eutrophication and Acidification
         1.3.2    Eutrophication, Acidification and Pollution
         1.3.3    General Definitions of 'Pollution'
         1.3.4    'Pollution' in National Criminal Law
         1.3.5    'Pollution' in National Civil Law
         1.3.6    The Legal Relevance of 'Pollution'
         1.3.7    Toxicity
         1.3.8    Direct Toxicity Assessment

1.4    **Water Quality**
         1.4.1    The Royal Commission Standard
         1.4.2    The Traditional Application of Water Quality Standards
         1.4.3    Water Quality Objectives and Standards
         1.4.4    National Use of Water Quality Objectives and Standards
         1.4.5    Formalising Water Quality Objectives and Standards
         1.4.6    Implementing European Community Water Quality
                     Standards

1.5    **Competing Objectives in Aquatic Protection**

1.6    **Problematic Activities**
         1.6.1    Treating Sewage Effluent
         1.6.2    Industrial Activities
         1.6.3    The Worcester Drinking Water Incident
         1.6.4    Agricultural Activities
         1.6.5    Road Transport
         1.6.6    Mining and Contaminated Land
         1.6.7    Shipping Activities and Sea Dumping

## Chapter 15 FISHERIES AND NATURE CONSERVATION

# FOREWORD

## by David Kinnersley

It was a fire at a riverside chemical factory in Switzerland that gave the seemingly far-away Dutch urgent cause to close for a while their water intakes from the River Rhine. How many people in either country would have readily seen the Swiss and the Dutch as water neighbours, one able to do serious harm to the other without at all intending to do so? It is one of the awkward features of river pollution that the damage often happens some way from its cause or source, but still has to be remedied there and downstream.

This book on water pollution and water quality law shows that it is not only of interest or relevance for lawyers or other experts, but of concern to all sorts of rural and urban communities and their citizens. Wherever we depend on rivers for water for all sorts of purposes including water supply and waste disposal, as well as fishing and irrigation, we depend on upstream neighbours observing care and limits in any activity that can do harm to the river's health and quality as natural and man-made conditions generate their endless variations.

In our own technological age, it should be no surprise that across the world laws related to the sharing of rivers as common assets grow more complex. That reflects the many more different uses for which communities wish to use water, including the sheer pleasure and amenity it brings to them.

From this book we can glean much of the principles as well as the practical rules to be good sharers of water. This is a world-wide concern as well as a local one. It is crucial where rivers serve as national boundaries. The authors have generously donated their royalties to WaterAid, a charity founded in Britain which helps poor communities across the world to improve their own sharing of water and access to it. This is of real value in drawing attention to WaterAid's work.

I am very pleased to commend this book to what I hope will be a wide global readership.

**David Kinnersley**

# PREFACE

The title of this book, *Water Pollution and Water Quality Law,* is a purposeful attempt to stress the two themes that run throughout its length and underlie the diverse and detailed legal provisions that are considered. Of the two themes, the first concerns the role of the law in prohibiting particular kinds of behaviour which have an unacceptable environmental impact on waters and the aquatic ecosystems which they support. The second relates to the environmental objectives that are, or may be, set for water and the aquatic environment and the role of the law in the realisation and maintenance of these objectives. Although at many points the two themes are closely interwoven and largely inseparable, at others the bifurcation between the concerns is more readily apparent. Nevertheless, the distinction between negative prohibitions and positive objectives is a fundamentally important one which pervades both environmental law and popular preconceptions about environmental protection.

Relatively early experience of industrialisation has meant that the major impacts of industrial activities upon the waters of England and Wales have needed to be confronted by a national legal response long before legislative intervention was necessary in other jurisdictions. Much of the present national law has retained the legacy of early legislation. However, the first response of environmental legislators, that there are certain kinds of activities and events which must be made unlawful, is increasingly inadequate to address present-day problems. The second response is to raise the more challenging issue of what positive goals for the water environment should be sought by legal means and what legal mechanisms are best suited to securing those objectives. It is the tension between what is to be prohibited and what is to be facilitated, and the respective legal strategies that these entail, that most acutely characterises water pollution and water quality law at the time of writing.

The tension between prohibiting and providing is reflected across the fields of water legislation in the discussion that follows. The bewildering collage of criminal, civil, administrative, European Community and international law that has a bearing upon the protection and improvement of the water environment seems to be guided by a diverse, conflicting and, sometimes, seemingly irreconcilable collection of purposes. The aim of this work is place the detail of these areas of law into perspective alongside consideration of the underlying environmental problems, the nature of the principal areas of activity that are subject to regulation and the range of potential legal strategies by which they may be addressed.

The first rule in writing a book of this kind must be to think of the readers. This might not be thought too difficult in a relatively specialised branch of environmental law where 'best seller' status is unlikely to be secured. However, we hope that this work will be as useful as possible to at least three distinct kinds of reader. First, there are the specialised legal practitioners working within public bodies and private water-related enterprises for whom water legislation is an everyday matter of practical concern. Second, there are an increasing number of academic researchers concerned with the more theoretical background to water legislation and the insights that it provides into wider debates in environmental regulatory strategy. Third, there is a range of environmental practitioners, engaged in assessing or advising on water quality issues or campaigning for water quality improvements, who need to understand the legal implications of their roles.

Clearly, these different kinds of reader have markedly different kinds of need. The practitioner will want an authoriative and comprehensive statement of all the relevant legal provisions along with discussion of the more practically important or problematic issues. The academic researcher will be interested in water pollution and water quality law in the context of a wider body of theoretical literature on how particular legal provisions are intended to realise broader objectives for environmental protection and the respective merits and failings of different regulatory approaches in this respect. The environmental practitioner, possibly approaching the subject from an environmental science background, will need to relate the scientific principles and practice of water management to the legal and administrative context in which they operate.

Pleasing all three categories of reader throughout the book is no easy task. Realistically, some of the legal discussion which follows may be regarded by specialist legal practitioners and legal academics as 'general knowledge' which may justify only a cursory reading before progressing into the more technical legal aspects of the different subject areas. By contrast, for the environmental practitioner, the 'broad brush' introductions to different areas of law and policy are intended to be of value in placing practical environmental activities alongside their detailed regulatory and institutional contexts and to introduce some of the more intricate areas of law to non-specialists. Contrasts also will be seen between those areas where essentially practical matters are under consideration and those places where discussions of the historical or theoretical issues predominate and where 'food for thought' and topics for further research are being provided with an academic reader in mind. Almost unavoidably, individual readers will be inclined to 'pick and choose' according to their preferences and these will differ significantly. What follows is our best effort to balance the discussion at a level which is as useful as possible for each of the three kinds of reader.

The original idea for the book came as a request to revise *Water Pollution Law*, published by Shaw & Sons in 1988, a time when environmental protection had acquired nothing like its present significance or complexity. On reconsideration, however, this earlier work no longer seemed to provide an adequate structure in which to accommodate subsequent legal and policy developments. Clearly, over the decade, a range of developments had assumed an importance which it would have been difficult to have foreseen: the expansion and ever-increasing impact of European Community water quality law, culminating in the recent adoption of the Water Framework Directive; the growing importance of the international arena, especially the Convention for the Protection of the Marine Environment of the North East Atlantic (OSPAR); nationally, the establishment of the Environment Agency for England and Wales as an integrated environmental regulatory authority; and, generally, the spawning of a range of preventative, precautionary and strategic measures to anticipate water quality problems. To take account of all these developments, a comprehensive new formula was needed to allow more appropriate co-ordination of the diverse themes that characterise the present scope of the subject. Doing justice to all these significant developments, and doing so for all the intended readership, has necessarily required a book of considerable length.

Despite the length needed to secure a reasonable claim to comprehensiveness of coverage, some of the boundaries which have had to be drawn may still disappoint some readers. In terms of jurisdictions, the book covers only England and Wales, and the European Community and international law which is relevant to them. Apart from occasional points of comparison, no attempt has been made to cover the corresponding provisions applicable in Scotland and Northern Ireland. In terms of subject matter, 'water pollution and water quality' has been construed to exclude a range of water quantity issues which are potentially relevant. Hence, activities such as water abstraction and land drainage, which in some contexts are capable of having significant effects upon water quality, have been touched upon only incidentally.

The law is generally stated as at 1 January 2001, though it has been necessary to consider some changes to the law which took place immediately prior to that date on the basis of provisional information; discussion of the Water Supply (Water Quality) Regulations 2000 which herald important changes to the law on drinking water falls into this category. However, it has also been possible to add brief coverage of subsequent developments at proof stage and where these are not discussed in the text they are indicated in footnotes. Almost inevitably, the prospect of changes in the law has been apparent in many areas and attempts have been made to indicate what is in prospect in relation to the most significant of the changes by discussing legislative proposals. Hopefully, this will prevent the work going out of date too rapidly, but readers are advised to check that the final form of actual legal developments corresponds with the proposals that are discussed.

And finally . . .

The completion of this book owes a great deal to a large number of people who have helped and contributed in various ways. We are extremely grateful to Crispin Williams of Shaw & Sons for his patience on the belated submission of the manuscript, and also for his invaluable guidance on the eventual submission. A major debt of gratitude is also due to Stuart Bell, with whom both authors have collaborated on water law issues prior to writing this book and who provided extensive and constructive comments and suggestions on a draft of the complete text which helped greatly in clarifying our thinking in many respects.

Thanks are also due to David Clapham, Cosmo Graham, Wyn Jones, John Wightman, Huw Williams and David Withrington for comments on draft chapters. Will Tipper provided invaluable help during a period as a research assistant in tracking down some of the less readily available sources, commenting on the manuscript, and providing a substantial input into the first draft of Chapter 8. Other past students – Eddie John, Mary Walters, Antonis Sifakis and Karin Bieback – were helpful in providing informed discussion on particular issues which have enhanced the coverage alongside the far larger number of students who have stimulated thought by raising incisive questions about the subject. Similar thanks for helpful discussions on diverse water management issues must be offered to Mike Averill, Alan Boyle, Lord Cranbrook, Maria Cull, Laurence Etherington, John Faulks, Sarah France, Ross Hilliard, Wendy Le-Las, Yvonne Rees, Peter Scott, Graham Setterfield, Peter Spillett and Tom Zabel. Gratitude also extends generally to the past and present editorial team of the journal *Water Law*, and particularly to the late Simon Ball who made an outstanding contribution to the journal over many years and whose untimely death was a tragic loss of a highly respected academic, a good friend of both of the present authors and an ardent champion of the water environment.

Staff at the public information department of the Environment Agency were outstanding in tracking down obscure and sometimes imprecisely referenced publications of the Agency, and help was also forthcoming from other quarters of the Agency, especially Martin Davies, Dave Foster, Geoff Mance, Joe McHugh and, again, Huw Williams. Valuable sources of information were provided by the Office of Water Services, the Department of the Environment, Transport and the Regions, the Maritime and Coastguard Agency, the Drinking Water Inspectorate, English Nature, the National Assembly for Wales, the Planning Inspectorate, Water UK, staff at Severn Trent Water and Southern Water (especially Mike Warren), the Chartered Institute of Environmental Health, the Water Working Group of the UK Environmental Law Association, the Food Standards Agency and the Secretariats of the International Maritime Organisation and OSPARCOM.

Sarah Carter, Jane Venis, Angela Faunch and other staff of the Templeman Library at the University of Kent at Canterbury were excellent in supporting and enhancing the gathering of materials, not least through the superb LawLinks portal (*library.ukc.ac.uk/library/lawlinks*). Invaluable administrative and secretarial support was provided by the team in the Kent Law School office who all contributed in different ways (not least Maggie Davis who bore the brunt of retyping sections of text). More general support was provided by colleagues in the Kent Law School and at Birkbeck College and we are deeply appreciative for much useful discussion and the provision of a strongly supportive environment at both places in which to undertake this project.

Closer to home, William Howarth would like to offer heartfelt thanks to Carol Sturgeon for her unfailing support and superhuman toleration of his seemingly endless immersion in 'dirty water'. Donald McGillivray would like to thank a motley selection of exceptional friends who, over the period of writing, provided much needed (and much undervalued) support, encouragement and fun.

Despite all this greatly valued help, the faults and omissions which remain are ours alone. Although we hope that a revised edition will not be necessary for some years, comments and suggestions, to *w.howarth@ukc.ac.uk* and *d.mcgillivray@bbk.ac.uk*, would be most welcome.

Last, but certainly not least, we are extremely grateful to David Kinnersley for agreeing to write a foreword to the book and appreciative of the kind words of support offered by such an insightful and distinguished commentator on water policy at home and abroad. As a founder of WaterAid, the UK based charity that works to provide access to safe drinking water and sanitation in Africa and Asia, few can have done more to bring home to those of us who might be preoccupied with our own water use dilemmas the far greater problems experienced elsewhere. It is a sobering statistic that around 80% of all diseases and one third of deaths in developing countries are caused by consuming contaminated water, and that as much as one tenth of each person's productive time is sacrificed to water-related diseases. All authors' royalties from sales of this book will be donated to WaterAid, more details about which can be found at *www.wateraid.org.uk*.

**William Howarth**
University of Kent at Canterbury

**Donald McGillivray**
Birkbeck College, University of London

# THE AUTHORS

**William Howarth** is Professor of Environmental Law at the University of Kent at Canterbury and the author of several books and reports, and numerous articles in academic journals, on diverse aspects of water and environmental law. He is the General Editor of the journal *Water Law* and has acted as an advisor on water and fisheries legislation to governments and regulatory bodies at national and international levels.

**Donald McGillivray** is a Lecturer in the School of Law, Birkbeck College, University of London. Previously he lectured at the University of Kent, collaborating with William Howarth on a number of water law-related projects at home and overseas. He is on the editorial committee of the *Journal of Environmental Law* and, with Stuart Bell, is the co-author of the 5th edition of *Ball and Bell on Environmental Law.*

# TABLE OF STATUTES

## United States

## New South Wales

# TABLE OF STATUTORY INSTRUMENTS

# TABLE OF EC SECONDARY LEGISLATION

## Regulations

### Decisions

# TABLE OF CASES

# ACRONYMS AND UNITS OF MEASUREMENT

| | |
|---|---|
| ALARA | as low as reasonably achievable |
| AMP | asset management plans |
| BAT | best available techniques |
| BATNEEC | best available techniques not entailing excessive cost |
| BEP | best environmental practice |
| BNFL | British Nuclear Fuels Ltd |
| BOD | biochemical oxygen demand |
| BPEO | best practicable environmental option |
| Bq | becquerel |
| CAP | common agriculture policy |
| CCW | Countryside Council for Wales |
| COD | chemical oxygen demand |
| CRISTAL | contract regarding an interim supplement to tanker liability for oil pollution |
| DDT | dichlorodiphenyltrichloroethane |
| DETR | Department of the Environment, Transport and the Regions |
| DoE | Department of the Environment |
| DoE(NI) | Department of Environment (Northern Ireland) |
| DWI | Drinking Water Inspectorate |
| EARP | enhanced actinide removal plant |
| EC | European Community |
| EEC | European Economic Community |
| EIONET | European Environment Information and Observation Network |
| ESA | environmentally sensitive area |
| EURATOM | European Atomic Energy Community |
| GT | gross registered tonnage |
| HCH | hexachlorocyclohexane (lindane) |
| HMIP | Her Majesty's Inspectorate of Pollution |
| HNDA | high natural dispersion area |
| HNS | hazardous and noxious substances |
| HSE | Health and Safety Executive |
| IAEA | International Atomic Energy Agency |
| ICRP | International Commission on Radiological Protection |
| IMDG | international maritime dangerous goods |
| IMO | International Maritime Organisation |
| IMPEL | European Community Network for the Implementation and Enforcement of Environmental Law |
| INSC | International North Sea Conference |
| IOPC Fund | International Oil Pollution Compensation Fund |
| IOPP | international oil pollution prevention |
| IPC | integrated pollution control |
| IPPC | integrated pollution prevention and control |
| LEAP | local environment agency plan |
| LNR | local nature reserve |

| | |
|---|---|
| LOS | law of the sea |
| MAFF | Ministry of Agriculture, Fisheries and Food |
| MARPOL | International Convention for the Protection of Pollution from Ships (1973/78) |
| MCA | Maritime and Coastguard Agency |
| MEHRA | marine environmentally high risk area |
| MEPC | Marine Environment Protection Committee (IMO) |
| mg/l | milligrammes per litre |
| MNR | marine nature reserve |
| mSv | millisievert |
| NEA | Nuclear Energy Agency |
| NRPB | National Radiological Protection Board |
| NVZ | nitrate vulnerable zone |
| Ofwat | Office of Water Services |
| OILPOL | International Convention for the Prevention of Pollution of the Sea by Oil (1954) |
| ONCC | Ofwat National Customer Council |
| OPRC | International Convention on Oil Pollution Preparedness, Response and Co-operation (1990) |
| OSPAR | Convention for the Protection of the Marine Environment North East Atlantic (1992) |
| OSPARCOM | OSPAR Commission |
| PAH | polycyclic aromatic hydrocarbon |
| PCB | polycarbonatedbiphenol |
| PCE | perchloroethene |
| PCP | pentachlorophenol |
| PPG | Planning Policy Guidance Note |
| REPAC | Regional Environment Protection Advisory Committee |
| RWMAC | Radioactive Waste Management Advisory Committee |
| SAC | special area of conservation |
| SDR | special drawing rights |
| SO | Scottish Office |
| SPA | special protection area |
| SSSI | site of special scientific interest |
| TBq | terabecquerels ($10^{12}$ becquerels) |
| TBT | tributyl tin |
| THORP | thermal oxide reprocessing plant |
| TOVALOP | Tanker Owner's Voluntary Agreement concerning Liability for Oil Pollution |
| UKOPP | United Kingdom oil pollution prevention |
| UN | United Nations |
| UN/ECE | United Nations Economic Commission for Europe |
| WO | Welsh Office |
| ìg/l | microgrammes ($10^{-6}$ grammes) per litre |

# INTRODUCTION

Given the diverse perspectives upon water pollution and water quality law that are considered within the following chapters, it may be helpful briefly to summarise the coverage and approach. Chapter 1 seeks to introduce the conceptual themes of water pollution and water quality in an environmental management context and to identify the most problematic activities for the aquatic environment alongside the range of regulatory mechanisms that are available. Chapter 2 then places the present law in its historical context by examining past attempts to address water quality problems by legislative means and the failings of many of these measures, amongst other things, through inadequacies in enforcement machinery. Further coverage of the development of the law is provided in Chapter 3 which covers the long-standing provisions of the civil law that have allowed certain private rights to be exercised through a range of procedures and remedies which have been progressively applied to provide compensation for certain kinds of private harm. The development of modern regulatory law cannot be fully understood without appreciating the historical role and limitations of the civil law.

Chapters 4 and 5 cover detailed background discussion to what is now a central body of European Community legislation and an overview of the key water quality directives and their implementing provisions. This culminates in fairly extensive coverage of the recent Water Framework Directive which will be progressively implemented in the years ahead. Opportunity is also taken, in Chapter 4, to explore some of the central principles of EC environmental law and policy with which water pollution and water quality law is now inseparably connected. Chapter 4 also explains in some detail the range of ways in which compliance with EC water directives might be secured, including the scope for individually-initiated action and the response of the national courts to Community environmental law.

Chapter 6 and the two following chapters continue the institutional perspective initiated in the discussion of the enforcement role of the Commission in Chapter 4. Initially, this is through an examination of the constitution and functions of the main regulatory authority at national level, the Environment Agency, and discussion of how broadly-formulated strategic obligations upon the Agency are to be translated into practical law enforcement policies and actions. Chapter 7 then looks at the economic regulation of the water industry, outlining the way in which the activities of water and sewerage undertakers are regulated by the Office of Water Services through mechanisms to control the way in which undertakers raise the finances necessary to secure water quality improvements, such as the upgrading of sewage treatment works. Chapter 8 combines an outline discussion of the constitutional structures and workings of local authorities with a survey of one of their more important functions, the focus here being on the role of local government in regulating statutory nuisances in the interests of public health.

Thereafter attention shifts to the licensing of potentially polluting activities and the offences to which licensing provides a defence. Hence, Chapter 9

provides an account and analysis of the main water pollution offences arising
in relation to inland and coastal waters, as these are provided for under the
Water Resources Act 1991. These offences are considered alongside discussion
of an extensive body of caselaw which has illuminated the statutory provisions
and consideration of associated sentencing and enforcement issues. The
following three chapters cover the regulation of discharges into the natural
water environment and into the sewer system, discussing first (in Chapter 10)
the powers and duties of the Environment Agency in relation to discharge
consents under the Water Resources Act 1991; second (in Chapter 11) the
granting of trade effluent consents by sewerage undertakers under the Water
Industry Act 1991 allowing for discharges into sewers, subject to oversight by
the Agency for the more polluting substances; and, third (in Chapter 12)
looking at a range of further environmental and other rather miscellaneous
legislation, and considering the possibilities for water pollution and water
quality offences to arise outside the Water Resources Act 1991.

Chapter 13 then contrasts the essentially reactive and punitive measures
against water pollution, previously discussed, with a range of legal mechanisms
which are primarily intended to prevent deterioration in water quality or to
restore water to a satisfactory state. This is followed by discussion (in Chapter
14) of the role of land-use planning law in relation to the protection of the water
environment and a range of other mechanisms by which strategic objectives
for water quality are formulated and legal mechanisms used as a purposeful
means of achieving those objectives. The land-use theme continues into
Chapter 15 which, in addition to looking at a range of fishery-related offences
and strategic provisions, examines the respect in which legal mechanisms
intended to safeguard natural habitats influence water quality regulation.

Chapter 16 recognises that various kinds of legal action are intimately
dependent upon the availability of information about water quality and
considers the range of duties upon regulatory authorities to gather this
information alongside the scope of public rights to obtain access to it.
Nowhere is the monitoring of water quality more critical than in relation to
human health, and Chapter 17 considers the law relating to the monitoring of
drinking water quality alongside the range of regulatory provisions intended
to ensure that supplies of drinking water – public, private and bottled – meet
certain standards.

The final three chapters of the book focus upon international law and its
national impacts in a range of areas. Chapter 18 provides background
discussion, including an outline of the OSPAR treaty regime which is gaining
in practical influence. The following chapter looks at two areas of activity,
discharges from shipping and dumping at sea, where the development of the
present legal controls has been heavily influenced by international legal
agreements. A similar theme is seen in the distinct body of law regulating the
discharge of radioactive contaminants into the water environment, considered
in Chapter 20. The law concerning radioactive contamination is influenced by
a diverse range of bodies and concerns, some of which have little

interrelationship with the control of other aspects of water quality management, and which set the control of this particular form of water contamination apart from others discussed in this book.

# Chapter 1

# WATER POLLUTION AND WATER QUALITY: ISSUES AND THEMES

## 1.1 Introduction

Understanding any branch of environmental law involves an appreciation of not only what the law is but also the nature of the underlying problems and the legal options which exist to address them. Water pollution and water quality law is no different. Underlying the substantive law there are negatively and positively formulated environmental objectives which different parts of the law strive towards. Broadly, avoiding 'pollution' of water is one of these imperatives, and achieving 'satisfactory' water quality the other. However, the supposition that the underlying environment and ecological concepts may be taken 'off the peg' and translated into neatly corresponding legal obligations proves to be a mirage. Many of the legal difficulties, in determining what is meant by water 'pollution' or 'satisfactory' water quality, arise because the underlying environmental concepts lack sufficient precision to allow their ready use as a basis for ascribing legal rights and duties. Both environmental science and environmental values are tested by the exercises of formulating and applying laws which accurately and fairly reflect the underlying objectives. The starting point for this work, therefore, is an attempt to explain the purposes of water pollution law and water quality law and relate this to relevant activities and options for legal control.

The purpose of this chapter is to introduce and examine the central themes that run through the body of this work: water pollution and water quality, and the legal implications to which these concerns give rise. The contrast between water pollution and water quality is examined in relation to the fundamental concepts involved, the practical difficulties in relating these concepts to the regulation of problematic activities and the range of regulatory approaches involved in the protection of the quality of the aquatic environment. Whilst many of the individual topics raised in this chapter are considered in more detail later in the work, the objective is to explain the general background and practical context in which the law operates and to emphasise and contrast the strategic role which different legal provisions play in the overall exercise of protecting the water environment.[1]

---

[1] General reading on water pollution and water quality includes: Turing (1952) Chs.I and II; Klein (1957) Ch.3; Klein (1962) Ch.3; Newsom and Sherratt (1972) Part Two; Mills (1972) Ch.10; Wood and Sheldon (1980); Institute of Fisheries Management (1981); Newson (1992); Newson (1994); Boon and Howell (1997); and Cook (1998).

1

## 1.2 Water

By definition, 'water' is a transparent, colourless, odourless liquid (at standard conditions of temperature and pressure) constituting the normal oxide of hydrogen and given the chemical formula $H_2O$. Although it may be technically possible to produce this substance in an almost pure form by distillation in a scientific laboratory, all water found in the natural state contains some amounts of dissolved and suspended substances which render it chemically less than pure, but environmentally no less valuable because of that.[2] Even water falling as natural precipitation is impure in the sense that it is acidic, rather than neutral as chemically pure water would be, due to dissolving gases such as carbon dioxide and sulphur dioxide and particulates which are naturally present in the atmosphere.[3]

In the most general terms, the quality of water can be viewed in terms of its physical, chemical and biological characteristics.[4] Physical characteristics of water include its temperature and colour, and its opacity which is largely determined by the suspended solids content of the water. Chemical characteristics include features such as acidity (pH) and hardness, which in natural water are the result of water-dissolving chemicals such as ammonia, nutrients such as nitrogenous or phosphorous compounds and a wide range of other substances. Because of the high solubility of various gases in water, such as oxygen and carbon dioxide, it provides a medium for the support of a range of aerobic aquatic life. Biological factors encompass matters such as the bacteriological content of water and the aerobic process by which organic constituents cause the removal of oxygen from the water, usually measured in terms of biochemical oxygen demand (BOD).

The natural ecological character of any body of water will be largely determined by the combination of its physical, chemical and biological features which may themselves be affected by the ecosystem supported by the water and the character of surrounding areas of land. Modifications of any of these characteristics, or combinations of them, are capable of arising for purely natural reasons, such as where seasonal fluctuations in water quality are found due to variations in ecological activity.[5] Similarly, the human uses that can be made of water are, to varying degrees, dependent upon the natural characteristics of water. Paradoxically perhaps, many of the characteristics commonly attributed to 'water', where water quality is at issue, are actually the result of substances or things other than water which are present in it either by human agency or as a natural occurrence. In a sense, all water is 'contaminated' in that it falls short of the standard of absolute purity by which, chemically, it is defined. In some

---

[2] Hence, it has been judicially observed that the strict scientific definition of 'water' as a colourless liquid is not always appropriate, *John S Deed & Sons Ltd v British Electricity Authority and Croydon Corporation* (1950) 66 TLR 567 at p.572 per Lloyd Jacobs J. Also see 17.1 below for a judicial observation on the unpalatability of absolutely 'pure' water.
[3] Newson (1994) p.155.
[4] See Templeton (1984) s.1.2; Fort and Brayshaw (1961) Chs.I and VIII; and Mills (1972) Ch.1.
[5] Generally see Royal Commission on Environmental Pollution (1992) Ch.2, on chemical and biological characteristics of freshwaters.

respects this 'contaminated' state of water arises as an impact of diverse human activities, but in other respects it is a natural and ecologically beneficial occurrence.

## 1.3 Water 'Pollution'

Although natural water quality may vary considerably for geographical, hydrological and ecological reasons, the concept of 'pollution' is usefully restricted to extremes of adulteration attributable to human activities. To recognise that water which is not absolutely pure is not necessarily 'polluted' it is helpful to term lesser degrees of impurity 'contamination' rather than pollution.[6] Hence, the broad spectrum of water quality extends from extreme adverse states resulting from human agency, properly characterised as 'pollution', to lesser degrees of adulteration of anthropogenic origin, and to natural states of water quality which are 'contaminated' in the sense of falling short of absolute purity.

Normally, the main environmental concern arises where water is polluted or contaminated by human agency. In an extreme case of water pollution, the likely consequence of this is that the water will become unsuitable for any use which might normally be made of it. In a less extreme case of water contamination, detectable quantities of substances which are present as a result of human activities may only make the water less suitable for a particular use. In a situation where water is contaminated as a result of natural processes, it is unlikely to be regarded as environmentally problematic. Nonetheless, naturally occurring contaminants may be present in significant quantities, such as where oil naturally seeps into waters around many parts of the British coast.[7] However, each assessment of the problematic nature of a contaminant depends on the actual or potential uses for which the water is intended. In some circumstances water might naturally become enriched with minerals to the extent that it is unsuitable for abstraction for water supply purposes whereas, for any other purpose, the same degree of contamination would be regarded as unproblematic.[8]

It must be acknowledged that the two expressions, 'pollution' and 'contamination', are not always clearly distinguished,[9] and doubts have been expressed as to how precisely the distinction is capable of being drawn for scientific purposes.[10] Despite these reservations, the contrast between extreme kinds of damage to the aquatic environment and lesser degrees of water quality impairment is useful both in indicating the different kinds of legal problem that arise and in reflecting the perception

---

[6] See Royal Commission on Environmental Pollution (1984) paras.1.9-1.13 and Clark (1987) p.215.

[7] See Clark (1997) p.5 and see Ch.19 on oil contamination generally.

[8] See Drinking Water Abstraction Directive (75/440/EEC) Annex II which lists the characteristics of water intended for abstraction as drinking water and see 17.6 below on this.

[9] See the discussion of provisions concerning 'contaminated' land at 13.7 below.

[10] Royal Commission on Environmental Pollution (1998) para. 2.58.

that not every measurable degree of water contamination should be categorised as 'pollution'.

However useful the distinction between 'pollution' and 'contamination' is in an exposition of the different legal approaches to water quality, this distinction is frequently conflated in authoritative legal sources. 'Pollution' is not uncommonly used in a undiscriminating sense to encompass almost any degree of deterioration in water quality which renders it, in some respect, less useful, thereby failing to distinguish between different kinds of underlying environmental problem which may require markedly different kinds of legal approach. For this reason, the contrasts between water 'pollution' and lesser degrees of 'contamination' which may constitute water quality concerns are emphasised in those contexts where this distinction is of importance.

Typically, pollution arises as the result of an extreme contamination event where a large quantity of a toxic substance enters receiving waters causing catastrophic damage to aquatic flora and fauna. Alternatively, water which has become chronically adulterated with effluent that it is of insufficient quality to be used for any practical purpose may be fairly described as 'polluted'. In either the acute or the chronic case, however, it is the extremity of the degraded state which characterises 'pollution', making the water unsuitable for all, or almost all, normal uses.

However, many of the situations under consideration in this work do not fall within the extreme of pollution. Where, for example, water fails to meet quality parameters specified for water to be used for a particular purpose it is fair to describe it as giving rise to a water quality problem, but not necessarily as 'polluted'. Again, use or potential use is the paramount consideration. Water which is of unsatisfactory quality in a domestic supply system may be regarded as excellent in a fishery. The key legal issue is the relevant standard against which quality is to be judged and, in relation to this, the disjunction between polluted and not-polluted is an unhelpfully crude and misleading guide as to the legal situation.

## 1.3.1 *Eutrophication and Acidification*

Examples of present water quality concerns which are better characterised as 'contamination' rather than 'pollution' are the problems of eutrophication and acidification of freshwaters.[11] 'Eutrophication' is the process of enrichment of water by nutrients, primarily nitrogen and phosphorus, which determine the rate of plant and algal growth.[12]

---

[11] Generally, see Royal Commission on Environmental Pollution (1992) Ch.6: Mason (1996) Chs.4 and 5; and Hardman, McEldowney and Waite (1993) Chs.8 and 11.

[12] In European Community law, 'eutrophication' has been defined as 'the enrichment of water by nutrients, especially the compounds of nitrogen and/or phosphorus, causing an accelerated growth of algae and higher forms of plant life to produce an undesirable disturbance to the balance of the organisms present in the water and to the quality of the water concerned' (Art.2(11) Urban Waste Water Treatment Directive (91/271/EEC) and see 5.6.2 below; and similarly see Art.2(i) Nitrates Directive (91/676/EEC) and see 5.6.3 below.

Although the phenomenon of eutrophication is an important concern,[13] it falls into a quite different environmental and legal category from that of industrial 'pollution' incidents and their environmental impacts. Typically, eutrophication is the consequence of a gradual and long-term process contributed to by various diffuse emissions rather than a particular or discrete entry of polluting matter into the waters concerned. Moreover, it is not possible to relate the problem directly to any single water quality parameter since the adverse effect of any concentration of a particular nutrient is so greatly dependent upon the individual characteristics of the receiving waters. A small amount of nutrient addition to an oligotrophic water may have a highly damaging effect on a rare species of aquatic flora and fauna, whereas a relatively large amount of nutrient may have little effect upon water that is already naturally eutrophic. Hence it has been stated,

> [e]utrophication describes a process rather than a state and studies have shown that it is controlled by a number of factors. These include nutrients, flow rate of waters, shading and turbidity, depth, temperature and turbulence. The relationship of many of these factors to eutrophication is not easily quantified. The assessment of whether a stretch of water actually or potentially is eutrophic is not possible simply by reference to numeric chemical criteria. A number of symptoms should be considered in order to come to a judgement as to whether an individual stretch of water is suffering or likely to suffer from eutrophication. The importance of particular symptoms will depend on local circumstances.[14]

Equally, any effective legal response to the problem will clearly need to address the mechanisms by which nutrients enter waters and the nature of the agricultural and effluent treatment activities which are responsible. Clearly, a legal approach which involved bringing prosecutions against those allowing the entry of 'polluting' substances into the affected waters would be difficult to maintain[15] and other approaches are needed.

A second example of a water quality issue which does not readily fit into the conception of 'pollution' is that of acidification of waters. Rainfall, as has been noted, is naturally acidic, but this feature has been significantly enhanced in some areas by emissions of gaseous and particulate emissions from industrial processes and energy generation. Although acidification has been recognised as a local problem in industrial areas for many years,

---

[13] See National Rivers Authority, *Toxic Blue-Green Algae* (1990), Moss, Madgwick and Phillips (1996) and Environment Agency, *Aquatic Eutrophication in England and Wales; A Proposed Management Strategy* (1998).

[14] *Government Response to Consultation on Criteria and Procedures for Identifying Sensitive Areas and Less Sensitive Areas (Urban Waste Water Treatment Directive) and 'Polluted Waters' (Nitrates Directive) in England and Wales* (incorporated in DoE, MAFF and WO, *Methodology for Identifying Sensitive Areas (Urban Waste Water Treatment Directive) and Methodology for Designating Vulnerable Zones (Nitrates Directive) in England and Wales* (1993) Annex B para.9).

[15] Although there is one recorded instance of a conviction of a water services company for the introduction of water contaminated by blue-green algae into a watercourse (Environment Agency, *Water Pollution Incidents in England and Wales 1998* (1999) para.7.7.6).

it is now understood to have a major global dimension. Typically, anthropogenic acid deposition originates from sulphur dioxide as a by-product of the combustion of fossil fuels, from nitrogen oxides originating in motor vehicle emissions and from gaseous ammonia originating in livestock wastes. As a result of atmospheric turbulence, these emissions may be dispersed over wide areas before deposition, hence the strongly international dimension to the problem. The impact of these atmospheric emissions upon water arises with the eventual precipitation of acidic rainfall or the deposition of particulate matter upon land which is eventually washed into watercourses. The effect of this is to cause the receiving waters to become more acidic, with consequent increases in the solubility of toxic metals such as aluminium, and for significant changes to take place in aquatic flora and fauna, with more acid-tolerant species progressively replacing those that are less tolerant.[16]

Although the legal solution to the acidification problem clearly lies in the reduction of the offending atmospheric emissions and a programme of internationally coordinated measures which are largely beyond the scope of this work,[17] the environmental issue again demonstrates the disparity between pollution and water contamination. Acidification is a gradual but progressive phenomenon which is highly variable in its impact with different areas showing markedly different levels of susceptibility depending upon the naturally acidic or alkaline nature of the soil and the corresponding buffering capacity against acid deposition. Contamination of this kind clearly causes a change in water quality which favours some species at the expense of others, but does not necessarily affect the range of uses which may be made of the water. To assimilate the process of acidification, and its environmental impacts, to traditional kinds of 'polluting' incident fails to recognise the distinctive nature of the problem and the specialised nature of the legal controls that are needed to address it.

Eutrophication and acidification are important examples of water quality problems which do not correspond with the traditional conception of 'pollution' either in terms of their mechanism or environmental impact. In both instances the mechanism of contamination tends to be indirect and diffuse, without an obvious link between a particular emission or discharge and its consequences. More importantly, the resulting environmental impact is much more difficult to ascertain since, as has been noted, many waters are naturally eutrophic or acidic in character. Comparison between degrees of contamination, judged relatively to the natural state of the receiving waters, is a crucial consideration and, therefore, assessments of the 'polluting' character of emissions or the 'polluted' state of the receiving waters are placed out of context.

---

[16] Generally see *Communication on a Community strategy to combat acidification* Com (97) 88.
[17] See 19.10 below on acidification in international marine pollution law.

### 1.3.2  Eutrophication, Acidification and Pollution

Consideration of eutrophication and acidification problems is also useful in emphasising the relatively subtle and complex nature of many contemporary water quality problems. The language of 'water pollution' tends to suggest dramatic incidents involving catastrophic deterioration in water quality. In practice, however, many of the most pervasive and intractable water quality problems lie in the gradual transmission of contaminants into the aquatic environment with a consequent need to rethink legal mechanisms to address the activities giving rise to these.

The term water 'pollution' tends to deflect attention from, perhaps, more pervasive and intractable kinds of water quality problem. Other ambiguities arise because the word 'pollution' is frequently used in grammatically different senses. 'Pollution' is sometimes used to refer to the offending activity, sometimes to refer to the substance which has the harmful effect and sometimes to refer to the resultant impact upon water quality and the aquatic environment. In this discussion it is the last of the three senses is most important since distinctions need to be drawn between *pollutants* and pollution. Specifically, the effects of a contaminating substance on water depends upon the chemical, physical and biological properties of the substance, its concentration and the duration for which the substance is present in any body of water, and the capacity of the water and its ecosystem to restore itself to its former state. Some substances are toxic or carcinogenic or give rise to serious concerns because of their resistance to degradation or their propensity for bioaccumulation in particular organisms. Other substances lack these characteristics and are biodegradable but this process is capable of having adverse effects upon water quality through depletion of oxygen and serious, frequent or long-lasting introductions of such substances may produce significant harm to ecosystems. The point to emphasise is that the water quality and ecological impacts of any introduction of a particular substance depend greatly upon the physical, chemical and biological characteristics of the receiving waters.[18] The association between pollutants and pollution, therefore, has to be treated with some caution.

### 1.3.3  General Definitions of 'Pollution'

Despite the environmental rationality and legal justification for distinguishing between the 'pollution' and 'contamination' of water, the fact remains that this distinction is widely conflated in legal terminology. 'Pollution' has been construed in the broadest possible sense to mean the human modification of water which renders it less suitable for use than it would be in its natural state.[19] Hence, an early but commonly accepted definition of 'pollution' is,

---

[18] See Royal Commission on Environmental Pollution (1992) para.3.5.

[19] See Smith (1972) p.170; McLoughlin (1972) Ch.1; and Hawkes (1979).

the introduction by man, directly or indirectly, of substances or energy into the environment resulting in deleterious effects of such a nature as to endanger human health, harm living resources and ecosystems, and impair or interfere with amenities and other legitimate uses of the environment.[20]

A general international definition of 'pollution of the marine environment' is that adopted under the United Nations Convention on the Law of the Sea of 1982,[21] which states that,

'pollution of the marine environment' means the introduction by man, directly or indirectly, of substances or energy into the marine environment, including estuaries, which results or is likely to result in such deleterious effects as harm to living resources and marine life, hazards to human health, hindrance to marine activities, including fishing and other legitimate uses of the sea, impairment of quality for use of sea water and reduction of amenities.[22]

A similar definition is to be found in the 1992 Convention for the Protection of the Marine Environment of the North East Atlantic (the OSPAR Convention),

'pollution' means the introduction by man, directly or indirectly, of substances or energy into the maritime area which results, or is likely to result, in hazards to human health, harm to living resources and marine ecosystems, damage to amenities or interference with other legitimate uses of the sea.[23]

Likewise, similarly formulated definitions have been used for the purposes of various European Community environmental directives[24] and the most recent example is to be found in the Water Framework Directive.[25] This defines 'pollution' as,

the direct or indirect introduction, as a result of human activity, of substances, heat into the air, water or land which may be harmful to human health or the quality of aquatic ecosystems or terrestrial ecosystems directly depending on aquatic ecosystems, which result in damage to material property, or which impair or interfere with amenities and other legitimate uses of the environment.[26]

---

[20] OECD Council Recommendation C(74) 224 of 14 November 1974, similarly see Holdgate (1979) p.17.

[21] Art.1(4) and see 18.7 below on the United Nations Convention on the Law of the Sea 1982.

[22] A similar definition had been formulated by the United Nations Joint Group of Experts on the Scientific Aspects of Marine Pollution (GESAMP), see UNESCO doc. SC/MD/19, 1 June 1970, Annex IV p.12.

[23] Art.1(4) OSPAR Convention and see 18.8 below on the OSPAR Convention.

[24] See, for example, Art.1(2)(e) Dangerous Substances Directive (76/464/EEC) and see 5.4.1 below on this Directive.

[25] See 5.7 below on the Water Framework Directive (2000/60/EC).

[26] Art.2(33) Water Framework Directive. Note also that the proposal defines 'pollutant' to mean any substance liable to cause pollution, in particular those listed in Annex VIII.

Although slight differences in wording are to be found in each of these definitions, some common features are usefully noted. Perhaps most significant is the consciously anthropocentric characterisation of 'pollution'. However greatly water quality may vary, for diverse natural reasons, the resulting state of the water is excluded from the meaning of 'pollution' insofar as it is not the result of human activities. Hence, the definition in the Water Framework Directive requires that the 'introduction' of the offending substance or thing is brought about, directly or indirectly, by human agency. Whilst the term 'introduction' encompasses both purposeful 'discharges' and accidental 'emissions'[27] of pollutants, it raises potentially difficult questions as to when the mechanism of the introduction is to be regarded as natural rather than the result of a human agency. Where a pollutant is carried into water by the action of wind, or surface water runoff from land, there must come a point at which this is regarded as a natural occurrence rather than a 'human activity'.

Even where a human activity is involved, the requirement that there is an 'introduction' of a substance into water may be capable of excluding situations where a pollutant is already present in water, perhaps for natural reasons, but disturbed or redistributed by human intervention as where sub-aquatic operations are undertaken.[28] Again, the activity-specific emphasis within the definition may raise problematic situations where water quality declines significantly without it being possible to identify any particular 'introduction' of the kind that the definition envisages.

Beyond showing that there is an 'introduction' as a result of 'human activity', the definition is limited to introducing certain substances or things which may be 'harmful' to human health or the quality of the environment. Clearly, a range of complexities underlie the concept of 'harmfulness', to either human health or the environment, and it is rather unhelpful to have to identify particular introductions as either 'harmful' or not harmful where, in reality, the issue is a matter of degree.[29] In environmental contexts, for example, natural populations will usually demonstrate progressive intolerance to the presence of a particular pollutant, but the precise concentration at which its presence becomes 'harmful' is far from clear. Likewise, a difficulty arises where a substance which is 'harmful' to one of the recognised interests is actually beneficial to another, such as where the control of insects for public health reasons is undertaken at potential ecological cost. The rather categorical wording of the definition of 'pollution' appears evasive when undertaking these rather intricate balancing exercises involved in reconciling competing interests in the state of the aquatic environment.

---

[27] See the discussion of 'entry' and 'discharge' at 9.10 below.

[28] For an illustration of this difficulty, see *National Rivers Authority* v *Biffa Waste Services Ltd* (1995) *The Times*, 21 November 1995 and see 9.10 below for a discussion of this case.

[29] See Alder and Wilkinson (1999) who suggest that definitions of 'pollution' tend to push the discussion back to determining the meaning of terms such as 'deleterious' or 'harmful' (at p.181).

Another aspect of the harmfulness requirement is the wording that the substance or thing which is introduced 'may be' harmful to human health or the quality of the environment. 'May be' seems to allow the possibility that 'pollution' may be found to exist without any actual deterioration in water quality being established. Whilst it seems odd to conclude that there has been 'pollution' without the need to show any *actual* adverse impact, there may be a justification for this wording insofar as it appears to allow a precautionary approach to be taken.[30] That is, the definition incorporates a precautionary approach if 'may be' is interpreted as meaning that there is some, albeit inconclusive, evidence that the introduced substance is harmful. Nonetheless, the wording is ambiguous since it seems to allow the possibility of encompassing introductions where even minimal grounds for suspecting harmfulness are unsatisfied.

However, the possibility of pollution without actual damage appears to be excluded by the final words of the definition which restrict its application to introductions which actually result in specified kinds of damage. Hence, 'pollution' generally requires that certain consequences ensue: that the introduction results in damage to material property, or the impairment or interference with amenities and other legitimate uses of the environment. In the first place, the need for damage to 'material property' seems particularly problematic if the concern is to protect wild species and ecosystems dependent upon the aquatic environment. It is difficult to conceive of these as 'property' since, as a matter of common law at least, they are usually unowned, but no less in need of protection because of this.[31] In the second place, the alternative is that of showing impairment or interference with amenities and legitimate uses of the environment but, again, this falls some way short of recognising an intrinsic value of uncontaminated water and the flora and fauna which this supports. There is, therefore, a heavy emphasis placed upon a human-utility rationale underlying water 'pollution' control, perhaps at the expense of recognising the value of ecosystems for reasons other than for human amenity or use.

Despite these reservations, a strength of the kind of definition of 'pollution' found in the Water Framework Directive lies in the broad association which it draws between activities and impacts. Increasingly, approaches towards 'pollution' have focussed upon the need for three elements to be shown: a source, a target and a pathway between the two, such that the presence of all the three elements will be needed to determine that 'pollution' exists. Whilst this approach has been adopted by environmental scientists for some years,[32] it is only gradually becoming assimilated into legal thinking about pollution. A good example of the approach is to be found in the national legislation and guidance concerning remediation of contaminated land[33] where it is advised that before any

---

[30] See 4.7.1 below on the precautionary principle.

[31] Generally see Howarth and McGillivray (1996) p.33.

[32] Generally see Holdgate (1979); Newson (1994) Ch.8; and Royal Commission on Environmental Pollution (1998) Ch.2.

[33] See 13.7 below on contaminated land generally.

determination is made that land is 'contaminated'[34] three elements must be found:

(a) a contaminant or pollutant, which has the potential to cause harm or pollution of controlled waters;[35]
(b) a receptor or target, consisting of a living organism or group of living organisms, an ecological system, some piece of property of a specified kind or controlled waters; and
(c) a pathway, consisting of one or more routes or means by or through which the receptor could be exposed to, or affected by, the contaminant identified either through general scientific knowledge or the nature of the contaminant or the circumstances of the land in question.[36]

By contrast, earlier attempts to define the meaning of 'pollution', particularly in national law, suffered from a failure explicitly to identify the three distinct elements or to indicate their respective roles in identifying the existence of 'pollution' in particular situations.

### 1.3.4 'Pollution' in National Criminal Law

The relatively sophisticated appreciation of the mechanism of 'pollution' found in the contaminated land legislation may be contrasted with the traditional approach of leaving the concept largely undefined in national criminal and civil law. In the criminal context, it will be seen that a principal water pollution offence involves causing or knowingly permitting the entry of poisonous, noxious or polluting matter into controlled waters.[37] Significantly, the offence is *not* formulated as causing the pollution of water, but as causing the *entry* of polluting matter into water, thereby leaving unspecified what impact, if any, such an entry must actually have upon the receiving waters for the offence to be committed. This ambiguity as to the distinction between emission and impact has generated some uncertainty in relation to the meaning of the offence and it has been suggested that the legislative failure to define 'pollution' is extraordinary in failing to give notice to those concerned as to what it is they are to avoid doing.[38]

---

[34] Note that 'contaminated' is here used in a sense that encompasses 'polluted' since it covers situations where 'pollution of controlled waters is being, or is likely to be caused' (s.78A(2)(a) Environmental Protection Act 1990, as amended).

[35] See 9.4 below on the definition of 'controlled waters'.

[36] See DETR, Circular 02/2000, *Environmental Protection Act 1990: Part IIA Contaminated Land* (2000) Annex 3 paras. 11 and 19 and also see DoE, *A Guide to Risk Assessment and Risk Management for Environmental Protection* (1995) for a general discussion of risk assessment methodology.

[37] Under s.85(1) Water Resources Act 1991, and see 9.3 below on this.

[38] Taylor (1928) p.82, commenting on the Rivers Pollution Prevention Act 1876. The concept of 'pollution' was first defined, rather uninformatively, in national legislation relating to integrated pollution control in s.1(2)-(4) Environmental Protection Act 1990: 'pollution of the environment' means pollution of the environment due to the release (into any environmental medium) from any process of substances which are capable of causing harm to man or any other living organisms

A contradiction within the principal water pollution offence is that the terms 'poisonous, noxious or polluting'[39] seem only to be understandable in terms of certain impacts of offending substances and yet those impacts are not strictly relevant to the offence: providing the entry of the poisonous, noxious or polluting matter takes place the offence is complete whatever the impact of that entry. Whilst the words 'poisonous, noxious or polluting' each have different meanings,[40] there is some markedly contrasting reasoning to be found in the case law on the interpretation of the words which may be attributable to the opaque formulation of the offence and/or the lack of relevant definitions. Hence, in one instance where a prosecution was brought for having caused 'deleterious or poisonous liquid' to flow into a watercourse, it was determined that the character of the matter was to be determined at the instant when it entered the river and its subsequent effect upon the receiving water was immaterial. As one of the judges put the point,

> the section excludes from consideration any results of the prohibited act . . . . If the act would be criminal in fair weather when a river was low, it does not become innocent because rainfall causes a flood. To throw in lime or spurge is made absolutely unlawful, irrespective of effect.[41]

Alternatively, in another prosecution for conveying into a stream water 'not freed from . . . noxious matter', it was stated that,

> it was impossible to conclude that there had been an offence against the prohibition unless that special purity and quality [of the watercourse] had been shown to be deteriorated . . . [and] . . . in judging the effect of [the defendants'] operations one must regard this stream as a whole, and that if, regarded as a whole, the water in the stream or watercourse has not been deteriorated, no offence has been or can be established.[42]

Whilst different words, under different statutes, were being construed in the passages cited, essentially the same problem is being addressed: are 'poisonous, noxious or polluting' to be regarded as intrinsic qualities of a substance entering the watercourse, or are they matters which are to be

---

supported by the environment. The 'environment' consists of all, or any, of the following media, namely, the air, water and land. 'Harm' means harm to the health of living organisms or other interference with the ecological systems of which they form part and, in the case of man, includes offence caused to any of his senses or harm to his property.

[39] See 9.8 below on the interpretation of 'poisonous, noxious or polluting'.

[40] Simes and Scholefield (1954) p.5158 note e; Newsom and Sherratt (1972) p.30; and Howarth (1993).

[41] *R* v *Justices of Antrim* (1906) 2 IR 298, per Gibson J. at p.319. Similarly, see *R* v *Dovermoss Ltd* [1995] Env LR 258 where it was submitted that the prosecution have to show some harm has resulted to the water but the Court refused to accept this submission (at p.265 per Stuart Smith LJ) and see 9.8 below for further discussion of this case.

[42] *Attorney-General* v *Birmingham Tame and Rea District Drainage Board* [1908] 2 Ch 551, per Kekewich J. at p.556.

determined by reference to the environmental impact to which the substance actually gives rise when it enters particular waters? The answer is far from clear. Hence, insofar as national criminal law does utilise a concept of 'pollution' it is incomplete in its specification. In the terminology that has previously been introduced, it seems to envisage a source, and perhaps a pathway, but is silent as to what target is envisaged and what degree of impact upon that target is needed for an instance of 'pollution' to be established.

### 1.3.5 'Pollution' in National Civil Law

Turning to national civil law,[43] although various remedies may be available to the victim of what might ordinarily be regarded as 'water pollution', the concept of 'pollution' is not recognised as an explicit legal basis for a remedy to be provided. Hence, where the owner of waterside land brings an action against an upstream riparian owner for an interference with the flow of water in a watercourse, the basis upon which recovery is allowed is that a claimant is entitled to the water, 'in its natural flow, without sensible diminution or increase, and without sensible alteration in its character or quality'.[44] Moreover, liability for causing deterioration of water quality arises as a consequence of 'sensible alteration' of the natural quality of a stream irrespective of whether the natural quality of the stream was previously good or bad in relation to the purpose for which the water is used.

Whilst in some instances judges in civil proceedings have sought to formulate definitions of 'water pollution',[45] it is thought that these are largely redundant in the sense that the key question remains whether 'sensible alteration' of water quality has been brought about, not whether the water has been 'polluted' in any other sense. The test as to what is to count as 'sensible alteration' in a particular context recognises the inherent variability of water in the natural state, in that the standard is not formulated in terms of any absolute scientific parameters of unacceptable deterioration in water quality but, rather, by reference to the degree of variation from the quality of the water naturally present in the watercourse.

Similarly, where civil litigation is based upon the tort of private nuisance,[46] rather than the infringement of riparian rights, the fundamental question to be addressed by the court is whether the offending actions have resulted in 'unreasonable interference with the use or enjoyment of land'.

---

[43] See Ch.3 below on civil law generally.

[44] Per Lord Macnaghten in *John Young and Co v Bankier Distillery Co* (1893) [1891-4] All ER Rep 439, at p.441; and see 3.5.1 below.

[45] See, for example, *Cook v South West Water plc* (unreported, Exeter County Court 15 April 1992, discussed [1992] *Water Law* 103) where the Court expressed a preference for a definition of 'pollution' as 'a change in water quality which produces damage to a legitimate user of the water, such as fishing'. Alternatively, in criminal proceedings, the *Oxford English Dictionary* definition of 'pollute' has been cited with approval, 'to make physically impure, foul or filthy; to dirty, stain, taint, befoul' (*R v Dovermoss Ltd* [1995] Env LR 258 per Stuart Smith LJ at p.265).

[46] See 3.8 below on private nuisance.

There have been many instances where causing the foreseeable deterioration of water quality has been found to constitute such an interference, but whether the degree of deterioration of water quality is sufficient to constitute 'pollution' is not strictly relevant to the issue to be decided. The nature and extent of the interference with use or enjoyment are determinative of the issue to be decided, without it being necessary, or relevant, for the court to enquire as to the status of the deterioration of water quality as 'pollution' or otherwise.

### 1.3.6  The Legal Relevance of 'Pollution'

The fundamental question may be posed as to how significant the concept of 'pollution' is in relation to the legal protection of the aquatic environment. Although the concept features in international and European Community legislation, and in national criminal and civil law, the legal significance of the concept is actually relatively limited or is so obscurely formulated as to be unhelpful. For many, 'water pollution' is a readily comprehensible idea which raises no profound conceptual difficulties. However, like many environmental intuitions, the translation of the popular idea into a precisely defined concept to which legal rights and duties may be satisfactorily associated is a matter of some difficulty. Perhaps for this reason, recent legal developments place a greater emphasis upon the more specific issue of whether water is of sufficient quality for a defined use. Hence, for legal purposes, the idea of 'pollution' is increasingly being overshadowed by the more sophisticated concept of 'water quality', expressed in terms of different standards for different waters in relation to the uses to which they may be put.

Despite the progressive overshadowing of water pollution by water quality concerns, there may be instances where the idea of 'pollution' continues to serve a useful purpose. This is to identify those extreme incidents which involve dramatic changes in water quality attributable to an isolated and identifiable entry of matter which has a visibly damaging effect upon the aquatic environment, typically involving sudden and extensive mortality of fish or other aquatic flora and fauna. Such 'pollution incidents' are a regrettably common occurrence,[47] and are likely to be well illustrated by those situations which actually result in criminal proceedings being brought by the regulatory authorities. Clearly, it is essential that criminal sanctions should apply to such activities though doubts previously expressed remain in that it is not altogether clear that the concept of 'pollution' is a necessary part of the legal definition of the offending activities.

Increasingly, it is recognised that pollution incidents constitute only a small part of the challenge of protecting the water environment which the law needs to address. A more widespread problem is that of unsatisfactory water quality commonly resulting from the gradual and sustained input of substances which cumulatively result in water quality falling below an

---

[47] See 9.2 below on statistics relating to pollution incidents.

acceptable standard. Such inputs are more likely to arise, not from dramatic pollution incidents, but from a succession of much more mundane activities which involve relatively commonplace discharges or the gradual transmission into watercourses or groundwater of substances from a range of land uses by surface water runoff without any contribution from polluting events being identifiable.

Significant parts of the remainder of this work are concerned with the problems of unsatisfactory water quality resulting from gradual and diffuse contamination. However, pollution-centred approaches are of limited relevance to their resolution. 'Pollution', insofar as it is relevant, focusses upon a conception of what one branch of the law is striving to prohibit. The increasing realisation is that it is necessary to undertake a more positive and purposive approach to the issues in determining what quality is reasonably required of various categories of waters and the aquatic environment, expressing those requirements in terms of objective and precise parameters and using the law in a more strategic fashion for the purpose of realising necessary water quality improvements.

### 1.3.7  Toxicity

The imprecision and uncertainty of the legal concept of 'pollution' may usefully be contrasted with the more rigourous scientific idea of 'toxicity' as a measure of the degree of harmfulness of a substance to living organisms. The concept of 'toxicity' seems capable of a greater degree of precision which, potentially, makes it more useful as a means of specifying legal objectives and prohibitions.[48]

'Toxicity' has the characteristic of being relatively precisely specifiable in the sense that, under laboratory conditions, a population of test organisms may be subjected to a measured concentration of a substance and the impact of that exposure quantitatively expressed. Hence for a particular substance, in relation to a target species, it is technically possible to ascertain what concentration of that substance will cause half that population to die within a specified time and to express this as the 'median lethal concentration' (expressed as $LC_{50}$) for that substance in relation to that species. Alternatively, the result may be expressed in terms of the 'median survival time' within which a given species may survive at a given concentration of a substance. Whilst this kind of experiment may give rise to significant ethical concerns, it allows, within defined parameters, the toxicity of a substance to be expressed with an exactness which has seen to be lacking in respect of the concept of 'pollution'.

The limitations of the methodology which allows precise toxicity values to be expressed, however, must also be recognised. First, there is the methodological objection that the death of half of a test population is not always an ecologically meaningful measure of the different kinds of harm

---

[48] Newson (1994) Ch.8; Royal Commission on Environmental Pollution (1998) Ch.2; and Mason (1996) Ch.2.

that might arise through exposure to a particular chemical. Whilst lethal tests have the experimental advantage of reasonably precise measurability, lesser, sub-lethal or 'chronic' impairments which might be identified, such as the capacity of the test species to reproduce, might be particularly relevant.[49] A better indication might take account of a wider range of impacts which would make the concept more ecologically meaningful, though there is no reason in principle why this should not be done. Second, there is an underlying assumption of uniformity of toxic effect within a species which is also assumed to be consistent in its susceptibility to a toxic substance. However, a uniformity of result will only be given where the test species is of a consistent genetic composition and, for this reason, species to be tested will need to be specially bred to ensure consistency between different experiments and between different laboratories. Whilst consistency in the genetic make up of the test species will allow a precise toxicity value to be reached to a distinct genetically-defined population, it may not reflect the impact of the substance upon wild populations with a potentially wide genetic diversity. Even within animal species, susceptibility to a particular substance has been found to vary greatly, and between mammals, fish and other aquatic organisms the range of variation would be even greater still. Third, the susceptibility of particular individuals within a species to a test substance will vary and, for this reason, a sufficiently large population of a species will need to be tested and the result expressed as a median for that species, rather than the impact upon any particular specimen. Clearly, this will be experimentally problematic where there is a need to determine appropriate levels of protection for a species which is scarce or endangered in the wild or where, for ethical reasons, experimental determination of precise toxicity levels is not feasible.

More broadly, the precision of the concept of 'toxicity', expressible in terms of median lethal concentration, is achieved at the cost of comprehensiveness and practicality. The levels of a substance which are found to be toxic, in this sense, are those found in highly specific laboratory conditions which may fail to reflect the range of toxic effects actually found in different individual specimens and species present in different aquatic ecosystems. To have practicable application, therefore, it is necessary that any value of toxicity should take account of a wide range of potential impact species. Clearly, the experimental implications of arriving at a toxicity value, which would provide optimum protection to the whole range of relevant species, upon which the ecological well-being of the aquatic environment depends, are immense.

---

[49] See, for example, discussions of potentially harmful effects of endocrine-disrupting substances upon fertility, Environment Agency, *Endocrine-disrupting substances in the environment: What should be done?* (1998) and Environment Agency, *Endocrine-Disrupting Substances in Wildlife: A review of the scientific evidence and strategic response* (1998). Generally see *Communication on a Community Strategy for Endocrine Disruptions* Com (99) 706.

### 1.3.8 Direct Toxicity Assessment

Despite the range of methodological reservations that have been raised, the issue remains whether the concept of 'toxicity' has inherent advantages over that of 'pollution' for practical legal purposes. One context where this is apparent is in relation to the determination of parameters in effluent discharge consents authorising the discharge of substances into the aquatic environment.[50] In this context it has been suggested that the traditional approach of setting parameters for the amounts of substances that may lawfully be discharged, according to the recognised pollution potential of particular substances, has significant limitations. Hence, it has been argued that,

> some discharges – especially those arising from industrial batch production processes – can contain a complex and variable cocktail of toxic chemicals which it is impractical or even impossible to identify and control by means of individual limits. For significant discharges of this sort, toxicity testing provides an effective control of their overall impact on the receiving water. In such cases the consent should specify the maximum acceptable level of toxicological response, and also stipulate the frequency with which this limit should be tested using one of the routinely available tests. Thus we recommend . . . for environmentally significant discharges of complex composition where not all important constituents can be individually identified and numerically limited, consents should specify a clearly-defined toxicity limit, the appropriate form of toxicity test to be used, and the minimum frequency with which it should be applied.[51]

The emphasis here is placed upon the difficulty of establishing the environmental impact of complex chemical discharges, and determining consent parameters accordingly, at the point of discharge. However, it might also be argued that the traditional, chemical-specific, approach fails to take sufficient account of the potential synergistic effects which arise where two substances interact to produce a higher level of toxicity than either would produce alone.[52] If synergistic effects are a cause of enhanced toxicity, then the failure to take account of these is a serious difficulty, in that substance-specific discharge consent parameters will not be representative of the environmental harm that a discharge actually produces.

Moreover, if synergistic effects are environmentally problematic, they need to be taken account of, not merely at the point of discharge, but in relation to the wider aquatic environment. That is, two or more discrete discharges may be introducing substances into the aquatic environment which, though benign when separate, result in a significant toxic effect

---

[50] See Ch.10 below on discharge consents.

[51] National Rivers Authority, *Discharge Consents and Compliance Policy: a Blueprint for the Future* (1990) (*'The Kinnersley Report'*) p.27.

[52] Wharfe and Tinsley (1995).

when combined in the receiving waters. If this impact is capable of arising, the implication is that it is not sufficient to control individual discharges in isolation but account must be taken of their combined effects. Although the assessment of synergistic effects of substances which may be separately discharged into the aquatic environment raises immense scientific and legal difficulties,[53] the possibility of such effects highlights the potential limitations of the traditional approach to formulation of discharge consent conditions and the means by which a more toxicologically-based approach might allow consent parameters to be more closely aligned with environmental impact.

The practical introduction of 'direct toxicity assessment' and the corresponding regulation of discharges raises difficulties in scientific methodology legal implementation. The scientific difficulty involves a selection, from the infinite variety of toxicity tests are potentially available, of those which are best applied against criteria such as ease of use, cost, rapidity, sensitivity, spectrum of response, consistency and precision. [54]

A final reservation about toxicity assessment and biological impact monitoring is the need for some caution in respect of the general association between the state of aquatic ecosystems and the state of the waters which support these ecosystems. The potential difficulty lies in the fact that natural populations of any species are subject to wide demographic variation due to a range of factors other than water quality. Populations of many aquatic organisms will show significant seasonal variation, variations due to site-specific conditions and variations perhaps for largely unknown reasons which are not necessarily related to water quality.[55] The assumption that particular waters are of poor biological status due to the introduction of particular substances, or because of any particular anthropogenic influence, need not, therefore, always be well founded. Likewise, the supposition that improvement in the quality of discharges into particular waters is guaranteed to secure a corresponding improvement of the ecological status of those waters, perhaps to realise a particular ecological quality standard, is far from conclusively established. These kinds of reservation have been a reason for reluctance to impose statutory ecological water quality objectives, at least until the methodology for ecological assessment of waters is sufficiently well established to allow greater objectivity in judging the relationship between discharges, water quality and ecological impacts.[56]

---

[53] See Teubner (1994) p.22.

[54] Environment Agency, *The application of toxicity-based criteria for the regulatory control of wastewater discharges* (1996) and Hunt, Johnson and Milne (1992).

[55] See Edwards (1997) p.3, and Pugh (1997) p.20.

[56] See DoE, *Freshwater Quality: Government Response to the Sixteenth Report of the Royal Commission on Environmental Pollution* (1995) p.10, and see 14.8 below on statutory water quality objectives.

## 1.4 Water Quality

Although 'water pollution', however defined, is the thing that is to be avoided in relation to the protection of the aquatic environment, satisfactory water quality, measured according to the appropriate standard, is the objective to be realised. However, the concept of 'water quality' is capable of a number of different interpretations which must be distinguished.[57] Most uses of the term 'water quality' intend this to refer to the contamination status, physical modification, catchment land use, biological and geomorphological nature, and conservation value of water. However, it is also commonly used in a broader sense to encompass landscape, recreational, economic and cultural attributes.[58] Clearly, a range of characteristics may be encompassed in judgements concerning water quality, ranging from those matters which can be assessed with a fair degree of objectivity, such as the degree of chemical contamination, to matters which seem to be strongly subjective such as the aesthetic value of a particular water. In the discussion which follows some narrowing of the potential breadth of the concept is needed and, for that reason, emphasis is placed upon physical, chemical and biological characteristics of water, whilst not contesting that there are important considerations which fall outside these matters.

An initial issue in relation to water quality is as to *what* water quality is under consideration, given the contrast previously drawn between cause and effect, that is, between the substance that is introduced and its impact upon the aquatic environment. Another important distinction which needs to be stressed is that between categorisation of waters according to their potential uses and the determination of minimum physical, chemical and biological parameters which enable water to be used for a particular use. Significant differences exist between the exercises, first, of allocating particular waters to potential use categories and, second, the scientific determination of qualitative requirements for such categories. The contrast between these exercises is not always aided by the terminology in which water quality issues are discussed by different commentators, but a broadly historical explanation of the issues is illuminating.

### 1.4.1 The Royal Commission Standard

Although nineteenth century water pollution legislation created various criminal offences concerning the discharge of polluting matter into watercourses,[59] important work had also been undertaken to refine the understanding of what quality of effluent discharge would be environmentally acceptable. The Royal Commission on Rivers Pollution of 1870 had recommended the adoption of prescribed standards of effluent purity by statute, and proposed a set of chemical criteria for this purpose,[60]

---

[57] Generally, see Boon and Howell (1997a).
[58] See Boon and Howell (1997b).
[59] See Ch.2 below on legislative history generally.
[60] Royal Commission on Rivers Pollution (1870) p.130.

but this early attempt to incorporate discharge quality criteria in legislation was resisted by the legislature. It was not until the Royal Commission on Sewage Disposal published its Eighth Report, in 1912, dealing with the standards to be applied to effluents discharged into rivers and streams, that a non-statutory standard came to serve as a general measure for acceptable effluent quality.[61] The so-called 'Royal Commission Standard' continued to serve as a reference point for much subsequent discussion of water quality issues and the methodology underlying it remains pertinent to any contemporary discussion as to how these issues may best be addressed.[62]

The Royal Commission of 1912 recognised that there were no graduated standards of purity for sewage effluents according to the law of that time. The Rivers Pollution Prevention Act 1876 merely imposed an operational duty to adopt the best practical and available means to render sewage harmless before being discharged.[63] The Commission concerned itself with the standard of purity which was necessary to obviate the risk of actual nuisance arising from a discharge of sewage effluent and, in particular, with the chemical tests which would best indicate at what point that degree of purity had been achieved. This investigation concluded that the nuisance-producing power of sewage effluent was broadly proportional to its de-oxygenating effect upon the water of a stream. To measure the speed at which oxygen was removed from water as a result of bacterial decomposition, the Commission proposed a test, known as the Biochemical Oxygen Demand (BOD) test, which remains one of the principal means by which the quality of water is assessed.

The Commission noted that if the amount of oxygen utilised from a watercourse in assimilating effluent is more than 4 parts per million then signs of pollution will be evident, other than in cold weather when the solubility of oxygen in the water will be greater. Hence, at a standard temperature of 65 degrees Fahrenheit, 4 parts per million was taken as the 'limiting figure' serving as the foundation upon which the scheme of standards was to be constructed. Accordingly, the Biochemical Oxygen Demand test, measuring the absorption of oxygen over a five day period under standard conditions, allowed watercourses to be classified according to their purity. On this scale it was suggested that river quality could be related to average BOD in the following way.[64]

| Very Clean | 1 part per million dissolved oxygen in 5 days |
|---|---|
| Clean | 2 parts per million dissolved oxygen in 5 days |
| Fairly Clean | 3 parts per million dissolved oxygen in 5 days |
| Doubtful | 5 parts per million dissolved oxygen in 5 days |
| Bad | 10 parts per million dissolved oxygen in 5 days |

[61] Royal Commission on Sewage Disposal (1912).

[62] See Garnett (1981) p.173 and Hammerton (1987) p.336.

[63] s.3 Rivers Pollution Prevention Act 1876 and see 2.6 below.

[64] Royal Commission on Sewage Disposal (1912) para.17.

Given biochemical oxygen demand as the central measure of contamination of watercourses, the Commission recognised the important contrast between chemical standards being applied to a contaminating discharge itself and to the watercourse which receives that discharge, that is, between the emission and its environmental impact. The view of the Commission was that the primary objective should be the improvement of the quality of watercourses and that the improvement of effluents should be regarded as a secondary consideration as a means to that end. In this respect, the Commission demonstrated a remarkable degree of prescience in confronting a debate which remains topical.[65] Accordingly, quality standards should be applied not to sewage effluents alone but to the quality of such discharges when mixed with the river water under ordinary conditions. It followed that it would be necessary to apply the BOD test to the water of the receiving watercourse at a point where it had received and mixed with the effluent discharge. At that point, the standard would be fixed at 4 parts per million so that if the mixture yielded a figure in excess of that figure the sewage liquor or effluent would be in need of improvement.[66] Essentially, the exercise was conceived of as a 'working back' from the state of the ambient environment to a determination of what quality of discharge would ensure that a satisfactory state of receiving waters was achieved.

Two further aspects of the BOD test which deserve comment are, first, the relevance of the state of the watercourse before any discharge is made, and, second, the significance of the level of dilution of the effluent. Clearly, if the state of receiving waters is not to fall below an acceptable standard, account has to be taken of the pre-existing water quality of a watercourse in assessing a discharge into it. Rivers receiving successive discharges of effluent throughout their course will tend to deteriorate in quality from source to mouth. In theory at least, this meant that the maintenance of river quality at the standard specified by the Commission would require the quality of discharges to vary inversely with river quality, with stricter discharge standards being applied to poorer quality lengths of rivers. The Commission resisted this conclusion, however, because of the inequities that variable standards of effluent quality would inflict upon dischargers at different points on a river, and because of the lack of any incentive that this would offer to dischargers into clean rivers to take effective measures to treat effluent. In preference, the Commission recommended that one normal standard should be fixed which would be suitable for the majority of locations, whilst special provision might be made for higher or lower standards to meet exceptional situations where variation could be justified.[67] To some extent, therefore, location-specific problems were subsumed to the perceived greater need for national uniformity of approach. Clearly, a delicate balance was being drawn here since the implication was that particular lengths of watercourse would be allowed to fall below what had been recognised as an acceptable standard.

---

[65] See the discussion of emission limits and environmental quality objectives at 1.4.5 below.

[66] Royal Commission on Sewage Disposal (1912) para.12.

[67] *Ibid* para.15.

It was also clear that the degree of dilution of an effluent discharge would be an important factor in determining the effect of a discharge upon the quality of the receiving water. The Commission made the assumption that the great majority of effluents are diluted by more than eight times their volume of river water. On that basis, it was possible to calculate that the contamination of the effluent discharged must not be worse than that which would absorb more that 20 parts of oxygen per million under the standard conditions of the BOD test. Such effluent was, at worst, to contain a maximum of 30 parts per million of suspended solids.[68] The combination of 30 parts per million of suspended solids and 20 parts per million biochemical oxygen demand, referred to as '30:20 effluent', came to be regarded by pollution control authorities as the normal minimum requirement for satisfactory sewage effluent.[69] Again, the underlying reasoning was that emission limits should be determined by consequent environmental impacts.

Although the 'Royal Commission Standard' was never enacted into law, it was nonetheless widely applied to evaluate particular effluent discharges both by regulatory authorities and in legal proceedings. Thus discharge consent parameters for sewage treatment works and for the discharge of industrial effluent were related to the standard. In the leading criminal case of *Alphacell Ltd* v *Woodward*[70] there was no dispute that 'pollution' had occurred where the biochemical oxygen demand of effluent was found to be 160 parts per million under the standard test. With the passage of time, however, the imperfections of the standard became more evident, in that it failed to reflect the increasing range of substances that are recognised to be harmful to the aquatic environment and oversimplified the mechanisms by which effluent impacts upon the aquatic environment. Nonetheless, the basic methodology established by the Royal Commission, in distinguishing impacts and emissions and using a determination of acceptable environmental quality as a means to ascertain an emission limit, remains a fundamental element of the legal approach towards securing an acceptable quality of water, and the environment generally.

### 1.4.2  The Traditional Application of Water Quality Standards

Despite the widespread adoption of the Royal Commission Standard by discharge consenting authorities as a matter of administrative practice, a distinctive feature of the national history of water quality regulation is the reluctance of the legislature to impose statutory standards upon the quality of effluent discharges or for receiving watercourses.[71] It might be argued that early legislative attention given to water pollution,[72] by the imposition of a broadly formulated prohibition upon the introduction of certain kinds

---

[68] *Ibid* para.22.

[69] Ministry of Housing and Local Government, *Taken for Granted: Report of the Working Party on Sewage Disposal* (1970) para.39.

[70] [1972] 2 All ER 475 and see 9.6.1 below. Similarly see *Price* v *Cromack* [1975] 2 All ER 113.

[71] See Richardson, Ogus and Burrows (1982) Ch.3.

[72] See Rivers Pollution Prevention Act 1876 discussed at 2.6 below.

of polluting matter into watercourses, represented a crude kind of discharge standard. However, the relatively unqualified prohibition failed to reflect the gradations of impact involved in the manner so effectively conceptualised by the Royal Commission and, for this reason amongst others, proved to be largely ineffective.

Recognising the unworkability of absolute prohibitions, and the need for a more refined approach, numerous illustrations exist of local enactments seeking to impose more sophisticated restrictions upon discharges, in some instances by the local enactment of the Royal Commission Standard.[73] In a similar vein Parliament attempted, for a period, to delegate the power to create legislative standards for water quality to river boards under the Rivers (Prevention of Pollution) Act 1951.[74] In each case, however, the outcome was unsatisfactory and, historically at least, standards of water quality were found to operate most effectively without the force, and concomitant inflexibility, of a statutory status.

Those standards relevant to water quality which have traditionally been incorporated in legislation are of an imprecise character in that they fall far short of providing an explicit specification of the quantities of particular substances which may be discharged into a watercourse. Typically standards of this character have been imposed to require effluent discharging activities to be conducted 'so as not to become a nuisance'[75] or so as not to be 'injurious to health'[76] with no further indication as to what qualitative levels of discharge are likely to give rise to these. Alternatively, standards of an operational kind were sometimes enacted to require persons to adopt 'the best practical means within a reasonable cost',[77] or 'the best practical and reasonably available means'[78] to render polluting material harmless.[79] Again, however, the translation of these rather vague kinds of operational requirements into more precise and explicit statements of acceptable levels of emission and environmental impact was not pursued by the legislature.

Even in relation to the quality of drinking water, where it might be thought that definite physical, chemical and biological quality criteria might be most readily applied, the specification of quality standards was resisted. Until relatively recently, the only legal requirement upon drinking water quality was that it should be 'wholesome', a requirement that was not technically defined. 'Wholesomeness', at least in the days before accurate

---

[73] s.13(1) of the Middlesex County Council Act 1931; s.32(3) Wimbledon Corporation Act 1933; and s.46 Hertfordshire County Council (Colne Valley Sewerage, etc) Act 1937; and generally see Wisdom (1966) pp.32-33.

[74] s.5(1)(a), repealed by Rivers (Prevention of Pollution) Act 1961, see 2.10 below.

[75] s.24 Towns Improvement Clauses Act 1847 and ss.27 and 29 Public Health Act 1875.

[76] s.91 Public Health Act 1875.

[77] s.5 Salmon Fisheries Act 1861.

[78] ss.3-5 Rivers Pollution Prevention Act 1876.

[79] Generally, see Guruswamy and Tromans (1986).

analytical tests for water were available, was understood as 'the criterion as to whether cattle would drink from it or fish survive therein'.[80]

'Wholesomeness' is now defined with reference to European Community law, which prescribes mandatory limits for certain substances, and there are now also binding specification standards which govern the kinds of material which may come into contact with water in the supply network or specific steps that must be taken to reduce the risk of cryptosporidium outbreaks.[81] Nevertheless, some uncertainties continue in relation to the quality of water that must be supplied. As well as the offence of supplying water which is not 'wholesome', it is an offence to supply water which is 'unfit for human consumption'. The extent to which this criminalises the supply of water that is merely discoloured or has an unusual smell, but which is not injurious to public health, is a matter of ongoing dispute.[82]

To an extent, the national tradition of abstaining from statutory specification of water quality standards continues in that the principal enactment now concerned with the quality of natural watercourses, the Water Resources Act 1991, provides no explicit statement of the criteria to be applied in determining the effluent quality parameters of a discharge consent. Provision is made under the 1991 Act for establishing water classification schemes and the specification of statutory water quality objectives for particular waters such that regulatory powers are to be exercised to ensure that, so far as practicable, such objectives are met and maintained.[83] However, for reasons to be explained, the facility for precise specification of the quality of those natural waters made subject to statutory water quality objectives arises not because of any radical national legislative initiative towards the incorporation of water quality standards into legislation, but rather because of the need to give effect to European Community water directives[84] which necessitate certain water quality parameters to be incorporated into national law.

### 1.4.3 Water Quality Objectives and Standards

A meaningful discussion of 'water quality objectives' and 'water quality standards' must commence by clarifying these terms. The term 'environmental standard' is capable of being used in a narrow sense to encompass numerically stated values for contaminant parameters which are subject to legal requirements. More broadly construed, 'standard' may encompass non-mandatory standards contained in guidelines, codes of practice or criteria for making individual determinations along with standards, such as the Royal Commission Standard referred to above, which are established by scientific or industrial bodies and which carry

---

[80] Wisdom (1966) p.30.

[81] Water Supply (Water Quality) Regulations 1989 (SI 1989 No.1147) as amended, and see 17.7.2 below.

[82] s.70 Water Industry Act 1991 and see 17.7.7 below.

[83] ss.82-84 Water Resources Act 1991, and see 14.8 below.

[84] See 5.5 below on European Community water directives concerned with quality objectives.

weight because of the eminence of the body establishing them. In this broad sense, an environmental standard may be characterised as any judgement about the acceptability of environmental modification resulting from human activities which is formally stated, after appropriate consideration, intended to apply to a defined range of circumstances and because of its relationship to certain sanctions, rewards or values can be expected to exert a direct or indirect influence upon activities that affect the environment.[85]

Although a broad notion of 'environmental standards' may usefully be adopted for some purposes, a far narrower meaning is adopted in the discussion of water quality objectives and water quality standards which follows. In the terminology commonly adopted in the United Kingdom, a 'water quality objective' is a general statement as to the short or long-term aims for the use of a particular water, usually to be pursued through a management programme for that water. The realisation of a particular water quality objective is secured by the achievement of the relevant, technically and numerically expressed 'water quality standard' required to ensure that a water is of sufficient quality to meet the particular use identified as its objective. Hence, whilst water quality objectives are likely to be general statements of activities constituting intended uses, such as drinking water supply, fishery use or use for industrial abstraction purposes, water quality standards will usually comprise a technically-expressed set of physical, chemical and biological parameters which represent the minimum quality which must be satisfied for water to be acceptable for a particular use.

It must be emphasised that this terminology is not always uniformly applied and the terms 'water quality objective' (or 'environmental quality objective') and 'water quality standard' (or 'environmental quality standard') are used interchangeably in some contexts. Particularly in relation to European Community legislation, the distinction between the use to which a water is to be put and the level of water purity required for that use is not always clearly drawn and the terms 'objective' and 'standard' tend to be used synonymously.[86] This conflation of terminology has been criticised as 'inappropriate and inaccurate' and the present discussion seeks to maintain the nationally-employed distinction between 'objectives', as general descriptive statements of intended water uses, and 'standards', as numerically defined minimum values for physical, chemical and biological water quality parameters.[87]

The water quality management significance of objectives and standards is that the identification of a particular quality objective for an individual water means that, within a specified duration, the corresponding quality standard should be met. This, in turn, determines what actions will need to be taken to ensure that the standard is met by the deadline. For example, if

---

[85] Royal Commission on Environmental Pollution (1998) paras.1.15-1.16.
[86] See House of Commons Environment Committee, Pollution of Rivers and Estuaries (1987) *Department of the Environment, Evidence* note at p.4.
[87] See Environmental Protection Agency (Ireland) (1997) p.9.

a watercourse is designated as having the objective of use as potable supply, and it is not of sufficient quality to meet the relevant standard for that use, then action will be needed to ensure that the necessary improvement is secured. What action is pursued will clearly depend upon the circumstances, and reasons for the unsatisfactory quality. Typically, however, quality improvement may require stricter parameters to be imposed upon discharges made into the watercourse or the imposition of more stringent controls upon land uses which have an adverse effect upon the water. The key point is that identifying a water quality objective for a particular water has an important strategic function in determining how a range of regulatory powers are to be used in improving or maintaining water quality at a particular location.

Having distinguished water quality objectives and water quality standards, a further distinction must be introduced according to whether such objectives and standards are introduced as statutory requirements, subject to a legal duty upon the regulatory body to secure their enforcement, or as lesser kinds of water management obligation. Again, the preference in the UK has been to make use of water quality objectives and standards for strategic management purposes, but to do so without elevating them into mandatory legal requirements.

### 1.4.4 National Use of Water Quality Objectives and Standards

There are many early instances of national courts making implicit use of water quality objectives in requiring that water should be maintained in a satisfactory condition for a particular purpose such as human consumption, to support a fishery, or so as not to endanger public health. However, this informal approach of determining water quality objectives by reference to water use invariably lacked an associated, and precisely formulated, water quality standard. Having decided, for example, that water should be sufficient to support a fishery, the quality of water necessary to achieve that objective was left to the broad discretion of the judge to determine.

The national origins of the systematic association between water uses and corresponding water quality standards lie in a 1978 report of the National Water Council, *River Water Quality, The Next Stage. Review of Discharge Consent Conditions*. This Report constituted a statement of the intention of the water authorities, with ministerial approval, to embark upon a programme of specifying water quality objectives for all surface waters. The programme envisaged each water authority[88] formulating detailed statements of short- and long-term objectives for every inland water in its area, relating these objectives to categories within a defined water quality classification system and using this information as a basis for the determination of individual applications for discharge consents.

The application of water quality objectives to inland waters was brought about in accordance with a five-category system of quality classification of

---

[88] On regional water authorities see 2.14 below.

waters suggested in the National Water Council's Report.[89] This quality classification system related precisely specified quality criteria, concerning matters such as dissolved oxygen content, biochemical oxygen demand and ammonia concentration, to the current and future uses to which water may be put, such as potable supply abstraction, game or coarse fisheries or low grade industrial abstraction purposes. The water quality criteria associated with each classification were set at 95% compliance, so that only those waters falling below a specified standard for more than 5% of samples would be placed in a lower class. Broadly the classifications, subject to subsequent modifications, were identified as the following.

| | |
|---|---|
| Good Quality – 1A | Water of high quality suitable for potable supply; game or other high class fisheries; high amenity value. |
| Good Quality – 1B | Water of less high quality than Class 1A but usable for substantially the same purposes. |
| Fair Quality – 2 | Waters suitable for potable supply after advanced treatment; supporting reasonably good coarse fisheries; moderate amenity value. |
| Poor Quality – 3 | Waters which are polluted to such an extent that fish are absent or only sporadically present; may be used for low grade industrial abstraction purposes; considerable potential for further use if cleaned up. |
| Bad Quality – 4 | Waters which are grossly polluted and likely to cause a nuisance.[90] |

Whilst the relationship which had been drawn between water uses and corresponding quality parameters represented a considerable advance in water quality management, the issue remained that water quality objectives and standards were informal mechanisms for water quality management and did not have any authoritative legal status. The need for waters to reach and be maintained at a specified quality may have had implications insofar as it was supposed to influence the determination of particular discharge consents. However, because of the degree of informality involved, it was not possible to ascertain how strictly the need to realise quality standards had to be adhered to in individual discharge consent determinations.

---

[89] See National Water Council (1978) and Wood and Sheldon (1980).

[90] DoE, *Water Quality in England and Wales* 1985 (1986) para.3. For subsequent developments in water quality classification see 16.5 below on water quality monitoring.

## *1.4.5 Formalising Water Quality Objectives and Standards*

Having recounted the development and refinement of the concepts of
water quality objectives and water quality standards in national practice,
and noted the traditional resistance to the elevation of these into formal
legal requirements, the final part of the discussion must account for the
transition from objectives and standards as informal tools of water quality
management to their present status. Essentially, the explanation for the
translation of water quality objectives and standards into formal legal
requirements lies in the obligations to which the UK became committed, as
a Member State of the European Community, to implement a body of
legislation which took a quite different approach towards the protection of
the aquatic environment to that previously provided for in national law.

Whilst national law had been largely focussed upon the prohibition of
pollution, Community water directives, frequently, have taken the
approach of identifying particular substances needing to be controlled to
protect the aquatic environment and imposing specific limits upon
discharges or upon the concentration of those substances in receiving
waters. These requirements needed to be given effect in national law, but
since the UK had no legislation for this purpose it was necessary to embark
upon an extensive programme of identifying relevant discharges, and
waters, and defining precise quality parameters for these which were at
least as stringent as required by Community water directives.

Although European Community water policy and legislation are discussed
in detail later in this work,[91] as are the national implementing measures
which have been enacted to give effect to it, some brief general
observations are warranted here about the shifting of emphasis from water
pollution law to water quality law that has ensued. The Community's
successive Environment Action Programmes have had the general
objective of improving the quality of life in all the Member States.[92]
Pursuant to this, a series of directives have been adopted concerned with
the quality of water throughout the Community. These water directives
take different approaches in seeking to regulate emissions, realise
environmental quality objectives and to restrict activities which are
potentially harmful to the aquatic environment. Consequently, they
envisage or provide for emission standards, water quality standards and
activity standards in the form of restrictions upon certain activities. Whilst
the interrelationship between these different kinds of approach is not
always clear, it is evident that the respective standards determined at
Community level need to be comprehensively and precisely transposed
into national law.[93] Some examples illustrate this impact.

In relation to a number of Community water directives, the approach taken
is centred upon realising environmental quality standards for a range of
particular waters. Hence, directives have been enacted which specify the

---

[91] See Chs.4 and 5 below.

[92] See 5.2 below on environmental action programmes.

[93] See 4.12 below on the transposition of directives.

quality standards which must be met by waters which are identified as being suitable for bathing,[94] for freshwater fish and for shellfish[95] and for drinking.[96] In these examples, the detailed physical, chemical and biological parameters which are established relate to the relevant waters rather than any particular emissions which enter those waters. Although clearly it may be necessary for Member States to address individual emissions to realise water quality standards in particular situations, essentially the directives adopt an ambient water quality standard approach.

By contrast, other water directives are primarily focussed upon the standards which must be applied to emissions. Of central importance, as an example of an emission-centred directive, is the Dangerous Substances Directive.[97] In general terms, this Directive identifies 'black list' substances, the regulation of which is necessary on grounds of toxicity, persistence and bio-accumulation, and 'grey list' substances the regulation of which was desirable in the interests of diminishing or avoiding water pollution. In respect of black list substances, the Directive provides that control should be brought about by the application of uniform baseline emission standards. However, emission standards may be dispensed with where ambient water quality standards established at Community level are met. Under this 'parallel' approach, Member States may opt for their preferred system of control, but in either case the standards and objectives determined for each black list substance are intended to be set out in further 'daughter' directives. Discharges of substances in either the black or grey lists of the Directive have to be authorised by consent of the appropriate national authority, termed the 'competent authority'.

Although the detail of the parallel approach to the regulation of emissions and ambient water quality is discussed elsewhere, it should be noted here that it will soon be superseded by the application of a 'combined approach' to the regulation of emissions and water quality. Under the Water Framework Directive[98] all Member States will be required to implement measures necessary to achieve 'good status' for all surface and groundwaters within the scope of the Directive. Achievement of this objective involves, within comprehensive river basin plans, a programme of measures which encompass both the elimination of pollution by certain pollutants in accordance with emission limits and the application of water quality standards where these are provided for. Most significantly, the combined approach requires that, as between emission limits and water quality standards, the two approaches must be applied cumulatively so that, in practice, the more stringent of the two standards is always met. This is curious in that it would seem to allow for situations where receiving waters are of a satisfactory environmental quality, insofar as they

---

[94] Bathing Water Directive (76/160/EEC) and see 5.5.2 below.

[95] Freshwater Fish Waters Directive (78/659/EEC) and Shellfish Waters Directive (79/923/EEC) and see 15.3.1 below.

[96] Drinking Water Quality Directive (80/778/EEC) and see 17.7.1 below.

[97] 76/464/EEC and see 5.4.1 below.

[98] See 5.7 below on the Water Framework Directive (2000/60/EC).

meet all relevant water quality standards but, despite this, further environmental improvement is still needed if relevant emission limits are being exceeded.[99] In theory at least, emissions will need to be regulated regardless of their environmental impact.

Clearly, the formulation of a range of different kinds of water quality standard under Community water directives, and the precise statement of physical, chemical and biological parameters in relation to these, represent a fundamental departure from the national practice of avoiding statutory specification of such matters. Beyond that, a significant difference of purpose in establishing standards is discernable. For example, the 1912 Royal Commission conceived of its task as of ensuring that receiving waters were of a satisfactory quality, and regarded the control of effluent discharges as a means to that end, and subsequent national approaches tended to follow this 'working back' approach. By contrast, the recent developments at Community level seem to conceive of the meeting of harmonised maximum emission limits as an equally valid objective to pursue alongside the realisation of acceptable standards of receiving water quality.

### 1.4.6 Implementing European Community Water Quality Standards

Notwithstanding the methodological contrasts that have been seen in the Community strategy towards water protection, the legally unavoidable consequence is that water quality standards for emissions and receiving waters provided for under water directives need to be implemented as precise and transparent legal obligations within all Member States. Nationally, there was some initial hesitation in recognising this, in that, before water privatisation in 1989, it was regarded as sufficient for implementation purposes for water quality obligations to be imposed upon water authorities by means of administrative directions, issued in circulars from the Secretary of State.[100] Increasingly, however, the legal inadequacy of this approach, and the need to place implementation upon a more formal legal footing, came to be recognised.

Powers to make provision for statutory water quality objectives and standards were eventually provided for under the Water Act 1989[101] which formalised the mechanisms by empowering the Secretary of State to prescribe systems for classifying waters according to criteria set out in regulations. In accordance with such water classification systems, it was then possible to specify statutory water quality objectives in relation to particular waters and, where this was done, it became a legal duty upon the Secretary of State and the regulatory authority to use available legal powers to ensure, so far as practicable, that water quality objectives are achieved and maintained. In legal terms, this development was of momentous significance in elevating water quality objectives and

---

[99] See Howarth (1999).

[100] DoE, *The Water Environment: The Next Steps* (1987) paras.3.1 and 3.6.

[101] ss.104-106 Water Act 1989, and see now ss.82-84 Water Resources Act 1991 and 14.8 below.

standards into matters of legal obligation, since it carried the implication that failure, by the Secretary of State or the regulatory authority, to use any of the available water protection powers to ensure a water quality objective was met and maintained, where practicable, would be capable of giving rise to enforcement action.

However, the national provisions relating to water quality classification systems and the specification of statutory water quality objectives were legally formulated as *powers* of the Secretary of State rather than *duties* to act. Whilst initial aspirations were that the powers would be used for the purpose of an extensive programme of specifying statutory water quality objectives for almost all natural waters, including groundwater, and that these objectives would need to be secured with specified durations, this has not transpired.[102] Likewise, suggestions that statutory water quality objectives might incorporate general requirements relating to matters such as aesthetic amenity and general and special ecosystems have not been pursued.[103] Where statutory objectives have been established this has been purely for the purpose of implementing Community obligations and the aspiration that the mechanism would be used to give effect to objectives formulated for national purposes has not been met. This may be accounted for by the perceived costs of realising statutory objectives, which would have to be transmitted to dischargers who would be required to secure improvements in effluent quality to ensure relevant standards were met. Alternatively, a nationally motivated programme of statutory water quality objectives may be seen as potentially inflexible, as opposed to the option of formulating similar levels of quality requirement within informal mechanisms such as Local Environment Agency Plans.[104] Whatever the reason, the prospect of comprehensive designation of statutory water quality objectives seems, at the time of writing, a remote prospect.

On the other hand, the implementation of statutory requirements for water quality in relation to discharges and receiving waters has brought about a significant change in approach. Implementing regulations have been enacted in respect of a range of waters falling within Community water directives, though in many respects initial designations have not been as extensive as has been found to be necessary for comprehensive implementation of certain directives.[105] Hence, the theoretical need for precise and complete transposition of directives by specified deadlines has, in practice, become a process of 'progressive' implementation as the imperfections of initial attempts at implementation have become apparent.[106] Nonetheless, the quality of the waters that have been designated now possesses an important status in both national and European Community Law, whereas, by contrast, activities giving rise to

---

[102] See Royal Commission on Environmental Pollution (1992) paras.4.41-4.49.

[103] National Rivers Authority, *Proposals for Statutory Water Quality Objectives* (1991).

[104] See 14.9 below on Local Environment Agency Plans.

[105] See discussion of implementation of the Bathing Water Directive (76/160/EEC) at 5.5.2 below for example.

[106] See 2.2.2 below on progressive transposition.

criminal offences concerning pollution of water are generally provided for under national law alone.

## 1.5 Competing Objectives in Aquatic Protection

The achievements of the European Community have been creditable in transforming rather vaguely expressed national concerns about 'pollution' into precisely formulated parameters for the quality of water required for a range of uses. Beyond this, the requirement that parameters should be provided for as formal legal requirements represents a major departure from the national approach in elevating the realisation of satisfactory water quality into a matter of legally enforceable rights and duties, rather than the lesser kinds of obligation that may previously have existed. Nonetheless, the overall task of protecting water quality raises a range of competing and conflicting interests in water use, between which preferences must be selected.[107] The use of a watercourse, for example, for the discharge of effluent from a sewage treatment works is likely to be in conflict with the use of the water for downstream water supply abstraction or for water recreation which may involve immersion. As has been commented,

> [r]esolving such conflicts is an essential part of the process of controlling water pollution and, more generally, of managing water resources. It is an area where competing interest groups may take different views and where value judgments may have to be applied. A framework for making such judgments must incorporate three elements: rational criteria, public involvement and proper accountability.[108]

In relation to these criteria, it has been suggested that establishing a system of water quality objectives enables some competing demands to be evaluated. The setting of such objectives will normally involve a statutory process involving public consultation, and the existence of a specialised environmental regulatory body with responsibility for the aquatic environment, provides a greater degree of accountability than existed previously.[109]

Despite this optimism, it is not apparent that the formulation of explicit quality standards relating to the various uses, in itself, necessarily resolves the potential for conflict between the wide range of potential water uses. In relation to a particular water, a non-exhaustive list of potential uses which might encompass any of, or any combination of, the following:[110]

(a) to serve as a source of drinking water supply;
(b) to serve as a source of irrigation for agriculture;

---

[107] Generally, see Parker and Penning-Rowsell (1980).
[108] Royal Commission on Environmental Pollution (1992) para.1.26.
[109] *Ibid.*
[110] Werritty (1997).

(c) to serve as an industrial resource for cooling and other processes;

(d) to receive, disperse and assimilate effluents from industry and sewage treatment;

(e) to serve as a source of hydro-electrical power generation;

(f) to support recreational and commercial fisheries, and shellfisheries;

(g) to facilitate recreational and commercial navigation;

(h) to facilitate bathing and a range of water-related recreational activities;

(i) to support aquatic, and riparian, ecosystems; and

(j) to enhance aesthetic value of the landscape.[111]

From amongst this list of broadly-formulated categories of consumptive and non-consumptive water uses it is possible to identify purposes grounded in concerns relating to public health, industrial productivity, recreation and ecological protection, and it is not apparent that any hierarchy exists between these purposes. The difficulty is that allowing water to be used for one purpose may effectively preclude its use for others and, therefore, an evaluative choice must be made between competing water uses in situations of incompatibility. It is far from clear on what basis such choices should be made.

Whilst water quality objectives and standards serve to identify the quality criteria which are needed for each particular use, they do not necessarily resolve the issue as to which set of water quality criteria are to be applied to any particular body of water. There may not be a great deal of national discretion allowed in this matter where a Member State is obliged to designate or identify a particular water as coming within the scope of a water directive,[112] since the directive may largely determine the waters to which it applies. In such situations, conflicts between competing water uses are implicitly resolved by the operation of Community law. For example, the identification of waters as falling within the Bathing Water Directive[113] carries the implication that activities which may cause a deterioration of the water quality below those standards provided for in relation to bathing will not be an acceptable water use in the vicinity of a bathing water. Outside those waters governed by Community directives, however, the problem of allocating water quality objectives and standards remains, and the need to make such allocations involves essentially the same need to exercise preference between competing, and potentially inconsistent, water uses that has been alluded to, with the same opaqueness as to how such decisions are to be made.

An important recent discussion of the issues which arise in relation to the establishment and application of environmental standards generally is provided in the Twenty-first Report of the Royal Commission on Environmental Pollution.[114] In the view of the Commission, more

---

[111] See Tunstall, Fordham, Green and House (1997); Swanwick (1997); and Spray (1997).

[112] Generally see 1.7.5 below on area designation under EC directives.

[113] See 5.5.2 below on the Bathing Water Directive (76/160/EEC).

[114] Royal Commission on Environmental Pollution (1998).

transparent ways need to be developed for articulating the values of ordinary people and incorporating these into the, hitherto, rather technocratic process of establishing environmental standards. That is, although scientific understanding of an environmental problem under consideration should serve as a starting point, a distinction should be drawn between the scientific evidence and the ethical and social issues which fall outside the scientific arena. Where standards incorporate elements relating to risk and uncertainty, again, it is necessary that the methodology used to assess these is transparent to those without a specialist knowledge. Also, economic appraisal of environmental policies and standards should be undertaken insofar as this is possible and, where it is not, consequences which cannot be expressed in money terms should be otherwise indicated. Perhaps most prominent in the Commission's report, however, is the emphasis which is placed upon public participation in the formulation and application of standards. In relation to this, the past tendency to neglect public attitudes to environmental concerns is criticised and the need for better mechanisms for these to be taken into account, alongside technical and scientific considerations, is recommended. Whilst these views were expressed in relation to environmental standards generally, they have clear implications in relation to those standards applicable to water quality and the resolution of competing objectives in aquatic protection.[115]

## 1.6 Problematic Activities

Although achieving satisfactory water quality now stands alongside the avoidance of pollution as a central aim of water protection law, the fact remains that specifying of water quality objectives and standards represents the goal to be achieved rather than the mechanism by which that goal is to be achieved. A large part of the remainder of this work is concerned with a variety of legal mechanisms which are directed towards the realisation of water quality standards by the use of different kinds of legal control being applied to a range of activities which are potentially harmful to the aquatic environment. However, the appropriateness of these mechanisms must depend upon the nature of the activities that are to be regulated, and different control mechanisms are appropriate in relation to different kinds of activity and different kinds of water quality problem. In respect of this, it is useful to identify the main kinds of activity adversely impacting upon the aquatic environment and to offer brief observations on the way in which the water pollution and water quality problems to which they give rise are addressed.

Given the previous discussion about the contrasts between pollution, contamination and water quality, it is apparent that there are difficulties in identifying those activities which are most problematic. Whilst reasonably

---

[115] For an example of the practical application of suggestions from the Royal Commission Report, see the discussion of strategic licence applications in 20.10.12 below.

objective records are available of substantiated pollution incidents,[116] it must be stressed that these represent the 'tip of the iceberg' in relation to water quality concerns. Many serious water quality concerns do not feature in the statistics of pollution incidents, and it is, therefore, necessary to be speculative in relation to some activities which are known to be problematic but where it is not possible accurately to assess the extent of the contribution that is made to water contamination.

### 1.6.1 Treating Sewage Effluent

The wastewater originating from domestic and industrial premises which is discharged into sewers, normally to be processed at sewage treatment works operated by sewerage undertakers, and discharged into watercourses and coastal waters is properly referred to as 'sewage effluent'.[117] Clearly, the harmfulness of this effluent to the quality of the waters into which it is discharged is largely dependent upon the premises and activity from which it originates. In the case of industrial premises certain chemical effluents are likely to be so toxic to the aquatic environment that specialised treatment is necessary. For that reason a special authorisation procedure will be needed for the transmission to sewage treatment works of trade effluent containing certain prescribed substances or substances from a prescribed process.[118]

Sewage of domestic origin also produces an effluent which, if not properly treated, may have a dramatic biological effect on water quality. The essential character of inadequately treated domestic sewage is that of a primarily organic contaminant which is subject to a process of bacteriological decay, the progress of which requires large quantities of oxygen which are extracted from the water into which the effluent is discharged. In serious cases, the effect of this removal of oxygen is to asphyxiate fish and other aquatic creatures living in the watercourse and in the longer term to cause the water to become anaerobic. Hence, a key objective in treating this kind of effluent is to encourage the process of bacteriological decay, involving the highest oxygen demand, to take place *before* the effluent from the treatment works is discharged into the aquatic environment.

Watercourses have a natural, though limited, capacity to assimilate amounts of organic contamination such as sewage effluent without extensive or long-term damage. Although dissolved oxygen is removed by a contaminant in the process of bacteriological decay, it is replaced by oxygen from the air and by the photosynthetic activity of algae and other plants, and, in manageable quantities, the end-products of decay contribute

[116] Environment Agency, *Water Pollution Incidents in England and Wales 1998* (1999) and see 9.2 below for a discussion of statistics on water pollution incidents.

[117] Hence, 'sewage effluent' is statutorily defined to include any effluent from the sewage disposal or sewerage works of a sewerage undertaker but does not include surface water (s.221(1) Water Resources Act 1991).

[118] See Trade Effluents (Prescribed Processes and Substances) Regulations (SI 1989 No.1156) as amended, discussed in 11.10 below.

nutrients to the ecosystem.[119] Nonetheless the purification capacity of receiving waters is subject to inevitable limitations, especially where the water is slow moving or aeration low, and the tendency of sewage dischargers has been to exceed the receiving capacity of watercourses into which effluent is discharged. Since the commencement of mains drainage in the last century, sewage pollution has been amongst the most frequent sources of water pollution incidents and this trend continues to the present.[120]

The primary responsibility for treatment of sewage effluent lies with sewerage undertakers who are under a general duty to provide public sewers, to ensure that sewers are effectually drained and to deal with the contents of sewers by means of sewage disposal woks or otherwise.[121] The usual process of treatment adopted by undertakers involves *primary treatment* in the form of detritus removal and an initial screening of effluent through grids to remove solid objects. This is followed by a process of passing effluent through settlement tanks, at a controlled rate of flow, to remove solid matter, termed 'sludge', from liquid effluent. In *secondary treatment* processes the effluent is then subjected to biological purification to secure the decomposition of remaining organic matter present by oxidation and remove harmful organisms. Traditionally, this is undertaken by a 'trickling filter' allowing settled sewage sediment to pass over stones on which a film of micro-organisms grow. *Tertiary treatment* involves any further treatment process designed to achieve higher standards than can be achieved by the combination of the first two processes. This may encompass 'passive' methods of treatment such as the passage of effluent through reed beds or lagoons, or active systems such as sand filters, microstrainers or ultra-violet irradiation. Nutrient removal is likely to be required if the effluent is intended to be used for a purpose necessitating a high quality of effluent, as where the receiving water is a source of potable water supply.[122]

A major difficulty in relation to the treatment of effluent at treatment works is the variability in the quality of incoming effluent and the relatively unpredictability of when effluent of a problematic character will be received. Perhaps because of this, discharge consents for sewage treatment works, historically, required compliance in relation to only 95% of samples. By contrast, consents for industrial discharges are usually absolute in the sense that their parameters must be complied with at all times. The problem with the percentile specification was that effluent of extremely poor quality could lawfully be discharged for 5% of any one-year period, resulting in serious environmental damage, providing that the parameters were met for the remaining 95% of the time. Amongst other

---

[119] See Royal Commission on Environmental Pollution (1985) para.7.49.

[120] *ENDS Report* 295 (1999) p.49 and see 9.2 below on water pollution incident statistics.

[121] s.94(1) Water Industry Act 1991, see Part IV of this Act on sewerage services generally and see Ch.11 below.

[122] Generally, see Wood and Sheldon (1980); Rhoades (1997); Royal Commission on Environmental Pollution (1992) p.89; Mason (1996) Ch.3; and House of Commons, Environment, Transport and Regional Affairs Committee, *Sewage Treatment and Disposal* (1998) paras.48-63.

matters concerning discharge consents for treatment works, this matter was addressed in the *Kinnersley Report* which recommended that such consents should contain absolute limits to protect receiving waters against extremely poor effluent quality.[123] In response to the report, the National Rivers Authority accepted that both absolute and percentile limits should be set on all relevant consents, such that at all times the effluent quality must stay below the absolute limit and must be maintained within the lower limit for 95% of samples.[124] It was hoped that the introduction of absolute parameters in discharge consents for sewage treatment works would address the worst excesses of inadequate performance by treatment works.[125]

Particular problems remain in relation to combined sewer overflows which receive both sewage effluent and surface water and are designed to over-spill in times of heavy rain when the capacity of sewers are exceeded. Where separate systems of sewerage for effluent and surface water runoff are not provided, intermittent overflowing discharges are capable of being of poor quality and having a significant adverse effect upon watercourses into which they discharge without treatment. The lack of screening of combined sewer overflows means that significant amounts of non-biodegradable litter and offensive detritus bypass the normal treatment process and are often deposited on the banks of watercourses and bathing areas.[126] The solution to this problem lies in either a separate systems of sewers, for effluent and surface water runoff, or in constructing holding tanks of sufficient capacity to take the highly contaminated 'first flush' of water following heavy rainfall, but the cost of these measures is considerable and as a consequence the problem of combined sewer overflows remains significant. For the present, combined sewer overflows remain a serious problem with some 7,000 such overflows being regarded as unsatisfactory by the Environment Agency.[127]

Despite the improvements over the last decade, it is evident that sewage treatment remains amongst the most problematic activities in relation to the state of the aquatic environment both in relation to numbers of recorded pollution incidents and in relation to the more general adverse effect upon water quality.[128] Whilst nutrient enrichment, or eutrophication, may not have been traditionally conceived of as a water '*pollution*'

---

[123] National Rivers Authority, *Discharge Consents and Compliance Policy: A Blueprint for the Future* (1990) Recommendations 8 and 9.
[124] National Rivers Authority, *Discharge Consents and Compliance Policy: A Blueprint for the Future – The NRA's Response to the Public Consultation* (1991).
[125] Royal Commission on Environmental Pollution (1992) para.7.40.
[126] See the discussion of *R v Carrick District Council ex parte Shelly and Another* [1996] Env LR 273 at 8.5.7 below.
[127] Royal Commission on Environmental Pollution (1992) para.7.43-7.55, House of Commons, Environment, Transport and Regional Affairs Committee, *Sewage Treatment and Disposal* (1998) paras.32-44. Notably also combined sewer overflows constitute on of the major heads of expenditure in the recent water industry price review, see 7.8.3 below on this.
[128] See the discussion of *Cook v South West Water PLC*, unreported, Exeter County Court 15 April 1992, noted [1992] *Water Law* 103, at 3.18.5 below.

problem, it needs increasingly to be addressed by sewerage undertakers as a water *quality* concern.

Another emerging cause for water quality concern relating to the sewage treatment process concerns the presence of a range of endocrine disrupting substances in sewage, such as oestogens, steroids, dioxins, phthalates and alkyl phenol exylates. There is growing evidence of the gender-transforming effect of endocrine disrupters on fish, and considerable public anxiety that these substances might also impact upon human health. A strong link has also been suggested between the presence of the substances in watercourses and sewage effluent discharges, though it is recognised that further research is needed to find out precisely which substances are implicated and the mechanism by which they cause hormone disruption.[129]

### 1.6.2 Industrial Activities

Industrial effluent is as diverse in character as the industrial enterprises that produce it and includes a wide range of physical, chemical and biological contaminants.[130] This kind of effluent may be either discharged directly into a watercourse by the producer, usually subject to a discharge consent, or discharged through a sewer, under a trade effluent consent, to a sewage treatment works before being discharged as treated effluent by the sewerage undertaker.[131] Direct discharges of industrial effluent into watercourses have been particularly problematic in the past, with traditional problem industries including coal gas production, chemical industries and paper making, each of which produced large quantities of highly noxious liquids.[132] Modern industries produce a wide range of acids, alkalis, organic chemicals and toxic metals, along with oil, radioactive and thermal pollution, each of which has its own distinctive effect upon the aquatic environment and the suitability of the receiving water for subsequent use. Moreover, the range of potential water contaminants is far from being fixed, with new substances being produced and used in industrial processes at a remarkable rate, often with little knowledge as to the adverse effects that these substances may have upon the aquatic environment. The introduction of such substances into the aquatic environment raises particular problems, especially where they feature as part of a complex discharge of chemicals, since the

---

[129] House of Commons, Environment, Transport and Regional Affairs Committee, *Sewage Treatment and Disposal* (1998) paras.79 to 81. See also European Community Strategy for Endocrine Disrupters (Com (99) 706) see *ENDS Report* 306 (2000) p.42. See also the discussion of the precautionary principle at 4.7.1 below.

[130] General reading on industrial effluent treatment includes: Klein (1957) Ch.4; Klein (1962) Ch.4; Royal Commission on Environmental Pollution (1971) paras.45, 46 and 58; House of Commons Environment Committee, *Pollution of Rivers and Estuaries* (1987) Ch.7; Royal Commission on Environmental Pollution (1992) paras.7.9-7.21; and Rhoades (1997).

[131] See the discussion of trade effluent consents at Ch.11 below.

[132] See Royal Commission on Salmon Fisheries (England and Wales) (1861) p.xxi and see Ch.3 below on the civil law for a range of illustrations of civil proceedings being used in relation to water contamination arising from many of these industries.

environmental impacts of such discharges are extremely difficult to monitor particularly where the composition of the discharge is of variable quality and the synergistic effects between component substances unknown.[133]

As indicated by the pollution incident figures, industrial incidents represent the largest category of major incidents.[134] The manufacture, storage and distribution of the most polluting substances which are involved in many industrial activities provides the greatest potential for the most disastrous kinds of incident. A dramatic example of this was the Sandoz fire, which occurred in November 1986 at a chemical warehouse at Basel in Switzerland, and caused 30 tonnes of agricultural chemicals, including insecticides, along with 150kg of mercury, to pass into the Rhine causing gross contamination of a considerable length of the river. The event gave rise to international concerns about the need to regulate industrial installations to prevent water pollution and was influential in the initiation of a range of preventative approaches to pollution control which have been adopted in the United Kingdom.[135]

Although environmental catastrophes of the scale of the Sandoz fire are fortunately uncommon, the water quality concerns associated with industrial activities are not confined to isolated pollution incidents. Routine discharges of industrial effluent to controlled waters are recognised to be capable of causing significant harm to the aquatic environment and need to be closely regulated. Presently there are about 6,000 significant discharges of industrial effluent authorised to be discharged into watercourses and other natural waters under discharge consents.[136] The parameters in each discharge consent seek to reflect the nature of the industrial activity taking place, the substances which are likely to be produced in effluent and any especially harmful constituents present in it which need to be the subject of explicit control.[137]

Where discharges of industrial effluent are made to sewer they will need to be subject to a trade effluent consent granted by a sewerage undertaker subject to conditions regulating the quality and quantity of discharge allowed to be made.[138] Whilst for most industrial effluent the terms of the trade effluent consent will be agreed between the industrial discharger and the sewerage undertaker,[139] in respect of 'special category effluent'[140] authorisation must be approved by the Environment Agency.[141]

---

[133] See the discussion of direct toxicity assessment at 1.3.8 above.

[134] See statistical information on pollution incidents at 9.2 below.

[135] See Department of the Environment (1986) para.5.7, and see Ch.13 below on preventative approaches to water pollution control.

[136] Environment Agency, *Discharge Consents: Monitoring and Compliance* (1997).

[137] See the discussion of discharge consents and undisclosed pollutants at 10.6.5 below.

[138] See Ch.11 below on discharges to sewers generally.

[139] Under ss.119 and 120 Water Industry Act 1991 and see 11.4 below.

[140] See 11.10 below on 'special category effluent'.

[141] s.120 para.105 Sch.22 Environment Act 1995.

### 1.6.3  The Worcester Drinking Water Incident

The legal relationship between the industrial discharger to sewer, the sewerage undertaker, and the Environment Agency which regulates the eventual discharge from the sewage treatment works is intricately provided for in legislation.[142] The relationship between trade effluent discharges to sewer and sewage effluent discharges to controlled waters, and the subsequent use of such waters, is well illustrated by the circumstances of the *Worcester Drinking Water Incident*[143] where extensive chemical contamination of the River Severn at Worcester was traced, by sense of smell, to a discharge from a sewage treatment works at Wem, in Shropshire. The effect of this contamination was that drinking water supplies at Worcester, 80 miles downstream, had become contaminated and drinking water treatment plants abstracting the river water for supply purposes had to be closed down. The ultimate source of the incident was traced to a discharge of trade effluent to sewer made from a waste recovery operation on an industrial estate at Wem. The circumstances of the incident required three distinct legal issues to be considered: first was the legality of the initial discharge to sewer; second the legality of the discharge made from the Wem sewage treatment works; and third, the legality of the supply of the contaminated drinking water to consumers in Worcester.

In respect of the first issue, the discharge of trade effluent to sewer took place from the premises of a waste management firm which operated under a waste disposal licence, granted by the waste regulatory authority.[144] However, there was some uncertainty as to whether the firm was in possession of a trade effluent consent and, if so, whether this authorised the discharge that had been made. This was because it was alleged that, at the time of the incident, there was no record of the consent on the register of trade effluent consents which the sewerage undertaker was obliged to maintain.[145] On the other hand, it was reported that the discharger had been granted the necessary authorisation for the discharge by the undertaker. Perhaps because of the uncertainty concerning the trade effluent consent, and the conditions to which it was subject, proceedings by the sewerage undertaker against the firm[146] were discontinued.

In respect of the second legal issue, the lawfulness of the discharge from the Wem sewerage treatment works, the matter was investigated by the National Rivers Authority, but it was concluded that it would not be possible to bring proceedings against the sewerage undertakers. The reason for this was that the wording of the sewage treatment works' discharge consent did not make reference to the discharge of substances not

---

[142] Under s.118 Water Industry Act 1991, and see 11.11.1 below and s.87(2) Water Resources Act 1991, and see 9.14 below.

[143] The discussion of this incident is based upon information provided in Ives, Hammerton and Packham (1994); *ENDS Report* 235 (1994) p.18; *ENDS Report* 240 (1995) p.9; and *ENDS Report* 243 (1995) p.45.

[144] Under Part II Environmental Protection Act 1990.

[145] Under s.196 Water Industry Act 1991, and see 11.4 below on this.

[146] Under s.118(5) Water Industry Act 1991, and see 11.11.1 below on this.

explicitly identified in the consent and it was ambiguous as to whether or not the consent authorised the discharge of the contaminating substance.[147] Had the offending substance been explicitly covered by the consent, there may still have been legal difficulties in bringing a prosecution because of the special defence provided to sewerage undertakers where a contravention of a discharge consent is attributable to a discharge which another person made to a sewer which the undertaker was not bound to receive and could not reasonably have been expected to prevent.[148] That is, even if the discharge consent for the sewage treatment works had explicitly prohibited the discharge of the contaminant, the undertaker might have been able to show that the discharge to sewer had been unlawful and it had done everything reasonable to prevent it and was, therefore, entitled to the benefit of the defence.

In respect of the final issue, the eventual contamination of the Worcester drinking water supply, the water supply undertaker was convicted of supplying water which was unfit for human consumption,[149] fined £45,000 and ordered to pay costs. The water undertaker also agreed to pay compensation to water consumers in the supply zone concerned,[150] who claimed that they had suffered vomiting and diarrhoea as a result of consuming the water, at £25 per household for 35,000 households in the supply zone, totalling £875,000.

The final legal outcome of the *Worcester Drinking Water Incident* is, therefore, remarkable, in that the industrial discharger making the original offending discharge to sewer and the sewerage undertaker which failed to prevent the subsequent discharge to controlled waters both escaped prosecution. However, the water supplier, who was remotely placed from the original sewer discharge, was convicted of a water supply offence. Clearly, this outcome raises concerns as to the need for both trade effluent consents and discharge consents to be carefully formulated and to encompass sufficiently stringent parameters to prevent extraordinary discharges containing substances which were not envisaged at the time when the consents were granted. It also demonstrates the need for close co-ordination between trade effluent controls and sewage effluent discharges to avoid an undertaker being put in a position where it is unable to treat industrial effluent to the standard required by a sewage treatment works' discharge consent. More generally, the incident demonstrates the interrelationship between the different systems of control to which industrial discharges may be subject.

### 1.6.4 Agricultural Activities

The intensification of agricultural production methods over recent years has brought major water pollution and water quality problems for rivers in

---

[147] See 10.6.5 below on the problem of undisclosed pollutants and discharge consents.

[148] s.87(2) Water Resources Act 1991, and see 9.14 below on this defence.

[149] s.70 Water Industry Act 1991, and see 17.7.7 below on this offence.

[150] See 7.6.6 below on the Guaranteed Standards Scheme.

rural areas that have previously been spared from the worst impacts of industrial water pollution.[151] Under traditional farming methods, the relatively small numbers of animals which could be kept on an area of land meant that the capacity of that land to assimilate the resulting waste was environmentally unproblematic. However, with the increased stocking densities which characterise modern agricultural practice, the capacity of the land to assimilate waste without environmental harm has been exceeded. Hence, methods of animal husbandry, involving the keeping of stock indoors to a greater extent than in traditional agricultural practice, have greatly increased the need for containment of animal slurry and the scope for water pollution incidents where it is not properly contained.

A large proportion of agricultural water pollution incidents occur because slurry containment tanks are improperly constructed, or maintained, and permit effluent to escape into watercourses.[152] The deoxygenating effect of slurry is considerable, and it may be as much as 100 times as polluting as untreated domestic sewage. A related problem stemming from agricultural intensification is the developing trend of farmers to produce a greater amount of silage rather than hay for animal fodder, partially because of its higher nutritional value, and partially because of the greater need for food for those animals over-wintering indoors. Silage production is also capable of producing a highly deoxygenating liquid effluent, which is capable of being as much as 200 times as polluting as untreated domestic sewage.[153] Other water quality problems of agricultural origin arise because of the use of a wide range of chemicals used in modern farming, as fertilisers, pesticides and veterinary medicines, which are capable of being transmitted into water either in diffuse form or as a result of spillages resulting in pollution incidents. Although not unique to agriculture,[154] another problem which has frequently arisen in agricultural contexts is the contamination of water due to inadequate storage of oil where this is for use on today's highly-mechanised farms.[155]

Whilst water pollution incidents from agricultural activities have been recognised to be problematic for some years, increasing attention has also been directed to the problems of diffuse contamination of water by manure application and a range of substances used in modern farming. The potential dangers arising from the application of nitrogen and phosphorous chemical fertilisers, and similarly the use of pesticides and veterinary medicines in agriculture, have been recognised for some time.[156] The

---

[151] General reading on agricultural pollution of water includes Royal Commission on Environmental Pollution (1971) paras.47-52; Royal Commission on Environmental Pollution (1974) paras.86-91; Royal Commission on Environmental Pollution (1979); and Royal Commission on Environmental Pollution (1992) paras.7.86-7.158. For further general reading see 13.5 below.

[152] See 9.2 below for statistics relating to agricultural water pollution incidents.

[153] House of Commons Environment Committee, *Pollution of Rivers and Estuaries* (1987) para.65.

[154] See 13.3.2 below on proposed oil storage regulations for non-agricultural premises.

[155] See Control of Pollution (Silage, Slurry and Agricultural Fuel Oil) Regulations 1991 (SI 1991 No.324, as amended) and see 13.3.1 below for a discussion of these Regulations.

[156] Organisation for Economic Co-Operation and Development (1986).

eventual seepage of these chemicals into watercourses, with rainwater run off or percolation through soil, has been identified as having a major impact upon water quality, and the presence of nitrate, in particular, has been a special cause of environmental and public health concern.[157] Nitrate is especially problematic in relation to waters that are to be used for drinking water supply purposes, and particularly groundwater, because of public health implications of excessive nitrate concentrations. Both nitrate and phosphate, as nutrients, are directly implicated in problem of eutrophication of natural waters, referred to previously. Pesticides are also a matter of concern both in relation to the natural environment and in respect of waters to be used for drinking water supply purposes.[158]

The control of diffuse contaminants originating from agriculture clearly needs a different legal approach from that applied in relation to agricultural pollution incidents. The presence of an excessive concentration of nitrate in a drinking water supply does not relate to any particular entry of nitrate at any particular time or from any particular farm. The effect upon water quality is usually the result of fertiliser being applied over a wide area, perhaps over many years, and gradually accumulating in surface water or groundwater.[159] For this reason, the approach to the problem that has been adopted in both national and European Community law is to seek to control agricultural land use by limiting applications of nitrate in the catchment areas of waters that are particularly susceptible to contamination.[160]

Similarly, the control of diffuse contamination from pesticides used in agriculture, and the impact of these upon the aquatic environment and drinking water supplies,[161] raises distinct issues which need to be specially addressed. One aspect of this is the need to prevent agricultural pesticides from entering groundwater and to ensure that practices such as the disposal of waste sheep dip, containing particularly harmful organophosphorus compounds, should not be disposed of to land without strict control.[162] Another aspect of pesticide control is the need to eliminate particularly hazardous chemicals from the environment completely, for example through product controls.[163]

---

[157] See Royal Commission on Environmental Pollution (1979) Chs.III and IV; and DoE, *Nitrate in Water* (1986).

[158] Generally, see Ch.17 on drinking water quality.

[159] Although in some instances nitrate may contaminate water from activities other than farming: see Case C-293/97 *R* v *Secretary of State for the Environment and the Ministry of Agriculture, Fisheries and Food, ex parte Standley and Others and Metson and Others and National Farmers Union (Intervener)*, European Court of Justice [1999] Env LR 801, discussed at 13.5.6 below.

[160] Provided for under ss.94 and 95 Water Resources Act 1991, and see 13.5.1 below on nitrate sensitive areas, and the Nitrates Directive (91/676/EEC) and see 13.5.5 below on nitrate vulnerable zones.

[161] See, for example, Case C-340/96 *Commission* v *United Kingdom* [1999] ECR I-2023, relating to the implementation of the Drinking Water Quality Directive (80/778/EEC) and see 4.15 below on this.

[162] Directive 80/68/EEC and see 13.6 below on groundwater controls.

[163] Council Directive concerning the placing of plant protection products on the market (91/414/EEC) and see 1.7.4 below on product controls. See also Part III Food and Environmental

More generally, it has been suggested that further measures to address the control of water contamination by fertilisers and pesticides could take the form of levies, which might reduce total usage and ensure that more care was taken to avoid wasteful or excessive application. [164] A proposal to impose a tax or charge scheme upon pesticides has recently been considered which would have sought reductions in pesticide use by providing incentives for substitution of less environmentally harmful substances or techniques.[165] However, it is understood that the Government does not intend to proceed with the introduction of a pesticide tax, but to rely upon voluntary mechanisms for pesticide reduction.[166]

### 1.6.5  Road Transport

Another activity which features prominently amongst the statistics relating to serious water pollution incidents is road transport[167] where, again, the nature of the activity must determine the legal response which is required. In fact, the general heading of 'road transport' encompasses quite a wide range of water quality concerns, ranging from road construction operations, frequently involving the transmission of suspended solids into nearby watercourses; maintenance activities, such as the application of de-icing chemicals and herbicides; spillages resulting from road traffic accidents, particularly where container-vehicles are involved; the routine runoff of oil, fuel, heavy metals (such as lead) and other debris from general road use; and the eventual impact on the aquatic environment of nitrogen oxides and other gaseous vehicle emissions.[168] Clearly this range of environmental problems requires a range of different kinds of legal response.

At the most extreme end of the scale, pollution incidents arising in relation to transport typically occur following the spillage of chemicals as a result of traffic accidents. This situation is partially addressed by general requirements for roadworthiness of vehicles under road traffic legislation,[169] whilst more specific requirements relating to road transport of hazardous substances are provided under health and safety legislation.[170] In relation to the latter, regulations have been enacted which impose duties upon operators, consignors and drivers of vehicles used to

---

Protection Act 1985 and Control of Pesticides Regulations 1986 (SI 1986 No.1510, as amended by SI 1997 No.188). Similarly, see the Medicines Act 1968 which provides for a system of product licensing in relation to veterinary medicines.

[164] Royal Commission on Environmental Pollution (1992) para.7.88.

[165] DETR, WO, DoE(NI) and SO, *Economic Instruments for Water Pollution* (1997) Ch.5 and DETR, *Design of a Tax or Charge Scheme for Pesticides* (1999).

[166] The Government now intends to consult on proposals from the British Agrochemicals Association on an alternative package of voluntary measures, see *ENDS Report* 302 (2000) p.26.

[167] See statistical information on transport-related water pollution incidents at 9.2 below.

[168] Royal Commission on Environmental Pollution (1992) paras.7.76 to 7.85 and Construction Industry Research and Information Association (1994).

[169] Road Traffic Act 1988.

[170] ss.15 and 82(3) Health and Safety at Work etc Act 1974.

carry dangerous substances to ensure that the vehicles are suitable for the purpose, regularly tested and labelled properly and also to impose other safety precautions against fire and explosion. [171] Subject to a due diligence defence, it will be a criminal offence to infringe these requirements.[172]

Despite the important controls imposed upon vehicles which give rise to exceptional pollution hazards, the reality is that most traffic accidents arise from human error and, in the aftermath of an incident of this kind, a key practical environmental task is preventing spillages of hazardous substances from entering watercourses and causing harm. [173]

By contrast with the need to deal with spillages from traffic accidents after the event, some scope exists for a preventive approach. This involves the use of highway drainage systems capable of containing spillages of harmful substances, particularly petrol and oil, and preventing transmission to surface water or groundwater. However, the use of such interceptive drainage systems will normally need to be provided for at the time that a road is constructed and, therefore, needs to be required as a part of the planning permission or other authorisation allowing the road to be constructed.[174] In relation to the imposition of such requirements, the role of the Environment Agency will be important in identifying areas where the threat to surface waters and groundwater is particularly serious because of local hydrological or geological conditions, or because the groundwater is particularly vulnerable as a source of water supply.[175]

Whilst road transport certainly gives rise to the kind of dramatic polluting event envisaged by the foregoing discussion, it is increasingly recognised that the routine surface water run off from roads is often of poor quality and likely to have significant impacts upon the quality of receiving waters.[176] In the past, it tended to be assumed that surface water run off was uncontaminated, or at least unharmful to the aquatic environment, and for that reason many highway drains transmit surface run off directly into surface waters or ground waters without treatment. In theory, the Environment Agency has legal powers to address problematic discharges from highway drains,[177] but in practice the power is only likely to be used where a particular problem is highlighted, not as a general means of regulating the quality of surface water run off from extensive lengths of road.

---

[171] Carriage of Dangerous Goods by Road Regulations 1996 (SI 1996 No.2095).

[172] s.33 Health and Safety at Work etc Act 1974, and see also s.47 which states that a breach of relevant regulations may give rise to civil liability.

[173] Environment Agency and Local Government Association, *Protocol between the Local Government Association and the Environment Agency on Fire Services Issues* (1999).

[174] Generally, see Ch.14 below on town and country planning and water quality. In relation to major road construction projects the Town and Country Planning (Environmental Impact Assessment) (England and Wales) Regulations 1999 (SI 1999 No.293) or the Highways (Assessment of Environmental Effects) Regulations 1999 (SI 1999 No.369) may be applicable.

[175] See Environment Agency, *Policy and Practice for the Protection of Groundwater* (1998).

[176] Construction Industry Research and Information Association (1994) Ch.2.

[177] s.86 Water Resources Act 1991, and see 9.11 below on prohibition notices.

Important innovations in practice have taken place over recent years in addressing the problem of contamination from run off by channelling water from roads through reedbeds to bring about significant improvements in water quality, and some very successful projects of this kind have been undertaken both in relation to road run off and run off from areas of contaminated land.[178] However, a better solution may lie in source control by reducing the amount and harmfulness of substances originating from road use. The phasing out of leaded petrol has brought about significant improvements in this respect, but it is evident that more needs to be done to address the problem of contamination from roads and water quality problems from transport generally.

### 1.6.6 Mining and Contaminated Land

The excavation and processing of minerals has been a major source of water pollution since the earliest times[179] due to the discharge of large amounts of sediment released in washing coal and other minerals.[180] The typical effect of this is to cause an increase in levels of suspended solids present in the receiving watercourse, which discolours the water and has harmful effects upon aquatic life. In the longer term, this may result in the accumulation of sediment, obstruction of water flow and interference with navigation in some instances. However, there are many instances where the effluent produced by mining activities is seriously toxic to aquatic flora and fauna.

At an international level the potentially catastrophic consequences of failure to control waste generated by mining operations are dramatically illustrated in the recent Danube pollution incident arising from operations at the Baia Mare goldmine in Romania in 2000.[181] In this incident a dam burst causing an estimated 100,000 cubic meters of silt, containing high concentrations of cyanide, to enter a tributary of the Danube. This resulted, on first estimates, in the wiping out of flora and fauna along a 30 to 40 kilometre length of river that had previously supported rare and unique species and dangerously high cyanide concentrations being recorded in Hungary and Yugoslavia.[182]

At a national level, emissions from the Wheal Jane tin mine in Cornwall in 1991 brought the problem of mine pollution graphically to the public attention. Here mining operations ceased and pumps which had previously

---

[178] See Simmons (1999).

[179] See Royal Commission on Salmon Fisheries (England and Wales) Report (1861) pp.xix to xxi.

[180] General reading on pollution from mines includes Klein (1957) Ch.4; Klein (1962) Ch.4, but see also material referred to in 9.17.3 below.

[181] Another serious incident arose in 1998 where there was a breach of a dam at the Aznancollar mine in Spain which created a flow of 5 million cubic metres of toxic waste which polluted a large area on the border of a national park.

[182] See European Commission press releases: *Danube Pollution*, 16 February 2000; *Cyanide Pollution Statement by Commissioner Wallstrom*, 18 February 2000; *The Baia Mare Task Force now Established*, 6 March 2000; and *Results of the First Meeting of the Baia Mare Task Force*, 14 March 2000 (http://europa.eu.int/comm/environment/press/index.htm).

been used to remove water from the mine were switched off. As a result, water levels in the mine, containing significant levels of cadmium, zinc, nickel, arsenic, copper and iron, rose to a level where emissions entered a nearby river and estuary causing dramatic peaks in heavy metal concentrations such that recreational users of the water were advised to keep away from the area. Initially, a temporary treatment plant was funded by the National Rivers Authority, but funding of £8 million was subsequently provided by the Department of the Environment to develop a long term solution to the problem of treating the effluent. Because of the complicated history of the mine, and legal difficulties as to whether the abandonment which had occurred placed the circumstances outside the principal water pollution offences,[183] no legal proceedings were taken against the former operators of the mine.[184]

Discharges from mining operations are likely to be subject to a discharge consent incorporating appropriate parameters to control amounts of suspended solids and other harmful substances which may be present. However, with the decline of the coal mining industry, and other mining activities, increasingly the problem is not with active mining operations but the persistent water quality problems that originate from mines that have ceased to operate or have been abandoned.[185] Previously, a defence to a water pollution offence existed where water from an abandoned mine was permitted to enter controlled waters,[186] but it became increasingly apparent that the extent of the problem of contamination from abandoned mines was such that duties should be imposed to execute works to ameliorate the environmental impacts which followed abandonment.[187] The legal response to this has been the prospective removal of the exemption to the water pollution offences in relation to abandoned mines.[188] Whilst this may address the problem of water contamination from mines which are abandoned in future, the greater problem of mines which were abandoned before the new measures were introduced remains.

A related problem of 'historic' pollution arises in relation to land which has been contaminated from past industrial use but continues to have a damaging effect upon the environment.[189] Typically, this arises through the transmission of contaminating substances to receiving waters in surface water runoff or by percolation through groundwater. In a country that was heavily industrialised at a relatively early time, the environmental problems are of potentially immense proportions though extremely difficult to quantify with accuracy. The legal difficulties are also considerable, in that the contamination of many sites is attributable to activities which took place long ago and consequently those responsible

---

[183] See 9.17.3 below on abandoned mines under the principal water pollution offences.

[184] National Rivers Authority, *Abandoned Mines and the Water Environment* (1994) paras.5.8-19.

[185] For general literature on abandoned mines see 9.17.3 below.

[186] s.89(3) Water Resources Act 1991.

[187] National Rivers Authority, *Abandoned Mines and the Water Environment* (1994) p.37.

[188] s.60 Environment Act 1995, and see 9.17.3 below on abandoned mines generally.

[189] For general literature on contaminated land see 13.7 below.

are no longer available to take responsibility for the environmental harm that their actions continue to cause.

Whilst a consensus exists that continuing problems originating from land contamination should be addressed, even where this involves considerable remediation costs, it has been resolved that cleaning up problematic sites should not normally be undertaken at public expense.[190] The consequence of this is that remediation action will be required, in the first instance, of the person who caused the land to be contaminated and, if that person cannot be found, the present owner or occupier of the land.[191] The legislation providing for this has only recently been given effect by secondary legislation and it is apparent that there are a range of major difficulties. Not least significant amongst the problems is the imposition of retrospective liability upon certain landowners for the clean up of contamination brought about by others and which, in many instances, has been the result of activities which were not thought to be environmentally harmful at the time they took place. The legal objective is to provide a system of controls which address the environmental problems with the maximum degree of fairness in relation to those upon whom the burden of meeting remediation costs must fall. It remains to be seen whether the implementation of the contaminated land legislation will realise this objective.

### 1.6.7 Shipping Activities and Sea Dumping

Beyond freshwater and coastal water quality concerns, various maritime activities must be regulated because of their impacts on water quality. Most notable amongst these are operational and accidental discharges from shipping, especially discharges of oil, and the use of the seas as a repository for certain types of waste, especially dredging material and sewage sludge, and the disposal of bulky installations such as drilling platforms. Although the dumping of sludge at sea has now been terminated under international and European Community law,[192] both shipping and dumping have given rise to high profile incidents over recent years, and the *Sea Empress* incident and the *Brent Spar* episode now need little introduction.[193]

Despite the high level of media attention which surrounded these events, there is a clear contrast between them. In the former case, the grounding of the *Sea Empress* off Milford Haven in 1996 gave rise to a widespread and serious water pollution incident, which ultimately led to the second highest fine for a water pollution offence.[194] From the perspective of combating

---

[190] DoE, *Framework for Contaminated Land* (1994).

[191] Part IIA Environmental Protection Act 1990, introduced by s.57 Environment Act 1995 and see 13.7 below on contaminated land.

[192] See 19.17 below.

[193] See 9.19.3 on the *Sea Empress* incident and 19.19.4 below on the *Brent Spar* episode.

[194] *R v Milford Haven Port Authority* [2000] Env LR 632, Court of Appeal and see discussion of sentencing at 9.19.3.

water pollution, therefore, there is a clear need to prevent such incidents occurring and to provide for legal mechanisms which can facilitate a swift and effective response to shipping casualties. If damage is caused, there is a need to provide sufficient funds for restoration and compensation after the event. To an extent, there are now provisions of international law which go some way towards meeting all these objectives, through specification standards for oil tankers, provisions for international co-operation in the event of a shipping casualty posing a hazard to the marine environment, and through liability provisions to compensate for losses incurred.[195]

Whether it is possible to 'restore' the marine water environment when there has been a major oil spill, however, or whether the most appropriate course is simply to let the oil be assimilated into the sea over time, remains an open question.[196] The adequacy of current provisions has again been called into question following the loss of the *Erika* off the Brittany coast in December 1999. Nevertheless, the fact remains that international shipping poses a direct hazard to the maritime environment and particularly the coastal zone. Shipping casualties have been seen to have devastating consequences for other legitimate 'uses' of this zone, such as shellfish or aquaculture production, or even the 'use' that the tourist industry makes of clean waters and beaches.

By contrast, it is difficult to present the proposed sea disposal of the *Brent Spar* oil platform, in 1995, and the successful campaign by Greenpeace to prevent this happening, as a water 'pollution' issue in the sense used here. Although this is not to say that dumping the installation would not have had localised impacts on the surrounding aquatic environment. Indeed, only in an indirect sense can the events of that time, and the subsequent decision at international level to prohibit the dumping of all but the most inert parts of the largest platforms,[197] be fairly described as a water 'quality' issue. Not least this is because, in contrast to the freshwater environment, knowledge of the marine environment is probably still too limited to set meaningful water quality standards for the marine environment, and quality standards have never featured in its regulation.[198]

The issue of sea dumping, though, is a water quality issue in the indirect sense that recent years have seen a general shift away from using the marine environment as a general waste repository, even where no harm to humans or the environment has resulted. While there are still some remaining aspects of this 'dilute and disperse' approach,[199] there is now a policy and legal presumption against dumping at sea. This is given effect through a 'reverse listing' approach under which only a narrow range of

---

[195] See generally Ch.19 below.

[196] See 19.13.1 below.

[197] See 19.19.3 and 19.19.4 below.

[198] Although see 20.6.3 below and what are, in effect, water quality standards for certain ionising radiations.

[199] Long sea outfalls for sewage effluent being the classic case.

defined categories of waste may be dumped.[200] In this sense, developments at international level illustrate the way in which law and policy has progressed from the time when the water environment was used as a conduit and dumping ground for industrial and sewage effluent.[201]

Now, the policy emphasis is not on the 'end of the pipe' but 'up the pipe', that is, looking higher up the production chain to emphasise ways in which wastes can be minimised, rather than seeking ways of using the water environment as a disposal option. One outstanding difficulty, though, is that this approach has yet to be cast in terms of legal obligations, in the way that national and European Community waste law revolves around what, on some levels, are legal as well as policy principles which place waste minimisation at the pinnacle of the waste hierarchy.[202] Indeed, a similar criticism relating to the lack of broader responsibility across the supply chain may be made in relation to the transport of oil and other hazardous substances, where neither the owner of the cargo, nor the charterer, are held liable for any resulting environmental damage.[203]

## 1.7  The Range of Regulatory Approaches

The preceding discussion of problematic activities has emphasised that the distinct characters of the activities involved is important in determining the appropriate legal response. Equally, the observations concerning the regulation of the different activities have served to provide some examples of the range of legal approaches that may be used in preventing water pollution incidents and meeting water quality requirements. It is convenient here to identify and summarise the range of regulatory approaches that may be applied to the protection of the aquatic environment.[204] In doing so, however, it must be appreciated that the concept of 'regulation' is capable of being used in widely different senses.

Broadly, 'regulation' may be characterised as encompassing that body of public law by which the state seeks to secure collective or community objectives by means of directions of various kinds which require or encourage particular actions to be taken by those subject to such mechanisms. The potentially open-ended nature of this characterisation will be appreciated and the theoretical difficulties with the boundaries of the concept will not be dwelt upon.[205] The more important task, for present purposes, is to identify those legal strategies which are of greatest relevance to the protection of the aquatic environment. In doing so, regulatory approaches may be contrasted according to the degree of intervention or compulsion involved.[206] The maximum degree of

---

[200] See 19.19 below on international legal prohibitions on dumping at sea.

[201] See 2.4 below on early public health law.

[202] See 12.2.1 below on the waste hierarchy.

[203] See 19.13 below.

[204] Generally see Haigh (1992) Ch.3; Alder and Wilkinson (1999) Ch.7; and Bell and McGillivray (2000) Ch.19.

[205] Generally see Ogus (1994a) Ch.1 and Rowan-Robinson, Watchman and Barker (1990).

[206] See Ogus (1994) Ch.8.

compulsion arises in relation to the unqualified prohibition of an activity and the minimum where 'voluntarily' mechanisms are used to discourage participation in the activity. Hence, the use of the criminal law is placed at one end of the regulatory spectrum whereas education and information provision lie at the other. As will be seen, the law relating to water quality illustrates the full range of regulatory approaches. However, it also seeks to relate the degree of compulsion to the perceived gravity of the environmental problem being addressed, with the underlying intention that the degree of compulsion is no greater than needed to address the problem at issue.

### 1.7.1 Prohibition

Perhaps the most centrally important kind of regulatory approach is the legal prohibition of those activities which must be avoided if the public interest in the protection of the aquatic environment is to be effectively protected sometimes, perhaps ambivalently and misleadingly, termed the 'command and control' approach.[207] Naturally, the criminalisation of certain water contaminating activities has considerable intuitive appeal. However, as a mechanism for the imposition of a sanction and the public identification of a misdeed that this may entail, the practicalities involved in formulating an appropriate criminal offence are considerable. The proscribed activities need to be identified with sufficient precision to permit those involved to know what behaviour will constitute an offence and this raises significant challenges where the definition of the offence relates to the degree of environmental harm involved. An offence of 'causing water pollution', for example, would presuppose that some objective definition of 'pollution' is available and, as has been seen, this concept is legally problematic.[208] It is perhaps for this reason that the principal water pollution offences[209] are formulated in terms of activities causing or knowingly permitting the *entry* or *discharge* of matter or effluent, rather than activities that necessarily have any specified *impact* upon the aquatic environment.

Moreover, the enactment of any offence concerning water contaminating activities presupposes that the capacity exists to enforce the prohibition in practice. Therefore, enforceability must be an important factor in the formulation of the offence and the form of the regulatory structure within which it is placed. In this respect, the relatively long history of water quality legislation in this country has demonstrated the vital importance of an appropriately empowered and resourced regulatory authority with the specialised expertise needed to monitor and evaluate activities which adversely impact upon the aquatic environment.[210] In addition, important historical lessons have been learnt as to the importance of independence of

---

[207] Royal Commission on Environmental Pollution (1998) para.6.34.

[208] See 1.3 on the definition of 'pollution'.

[209] s.85 Water Resources Act 1991, and see 9.3 below on the principal water pollution offences.

[210] Royal Commission on Environmental Pollution (1998) para.6.37.

a regulatory authority from the bodies that it is bound to regulate.[211] Hence, prohibition approaches to water quality are intimately dependent upon enforcement capacity and are of limited value where that capacity is lacking.[212]

## 1.7.2 Discharge Consenting

The criminalisation of activities which result in water contamination might be regarded as an end in itself. However, it is also a mechanism by which such activities may be controlled in ways which relate more specifically to the hazards involved and the circumstances and location in which activities are conducted. The existence of a criminal offence relating to water polluting activities allows for the provision of specific defences which may be provided for to identify situations where the offence should not apply. These may be of a general kind, such as where water contamination results from action taken in an emergency, or may be specific to the circumstances where a potentially polluting substance is permitted to be introduced into the aquatic environment under specified conditions. Specific permissions of this kind may authorise particular activities to be undertaken over a short duration, such as the disturbance of sediment or the removal of vegetation in rivers,[213] or may be provided for by way of environmental licences[214] allowing a continuing activity to be conducted over a longer period of time. In the water context, the most important authorisation of this kind is the discharge consent.[215]

Discharge consents contrast with other kinds of environmental licences. In relation to waste management, for example, it is necessary for a prospective licensee to establish the status of being a 'fit and proper person' in the sense of showing technical capacity in waste management, financial soundness in being able to meet possible environmental liabilities and lack of antecedence in respect of past environmental offences.[216] By comparison, discharge consents are primitive and unsophisticated in requiring none of these things to be shown by an applicant. The assumption is made that the applicant has the technical and financial capacity to meet the requirements of any consent that is granted and past convictions for failing to do so are no bar to a consent being granted. Perhaps the explanation for this contrast lies in the fact that discharge consents were first introduced at a time when the most significant effluent discharges, from sewage treatment, were the responsibility of public bodies.[217] In that context, the impersonal assumptions underlying

---

[211] See the discussion of the Water Act 1973 and the law enforcement problems to which it gave rise in 2.14–15 below.

[212] See the discussion of the Rivers (Prevention of Pollution) Act 1951 at 2.10 below.

[213] s.90 Water Resources Act 1991, and see 9.15 below.

[214] See s.56(1) Environment Act 1995, identifying a range of environmental licences.

[215] See Ch.10 below on discharge consents.

[216] See 12.2.6 below on waste management licensing.

[217] See the discussion of the Rivers (Prevention of Pollution) Acts 1951-61 at 2.10 below.

discharge consenting may not have been so remarkable. Nonetheless, there is scope for reconsidering the assumptions in modern circumstances.

The legal status of a discharge consent, as a defence to what would otherwise be a criminal offence, is of great practical importance because it effectively allows a broadly-formulated prohibition against the entry of any polluting matter into waters to be modified to take account of particular circumstances. Hence, despite the general prohibition, the permissible amount of substances which may be discharged from a particular installation may be determined according to a range of matters. These may encompass the substances involved, the quantity and quality of the receiving waters, their ecological sensitivity and any water quality requirements to which they are subject. Discharge consents have the capacity to modify the impact of a prohibition so that its practical effect is highly specific to individual situations.

Moreover, the facilities for modification and revocation of discharge consents allow longer-term changes in effluent quality requirements to be taken into account, for example, where increasingly stringent quality requirements for receiving waters are imposed. More immediate concerns may also be addressed through the discharge consent system insofar as enforcement notices may be served where a particular discharge is proving problematic specifying actions which are required to rectify contravention of a consent.[218] The general advantages of environmental licensing of this kind over comprehensive prohibition, in respect of location and operation specificity and general flexibility, are readily apparent.

A key limitation of discharge consenting, however, is that, in practice, it depends upon there being a readily identifiable point of discharge. In effect, this allows regulation only in relation to effluent entering waters from pipes or similarly discrete points of entry where effluent quality can feasibly be monitored. Hence, discharge consents will be of no assistance in addressing the range of water quality concerns relating to diffuse forms of contamination where entry takes place other than through a pipe of some kind. Also, there are situations where an effluent discharge is better regarded as the end point of an industrial process and where the preferable regulatory strategy is to control the process itself rather than its eventual environmental emission.[219] Although the imposition of conditions upon the quality of effluent may have important implications for the manner in which an industrial process is conducted, it can only be an indirect way of regulating the process is itself.

### 1.7.3 Process Authorisation

The regulation of processes, rather than their environmental emissions, is capable of being more intrusive than discharge controls insofar as it may allow a regulatory authority significantly more control over the manner in

---

[218] s.90B Water Resources Act 1991, and see 10.11.1 below.
[219] Royal Commission on Environmental Pollution (1998) Appendix C paras.54 to 62.

which an industrial activity is conducted. Traditionally, mechanisms for controlling industrial processes have been provided for by the imposition of general requirements such as the requirement of using the 'best practicable and reasonably available means'[220] to render polluting material harmless. However, the most important practical application of process authorisation now lies in the system of integrated pollution control[221] presently applicable to the most environmentally hazardous industrial activities.

Process authorisation, as it is provided for in relation to integrated pollution control, has important advantages over sector-specific environmental controls such as discharge consents. Process authorisation, at national level, allows more comprehensive consideration of the overall environmental impact of an industrial activity and is more conducive to the realisation of the 'best practical environmental option' for the environment as a whole (BPEO) and the imposition of requirements that the 'best available techniques not entailing excessive cost' (BATNEEC) should be used. However, the integration of approaches to controlling environmental emissions which process authorisation allows also gives rise to difficulties in translating these, rather abstractly stated, objectives into specific, cost-effective, regulatory requirements for individual operations. For this reason, integrated pollution control is an approach which has been restricted to the most polluting industrial activities, or activities involving the most polluting substances, and has not been applied to all industrial emissions. Whilst the objective of integrating approaches to emissions to the environmental media of water, air and land has much to commend it in terms of regulatory coherence, the physical differences between the different media give rise to practical limitations as to the extent to which this approach may be followed.

For the future, however, the national approach to process authorisation, by way of integrated pollution control, is being overtaken by the system of controls which are needed to implement the European Community Integrated Pollution Prevention and Control Directive.[222] Although similarities may be noted between the national and Community systems, contrasts may be drawn in the broader scope of the Community approach which applies to a wider range of emissions including vibrations, heat and noise. Also encompassed within the Community regime are regulation of waste reduction and energy use in industrial installations, and requirements for the aftercare of sites after an industrial activity has ceased. Perhaps most important in practice is the fact that the Community controls apply to a far greater number of installations, including intensive animal rearing units and food and drink plants, than the national integrated pollution control system. Within the regulated activities, it is clear that significant

---

[220] See ss.3, 4 and 5 Rivers Pollution Prevention Act 1876, discussed in 2.6 below. Similarly, see the defence of 'best practicable means' as provided for in relation to statutory nuisances under s.79(9) Environmental Protection Act 1990 and see 8.5.10 below on this.

[221] Provided for under Part I Environmental Protection Act 1990, and see 8.5.10 below on this.

[222] (96/61/EC) and regulations to be enacted under the Pollution Prevention and Control Act 1999, and see 12.3 below on integrated pollution prevention and control.

environmental benefits are capable of being realised. However, the difficulties remain in resolving how best to direct unavoidable environmental impacts in achieving a high level of protection of the environment as a whole. Is greater contamination of air, from increased atmospheric emissions, a price worth paying for cleaner water, through reduction of liquid effluent discharges, or *vice versa*? For all its merits, integrated pollution control does not necessarily provide an answer.

### 1.7.4 Product Control

Controlling discharges and activities through prohibitions and environmental licensing systems both assume that the discharge or activity are, in principle, capable of being regulated with sufficient stringency to avoid unacceptable environmental consequences. In some instances, this requires the imposition of highly substance-specific or activity-specific regulation to reflect the exceptional kinds of environmental hazard that may arise. Examples of 'specification standards' of this kind are to be found in the regimes relating to the control of radioactive contamination and in respect of maritime transport of oil and other hazardous substances.[223] In the most extreme cases, however, the approach that has been adopted has been to prohibit the manufacture, sale or use of commodities that are not capable of being effectively environmentally regulated by other means.[224]

Consumer products are increasingly being viewed in respect of their life cycle impact upon the environment: from the collection of raw materials, the manufacturing and distribution processes, to the environmental impacts of use and eventual disposal.[225] This product-focussed approach allows attention to be directed to those products which need to be made subject to environmental standards, authorisation processes and, in the last resort, a complete ban. Whilst prohibiting the production, sale or use of a substance or product is an approach which is inevitably restrictive of consumer choice, it is an option that may need to be pursued where other regulatory mechanisms will not be of sufficient stringency to provide an adequate degree of environmental protection.

Another distinct aspect of the use of the product-control regulatory approach arises where water itself is conceived of as a product. Potable water which is supplied to consumers by water undertakers for domestic purposes is a different kind of commodity from other kinds of consumer goods and this is reflected in the public law character of the transaction under which water is supplied.[226] Nonetheless, the water quality obligations which relate to drinking water supplies contain a significant

---

[223] See Chs.20 and 19 below respectively on this.

[224] See s.140 Environmental Protection Act 1990 discussed at 12.4.6 below, and see Royal Commission on Environmental Pollution (1998) Appendix C paras.47 to 53.

[225] See Council Regulation on a Community eco-label and award scheme (880/92/EEC) and see also the 'cradle to grave' approach to waste management contained in Part II Environmental Protection Act 1990.

[226] See Stiff (1996), though contrast Kaye (1996).

product quality element.[227] The analogy is even stronger where bottled water is supplied for drinking, where the relationship between the seller and consumer is purely contractual in nature, and subject to important water quality requirements in relation to the quality of the bottled water for consumer safety purposes.[228]

### 1.7.5  Land Use and Area-based Controls

Although the use of prohibitions against the contamination of water has been noted, increasing scope is being found for the use of regulatory law in an 'anticipatory' manner as a means of requiring action to be taken to prevent, or as a precaution against, water contamination. This use of the criminal law relates to activities which do not necessarily involve any harm to water quality but are nonetheless justifiably regulated as a preventative or precautionary measure. Examples of this kind of approach are multifarious, but typically might involve the imposition of requirements upon persons who have custody of potentially polluting substances to ensure that those substances are contained, transported or used in a particular manner.[229] Notably, criminal offences are generally provided for where such requirements are disregarded, or related licensing conditions contravened, irrespective of whether this has given rise to any actual water quality problem.

A similar need to control land use for the purpose of protecting water quality is to be seen in controls imposed under town and country planning law. The progressive assimilation of these concerns into planning law has been such that the water quality impacts of a particular development have become an increasingly important element in determining whether a planning permission will be granted.[230] Although, ultimately, planning law rests upon the existence of a criminal sanction, the practical impact is normally that a development proposal will be modified to ensure the amelioration of a perceived water quality problem. Again, the preventative or precautionary theme is prominent.

Other kinds of control upon land use may also be effective in reducing adverse impacts upon water quality in a way that could not be effectively undertaken through discharge consent control, particularly where diffuse forms of water contamination are involved. Hence, a range of land and water designations, and the associated control systems related to these, are of major importance to water quality: nitrate vulnerable zones,[231] water protection zones,[232] sensitive areas in relation to wastewater treatment,[233]

---

[227] See Ch.17 below on drinking water quality.

[228] See 17.13.2 below on requirements for bottled water.

[229] See, for example, Control of Pollution (Silage, Slurry and Agricultural Fuel Oil) Regulations 1991 (SI 1991 No.324, as amended) discussed in 13.3.1 below. In an international context, see the discussion of the 'double-hull' requirement in relation to oil tankers at 19.5.3 below.

[230] See Ch.14 below on town and country planning law and water quality.

[231] See 13.5 below on nitrate vulnerable zones.

[232] See 13.4 below on water protection zones.

sites of special scientific interest, environmentally sensitive areas and other conservation and landscape areas.[234] In most respects, area designation provides a valuable mechanism for controlling land use, for the purpose of securing water quality improvement. This is normally done to recognise the special vulnerability of the waters which are impacted upon and where a satisfactory level of protection cannot be so effectively provided for by other means. Notably, also, area-based controls are emerging in international marine protection law to protect areas which are sensitive because of their ecological characteristics or because of their vulnerability to shipping casualties.[235]

### 1.7.6 Anti-Pollution and Remediation Works

Although anticipatory controls upon land use serve the purpose of restricting present activities to prevent deterioration of water quality, the counterpart of this is the need to address past activities which give rise to continuing water quality problems. In the immediate aftermath of a pollution incident this may involve anti-pollution works and operations being undertaken by the Environment Agency to minimise harm to the aquatic environment or action to restore a water to its former state where this is possible. Alternatively, it may be more appropriate to require the person responsible for the contamination to undertake works for restorative purposes or to prevent further pollution. In either instance, the cost of works reasonably undertaken for these purposes will fall upon the person who caused the polluting matter to be present in the waters.[236] Whilst the capacity exists for such costs to overlap with matters that might be the subject of a compensatory award in civil proceedings,[237] the public interest in ameliorating pollution and restoring waters to an unpolluted state necessitates swift action to be taken without the need for civil liability to be established.[238] Punishing water pollution as a crime, by itself, is not sufficient to meet the need for restoration which arises in such situations.

Similar purposes can be seen to lie behind the contaminated land legislation, noted above, where an intricate range of provisions is being introduced to impose requirements upon those responsible for contamination, and in some cases innocent landowners, to restore contaminated land to a satisfactory state. Again, the distinctive feature of this body of law is that, rather than punishing past offenders, it seeks to impose present liabilities in relation to past acts which continue to give rise

---

[233] See 5.6.2 below on sensitive areas under the Urban Wastewater Treatment Directive (91/271/EEC).

[234] Generally see Ch.15 below on conservation designations.

[235] See the discussion of special areas and of routeing controls at 19.6.4 and 19.5.6 below.

[236] See 13.2.3 below on anti-pollution works powers and works notices.

[237] See Ch.3 on the civil law generally.

[238] Although the availability of compensation orders in criminal proceedings under the Powers of the Criminal Courts Act 1973, discussed in 9.2.1 below, and the provision of statutory civil liability, discussed in 3.18 below, should be noted as mechanisms by which the complex and protracted proceedings involved in bringing a civil action may be mitigated.

to environmental harm. Clearly, distinctions may be drawn between clean-up operations in respect of water and of land, and contrast drawn between restoration being commenced immediately after a polluting event as opposed to being undertaken perhaps many decades after contamination has occurred. However, the retrospective and restorative themes are common to both areas of law and are an important counterpart to the punitive and restrictive approaches adopted by other legal provisions.

### 1.7.7 Strategic Use of Controls

The nature of regulatory law, in environmental contexts as elsewhere, is such that it is capable of being effective in prohibiting and punishing extremes of unacceptable behaviour but less effective in realising positively formulated aspirations. Hence, whilst the proscription of extreme kinds of water contamination incident is appropriately provided for through a criminal offence, the realisation of broader strategic objectives for the aquatic environment as a whole is not necessarily capable of being achieved by regulating the worst kinds of polluting activity alone. Increasingly, the range of regulatory powers previously mentioned must be used in a co-ordinated and purposeful manner to secure an integrated approach towards water quality management.

It is convenient to classify waters according to their hydrological characteristics and potential uses, for the purpose of identifying the regulatory regime to which they are subject. Flowing and still surface waters, groundwaters, estuarial, coastal and certain marine waters are identified and collectively termed 'controlled waters'. Domestic supplies of water are classified as 'drinking water' and waste waters from certain premises are classified as 'effluent'. In each case hydrological or intended use classification serves the purpose of determining the associated legal obligations.

However, the classification of individual waters for regulatory purposes is undertaken at different levels and in respect of different geographical areas. Effluent quality and abstracted water quality are respectively identified at their particular points of introduction or removal. Water quality standards are established for a length of watercourse, water quality objectives may be coordinated in relation to a whole catchment and the water quality required where a supply is actually made to water consumers is set as a national requirement. A further distinction may be drawn between those standards which are of point-specific, local, water catchment or national applicability and those which originate from European Community water legislation, where the geographical scope is Community-wide.[239] Beyond these, international agreements such as the 1992 OSPAR Convention may set 'North Atlantic'-wide standards spanning an enormous area from the North Pole to the Straits of Gibraltar, which is one reason that the emphasis is on process controls and the broad concept of 'best environmental practice', rather than meeting water quality

---

[239] Although see the discussion of subsidiarity at 4.4.2 below.

standards.[240] Whilst each of these methods of classification serves a useful regulatory purpose, the interdependence between the different levels of classification and their regulation must also be recognised.

The practical reality is that the quality of water at any particular location is unlikely to be achievable by regulatory powers which apply to that place in isolation from interconnected waters. A more extensive system of controls is needed, for example, to ensure that water reaching a particular abstraction point is of sufficient quality for supply purposes. This interdependence between the quality of different categories of waters at different locations is recognised in the increasing emphasis which is placed upon integrated catchment management emphasising the need for regulation of interconnected watersheds as a whole. Hence, from a geographical perspective, it has been argued,

> [t]here are many merits in addressing water quality problems at the catchment scale rather than in terms of individual rivers, lakes and wetlands. First, such an approach explicitly acknowledges the hydrological cycle as a cascade in which fluxes of water, sediment, nutrients and pollutants steadily move downstream through a series of interconnected storages. Second, it focusses attention on the nature of the physical environment and the ways in which topography, lithology, vegetation, soil and land use collectively determine both flow regime and water quality. Third, it stresses the importance of embracing a 'holistic' approach to water quality issues, rather than addressing each question in terms which are site-specific or largely driven by narrow sectoral interests.[241]

Integrated catchment planning has been progressively adopted nationally by the formulation of catchment management plans for major watercourses, by the Environment Agency, to be used as guides to the exercise of its particular powers in relation to water protection.[242] However, a more rigorous legal approach is in prospect under the European Community Water Framework Directive[243] which requires that river basin management plans, encompassing a range of specified matters, are produced for each river basin district. These plans will be used as the basis for programmes of measures which are necessary to achieve the environmental objectives of the Directive.

In the future, the comprehensive river basin management plans envisaged by the Directive are likely to be the means by which particular legal actions are guided in relation to interrelated categories of waters within a catchment. For the present, the need for particular legal powers and duties to be used strategically is provided for by the incorporation of water quality requirements into law. In most instances quality objectives are formulated in relation to extensive areas of water, rather than the location

---

[240] See 18.8.2 below, though note that for some substances there are, in effect, quality standards.
[241] Werritty (1997) at pp.491-492, see also Gardiner (1991) and Gardiner (1994).
[242] See 14.9 below on integrated catchment planning.
[243] See 5.7 below on the Water Framework Directive (2000/60/EC).

of a particular discharge or abstraction point. Nonetheless, the realisation of a broadly-formulated objective requires coordination of particular legal actions, applied in individual locations, for the purpose of meeting the required objective. It is this orchestration of particular legal powers and duties as component elements in meeting strategically formulated environmental goals which is perhaps the defining feature of water quality law. Moreover, it is an approach which extends beyond the range of legally-compulsive powers that have been noted into a range of 'voluntary' approaches to water quality protection.

### 1.7.8 Voluntary Approaches

In terms of the degree of intervention involved,[244] the prohibition of an activity or product stands at one extreme of the spectrum of regulatory possibilities. At the other, least mandatory, extreme are placed economic and educational approaches, the possibility of 'self regulation' and the encouragement given to industrial concerns to put in place improved systems of environmental management.[245] These 'voluntary' approaches are generally characterised by being influential upon those involved in water contaminating activities without being legally compulsive. An example falling into this category is the use of voluntary undertakings, which may be illustrated in the water context by the provisions for agreements to be entered into by farmers to reduce nitrate applications to land in areas originally designated as nitrate sensitive areas in national law.[246] Whilst there was no compulsion upon farmers to enter such agreements, the availability of compensation for changes in farming practice was clearly an effective incentive to do so, and the result was that uptake of agreements was good, and consequent improvement in water quality was achieved as a result. Moreover, this improvement was achieved without legal compulsion being imposed, though the general use of subsidies of this kind does raise problems in respect of compatibility with the polluter pays principle.[247]

Another approach, which must be placed somewhere towards the least-compulsive end of the regulatory spectrum, is the treatment of environmental information. Information about water discharges, and related activities, must be entered onto registers which are open to public inspection and more general rights are provided to the public to have access to environmental information held by public bodies.[248] To an extent, this involves a compulsion upon dischargers to provide information, and an obligation upon regulatory authorities to make such information available on request. However, it does not involve any compulsion upon a discharger to change the nature of the activity being

---

[244] See Ogus (1994) Ch.8.

[245] See 16.8 below on self regulation.

[246] s.95 Water Resources Act 1991 (though the nitrate sensitive areas scheme is now closed to new applicants) and see 13.5.1 below on nitrate sensitive areas.

[247] See 4.7.3 below on the polluter pays principle.

[248] See Ch.16 on information provisions.

undertaken, merely to report upon that activity. Nonetheless, the placing of information in the public domain is capable of being highly influential where it serves to expose an unsatisfactory activity and is capable of prompting improvement simply by being generally known. Access to water quality information has been precocious in this respect with public access being provided for before the approach was more generally applied in other environmental sectors.[249] Arguably, this has been a significant factor in encouraging improvements which have been secured by the application of a less compulsive legal mechanism.

These examples of voluntary approaches show the effectiveness of non-compulsive measures in some contexts and may be particularly effective where water quality, as opposed to water pollution, is at issue. However, they must be seen as mechanisms which complement the other legal approaches which have been described rather than operating in isolation from them. It is suggested that whilst voluntary approaches may sometimes provide a valuable complement to more compulsive kinds of regulatory control, the extension of voluntary approaches beyond a supplementary mechanism for protection of the aquatic environment may be problematic.

### 1.7.9 Economic Instruments

A good final illustration of the limitations which apply with regard to voluntary measures may be seen in relation to the proposals to apply economic instruments to discharges of wastewater which were formulated in a consultation paper, *Economic Instruments for Water Pollution*, issued by the relevant government departments.[250] The general approach of applying market mechanisms such as economic instruments to pollution control continues to be favourably viewed by government as a means towards sustainable development through the better implementation of the polluter pays principle.[251] The consultation paper emphasised economic arguments to the effect that traditional approaches to pollution control may not meet environmental objectives at lowest cost; may not make those responsible for pollution pay fully for the effect of their activities; and may not necessarily encourage dischargers to go beyond the minimum requirements of discharge consents. Hence, the proclaimed benefits of economic instruments were seen to be greater efficiency in achieving water quality objectives; more cost-effective improvements in water quality generally; and improved implementation of the polluter pays principle.

---

[249] See 2.13 below on the delay and eventual introduction of information provisions under the Control of Pollution Act 1974.

[250] DETR, WO, DoEII(NI) and SO, *Economic Instruments for Water Pollution* (1997). For discussion of these proposals see Jewell and Pontin (1998); *ENDS Report* 274 (1997) p.17; Zabel and Rees (1998); and Howarth (2000).

[251] HM Government, *A Better Quality of Life: A strategy for sustainable development for the United Kingdom* (1999) para.5.7. and see 4.4.1 below on sustainable development and 4.7.3 below on the polluter pays principle. See also Royal Commission on Environmental Pollution (1992) para.10.56.

The more detailed implications of applying economic theory to water pollution charges were that, for point sources of industrial and sewage discharges to watercourses, a charge would be imposed relating to the quantity and nature of pollutants contained in each particular discharge. In principle, this charge would reflect the value to society of improved water quality, and this valuation could be formulated so as to reflect, for each area, the amount to be paid by each discharger. However, difficulties were recognised to arise in relation to the problem of placing a valuation upon water quality[252] in equating the charge per unit of discharge to the value of the marginal environmental damage inflicted by that unit. Given the methodological difficulty, a more feasible alternative was thought to be to concentrate upon the relevant abatement costs, such that environmental charges were related to the marginal abatement costs at the level required to achieve a particular water quality objective. Again, however, there are methodological difficulties, given that any estimation of abatement costs is likely to be speculative and greatly dependent upon location.

Conceivably, all these methodological and practical difficulties might be overcome. Nonetheless, the key question raised by the consultation paper was whether a scheme of economic instruments for water discharges offers any significant advantages over the existing regulatory regime either as a means of meeting existing standards or as a means of meeting higher water quality objectives. Reliance upon economic instruments alone might allow overall water quality improvements to be made more cheaply, but it could mean that watercourses in some localities might become more polluted in the interests of national cost-effectiveness. The underlying problem is that aggregation of the benefits of cost-effectiveness involves some loss of location-specific controls. The objectionable aspect of this is that economic instruments alone provide no guarantee for water standards where, for example, there is a concentration of discharges into receiving waters which are unable to receive effluent without an unacceptable deterioration in water quality.

The possibility of water pollution being concentrated in particular areas is clearly a difficulty if economic instruments could ever be used to allow water quality requirements under European Community water directives to be breached. At a national level, the inherent unpredictability of the effect of economic instruments upon water quality would also be a difficulty in relation to the realisation of statutory water quality objectives[253] if economic instruments were introduced without regulatory safeguards. It has also been pointed out that the possibility that economic instruments could lead to local pollution might render dischargers liable to civil litigation which might, through the common law, undercut any statutory system for pricing pollution.[254]

---

[252] See Hanley (1997) on valuation of freshwaters.

[253] See ss.83–84 Water Resources Act 1991, and see 14.8 below.

[254] See Jewell and Pontin (1998) at p.33.

One conclusion upon the consultation exercise was that, even if all the other difficulties that have been noted could be overcome, there would be little, if any, actual benefit to be secured from using economic instruments as opposed to existing regulation.[255] To some extent this is because most of the supposed benefits of economic instruments are already provided for by existing regulation: first, by the Environment Agency being already obliged to take account of costs and benefits in setting discharge consents;[256] second, because existing charging schemes for both discharge consents and discharges of trade effluent to sewer already take some account of the environmental impact or the difficulties in treating the wastewater being discharged;[257] and, third, because it is not entirely clear why a discharger should be required to improve the quality of effluent which is shown not to be harmful to the environment.

However, perhaps the most remarkable aspect of the consultation paper concerned the relationship between legal and economic systems of regulatory control. It was suggested that 'the introduction of an economic instrument has potential to reduce the cost of achieving current levels of water quality – if the introduction of such an instrument allows for relaxation of some regulatory controls'. Accordingly, it was enquired 'whether existing regulatory controls can be reduced in scope and effect'.[258] The implication of this was that economic instruments should be considered, not merely as a supplement to present regulatory controls, but as a means of displacing those controls. This contrasted markedly with views previously expressed by the Royal Commission on Environmental Pollution:

> [I]t would, however, be unacceptable to introduce a system of market mechanisms which did not provide at least as much confidence that water quality standards would be achieved as the present system of regulation, or which could not ensure compliance with EC obligations. For point discharges into freshwater, therefore, economic instruments by themselves do not offer an acceptable approach; more traditional forms of regulation, operating with due flexibility, must remain in place. The principal role of any market mechanism should therefore be to reinforce the regulatory system to ensure that it works as cost-effectively as possible.[259]

For the reasons that have been summarised, amongst others, the responses in the consultation exercise were strongly critical and the proposals have come to nothing.[260] In his 1999 Budget speech the Chancellor of the

---

[255] Environmental Resources Management (1999) p.xi.

[256] Under s.39 Environment Act 1995, see also s.4 on the principal aim and objectives of the Agency, and see 6.7 and 6.14 below.

[257] See 10.7 on charges for discharge consents and 11.6 below on charges for trade effluent discharges.

[258] DETR, WO, Doe(NI) and SO, *Economic Instruments for Water Pollution* (1997) at p.13.

[259] Royal Commission on Environmental Pollution (1992) para.10.54, and see similarly Royal Commission on Environmental Pollution (1998) para.6.59.

[260] *ENDS Report* 277 (1998) p.20.

Exchequer indicated that the Government was not inclined to proceed with national water pollution charges for the reason that this would not be as efficient at delivering environmental benefit as targeted improvements in regulatory control. Whilst the possibility of economic instruments relating to water pollution has not been totally ruled out for the future,[261] the theoretical and practical difficulties involved in introducing charges in relation to wastewater discharges are clearly considerable. Not least significant amongst these is the problem of lack of consensus about the methodology to be used in quantifying the economic value of the aquatic environment and whether, in principle, the incommensurability of environmental and economic valuation prevents this being achieved.[262]

---

[261] See, in particular, the discussion of cost recovery pricing for water services under the Water Framework Directive (2000/60/EC) at 5.8.6 and 5.9.9 below.
[262] Generally see Royal Commission on Environmental Pollution (1998) Ch.5.

# Chapter 2

# HISTORY AND DEVELOPMENT

## 2.1 Introduction

England and Wales have a remarkably long history of water pollution legislation. To a great extent, this is attributable to relatively early industrialisation, as compared with other countries, and the need to regulate the worst excesses from 'dark satanic mills'. However, many provisions may be traced back to pre-industrial times and show the enduring nature of concerns about water quality for reasons of public health and amenity, rather than the modern tendency to emphasise environmental quality for its own sake. Remarkably also, is the durability of much of the legislation which has been enacted over the last century and a half. Many of the provisions of modern water pollution and water quality legislation may be traced back to public health and water pollution legislation of the nineteenth century.[1] Whilst society has changed dramatically over this period, the character of many of the legal key elements has shown amazing resistance to change.

This chapter traces the evolution of water pollution and water quality controls as these have been provided for in legislative measures dating from the earliest legal records to the present day.[2] Concern for the protection of potable water supplies and the prevention of water-borne disease have been enduring purposes in prompting legislative action on sanitary matters. These concerns became especially pressing in the nineteenth century, with the concentration of population in manufacturing centres, and it is in this era that the foundations of much of the modern legislation are to be found. Although well-intentioned, much of the legislation of this period sought to 'legislate away' water pollution by proclamation and little else. The lack of an effective means of monitoring pollution and specialised mechanism for enforcement of the law resulted in uneven or ineffective restraint being imposed upon those causing pollution.

The major contribution of the legislation enacted over the last century and a half has been a series of attempts to devise an optimum formula for the

---

[1] Postscript: although some care has to be exercised in construing present legislation in accordance with previous enactments. Particularly where construing a consolidation Act, such as the Water Industry Act 1991, a court should look for the intention expressed in that Act and should not interpret it by reference to repealed statutes which have been consolidated unless this is necessary because of ambiguity or other factors. See *R v Secretary of State for Environment, Transport and the Regions, ex parte Spath Holme Ltd* [2001] 2 WLR 15, applied in *British Waterways Board* v *Severn Trent Water Ltd* [2001] EWCA Civ 276, 2 March 2001 and see 2.20 below on the water consolidation legislation.

[2] General reading on the history of water pollution law includes: Royal Commission on Sanitary Laws, Second Report (1871) Vol.I pp.4 to 11; Klein (1957) Ch.1; Rosen (1958); Klein (1962) Ch.1; Porter (1978) Ch.2; Smith (1979) Ch.4 Part 1; Wohl (1983) Ch.9; Maloney and Richardson (1995) and Hassan (1998).

effective administrative organisation of water quality control and the enforcement of water pollution law. Hence, major national developments have taken place in the administration of water management with progressive legislative recognition of the specialised role of regulatory authorities with responsibility for the aquatic environment. Alongside this there has been substantial reconsideration of the nature of water pollution and the appreciation that diverse water quality concerns are greatly dependent upon the use to which water is to be put. Finally, over a relatively recent period, the influence of international law, and particularly of European Community law, on water quality has become of profound importance in shaping almost all aspects of water quality law.

## 2.2 Water Quality Law in Earliest Times

The earliest recorded enactment prohibiting water pollution was the Act for Punishing Nuisances which Cause Corruption of the Air near Cities and Great Towns, dating from 1388.[3] The wording of the preamble to the Act, though couched in the rather convoluted statutory phraseology of the period, makes its purpose clear:

> ...so much dung and other filth of the garbage and entrails as well of beasts killed, as of other corruptions, be cast and put in ditches, rivers and other waters, and also many other places, within, about, and nigh unto divers cities, boroughs, and towns of the realm, and the suburbs of them, that the air there is greatly corrupt and infect, and many maladies and other intolerable diseases do daily happen, as well to the inhabitants and those that are conversant in the said cities, boroughs, towns, and suburbs, as to others repairing and travelling thither, to the great annoyance, damage, and peril of the inhabitants, dwellers, repairers, and travellers aforesaid.

The legislative solution to this collection of problems was that,

> proclamation be made as well in the City of London, as in other cities, boroughs, towns, throughout the realm, where it shall be needed, as well within franchises as without, that all they which have cast and laid such annoyances, dung, garbage, entrails, and other ordure in ditches, rivers, waters, and other places aforesaid, shall cause them utterly to be removed, avoided, and carried away betwixt this and the feast of Saint Michael next ensuing after the end of this present Parliament, every one upon pain to lose and to forfeit to our Lord the King twenty pounds; and that the mayors and bailiffs of every such city, borough, and town, and also the bailiffs of franchises, shall compel the same to be done upon a like pain.

Despite wide scope of the enactment of 1388, and the relatively high financial penalty that accompanied it, the problem of water pollution remained sufficiently pressing for the legislature to return to the matter in

---

[3] 12 Ric 2 c.13 (1388).

another Act of 1488.[4] On this occasion the complaint was primarily grounded in the practice of slaughtering animals within the walls of the City of London causing,

> corrupt airs . . . by whose corruption and foul ordure, by violence of unclean, corrupt, and putrified waters, is borne down through . . . parts of the palace where the King's most royal person is wont to abide when he cometh to the Cathedral Church.

The resolution of the legislature was that the slaughtering of animals should be prohibited in *every* walled city, borough, and town within the realm upon pain of a fine, which in each case depended upon the kind of animal which had been slaughtered in breach of the Act. Despite these early enactments it is evident from the continuation of water pollution problems that the difficulties were not so simply solved.

A subsequent statute sought an administrative solution to the problem of water pollution. The 'Bill of Sewers',[5] enacted in 1531, provided for the establishment of Commissions of Sewers to allocate responsibility for watercourses, sea defences and related matters. Amongst their responsibilities persons charged with such commissions were to undertake certain public health duties including 'to cleanse, and purge the trenches, sewers, and ditches, in all places necessary'.[6] Another enactment of around the same period, an Act for the Preservation of the River of Thames,[7] created offences, 'if any person do or procure any thing to be done, to the annoying of the stream of the river of Thames'. Amongst the acts causing 'annoyance' to the river was the casting of dung, rubbish or other things in the River, for which the penalty was the forfeiture of a hundred shillings to the King, and to the Mayor and Commonalty of London.

Along with the perceived danger to public health constituted by the pollution of waters, an associated matter that prompted early legislative attention was the discharge of waste into harbours in such accumulations as to become a hazard to shipping. An example is to be found in an Act of 1531[8] which noted that as a result of tin works certain ports and havens in the west country had become 'utterly decayed and destroyed' due to the carrying by rivers of 'a marvellous great quantity of sand gravel stone robel earth slime and filth into the said ports and havens'. The solution to the problem was that tin working should cease unless measures were taken to keep the waste out of the streams flowing into the affected harbours, and a fine of £10 was imposed for failure to do this.[9] Essentially the same problem was returned to in a sequence of later enactments.[10] Although,

---

[4] 4 & 5 Hen 7 c.3.

[5] Officially entitled 'A General Act concerning Commissions of Sewers to be directed in all Parts within this Realm', 23 Hen 8 c.5; and see Callis (1622).

[6] *Ibid* s.3.

[7] 27 Hen 8 c.18 (1535).

[8] 23 Hen 8 c.8 (1531).

[9] The fine was increased to £20 under 27 Hen 8 c.23 (1535-6).

[10] 34 & 35 Hen 8 c.9 (1542-3), 19 Geo 2 c.22 (1745) and s.11 of the Harbours Act 1814.

primarily these were intended to address the entry of matter which constituted an obstruction to navigation, in many instances it was apparent that a water quality dimension was also envisaged in that the entry of 'filth' from vessels fell within the scope of the offences.

## 2.3 The Clauses Acts

Although the preceding citations illustrate the intermittent concern of the legislature with primarily local problems of pollution of water, this first became an important general issue with the growth of industrialisation in the early nineteenth century. A precursor of much industrial water pollution, and the associated problems of providing adequate sanitation for new populations concentrated in manufacturing areas, was the widespread pollution of water caused by the making of gas. Prohibition of this kind of water contamination was first provided for by the Lighting and Watching Act 1830. Where this Act was adopted by a poll of the rate-payers of a parish, it became an offence to foul a watercourse with washings or other waste matter from any gasworks. The offence was committed where any person making, furnishing or supplying gas, within the limits of a parish which had adopted the Act, caused or suffered to be emptied, drained or conveyed, or to run or flow, into any waters any washings or waste liquids, substances, or other things arising in the manufacture of gas. The waters in respect of which the offence were committed were comprehensively defined to include any river, brook, or running stream, reservoir, canal, aqueduct, waterway, feeder, pond or springhead, or well, or any drain, sewer, or ditch communicating with any of them.[11]

A series of 'Clauses' Acts enacted in 1847 provided a standard form for water pollution offences in respect of a range of different enterprises. The procedure involved the specification of the offences in a general 'consolidating' Act passed by Parliament which was given effect within a particular district where the provisions of the Act were incorporated into local legislation authorising particular persons, termed 'undertakers', to pursue specific enterprises in accordance with the consolidating Act.

During 1847 a range of Clauses enactments of this kind were passed to allow general regulation of gasworks, waterworks, harbours, docks and piers, town improvement and cemeteries. In each case the consolidating Act included explicit measures to regulate water pollution. Thus the Gasworks Clauses Act 1847 stated that in respect of any 'special Act', authorising the construction of a particular gasworks, in which the provisions of the Gasworks Clauses Act were incorporated, the undertakers authorised to construct the gasworks would be subject to express prohibition in respect of the corruption of water. The prohibition was that if the undertakers at any time caused or suffered to be brought or to flow into any stream, reservoir, or aqueduct, pond or place for water, or into any drain communicating therewith, any washing or other substance produced in making or supplying gas, or wilfully did any act connected

---

[11] s.38 Lighting and Watching Act 1830 and subsequently s.50 Lighting and Watching Act 1833.

with the making or supplying of gas whereby such waters were fouled, they would be guilty of an offence.[12]

On a similar basis, the Waterworks Clauses Act 1847 provided a consolidation of those provisions usually contained in particular 'special Acts' authorising the establishment of waterworks supplying water for domestic and industrial consumption in a particular locality. Where the 1847 Act was applied, a duty was imposed upon water undertakers to provide a constant supply of 'wholesome' water for domestic purposes supplied to all inhabitants of the district willing to pay a water rate for receiving the supply. Domestic water supplies were to be provided at "high" pressure, such as would make the water reach the top storey of the highest houses within the undertaker's district.[13] For the purpose of fulfilling the duty to supply water for domestic purposes, a range of powers were given to water undertakers allowing them, amongst other things, to construct waterworks, lay pipes and levy rates upon the owners of properties receiving water supplies.[14]

In addition, criminal offences were created under the Waterworks Clauses Act 1847 in relation to activities causing the water supplies to be fouled. Specifically, it was an offence to bathe in any stream, reservoir, aqueduct or other waterworks belonging to the undertakers, or to wash, throw, or cause to enter therein any dog or other animal; to throw any rubbish, dirt, filth, or other noisome thing into any such waters, or wash or cleanse therein any cloth, wool, leather, or skin of any animal, or any clothes or other thing; or for a person to cause the water of any sink, sewer, or drain, steam engine boiler, or other filthy water belonging to him or under his control, to run or to be brought into any such waters, or to do any other act whereby such waters are fouled.[15] Separate provision was also made for an offence where a person caused or suffered to be brought into any stream, reservoir, aqueduct or waterworks belonging to an undertaker, or any communicating drain, any washing or other substance produced in making or supplying gas.[16]

The Harbours, Docks, and Piers Clauses Act 1847 provided for the consolidation of provisions contained in local Acts authorising the making and improving of harbours, docks and piers. This enactment created an offence where any person threw or put any ballast, earth, ashes, stones, or other thing into a harbour or dock. The offence was subject to the proviso that it was not to prevent any person adopting any lawful measure for recovering land which had been lost, or severed from other land, by reason

---

[12] s.21 Gasworks Clauses Act 1847.

[13] s.35 Waterworks Clauses Act 1847. In relation to the obligation to supply 'wholesome' water for domestic purposes it was held that the duty was met where the water in the undertaker's service pipes was wholesome, notwithstanding that it was subsequently contaminated by lead from a consumer's service pipes (*Milnes* v *Huddersfield Corporation* (1886) 11 App Cas 511, but contrast *Read* v *Croydon Corporation* [1938] 4 All ER 631) and see Ch.17 below on present requirements for drinking water quality.

[14] See ss.6, 28 and 68 Waterworks Clauses Act 1847.

[15] s.61 Waterworks Clauses Act 1847.

[16] *Ibid* s.62.

of the overflowing or washing of any navigable river, or for the protection of land from further loss or damage.[17]

The Towns Improvement Clauses Act 1847 brought about the consolidation of diverse measures for paving, draining, cleansing, lighting, and improving towns. Amongst these measures were provisions vesting public drains and sewers, within the limits of the Act, in Commissioners and requiring them to construct whatever other sewers were necessary for the effectual draining of any town or district subject to a special Act incorporating the Towns Improvement Clauses Act 1847. The Commissioners were to cause such sewers to communicate with, and empty into, the sea or any public river, or to cause the refuse from such sewers to be conveyed by a proper channel to the most convenient site for its collection and sale for agricultural or other purposes. In no case, however, were these things to be done in such a way as to become a nuisance.[18]

The Cemeteries Clauses Act 1847 consolidated provisions to be incorporated in particular Acts authorising the making of cemeteries. Amongst the provisions of the Act, which came into effect when incorporated into a 'special Act' authorising the making of a particular cemetery, was the stipulation that any cemetery company authorised to construct a cemetery would commit an offence by permitting any offensive matter from the cemetery to be brought or to flow into any stream, canal, reservoir, aqueduct, pond or watering place whereby the water would be fouled.[19]

## 2.4 Early Public Health Legislation

The first Public Health Act, enacted in 1848, sought to bring about more effectual provision for the improvement of the sanitary conditions of towns and 'populous places' in England and Wales. Amongst other things this objective was to be accomplished by placing water supply, sewerage, drainage and cleansing under a single local management body which was to be subject to general supervision at a national level. Pursuant to this, elected local boards of health were empowered to implement a range of measures for the improvement of sanitation under the overall supervision of the General Board of Health.

Amongst the wide range of duties and powers given to local boards of health under the 1848 Act were a collection of responsibilities arising from the vesting of all sewers and sewerage works in the boards.[20] The local boards were obliged to repair sewers vested in them and to construct such sewers as were necessary for the effectual drainage of their district. The obligations to provide and maintain sewers were subject to the constraint that sewers were to be constructed, covered and kept in such a state as not

---

[17] s.73 Harbours, Docks and Piers Clauses Act 1847.
[18] s.24 Towns Improvement Clauses Act 1847.
[19] s.20 Cemeteries Clauses Act 1847.
[20] s.43 Public Health Act 1848.

to be a nuisance or injurious to health. For the purpose of clearing, cleansing and emptying such sewers, local boards were authorised to construct such places and works as were necessary so that sewers would communicate with and be emptied into such places. Sewage and refuse were then to be collected for sale for any purpose whatsoever providing that no nuisance was created. Allowing any private sewer or drain to communicate with that of the local board was not permissible unless the written consent of the board had been obtained and, in the case of an owner or occupier of premises outside the district of the board, communication with the board's sewer was only permissible upon terms agreed with the board.[21]

As a forerunner of the modern power of local authorities to deal with nuisances,[22] the local boards of health were placed under a duty to require the owner or occupier of premises to put an end to any nuisance of a kind likely to be prejudicial to health. As a last resort the boards were empowered to carry out any necessary work themselves and charge the cost of so doing to the owner or occupier of the premises. In particular, boards were under a duty to drain, cleanse, cover, or fill up ponds, pools, open ditches, sewers, drains, and places containing or used for the collection of any drainage, filth, water, matter, or thing of offensive nature likely to be prejudicial to health.[23]

Also amongst the powers given to the local boards was that of providing their district with a supply of water for private use.[24] Where this was done, special provision was made for the protection of water belonging to, or under the management or control of, the local board in any stream, reservoir, conduit, aqueduct or other waterworks. In respect of such water it was an offence to bathe in, or wash, cleanse, throw, or cause to enter therein any animal, rubbish, filth, stuff, or thing of any kind whatsoever, or cause or suffer to run or be brought therein the water of any sink, sewer, drain, engine, or boiler, or other filthy, unwholesome, or improper water, or to do anything whatsoever whereby the water would be fouled. Although apparently within the scope of this broadly worded general offence relating to water pollution, explicit provision was also made for a more specific and more serious offence of pollution of water by any washing or other substance produced by persons engaged in the manufacture or supply of gas.[25]

The powers of the local boards in respect of public health matters were extended by the Local Government Act 1858 which brought about amendments of the Public Health Act 1848. In particular, the 1858 Act enlarged the powers of the local boards in respect of sewage by conferring

---

[21] ss.45 to 48 Public Health Act 1848, and see 11.3.2 below on the corresponding present provisions concerning sewer connection.

[22] See 8.4 below on statutory nuisances.

[23] s.58 Public Health Act 1848 and subsequently the Nuisance Removal Acts 1855, 1860 and 1863.

[24] *Ibid* s.75.

[25] *Ibid* s.80.

upon them the power to construct works outside their districts, if necessary, for the purposes of creating outfalls and enabling appropriate removal of sewage. In pursuance of this, they were entitled to contract with any person for the sale or distribution of sewage, and to acquire any lease or lands for the purpose of receiving, storing, disinfecting or distributing sewage. In each case these powers were to be exercised so as not to create a nuisance.[26]

In 1861 an amending Act to the Local Government Act 1858 imposed a significant restriction to the powers of local boards in stipulating that no local board had the power to construct or use any outfall, drain or sewer for the purpose of conveying sewage or filthy water into any natural watercourse or stream until such water was freed from all excrementitious or other foul or noxious matter as would affect or deteriorate the purity and quality of the water in the stream of watercourse.[27] It was clear, therefore, that the duty of the local boards was not merely to dispose of sewage effluent, but also to purify that effluent before disposal into watercourses where this was necessary.

The Sewage Utilisation Act 1865 removed certain difficulties encountered by the local boards in exercising their duty of sewage disposal without creating a nuisance. Specifically the Act extended the powers of such boards to make arrangements for the application of sewage to land for agricultural purposes. The Act permitted sewerage authorities to combine together for the purpose of executing and maintaining works for the benefit of their respective districts. In addition a sewer authority was, with the sanction of the Attorney-General, empowered to take proceedings for the protection of a watercourse within its jurisdiction from pollution arising from sewage, either within or outside the district. Another provision of the Act prohibited the draining of a sewer directly into a stream or watercourse by a sewer authority.[28] The 1865 Act was amended in 1867 to make additional provision for the distribution of sewage matter over land, and facilitate the formation of joint sewerage boards where two or more sewage authorities within the same drainage area combined in providing sewage services.[29]

Further amendments to the law on sewerage provision were made under the Sanitary Act 1866. This specified that the owner or occupier of premises within the district of a sewer authority was entitled to cause his drains to empty into the sewers of the authority, on condition that the authority was given such notice as was required of his intention to do so, providing that the regulations of the authority concerning the mode of such communications was complied with and subject to any superintendence by the authority.[30] Where a complaint was made to the Secretary of State that the sewer authority was in default in failing to provide or maintain sewers

---

[26] s.30 Local Government Act 1858.
[27] s.4 Local Government Amendment Act 1861.
[28] ss.9 to 11 Sewage Utilisation Act 1865.
[29] Sewage Utilisation Act 1867.
[30] s.8 Sanitary Act 1866.

in its district and, after due inquiry he was satisfied that the authority were guilty of the default, an order could be made to compel the authority to perform its duty.[31]

The Public Health Act 1872 brought about the division of England into urban and rural sanitary districts in which responsibility for sewage was to be undertaken by corresponding local authorities. The Public Health Act 1875 consolidated earlier legislation relating to public health and introduced a number of minor amendments. It was the 1875 Act which served as the legal basis for the provision of sanitary services up until the enactment of the Public Health Act 1936.

## 2.5 The Salmon Fisheries Act 1861

Alongside the general pressure for improvement in water quality prompted by public health concerns, it is incongruous that the first general legislation making the pollution of water a criminal offence was motivated by quite different considerations. The Commissioners appointed to Inquire into Salmon Fisheries in England and Wales in 1860 found a marked decline in the productivity of salmon fisheries in many districts where rivers were polluted, especially where pollution was from mines, factories and gasworks.[32]

The legislative response to the Commissioners' Report was the Salmon Fisheries Act 1861 which made it an offence to pollute certain waters.[33] Specifically, it became an offence for a person to cause or knowingly permit to flow, or put or knowingly permit to be put into any waters containing salmon, or into any tributaries thereof, any liquid or solid matter to an extent as to cause the waters to poison or kill fish. The maximum penalties provided for in respect of this offence were, on first conviction, a fine of £5 and, on second conviction, a fine not exceeding £10, and a further penalty of £2 for every day on which the offence continued. On third or subsequent conviction a fine of £20 a day was provided for in relation to every day during which the offence continued, commencing with the date of the third conviction. The offence of poisoning salmon waters was restricted by the qualification that it was not to apply to anything done in the exercise of a legal right if it was proved that the best practicable means within a reasonable cost had been used to render harmless the liquid or solid matter permitted to flow or be put into waters. Perhaps because of these exceptions, however, the offence under the 1861 Act proved to be of limited effectiveness and appears to have been little used in practice. In part also, the reason for this abeyance may have been the more comprehensive approach to prohibition of water pollution provided for a few years later under the Rivers Pollution Prevention Act of 1876.

---

[31] *Ibid* s.49.

[32] Royal Commission on Salmon Fisheries (1861) pp.xix-xxi; and see Howarth (1987) Ch.2.

[33] s.5 Salmon Fisheries Act 1861; see now s.4 Salmon and Freshwater Fisheries Act 1975 and Ch.15 below.

## 2.6 The Rivers Pollution Prevention Act 1876

Although the early public health legislation largely achieved its first purpose of removing sewage from the centres of industrial towns, it frequently secured this objective by encouraging the wholesale dumping of untreated wastes into convenient watercourses.[34] In the later part of the nineteenth century it came to be realised that it was both feasible and necessary to treat sewage and other effluents if waterborne diseases were to be eradicated.

Royal Commissions had been established in 1865 and 1868 to inquire into the pollution of rivers and the means of preventing such pollution. Their eventual conclusions were that legislation was urgently necessary to prevent river pollution caused by sewage, mining and industrial pollution. If the prevention of river pollution was to be achieved, it was suggested[35] that it would be necessary, first, absolutely to forbid the casting of solid matter into river channels.[36] Second, it would be necessary to enact standards of purity below which any liquid discharges into a watercourse would be forbidden,[37] and for that purpose upper limits were formulated for suspended matter, organic carbon and nitrogen, colouration, metals, arsenic, chlorine, sulphur, acidity, alkalinity, and oil.[38] Third, with certain exceptions involving especially noxious effluents, manufacturers in towns should be given the power to discharge their drainage waters in the town sewers under suitable conditions.[39] These relatively radical proposals of the Royal Commission, in so far as they concerned the imposition of legislatively prescribed standards, never passed into law. Either because of the hostile response of manufacturing industry, or because of anticipated difficulties in administration of absolute standards for effluent,[40] the legislative response was the more cautious approach embodied in the Rivers Pollution Prevention Act 1876.

The Rivers Pollution Prevention Act 1876[41] was the first general enactment to be concerned directly and exclusively with the prevention of water pollution. Broadly, it imposed three categories of prohibition relating to pollution by solid matter, sewage pollution, and pollution from manufacturing and mining. In respect of solid matter it was made an offence under Part I of the Act for any person 'to put or cause to be put or to fall or knowingly permit to be put or to be carried into any stream'[42] any

---

[34] See Wohl (1983) p.234.

[35] See Royal Commission on the Pollution of Rivers (1874) p.50.

[36] A precedent for such a measure existed under s.18 Newport (Monmouthshire) Harbour Act 32 & 33 Vict c.118 (1869).

[37] A precedent for standards of forbidden discharges existed under the Alkali Act 26 & 27 Vict c.124 (1863).

[38] See Royal Commission on the Pollution of Rivers (1874) p.49; and Hammerton (1987) p.334.

[39] A precedent forbidding foul discharges into sewers existed under s.205 of the Metropolis Management Act 18 & 19 Vict c.120 (1855).

[40] See Richardson, Ogus and Burrows (1982) p.42.

[41] Generally see Hobday (1952) pp.207-10.

[42] For discussion of the present formula of 'cause or knowingly permit' in relation to the principal water pollution offences see 9.5-7 below.

of a range of matter which, 'either singly or in combination with other similar acts of the same or any other person, interfered with its due flow, or polluted its waters'. The solid matter in respect of which this offence was committed was stated to include the solid refuse of any manufactory, manufacturing process or quarry, or any rubbish or cinders, or any other waste or any putrid solid matter. Moreover the problem of cumulative sources of pollution[43] was addressed by means of a stipulation that, in proving interference with the due flow of any stream, or in proving the pollution of any stream, evidence may be given of repeated acts which together caused interference or pollution though each act taken by itself might not be sufficient for that purpose.[44] Thus the offence provided for in respect of pollution by solid matter could be committed by concurrent polluting acts by different persons, or consecutive polluting acts by the same person, wherever the end result was an interference with flow or the pollution of water.

Under Part II of the 1876 Act an offence was created where any person caused to fall or flow or to be carried into any stream any solid or liquid sewage matter. This general statement of the offence was circumscribed by qualifications which served significantly to limit its practical effect. Thus where any sewage matter fell, flowed or was carried into any stream along a channel used or constructed for the purpose of conveying sewage matter, the person causing or knowingly permitting this did not commit an offence if he was able to show that he had used the 'best practicable and available means' to render harmless the sewage matter passing into the stream.[45] The extent of this 'best practical means' defence was extended by the power of the Local Government Board to make an order to suspend the operation of this offence to permit a sanitary authority time to adopt the best practical and available means for rendering sewage matter harmless. It appears to have been envisaged that the most likely culprits in respect of the offence would be the local sanitary authorities. Thus the offence was stated not to be committed by a person other than a sanitary authority in respect of the passing of sewage matter into a stream along a drain communicating with any sewer provided by, belonging to, or under the control of any sanitary authority provided he had the sanction of the sanitary authority. That is, sanitary authorities were to take legal responsibility for the treatment of sewage lawfully passed to them for treatment.[46]

Part III of the 1876 Act was concerned with pollution caused by manufacturing and mining pollution. The basic offence concerning industrial pollution was committed by any person who caused to fall or flow or knowingly permitted to fall or flow, or to be carried into any stream any poisonous, noxious, or polluting liquid proceeding from any

---

[43] See *Crossley* v *Lightowler* (1867) 36 LJ Ch 584; *Blair and Sumner* v *Deakin* (1887) 52 JP 327; and see 3.2.5 below.

[44] s.2 Rivers Pollution Prevention Act 1876.

[45] *Ibid* s.3.

[46] On the present provisions relating to this, see s.87 Water Resources Act 1991 and see 9.14 below.

factory or manufacturing process.[47] This offence was made subject to the exception that it was not committed where industrial pollution flowed into a stream along a channel that was used or constructed for that purpose providing that it could be shown that the best practicable and reasonably available means was used to render harmless the polluting liquid passing into the stream. Similarly in respect of the prohibition imposed upon drainage into a stream from a mine, the basic offence was committed where a person caused to fall or flow, or knowingly permit to fall or flow or to be carried into any stream, any poisonous, noxious, or polluting solid or liquid matter proceeding from any mine, other than water in the same condition as that in which it had been drained or raised from the mine.[48] The offence was again circumscribed by the proviso that it was not committed where it was shown that the best practicable and reasonably available means had been used to render harmless the polluting matter passing into the stream.

Despite the apparent breadth of the measures provided for under the 1876 Act, it is generally accepted that the Act was largely ineffective in its objective of preventing the pollution of rivers.[49] Primarily, this was due to the extensive limitations imposed upon enforcement of the Act. In respect of Part III of the Act, concerned with manufacturing and mining pollution, proceedings were not to be taken except by a sanitary authority, and only then with the consent of the Local Government Board.[50] The Local Government Board were empowered to direct a sanitary authority to take proceedings on the application of an interested person alleging an offence had been committed. However, the Local Government Board, in giving or withholding their consent to proceedings, were to have regard to the industrial interests involved in the case and to the circumstances and requirements of the locality. In particular, it was specified that the Board were not to give their consent to proceedings by a sanitary authority, of any district which was the 'seat of any manufacturing industry', unless they were satisfied, after due enquiry, that means for rendering harmless the poisonous, noxious, or polluting, liquids proceeding from the processes of such manufacture were reasonably practicable and available, and that no material injury would be inflicted on the interests of industry by instigating proceedings. Notwithstanding the breadth of this exception, no proceedings could be brought in any case until two months after notice had been given of the intention to take such proceedings.[51] In effect, therefore, an Act which purported to outlaw the main forms of river pollution was emasculated by excessive restraints upon enforcement which in practical terms rendered the law a dead letter.

A significant shift of the burden of showing the offence of causing pollution by sewage matter, under the 1876 Act, was brought about under

---

[47] s.4 Rivers Pollution Prevention Act 1876, and for a discussion of the meaning of "poisonous, noxious or polluting" see **** below.

[48] s.5 Rivers Pollution Prevention Act 1876.

[49] See Turing (1952) p.72 and Hammerton (1987) p.333.

[50] s.6 Rivers Pollution Prevention Act 1876.

[51] *Ibid* s.13.

the Rivers Pollution Prevention Act 1893. This provided that where any sewage matter fell or flowed or was carried into any stream after passing through or along a channel which was vested in a sanitary authority, the sanitary authority would be deemed to have knowingly permitted the sewage matter to fall, flow or be carried into the water.[52] As a result sanitary authorities were to be strictly liable for failing to treat discharged sewage effluent adequately.

Between the enactment of the Rivers Pollution Prevention Act 1876 and its eventual repeal in 1951, a number of minor amendments were made to improve the effectiveness of the Act. Under s.14 of the Local Government Act 1888, a county council was given the power, in addition to other enforcement authorities, to enforce the 1876 Act in relation to so much of any stream as was situated within, or passed through or by, any part of its county. For the purpose of enforcement county councils were to have the same powers and duties as sanitary authorities.[53] A later amendment, under the Salmon and Freshwater Fisheries Act 1923, permitted fishery boards to institute proceedings under the 1876 and 1893 Acts in the same way as sanitary authorities with respect to the protection of fisheries in their districts.[54] In respect of the protection of fisheries, the Acts were to extend in their operation to the sea and tidal waters to an extent determined by the Minister of Health, though proceedings in respect of the pollution of such waters were not to be instituted without the consent of the Minister.

### 2.7 Public Health Legislation 1890 to 1937

Those parts of the Public Health Act 1875 concerned with the provision of sanitation and water pollution underwent a number of amendments concerned with the uses that could be made of sewers. The Public Health Acts Amendment Act 1890 created an offence where any person threw, or suffered to be thrown, or to pass into any sewer of a local authority, or any drain communicating therewith, any matter or substance which might interfere with the free flow of the sewage or surface water or storm water, or which might injure the sewer or drain.[55] In addition the Amendment Act made it unlawful for any person to throw or to suffer to be thrown, or to pass into the sewer of a local authority or any drain communicating thereto, certain harmful matter. Specifically, an offence was committed where a person turned into a public sewer, or communicating drain, chemical waste, or waste steam, condensing water, heated water or other liquid of a higher temperature than 110 degrees Fahrenheit which either alone or in combination with sewage caused a nuisance or was dangerous or injurious to health.[56]

---

[52] s.1 Rivers Pollution Prevention Act 1893, and see now s.87 Water Resources Act 1991 and 9.14.2 below on this.

[53] s.14 Local Government Act 1888.

[54] s.55 Salmon and Freshwater Fisheries Act 1923.

[55] s.16(1) Public Health Acts Amendment Act 1890, and see 11.3.5 below on the corresponding provisions in the present legislation.

[56] s.17(1) Public Health Acts Amendment Act 1890.

Further restrictions upon the permitted uses of sewers were introduced under the Public Health Act 1925 which prohibited the wilful or negligent emptying of calcium carbide or petroleum spirit into sewers or drains connecting therewith.[57] Part V of the 1925 Act empowered urban authorities to require watercourses and ditches abutting on land laid out for building to be covered in, culverts to be maintained and cleansed by the owners and occupiers thereof, and choked or silted up watercourses to be treated as statutory nuisances.[58] The sanitary provisions of the Public Health Act 1875 and the numerous Amending enactments were consolidated in the Public Health Act 1936.

In particular, Part IV of the Public Health Act 1936 consolidated provisions relating to water supply by local authorities. These provisions imposed duties upon local authorities to ascertain the sufficiency and wholesomeness of water supplies within their districts, insofar as reasonably practicable, to provide a piped supply of wholesome water to every part of their district and to provide a supply of water otherwise than in pipes where piped water could not be provided at a reasonable cost and where existing supplies were inadequate.[59] A local authority supplying water in accordance with these provisions was bound to secure that any water in any waterworks from which water was supplied for domestic purposes was wholesome.[60] In relation to the water supply duty upon local authorities, a range of powers were provided to allow authorities to acquire waterworks and rights to abstract and convey water, to construct reservoirs and to undertake various works concerned with the laying and maintaining of water mains.[61] Local authorities were also empowered to make byelaws for preventing waste, misuse or contamination of water supplied by them.[62]

Local authorities were also given powers in relation to water obtained from any well, tank or other source of supply not vested in a local authority where such water was, or was likely to be, used for domestic purposes or in the preparation of food or drink for human consumption and was, or was likely to become, so polluted as to be prejudicial to health. In these circumstances, the local authority was empowered to apply to a magistrates court for a summons to be issued to the owner or occupier of the premises requiring the source of supply to be permanently or temporarily closed or cut off, or that the water should be used for only for specified purposes. Alternatively, a court was empowered to make any other order necessary to prevent injury or danger to the health of persons using the water, or consuming food or drink prepared using the water. Where a person failed to comply with such an order, a court was

---

[57] s.41(1) Public Health Act 1925, and see 11.3.5 below on the corresponding provisions in the present legislation.

[58] ss.51-54 Public Health Act 1925, and see 8.4 below on the present provisions concerning statutory nuisances.

[59] s.111 Public Health Act 1936.

[60] s.115 Public Health Act 1936, previously provided for under s.35 Waterworks Clauses Act 1847, and see Ch.17 on present requirements for drinking water quality.

[61] ss.116, 118 and 119 Public Health Act 1936.

[62] *Ibid* s.132.

empowered, on application of the local authority, to authorise the authority to do whatever was necessary to give effect to the order and any expenses incurred in so doing could be recovered by the authority from the person in default.[63]

Although the Public Health Act 1936 had conferred upon the owner or occupier of any premises the right to have a drain or sewer communicate with a public sewer of the local authority, this right had specifically excluded the discharge of liquid from a factory or a manufacturing process.[64] Industrial effluent discharges were separately provided for under the Public Health (Drainage of Trade Premises) Act 1937, which reaffirmed the principle that the occupier of trade premises was entitled, subject to the control of the local authority, to discharge trade effluent into public sewers of the local authority.[65] Thus, the occupier of any trade premises within the district of a local authority could, with the consent of the authority or, so far as was permitted by byelaws made by the authority, discharge into public sewers any trade effluent proceeding from the premises.[66] 'Trade effluent' was defined to mean any liquid, either with or without particles or matter in suspension therein, which was wholly or in part produced in the course of any trade or industry carried on at any premises used, or intended to be used, for those purposes.[67]

Discharges which had commenced before the 1937 Act came into force, and certain other discharges, were exempt from the requirement of obtaining trade effluent consents. Otherwise, consent for a discharge of trade effluent into a public sewer required the owner or occupier of trade premises seeking to make the discharge to serve the local authority with a 'trade effluent notice'. This notice contained information about the nature and composition, maximum quantity and highest rate of the proposed discharge. Upon receipt of a trade effluent notice, and subject to the approval of certain interested bodies, the local authority could give consent either unconditionally or subject to conditions as to the receiving sewer, the nature and composition of the effluent, the maximum quantity of effluent, the highest rate of discharge and any other matter provided for by byelaws under the Act. Persons aggrieved by a decision of a local authority in relation to a trade effluent notice or the terms of a discharge consent were given a right of appeal to the Minister.[68]

Another aspect of the relationship between a discharger of trade effluent and the local authority provided for under the 1937 Act was the possibility of payment being made to defray the cost of effluent treatment. The Act

---

[63] s.140 Public Health Act 1936. A power had previously been provided for under s.70 Public Health Act 1875 to take action in relation to polluted private water supplies, but this power had only been available where water was actually found to be polluted, rather than 'likely to become' polluted.

[64] s.34 Public Health Act 1936.

[65] Previously provided for under s.21 Public Health Act 1875, and for the present provisions concerning this see 11.3 below.

[66] s.1(1) Public Health (Drainage of Trade Premises) Act 1937.

[67] *Ibid* s.14(1).

[68] *Ibid* ss.2 to 4.

provided that agreements could be entered into between the occupier of any trade premises and a local authority, with the approval of any interested body, regarding the reception and disposal of any trade effluent produced from the premises. In particular, agreements of this kind could provide for the construction by the local authority of any works that might be required for the reception or disposal of effluent, and the repayment by the owner or occupier of premises of any expenses incurred by the local authority in carrying out their obligations under the agreement. Similarly, local authorities were empowered to enter into agreements with the owner or occupier of trade premises, whereby the local authority undertook to remove and dispose of substances produced in the course of treating trade effluent on, or in connection with, those premises.[69]

The 1937 Act empowered local authorities to make byelaws in respect of trade effluent discharges covering a range of specified matters. Amongst other things, byelaws could determine the periods of the day during which discharges could be made; could require the exclusion from trade effluent of condensing water; or could require the exclusion from the effluent of specified constituents which might injure or obstruct sewers or make specially difficult or expensive the treatment or disposal of the sewage from those sewers. Trade effluent byelaws were subject to ministerial confirmation and, in the event of a local authority failing to make a byelaw when required to do so by the Minister, the Minister himself was entitled to make a byelaw which would have the same effect as if made by the local authority.[70]

Another power given to local authorities under the 1937 Act was that of taking samples of trade effluents. This permitted officers of the authority to obtain and take away samples of any trade effluent which was passing from premises into a public sewer of the authority. The admissibility of analysis of the sample in legal proceedings was, however, subject to compliance with formalities which required the officer taking the sample to notify the occupier of the premises of the intention to have the sample analysed. Thereafter the sample was to be divided into three parts, each sealed and marked, and one part delivered to the occupier of the premises, one part retained for future comparison and one part submitted for analysis.[71]

## 2.8 The Water Act 1945

A Government White Paper entitled, *A National Water Policy*,[72] was published in 1944 identifying a range of defects in the existing system of arrangements relating to water supply. Water supply was then provided for by 'statutory undertakers' consisting of local authorities, acting singly or in combination, and statutory water supply companies. In some instances

---

[69] *Ibid* s.7, and see 11.8 below on the present provisions concerning trade effluent agreements.

[70] ss.5 and 6 Public Health (Drainage of Trade Premises) Act 1937.

[71] s.10 Public Health (Drainage of Trade Premises) Act 1937, and see 16.9 below on the repeal of the tripartite sampling requirement.

[72] HM Government, *A National Water Policy* (Cmd.6515, 1944).

local authorities derived their powers from public health legislation, otherwise local authorities and all statutory companies derived their powers from local Acts of Parliament individually regulating the management of particular undertakings. It was recognised that the law relating to water supply was rather vague and inconsistent and that there was a general lack of ministerial supervision to ensure that powers were properly exercised.

A key weakness in the administrative arrangements lay in the multiplicity of water undertakers, which amounted to over 1,000 bodies, operating under different statutory powers and varying greatly in size, resources and efficiency. Other identified problems lay in the lack of information about surface and underground water sources, the uses which could be made of these and the lack of control over the exploitation of such sources. Along with this, it was recognised that there was a need for greater stringency in the protection of public water supplies against contamination. More broadly, the need was perceived for a thorough overhaul of the water supply system to take account of increasing water consumption and the need to raise standards to meet future needs.

For the most part,[73] the White Paper proposals were given effect to by the Water Act 1945.[74] Part I of this Act placed a duty upon the Minister of Health to promote the conservation and proper use of water resources and the provision of water supplies and to secure the effective execution by water undertakers, under his control and direction, of a national policy relating to water.[75] Statutory provision was made for a Central Advisory Water Committee to advise the Government on general questions in relation to water and for Joint Advisory Water Committees to be constituted by ministerial order where these were necessary in any area.[76] Ministerial powers were greatly extended to allow information to be obtained in relation to surface and underground water resources and use. For this purpose, local authorities and statutory water undertakers could be required to carry out surveys and formulate proposals relation to water consumption and demand. Also, provision was made for the supply of records and information from persons abstracting water from any source or where certain boreholes for the abstraction of groundwater were proposed.[77]

Part II of the 1945 Act dealt with the local organisation of water supplies and included machinery for securing, if necessary by compulsion, the combination of water undertakers and the transfer of undertakings, the variation of areas in which supply could be provided and the supply of

---

[73] See also the River Boards Act 1948 at 2.9 below.

[74] See also the Water Act 1948 which amended the 1945 Act.

[75] s.1 Water Act 1945.

[76] *Ibid* ss.2 and 3.

[77] *Ibid* ss.5 to 7. Note also s.9 River Boards Act 1948, discussed at 2.9 below, which placed a duty upon river boards to conserve the water resources of their area and enables the Minister to direct a river board to furnish information as to the abstraction of water from rivers and other inland water and to provide information as to the water resources generally.

water in bulk.[78] Default powers were given to the Minister in relation to various types of complaint concerning water undertakers. Hence, where it was alleged that a local authority had failed to discharge a duty of water supply[79] or a statutory water undertaker had failed to provide an adequate supply of water, either in respect of quantity or quality, and there had been a failure to take reasonably practicable steps to remedy the failure, the Minister was entitled to investigate the complaint and to hold a local inquiry into the matter. If satisfied that the complaint was well-founded, the Minister was empowered to make an order declaring a water undertaker to be in default and directing it to remedy the matter within a reasonable time. Failure to comply with such a direction would allow relevant functions of the undertaker to be transferred to the Minister and any expenses incurred by the Minister in discharging those functions charged to the body in default.[80]

Part III of the 1945 Act provided for the conservation and protection of water resources and the prevention of waste. This allowed the Minister to impose special measures for water conservation by the imposition of a licensing requirement for new or increased abstractions of water within a designated area. Water undertakers were able to make agreements with land owners or occupiers, or local authorities, for carrying out drainage and other works intended to safeguard the purity of supplies and to execute works for the protection of water sources. Alternatively, a specific power was given to allow statutory water undertakers to acquire land for the purpose of protecting water against pollution.[81] Undertakers were also given general powers to make byelaws, subject to ministerial approval, imposing penalties for preventing waste, misuse, contamination and pollution of water, with a power given to the Minister to require the making of such byelaws and to make byelaws himself in a case of default.[82] In addition, a specific offence was created where a person was found guilty of any act or neglect by which any spring, well or adit, from which water was used or likely to be used for human consumption, was polluted or was likely to be polluted. However, it was stated that this offence was not to be construed as prohibiting or restricting any method of cultivating land according to the principles of good husbandry or the reasonable use of oil or tar on public highways so long as the highway authority took reasonable steps to prevent water pollution.[83]

Part IV of the 1945 Act allowed water undertakers to construct works, to acquire land, to obtain and to supply water and to deal with various other matters essential or incidental to their undertakings. Another significant innovation in the 1945 Act was the provision, under Schedule 3 to the Act, of a series of standard clauses concerning the activities of water undertakers, for incorporation, with or without modification, in orders

---

[78] ss.8-12 Water Act 1945.
[79] Under s.111 Public Health Act 1936.
[80] s.13 Water Act 1945.
[81] ss.14,15 and 22 Water Act 1945, see now Part VI Water Industry Act 1991, and 7.6.2 below.
[82] ss.17-20 Water Act 1945.
[83] s.21 Water Act 1945, see now s.72 Water Industry Act 1991, and 17.10 below.

made under the Act. These clauses dealt with the relations of water undertakers with consumers, with highway and other authorities and bodies and related matters. A mechanism was provided for by which the new 'waterworks code' could be applied to existing acts and orders, subject to such modification and adaptations as were specified in ministerial orders. Hence Schedule 3 progressively superseded the original waterworks code, governing the day to day operation of water undertakings, which had been provided for under the Waterworks Clauses Act 1847.

## 2.9 River Boards Act 1948

The Central Advisory Water Committee, formally provided for under the Water Act 1945 to advise the Government upon matters connected with the conservation and use of water resources, submitted a series of reports having a profound effect upon the development of water pollution law. The Third Report of the Committee drew attention to the shortcomings in the administration of water law in observing:

> [t]he defects of the system are most apparent when the mitigation of pollution is considered. The boundaries of the larger local government areas necessarily bear no relation to watershed areas. There are in consequence many separate Authorities with responsibilities in relation to the same river basin even if, which is not always the case, the County Councils exercise a general control. Moreover, the larger rivers run through several counties or may form county boundaries, so that, even though one County Council may actively administer the powers of the Acts, there is no guarantee that the work will be effectively carried out throughout the river basin. There is thus a patchwork system of control, with several Authorities, possibly with differing ideas of the desirable standard of purity, dealing with the one river, or, what is worse, neglect arising from the fact that with so many responsible Authorities, each Authority may be inclined to leave the duty of enforcing the Acts to others. With divided responsibility, moreover, the failure of one Authority to administer the law may well nullify the work of those Authorities who take their duties more seriously.[84]

The solution to the defective system of river pollution control generated through the overlap of functions of different bodies, was that the number of authorities should be greatly reduced by the formation of new 'river boards' taking responsibility for the pollution control functions of all the existing bodies within watershed areas.[85]

The proposal to reallocate administrative responsibility for river pollution control was given effect by the River Boards Act 1948 which established river boards and conferred upon them comprehensive responsibility for

---

[84] Central Advisory Water Committee, *River Boards* (Cd.6465, 1943) para.57.
[85] *Ibid* para.59.

river pollution control. Each river board area was to consist of an area the drainage of which was related to a river, or group of rivers, and defined by watersheds or catchment areas. Within their respective areas, each river board was to assume the pollution control functions previously exercised by a range of authorities.[86] Hence powers previously enjoyed by local authorities to bring proceedings to protect a watercourse from pollution,[87] were henceforth to be exercised by river boards. Similarly, the power of a sanitary authority to bring proceedings for pollution,[88] were to be exercised by river boards. Likewise, any local Act or statutory order, conferring functions relating to river pollution on any local authority or any joint board of local authorities, was to have effect as if reference to those authorities were replaced by references to the river authority for the area. The effect of this was that the multiplicity of bodies which had previously possessed concurrent responsibility over the administration of water pollution law were to be superseded, and each part of England and Wales, other than the Thames and Lee catchment areas (which were excluded from the operation of the Act) was to have its river pollution law administered by a single body with comprehensive powers of enforcement.

A substantive innovation brought into effect under the River Boards Act 1948 was the empowering of river boards to take samples of effluent passing from any land or vessel into any river, stream, watercourse or inland water in their area. As with the analogous provisions applicable to the sampling of trade effluent by local authorities, under the Public Health (Drainage of Trade Premises) Act 1937, the admissibility of samples of effluent depended upon the compliance with a formal sampling procedure. This involved threefold division of the sample into sealed and marked containers with one part delivered to the occupier of the land, another part retained for future comparison, and the third part submitted for analysis.[89] An offence was committed where any person wilfully obstructed a person exercising a right to take a sample in accordance with these provisions.[90]

## 2.10 The Rivers (Prevention of Pollution) Acts 1951 to 1961

Despite the administrative rationalisation which had been accomplished in making water pollution law enforcement the responsibility of the newly established river boards, shortcomings remained with the substance of the law, the central enactment of which remained the Rivers Pollution Prevention Act 1876. A Central Advisory Water Committee sub-committee with a remit to investigate measures for strengthening the law regarding the prevention of pollution of rivers and streams recommended replacement of the 1876 Act by a comprehensive code making it an offence to allow offensive matter, solid or fluid, to enter a stream. It was proposed that the river boards should prescribe minimum standards for

---

[86] ss.2(1) and 4(1) and para.14 Sch.3 River Boards Act 1948.
[87] Under s.69 Public Health Act 1875.
[88] Under ss.6 and 8 Rivers Pollution Prevention Act 1876.
[89] s.15 River Boards Act 1948, and see 16.9 below on the repeal of the tripartite sampling procedure.
[90] s.17 River Boards Act 1948.

purity, temperatures, and colouration by byelaws, subject to confirmation by the Minister, on the basis of surveys of the streams concerned, and new discharges into streams should be subject to control. Although these proposals were never fully implemented, the need for repeal of the 1876 Act was conceded and it was replaced by the Rivers (Prevention of Pollution) Act 1951.[91] This enactment was to be enforced by the river boards, along with the two Catchment Boards for the Thames and Lee areas, and certain local authorities in and around London that had been excluded from the 1948 River Boards Act.

A key provision of the Rivers (Prevention of Pollution) Act 1951 was the general prohibition on use of a stream for the disposal of polluting matter. Hence it was an offence for a person to cause or knowingly permit to enter a stream any poisonous, noxious or polluting matter. Alternatively, it was an offence to cause or permit matter to enter a stream so as to tend, either directly or in combination with similar acts, to impede the proper flow of the water of the stream in a manner leading, or likely to lead, to a substantial aggravation of pollution due to other causes.[92] For these purposes, a local authority was deemed to cause or knowingly permit to enter a stream any poisonous, noxious or polluting matter which passed into the stream from any sewer or sewage disposal works vested. This situation arose where either the authority was bound to receive the matter into the sewer or sewage disposal works, or it consented to do so unconditionally, or it consented to do so subject to conditions which were observed. The offence of using a stream for the disposal of polluting matter was subject to the defence that it was not reasonably practicable to dispose of the effluent in any other way. The effect of the new offence was, amongst other things, to bring to an end the distinctions previously drawn between sewage pollution and industrial pollution, and between solid and liquid pollution, and to replace them by a comprehensive offence covering all kinds of pollution. The position of local authorities who had responsibility for sewage treatment was that failure to discharge their duty in such a way as to avoid pollution would make them guilty of the offence as a matter of strict liability.[93]

The central water pollution offence of using a stream for the disposal of polluting matter contrary to the 1951 Act was made subject to a number of significant qualifications. Of greatest practical importance amongst these was the innovation of subjecting *new* discharges of trade or sewage effluent to a system of licensing whereby the discharge of such effluent into a stream from a new or altered outlet was permitted where the consent of the appropriate river board had been obtained. Similarly, discharges of

---

[91] General reading on the Rivers (Prevention of Pollution) Act 1951, the Clean Rivers (Estuaries and Tidal Waters) Act 1960 and the Rivers (Prevention of Pollution) Act 1961 (cited together as 'The Rivers (Prevention of Pollution) Acts 1951 to 1961') includes Klein (1957) Ch.2; Fort and Brayshaw (1961) Ch.VIII; Klein (1962) Ch.2; McLoughlin (1972) Ch.2; Newsom and Sherratt (1972) Ch.II; Bigham (1973) Ch.7; Garner (1974); and Walker (1979) Ch.2.

[92] s.2(1) Rivers (Prevention of Pollution) Act 1951, and see now s.85 Water Resources Act 1991 and 9.3 below.

[93] See now s.87 Water Resources Act 1991 discussed at 9.14.2 below.

trade or sewage effluent begun or substantially increased, in respect of their temperature, rate of discharge or volume, or altered in their nature or composition, after the Act came into force, were made subject to a discharge consent granted by the river boards.[94] Consent to such discharges, which could not be unreasonably withheld, could be made subject to conditions as to the point of discharge into the stream, the construction of the outlet, the use of the outlet or any other outlet for trade or sewage effluent from the same land or premises. In the case of a new discharge, conditions could be imposed as to the nature and composition, temperature, volume or rate of discharge of effluent from the land or premises from which the discharge was to be made. Another qualification to the offence of using a stream for the disposal of polluting matter was that, initially, ministerial consent was required for a prosecution involving pollution by trade or sewage effluent.[95]

It was anticipated that the role of river boards in relation to the implementation of the 1951 Act would be wide ranging in that they were empowered to take pre-emptive action to prevent pollution. Hence, where a river board apprehended that use of a stream for the disposal of polluting matter was likely to occur, it could take action by applying for a court order to prohibit a proposed use of a stream, land or a vessel.[96] Also river boards were able to make byelaws, in respect of any stream in their area, prescribing standards for determining when matter was to be treated as poisonous, noxious or polluting; for prohibiting or regulating the use of a stream for washing or cleansing things of any description; and for prohibiting or regulating the keeping on a stream of vessels with sanitary appliances.[97] The consent of a river board was also required before a person was allowed to cleanse any part of the channel or bed of a stream of a deposit accumulated by reason of any dam in such a way as to cause the deposit to be carried away in suspension in the water of the stream. Likewise, it was an offence for a person, wilfully and without the consent of the river board, to cut or uproot any substantial amount of vegetation in a stream, or so near the stream that it fell in, and to allow the vegetation to remain in the stream.[98]

The main provisions of the 1951 Act were only stated to apply to the pollution of 'streams', though this term was defined to include any river, watercourse or inland water, whether natural or artificial, except that it did not include any lake or pond which did not discharge into a stream, or any sewer vested in a local authority, or tidal waters.[99] It was, however, possible for a ministerial order to be made to the effect that provisions of the Act should apply to any tidal waters or parts of the sea as specified in the order. In such a case application for an order had to be made by either a

---

[94] s.7 Rivers (Prevention of Pollution) Act 1951, and see now s.88 Water Resources Act 1991 and Ch.10 below.

[95] s.8(2) Rivers (Prevention of Pollution) Act 1951.

[96] *Ibid* s.3(1).

[97] *Ibid* s.5(1)(a).

[98] *Ibid* s.4(1) and see 9.15 for discussion of the present counterpart of this offence.

[99] *Ibid* s.11(1) and see 9.4 below for a discussion of 'controlled waters'.

river board or a person appearing to have an interest in the matter and the making of the order was subject to certain requirements concerning advance publicity.[100]

The Clean Rivers (Estuaries and Tidal Waters) Act 1960 amended the Rivers (Prevention of Pollution) Act 1951 in order to give river boards powers to deal with new outlets and discharges of trade or sewage effluent into tidal waters or parts of the sea. This was accomplished by extending the 1951 Act to the use of new or altered outlets for the discharge of trade or sewage effluent into streams, and the making of new discharges into streams, to tidal waters or parts of the sea within certain seaward limits.[101] In respect of these 'controlled waters' the requirements of the discharge consent system applied, as for freshwater 'streams' under the 1951 Act.

A major reform brought about under the Rivers (Prevention of Pollution) Act 1961 was the subjection of discharges of trade and sewage effluent which had been in existence since before 1951 to the system of discharge consents applicable to post-1951 discharges under the 1951 Act. The continuation of pre-1951 discharges was to be subject to consents, applications for which had to state the nature and composition, maximum temperature, maximum quantity and highest rate of discharge of effluent. With the exception of certain discharges of water from certain mines, the practical effect of this was that it became unlawful to make a discharge of any trade or sewage effluent brought under the consent system by the 1961 Act without river board consent.[102] Consents given under the 1961 Act, along with those under the 1951 Act, were to be subject to review from time to time, and were subject to variation or revocation, but a consent would not normally be altered before the expiry of a reasonable period of not less than two years.[103]

The 1961 Act brought about several further amendments to the 1951 Act, including removing the need for ministerial consent before a prosecution could be brought for use of a stream for disposal of polluting matter. However, a new restriction imposed upon proceedings under either Act was that proceedings could not be instituted except with the consent of the Attorney-General or by a river board.[104] A second amendment, in respect of the offence of using a stream for the disposal of polluting matter, was the removal of the defence under the 1951 Act that it was not reasonably practicable to dispose of the effluent in any other way.[105] A third amendment was the introduction of new provisions relating to the taking of samples of effluent, and restrictions upon the disclosure of information obtained in connection the Acts.[106] A fourth amendment was that the power

---

[100] *Ibid* s.6.

[101] s.1 and Sch.1 Clean Rivers (Estuaries and Tidal Waters) Act 1960.

[102] s.1 Rivers (Prevention of Pollution) Act 1961.

[103] *Ibid* s.5(1) and (2).

[104] *Ibid* ss.8(2) and 11(1).

[105] *Ibid* s.8(3) (given the establishment of a discharge consent system which allowed matters of this kind to be taken into account).

[106] *Ibid* ss.10 and 12.

of river boards to make byelaws to prescribing standards for the purpose of determining whether an effluent is polluting was to cease to have effect.[107] It appeared that this power had proved to be an impractical means of regulating discharges.[108]

## 2.11 The Public Health Act 1961

Part V of the Public Health Act 1961 made a number of important amendments to the Public Health (Drainage of Trade Premises) Act 1937 concerning the discharge of trade effluents into public sewers. For certain 'exempted' discharges[109] which pre-dated the 1937 Act, or where discharges had been subject to an alteration in the sewage system brought about by the local authority,[110] a local authority was able to impose charges for the discharge of trade effluent into a public sewer. In particular, the charges made by the local authority were to have regard to the nature and composition and to the volume and rate of discharge of the trade effluent, to any additional expense incurred or likely to be incurred by a sewerage authority in connection with the reception or disposal and to any revenue likely to be derived by a sewage authority from the trade effluent.[111] In respect of the exempted discharges, the 1961 Act empowered the local authorities to impose conditions relating to a number of matters including the provision and maintenance of inspection chambers to facilitate sampling of effluent passing from trade premises into a sewer, and meters to measure the volume and rate of discharge of effluent. Further conditions could be imposed to require records to be kept of the volume and rate of discharge of trade effluent, and to require returns to be made to the local authority in respect of the volume, rate of discharge, nature and composition of trade effluent discharged.[112]

The power of local authorities to make byelaws regulating the discharge of trade effluents provided for by the 1937 Act[113] was abolished by the 1961 Act. In fact this amounted to a formality since the byelaw making power had proved to be impractical and no byelaws were actually made under it. In lieu of the abandonment of byelaw regulation, certain matters upon which a local authority had previously been empowered to make byelaws, could, in future, be the subject of conditions imposed in trade discharge consents.[114]

Two amendments in the scope of trade discharge licensing by local authorities involved the expansion of the consent system to new fields of enterprise. The first of these was that effluents from farms and horticultural

---

[107] *Ibid* s.4(2).

[108] See Richardson, Ogus and Burrows (1982) p.42 n.36.

[109] Under s.4 Public Health (Drainage of Trade Premises) Act 1937.

[110] Under s.42 Public Health Act 1936.

[111] s.55(2) Public Health Act 1961.

[112] s.57 Public Health Act 1961, and see now s.121 Water Industry Act 1991, discussed at 11.5 below.

[113] Under s.5 Public Health (Drainage of Trade Premises) Act 1937.

[114] ss.58 and 59 Public Health Act 1961.

premises and premises used for scientific research or experiment were brought within the definition of 'trade effluent' and became subject to trade discharge consent.[115] The second extension of the trade discharge consent system concerned the removal of exemption from consent which had previously applied in relation to laundry premises.[116]

## 2.12 The Water Resources Act 1963

Reports of a Central Advisory Water Committee Sub-committee, established to consider the extent of the increasing demand for water, were followed by a White Paper on *Water Conservation in England and Wales*[117] the proposals in which were implemented in the Water Resources Act 1963.[118] The 1963 Act was intended to promote the conservation and proper use of water resources through the extension of the national policy for water in England and Wales. Under the Water Act 1945 it had become the duty of the Minister of Health to promote the conservation and proper use of water resources and the provision of water supplies, and to formulate and effectively execute a national policy relating to water.[119] The 1963 Act extended this duty to require the Minister of Housing and Local Government and the Minister of Health, acting jointly, to include in the national policy for water such measures as they considered necessary or expedient for augmenting and redistributing water resources, and to secure that the policy would be effectively executed by 'river authorities' in so far as the policy related to matters falling within their functions.[120] The 27 new river authorities were to succeed the 32 river boards which had been established under the River Boards Act 1948, and to take over a range of functions including those relating to river pollution control.[121] In addition to important new powers in relation to the licensing of water abstraction,[122] the new river authorities were to acquire additional functions concerned with water pollution control.

Amongst the new pollution control functions acquired by river authorities under the Water Resources Act 1963 was the control of discharges into underground strata. Subject to a discharge consent being obtained, it became an offence to discharge any trade effluent or sewage effluent or any other poisonous, noxious or polluting matter into any underground strata within a river authority area by means of any well, borehole or pipe. In effect, underground discharges became subject to an analogous system of discharge consents to that operating in respect of discharges into surface watercourses. In the same way, consent to an underground discharge could be given by a river authority, either unconditionally or subject to

---

[115] s.63 Public Health Act 1961.

[116] s.65 Public Health Act 1961 (previously exemption had been provided for under s.4(4) Public Health (Drainage of Trade Premises) Act 1937).

[117] HM Government, *Water Conservation in England and Wales* (Cmnd.1693, 1962).

[118] Generally see Craine (1969) and Trice and Godwin (1974).

[119] s.1 Water Act 1945.

[120] s.1(1) Water Resources Act 1963.

[121] *Ibid* s.5(1).

[122] *Ibid* s.63.

reasonable conditions as to the nature, composition and volume of the effluent to be discharged, the strata into which could be discharged, the measures to be taken for the protection of underground water, and the provision of facilities for inspection.[123] Consents so granted could be revoked or varied by the river authority and a person aggrieved by a revocation or variation, or refusal of the river authority to vary the terms of a consent, was entitled to appeal to the Minister. The river authority was bound to keep a register containing particulars of all consents granted in respect of underground discharges of effluent.[124]

In accordance with the extended powers of river authorities under the 1963 Act, powers to take samples of effluent, which had been granted to river boards under the River Boards Act 1948, were also extended. River authorities could obtain and take away samples of effluent passing from any land or vessel into any inland water in the authority area, any tidal water or part of the sea adjoining the coast of the authority's area or any controlled waters[125] adjoining that area or any underground strata in that area. This power to take samples was subject to the same formalities relating to threefold division as under the 1948 Act if the results of analysis were to be admissible in evidence, and an offence was similarly committed in respect of wilful obstruction of a person exercising a right to take an effluent sample.[126]

Another new function arising under the 1963 Act concerned the powers given to river authorities to take emergency measures in situations involving water pollution. These powers were to be exercised where it appeared to a river authority that any poisonous, noxious or polluting matter was present in an inland water, in the area of the authority, and had entered that water in consequence of an accident or other unforeseen act or event. In these circumstances, the authority was to carry out such operations as were necessary to remove the matter from the water and dispose of it in such a manner as it considered appropriate, and to remedy or mitigate any pollution caused by its presence in the water.[127] The 1963 Act also introduced powers to make byelaws for the protection of water resources.[128]

## 2.13  The Control of Pollution Act 1974

Although out of precise chronological order, it is convenient at this point to consider the further amendment of water pollution legislation that was brought about by the Control of Pollution Act 1974[129] and, as a

---

[123] *Ibid* s.72.

[124] *Ibid* ss.74 and 75.

[125] Within the meaning of the Clean Rivers (Estuaries and Tidal Waters) Act 1960.

[126] s.113 Water Resources Act 1963.

[127] *Ibid* s.76.

[128] *Ibid* s.79.

[129] For general reading on the Control of Pollution Act 1974 see Garner (1975); Walker (1979) Ch.2; McLoughlin (1975); Burton and Freestone (1986); and House of Commons Environment Committee, *Pollution of Rivers and Estuaries* (1987).

consequence, the almost complete repeal of the Rivers (Prevention of Pollution) Acts 1951 to 1961. The 1974 Act contained provisions which applied to almost all inland waters, including some underground waters, and estuaries and coastal waters within a three nautical mile limit.[130] In relation to these waters, two key offences were provided for in respect of water pollution. The first offence arose where there was an entry of poisonous, noxious or polluting mater into water, whereas the second arose where that was an unauthorised discharge of effluent into waters.[131] Between the two offences, a distinction was envisaged between spontaneous or casual incidents giving rise to pollution as opposed to continuing activities where emissions were regulated by a discharge consent. Under the 1974 Act general restrictions were imposed upon the defences available to persons causing pollution.[132] Controls were applied to trade effluent discharges into public sewers which commenced before the Public Health (Drainage of Trade Premises) Act 1937 came into effect, thereby extending the trade effluent consent system to all discharges of relevant effluent.[133] New duties and powers were given to water authorities, established under the Water Act 1973,[134] to remedy and forestall pollution and, where the flora or fauna of a stream had been damaged as a result of a discharge made under a consent granted by them, a requirement to carry out operations to remedy the situation.[135] New powers were given to control the use of sanitary appliances on vessels, and for the Secretary of State to make regulations to prohibit or restrict activities which were likely to result in the pollution of water.[136]

Perhaps the most significant general reform under the 1974 Act was the 'opening up' of access to environmental information provided for under the Act.[137] This was introduced by a requirement that discharge consent applications should, generally, be advertised, permitting third party representation to be made. Further provision was made for 'call-in' powers by the Secretary of State, allowing the consideration of an application for a consent at a public inquiry.[138] Public involvement was further provided for by the establishment of a general right of access to information about

---

[130] s.56(1) Control of Pollution Act 1974: putting to an end the previous distinction between pollution control in tidal and non-tidal waters under the Rivers (Prevention of Pollution) Acts 1951 to 1961, and see now s.104 Water Resources Act 1991, and discussion of 'controlled waters' at 9.4 below.

[131] s.31(1) and (2) Control of Pollution Act 1974, see now s.85 Water Resources Act 1991 on the principal water pollution offences and discussion in 9.3 below.

[132] Under s.31(2) and (3) Control of Pollution Act 1974.

[133] *Ibid* s.34.

[134] See 2.14–15 below on the Water Act 1973.

[135] s.46 Control of Pollution Act 1974, and see now s.161 Water Resources Act 1991, though note that the provisions concerning anti-pollution works and operations are now formulated as a power, rather than a duty, of the regulatory authority, and see 13.2 below on anti-pollution works and operations.

[136] s.33 Control of Pollution Act 1974, see now s.210 Water Resources Act 1991, and see 12.4.9 below.

[137] See Ch.16 below on environmental information generally.

[138] ss.34-40 Control of Pollution Act 1974, and for a discussion of the present provisions see Ch.10 below.

discharge consents contained in public registers.[139] However, whilst the provisions in the Act allowing for greater openness and public access to information had become enacted in law, there was an extensive period of delay before the information-related provisions of the Act were actually implemented and this was the subject of criticism. In 1984, some ten years after enactment, the Royal Commission on Environmental Pollution expressed the regret that the 1974 Act had become an example of 'optional' legislation whereby Ministers' unfettered discretion over commencement dates had effectively frustrated Parliament's intentions.[140] Eventually, in 1985, the key provisions relating to information were brought into effect.[141]

### 2.14 The Water Act 1973

The Water Act 1973 marked a major turning point in the modern history of water pollution legislation.[142] A key purpose of the enactment was that of administrative rationalisation and to appreciate the significance of this it is necessary to recognise the rather complicated administrative arrangements that had arisen through the cumulative effect of the legislation previously described. On the eve of implementation of the 1973 Act, the structure of water supply and sewage treatment responsibilities in England and Wales demonstrated a remarkable degree of fragmentation. Water supply rested with 198 different undertakings including 64 local authorities, 101 joint water boards consisting of groupings of local authorities and 33 private statutory water supply companies. Sewerage responsibilities lay with over 1,300 county boroughs and county district councils and 24 joint sewerage boards. Alongside these, water conservation and the control of pollution was primarily the responsibility of 29 river authorities. The multiplicity of bodies involved was generally recognised to be unsatisfactory and it was thought necessary to reduce their number and to secure a greater degree of co-ordination between them so as to reduce conflicts between water users. Hence, administrative simplification in the allocation of water responsibilities was a principal objective of the 1973 Act.[143]

The criticism of fragmentation of responsibility had been confirmed in a report of the Central Advisory Water Committee, *The Future Management of Water in England and Wales*,[144] which affirmed the need for mechanisms for resolution of conflicts between the different bodies

---

[139] s.41 Control of Pollution Act 1974, see now s.190 Water Resources Act 1991, and see 16.15 below on the pollution control register.

[140] See Royal Commission on Environmental Pollution (1984) paras.2.56 and 3.50 and similarly see Royal Commission on Environmental Pollution (1981) para.5.47.

[141] On the practical operation of the provisions of a public register see DoE, Circular 17/84, *Water and the Environment: the Implementation of the Control of Pollution Act 1974* (1984); Burton and Freestone (1986); Burton (1987); Burton (1989) and see the discussion of the pollution control register at 16.15 below.

[142] Generally, see Telling (1974) and McLoughlin (1973).

[143] For general discussions of the policy background see Funnell and Hey (1974); Okun (1977); Porter, (1978); Jordan, Richardson and Kimber (1977); and Hassan (1998) Ch.5.

[144] Central Advisory Water Committee, *The Future Management of Water in England and Wales* (1971).

involved. The report concluded with the recommendation that the number of operating units should be reduced and a change in the relationships between authorities was necessary to permit the formation and implementation of comprehensive water management plans. The response of the Government was announced in a Circular from the Department of the Environment which stated,

> [t]he Government are satisfied that the full integration of water services is now essential . . . there is an urgent need for Regional Water Authorities[145] with a clear sense of purpose, able to take a comprehensive and long-term view of all the relevant aspects of water management, and at the same time capable of taking successful and cost-effective action to safeguard water supplies and protect the environment. This entails these authorities replacing virtually all the diverse public authorities at present responsible for water services.[146]

Although the 1973 Act retained executive supervision of water by means of Ministerial responsibilities to promote a national policy for water,[147] a key change in administration was to reduce the number of bodies with significant water responsibilities to just ten water authorities, with areas determined primarily by reference to pre-existing river authority areas. The corollary of this was the demise of the other organisations previously mentioned in relation to their water functions. In the words of one commentator,

> it is difficult to exaggerate the magnitude of this change. The three main groups of water interests – river management, water supply and sewage disposal – [came] together for the first time, with a simultaneous increase in the territory covered by each management unit.[148]

The ten water authorities were to be responsible for water supply[149] and to take over the water undertakings of local authorities and joint water boards, but statutory water companies would remain in existence to supply water in particular localities. In relation to sewerage and sewage disposal, it became the responsibility of each water authority to provide such public sewers as were necessary for effectually draining its area and to make such provision as might be necessary, by means of sewage disposal works or otherwise, for effectually dealing with the contents of sewers.[150] However,

---

[145] Although commonly referred to as 'regional water authorities' nine regional water authorities were provided for in England, whereas a *national* water authority was constituted for Wales, the Welsh Water Authority.

[146] DoE, *Reorganisation of Water and Sewerage Services: Government Proposals and Arrangements for Consultation*, Circular 92/71 (1971).

[147] s.1(1) Water Act 1973.

[148] Porter (1978) p.28.

[149] s.11(1) Water Act 1973.

[150] *Ibid* s.14(1).

provision was made for local authorities to continue to have local sewerage functions when acting as agents on behalf of water authorities.[151]

Other key responsibilities entrusted to water authorities included land drainage, so that the functions in respect of land drainage previously exercised by river authorities and other statutory bodies became the responsibility of the water authorities, with each authority being required to exercise a general supervision over all matters relating to land drainage in their area.[152] In addition, the responsibilities of river authorities in relation to fisheries and pollution of rivers passed to the water authorities. The latter was particularly significant in that it made water authorities responsible for implementation of legislation dealing with water pollution and the control of discharges to rivers and other watercourses.[153]

Beyond the major objective of administrative simplification, however, there were other key policy principles determining the shape of the 1973 Act. Uppermost amongst these were the ideas of hydrological rationality and regionalisation. 'Hydrological rationality' refers to the objective of imposing an administrative structure which reflected the natural progression of water from source to sea and the control of water related activities as they impact upon this progression. The guiding idea, in this respect, was that of 'integrated management of the water cycle', or 'integrated river basin management', whereby a single body would undertake responsibility for all water-related matters within a natural watershed. The advantages of this were expressed as follows.

> The water cycle is the natural system wherein water circulates between land, air and sea, while catchment areas are those areas of land that drain to a particular river. The importance of the utilization of these principles lies in the fact that the regional boundaries of the water authorities are determined by catchment areas, and that each water authority therefore deals with self-contained water cycles. The water authorities can thus manage and plan water resources as a totality, and can assess conflict in the catchment area. The previously fragmented system, based predominantly on administrative rather than hydrological boundaries, was usually concerned with only one part of the water-cycle – either water supply, sewerage, or land drainage – and with only one part of a catchment area. This geographical and functional separation of responsibilities for water resources had led to concern over the ability of the water industry to meet future demands and to resolve conflicts over different uses of water, and was a motivating force behind reorganization.[154]

In some respects the move towards regionalism follows from the principle of hydrological integration of functions. Recognition of river catchments as the appropriate unit for administration of water functions ran contrary to

---

[151] *Ibid* s.15(1).
[152] *Ibid* s.19(1).
[153] *Ibid* s.9.
[154] Gray (1982) at p.147.

the previous organisation of functions according to local authority boundaries which bore little, if any, relationship to the hydrological features of the area being administered. The implication of this was a considerable shift away from the use of local authorities as the key providers of water services towards new, comprehensively-empowered, bodies established specifically for this purpose: the regional water authorities.

The upshot of all this was that the 1973 Act provided for ten regional water authorities in England and Wales as multi-functional administrative units with responsibility for activities extending across the whole of the hydrological cycle encompassing water conservation, water supply, wastewater treatment, land drainage and flood defence, and the management of fisheries. More generally, the emphasis of the enactment was upon planning in a markedly technocratic sense. As later commentators have noted,

> The 1973 Act implies a belief in planning, a preference for efficiency rather than participation: it presents a design to meet technical rather than political criteria and which attempts to solve conflict by intra-organizational methods.[155]

A final point to emphasise about this transition is that a substantially public sector mechanism for water services was retained under the new structure for water administration. The shift from local to regional administration did not trespass across the public-private sector divide to any extent greater than previously existed. Private water supply companies remained in operation in some areas, but for the most part the reforms were entirely within the public domain. The significance of this is that control by central government did not undergo any fundamental changes. Ministerial responsibility for water resided with the same Ministers as previously, though the links with local authorities were greatly diminished.

## 2.15 Problems with the 1973 Act

The achievements of the 1973 Act were to place the administration of water on a more unified basis and to translate into law a more rational approach to the co-ordination of different water functions. Having a single body to manage water resources, to secure essential supplies and to treat effluent so that it did not contaminate those supplies has much to commend it. The failings of this approach were, most crucially, that it transferred too broad a range of powers to the regional water authorities and provided too little by way of an external mechanism to scrutinise and regulate their activities. Water quality regulators and effluent dischargers are inevitably placed in a position of conflict of interest, and the location of both functions within a single body necessitates a sophisticated mechanism for the resolution of conflicting concerns. A key shortcoming of the Act lay in the lack of an effective mechanism of this kind.

---

[155] Jordan, Richardson and Kimber (1977) p.318.

To an extent, the fundamental problem of conflict of interests was recognised in the 1973 Act. In order to prevent water authorities being seen to be partial in determining consents for discharges from their own effluent treatment plants, the Act incorporated provision to make new outlets and discharges by water authorities subject to the control of the Secretary of State.[156] The effect of this was, therefore, to bring the discharge of effluent by water authorities under the control of the Secretary of State. However, the practical operation of this proved to be seriously unsatisfactory.

A telling indication as to the longer-term consequences of a general lack of external control of water authorities in relation to water pollution was noted by the House of Commons Environment Committee, in its 1987 Report on *Pollution of Rivers and Estuaries*. One passage from this Report, focusing upon sewage treatment, is worth quoting at length.

> One of the reasons for the general deterioration in river quality is the poor quality of effluent discharged from sewage treatment works. The failure by water authorities to comply with their formal discharge consents is a matter for considerable concern. . . . At our request, the Water Authorities Association provided us with figures which show that in 1986, of the 4,355 numerical discharge consents issued by the Department of the Environment to water authority sewage treatment works, no less than 22% were breached or in the Water Authorities Association's own words were 'unsatisfactory'. That is, in 1986, 22% of all sewage works failed to meet the requirement to comply with their discharge consents for 95% of the time. This is not an acceptable state of affairs.[157]

Beyond the immediate threat to water quality posed by 'unsatisfactory' sewage discharges from water authority treatment works, it was observed that there was another serious consequence of this unacceptable state of affairs. This was that their status amongst the worst polluters of rivers placed water authorities in an invidious position where they sought to exercise their regulatory powers against other polluting dischargers. That is, where a water authority was amongst the worst polluters of a watercourse, that authority seeking to prosecute an industrial discharger for causing pollution inevitably had an air of hypocrisy about it. In practice the law on water pollution was rarely enforced using formal enforcement mechanisms,[158] with inevitable consequences for the aquatic environment.

There were various reasons why water authorities were failing in their duties to treat effluent to an acceptable standard. Perhaps the most

---

[156] s.17 Water Act 1973.

[157] House of Commons Environment Committee, *Pollution of Rivers and Estuaries* (1987) at para.25. Contrast the situation in 1970, when it was found that *60%* of sewage treatment works were discharging effluent in breach of consent requirements (Ministry of Housing and Local Government and WO, *Taken for Granted: Report of the Working Party on Sewage Disposal* (1970) (the *'Jeger' Report*)).

[158] Generally see Richardson, Ogus and Burrows (1982); Brittan (1984); and Vogel (1986).

significant of these was directly financial. There had been a steady decline in water infrastructure investment from the mid-1970s to the early 1980s and this translated into many instances of sewage treatment works being overloaded, particularly by new development, and suffering operational impairment or failure. Despite the modest upturn in investment in this sector which took place after 1981, the long lead times between investment in sewerage facilities and tangible improvement in river water quality meant that positive benefits from this investment would not be experienced until the end of the decade.[159]

The state of sewage treatment by water authorities in the late 1980s was perhaps the clearest example of the failings of the system of regulation founded upon the Water Act 1973. The provision of water utility functions depended upon funding from government to meet vital infrastructure improvements and this made such improvements extremely vulnerable to deterioration in the general state of the economy. Beyond that, the system of regulation that it imposed, whereby water regulators were themselves amongst the worst offenders, proved to be fundamentally misconceived. Whilst co-ordination of functions may have demonstrated its benefits at an operational level, its regulatory shortcomings were patent.

### 2.16 The Water Act 1989

The Water Act 1989[160] had roots in a mixture of ideological preconception and financial exigency and must be seen alongside a range of utility privatisations which had taken place throughout the 1980s.[161] Its central purpose was to implement the Government policy of privatising the water sector, to the greatest possible extent, by transferring as many of the functions of the regional water authorities into the private sector as was feasible. A key statement of the policy basis for privatisation is to be found in the Government's initial White Paper of 1986, *Privatisation of the Water Authorities in England and Wales*.[162] This emphasised the Government's belief that the privatisation of water authorities would benefit their customers and employees, and the nation as a whole, in the following ways:

(1) the authorities would be free of Government intervention in day to day management and protected from fluctuating political pressures;

(2) the authorities would be released from constraints on financing which public ownership imposes;

(3) access to private capital markets would make it easier for the authorities to pursue effective investment strategies for cutting costs and improving standards of service;

---

[159] House of Commons Environment Committee, *Pollution of Rivers and Estuaries* (1987) para.27.
[160] Generally, see Macrory (1989) and (1990); Gordon (1989); Kinnersley (1988) and (1994); Maloney and Richardson (1995); and Hassan (1998) Ch.6.
[161] Generally see Graham and Prosser (1991).
[162] See HM Government, *Privatisation of the Water Authorities in England and Wales* (Cmnd.9734, 1986) and DoE, *The Water Environment: the Next Steps* (1986).

(4)   the financial markets would be able to compare the performance of individual water authorities against each other and against other sectors of the economy and this would provide the financial spur to improved performance;

(5)   a system of economic regulation would be designed to ensure that the benefits of greater efficiency were systematically passed on to customers in the form of lower prices and better service than would otherwise have occurred;

(6)   measures would be introduced to provide a clearer strategic framework for the protection of the water environment;

(7)   private water authorities would have greater incentive to ascertain the needs and preferences of customers, and to tailor their services and tariffs accordingly;

(8)   private water authorities would be better able to compete in the provision of various commercial services, notably in consultancy abroad;

(9)   privatised authorities would be better able to attract high quality managers from other parts of the private sector;

(10)  there would be the opportunity for wide ownership of shares both among employees and among local customers; and

(11)  most employees would be more closely involved with their business through their ownership of shares, and motivated to ensure its success.

Clearly, the 1986 policy statement on water privatisation followed the rationale for previous utility privatisations in heavily emphasising the importance of essentially commercial objectives in the provision of water services. To a great extent, underfunding and lack of competitiveness were perceived to be the problems, and private investment and private sector styles of management were perceived to be the solutions. However, it is notable that amongst the stated objectives was that of 'a clearer strategic framework for the protection of the water environment'. This matter proved to be a serious difficulty in the initial plan for privatisation. The original idea of transferring into the private sector all the functions of the regional water authorities would have resulted in regulatory responsibilities for the aquatic environment being discharged by a private sector body and exercised over other private sector bodies. This approach would have effectively reintroduced, in a privatised form, the 'poacher-gamekeeper' problem of conflict of interest previously discussed in relation to the regional water authorities under the 1973 Act.

Beyond national concerns about the establishment of a privatised system of regulating the aquatic environment, the issue was also a matter of European Community significance. Objections founded upon EC requirements for a satisfactory 'competent authority' to implement water quality directives were influential in redirecting initial plans for the privatisation of the water industry. Specifically, legal opinion suggested that a private regulatory body would not have the legal capacity to act as a competent authority for the purposes of implementing European Community directives. Perhaps because of this objection, and the more general difficulties with private regulation, the necessity for a public regulatory authority was eventually conceded.[163] The Government revised the initial proposals to provide for a public body to undertake regulatory responsibilities with respect to the aquatic environment and privatisation only took place in relation to the water utility functions of water supply and effluent treatment.[164] Probably for the first time, therefore, external legal constraints played a significant part in shaping the national administrative arrangements for water quality regulation.

## 2.17 Water and Sewerage Undertakers

The Water Act 1989 provided for the comprehensive transfer of the public water utility functions of water supply and wastewater treatment into the private sector as the responsibilities of the water and sewerage undertakers, termed 'water service companies', though private statutory water supply companies which previously existed were retained.[165] This transfer of ownership incorporated a transfer of control, and with that a fundamental need to rethink the legal mechanisms by which the new companies would be regulated. The freedom given to undertakers to organise their affairs according to commercial priorities carried with it the clear danger that profit motives would override the needs of water service consumers and the protection of the environment. So long as the water industry had been located in the public sector these concerns had not been prominent since Ministerial control had provided a policing function and profitability was not an issue. The relinquishment of public ownership, however, necessitated an innovative approach to regulatory control. These arrangements have been modified slightly following Welsh devolution and the creation of the Competition Commission, but for the most part they remain little changed since privatisation. Accordingly, this and the following section outline only briefly the legal framework for the water and sewerage undertakers, with more detailed consideration being provided later in this work.[166]

Ultimately, responsibility for the provision of sewerage services in England and Wales remained with the Secretary of State under the 1989 Act, with particular duties in relation to economic regulation, customer services and determination of appeals in relation to specified kinds of dispute being the responsibility of the Director General of Water Services appointed by the Secretary of State.[167] Hence, the two overriding duties of the Secretary of State and the Director were to secure that the functions of

---

[163] See Haigh (1992 updated) 4.1-5; Gordon (1989) p.138; and generally see Maloney and Richardson (1995) Ch.3.

[164] See DoE, *The National Rivers Authority: the Government's Proposals for a Public Regulatory Body in a Privatised Water Industry* (1987).

[165] Statutory water companies are now provided for under the Statutory Water Companies Act 1991.

[166] For the present position regarding the regulation of water and sewerage undertakers see Chs.7, 11 and 17 below.

[167] ss.5-10 Water Act 1989, and see now Part I Water Industry Act 1991, and see 7.4 below on the regulatory role of the Office of Water Services.

water and sewerage undertakers are properly carried out throughout England and Wales and that undertakers were able to finance the proper carrying out of their functions.[168] The functions of both the Secretary of State and the Director were therefore central in the control of funding for improvements to water quality, through programmes for sewerage infrastructure improvement and measures for improving drinking water quality.

Amongst the more important obligations imposed on the water service companies were general obligations on water undertakers to provide a supply of water to domestic consumers.[169] Specifically, water undertakers were made subject to broad obligations to maintain, improve and extend their water mains and other pipes; to develop and maintain an efficient and economical system of water supply; and to enable the provision of water to premises, and to supply water if requested. For these purposes the Secretary of State was authorised to prescribe standards of performance relating to the provision of water supplies and demand that an undertaker make payments to a person who was affected by a failure of an undertaker to meet such standards.[170]

In relation to sewerage undertakings,[171] the general duties imposed upon an undertaker were to provide and improve upon a system of public sewers, to cleanse and maintain them to ensure that the area was effectively drained, and to make provision for emptying sewers and dealing with their contents by means of sewage treatment works or otherwise.[172] In relation to these matters, the Secretary of State was empowered to impose regulations setting standards of performance relating to sewerage services, and any failure to meet such a standard may require the undertaker to pay a specified amount to a person affected by the failure.[173]

For the first time, the 1989 Act also imposed on the providers of water and sewerage services, and those regulating them, specific environmental duties. Hence, it became the duty of every water or sewerage undertaker, in formulating or considering any proposals relating to any of its functions, to exercise any power with respect to the proposals so as to further the conservation and enhancement of natural beauty and the conservation of flora, fauna and geological or physiographical features of special interest so far as is consistent with the purposes of any enactment relating to the functions of the undertaker. The exercise of these duties was made subject to a statutory Code of Practice.[174]

---

[168] s.7 Water Act 1989, and see now s.2(2) Water Industry Act 1991.

[169] For the present position regarding drinking water supply see Ch.17 below.

[170] s.37 Water Act 1989, and see now ss.37 and 38 Water Industry Act 1991.

[171] For the present position on sewerage responsibilities see 11.3 below.

[172] ss.67 and 68 Water Act 1989, and see now s.94 Water Industry Act 1991.

[173] s.69 Water Act 1989, and see now ss.95 and 96 Water Industry Act 1991.

[174] See 6.12 below on the code of practice.

Outside of general controls on price setting,[175] the Water Act 1989 established a graduated regime for securing compliance by the undertakers with their obligations. Formerly, the Secretary of State or the Director was empowered to issue 'enforcement orders' to any undertaker in breach of any condition of its licence or a range of other statutory obligations. In practice, however, far greater use was made of 'undertakings' agreed between the undertaker and the Secretary of State, in effect, negotiated timetables under which an undertaker would come into compliance within an agreed period. Where an undertaker had seriously contravened a principal duty, however, the 1989 Act provided the ultimate sanction of allowing water services duties to be transferred to the administration of another person.[176]

Finally, a remarkable feature of the powers of the privatised sewerage undertakers was that they included certain powers to act in a regulatory capacity in instigating criminal proceedings in respect of offences involving unlawful discharges being made to sewers by industrial dischargers. Such offences were not normally to be prosecuted other than by the appropriate sewerage undertaker.[177] These arrangements are notable for being a rare instance where statute has specifically entrusted a private commercial body with criminal enforcement powers. While the conflation of 'poacher' and 'gamekeeper' roles was generally dispensed with, in respect of trade effluent law enforcement a private company may still resort to the criminal law to enforce obligations owed by another private company.

## 2.18 Regulation of Water Services Companies

A range of regulatory powers apply to water services companies on a day to day basis. As provided for under the 1989 Act, regulatory functions of different kinds were allocated to the Director General of Water Services,[178] the Drinking Water Inspectorate,[179] the National Rivers Authority, Her Majesty's Inspectorate of Pollution, Local Authority Environmental Health Departments, the Office of Fair Trading and the Monopolies and Mergers Commission.[180] Alongside these were the important regulatory powers retained by the Secretary of State for the Environment, other ministerial powers which may impact upon the functioning of the industry and the expanding body of legislation originating from the European Community. The general roles of the first three regulators deserve to be briefly outlined.

---

[175] See 7.8 below on price setting.

[176] s.23 Water Act 1989, and see now s.24 Water Industry Act 1991.

[177] s.182 Water Act 1989, and see now s.211 Water Industry Act 1991, and for illustrations of the use made of this regulatory power see *ENDS Report* 267 (1997) p.42.

[178] For the present position concerning the Office of Water Services see 7.4 below.

[179] For the present position concerning the Drinking Water Inspectorate see 17.5 below.

[180] Now the Competition Commission.

## 2.18.1 The Director General of Water Services

The perception of the Conservative Government in enacting the privatisation legislation was that improvements in the provision of water services would naturally follow as a consequence of market regulation. Accordingly, it would be pointless to replace a state-owned water monopoly of water services with a privately-owned one. There had to be a mechanism to ensure that water undertakers did not abuse the natural monopoly which water infrastructure provided to the detriment of consumers and the environment. To the extent that such abuses were capable of being economic in character, the central regulatory role was allocated to the Office of Water Services with its Director General ('the Director') entrusted with extensive powers to oversee the prices that water and sewerage undertakers may charge their customers.

Beyond ensuring that water and sewerage companies operated within their instruments of appointment, and adhered to a pricing formula[181] imposed by the Director, the Director was entrusted with a range of regulatory duties for the purpose of protecting the interests of consumers and the quality of water services provided. The primary obligations upon the Director required him to exercise various powers and duties in the manner best calculated to secure that the functions of a water or sewerage undertaker are properly carried out and to secure that undertakers are able, by securing a reasonable return on their capital, to finance the proper carrying out of their functions.[182]

Customers' interests were required to be taken into account in various ways, as secondary obligations.[183] Additionally, the Director was to establish and maintain customer service committees to carry out specified functions and other functions required to be carried out by the Director.[184]

## 2.18.2 The Drinking Water Inspectorate

Under the 1989 Act a separate system of regulation was established for drinking water quality. In relation to this, the main regulatory responsibility rested with the Secretary of State, who was advised by the Drinking Water Inspectorate, based within the Department of the Environment.[185] The Secretary of State was bound to take enforcement action against a water company if it failed to supply wholesome water,[186] though no such action was required where the breach was trivial or if the

---

[181] On the pricing formula see 7.8 below.

[182] s.7 Water Act 1989, and see now s.2(1) and (2) Water Industry Act 1991.

[183] s.26 Water Act 1989, and see now s.27(1) Water Industry Act 1991.

[184] s.6 Water Act 1989, and see now s.28 Water Industry Act 1991 and see 7.4.2 on customer services committees..

[185] s.60 Water Act 1989, and see now s.86 Water Industry Act 1991, though local authorities also have powers in relation to drinking water (under s.77 Water Industry Act 1991), see 17.9 below.

[186] s.65 Water Act 1989, and see now s.67 Water Industry Act 1991.

company had given an undertaking to facilitate compliance within a timescale acceptable to him.[187]

The requirement that drinking water should be 'wholesome' at the time of supply was defined by reference to standards and requirements set out in Regulations[188] made to give belated effect to the EC Drinking Water Quality Directive,[189] and the requirement that it did not contain any element, organism or substance at a concentration or value which would be detrimental to public health. Local authority environmental health departments also possessed a role in monitoring water quality and powers to take samples of drinking water and were placed under a duty to notify water undertakers and the Secretary of State where a supply was, or was likely to become, unwholesome.[190] However, legal proceedings for supplying water of unsatisfactory quality could only be brought by the Secretary of State or the Director of Public Prosecutions.[191]

The 1989 Act also made it a criminal offence for a water company to supply water that was 'unfit for human consumption', though a defence arose where the undertaker could show that there were no reasonable grounds for suspecting that the water would be used for human consumption or that the undertaker took all reasonable steps and exercised all due diligence to secure that the water was fit for human consumption.[192] This origins of this provision lay not in privatisation, nor in EC water law, but rather in the concerns following the serious drinking water contamination incident at Camelford in 1988.[193]

## 2.19 The National Rivers Authority

Under the Water Act 1989 the National Rivers Authority was established as the regulatory authority in relation to the protection of the aquatic environment.[194] The principal functions of the Authority were provided for as follows:

(a) functions with respect to water resources;
(b) functions with respect to water pollution;
(c) functions with respect to flood defence and land drainage;
(d) functions with respect to fisheries;
(e) functions as a navigation authority, harbour authority or conservancy authority which were transferred to the Authority; and

---

[187] See s.54 Water Act 1989, and see now s.70 Water Industry Act 1991 on the offence of supplying water unfit for human consumption. On the legal significance of undertakings given by water companies see 4.15.1 and 17.7.6 below.

[188] See Water Supply (Water Quality) Regulations 1989, SI 1989/1147 as amended, and see 17.7.1 below.

[189] Directive 80/778/EEC.

[190] ss.55-59 Water Act 1989, and see now ss.77-85 Water Industry Act 1991.

[191] s.54(4) Water Act 1989, and see now s.70(4) Water Industry Act 1991.

[192] s.54 Water Act 1989, and see now s.70 Water Industry Act 1991.

[193] See 17.7.7 below.

[194] For the present position see the discussion of the Environment Agency at Ch.6 below.

(f) functions assigned to the Authority by any other enactment.[195]

Although not statutorily listed amongst the principal functions, the Authority also had a significant role as the competent authority in England and Wales for the purposes of certain European Community directives concerned with water quality.[196] In most respects obligations originating under Community law were directly provided for in national legislation. However, a reserve power allowed for Ministerial directions of a general or specific nature to be given to the Authority relating to the carrying out of its principal functions. Specifically, a direction of this kind might include requirements considered appropriate to give effect to any Community obligations. In the event of a direction of this kind being given, the Authority was placed under a legal duty to comply with it.[197]

Alongside its principal functions, the Authority had important responsibilities in relation to conservation and recreation which extended comprehensively across its particular powers and duties. In respect of conservation, it was specified to be the duty of the Authority generally to promote the conservation and enhancement of the natural beauty and amenity of inland and coastal waters and of land associated with such waters, and the conservation of flora and fauna dependent on an aquatic environment.[198] Further duties of the Authority in respect of conservation were provided for under a general environmental duty which required the Authority, in formulating or considering any proposals, to exercise any power conferred on it so as to further the conservation and enhancement of natural beauty and the conservation of flora, fauna and geological or physiographical features of special interest.[199]

Part III of the Water Act 1989, concerning the protection and management of rivers and other waters, re-enacted much of the substantive law concerning water pollution previously provided for under Part II of the Control of Pollution Act 1974. However, some innovations were introduced including provisions allowing for water quality objectives to be placed on a statutory footing,[200] for the establishment of nitrate sensitive areas[201] and for charges to be made in relation to discharge consents.[202]

---

[195] Para.23(3) Sch.13 Water Act 1989, subsequently s.2(1) Water Resources Act 1991 and see now s.2 Environment Act 1995 discussed in 6.3 above.

[196] See the discussion of the need for a public competent authority in 2.16 above, and see the discussion of European Community Law in Ch.4 below generally.

[197] s.146 Water Act 1989, subsequently s.5 Water Resources Act 1991 and see now s.40 Environment Act 1995 discussed in 6.2 below.

[198] s.8 Water Act 1989, subsequently s.2(2) Water Resources Act 1991 and see now s.6(1) Environment Act 1995, and see the discussion of the Environment Agency at 6.10 below.

[199] s.8 Water Act 1989, subsequently s.16(1)(a) Water Resources Act 1991 and see now s.7(1) Environment Act 1995.

[200] ss.104-106 Water Act 1989, see now ss.82-84 Water Resources Act 1991, and see 14.8 below on water quality objectives.

[201] s.112 Water Act 1989, and see now ss.94 and 95 Water Resources Act 1991, and see 13.5 below on nitrate control generally.

[202] Para.9 Sch.12 Water Act 1989, subsequently ss.131 and 132 Water Resources Act 1991 and see now ss.41 and 42 Environment Act 1995, and see 10.7 below on discharge consent charging schemes.

Some rationalisation of the main water pollution offences was also brought about, in that the distinction between isolated pollution incidents and breaches of discharge consents, which was introduced under the 1974 Act,[203] was consolidated by the principal water pollution offences being brought together in a single section[204] and generally made subject to the same defences. Another modification was the use of prohibitions under the 1989 Act to determine the circumstances in which discharge of effluent on to land would constitute an offence.[205]

Although law enforcement powers had previously been given to water authorities, a dramatic consequence of establishing the National Rivers Authority, as an *independent* environmental regulator, was the significantly greater use of legal proceedings in relation to water pollution than ever previously. During the early years of the Authority convictions for water pollution incidents ranged between about 300 and 500 per annum.[206] Despite this considerably more frequent use of prosecution powers, however, the number of water pollution convictions remained relatively small compared with the number of reported incidents. For example, during 1995, 35,891 reported incidents (23,463 of which were substantiated) gave rise to only 149 convictions, with 151 prosecutions pending.[207] Nevertheless, this contrasted markedly with the relatively less litigious approach of other environmental authorities,[208] and with a long-standing British tradition of not prosecuting environmental offences.[209]

Despite the relatively greater use of water pollution prosecution powers, and the frequent prosecution of sewerage undertakers for exceeding discharge consent conditions for sewage treatment works, the problem of unsatisfactory sewage effluent discharges remained a serious one. Sewerage undertakers continued to be the most frequently prosecuted businesses for water pollution offences, with eight of the ten privatised water services companies amongst the most prosecuted 20 industrial concerns during the period of existence of the National Rivers Authority.[210]

## 2.20 The Water Consolidation Legislation 1991

The Water Act 1989 brought about the privatisation of the water industry by the transfer of utility functions to the water services companies, and the establishment of an independent environmental regulatory body in the form of the National Rivers Authority. It also left the law relating to water in rather an untidy state with related provisions enacted within a diverse

---

[203] Under ss.31 and 32 Control of Pollution Act 1974.

[204] s.85 Water Resources Act 1991, and see 9.3 below on the principal water pollution offences.

[205] s.85(4) Water Resources Act 1991, and see 9.11 below on prohibitions.

[206] See National Rivers Authority, The State of the Water Environment Six Year Trends Report (1995).

[207] See Environment Agency, *Water Pollution Incidents in England and Wales 1995* (1996).

[208] See Her Majesty's Inspectorate of Pollution, *Her Majesty's Inspectorate of Pollution Annual Report 1995-96* (1996).

[209] Generally, see Richardson, Ogus and Burrows (1982); Brittan (1984); Vogel (1986); and Rowan-Robinson, Watchman and Barker (1990).

[210] See *ENDS Report* 225 (1996) p.50.

collection of statutes. To remedy this situation, the Law Commission proposed a rationalisation of water enactments to consolidate the legislation within separate enactments dealing with the distinct areas of water law.[211] The consolidation process, which took place in 1991, brought about only minor substantive amendments, where these were needed to avoid anomalies in the law, but sought to achieve greater consistency in the presentation of water legislation.

The enactments resulting from the consolidation process were as follows:

(a)  the Water Resources Act 1991;
(b)  the Water Industry Act 1991;
(c)  the Land Drainage Act 1991;
(d)  the Statutory Water Companies Act 1991; and
(e)  the Water Consolidation (Consequential Provisions) Act 1991.

These statutes came into force on 1 December 1991, and are collectively known as 'the consolidation Acts'.[212]

Although incidental provisions from each of the consolidation Acts may have considerable significance in particular contexts, the first two listed are of greatest relevance to the topics covered by this work. The Water Resources Act 1991 detailed the powers, duties and structure of the National Rivers Authority, providing for its principal functions in respect of water resources, control of pollution, flood defence and fisheries, its general responsibilities in respect of conservation and the protection of the aquatic environment, and incidental matters. The Water Industry Act 1991 provided for the appointment and regulation of water undertakers, responsibilities for water supply, sewerage services encompassing trade effluent controls and related matters including the responsibilities of the Director General of Water Services. Specifically, in relation to water pollution control, the main powers and duties are to be found in Part III of the Water Resources Act 1991, the responsibilities of sewerage undertakers in respect of sewage services and trade effluent in Part IV of the Water Industry Act 1991, and the responsibilities of water undertakers for water supply in Part III of the Water Industry Act 1991.

## 2.21  The Environment Act 1995

A final key development in the history of national water legislation is the major change in environmental regulatory administration brought about by the Environment Act 1995.[213] The fundamental effect of this was that, on 1

---

[211] See Law Commission (1991).

[212] s.1 Water Consolidation (Consequential Provisions) Act 1991 and on the interpretation of the consolidation legislation see *British Waterways Board* v *Severn Trent Water Ltd* [2001] EWCA Civ 276, 2 March 2001.

[213] For general discussion of developments leading up to the establishment of the Environment Agency, see House of Commons Environment Committee, *The Government's Proposals for an Environment Agency* (1992); Howarth (1992); Carter and Lowe (1995); and Gallagher (1996). For general discussion of the Environment Act 1995 see Lane and Peto (1995); Tromans (1996); and Jewell and Steele (1996).

April 1996, the functions of the National Rivers Authority were transferred to the newly-created Environment Agency.[214] This development took place as a consequence of the consolidation of environmental regulatory authorities which resulted in the new Agency acquiring functions previously possessed by the National Rivers Authority, Her Majesty's Inspectorate of Pollution (in relation to the authorisation of processes subject to integrated pollution control)[215] and the waste regulation functions of local authorities. The purpose of this reorganisation was to create an Agency with a greater capacity to achieve sustainable development through integration of systems of control and harmonisation of pollution regulation.

Prior to the establishment of the new Agency, the administratively fragmented system of pollution controls was subject to criticism in environmental management terms in that it lacked a coherent and holistic approach to environmental regulation. It was suggested that consolidation of pollution regulation authorities was needed to achieve greater integration of pollution control in relation to the environment *as a whole*, as contrasted with the previously sectoral approach to the different environmental media.[216] In addition, it was recognised that establishing a unified environmental authority would make it easier for regulated bodies to have only one inspectorate to approach (the so-called 'one stop shopping' argument); that this would avoid overlap or duplication of effort which might arise with separate regulatory authorities; and that combining authorities under one management would lead to greater consistency of approach across all pollution types and environmental media.[217]

The Environment Act 1995 consolidates, in a single regulatory authority for England and Wales, a wide range of functions previously exercised by environmental regulators including the former National Rivers Authority. Whilst the remit of the former Authority tended to be used as a baseline,[218] some potentially important additional obligations were imposed upon the Agency as compared with its predecessors. In particular, the Agency is given an explicit duty in relation to sustainable development[219] and is made subject to a reformulated general environmental duty[220] and a new statutory

---

[214] See Ch.6 below on the Environment Agency.

[215] See 12.3 below on integrated pollution control.

[216] See Royal Commission on Environmental Pollution (1976) and see Royal Commission on Environmental Pollution (1988) suggesting that regulatory and administrative controls should seek the best practicable environmental option for the environment as a whole.

[217] See HM Government, *This Common Inheritance* (Cm.1200, 1990) p.232; and DoE, *Improving Environmental Quality – the Government's Proposals for a New Independent Environment Agency* (1991).

[218] See Part I Water Resources Act 1991.

[219] s.4(1) and (2) Environment Act 1995; DoE, MAFF and WO, *The Environment Agency and Sustainable Development* (1996); DoE, MAFF and WO, *The Environment Agency Management Statement* (1996); generally on sustainable development, see HM Government, *A Better Quality of Life* (1999) and see 4.4.1 and 6.7 below on sustainable development.

[220] s.7(1) Environment Act 1995, which contrast the wording of the previous environmental duty imposed upon the National Rivers Authority under s.16 Water Resources Act 1991.

duty to have regard to costs and benefits.[221] Alongside these, the Agency has acquired an increasing range of responsibilities in relation to prevention of deterioration in water quality and powers to require works or remediation where this is necessary to protect water quality, particular where harm arises from contaminated land.[222] The Agency has also developed an increasingly explicit and strategic approach to the discharge of many of its functions in publishing a range of policy documents, amongst other things, explaining how it intends to use its law enforcement powers.[223] The details and impact of these responsibilities, and other matters relating to the functions of the Agency in relation to water quality, are considered more fully in Chapter 6.

## 2.22 The 'Europeanisation' of Water Quality Legislation

Whilst the main contrasts which have been drawn between water administration under the Water Act 1973, and the Water Act 1989 and subsequent legislation may be largely attributable to the transfer of water services from the public to the private sector, other factors have also had a significant impact in distinguishing the two enactments. One of the most prominent of these is the progressive influence of the European Community upon national water policy and legislation over the years between the two Acts.[224] The 1973 Act predated an extensive collection of European Community directives concerned with water quality[225] which needed to be transposed into national law by appropriate legislation. By contrast, the Community law dimension to the 1989 Act is more pronounced as a mechanism for securing fulfilment of Community obligations, for example, in respect of the legal mechanisms that are provided for establishing statutory water quality objectives[226] particularly where these are necessary for securing water quality standards required under Community water directives and in relation to enforcement matters generally.

The approach taken by the 1989 Act in respect of implementing water quality standards originating from Community law was in marked contrast with the informal or administrative use of standards in previous legislation and practice. Previously, transposition of water directives tended to be done rather unsatisfactorily by administrative rather than legal mechanisms of the kind that are formally required under Community law.[227] A partial explanation for the use of 'informal' methods of implementation in England and Wales may lie in the fact that the regional water authorities,

---

[221] s.39 Environment Act 1995, and see 6.14 below on costs and benefits.

[222] Generally see Ch.13 on preventative and remedial approaches to water quality.

[223] See 6.18 below on law enforcement by the Environment Agency.

[224] See 4.3 below on the development of European Community competence in relation to the environment.

[225] On European Community water directives see Ch.5 below.

[226] See ss.82-84 Water Resources Act 1991 and discussion at 14.8 below.

[227] For an early example of the need for legal transposition, see Case 96/81 *Commission* v *Kingdom of the Netherlands* [1982] ECR 1791, concerning the implementation of the Bathing Water Directive (76/160/EEC).

as public bodies, were duty bound by circulars issued by the Department of the Environment.[228] The 'official' view, stated as late as 1986, was that duties to meet obligations arising under Community directives were 'imposed upon themselves, voluntarily, by water authorities'.[229] However, notwithstanding the privatisation of water utility functions, this is no longer a tenable view of what is required to secure formal implementation of requirements arising under Community directives. Transposition clearly requires a legislative act by the Member State to meet the now-acknowledged requirement of transparency, perhaps, for the purpose of giving enforceable rights to individuals.[230]

The challenges involved in securing formal transposition of Community water directives into national law was compounded by the markedly contrasting style of Community water regulation, as compared with the national approach, in respect of the emphasis placed upon formal environmental quality standards. This represented a significant departure from the British tradition of pollution control, which conscientiously avoided the setting of statutory standards, either for emissions or for the ambient environment, preferring the application of more generalised approaches such as a requirement that dischargers use the 'best practical means' of reducing pollution or the application of discretionary and locally negotiated standards.[231]

In respect of the national impact of Community water legislation, the historical progression has been from a characterisation of this as a remote and imprecise body of obligations to a much more direct and practical concern. Not least, this has been because of a succession of important decisions by the European Court of Justice which have brought home to Member States the direct impact of Community legislation upon matters which were previously conceived of as purely national concerns. The national appreciation of this impact, however, was not always as swift as it should have been. This may be illustrated in two contexts: the transposition of Community water directives and the judicial consequences in relation to non-compliance with directives.

In relation to transposition of water directives, as has been stated, in the early period the need for explicit implementation in national law was not fully appreciated. In respect of the first water directives, misunderstandings as to their legal significance may have been the reason for unsatisfactory implementation but, more recently, the difficulties may have been attributable to more substantial reasons.

Although the theory of transposition requires the precise and complete implementation of the obligations of a directive in national law by a

---

[228] s.5(2) Water Act 1973.

[229] See DoE, *The Water Environment: the Next Steps* (1986) para.2.5.

[230] On the requirement for implementation by way of legally binding rules see Jans (1995) pp.125-127. On the acquisition of rights by individuals see 4.16 below.

[231] Generally see Richardson, Ogus and Burrows (1982) pp.62-64; and Brittan (1984); and Vogel (1986) pp.87-90.

specified date, the practical reality is that for many directives implementation has taken place 'progressively' sometimes over a remarkably lengthy period of time. Hence, the national Surface Waters (Fishlife) (Classification) Regulations 1997,[232] prescribing a system for classifying the quality of water needing protection or improvement in order to support fish life, have recently been enacted to give effect to the *1978* Freshwater Fish Waters Directive.[233] Similarly, the Surface Waters (Shellfish) (Classification) Regulations 1997,[234] prescribing a system for classifying the quality of coastal or brackish waters needing protection to support shellfish life, have been enacted to give effect to the *1979* Shellfish Waters Directive.[235] Another example of late transposition is to be found in the 1998 Groundwater Regulations[236] which, amongst other things, require the prior investigation of the effect on groundwater of discharges and activities upon the ground, which implement the *1980* Groundwater Directive.[237] Although implementation of this Directive was previously thought to have been accomplished under Parts I and II of the Environmental Protection Act 1990 (concerned with integrated pollution control and the management of waste) and Part II of the Water Resources Act 1991 (concerned with water pollution) it was subsequently recognised that these provisions would not cover certain activities, such as the disposal of agricultural pesticides, which fell outside these regulatory regimes. Hence, 'completion' of transposition was necessitated, nearly twenty years after the Directive was adopted.

These illustrations of progressive implementation of Community water directives contrast markedly with the theory of precise and complete transposition by the two year deadline provided for in most directives. In part, they may demonstrate an initial lack of punctiliousness on the part of the United Kingdom Government in satisfying itself that all situations covered by directives were fully met by national legislation and administrative practice. In part also, they may demonstrate some of the difficulties which arise in implementation. Completeness of transposition requires that there is no possible situation covered by a directive which is not similarly provided for in national law. Literal transposition of a directive might seem to satisfy this requirement, but literal transposition may not always be possible where national legislation is required to take account of allocations of administrative and regulatory responsibilities and the peculiarities of the national legal order. The practical difficulty in achieving comprehensive transposition is that national legislators are required to enact legislation which anticipates every possible situation which falls under a directive and this involves a challenging degree of foresight. Historically, therefore, it may be concluded that the national implications of transposition are better understood than in the past and that

---

[232] SI 1997 No.1331.

[233] Directive 78/659/EEC and see 15.3 below for a discussion of this Directive.

[234] SI 1997 No.1332.

[235] Directive 79/923/EEC and see 15.3 below for a discussion of this Directive indicating continuing uncertainties as to whether its obligations have been fully met.

[236] SI 1998 No.2746.

[237] Directive 80/68/EEC and see 5.4.2 below for a discussion of this Directive.

the activity of implementing directives is now undertaken more carefully than previously, but the need for subsequent rectification cannot ever be completely discounted.

The second respect in which the national significance of Community water legislation has come to be appreciated is through the instigation of judicial proceedings against the United Kingdom in respect of non-compliance with obligations under water directives and, more generally, with developments by the European Court of Justice as regards procedural implementation of directives.[238] In the early period there may have been a national preconception that Community law was not of equivalent status to national law, perhaps because of the lack of a power of the European Court of Justice to impose formal sanctions in respect of breach of Community law[239] or perhaps because of a common belief that water and environmental quality in the UK was generally good and that adherence to Community requirements did not require particularly burdensome further national obligations to be assumed. As later commentators put it, "the idea that British water might not be clean enough to pass tests which would also have to be met by continentals with supposedly dirtier water probably did not occur to the British Government".[240]

The early water directive cases before the European Court of Justice involving the United Kingdom are considered elsewhere in this work.[241] Although the findings against the UK did not demonstrate any substantially novel points of law, they were, nonetheless, notable in making it transparent to all what compliance with Community water directives required.[242] In this respect the adverse decisions of the Court against the United Kingdom in relation to the implementation of the Drinking Water Quality Directive[243] and the Bathing Water Directive[244] are significant. Not only did they emphasise the tangible judicial impact of Community water legislation, they also generated significant national debate as to the status, and cost, of water quality generally. Historically, it is suggested that the initial cases against the United Kingdom significantly contributed to a change of outlook towards Community water legislation, from an abstract and somewhat remote body of legal theory into a far more direct and practical concern.

---

[238] See 4.16 below on the developments in the European Court of Justice in respect of the procedural implementation of directives.

[239] On the present position in relation to this see 4.13.2 below.

[240] Haigh and Lanigan (1995) p.22.

[241] Generally see 4.15 below.

[242] See Jordan and Greenaway (1998) and generally see 4.12 below.

[243] Case C-337/89 *Commission* v *United Kingdom* [1993] Env LR 299 and see 4.15.1 below for a discussion of this decision.

[244] Case C-56/90 *Commission* v *United Kingdom* [1993] Env LR 472 and see 4.15.2 below for a discussion of this decision.

## 2.23  The Impact of International Law

Alongside European Community law, national water quality law has also been significantly influenced, though perhaps to a lesser degree, by international law. In particular, since the early 1970s the United Kingdom has been a party to two important regional Conventions covering the North Sea and North East Atlantic area. Respectively, these regimes related to the prevention of land-based sources of pollution and water pollution from dumping from ships and aircraft.[245] The Conventions were subsequently amended to include, respectively, pollution of the sea from atmospheric sources and incineration of waste at sea. More recently, these Conventions have been consolidated and updated in the 1992 Convention for the Protection of the Marine Environment of the North East Atlantic, referred to as the 'OSPAR' Convention, which came into force in March 1998. Concurrently with these developments a fairly sophisticated body of law has developed, aimed at preventing, and dealing with the consequences of, contamination from the maritime transport sector, particularly pollution by oil.[246] While international law is covered in more detail later, it is worth mentioning a few of the more important consequences for national water law which have originated from the international arena.

Compared with European Community water directives, the impact of international law displays some similarities but also some significant contrasts. Thus, in broad terms both Community and international law have focused on the prevention of water pollution, for example, through standards which require double hulls for oil tankers or the use of best available techniques for reducing industrial pollution emissions.

Both Community and international law, especially the OSPAR regime, have also advanced the development of a number of the more important principles of environmental regulation. Specifically, the development of the precautionary principle[247] may be traced back to Declarations of the International North Sea Conferences from the late 1980s. These conferences, in reality ministerial meetings which paralleled the development of the North Sea and North East Atlantic Conventions, have been an important driving force in the development of principles of environmental regulation generally, but have also acted as a catalyst for some important domestic policy changes in relation to the water environment. For example, the imposition of a ban on the dumping of sewage sludge at sea after 1998 can be traced back to agreements reached at the Third Ministerial Meeting, in 1990. This period marked an important turning point in the 'marine treatment' approach to contamination which had been accepted scientifically and followed politically until then.[248] The sewage sludge ban also neatly illustrated the impact of international law on

---

[245] The 1974 Paris Convention for the Prevention of Marine Pollution from Land-Based Sources, and the 1972 Oslo Convention for the Prevention of Marine Pollution by Dumping from Ships and Aircraft. See 18.8 below on these Conventions.

[246] See Ch.19 below.

[247] See 4.7.1 below on the precautionary principle.

[248] See Jordan and Greenaway (1998).

Community law, since the ban was included in the Urban Waste Water Treatment Directive[249] which was then in the process of securing political agreement within the Community.

The example of the sewage sludge ban, and other examples such as the imposition of international standards governing the discharge of wastes and requiring the labelling of potentially hazardous cargoes being transported at sea, illustrate that international law may impose obligations which are at least as prescriptive as those imposed under Community law. Generally, international law is characterised by its non-binding nature, in that sanctions are rarely specified or available for any breach of its obligations and institutional enforcement arrangements revolve around political pressure to realise compliance rather than penalties of the kind normally used at national level. This contrasts markedly with the relatively exacting legal requirements and sophisticated enforcement mechanisms, for international law at least, that are provided for under Community law.[250] On the other hand, it should be noted that the OSPAR regime adopts a 'reverse listing' approach to the disposal of wastes at sea; only a limited number of expressly prescribed substances may be dumped, as opposed to the previous position where dumping was generally permissible subject to exceptions.[251] OSPAR also displays a preference for emission-based standards through promotion of the use of best available techniques. This is a trend which is becoming increasingly apparent in the Community, albeit with an increasing tendency for emission standards to be tempered by a need to have regard to local environmental conditions.

Compared to Community law, international law is strictly non-enforceable in the absence of specific transposing legislation. In the case of some conventions, however, the international law rules have been transposed into national legislation, and in this sense decision-makers and affected parties may rely on the national legislation. An example of this is to be found in the Merchant Shipping Act 1995, and related regulations, which gives effect to United Kingdom obligations under the 'MARPOL' Treaty relating to pollution by oil and other hazardous and noxious substances.[252] Similarly, Part II of the Food and Environment Protection Act 1985 gives effect to international treaty law on dumping of waste at sea.[253] In such cases, the national legislation assumes the greatest practical relevance, with the relevant international convention serving only as a background aid to the interpretation of the national law.

However, many international obligations, such as those contained in the OSPAR Convention and key parts of the 1982 Law of the Sea

---

[249] Directive 91/271/EEC and see 5.6.2 below on this Directive.

[250] See 4.13–4.18 below on the enforcement of European Community law.

[251] See also the 1996 Protocol to the 1972 Convention on the Prevention of Marine Pollution by Dumping of Wastes and Other Matter (the 'London Convention'), see 19.19.3 below.

[252] 1973/78 International Convention for the Prevention of Pollution from Ships ('MARPOL'). See 19. 5 below.

[253] Under the OSPAR and London Conventions see 19.20 below.

Convention[254] relating to marine pollution, have not been transposed into national legislation, and the prospect of their transposition is unlikely.[255] These obligations, therefore, can only be given effect to by the actions of national decision-makers such as the Environment Agency or central government in their practical deliberations, and provision is generally made for this in national legislation.[256] For example, the obligation under the OSPAR Convention to achieve concentrations in the environment near background values for naturally occurring radioactive substances and close to zero for artificial radioactive substances[257] will only be realised through appropriate licence determinations for installations emitting relevant substances.[258] However, there is an important contrast with the national enforcement of Community law, in that the scope for individual enforcement of international obligations at national level is not provided for.[259] In short, therefore, many international obligations are binding only in the sense of being material considerations for bodies like the Environment Agency in the determination of individual licence or consent applications. Nevertheless, as with many Community obligations, an important practical impact has been provided by the development of a further baseline against which national practice may be judged.

Two final contrasts between Community and international law may also be noted. First, the difficulty of establishing quality standards for the marine environment means that, to date, standard setting under international law has tended to revolve around emission controls rather than environmental quality objectives and standards. Second, the need to find acceptable mechanisms for dealing with the consequences of major oil pollution spills in particular has led to the development of civil liability regimes under international law. These have provided a means whereby pollution compensation funds have been established under international law, of the kind that have been called upon to compensate for environmental and economic losses following incidents such as those involving the *Braer* in 1993 and the *Sea Empress* in 1996.[260] One consequence of this is that disputes about liability arising under the funds are taken directly in the national courts,[261] again emphasising that in certain contexts international law can have a direct impact on national water law. By contrast, EC law

---

[254] See 18.7 below on the Law of the Sea Convention.

[255] Although key features of the OSPAR-type approach are reflected in the European Community Water Framework Directive (2000/60/EC), see 5.7.1 below.

[256] See, for examples, s.156 Environmental Protection Act 1990, s.102 Water Resources Act 1991 and s.40 Environment Act 1995.

[257] Under the OSPAR Strategy for Radioactive Substances, adopted under the Convention in 1998, see 20.6.3 below.

[258] See, for example, the discussion of the Sellafield emissions of technetium-99, at 20.10.12 below.

[259] See 4.16 below.

[260] See 19.13–14 below on civil liability for oil pollution.

[261] See, for example, the series of cases heard in the Scottish courts following the *Braer* incident, discussed at 19.15.2 below.

has yet to adopt a regime for dealing with compensation or remediation for environmental damage.[262]

In summary, therefore, international treaty law and international agreements more generally have had important consequences for the development of water quality law at the national level. This influence may have been less direct in its legal impact than Community water directives, and less comprehensive. Nevertheless, it has acted as a spur to a number of important developments at Community level, and has also provided a framework of controls for water quality concerns, particularly those relating to marine shipping, that are most significantly international in character.

---

[262] Although see 3.20 below for a discussion of recent Community proposals on environmental liability.

# Chapter 3

# THE CIVIL LAW

## 3.1 Introduction

The civil law concerning water pollution and water quality is primarily comprised of judicially-constructed common law rules governing the relationship between those whose activities result in deterioration of water quality and those who have a recognised interest in the use of the water which is thereby infringed.[1] A person wishing to secure compensation for the contamination of a supply of water, or to restrain the continuation of such contamination, must generally turn to the civil law to protect private interests, notwithstanding the enactment of numerous statutory provisions making the pollution of water a criminal offence.[2] Although, in narrowly defined circumstances, the civil law does treat damage to water quality as a quasi-criminal matter,[3] for the most part, the civil law is concerned with the provision of redress for those who suffer infringements of private rights as a result of water quality deterioration, and sometimes the prevention of its continuation, rather than the punishment of those who cause it. Hence, compensatory and rectificatory themes feature more prominently than that of punishment in this chapter.

Initially, the contrast between the role of private rights and public interests must be emphasised. The prospect of being sued for water polluting activities may well serve as a useful incentive, alongside the criminal law, to encourage those discharging effluent into natural waters to ensure that the quality of that effluent is of sufficient quality to avoid liability, thereby bringing a general benefit to the aquatic environment. In those cases where an injunction is granted against a polluter as a result of civil proceedings a continuing water quality improvement may be secured, which will also be of general benefit. Beyond that, however, the areas of overlap between private rights and the public interest in the state of the aquatic environment are limited and contingent. An award of damages in civil proceedings is likely to provide a clear financial benefit to the recipient, but is not necessarily beneficial to the environment that has been damaged by contamination. The claimant is not bound to use the award to redress the harm that has been done, and in many instances there is a limited amount that can feasibly be done to restore polluted waters to their former state. Damages are awarded in civil proceedings to recognise infringements of

---

[1] General reading on the civil law on water pollution and related aspects of environmental civil liability includes Hobday (1952) pp.191 to 220; Newsom and Sherratt (1972) Ch.I; Bates (1990, updated) Ch.2; Howarth (1992a) Chs.3 and 11; Brubaker (1995); and Pugh and Day (1995).

[2] See Ch.9 below for a discussion of the criminal offences concerning water pollution. See 9.21 below on the powers of a criminal court to make a compensation order under the Powers of the Criminal Courts Act 1973. See also 19.13–14 below concerning the provision for civil liability for oil contamination in international law and the national implementing measures relating to this.

[3] See 3.17 below on public nuisance.

private rights, but not necessarily for the purpose of restoring waters to their former state and not for securing any benefit to the public at large.[4]

Moreover, civil protection of private rights in water falls some way short of securing protection of the aquatic environment for its own sake. Whilst compensation may be awarded for financial loss to the claimant, damage to the flora, fauna and ecosystem of a watercourse will rarely be quantifiable in monetary terms. Only where the claimant is able to show some tangible interest in the waters, such as the loss of income from the amenity of a fishery, will compensation be payable. The equation between the private amenity value of waters and the non-quantifiable value of the 'unowned' environment which they support demonstrates the crudity and limitations of the civil law as a mechanism for giving effect to broader environmental concerns.

Because the civil law has environmental protection, at best, only as a secondary purpose, it contrasts with certain aspects of regulatory law[5] in being almost entirely lacking in overall strategic objectives for environmental quality. The civil law serves to provide private redress for particular kinds of harm in a piecemeal way, without any significant attempt to formulate or adhere to general objectives for water quality or aquatic ecosystems. The general public interest in the satisfactory state of the aquatic environment, therefore, is intended to be secured through the criminal or regulatory law, not the civil law.

This chapter provides a discussion of the water quality rights which arise between waterside 'riparian' land owners as these have been provided for through case law, and details the extent to which the law provides for civil remedies against those causing deterioration of water quality, and the waters in respect of which such claims can be maintained. The discussion then turns to consider those parts of the general law of tort which may be of especial relevance to civil claims for water contamination, encompassing trespass, private nuisance and negligence. The factual and legal background and the main implications of the important decision in *Cambridge Water Company* v *Eastern Counties Leather plc*[6] are then considered. This is followed by an account of the various general exceptions and defences which arise in relation to civil claims and the principal remedies that are likely to be relevant in water quality litigation, the award of damages and the injunction. Discussion is then provided of the criminal and quasi-criminal elements of the common law as they feature in actions founded upon public nuisance, the circumstances where civil liability is statutorily provided for and the interrelationships between the civil and statutory law on water quality. The chapter provides some general observations on the limitations and practicalities of civil litigation and concludes with a discussion of proposals for establishing environmental liability at European Community level. It should be noted

---

[4] Generally see Steele (1995a).

[5] See, by contrast, the discussion of water quality objectives at 14.8 below.

[6] [1994] 1 All ER 53.

that the regulation of 'statutory nuisances', as an alternative mechanism for the control of specific kinds of nuisance, is considered elsewhere in this work.[7] Also considered elsewhere are international law provisions governing civil liability following damage from the marine transport of oil and hazardous substances,[8] and civil liability arising from radioactive contamination.[9]

## 3.2 The Case Law Legacy

Private legal proceedings have been brought for many centuries for interferences with amenity that would today be regarded as 'environmental' in character. However, the modern common law conception of 'water pollution', insofar as this is recognised as a basis for civil proceedings, is largely a product of case law decisions of the last century and a half. By contrast with regulatory approaches to water quality, where statutory definitions go into extensive detail as to the physical and chemical requirements for water to be used for particular purposes, no correspondingly detailed or explicit definition of 'water pollution' has ever been formulated in civil law. As a consequence, the meaning of the expression has been, and continues to be, determined through the extensive collection of judicial decisions in which courts have determined whether diverse kinds of water contamination are to be categorised as 'pollution' insofar as they are deserving of a civil remedy.

Despite the rather motley character of past litigation on water pollution and water quality, the system of precedent which permeates common law reasoning has provided useful general principles which indicate where a civil remedy is likely to be available. Although the civil law has provided remedies for interference with water rights for many centuries many of the leading authorities illuminating the key principles are the work of Victorian judges confronted with the first wave of industrial pollution litigation and acutely conscious of the value of manufacturing industry to the economic state of the nation. This was at a time when major industrial development placed great demands upon water resources and when local authorities first assumed responsibility for implementing extensive programmes of sanitation improvement. Unavoidably, these activities placed new pressures upon the aquatic environment and caused judges to draw analogies with established principles for the protection of land from actual damage.[10]

Despite the age of some of the key decisions on civil liability for contamination of water, many of the fundamental principles that were established remain authoritative as statements of the present law. On the

---

[7] See 8.5 below.

[8] See 9.13–14 below.

[9] See 20.11 below.

[10] See *St Helens Smelting Co* v *Tipping* (1865) 11 HLC 642 for an early illustration of the protection of land rights from harm cause by atmospheric industrial emissions, discussed in 3.8.3 below.

other hand, some caution may be needed in the evaluation of some of the reasoning applied in older cases given the changes of circumstances which have taken place since they were decided.[11] It must be recognised, for example, that modern civil litigation takes place against the background of a relatively sophisticated system of regulatory controls governing discharges of effluent into waters which did not exist at the time of earlier decisions. Also notable are the advances which have taken place in scientific understanding and the appreciation of environmental impacts. Hence, the tendency for Victorian judges to be sceptical of scientific information when assessing deterioration in water quality may not be shared by modern judges who may be more willing to embrace water quality evidence which goes beyond that of the human senses.

## 3.3 Riparian Interests in Land

Traditionally, the basis for a civil claim relation to the contamination of water lay in the relationship between the claimant and the defendant as 'riparian' owners of land adjoining a watercourse. Whilst civil remedies for water contamination outside the sphere of riparian rights are otherwise provided for,[12] insofar as riparian rights are concerned a claimant's claim to a civil remedy for water contamination is entirely dependent upon the possession of such rights and the existence of a corresponding duty to avoid contamination being incumbent upon another riparian owner.

The expression 'riparian rights' refers to those common law rights relating to the use of water associated with the ownership of the bank or bed of a watercourse. The extent of these rights was examined in the judgment of Lord Wensleydale in *Chasemore* v *Richards* where it was said,

> [i]t has been now settled that the right to the enjoyment of a natural stream of water on the surface *ex jure naturae* belongs to the proprietor of the adjoining lands as a natural incident of the soil itself; and that he is entitled to the benefit of it, as he is to all the other advantages belonging to the land of which he is the owner. He has the right to have it come to him in its natural state, in flow, quantity and quality, and to go from him without obstruction, upon the same principle that he is entitled to the support of his neighbour's soil for his own in its natural state. His right in no way depends on prescription or the presumed grant of his neighbour.[13]

---

[11] See, for example, the dismissal as a binding authority of *Ballard* v *Tomlinson* (1885) 29 Ch D 115 in the House of Lords in *Cambridge Water Company* v *Eastern Counties Leather plc* [1994] 1 All ER 53 discussed at 3.10 below. See also the disapproval of the Court of Appeal on the reapplication of *Durrant* v *Branksome Urban District Council* [1897] 2 Ch 291 in the context of the Water Industry Act 1991, in *British Waterways Board* v *Severn Trent Water Ltd*, [2001] EWCA Civ 276, Court of Appeal, 2 March 2001.

[12] See the discussions of trespass, private nuisance and negligence below.

[13] (1859) 7 HL Cas 349, at p.382. See also *Embrey* v *Owen* (1851) 6 Ex 353, per Parke B. at p.369; and *Miner* v *Gilmour* (1859) 12 Moo 131, per Lord Kingsdown at p.126.

Riparian rights depend on the ownership of riparian land, meaning land which is contiguous to the bank or bed of a watercourse or, in the case of tidal waters, land which is in contact with water during ordinary high tides.[14] It follows that land which is separated from a river by a strip of land in separate ownership will not be sufficiently proximate to found a claim based upon riparian rights.[15] Similarly, where a riparian owner grants away part of his estate not abutting the watercourse the grantee acquires no riparian rights,[16] and a contractual right against a riparian owner to extract water from a watercourse will not amount to a riparian interest against other riparian owners.[17] Thus in *Kensit* v *Great Eastern Railway Co*[18] a riparian owner granted a licence to a factory owner, who was not a riparian owner, to draw water from the river across his land via a pipe. A lower riparian owner brought an action against the upper riparian owner and the factory owner. It was held that the claimant was not entitled to an injunction against the factory owner making use of the water because he was not a riparian owner. Moreover, since it was found that the water which was eventually discharged was undiminished in quality or quantity, the claimant was not entitled to an injunction against the upper riparian owner either.

Most commonly, the ownership of riparian land arises simply through the ownership of the bank of a watercourse. Alternatively, it can arise through ownership of the bed of a river where this is in separate ownership from the banks. Unless it is expressly provided otherwise, the ownership of both banks of a river carries with it the ownership of the river bed,[19] or, in a situation where a single bank is owned, the river bed up to the centre line ('*medium filum*') of the stream.[20] This presumption, that the owner of a bank of a river owns the river bed, may be rebutted by sufficient contrary evidence.[21] In every case, however, it is essential that the land which is possessed abuts the water over which rights are claimed.[22] Riparian rights, therefore, arise exclusively from an interest in land,[23] and where a riparian owner permits another person to exercise rights over his land, for example under contract or licence, this will not convey any riparian interest in the land.[24]

Riparian rights may be possessed by a freeholder or leaseholder of waterside land and are presumed to be passed by a conveyance of the

---

[14] *North Shore Railway* v *Pion* (1889) 14 AC 612 at p.621; and *Stockport Waterworks Co* v *Potter* (1864) 10 LT 748.

[15] *Attorney-General* v *Rowley Bros and Oxley* (1910) 75 JP 81.

[16] *Stockport Waterworks Co* v *Potter* (1864) 10 LT 748; and see Hobday (1952) pp.196 to 198.

[17] *Crossley* v *Lightowler* (1867) 16 LT 438.

[18] (1884) 51 LT 862.

[19] *Blount* v *Layard* (1888) [1891] 2 Ch 681.

[20] *Bickett* v *Morris* (1866) 30 JP 532; and *Bristow* v *Cormican* (1878) 3 AC 641, at p.666 to 667, and on the *medium filum* rule generally Howarth (1992a) pp.17 to 20.

[21] *Micklethwait* v *Newlay Bridge Co* (1886) 51 JP 132.

[22] *Stockport Waterworks Co* v *Potter* (1864) 10 LT 748.

[23] *Portsmouth Waterworks Co* v *London Brighton and South Coast Railway Co* (1906) 26 TLR 173, at p.175.

[24] *Ormerod* v *Todmorden Joint Stock Mill* (1883) 11 QBD 155.

land.[25] The category of riparian ownership also extends to encompass a person having merely a reversionary interest in such land. Thus in *Jones v Llanrwst Urban District Council*[26] it was held that the claimant was not prevented from bringing an action through having leased fields adjoining the river to a tenant on an annual lease where the infringement of rights which had arisen was of a sufficiently permanent nature in that it would cause damage to the reversionary interest in the property by reducing its value. Although the decision may have been otherwise if the pollution had been only temporary and of such short duration as not to detract from the value of the reversionary interest, the court took the view that 'permanent' meant 'such as will continue indefinitely unless something is done to remove it', and it was clear that the discharge of sewage effluent in question was 'permanent' in that sense.

A limited range of persons, apart from riparian owners, are recognised to have sufficient interests in a watercourse to bring a civil action for water contamination in their own right. An example within this category is that of persons who possess a right of fishery in a water. Such persons will be entitled to bring an action against a person who interferes with the right of fishery by causing contamination which kills or drives away fish. Thus in *Fitzgerald v Firbank*[27] it was held that a body having the grant of an exclusive right of fishery for a specified term of years was possessed of a *profit a prendre* involving a right to take away any fish caught. This right was distinguished from a mere revocable licence from the fishery owner, in that it conferred the right to bring an action against a person who had allowed dirty water containing a quantity of silt to pass into the stream and so caused fish to be driven away from the water. Similarly in *Nicholls v Ely Beet Sugar Factory Ltd*[28] it was held that the owner of a right of fishery, owned without any ownership of the soil of waterside land or the bed of the river, was nonetheless entitled to bring an action for infringement of the right where the operator of a factory discharged large quantities of refuse and effluent into the river causing fish to be killed. The same reasoning was applied where a claimant, as a lessee in occupation of oyster beds situated in a river estuary, was granted an injunction to prevent the discharge of untreated sewage by local authority which had caused pollution of the beds.[29]

Conversely, a person who has no riparian, or other legally recognised, interest in an unpolluted supply of water cannot maintain a civil action for water contamination. This principle is illustrated by *Paine and Co Ltd v St Neots Gas and Coke Co*[30] where the claimant's well became contaminated

---

[25] See s.62(1) and (4) Law of Property Act 1925, which provides that a conveyance of land will convey all waters and watercourses in so far as a contrary intention is not expressed; and *Marshall v Ulleswater Steam Navigation Co* (1871) LR 7 QB 166.

[26] (1910) [1908-10] All ER Rep 922.

[27] [1897] 2 Ch 96.

[28] [1936] 1 Ch 343.

[29] *Hobart v Southend-on-Sea Corporation* (1906) 75 LJKB 305; and see also *Owen v Faversham Corporation* (1908) 73 JP 33.

[30] [1939] 3 All ER 812.

by ammonia escaping from the defendant's works discharging into the gravel and sub-soil and percolating into a well which had been sunk on common land. It was found that the claimant's right to create the well had been granted by persons who actually had no legal right to grant any lease of the common for this purpose, and though the claimant may have been given a licence this did not amount to an easement sufficient in law to substantiate the action which had been brought. Even if the claimant had been able to establish possession and use of the well, this would have been insufficient to show the existence of a recognised riparian interest in the supply of water, and the claimant's action failed.[31]

Whilst many of the riparian rights which arise in civil law have been modified or overridden by statutory provisions, in general terms the common law provides that,

> the possessor of land through which a natural stream runs, has a right to the advantage of that stream flowing in its natural course, and to use it when he pleases for any purpose of his own not inconsistent with the similar rights in the proprietors of the land above and below.[32]

In particular, riparian ownership imports:

(a)  the right to discharge effluent into a watercourse;
(b)  the right to abstract water from a watercourse for domestic and agricultural use;
(c)  the right to impound or divert the flow of water by placing obstructions in the watercourse;
(d)  rights of fishery; and
(e)  rights of navigation.

However, the nature of the uses which can be made of riparian land is to some extent open-ended and may encompass other rights which might qualify as 'riparian' to the extent that they are dependent upon the use of waterside land.[33]

## 3.4  Watercourses and Other Kinds of Waters

Most fundamentally, riparian rights are dependent upon the ownership of waterside land. However, different treatment is given to different categories of water for these purposes. The following subsections contrast the rights arising in relation to different kinds of waters.

---

[31] Contrast *Ballard* v *Tomlinson* 52 LT 942, and see 3.10 below on groundwater contamination.

[32] Per Denman CJ in *Mason* v *Hill* (1833) 5 B&Ad 1, at p.17.

[33] *Pennington* v *Brinksop Hall Coal Co* (1877) 5 Ch D 769.

## 3.4.1 Natural Streams and Watercourses

The civil law concerning riparian rights is formulated in terms of the relationship between persons owning interests in the banks or bed of a 'stream' or 'watercourse'.[34] At common law a 'stream' is defined as a flowing quantity of water which runs in a defined course in such a way as to be capable of diversion.[35] Providing that there exists such a channel, having reasonably defined banks, it need not be shown that water is present continuously. Thus, it will not matter that it may occasionally become dry,[36] or even if it ceases to flow during a considerable part of the year.[37] Similarly, a 'watercourse' envisages a relatively permanent course for moving water with reasonably determined boundaries, though not necessarily a permanent flow of water. Thus, the element of a permanent course was found to be lacking where an artificial marsh of a temporary character, which was only present during the times when it was required by mine owners, was found not to be a 'watercourse'.[38] Similarly, surface water which was intermittently present over an undefined area, without a definite or regular course was held not to constitute a watercourse,[39] and natural 'bourne flows' of underground water from chalk which at times of flood flowed over the surface of land, have been held not to constitute 'watercourses'.[40] Likewise it has been found that water which percolates through marshy ground did not constitute a 'stream'.[41]

Another defining feature of a 'stream' or 'watercourse' is the existence of a flow of moving water. Hence, this feature will be lacking where water is stationary, as was held in a case concerning abstraction of water from a canal where no flow of water existed.[42] Although not within the definition of 'watercourse', however, it has been suggested that if the waters of a stillwater lake or pond are polluted the owner will have the same remedies as those that are available to a riparian owner of a stream or watercourse.[43]

---

[34] 'Watercourse' may have a different interpretation in statutory contexts. See *R v Falmouth and Truro Port Health Authority ex parte South West Water Ltd* ([1999] Env LR 833 and unreported, Court of Appeal, 30 March 2000) where, in interpreting s.259(1) Public Health Act 1936, it was held that rivers and estuaries would not be 'watercourses' within the meaning of this section see 8.5.4 below. See also 9.4 below on the statutory definition of 'watercourse'.

[35] *Taylor v St Helens Corporation* (1877) 6 ChD 264, at p.273.

[36] *R v Oxfordshire (Inhabitants)* (1830) 1 B&Ad 289, at p.301.

[37] *Stollmeyer v Trinidad Lake Petroleum Co* [1918] AC 485.

[38] *Arkwright v Gell* (1839) 5 M&W 203.

[39] *Rawstron v Taylor* (1855) 156 ER 873.

[40] *Pearce v Croydon Rural District Council* (1910) 74 JP 429.

[41] *M'Nab v Robertson* [1897] AC 129 HL.

[42] *Staffordshire Canal Co v Birmingham Canal Co* (1866) LR 1 HL 254.

[43] Wisdom (1979) p.56; though there does not appear to be any direct authority on this point, and it is not entirely clear whether such remedies arise by virtue of riparian rights or because of other civil law remedies (on this, see the discussion of trespass, nuisance and negligence 3.7–8 and 10 below).

### 3.4.2 *Artificial Watercourses*

Whilst riparian rights arise as a natural incident of the ownership of waterside land, such rights will not normally exist in relation to artificially constructed channels through which water flows. Hence, where water flows through an artificial watercourse the existence of riparian rights, if any, will rest upon a very different basis to that in respect of natural watercourses.[44] This distinction was emphasised in the observation that,

> [t]he right to the water of a river flowing in a natural channel through a man's land, and the right to water flowing to it through an artificial watercourse constructed on his neighbour's land, do not rest on the same principle. In the former case each successive riparian owner is prima facie entitled to the unimpeded flow of the water in its natural course, and to its reasonable enjoyment as it passes through his land, as a natural incident of his ownership of it. In the latter case any right to the flow of the water must rest on some grant or arrangement, either proved or presumed, from or with the owners of the lands from which the water is artificially brought, or on some other legal origin.[45]

In principle, therefore, natural watercourses and artificial watercourses have a different status with regard to the existence of riparian rights. However, the possibility exists that riparian rights may arise in respect of a permanent artificial watercourse where the claimant of such rights is able to establish an actual or presumed grant of such rights in the watercourse, or the acquisition of such rights through long use.[46] Hence, it has been held that a non-riparian owner abstracting water from a stream by means of conduits had no riparian status to bring an action against a riparian owner who had polluted the stream which served as the ultimate source of the water supply.[47] Likewise where the artificial channel is intended to be of only a temporary nature it will not give rise to riparian rights, as with a channel used to remove mine waste at the convenience of the mine owners,[48] or an agricultural ditch or drain the operation of which was dependent upon the mode of draining land adopted by the defendant.[49] More remarkably perhaps, in *Burrows* v *Lang*[50] an ancient, though artificial, watercourse maintained solely for the purpose of a mill was held to have been constructed for a temporary purpose and consequently the mill owner acquired no riparian right to use the water of the watercourse.

The intention with which an artificial channel is constructed, or subsequently used, is of crucial importance. Where it is shown that a

---

[44] Generally see Hobday (1952) pp.194 to 195.

[45] Per Sir Montague Smith in *Rameshur Pershad Narain Singh* v *Koonj Behari Pattuk* (1878) 4 AC 121.

[46] See 3.13.3 below on prescriptive rights.

[47] *Ormerod* v *Todmorden Joint Stock Mill Co* (1883) 11 QBD 155; and *Paine and Co Ltd* v *St Neots Gas and Coke Co* [1938] 3 All ER 812.

[48] *Arkwright* v *Gell* (1839) 5 M&W 203.

[49] *Greatrex* v *Hayward* (1853) 8 Ex 291; and *Bartlett* v *Tottenham* [1932] 1 Ch 114.

[50] [1901] 2 Ch 503.

watercourse has been created and used in such circumstances as to generate riparian rights in favour of the waterside owners then such owners will be in the same legal position as the owners of land adjoining a natural watercourse.[51] In particular, the acquisition of riparian status by the owner of a bank of an artificial watercourse may be achieved either by an express grant,[52] or by means of a prescriptive right[53] acquired through long use of the channel either to receive water or to discharge it,[54] or by statutory authorisation.[55] In each of these situations the extent of the riparian interest acquired will depend upon the scope of the grant, prescriptive use or statutory authority, as the case may be.

### 3.4.3 Tidal Waters

As a matter of common law, water which is affected by the regular ebb and flow of the highest tides is termed 'tidal water'.[56] This includes waters where tides have a lateral effect, or a vertical effect due to the arresting of water passing down an estuary into the sea.[57] With the exception of certain differences in respect of public rights of navigation, the owner of land on the bank of a tidal river has the same riparian rights as those possessed by a riparian owner whose land abuts non-tidal water.[58] In some exceptional instances, the ownership of the foreshore may be vested in a private individual,[59] and where this exists the foreshore owner will have the same rights in the sea as possessed by a riparian owner in respect of an inland watercourse.[60]

It follows from the common character of riparian ownership on tidal and non-tidal watercourses that contamination of salt or brackish water will, in principle, be actionable by the owner of tidal riparian land. Thus the lessee of oyster beds in a river estuary was awarded damages and an injunction against a sanitary authority which had discharged crude sewage into the estuary causing the oysters to become contaminated.[61] In another case it was held that no prescriptive right could be acquired by a district council

---

[51] *Sutcliffe* v *Booth* (1863) 32 LJQB 136.

[52] *Wood* v *Saunders* (1875) 10 Ch App 583.

[53] *Gaved* v *Martyn* (1865) 13 LT 74.

[54] A distinction noted by Bowen LJ in *Chamber Colliery Co* v *Hopwood* (1886) 55 LT 449, at p.452.

[55] See 3.13 below on general defences in civil proceedings.

[56] *Reece* v *Miller* (1882) 8 QBD 626, and generally see Newsom and Sherratt (1972) Appx.II; and Ch.18 below on marine pollution.

[57] *West Riding of Yorkshire Rivers Board* v *Tadcaster Rural District Council* (1907) 97 LT 436; and *Ingram* v *Percival* [1968] 3 All ER 657.

[58] See *Attorney-General* v *Lonsdale* (1868) 20 LT 64; *Lyon* v *Fishmongers' Co* (1876) 35 LT 569; and *North Shore Railway Co* v *Pion* (1889) 14 AC 612.

[59] *Blundell* v *Caterrall* (1821) 5 B & Ald 268, and see Howarth (1992d) p.11.

[60] See Payne (1994).

[61] *Hobart* v *Southend-on-Sea Corporation* (1906) 75 LJKB 305; though contrast *Somersetshire Drainage Commissioners* v *Bridgwater Corporation* (1899) 81 LT 729 where a grant was presumed to permit a corporation to discharge sewage into a tidal river. More recently, on the quality required of waters for shellfish under European Community law see *Bowden* v *South West Water Services Ltd* [1999] Env LR 438 discussed at 15.3.4 below.

to discharge sewage so as to contaminate oyster beds.[62] The discharge of oil onto coastal land will also be civilly actionable by the owners of that land.[63]

### 3.4.4 Underground Water

In most cases where civil litigation for water contamination is in prospect the claimant and defendant are likely to be downstream and upstream owners of riparian land adjoining a surface watercourse. However, in some circumstances riparian rights are capable of arising in respect of underground water. An underground flow of water is capable of giving rise to riparian rights where it constitutes a stream or watercourse, that is, providing that it has a reasonably well defined channel and a flow of water. Hence, where a surface watercourse sank below ground, where it continued its course for a distance, and then emerged above ground it was held that it did not cease to be a stream because of the subterranean flow.[64] In another case,[65] an action was sustained when polluted water from lead extraction operations was discharged into drains which passed into natural underground passages which communicated with a stream from which water was abstracted for use in the manufacture of paper.[66]

Although underground water following a defined channel is regarded in the same way as surface water for the purposes of establishing riparian rights, in respect of abstraction and diversion of water at least, different conclusions have been reached in situations where underground water lacks a definite channel of flow. Hence, it has been held that the principles relating to underground water in a defined channel, are 'inapplicable to the case of subterranean water not flowing in any definite channel . . . but percolating or oozing through the soil, more or less according to the quantity of rain that may chance to fall'.[67] It appears, therefore, that riparian rights may be exercised only where a defined underground channel is identified, though establishing this may give rise to some practical difficulty, but riparian rights will not arise where water merely percolates through soil or where no definite watercourse can be shown to exist.

Despite the absence of riparian rights in underground water which does not follow an identifiable course, it has been established that a right of action may exist against a person who causes the contamination of a supply of

---

[62] *Foster* v *Warblington Urban District Council* [1906] 1 KB 648; and see 3.13.3 below on prescription.

[63] *Esso Petroleum Co Ltd* v *Southport Corporation* [1956] AC 218; and see 19.13 below on oil contamination.

[64] *Dickinson* v *Grand Junction Canal Co* (1852) 16 Jur 200.

[65] *Hodgkinson* v *Ennor* (1863) 122 ER 446.

[66] See also *Tenant* v *Goldwin* (1703) Salk 21.

[67] Per Lord Chelmsford LC in *Chasemore* v *Richards* (1859) 7 HL Cas 349, at p.367; *R* v *Metropolitan Board of Works* (1863) 3 B&S 229; and *Rugby Joint Water Board* v *Walters* [1966] 3 All ER 497.

underground water. Thus in *Womersley* v *Church*[68] an injunction was sought to prevent the defendant from using a cesspool in such a manner as to pollute a well belonging to the claimant who occupied an adjoining property. It was held that, although sewage matter had percolated rather than flowed through an underground channel, it had rendered the water from the well unfit to drink and an injunction would be granted to restrain the defendant from making further use of the cesspool.[69] Whilst not strictly a riparian right, the protection of the natural right to percolating water, in private nuisance and under the rule in *Rylands* v *Fletcher*, was extensively and authoritatively considered in *Cambridge Water Company* v *Eastern Counties Leather plc.*[70]

### 3.4.5 'Ownership' of Water

Although a range of uses of water are permitted to riparian owners, remarkably, ownership of riparian land does not normally carry with it the *ownership* of flowing water. This is regarded as being in public and common ownership in that,

> all may reasonably use it who have a right of access to it, and that none can have any property in the water itself, except in the particular portion which he may choose to abstract from the stream and take into his possession, and that during the time of his possession only.[71]

As a consequence of this, flowing water is not capable of being stolen unless it has been removed from a stream for some purpose.[72] Water which is appropriated from a stream would then become the property, but only for so long as it was stored, and an 'owner' of such water who decided to return it to a stream would relinquish his right of ownership by so doing, and the water would be restored to public ownership.[73] Since riparian owners generally have a limited capacity to take water into their possession for any length of time, it follows that riparian rights are normally concerned with those activities which may legitimately be undertaken by the owners of waterside land. They are not normally concerned with the establishment or exercise of anything more than a transient or qualified right of property in the water itself.

As will be seen in discussion of other areas of civil law relating to water quality, the peculiar status of water as 'unowned' has implications for torts which are primarily concerned with the protection of interests in *land*.

---

[68] (1867) 17 LT 190.

[69] Similarly, see *Ballard* v *Tomlinson* (1885) 29 Ch D 115.

[70] [1994] 1 All ER 53 and see 3.10 below.

[71] Per Parke B in *Embrey* v *Owen* (1851) 6 Ex 353, at p.369; and see *Williams* v *Morland* (1824) 2 B&C 910; and *Mason* v *Hill* (1833) 5 B&Ad 1 at p.24. Similarly, ownership of fish and other flora and fauna in flowing waters are not the property of the landowner until they are appropriated into possession, see *R* v *Hudson* (1781) 3 East PC 611, but see para.2 Sch.1 Theft Act 1968 which creates an offence in relation to the taking or destroying of fish in certain waters.

[72] *Freans* v *O'Brien* (1883) 47 JP 472.

[73] *Liggins* v *Inge* (1831) 7 Bing 682, at p.693.

Arguably, the protection of the *enjoyment* of land provided by private nuisance[74] may be construed to encompass the quality of water since deterioration in water quality may impact on the enjoyment of the land. In a derivative sense, therefore, the protection of water falls within nuisance despite its central concern with interests in land. Perhaps more problematic, however, is the situation with regard to liability for trespass[75] to land where the emphasis is placed upon the protection of land ownership and the associated rights to possession of land. Here, it is less certain that interference with unowned water is, without more, a basis for liability.

## 3.5 Riparian Rights and Water 'Pollution'

Having considered the general nature of riparian rights and the kinds of water in which they may subsist, the critical issue is the quality of water which they may serve to protect. Hence, consideration must be given to the degree of protection given to riparian owners and the underlying concept of water 'pollution' which serves as a basis for granting a remedy for infringement of riparian rights.

### 3.5.1 Lord Macnaghten's Principle

Insofar as the civil law concerning riparian rights does approach a definition of water 'pollution', its most authoritative exposition is to be found the statement of the entitlements of riparian owners to clean water formulated by Lord Macnaghten in *John Young and Co v Bankier Distillery Co*,[76] where it was said:

> A riparian proprietor is entitled to have the water of the stream, on the banks of which his property lies, flow down as it has been accustomed to flow down to his property, subject to the ordinary use of the flowing water by upper proprietors, and to such further use, if any, on their part in connection with their property as may be reasonable under the circumstances. Every riparian owner is thus entitled to the water of his stream in its natural flow, without sensible diminution or increase, and without sensible alteration in its character or quality. Any invasion of this right causing actual damage, or calculated to found a claim which may ripen into an adverse right, entitles the party injured to the intervention of the court.

Several features of Lord Macnaghten's principle deserve special note.[77]

---

[74] See the discussion of private nuisance at 3.8 below.

[75] See the discussion of trespass at 3.7 below.

[76] (1893) [1891-4] All ER Rep 439, at p.441; see also *Mason v Hill* (1833) 110 ER 692; and *Wood v Waud* (1849) 154 ER 1047.

[77] See Newsom and Sherratt (1972) pp.3-9.

### 3.5.2 *Water Quality and Quantity*

First, the rights of a riparian owner arise in respect of both the quantity and the quality of water which flows past his land.[78] Normally, where pollution of water is alleged, the court will be concerned with the deterioration in water quality, but in some situations the quantity of water may become an issue. This may either be because the improper abstraction of water results in contamination otherwise present in a water becoming harmful through insufficient dilution, or because the addition of effluent to the stream causes an increase in the flow which is itself actionable under the principle. Hence the principle incorporates the possibility that a complaint can be grounded in a variation of the quantity of water in a watercourse without the need for deterioration in water quality actually to be shown.

*John S Deed & Sons Ltd* v *British Electricity Authority and Croydon Corporation*[79] is an instructive, if extraordinary, decision on the right of riparian owners to a continued flow of water. Here the claimant riparian owners claimed entitlement to receive the flow of a watercourse *including sewage effluent* discharged from the Corporation's sewage treatment works and were objecting to proposals to divert the effluent from the river to be used in cooling towers at an electricity generating station. The claim was based, first, upon a local Act which prevented the Corporation from taking water which diminished the flow of the river and, second, upon their entitlement as riparian owners to the flow, including the effluent, based upon prescription and equitable principles of acquiescence and estoppel, on the basis of expenditure having been made in reliance upon statements as to continued flow made by the Corporation. However, it was held that there were no grounds for inferring an easement or grant which would require the Corporation to maintain the flow of effluent since the local Act only applied to naturally occurring water and there were no grounds for relief in respect of acquiescence or estoppel. The right of a riparian owner to discharge effluent does not give a right to other riparian owners to compel its continuing discharge. There is no right to a non-natural flow of water even in unusual circumstances where contaminated water is actually desired by a riparian owner.

### 3.5.3 *Ordinary and Reasonable Use of Water*

A second notable feature of Lord Macnaghten's principle is that it makes a riparian owner's right to the flow of water subject to the 'ordinary' use of upper proprietors and such further use 'as may be reasonable in the circumstances'. The implicit contrast between 'ordinary' and 'extraordinary' uses of water was elaborated upon in a later case, in a speech by the same judge, where it was said:

> [t]here are, as it seems to me, three ways in which a person whose lands are intersected or bounded by a running stream may use the

---

[78] See 3.3 above on riparian rights.
[79] (1950) 114 JP 533.

water to which the situation of his property gives him access. He may use it for ordinary or primary purposes, and the wants of his cattle. He may use it also for some other purposes – sometimes called extraordinary or secondary purposes – provided those purposes are connected with or incident to his land, and provided that certain conditions are complied with. Then he may possibly take advantage of his position to use the water for purposes foreign to or unconnected with his riparian tenement. His rights in the first two cases are not quite the same. In the third case he has no right at all.[80]

The difference between 'ordinary' and 'extraordinary' uses of water by a riparian proprietor was explained in a later passage in the speech:

> [i]n the ordinary or primary use of flowing water a person dwelling on the banks of a stream is under no restriction. In the exercise of his ordinary rights he may exhaust the water altogether. No lower proprietor can complain of that. In the exercise of rights extraordinary but permissible, the limit of which has never been accurately defined and probably is incapable of accurate definition, a riparian owner is under considerable restrictions. The use must be reasonable. The purposes for which the water is taken must be connected with his tenement, and he is bound to restore the water which he takes and uses for those purposes substantially undiminished in volume and unaltered in character.[81]

It has been suggested that the use of water for secondary purposes might include water 'used for producing power, or for a fish farm, or for cooling, or for such irrigation as does not affect the quantity of the flow reaching the lower tenement'.[82] Conversely, it has been held that the use of water for spray-irrigation is an example of an extraordinary purpose[83] and, because it results in only a small amount of the water which is used returning to the watercourse, it will be impermissible as a matter of civil law.[84] More pertinently, the use of water to dispose of contaminating effluent will fall into the category of extraordinary use of water and will be permissible only to the extent that the water which is used for this purpose is returned to the watercourse from which it was abstracted 'without sensible diminution or increase, and without sensible alteration in its character or quality'.[85]

---

[80] *McCartney* v *Londonderry and Lough Swilly Railway* [1904] AC 301, at p.306.

[81] *Ibid* at p.307.

[82] Newsom and Sherratt (1972) p.6; though water abstraction may require a licence under Chapter II Part II Water Resources Act 1991.

[83] Special licensing provisions apply to spray irrigation: see ss.127 to 129 Water Resources Act 1991 and Spray Irrigation (Definition) Order 1992 (SI 1992 No.1096).

[84] *Rugby Joint Water Board* v *Walters* [1966] 3 All ER 497.

[85] Per Lord Macnaghten in *John Young and Co* v *Bankier Distillery Co* (1893) [1891-4] All ER 439, at p.698, quoted above.

### 3.5.4 *Damage and Sensible Alteration*

A third notable aspect of Lord Macnaghten's principle is that infringement of a riparian owner's right to a flow of water is actionable only where infringement results in 'actual damage' or gives rise to the basis of a future claim for an adverse right.[86] It is implicit, therefore, that it is the combination of sensible alteration of the flow of water in conjunction with damage to interests of the riparian owner that is the basis of a civil claim based upon riparian rights.[87]

The reference to a 'future claim for an adverse right' seems to envisage an action being brought to prevent a discharger gaining a prescriptive right to continue the discharge through continued long use.[88] In a situation of this kind, the disjunctive wording suggests that the 'actual damage' requirement does not need to be met. This possibility is likely to be of less practical importance today because of the difficulty of establishing prescriptive rights in relation to unlawful discharges and the fact that most lawful discharges would need to comply with regulatory requirements, including the requirements of discharge consents.[89] Hence, the possibility of a seriously contaminating discharge becoming justified by prescription would normally be precluded by the fact that it would be unlawful.

Other than situations where adverse rights are at issue, however, the claimant will need to show 'actual damage' to the party injured. The meaning of this term is not specified and this raises significant issues as to what kinds of damage will be sufficient. However, the suggestion that only harm to the claimant will suffice seems to rule out a remedy for harm to water quality or to the aquatic ecosystem alone, unless this can be shown to have adverse consequences upon the claimant. It follows that the availability of a remedy will be greatly dependent upon the *use* made of the water, as much as the degree of deterioration in its quality.

Another key issue in the characterisation of 'water pollution', as it features in claims based upon riparian rights, is the meaning of 'sensible alteration in the character or quality' of water. In relation to the requirement that damage must be 'sensible' it has been noted that a contrast is to be drawn between what is 'sensible', in the sense of being capable of being detected by the senses, and things which are capable of detection by scientific means. Hence, it has been stated that the principle is that:

> although when you once establish the fact of actual substantial damage it is quite right and legitimate to have recourse to scientific evidence, such as the microscope of the naturalist, or the tests of the chemist, for the purposes of establishing the damage itself, that

---

[86] See 3.13.3 below on prescriptive rights.

[87] Contrast the position in relation to trespass, see 3.7 below.

[88] See 3.13.3 below on prescription.

[89] See Ch.10 below on discharge consents.

evidence will not suffice. The damage must be such as can be shewn by a plain witness to a plain common juryman.[90]

Hence, the common law has tended to take a somewhat sceptical view of scientific evidence as to 'sensible alteration' of water quality.[91] In another case it was observed that 'the scientific evidence ought to be construed as secondary only to the evidence as to the facts'.[92] By contrast, several cases have made reference to the test of whether animals are willing to drink water which is alleged to have undergone 'sensible alteration'. One notable quote from a relatively early case seems to attribute horses a superior capacity in the assessment of water quality:

> [t]he primary use is not for carrying off impurities, but for drinking; and it is here of consequence that not only was the water tainted, but the air also. The taste of men is said to be various, and no doubt it is so, but that of horses is unvitiated. It is proved here that at least one horse refused to drink the water.[93]

The practical interpretation of 'sensible alteration' is to be discerned from examination of some of the leading authorities. The facts of *John Young and Co v Bankier Distillery Co* are an instructive starting point. Here, the claimants were the owners of a distillery situated on the banks of a stream, the waters of which were used for the purposes of their business. The respondents were the owners of a coal mine higher up the stream who, in the course of working their mine, pumped large quantities of water from lower strata into the stream. Although the pumped water discharged into the stream was 'pure', in the sense that it was thought usable to ordinary purposes, it was 'hard' in quality and this made the water of the stream less suitable for use by the respondents for the purpose of distilling.

On these facts, the House of Lords found that the lower riparian owner was not bound to receive the water pumped from the mine by artificial means, and which would never have reached his land otherwise. Moreover, the owner of the distillery had the right to the continuing flow of water without alteration of its natural character and, specifically, without change to the particular chemical composition of the stream which made the water suitable for distilling. The decision serves to emphasise the point that at civil law any 'sensible alteration' in the quality of a flow of water is actionable, notwithstanding that the stream remained 'pure' in the sense of being suitable for most ordinary purposes. As a matter of common law, therefore, actionable deterioration in water quality is regarded as a relative

---

[90] Per James LJ in *Salvin v North Brancepeth Coal Co* (1874) 9 Ch App 705, at p.708, quoted by Kennedy L in *Cambridge Water Company v Eastern Counties Leather plc and Hutchings and Harding Ltd* [1992] *Journal of Environmental Law* 81 at p.101.

[91] Contrast the approach taken in relation to statutory civil liability, see the discussion of *Blue Circle Industries plc v Ministry of Defence* [1999] Env LR 22 at 20.11.5 below.

[92] *Goldsmid v Tunbridge Wells Improvement Commissioners* (1866) 14 LT 154, at p.156.

[93] Per Lord Monboddo in *Russel and Others v Haig* (1791) Mor Dict 12823 and reported as *Jamieson v Haig*, House of Lords, 3 Pat 403, see also *Smith v Cameron* (1900 2 F 1179) and *Oldaker v Hunt* (1854) 19 Beav 425 (concerning the willingness of cattle to drink water) and generally see Taylor (1928) pp.16 to 19.

measure of the present state of water compared with its natural state, rather than a matter to be gauged by reference to any absolute physical, chemical or other criteria of contamination or water quality.

Subsequent case law has established that the civil law conception of actionable water pollution encompasses all the types of water contamination which are commonly encountered. Innumerable examples are to be found of actions being brought by complainants seeking to remedy industrial pollution caused by such matters as 'alkali refuse',[94] 'blotches of tarry matter',[95] 'deposits of mud',[96] 'water mixed and impregnated with injurious mineral substances',[97] and 'sulphuric acid and other deleterious matters'.[98] Successful actions were also brought where pollution resulted from the discharge of crude sewage, or inadequately treated sewage effluent, into watercourses where this resulted in a sensible diminution of the purity of the river or rendered it less fit for watering cattle or for other purposes for which a riparian owner would be entitled to use it.[99]

In addition to industrial and sewage contamination, the broad characterisation of actionable deterioration in natural water quality encompasses merely physical qualities of water. Hence, alteration of the temperature of water, or 'thermal contamination', has long been recognised as a ground upon which remedy can be given. In *Tipping* v *Eckersley*,[100] for example, the defendant operated a steam-engine which caused water discharged into a stream to become heated to such an extent that the claimant, who abstracted water downstream for condensing, was unable to operate his machinery to its normal level of efficiency. It was held that the claimant was entitled to so much of the stream in its natural state as was required for his works, that is, at its natural temperature. Accordingly, the claimant was granted an injunction restraining the defendant from discharging any heated water into the stream so as to cause an increase in the water temperature at the claimant's premises.[101]

Similarly, the addition of matter to water which changes its colour or clarity will be actionable in civil law, insofar as the addition amounts to a 'sensible alteration' of the natural quality of the water. However, there have been a number of cases where courts have been reluctant to conclude that trivial or transient interference with a watercourse should be regarded as having this effect. Thus the effect of contamination on the natural

---

[94] *Fletcher* v *Bealey* (1885) 61 ER 303.

[95] *Marquis of Granby* v *Bakewell Urban District Council* (1923) 87 JP 105.

[96] *Tatton* v *Staffordshire Potteries Waterworks Co* (1879) 44 JP 106.

[97] *Hodgkinson* v *Ennor* (1863) 122 ER 446.

[98] *Pennington* v *Brinksop Hall Coal Co* (1877) 5 Ch D 769.

[99] *Jones* v *Llanrwst Urban District Council* [1908-10] All ER Rep 922; *Haigh* v *Deudraeth Rural District Council* [1945] 2 All ER 661; and *Pride of Derby Angling Association Ltd* v *British Celanese Ltd* (1952) [1953] 1 All ER 179.

[100] (1855) 69 ER 779; see also *Ormerod* v *Todmorden Joint Stock Mill* (1883) 11 QBD 155; and *Pride of Derby and Derbyshire Angling Association Ltd* v *British Celanese Ltd* [1953] 1 All ER 179.

[101] See 3.16 below on injunctions.

opacity of water was regarded as insignificant in *Taylor* v *Bennett*[102] where it was held that the effect of throwing rubbish in a well was merely to make the water temporarily muddy and was too minute a damage to support the action. Likewise, in *Durrant* v *Branksome Urban District Council*[103] a drainage scheme conveyed flood-water containing silt and sand into a stream which was already charged with the same kind of impurities through natural causes. It was held that, since there was no apparent overall increase in the amount of suspended matter, no action would lie. Following analogous reasoning, it has been held that not every disagreeable smell which results from the discharge of matter into a stream will necessarily ground a civil action. Thus in *Ridge* v *Midland Railway*[104] where a discharge from a gas works into a river produced no appreciable effect on the water, and the associated smell did not appear to have caused serious inconvenience, the court declined the claimant's request for an injunction and damages. In summary, it is apparent that the notion of 'sensible alteration' of water quality involves a change in character which is neither transient nor insubstantial and lesser impairment will be regarded by a court as *de minimis*.[105]

### 3.5.5 Sensible Alteration and Multiple Discharges

A particular difficulty, which has arisen in a number of cases in the past, concerns situations where it is alleged that 'sensible alteration' to water quality has arisen where the contamination of a watercourse has been brought about by the combined activities of a number of dischargers each of whom claims to have made an insignificant contribution to the overall state of the receiving waters. This situation arose in *Blair and Sumner* v *Deakin*[106] where the defendants, who had discharged refuse and foul water into a watercourse, claimed in their defence that the injury that they might have caused was slight and inappreciable. This, it was alleged, was because the damage to the claimants was actually occasioned by the cumulative effects of discharges made by the defendants and several other manufacturers and mill owners higher up the watercourse. Although it was found that the activities of the defendants did in fact contribute in a material degree to the fouling of the stream, and so caused damage to the claimants, the court held as a general matter that where a number of persons contribute an infinitesimally small share to something which becomes a serious nuisance none of them can claim that his share is itself inconsiderable.[107] It follows that a riparian owner may bring an action against a discharger into a watercourse, however minor the discharge may

---

[102] (1836) 173 ER 146.

[103] (1896) [1897] 2 Ch 291.

[104] (1888) 53 JP 55.

[105] *Staffordshire County Council* v *Seisdon Rural District Council* (1907) 71 JP 185; and *Attorney-General* v *Gee* (1870) 23 LT 299.

[106] (1887) 52 JP 327; see also *Staffordshire County Council* v *Seisdon Rural District Council* (1907) 71 JP 185, which considered the problem of cumulative pollution in a statutory context.

[107] *St Helens Smelting Co* v *Tipping* (1865) 11 HLC 642; and *Thorpe* v *Brumfit* (1873) 8 Ch Ap 656 were cited as authority for this proposition.

be when considered in isolation, where waters become polluted through the cumulative effect of such discharges.[108]

## 3.6 Other Civil Claims for Water Contamination

Whilst the relationship between riparian owners in a watercourse gives rise to some rather distinctive kinds of legal rights and duties which arise as natural incidents of land ownership, the absence of a riparian relationship between a discharger and the recipient of contamination does not prevent civil proceedings being brought. However, where an action which is not based upon riparian rights arises, the claimant will only be entitled to a remedy where it can be shown that the action which is the subject of the proceedings falls within the parameters of a recognised tort action.[109] Although it is conceivable that water contamination may arise from a breach of a contractual obligation between parties,[110] it is more likely that redress for civil wrongs will arise in the law of tort, independently of any contract between the parties. Outside the principles concerning riparian rights, the main tortious actions which are potentially relevant in providing a means of redress for injury caused by water contamination: trespass, private nuisance[111] the rule in *Rylands* v *Fletcher*, negligence and breach of statutory duty. The elements of these different actions which are likely to be relevant in relation to water contamination proceedings are considered in the following sections.

## 3.7 Trespass

In general terms, the tort of trespass may provide a remedy where there is an interference with rights associated with the ownership of land. Typically, this may arise where an unauthorised person brings about the direct entry[112] of contaminating matter into the property of another person, without justification. Hence, trespass might be particularly appropriate if one person were to deposit contaminating matter directly upon the land of another. This might arise, in a situation where riparian rights were not at issue, where a deposit is made into an enclosed pond owned by another. By contrast, the indirect transmission of pollutants, perhaps by being blown in the wind, would be unlikely to form a basis for the action.

However, the essential purpose of trespass as a means of protecting interests in *land*, may give rise to difficulties where damage to *water* quality is concerned. As has been noted, water flowing in a watercourse is

---

[108] See also *Wood* v *Waud* (1849) 154 ER 1047; *Crossley* v *Lightowler* (1867) 36 LJ Ch 584; and *Nixon* v *Tynemouth Union Rural Sanitary Authority* (1888) 52 JP 504.

[109] Generally see Howarth (1995); Rogers (1998); Jones (1998); and Brazier and Murphy (1999).

[110] Similarly a contract may serve as a defence to a tortious action; see the discussion of the defence of 'grant' at 3.13.2 below. See also the discussion of whether drinking water is supplied under a contract at 7.6.7 below.

[111] More strictly termed 'private nuisance': contrast 'public nuisance' considered in 3.17 below.

[112] 'Direct entry' as opposed to *indirect* or consequential entry which is more appropriately addressed under private nuisance, discussed in 3.8 below.

not normally the subject of private ownership.[113] This is not problematic in relation to actions based upon riparian rights, since rights to water are conceived of as an incident of ownership which are, therefore, capable of protection. In relation to trespass, however, the position is less clear since the firm emphasis of the tort upon ownership and possession of land raises doubts as to whether protection of unowned water is strictly within the compass of the tort. In practice, this may not be an insuperable problem where harm to water quality impacts upon surrounding land or the bed or banks of a watercourse. However, there may be a difficulty in relation to the application of trespass to a situation where the harm is to water quality alone.

A contrasting situation arose in the recent case of *British Waterways Board v Severn Trent Water Ltd*[114] which was principally concerned with the existence of an implied power of a sewerage undertaker to discharge drained surface water into a privately owned canal.[115] Here the canal into which the discharge took place was taken to be an artificial watercourse so the riparian rights found in natural watercourses did not arise and the canal owners may have had rights of ownership over the water which would not normally exist in running watercourses. The point was conceded between the parties that a discharge into the canal would be a trespass unless statutory authority could be implied. It was, therefore, accepted as common ground that discharging into privately owned waters would constitute trespass where the entry is directly onto land and it seemed to be accepted that the facts involved such a discharge.

A distinctive feature of trespass is that the tort is committed whether or not the deposit or entry of offending matter actually results in any damage being caused. This is because where damage is absent the presence of polluting matter is regarded as constituting an infringement of the owner's right to possession, and this, without more, is sufficient to ground an action for trespass. In a case where no damage is shown, however, only a token sum of 'nominal damages' may be awarded in recognition of the infringement of the landowner's interest. Several aspects of the tort of trespass are of especial relevance in relation to water contamination. These are: the claimant's interest in land; the behaviour of the defendant; actionability *per se*; and the directness of the injury.

### 3.7.1 The Claimant's Interest in Land

The action for trespass, in the context of water contamination, arises from the right to possession of land or the protection of certain kinds of interest in land. It follows that trespass will only be available to a person who occupies land as a freeholder or as a leaseholder during the duration of a

---

[113] See the discussion of 'ownership' of water at 3.4.5 above.

[114] Postscript: [2001] EWCA Civ 276, 2 March 2001, paras 37-38.

[115] Under s.159 Water Industry Act 1991, concerned with the power of an undertaker to lay pipes.

lease.[116] Since the action is founded on the violation of a right to possession it will not normally be available to a landlord whilst he has relinquished his right to possession during the subsistence of a lease. By way of exception to this principle, however, a landlord will be able to bring an action for trespass if the injury complained of is of such a permanent nature that the reversionary interest in the land is likely to be affected. Thus a landlord was entitled to bring an action for trespass where it was found that sewage would continue to be discharged into a river 'unless and until something is done to divert it elsewhere', that is, beyond the duration for which the property was subject to a lease.[117]

Another consequence of trespass serving to protect interests in land, rather than the unqualified ownership of land, is that it will not be a defence to challenge the legitimacy of a claimant's claim to ownership. Hence it will not be a defence to an action for trespass for the defendant to argue the existence of third party rights, that is, that some other person has a stronger claim to possession of the property than the claimant.[118] Trespass, therefore, serves to protect actual possession, and even possibly wrongful possession by the claimant, against persons others than a person with a better title to the right which has been infringed.

The interest necessary for an action for trespass to be brought must be a legal right usually involving the exclusive possession of the land. Consequently the action will not be available to a lodger, without exclusive possession, who has only the use of property,[119] or a person with a mere contractual licence or permit to use a watercourse for a particular purpose such as angling. Thus in *Hill* v *Tupper*[120] the claimant had been granted a concession by the owner of a canal amounting to the exclusive right to hire out pleasure boats on the canal. He brought an action for trespass when the defendant established a business in direct competition, but failed when the court ruled that his interest was a mere licence which did not grant a legal right to the exclusive possession of the canal for boating purposes. Likewise trespass will not be available for interference with lesser kinds of legal interest such as an easement or a right to take water.[121]

It is established that trespass will be available where there is interference with a proprietary interest of a kind which, if created by deed or prescription,[122] would amount to a *profit a prendre* permitting the holder to enter and to take something from the servient land. Hence in *Mason* v

---

[116] Trespass has also been held to be available to a person who is a licensee of the owner of property to bring an action to remove persons who were occupying the land without permission, *Manchester Airport plc* v *Lee Dutton and others* (1999) 3 WLR 524, though contrast the outcome in *Countryside Residential (North Thames) Ltd* v *Tugwell* (2000) *The Times* 4 April 2000.

[117] Per Parker J in *Jones* v *Llanrwst Urban District Council* [1908-10] All ER Rep 922, at p.927.

[118] *Nicholls* v *Ely Beet Sugar Factory Ltd* [1931] 2 Ch 84.

[119] *Allen* v *Liverpool Overseers* (1874) LR 9 QB 180, at pp.191 to 192.

[120] (1863) 2 H&C 121.

[121] *Paine and Co Ltd* v *St Neots Gas and Coke Co* [1939] 3 All ER 812; and *Race* v *Ward* (1855) 4 E&B 702.

[122] See 3.13.3 below on prescriptive rights.

*Clarke,*[123] where the claimant had made an oral agreement amounting to a *profit a prendre* entitling him to catch rabbits on an estate, it was held that he could succeed in an action against the defendant who had interfered with the exercise of this right. Similarly, it has been held that a person possessed of a legal rights of fishery, a *profit of piscary,* will be able to sue in trespass for the direct interference with a right of fishing and taking fish.[124] It must be stressed, however, that the interest granted must be more than a mere licence to be present on the land and, beyond conveying the legal right to fish, it must convey a right to the property in captured fish so that the possessor of the profit is entitled to keep and take away any fish caught.

### 3.7.2 The Directness of Injury

A somewhat peculiar, feature of the action for trespass descends from a historical division between acts causing direct damage and those where damage is caused indirectly or consequentially. Traditionally, where a person suffered a direct injury his action was properly brought as a trespass whereas where the injury was suffered indirectly the appropriate action was that of 'trespass upon the case', or simply 'case', from which the modern actions for nuisance and negligence originate.[125] The same distinction between direct and indirect injuries survives, in that the action for trespass continues to require a direct interference with possession of land. For example, in *Reynolds* v *Clarke*[126] a landowner was unable to succeed in an action for trespass brought against his neighbour for causing water to run onto his land from a spout draining water away from the eaves of the neighbour's house. It was held that the transmission of the water in this case was insufficiently direct to ground an action in trespass. The facts may have supported a tortious action of another kind, but for an action in trespass to be successful it had to be shown that the defendant placed something directly upon the claimant's land rather than merely permitting it to enter the land by some indirect means.

A leading authority illustrating the operation, and limitations, of the tort of trespass in the sphere of water contamination is *Esso Petroleum Co Ltd* v *Southport Corporation,*[127] which arose out of an oil tanker belonging to the defendants running aground on a revetment wall. In order to save the vessel and crew from danger, the master of the vessel discharged a considerable quantity of oil to lighten the vessel. The oil which was discharged became deposited on the respondents' foreshore causing

---

[123] [1955] AC 778.

[124] *Nicholls* v *Ely Beet Sugar Factory Ltd* [1931] 2 Ch 84; and *Fitzgerald* v *Firbank* [1897] 2 Ch 96.

[125] See *Prior of Southwark's Case* (1498) YB 13 Hen 7 p.26; cited in Fifoot (1949) p.87, also cited by Denning LJ in *Southport Corporation* v *Esso Petroleum Co* [1954] 2 All ER 561, at p.570, and discussed at 3.8 below.

[126] (1725) 2 Ld Raym 1399.

[127] [1953] 2 All ER 1204, Queen's Bench Division; [1954] 2 All ER 561, Court of Appeal; and [1955] 3 All ER 864, House of Lords.

damage. Amongst other grounds for redress,[128] the respondents brought an action for trespass. In the Court of Appeal, Denning LJ was of the opinion that an action for trespass would not lie, since the discharge of oil was not made directly onto the foreshore, but outside in the estuary, and oil was carried by the tide onto the foreshore. Because of the indirect mechanism of transfer of the oil the damage was regarded as consequential and not direct. Similarly in the appeal to the House of Lords,[129] Lord Radcliffe doubted whether trespass would be a relevant action where the oil had been jettisoned at sea, 'committed to the action of wind and wave', such that there was no certainty when or under what conditions it might come ashore.[130] The decision, therefore, is an important affirmation of the need for directness of injury as a prerequisite for trespass to be successful in water contamination situations.

There are, however, several important examples of decisions on water contamination where courts have allowed the tort of trespass as an appropriate basis for redress. Thus in *Jones* v *Llanrwst Urban District Council*[131] it was found that where the defendant discharged crude sewage into a river from a sewer on the claimant's bank onto the bed of the river, which was also owned by the claimant, an action for trespass could be maintained. Moreover the view was expressed that, 'anyone who turns faecal matter or allows faecal matter collected by him or under his control to escape into a river in such a manner or under such conditions that it is carried, whether by the current or the wind, on to his neighbour's land is guilty of a trespass'.[132] Although this statement may be over-wide, in that it appears to encompass cases of indirect contamination caused by matter being transmitted by natural forces,[133] it was evident that the matter in question did fall directly onto the claimants land without the assistance of water or wind currents, and in such a situation the element of direct damage would seem to be undeniably present. Nonetheless, there are clear difficulties in drawing a clear line between direct and indirect damage in situations of this kind.

The re-emphasis of the requirement of direct injury, in *Esso Petroleum Co Ltd* v *Southport Corporation*, casts some doubt upon earlier suggestions that an action for trespass can be maintained on account of water contamination without direct injury.[134] In one such case the claimant complained that effluent which had been discharged from the defendant's

---

[128] Public nuisance, private nuisance and negligence.

[129] Where the action for negligence was the sole ground of appeal.

[130] [1955] 3 All ER 864, at p.872; and see Lord Tucker at p.873, though it is recognised that these remarks were *obiter*.

[131] (1910) [1908-10] All ER Rep 922, and see Payne (1994).

[132] *Ibid* at p.926.

[133] Although in *Southport Corporation* v *Esso Petroleum Co Ltd* discussed above, Morris LJ thought that there may be trespass if the force of the wind or of moving water is employed to cause a thing to go on to land (Court of Appeal at p.576), and Lord Radcliffe stated that he did not regard the decision in *Jones* v *Llanrwst Urban District Council* as having any bearing on the case of oil being jettisoned at sea (House of Lords at p.872).

[134] See *Fitzgerald* v *Firbank* (1897) 76 LT 584, at p.587; and *Foster* v *Warblington Urban District Council* (1906) 70 JP 233, at p.237.

factory into a river and conveyed by the current more that four miles downstream to pollute the claimant's fishery amounted to trespass.[135] Farwell J. recognised the difficulty involved in this contention and expressed the view that,

> [t]his is not strictly speaking an action of trespass. In the old days it would have been trespass on the case. The defendants are not discharging anything directly on to the [claimant]'s property, but on to an intermediate property, and the discharge is carried down to the [claimant]'s property. That is not strictly speaking trespass. It is nuisance.[136]

Nevertheless he apparently chose to assimilate the situation to one of trespass in saying, 'in this case I am dealing with a nuisance action of a kind peculiar to itself and to other pollution actions. It is not trespass, but it is very analogous to trespass'.[137] Following the same 'analogy' it has, on occasions, seemed as if the difficulty with regard to directness of damage has been overlooked.[138] These attempts to side-step the requirement of directness of injury in an action for trespass in respect of water contamination look incongruous alongside uncompromising statements to the effect that direct damage is a prerequisite for an action in trespass.[139]

### 3.7.3 The Behaviour of the Defendant

Another key feature of an action for trespass is that the actionable behaviour arises through a negligent or intentional act of the defendant. In most situations the behaviour of the defendant amounts to an intention to do the tortious act, but it is apparent that negligence on the part of the defendant is sufficient.[140] Hence it has been long established that an occupier of premises adjoining a highway cannot bring an action against a lawful user of the highway in trespass unless negligence, at least, can be shown.[141] Although there are some indications that 'consequential directness' may be sufficient,[142] no decisive authority on the matter exists,

---

[135] *Nicholls* v *Ely Beet Sugar Factory* [1931] 2 Ch 84 and [1936] 1 Ch 343.

[136] *Ibid* at pp.86 to 87.

[137] *Ibid* at p.87.

[138] See Devlin J in *Southport Corporation* v *Esso Petroleum Co* [1953] 2 All ER 1204 at p.1208.

[139] See the speech of Denning LJ in *Southport Corporation* v *Esso Petroleum Co* [1954] 2 All ER 561, at p.570 in the Court of Appeal, and Lord Tucker [1955] 3 All ER 864 at p.873 in the House of Lords, affirming the need for directness of injury before an action for trespass will be successful. Similarly, in *Pride of Derby and Derbyshire Angling Association Ltd* v *British Celanese Ltd* [1952] 1 All ER 1326 and [1953] 1 All ER 179, it was notable that although the lower court had awarded damages for trespass and nuisance, the Court of Appeal confined the remedies to the latter ground alone.

[140] *Fowler* v *Lanning* [1959] 1 QB 426; see also *Letang* v *Cooper* [1965] 1 QB 232; and *Stanley* v *Powell* [1891] 1 QB 86.

[141] See Lord Blackburn in *River Wear Commissioners* v *Adamson* (1877) 2 App Cas 743 at p.767; and *Esso Petroleum Co* v *Southport Corporation* [1955] 3 All ER 864, per Lord Radcliffe at p.872 and Lord Tucker at p.873.

[142] In *League Against Cruel Sports* v *Scott* [1986] QB 240 the question arose as to whether the entry on land of hounds in pursuit of a stag amounted to trespass. It was held that the master of

it is likely that an unintentional act will not amount to trespass.[143] Thus a claimant seeking to bring an action for trespass on account of water contamination is obliged to show the presence of intention on the part of the defendant in causing the contamination.

### 3.7.4 Actionability per se

Trespass is distinguished from the other tortious actions which may be pursued on account of water contamination in that it is actionable *per se*, that is, without the need for proof of damage.[144] Normally, of course, trespass will result in damage and it may not matter whether the action for contamination of water is brought on this ground or another. However, in a situation where no loss can be shown, it may be important to pursue an action for trespass to establish the claimant's right not to have water contaminated in order to prevent the discharger acquiring a legal right to pollute through continuation of the practice,[145] or to serve as a ground for an order to prevent future contamination.[146] In the absence of a provable loss being suffered as a consequence of water contamination, however, the existence of trespass would be recognised by an award of merely nominal damages.[147]

## 3.8 Private Nuisance

'*Private* nuisance', so called to distinguish it from actions brought on behalf of the public at large as 'public nuisance',[148] is a common basis for a civil action in relation to water contamination.[149] The tort of nuisance arises where there has been an unreasonable interference with a landholder's interest in the enjoyment of land.[150] In common with trespass, nuisance is concerned with the protection of interests in land[151] and, as with trespass, the interest in land which must be shown by the claimant

---

hounds was liable if he had intended the hounds to enter or, knowing there was a risk that they would enter, their entry was caused by his failure to exercise proper control over them.

[143] See Brazier and Murphy (1999) pp.83 and 472.

[144] *Entick* v *Carrington* (1765) 2 Wils KB 275, at p.291.

[145] See 3.13.3 below on prescriptive rights.

[146] See 3.16 below on injunctions.

[147] See 3.15 below on damages.

[148] See 3.17 below on public nuisance.

[149] For general reading on nuisance and pollution control see Newark (1949); McLaren (1972); and (1983); Ogus and Richardson (1977); Gearty (1989); and Steele (1995).

[150] Generally, on the scope of nuisance, see *Cambridge Water Company* v *Eastern Counties Leather plc* [1994] 1 All ER 53 discussed at 3.10 below. Previously, see *Esso Petroleum Co Ltd* v *Southport Corporation* [1955] 3 All ER 864, House of Lords, which had suggested that a requirement of negligence was necessary for an action for nuisance.

[151] See the discussion of 'ownership' of water at 3.4.5 above. Technically, a contrast may be drawn between the ownership of land and the non-ownership of flowing water but, since nuisance is concerned to protect the *enjoyment* of land, the right to water of a particular quality is usually construed to come within this. Contrast the difficulties in using trespass to land to protect water quality discussed at 3.7 above.

will include that of a freehold owner or a leaseholder, but will also include other legal interests in land, or water, such as a legal right of fishery. Where nuisance can be established, and consequent damage shown, the remedies which are available to the claimant are an injunction to restrain the defendant from commencing or continuing the activity which constitutes the nuisance, and/or an award of damages to compensate the claimant for the injury which he has suffered in consequence of the nuisance.[152]

The rather open-ended nature of the interest in the 'enjoyment of land' protected by nuisance deserves emphasis. Whilst innumerable actions have been successfully brought concerning water contamination incidents involving a variety of environmentally harmful substances, the scope for nuisance proceedings for the protection of water extends well beyond these. Hence, an action in nuisance was successfully brought where rainbow trout escaped from a fish farm into a river that was preserved as a brown trout fishery and loss of angling amenity was shown as a consequence.[153] In another case, the removal of a large part of the river flow for abstraction purposes, resulting in the death of fish in a downstream fish farm due to a lack of oxygen, was held to be actionable.[154] More remarkably, nuisance proceedings were successful in a Scots court where owners of a fishery alleged that 'light pollution' from tennis court floodlights substantially interfered with the amenity of the fishery.[155] Whilst, at most, these situations are placed at the periphery of what might ordinarily regarded as 'water pollution', they usefully demonstrate the emphasis placed on 'enjoyment of land' and a refusal to confine remedies to water contamination incidents of a more customary kind.

Another general observation about nuisance concerns the antiquity of the action. Whilst some modern commentators may be swift to characterise nuisance as an 'environmental' tort, it should be noted that the action predates modern concepts of 'the environment' or even 'pollution' by many years. Although examples of early proceedings can be found, classically illustrating what today would be regarded as environmental complaints, these proceedings were probably conceived of at the time as being grounded in less abstract concerns. Hence in proceedings brought in 1498,[156] the Prior of Southwark brought a writ of *Trespass sur le cas* (the forerunner of the modern action in nuisance) and alleged that he had been

---

[152] See 3.14 below on remedies.

[153] *Broderick* v *Gale and Ainslie Ltd*, unreported Swindon County Court, 29 March 1993, but see [1993] *Water Law* 127. Notably, these proceedings were successful in both nuisance and negligence.

[154] *Swan Fisheries Ltd* v *Holberton*, unreported, Queen's Bench Division, 14 December 1987, but see Howarth (1990) p.91. Again, the proceedings were successfully brought in both nuisance and negligence.

[155] *Stonehaven and District Angling Association* v *Stonehaven Recreation Ground Trustees and Stonehaven Tennis Club* (1997) 60 SPEL 36, noted at [1997] *Water Law* 200 and [1997] *Environmental Law and Management* 117. See also Jewkes (1998).

[156] *The Prior of Southwark's Case* (1498) Year Book Trinity, 13 Hen 7, f.26, pl.7, and see Fifoot (1949) p.87.

possessed of certain houses and gardens in Southwark. The tenants of the houses had a watercourse running between the houses and gardens, and this water was used to dye clothes, to water beasts, to bake and brew and for other easements. The Prior's complaint was that the defendant had made a lime pit for tanning calf-skins so close to the stream that the lime pit had 'corrupted' the stream and because of this the tenants had left the houses. The writ was challenged on behalf of the defendant because the defendant had made the lime pit on the claimant's soil and the appropriate writ was that of *Trespass quare vi et armis* (the forerunner of the action in trespass) and not a *writ sur le cas*. It was also argued that the claimant had no rights in the water except in common with others and that the claimant's plea was not good for that reason. In determining the dispute Brian CJ said,

> I put the case that I and a stranger are tenants in common of a stream, and I have houses adjoining for which I have an easement of such water, as in the case here, and my companion commits such a nuisance as this and corrupts the water; shall I not have an action *sur mon cas* against him? I think so: for the nuisance is done to my soil, since he has no rights in the houses to which the nuisance is done.

### 3.8.1 The Proof of Damage

Actual damage must be shown for an action in nuisance to be established. In some situations, however, it is considered that damage is so likely to arise that it is considered unnecessary for the claimant to prove the matter specifically. Thus in *Fay v Prentice*[157] a cornice of the defendant's house projected over the claimant's garden causing rain water to run from it on to the garden. It was held that injury to the claimant would be inferred without the need for proof of it to be provided. Other exceptions to the need for actual proof of damage arise in respect of interference with third party rights in land, where an action in nuisance may be brought to prevent the acquisition of rights by another without the need to show actual damage.[158] Moreover, it has been suggested that actions in nuisance on account of interferences with fishery rights are protected to the extent of importing the rule of trespass that no specific damage need be shown.[159] Although contrary to the general principles governing the availability of the action for nuisance, this feature is likely to be of particular importance with respect to water contamination litigation.

### 3.8.2 The Interest in Land

An action for nuisance can only be brought where the claimant has a sufficient legal interest in land. Thus it has been stated that 'to give a cause

---

[157] (1845) 1 CB 828.

[158] *Harrop v Hirst* (1868) LR 4 Exch 43; and see 3.13.3 below on prescription.

[159] *Nicholls v Ely Beet Sugar Factory Ltd* [1936] 1 Ch 343 at p.349, per Lord Wright and see 3.7 above on trespass.

of action for private nuisance, the matter complained of must affect the property of the [claimant]'.[160] Hence, sufficient legal interest will not be established where the claimant's interest is a mere personal right such as a contractual right to fish a particular water, or a permission which conveys no proprietary interest in the water. For this reason an angler or angling association or an environmental pressure group or any other body seeking to bring an action on account of water contamination will find themselves without redress in nuisance where they lack the necessary legal interest in the land adjoining the waters which have been contaminated.

The issue of the interest required for a nuisance action was authoritatively considered in *Hunter and Others* v *Canary Wharf Ltd and London Docklands Development Corporation*,[161] where an action was pursued in nuisance on account of interference with television reception in the homes of various persons in the shadow of the Canary Wharf Tower. It was held that an action in nuisance would only lie where the claimant had a right to the land affected and this would only be established where that person had a right to exclusive possession as a landlord or tenant. Hence, contrary to previous indications,[162] a mere occupier or licensee without exclusive possession of the land would not have the legal capacity to pursue an action in nuisance.[163]

Another feature of the action for private nuisance concerns the source of the nuisance in relation to the land of the defendant. Thus it has been said that, '[t]he ground of responsibility is the possession and control of the land from which the nuisance proceeds'.[164] Similarly, it has been emphasised that the function of nuisance is 'to control the activities of the owner or occupier of property within the boundaries of his land which may harm the interest of the owner or occupier of other land'.[165] For this reason it was held that a discharge of oil from a tanker onto the claimant's land did not amount to nuisance because it did not involve any interest of the defendants in land where the discharge was made from a ship at sea.[166] It follows that, normally at least, an action in nuisance must not only be brought by a landholder, but must also be brought *between* landholders.

---

[160] *Southampton Corporation* v *Esso Petroleum Co* [1953] 3 WLR 773, at p.776 per Devlin J.

[161] [1997] Env LR 488 and see Steele (1997).

[162] *Khorasandjian* v *Bush* [1993] QB 727.

[163] Similarly see *Malone* v *Laskey* [1907] 2 KB 141, though contrast *Foster* v *Warblington District Council* [1906] 1 KB 648 where it was established that a person with actual exclusive possession of oyster beds could maintain an action in nuisance even though he was unable to establish a formal title.

[164] Per Lord Wright in *Sedleigh-Denfield* v *O'Callaghan* [1940] 3 All ER 349, at p.364.

[165] *Hunter and Others* v *Canary Wharf Ltd and London Docklands Development Corporation* [1997] Env LR 488, per Lord Hope at p.536 and, similarly, see Lord Goff at p.494 and Lord Lloyd at p.510.

[166] *Southport Corporation* v *Esso Petroleum Co* [1954] 2 All ER 561, at p.570 per Denning L.J., Court of Appeal; approved by Lord Radcliffe in the House of Lords in *Esso Petroleum Co Ltd* v *Southport Corporation* [1955] 3 All ER 864, at p.871.

### 3.8.3  The Nature of the Damage and the Locality

Although concerned with the contamination of air rather than water, a leading case illustrating the scope of the action for nuisance is *St Helens Smelting Co* v *Tipping*.[167] The facts were simply that the claimant had acquired an estate in a manufacturing area and found that vapours emanating from a nearby smelting works caused damage to the trees on the estate and general disamenity. On appeal to the House of Lords, it was established that a distinction should be drawn between nuisances causing material injury to the value of property and lesser nuisances causing 'sensible personal discomfort' without damage to property. Although the former type of damage would invariably provide a ground for an action in nuisance, the possibility of an action being grounded upon the latter depended upon the nature of the locality. Hence where non-physical injury is the basis of a claim in nuisance,

> [i]f a man lives in a town, it is necessary that he should subject himself to the consequences of those operations of trade which may be carried on in his immediate locality, which are actually necessary for trade and commerce, and also for the enjoyment of property, and for the benefit of the inhabitants of the town and of the public at large.[168]

Similarly, in another case it was said that '[w]hat would be a nuisance in Belgrave Square would not necessarily be so in Bermondsey'.[169] On the facts of *St Helens Smelting Co* v *Tipping*, however, the effect of the smelting works was such as to cause 'sensible injury to the value of the property'. In such circumstances, the suitability of the locality for smelting operations did not assist the defendant's case and the court held that the claimant was only entitled to recover damages for the physical damage which had arisen.[170]

Notwithstanding the distinction which is drawn between material injury to property and sensible personal discomfort in determining the relevance of locality, it has recently been emphasised that this does not detract from the essential purpose of nuisance in protecting interests in land. Hence, where damages are to be assessed for sensible personal discomfort, the emphasis remains upon the harm caused to the land rather than the person discomfort caused to those occupying it. 'Loss of amenity', in this context, may therefore encompass diminution in the value of the land and consequential losses such as business profits. It is not quantified on the basis of inconvenience, annoyance or person injury to owners, and is certainly not multiplied by the number of occupants suffering personal discomfort.[171]

---

[167] (1865) 11 HLC 642; and see also *Halsey* v *Esso Petroleum Co Ltd* [1961] 2 All ER 145 and *Graham* v *ReChem International Ltd* [1996] Env LR 158.

[168] (1865) 11 HLC 642 at p.650.

[169] *Sturges* v *Bridgman* (1879) 11 Ch D 852, at p.865 per Thesigner LJ.

[170] Similarly, see *Halsey* v *Esso Petroleum Co* [1961] 1 WLR 683.

[171] *Hunter and Others* v *Canary Wharf Ltd and London Docklands Development Corporation* [1997] Env LR 488, per Lord Hoffman at pp.517-18.

It is no defence in nuisance for a defendant to argue that the claimant came to the source of a pre-existing nuisance since, first, the locality would be of no relevance where the action is for physical damage to property, and, second, it has been held that where an annoyance is unreasonable in a particular district the claimant can recover even if the activity has been going on before he arrived. Hence in *Bliss* v *Hall*[172] it was found that a tallow-chandlery emitted 'diverse noisome, noxious, and offensive vapours, fumes, smells and stenches', causing the discomfort of the claimant who lived near to it. Notwithstanding that the business had been in operation before the claimant moved to the locality, it was held that this was no defence where the defendant had infringed the claimant's 'right to wholesome air'.[173] The water-related implications of this are that there may be potential, for example, for actions to be brought where smelly operations take place at sewage treatment works, and it would be no defence for a sewerage undertaker to maintain that houses occupied by claimants had been recently built around a treatment works which had previously located at a sufficient distance from residential properties to avoid odour nuisance.

### 3.8.4 Locality and Environmental Licences

The issue of whether a use of land in a particular locality constitutes an actionable nuisance has arisen most recently in relation to situations where a development has been undertaken pursuant to a grant of planning permission. Hence, it has been alleged that a planning permission is sufficient to change the nature of the locality and to permit land uses that would otherwise have constituted a nuisance. For example, in *Gillingham Borough Council* v *Medway (Chatham) Dock Co Ltd*,[174] it was held that a planning permission allowing the development of a commercial port served as a defence to an action for public nuisance in relation to noise generated by vehicles using the port. This decision was reached on the basis that the nature of the locality in which the alleged nuisance arises is to be assessed by reference to the neighbourhood with the authorised development or use, rather than as it was previously.

However, the suggestion that a planning permission is akin to a statutory authority[175] in allowing what would otherwise be a nuisance would seem to be of narrow application and has not been followed. A subsequent decision resolved that a planning application allowing a pig farm to be constructed did not serve as any defence to the consequent odour nuisance generated by the pig rearing activities.[176] That is, the development of the land in accordance with the planning permission did not serve to change the locality to such an extent that the operation of the development was immune from proceedings in nuisance. Similarly, in the *Canary Wharf*

---

[172] (1838) 4 Bing NC 183.

[173] Similarly, see *Miller* v *Jackson* [1977] QB 966.

[174] [1993] QB 343, and see Crawford (1992).

[175] See the discussion of statutory authority at 3.13.4 below.

[176] *Wheeler* v *J J Saunders Ltd* [1996] Ch 19, and see Ball (1995).

case, discussed above, the Court of Appeal found that the designation of an enterprise zone in an urban development area[177] did not change the nature of the locality so that the tower which was constructed within the area enjoyed an immunity from actions based on nuisance.[178]

Whilst those situations that have been considered by the courts have concerned the effect of a planning permission upon the character of a locality, analogous issues are capable of arising in relation to activities conducted pursuant to other kinds of environmental licence. In particular, whilst the grant of a discharge consent does not preclude civil proceedings being brought in relation to that discharge,[179] conceivably the existence of the discharge consent, or a number of such consents, may result in a deterioration in the quality of the receiving waters. The uncertain issue in such circumstances, would be whether the 'locality' of the watercourse should be ascertained in relation to the natural or actual state of the receiving waters.[180]

### 3.8.5 Unusual Susceptibility

Closely related to the assessment of nuisances which give rise to 'sensible personal discomfort' according to locality, is the principle that an action will not be available to a claimant who is unusually susceptible to the nuisance which is complained of. The question as to what is to count as 'unusual susceptibility' will to some extent depend upon the locality in which the nuisance is alleged to arise[181] but, nonetheless, there are instances where courts have denied recovery in nuisance on this ground.[182]

In relation to the position of the unusually susceptible claimant and the locality doctrine generally, a contrast may be drawn between proceedings for water contamination based upon nuisance and proceedings based upon riparian rights in relation to which issues of locality and sensitivity do not arise. Hence, in *John Young and Co v Bankier Distillery Co*, discussed previously,[183] questions as to whether the claimant was involved in a hyper-sensitive activity in distilling whisky, or whether the fact that mining took place in the locality justified the discharges which had taken place, were not relevant.

---

[177] Under s.134 Local Government Planning and Land Act 1980.

[178] See *Hunter and others v Canary Wharf Ltd* and *Hunter and others v London Docklands Development Corp* [1996] 1 All ER 482.

[179] s.100 Water Resources Act 1991, and see discussion at 3.18.5 below.

[180] See Payne (1994) and Ball (1995).

[181] See Howarth (1995) p.510.

[182] See *Robinson v Kilvert* (1889) 41 Ch D 88, and *McKinnon Industries v Walker* (1951) 3 DLR 577.

[183] (1893) [1891-4] All ER 439, and see 3.5 above.

### 3.8.6 The Appropriateness of Private Nuisance

Relating these general principles to the action for private nuisance in the context of water contamination, it follows that a remedy in nuisance will be possible where water, in which the claimant has a sufficient legal interest, is contaminated if either this amounts to material injury to property or the activity which causes merely sensible discomfort is conducted unreasonably given the nature of the locality and the other circumstances. Since many cases of water contamination will result in material injury to property, in the sense of materially diminishing the enjoyment of the neighbouring land, it is likely that they will amount to nuisance without a court needing to enquire whether the activity is a reasonable one in the circumstances.[184] It is for this reason that the tort of nuisance is usually the most appropriate tortious action to pursue in the case of water contamination providing the claimant has sufficient interest in affected land to maintain the action.

Where the basis of a claim is sensible discomfort, rather than material damage to property, the need to take account of locality is more problematic for the claimant. Although it is difficult to conceive of a typical discharge consent changing the 'locality' of the receiving waters, the possibility is not ruled out that consent for discharge by a major effluent treatment plant might have this consequence. The effect of this would be that the claimant would not be able to succeed in private nuisance unless the claim could be based upon material damage to property.

## 3.9 Rylands v Fletcher

Although the rule in *Rylands* v *Fletcher*[185] was previously regarded as a distinct tort, distinguished from the general law of private nuisance by the application of strict liability for especially hazardous activities, present thinking is that the rule is better regarded as an aspect of nuisance rather than a separate grounds of action.[186] Nonetheless, the rule has some peculiar features which are usefully considered here.

In *Rylands* v *Fletcher* the defendant employed independent contractors to construct a reservoir on his land. The contractors failed to seal off certain disused mine shafts and, when the reservoir was filled, water escaped through the shafts and flooded the claimant's mine. Notably the defendant had not been negligent and could not be held liable for the negligence of the reputable contractors he had employed. Nonetheless, the House of Lords held that the claimant should succeed. The basis of this decision was

---

[184] Although the 'balance of convenience' in allowing an activity to continue may be considered in deciding whether to grant an injunction to restrain water contamination see 3.16.1 below.

[185] See *Fletcher* v *Rylands* (1866) LR 1 Ex 265, Court of Exchequer Chamber; and *Rylands* v *Fletcher* (1868) LR 3 HL 330, House of Lords.

[186] See discussion of *Cambridge Water Company* v *Eastern Counties Leather plc* ([1994] 1 All ER 53) at 3.10 below.

the principle enunciated by Blackburn J in a lower court and reaffirmed on appeal,

> [w]e think that the rule of law is, that the person who for his own purposes brings on his lands and collects and keeps there anything likely to do mischief if it escapes, must keep it at his peril, and, if he does not do so, is prima facie answerable for all the damage which is the natural consequence of its escape.[187]

Although it was not alleged, on the facts of the case, that the water which escaped was contaminated in any way, the implications of this principle in cases of water contamination are clear. A considerable proportion of water contamination incidents arise through persons bringing on to their land or accumulating noxious matter which subsequently 'escapes' and causes damage in so doing.

Whilst it is now accepted that the rule in *Rylands* v *Fletcher* does not give rise to any liability that is more strict than liability in the tort of nuisance, it has certain distinctive features. Specifically, it is particularly appropriate to isolated contamination incidents in which an escape of contaminating matter from certain kinds of premises causes damage, rather than a continuing state of affairs giving rise to contamination of the sort that is customarily proceeded against in an action for nuisance. Despite the apparent relevance of the rule to situations involving water contamination, however, it will be seen that its scope is limited by a number of restrictions.

In the first place, the rule is concerned with things which are brought onto land and collected there. Implicitly this excludes damage caused by things which are naturally present on the land, so that liability is unlikely to arise due to the spontaneous accumulation of water,[188] or even the accumulation of matter as an undesired by-product of the normal working of the land.[189] Since most of the materials that are likely to cause the contamination of water fall into the category of accumulated matter, this factor is not likely to be especially problematic for a claimant seeking to bring an action under the rule.

A second aspect is that the rule is concerned with a thing 'likely to do mischief if it escapes'. Although this formulation envisages things of a inherently hazardous nature, it extends beyond that to include things that would not normally be thought of as dangerous but become capable of 'mischief' due to the circumstances of their accumulation, as with the impounded water in the case of *Rylands* v *Fletcher* itself. There is little doubt that most of the materials that are capable of causing water contamination are within the scope of this requirement. The propensity of industrial or sewage effluent to cause harm if it is allowed to escape is self

---

[187] Court of Exchequer Chamber at pp.338 to 40.
[188] *Wilson* v *Waddell* (1876) 2 App Cas 95.
[189] *Giles* v *Walker* (1890) 24 QBD 656.

evident, and decided cases have held noxious gases or fumes,[190] gas likely to pollute water supplies,[191] and sewage[192] to be within the rule.

The third requirement of the rule is the need to establish that there has been an 'escape' of the thing likely to cause damage, that is, an 'escape from a place where the defendant has occupation of or control over land to a place which is outside his occupation or control'.[193] Thus in *Ponting* v *Noakes*[194] it was held that an action under the rule must fail where a horse died after eating the poisonous leaves of a yew tree by reaching over a fence onto the land of the defendant, since the tree did not extend beyond the defendant's boundary and there had been no 'escape' of the poisonous vegetation. Similarly in *Read* v *Lyons and Co*[195] the claimant, who was employed as an inspector of munitions at an explosives factory, failed to recover for injuries sustained in an explosion at the factory because she had been within the grounds of the factory when her injuries were sustained and there had been no escape of the thing that caused the injuries. The requirement of an escape is unlikely to be problematic in cases of water contamination since the usual substance of the complaint is that a generator or accumulator of polluting matter has failed to contain it on his premises and an unjustified discharge has resulted in damage to others outside the place where the noxious material should have been contained.

The final condition for the application of the rule in *Rylands* v *Fletcher* is perhaps the most significant obstacle for a claimant seeking to apply the rule to a water contamination incident. This is the requirement that the activity complained of must constitute a 'non-natural use of land'.[196] This rather vague expression has been interpreted to mean that the use of land involved 'must be some special use bringing with it increased danger to others, and must not merely be the ordinary use of the land or such a use as is proper for the general benefit of the community'.[197] The meanings of 'ordinary use of land' and 'general benefit to the community' have been broadly construed in later considerations of the rule in such a way as to place considerable restrictions upon the scope of what is regarded as a 'non-natural' use of land. In *Read* v *Lyons and Co Ltd* it was doubted whether building and operating a munitions factory in time of war constituted a non-natural use of land.[198] Likewise, courts have ruled that the working of mines and minerals[199] and the accumulation of industrial waste[200] do not constitute non-natural uses of land, and have doubted

---

[190] *Halsey* v *Esso Petroleum Co Ltd* [1961] 2 All ER 145, concerning the release of acid smuts.

[191] *Batcheller* v *Tunbridge Wells Gas Co* (1901) 84 LT 765.

[192] *Humphries* v *Cousins* (1877) 2 CPD 239.

[193] *Balfour* v *Barty-King* [1956] 2 All ER 555, affirmed [1957] 1 All ER 156.

[194] [1894] 2 QB 281.

[195] [1946] 2 All ER 471.

[196] See Lord Cairns in *Rylands* v *Fletcher* (1868) LR 3 HL 330 at pp.337 to 40

[197] See Lord Moulton in *Rickards* v *Lothian* [1913] AC 263, at p.280.

[198] [1947] AC 156 Contrast *Rainham Chemical Works Ltd* v *Belvedere Fish Guano Co* [1921] 2 AC 365.

[199] *Rouse* v *Gravelworks Ltd* [1940] 1 KB 489.

[200] *British Celanese Ltd* v *A H Hunt (Capacitors) Ltd* [1969] 2 All ER 1252.

whether the provision for sewage disposal by a local authority constitutes a non-natural use.[201] On the other hand, some broadening of the concept of non-natural use of land may be inferred from the decision in *Cambridge Water Company v Eastern Counties Leather*,[202] where it was concluded that the storage of industrial chemicals in substantial quantities was a 'classic' example of non-natural use of land.

Where a claimant is able to surmount the various limitations that have been noted upon the applicability of the rule in *Rylands v Fletcher*, an action under the rule may still fail if the defendant is able to establish any one of a number of recognised defences to the rule. This may arise where the defendant shows that his activity is made exempt from liability by specific statutory provision.[203] It will also be a defence for the defendant to establish that the claimant gave his express or implied consent to the activity complained of. Thus, in *Kiddle v City Business Properties Ltd*[204] the claimant was deemed to have knowledge of the state of a property which he leased, and for that reason was unsuccessful in an action brought when an overflow of rainwater from a blocked gutter caused damage to stock in the premises. Another defence is that the escape which occurs is the unauthorised act of a third party,[205] though in such a case the availability of the defence will depend upon the precise circumstances, so that the defendant will 'avoid liability unless the claimant can go on to show that the act which caused the escape was an act of the kind which the owner could reasonably have contemplated and guarded against'.[206] A final possibility is that a defence can arise in extraordinary circumstances through an Act of God,[207] that is, in 'circumstances which no human foresight can provide against, and of which human prudence is not bound to recognise the possibility'.[208] The scope of this defence is, however, strictly limited to the extent that it is doubtful that even an unprecedented amount of rainfall[209] or an exceptional drought[210] will amount to an Act of God.

---

[201] *Pride of Derby and Derbyshire Angling Association Ltd v British Celanese Ltd* [1953] 1 All ER 179 at p.203; though contrast *Smeaton v Ilford Corporation* [1954] 1 All ER 923, where it was held that the defendants could not claim exemption from the principle on the ground that the use of the land for sewage collection was for the general benefit of the community or that such collection was a natural user of the land.

[202] [1994] 1 All ER 53 and see 3.10 below for discussion of this case.

[203] See *Smeaton v Ilford Corporation* [1954] 1 All ER 923; though by contrast it is notable that liability under *Rylands v Fletcher* is expressly preserved in the s.28 and Sch.2 of the Reservoirs Act 1975 in respect of civil actions for defective reservoirs; and see the discussion of the defence of statutory authority at 3.13.4 below generally.

[204] [1942] 2 All ER 216.

[205] *Rickards v Lothian* [1913] AC 263.

[206] *Perry v Kendricks Transport Ltd* [1956] 1 All ER 154, at p.161.

[207] See also the defence of 'Act of God' in relation to criminal proceedings discussed at 9.6.3 below.

[208] Per Lord Westbury in *Tennent v Earl of Glasgow* (1864) 2 Macph 22 at p.26 to 7; approved by the House of Lords in *Greenock Corporation v Caledonian Railway Co* [1917] AC 556.

[209] See *Greenock Corporation v Caledonian Railway Co.* [1917] AC 556; though contrast *Nichols v Marsland* (1876) 2 Ex D 1.

[210] See *Chesham (Lord) v Chesham Urban District Council* (1935) 79 Sol Jo 453.

The overall effect of these various restrictions upon the operation of the rule in *Rylands* v *Fletcher* is that there are few instances of a claimant being successful in an action of this kind in recent years. On the other hand, the litigation in *Cambridge Water Company* v *Eastern Counties Leather plc*[211] has served to clarify the nature of the action and perhaps provided some basis for its revival. The reaffirmation that the rule in *Rylands* v *Fletcher* gives rise to 'strict liability' only in the sense that fault or negligence on the part of the defendant need not be shown, though reasonable foreseeability of harm must be shown, tends to assimilate the rule to the general basis for liability in nuisance. However, the recognition that the rule is most appropriately applied to isolated escapes of polluting matter,[212] and that an escape of a pollutant from industrial premises where a substantial quantity of chemicals are stored is a non-natural use of land, are factors which may provide a helpful clarification of the circumstances where the rule is appropriately applied in future proceedings.

## 3.10 The Cambridge Water Company Litigation

Whilst several references have been made in the previous discussion to the important litigation in *Cambridge Water Company* v *Eastern Counties Leather plc*,[213] which represents the most recent authoritative consideration of the civil law on groundwater contamination, it is convenient here to discuss the case in some detail and to consolidate the discussion of a range of issues concerning civil litigation in respect of water contamination. The culmination of the litigation was a ruling of the House of Lords that foreseeability of damage of the relevant kind is a prerequisite of establishing civil liability either in private nuisance or under *Rylands* v *Fletcher*. Hence, liability under the rule in *Rylands* v *Fletcher* will only arise if the defendant making a non-natural use of land knew, or ought reasonably to have known, that things likely to do mischief if they were to escape would cause damage if they actually escaped. Accordingly, the rule is one of 'strict' liability in the sense that a defendant will be liable for the escape even if he has taken all due care to prevent the escape from occurring, providing that damage of the relevant kind is foreseeable. In reaching this eventual decision, however, the three levels of court considering the issues made numerous observations concerning the civil law relating to water contamination which are usefully considered alongside the situation which gave rise to the litigation.

---

[211] [1994] 1 All ER 53 and see 3.10 below for discussion of this.

[212] Contrast the reluctance of the courts to find the existence of a nuisance where the matter complained of is of an isolated or temporary character, see *Harrison* v *Southwark and Vauxhall Water Co* [1981] 2 Ch 409.

[213] *Cambridge Water Company* v *Eastern Counties Leather plc and Hutchings and Harding Ltd* [1992] *Journal of Environmental Law* 81 (Queen's Bench Division) and *Cambridge Water Company* v *Eastern Counties Leather plc* [1994] 1 All ER 53 (Court of Appeal and House of Lords). See also commentaries on this case: Atkinson (1992) and (1993); Ogus (1994); Shelbourne (1994); Ward and Parpworth (1994); Ball (1994); Cross (1995); and Hilson (1996).

*3.10.1  The Facts*

The defendants, Eastern Counties Leather plc, had conducted business as a leather tannery at Sawston, Cambridgeshire, for over a century. The tanning process required the degreasing of pelts and, since the early 1950s, this was done by the use of organochlorine solvents, primarily perchloroethene (PCE), a substance which is highly volatile but not readily soluble in water. Until 1976, this solvent was delivered to the tannery in 40 gallon drums which were tipped into a tank at the base of the machine in which the degreasing operations took place. From 1976 onwards, the solvent was delivered to the premises in bulk and piped directly into the machine. Whilst no direct evidence was provided as to the manner in which spillages took place, the trial judge concluded that relatively small spillages of PCE had occurred before 1976 during the topping up process. The spillages had seeped through the concrete floor of the tannery into the chalk aquifer below to the extent that an estimated minimum of 1,000 gallons of PCE had entered the aquifer.

The claimant, Cambridge Water Co Ltd, was a statutory water company which supplied water to over a quarter of a million people in the area. As demand for water increased, the company had to find new sources of water, and purchased a borehole at Sawston Mill, some 1.3 miles away from the tannery, in 1976. The water from the borehole was found to be 'wholesome'[214] and suitable for drinking supply, and in 1979 a pumping station was built to abstract the water and pump it into the main supply system.

Following the adoption of the European Community Drinking Water Quality Directive[215] in 1980, Member States were bound to achieve, by 1985, compliance with 'maximum admissible concentration' values for specified substances in drinking water and to endeavour to achieve compliance with 'guide' values. In particular, a guide value for PCE was initially set at $1\mu g/l$, though, subsequently, prescribed maximum concentration and guide values were set at $30\mu g/l$ and $10\mu g/l$ respectively.[216] Following sampling of water supplied by the Cambridge Water Company, it was discovered that these parameters were being exceeded and an investigation took place as to the source of the contamination. The result of this investigation was the identification of the Sawston Mill borehole as the source and, following this discovery, the borehole was taken out of use. A further exhaustive investigation, undertaken by the British Geological Survey, sought to ascertain the origin and route by which the PCE reached the abstraction point. It was concluded that the contaminant formed pools at the base of the chalk aquifer beneath Eastern Counties Leather's premises and that these were dissolving slowly in groundwater which gradually flowed to the

---

[214] See 17.7.3 on the meaning of 'wholesome' in relation to drinking water.

[215] Directive 80/778/EEC, and see 17.7.1 below on this Directive.

[216] See Water Supply (Water Quality) Regulations 1989 (SI 1989 No.1147), and see Ch.17 below on drinking water quality generally.

abstraction point, some 1.3 miles distant, at a rate of about 8 metres per day.

In seeking to find a way of mitigating the impairment of water quality, Cambridge Water Company considered various methods of treatment of the contaminated water but all of these were found to be uneconomical or otherwise unsatisfactory. As a consequence of the decommissioning of the borehole, the company was obliged to locate and commission a new source of supply. The cost of the replacement source was almost £1 million, and the water company sought to recover this amount, along with certain incidental expenses, from Eastern Counties Leather plc.

### 3.10.2 The Proceedings in the Queen's Bench Division

The initial proceedings, before Kennedy J in the Queen's Bench Division, involved a claim for damages in negligence, nuisance[217] and under *Rylands* v *Fletcher* and an injunction against Eastern Counties Leather plc and a second defendant, another leather tannery company, Hutching and Harding Ltd, which was also alleged to have contributed to the contamination. However, the conclusion was reached, following a detailed examination of the hydro-geological evidence, that the spillages which had taken place at the premises of Hutchings and Harding Ltd had not had any sensible impact upon the quality of water at the Sawston Mill borehole. Even in relation to the argument that an injunction should be given against the second defendants, lest their contribution give rise to an adverse right to continue contaminating activities,[218] it was ruled that any contribution that had been made by the second defendants was, at most, *de minimis* and injunctive relief was refused.

The claimants based the claim against Easter Counties Leather upon negligence, nuisance and the rule in *Rylands* v *Fletcher*. In respect of the claims in nuisance and negligence, the claimant's claim failed at first instance because it was found that the defendant's employees could not have reasonably foreseen in 1976, or before, that the spillages would result in detectable quantities of PCE being present in the aquifer, or that those quantities would have a sensible effect upon the quality of water abstracted at Sawston Mill. In relation to the claim based upon *Rylands* v *Fletcher*, it was noted that the strictness of the rule that was provided for had been mitigated over the years by the qualification that the rule was only applicable in relation to 'non-natural' uses of land. In relation to this, somewhat surprisingly, it was thought that Sawston was properly characterised as 'an industrial village' and the employment that it provided was clearly of benefit to the local community. Therefore, it was found that the siting of Eastern Counties Leather was not inappropriate and did not amount to a 'non-natural' use of land. Consequently, the claimant's claim failed on all three counts.

---

[217] See 3.11 below on negligence.
[218] See 3.13.3 below on prescriptive rights.

### 3.10.3  The Proceedings in the Court of Appeal

The claimants pursued an appeal in the Court of Appeal on the basis of the rule in *Rylands* v *Fletcher* alone and the Court found in their favour on the basis of the decision of *Ballard* v *Tomlinson*.[219] In this case, neighbouring properties each had wells sunk into a chalk aquifer. The claimant used water from his well for the purpose of brewing. The defendant allowed sewage and refuse to enter his well and these found their way into the common source of underground water with the consequence that the water became unusable for the claimant's brewing purposes. It was held that the claimant was entitled to extract water percolating beneath his land and the defendant had no right to contaminate this. Accordingly, the claimant was awarded an injunction and damages. In the opinion of Mann LJ,

> *Ballard* v *Tomlinson* decided that the where the nuisance is an interference with a natural right incident to ownership then the liability is a strict one. The actor acts at his peril in that if his actions result by the operation of ordinary natural processes in an interference with the right then he is liable to compensate for any damage suffered by the owner.[220]

In the opinion of the Court of Appeal, the action brought by the Cambridge Water Company was indistinguishable from the situation in *Ballard* v *Tomlinson*, and the precedent should be applied. It was immaterial that the contamination of the well in the earlier case was deliberate, whereas the entry of PCE into the groundwater used for water supply purposes was accidental. The relevant principle did not distinguish between deliberate and accidental acts, since it is sufficient that the defendant's act caused the contamination. Similarly irrelevant, in the view of the Court of Appeal, was the fact that Eastern Counties Leather was unable to foresee that the spillages would have the consequences that they did, since the situation was one in which negligence played no part. *Ballard* v *Tomlinson* determined that where the matter complained of is an interference with a natural right incident to ownership then the liability is strict, and on that same basis Eastern Counties Leather should be held liable.

### 3.10.4  The Proceedings in the House of Lords

In reversing the decision of the Court of Appeal and deciding the final appeal in favour of the defendants, the House of Lords made some wide-ranging observations about the nature of civil litigation in environmental situations generally. The significance of *Ballard* v *Tomlinson* was noted in recognising that the right to abstract percolating water is a natural right incident to the ownership of land which may be protected by an injunction or action for damages in nuisance, despite there being no natural right to percolating waters such as exists in relation to water running in a defined

---

[219] (1885) 29 Ch D 115, and see 3.4.4 above.
[220] [1994] 1 All ER 53, at p.61.

channel.[221] However, the House of Lords took a different view of the nature of the 'strict' liability that existed in relation to the protection of groundwater from contamination. The case did not establish that the defendant would be liable for damage that could not reasonably have been foreseen, and the liability at issue was no stricter than otherwise provided for in nuisance or under the rule in *Rylands* v *Fletcher*.

In relation to liability in nuisance and under *Rylands* v *Fletcher,* Lord Goff noted the historical origins of nuisance as a tort to land, and its subsequent application to personal injuries and 'cross-infection' by concerns such as the need for reasonable care, or for fault to be shown, that were only genuinely relevant to the tort of negligence.[222] As a historical matter, the decision in *Rylands* v *Fletcher* should not be seen as creating any stricter liability than already was provided for in nuisance. That is, reasonable foreseeability of harm[223] is a prerequisite of liability for damages in nuisance and whether the defendant has exercised reasonable care is irrelevant. Similarly, under *Rylands* v *Fletcher*, the question as to whether an escape of a mischievous thing is negligent or not is irrelevant, since the issue to be addressed is whether the risk was reasonably foreseeable. The liability is 'strict', therefore, in the sense that a defendant may be held liable despite the fact that all due care has been exercised to prevent the relevant escape, but liability is not absolute because reasonable foreseeability on the part of the defendant always needs to be shown. Possibly, *Rylands* v *Fletcher* may be seen as an extension of the pre-existing law of nuisance insofar as it allowed liability to be established in relation to an isolated escape, as opposed to continuing states of affairs previously provided for in nuisance, but it should not be seen as creating any fundamentally new basis for liability. Although it might be open to the common law to establish some new basis for liability arising from abnormally dangerous activities, *Rylands* v *Fletcher* did not establish any basis for such liability beyond that already provided for in nuisance. Moreover, the view of Lord Goff was that imposing strict liability in relation to ultra-hazardous activities was a matter better dealt with by Parliament than the courts.[224]

In relation to the facts of the *Cambridge Water* case, the key question to be addressed was whether anyone at Eastern Counties Leather, before 1976, could reasonably have foreseen the subsequent impairment of water quality at the Sawston Mill borehole. The conclusion reached by Lord Goff was that,

> [t]o impose strict liability on Eastern Counties Leather in these circumstances, either as the creator of a nuisance or under the rule in *Rylands* v *Fletcher*, on the ground that it has subsequently become

---

[221] *Chasemore* v *Richards* (1859) 7 HL Cas 349, at p.379, was cited as authority for this, see 3.3 above.

[222] Citing Newark (1949).

[223] Citing *Overseas Tankship (UK) Ltd* v *Miller Steamship Co Pty (The Wagon Mound) (No 2)* [1967] 1 AC 617 as authority for this proposition.

[224] [1994] 1 All ER 53, at p.76.

reasonably foreseeable that PCE may, if it escapes, cause damage, appears to me to go beyond the scope of the regimes imposed under either of these two related heads of liability.[225]

It was also observed that, had reasonable foreseeability of damage been established, it would also be necessary for the claimants to show that the circumstances came within the rule in *Rylands* v *Fletcher* insofar as it needed to be established that Eastern Counties Leather were making a 'non-natural' use of their land. As Lord Goff noted, 'non-natural use' of land involves a 'special use of land bringing with it increased danger to others, and must not merely be the ordinary use of land or such a use as is proper for the general benefit of the community'.[226] However, the conclusion reached was that the storage of chemicals in substantial quantities, and their use in the manner employed at Eastern Counties Leather's premises, was not a natural use of land, despite any general benefits that it might have brought to the local community such as the creation of employment. Indeed, the judge went so far as to say that 'the storage of substantial quantities of chemicals on industrial premises should be regarded as an almost classic case of non-natural use'.[227] Nonetheless, because of the lack of reasonable foreseeability of harm, the claimants action failed.

### 3.10.5 General Comments

Perhaps the greatest difficulty with the final decision in the *Cambridge Water* case is that of reconciling the outcome with the polluter pays principle.[228] This principle involves a person whose actions result in damage to the environment paying the cost of restoring the environment to its former state, or paying the cost of preventing pollution, the outcome in this case amounted to the opposite of this.[229] In effect the recipients of the contamination, the water company or perhaps ultimately the water consumers of Cambridge, were being obliged to meet the costs arising from the contamination and litigation,[230] rather than those whose actions had caused it. It may be concluded, that the civil law places a greater weight upon the avoidance of retrospective liability for 'historic' pollution (where the polluting action precedes legislative control) than the need to meet more abstract principles of environmental policy in circumstances

---

[225] [1994] 1 All ER 53, at p.77.

[226] Quoting Lord Moulton in *Rickards* v *Lothian* [1913] AC 263, at p.280, and see Newark (1961).

[227] [1994] 1 All ER 53, at p.79.

[228] See 4.7.3 below on the polluter pays principle.

[229] Although it is recognised that an agreement was subsequently made between the National Rivers Authority and Eastern Counties Leather plc whereby the tannery undertook to abstract groundwater from the most contaminated area and to remove the contamination by the use of a dissolved air flotation plant. This was acknowledged to be a less than ideal solution, but was constrained by the means of the tannery to afford a more extensive remediation strategy. See *ENDS Report* 233 (1994) p.7.

[230] Subject to insurance cover, the legal costs of both sides had to be paid by Cambridge Water Company and were estimated to be in excess of £500,000, see Rodgers and Durman (1993).

where adherence to such principles would involve the imposition of liability without either fault or reasonable foreseeability being established.

Whilst the non-adherence to the polluter pays principle caused the *Cambridge Water* decision to be condemned by environmentalists,[231] the obverse of this is the appreciation that levels of environmental awareness improve over time and it would be harsh to impose liability on the basis of a higher standard than would be accepted as 'good practice' at the time when an action giving rise to environmental harm took place.[232] An advantage of applying the standard of reasonable foreseeability as a basis for determining liability is that it is a standard that is continually rising as knowledge of environmental hazards expands. Were a tannery today to allow the escape of PCE into water supplies, it is likely that it would be legally liable for the consequent damage, since contamination of water supplies is now a risk which a tannery operator should reasonably foresee.

However, some caution is needed with the concept of 'reasonable foreseeability' since it begs the question, reasonable foreseeability *of what?* There are various possibilities: reasonable foreseeability that there would be spillages of PCE, that these would seep through the floor of the tannery, that they would enter the aquifer, that they would be transmitted to an abstraction point, and that they would have an adverse impact upon the use of the abstracted water. In theory, the lack of reasonable foreseeability in relation to any link in this chain might have provided a basis for determining that the eventual harm or damage could not have been foreseen and ruling against the claimants.

In the actual circumstances, most of the discussion concerned the reasonable foreseeability of the impacts of PCE contamination of the abstracted water. However, another element of foreseeability which was at issue in the case concerned the mechanism by which the contaminant was transmitted through the groundwater to the point of abstraction. In relation to this, it is not so clear that reasonable foresight could now be assumed to be possessed by a reasonable tannery supervisor.[233] The *Cambridge Water* case, at first instance, provided a major innovation in advancing hydro-geological knowledge of questions of causation in relation to the contamination that had arisen. Whilst this evidence served to convince the courts, on the balance of probabilities, that cause and effect were established between the tannery activities and the water quality deterioration, the magnitude and technical complexity of the exercise involved should not be underestimated. In civil environmental litigation generally,[234] and in litigation concerning the contamination of groundwater

---

[231] See Rodgers (1993).

[232] Similarly, in relation to the application of historic environmental standards see *Margereson* v *J W Roberts Ltd* [1996] Env LR 304 noted at 3.11 below, though it was concluded in this case that the standard of environment performance at issue fell below that required at the time the offending actions took place.

[233] See Hilson (1996).

[234] For another example of the difficulties of establishing causation in an environmental context see *Graham* v *ReChem International Ltd* [1996] Env LR 158. Generally, on causation issues, see Holder (1994) and Reece and Freeman (1998).

in particular, the task of establishing a source and pathway[235] for a pollutant is likely to remain a significant challenge for a claimant seeking to establish civil liability.

A useful illustration of the difficulties which may arise in showing reasonable foreseeability is provided by the recent decision in *Savage & Another* v *Fairclough & Others*.[236] Here, the claimants claimed that the defendant's pig farming activities, involving the spreading of manure and inorganic fertilisers on nearby land, had resulted in the contamination of their private drinking water supply by excessive quantities of nitrate.[237] Having regard to what was 'good agricultural practice'[238] at the time when the applications of manure and nitrate took place, and taking the perspective of a 'hypothetical good farmer', it was held that the contamination of the drinking water supply could not reasonably have been foreseen and the claimant's action must fail.

Another peculiarity of the *Cambridge Water* case was the kind of harm which was at issue. Essentially, the claimant's were seeking compensation for financial expenditure which they had been obliged to undertake to commission an alternative source of water supply. Compensation was not being sought for the cost of purification of the contaminated groundwater, which would have been considerably more than the amount actually claimed, and would probably not have been recoverable because of the obligation upon a civil claimant to mitigate a loss by adopting the most cost-effective means of rectifying the tortious harm that has been inflicted.[239] Moreover, the peculiarity of this is that no 'harm' would have arisen had not the quality of drinking water become subject to the precautionary requirements of the EC Drinking Water Quality Directive and the national regulations implementing this. As the point was stressed, there was no evidence that the concentration of PCE present in the water abstracted at Sawston Mill was injurious to health, it was merely that it was unfit to be supplied for human consumption within the legal requirements that had been imposed.[240] Whilst the judgments make numerous references to the water being 'polluted' it is not at all clear in what sense this is meant. Perhaps the more pertinent observation is that a degree of *contamination* of water is capable of becoming civilly actionable due to a change in regulatory requirements rather than any intrinsic feature of the water itself or the harm to which contamination may give rise. If so, the decision is better regarded as one concerning the suitability of water for a particular use, rather than establishing any broader or unqualified principles as to the meaning or actionability of water 'pollution' generally.

---

[235] See 1.3.3 above on the source-pathway-receptor approach to environmental contamination.
[236] [2000] Env LR 183.
[237] See 13.5 below on nitrate control generally.
[238] See 13.5.7 below on 'good agricultural practice'.
[239] See Brazier and Murphy (1999) p.530.
[240] See Kennedy J *Cambridge Water Company* v *Eastern Counties Leather plc and Hutchings and Harding Ltd* [1992] *Journal of Environmental Law* 81, at p.90.

Finally, the House of Lords declined to develop the common law towards stricter forms of liability for ultra-hazardous activities or to impose retrospective liability for historic pollution, since these matters could and should be more precisely provided for in legislation. To some extent, the implicit invitation to Parliament to enact legislation to address the difficulties has been responded to by the enactment of a regime establishing liability for the remediation of historically contaminated land provided for under the Environment Act 1995.[241]

Although, as will be seen, the contaminated land regime is capable of imposing liability for remediation of historically contaminated land, there will continue to be significant differences between the bases for civil liability and regulatory obligations for remediation. Whilst foreseeability of damage is the vital factor in establishing civil liability, it is not a consideration in determining whether remediation may be required under the contaminated land regime which will thereby allow problems of historic pollution to be addressed. However, there may be respects in which the civil law remains significantly wider in compass than the contaminated land regime. For example, regulatory remediation requirements are limited to restoring land to a 'suitable for use' standard, determined by the purpose for which it is intended the remediated land is to be used. The contrast is that no 'suitable for use' limitation will arise in civil proceedings, since a claimant will be entitled to civil recompense for a loss suffered as a result of contamination which involves unreasonable interference with enjoyment of the land. Indeed, the fact that remediation has been accomplished to a suitable for use standard will not necessarily serve as any defence in civil proceedings where it is shown that the state of contamination continues to impair reasonable enjoyment of the land.

## 3.11 Negligence

A final category of tortious action which may be relevant in relation to civil liability for water contamination is that of negligence. The origin of negligence as a distinct kind of tortious action is usually acknowledged to be the renowned case of *Donoghue* v *Stevenson* where, in a speech which is generally regarded as laying the foundations of the modern action for negligence, Lord Atkin put forward the general principle that 'you must take reasonable care to avoid acts or omissions which you can reasonably foresee would be likely to injure your neighbour'.[242] Clearly Lord Atkin's 'neighbour' principle is of considerable breadth and generality. As another judge in the same case put the point, 'the categories of negligence are never closed'.[243]

---

[241] Inserting a new Part IIA in Environmental Protection Act 1990, and see 13.7 below on the contaminated land regime generally.

[242] [1932] AC 562 at p.580.

[243] Per Lord Macmillan at p.619. However, courts will be guided by previous cases in which liability has been established, and the reasonableness or otherwise of imposing a duty between the parties, see *Caparo Industries plc* v *Dickman and others* [1990] 1 All ER 568.

Subsequent decisions have clarified the situations in which a duty to avoid negligence arises such that it may now be understood as having three elements. The first feature is a requirement upon the defendant to exercise care in conduct which it is reasonably foreseeable will case consequent damage to the claimant; second, there must be sufficient proximity between the parties; and, third, the situation must be one in which the court considers it fair, just and reasonable that a duty should be imposed and there is no ground of public policy[244] for excluding such a duty.[245]

Despite the diversity of situations where negligence arises, the general application to situations where water contamination is at issue is that care must be exercised by the defendant to avoid reasonably foreseeable harm to water quality which will cause consequent damage to a claimant who is sufficiently proximate where it is fair, just and reasonable for such liability to be imposed. Alternatively, the existence of negligence has been characterised in terms of the defendant having failed to adhere to the standard of conduct of a 'reasonable person'. Hence negligence has been defined as, 'the omission to do something which a reasonable man, guided upon those considerations which ordinarily regulate the conduct of human affairs, would do, or doing something which a prudent and reasonable man would not do'.[246]

Whatever general formulation of the tort of negligence is adopted, it is clear that the action holds potential in respect of civil proceedings for the contamination of water. Moreover, if negligence is pursued as the ground of liability, it holds certain advantages for the claimant over other tortious actions. In particular, negligence is not a tort which is inextricably linked with interests in land, as are the others that have been discussed in this chapter. Consequently, negligence may be open to persons who lack a direct legal interest in land, providing they are able to show that the other elements of the tort are present including consequent damage to an interest other than land.

Another advantage of the action for negligence is that where contamination occurs in circumstances which are solely within the knowledge of the defendant it may be possible for the claimant to invoke the plea of *res ipsa loquitur,* or 'the thing speaks for itself'. If this plea is accepted, a court will draw the inference that the defendant was negligent without the need for conclusive evidence to that effect to be presented by the claimant. *Res ipsa loquitur* will only be accepted, however, where a number of factors are satisfied.[247] First, the circumstances in which the

---

[244] On public policy generally see *Barret* v *London Borough of Enfield* [1999] 3 All ER 193 and contrast the more restrictive approach in *X (Minors)* v *Bedfordshire County Council* [1995] 2 AC 633.

[245] Generally see Brazier and Murphy (1999) pp.97 to 98 and Ch.5 generally.

[246] Per Alderson B in *Blythe* v *Birmingham Waterworks Co* (1856) 11 Exch 781, at p.784.

[247] Identified in the judgement of Erle CJ in *Scott* v *London and St Katherine Docks Co* (1865) 3 H&C 596, at p.601: 'There must be reasonable evidence of negligence. But where the thing is shown to be under the management of the defendant or his servants, and the accident is such as in the ordinary course of things does not happen if those who have the management use proper care, it affords reasonable evidence, in the absence of explanation by the defendants, that the accident

accident arose were in the control of the defendant. Second, the accident was of a kind which would not happen in the ordinary course of events without the presence of negligence. Third, no evidence is presented as to the actual cause of the accident. Where the claimant is able to satisfy the court of these three matters, it will be sufficient to support an inference of negligence on the part of the defendant unless the defendant is able to produce evidence to show that he was not in fact negligent. In a frequent situation involving water contamination, where a defendant has the exclusive management of the source of contamination and declines or is unable to offer an explanation as to how it came to be discharged into a watercourse, the potential of *res ipsa loquitur* in establishing a claim of negligence is considerable.[248]

Given the apparent advantages of a claim being brought in negligence for the contamination of water it is somewhat surprising that direct authority on the use of this kind of action in this context is scanty in the UK. In *Overseas Tankship (UK) Ltd* v *Morts Dock and Engineering Co Ltd (The Wagon Mound)*[249] a negligent spillage of oil from a ship spread to the claimants' wharf where welding was taking place and, contrary to the best scientific opinion, caused a fire when molten metal fell on a piece of floating waste and ignited the oil. In an action for negligence against the persons having control of the ship, it was held that the damage to the wharf was not recoverable because it was too remote. However, had the fire not occurred, and an action been brought due to damage caused by the negligent oil pollution alone, it is unlikely that the problem of remoteness would have presented an obstacle to the claimants' recovery.

Another situation in which an action for negligence was considered in relation to water contamination arose in *Scott-Whitehead* v *National Coal Board*[250] where the defendants discharged a saline solution into a watercourse. Insufficient dilution of the effluent occurred, because of drought conditions, and as a result damage was caused to the crops of a downstream farmer who abstracted water for irrigation purposes. The defendants were held not liable because they had no knowledge that the concentration of salinity in the effluent was so great as to be harmful to irrigated crops, and also because they were entitled to rely on the water authority for the area to issue warning of the hazard to abstractors. The water authority, which was the second defendant in the case, was held liable in negligence in failing to warn the claimant of the danger to crops due to the use of abstracted water, the removal of which they had

---

arose from want of care.' See also *Roe* v *Ministry of Health* [1954] 2 QB 66 per Morris LJ at pp.87 to 88.

[248] See the discussion of this plea by Denning LJ in *Southport Corporation* v *Esso Petroleum Co Ltd* [1954] 2 All ER 561, at p.573 to 4; though his opinion was not accepted in the appeal to the House of Lords [1955] 3 All ER 864.

[249] [1961] 1 All ER 404, and see also *Overseas Tankship (UK) Ltd* v *Miller Steamship Co Pty (The Wagon Mound (No 2)* [1967] 1 AC 617.

[250] (1987) 53 P&CR 263; and see Tromans (1987) contrast Ball (1990).

licensed[251] under the Water Resources Act 1963. However it is doubtful whether the same conclusion would be reached if a similar situation was to arise today because of an increasing reluctance of the courts to find public bodies liable for the negligent exercise of statutory administrative functions.[252] By contrast, the decision in *Dear* v *Thames Water plc*,[253] is a better illustration of what is likely to be the present approach. In this case foul water from sewers overflowed into the claimant's house and garden. However, it was held that the statutory powers and duties possessed by the water authority, sewerage undertaker and local authority, against whom the action was brought in negligence and nuisance, were owed to the public at large and no actionable duty of care was owed to the claimant to prevent the flooding.[254]

Although actions in negligence have been successfully pursued in other environmental contexts,[255] the limited use of negligence in the context of water contamination may reflect the fact that the usual kind of harm associated with such incidents is normally related to interests in land and, for this reason, nuisance is a preferable form of action. By contrast, harm in the form of personal injury or damage to property other than land would typically be pursued by an action in negligence, but these kinds of harm are less characteristic of water contamination incidents. Another contrast that may be relevant is the potential difficulty of showing fault, or the failure to take reasonable care, where negligence is claimed, as opposed to the need to show only reasonable foreseeability of harm arising where nuisance is pleaded.[256] Nonetheless, in an appropriate case, the possibility of an action in negligence for water contamination remains.

### 3.12 Breach of Statutory Duty

Alongside the torts that have been previously considered, a civil claim for breach of statutory duty may also be possible in relation to unsatisfactory water quality. The general basis of this kind of claim is that there has been a breach of a statutory obligation and, as a result of this, a claimant suffers

---

[251] Under Water Resources Act 1963, now see Part II Chapter II Water Resources Act 1991.

[252] See *Murphy* v *Brentwood District Council* [1990] 2 All ER 908, and *X (Minors)* v *Bedfordshire County Council* [1995] 3 All ER 353; but contrast the European Court of Human Rights' ruling in *Osman* v *United Kingdom* [1999] 1 FLR 193, where it was held that there had been a breach of Art.6 of the European Convention on Human Rights (concerning the right to a fair trial) in relation to a blanket exclusion of liability by a public body, similarly see *Barret* v *London Borough of Enfield* [1999] 3 All ER 193.

[253] 33 Con LR 43, and see [1993] *Water Law* 116.

[254] Contrast *Stretton's Derby Brewery Co* v *Derby Corporation* [1894] 1 Ch 431.

[255] See *Margereson* v *J W Roberts Ltd* [1996] Env LR 304 where it was held that the owner of an asbestos factory owned a duty of care to children who played in the dust near to the factory and subsequently suffered illness as a result (discussed in Steele and Wikely (1997)). See also *Tutton* v *A D Walter Ltd* [1986] QB 6, where, contrary to official advice, the defendant farmer was found to have negligently sprayed a crop of oilseed rape at a time when it was flowering and, as a consequence, the bees owned by the claimant were killed (discussed in Spencer (1986)). Generally see Pugh and Day (1995) Ch.12.

[256] See the discussion of *Cambridge Water Company* v *Eastern Counties Leather plc* [1994] 1 All ER 53 at 3.10 above.

a loss for which a remedy, either an injunction or more usually damages, may be given.[257] Notably, there does not have to be any finding of negligence by the defendant for liability to be established.

In practice, however, the tort of breach of statutory duty is relatively little used because the courts have held that an action will succeed only if it can be established that Parliament intended the claimant to have a civil remedy in the event of breach of the duty. In many instances it is clear from the wording of the relevant statute that Parliament has specifically excluded the possibility of a remedy of this kind. For example, the Water Resources Act 1991 makes it clear that a breach of discharge consent *by itself* will not provide the basis of a civil action.[258]

Where a statute is unclear as to whether a breach of duty is to give rise to civil liability, then this must be ascertained by interpreting the relevant provision. Particularly where a statute involves general public law duties, the broader the exercise of discretion involved the less likely will be a right of action for breach of statutory duty.[259] Another factor which is important in ascertaining whether breach of a statutory provision gives rise to liability is the existence of other mechanisms for enforcement. The general view is that if the statute provides for criminal enforcement then this rules out civil claims under breach of statutory duty. This is explicable on the basis that the criminal sanctions show that the interests of those affected are sufficiently protected by the provision for punishment where a duty is not adhered to.

Another important element in construing statutory provisions is that the action for breach of statutory duty is only likely where rights are given to a limited class of persons, rather than to the public in general. This factor makes the application of breach of statutory duty particularly unlikely in relation to environmental quality legislation which usually has as its objective the protection of the public at large, rather than any distinct group of individuals. By contrast, breach of statutory duty is used most frequently in relation to industrial safety legislation, where protection of employees is a key objective.

Despite these difficulties in establishing breach of statutory duty as a basis for a water quality claim, there are a few illustrations of this possibility. One such example of breach of statutory duty being claimed in an environmental context followed the incident at Camelford in 1988 when a large quantity of aluminium sulphate was wrongly introduced into the public water supply.[260] The water authority eventually settled the case out of court on the basis of a breach of their statutory water supply duties.[261]

---

[257] Generally see Rogers (1998) Ch.7.

[258] s.100(b) Water Resources Act 1991, see 3.18.5 below.

[259] *X (Minors)* v *Bedfordshire County Council* [1995] 2 AC 633.

[260] See 17.11 below.

[261] See also *Read* v *Croydon Corporation* [1938] 4 All ER 631.

Breach of statutory duty was also argued in *Bowden* v *South West Water Services Ltd*,[262] an action brought by a shellfisherman following contamination of shellfish beds which the claimant alleged was attributable to unlawful discharges by a sewerage undertaker. The claim was initially rejected in the High Court because the judge thought that the three European Community directives upon which liability was alleged to be based (concerning Shellfish Waters, Bathing Waters and Urban Waste Water Treatment)[263] were all too general in their application to support a private law claim of this kind. However, the High Court decision was overturned by the Court of Appeal[264] which held, at least in relation to the Shellfish Waters Directive, that failure to adhere to its requirements could form the basis of a state liability claim.[265] Most significantly, this was because the Directive was adopted for the direct benefit of a limited class of persons, shellfishermen, rather than for general public benefit, and the claimant fell within that class.

Where the substantive breach of a Community water directive is at issue, therefore, and the claimant shows membership of the class of persons intended to benefit from the directive, it may be possible for the claimant to succeed on the basis of breach of statutory duty. However, in other circumstances where liability of a public body is contended, the scope for showing breach of statutory duty may be limited. Recent decisions on liability of public bodies indicate a greater willingness to allow liability,[266] or not to allow the blanket exclusion of liability,[267] but this seems to be most relevant in situations where the body has a continuing responsibility of some kind towards the claimant. By contrast, the possibility of establishing breach of liability against the Environment Agency, perhaps in a situation where it has failed to take insufficient action in the aftermath of a pollution incident, appears limited. Distinctions here may be drawn in terms of the 'one-off' nature of the Agency's potential involvement and the fact that it has a power, rather than a duty, to take action. Ultimately, however, legislation intended to protect general environmental interests, and giving authorities a discretion in implementing public law duties, is unlikely to lead to a successful claim for breach of statutory duty.

### 3.13 General Defences in Civil Proceedings

The preceding sections, which have described the bases on which civil actions may be brought on account of water contamination, must be read subject to the possibility that a person causing the contamination possesses a right to do so which will serve as a general defence to a civil action.

---

[262] [1998] Env LR 445 and see 15.3.4.

[263] See 15.3.1, 5.5.2 and 5.6.2 on these directives.

[264] [1999] Env LR 438.

[265] Under the *Francovich* principle, discussed at 4.16.6 below.

[266] On the general trend towards limiting the extent of liability of public bodies see, most recently, *Phelps* v *Hillingdon London Borough Council*, [2000] 4 All ER 504.

[267] *Barret* v *London Borough of Enfield* [1999] 3 All ER 193, where a blanket exclusion of liability for negligence was found to be contrary to Art.6 of the European Convention on Human Rights.

Such a right is capable of arising under four headings: custom, grant, prescription and statutory authority.

### 3.13.1 Custom

The right to pollute can be acquired by immemorial custom providing that it can be shown that the custom which is claimed is sufficiently definite, not unreasonable and confined to the necessary working of the enterprise. Thus in *Carlyon* v *Lovering*[268] the defendants were alleged to have wrongfully thrown sand, stones, rubble and other matter into a natural stream of water flowing through the claimant's land causing the channel to become obstructed and water to flood over the claimant's land and destroy produce. In their defence the defendants stated that the stream and land in question were within the Stannaries of Cornwall and subject to the customs thereof, amongst which there was an immemorial custom of those working in the tin mining industry to make use of streams to wash away material which became dislodged in the course of working a mine. The court accepted this plea since the use was not indefinite or unreasonable, and was limited to the necessary working of the mine.[269] By contrast, in *Attorney-General* v *Richmond*[270] a court restrained a local authority highway board from allowing additional matter to pass down a sewer occasioning a nuisance by polluting a stream. It was held that the ground of ancient custom and privilege could not be accepted as a justification for the nuisance, since to discharge the sewage into the stream in such a quantity that it was not sufficiently diluted was 'to create an evil which is illegal, and which is such as no custom can authorize'.[271]

A custom may be extinguished by statute as in *Evans* v *Birmingham Corporation*[272] where it was decided that the custom of the inhabitants to clean the streets and to dispose of the rubbish into sewers and streams, which was claimed on behalf of the inhabitants by the Corporation, was put to an end by the Towns Improvement Clauses Act 1847.[273] However, where a statute has been repealed which had enacted a right which had previously been exercised as a custom, the custom is not revived.[274]

### 3.13.2 Grant

A second defence to an action for water contamination is founded upon the existence of a right arising through an express or implied grant of permission to do so. In principle, it is clear that where one person gives another permission to contaminate a watercourse, the person who has

---

[268] (1857) 1 H&N 784.

[269] See also *Wright* v *Williams* (1836) 1 Gale 410; *Gaved* v *Martyn* (1865) 13 LT 74; and *Ivimey* v *Stocker* (1866) 14 LT 427.

[270] (1866) 30 JP 708.

[271] *Ibid* at p.708.

[272] (1853) 17 JP 422.

[273] See 2.3 above on the 'Clauses Acts'.

[274] *New Windsor Corporation* v *Taylor* (1899) 63 JP 164.

given permission will be unable to succeed in a tortious action, since the agreement will amount to a defence of consent. Similarly, the defence will arise between the original covenantors and their successors in title where the agreement is contained in a deed which creates an easement allowing the discharge of polluted water.[275] Clearly, the scope of the defence provided by the existence of a deed granting an easement will depend upon its precise construction, and it may be that an easement permitting the discharge of water in a natural state into a stream will not provide any defence to an action for the discharge of contaminated water.[276] In *Hall* v *Lund*[277] the claimant had occupied a mill which was used as a bleaching works and had made discharges of refuse into a nearby stream. Subsequently the defendant entered into a lease of the premises from the claimant and used them for the same purpose and made similar discharges. The claimant then brought an action against him for fouling the stream by discharging refuse into it. It was held that the lease, interpreted in the light of the surrounding circumstances including the previous use of the mill, amounted to an implied grant to continue to discharge matter into the stream and so to a defence against the action brought by the claimant.

### 3.13.3 *Prescription*

A third defence to an action for the contamination of water lies in the claim that the polluter has gained an easement, amounting to a legal right to pollute water, by prescription. The fundamental basis of the doctrine of prescription is that, where long enjoyment of a right is established, a court will uphold the continuation of the right by a presumption that it is of lawful origin. It is theoretically possible to establish a prescriptive right to pollute water in three ways: at common law; under the doctrine of 'lost modern grant'; and under the Prescription Act 1832.[278]

The common law required, traditionally at least, for it to be shown that a right existed since 'time immemorial' or the limit of legal memory, which was fixed at the year 1189 by the Statute of Westminster I of 1275. The difficulty of showing this was often insuperable but was circumvented by the courts adopting a presumption that long use of a right was evidence of it having been exercised since time immemorial. The difficulty remained, however, that a prescriptive right could not be established where it could be shown that at some time since 1189 the right which was claimed could or did not exist. To meet this problem the courts devised the doctrine of 'lost modern grant' which involves a presumption that long use of a right was based upon a grant which had authorised the use but has since been lost. Where this plea is raised in defence in an action for water contamination, it has been held that the defendant is entitled to know whether the lost grant, which is presumed to serve as a basis for the

---

[275] See *Hewlins* v *Shippam* (1826) 5 B&C 221; *Fentiman* v *Smith* (1805) 4 East 107; and *Nuttall* v *Bracewell* (1866) 15 LT 313.
[276] *New Windsor Corporation* v *Stovell* (1884) 51 LT 626.
[277] (1863) 158 ER 1055.
[278] Generally, see Gray (1993) pp.1106 to 1115.

prescriptive right, was granted before or after certain dates.[279] The date of a lost grant becomes significant if at the time it is presumed to have been created it could not have been made lawfully.

A further basis for prescriptive claims lies under the Prescription Act 1832,[280] which provides that a right to contaminate a watercourse can be claimed by a person who has actually enjoyed the use of the watercourse for this purpose for 20 years, as of right and without interruption, even though the use is not of immemorial antiquity. If the use has been enjoyed for 40 years it is deemed to be absolute and indefeasible unless it is enjoyed by consent or agreement in writing. Hence the long use of a stream may result in the acquisition of a right to discharge effluent into the stream even though the discharger may have no ownership in relation to the stream.[281]

The acquisition of a right to discharge effluent into a stream by prescription requires the use of the watercourse for the necessary period involving continual and perceptible injury to those against whom the legal right is claimed. The continued presence of perceptible injury over the prescriptive period must be shown, since until some injury is suffered, as a consequence of the use of the watercourse for the discharge of effluent, the prescriptive period does not begin to run and no easement to pollute can be acquired.[282] Moreover no prescriptive right will be established where the use which is made of a stream to discharge effluent is conducted in secret and is unknown to those against whom the right is later asserted. Thus in *Liverpool Corporation* v *Coghill and Son*[283] the defendant had for more that 20 years discharged into the claimant's sewers waste liquors from his borax works, but it transpired that the waste had been discharged intermittently and usually at night, and the claimants had no notice of it. The court declined to accept that any prescriptive right to pollute had been acquired because the enjoyment claimed was secret and unknown and not of such a character as would establish a prescriptive right. Today, many of the details of discharges into watercourses are made publicly accessible in public registers,[284] but it might still be possible to argue that the contaminating effect of a discharge was unknown on the basis that the content of the relevant register was not known to the claimant.[285]

In circumstances where an easement to pollute has been acquired by prescription, the scope of the easement cannot be extended beyond the use made over the period during which the right was acquired. Hence it has been held that the right to use a drain for ordinary waste water may not be

---

[279] *Tremayne* v *English Clays Lovering Pochin and Co Ltd* [1972] 2 All ER 234.

[280] See s.2 Prescription Act 1832.

[281] *Wright* v *Williams* (1836) 1 Gale 410; *Carlyon* v *Lovering* (1857) 1 H&N 784; and *Wood* v *Sutcliffe* [1851] 21 LJ Ch 235.

[282] *Murgatroyd* v *Robinson* (1857) 119 ER 1292; *Goldsmid* v *Tunbridge Wells Improvement Commissioners* (1866) 14 LT 154; and *Scott-Whitehead* v *National Coal Board* (1987) 53 P&CR 263, and Tromans (1987).

[283] [1918] 1 Ch 307.

[284] See 16.15 below on the pollution control register.

[285] Tromans (1987) p.372.

enlarged to permit the drain to be used for foul water drainage,[286] nor may a right to foul a stream be enlarged to permit an increased amount of foul water to be discharged.[287] However, it has been held that where a factory has a prescriptive right to pollute a stream this may permit the discharge of a new substance used in the same manufacturing process, providing that it does not increase the contamination to any substantial degree.[288] By contrast, however, a factory with a prescriptive right to discharge effluent into a stream as a result of a particular trade, may not change to another trade, though the contamination of the later trade is less in degree than that caused by the former trade.[289] In summary, to justify contamination of a stream on ground of prescription, it must be shown that over the prescriptive period a right has been asserted to introduce contaminating matter of a kind, and in a quantity, which produces the effect upon the stream which the claimant claims to be entitled to continue.[290]

A prescriptive right to pollute a stream is capable of coming to an end through abandonment where the possessor of the right acts in such a way as to indicate his unequivocal intention to relinquish it, though a mere suspension of the exercise of the right is not sufficient to prove an intention to abandon it. Thus in *Crossley* v *Lightowler*[291] it was held that where a prescriptive right to foul a stream by a dye works was not exercised for a 25 year period, and the works were dismantled without any intention of erecting a new building on the site, there was evidence to establish the abandonment of the prescriptive right.[292]

The scope of the defence of prescription to an action for water contamination is narrowed considerably by the constraint that prescription can only be claimed in respect of a use of the watercourse, during the prescriptive period, which is not otherwise unlawful. It follows that many prescriptive claims to pollute water arising in recent times are likely to be declined for the reason that the pollution of rivers by sewage or trade refuse has been an offence under the Rivers Pollution Prevention Act 1876 and succeeding legislation since 15th August 1876.[293] It has been noted, however, that the 1876 Act prohibited the discharge of polluting matter into 'streams',[294] which were defined by s.20 to include the sea and tidal waters only to the extent determined by the Local Government Board. It follows from this that there was no general prohibition of polluting discharges into tidal waters under the 1876 Act and, therefore, the Act may not operate as a bar to prescriptive claims relating to tidal waters in the

---

[286] *Cawkwell* v *Russell* (1856) 26 LJ Ex 34.

[287] *Crossley* v *Lightowler* (1867) 16 LT 438.

[288] *McIntyre* v *McGavin* (1867) 31 JP 821.

[289] *Clarke* v *Somerset Drainage Commissioners* (1888) 52 JP 308.

[290] *Cargill* v *Gotts* [1981] 1 All ER 682, at p.687.

[291] (1867) 2 Ch App 478.

[292] See also *Magor* v *Chadwick* (1840) 11 A&E 571.

[293] *George Legge and Son Ltd* v *Wenlock Corporation* [1938] 1 All ER 37; and *Green* v *Matthews* (1930) 46 TLR 206.

[294] See 2.6 above on the Rivers Pollution Prevention Act 1876, and see 3.4 above on the meaning of 'stream'.

same way as for freshwater discharges.[295] Other offences relating to water pollution have existed for a considerable time under fisheries and public health legislation,[296] and for the same reason, pollution of water in contravention of these Acts could not be used as the basis of a prescriptive right.[297] The same reasoning has been applied where the activity upon which the prescriptive right has been based amounts to a public nuisance,[298] or it has been conducted in such a manner as to be injurious to health.[299]

As a consequence of the requirement that a prescriptive right to contaminate water must be founded upon a lawful activity, a defence based upon prescription is less likely to succeed today than previously. Nonetheless, some caution must be exercised in reaching this conclusion which rests on the questionable assumption that the criminal and civil law are co-extensive in what they regard as 'water pollution'. The possibility remains that a discharge or emission which does not amount to a criminal offence might still ground an action for civil redress.[300] In a situation of this kind, the defence of prescription may remain of significance.

### 3.13.4 Statutory Authority

The final matter which may be pleaded in a tortious action for water contamination is that of statutory authority.[301] As has been noted, the failure of a person or body to act in accordance with a statutory duty may also be regarded as constituting a distinct ground of action under a separate tort of breach of statutory duty.[302] Alternatively, statutory authority may serve as a defence to liability which would arise under the torts considered above. However, whether the relevant statute imposes a duty or serves as a defence, the essential issue remains the same: does the enactment authorise the contamination of water which has occurred? If, properly construed, an enactment does authorise the contamination, then the conclusion is either, that there is no breach of statutory duty, or that the statute authorises the contamination of water which has occurred. Having noted the two distinct approaches which may be taken to claims of statutory authority to contaminate water, however, it appears from past cases that the more common use to which this feature has been put is as a defence to actions based upon other torts.

Since both general and private Acts of Parliament override the common law, it follows that if an otherwise tortious action can be justified by

---

[295] See Newsom and Sherratt (1972) Appx.II.

[296] Generally see Ch. 2 above.

[297] *Foster* v *Warblington Urban District Council* (1906) 21 TLR 214.

[298] *Attorney-General* v *Barnsley Corporation* (1874) WN 37; *Hulley* v *Silversprings Bleaching Co* (1922) 86 JP 30; and see 3.17 below on public nuisance.

[299] *Blackburne* v *Somers* (1879) 5 LR Ir 1; and *Traill* v *McAllister* (1895) LR 25 Ir 524.

[300] See 3.18.5 below on the interrelationship between the civil and criminal law.

[301] Statutory authority may also serve as a defence to a criminal charge under s.88(1)(f) and (g) Water Resources Act 1991, and see 9.16 below.

[302] See 3.12 above on breach of statutory duty.

reference to statute this will provide a defence. Inevitably the extent of the defence of statutory authority depends upon the permissive scope provided by the particular statute relied upon by the defendant, and this is primarily a matter of statutory interpretation.[303] Examples are to be found, however, of past cases where statutes have had the effect of overriding civil liabilities in respect of water contamination.

An instructive illustration is *Edinburgh Water Trustees* v *Sommerville and Son*[304] where the appellants were statutorily entrusted with the management of a water supply reservoir.[305] Statutory provision imposed a duty upon them to maintain a flow of a specified quantity of water from the reservoir as compensation to the riparian proprietors lower down the stream. In an exceptionally dry summer the water level in the reservoir fell so low that a portion of the bed, composed of accumulated silt, became exposed, and when rain eventually fell the water which was discharged down the stream was impregnated with silt. The quality of water discharged was unsuitable for use in the manufacture of paper, a process conducted at the respondent's mill lower down the stream. In the respondent's action for a declaratory judgment that they were entitled to water of a certain quality and damages for their loss, it was said that,

> [i]n the present case the private Acts do not obliterate the original right of the riparian proprietor to the natural quality of the water, but they impose upon it a qualification - viz, that if the proper construction of the works authorised, or the reasonable use of those works for the purpose specified by Parliament, leads to a deterioration in the quality of the water, the riparian proprietors have no remedy."[306]

On the facts, it was held that the Water Trustees had used reasonable skill and care so as to avoid deterioration in the quality of the water passing down the stream and were found not to be liable.

Another example is *Harrison* v *Southwark and Vauxhall Water Co*[307] where a complaint of nuisance arose from the noise generated by a water pump at the premises of a water supply company. The claimant contended that it would have been possible for the company to have installed pumps which would have considerably diminished the amount of noise. It was held that the authority conferred by statute[308] upon the company to do all things necessary for the purpose of supplying water, along with its use of reasonable skill and care and the absence of negligence, were a defence in nuisance.

---

[303] Generally see Bell and Engle (1995).
[304] (1906) 95 LT 217.
[305] Under the Edinburgh and District Waterworks Act 1869.
[306] Per Lord Loreburn at p.218.
[307] (1891) 2 Ch 409.
[308] Under the Vauxhall Water Act 1866, which incorporated the Waterworks Clauses Act 1847, and see 2.3 above on the 1847 Act.

Statutory provisions may have the effect of modifying or preserving specific common law obligations from the effect of general amending enactments. Thus in *Lee Conservancy Board* v *Hertford Corporation*[309] the defendants were authorised by statute to construct and maintain a works for the purification of sewage and convey the effluent sewage water along a specified watercourse. These operations were to be conducted subject to a provision to the effect that the defendants should not at any time discharge or permit any sewage to flow into the watercourse until it had been subjected to a process of purification specified in the statute. Alternatively, the sewage had to be subjected to such other process of purification as was 'the best then known practicable process for the purification thereof'.[310] The process of purification employed was improved several times over the years as better processes became known. Nevertheless, the purity of the discharge from the works failed to satisfy the claimants who sought an injunction to prevent further discharges. It was held that the intention of the legislature was not to require complete purification of the water, and so long as the defendants treated the sewage thoroughly and effectively according to the best known practicable process of purification, no action could be brought against them. Hence, the statutory proviso superseded the common law duty of the defendants.

Conversely, a statutory provision may have the effect of preserving common law rights. In *Somersetshire Drainage Commissioners* v *Corporation of Bridgwater*[311] a private Act of Parliament, prohibiting the opening of new drains carrying discharges of polluting water, was construed to permit the continuation of existing discharges where a legal right to discharge existed. The effect of this was to permit the local sanitary authority to remodel their system of drainage and replace a pre-existing drainage outfall with a new outfall without committing any offence under the Act.

The scope of the defence of statutory authority has, in each case, to be determined by the construction of the authorising Act. In *Smeaton* v *Ilford Corporation*[312] the obligation upon a local authority to discharge its sewerage functions without creating a nuisance was considered in circumstances where sewage effluent had flooded the claimant's house and garden. In this situation the court declined to find any liability on the part of the local authority because the flooding from the sewer arose not from any act of the local authority, but from its statutory obligation[313] to permit occupiers of its area to discharge their sewage into its sewers which had resulted in the sewerage system becoming overloaded. This was regarded

---

[309] (1884) 48 JP 628.
[310] Under s.8 New River Company's (Hertford Sewage Diversion) Act 1854, *ibid* p.628.
[311] (1899) 81 LT 729.
[312] [1954] 1 All ER 923, under s.31 Public Health Act 1936.
[313] Under s.34(1) Public Health Act 1936, now see s.106 Water Industry Act 1991.

as a matter over which the local authority had no control since it had not created or continued the nuisance which had arisen.[314]

However a contrasting conclusion was reached in *Pride of Derby Angling Association* v *British Celanese Ltd*[315] where the co-defendants, Derby Corporation, claimed that they were authorised to discharge insufficiently treated sewage matter from their sewage works into a river by the Derby Corporation Act 1901, under which they were empowered to construct and maintain the works. A close reading of the provisions of that Act, however, revealed that the authorisation to discharge effluent from the sewage works was subject to a specific prohibition against allowing noxious or offensive effluvia to escape therefrom, or doing anything which amounted to a contravention of the Rivers Pollution Prevention Act 1876, under which it was an offence to cause any solid or liquid sewage matter to fall or flow into any stream.[316] As a consequence of the Corporation having acted outside their statutory powers, their defence of statutory authorisation failed, and they were held liable for nuisance in causing the pollution of the claimants' fishery.[317]

The present provisions requiring sewerage undertakers to discharge relevant functions without creating a nuisance[318] are likely to be similarly construed. Hence, the statutory obligation upon sewerage undertakers not to create a nuisance will apply except in relation to those matters which arise as an inevitable result of the activities concerning sewage treatment that undertakers are authorised to undertake.[319]

## 3.14  Civil Law Remedies

The main remedies likely to be sought in a civil action for water contamination are, first, an award of damages and, second, an injunction. Normally a substantial award of damages will be sought to compensate the claimant for losses suffered as a consequence of the contamination, but there may be circumstances where a nominal award is sought in recognition of the infringement of a legal right. An injunction will normally be sought to restrain the continuation of a contaminating discharge and to prevent future injury to the claimant. Although both remedies may be pursued in a particular action, the appropriateness of the different remedies depends upon the circumstances of the case. In particular, the choice between damages and an injunction, or both, may

---

[314] Postscript: on the issue of civil liability of public bodies for matters beyond their control, see the recent decision in *Bybrook Barn Garden Centre Ltd* v *Kent County Council* [2001] Env LR 30.

[315] [1953] 1 All ER 179.

[316] Under s.3 Rivers Pollution Prevention Act 1876, see 2.6 above on the 1876 Act, and see 9.3 below on s.85(1) Water Resources Act 1991 which provides the present counterpart of this offence.

[317] In relation to the use of statutory authority as a defence in respect of air contamination see *Allen* v *Gulf Oil Refining Ltd* [1979] 3 All ER 1008.

[318] Under s.117(6) Water Industry Act 1991, and see also s.209(1) which provides for liability for escapes of water from pipes vested in water undertakers.

[319] *Allen* v *Gulf Oil Refining Ltd* [1981] 1 All ER 353, and see Payne (1994).

depend on whether the situation at issue constitutes an isolated and discrete incident of contamination or a continuing state of affairs. An isolated escape of polluting matter can devastate the ecosystem of a watercourse, which may take a considerable period of time to recover, but in such a case there would be little prospect of securing an injunction unless there was good reason to suppose the escape would be likely to be repeated. Conversely, a relatively small amount of a contaminant discharged over a period of time may become harmful through its cumulative effect upon a watercourse. Although the initial damage may be small, the prospect of continuation of the discharge causing uncompensatable losses, or the acquisition of a legal right to discharge in the future, will be sufficient to ground a claim for an injunction.

Another possible remedy is that of abatement, whereby the victim of a nuisance is entitled to exercise self-help insofar as this is necessary to put an end to the nuisance and this is done with the least possible injury commensurate with the abatement.[320] However, this is a remedy which needs to be exercised with some caution to ensure that the self-help does not exceed what is reasonable to secure abatement of the nuisance and to ensure that entry on the land of another does not take place until reasonable notice has been given requesting the removal of the nuisance.[321] In practice, perhaps because of the practical dangers of exceeding the limits which are imposed upon the remedy of abatement, it appears that the remedy is little used in relation to water contamination.

## 3.15 Damages

As has been noted, nominal damages may be awarded as a recognition that an interference with the claimant's interest in water has taken place without significant injury having been shown. In such a case it would be customary for the claimant to seek an injunction to prevent the continuation of the contamination if this is threatened, but an award of nominal damages by itself often serves as a declaration of the rights of the parties which may serve to bring about the end of a discharge which the defendant had previously maintained he was lawfully entitled to make. In *Nixon* v *Tynemouth Union Rural Sanitary Authority*[322] it was held that the defendants, by failing to maintain a tank in a proper state to contain sewage, had polluted the claimant's stream entitling him to an injunction to compel the authority to discontinue the pollution. In respect of the claimant's claim for substantial damages, it was found that the stream in question had been polluted by others to such an extent that the defendant had suffered no substantial injury on account of the additional pollution brought about by the defendants[323] and was, therefore, entitled only to an

---

[320] See *Greenslade* v *Halliday* (1830) 6 Bing 379 and *Hill* v *Cock* (1872) 26 LT 185.

[321] See *Lemmon* v *Webb* (1895) 59 JP 564 and *Jones* v *Williams* (1843) 12 LJ Ex 249.

[322] (1888) 52 JP 504.

[323] However, see 3.2.5 above on the legal position where water contamination arises due to cumulative discharges from several dischargers.

award of nominal damages in recognition of the infringement of his rights.[324]

More commonly, the purpose of civil proceedings for water contamination is to secure for the claimant a substantial sum as compensation for loss suffered as a result of water contamination.[325] The objective of such an award is to place the claimant in the financial position he was in before the injury was inflicted. The practicalities involved in calculating the amount of an award which is necessary to achieve this are often highly complex. An instructive decision illustrating some of the general difficulties in assessment of damages is *Marquis of Granby* v *Bakewell Urban District Council*.[326] where the defendants' gasworks was found to have discharged noxious waste into a river, in which the claimant had rights of fishery, on two occasions. It was held that the claimant was entitled to an injunction to prevent repetition of the incidents. In addition he was entitled to an award of damages. The general basis for quantification of damages was that the court was to consider what pecuniary sum would make good the loss suffered as a natural and probable consequence of the defendants' acts. The heads under which losses were claimed in the circumstances of the case illustrate some of the difficulties occasioned in ascertaining loss in situations of this kind.

On the facts, it was evident that a large number of fish had been killed as a result of the pollution incidents and, though the claimant had no property in the fish in his fishery until they were caught,[327] it was clear that the destruction of the fish had prejudicially affected the fishery. In calculating the number of fish killed it was accepted without challenge that it was safe to assume that for every dead fish which had been seen at least two more dead fish would not have been seen. On this basis it was ascertained that the numbers of fish killed were 300 in the first incident and 150 in the second. However, the value of those fish to the fishery could not be equated with the cost of replacement with bought fish of the same average size, since,

> [t]he bought fish would from the time of their hatching have been hand-fed in a stew and would never have had to find their own food under natural conditions. Such fish, when turned out in strange waters would be liable to move away from the place where they were put into the river, and would be subject to some casualties; therefore, if the loss is to be replaced by bought fish more than the number killed would have to be turned out.

Moreover,

---

[324] See also *Holland* v *Lazarus* (1897) 61 JP 262, where the claimant was awarded a farthing damages, and made to pay costs.

[325] See also the discussion of exemplary damages at 3.17 below.

[326] (1923) 87 JP 105 and see Howarth and McGillivray (1996) at p.39.

[327] See s.4(4) Theft Act 1968 and Howarth (1987) p.111.

such of the bought fish as remained in the [claimant]'s fishery and survived the casualties . . . would not be of the same value to the users of the fishery as the fish which have been killed, which latter fish were all naturally bred wild fish, well able to fend for themselves and therefore calculated not only to keep in better condition, but also to be more wary and to give better sport than the bought fish.[328]

Consequently, the lower value of the stocked fish had to be taken into account. Along with the fish mortality, it was also shown that the poisoning of the river had caused the loss of a quantity of the food supply, especially crustaceans and, to a lesser degree, molluscs and nymphs. This was also held to be legitimately taken into account in assessing the amount of damages. In addition, the locality where the fish were poisoned had to be taken into the assessment. In part of the polluted length the river was flanked by trees which provided food and shelter and formed a sanctuary for fish which were of especial value to the fishery for breeding purposes, and fish occupying this region were held to of greater value to the fishery than fish in open stretches of the river, and allowance for this was made in the assessment of damages.

On the other side of the calculation of damages, the claimant claimed that, as a consequence of the poisoning, fish from a lower part of the fishery, which had not been affected by the pollution, would migrate upstream to take the places of those which had been lost. In respect of this head of the claim, however, it was held that the claimant could not have it both ways. If he was to be awarded damages to meet the cost of re-stocking the upper part of the fishery he could not also be compensated for the diminution of fish in the lower part of the fishery since this would amount to double compensation for the same loss. In addition, the claimant claimed entitlement to a sum of compensation on account of the loss of reputation suffered by the fishery, which previously had enjoyed a high reputation as a trout fishery. On this head of the claim it was found that, in respect of the lower part of the fishery on which the claimant charged anglers wishing to fish, the evidence did not justify the conclusion that the fishery had actually suffered any loss of reputation. No reasonable angler knowing the locality would be deterred from fishing the lower part of the fishery because of the damage occasioned to the upper part by the incidents which had occurred, and the consequent effect upon the anglers who did not know the locality was held to be too remote. All these factors taken into account, the claimant was awarded damages of £100 for the first incident of pollution and £50 for the second.

Other cases have resulted in claimants being able to recover damages for a variety of losses resulting from water contamination. In *James* v *Bedwellty Urban District Council.*[329] the claimant was able to recover an award of damages for losses incurred when a turbine became clogged and rendered useless by sewage matter emanating from the defendant's sewer. In *Tatton*

---

[328] Per Lawrence J. (1923) 87 JP 105 at p.108.
[329] (1916) 80 JP 192.

v *Staffordshire Potteries Waterworks Co*[330] the claimant's supply of water became unfit for use by his works due to a deposit of mud created as a result of the construction of a reservoir. Whilst the claimant was allowed to recover damages for loss of profits consequent upon the pollution, he was not permitted to recover for depreciation in the value of his property since, it was reasoned, such damage was already compensated for in the amount awarded for loss of profits.

Another instructive case is *Harrington (Earl)* v *Derby Corporation*[331] where the claimant's land was situated along the course of a river and water from the river was used to supply a lake in the grounds. At the outflow from the lake a water wheel had been installed from which power was generated to pump water from an adjacent well up to the claimant's castle for domestic and agricultural purposes. Sewage was discharged into the river by the Corporation a number of miles above the claimant's estate and, as new houses contributed to the Corporation's sewer, the amount of effluent increased to such an extent that the lake became foul. As a result fish and weed in the lake died and residence at the castle became unpleasant and dangerous due to the presence of cholera in the locality, and the claimant was obliged to close off the supply of water from the river. Damages were awarded under various heads:

> the expense of procuring an alternative supply of pure water to replace that of which he had been deprived;
> losses suffered in consequence of the interruption of power the claimant generated from the water supply;
> the cost of providing an alternative supply of water for agricultural use;
> the amount of depreciation suffered in the rental value of a house on the estate; and
> an amount due to the injury to fishing in the river and lake.

Damages were not allowed, however, on account of injury to the amenities of the castle on the ground that no pecuniary damage could be attributed to the fact that the residence became more disagreeable as a consequence of the loss of the lake. In total the damages were assessed at £500.

### 3.16 The Injunction

The appropriate remedy where water contamination is of a continuing character is an injunction to restrain the defendant from persisting with the behaviour which is causing the contamination. The injunction, as an equitable remedy, is granted at the discretion of the court only where it is proper to do so in all the circumstances. Where the contamination is substantial and likely to continue and cause serious injury, or to lead to the acquisition of a legal right,[332] an injunction is likely to be granted.

---

[330] (1879) 44 JP 106.
[331] [1905] 1 Ch 205.
[332] See 3.13.3 above on prescriptive rights.

However, an injunction will not be granted where it is considered that damages are a proper and adequate remedy. Hence, an injunction will be declined if there is no likelihood that the nuisance will persist, as where the nuisance complained of has already ceased after the action has been brought due to remedial action by the defendant.[333] Similarly, an injunction is likely to be declined if the nuisance is of a temporary character,[334] or occurs only occasionally,[335] or is too trivial.[336]

### 3.16.1 The Balance of Convenience

As a general principle, it has been suggested that the approach adopted by the courts in determining applications for injunctions to prevent water contamination should be determined according to the 'balance of convenience' in granting an injunction.[337] Thus in *Lillywhite* v *Trimmer*[338] the claimant sought an injunction to restrain a local board of health from allowing its sewers to discharge into a river above his mill. It was acknowledged that where works of great public importance, such as the sewerage scheme at issue, this must be weighed into the balance. However, if those works could not be effected without interfering with private rights, those private rights must prevail. Hence public works are to be carried out by those who are undertaking them as best they can without interference to private rights.[339] This general principle was, however, to be applied with regard to the balance of convenience of the parties, and if the inconvenience of the claimant is trifling and such as may readily be compensated by payment of money, and the inconveniences of others are as considerable as would arise if the operation of the drainage system of a sizeable town were made unlawful, then the balance of convenience will be opposed to the granting of an injunction. On the facts it was found that the works which had given rise to the complaint were not so serious as materially to interfere with or reduce the comfort or value of the claimant's property and, on balance of convenience, the injunction was declined.[340]

In *Goldsmid* v *Tunbridge Wells Improvement Commissioners*[341] the balance of convenience was found to be weighted against the Commissioners who had constructed a sewer through which sewage was discharged into a brook which ran across the claimant's estate. The

---

[333] *Batcheller* v *Tunbridge Wells Gas Co* (1901) 65 JP 680 and *Attorney-General* v *Dorchester Corporation* (1903) 69 JP 363.

[334] *Attorney-General* v *Metropolitan Board of Works* (1863) 27 JP 597.

[335] *Attorney-General* v *Preston Corporation* (1896) 13 TLR 14.

[336] *Llandudno Urban District Council* v *Woods* (1899) 63 JP 775.

[337] *Pride of Derby and Derbyshire Angling Association Ltd* v *British Celanese Ltd* [1953] 1 All ER 179, per Evershed M.R. at p.197. The expression is referred to as the 'balance of inconvenience' in many of the earlier cases.

[338] (1867) 16 LT 318.

[339] *Attorney-General* v *Birmingham Borough Council* (1858) 4 K&J 528; see also *Kennaway* v *Thompson* [1981] QB 88.

[340] See also *Attorney-General* v *Dorking Union* (1882) 46 LT 573; and *Attorney-General* v *Metropolitan Board of Works* (1863) 27 JP 597, but contrast the decision in *Pride of Derby Angling Association Ltd* v *British Celanese Ltd* [1953] 1 All ER 179.

[341] (1866) 14 LT 154.

discharge rendered the brook unfit for use by the residents of the estate. This in turn diminished the value of the estate and the prospect of selling it advantageously. The court conceded that an injunction should not be granted in a case where the injury is merely temporary and trifling, but thought that an injunction should be granted where the injury is permanent and serious. On the facts, it was held that the balance of convenience in this case lay in the claimant's favour. The proof of both nuisance and injury justified the injunction being granted notwithstanding the inconvenience involved for the Commissioners who were charged with responsibility for sewage treatment for the locality.

### 3.16.2 Delay

Because the award of an injunction is an equitable remedy its availability is subject to the claimant not having delayed in seeking the remedy. Such delay is subject to the equitable doctrine of laches by which a claimant will lose his right to a remedy if he does not pursue it with sufficient expedition.[342] The presence of delay does not put an automatic end to a claimant's right to an injunction, and it has been held that a delay of a few months will not act as a bar to equitable relief by way of an injunction.[343] Nor will a period of time spent in negotiations between the parties be taken to constitute acquiescence on the part of the claimant.[344] Similarly delay did not act as a bar to relief where the claimant had refrained from pursuing legal proceedings in the hope that a local authority would conduct remedial works to deodorise sewage and render it fit for agricultural purposes.[345]

### 3.16.3 Anticipatory Injunctions and Suspension

Where there is imminent danger of water contamination of a substantial character it is possible for an anticipatory injunction to be sustained to restrain water contamination.[346] Environmentally, this remedy has much to commend it in that it is invariably better to use the law to prevent harm to the aquatic environment, rather than to secure a remedy after the event. Hence, the anticipatory injunction may be seen as reflecting a preventative approach[347] to maintaining water quality. It might be thought environmentally better still if injunctions were available as a precaution[348] against environmental damage, that is, where there was some, though not conclusive, evidence that harm would arise without an injunction being

---

[342] On the doctrine of laches generally, see Martin (1997) Ch 23 4E, though note that this doctrine is superseded where the Limitation Act 1980 provides a relevant limitation period.

[343] *Turner* v *Mirfield* (1865) 34 Beav 390, where a delay of six months was held not to act as a bar to relief by injunction.

[344] *Attorney-General* v *Colney Hatch Lunatic Asylum* (1868) 33 JP 196.

[345] *Attorney-General* v *Birmingham Corporation* (1858) 22 JP 561.

[346] See Martin (1997) p.373, and see *Attorney-General* v *Wellingborough Urban District Council* (1974) 72 LGR 507.

[347] See 4.7.2 below on the preventive principle.

[348] See 4.7.1 below on the precautionary principle.

granted. However, it is evident that the possibility of environmental damage, as opposed to its probability, will not be a sufficient basis for an anticipatory injunction to be granted. Thus an anticipatory injunction will not be granted where it is merely shown that a risk of accidental contamination exists, without showing that such an accident is imminent or providing any reason to suppose such an accident will produce serious consequences.[349] Similarly a court will not be justified in interfering if it is possible and practicable for the defendant to take measures to prevent contamination entering a watercourse.[350]

Providing that the claimant is able to establish grounds for an injunction he should, as a matter of theory, be entitled to the injunction immediately, unless the removal of the nuisance is physically impossible, and it is for the defendant to remove the nuisance in the best practicable manner, at whatever cost or inconvenience this may involve. In practice, however, it is open to a court to suspend the operation of the injunction for a period, possibly permitting the defendant to request an extension of the period of time if the circumstances require it. For example, if the removal of the nuisance is a substantial project such as the reconstruction of a sewage system the court will permit time for the necessary work to be undertaken and suspend the operation of the injunction accordingly.[351] In *Pride of Derby and Derbyshire Angling Association Ltd v British Celanese Ltd*[352] the operation of an injunction was suspended for two years and the defendants were allowed the liberty to apply for further suspension. It was stressed, however, that a further suspension of the operation of the injunction would not be granted automatically, and the applicants would have the onus of satisfying the judge that they had, in all sincerity, done all that was reasonably within their power to remedy the injury caused to the claimant.[353]

### 3.16.4 Disobeying an Injunction

Disobedeying the terms of an injunction restraining water contamination amounts to contempt of court for which imprisonment may ultimately be imposed.[354] In past cases, however, it has been thought appropriate to impose the penalty of sequestration of property in the cases of local authorities who commit a breach of the terms of an injunction. The strictness of the duty to obey an injunction is illustrated by *Spokes* v *Banbury Board of Health*[355] where it was held that, despite the unsuccessful attempts of the defendants to deodorise sewage and render it

---

[349] *Attorney-General* v *Dorchester Corporation* (1903) 69 JP 363.

[350] *Fletcher* v *Bealey* (1885) 52 LT 541.

[351] See *Attorney-General* v *Colney Hatch Lunatic Asylum* (1868) 33 JP 196; and *Attorney-General* v *Birmingham Corporation* (1880) 43 LT 77, where the operation of an injunction was suspended for five years in order to give the defendants time to carry out works for the prevention of pollution of a river by sewage.

[352] (1953) 117 JP 52.

[353] See speech of Romer L.J. at p.77.

[354] Under the Contempt of Court Act 1981; generally see Martin (1997) p.739.

[355] (1865) 30 JP 54.

innocuous, if the effluent could not be discharged into a river in accordance with the terms of an injunction it should not be discharged at all, and sequestration of the property of the Corporation was granted for breach of the injunction. In the event of a local authority failing to abide by the terms of an injunction it will not be able to escape punishment by showing that the infringement was done by the act of its servant or agent through carelessness, neglect or dereliction of duty.[356] However, it has been held that a writ of sequestration will not lie against a local authority for its failure to comply with an undertaking not to pollute a river where the breach was accidental.[357] In *Marsden and Sons Ltd* v *Old Silkstone Collieries*,[358] where an action for an injunction to restrain pollution had been brought, the defendants gave an undertaking to refrain from further pollution. Subsequently the defendants failed to adhere to the terms of their undertaking by wilfully allowing waste oil and tar to escape into a river. In the sequestration proceedings which followed it was decided that, though the court may have been justified in making a sequestration order, in the circumstances it would be sufficient to penalise the defendants by granting an injunction and ordering them to pay all the costs of the application.

### 3.16.5  Use of Injunctions in Support of Criminal Proceedings

Although the preceding discussion has characterised injunctions as a 'remedy' for a litigant in civil proceedings, there are some circumstances where they may actually be used as a mechanism to support criminal proceedings. In particular, this arises where a criminal penalty is not thought to offer sufficient deterrent to cause the offending behaviour to cease.

An example of the use of an injunction in this manner is *Attorney-General* v *Wellingborough Urban District Council*,[359] where a local authority sought to bring a new sewage treatment works into operation before construction of the works was complete. The reason for this was to enable the decommissioning of the old sewage treatment works so that its site could be developed for residential use. The decommissioning needed to be accomplished by the local authority before the Water Act 1973[360] came into effect and transferred ownership of the old treatment works to the newly established water authority. An action was brought by the Attorney-General, at the relation of the water authority, for an injunction to restrain the use of the new works until they were capable of dealing with effluent to a standard required by a discharge consent.[361] On appeal, the granting of an injunction was upheld on the basis that it was the only method of

---

[356] *Stancomb* v *Trowbridge Urban District Council* (1910) 74 JP 210.

[357] *Monckton* v *Wolverhampton Corporation, The Times* 26 November 1960.

[358] (1914) 78 JP 220.

[359] (1974) 72 LGR 507.

[360] See 2.14 above on the Water Act 1973.

[361] Discharge consents were then provided for under s.7(1) Rivers (Prevention of Pollution) Act 1951, as amended, and see 2.10 above on the 1951 Act.

preventing a discharge of effluent from the uncompleted sewage treatment works and the consequent pollution of the receiving waters.

The power of the Environment Agency to seek injunctions, under its general incidental function[362] to do anything calculated to facilitate, or which is conducive or incidental to, the carrying out of its functions, is noted elsewhere.[363] However, unless otherwise provided for, the granting of an injunction remains subject to the guiding principle in the previous case. That is, an injunction is only likely to be granted in circumstances where criminal proceedings are shown to be insufficient to prevent a water pollution offence.

An example of an analogous use of an injunction, by a private litigant, to support criminal proceedings is provided by *Whitham* v *Wansford Trout Farm Ltd.*[364] Here undertakings were given, in settlement of legal proceedings,[365] as to the quality of water to be discharged from a trout farm. The water quality undertakings were identical to the requirements imposed by a discharge consent[366] for the premises. The subsequent contempt proceedings, brought by representatives of an angling club, arose because of breaches of these undertakings which, it was found, had occurred persistently over a significant period of time. Mitigating factors were established, in that the defendants had installed expensive equipment in an attempt to avoid breaches of the undertakings and, perhaps because of this, it was not thought appropriate to commit the owner of the fish farm to prison. Nonetheless, penalties of £500 each were imposed in relation to 15 breaches of the undertakings.

### 3.17 Public Nuisance

The civil law provisions which have been discussed so far have been concerned with the rights of individuals and corporate bodies to bring actions against one another for redress for the contamination of water. The common law also gives rise to a distinctive form of quasi-criminal action which may be pursued in order to punish offenders who cause water contamination amounting to a public nuisance.[367] Although public nuisance is a crime, punishable by life imprisonment and an unlimited fine, civil proceedings may be brought where a private individual has suffered physical damage beyond the inconvenience suffered to the public in general. In such a case a court may grant an order restraining the nuisance or awarding recompense for consequential injuries.

---

[362] Under 37(1) Environment Act 1995.

[363] See 3.16.5 below on the use of injunctions to support enforcement of the criminal law.

[364] Unreported, Queen's Bench Division 12 April 1991, see [1991] *Water Law* 143.

[365] See *Wansford Trout Farm Ltd* v *Yorkshire Water Authority,* unreported, Queen's Bench Division, 23 July 1986, see Howarth (1990) p.142.

[366] See Ch.10 below on discharge consents.

[367] For water-related examples of the use of public nuisance see *Overseas Tankship (UK) Ltd* v *Miller Steamship Pty Ltd (the Wagon Mound) (No 2)* [1967] 1 AC 617 (oil discharged into navigable waters causing a fire which destroyed a ship) and *Southport Corporation* v *Esso Petroleum Co Ltd* [1953] 2 All ER 1204 (oil contamination of claimant's foreshore).

Public nuisance 'covers a multitude of sins, great and small'[368] unified by the common feature that they involve injuries suffered by the general public in the locality of the troublesome operation. A definition of public nuisance customarily cited is that of any unwarranted act or omission 'which obstructs or causes inconvenience or damage to the public in the exercise of rights common to all Her Majesty's subjects'.[369] Examples of public nuisances have included keeping a disorderly house, selling food unfit for human consumption, carrying on an offensive trade, and obstructing of public highways.[370]

More pertinently to present concerns, a number of decisions are to be found where an action for the contamination of water has been founded on public nuisance. Thus it was held that a public nuisance was committed where a gas company conveyed gas refuse into a river, rendering the water unfit for drinking and causing the mortality of fish.[371] In another case a canal company was authorised by statute to take water from certain brooks for the purposes of the canal. Due to the discharge of factory waste into the brooks the water became foul, and when it was impounded in the canal 'noisome and unwholesome smells and stenches' arose in the neighbourhood of nearby dwelling houses and public streets. The canal company was found to have committed a public nuisance in accumulating the water in the manner complained of and their defence of statutory authority was no answer to the charge.[372]

Whilst in most cases the purpose of public nuisance proceedings is to obtain an injunction to prevent the continuation of offending behaviour, the possibility that an individual has suffered special damage, above that of the public generally, allows damages to be awarded. Hence, in one instance damages were awarded for the claimant's costs incurred in dredging out a navigable river which had been silted up due to the defendant's actions in constructing a ferry terminal.[373] However, an application was declined for exemplary damages to be awarded in public nuisance to a group of 180 claimants who had drunk water which had been contaminated in the drinking water system of a water supplier at Camelford in 1988.[374] Despite claims that the tardy response of the supplier in informing the water consumers of the contamination had caused water to be drunk which would not otherwise have been, the situation did not fall within those where oppressive, arbitrary or unconstitutional action had been shown by public officials or where the defendant's action had

---

[368] Per Denning LJ *Southport Corporation* v *Esso Petroleum Co Ltd* [1954] 2 QB 182, at p.196.

[369] *Attorney-General* v *P Y A Quarries Ltd* [1957] 2 QB 169, per Romer LJ at p.184.

[370] Generally see Spencer (1989) and Kodilinye (1986).

[371] *R* v *Medley* (1834) 6 C&P 292.

[372] *R* v *Bradford Navigation Co* (1865) 29 JP 613; and see 3.13.4 above on the defence of statutory authority.

[373] *Tate & Lyle Industries Ltd* v *Greater London Council* [1983] 2 AC 509, and see Howarth (1992a) p.144.

[374] *Gibbons and Others* v *South West Water Services Ltd* [1993] QB 507. See Ghandhi (1993) and Cane (1993), and see Ch.17 below on drinking water quality generally.

been calculated to make a profit which might exceed any compensation payable.[375]

Although public nuisance has much in common with private nuisance, there are important differences between the two kinds of action. An action for private nuisance is inseparably concerned with the enjoyment of land, and for that reason only available to persons with an interest in land. The action for public nuisance is concerned with nuisances affecting members of the public present in a locality regardless of their interests in the land of that locality. Public nuisance is primarily a criminal offence involving the prosecution of the wrongdoer, for the benefit of the public as a whole, usually by proceedings instituted by the Attorney-General as the representative of the public. Where he considers it proper, the Attorney-General may also, upon the information of a particular member of the public, bring an action, termed a 'relator' action, for an injunction to prevent the continuation of the nuisance.[376] However, if it can be shown that a particular person suffers a direct and substantial injury due to a nuisance, beyond that suffered by the public of the locality in general, then that person will be entitled to pursue a civil action, without the need for the permission of the Attorney-General.[377]

The issue has arisen on several occasions whether special injury of a kind beyond that suffered by the general public can be shown where a person who earns a living as a fisherman in a water suffers loss of livelihood due to pollution of the water causing fish mortality.[378] In *R v Medley*[379] it was alleged that pollution of a river by gas company waste had caused a diminution of fish by which a considerable number of fishermen lost their employment. It was held that this would not be sufficient ground on which to sustain the action for public nuisance since, 'if it were sufficient, every successful speculation in trade might be the subject of a prosecution',[380] but nonetheless the defendants were found guilty of the crime of public nuisance.[381]

The great majority of cases concerning public nuisance by water contamination have involved the Attorney-General, with or without another person as a relator, acting on behalf of the public to obtain an injunction to restrain the continuation of the nuisance which constitutes an infringement of a general public right.[382] In past cases where the action has been brought on the information of an individual as relator, that person has

---

[375] Citing *Rookes v Barnard* [1964] AC 1129 and *Broome v Cassell & Co Ltd* [1972] AC 1027.

[376] *Attorney-General v P Y A Quarries Ltd* [1957] 2 QB 169.

[377] *Benjamin v Storr* (1874) 30 LT 362.

[378] See Abecassis and Jarashow (1985) pp.398-400.

[379] (1834) 6 Car &P 292.

[380] Per Denman CJ at p.298.

[381] See also *Cattle v Stockton Waterworks Co* (1875) LR 10 QB 453, at p.457.

[382] See for examples, *Attorney-General v Cockermouth L B* (1874) 38 JP 660; and *Attorney-General v Dorchester Corporation* (1903) 69 JP 363.

been a riparian proprietor,[383] a local authority,[384] a former water authority,[385] or another person regardless of whether they reside near the nuisance or not or whether or not they possess an interest in the property on which the nuisance exists.[386]

### 3.18 Civil Liability and Statutory Provisions

Although, for the most part, the preceding discussion in this chapter has concerned the scope of civil liability under the common law, there are also a range of situations where civil liability is specifically provided for by statutory provisions. Key examples of this arise in relation to radioactive contamination, oil contamination and waste.[387]

*3.18.1 Statutory Liability for Radioactive Contamination*

In relation to radioactive contamination, the Nuclear Installations Act 1965 provides for strict and extensive civil liability for exposure to nuclear matter by making operators of nuclear installations subject to a duty to prevent occurrences causing injury to any person or damage to any property.[388] However, liability for economic loss may only be recovered where there is actual physical harm caused to land. Hence, where claimants sought to recover for a decline in value of a property in the vicinity of a nuclear installation, resulting from radioactive contamination, this was refused on the basis that no physical harm was established in relation to the property.[389] Subsequently, however, a successful claim arose out of the contamination of land arising from a flood of water from the Atomic Weapons Establishment which caused radioactive contamination of the claimant's land. Here, although the contamination did not exceed a level which was considered dangerous, and remediation works were carried out by the defendant to remove the contamination, compensation was payable for the diminution in value and saleability of the claimant's property due to blight resulting from the contamination.[390]

---

[383] *Attorney-General* v *Lonsdale* (1868) 33 JP 435, where an injunction was granted to restrain a public nuisance caused by the erection of a jetty upon the bed of a tidal river extending into the river so far as to interfere with navigation.

[384] See s.222 Local Government Act 1972 to the effect that a local authority which takes proceedings in respect of a public nuisance is bound to sue on the relation of the Attorney-General; *Attorney-General* v *Grand Junction Canal Company* (1909) 73 JP 421; *Attorney-General* v *Logan* (1891) 55 JP 615; *Solihull Metropolitan Borough Council* v *Maxfern Ltd* [1977] 1 WLR 127; and *Kent County Council* v *Bachelor (No 2)* [1979] 1 WLR 213.

[385] *Attorney-General* v *Wellingborough Urban District Council* (1974) 72 LGR 507.

[386] *Attorney-General and Domes* v *Basingstoke Corporation* (1876) 24 WR 817.

[387] Generally, see Ch.20 below on nuclear contamination, Ch.19 below on oil contamination and 12.2 below on waste management.

[388] s.7 Nuclear Installations Act 1965.

[389] *Merlin* v *British Nuclear Fuels plc* [1990] 2 QB 557, discussed at 20.11.5 below.

[390] *Blue Circle Industries plc* v *Ministry of Defence* [1999] Env LR 22, discussed at 20.11.5 below.

### 3.18.2  Statutory Liability for Oil Contamination

In relation to oil contamination, the Merchant Shipping Act 1995 provides for compensation for oil contamination damage in civil proceedings. Hence, where, as a result of any occurrence taking place whilst a ship is carrying a cargo of oil in bulk, any oil carried by the ship is discharged or escapes, the owner will be liable for specified kinds of loss. Specifically, liability will arise for damage caused by contamination resulting from the discharge or escape and for any measure reasonably taken for the purpose of preventing or reducing such damage.[391] Liability, for such damage is strict, in the sense that negligence on the part of the owner does not need to be shown, except where otherwise provided for under the Act as where, for example, contributory negligence is found.

### 3.18.3  Statutory Liability for Waste

Another example of statutory civil liability for environmental harm being provided for arises in waste management legislation, without prejudice to other civil liability which may arise. Where any damage is caused by waste being deposited in or on land, any person who deposited it, or knowingly caused or knowingly permitted it to be deposited, so as to commit an offence,[392] is liable for the damage. This statutory liability is subject to two exceptions, that the damage was due wholly to the fault of the person who suffered it or was suffered by a person who voluntarily accepted the risk of the damage being caused.[393]

### 3.18.4  Statutory Liability and Water Pollution Offences

By contrast, however, the regulatory provisions concerning the pollution of controlled waters[394] make no provision for civil liability arising out of a water pollution offence. Statutory provision is made for compensatory awards to be made to the Environment Agency in relation to the reasonable costs arising from anti-pollution works and operations undertaken in the aftermath of a pollution incident,[395] and it is possible for criminal courts generally to make a compensation order for the benefit of a victim of contamination.[396] However, the more general matter of the civil liability of a person who has committed a criminal offence in relation to the pollution of water is not statutorily provided for, raising the question as to when the circumstances of a criminal conviction for water pollution will also provide grounds for a civil action and *vice versa*.

Historically, the approach towards the relationship between criminal provisions concerning water pollution and civil liability for adverse

---

[391] s.153(1) Merchant Shipping Act 1995.

[392] Contrary to s.33(1) or 63(2) Environmental Protection Act 1990.

[393] s.73(6) Environmental Protection Act 1990.

[394] Under Part III Water Resources Act 1991, and see 9.3–4 below.

[395] Under s.161 Water Resources Act 1991, and see 13.2 below.

[396] Under the Powers of the Criminal Courts Act 1973, and see 9.21 below.

impacts upon water quality has been to construe the two matters quite separately. Hence in *Brocket* v *Luton Corporation*[397] the point was raised as to whether the discoloration of a river was, by itself, a ground of civil complaint based upon riparian rights. Vaisey J said,

> [i]n the Rivers Pollution Prevention Act 1876 it is provided that the word 'pollution' shall not, for the purposes of that Act, include 'innocuous discoloration', but in connection with riparian rights I incline to the view that this, like so many other matters, must be a question of degree. I cannot believe that a riparian owner would be obliged to submit to the conversion of clear water into a water dyed, for example, bright crimson with cochineal, which I believe to be a perfectly harmless ingredient.

Hence, the characterisation of water 'pollution' for regulatory purposes may not be determinative of what kinds of deterioration in water quality give grounds for civil redress.

Indeed, the regulatory regime for protection of water quality from pollution, under Part III of the Water Resources Act 1991, is explicitly insulated from the civil law. Hence, except insofar as otherwise provided for,[398] nothing in Part III of the Act

(a) confers a right of action in any civil proceedings (other than proceedings for the recovery of a fine) in respect of any contravention of Part III or any subordinate legislation, consent or other instrument made, given or issued under Part III;

(b) derogates from any right of action or other remedy (whether civil or criminal) in proceedings instituted otherwise than under Part III; or

(c) affects any restriction imposed by or under any other enactment, whether public, local or private.[399]

The natural interpretation of this separation between criminal and civil proceedings is that, first, a criminal conviction for a water pollution offence will not serve to establish civil liability and, second, successful civil proceedings will not justify a finding that the defendant has committed any criminal offence. The first proposition would seem to be justified by the differences in the nature of what needs to be established in relation to the two kinds of proceedings. Doubtless, the fact that criminal proceedings have been successful in relation to a particular incident may make evidentiary issues less burdensome for a claimant in subsequent civil proceedings. However, showing that a person has caused the unlawful entry or discharge of polluting matter, for the purpose of establishing a criminal conviction,[400] is a distinct issue from showing that a particular

---

[397] [1948] WN 352 and see McDowell and Chamberlin (1950) p.222.

[398] Subject to s.18 Interpretation Act 1978, relating to offences under two or more laws.

[399] s.100 Water Resources Act 1991.

[400] See s.85 Water Resources Act 1991, and the discussion of the principal water pollution offences at 9.3 below.

claimant has suffered loss as a result of the entry which would need to be established in civil litigation. The second proposition would seem to be justified by the different burdens of proof in civil and criminal proceedings. Hence, establishing that 'on the balance of probabilities', the claimant's loss has resulted from the defendant's action, for the purposes of civil proceedings, does not necessarily justify a finding that it is 'beyond reasonable doubt' that the defendant caused the entry of polluting matter for the purposes of a criminal conviction.

### 3.18.5 Interrelationships between Civil and Regulatory Law

Despite the statutory separation of the civil and regulatory law concerning water pollution, there are situations where their interrelationship becomes a contentious issue. A good example of this is *Cook* v *South West Water*[401] where the claimant was the owner of fishing rights downstream from where the defendant sewerage undertaker operated three sewage treatment works discharging effluent into the river under a discharge consent. These discharges contained surfactants from detergents[402] which resulted in a foam forming on the surface of the river for significant periods of time, and phosphates which caused excessive algal growth, which detrimentally affected the aquatic ecosystem and seriously interfered with angling. The claimant brought a civil action against the sewerage undertaker, seeking damages and an injunction in nuisance for diminution in the amenity value of the fishery. He was awarded damages of £2,500 and £1,500 costs, and an undertaking was also given by the sewerage undertaker that it would pay £5,000 for the Institute of Freshwater Ecology to carry out a study of the effects of surfactants on the rivers. However, no injunction was granted.

Whilst the final outcome of the litigation provides a clear illustration of the right of a riparian owner to receive water without sensible alteration in its natural quality,[403] the remarkable aspect of the proceedings was an argument raised by the defendants. This was that, since the discharges made from their sewage treatment works were, at all times, within the terms of their discharge consents in relation to the substances which were the subject of the complaint, and the river had actually attained a 1B quality classification,[404] no liability could arise. This argument was remarkable because the relevant discharge consents contained no conditions relating to surfactants or detergents which, on one interpretation,[405] meant that the undertaker was permitted to discharge unlimited quantities of these substances without contravening the consents. The judge was not prepared to accept the argument, and found that the surfactants did have a damaging impact on the amenity of the fishery and

---

[401] Unreported, Exeter County Court 15 April 1992, see [1992] *Water Law* 103.

[402] Generally see 5.4.3 below on the Detergents Directives.

[403] See *John Young and Co* v *Bankier Distillery Co* [1893] AC 691, and see discussion at 3.5 above.

[404] See 1.4 above on general water quality classification.

[405] See 10.6.5 below on the status of substances not identified in a discharge consent.

an appreciable effect upon the receiving waters. Thus, whether or not a defendant complies with regulatory requirements, the fact that a discharge gives rise to sensible alteration of water quality should allow civil proceedings to be maintained.

However a contrasting approach was taken in *Hughes* v *Dwr Cymru Cyfyngedig*,[406] where an action was brought by an angling association in relation to the quality of effluent discharged from a sewage treatment works. It was alleged that the effluent contained excessive amounts of phosphates which resulted in eutrophication[407] of the receiving waters of Llyn Padarn. The action was brought in nuisance and negligence seeking damages and an injunction for damage to the fishery. However, whilst conceding that the phosphate input from the treatment works had caused algal blooms, it was not accepted that this resulted in harm to the fish population of fishery. Because no connection between the eutrophication and the low fish catches had been established, it was ruled that no recoverable damage had been caused. In addition, however, observations were offered in relation to the discharge having been made in accordance with a discharge consent, albeit a consent which did not include any parameter governing phosphates, which the undertaker maintained should be a defence to the action. The judge stated that,

> [i]f the consents provide the defendant with the statutory authority to do what is set out in the consents, this, in the absence of negligence or want of care and reasonable regard for the interests of other persons, protects them from actions in nuisance or negligence, and this would be the end of the [claimant]'s case.

This assertion that compliance with a discharge consent amounts to a defence to a civil action seems impossible to reconcile with the statutory statement that nothing in Part III of the Water Resources Act 1991 derogates from any civil right of action in proceedings instituted otherwise than under Part III of the Act.[408] It must, therefore, be of dubious authority. Between the two decisions, the approach taken in the *Cook* case must be regarded as the more preferable but, as both are decisions made only at county court level, neither may be regarded as an authoritative statement of the law.

The basic approach of separating the grounds for civil and criminal liability for water contamination has important consequences where the harm at issue is not subject to effective regulatory control. Moreover, the distinct grounds for the different proceedings recognises the differences between private and public interests in the aquatic environment.

---

[406] Unreported, Llangefni County Court, 21 June 1995, see [1996] *Water Law* 40 and *ACA Review* 1999 p.27 for an account of subsequent difficulties.
[407] See 1.3.1 above on eutrophication.
[408] s.100(b) Water Resources Act 1991.

### 3.19  Practicalities of Civil Law Proceedings

In concluding the discussion of national civil law relating to water
pollution and water quality, it is appropriate to place litigation of this kind
in context by offering some observations on the practical difficulties that a
litigant is likely to face. There is a temptation to suppose that the legal
rules that have been described operate mechanically to produce the
consequence that they indicate whereas, in practice, there are many other
considerations which determine whether a remedy will be gained or
proceedings for water contamination even brought.

The practical shortcomings of the common law, and the pitfalls of civil
litigation on water pollution, were succinctly expressed in the Third Report
of the Royal Commission on the Pollution of Rivers in 1867.[409] Despite the
passing of time and the extensive development of regulatory laws
concerning water quality, a passage from the Report entitled *Defects of
Existing Law Relating to Rivers Pollution* remains such an incisive account
of the difficulties confronting a claimant considering civil proceedings that
it justifies substantial citation.

> So far as river abuses affect only private rights, each individual is left
> to protect himself by putting the law in motion. An aggrieved
> proprietor has the option of bringing an action for damages in the
> Common Law Courts or of filing a bill in Chancery for an
> injunction.[410] Either course is necessarily invidious, expensive, and
> doubtful in its result. It is invidious because neighbour is set against
> neighbour, and because it must seem unjust that one manufacturer
> should be proceeded against and mulcted [i.e., fined] for doing that
> which hundreds of others, who do not happen to offend a powerful
> neighbour, are doing with impunity. It is an expensive remedy. For
> the same money which is spent over a hardly fought litigation against
> a single manufacturer, a Conservancy Board, armed with proper
> powers, might for years keep safe from all abuse, a long extent of
> river with hundreds of manufactories situated on its banks . . . . Legal
> proceedings are also a very doubtful remedy. The [claimant] may
> prove that he has suffered injury from the pollution of the river and
> that the defendant has polluted the river above him; but this is not
> enough. The [claimant] has also to prove that what he has suffered
> has been caused wholly or in part by the special act of the defendant,
> which is always difficult - often impossible. For besides the
> defendant there is probably a multitude of manufacturers who, at
> various points higher up the stream, cast in liquid refuse from their
> works; these impurities are carried down by the current, and by the
> time they reach the [claimant]'s works they are all mingled
> confusedly together, and the offence of the defendant has ceased to
> be distinguishable. The [claimant] accordingly fails to establish his
> case.

---

[409] Royal Commission on the Pollution of Rivers (1867) pp.li-liii.

[410] Today both of these remedies are granted by the same courts.

Even where successful these private attempts to protect the river are but little gain to the public. Several instances have come before us where a manufacturer, sued for polluting running water, has brought the litigation to a close, not by ceasing to foul the river, but by simply removing the discharge into the river to a point below the works of the complainant.

Further, the law recognises prescriptive rights to pollute running water and obstruct its flow, provided such abuses fall short of public nuisance. Such rights we do not hesitate to call privileged abuses. A manufacturer who, in the exercise of a right so acquired, discharges into the river the solid and liquid refuse from his works may thereby do injury to the river to the extent of many times the money value of the right. But the loss to the public is too serious to be measured by a money standard. If some are permitted to pollute or obstruct the river, it is in vain that others abstain from abusing it. Thus by the maintenance of exceptions the law discourages those who are well disposed, and renders ineffectual voluntary combination, even upon a large scale, amongst manufacturers, to preserve the river. More that this, the law actually holds out a premium to those who abuse the river. A manufacturer is tempted to go on casting solid and liquid refuse into the river in order to establish a new right or to keep alive an old one.

The law prohibiting river abuse, when it amounts to a public nuisance, is not open to the same objection, because no length of toleration is held to justify a public nuisance. But the term "public nuisance" is a very equivocal one. In a manufacturing district no manufacturer is in danger of being indicted, still less of being convicted of causing a public nuisance, on the ground that the discharge of his dye waste renders the water of the river opaque, discoloured, unsightly, and quite unfit to drink, provided no smell is occasioned and there is no danger to public health. Again, in the neighbourhood of large towns it has come to be thought that a river foul with sewage is inevitable; inhabitants are reluctant to come forward as witnesses to denounce that to which they have become long familiar, and in like manner jurymen are slow to find such things to constitute a public nuisance. In the case of sewage pollution it is not usually difficult (as it is in the case of pollution from manufactory refuse) to trace the offence home, but, however serious the evil, it is very difficult to find a prosecutor. For the principal offenders are the governing bodies of large towns. These do not prosecute one another for the reason that each is guilty of the same offence towards his neighbour, and that they are rarely prosecuted by private persons because few are willing to bear the expense and odium of acting as public prosecutors. To institute legal proceedings against a large town with a view to compel it to adopt a different mode of disposing of its sewage, at a cost perhaps of many thousand pounds, is to provoke a wealthy adversary to a conflict in which every step will be contested. The expense of such a litigation generally far exceeds the value of the personal interest of any individual in the stoppage of the nuisance. Accordingly, whatever the inconvenience to the public, the nuisance continues unabated. Rich and poor alike submit to it as a sort of destiny.

Regrettably, many of the problems identified by the Royal Commission Report of 1867 remain difficulties for prospective civil litigants of today.[411] Instigation of proceedings relies upon the initiative of a committed claimant who is willing to take the 'invidious, expensive and doubtful' step of bringing a civil action and bearing an expense which 'generally far exceeds the value of the personal interest of any individual in the stoppage of the nuisance'. Fortunately, present criminal offences concerning water pollution[412] make civil litigation less necessary as a general means of protecting the aquatic environment than at the time when the Commission reported, but the expense and uncertainty of outcome of civil litigation continues to be a deterrent to many potential litigants.

On the other hand, a significant development in civil litigation concerning water contamination was the establishment of the Anglers' Co-operative Association in 1948 (now renamed the 'Anglers' Conservation Association'). This voluntary organisation is an association of some 15,000 anglers, angling clubs and riparian owners committed to using the law against water pollution and providing legal support in relation to pollution incidents and water quality concerns impacting upon fisheries. Over the years it has brought legal proceedings, or achieved out-of-court settlements, in several hundred cases and many of the leading legal decisions concerning water contamination have been brought with the support and expertise of the Association.[413] Hence, the Annual Report of the Association for 1998 indicates that at the start of the year 42 legal actions against polluters were being conducted on behalf of members and during the year the Association settled or won 18 cases.[414] Whilst in 1867 bringing water pollution proceedings may have rested entirely upon the initiative of the victim of pollution, the Anglers' Conservation Association has provided important legal support which has allowed proceedings to be brought, or a settlement to be reached, in circumstances where, in times past, this would not have been a financial or practical possibility.

## 3.20 European Community Proposals on Environmental Liability

Having considered the civil law, and the private rights provided to individual claimants to bring actions in relation to water contamination, the close relationship between this body of law and other mechanisms by which those responsible for environmental harm may be required to rectify

---

[411] Although see Tromans (1999) for commentary on the environmental law implications of reforms in civil procedure (reviewing, Lord Chancellor's Department, *Civil Procedure Rules (with Practice Directions, Pre-action Protocols and Forms)* (1999)).

[412] See Ch.9 below.

[413] See Sutton (1988).

[414] See James (2000) and *ibid* p.26 for an account of some 37 instances where legal proceedings may be brought or are in prospect concerning contamination affecting fisheries.

that harm must be noted. Three of the most important aspects of this are considered elsewhere in this work: first, the powers of criminal courts to make compensation orders to victims of crimes including that of water pollution;[415] second, the obligations imposed upon a person responsible for a water pollution incident to undertake anti-pollution works or operations or to bear the cost of such works;[416] and, third, the duty of appropriate persons to secure the remediation of certain contaminated land.[417]

In a broad sense each of these mechanisms is concerned with 'liability' for environmental harm, though a contrast may be drawn between the civil law and compensation orders, which are primarily directed providing the victim of water pollution with private redress, whereas anti-pollution works and contaminated land obligations are mainly concerned with public law requirements to undertake remediation activities or to meet the costs of such work. Nonetheless, the common theme is that of imposing 'liability', as opposed to punishment, upon those responsible for deterioration in water quality. In this broader sense of 'liability' it is evident that changes in the law are in prospect as a consequence of international and European Community developments.

### 3.20.1  The Lugano Convention

Principle 13 of the Rio Declaration on Environment and Development requires that

> States shall develop national law regarding liability and compensation for the victims of pollution and other environmental damage; they shall also co-operate in an expeditious and more determined manner to develop further international law regarding liability and compensation for adverse effects of environmental damage caused by activities within their jurisdiction or control to areas beyond their jurisdiction.[418]

One development which has followed from this principle is the 1993 Council of Europe Convention on Civil Liability for Damage Resulting from Activities Dangerous to the Environment, the 'Lugano Convention'.[419] This Convention aims to ensure that adequate compensation is provided for transboundary damage resulting from activities dangerous to the environment and also to provide for a means of

---

[415] See s.35(1) Powers of the Criminal Courts Act 1973 and see 9.2.1 below on compensation orders.

[416] Under ss.161-161D Water Resources Act 1991 and see 13.2 below on anti-pollution works and operations.

[417] Under Part IIA Environmental Protection Act 1990, as inserted by the Environment Act 1995, and see 13.7 below on the contaminated land regime.

[418] 31 ILM 874 (1992). Note also Principle 16 which states "[n]ational authorities should endeavour to promote the internalization of environmental costs and the use of economic instruments, taking into account the approach that the polluter should, in principle, bear the cost of pollution, with due regard to the public interest and without distorting international trade and investment" and see 4.7.3 above on the polluter pays principle.

[419] 32 ILM 1230 (1993).

prevention and reinstatement of environmental damage. The Convention provides for strict liability for personal injury and damage to property in relation to injury caused by hazardous activities on the part of persons responsible for these, subject to specified exceptions. This liability extends to damage involving impairment of the environment so far as that damage takes the form of costs incurred in taking remedial action to restore the environment to its previous state. However, the Convention does not indicate what kinds of remedial action will be within the scope of this requirement beyond the indication that they should be 'reasonable'. Perhaps because of this uncertainty, and other ambiguities in the Convention, there is ambivalence amongst the Member States of the European Community towards signing the convention and implementing its provisions in national laws.[420]

### 3.20.2 *European Community Environmental Liability*

At European Community level, a Commission Green Paper, *Remedying Environmental Damage,*[421] was published in 1993 providing a discussion of the possibilities for harmonisation of the approach to remedying environmental damage provided for in the Community. This has been followed, after extensive consultation with Member States and at Community level, by the recent publication by the Commission of a *White Paper on Environmental Liability*.[422] Broadly, the White Paper discusses various mechanisms for establishing a Community-wide environmental liability regime as a means of improving application of Community environmental policy[423] and ensuring adequate restoration of the environment. The overall objective is to make persons who cause environmental damage meet the cost of that damage. It is maintained that the introduction of a Community regime for environmental liability would improve implementation of environmental principles such as the polluter pays principle and the prevention and precaution principles, serve as an incentive towards more responsible behaviour, secure decontamination and restoration of the environment and provide better implementation of Community environmental legislation generally.

However, the White Paper is relatively non-committal as to the precise basis upon which Community environmental liability should be imposed and seeks only to indicate some *possible* features of a Community regime. The basic principles which might govern such liability are identified as the following:

(a) no retroactivity (application to future damage only);

---

[420] European Commission, *White Paper on Environmental Liability*, 9 February 2000, COM (2000) 66 final, para.5.1.

[421] COM(93) 47 final, 14 May 1993 and see House of Lords Select Committee on the European Communities, *Remedying Environmental Damage* (1993).

[422] European Commission, *White Paper on Environmental Liability*, 9 February 2000, COM (2000) 66 final, and generally see Poli (1999).

[423] See Ch.4 below on European Community environmental policy generally.

    (b)  coverage of both environmental damage (site contamination and damage to biodiversity) and traditional damage (harm to health and property);

    (c)  a closed scope of application linked with Community environmental legislation;

    (d)  coverage of contaminated sites and traditional damage only where caused by a hazardous, or potentially hazardous, activity regulated under Community law;

    (e)  damage to biodiversity give rise to liability only if protected under the Natura 2000 network;[424]

    (f)  strict liability for damage caused by inherently dangerous activities, fault-based liability for damage to biodiversity caused by non-dangerous activities;

    (g)  liability subject to commonly-accepted defences, allowing some alleviation of the claimant's burden of proof and some equitable relief for defendants;

    (h)  liability focussed on the operator in control of the activity which causes the damage;

    (i)  criteria for assessing and dealing with different types of damage;

    (j)  an obligation to spend compensation paid by the polluter on environmental restoration;

    (k)  enhanced access to justice in environmental damage cases;

    (l)  co-ordination with international conventions; and

    (m) financial security for potential liabilities, working with markets.

Although the White Paper considers various options for Community action in relation to environmental liability, it is concluded, on the basis of concerns for subsidiarity and proportionality,[425] that the most preferable option would be the enactment of a framework directive. A directive of this kind would provide for strict liability for damage caused by dangerous activities, regulated at Community level, and fault-based liability for damage to biodiversity resulting from non-dangerous activities.

### 3.20.3 Implications and Limitations

Given the relatively provisional stage of deliberations, it is difficult to be categorical about the implications of the proposals upon the existing scheme of national environmental civil liability. However, some tentative observations are possible with particular reference to liability for damage to water quality. Most notably, it is evident that there will be broad areas of potential liability which will not be addressed by, or are likely to be excluded from, the Community regime. For example, intractably difficult practical issues, such as the identification of a person responsible for an action which is causally linked to quantifiable environmental damage, are not addressed. Hence much water contamination of a diffuse kind will fall outside the scope of the Community regime. The exclusion of retroactive measures leaves to Member States the task of addressing the problem of

---

[424] On Natura 2000 see 15.8.1 below.
[425] See 4.4.2 below on subsidiarity and 4.4.3 below on proportionality.

dealing with 'historic' contamination of land and water through regimes for contaminated land remediation such as that which has recently been adopted nationally.[426] As will be seen, the national contaminated land regime appears to meet the requirements for effective decontamination, restoration or replacement of the environment which are envisaged by the Community liability proposals.

Other features of the proposals which will limit their impact upon national civil law have been formulated purposefully to place boundaries upon the extent of the Community environmental liability regime. Liability is confined in two main ways, first, by restriction to specified kinds of environmentally hazardous activities and, second, to harm to limited biodiversity interests however such harm is caused. Hence, in relation to hazardous activities, the proposals are restricted in coverage to those activities which are subject to identified categories of Community legislation:

(a) imposing discharge or emission limits for hazardous substances;

(b) otherwise regulating such substances for the protection of the environment;

(c) preventing and controlling risks of accidents and pollution such as the Integrated Pollution Prevention and Control Directive[427] and the revised 'Seveso II' Directive;[428]

(d) governing the production, handling, treatment, recovery, recycling, reduction, storage, transport, trans-frontier shipment and disposal of hazardous and other waste; and

(e) regulating the field of biotechnolgy.

The general emphasis which is placed upon hazardous substances legislation would seem to leave quite a broad range of potential water contaminants outside the scope of the liability proposals. Looking back over the cases that have been reviewed in this chapter, there would seem to be quite a large proportion which did not involve inherently hazardous substances or activities which, were the facts to arise in future, would not fall within the scope of the Community proposals.

The other respect in which the proposals provide for liability is in regard to, damage to biodiversity, where liability will arise irrespective of the activity which gives rise to such damage. Here the scope of liability is bounded by the restriction that such liability will only arise in relation to 'European sites' within the Natura 2000 network designated under the Wild Birds and Habitats Directives.[429] Hence damage to wildlife resources outside the protection offered by these Directives, or to other areas designated at EC level for their environmental sensitivity,[430] will not be the

---

[426] See 13.7 below on contaminated land.

[427] Directive 96/61/EC and see 12.3.3 below on this Directive.

[428] The Control of Major Accident Hazards Directive (96/82/EC) ('Seveso II').

[429] Directives 79/409/EEC and 92/43/EEC and see 15.8 below on these Directives.

[430] See for example nitrate vulnerable zones and environmentally sensitive areas, discussed at 13.5 below.

subject of liability except where this is provided for under national law. Whether liability is provided for at Community level or under national law alone, however, the general difficulty with biodiversity damage lies in the supposition that the harm is capable of financial quantification and that payment of damages is genuinely a means of restoring a habitat to its former state.

### 3.20.4 Strict Liability and Significant Damage

The limitation of the proposals to hazardous activities and biodiversity damage serves to address the problem of 'environmental liability' being, otherwise, a rather open-ended concept. The contrast between hazardous activity liability and liability for biodiversity damage is also important in distinguishing between two distinct types of liability that are envisaged. Amongst the most fundamental changes to national civil liability that is being proposed is the imposition of strict liability for certain kinds of environmental harm, that is, the fault of the actor need not be established only the fact that the act or omission actually caused the damage. However, the extent of strict liability which is proposed is limited to inherently hazardous activities and will not apply in relation to biodiversity damage where fault-based liability will be applied unless particular damage is attributable to a dangerous activity. Moreover, even where strict liability does apply to hazardous activities it is, nonetheless, envisaged that certain defences will be allowed. Hence, Acts of God, a contribution to the damage by the claimant and intervention of a third party are suggested as defences. Possibly, also defences might be allowed where releases are made under authorisation or in accordance with the 'state of the art'. Depending upon the final outcome of discussions on the defences which are to be allowed, the form of 'strict liability' that is eventually adopted may well fall significantly short what is commonly understood by that phrase.

Perhaps the most important practical matter surrounding the environmental liability proposals is the issue of what kinds of damage are to be the subject of liability and how the extent of that liability to be quantified. In respect of 'significant' contamination impacts, the proposals anticipate a degree of harmonisation in relation to remediation standards and the objectives. Such standards would need to indicate the circumstances in which remediation of a contaminated site would be necessary. Standards would also define the quality of soil and water which would need to be achieved to remove any serious threat to human beings and the environment and to make the contaminated area fit for actual or plausible future uses. As national experience has shown,[431] the task of expressing requirements of this kind in quantified numerical standards indicating the required soil and water quality represents a significant technical challenge, even assuming some consensus can be reached as to the prospective use of an area of land.

---

[431] See the discussion of the national contaminated land regime at 13.7 below.

The difficulties are perhaps even greater where the damage involved is of an ecological kind. In this respect it is envisaged that there will be a minimum threshold for activating liability so that only 'significant' damage to habitats and wildlife will be covered. Where this significance threshold is exceeded, and it is determined that restoration is not technically feasible, the suggested approach is that of assessing the cost of provision of an 'alternative' to that which has been damaged. This raises profoundly difficult issues as to the extent to which provision of an 'alternative' area of land is capable of serving as a 'equivalent' for an acknowledged area of biodiversity importance which has been damaged or lost. Even more problematic is the question whether species, rather than habitats, are capable of 'restoration' in any meaningful sense. Supposing that restoration is feasible, however, it is proposed that this will be subject to a cost-benefit or reasonableness test in assessing restoration costs against the consequent valuation of the benefits of the natural resource at issue. Contingent valuation and other forms of revealed preference techniques are indicated as a mechanism for quantification of the values of natural resources. Again, the national experience of formulating a methodology for assessing the value of the unowned environment, and the ecosystems which this supports, has not been especially encouraging.[432]

### 3.20.5 Compensation and Access to Justice

Under national law, the practical purposes for which an award of damages are used is a matter entirely within the discretion of the successful claimant. There is no general obligation that damages should be used for the purpose of environmental or ecological restoration or for any other particular purpose. This contrasts markedly with the Community's environmental liability proposals which suggest that compensation which is paid in respect of biodiversity damage or site contamination would have to be actually expended for that purpose.[433] If restoration of the particular damage is not possible, for technical or cost-benefit reasons, the 'compensation' paid must be expended upon 'comparable' projects involving the restoration of natural resources. Such projects would be determined by competent authorities by reference to consequent environmental benefits. Echoing previous observations, it is likely that there will be many situations where environmental or ecological harm is not amenable to rectification merely by monetary expenditure and these will probably be situations where damages which have been awarded will need to be redirected to 'comparable' projects. The difficulty underlying this is that the removal of the discretion given to successful claimants to use awards of damages as they think fit is likely to increase the disincentives to instigation of costly and perhaps uncertain civil proceedings. Given the significant difficulties that already need to be

---

[432] See the discussion of the cost-benefit duty imposed upon the Environment Agency under s.39 Environment Act 1995 at 6.14 below and the discussion of economic instruments for water pollution control at 1.7.9 above.

[433] Although compare the requirements for expenditure of compensation payable from oil pollution funds, discussed at 19.13 below.

surmounted by a civil claimant,[434] the prospect of effective 'appropriation' of any eventual award of damages by an environmental regulatory authority may be seen by claimants as a final reason for not pursuing such litigation.

To some extent these concerns are met by proposals in relation to access to justice. Although 'traditional' damage, comprising personal injury, property damage and possibly economic loss, is acknowledged to be a private law matter left within the jurisdiction of the Member States, environmental damage, such as site contamination and biodiversity damage, is recognised to be a matter of public interest. In relation to environment damage, therefore, the State is identified as having the primary responsibility to take action. Presumably, in the national context, this would involve the appropriate regulatory authority acquiring the status of a civil litigant albeit with the capacity to recover damages for pure environmental loss. However, given increasing concerns to secure enhancement of access to legal proceedings by the public generally,[435] it is proposed that certain public interest groups promoting environmental protection should have the right to pursue proceedings where the State does not act, or does not act effectively or sufficiently swiftly, in ensuring decontamination or restoration of biodiversity damage. Where proceedings of this kind are pursued, the difficulties arising from the requirement that an award of damages are actually used for the purposes of environmental or biodiversity restoration may be less significant that in litigation pursued by private individual. However, difficulties may remain as to the allocation of a responsibility to ensure that an award of damage is actually used for the purpose of restoration and the question of who will exercise supervision over this. Essentially though, the contrast with the customary use of the national civil law by private individuals is that the proposals envisage the use of the civil law to provide remedies to the public generally rather than to individuals whose private rights are infringed.

### 3.20.6 Fundamental Limitations

The Community's environmental liability proposals illustrate and reaffirm many of the fundamental limitations, indicated at the commencement of this Chapter, which underlie any system of civil liability when applied to environmental contexts. An award of civil compensation serves a useful restorative purpose where private rights have been infringed and a payment of money or other remedy provides a means of making good the consequent harm to the victim. Where, however, the harm is inflicted upon the environment, and the ecosystems which it supports, it is far from clear whether payment of money alone serves any useful compensatory purpose, though it may be easier to defend the imposition of a regulatory

---

[434] See 3.19 above on the practicalities of civil litigation in relation to water quality matters.

[435] See European Commission, *Implementing Community Law*, COM(96) 500 final, discussed at 4.18 below and the 1998 Aarhus Convention (UN/ECE Convention on Access to Information, Public Participation in Decision-Making and Access to Justice in Environmental Matters), which the European Community is a signatory to, and see 16.18 below on this.

remediation obligation such as those imposed in relation to land or water contamination. If deterrence, rather than compensation, is the object of imposing environmental civil liability then, properly enforced, the criminal law might be more appropriately applied since payment of a substantial fine, in many instances, is likely to bring as much environmental benefit as paying civil damages through having a greater deterrent effect.

The central problem remains, that the civil law is largely concerned with securing compensation for quantifiable kinds of loss. In national law, injury to private rights has provided a workable mechanism for the quantification of such loss, but where damage is to the unowned environment it is far from clear what the basis for quantification of loss should be or whether any payment of 'compensation' is genuinely a means of providing redress for harm to the public interest in the environment.

# Chapter 4

# EUROPEAN COMMUNITY WATER LAW AND POLICY

## 4.1 Introduction

Membership of the European Economic Community, and now the European Community,[1] has had a dramatic effect upon the general environmental law of the United Kingdom, and particularly upon the nature and scope of water pollution and water quality law. This Chapter seeks to outline the general background to Community environmental policy and legislation and its application in the UK. In particular, it briefly charts the development of Community environmental law in order to illustrate the extent to which this can be seen as being tied to the functioning of the original European Economic Community, and the extent to which it might be said to have established more free-standing public health or environmental objectives. Particular attention is given to the development, first, of specific principles of Community environmental policy and law, and then the more general acceptance of principles with an environmental heritage in the functioning of the Community more generally. Amongst the latter are the objectives of 'sustainable development' and of integrating environmental considerations into other aspects of Community policy, both of which are now general principles of the EC Treaty governing the Community as a whole.

The Chapter also looks in some detail at the mechanisms for enforcing Community environmental law. Partly this is because of the difficulties of enforcing EC environmental law generally, which has often appeared to be something of a weakness. But it is also because the mechanisms for enforcing EC law differ from those that are used to enforce purely domestic legislation. Accordingly, this involves looking both at enforcement by the European Commission and at the scope for individuals to ensure that Member States comply with their Community obligations. It is hoped that this survey will be helpful when the substance of EC water

---

[1] Although the expression 'European Communities' was used to refer to the European Coal and Steel Community, the European Atomic Energy Community and the European Economic Community (the last of these established under the 1957 Treaty of Rome), reference to the 'Community' was commonly used to refer to the European Economic Community alone. The European Union was established under the 1992 Treaty on European Union (the Maastricht Treaty), which changed the name of the European Economic Community to the 'European Community'. The terms 'European Union' and 'European Community' are often used indiscriminately but, more precisely, the Union encompasses the Community but also extends to encompass a common foreign and security policy and co-operation in the fields of justice and home affairs. As environmental law falls primarily within the 'Community' part of the Union's activities, reference is to Community or 'EC' law and policy, and references are generally to the EC Treaty (which, following the 1997 Treaty of Amsterdam is now abbreviated to 'EC', e.g. 'Article 175 EC').

legislation, and the various Environmental Action Programmes on which it is based, are considered in the following chapter.

As far as references to the European Community Treaty are concerned, this was amended and renumbered under the 1997 Treaty of Amsterdam, which came into force on 1 May 1999. As a rule, references are generally to the new Articles of the EC Treaty with the old Article numbers in brackets. Where the discussion is of a historic nature, however, this is reversed so that reference is made to the original Article number of the Treaty, with the new number referred to in brackets afterwards.[2]

## 4.2 The Origins of Community Environmental Law

Remarkably, the original Treaty of Rome of 1957, establishing the European Economic Community, did not provide for a Community policy in the field of the environment and did not even contain the word 'environment' or any synonym of this. Clearly, the immediate post-war need for improvement of relations between the nations of Europe, which it was envisaged could be secured by greater economic interdependency, overshadowed any need for environmental provisions in the Treaty. Accordingly, the fundamental objectives of the European Economic Community were stated as follows.

> The Community shall have as its task, by establishing a common market and progressively approximating the economic policies of member states, to promote throughout the Community a harmonious development of economic activities, a continuous and balanced expansion, an increase in stability, an accelerated raising of the standard of living, and closer relations between the states belonging to it.[3]

Despite the absence of any explicit provision in respect of environmental policy, it subsequently became apparent that the objectives of the Community should be interpreted to encompass environmental matters. Environmental degradation does not respect national boundaries and was, therefore, of general concern to the Member States of the Community. An initial basis for an implicit environmental policy lay in the economic need for realisation of the internal market as 'an area without frontiers in which the free movement of goods, persons, services and capital is ensured'.[4] In relation to this, a significant concern was the need to avoid trade barriers by harmonising national environmental legislation and to avoid distortions of competition between industrial operations based in different Member

---

[2] With some changes, the Amsterdam Treaty renumbered the following Articles of the Treaty which are most widely cited below. Article 100 became Article 94; Article 100A became Article 95; Articles 130R-T became Articles 174-176; Articles 169-173 became Articles 226-230; and Article 235 became Article 308. Reference to the Treaty following Amsterdam are to Article 174 EC and so on.

[3] Art.2 Treaty of Rome 1957.

[4] Art.7a European Community Treaty.

States.[5] Without a co-ordinated approach to environmental policy, it was thought that industries in more environmentally conscious Member States would be subject to higher production costs, as a result of more stringent pollution control legislation, and competitive pressure might prevent improvement of environmental protection requirements.

Alongside internal market and competition concerns, a further reason for a Community environmental policy was derived from the objective of improving the quality of life of the citizens of the Community and the interrelationship between economic development and environmental protection. Accordingly, the Council of Ministers found a justification for the establishment of an environmental policy in that combination of concerns in stating, following the 1972 Stockholm Conference on the Human Environment, that

> Economic expansion is not an end in itself. Its first aim should be to enable disparities in living conditions to be reduced. It must take place with the participation of all the social partners. It should result in an improvement in the quality of life as well as in standards of living. As befits the genius of Europe, particular attention will be given to intangible values and to protecting the environment, so that progress may really be put at the service of mankind.[6]

Relatively early endorsement of the need for environmental protection in the Community was also provided by the European Court of Justice. The conflict between realising trade freedom and securing adequate environmental protection is one of the fundamental tensions within the Community and is likely to remain so for the foreseeable future.[7] Nevertheless, at a relatively early stage the Court held, in 1980, that provisions which are necessary on environmental protection grounds are justified for reasons of trade harmonisation to prevent distortions of competition in a common market.[8] Similarly, in determining the *ADBHU* (*Used Oils*) case,[9] the Court found that environmental protection was one of the 'essential objectives' of the Community which could be used to justify exceptions to principles governing freedom of trade and competition.

---

[5] Joined Cases 91-92/79 *Commission* v *Italy* [1980] ECR 1099 and 1115.

[6] For the text of the communiqué of the Paris meeting on 19 and 20 October 1972 see Cmnd 5109.

[7] This conflict is perhaps best illustrated by the interrelationship between Art.28 EC (ex Art.30), which guarantees free movement of goods by prohibiting imposition of import quotas ('quantitative restrictions') and other trade measures having equivalent effect, and Art.30 EC (ex Art.36) which justifies measures which may have the effect of hindering imports on grounds of public morality, policy or security; the protection of health and life of humans, animals and plants; the protection of national treasures possessing artistic, historic or archaeological value; or the protection of industrial and commercial property. Notable in the list of justifications for impeding the free movement of goods is the absence of any explicit environmental justification.

[8] See Case 91/79 *Commission* v *Italy* [1980] ECR 1099.

[9] Case 240/83 *Procureur de la République* v *Association de Défense des Brûleurs d'Huiles Usagées* [1985] ECR 531 at 549.

## 4.3  Environmental Legislative Competence

### 4.3.1  Early Environmental Legislative Competence

The development of a significant body of Community environmental law can be traced back to the early 1970s and the adoption of the first of six Environmental Action Programmes.[10] The adoption of legislation was usually on the basis of Article 100 of the EEC Treaty (now Article 94 EC) harmonising laws on the common market and occasionally Article 235 EEC (now Article 308 EC), a residual provision. As amended, Article 94 EC now provides that

> The Council shall, acting unanimously on a proposal from the Commission and after consulting with the European Parliament and the Economic and Social Committee, issue directives for the approximation of such laws, regulations and administrative provisions of the Member States as directly affect the establishment or functioning of the common market.

Article 308 EC now provides that

> If action by the Community should prove necessary to attain, in the course of the operation of the common market, one of the objectives of the Community and this Treaty has not provided for the necessary powers, the Council shall, acting unanimously on a proposal from the Commission and after consulting the European Parliament, take the appropriate measures.

The close link between these Articles and the realisation of a common market is to be noted. However, because of the perception that meeting environmental concerns was an aspect of the common market, this was not seen as problematic. Nevertheless, the European Court did emphasise the need for a link with the common market in such legislation:

> It is by no means ruled out that provisions on the environment may be based on Article 100 [now Article 94] of the Treaty. Provisions which are necessary by considerations relating to the environment and health may be a burden upon the undertakings to which they apply and if there is not harmonisation of national provisions on the matter, competition may be appreciably distorted.[11]

The link with Community objectives which was required under both Articles 100 and 235 might have been problematic at a time when the status of environmental matters as an objective of the Community was unclear. But in part because during this early period all Community legislation was enacted unanimously, no formal constitutional objections were raised and no significant hindrance emerged to the adoption of a

---

[10] See 5.2 below on the Environmental Action Programmes.
[11] Case 91/79 *Commission* v *Italy* [1980] ECR 1099, at p.1106.

number of water quality directives in the period before the Community's legislative competence in the environmental sphere was first addressed.

One obvious difficulty prior to the Single European Act 1986, however, was that attempts to characterise environmental concerns as being grounded in the needs of the common market were sometimes uneasily accomplished. In relation to the early water directives, the problem is well illustrated by the Freshwater Fish Waters Directive of 1978[12] which, despite its reasonably clear environmental objectives, needed formally to be founded on the Articles cited above. To accomplish this, recitals stated the following.

> Whereas differences between the provisions already in force or in preparation in the various member states as regards the quality of waters capable of supporting the life of freshwater fish may create unequal conditions of competition and thus directly affect the functioning of the common market; whereas laws in this field should be approximated as provided for by Article 100 [now Article 94] of the Treaty.

> Whereas it is necessary to couple this approximation of laws with Community action aiming to achieve, by means of wider-ranging provisions, one of the Community's objects in the field of environmental protection and the improvement of the quality of life; whereas certain specific provisions must be laid down in this connection; whereas, since the specific powers of action required to this end have not been provided for in the Treaty, it is necessary to invoke Article 235 [now Article 308] thereof.

Although the environmental justification for the Directive was clear and unanimously endorsed, the link between protecting the qualify of water for fish and the creation of unequal economic conditions in the common market looks far from convincing, and has led to confused interpretation by the Court of Justice.[13]

### 4.3.2 The Evolution of Environmental Competence

Insertion of a specific Environmental Title to the EEC Treaty came with the Single European Act 1986[14], and successive amendments to the Treaty have continued the evolution of Community competence in this area.[15]

---

[12] Directive 78/659/EEC and see 15.3.1 below.

[13] See the later characterization of this Directive by the European Court of Justice as a public health measure, at 15.3.3 below. See also the national courts characterisation of the sister Shellfish Waters Directive 79/923/EEC as economic, see 15.3.4 below.

[14] Generally on the environmental aspects of the Single European Act see Vandersmeerch (1987), Krämer (1992) and Golub (1996).

[15] On the evolution of EC environmental law see Jans (2000) pp.3-10

*4.3.2A  The Single European Act 1986*

Following the matters identified as priorities in earlier environmental action programmes,[16] amendments to the Treaty specified that Community policy on the environment should contribute to the following objectives:

(a)  preserving, protecting and improving the quality of the environment;
(b)  protecting human health; and
(c)  prudent and rational utilisation of natural resources.[17]

Community policy on the environment was also to be based on the principles that preventative action should be taken, that environmental damage should as a priority be rectified at source and that the polluter should pay.[18]

Whilst these provisions served to formalise the status of the environmental policy of the Community, further amendments were specifically concerned with the jurisdiction and legislative procedure of the Community in relation to the enactment of environmental legislation.[19] Further constraints arose in relation to the principle of subsidiarity[20] and limitations upon the legal instruments that could be used and the financing of implementation.[21] The Single European Act therefore placed the enactment of environmental legislation upon an explicit footing, established the environment as a component of the Community's other policies and removed the requirement that it should serve the purposes of the common market. But for legislation adopted under the Environmental Title, unanimous voting remained.

*4.3.2B  The Treaty on European Union 1992 ('Maastricht Treaty')*

The Treaty on European Union 1992[22] provided for further amendments of the environmental provisions of the (renamed) European Community Treaty. Many of these changes enhanced the commitment of the Community to environmental protection at a policy level, including:

(a)  inserting the precautionary principle into Community environmental law;[23]
(b)  stipulating that environmental protection requirements must be integrated in the definition and implementation of other Community policies;

---

[16] See further 5.2 below.
[17] Art.130r(1) (now Art.174(1) EC).
[18] *Ibid.* Art.130r(2) (now Arts 174(2) EC) and see 4.7 below.
[19] Under *ibid* Art.130s (now Art.175 EC).
[20] Art 130r(4) (now Art.174(4) EC) and see 4.4.2 below.
[21] *Ibid.*
[22] Generally on the environmental aspects of the Treaty on European Union see Wilkinson (1992); Somsen (1992); Freestone (1994); and Hession and Macrory (1994).
[23] See 4.7.1 below.

(c) promoting measures at international level to deal with regional or worldwide environmental problems; and

(d) aiming at a high level of protection taking into account the diversity of situations in the various regions of the Community (as opposed merely to taking economic and social differences into account as had previously been the case).[24]

In addition, qualified majority voting was provided for in relation to environmental legislation along with an extension of the legislative role of the Parliament[25] and for temporary derogations from environmental measures where costs were disproportionate for the public authorities of a Member State.[26] Hence, the cumulative effect of the amendments introduced under the Single European Act and the Treaty on European Union is that Community environmental legislation is now primarily based upon either Article 130s (now Article 175 EC) or Article 100a (now Article 95 EC) governing the internal market.[27]

### 4.3.2C The Treaty of Amsterdam 1997

The Treaty of Amsterdam 1997 came into effect on 1 May 1999.[28] This gives a greater role for the Parliament in the legislative process, requiring co-decision with the Council for nearly all environmental measures under Article 175 EC, thus applying broadly similar voting procedures to directives adopted as environmental and as internal market measures. However, disputes over the legal basis of 'environmental' measures may continue where, for example, a legal basis outside these areas is relied upon, since different degrees of influence for the institutions are preserved in some of these (e.g. the Parliament still has only a consultative role in relation to agriculture policy).[29]

Other matters of note introduced in the Amsterdam Treaty are that the objectives of the Community now specifically include promoting a 'balanced and sustainable development of economic activities' and 'a high level of protection and improvement of the quality of the environment'.[30] Environmental protection requirements must be integrated into the definition and implementation of all Community policies and activities,[31]

---

[24] Article 130r(2) EEC (now Art. 175(2) EC)

[25] Discussed at 4.10.1 below.

[26] Under Art.130s(5) of the EC Treaty (now Art.175(5) EC).

[27] Although Arts 175 and 95 EC are the main basis for environmental legislation, Community legislation in other sectors may have increasing importance in the future because of the new emphasis given to integrating environmental policy across other all sectors of Community policy (see 4.6 below on the integration principle). Accordingly, Community acts affecting the environment may also be provided for in relation to agriculture (under Article 37 EC (ex Article 43)); transport (Article 80 EC (ex Article 84)); commercial policy (Article 133 EC (ex Article 113)); and research (Article 172 EC (ex Article 130o)).

[28] Generally, see Bar and Kraemer (1998); van Calster and Deketelaere (1998) and Macrory (2000).

[29] For an example see Cases C-164 and 165/97 *Parliament* v *Council* [1999] ECR I-1139.

[30] Art. 2 EC, and see discussion of sustainable development at 4.4.1 below.

[31] Including a policy in the sphere of the environment (Art. 3(1)(l) EC).

in particular, with a view to promoting sustainable development,[32] thus elevating the integration principle into a general principle of Community law rather than applying only where measures are being adopted under the Environmental Title.[33]

## 4.4 Fundamental Concepts of Community Environmental Legislation

Various principles of environmental policy have been established in amendments to the EC Treaty as requirements for Community environmental legislation. As these are now provided for, the key concepts, objectives and principles are summarised in the following sections. However, from the outset it must be noted that there are some uncertainties as to the interpretation and status of these. In many respects it is far from clear whether the concepts at issue are to be regarded as stating political, policy or legally justiciable principles, and their relative priority and relationship to specific legal enactments is often rather obscure.[34]

### 4.4.1 Sustainable Development

Paramount amongst the objectives which govern EC environmental policy is the concept of 'sustainable development', which has been popularly defined, at international level, as 'development that meets the needs of the present without compromising the ability of future generations to meet their own needs'.[35]

The present international legal basis of the principle of sustainable development lies in the United Nations Conference on Environment and Development, 'The Earth Summit', held at Rio de Janeiro, Brazil, in June 1992. This Conference was convened for the purpose of promoting the further development of international environmental law and specifically to examine the feasibility of elaborating general rights and obligations of States in the field of the environment.[36] Amongst the products of the Conference,[37] the Rio Declaration on Environment and Development was most significant in emphasising the importance of the concept of sustainable development and, though the expression is not formally defined at any point in the Declaration, it is a theme which runs through the initial principles and which, cumulatively, serve to indicate its meaning in international law.

Nevertheless, Principle 1 of the Rio Declaration states that human beings are at the centre of concerns for sustainable development, and that they are

---

[32] Art. 6 EC.

[33] Arts 174-176 EC (ex Article 130r-s).

[34] Generally see Wilkinson (1992), McIntyre (1994) and Tromans (1995).

[35] World Commission on Environment and Development (1987).

[36] For an overview see Johnson (1993). For a critical response see Pallemaerts (1993).

[37] The Conference produced five distinct instruments: the Rio Declaration on Environment and Development; the Framework Convention on Climate Change; the Convention on Biological Diversity; a non-binding Declaration on Forests; and Agenda 21.

entitled to a healthy and productive life in harmony with nature. Principle 3 requires that the right to development must be fulfilled so as equitably to meet developmental and environmental needs of present and future generations. Principle 4 asserts that in order to achieve sustainable development, environmental protection must constitute an integral part of the development process and cannot be considered in isolation from it. Principle 5 requires that all states and all people must co-operate in the essential task of eradicating poverty as an indispensable requirement of sustainable development, in order to decrease the disparities in standards of living and better meet the needs of the majority of the people of the world. Principle 8 states that to achieve sustainable development and a higher quality of life for all people, states should reduce and eliminate unsustainable patterns of production and consumption and promote appropriate demographic policies. Thus, despite the absence of any precise definition of 'sustainable development', the concept is placed at the centre of the stage in global international environmental law. As a policy commitment, therefore, if not as a matter of law, the task falls to the EC[38] and the Member States to interpret the concept in a way that permits practical application to specific issues such as the protection of water quality.

In EC environmental policy, achieving sustainable development is construed as entailing the preservation of

> the overall balance and value of natural capital stock, redefinition of short, medium and long-term cost-benefit evaluation criteria and instruments to reflect the real socio-economic effects and values of consumption and conservation, and the equitable distribution and use of resources between nations and regions over the world as a whole.[39]

The all-encompassing nature of the task of achieving the desired balance between development and the protection of the environment for the future entails a need to give effect to these concerns. In particular, this must be done through formulating economic and sectoral policies, in the decisions of public authorities, in the conduct and development of production processes and in individual behaviour and choice.[40] Clearly, the status of sustainable development as a legal imperative lies at the centre of a very much more broadly-based collection of policy initiatives.

Whilst the need to progress towards a state of sustainable development is frequently recognised in Community documentation, it is only very recently that this has become a foundational objective of the Community. Following amendments made under the Treaty of Amsterdam, the EC Treaty now includes amongst the objectives of the Community the promotion throughout the Community of a 'harmonious, balanced and sustainable development of economic activities', together with 'sustainable and non-inflationary growth respecting the environment' and 'a high level

---

[38] The EC is a signatory to both the Rio Declaration and Agenda 21.

[39] *Towards Sustainability*, COM(92)23 final, para.5.

[40] *Ibid* para.4.

of protection and improvement of the quality of the environment'.[41] It is debatable whether objectives relating to sustainable development and sustainable growth are mutually consistent. More generally, even within the concept of sustainable development there is an inherent vagueness because of the impossibility of predicting the impact of present measures upon future generations. Nevertheless, it is worth mentioning here that the principle that environmental considerations be integrated into all other Community policy areas is specifically stated to be 'with a view to promoting sustainable development'.[42] This has led the Court of Justice to emphasise the extent to which sustainable development involves a balancing of environmental and non-environmental considerations.[43] Nevertheless, the difficulty remains that the concept itself offers little guidance on the respective weight to be given to these respective interests.

### 4.4.2 Subsidiarity

The requirement now referred to as 'subsidiarity' was originally introduced into the EEC Treaty specifically to address environmental actions. Thus, the Treaty, as amended by the 1986 Single European Act, stipulated that 'the Community shall take action relating to the environment to the extent to which the objectives . . . can be attained better at Community level than at the level of the individual Member States'.[44] However, the Treaty on European Union extended the application of the subsidiarity principle to make it operative in all areas which do not fall within the exclusive competence of the EC. Hence, the EC Treaty now provides that

> in areas which do not fall within its exclusive competence, the Community shall take action, in accordance with the principle of subsidiarity, only if and in so far as the objectives of the proposed action cannot be sufficiently achieved by the Member States and can, therefore, by reason of the scale or effects of the proposed action, be better achieved by the Community.[45]

Accordingly, it is now necessary that this requirement is complied with before any action is taken by the Community either in relation to the environment or any other matter within its non-exclusive competence.

However, the formal necessity that subsidiarity should be respected before action is taken by the EC does not elucidate the critical issues as to when a proposed objective cannot be 'sufficiently achieved' by a Member State or

---

[41] Art.2 EC.

[42] See further 4.6 below.

[43] Case C-371/98 *R* v *Secretary of State for the Environment, Transport and the Regions, ex parte First Corporate Shipping Ltd*, [2001] 1 CMLR 19, per Advocate General.

[44] Art.130r(4) EEC Treaty, as amended by the Single European Act.

[45] Art.5 EC (ex Art.3b).

when that objective can be 'better' achieved by the Community.[46] In some contexts, environmental problems are recognised to have transboundary characteristics, or environmental action by individual Member States may generate distortions of competition and barriers to trade of a kind that EC environmental policy was initiated to avoid, and 'better' might then be understood to mean preferable in avoiding these consequences. Alternatively, 'better' could be interpreted to mean 'quicker, more effective, cheaper, more efficient, closer to the citizen . . ., more democratic, more uniform, more consistent with other measures in parts of the industrialised world, or the global or the European Community' without any of these interpretations necessarily being inappropriate.[47] Presumably, however, an environmental problem which could be characterised as purely national, regional or local would not justify action by the Community because of the subsidiarity requirement. Whether there are actually any aspects of water quality management which fall into this category however, is a matter of argument.[48]

At the meeting of the Council at Edinburgh in 1992,[49] it was resolved that the Commission should provide detailed justification for all new legislative proposals and that proposals which were not justified under the subsidiarity requirement should be withdrawn.[50] Following this, there was speculation about an extensive programme of repealing earlier directives which, it was alleged primarily by the Governments of the UK and France, failed to comply with the subsidiarity requirement, and the 'repatriation' of the substance of these measures into matters of national law of the Member States. Prominent candidates for repatriation were environmental directives in the area of water quality.[51]

However, when the implications of subsidiarity came to be formally considered at national level the arguments for 'subsidiarisation' were not accepted. In considering a proposal for a revised directive concerning the quality of bathing water,[52] the House of Lords Select Committee on the European Communities[53] noted the ambivalent stance of the Government on the matter: whilst the Government did not consider that there was a

---

[46] Not least because of the diffusion of power from local to international level; see de Búrca (1999). There is a Protocol to the Amsterdam Treaty on Application of the Principles of Subsidiarity and Proportionality, but this provides little further guidance, at least on subsidiarity.

[47] See Krämer (2000) p.13.

[48] The closest example is probably drinking water supplies, on which see 17.7 below.

[49] COM(93)47 final.

[50] See European Commission report to the European Council on the adaptation of Community legislation to the subsidiarity principle, COM(93)545 final.

[51] Generally see Axelrod (1994), Wils (1994) and Jewkes (1994).

[52] COM(94)36 final and see 5.5.2 below.

[53] House of Lords Select Committee on the European Communities, *Bathing Water* (1994), paras 59-65, and see also House of Lords Select Committee on the European Communities, *Drinking Water* (1996) paras 77-80 where the Committee considered a proposal for revisions to the Drinking Water Quality Directive (80/778/EEC) (see COM (94) 612 final) and expressed the view that legally binding minimum standards for drinking water in the Community were highly desirable and the proposal was well-justified in drawing proper distinctions between matters for action by Member States and by the Community. On revisions to the Drinking Water Quality Directive see 17.7.8 below.

'strong' case for the Community to set minimum standards for bathing waters, there was no support for outright repeal of existing Community legislation on bathing waters, and to do so would be 'politically unrealistic'. Hence, pragmatism prevailed on the question of subsidiarity, although concerns were raised as to whether the cost of the proposed directive was proportionate to the potential benefits which might be secured.

While subsidiarity may have had little impact on the division of competences between the Member States and the Community in the environmental field, it has certainly affected the content of Community environmental law. As one commentator has put it, there has been a move from concerns focusing on 'who does what' to the different issue of 'what it is they actually do', thus conflating subsidiarity with pressures towards deregulation.[54] A particular impact has been the subtle reorientation of new proposals towards greater flexibility. This is seen most clearly in the exercise of discretion, primarily at national level, and both legislatively and judicially: changes to the form and intensity of legislation, and a greater willingness to apply and interpret this flexibly and to bolster this approach through a preference for decentralised enforcement methods.[55] For example, there has been some shift in the Drinking Water Quality Directive towards regulating only for essential quality and health-related parameters, and Member States are now given greater flexibility in monitoring water quality.[56] Similarly, there is the prospect that amendments to the Bathing Water Directive might, for the first time, make distinct provision for different waters depending on natural differences in, e.g., pH, turbidity and salinity, requiring standards to be set with respect to what is 'normal', which will vary across the EC.[57]

The impact of subsidiarity can also be seen in relation to enforcement and liability issues. There can be little doubt that the climate of subsidiarity has acted to prevent any major shift in enforcement functions from the Member States to the Community, and proposals for an environmental liability directive are, in essence, limited in the sites to be protected to areas of 'Community' biodiversity interest.[58] Subsidiarity has also had an impact on how strict the obligations on the Member States are, that is, how much flexibility they are given in meeting objectives. Generally, the trend has been away from the setting of very prescriptive standards to the use of more flexible mechanisms such as the use of 'best available techniques' or, in relation to water quality, achieving 'good status'.[59] On the other hand, for priority substances the Water Framework Directive takes a more absolutist approach, requiring that discharges cease or be phased out over a

---

[54] Flynn (1997).

[55] See generally Scott (1998) Chs. 1 and 2.

[56] See 17.7.8 below on revisions to the Drinking Water Quality Directive.

[57] See 5.5.2 below on revisions to the Bathing Waters Directive.

[58] See, respectively, 4.14 below and 3.20.2 above.

[59] See, respectively, 12.3.3 below on best available techniques in integrated pollution prevention and control, and 5.8.2 on good status under the Water Framework Directive.

set period of time, albeit that the language of the requirement to do so is somewhat vague.[60]

### 4.4.3 Proportionality

Closely associated with the idea of subsidiarity is what may be termed the 'proportionality principle'[61] though, again, this principle is not peculiar to the environmental policy and legislation of the Community. The proportionality principle is provided for by the requirement that action by the Community 'shall not go beyond what is necessary' to achieve the objectives of the Treaty.[62] Because of the generality at which the environmental objectives of the Treaty are stated, however, it may be difficult to establish whether a particular piece of legislation offends this requirement.

The approach taken by the Member States has been to assert that proportionality requires Community action to be 'as simple as possible, consistent with satisfactory achievement of the objective of the measure and the need for effective enforcement' and that 'other things being equal, directives should be preferred to regulations and framework directives to detailed measures'. In addition, 'Community measures should leave as much scope for national decision as possible, consistent with securing the aim of the measure and observing the requirements of the Treaty'. Both subsidiarity and proportionality generally require wide consultation and reasoned justifications for legislating.[63]

The European Court of Justice has considered the principle of proportionality in a water law context. A recent reference from the English High Court[64] raised questions about the validity of the Nitrates Directive[65] on the basis, amongst other things, that the way in which the Directive imposed obligations on farmers in designated nitrate vulnerable zones imposed disproportionate burdens on them, since the farmers might not be solely responsible for excessive nitrate concentrations in the designated zones. However, the Court of Justice did not support this line of argument, and to some extent equated the principle of proportionality with a flexible reading of the polluter pays principle[66] in observing that:

> the directive contains flexible provisions enabling the Member States to observe the principle of proportionality in the application of the

---

[60] See 5.7 below on the Water Framework Directive. It is not clear whether the obligation is an absolute one, or an obligation on the part of the Community to 'aim to achieve' it, see 5.7.3(c).

[61] See generally McIntyre (1997).

[62] Art.5 EC (ex Art.3b).

[63] See Protocol to the Amsterdam Treaty on Application of the Principles of Subsidiarity and Proportionality, and see 4.9 below on the legal status of directives and regulations.

[64] Case C-293/97 *R* v *Secretary of State for the Environment and Minister of Agriculture, Fisheries and Food, ex parte Standley* [1999] ECR I-2603.

[65] Directive 91/676/EEC, see 5.6.3 below.

[66] On the polluter pays principle see 4.7.3 below.

measures which they adopt. It is for the national courts to ensure that
that principle is observed.

Elsewhere in a water context, the Court of Justice has held that the
principle of proportionality, in the sense that it requires some consideration
of costs as against benefits, was not applicable to the Drinking Water
Quality Directive, since the aim of the Directive is to lay down a uniform
minimum public health standard.[67] In the Water Framework Directive,
however, proportionality can be seen in the provision that where a body of
water is in such a condition that it would be infeasible or unreasonably
expensive to achieve 'good status', less stringent environmental objectives
may be set.[68]

Additionally, the idea of proportionality has been analogously applied to
scrutinising national legislation in particular environmental contexts.
Hence, where common rules on the marketing of products do not exist,
obstacles to the free movement of goods resulting from disparities in
national laws have been found to be acceptable providing the rules are not
discriminatory, are necessary in order to satisfy 'mandatory requirements'
and are *proportionate* to the aim to be achieved.[69] In reality, what this
amounts to is something of an imprecise balancing of various factors,
including the deemed necessity of the national measure, its proportionality
to the objective to the pursued, and pursuing the least restrictive means of
attaining the objective.[70] Thus, for example, a measure banning the import
of live crayfish into Germany in the interests of protecting native species
from crayfish plague was held to be in violation of Articles 30 and 36 of
the EC Treaty (now Articles 28 and 30 EC), because there were less
restrictive means of preventing the spread of disease, such as health
checks.[71] It is significant that this case was exclusively concerned with
crayfish plague and not with arguments about habitat competition between
imported crayfish and native species. This has been a particular concern in
the UK, and it might be more difficult to hold that less restrictive measures
could be taken where competition rather than disease was at issue.

No examples are known of national water legislation being challenged by
the Commission for unduly restricting the free circulation of goods by
being disproportionately restrictive to the objectives being pursued.
However, national measures regulating anglers' lead weights due to
ecological concerns were amended so that they only prohibited their
supply rather than also banning their import.[72] Presumably, however, it

---

[67] Case C-237/90 *Commission* v *Germany* [1992] ECR I-5973.

[68] Art. 4(5) Water Framework Directive, and see 5.9.4 below.

[69] Case 120/78 *Cassis de Dijon* [1979] ECR 649 and, in an environmental context, Case 302/86
*Commission* v *Denmark* ('Danish Bottles') [1988] ECR 4607.

[70] Scott (1998) p.69.

[71] Case C-131/93 *Commission* v *Germany* [1994] ECR I-3303. Note that the case was brought
before a harmonising directive on fish health (91/67/EEC) was adopted, after which the scope for
Member States to take unilateral action of this kind would have been reduced to those limited
protections contained in Art.100a(4) (now Art.95(5)-(9) EC).

[72] See the Control of Pollution (Anglers' Lead Weights) (Amendment) Regulations 1993 (SI 1993
No. 49), discussed at 12.4.6 below.

would be open to national governments to establish stricter regulation in this area within the scope of the proportionality requirement.

### 4.5 Objectives of Community Environment Policy

It is stated that Community environment policy 'shall contribute to the pursuit of' four objectives:

(a) preserving, protecting and improving the quality of the environment;
(b) protecting human health;
(c) prudent and rational utilisation of natural resources; and
(d) promoting measures at international level to deal with regional or worldwide environmental problems.[73]

The first of these objectives leaves open the question of how the 'environment' is to be defined[74] and, specifically, whether the concept is to be confined to the three environmental media of water, air and land,[75] or whether it is to be more broadly construed to encompass the species and ecosystems which are dependent upon those media. Similarly, the lack of an explicit definition of the key expression leaves it uncertain whether landscape features or man-made features fall within the concept. For example, it is not clear whether it would include aesthetic qualities associated with reservoirs, or just the ambient quality of the water in them.[76] Beyond the definition of 'environment', however, there are a number of potentially intractable policy issues as to what is to count as 'preserving', 'protecting' and 'improving' and how these are to be reconciled in instances of conflict.[77]

The second objective, of protecting human health, is again broadly formulated in that it might be construed to encompass diverse matters that might not be thought to have any particular environmental dimension. These might include, for example, the protection of consumers from products which are damaging to health or otherwise dangerous, or matters of general public health concern such as the spread of disease. It would

---

[73] Art.175(1) EC (ex Art.130r(1)).

[74] No definition of 'environment' is provided elsewhere in the EC Treaty, but the term is defined in various secondary legislation; see, for example, the Environmental Impact Assessment Directive (85/337/EEC), Art.3 of which requires assessments to identify, describe and assess the direct and indirect effects of a project on the following factors: 'human beings, fauna and flora; soil, water, air, climate and the landscape; the interaction between [these] factors; material assets and the natural heritage' (see 14.6.1 below).

[75] This is the approach taken in the Pollution Prevention and Control Act 1999, which states that ' "environmental" pollution means pollution of the air, water or land', although it is further provided that environmental pollution arises if there is 'harm', which includes harm to ecological systems from pollution of the environmental media (s.1(2) and (3)). See 12.3.5 below.

[76] Generally, Community law has not ventured greatly into matters of landscape, for the twin reasons that it concerns land and because of the subjectivity involved.

[77] Useful illustrations of how this provision is interpreted in practice can be seen in the Water Framework Directive, which contains a wide variety, and hierarchy, of objectives; see 5.7–9 below.

seem sensible, however, to interpret the objective as being limited to the protection of human health *from adversities of an environmental kind*.[78] Hence, for example, in water-related contexts, directives concerned with the quality of bathing water and drinking water[79] have cited the need for protection of human health as being amongst their justifications.

The third objective, of securing prudent and rational utilisation of natural resources, appears to be closely linked with the idea of sustainable development, previously discussed. However, its extent is unclear due to the lack of a definition as to what counts as a 'resource' for these purposes. The concept of a 'resource' is usually taken to encompass some kind of raw material or facility that is capable of utilisation, commonly for economic advantage. Most characteristically, vegetable and mineral materials and natural capacities for the generation of energy might fall into this category.[80] The inherent difficulty is whether, or in what sense, natural flora and fauna, and the ecosystems of which they form a part, can be conceived of as being 'utilised' as a 'resource', either in the sense of being consumed for use, as with the abstraction of groundwater beyond natural recharge levels, or even by 'using' the natural capacity of the environment to assimilate a degree of pollution or contamination. In some instances, such as fisheries, the terminology is unproblematic; in others, where the real objective is that of nature conservation or environmental protection for its own sake, the wording seems inappropriate.[81]

The fourth objective, of promoting measures at international level to deal with regional or worldwide environmental problems, was introduced under the Treaty on European Union to clarify what appears to have been the long and well-established practice of the Community being a party to conventions with intra- and extra-territorial objectives. Specific water-related examples of this include the 1974 Paris Convention on the prevention of marine pollution from land-based sources[82] and, more recently, its successor treaty the 1992 'OSPAR' Convention for the Protection of the Marine Environment of the North East Atlantic.[83]

Generally, in relation to the four stated objectives of Community environment policy, no indication of priority or relative status is given, and no indication as to how conflicts between the objectives might be resolved. Moreover, the objectives provide no guidance as to how Community

---

[78] Similarly, see Vandermeersch (1987), at p.414.

[79] Directive 76/160/EEC and Directive 80/778/EEC, see respectively 5.5.2 and 17.7.1 below.

[80] Although it must be noted that an annex to the Single European Act, which originally introduced this objective, stated that 'the Community's activities in the sphere of the environment may not interfere with national policies regarding the exploitation of energy resources'. However, there is some uncertainty as to the legal status of this declaration and, perhaps significantly, it was not reiterated in the Treaty on European Union. However, matters significantly affecting a Member States choice of energy supplies may only be agreed by a unanimous vote (Art.175(2) EC).

[81] The Water Framework Directive, Recital 28, remarks that 'Surface waters and groundwaters are in principle renewable natural resources'.

[82] Decision 75/437/EEC.

[83] Decision 98/249/EC. On the OSPAR Convention see 18.8 below.

environment policy is placed alongside other tasks of the Community and how conflicts between objectives are to be resolved.

Alongside the four stated objectives, the Treaty provides that 'Community policy on the environment shall aim at a high level of protection taking into account the diversity of situations in the various regions of the Community'.[84] Again the generality and imprecision of this objective is notable. 'A high level of protection' might be conceived as requiring the highest level of protection imaginable, though this approach has not been followed in other policy areas.[85] Alternatively, it can be seen as a relative measure of the level of environmental protection as compared with the position in Member States. The requirement that this should 'take into account the diversity of situations in the various regions of the Community' might indicate that the latter is the more appropriate interpretation. If this is so, a 'high level of protection' would refer to the level of protection in those Member States with more stringent environmental protection requirements, though not necessarily the Member State with the *highest* level of environmental protection. However, it is submitted that a high level of protection requires going beyond current best practice in the Community, and is more aspirational in character. It could involve looking in practice in non-EC European countries (such as Switzerland or Norway),[86] but there appears no reason in principle why it should be limited to what is presently achievable. Indeed, there are many obligations which aim for improvements over long periods of time, which are presently impossible to achieve.[87]

### 4.6 The Principle of Environmental Integration

Following the Amsterdam Treaty, Article 6 of the EC Treaty provides that environmental protection requirements must be 'integrated into the definition and implementation of' all other Community policy areas listed in Article 3 EC, 'in particular with a view to promoting sustainable development'.[88] One of the most significant changes made to EC environmental law by the Amsterdam Treaty was to elevate this 'integration' principle from its previous location in the Environmental Title of the EC Treaty,[89] and explicitly to link it with the pursuit of sustainable development. This has the consequence that, unlike the other environmental policy principles, the integration principle operates when *any* Community proposals are being considered or adopted, not simply when a measure is proposed for adoption under the Environmental Title. A further consequence is that it also provides some guidance on what sustainable development might require. The integration principle is

---

[84] Art.175(2) EC (ex Art.130r(2)). See also Art.95(3) EC (ex Art.100a(3)) which provides for a similar requirement in relation to the approximation of laws.
[85] Case C-233/94 *Germany* v *Parliament and Council* [1997] ECR I-2405 (consumer protection).
[86] See Krämer (2000) p.8.
[87] See, e.g., the phased implementation of the Water Framework Directive, at 5.9.21 below.
[88] See also 4.4.1 above on sustainable development.
[89] See previously Art.130r(2) EC Treaty.

potentially the most wide-ranging of all the environmental principles and for that reason, perhaps, the most significant.[90]

A legal analysis of the integration principle suggests that integration is primarily a procedural requirement.[91] Although not purely exhortatory,[92] neither is it clearly justiciable.[93] And while the legal status of the principle of integration has been debated in disputes over the legal base of a measure,[94] it remains an open question whether the principle can constrain Community activities if they fail to reflect the integration concept, or even if it requires positive steps to be taken.[95]

Recognising its limited legal enforceability, the extent and mechanism for applying the integration principle is far from clear. It is doubtful whether the need for 'integration' could be construed as an allocation of any priority to the environment over other matters.[96] More likely, what is envisaged is that environmental factors should be considered at the stages when other Community policies are being formulated and put into effect, and in this respect a further development under the Amsterdam Treaty was a Declaration noting that 'the Commission undertakes to prepare environmental impact assessment studies when making proposals which may have significant environmental implications'.[97] This formulation, however, falls short of a guarantee that a more strategic form of environmental assessment procedure will be applied to policy formulation to ensure environmental acceptability.[98]

The need for greater integration in Community policy can be seen from the many examples of *disintegration* between the EC's environmental policy and its other policy areas, including the completion of the internal market, structural funding and transport policy,[99] all of which have had a direct, and adverse, effect on Community water quality. To give one specific example of institutional disintegration, EC funding was once provided to

---

[90] Macrory (2000).

[91] Hession and Macrory (1998).

[92] The conclusion of the Court in Case C-62/88, *Parliament* v *Council* [1990] ECR I-1527 ('Chernobyl I') was that the integration principle in its slightly weaker pre-Maastricht version implied that 'all Community measures must satisfy the requirements of environmental protection' has been taken as hinting at 'more than a mere enabling provision', Hession and Macrory, *ibid*.

[93] Notwithstanding the Opinion of Advocate General Cosmas in Case C-321/95P *Stichting Greenpeace Council* v *Commission* [1998] 3 CMLR 1 who was prepared to find that the integration principle was capable of direct effect, although the Court was silent on this point. Contrast transport policy: Case C13/83 *Parliament* v *Council* [1985] ECR 1513.

[94] For example, in Case C-300/89 *Commission* v *Council* ('Titanium Dioxide') [1991] ECR I-2867 the Court considered that the principle of integration implied that 'a Community measure cannot be covered by Art.130s [now Art.175] merely because it also pursues objectives of environmental protection'.

[95] Hession and Macrory (1998).

[96] See further Case C-371/98 *R* v *Secretary of State for the Environment, Transport and the Regions, ex parte First Corporate Shipping Ltd*, Opinion of A-G Léger, 7 March 2000.

[97] Declaration 12 to the Treaty of Amsterdam.

[98] On strategic environmental assessment see http://europa.eu.int/comm/environment/eia/home.htm

[99] See, e.g. Sheate (1997) and Nollkaemper (1997).

support intensive fish farming projects in areas in the Mediterranean whilst the Commission was, at the same time, providing financial assistance to environmental groups seeking to purchase those areas to protect them from over-exploitation.[100] The Court of Auditors has also raised more specific concerns about the extent to which Community structural funding has been given for projects that fail to meet EC water quality standards, in particular under the Directives on Urban Waste Water Treatment, Nitrates and Sewage Sludge.[101]

As to the legal enforceability of the integration principle, the principle has been prominent in cases where it was argued that insufficient account was taken of environmental considerations by the Commission wrongfully allocating funding to projects with adverse environmental consequences.[102] A good example of this was the dispute about the allocation of structural funds for a visitors', or 'interpretative', centre in a nature reserve at Mullaghmore in Ireland which, amongst other concerns, involved the construction of a waste water treatment plant which may have had adverse impacts upon groundwater quality.[103] Specifically, the objectives of providing structural funds require that the project concerned must be in keeping with Community policy on environmental protection.[104] However, following an investigation into the matter, the Commission announced that the project did not infringe Community environmental law and there was no obstacle to the grant of structural funding to assist the project. Legal proceedings challenging this substantive decision were unsuccessful as, to some extent, were further proceedings on access to information upon which the funding decision was based.[105] The basis on which the European Courts dismissed the application by the challengers was because, it was alleged, there was no 'legal act' by the Commission to be challenged. The Commission had merely approved, in conjunction with national partners, the funding of a more general 'Operational Programme' for tourism in Ireland, while it was the Irish Government that had put forward plans for the visitors' centre and therefore taken 'the decision'. This was notwithstanding the fact that the Commission reserved the right to veto any Operational Programme. The Mullaghmore case, and a later challenge by Greenpeace to Community funding for two power stations in Spain,[106]

---

[100] Court of Auditors *Special Report No.3/92 concerning the environment*, OJ C245/1, 1992.

[101] *Special Report No. 3/98 concerning the implementation by the Commission of EU policy and action as regards water pollution, together with replies by the Commission* OJ C191/2, 1998. On the Directives mentioned see 5.6 below.

[102] Generally see Scott (1996).

[103] See Case T-461/93 *An Taisce and WWF (UK)* v *Commission* [1994] ECR II-733 at para.9 and, on appeal, Case C-325/94 [1996] ECR I-3727. On the Groundwater Directive see 5.4.2 below.

[104] Regulation 2052/88/EEC on the objectives of structural funds, Art.7. See now Regulation (EC) 1260/1999 laying down general provisions on the Structural Funds, which now provides for greater procedural scrutiny of environmental compatibility (see Arts 2(5), 12, 26(1)(g) and 41(2)(b) and see also 4.7.3(a) below.

[105] Case C-325/94P *An Taisce and WWF (UK)* v *Commission* [1996] ECR I-3727; and Case T-105/95 *WWF (UK)* v *Commission* [1997] Env LR 242.

[106] Case C-321/95P *Stichting Greenpeace Council* v *Commission* [1998] 3 CMLR 1. An action was brought to annul the Commission funding because of infringement of the integration principle, but declared inadmissible because the applicants were held to lack sufficient legal standing under Art.173 (now Art.230 EC) and the European Court did not determine the integration issue.

demonstrates the extent to which effective environmental integration requires more than a commitment to policy integration, but also a wider recognition of environmental interests in the practical process of Community administration.

Although the potential benefits of incorporating environmental requirements in other sectors of Community policy are immense, the results so far remain limited. Nevertheless, there have been some positive developments, including the adoption of legislation intended to integrate environmental protection into the Community Agriculture Policy (CAP). In this area, the potential conflicts between agricultural production and environmental damage are immense,[107] and yet the early history of the CAP[108] demonstrated support for various kinds of agricultural intensification that are now recognised to have caused incalculable harm to the environment. To a very limited extent, these negative impacts were addressed in reforms to the CAP which ushered in the enactment of a number of instruments for various purposes concerning environmental improvement in agricultural practice.[109]

Perhaps the best example of this kind was the replacement of the previous legislation on agricultural structures[110] by a Regulation on agricultural production methods compatible with the maintenance of the countryside.[111] This 'Agri-Environment' Regulation aimed at a reduction of pollution caused by agriculture and took into account the function of farmers in nature conservation and the protection of landscapes. Specifically, it provided incentives for reducing the use of fertilisers and plant protection products, including the provision of support for organic farming, for the extensification of crop and livestock production and the voluntary long-term set aside of areas of farmland. These reforms have been continued, again in incremental steps, by further reform of the CAP which moves policy away from price support for agricultural produce towards direct payments by benefiting environmental improvements, a more balanced use of polluting inputs and less intensive use of sensitive land,[112] although the long-term impact of these measures remains to be seen.

From within the body of Community water quality legislation,[113] perhaps the most significant measure, concerning the interrelationship between agriculture and the aquatic environment, is the Nitrates Directive[114] which

---

[107] Generally see Jones (1993) and Gardner (1996) ch.8.

[108] Based on Arts.38-47 of the EEC Treaty (see now Arts.32-38 EC). See generally Wathern (1992) and Hawke and Kovaleva (1998).

[109] See, for example, Regulation 1765/92/EEC linking compensatory payment with obligations to set-aside agricultural land; and Regulation 2092/91/EEC defining organic practices for the production of crops.

[110] See Directive 75/268/EEC on Mountain and Hill Farming in Certain Less Favoured Areas; and Regulation 797/85/EEC on Improving the Efficiency of Agricultural Structures.

[111] Regulation 2078/92/EEC.

[112] See generally Chapter V of the 'Rural Development Regulation', Regulation 1257/1999/EC.

[113] See Ch.5 below.

[114] Directive 91/676/EEC; see 5.6.3 and 13.5.4 below.

seeks to protect waters against contamination from nitrate used in agriculture. It is noted in the recitals to this Directive that

> the reform of the common agricultural policy set out in the Commission's green paper *Perspectives for the common agricultural policy* indicated that, while the use of nitrogen-containing fertilisers and manures is necessary for Community agriculture, excessive use of fertilisers constitutes an environmental risk, that common action is needed to control the problem arising from intensive livestock production and that agricultural policy must take greater account of environmental policy.

Accordingly, this key Directive makes extensive inroads into the regulation of agricultural activities through action programmes and other measures for the purpose of reducing water pollution by nitrates from agricultural sources particularly where areas are identified as nitrate vulnerable zones under the Directive. This serves as a good example of another sector of Community policy being made more responsive to environmental concerns. However, it is notable that it illustrates 'integration' of environmental policy by the imposition of an environmental measure[115] upon agriculture, rather than measures enacted under the Agriculture Title of the Treaty incorporating environmental policy.

Since political agreement was reached on elevating the integration principle into a general principle of the EC Treaty, a notable development has been publication by the Commission of a number of documents fleshing out bilateral environmental integration in other policy sectors or taking a multilateral approach involving more complex and complete patterns of co-operation. In relation to the former, a number of policy documents have been produced relating to sectors including agriculture and the single market.[116] In relation to the latter, the central document is a Commission Communication on *Partnership for Integration*.[117] This Communication recognised that practical steps towards the better implementation of the integration principle are needed within the daily work of the Community institutions involving a departure from the traditional sectoral approach to decision making. More specifically, the Communication invites the Council to recognise that implementation of the integration principle is a joint responsibility which involves a partnership between the Council, Parliament and Commission to enable integration of environmental concerns into other Community policies. It is suggested that this partnership should be based upon a number of specific guidelines, including amongst other things undertaking environmental assessments for all key policy initiatives, reviewing existing policies and

---

[115] Enacted under Art.130s of the EC Treaty (now Art.175 EC).

[116] See, respectively, *Indicators for the Integration of Environmental Concerns into the Common Agricultural Policy*, COM(2000)20 final and *Single Market and Environment*, COM(99)263 final.

[117] *Partnership for Integration – A Strategy for integrating Environment into European Union Policies*, COM(98)333 final.

generally reviewing the mechanisms of Community decision-making to ensure that the objective of integration is effectively pursued.

Despite the 1997 Treaty amendment, the uncertain status of the integration principle in dictating particular courses of legal action remains. However, the need to integrate environmental protection considerations into other areas suggests both a commitment to substantive legal and policy integration as well as procedural integration through such techniques as greater use of environmental impact assessment[118] and wider access to decision-making for bodies like environmental interest groups.[119] In some areas such as agriculture, however, policy commitments along these lines are some way off, and the emphasis at this stage is on developing what seem to be little more than weakly-worded 'indicators' of integration.[120]

### 4.7 Other Principles of Community Environment Policy

In addition to the principle of environmental integration, the Treaty specifies a number of further principles upon which EC environment policy is to be founded. Specifically, it is stated that Community environmental policy (as opposed to Community policy more generally):

> shall be based on the precautionary principle and on the principles that preventive action should be taken, that environmental damage should as a priority be rectified at source and that the polluter should pay.[121]

Accordingly, the following sections discuss the different characteristics of the three further policy principles:

(a)  the precautionary principle;
(b)  the prevention principle; and
(c)  the polluter pays principle.

It is significant that these are stated to be principles which must be adhered to in the environmental *policy* of the Community. Only where EC legislation has been adapted following a 'manifest error of appraisal' will it be susceptible to annulment by the Court of Justice.[122] This suggests that there may be some, albeit extreme, circumstances where Community secondary legislation can be challenged as not being compatible with the environmental policy principles, although for the more important measures the lengthy legislative process makes this possibility somewhat unlikely.

---

[118] On which see Declaration 12 Treaty of Amsterdam, strengthening Declaration 20 Maastricht Treaty.

[119] See the 1998 Aarhus Convention on access to information, public participation in decision-making and access to justice in environmental matters, and see 16.18 below.

[120] *Indicators for the Integration of Environmental Concerns into the Common Agricultural Policy*, COM(2000)20 final.

[121] Art.175(2) EC (ex Art.130r(2)).

[122] Case C-341/95 *Bettati* v *Safety Hi-Tech Srl* [1998] ECR I-4355.

The principles relating to precaution, prevention and to the polluter paying are stated to be subject to any 'safeguards' introduced by Member States. Hence, harmonisation measures meeting the environmental policy principles must include, where appropriate, a safeguard clause allowing Member States to take provisional measures, for non-economic environmental reasons, subject to a Community inspection procedure.[123] The significance and purpose of this is difficult to ascertain. It might be construed as allowing Member States to take particular actions in extraordinary conditions to secure environmental protection despite such actions being contrary to the requirements of a particular directive. However, in part, the need for this would seem to be limited by the fact that directives frequently make explicit provision for departure by way of exceptions. Thus, for example, the Bathing Water Directive may be 'waived' in certain respects because of exceptional weather or geographical conditions or where natural enrichment occurs,[124] and the present Drinking Water Quality Directive provides for derogations to take account of the nature and structure of the ground, exceptional meteorological conditions and emergencies.[125] Whilst directives commonly provide 'safeguards' in the sense of allowing relaxation of controls in exceptional circumstances, 'safeguards' may also be allowed in the sense of allowing Member States the power to enact environmental requirements that are stricter than provided for in Community legislation. In that respect it may be noted that, in general, Member States may maintain or introduce more stringent environmental protection measures where these are compatible with the Treaty and notified to the Commission.[126]

### 4.7.1 The Precautionary Principle

Whilst Community policy on the environment should be based on the 'precautionary principle',[127] no definition is provided of this principle in the Treaty and interpretations of its meaning differ. The general idea is that action should be taken to address an environmental problem where some scientific evidence indicates that environmental harm will otherwise arise, without the need for that evidence to establish a conclusive causal link. Alternatively, a precautionary approach requires that some degree of scientific uncertainty should not be used as a justification for inaction. This contrasts with the preventive principle which is applicable to the prospect of those kinds of environmentally harmful consequences which are regarded as conclusively established.

---

[123] Art.175(2) EC (ex Art.130r(2)), and see also Art.95(10) EC (ex Art.100a(5)) which deals with similar safeguard measures in relation to the approximation of laws.

[124] Directive 76/160/EEC, Art.8 and see 5.5.2 below.

[125] Directive 80/778/EEC, Arts.9 and 10, although note that the scope for derogations is significantly altered under the revised Drinking Water Quality Directive 98/83/EC; see 17.7 below.

[126] Art.176 EC (ex Art.130t) and see also Art.95(4)-(9) EC which allows Member States to maintain or introduce higher environmental standards in relation to the approximation of laws. See 4.10.2 below.

[127] On contested meanings of the precautionary principle see O'Riordan and Cameron (1994).

The origins of the precautionary approach to environmental policy is generally traced to the national law of West Germany and the adoption of the *Vorsorgeprinzip*, the principle of precaution of foresight, in the 1970s.[128] However, different kinds of precautionary approach have been adopted in international law from a relatively early period.[129] Hence, the 1974 Paris Convention on the prevention of marine pollution from land-based sources allowed the parties to take additional measures 'if scientific evidence has established that a serious hazard may be created in the maritime area by that substance and if urgent action is necessary'.[130] In the Preamble to the 1984 Ministerial Declaration of the First International Conference on the Protection of the North Sea it was affirmed that states 'must not wait for proof of harmful effects before taking action' because damage to the marine environment can be irreversible or remedial only at considerable expense and over long periods.[131]

More recently, the 1992 OSPAR Convention for the Protection of the Marine Environment of the North East Atlantic, which the EC has ratified,[132] requires the parties to apply the precautionary principle, by virtue of which 'preventive measures are to be taken when there are reasonable grounds for concern' that pollution will arise, 'even where there is no conclusive evidence of a causal relationship between the inputs and the effects.' The OSPAR Convention also adopts a precautionary approach to the definition of pollution,[133] while the Esjberg Declaration to the Fourth North Sea Conference in 1995 agreed that the precautionary principle be adopted as the 'guiding principle' for achieving a clean North Sea, with reference to reducing discharges, emissions and hazardous substances with a goal of zero emission within 25 years.[134] This approach to precaution is more in line with its earlier formulation in the 'Vorsorgeprinzip', which emphasised that pollution reduction standards should be based on the use of best available reduction technology.[135]

Principle 15 of the Rio Declaration, however, takes a slightly more tentative approach, providing that

> in order to protect the environment, the precautionary approach shall be widely applied by States according to their capabilities. Where there are threats of serious or irreversible damage, lack of full scientific certainty should not be used as a reason for postponing cost-effective measures to prevent environmental degradation.[136]

---

[128] See von Moltke (1988).

[129] Generally see Freestone (1991); Hohmann (1994); Sands (1995) pp.208-13; Freestone and Hey (1996); and McIntyre and Mosedale (1997).

[130] Art.4(4).

[131] A7 Bremen Declaration, 1 November 1984, contained in Freestone and IJlstra (1990) p.6.

[132] Decision 98/249, OJ L104/1, 1998; see 18.8 below.

[133] OSPAR Convention, Art.2(2)(a) see 18.8.3 belo.

[134] A similar approach has been taken in relation to the reductions of radioactive substances under the OSPAR Convention, see 20.6.3 below.

[135] On the use of 'best available techniques' and similar formulations see 12.3.2–3 below.

[136] See further Freestone (1994).

By contrast, the elaboration at EC level of the precautionary principle has been relatively undeveloped. A first attempt at a detailed explanation of the policy, however, came early in 2000 with the publication of a Communication from the European Commission which sets out the Commission's guidelines to using the precautionary principle.[137] The Commission sets out the risk-based context of the precautionary principle emphasising the relationship between the principle and the management of risks which might impinge upon the environment, or human, animal or plant health. The Communication also makes it clear that the precautionary principle is not to be invoked defensively, (i.e. as a 'disguised form of protectionism') reflecting the fact that the principle has been invoked as a justification of what might more appropriately be called a 'trade ban'.[138]

In particular, the policy makes it clear that identifying an 'acceptable' level of risk is an essentially political decision, which must take into account such things as proportionality, in the sense that the steps taken must be in proportion to the risks involved,[139] an analysis of the costs and benefits associated with the measure (involving non-economic considerations such as public acceptability of other options and their effectiveness), and consistency (in relation to the measures taken in similar areas). The requirement of a cost-benefit justification for precautionary action, however, raises some difficult questions as to how cost-benefits are to be assessed given that the circumstances under consideration are necessarily uncertain and the risks involved are, therefore, difficult if not impossible to quantify.[140]

Within European Community water legislation, it has been suggested that the precautionary approach played an important part in setting some of the parameters in the Drinking Water Quality Directive, where, for example the parameter concerning pesticides amounts to a surrogate zero in the context of the detection limits at the time of enactment of the Directive.[141] Perhaps a stricter precautionary approach is to be found in the Urban Waste Water Treatment Directive which allows certain waste water discharges to be subject to less stringent treatment than is generally required by the Directive providing that 'comprehensive studies indicate that discharges will not adversely effect the environment'.[142] In this formulation, there is a shifting of the burden of proof whereby it needs positively to be shown on the basis of 'comprehensive' evidence that harm will *not* arise, as opposed to other formulations which rest upon it being shown that there is some evidence that harm *will* arise.

---

[137] *Communication on the Precautionary Principle*, COM(2000)1.

[138] E.g., in relation to the French and German ban on British beef, although this might be contrasted with the EC's own use of precaution in relation to beef hormones, on which see *EC Measures Concerning Meat and Meat Products (Hormones)* WT/D526/AB/R and WT/D548/AB/R.

[139] On proportionality more generally see 4.4.3 above.

[140] On costs and benefits issues generally see 6.14 below.

[141] Directive 80/778/EEC; see 17.17.1 below.

[142] Directive 91/271/EEC, Art.6(2) and see 5.6.2 below.

The precautionary approach may also be illustrated by controls upon products to prevent environmentally harmful substances being sold: a strategy that is capable of being more effective than attempting to regulate the emission of diffuse pollutants.[143] This approach is exemplified by a Directive requiring the classification, packaging and labelling of chemical products and which has been amended to require substances to be notified to the Commission before they are placed on the market.[144] The notification must be supplemented by the results of tests conducted by the manufacturer or importer to evaluate the risk posed by the substance to human beings and the environment, and products may not be marketed until Member States have had the opportunity to consider the proposal. Even where these procedures have been complied with, a Member State may provisionally prohibit the sale of the substance where new evidence provides a justification that the substance may constitute a hazard to human beings or the environment.

Hence, it may be generally concluded that whilst a number of instruments demonstrate the application of a precautionary approach and allow or require environmental action to be taken in circumstances of scientific uncertainty, the meaning and status of the principle remains obscure. The questions as to what degree of certainty is needed to justify action in accordance with the principle, and what kind of action should be taken, remain problematic. The requirement that Community policy should be based on the precautionary principle, and the relationship between this and the incorporation of precautionary elements in particular legislation, still leaves a good deal of scope for interpretation.

### 4.7.2  The Preventive Principle

The 'prevention rather than cure' approach has the economic attraction of avoiding environmental harm rather than seeking to undertake costly, or perhaps impractical, clean-up operations after a pollutant has been dispersed into the wider environment, and the further economic advantage of internalising external costs. However, the approach raises weighty issues as to what levels of emission into the wider environment are acceptable, to the extent that these do not give rise to 'pollution', and to what extent it is legitimate to use the capacity of the environment to dilute, disperse and assimilate contaminants. These issues lead to an intractable, and seemingly circular, debate about the respective advantages of emission limits and environmental quality objectives in environmental protection policy.[145] The priority that environmental damage should be 'rectified at source' would seem to imply a preference for emission controls, but this is only required where there would otherwise be environmental 'damage' and

---

[143] See 1.7 above on controlling diffuse sources of contamination.

[144] Directive 67/548/EEC on the approximation of laws, regulations and administrative provisions relating to the classification, packaging and labelling of dangerous substances, as amended. See also Regulation 793/93/EC on the evaluation and control of the risks of existing substances.

[145] On this tension see 1.4.5 above and 5.7.2(d) below.

the identification of this seems to require environmental quality objectives to be formulated as a priority.

The need for preventive environmental measures was a prominent theme of the *Third Action Programme on the Environment*,[146] which stressed the need for environmental information to be made more readily available and for this information to be taken into account by decision-makers regulating activities likely to have a significant effect upon the environment. This approach is well-illustrated by the Environmental Impact Assessment Directive, which reaffirms the need to prevent the creation of pollution or nuisances and requires any private or public project which is likely to have significant effect upon the environment to be the subject of prior environmental assessment of its consequences before authorisation is given for the project.[147]

Within the body of EC water legislation, the preventive approach is well-illustrated by the Groundwater Directive which imposes extensive monitoring and investigation requirements which must be adhered to before a competent authority may grant an authorisation for the discharge of certain substances to groundwater.[148] More generally, perhaps, the numerous directives that require limitations upon emissions or seek to realise environmental quality objectives may be seen as being based upon a preventive approach.[149]

Perhaps better still, as an example of the preventive approach, are controls upon the manufacture, distribution or use of products which have environmentally adverse effects. The advantage of controlling these commodities at source, as opposed to 'end-of-pipe' regulation of emissions, is clear where emissions are of a diffuse kind and difficult to regulate. At a Community level, this may be illustrated by legislation relating to the environmental impacts of pesticides such as the Directive prohibiting the placing on the market and use of certain plant protection products containing certain active substances, which requires Member States to ensure that plant protection products containing certain specified substances may neither be placed on the market nor used.[150] Amongst the prohibited substances are mercury compounds, nine persistent organo-chlorine compounds including aldrin, dieldrin, endrin, isodrin, DDT and other substances.[151]

---

[146] OJ C 1983 46/1 see 5.2 below.

[147] Directive 85/337/EEC, as amended by Directive 97/11/EC; see 14.6.1–2 below. Some attempts to characterise the EIA *Directive* as a precautionary directive (Peters, 1996) are unconvincing (Sifakis, 1998), though impact assessment *per se* is a core component of precaution.

[148] Directive 80/68/EEC discussed at 5.4.2 below.

[149] See 5.4–5 below. For national examples of preventive controls see 13.2–6 below.

[150] Directive 79/117/EEC, as amended.

[151] This is to be replaced by a system of Community-wide authorisation of plant protection products under Directive 91/414/EEC concerning the placing of plant production products on the market which includes a list of authorised ingredients and requires it to be established that a product has, amongst other things, no harmful effect, directly or indirectly on groundwater and no unacceptable influence on the environment.

In practical terms, there is much common ground between the prevention principle and the principle that environmental damage should, as a priority, be rectified at source. The 'source' principle is commonly further sub-divided into what are known as the self-sufficiency principle and the principle of damage rectification at source (or the 'proximity' principle). In practice, however, these further principles have more application to sectors like waste management, where it is provided that the Community as a whole, and increasingly the Member States individually, must be self-sufficient in waste disposal, in order to reduce the risks from the transportation of hazardous and non-hazardous waste.[152] In a sector such as water, where the release of pollutants into the aquatic environment is a process that cannot easily be reversed, the rectification at source principle may add little to the principle that pollution should be prevented.

### 4.7.3  The Polluter Pays Principle

#### 4.7.3A  Interpretations of the polluter pays principle

The requirement that environment policy should be based on the principle that the polluter should pay has considerable intuitive attractiveness but it is a principle that is immensely difficult to state with any degree of precision. It presupposes that there is a consensus of agreement about the answers to questions such as what is 'pollution'?[153] who is a polluter? what should polluters be paying for? and, perhaps most crucially, *why* should they be paying for it? Differences of view about each of these questions demonstrates the elusive foundations upon which the polluter pays principle is based.[154] Whilst, on first impression, it might be thought to be a general statement as to where responsibilities should lie in environmental cost allocation, it might alternatively be interpreted as a statement as to who should *not* be meeting costs arising from pollution, that is, non-polluters and specifically *not* the public in general. More generally, the punitive or remedial, incentive or deterrent, economic or legal status of the principle is difficult to ascertain.

An early statement of the polluter pays principle was provided by the Organisation for Economic Co-operation and Development in 1972, which suggested that

> the polluter should bear the expenses of carrying out the measures decided by public authorities to ensure that the environment is in an acceptable state. In other words, the cost of these measures should be reflected in the cost of goods and services which cause pollution in production and/or consumption. Such measures should not be

---

[152] Directive 75/442/EEC on waste, as amended by Directive 91/156/EEC, Art.5, and see Case C-2/90 *Commission v Belgium* [1992] ECR I-4431 ('Walloon Waste').

[153] On different understandings of 'pollution' see 1.3.3–6 above.

[154] Generally see Vandekerchove (1993).

accompanied by subsidies that would create significant distortions in international trade and investment.[155]

As a principle of general Community environmental policy, the polluter pays principle originates from a 1975 Council Recommendation regarding cost allocation and action by public authorities on environmental matters.[156] The Recommendation endorsed the principle in the following form:

> natural or legal persons governed by public or private law who are responsible for pollution must pay the costs of such measures as are necessary to eliminate that pollution or to reduce it so as to comply with the standards or equivalent measures which enable quality objectives to be met or, where there are no such objectives, so as to comply with the standards or equivalent measures laid down by public authorities . . . [and] measures taken by such authorities to avoid pollution should also be paid for by the polluters.

The Recommendation noted the value of charging polluters the cost of action taken to combat pollution in encouraging them to reduce pollution and in finding less polluting products and technologies. It was also noted that these costs should be allocated according to the same principles throughout the Community to avoid distortions of competition and the location of investment which would be incompatible with the proper functioning of the common market. Accordingly, it was recommended that Member States apply the polluter pays principle in national legislation by requiring persons who are responsible for pollution to pay the costs of measures which are necessary to eliminate pollution or to reduce it so as to enable environmental quality objectives to be met. Consequently, environmental protection should not, in principle, be dependent on grants of aid which place the burden of combating pollution on the Community.

However, the Council Recommendation recognised some of the difficulties involved in implementing these objectives. Whilst a 'polluter' was defined as someone who directly or indirectly damages the environment or creates conditions leading to such damage, it was recognised that pollution may be cumulative in arising from several simultaneous or consecutive causes. In such circumstances it was suggested that costs should be borne at the point in the pollution 'chain' which offers the best solution, from administrative and economic perspectives, and makes the most effective contribution towards environmental improvement. Inherently, therefore, there is some expediency, and perhaps arbitrariness, in identifying 'polluters' for the purpose of imposing expenditure costs for pollution control measures and charges which are envisaged as incentives or redistributive costs.

---

[155] OECD, *Council Recommendation on Guiding Principles concerning International Economic Aspects of Environmental Policies*, 26 May 1972, C(72)128, 14 ILM 236 (1975).
[156] Council Recommendation 75/436/Euratom, ECSC, EEC regarding cost allocation and action by public authorities on environmental matters. On the interpretation of the principle in EC environmental law generally see Krämer (1992) ch.11.

Exceptions to the polluter pays principle were envisaged where the application of 'very stringent' environmental standards is likely to lead to 'serious' economic disruption or where investment affecting environmental protection benefits from aid intended to address industrial, agricultural or regional structural problems.

In the *ex parte Standley* case,[157] a further argument advanced on behalf of the applicants was that the Nitrates Directive[158] violated the polluter pays principle because farmers in the designated nitrate vulnerable zones were having restrictions imposed upon them because of nitrate pollution, not all of which could be traced to agricultural activities. In this sense the farmers argued that they were effectively paying for pollution caused by others or, alternatively put, the non-agricultural polluters were *not* paying for water pollution by nitrate. The European Court of Justice, however, rejected this line of argument, and upheld the Directive on the basis that it only required the designation of vulnerable zones where agricultural activities made a 'significant contribution' to nitrate pollution. On reasoning which followed closely that used in relation to arguments about incompatibility with the proportionality principle, the Court in effect referred the question of whether in fact agriculture made a significant contribution to nitrate pollution back to the national courts to decide. In finding that the Nitrates Directive did not infringe the polluters pays principle, therefore, the Court suggested that a fairly wide latitude should be given in applying the principle, so that it does not require a precise attribution of responsibility for pollution but can be tempered by discretion which reflects administrative realities.

### 4.7.3B  The polluter pays principle and subsidies to polluting activities

Despite the stated need for Member States to implement the polluter pays principle, difficulties remain, both at Community and national levels, as to how funding for environmental improvement may be given without contravening the principle. At a Community level funding may be provided under the Structural Funds,[159] LIFE,[160] the Cohesion Fund[161] and

---

[157] Case C-293/97 *R* v *Secretary of State for the Environment and Minister of Agriculture, Fisheries and Food, ex parte Standley* [1999] ECR I-2603 and see 5.6.3 and 13.5.6 below.

[158] Directive 91/676/EEC, see 5.6.3 below and 13.5.4 below.

[159] Structural funds are provided for under the European Regional Development Fund, the European Social Fund, the European Agricultural Guidance and Guarantee Fund and the Financial Instrument for Fisheries Guidance. These are subject to Regulation (EC) 1260/1999 which requires that measures receiving assistance are to be in keeping with the Treaty and Community policies including environmental protection (see also 4.6 above). For a critique of structural funding and environmental protection see Scott (1996).

[160] LIFE is the Community Financial Instrument on the Environment established under Regulation 1973/92/EEC which is intended to contribute to the development and implementation of Community environmental policy and legislation by financing priority environmental actions in the Community, technical assistance for certain third countries and, exceptionally, actions concerning regional or global problems provided for under international agreements. The fields of action eligible for financial assistance under this Instrument include the promotion of sustainable development and the quality of the environment in the Community, amongst other things, by actions to reduce the discharge into the aquatic environment of nutritive substances and potentially

under other budgets. In each case the balance between securing environmental benefits on the one hand and 'paying polluters' on the other is an immensely difficult one to draw.

In relation to the polluter pays principle, the Community has recognised that subsidies to national industries to reduce emissions represent a 'second-best solution' from the perspective of the polluter pays principle, against a background of a general Treaty prohibition on state aids subject to various, largely non-environmental, exceptions.[162] However, Community guidelines lay down rules governing the extent to which Member States may assist national industries to improve their environmental protection capacities. These allow for a certain measure of subsidies to adapt existing plant, or invest in new plant, to meet existing environmental standards, or to go beyond mere compliance.[163]

*4.7.3C  The polluter pays principle and other environmental policy principles*

A more fundamental point about the polluter pays principle is that the justification of the principle might be brought into question insofar as it is inconsistent with other principles and objectives of Community environment policy. In the first place the polluter pays principle seems inconsistent with the preventive principle, and the requirement that environmental damage should 'as a priority' be rectified at source. If this priority is fully observed there should be little scope for requiring polluters to be paying for pollution, since 'pollution' simply would not arise; the 'polluter' would only pay for any abatement costs.

Second, the idea of 'paying' for polluting activities seems difficult to reconcile with the ultimate objective of realising sustainable development.[164] If sustainable development requires present needs to be met without compromising the ability of future generations to meet their own needs, paying for pollution would not seem to provide a justification for allowing unacceptable levels of persistent environmental damage. The supposition that environmental quality is a commodity to be bought by

---

bio-accumulative toxic, and persistent pollutants (Annex). However, it is specifically stated that financial assistance may be provided for actions which contribute significantly to the implementation of Community environmental policy and meet the conditions for implementing the polluter pays principle (Art.2).

[161] The Cohesion Fund is provided for under Art.161 EC (ex Art.130d) and the Regulation establishing a Cohesion Fund 1164/94/EC, and provides for financial contribution to projects in the field of the environment and trans-European transport infrastructure, though funding is only available to member states with lower per capita gross national products, and the UK does not qualify. Funding is provided under the Fund for projects established as a consequence of Community legislation where this involves a disproportionate cost for public authorities in particular Member States.

[162] Art 87 EC (ex Art.92).

[163] *23rd Competition Report from the Commission: 1993*, COM(94)161.

[164] See 4.4.1 above on sustainable development.

polluters, at any price, is morally difficult to reconcile with the achievement of sustainable development.[165]

Third, where pollution has occurred, it is increasingly recognised that remediation is necessary and the need for remediation exists whether or not a polluter can be identified or made to pay remediation costs.[166] It would be unfortunate if the prohibition on allocation of environmental costs to society at large, which would follow from an extreme reading of the polluter pays principle, justified inaction in such contexts.[167]

### 4.8 Matters to be Taken into Account

In preparing its policy on the environment, the Community must take account of:

(a) available scientific and technical data;
(b) environmental conditions in the various regions of the Community;
(c) the potential benefits and cost of action or lack of action; and
(d) the economic and social development of the Community as a whole and the balanced development of its regions.[168]

In relation to the first of these matters, the need to take account of 'available scientific and technical data', there would appear to be a link between this and the precautionary principle, discussed above. 'Taking account' of scientific and technical data would seem to fall far short of establishing scientific certainty on a matter before taking action if the precautionary principle is not to be contradicted. Therefore, it must be construed as meaning taking account of *available* data, *however incomplete that may be*. Also, it must be recognised that the Community has been active in improving the availability of environmental data, perhaps most significantly by the establishment of the European Environment Agency which has as its remit the co-ordination of the European Environment Information and Observation Network.[169] It is likely that information gathered and disseminated by the Agency will gain increasing importance in providing the scientific and technical information which must be taken into account in Community environment policy.

The need to take account of 'environmental conditions in the various regions of the Community' seems, on first impression, somewhat difficult

---

[165] See 1.7.9 above on economic instruments for water quality and 6.14 below on balancing costs and benefits.

[166] See 13.7 below on remediating historically contaminated land.

[167] On the costs of remediation see the proposal for a Community measures on environmental liability, discussed at 3.20.2 above, and see also the national regime for dealing with historically contaminated land at 13.7 below.

[168] Art.175(3) EC (ex Art.130r(3)).

[169] Regulation 1210/90/EEC on the establishment of the European Environment Agency and the European Environment Information and Observation Network, as amended, and see 16.3 below on the Agency.

to reconcile with the central purpose of EC environmental law under Article 175 EC (ex Article 130r), namely a collective endeavour of pursuing higher environmental standards throughout the Community. Beyond that, it raises the question as to the *manner* in which different states of the environment are to be taken into account. Does a cleaner environment in a particular region require stricter environmental protection in order to maintain its relatively pristine state, or does it provide a justification for less strict controls on emissions so that Community-wide environmental quality objectives are thereby met to the same extent as would be achieved by stricter emission controls in more degraded regions? It has been suggested that the original purpose of the provision was to meet the concerns that those regions with ample natural capacity for absorption of emissions without adverse environmental consequences should not be prevented from using that capacity by the imposition of, allegedly unnecessary, fixed limits on emissions.[170] If so, it would seem that the original intention was to allow the existence of a cleaner or more resilient environment in a particular region to provide a justification for less strict controls upon emissions. However, that approach would seem to show a preference for harmonisation of environmental quality objectives over harmonisation of emission limits which seems difficult to reconcile with the prevention principle, previously discussed.

The need to take account of 'the potential benefits and cost of action or lack of action' raises the insuperable difficulties in quantifying the value of an environmental improvement, as opposed to the cost of undertaking improvement work.[171] Also, it has been suggested that cost-benefit assessment of proposals could be seen as an application of the proportionality principle which is already provided for in the Treaty.[172] However, the need to assess the economic impact of proposed Community legislation, including environmental proposals, is tangibly provided for in that the Commission has undertaken to evaluate the costs to public authorities and all parties concerned.[173] The practicalities of undertaking such an economic assessment of legislative proposals raises serious methodological difficulties in relation to particular proposals and has been difficult to apply in practice.[174] There is also the view, which the

---

[170] The provision was inserted at the request of the UK following the controversy on Community-wide limit values for emissions into the aquatic environment raised by the Dangerous Substances Directive 76/464/EEC, on which see 5.4.1 below. Indeed, all the matters to be taken into account under Art.175(3) EC can be said to reflect a characteristically 'British' approach to pollution control; see Golub (1996). On the 'British' approach generally see Bell and McGillivray (2000) ch.7.

[171] This problem is discussed elsewhere in this work, see 4.7.2 above.

[172] Jans (1995) p.34. On the proportionality principle see 4.4.3 above.

[173] This was provided for in Declaration 18 annexed to the European Community Treaty by the Final Act of the Treaty on European Union.

[174] The House of Lords Select Committee on the European Communities in its report *Bathing Water* (1994) considering proposals to revise the Bathing Water Directive (COM(94)36 final) expressed strong criticism of the initial failure to undertake an economic assessment of the proposal: 'we think it unacceptable for policy formulation to have reached the stage of a proposal being formally adopted by the Commission for consideration by the Council without a menu of individually costed measures attached. We deplore that a soundly-based cost-benefit analysis has

Commission has as yet given little weight to, that costs and benefits should not be considered only from an economic perspective, but should also seek to take other values into account, for example values associated with public participation and perhaps even higher aspirational values.[175]

A pertinent recent illustration of the difficulties in assessing costs and benefits of proposals is to be found in relation to the Water Framework Directive.[176] In relation to the proposal the Commission identified costs in relation to administration in Member States; monitoring costs; costs to private households; costs to industry and agriculture; costs of physical improvement of water infrastructure; and job losses in relevant industries. As advantages, the Commission identified improved efficiency in water policy; reduced water treatment costs; improved sustainability of water supply; increased amenity value of surface water; conservation advantages for habitats and species; and job creation advantages. Ultimately, however, it proved impossible for the Commission to give any overall economic assessment of the cost of the proposal. In part, this was because of the difficulty of ascertaining the extent to which the improvements that would be required to implement the proposal would already be required by other directives.[177] Nonetheless, the Commission concluded that the overall advantages of the proposal outweighed the costs, particularly when so many of the costs amounted to internalisation of costs presently constituting resource depletion and deterioration or causing damage to aquatic and wetland habitats.

The requirement that account should be taken of 'economic and social development of the Community as a whole and the balanced development of its regions' raises similar issues to those previously discussed in relation to the need to take account of environmental conditions in various regions of the Community. It is unclear from the wording that is used whether a lower level of economic and social development is to be used as a justification for more or less strict environmental legislation, or whether the predominant objective of Community environmental policy is the harmonisation of emission limits or environmental quality objectives. However, the illustrations that are cited as applications of this requirement all seem to demonstrate that lower levels of development justify the application of lower environmental standards or, perhaps, that greater cost of implementation will justify this. In that respect the requirement would seem to be closely linked both to the power of the Council to make appropriate provisions for temporary derogations and/or financial support from the Community's Cohesion Fund where environmental legislation is

---

not been produced' (para.67). The matter of the cost of the Proposal was reconsidered in a subsequent report by the same committee (*Bathing Water Revisited* (1995)).

[175] See the discussion in Lange (2000) at p.298. See also 6.14 below on valuation techniques used at national level.

[176] See 5.7 below.

[177] Specifically, the Urban Waste Water Treatment Directive (91/271/EEC), the Bathing Water Directive (76/160/EEC), the Nitrates Directive (91/676/EEC) and the Integrated Pollution Prevention and Control Directive (96/61/EC).

enacted which involves disproportionately high costs for the public authorities of a Member State,[178] and to the actual content of directives.[179]

## 4.9 Categories of EC Legislation

Turning to the sources of EC law, these can be placed into four categories. First, there is the 'primary' legislation consisting of the EC Treaty, as this has been amended, along with treaties providing for the accession of different Member States. Second, there is 'secondary' legislation enacted by the Community institutions in the form of regulations, directives and decisions.[180] Third, there are international agreements entered into by Community institutions on behalf of the EC where appropriate powers are provided under the Treaty. Finally, the jurisprudence of the European Court of Justice may be considered as a source of law where, in deciding particular cases, the Court establishes distinct principles for the interpretation of Community legislation.[181] According to Article 10 of the EC Treaty, each of the sources of law is binding upon a Member State insofar as it will be bound to 'take appropriate measures, whether general or particular, to ensure fulfilment' of Community obligations and must 'abstain from any measure which could jeopardise the attainment of the objectives of the Treaty'.

Insofar as environmental legislation is specifically provided for, it is located, for the most part, in EC secondary legislation. In respect of secondary legislation, the Council and the Commission shall, in accordance with the provisions of the Treaty, make regulations, issue directives, take decisions, make recommendations or deliver opinions.[182]

### 4.9.1 Regulations

Regulations have general application and are binding in their entirety and directly applicable in all Member States. Because they have 'general application' they apply in a uniform manner throughout the Community and do not, as a matter of Community law, require further national implementing legislation to take effect. That they are 'binding in their entirety' means that regulations are capable of creating individual rights which national courts must recognise, and this distinguishes them from directives in which obligations are formally addressed to Member

---

[178] Art.175(5) EC (ex Art.130s(5)).

[179] On subsidiarity and the content of directives see 4.4.2 above.

[180] The legal status of each of these is provided for in Art.249 EC (ex Art.189) and discussed further below.

[181] This jurisprudence now views the principles of the European Convention on Human Rights as general principles of law which the Court must observe. For an illustration see the arguments in Case C-293/97 *R v Secretary of State for the Environment and Minister of Agriculture, Fisheries and Food, ex parte Standley* [1999] ECR I-2603 concerning whether the Nitrates Directive (91/676/EEC) breaches the Convention's protection of property.

[182] Art.249 EC (ex Art.189). Recommendations and opinions have no binding force and are not considered further here.

States.[183] Moreover, regulations cannot be derogated from by national law which subtracts from provisions in regulations,[184] and national law cannot be used to prevent their application even if enacted subsequently.[185] As a matter of Community law, regulations are directly applicable without the need for any further action by the national legislatures. Within the United Kingdom, direct applicability is explicitly provided for by s.2(1) European Communities Act 1972 which states:

> All such rights, powers, liabilities, obligations and restrictions from time to time created or arising by or under the Treaties, and all such remedies and procedures from time to time provided for by or under the Treaties, as in accordance with the Treaties are without further enactment to be given legal effect or used in the United Kingdom shall be recognised and available in law, and enforced, allowed and followed accordingly.

In relation to the implementation of environmental policy, regulations are rarely used. The exceptions to this are where matters are subject to international agreement which need to be consistently implemented throughout the Community[186] or where the Community provides for the establishment of a Community body with environmental responsibilities.[187] The preference for directives over regulations may be justified by the need to allow Member States to interpret Community requirements to meet particular environmental conditions and to accord with national and local legal and administrative arrangements, in accordance with the subsidiarity principle.[188]

### 4.9.2 Directives

Directives are the principal means by which the environmental policy of the EC has been pursued and a relatively large number of these have been enacted in relation to water quality.[189] However, some general observations may be offered here about the legal status of directives as an instrument of EC law.

Directives are binding as to the result to be achieved upon each Member State to which they are addressed, but leave to the national authorities the choice of form and methods. This leaves to the Member States a degree of

---

[183] Although note the possibility of individual rights being enforceable in national courts, see 4.16.3 below.

[184] Case 93/71 *Leonesio* v *Ministero dell'Agricoltura a delle Foreste* [1972] ECR 287.

[185] Case 230/78 *Eridania* v *Ministry of Agriculture* [1979] ECR 2749.

[186] For examples of this see Regulation 259/93/EEC, which implements the Basel Convention on the transfrontier movement of hazardous waste, and Regulation 338/97/EC which implements the international Convention on trade in endangered species ('CITES').

[187] For examples of this see Regulation 1210/90/EEC establishing the European Environment Agency (see 16.3 below); Regulation 880/92/EEC creating the Community ecolabel; and Regulation 1836/93/EEC which establishes a Community ecoaudit scheme.

[188] See 4.4.2 above on subsidiarity.

[189] The range of EC directives relating to water are considered in Ch.5 below.

flexibility or discretion in relation to the choice of mechanism for implementation which is most appropriate to meet the obligations arising under a directive where existing national legislation must be modified or new national law enacted. Transposition does not require that precisely the same words must be used in the national implementing measure,[190] but it must be clear that it actually ensures the full application of the directive and that the measure is sufficiently binding to meet the requirement of legal certainty.[191] In relation to the UK, the implementation of a directive may be brought about by the enactment of an Act of Parliament where new primary legislation is necessary. Alternatively,[192] directives can be implemented by means of delegated legislation and, in some instances,[193] by the use of a statutory power to give directions to national authorities.[194] The important point in relation to the use of national regulations is that they cannot be used to go further than the directive requires, which can have the practical effect of limiting the development of national law in EC-driven areas.[195]

Difficulties have arisen in the past in relation to the national legal mechanisms which have been used to implement environmental directives. In the early period it was not uncommon for directives to be implemented by administrative directions to the responsible national authorities, and even where powers existed to exercise formal legal powers these were not always used.[196] Hence, in England and Wales, prior to water privatisation, the Secretary of State possessed a power to issue a formal direction to a water authority for various purposes.[197] However, this power was not used in relation to the implementation of Community water directives because 'it has never been necessary for the Secretary of State to give such a direction because water authorities have readily responded to advice and guidance given less formally'.[198] As a matter of Community law, this approach appeared of dubious legality in the light of the European Court ruling[199] that the Netherlands had failed to implement the Bathing Water Directive[200] where it had sought to do so merely by changes in

---

[190] Case C-339/87 *Commission* v *Netherlands* [1990] ECR I-851.

[191] Case 239/85 *Commission* v *Belgium* [1986] ECR 364.

[192] Under s.2(2) European Communities Act 1972.

[193] See, for example, s.40(2)(a) Environment Act 1995, and see 6.2 below.

[194] On national mechanisms for implementation of directives, see Noble (1996).

[195] See the discussion of the background to the Pollution Prevention and Control Act 1999 at 12.3.4–5 below.

[196] 'The early phase was characterized by a tendency towards regarding EEC Directives as helpful if eccentric recommendations to be gently eased into the United Kingdom scheme of things, ideally by government circular rather than legislation, and ideally without cost', Wyatt (1998) p.10. See also Macrory (1992) p.350.

[197] s.5(2) Water Act 1973.

[198] *Privatisation of the Water Authorities in England and Wales* Cmnd.9734 (1986) para.86. Contrast the presently position whereby the UK Government has 'generally' ceased to rely on directions to implement Community legislation, see House of Lords Select Committee on the European Communities, *Implementation and Enforcement of Environmental Legislation* (1992) Vol.1 para.100.

[199] Case 96/81 *Commission* v *Netherlands* [1982] ECR 1791. See also Case 145/82 *Commission* v *Italy* [1983] ECR 711.

[200] Directive 76/160/EEC, and see 5.5.2 below.

administrative practice. It was found to be necessary to implement directives by means of a national provision of a *binding legal nature*. Similarly, it has been held in later cases that directives may not be implemented by administrative circulars but must be transparently implemented by binding legal measures which are sufficiently clear and precise to be enforceable by individuals in national courts.[201] Hence, in relation to particular parameters in environmental directives, the transposition obligation extends to the incorporation of the same emission limits or environmental quality standards into national legislation.[202]

### 4.9.3 Decisions

Decisions are binding 'in their entirety' upon those to whom they are addressed, but are usually addressed to a specific Member State or person without requiring implementation in national law. Their more specific nature means that they are appropriate for the granting of authorisations or administrative matters which do not justify a more stringent kind of legislative act. In the water context, an example is provided by the Information Exchange Decision[203] which establishes a common procedure for the exchange of information on the quality of surface waters to ascertain levels of pollution of rivers in the Community and to monitor long-term trends in water quality.

### 4.10 The Legal Bases for EC Water Law

The Community has certain powers to translate EC environmental policy into specific legal enactments. The fundamental idea is that of 'attribution': that the Community must act within the powers and objectives conferred upon it by the EC Treaty[204] and that any action which is not capable of justification by reference to the Treaty will be invalid. The first concern, therefore, is the extent of the power of the Community to legislate in relation to the environment (and the mechanisms by which it does so).

As has been discussed, there is now an Environmental Title in the EC Treaty which spans Articles 174-176 (ex Articles 130r-130t) and which contains the 'cascade' of policy objectives, policy principles and criteria for policy-making.[205] Article 175 is therefore now the principle legal base for 'pure' environmental legislation. Legislation with an environmental dimension may, however, also be adopted under other Articles of the Treaty, of which the most notable is Article 95 (ex Article 100a) which is concerned with the single market and the free movement of goods. It is

---

[201] Case C-131/88 *Commission* v *Germany* [1991] ECR I-825; and Case C-58/89 *Commission* v *Germany* [1991] ECR I-4983.

[202] Case C-361/88 *Commission* v *Germany* [1991] ECR I-2567.

[203] Decision 77/795/EEC, as amended by Decision 86/574/EEC. See 16.2.5 below.

[204] Hence, Art.5 EC (ex Art.3b) provides that 'The Community shall act within the limits of the powers conferred upon it by this Treaty and the objectives assigned to it therein'.

[205] See 4.5–8 above.

also possible, however, that legislation impacting on Community water quality might also be adopted under other Articles of the Treaty, for example Article 37 EC (ex Article 43) which deals with agriculture policy.

The legal basis for any item of EC water law may, however, be contentious. For example, a directive laying down quality standards for specified Community waters will most likely be adopted under Article 175. However, it may be more problematic to determine whether legislation relating to the toxicity or labelling of pesticides which may end up in the aquatic environment should be adopted under the Environmental Title, should be classified as a single market measure and therefore adopted under Article 95, or even regarded as an agricultural measure and adopted under Article 37.

The approach of the European Court of Justice in deciding the correct basis for legislation is now, however, fairly well settled. This is to identify the 'centre of gravity' of a proposal. In this respect, Article 95 is probably the appropriate basis for measures which approximate environmental provisions by seeking to remove distortions of competition in a particular industry, classically where harmonised product standards are concerned. For more general environmental measures which have a wider, more diffuse effect, Article 175 is generally upheld as the proper basis despite any incidental effect legislation may have on other Community activities, such as the single market[206] or agricultural policy.[207]

There are various reasons why the specific Article under which EC legislation is adopted is of importance. These are:

(a) Each legal base for legislation is assigned a specific procedure under which legislation is adopted ('legislative procedure').
(b) Each legal base has specific rules governing the scope for Member States to adopt higher standards.
(c) Each legal base has different rules about the scope for Member States to derogate from agreed standards in defined cases (i.e. to adopt lower national standards).

### 4.10.1 Legislative Procedures

Since the Amsterdam Treaty, the *co-decision procedure* is now used for the majority of proposals in relation to environmental protection and the internal market.[208] Following proposals by the Commission, this procedure involves both the Council and the European Parliament in the decision-making process, with decisions of the Council being taken by a qualified

---

[206] Case C-155/91 *Commission* v *Council* [1993] ECR I-939, concerning Directive 91/156/EEC on waste, and see also Case C-187/93 *Parliament* v *Council* [1994] ECR I-2857 (the 'Basel Regulation case').

[207] Case C-303/94 *Parliament* v *Council* [1996] ECR I-2943; Joined Cases C-164/97 and C-165/97 *Parliament* v *Council* [1999] ECR I-1139. For criticism of the current approach of the Court of Justice, and arguments for greater use of Article 95 as a legal base for measures relating to the environment, see Krämer (2000) pp.56-63.

[208] Provided for under Art.251 EC (ex Art.189b).

majority vote. The balance of power, however, rests with the Council, and formally the Parliament has only a negative power to prevent adoption of proposals. There is provision, though, for a Conciliation Committee of members of both Council and Parliament to resolve differences, and this has been used on a number of occasions in relation to environmental directives, including the Water Framework Directive.[209]

An important exception to majority voting is that, for proposals in certain environmental policy areas, legislation under Article 175 must be adopted unanimously by the European Council, and the Parliament enjoys a lesser, consultative, role. These concern provisions primarily of a fiscal nature; measures concerning town and country planning, land use with the exception of waste management and measures of a general nature, and management of water resources; measures significantly affecting a Member State's choice between energy sources and the general structure of its energy supply. However, it is provided that, by unanimous decision, the Council may define those matters in relation to these areas where decisions may be taken by a qualified majority.[210]

The extent of the expression 'management of water resources' is not defined and the question arises whether it is intended to encompass purely quantitative aspects of water management, such as water supply and irrigation, or both quantitative and qualitative. The better view, it is submitted, is that only quantitative aspects are envisaged,[211] and this is supported by the fact that recent proposals for the amendment of water quality directives have been based upon Article 130s (and now Article 175) and no need for unanimous voting has been thought necessary.[212] It is also supported by the fact that the Water Framework Directive has been adopted under Article 175 EC since the bulk of the proposal is concerned with water quality issues, even though it does incorporate quantitative provisions intended to ensure a balance between abstraction and recharge of groundwater.[213] This view has now been supported by the Court of Justice.[214]

It is worth stressing that since 1987 and the insertion into the Treaty of an Environmental Title, most Community water legislation has been adopted under the Environmental Title, so in practice the distinction between Articles 175 and 95 is not greatly relevant. Prior to the Environmental

---

[209] See Tydeman (2000). On adopting the Water Framework Directive see 5.7.1(b) below.

[210] Art.175(2) EC (ex Art.130s(2)).

[211] Jans (1995) p.38. See Krämer (2000) p.185 for a summary of the arguments, and a compelling analysis why the 'quantitative' view is to be preferred.

[212] See discussion of the revised Drinking Water Directive (98/83/EC) at 17.7.8 below, and proposals for revisions to the Bathing Waters Directive (at 5.5.2 below).

[213] See the view of the Commission in COM(97)49 final, s.2.6. On the Water Framework Directive see 5.7 below.

[214] See Case C-36/98 *Spain* v *Council* in relation to Community adherence to the Convention for the Protection of the Danube, 30 January 2001, not yet reported, where the Court held that the Convention, being mainly concerned with water quality issues, should be adopted under Art.175(1) EC.

Title, however, water legislation was always adopted under a combination of Articles 100 and 235.[215]

### 4.10.2 Stricter National Standards

A further reason why the legal basis for adopting legislation matters is that there are different safeguards, or 'guarantees', allowing Member States to maintain or adopt national standards which are higher than those provided for in EC legislation. Where legislation is enacted under Article 175, it is subject to the safeguard provision of Article 176 (ex Article 130t), which provides that 'protective measure adopted pursuant to Article 175 shall not prevent any Member State from maintaining or introducing more stringent measures'. Such measures must be compatible with the Treaty and notified to the Commission.

This gives the Member States a considerable amount of discretion to maintain or introduce higher national standards, and certainly makes it easier to do so when compared to similar provisions which govern the discretion of Member States to set standards stricter than those contained in legislation adopted under Article 95 (ex Article 100a). This emphasises the distinction between Article 175 and Article 95, in that there is less justification for seeking uniformity of standards when the objective is environmental protection as opposed to the harmonisation of laws in the interests of establishing a single market.

For this reason, the environmental guarantee in relation to the single market gives Member States less scope to impose higher standards. Briefly, where a harmonisation measure has been enacted, a Member State can *maintain* a national provision on environmental protection grounds so long as it notifies the Commission of these provisions and the grounds for maintaining them. Member States can also *introduce* stricter national standards if this is based on new scientific evidence and relates specifically to the Member State in question. An example of the strict interpretation of this provision can be seen in the Decision of the Commission rejecting a request by Belgium to introduce a ban on organotin marine anti-fouling paints, which went beyond a harmonisation measure on this.[216] The Commission was able to show it had considered advice from the IMO, and Belgium was unable to show the required 'new scientific evidence'. The Decision also suggests, curiously, that humans will not be regarded as part of the environment.[217]

There is therefore oversight by the Commission. But where a matter has not been provided for under Community legislation, the availability of a power

---

[215] That is, the Drinking Water Abstraction Directive (75/440/EEC); Bathing Water Directive (76/160/EEC); Dangerous Substances Directive (76/464/EEC); Freshwater Fish Waters Directive (78/659/EEC); Shellfish Waters Directive (79/923/EEC); the Groundwater Directive (80/68/EEC) and the Drinking Water Quality Directive (80/778/EEC) were all adopted on this basis. No water directive was adopted only under one legal base.

[216] See Directive 1999/51/EC.

[217] See Commission Decision 2000/509/EC, OJ L205/7, 12 August 2000.

of derogation needs to be considered in relation to Articles 28 and 30 of the EC Treaty (ex Articles 30 and 36). Article 28 guarantees free movement of goods by prohibiting imposition of import quotas, or 'quantitative restrictions', and other trade measures having equivalent effect. However, Article 30 allows 'measures which may have the effect of hindering imports on specified grounds:

    (a)  public morality;
    (b)  public policy or public security;
    (c)  the protection of health and life of humans, animals and plants;
    (d)  the protection of national treasures possessing artistic, historic or archaeological value; or
    (e)  the protection of industrial and commercial property.

The omission should be noted, however, of any explicit environmental ground for derogation amongst these matters. Nevertheless, the European Court has interpreted the exceptions to allow 'mandatory requirements' in the public interest where the measure applies equally to domestic and imported products; and it is proportional to the objective to be achieved.[218] Moreover, the protection of the environment has been held to be a 'mandatory requirement' capable of limiting the free movement of goods. Accordingly, it has been stated that environmental protection 'is one of the Community's essential objectives', providing that proportionality and non-discrimination are observed.[219]

The scope for exceptions from trade-related measures being founded on environmental grounds has been clearly established where the requirements under Article 30 are met.[220] However, the scope for derogation on this ground in relation to the protection of water quality and the aquatic environment must be rather limited since most of the relevant legislation falls into the non-trade-related category.[221] Nevertheless, examples of derogations from trade, imposed for the purpose of protecting the aquatic environment, are illustrated by the right of a Member State to ban pesticides where these are not provided for under Community law,[222] and to limit the phosphate content in detergents in order to combat eutrophication of water.[223] Another example is provided by Community proceedings against Germany following the imposition of a complete prohibition upon the import of living crayfish, which it was argued was necessary to protect health and life of indigenous species. Here, the European Court applied Article 30 insofar as it concerned the health and

---

[218] Case 120/78 *Rewe* v *Bundesmonopolverwaltung* ('*Cassis de Dijon*') [1979] ECR 649.
[219] Case 240/83 *Procureur de la République* v *Association de Défense des Brûleurs d'Huiles Usagées* (ADBHU, or '*Waste Oils*') [1985] ECR 531 and see 4.2 above.
[220] Case 302/86 *Commission* v *Denmark* ('*Danish Bottles*') [1988] ECR 4607 and Case 2/90 *Commission* v *Belgium* ('*Wallonian Waste*') [1992] ECR I-4431.
[221] There are situations where water quality may *impact* on trade related measures. For example, it is a requirement of the Fish Products Directive (91/492/EEC) that fish are prepared with water which meets the standards of the Drinking Water Quality Directive (80/778/EEC, as amended). On the implications see Howarth (1999).
[222] Case 125/88 *Nijmann* [1989] ECR 3533.
[223] See the First Detergent Directive (73/404/EEC), and see 5.4.3 below.

life of animals, but held that the German measure was disproportionate because less restrictive measures could have been used to protect the indigenous species from disease.[224]

Because the early water directives were adopted on the basis of ex Articles 100 and 235 of the EEC Treaty, the only barrier to their setting higher national standards is provided by what is now Articles 28-30 of the EC Treaty. That is, the environmental guarantees only apply to measures adopted under those specific provisions, and not to measures adopted under treaty bases used previously.

### 4.10.3 Derogations: Lower National Standards

The third respect in which the legal base of a directive matters is in the scope it gives Member States to set standards at national level which are *lower* than those prescribed in directives. For internal market harmonisation measures, no provision is made in the Treaty to depart from these standards by allowing lesser environmental standards; that is, in theory they provide a strict baseline of regulation. In practice, however, there are quite a few examples where a directive adopted under Article 100 (now Article 95 EC) itself provides for a form of derogation by imposing different standards on different Member States, or providing that a particular Member State or States has longer to meet its obligations.[225] However, in principle Article 175 gives Member States the right to derogate from an environmental harmonisation measure where the costs of compliance are deemed to be disproportionate for the public authorities of the Member State concerned. In this case, specific provision may be made in the directive concerned allowing either for a temporary derogation or for financial support from the Cohesion Fund to be made available. Again, the reality is somewhat different, and what often happens is that the general provisions of the directive provide for some flexibility, allowing for economic and developmental differences between states to be taken into account (although this is probably a less pronounced characteristic of the water directives than it is of other environmental directives).[226]

### 4.11 The Status of Environmental Directives

The EC's environment policy has been pursued primarily through the enactment of numerous environmental directives[227] which impose obligations upon the Member States to achieve a specified environmental objective, whilst allowing a degree of flexibility in the manner of implementation through national law and administration. The enactment of

---

[224] Case C-131/93 *Commission* v *Germany* [1994] ECR I-3303 and see on proportionality also 4.4.3 above.

[225] See, e.g. Directive 94/62/EC on packaging and packaging waste.

[226] Although see the wording of the requirement to impose water charging schemes under the Water Framework Directive, discussed at 5.9.9 below.

[227] Global figures vary, but most commentators refer to upwards of 200 distinct measures; for a complete overview see Haigh (1992, updated).

an environmental directive, however, raises important questions about the competence of a Member State to legislate on the environment and, more broadly, the interrelationship between national and Community law.

### 4.11.1 Supremacy of Community Law

The overriding principle is that of supremacy: that Community law should always take precedence over national legislation. Whilst environmental competence is generally said to be shared between the Community and the Member States, and both the EC and the Member States are empowered to take action in relation to the environment, EC enactments should always take priority. Member States must take all appropriate measures to ensure fulfilment of obligations arising out of the EC Treaty or resulting from action taken by the institutions of the Community and are to abstain from any measure which could jeopardise the attainment of the objectives of the Treaty.[228] So Community provisions have priority over previous and subsequent national legislation in instances of conflict.

### 4.11.2 Extent of Harmonisation

Given the supremacy of EC law over national law, the question arises as to how much freedom a Member State has to enact environmental legislation in an area which is subject to EC environmental legislation. Alternatively, the issue may be formulated as whether the relevant EC legislation seeks to realise comprehensive harmonisation of the area or whether it seeks only partial harmonisation, leaving Member States to enact additional legislation on matters not covered by Community law.

Where a directive provides for complete regulation of a particular area of environmental activity, by way of an exhaustive set of rules, the Community regime will not permit national legislation extending the obligations which have been provided for. Hence, where a directive exhaustively provided for the circumstances in which solvents could be placed on the market,[229] it was not open to a Member State to impose more restrictive rules for its domestic market, or rules which were more detailed or different in respect of the classification, packaging or labelling, than those established by the Directive.[230] However, a critical issue in each case concerns the precise scope of the harmonisation provided for under the relevant Community directive. A directive which seeks to harmonise environmental standards in a particular area will not prevent a Member State regulating that area for non-environmental reasons[231] and, conversely, an activity which is regulated at Community level for non-environmental purposes will not prevent a Member State imposing environmental requirements upon that activity. In each case, it is a matter

---

[228] Art.10 EC (ex Art.5).

[229] Directive 73/173/EEC.

[230] Case 148/78 *Ratti* [1979] ECR 1629; see also Case 278/85 *Commission v Denmark* [1987] ECR 4069.

[231] Joined Cases 141 and 143/81 *Holdijk* [1982] ECR 1299.

of ascertaining the purpose for which the Community regulatory regime is imposed. [232]

### 4.11.3 Minimum Environmental Standards

Beyond product controls, comprehensive harmonisation is rarely encountered in Community water legislation and it is more common to find directives seeking to secure minimum environmental standards without restricting the freedom of Member States to enact more stringent environmental legislation. This is particularly the case where environmental legislation has a less direct impact upon the functioning of the common market and where minimum standards are sought without the need for complete uniformity.[233] For the most part, EC directives on water quality fall into this category in seeking to control emissions and secure minimum environmental standards without restricting the capacity of the Member States to legislate for higher standards. In many instances, this has been made explicit by provisions allowing for more stringent standards to be set by Member States.

An exceptional example of a directive imposing a restriction upon the imposition of a higher environmental standard than provided for under the directive is to be found in the Drinking Water Quality Directive.[234] This allows Member States to adopt more stringent national provisions for drinking water quality than those provided for in the Directive. However, Member States may not prohibit or impede the marketing of foodstuffs on grounds relating to the quality of water used where the quality of the water meets the requirements of the Directive unless it is shown that marketing such goods constitutes a hazard to public health. Hence, an upper limit is imposed upon water quality used in the preparation of food insofar as this is capable of being used as a restriction upon trade.

While early environmental directives commonly provided an explicit statement to the effect that only minimum harmonisation was required, this practice has now been made unnecessary by explicit provision in the Treaty. Article 176 EC (ex Article 130t) provides that protective measures adopted pursuant to Article 175 EC (ex Article 130s) will not prevent a Member State from maintaining or introducing more stringent protective measures, providing that they are compatible with the Treaty and notified to the Commission. Notably, this will be applicable only where the relevant Community measure is adopted under Article 175 and not where it is adopted under Article 95, although as noted above there is now an expanded 'environmental guarantee' in relation to Article 95 which allows Member States to both maintain *and* introduce higher national standards in

---

[232] *R* v *London Boroughs Transport Committee ex parte Freight Transport Association Ltd* [1990] 3 CMLR 495 (CA); overturned on appeal [1991] 1 WLR 828.

[233] Minimum harmonisation provisions are increasingly to be found in directives adopted under Art.95 EC (ex Art.100a).

[234] Directive 80/778/EEC, Arts.16 and 4(2). See 17.7.1 below.

defined circumstances.[235] Also, the requirement that the national measure is compatible with the Treaty raises the question whether more stringent national provision will be permitted where an area is intended to be comprehensively regulated by a directive.

### 4.11.4 Less Stringent Environmental Standards

Although, in principle, the national enactment of stricter environmental requirements is allowed by EC law, the enactment of less stringent environmental requirements in national law is not permissible. This principle is well illustrated in relation to the Drinking Water Quality Directive[236] which imposes maximum parameters for various substances that may be present in such waters. Following proceedings in Italy to determine the criminal liability of the Government for allowing a particular parameter to be exceeded, the European Court of Justice gave a preliminary ruling as to the competence of a Member State to derogate from the limit imposed by the Directive. It was held that derogation was only permitted where this was provided for by the Directive and this must be strictly interpreted.[237] Similarly in relation to the UK's failure to comply with the Bathing Water Directive,[238] a requirement was clearly set out in the Directive that bathing water must comply with limit values within a period of ten years. The submission of the UK Government that Member States were only required to take all practicable steps to comply with these requirements was not accepted. The obligation required Member States to take steps to ensure that certain results are achieved, and it is not possible to rely upon national administrative, political or institutional circumstances to excuse a failure to achieve a result required by a Directive.[239]

Despite the strictness of the obligation to meet the requirements of environmental directives, the obligation is not an absolute one. Specifically, narrow grounds for derogation may exist where greater interests prevail or where derogation provides for greater environmental benefit. Evidence for this is to be found in the interpretation of the Wild Birds Directive[240] in the *Leybucht* case,[241] where operations involving the construction of a dyke resulted in a reduction in a Special Protection Area under the Directive. The Court of Justice conceded that only exceptional circumstances would justify the reduction in the area, and emphasised that these must involve a general interest which is superior to the general interest represented by the ecological interest represented by the ecological objective of the Directive. In the circumstances, the Court held that the protection of the area from flooding and the protection of property and

---

[235] See 4.10.2 above.

[236] Directive 80/778/EEC, and see 17.7.1 below.

[237] Case 228/87 *Pretore di Torino* v *Persons unknown* [1988] ECR 5099.

[238] Directive 76/160/EEC, and see 5.5.2 below.

[239] Case C-56/90 *Commission* v *United Kingdom* [1993] ECR I-4109.

[240] Directive 79/409/EEC; see further 15.8 below, in particular changes made under the Habitats Directive (92/43/EEC).

[241] Case C-57/89 *Commission* v *Germany* [1991] ECR I-883 and see 15.8.2 below.

human safety were interests of sufficient gravity to justify the work which had been undertaken providing that only the least possible reduction in the special protection area resulted. Inherently, therefore, the existence of greater interests in exceptional circumstances may justify derogation from the strict requirements of a directive.

Another point raised, but less conclusively resolved, by the *Leybucht* case is the question whether derogation from an environmental directive may be justified to secure a greater environmental benefit. It was noted by the Court that the construction work involved might have positive ecological benefits in the establishment of new salt meadows of ecological importance. It has been suggested that here the Court was accepting a principle of offsetting ecological benefits as a basis for derogation from the Directive.[242] However, it is not clear what the legal basis for such a principle might be.

In relation to water quality directives, it is difficult to conceive of situations where greater interests are involved or greater environmental benefits might be secured by derogation other than those matters that are explicitly provided for in the Directives. The practical position, therefore, is that explicit provision for derogation is the only situation where derogation is likely to be available and this depends, in relation to each Directive, upon the precise extent of the provision which is made.

In relation to the use of derogations, however, their use is now perhaps slightly more prevalent than previously, which might suggest a political preference for mechanisms which explicitly allow the use of less strict standards, invariably for a time-limited period. That is, there is a political preference for agreeing derogations from generally-required standards at the time that a directive is adopted, rather than relying on a subsequent request to the Commission to derogate for exceptional reasons. These 'built-in' derogations might require a phased introduction of new standards, or that in the interests of flexibility certain requirements may not be required of a Member State at all.

### 4.11.5 *Implementation in Fact*

A final general implementation issue concerns situations where derogation may be allowed in law because implementation is secured in fact. This could arise, for example, in a situation where the activity which a directive seeks to regulate could not actually be undertaken within a particular Member State. To use an example,[243] Article 4(2) of the Urban Waste Water Treatment Directive[244] provides for measures in respect of discharges to high mountain regions over 1500m above sea level. Since the highest point in the Netherlands is only 300m above sea level, this requirement is clearly irrelevant to this Member State, and it is suggested

---

[242] Jans (1995) p.118.
[243] *Ibid* p.134.
[244] Directive 91/271/EEC, and see 5.6.2 below.

that this provides a justification for it not having to implement the provision. Similar reasoning is conceded by the Court of Justice where an activity *could not occur* in a Member State, but not where, as a matter of fact, it *does not actually occur.*[245]

The extent of 'compliance in fact' justification for non-implementation of a water quality directive has only rarely been directly considered by the Court of Justice. The argument was not accepted by the Court in relation to the claim of the Dutch Government that it had implemented Article 6 of the Groundwater Directive,[246] concerned with artificial recharges of groundwater, by allowing the relevant authorisation to be given by national authorities where those authorities were allowed greater latitude in granting authorisations than permitted by the Directive. Although the national authorities were to ensure the proper management of groundwater, this was not thought to be as strict as the Directive requirement that there should be no risk polluting groundwater. The *possibility* that the less strict national requirement might allow contravention of the Directive was therefore held to be a breach of Community law.[247] By contrast, in bringing proceedings against Belgium in respect of failure to implement the Drinking Water Abstraction Directive and the Drinking Water Sampling Directive,[248] the Commission accepted that no transposition was required in the Brussels Region since no surface water in that region was intended for drinking water. Accordingly, though the Court held that Belgium had failed to implement the Directives in the Flemish and Walloon Regions, it did not make any finding concerning the Brussels Region.[249]

In line with flexibility, it is possible to identify provisions of directives which, although formally framed as generally binding obligations, in fact mean that they impact differently on different Member States to the extent that some provisions may not apply to a particular Member State at all. This variant of 'non-implementation in fact' can be seen, for example, in the provision of the Water Framework Directive allowing Member States not to apply resource related water pricing if this would not be in accordance with established practices and does not compromise the purposes and achieving the objectives of the Directive.[250]

### 4.12 Implementing Environmental Directives

While the preceding section has considered the extent of discretion enjoyed by Member States when a directive is in force governing a particular policy area, a related issue is the duty on Member States to

---

[245] Case C-339/87 *Commission* v *Netherlands* [1990] ECR I-851. On the contention that the absence of water pollution removed the need for redirection programmes see Case C-184/97 *Commission* v *Germany* [1999] ECR I-7837, paras 51–61.
[246] Directive 80/68/EEC, and see 5.4.2 below.
[247] Case 291/84 *Commission* v *Netherlands* [1987] ECR 3483.
[248] Directive 75/440/EEC and Directive 79/869/EEC, and see 17.6 below.
[249] Case C-290/89 *Commission* v *Belgium* [1991] ECR I-2851.
[250] Art.9 Water Framework Directive, and see 5.9.9 below.

comply with EC law in practice. That is, in what circumstances can a Member State be found in breach of its obligations under the EC Treaty for failing to implement Community law? 'Failure to implement a directive', however, encompasses a diverse range of matters ranging from the failure to enact national legislation to the failure to adhere to the most detailed obligation arising under a particular directive. Recognising the potential complexities involved, however, this failure may arise in three broad categories of situation:

(a) 'formal' failure to transpose a directive;
(b) 'substantive' failure of implementation; and
(c) certain procedural and administrative requirements of directives not being fulfilled.

Although non-implementation can have a particular legal connotation, the importance of the wider process of implementing EC law should be appreciated. Hence it has been stated that,

> Implementation is the link between what is desirable and what is achievable; it provides the essential feedback for the improvement of new policy making. It also provides the link between Community policy and national policies and ensures, not only that Community policies really penetrate into each Member State, but also that an understanding of national and local policies informs the development of Community policies. EC policy only really comes to life when it is implemented in the Member States and has become inseparably intertwined with national policies.[251]

### 4.12.1 Formal Failure of Transposition

Formal failure to implement a directive arises where national legislative provisions for transposition have not been enacted by the required deadline, or fail to apply throughout the territory of the Member State, or only provide for the incomplete implementation of a directive. In respect of implementation, Member States are generally required to provide the Commission with information about national implementing measures and administrative arrangements either under a directive itself or under general requirements of Community law. Failure to enact implementing legislation will provide a fairly clear ground for the Commission to bring proceedings. Failure to secure timely implementation is relatively common, although infringement proceedings often pressure Member States into incorporating Community environmental provisions into law without resort to full Court proceedings.

---

[251] N. Haigh, *Effective Environment Protection: Challenges for the Implementation of EC Law*, Appendix 5 s.3 in House of Lords Select Committee on the European Communities, Second Report, *Community Environmental Law: Making it Work* (1997) (henceforth *Making It Work*).

## 4.12.2  Substantive Failure of Implementation

Substantive failure to implement an environmental directive arises where
an obligation under the directive, such as an environmental quality
standard or emission standard, is not actually met by a Member State. An
example of this was the finding of the Court of Justice that Belgium was
guilty of failing to fulfil its obligations under EC law[252] where it was
established that the supply of drinking water to one city did not meet the
standards required under the Drinking Water Quality Directive.[253]
Similarly, the UK was found by the Court to have failed to meet the
standards required for bathing water under the Bathing Water Directive.[254]
This conclusion was reached despite the claim of the UK Government that
it had taken all practicable steps to meet the required bathing water quality
parameters, since the Community obligation required that all necessary
measures to ensure that the quality objectives of the Directive were
actually met. That is, where quality objectives are required under a
directive they must actually be realised, and it is no defence for a Member
State to rely upon particular, national, circumstances, such as
administrative difficulties, to seek to justify a failure to do so.

## 4.12.3  Procedural Failure of Implementation

Procedural and administrative failures to implement an environmental
directive may take diverse forms depending, in each case, upon what
obligations the relevant directive imposes. Hence, environmental directives
incorporate a wide range of procedural requirements: drawing up plans;
designating areas; granting authorisations; providing information; making
assessments; conducting consultations; restricting marketing and use of
particular products; monitoring; and preparing reports.[255] In each case, the
terms of the relevant directive will determine the administrative and
practical matters that must be undertaken by each Member State.

A common illustration of this kind of failure would arise in the case of a
directive which imposes a reporting requirement of some kind, whereby a
Member State is required to provide information to the Commission about
specified matters by a stated deadline.[256] Here, the failure to adhere to the
required procedure by providing the specified information would be a
breach of the directive for which infringement proceedings could be
brought by the Commission whether or not any substantive breach of the
environmental quality requirements of the directive at issue had taken
place. Similarly, where a directive requires acts of an administrative nature
such as the establishment of plans or programmes for environmental

---

[252] Case C-42/89 *Commission* v *Belgium* [1990] ECR I-2821.

[253] Directive 80/778/EEC, and see 17.7.1 below.

[254] Case C-56/90 *Commission* v *United Kingdom* [1993] ECR I-4109, under Directive
76/160/EEC, and see 4.15.2 below.

[255] See N. Haigh, *Effective Environment Protection: Challenges for the Implementation of EC
Law*, Appendix 5 s.2.3 in *Making it Work*. On monitoring under EC law see16.2 below

[256] See, e.g., Directive 91/692/EEC on standardizing and rationalizing reports on the
implementation of certain Directives relating to the environment, discussed at 16.2.5 below.

improvement, licensing procedures or monitoring, these must be provided for in national legislation and actually given effect to. In particular, the Court has held that incomplete practical measures or fragmentary legislation cannot discharge the obligation of a Member State to draw up a comprehensive programme with a view to attaining certain objectives,[257] and measures which are merely ad hoc interventions will not amount to 'plans' insofar as they are disorganised and uncoordinated.[258] In addition, actual compliance with quality standards or limit values will not avoid any obligation to prepare and implement any required plans or programmes. Despite the formal and substantive implementation of a directive, transposition may be incomplete if obligations of a procedural and administrative kind are not adhered to.

### 4.13 Remedying Non-Implementation: the Role of the Commission

As a matter of EC Treaty law, addressing inadequate national implementation of Community directives is a matter for the Commission which, as the 'Guardian of the Treaty', may initiate proceedings against a Member State. It is the general duty of the Commission to ensure that the provisions of the EC Treaty, and the actions taken by Community institutions, are given effect.[259] This involves the Commission undertaking a monitoring role in relation to the application of Community law in the Member States and in bringing legal proceedings in the event of any of the categories of non-implementation. The procedure allowing the Commission to pursue enforcement proceedings is contained in Articles 226 and 228 EC (ex Articles 169 and 171).[260]

Enforcement proceedings brought before the Court of Justice should not be conflated with the facility, in certain situations, for national courts to refer to the Court questions about the interpretation of Community law under Article 234 EC (ex Article 177). It is arguable, however, that the result of national references is a form of 'indirect' or 'private' enforcement in the sense that such references are a further means to establishing the precise nature of Community obligations. Although national reference to the Court requires the co-operation both of individuals, parties and of the national courts, this procedure has advantages in the sphere of environmental law because the Court of Justice is obliged to clarify points of law, and so the property and other interests of those bringing the case are largely irrelevant to the matter the Court has to decide.[261] As a result, this avenue may be most appropriate where proceedings by environmental pressure groups are

---

[257] See the cases cited at 5.4.1(d) below in relation to Art.7 Dangerous Substances Directive (76/464/EEC).

[258] Case C-214/96 *Commission* v *Spain* [1998] ECR I-7661, para.30; Case C-387/97 *Commission* v *Hellenic Republic*, [2000] ECR I-3823, para.76.

[259] Art.211 EC (ex Art.155).

[260] Under Art.227 EC (ex Art.170) a Member State may bring infringement proceedings against another Member State, but this course of action is politically unpopular and almost never resorted to in practice. It has never been used in an environmental context.

[261] Although overcoming *national* procedural rules such as on standing or delay may be an issue.

at issue.[262] In practice, however, UK courts have been comparatively reluctant to refer questions to the Court of Justice in environmental cases,[263] and there is considerable pressure not to do so because of the present number of cases currently pending before the Court. There is also the practical problem that preliminary references attract much less publicity compared to adverse judgments against Member States, and environmental interest groups tend to litigate where general points of law can be established (and publicised). The lack of resources at Community level to ensure the implementation of EC law, however, is also one reason why the Court of Justice has developed a number of doctrines, discussed below, the purpose of which is to allow individuals to assert their rights under EC law before their national courts.[264]

### 4.13.1 Enforcement Proceedings by the Commission

Under Article 226 of the EC Treaty:

> If the Commission considers that a Member State has failed to fulfil an obligation under this Treaty, it shall deliver a reasoned opinion on the matter after giving the State concerned the opportunity to submit its observations.
>
> If the State concerned does not comply with the opinion within the period laid down by the Commission, the latter may bring the matter before the Court of Justice.

In practice, the procedure provided for under Article 226 involves a letter of formal notice being sent by the Commission to the Member State concerned, a reasoned opinion being provided by the Commission and, ultimately, a referral of the matter to the Court of Justice. Member States are allowed at least two months to reply to the letter of formal notice, and if the response is not satisfactory, the reasoned opinion of the Commission sets a further deadline for a response from the Member State. If that response is not satisfactory, the Commission can apply to have the case brought before the Court on the grounds stated in the formal notice and reasoned opinion, but may not introduce new grounds which the Member State has not been given the opportunity to respond to in the preliminary correspondence.[265] The final stage is the referral of the issue to the Court of Justice, where cases may be referred even if non-implementation has been remedied (since the critical date for assessing non-compliance is the

---

[262] E.g. Case C-44/95 *R* v *Secretary of State for the Environment, ex parte RSPB* [1996] ECR I-3805 ('Lappel Bank'). For an overview see Somsen (2000).

[263] The only three cases which have been referred at the time of writing are Case C-44/95 *R* v *Secretary of State for the Environment ex parte RSPB* [1996] ECR I-3805 ('Lappel Bank'); Case C-293/97 *R* v *Secretary of State for the Environment and Minister of Agriculture, Fisheries and Food, ex parte Standley* [1999] ECR I-2603 and Case C-371/98 *R* v *Secretary of State for the Environment, Transport and the Regions, ex parte First Corporate Shipping Ltd*, [2001] 1 CMLR 19.

[264] See 4.16 below.

[265] See Case C-337/89 *Commission* v *United Kingdom* [1992] ECR I-6103, discussed at 4.15.1 below, and see also 7.93 and 17.7.1 below.

end of the period stated in the reasoned opinion). Despite the large number of complaints about environmental matters received by the Commission,[266] however, the numbers of cases that actually come before the court are relatively small, certainly when compared to other areas of EC law.[267] The Commission has an absolute discretion whether to bring enforcement action.[268]

### 4.13.2 Compliance Requirements upon Member States

Following referral of a matter to the Court of Justice, Article 228 EC (ex Article 171) provides that if the Court finds that a Member State has failed to fulfil an obligation under the Treaty, the State shall be required to take the necessary measures to comply with the Court's judgment. As the Treaty has been amended the Commission may now bring a second application against a Member State, in the event of continuing non-compliance with a judgment of the Court, and specify an appropriate level of sanction. However, reservations have been expressed about the appropriateness of using financial sanctions in relation to the enforcement of EC environmental law. Three particular arguments have been advanced in this respect:

(a) that they will be unnecessary since, if the system for monitoring national compliance was made more effective and the findings published, the political embarrassment that would result from this would provide a better incentive to enforcement;

(b) that imposing fines will not assist environmental protection and might actually reduce the monies available for compliance; and

(c) that imposing a fine might be unfair, in that it would fall on all taxpayers, rather than those specifically responsible for the particular illegality proceeded against.[269]

Two communications have been issued by the Commission concerning the methods for calculating penalty payments.[270] These emphasise the seriousness and length of the infringement and the deterrent effect of the financial sanction and the outcome is determined by the financial capacity of the Member State. The seriousness of the violation will be evaluated on a case-by-case basis, taking into account such factors as the clarity of the rule which has been breached and the seriousness of the environmental damage or harm to human health involved. The duration of the violation

---

[266] See 4.13.3 below on the Commission's complaints procedure.

[267] For a survey of environmental cases brought before the European Court up to the end of 1995, see Krämer (1996).

[268] Case 48/65 *Lütticke (Alfons)* v *Commission* [1966] ECR 19; Case 247/87 *Star Fruit* v *Commission* [1989] ECR 291 and Case C-107/95P *Bundesverband der Bilanzbuchhalter* v *Commission* [1997] ECR I-947. See also comment on the exercise of discretion by the Commission at 4.13.3 below.

[269] See House of Lords Select Committee on the European Communities, *Implementation and Enforcement of Environmental Legislation* (1992) Vol.1 para.83 (henceforth *Implementation and Enforcement*).

[270] Memorandum 96/C 242/07, OJ 1996 C 242/6 and Communication 97/C 63/02, OJ C63/2.

runs from the date of the first court hearing and it is relevant to consider the co-operation of the Member State in seeking to resolve the matter after the hearing. In addition to these two variable factors, there is a degree of weighting which is applied taking into account the Member State's influence over the law which has been violated (i.e. the number of votes it has on the Council and its gross domestic product). If all of these factors resulted in the maximum daily penalty it could lead to significant fines (well in excess of €500,000 in some cases) which could be a serious deterrent.[271]

In practice, the majority of the cases where the Commission has requested payment have been settled before proceedings have been brought to the European Court of Justice. For example, the Commission sought daily fines of €264,000 and €158,400 respectively from Germany for non-compliance with the judgments in cases relating to the Groundwater Directive[272] and to the Drinking Water Abstraction Directive.[273] In both cases the dispute was resolved before any proceedings were brought,[274] suggesting that the prospect of substantial fines being imposed may have caused some Member States to take corrective action. Nevertheless, the suspicion remains that the 'embarrassment factor', generated by adverse publicity, may actually count for more than the monetary penalties imposed.[275]

In the first case to be decided by the Court of Justice on Article 228 EC (ex Article 171),[276] a daily fine of €20,000 was imposed on the Greek Government for non-compliance with an earlier ruling concerning waste management, as a result of which leachates were continuing to seep into the sea.[277] The judgment stressed that determining the appropriate fine level was ultimately a matter for the Court, and the Court essentially upheld the approach to calculating fine levels laid down by the Commission in the guidance documents noted above. In this respect, a significant aspect of the judgment is the extent to which the Court found that failure to implement waste management plans was to be regarded as seriously as actual mismanagement of waste on the ground. In particular, the fact that specific measures had been taken to reduce quantities of toxic and dangerous waste[278] was said not to have a bearing on the seriousness of the failure to comply with waste management planning obligations for these types of waste.[279] However, the Court also pointed out that the

---

[271] The Commission has also discussed the possibility of withholding EC funds provided for environmental matters in the event of non-compliance.

[272] Directive 80/68/EEC, see Case C-131/88 *Commission* v *Germany* [1991] ECR I-825 and on the Directive see 5.4.2 below.

[273] Directive 75/440/EEC, see Case C-58/89 *Commission* v *Germany* [1991] ECR I-4983 and on the Directive see 17.6 below.

[274] Krämer (2000), p.292.

[275] *Making it Work* para.98.

[276] Case C-387/97 *Commission* v *Hellenic Republic*, 4 July 2000, not yet reported.

[277] Case C-45/91 *Commission* v *Greece* [1992] ECR I-2509.

[278] Indeed, on the disposal of this kind of waste, the Commission could not establish any substantive breach (para.74).

[279] *Ibid* para.96.

penalties to be imposed were not strictly punitive, since their purpose was to influence future conduct. Therefore, while the Treaty allows for both lump sums and daily penalty payments to be imposed, the judgment suggests a judicial preference for the latter. As the cases which did not proceed to the Court indicate, this is in line with Commission behaviour in terminating cases where the Member State comes into compliance before the case is submitted to the Court of Justice.

### 4.13.3 The Complaints Procedure

As an enforcement provision, Article 226 EC is greatly reliant upon the capacity of the Commission to bring appropriate cases before the Court. However, the Commission does not have any formal competence to investigate environmental compliance within the territory of the Member States and, in part, it must base its decisions to instigate proceedings on information provided at Member State level. This may be by national governments passing on transposition or monitoring information. But a far greater number of potential contraventions of EC law are brought to its attention by concerned individuals and environmental action groups,[280] and matters raised for consideration by the Parliament, under its complaints procedure.

As a mechanism for dealing rationally and effectively with breaches of Community water law, however, the complaints procedure has many weaknesses. The Commission is directed to those matters which are the subject of complaint, rather than those that represent the most flagrant violations of Community environmental law or breaches leading to the greatest environmental harm. The Commission is also directed towards those issues and areas where the levels of environmental concern are greatest, rather than where breaches of the law are most serious or require the most urgent attention. The Commission itself downplays the importance of what may be serious breaches of quality or emissions standards on the ground, prioritising breaches of Community law *per se* rather than environmental harm.[281] It is also clear that decisions on complaints, and other questions related to Article 226, 'always contain an element of political decision'[282] and there is fairly compelling evidence of

---

[280] It has been estimated that 80% of complaints registered with the Commission are made by the public (see European Parliament, Committee on the Environment, Public Health and Consumer Protection, *Working Document on the Implementation of Community Environmental Law* (1996) para.6, published as Appendix 6 to *Making it Work*.

[281] Hence the guidelines advise Commission staff to deal with complaints in the following order of priority: first, 'infringements which cause the greatest damage to the Community legal order, i. e. failure to transpose legislation and failure of national legislation to comply with Community law'; second, 'horizontal cases of incorrect application, in particular when these are detected on the basis of a series of specific complaints by individuals' and, third, 'infringements which seriously harm the interests which the transgressed law is intended to protect' (*Making it Work* para.85, and see Appendix 13 which reproduces the Commission Guidelines).

[282] Krämer (1998) p.178. A stronger view is that "the overtly political nature of the grievance procedure at Community level is a massive hindrance to effective environmental protection. There is an astonishing degree of interference and non-cooperation by Member States who often appear to display a cavalier disregard for the rule of law which they themselves are duty bound to uphold"

political interference.[283] More fundamental doubts have been raised about the capacity of the Commission to function independently as a guardian of the public interest in relation to environmental litigation.[284] Alongside the unavoidably political role of the Commission, the legislation under which it must act gives rise to serious conflicts of interest. This might arise, for example, where a decision of the Commission is contested on environmental grounds.[285]

Finally, the procedure for bringing complaints to the Court of Justice is lengthy,[286] and some environmental actions have involved the Court taking five years to give a ruling.[287] Nevertheless, the formal registration of a complaint has often been sufficient to prompt a Member State to re-examine the matter at issue and led to the settlement of the majority of proceedings without the matter being judicially considered.[288] This was the case, e.g., when a complaint by an individual about the UK's implementation of the Groundwater Directive[289] led to the Commission issuing a reasoned opinion in March 1997, which was the trigger for enacting the Groundwater Regulations 1998.[290]

### 4.13.4 Information and the Co-operation Duty

Article 10 of the EC Treaty (ex Article 5) provides a general legal basis for requiring co-operation by the Member States where this is required by any of the institutions of the Community, and also imposes on Member States a duty to facilitate the achievement of the Community's tasks. One difficulty in enforcing Community law is delay by the Member States in dealing with requests for information from the Commission. Since 1999, the Commission has begun to make much greater use of Article 10 for such things as clarifying facts and confirmation of official positions, and there are a number of examples where this procedure has been used in relation to water directives.[291]

---

(European Parliament, Committee on the Environment, Public Health and Consumer Protection, *Working Document on the Implementation of Community environmental law*, (1996) section 4 para.7, published as Appendix 6 to *Making it Work*.

[283] See Williams (1994) and Kunzlik (1995).

[284] Krämer (1997) ch.14 at p.308.

[285] See, for example, Case C-321/95P *Stichting Greenpeace Council* v *Commission* [1998] 3 CMLR 1, and Case C-325/94 *An Taisce and WWF(UK)* v *Commission* [1996] ECR I-3727, discussed at 4.6 above.

[286] Krämer (2000) p.291.

[287] E.g. Case C-45/91 *Commission v Greece* [1992] ECR I-2509, cited by Macrory and Purdy (1997) p.35.

[288] Macrory (1992), although recently there has been a decline in the proportion of environmental complaints, see Macrory and Purdy (1997) p.38.

[289] Directive 80/68/EEC, see 5.4.2 below. See *ENDS Report* 275 (1997) p.40.

[290] On the Groundwater Regulations 1998 see 13.6 below.

[291] E.g., 'Commission again takes action against Italy, Ireland, Spain and France for failure to supply environmental information', RAPID, IP/00/344, 7 April 2000.

### 4.13.5 The Role of the European Ombudsman

Although a decision of the Commission not to follow the procedures leading to proceedings before the Court is not open to judicial review,[292] there are mechanisms allowing scrutiny of the Commission's procedures in declining to pursue enforcement proceedings. The European Ombudsman may receive complaints from persons in the Community concerning maladministration in the activities of the Community institutions or bodies, except where a judicial role is being exercised.[293] The Ombudsman may conduct inquiries where grounds are shown, either in response to a complaint or at his own initiative. Where an instance of maladministration is established, the matter must be referred to the institution concerned and time allowed for a response to be offered. This is followed by a report to the European Parliament and the institution concerned, which may incorporate the Ombudsman's recommendations.[294] The Ombudsman has no power to order an institution or body to change a decision or grant redress by annulling decision or by awarding damages. Nevertheless, the referral of a matter to the Ombudsman may be an effective mechanism of drawing attention to procedural improprieties where the Commission has declined to pursue an environmental complaint under Article 226 EC.[295]

The alternative to a complaint to the Ombudsman is the right of EU citizens to petition the European Parliament on any matter within the Community's fields of activity which directly affects them.[296] This is broader in scope than the areas that may be considered by the Ombudsman, whose remit is confined to matters of maladministration by EC institutions. It might, therefore, allow the investigation of political considerations which have influenced Commission decisions which fall short of maladministration.[297]

### 4.14 IMPEL and Minimum Criteria for Environmental Inspections

The European Environment Agency, established in 1993 and considered in detail elsewhere,[298] has no role in monitoring the application of Community environmental law, and acts only as a body charged with gathering Europe-wide environmental information. However, while there is clear resistance to formal Community-level control over the activities of national authorities with the responsibility to monitor and enforce Community environmental law, significant practical progress in the harmonisation of practice by informal means has been made. This has been

---

[292] See 4.13.1 above.

[293] See Arts.21 and 195 EC (ex Arts.8d and 138e). Generally see House of Lords Select Committee on the European Communities, *The European Ombudsman* (1997) and Magliveras (1995).

[294] Art.195 EC and Decision 94/262/ECSC, EC, Euratom on the regulations and general conditions governing the performance of the Ombudsman's duties.

[295] Kunzlik (1997).

[296] Under Art.194 EC (ex Art.138d), and see Marias (1994).

[297] Kunzlik (1997).

[298] On the European Environment Agency see 16.3 below.

through the 'European Community Network for the Implementation and Enforcement of Environmental Law', now referred to as IMPEL, comprising representatives of environmental regulatory bodies within the Member States.[299] The aim of IMPEL is to enhance the effectiveness of environmental legislation within the Member States by promoting the exchange of information and expertise between regulators and developing a more consistent approach to implementation and enforcement.[300]

While IMPEL has made good progress towards this end, one problematic limitation is that its membership is only open to representatives of environmental enforcement bodies concerned with industrial installations within the Member States. Consequently, it does not cover all Community environmental legislation and notable omissions are those bodies of legislation concerned with wildlife conservation and certain water directives, such as the Bathing Water Directive,[301] which are not directly concerned with industrial activities.[302] A proposal to address this is that IMPEL's scope should be extended to cover 'cross-cutting' regulatory aspects of Community environmental legislation concerning the environmental media, such as the licensing, monitoring and auditing of other non-industrial polluters, such as sewage treatment works.[303]

Although there is little prospect of a pan-EC environmental inspectorate, there are some steps in the direction of a greater role for the Community in relation to implementation. At a recent meeting of the Environment Council, broad agreement was reached on proposals which would establish minimum criteria for environmental inspections in Member States. Under these proposals Member States would be required to draw up plans covering both routine monitoring of industrial activities regulated under Community environmental law, and non-routine follow-up inspections.[304] While this indicates a continuing concern with the lack of uniformity in implementation and its enforcement, it clearly stops short of an 'inspectorate of inspectorates' along the lines that have previously been proposed for a strengthened European Environment Agency. As with IMPEL, however, the proposals would only apply to industrial activities, and not to environmental law more generally.

---

[299] See OJ 1993, C138/80.

[300] See Osborn, 'The Chester Network', Memorandum submitted to the House of Lords Select Committee on the European Communities, *European Environment Agency* (1995), Minutes of Evidence p.13.

[301] Directive 76/160/EEC and see 5.5.2 below.

[302] Haigh, *Effective Environment Protection: Challenges for the Implementation of EC Law*, Appendix 5 s.2.7, in *Making it Work*.

[303] *The future role and organisation of IMPEL*, a discussion paper prepared by the Environment Agency (for England and Wales) on behalf of the Department of the Environment for the Dublin Plenary meeting, 21 to 22 November 1996, published as Appendix 12 to *Making it Work*.

[304] Conseil 99/409, Brussels, 13/14 December 1999, at www.asser.nl/EEL/index4.htm

## 4.15 The United Kingdom Water Cases

Many of the key issues relating to the practical implementation of EC environmental law are well illustrated by Commission enforcement action concerning the implementation of EC water legislation in the UK. Of these, two judgments of the Court of Justice relate to the Drinking Water Quality Directive.[305] A third judgment of the Court related to the quality of bathing waters at Blackpool and Southport,[306] while there is in prospect the possibility of a further appearance before the Court for non-compliance with this Directive.[307]

### 4.15.1 The Drinking Water Cases

The 'Drinking Water' cases concerned the implementation by the UK of the Drinking Water Quality Directive,[308] which required that maximum admissible concentrations of certain parameters, specified in an Annex to the Directive, should not be exceeded. The Directive allowed the UK until 18 July 1982 to enact the necessary national laws to implement the Directive and until 18 July 1985 to ensure that drinking water in the UK complied with the substantive requirements of the Directive.

In August 1987, following a complaint from Friends of the Earth in 1986,[309] the Commission sent a letter of formal notice to the UK Government raising concerns about drinking water quality since, at this time, no formal implementing legislation had been enacted. An action was filed before the Court of Justice on 31 October 1989, but in the intervening period the Water Supply (Water Quality) Regulations 1989[310] had been enacted and had taken effect in England and Wales at the time the action was lodged. Nevertheless, in its first infringement action against the UK the Commission alleged breach of the Directive on the grounds that:

(a) the 1989 Regulations did not cover Scotland and Northern Ireland and did not fully cover the food industry as required by the Directive;

(b) the nitrate levels in 28 supply zones in England exceeded the maximum admissible concentrations allowed under the Directive; and

(c) lead levels in 17 supply zones in Scotland exceeded the maximum admissible concentration.

---

[305] Case C-337/89 *Commission* v *United Kingdom* [1992] ECR I-6103 and Case C-340/96 *Commission* v *United Kingdom* [1999] ECR I-2023.

[306] Case C-56/90 *Commission* v *United Kingdom* [1993] ECR I-4109.

[307] See now also Case C-69/99 *Commission* v *UK*, 7 December 2000, not yet reported, concerning the Nitrates Directive (91/676/EEC), see 13.5 below.

[308] Directive 80/778/EEC, and see 17.7.1 below.

[309] 'European Court 'Convicts' UK Government over Sub-Standard Drinking Water', Friends of the Earth press release, 25 November 1992.

[310] SI 1989 No.1147, on which see 17.7.2 below.

In effect, therefore, the bases of the proceedings were a combination of formal failures to enact comprehensive legislation implementing the Directive comprehensively across its territory and within all relevant sectors, and substantive failures to meet the requirements of the Directive in respect of the nitrate and lead parameters. The failure to make any provision for the formal implementation of the Directive until the 1989 Regulations were enacted, several years after the deadline for enactment of national implementing legislation, was not raised as an alleged infringement.

In its defence, the UK raised a series of procedural and substantive arguments:

(a) that the Commission had failed to follow proper procedures by adding to the original complaint which, it was contended, was only raised in relation to private water supplies;

(b) that enacting the Water Supply (Water Quality) (Scotland) Regulations 1990[311] and the Food Safety Act 1990 rendered the Commission's complaints concerning water in Scotland and in relation to the food industry irrelevant;

(c) that the delay in relation to Northern Ireland was justified because of difficulties relating to the organisation of public authorities in the province;

(d) that where a Member State takes all necessary steps to achieve the water quality requirements, then a failure to achieve them in isolated cases would not constitute an infringement of the Directive;

(e) that the UK was entitled to the benefit of derogations in the Directive concerned with peculiar geological conditions and exceptional cases;[312] and

(f) that the Commission had failed to prove its case concerning excessive levels of lead in water in Scotland.

In all but the last of these arguments, the Court of Justice found against the UK. In the first place the Commission had not infringed any rule of pre-litigation procedure because its letter of formal notice and its reasoned opinion had both been drafted with sufficient breadth to encompass all the specific allegations contained in the final complaint against the UK considered by the Court. Second, the failure to implement the Directive in relation to Scotland was an infringement of Community obligations. Third, the administrative problems in Northern Ireland did not justify a failure to implement the Directive. Fourth, the maximum admissible concentrations provided for in the Directive are binding legal obligations that Member States are bound to achieve. Fifth, the UK had failed to achieve the maximum admissible concentration for nitrate, and had not established that any of the derogations in the Directive applied. Finally, it was accepted that the Commission had failed to prove its case in relation to exceedence

---

[311] SI 1990 No.119

[312] As provided for under Arts.9 and 20 of the Directive, see 17.7.1 below.

of the maximum admissible concentration for lead in Scotland, since it could not establish that standards were being breached 'frequently or to an appreciable extent'.

Although the first Drinking Water case did not establish any significantly new principles of Community environmental law, it does provide a useful example of the strictness of the obligation upon Member States to secure timely, comprehensive and substantive compliance with all relevant parameters in a water directive. It was not accepted that late compliance with the Directive rendered the proceedings inadmissible. Moreover, it reaffirmed that a Member State may not plead provisions, practices or circumstances in its internal legal system in order to justify a failure to comply with the obligations or time limits imposed by a Directive. Similarly, the argument of the UK that it was sufficient to take 'all practicable steps' to achieve the resulted required by a directive was not accepted by the Court.

More recently, the Commission has taken further infringement proceedings against the UK over the Drinking Water Quality Directive. This second action related to the practice, in England and Wales, of accepting from water companies what in effect are timetables of agreed action, known as 'undertakings', in lieu of taking enforcement action against the companies for breaching the Water Supply (Water Quality) Regulations 1989.[313] In passing, it might be noted that these undertakings are drafted by the water companies and then agreed with the Drinking Water Inspectorate.[314] Part of the background to this second action was that, following the first Drinking Water case, Friends of the Earth had brought a judicial review action against the Secretary of State for the Environment.[315] In these proceedings it was argued that the Secretary of State acted unlawfully in accepting undertakings[316] from Thames Water and Anglian Water when they were in breach of the pesticide standard in the Drinking Water Quality Directive. The decision of the Court of Appeal, however, was that while the *primary* duty imposed by the Directive on the Government was absolute, in the sense that it was not an excuse to argue that all practicable steps had been taken to achieve the standards, this then gave rise to a *secondary* duty to comply with the judgment of the Court of Justice. This secondary duty, it held, was not absolute in the same way, but was capable of being qualified by practical considerations such as the cost of providing consumers with water of an acceptable standard as speedily as reasonably practicable.

In the second infringement proceedings brought by the Commission, it was argued that the practice of accepting undertakings from the water companies was in breach of the Directive, since in theory they gave unlimited time for the companies to comply with the mandatory standards

---

[313] See ss.18-22 Water Industry Act 1991 and see 7.9.2 below on undertakings.

[314] On the Drinking Water Inspectorate see 17.5 below

[315] *R* v *Secretary of State for the Environment, ex parte Friends of the Earth* [1996] Env LR 227.

[316] And, in the lead up to the oral hearing before the Court of Justice in the first Drinking Water case, revised undertakings.

laid down in the Directive. At a later stage in the proceedings, it was also argued that the use of undertakings prevented individuals from asserting their rights under the Directive. The UK Government, however, argued that the use of undertakings was a reasonable and legitimate response to remedying the problem after it was recognised that the deadline for complying with the Directive had been breached. Moreover, the UK Government raised the issue that when the enforcement provisions which are now contained in the Water Industry Act 1991[317] were first considered, at the time of privatisation, the Commission had been consulted on the compatibility of the draft legislation with Community law and changes had subsequently been made to the enforcement provisions in response to this consultation.

On the use of undertakings generally, the Court of Justice supported the Commission and found the UK Government to be in breach of its obligations.[318] In a sense, this decision was unsurprising, since the Water Industry Act 1991 does not specify the kinds of things to be covered in the compliance programme, nor indeed the timetable within which compliance should be attained. The Court also followed its settled position in holding that any prior negotiations there may have been between the UK Government and the Commission were immaterial to whether national legislation was in compliance with the Directive. However, the Court refused to consider the question of whether the UK was in breach of any duty it might have had to ensure that individuals could assert any rights derived from the Directive, since this issue had been raised too late in the proceedings to be considered.

The second action brought by the Commission illustrates the rather different approaches taken by the Court of Justice and the national courts to questions of implementation. For the latter, in the *ex parte Friends of the Earth* case, there was an obvious reluctance to interfere with the undertakings that had been accepted by government. For the Court of Justice, however, the undertakings were clearly incompatible with its established case law on implementation and the need for effective EC legislation. Following the second infringement case, it is notable that the Drinking Water (Undertakings) (England and Wales) Regulations 2000[319] were enacted. These are an explicit response to the judgment of the Court of Justice, and in effect require undertakings to be entered into only for the shortest possible period and only if no reasonable alternatives exist. It is debatable, however, whether the Regulations will in fact secure full compliance with the Directive, or whether they will merely make transparent what had already been agreed. What they may do, however, is ward off any attempt by the Commission to use the powers available to it

---

[317] See ss.20-22 Water Act 1989. On the drafting of the Water Bill (which became the Water Act 1989) see also 2.16 above.

[318] Case C-340/96 *Commission v United Kingdom* [1999] ECR I-2023.

[319] SI 2000 No. 1297 and see 7.9.4 below.

under Article 228 EC to seek financial penalties from the UK Government for non-compliance with the Directive.[320]

### 4.15.2 The Blackpool Bathing Water Case

The *Blackpool Bathing Water* case[321] concerned the failure of the UK to meet water quality requirements under the Bathing Water Directive[322] in relation to waters at Blackpool and Southport. The Directive had been adopted on 8 December 1975, and notified to the UK on 10 December 1975, and required that, within ten years of notification, the quality of bathing waters within the scope of the Directive must conform to the physical, chemical and microbiological parameters set out in the Directive.[323] However, under exceptional circumstances Member States were allowed to make derogations provided that such derogations were based upon plans for the management of the water and communicated to the Commission not later than 10 December 1981.[324]

Under the Directive, 'bathing waters' are defined as those waters where bathing is explicitly permitted, or where bathing 'is not prohibited and is traditionally practised by a large number of bathers',[325] but no criteria are provided as to what was meant by a 'large' number of bathers. Partially because of uncertainty in determining which waters needed to be identified, on 18 December 1979 the UK applied a restrictive identification test and notified the Commission of only 27 areas which fell within the scope of the Directive. This list did not include the waters at Blackpool or Southport.

Nothing more was heard from the Commission on this matter until 1986, when it drew the UK Government's attention to the quality of the waters at Blackpool and Southport which it regarded as bathing waters and which failed to meet the quality requirements under the Directive, the ten year period for implementation having elapsed.[326] The UK Government reconsidered the method of identifying bathing waters and 362 additional bathing waters were notified to the Commission in February 1987, including the waters at Blackpool and Southport. In February 1988 the Commission served a reasoned opinion upon the UK that there had been a breach of the Directive in relation to the waters at Blackpool and Southport and required a response within two months. In March 1990 the Commission initiated proceedings in the Court of Justice against the UK

---

[320] See 4.13.2 above.

[321] Case C-56/90 *Commission* v *United Kingdom* [1993] ECR I-4109, and see Geddes (1994).

[322] Directive 76/160/EEC, and see 5.5.2 below.

[323] *Ibid* Art.4(1).

[324] *Ibid* Art.4(3).

[325] *Ibid* Art.1(2)(a).

[326] Anecdotally, having been informed by a loosely-worded postcard from an irate bather.

for a declaration that it was in breach of the Directive in respect of the specified waters.[327]

Whilst the UK did not dispute that the quality of the bathing waters concerned failed to meet the requirements of the Directive, in essence, three arguments were raised in defence. First, it was argued that the action was inadmissible because the UK was entitled to infer the approval of the Commission to the original list of bathing waters, submitted in 1979, from the fact that the Commission had raised no objections to the list. Second, the UK maintained that the ten year time limit for implementation of the Directive ran from the time of identification of the waters, and not from the time of notification of the Directive. Third, it was argued that the Directive only imposed upon Member States an obligation to take all practical steps to comply and this duty had been complied with.

The Court of Justice found against the UK on all counts. In relation to the admissibility argument, the Court found that the Commission was not obliged to express any opinion on the initial list and that its approval could not be inferred from the absence of objection or from silence. The Commission was entitled to formulate objections at any time that it thought appropriate. Beyond this it was not accepted that it would be physically impossible to adopt the necessary measures within the two month period that the Commission had allowed for improvement in the reasoned opinion of 2 February 1988, because the same concerns had been raised in the earlier letters in 1986, almost two years prior to the reasoned opinion. In the circumstances the period was regarded as reasonable and, in any event, the UK could have prohibited bathing in the areas in question, an action which had been taken by other Member States.[328]

In respect of the second argument that the ten year period did not begin to run until bathing waters were identified, that is from February 1987, the Court held that the waters concerned should have been identified as bathing waters from the outset. Contrary to the supposition that identification of bathing water was a matter of discretion for each Member State, the Court regarded the matter as one of objective fact depending upon all the circumstances. Considering the objectives of the Directive as indicated by the recitals, and that the resorts concerned were equipped with bathing facilities such as huts, toilets and markers indicating bathing areas supervised by lifeguards, there was clear evidence that the waters should have been included in the original identification of bathing waters. The failure of the UK to designate the waters in 1979 could not be used as a justification for allowing a longer period for the waters to attain the required quality standards. The ten year time period began to run from the time that waters *should* have been designated.

---

[327] Part of the reason for this delay can be attributed to UK Government anxiety to delay infringement proceedings while water privatisation was ongoing: see Jordan and Greenaway (1998) p.681.

[328] On the absence of a specific requirement to prohibit bathing see 5.5.2(c) below.

In relation to the third argument raised by the UK, that the Directive imposed upon Member States an obligation only to take all practical steps to comply, the Court referred back to the wording of the Directive. This made it clear that the obligation was to take all necessary measures to ensure that, within ten years following the notification of the Directive, bathing water conforms to the limit values. Accordingly, Member States must ensure that certain results are attained, and apart from the provision for derogations, they cannot rely upon particular circumstances to justify a failure to fulfil this obligation. The point was raised by the UK that there might be circumstances where it was physically impossible to achieve the obligations required by the Directive. The Court left this possibility open[329] in suggesting that even if absolute physical impossibility did excuse a failure, as a matter of fact the UK had not succeeded in establishing the existence of such impossibility in the circumstances at issue.

Whilst the *Blackpool Bathing Water* case does not raise significantly new points of Community law, it does provide another pertinent illustration of the strictness of the obligations upon Member States actually to realise quality objectives provided for under water directives. Taking practicable steps will not be sufficient, and other than the unlikely possibility of absolute physical impossibility, Member States will be bound to ensure that substantive obligations under directives are met. Another consequence of failure to achieve this is the possibility that actions may be available to private individuals who have suffered injury to their individual rights, for example by suffering ill health as a result of bathing in water which fails to meet the requirements of the Directive, and who may be able to sue the Member State as a consequence.[330]

By way of a recent update on the *Blackpool* case, it is worth noting that despite substantial investment in clean-up, in January 2000 the Commission issued a Reasoned Opinion against the UK for continued breach of standards contained in the Bathing Water Directive at beaches around Blackpool.[331] The Reasoned Opinion was issued under Article 228 EC (ex Article 171), however, and thus the infringement proceedings relate to non-compliance with the earlier judgment of the Court of Justice in 1993. If this case is brought for a second time before the Court of Justice, then the UK may be liable for a daily fine.[332] Given that the Bathing Water Directive was agreed to unanimously, that the UK has a relatively high gross domestic product amongst the Member States, that the Directive relates to public health, that the breach of standards has continued for such a long time,[333] and that compliance is some way from

---

[329] But see now Case C-198/97 *Commission* v *Germany* [1999] ECR I-3257, at 5.5.2(c) below.

[330] See 4.16.6 below on state liability, where the limitations of direct effect when there are multiple effluent discharge points is noted.

[331] 'Bathing Water: Commission acts against several Member States', RAPID, IP/00/14, 11 January 2000.

[332] See 4.13.2 above.

[333] The case appears to be one of the oldest environmental infringements currently being handled by the Commission.

being achieved, it is possible that any fine sought by the Commission could be considerable.[334] This action is distinct from proceedings which have been taken to the European Court of Justice relating to general non-compliance with the Bathing Water Directive across the UK as a whole.[335]

## 4.16 Enforcing EC Water Law in National Courts

The mechanism that is formally required for implementing a directive involves the Member States enacting national legislation to give effect to the requirements of the directive. The consequence of this is that generally transparent legal obligations will be provided for in national law which will allow remedies in domestic courts in the event of a failure to implement a directive. However, a critical difficulty arises where this does not happen and national legislation fails to give effect to a directive or does so in an imperfect or incomplete manner. In particular, the issue then arises as to what remedies are available to persons who are disadvantaged by such shortcomings and seek redress either against the state or against other individuals. Additionally, can individuals or groups seek to 'enforce' other provisions of Community law where they have suffered no obvious personal detriment, or where the Community obligation is set at a high level of generality?

As with 'enforcement' by the European Court of Justice when infringement proceedings are taken by the Commission under Article 226 EC, enforcement before national courts has different dimensions. Classically, this has been through the doctrine of 'direct effect', whereby if certain conditions apply, directives can be enforced by individuals or companies before national courts regardless of whether there has been correct transposition by the Member State. Direct effect is therefore considered initially. As will be seen, there is some doubt as to whether there must be breach of an individual right for there to be 'direct effect'. This may be a particular difficulty in relation to environmental directives where the objective may be general improvements to environmental quality rather than protecting individual rights. However, there are various responses to this. As suggested below, there is a good case to be made that the doctrine of direct effect does not require individual rights (e.g. rights relating to human health) to have been breached. Hence, directives should be 'enforceable' in national courts in the sense that individuals may take actions at national level which, in effect, require the Member State to achieve compliance with the directive in question.

This is not 'enforcement' in same sense that a criminal prosecution by the Environment Agency for a national water pollution offence is 'enforcement' of the Water Resources Act 1991.[336] Rather, it is in the nature of a judicial review of the activities of central or local government

---

[334] See now 'Bathing water quality and impact assessment: Commission proposes fines against the UK and Germany', RAPID IP/00/1541, 22 December 2000.

[335] See 5.5.2(c) below.

[336] See 9.19 below on offences.

or some public authority such as the Environment Agency, alleging non-compliance with Community obligations. Nevertheless, it is an approach to Community law which is generally categorised as 'enforcement' since the origins of direct effect is a concern by the Court of Justice that Community law should be given effect to and not evaded by a Member State's failure to enact legislation giving force to Community obligations.[337] Likewise, further 'internalising doctrines' of the Court of Justice, the doctrines of sympathetic interpretation (or 'indirect effect') and of 'state liability' (or '*Francovich* liability'), have also been developed to give greater practical effect to EC law and may be important in relation to water directives.

### 4.16.1 Direct Effect

The doctrine of 'direct effect' enables EC law to be applied in national courts despite the absence of implementing legislation.[338] This doctrine, devised by the Court of Justice, is generally said to provide that EC law can confer rights[339] upon individuals directly and these may be invoked before national courts without the need for reliance on national legislation.[340] However, this is only possible where a Community measure, which has not been provided for in national law within the period allowed for transposition, is sufficiently clear and precise, unconditional and leaves no discretion as to the manner of implementation. Alternatively, it has been suggested that the crucial issue is whether a provision of Community law provides a national court with sufficient guidance to apply it without exceeding the limits of its judicial powers.[341] Essentially, therefore, direct effect permits an individual to compel a Member State to comply with a Community obligation where the requirements for direct effect have been satisfied, and to pursue an action of this kind before national courts.

---

[337] In this sense, there is a distinction between direct effect and references to the Court of Justice under Article 234 EC (ex Article 177), the latter being intended to provide a determinative mechanism to agree on the interpretation of Community law; see 4.13 above.

[338] Generally on the environmental aspects of direct effect see Krämer (1997) ch.4 and Wyatt (1998).

[339] Notably direct effect is said to confer *rights* on individuals (although see below) and not *obligations*. For example, the Natural Mineral Waters Directive (80/777/EEC) imposes a prohibition upon the sale of tap water as mineral water. Despite the failure of the Netherlands to transpose this into national legislation, the prohibition imposed obligations rather than rights upon individuals and for that reason could not be directly effective (Case C-80/86 *Officier van Justitie* v *Kolpinghuis Nijmegen BV* [1987] ECR 3969). See 17.13.1 below on this Directive.

[340] The doctrine of direct effect originated in Case C-26/62 *Van Gend en Loos (Algemene Transport – Expedite Onderneming Van Gend en Loos* v *Nederlandse Tarief Commissie)* [1963] ECR 1 where there was held to be an unconditional obligation on the part of a Member State to refrain from introducing new customs duties and this created corresponding rights in favour of citizens. In a frequently cited quotation it was stressed that: 'the Community constitutes a new legal order of international law for the benefit of which the states have limited their sovereign rights, albeit within limited fields, and the subjects of which comprise not only member states but also their nationals. Independently of the legislation of member states, Community law therefore not only imposes obligations on individuals but is also intended to confer upon them rights which become part of their legal heritage' (at p.29).

[341] Jans (1996) p.50.

Another limitation upon the availability of direct effect lies in the contrast between 'vertical' and 'horizontal' direct effect. Broadly, vertical direct effect is where an individual seeks to invoke a Community measure against the state or a public body, whereas horizontal direct effect is where a person seeks to invoke such a measure against another individual or private body. The general legal position is that vertical direct effect is permissible whereas horizontal direct effect is not[342] because the direct effect doctrine is based on the notion that Member States should not be able to evade their obligations under EC law because of their own failings (in effect, an 'estoppel' argument).

Because the doctrine of direct effect may normally only be invoked against a Member State, the extent of 'the state' is important in ascertaining whether the doctrine will be applicable. In particular, the status of various kind of public body and quasi-public body, such as utilities, is important in determining whether vertical direct effect is available against them. The issue was raised in *Foster* v *British Gas plc*,[343] a case contesting differential compulsory retirement ages for men and women. In a referral to the Court of Justice, it was held that a directive may be invoked against a body, whatever its legal form, which has been made responsible, pursuant to a national measure, for providing a public service under the control of the state and has for that purpose special powers beyond those which result from the normal rules applicable in relations between individuals.

In applying this so called 'emanation of the state' test in an employment case, a privatised water undertaker was similarly determined to be subject to direct effect because of the nature of the public functions that it undertook rather than the form of its commercial structure.[344] This functional approach seems conducive to consistent application of the doctrine of direct effect in different Member States, where utility functions are alternatively provided for by public and private sector bodies in different jurisdictions. The contingency that a utility undertaker operates in the private sector in one Member State should not be used to deprive individuals of rights that would be available in other Member States where the utility is provided by a public body.[345] Even within the same Member State utility services may be provided by the private and public sector in different regions, as is the case with the privatised water industry in England and Wales when compared to its non-privatised counterparts in Scotland and Northern Ireland. In practice, though the privatised water utility companies have on occasion sought to deny that they are public

---

[342] Case C-91/92 *Faccini Dori* v *Recreb Srl* [1994] ECR I-3325.

[343] Case C-188/89 *Foster* v *British Gas plc* [1990] ECR I-3313.

[344] *Griffin* v *South West Water plc* [1995] IRLR 15; see also *Unison* v *South West Water plc* [1995] IRLR 15.

[345] See Burnett-Hall (1995). See now also the opinion of A-G Mischo in Case C-340/96 *Commission* v *UK* [1999] ECR I-2023. For judicial comment emphasising the *private* nature of undertakers see, in a different context, *British Waterways Board* v *Severn Trent Water Ltd* [2001] EWCA Civ 276.

bodies for the purposes of EC law,[346] in other contexts, notably their status in relation to certain water quality directives, the point has been conceded before the courts.[347]

Although direct effect does not generally allow the horizontal enforcement of rights by private individuals against other individuals or bodies, this must be qualified in certain respects. The potential 'indirect horizontal impact'[348] on individuals of the direct effect doctrine in national law depends upon the form of the proceedings in which it is raised. In national administrative proceedings, for example, direct effect might be used by an interested individual to challenge the validity of an environmental licence, or a planning permission, which authorised an activity with adverse environmental consequences.[349] Here, if successful, the outcome of such proceedings would be the annulment of the administrative decision or the cancellation of a licence which is found to be contrary to EC law. The effect of this will clearly impact upon the person to whom the invalid licence had been granted. Hence, whilst the position remains that horizontal application of direct effect is not permissible, vertical application of direct effect is capable of having indirect consequences between individuals which go beyond the assertion of rights by individuals against the State.[350]

## 4.16.2 Direct Effect of Environmental Directives

In principle, the doctrine of direct effect is capable of being invoked in relation to any item of primary or secondary EC law. However, in environmental contexts it is usually most relevant in the context of secondary legislation. This is because the primary environmental legislation, under the Treaty, would not normally be amenable to the doctrine because of the need for a directly effective provision to be sufficiently precise and unconditional for individual rights to arise. As has been noted, the equivocally stated obligations provided for in the Treaty in matters such as the formulation of environmental policy allow the exercise of a considerable amount of discretion by EC institutions in determining how generally stated principles should be interpreted and applied.[351]

In practice, therefore, the important issues surround the interpretation of secondary EC environmental legislation, and the identification of circumstances where the doctrine of direct effect will allow for

---

[346] See 16.17.1 below.

[347] See, e.g., *Moase* v *Secretary of State for the Environment, Transport and the Regions and South West Water Ltd* [2000] Env LR 266 (HC); [2001] Env LR 13 (CA), where the undertaker's position as an emanation of the state for the purposes of the Bathing Water Directive and Urban Waste Water Treatment Directive was common ground between the parties.

[348] See Jans (1995) pp.171-173.

[349] Macrory and Purdy (1997) p.29.

[350] The permissibility of such an indirect horizontal effect action has been upheld by the Court of Appeal in *R* v *Durham CC, Sherburn Stone Company Ltd and Secretary of State for the Environment, Transport and the Regions, ex parte Huddleston* [2000] 2 CMLR 313.

[351] See 4.7 above on policy principles.

enforcement of an environmental directive, or more likely a particular obligation under a directive,[352] that has not been satisfactorily implemented in national law. Insofar as they concern EC water legislation, it has been suggested that, where timely provision has not been made for transposition into national law, provisions which are sufficiently precise and unconditional to be directly effective fall into two main categories:

(a) those where a numerical limitation is imposed upon emissions or concentrations of pollutants; and
(b) those where a prohibition is imposed.

In relation to numerical parameters for emissions or environmental quality the element of precision required for direct effect is clearly present. A number of other water-related examples are given in respect of emission values and quality objectives in relation to discharges of mercury, cadmium, hexachlorocyclohexane and other substances discharged to water.[353] It is also suggested that maximum concentrations of undesirable substances in drinking water also fall into this category.[354] There is some judicial authority to the effect that a minimum harmonisation directive which allows Member States to set higher standards (e.g. higher limit values) may not be sufficiently precise to be directly effective.[355] But notably this has not been endorsed by the Court of Justice and the better view is probably that any directive establishing either limit values or quality standards is, in principle, directly effective up to the level of minimum harmonisation provided for.

The technical specification of various kinds of parameter in the various directives referred to is in each case, therefore, so precisely specified that the precision requirement for direct effect must be met. What is not always so clear, however, is the requirement of unconditionality. In each case this depends upon the degree of discretion allowed to the Member State to designate or identify the particular waters or emissions to which the parameters are to apply. Presumably, if a Member State possessed such discretion, an issue of water or emission quality would fall into the third category of matters which involve an administrative judgment being made and, for that reason, would not be directly effective. In relation to some of the examples given, the extent of administrative discretion involved in determining the waters to which a parameter is be applied may not be entirely clear. But the Court of Justice has delivered a series of judgments in which the discretion of Member States to identify and designate areas for particular protection (e.g. bathing waters,[356] shellfish waters,[357] habitat

---

[352] Supposing that a particular provision is capable of being considered separately from the directive of which it forms a part: see Case C-8/81 *Becker* [1982] ECR 53.

[353] Specifically, these are respectively regulated under Directive 82/176/EEC; Directive 83/513/EEC; Directive 84/156/EEC; Directive 84/491/EEC and Directive 86/280/EEC.

[354] Under Directive 80/778/EEC, on which see 17.7.1 below.

[355] Case C-168/95 *Criminal Proceedings against Arcaro* [1996] ECR I-4705, per Advocate General Elmer.

[356] See Case C-56/90 *Commission v United Kingdom* [1993] ECR I-4109 (the *Blackpool Bathing Waters* case) and see discussion at 4.15.2 above and generally 5.5.2 below.

[357] See Case 322/86 *Commission v Italy* [1988] ECR 3995.

sites of Community nature conservation importance[358]) has been held to be narrow and only to be exercised on objective environmental criteria. Where waters or emissions are identified for the purposes of a directive this should not be problematic in invoking direct effect.

The second group of provisions in environmental directives thought to be directly effective arise where directives require a prohibition, for example, in relation to the use of certain substances or the discharge of substances into water or soil. Again, the requirements of precision and unconditionality need to be shown and the implication that such prohibitions are to protect the interests of individuals. A water-related example of this kind is the ban on direct discharges of certain chemicals under the Groundwater Directive,[359] and it is suggested that although derogations are possible, this does not detract from the applicability of direct effect where, in fact, no derogation is in force. Again, the underlying supposition is that the formulation of the relevant prohibition is precise, in defining what action must be made unlawful, and does not leave any discretion to the Member State about the form in which it is provided for in national law.

Although the direct effect of provisions in EC environmental directives has not been frequently considered by the Court of Justice, a relevant example is *Pretore di Salo*.[360] This case was a referral from an Italian court which raised the question whether the provisions of the Freshwater Fish Waters Directive[361] were sufficiently precise and unconditional to be used in criminal proceedings. In this instance the Advocate General advised against direct effect of the Directive since Member States had a discretion as to which national waters were to fall within the scope of the Directive.[362] Moreover, it was apparent that the national proceedings envisaged the use of direct effect to impose criminal sanction on an individual and, from previous discussion, it is clear that direct effect may only use to create individual *rights* and not to give rise to *obligations*.

Beyond these kinds of provisions in directives, it is often the case that environmental directives contain a range of what can be described as strategic obligations, for example obligations to establish emissions reductions programmes for Grey List substances in the Dangerous Substances Directive[363] or action programmes under the Nitrates

---

[358] See Case C-355/90 *Commission* v *Spain* [1993] ECR I-4221 ('Marismas de Santoña') and Case C-44/95 *R* v *Secretary of State for the Environment, ex parte RSPB* [1996] ECR I-3805 ('Lappel Bank') and Case C-3/96 *Commission* v *Netherlands* [1999] Env LR 147, discussed at 15.8.1 below. Different considerations may arise where a representative number of sites must be identified at national level, such as under the Habitats Directive (92/43/EEC), but this particularly difficulty does not arise in relation to any of the EC water directives.

[359] Directive 80/68/EEC, and see 5.5.2 below.

[360] Case C-14/86 *Pretore di Salo* [1987] ECR 2545.

[361] Directive 78/659/EEC, and see 15.3.1–3 below.

[362] Whether quite such an absolute position would now be taken in relation to this Directive must be doubted.

[363] Directive 76/464/EEC; see 5.4.1 below.

Directive,[364] or to disseminate environmental information through periodic reports.[365] On the basis of case law of the Court of Justice, there is some doubt whether provisions of this kind can be directly effective, because the Member States enjoy a certain amount of discretion in meeting these general obligations which makes them insufficiently precise.[366] This was the case in relation to Article 4 of the Waste Framework Directive, under which Member States must take necessary measures to ensure that waste is recovered or disposed of without endangering human health and without using processes or methods which could harm the environment including, amongst other things, without risk to water.[367] On the other hand, in the national case of *R v Bolton Metropolitan Council, ex parte Kirkman*,[368] the Court of Appeal held that an individual could, in challenging a planning permission for an incinerator, bring an argument based on essentially the same provision. The provision had been transposed almost word for word in the Waste Management Licensing Regulations 1994,[369] creating a sufficiently absolute obligation on the local planning authority that could be enforced by a judicial review. From this it is clear that whether a provision is sufficiently precise may depend in part on the context in which its application is being considered.

### 4.16.3 Direct Effect and Individual Rights

A further point on the possible direct effect of environmental directives is that while the two categories of environmental provisions noted above are said to be capable of being directly effective, some commentators argue that there is an important limitation on these. This limitation is that there is a category of measures which oblige the administration of a Member State to take action but will not have direct effect because they are unlikely to create individual rights.[370] This, in turn, has led to distinguishing between directives which confer *rights* on individuals and those which simply seek to protect the environment *per se*, or wider environmental *interests*.

On occasion, the Court of Justice has characterised direct effect as being about who is directly affected, that is who has personal rights. With most environmental quality and conservation directives, however, the Court seemed to suggest that only where human health is an objective of the directive (usually ascertained from the preamble) will the directive confer rights on individuals. This approach has been taken in relation to the Directives on Drinking Water Abstraction[371] and Sulphur Dioxide and Suspended Particulates in Air,[372] where the Court has emphasised the need

---

[364] Directive 91/676/EEC; see 5.6.3 and 13.5.4–6 below.

[365] Directive 90/313/EEC; see 16.16 below.

[366] Case C-236 *Comitato di Coordinamento per la Difesa della Cava* v *Regione Lombardia* [1994] ECR I-483.

[367] Directive 75/442/EEC, as amended by Directive 91/156/EEC.

[368] [1998] Env LR 719.

[369] SI 1994 No. 1056 and see 12.2.3 below.

[370] Krämer (2000) p.289 and Jans (1996).

[371] Case C-58/89 *Commission* v *Germany* [1991] ECR I-4983, para 14.

[372] Case C-361/88 *Commission* v *Germany* [1991] ECR I-2567, para 16.

for persons whose health is affected by non-compliance to rely on mandatory rules to assert their rights.[373] In this vein, those water directives which have as one of their stated purposes the protection of public health and, thereby, to bring benefit to individuals (such as the Bathing Water Directive[374] and the Drinking Water Quality Directive)[375] would be capable of direct effect. Here it is worth noting that public health is stated to be only an indirect justification for the Water Framework Directive.[376] In relation to the Groundwater Directive, however, the Court has held that individuals rights are created only for the companies concerned.[377] Under this approach, it is clear that conservation directives could never be enforced under direct effect and the programmatic nature of many of the water directives would be a significant limiting factor upon the recognition and enforcement of individual rights under this approach.

Alternatively, an approach might be taken allowing any citizen rights under EC law, whether or not the citizen is directly affected and whether or not the directive is intended to protect human health.[378] This approach would look more towards the legality of national decision-making, and the need for EC law to be effectively implemented, rather than only allowing claims to be made in the national courts where individual rights had been infringed. This is an approach which is more closely in line with the approach now being taken by the English courts in relation to judicial review and which therefore allows for claims to be brought by pressure groups rather than merely by affected individuals.[379]

It is suggested that, for a variety of reasons, this latter approach of allowing more general access for enforcement purposes is to be preferred (especially in relation to environmental directives) and is also emerging in recent decisions of the Court of Justice.[380] Thus, in two cases concerning the Environmental Impact Assessment Directive,[381] the Court has held that what matters is the obligation on the Member State (or its competent authorities or even national courts) to take all the appropriate measures to ensure that the Directive is faithfully implemented in practice and that any discretion that a Member State has is not unduly exceeded.[382] Also, some

---

[373] See also Case C-262/95 *Commission* v *Germany* [1996] ECR I-5729.

[374] Directive 76/160/EEC, see 5.5.2 below.

[375] Directive 80/778/EEC, and see 17.7.1 below and on the significance of human health concerns see 4.16 below.

[376] See Recital 24 Water Framework Directive.

[377] Case C-131/88 *Commission* v *Germany* [1991] ECR I-825, paras 6-7, and on the Groundwater Directive see 5.4.2 and 13.6 below.

[378] Hilson (1997). See also House of Lords Select Committee on the European Communities, *Implementation and Enforcement of European Community Environmental Law* (1992) para.45.

[379] See, e.g., *R* v *Secretary of State for the Environment, ex parte Friends of the Earth* [1996] Env LR 227 at 14.15.1 above and also *R* v *Somerset County Council, ex parte Dixon* [1998] Env LR 111.

[380] See generally Hilson and Downes (1999).

[381] Directive 85/337/EEC, and see 14.6 below.

[382] Case C-72/95 *Aannemersbedrijf PK Kraaijeveld BV* v *Gedeputeerde Staten van Zuid-Holland* [1996] ECR I-5403 and Case C-435/97 *World Wildlife Fund and Others* v *Autonome Provinz Bozen and Others* [2000] 1 CMLR 149. It is worth noting that the impact of these judgments has

of the ambiguity in relation to direct effect and individual rights is perhaps because the issue has arisen in the context of infringement proceedings by the Commission, where one of the grounds of complaint has been that national legislation has frustrated individuals' asserting their 'rights' under the directive being transposed. And other ambiguities have arisen because of a desire to make it clear that non-implemented directives should not directly impose duties (especially criminal liabilities) on individuals.

While the matter is not beyond doubt, it is suggested that what some have categorised as giving directives a 'public law effect',[383] or taking as a starting point the 'effet utile' or practical effectiveness of Community law, both has much to offer, and is an approach which appears to be finding some favour with the European Court. Not least, this is because it avoids finding that individuals enjoy rights under directives which, in theory, could expose the Member States to claims for damages under the *Francovich* principle discussed below. Following this 'public law effect' approach, therefore, a directive such as the Environmental Information Directive,[384] which provides that the rights conferred are intended for 'any legal or natural person at his request and without having to prove an interest', will be directly effective not because it appears to dispense with any need for individuals to show that they have 'rights' under the Directive, but because its provisions are clear, precise and unconditional and impose incontrovertible obligations on public authorities to give effect to them in practice.

An interesting example of what might be termed 'public law effect', or perhaps a variant of direct effect, is the case brought by two English local authorities challenging the economically-motivated decision of the Secretary of State to draw the boundaries of the estuaries of the Humber and Severn rivers at the Humber and Severn road bridges respectively.[385] This decision would have enabled less costly levels of sewage treatment under national provisions implementing the Urban Waste Water Treatment Directive[386] for treatment works alongside the rivers, since the estuaries could be categorised as 'less sensitive areas' or high natural dispersion areas. The decision of the Secretary of State was successfully challenged, essentially on the grounds that costs should not have been taken into account. What is significant for present purposes is that the Court did not insist that 'rights' were at issue before finding for the local authorities. Instead, it appears that this difficulty associated with direct effect was simply not raised either by the Secretary of State or by the High Court.[387]

---

been that English courts now routinely refer to the EIA Directive as being capable of 'direct effect'.

[383] Scott (1998) p.157.

[384] Directive 90/313/EEC, see 16.16 below.

[385] *R* v *Secretary of State for the Environment, ex parte Kingston upon Hull City Council* [1996] Env LR 248.

[386] Directive 91/271/EEC, see generally 5.6.2 below.

[387] See Scott (1998) pp.155-157.

## 4.16.4 Direct effect and national procedural rules

Even if there is a move, at national and Community level, to make it easier for the provisions of directives to be relied upon directly before national courts (so long as they are sufficiently clear, precise and unconditional) this does not mean that that national courts must always give effect to such provisions. This is because Member States enjoy a considerable amount of discretion to use national procedural rules relating to things like the period of time within which an action should be commenced, or the amount of money that an applicant in a judicial review case must pay into court in case a challenge is unsuccessful and the opposing party incurs costs as a result (known as a 'cross-undertaking in damages').[388] In essence, the position is that national courts need only set aside national rules on things like delay etc. where the national procedure makes it impossible or excessively difficult for either party to rely on directly effective EC law.[389] This means, for example, that if an application is considered to have been brought late, then the national courts may decline to grant the remedy which is sought; the seriousness of the breach of Community law will only be one factor to be taken into account.[390] Needless to say, this may act as a considerable practical and legal obstacle to giving effect to EC water directives at national level.

## 4.16.5 Sympathetic Interpretation

National courts must interpret national law consistently with EC obligations[391] and this is reaffirmed by the decision of the Court of Justice in *Marleasing*.[392] This established the principle of 'sympathetic interpretation' (or 'indirect effect') whereby the courts of the Member States must interpret national law to give effect to Community obligations. Indirect effect can be seen as a further response by the Court of Justice to the inadequacies of implementation, but also to the difficulties of direct effect, at least insofar as this was originally understood to require a breach of an individual right.

A fairly rare example of the UK courts interpreting an environment directive sympathetically was the High Court's decision that the 'justification' principle in radioactive waste management[393] must be considered in relation to the granting of authorisations and variations for releases from the THORP plant at Sellafield.[394] More recently, the principle of sympathetic interpretation was recognised in an environmental

---

[388] E.g. lost profits on costs associated with development. See *R v Secretary of State for the Environment, ex parte RSPB* [1996] ECR I-3805 ('Lappel Bank') at 15.8.1 below.

[389] Case C-188/95 *Fantask* [1998] All ER (EC) 1.

[390] Generally see Bell and McGillivray (2000) p.77.

[391] See Art.10 EC Treaty and s.2 European Communities Act 1972.

[392] Case C-106/89 *Marleasing* v *La Comercial Internacional de Alimentacion* [1990] ECR I-4135.

[393] On the jurisdiction principle see 20.5 and 20.10.6(b) below.

[394] *R v Secretary of State for the Environment, ex parte Greenpeace Ltd* [1994] 4 All ER 352. See 20.10.6(b) below.

context in a judgment of the Court of Justice[395] arising from national proceedings for infringement of rules intended to implement the Dangerous Substances Directive[396] and the Directive on limit values and quality objectives for cadmium discharges.[397] Here it was stated that the obligation to achieve a result envisaged by a directive is binding upon national courts, and a national court which is called upon to interpret a directive must do so, so far as possible, in the light of the wording and purpose of the directive in order to achieve the result intended by the directive. However, it was recognised that the sympathetic interpretation obligation on national courts reaches a limit where such interpretation leads to the imposition on an individual of criminal liability in relation to an obligation under a directive which has not been transposed into national law.[398]

In summary, the principle of sympathetic interpretation requires that, where there is an ambiguity about the meaning of a national implementing measure, national courts should resolve that ambiguity so as to give effect to the relevant directive. This approach should be adopted even where a directive has not been implemented in national law or where the directive is inconsistent with national law. Nevertheless, the principle of sympathetic interpretation is subject to limitations in respect of general Community requirements of legal certainty and non-retroactivity and should not be used to impose criminal liability on an individual unless this was already provided for in national law. Beyond this, it has been suggested that the principle seems to require at least some framework of national law to interpret, and where this is lacking it is difficult to see how it could be applied.[399] If direct effect develops along the lines suggested above, or a separate 'public law effect' doctrine develops, sympathetic interpretation is unlikely to provide much additional benefit.

### 4.16.6 State Liability

Although the significance of an individual being able to claim the benefit of *rights* under Community law in national proceedings may not be an imperative, it does form one of the foundations for 'state liability', or '*Francovich* liability' following the decision of the Court of Justice in the case of that name.[400] This provides for an action for damages against the Member State in order to give individuals remedies they would not otherwise have enjoyed, the underlying purpose being to strengthen Community law. Specifically, what is required for state liability to be established is that:

---

[395] Case C-168/96 *Criminal Proceedings against Arcaro* [1996] ECR I-4705, and see Wyatt (1998) p.13.

[396] Directive 76/464/EEC, see 5.4.1 below.

[397] Directive 83/513/EEC, see 5.4.1(c) below.

[398] In this sense, the limitations of indirect effect are no different from direct effect, as discussed above; i.e. it cannot be used *by* the State, only *against* it.

[399] Macrory and Purdy (1997) p.31.

[400] Cases C-6/90 and 9/90 *Francovich v Italy* [1991] ECR I-5357, and see Somsen (1996).

(a) the rule of law is intended to confer rights on the individuals concerned;

(b) the content of these rights is identifiable by reference to the directive;

(c) the breach is sufficiently serious; and

(d) there is a direct causal link between the breach of the obligation resting on the state and the damage sustained by the injured parties.

Subsequent case law has focused on what is required to establish a 'sufficiently serious breach'.[401] While *Francovich* was a case of failure to implement a directive, in the later cases the Court has held that there may be liability for incorrect transposition where the Member State has 'manifestly and gravely disregarded' the limits of its discretion. What will constitute this includes, for example, persisting with a breach in the face of a contrary Court of Justice ruling or other settled case law, and whether the breach was deliberate or involuntary. It will also depend on the breadth of discretion given to the state, so where (as in *Francovich* itself) the state effectively has no discretion then there will be liability provided all the other parts of the claim are satisfied. In this respect, the very prescriptive standards laid down in the Drinking Water Quality Directive, e.g., might be contrasted with more strategic obligations of the kind previously noted. Complete failure to implement a directive, or failure to take any measures to achieve the objectives of the directive, will always be a serious breach. In the case of environmental directives, the degree of non-implementation in practice (e.g., through non-enforcement of the law) that would amount to a sufficiently serious breach remains an open question.

A further issue is causation. Thus, the aggrieved parties in *Francovich* were claiming compensation for damage suffered through financial loss where compensation was directly provided for under the relevant directive. Under water quality directives the kind of loss that might result from non-implementation is less clearly identified and the link between non-implementation and harm to particular individuals may be less direct (i.e. establishing causation may be a particular difficulty). However, *Francovich* liability has the evidential virtue of not requiring the identification of the individual or individuals responsible for contributing to the breach of environmental standards complained of. Thus while water quality directives might be held to be effective as against Member States or competent authorities, *Francovich* liability might be imposed on the Member State itself where harm is caused by the cumulative impact of a large number of actions, such as in relation to directives which regulate the level of nitrate in drinking water quality.[402] However, it is clear that the extent of scientific uncertainty in respect of such questions as whether nitrate levels above those provided in the Drinking Water Quality

---

[401] Cases C-46/93 and 48/93 *Brasserie du Pecheur SA* v *Germany* [1996] ECR I-1029; Case C-392/93 *R* v *HM Treasury ex parte BT* [1996] ECR I-1613; Case C-5/94 *R* v *MAFF ex parte Hedley Lomas (Ireland) Ltd* [1996] ECR I-2553; and Cases C-178/94, 179/94, 189/94 and 190/94 *Dillenkofer* v *Germany* [1996] ECR I-4845).

[402] Notably, the Nitrates Directive (91/676/EEC), see 5.6.3 and 13.5.4 below.

Directive give rise to problems like gastric cancer or 'blue-baby syndrome' is considerable. At least in the English courts, proving environmental-type damage using epidemiological evidence can be extremely difficult.[403] Moreover, the possibility of the Court of Justice opening up a Member State to near-unlimited liability in the case of such general provisions as those relating to drinking water quality must be considered unlikely, and might explain the preference for seeking duty-based solutions of the kind discussed above.

The *Francovich* decision is of considerable importance in relation to the potential for state liability and individual redress where loss is suffered through a failure to implement EC law. But unlike direct effect it is clear that state liability requires the breach of an individual right. In this context, it is likely that the Courts would, for policy reasons, distinguish between individual *rights* and more general *interests* in law enforcement.[404] Therefore, the case law of the Court of Justice which has held that directives intended to protect human health can give rise to such rights, and that persons whose health is at issue should be able to enforce those rights, would be relevant here.[405] Specifically, amongst the water quality directives, the Drinking Water Abstraction Directive[406] and the associated Drinking Water Sampling Directive[407] have been held to fall into this category, and similarly other water directives where human health is a stated objective should be treated similarly.[408]

Where an environmental directive is intended to protect the environment but not, specifically, human health it is less clear that it will give rise to individual rights. On balance, the more likely view is that whilst Community directives concerned with the protection of human health give rise to individual rights which may be enforced in national courts, directives that are concerned purely with protection of the environment do not give rise to such rights. A consequence of this is that other water quality directives, such as the Groundwater Directive,[409] the Dangerous Substances Directive[410] and the Freshwater Fish Waters Directive[411] which do not refer to the protection of human health amongst their objectives, will not give rise to individual rights, and the same may also be true of the Water Framework Directive.[412] It has been argued that this distinction

---

[403] See, e.g. *Reay* v *BNFL plc* [1994] Env LR 320, and see also 3.10.5 above.

[404] Case 158/80 *Rewe* v *Hauptzollampt Kiel* [1981] ECR 1805; and generally Geddes (1995).

[405] Case 58/89 *Commission* v *Germany* [1991] ECR I-4983.

[406] Directive 75/440/EEC, see 17.6 below. See Case C-58/89 *Commission* v *Germany* [1991] ECR I-4983 para. 14. In Case C-337/89 *Commission* v *United Kingdom* [1992] ECR I-6103, Advocate General Lenz suggested that a ruling that the UK had failed to fulfil its obligations arising out of the Drinking Water Quality Directive (80/778/EEC) could provide a basis for actions for damages against the state.

[407] Directive 79/869/EEC, and see 17.6 below.

[408] See for example the Bathing Water Directive (76/160/EEC) and 5.5.2 below.

[409] Directive 80/68/EEC, and see 5.4.2 and 13.6 below.

[410] Directive 76/464/EEC, see 5.4.1 below, and see 5.4.1(c) below on daughter directives.

[411] Directive 78/659/EEC, see 15.3.3 below, where it is noted that in Case C-298/95 *Commission* v *Germany* [1996] ECR I-6747 where the ECJ held that this directive concerned human health.

[412] See Recital 23 Water Framework Directive.

reflects an excessively anthropocentric approach, and a fine distinction between those aspects of environmental quality which do and those which do not impact upon human health, which are difficult to defend.[413] On the other hand, it has been pointed out that there may be circumstances where environmental directives that do not include in their objectives the protection of human health may nevertheless give rise to individually enforceable rights in certain circumstances.[414] Hence, in proceedings against Germany concerning the Groundwater Directive,[415] Articles were at issue which required prior examination of the hydrogeological conditions, and further requirements, before authorisation of an activity involving certain discharges to groundwater and subsequent monitoring of groundwater quality. It was held that precise and detailed rules had been provided for and that these are intended to create rights and obligations for individuals. Thus a contrast may be drawn between the individual enforceability of the substantive environmental quality aspects and the procedural aspects of a Directive, with the latter being enforceable in circumstances where the former are not. However, there is little case law which bears directly on whether directives confer individual rights, and no case law yet from the European Court on *Francovich* liability in an environmental context.

Another potentially important point of contrast concerns the status of the individual who seeks to enforce a provision in a directive. An environmental directive which gives rise merely to unenforceable *interests* in members of the environmentally-concerned public might be construed as giving enforceable *rights* to commercial bodies, such as water undertakers, who possess an economic interest in the matter at issue which might justify individual enforcement. This matter has not been conclusively resolved as a matter of Community law, but there are dicta to suggest that enforceability might depend upon such differences in status.[416] At national level, however, the decision of the Court of Appeal in *Bowden v South West Water Services* seems to support this view.[417] In these proceedings, the claimant was a fisherman who harvested mussels. Pursuant to a Community Directive, the area in which he fished was classified by the Ministry of Agriculture, Fisheries and Food as being polluted and this made the mussel harvesting activity impossible. Alongside a number of other legal issues raised by the proceedings, it was held that insofar as there had been a failure to designate the relevant area under the Shellfish Waters Directive,[418] this could amount to an infringement of the rights of the claimant, a shellfisherman, since the Shellfish Waters Directive had as one of its legal bases trade harmonisation and was therefore intended to confer economic rights on

---

[413] See Hilson (1997) pp.57-58 and Miller (1995).

[414] Jans (1995) pp.186-87.

[415] Case C-131/88 *Commission* v *Germany* [1991] ECR I-825, concerning Directive 80/68/EEC, and see 5.4.2 below.

[416] See the Opinion of Advocate General. Jacobs in Case C-58/89 *Commission* v *Germany* [1991] ECR I-4983, noted by Hilson (1997) p.55.

[417] [1999] Env LR 438 and see 3.12 above and 15.3.4 below.

[418] Directive 79/923/EEC and see 15.3.1 below.

shellfishermen throughout the Community. Further claims in relation to the Directives on Bathing Water[419] and on Urban Waste Water Treatment,[420] however, were dismissed on the grounds that those directives could not be said to confer individual rights since their objective was general environmental improvement. Fundamentally, therefore, the question remains as to what, or who, is the directive provision at issue intended to protect. But this question does not preclude different conclusions in relation to different categories of individual or even, as the *Bowden* case illustrates, the same individual in relation to different directives.

## 4.17  Litigating EC Water Law at National Level

Bringing together the various individual enforcement possibility outlined above gives rise to a range of propositions. A relatively straightforward example might be that of a consumer who became ill as a result of drinking water from the public supply that did not comply with the standards laid down in the Drinking Water Quality Directive[421] (even if the water otherwise complied with national standards). Although there are certain remedies under national law,[422] if these were not provided for a claim might be brought against the water undertaker in tort, relying on the direct effect of the Directive. This might be pursued on the basis that the Directive was intended to protect human health or that it otherwise conferred rights on individual consumers of water. Alternatively, it might be argued that the effectiveness of the Directive would be unduly prejudiced if potential claimants could not assert claims against water suppliers before national courts.

Another possibility is of a claim under the *Francovich* doctrine against the state which might be taken on the basis that the Directive conferred rights on individuals. In both instances, it is suggested that there would be little difficulty in proving that the Directive conferred rights which would be breached by non-compliance with the parameters of the Directive. With *Francovich* liability, however, the more difficult issue is whether any level of breach would give rise to liability as being sufficiently serious. That is, given that the Directive incorporates safety margins, could it be argued that *any* supply of sub-standard water would be sufficient for there to a sufficiently serious breach, or would something more be required? Finally, there is the question of causation. Even in the case of a relatively straightforward illness this would still require proof, perhaps epidemiological, that the breach of a parameter in the Directive materially contributed to the illness. With other types of illness, however (e.g. gastric cancer) scientific uncertainty may be a much more significant hurdle to overcome. There is also the complication that many of the standards in the Directive are, in effect, precautionary standards, which might make it still more difficult to argue that their breach did, in practice, cause detriment.

---

[419] Directive 76/160/EEC, see 5.5.2 below.

[420] Directive 91/271/EEC, see 5.6.2 below.

[421] Directive 80/778/EEC, on which see 17.7.1 below and see 17.7.8 on amendments.

[422] Under both statute and common law, discussed at 17.11 below.

Further difficult issues arise with potential claims in relation to things like breach of ambient water quality standards or with failure to implement strategic obligations under a directive. In either instance, complaints could be lodged with the European Commission, either directly or through an organisation such as an environmental or public health non-governmental organisation. Regarding any possible breach of standards, however, the position in the UK may be different from that in other Member States. This can be illustrated by considering the Dangerous Substances Directive.[423] This Directive provides a regime for the elimination or reduction of certain polluting substances, known as Black List and Grey List substances. Uniquely, though, the Directive gives Member States the option of setting water quality standards for the substances to be controlled under it, or imposing maximum limit values on individual points of discharge. Only the UK has elected to implement the Directive by way of water quality standards[424] which means that for those Black List substances where the Community has agreed water quality and emissions standards (e.g., cadmium and mercury), the UK's obligation under the Directive is limited to establishing and meeting environmental water quality standards. As a matter of practice, therefore, individuals in other Member States might find it easier to establish a breach of the Directive for any individual discharge point by little more than comparing data on actual and permitted emission levels of specified Black List substances. This would not be sufficient in itself to establish an individually-enforceable right under Community law. But it would surmount the first hurdle of any claim (either under the direct effect or *Francovich* doctrines) by establishing non-implementation of the Directive, and provide the basis for a judicial review of any permit issued in breach of any such limit value. By contrast, a complainant in the UK would have to establish that there had been a breach of an ambient water quality standard. The claimant would therefore have to go beyond formally recording a discrepancy between actual and permitted emissions, and embark upon the more difficult task of investigating actual water quality for a particular area of water.[425] In must be doubted whether, in relation to any directive which establishes ambient water quality standards,[426] individual 'enforcement' mechanisms can realistically be relied upon, something which appears to be borne out by the lack of illustrative case law on this matter.[427]

There is some uncertainty about the status of 'minimisation' obligations in directives. Examples in the field of water directives would include the obligation on Member States under the Urban Waste Water Treatment Directive to minimise the risk of pollution from a discharge by selecting disposal routes for treated waste water which, as far as possible, minimise

---

[423] Directive 76/464/EEC, see 5.4.1 below.

[424] As to the reasons behind this feature of the Directive, and the UK choice, see 5.4.1(b) below.

[425] Somsen (2000) p.337. On information on environmental water quality see Ch.16 below.

[426] See generally 5.5 below, but see also the Water Framework Directive at 5.7 below.

[427] Somsen (2000) p.387 notes 'little or no' references for preliminary rulings under Art.234 EC (ex Art.177) on such points.

the adverse effects on receiving waters.[428] Also relevant are various obligations in the Water Framework Directive, for example the requirement that Member States reverse any significant and sustained upward trend in the concentration of any pollutant resulting from the impact of human activity in order to progressively reduce pollution of groundwater.[429] It is unclear what obligations of this kind require of national decision-makers. Arguably, though, they require an approach to decision-making which sufficiently reflects the purposive nature of the obligation. In requiring this, however, minimisation obligations may create a kind of procedural law obligation of a kind which national decision-makers (and, more so, national courts) deal with uneasily.

An illustration of the attitudes of the domestic courts in this respect is *R v Leicester County Council, Hepworth Building Products Limited and Onyx (UK) Ltd, ex parte Blackfordby and Boothorpe Action Group Ltd,*[430] where the legal status of the general objectives laid down in the Waste Framework Directive, which are similarly worded as minimisation objectives, were at issue.[431] The approach of Richards J in the High Court was to reject any suggestion that these should be given any special weight by the decision-maker. On this reasoning, it is enough that decision-makers take these objectives into account; they do not need to do all they can to achieve them. This gives minimisation obligations little more than the status of 'material considerations' as found in town and country planning law. That is, the decision-maker must have regard to them, but the weight that any consideration is given, if any, is a matter of judgment which will not be overturned by a court in reviewing a decision.[432] On this line of reasoning, therefore, the extent to which some of the key objectives of EC water law are realised at national level might be frustrated by the tendency of the courts, at national level, to resort to traditional ways of supervising discretion rather than develop new approaches to meet new challenges.

As far as general strategic obligations are concerned, where specific water quality improvement[433] or water pollution reduction[434] programmes and plans are involved, the duty on Member States to implement such obligations may be taken as seriously as obligations to effect actual environmental change.[435] When it comes to individual enforcement, however, it may be difficult to pursue a legal action if evidence that an

---

[428] On which see *Moase v Secretary of State for the Environment, Transport and the Regions* [2001] Env LR 13 and see 5.6 below.

[429] Art.4(1)(b)(iii) Water Framework Directive.

[430] [2001] Env LR 2. An appeal is pending.

[431] Under Art.4, the same duties as in Case C-236 *Comitato di Coordinamento per la Difesa della Cava v Regione Lombardia* [1994] ECR I-483 and *R v Bolton Metropolitan Council ex parte Kirkman* [1998] Env LR 719, although in a different context.

[432] See 4.18 below.

[433] E.g., Art.4(1)(b)(ii) Water Framework Directive concerning improving groundwater quality status.

[434] E.g., *ibid* Art.4(1)(b)(i) and (iii) concerning groundwater pollution reduction.

[435] See e.g. Case C-387/97 *Commission v Hellenic Republic* (4 July 2000, unreported), at 4.13.2 above.

individual right has been infringed is required, since it is not clear that such obligations are aimed at protecting individual rights so much as improving the state of the natural environment more generally. The national courts have accepted, it should be said, the obligation to review alleged non-compliance of designation duties.[436] However, establishing that an obligation to implement a pollution reduction plan or programme, which is contained in a directive but not transposed into national legislation (or, more likely, not given effect to in practice) would probably require an action to be brought on the basis that there has been a failure on the part of a national decision-maker to act in accordance with Community obligations.[437] As noted above, this may be desirable but is as yet insufficiently tested at national level. On the other hand, obligations to implement plans and programmes tend to be sufficiently clear and unambiguous to be amenable to review,[438] and this would undoubtedly assist any such review. As a matter of practice, the only example of individual legal action in relation to programmatic obligations in water directives that has reached the Court of Justice has been brought not by those arguing *for* compliance with such obligations but by those suffering adverse economic consequences *by* such obligations.[439]

In relation to all of the above, an additional consideration is whether any obstructive national procedural rule should be set aside to give individuals remedies. As noted, there is considerable scope for national rules on things like standing to bring actions, and time limits, to present an impediment. But as a matter of EC law these may be set aside where their exercise would make it impossible or exceptionally difficult to obtain a remedy. Where this is likely to lead to most practical difficulty is with judicial review actions (i.e. actions brought in public law against public bodies such as the Environment Agency, the Secretary of State for the Environment, Transport and the Regions, or local authorities). For example, it is still not established as a matter of principle that a national environmental pressure group may mount a challenge to any breach of EC water quality or emission standards, or whether an applicant (individual or group) with a more immediate, local concern must instigate the litigation.

Then there is the thorny problem of bringing actions on time. If a limit value or quality standard has been breached for a long time, it may be difficult to show that any judicial review has been brought within the time allowed. That is, it might be argued by the court that in the interests of good administration (e.g. because of costs incurred by polluting industries,

---

[436] See *R* v *Secretary of State for the Environment, ex parte Kingston Upon Hull CC* [1996] Env LR 248.

[437] That is, 'public law effect', see 4.16.3 above.

[438] Judgments of the Court of Justice in this context about what is required of Member States when implementing such obligations, although usually delivered in infringement proceedings brought by the Commission, have been fairly robust on this point; see, e.g., the obligations in relation to the Directives on Dangerous Substances at 5.4.1 below and on Urban Waste Water Treatment at 5.6.2 below.

[439] Case C-293/97 *R* v *Secretary of State for the Environment and Minister of Agriculture, Fisheries and Food, ex parte Standley* [1999] ECR I-2603. There are, however, examples of such national obligations being pursued through individual complaint to the Commission.

or which might be incurred by the Environment Agency in revoking discharge consents or integrated pollution control licences) that the challenge should be considered to have been brought out of time. So far at least, the English courts have shown something of a reluctance to allow actions which are technically out of time, unless they think that there has been a serious failure in implementing a directive and little prejudice.[440]

## 4.18 General Concerns on Implementation and Enforcement

General concerns about the implementation and enforcement of Community environmental law have been raised for a number of years. In relation to the water quality sector in particular, Community legislation creates considerable problems for the administrations of the Member States, many of whom have major difficulties in satisfactorily applying the relevant directives. In this respect the Dangerous Substances Directive,[441] the Bathing Waters Directive,[442] the Nitrates Directive[443] and the Drinking Water Quality Directive[444] are identified as being particularly problematic.[445] But it is quite clear from recent infringement proceedings brought by the Commission, and from decisions of the Court of Justice, that all the water directives have given rise to implementation difficulties.

To some extent the difficulties in implementing and enforcing EC water directives are attributable to the peculiarly challenging nature of environmental law, involving complex interdependencies between the environmental media and variations in environmental conditions in different parts of the Community. These considerations are compounded by a constantly changing state of scientific knowledge, the need for a delicate balancing exercise between the activities of a range of Community and national authorities, and involved individuals, and the fact that environmental protection relates to general concerns which often fall outside the scope of proprietary interests.[446]

At the institutional level, the Commission's limitations in enforcing EC environmental law are well recognised.[447] While these might be aided by, for example, developing Community-wide minimum inspection criteria,[448] or by improvements to the complaints procedure, there is increasing recognition of the importance of developing greater capacity for environmental cases to be dealt with by national courts. At national level,

---

[440] See generally Bell and McGillivray (2000) p.79.

[441] Directive 76/464/EEC, see 5.4.1 below.

[442] Directive 76/160/EEC, see 5.5.2 below.

[443] Directive 91/676/EEC, see 5.6.3 below and 13.13.5.4-7below.

[444] Directive 80/778/EEC, see 17.7.1below.

[445] Commission Communication, *Implementing Community Environmental Law*, COM(96) 500 (henceforth *Implementing Community Environmental Law*), Annex II: Implementation Problems by Sector. And see Council Resolution of 7 October 1997 (OJ 1997, C321/1) welcoming the Communication.

[446] *Ibid* Para.7

[447] *Ibid* para.13.

[448] See 4.16 above.

the right for environmental pressure groups to bring actions in judicial review is now fairly well established, although practical difficulties like the costs and time involved, as well as a certain continuing reluctance amongst some of the national judiciary not to interpret Community environmental law in a purposive way, pose practical hurdles. Resort to greater use of Ombudsman-type mechanisms has also been suggested. It remains to be seen what the effect of Community ratification of the 1998 Aarhus Convention on Access to Information, Public Participation in Decision Making and Access to Justice in Environmental Matters[449] will be on these matters.

A final general issue is the need for Member States to introduce effective, proportionate and dissuasive sanctions, and to apply these in practice, to ensure compliance with provisions of Community environmental law.[450] In the past, many environmental directives have contained no provisions concerning criminal or other mechanisms for enforcement,[451] but it is envisaged that future measures may require national implementing legislation to include appropriate administrative, civil or penal sanctions to ensure compliance.[452] The Water Framework Directive, in requiring Member States to provide for penalties which are 'effective, proportionate and dissuasive',[453] illustrates this development.[454] But the difficulty remains as to how such powers are actually used in practice, i.e. whether such fines are actually used, which in part is a matter of official enforcement policy and in part a matter of judicial discretion.

At a national level, the Commission's Communication on *Implementing Community Environmental Law* has been considered by the House of Lords Select Committee on the European Communities,[455] which stressed that more needed to be done in developing and putting Commission proposals into practice. Particular attention, though, was focused on seeking greater transparency in the regulatory process as a whole. These concerns are now being addressed at Community level, and a theme of the latest Environmental Action Programme is identifying ways to give citizens and other stakeholders 'greater ownership of efforts to protect the environment'.[456] Some of the continuing difficulties, however, can be seen in the passage of the Water Framework Directive. While the early stages of its evolution were characterised by a fair degree of openness and wide

---

[449] See 16.18 below.

[450] *Implementing Community Environmental Law* para.48.

[451] See Jans (1995) p.144.

[452] *Implementing Community Environmental Law* para.50.

[453] Art.23 Water Framework Directive. Having such provision may be an implicit obligation as a matter of Community law under Art 10 EC, but what the minimum requirement in practice under this would be could only be a matter of speculation.

[454] Postscript: see now the proposed Directive on the Protection of the Environment through Criminal Law, COM(2001)139.

[455] *Making it Work.*

[456] Postscript: see *Environment 2010: Our Future, Our Choice*, Sixth Environmental Action Programme, COM(2001)31. Contrast e.g. the extent to which the initial and revised Directives on Drinking Water Quality (80/778/EEC and 98/83/EC respectively) involved wider stakeholders (see 17.7 below).

stakeholder involvement, many central objectives and obligations were inserted only at the last minute in conciliation talks between the Council and Parliament.[457]

Addressing transparency and participatory concerns in the Sixth Action Programme is in addition to improving implementation of existing environmental legislation, if necessary by combining 'vigorous' legal action through the European Court of Justice with support for best practices and a policy of public information to 'name, fame and shame'. These developments, however, must be seen against a background of the emergence of Community water law which, at least in certain areas,[458] is less susceptible to enforcement by traditional mechanisms, a development common to EC environmental law where Member States are being given a degree of discretion at many stages in the process of implementing EC environmental law, subject in many cases to procedural, rather than substantive, oversight by the Community institutions.[459] What may be particularly important, therefore, is the extent to which Member States choose literally to transpose the provisions of directives into national legislation,[460] rather than engaging with the purposive objectives which lie behind the language in which directives are couched.

---

[457] On the conciliation process see Tydeman (2000).

[458] Compare the more discretionary Water Framework Directive (2000/66/EC) with the more mandatory Revised Drinking Water Quality Directive (98/83/EC).

[459] Scott (2000a).

[460] For UK examples of the 'copy-out' approach to transposition see the Directives on Environmental Information (90/313/EEC), Waste (91/156/EEC) and Habitats (92/43/EEC) and their transposing regulations, discussed at 16.17, 12.2.3 and 15.8.3 below respectively.

# Chapter 5

# THE EUROPEAN COMMUNITY WATER
# DIRECTIVES

## 5.1 Introduction

Water quality has traditionally provided a barometer as to the general state of the environment, with the aquatic sector tending to accumulate substances that are initially discharged into any of the three media of water, air and land. It is perhaps for this reason, and the relatively high profile of environmental problems that are manifested in the aquatic environment, that European Community environmental legislation has tended to be most precocious in relation to water pollution and water quality. Certainly, of the principal legal instruments relating to water quality, a number date from quite an early period in the evolution of Community environmental policy and these have been successively added to by measures which have reflected changes in policy and priorities over the subsequent years.[1] As a consequence of this, water quality legislation is one of the most highly developed sectors of Community environmental law.

Opinions differ as to precisely how many Community measures relate to water pollution and water quality since measures from sectors such as environmental health, industrial activities and wildlife conservation frequently possess a water dimension.[2] Equally, EC water legislation has important implications for other sectors. However, the following directives are generally regarded as being of central importance in that they are *primarily* concerned with water.

(a) Directives on the approximation of the laws of the Member States relating to detergents (referred to as the 'Detergent Directives').[3]

(b) Directive concerning the quality required of surface water intended for the abstraction of drinking water in the Member States (the 'Drinking Water Abstraction Directive'),[4] together with Directive concerning sampling and analysis of surface water for drinking (the 'Drinking Water Sampling Directive').[5]

---

[1] See the development of EC environmental law through successive action programmes, at 5.2 below.

[2] A useful source is Eur-Lex, at *http://europa.eu.int/eur-lex*, which contains the full text of all EC legislation in force, including a grouping of measures under the heading 'water protection and management' (which similarly tends to exclude 'marine' provisions).

[3] Directive 73/404/EEC, amended by Directive 82/242/EEC, Directive 82/243/EEC and Directive 86/94/EEC, see 5.4.3 below. See also Directive 73/405/EEC relating to methods of testing the biodegradability of anionic surfactants.

[4] Directive 75/440/EEC, see 5.5.3 and 17.6 below.

[5] Directive 79/869/EEC, see 5.5.3 and 16.2.1 and 17.6 below.

(c) Directive concerning the quality of bathing water (the 'Bathing Water Directive').[6]

(d) Directive on pollution caused by certain dangerous substances discharged into the aquatic environment of the Community (the 'Dangerous Substances Directive'), together with a number of 'daughter' directives enacted pursuant to it.[7]

(e) Directive on the quality of freshwater needing protection or improvement in order to support fish life (the 'Freshwater Fish Waters Directive').[8]

(f) Directive on the quality required for shellfish waters (the 'Shellfish Waters Directive').[9]

(g) Directive on the protection of groundwater against pollution caused by certain dangerous substances (the 'Groundwater Directive').[10]

(h) Directive on the quality of water intended for human consumption (the 'Drinking Water Quality Directive').[11]

(i) Directive concerning urban waste water treatment (the 'Urban Waste Water Treatment Directive').[12]

(j) Directive concerning the protection of waters against pollution caused by nitrates from agricultural sources (the 'Nitrates Directive').[13]

(k) Directive establishing a framework for Community action in the field of water policy (the 'Water Framework Directive').[14]

The influence of these directives, and other Community measures which impact on water quality,[15] can scarcely be overstated. Consequently, their wide impact, and thus relevance to many of the later chapters of this work, makes it convenient to avoid detailed discussion of all of the directives here. Instead, the focus in this chapter is with drawing out the contrasts in the general water protection strategies underpinning the directives, and charting the development of this body of legislation. Brief coverage is also

---

[6] Directive 76/160/EEC, see 5.5.2 below.

[7] Directive 76/464/EEC. On this and the daughter directives enacted under it see 5.4.1 below.

[8] Directive 78/659/EEC, see 5.5.3 and 15.3.1 below.

[9] Directive 79/923/EEC, see 5.5.3 and 15.3.1 below.

[10] Directive 80/68/EEC, see 5.4.2 and 13.6 below.

[11] Directive 80/778/EEC, replaced with effect from December 2003 by Directive 98/83/EC. See 17.7.1 and 17.7.8 below.

[12] Directive 91/271/EEC, see 5.6.2 below.

[13] Directive 91/676/EEC, see 5.6.3 and 13.5.4 below.

[14] Directive 2000/60/EC, see 5.7 below.

[15] Not included below as 'water directives' are measures adopted largely to prevent water pollution but which have a more general compass. These include Directive 78/176/EEC on titanium dioxide, which was passed primarily to prevent pollution of marine and coastal waters (a directive better classified as a waste management measure); Directive 87/217/EEC on the prevention and reduction of environmental pollution by asbestos, an early 'integrated pollution control' directive; and the more general Directive 96/61/EC on integrated pollution prevention and control, discussed at 12.3.3 below. Community directives (and proposals) aimed at reducing acidification are also excluded. Although the importance of curbing atmospheric emissions to improve water quality is recognised, these measures have a wider compass which extends to preventing more general environmental damage as a result of things like emissions of sulphur dioxide, nitrogen oxides and ammonia.

given to outlining the various implementing provisions. Some directives, though, are covered in detail, either because of their general impact on national law and practice or to illustrate the various protection strategies adopted and the legal issues which arise.

It must be stressed that the most recent measure mentioned above, the Water Framework Directive, will have significant implications for this body of legislation. In particular, many of the present water quality directives[16] will, by 2013, be repealed and replaced by the Water Framework Directive.[17]

Two further introductory points must be made. First, the focus of this chapter, and of the book as a whole, is on those directives and other measures which have greatest impact on the UK. Hence, Community measures such as those which involve the EC in protection of the Oder or the Elbe are not covered. Second, the directives covered in this chapter, though they may impact on the marine environment, or relate to coastal waters such as bathing waters, are essentially land-based. Those Community directives which more directly relate to the marine environment are considered elsewhere.[18]

## 5.2 Action Programmes on the Environment

Before looking in detail at the substance of Community water legislation, it is worth considering the general evolution of EC environmental policy through successive action programmes which have provided the policy foundations for the successive waves of legislative development relating to water quality.[19] Whilst the successive programmes have built upon the original objectives and principles relating to environmental protection, they have prompted distinct approaches to environmental legislation with significant changes of emphasis over the different periods. To a large extent, the specific directives enacted in relation to water quality reflect these evolving policy concerns with early legislation seeking to address pollution at source through the application of emission standards but tending, in later directives, to prefer ambient standards as a measure of environmental impacts and desired states of water for different uses.

Following the Stockholm Conference in 1972,[20] the (then) six Member States resolved that the Community should undertake a co-ordinated initiative on environmental policy,[21] and the Council formally adopted the

---

[16] On the classification of directives as water quality directives see 5.5 below.

[17] See 5.9.19 on those directives which will be replaced by the Water Framework Directive.

[18] See, e.g. discussion of the Vessels Directive (95/21/EC) at 19.8.1 below.

[19] These Action Programmes are not intended to have direct legal force, but rather shape Community environmental law and policy development during their duration; see (at least in relation to the Fifth Action Programme) Case C-142/95P *Associazone agricoltori della provincia di Rovigo and Others* v *Commission* [1996] ECR I-6669.

[20] UN Conference on the Human Environment, Stockholm, 5–16 June 1972.

[21] *Bulletin of the European Communities* (1972) No.10 p.21.

*First Action Programme for the Environment* in 1973.[22] The stated aim of the Programme was to bring about an improvement in the quality of life for citizens of the Community through securing an environment which provided the best conditions of life. In particular, it was affirmed that Community environment policy should be in accordance with the following principles.

(a) Pollution or nuisances should be prevented at source, rather than subsequently trying to counteract their effects.

(b) Effects on the environment should be taken into account at the earliest possible stage in all technical planning and decision-making processes.

(c) Any exploitation of natural resources or of a nature which causes significant damage to the ecological balance must be avoided.

(d) The standard of scientific and technological knowledge in the Community should be improved with a view to taking effective action to conserve and improve the environment and research in this field should be encouraged.

(e) The cost of preventing and eliminating nuisances must, in principle, be borne by the polluter.

(f) Activities carried out in one state must not cause any degradation of the environment in another state.

(g) Environment policy must take into account the interests of the developing countries with a view to preventing or reducing any adverse consequences as far as possible.

(h) The effectiveness of the Community's efforts at international level will be increased by a clearly defined long-term concept for a European environmental policy.

(i) The protection of the environment is a matter for all in the Community and all should therefore be made aware of its importance.

(j) In each different category of pollution, it is necessary to establish the level of action that befits the type of pollution.

(k) Major aspects of environmental policy in individual countries must no longer be planned in isolation. The individual national policies should be co-ordinated and harmonised as far as possible without hampering progress at national level.[23]

The initial environmental policy, covering the period 1973 to 1976, tackled the urgent problems of pollution control facing the Community, and some of the earliest water directives date from this period.[24] This was followed by four subsequent action programmes being approved by the Council. The *Second Action Programme*, which covered the period 1977 to 1981,[25]

---

[22] *First Community Action Programme on the Environment* OJ 1973, C112/1.

[23] *Ibid*, and see OJ 1977, C139/1 on Council Resolution for continuation and implementation.

[24] Examples include the Detergent Directives (73/404/EEC and 73/405/EEC), the Drinking Water Abstraction Directive (75/440/EEC), the Bathing Water Directive (76/160/EEC) and the Dangerous Substances Directive (76/464/EEC).

[25] OJ 1977, C39/1. Water directives enacted during this period were the Freshwater Fish Waters Directive (78/659/EEC), the Shellfish Waters Directive (79/923/EEC), the Drinking Water

had as its object ensuring that the first Programme was implemented in all its aspects and brought up to date to ensure the continuity of the projects already undertaken. On 26 June 1978 a Council resolution was passed setting up an additional action programme relating to the control and reduction of pollution caused by hydrocarbons discharged into the sea,[26] though to date this has not been a platform for the development of any significant body of legislation in this area.[27]

The *Third Action Programme,*[28] covering the period 1982 to 1986, set out new tasks to be undertaken. This Programme marked a change from the original central concern arising from the pursuit of very divergent national policies to an aim of protecting not only human health and the environment but also of ensuring that natural resources are well managed, in particular by introducing qualitative considerations into the planning and organising of economic and social development. To some extent, however, the Third Action Programme, in emphasising positive environmental provisions, did little more than recognise areas in which the Community had already begun legislating, using the powers to enact economic harmonisation measures under Article 100 (now Article 94 EC) and to adopt legislation on the basis of its 'residual' competence to legislate so as to further the Community's objectives under Article 235 (now Article 308 EC).[29] As importantly, this period marked the beginning of a period where greater emphasis was placed on implementing and enforcing environmental law. This is attributable in part to criticisms by the Parliament of both the Commission and the Member States for failing to implement EC environmental law adequately.[30] This may help explain the fact that no water directives were adopted during this period.

The principal aim of the *Fourth Action Programme* for the period 1987 to 1992[31] was the reduction at source of pollution and nuisances, taking particular account of the need to prevent the transfer of pollution from one part of the environment to another, and to combat transfrontier pollution. Specifically, it referred, amongst other things, to

(a) the need to control chemical substances and preparations;
(b) the harmonised implementation of existing directives on toxic and dangerous wastes;
(c) achieving the best use of technology;
(d) protection against radiation;[32]

---

Sampling Directive (79/869/EEC), the Groundwater Directive (80/68/EEC) and the Drinking Water Quality Directive (80/778/EEC).

[26] Council Resolution of 26 June 1978 setting up an action programme of the EC on the control and reduction of pollution caused by hydrocarbons discharged into the sea, OJ 1978, C162/1.

[27] See 19.4 below.

[28] OJ 1983, C46/1.

[29] See 4.3.1 above.

[30] Following the 1983 Seveso incident, see Haigh and Lanigan (1995).

[31] OJ 1987, C328/1. Water directives enacted during this period were the Urban Waste Water Treatment Directive (91/271/EEC) and the Nitrates Directive (91/676/EEC).

[32] See generally Ch.20 below.

(e)  improved management of resources including recycling;
(f)  active participation in international activities;[33] and
(g)  the development of appropriate instruments.

In line with the insertion of a new Environmental Title in the Treaty,[34] the *Fourth Action Programme* emphasised the inclusion of environmental protection policies in other Community policies. The contribution of environmental policy to improved economic growth and job creation was also stated.

Most recently, the *Fifth Action Programme*,[35] entitled *Towards Sustainability*, was adopted to cover the period 1993 to 2000,[36] subject to a review in 1995.[37] The Programme noted that, despite about 200 pieces of environmental legislation, the available information indicated a 'slow but relentless deterioration of the general state of the environment of the Community'.[38] In response, the Programme addressed a number of environmental issues which are regarded as being

> of particular seriousness and which have a Community-wide dimension, either because of the internal market, cross-boundary, shared resource or cohesion implications and because they have a crucial bearing on environmental quality and conditions in almost all regions of the Community.[39]

Areas identified as general priorities for action in the Programme included sustainable management of natural resources, soil, water, natural areas and coastal zones and integrated pollution control and prevention of waste.[40] In addition, certain target sectors were identified for special attention where a Community-wide approach was considered the most efficient level at which to tackle the problems involved. These were industry, energy, transport, agriculture and tourism.[41] It must be said, however, that action during this period in relation to these key sectors has been rather limited,[42] and arguably it is only with the elevation of the principle of integration is significant progress, at least at policy level, likely to be forthcoming.[43]

---

[33] See 4.3.2(b) above on the insertion of international level action into the Environmental Title of the Treaty.

[34] See 4.3.2(a) above.

[35] *Towards Sustainability*, COM(92)23 final (henceforth '*Towards Sustainability*') The Council approved the general approach and strategy of the Programme by a Resolution of 1 February 1993, OJ 1993, C138/1.

[36] Directives adopted during this period include the Directive on Integrated Pollution Prevention and Control (96/61/EC) and a major revision to the Drinking Water Quality Directive (98/83/EC).

[37] See COM(95)647 final and Decision 98/2179/EC.

[38] *Towards Sustainability* para.1.

[39] *Ibid* para.16.

[40] See, e.g., the adoption of the Integrated Pollution Prevention and Control Directive (96/61/EC) discussed at 12.3.3 below.

[41] *Towards Sustainability* para.18.

[42] See the 1995 review of *Towards Sustainability*, COM(95)647 final, and see Decision 98/2179/EC.

[43] On the integration principle see 4.6 above.

In relation to the realisation of objectives for action areas and target sectors, *Towards Sustainability* envisaged a broadening of the range of instruments, whereby legislative instruments are supplemented by other measures including market based instruments, horizontal supporting instruments and financial support mechanisms.[44] Again, developments here have been sluggish,[45] and to date it must be stressed that the body of EC water legislation, at least, continues to reflect a traditional 'command and control' approach to regulation. Ultimately, the emphasis of the Programme was on realising sustainable development[46] by ensuring that the objectives, targets and actions are implemented by appropriate national, regional and local efforts and initiatives, whilst taking account of the traditions and sensitivities of different regions of the Community. This involves a combination of the principle of 'subsidiarity'[47] with a wider concept of shared responsibility involving a mixture of actors and instruments which will operate in combination to secure the most relevant mechanism for the implementation of particular measures.[48] Again, a contrast may be drawn with previous Action Programmes which have tended to employ a legislative, or 'top-down', approach, whereas *Towards Sustainability* sought to ensure the involvement of all economic and social partners in a new, more collective, approach towards realising sustainable development.[49]

In particular, in relation to the management of water resources, the Programme stated that Community policies had to address the following objectives:

(a) preventing pollution of fresh and marine surface waters and groundwater, with particular emphasis on prevention at source;
(b) restoring natural ground and surface waters to an ecologically sound condition, thus ensuring, amongst other things, a suitable source for extracting drinking water; and
(c) ensuring that water demand and water supply are brought into equilibrium on the basis of more rational use and management of water resources.

Specifically, in relation to the qualitative aspects of water, the objectives for groundwater were to maintain the quality of uncontaminated groundwater; to prevent further contamination of contaminated groundwater and to restore contaminated groundwater to a quality required for drinking water production purposes. In relation to surface waters, the qualitative objective was to maintain a high standard of ecological quality with a biodiversity corresponding as closely as possible to the unperturbed state of a given water. For marine water, the corresponding objective was a reduction of discharges of all substances, which due to their toxic

---

[44] *Towards Sustainability* para.31.
[45] See the 1995 Review, COM(95)647 final.
[46] See 4.4.1 above on sustainable development.
[47] See 4.4.2 above on subsidiarity.
[48] *Towards Sustainability*, paras 32 and 33.
[49] *Ibid* para.34.

persistence or accumulating impact could negatively affect the environment, to levels which are not harmful to a high standard of ecological quality of all surface waters.[50] To some extent it was envisaged that these matters would be addressed by legal means, through the strict implementation of existing directives or by proposals for new directives.[51] Otherwise, extra-legal measures such as the progressive replacement of harmful pesticides, improved surveillance and monitoring and economic and fiscal measures were regarded as a more appropriate form of action. Finally, the review of *Towards Sustainability* stated that, in relation to the management of water resources, particular attention was needed in developing a comprehensive strategy setting out an integrated planning and management approach to groundwater and surface water resources, focus on both quantitative and qualitative aspects, a clear message in relation to the lack of progress then being made on the Water Framework Directive.

Finally, though not yet adopted, some clear indications are emerging as to the focus of any Sixth Action Programme.[52] Briefly, there are signs of a continuing emphasis on implementation, in the context of which measures to strengthen the Environmental Information Directive in line with the 1998 Aarhus Convention have been proposed.[53] Whether other aspects of this convention, which deal with access to justice and public participation in decision-making, will be given effect to remains to be seen. There is also likely to be continuing emphasis on integrating environmental considerations into other policy areas, and the prospect of environmental indicators playing a role in this respect.[54] While the Water Framework Directive will inevitably be a major focus, in general terms water matters have not figured as prominently as areas like climate change or waste management, and it remains to be seen how active the Community will be on areas which fall outside the Framework Directive, such as bathing waters.[55]

## 5.3 Water Protection Strategies

While the *Fifth Action Programme* and more recent developments give an indication of current policy thinking and directions, it remains the case that the bulk of Community water legislation was adopted under the previous action programmes. As noted, however, before 1993 there were policy and legal developments which shaped the content of the earlier legislation. This section looks at the central approaches which the Community has successively adopted in legislating on water quality.

---

[50] *Ibid* section 5.4.

[51] See the discussion of the Water Framework Directive at 5. 7 below.

[52] See now COM(2001)31.

[53] See 16.18 below on the Aarhus Convention, and 16.16 on the Environmental Information Directive.

[54] See Article 6 EC, at 4.6 above.

[55] Tornero (1999). See also McGillivray and Holder (2001).

There are significant differences in the underlying strategies adopted in the various EC water directives, and even within particular directives markedly different approaches to water protection are employed. However, some broad trends may be discerned, and the directives may be grouped into three broad categories according to the general approach they adopt:

(a)  imposing of emission controls;
(b)  establishing water quality objectives and standards; and
(c)  regulating activities.[56]

In the first category are those directives that are primarily concerned with emissions that cause the contamination of water by specified kinds of substances. Emission controls may take the form of an 'end-of-pipe' restrictions regulating the point of emission by the imposition of 'limit values' or, in relation to substances or products where this is not feasible, by prohibitions upon the production or marketing of environmentally hazardous products. In each instance, however, the objective is to limit or prohibit the emission or transfer of particular substances into the environmental media. Consequently, this approach tends to concentrate upon those substances identified as being most seriously harmful to the environment. At Community level, various measures relating to product and process controls are directed towards the limitation or prohibition of such emissions but, in terms of restrictions imposed at the point of emission, the approach is most clearly illustrated by the Dangerous Substances Directive[57] (and various subsidiary measures enacted to deal with particular kinds of dangerous substance) and the Groundwater Directive.[58]

In a second grouping, of those directives that establish environmental quality objectives or standards, the emphasis is placed upon environmental impacts rather than emissions. Hence, the objective is that particular waters should actually attain whatever level of environmental quality is needed for the purpose for which the water is to be used. This is illustrated by the quality of water for bathing, where a major concern is that bathing water should not be harmful to human health and parameters have been determined largely on that basis.[59] In other respects broader environmental concerns determine the values of water quality parameters, as where water provides the habitat for freshwater fish.[60] In each case, however, the concern extends beyond those substances which are regarded as intrinsically hazardous or polluting to substances which only become problematic where certain concentrations are exceeded in particular waters. In each directive, therefore, the task is that of determining levels of acceptability in relation to waters for particular purposes.

---

[56] See 1.4.3 above on objectives and standards for water quality, and 1.7 generally on regulatory approaches.
[57] See 5.4.1 below on the Dangerous Substances Directive.
[58] See 5.4.2 and 13.6 below on the Groundwater Directive.
[59] See 5.5.2 below on the Bathing Waters Directive.
[60] See 15.3.1 below on the Freshwater Fish Waters Directive.

The third grouping of directives are those measures which, primarily, seek to regulate activities which may give rise to water quality problems. Implicitly, this may be done by reference to emission controls and environmental quality objectives, but its distinctive feature is to go beyond these approaches in addressing environmentally harmful undertakings, processes and operations and restricting the ways in which they are conducted. This strategy is well illustrated in relation to the treatment of sewage by the Sewage Sludge Directive[61] and the Urban Waste Water Treatment Directive;[62] to agricultural activities by the Nitrates Directive;[63] and more generally to hazardous industrial activities by the Integrated Pollution Prevention and Control Directive.[64]

Despite the convenience of this threefold classification of strategies, which is used in the exposition below, it should be stressed that this is not strictly adhered to within particular directives, almost all of which generally rely upon more than one strategic approach. Also of note is the recent trend towards a consolidation of the different strategies, as is well illustrated by the recent adoption of the Water Framework Directive which seeks to combine emissions controls with the setting of water quality objectives.[65]

## 5.4 Directives Imposing Emission Controls

Those directives which impose emissions limits tend to date from the earlier period of Community involvement, and both the Dangerous Substances Directive and the Groundwater Directive (though not the Detergents Directives) will eventually be replaced by the Water Framework Directive.

### 5.4.1 The Dangerous Substances Directive

Currently, the best examples of primarily emission-centred directives are the Dangerous Substances Directive[66] and the Groundwater Directive.[67] The Dangerous Substances Directive applies to the pollution of inland surface waters, territorial waters and internal coastal waters,[68] and establishes a general legal mechanism for reducing and eliminating water

---

[61] See 5.6.1 below on the Sewage Sludge Directive.

[62] See 5.6.2 below on the Urban Waste Water Treatment Directive.

[63] See 5.6.3 below on the Nitrates Directive.

[64] Although not included in the list of Directives that are primarily concerned with water, it is clear that this Directive has major implications for the protection of water from pollution from the most hazardous industrial processes. See 12.2.3 below.

[65] See 5.7 below on the Water Framework Directive.

[66] Although originally the Directive also applied to groundwater, it has now ceased to apply to this category of water because of the implementation of a separate directive on groundwater (80/68/EEC) (see Art4(4) Dangerous Substances Directive).

[67] See 5.4.2 below on the Groundwater Directive.

[68] 'Inland surface water' means all static or flowing fresh water situated in the territory of one or more Member States. 'Internal coastal waters' means waters on the landward side of the base lines from which the breadth of territorial waters is measured, extending, in the case of watercourses, up to the fresh-water limit (Art.1 Dangerous Substances Directive).

pollution caused by specified dangerous substances, in particular persistent toxic and bioaccumulable substances. For this purpose two lists of polluting substances are provided for in the Annex to the Directive:

(a) *List I* comprising substances selected on the basis of their toxicity, persistence and bioaccumulation (and commonly termed the 'Black List'); and

(b) *List II* containing substances which have a deleterious effect upon the aquatic environment, but which can be confined to a given area depending on the characteristics and location of the water into which they are discharged (the 'Grey List').

Initially, however, Black List substances are to be regarded as featuring in the Grey List until limit values or quality objectives for these substances have been established.[69] As a framework directive, the Directive envisages the adoption of further subsidiary directives, or 'daughter directives', to provide for more specific control of individual List I substances.[70]

The ultimate objective of the Directive is to eliminate 'pollution by List I substances'[71] and to reduce pollution by List II substances. 'Pollution', for these purposes, is defined as the discharge by man, directly or indirectly, of substances or energy into the aquatic environment, the results of which are such as to cause hazards to human health, harm to living resources and to aquatic ecosystems, damage to amenities or interference with other legitimate uses of water.[72]

### 5.4.1A  The meaning of discharge

'Discharge' means the introduction into inland surface waters, territorial waters, inland coastal waters or ground water of any substance listed in List I or List II of the Annex to the Directive, with the exception of discharges of dredgings, operational discharges from ships in territorial waters, and dumping from ships in territorial waters.[73]

The Court of Justice has recently given the meaning of the term 'discharge' a broad interpretation in two cases referred from the Nederlands Raad van State for preliminary rulings.[74] In *Nederhoff*,[75] a company used wooden posts treated with creosote (which contains polycyclic aromatic hydrocarbons (PAHs), a Black List substance) for

---

[69] Annex, Dangerous Substances Directive.

[70] Although, uniquely, no specific date was set for transposition, see Art.12(2) and the sensible approach taken in Case C-206/96 *Commission* v *Luxembourg* [1998] ECR I-3368.

[71] Notably, the Directive does not strive to eliminate *emissions* of List I substances but only 'pollution' by such substances, which places further importance upon the definition of 'pollution' provided above.

[72] Art.1(2)(g) Dangerous Substances Directive, and see 1.3.3 above on the definition of 'pollution'.

[73] *Ibid* Art.1(2)(d).

[74] For comment and analysis in the UK context see Brumwell (2000).

[75] Case C-232/97 *L Nederhoff & Zn* v *Dijkgraaf en Hoogheemraden van het Hoogheemraadschap Rijnland* [1999] ECR I-6385.

shoring up river banks. Having placed the posts in a river, Nederhoff retrospectively applied to the competent national authority for an authorisation under the relevant transposing provisions. This was refused on the grounds that the competent authority had adopted a policy of combating the emission of PAHs at source by looking for alternative materials that were more environmentally acceptable. Nederhoff appealed against the refusal, submitting in essence that 'discharge' did not encompass diffuse sources of pollution. In *van Rooij*,[76] steam, containing the Grey List substances arsenic, copper and chromium, was released from a wood treatment business and was precipitated directly, and also passed indirectly by a storm drain, into nearby surface water. Van Rooij asked the local water authority, acting under national law, to protect surface water against the precipitation. On these two sets of facts, the Court of Justice was therefore asked to rule on whether the placing of the creosoted posts in the river could amount to a 'discharge' for the Dangerous Substances Directive, and whether 'discharge' could encompass the emission of contaminated steam and its subsequent precipitation and transmission into surface water.

The Court held that both situations involved a 'discharge' for the purposes of the Directive. In *Nederhoff*, 'discharge' could include placing the creosote-treated posts in surface water because, when placed in contact with water, the posts would release Grey List substances into the water. In *van Rooij*, 'discharge' was held to cover the emission of contaminated steam that precipitated into surface waters since an indirect discharge could also be covered. The distance between the place of emission and the waters into which the precipitation occurred was relevant only for determining whether the pollution of the waters could be regarded as foreseeable so that the entry could be attributable to the person causing the steam. Accordingly, 'discharge' could cover the emission of contaminated steam that first precipitated onto land and roofs and then reached the surface water via a storm water drain.

The *Nederhoff* case is also important because the Court further held that it was lawful for the competent authority to follow its policy even where this made the grant of an authorisation virtually impossible.[77] The Directive allowed Member States to make a discharge subject to additional licensing requirements not provided for in the Directive in order to protect the EC aquatic environment against pollution caused by certain dangerous substances.[78] The obligation imposed by the competent Netherlands authority to investigate or choose alternative solutions which had less impact on the environment amounted to such a requirement, even if it

---

[76] Case C-231/97 *AML van Rooij* v *Dagelijks bestuur van het Waterschap de Dommel ex parte Gebr van Aarle BV* [1999] ECR I-6355.

[77] This was alleged to violate Art.3 of the Directive, discussed below. Similarly, the Court held that the Directive gave sufficient flexibility to set higher national standards, even where these would in effect amount to a prohibition. This might also have been possible under the environmental guarantee applicable to harmonisation directives (Art.95(4)-(9) EC (ex Art.100a(4)).

[78] Art.5(2) Dangerous Substances Directive.

might have made the grant of an authorisation virtually impossible. While the marketing and use of creosote within the EC was governed by a separate Directive,[79] this did not preclude a Member State, when dealing with a consent or discharge to surface waters, effectively prohibiting the use of substances within the Dangerous Substances Directive where they would be discharged to surface waters.

### 5.4.1B  The parallel approach: limit values or quality standards

Under the Dangerous Substances Directive, elimination and reduction of pollution is to be brought about by a system of prior authorisation of discharges of substances in both lists by the appropriate competent authority.[80] Authorisations must contain emission limitations incorporating maximum concentrations of substances and maximum quantity of substances permissible during specified periods of time and competent authorities must take appropriate steps to ensure that conditions are fulfilled.[81] It is for the Council to establish limit values for emissions within List I,[82] under 'daughter directives', specifying maximum concentrations and quantities of such substances on the basis of their toxicity, persistence and bioaccumulation 'taking into account the best technical means available'.[83]

The main purpose of the regime so far described is clearly to restrict emissions of dangerous substances, rather than to impose water quality objectives. However, the Directive also provides for the Council to establish quality objectives[84] for List I substances on the basis of toxicity, persistence and accumulation in living organisms and sediment. As an alternative to the limit values, quality objectives set by the Council can be applied by a Member State where it can prove to the Commission that the quality objectives are being met and continuously maintained throughout an area affected by a discharge.[85] Hence the Directive, whilst largely concerned to limit emissions of specified substances, actually incorporates a 'parallel approach' whereby emissions are allowed if a Member State can maintain compliance with ambient water quality objectives.

The adoption of the parallel approach, and the respective appropriateness of emission standards as opposed to quality standards for receiving waters, was a matter of considerable controversy between the UK and the other (then) eight Member States when the Directive was adopted. Controlling water pollution by imposing emission standards alone may fail to utilise

---

[79] Directive 76/769/EEC on the marketing and use of certain dangerous substances and preparations.

[80] Art.2 Dangerous Substances Directive.

[81] *Ibid* Art.5.

[82] For List II substances, the Directive obliges Member States to establish programmes of quality objectives in order to reduce pollution by these substances (Art.7).

[83] *Ibid* Art.6(1). This provision has been described as a 'dead letter', with values being fixed 'on the basis of a political compromise' (Krämer (2000) p.194).

[84] These are provided for in the daughter directives, on which see 5.4.1C below.

[85] Arts. 6(2) and (3) Dangerous Substances Directive.

the assimilative capacity of ambient waters to disperse and neutralise pollutants. Alternatively, water quality objectives under-emphasise the need to prevent pollution at source by regulating discharges at the points of origin.[86]

Generally, the UK has tended to support the quality objective approach whilst the other Member States have preferred emission standards. There are various reasons for this. They include the considerable comparative advantages enjoyed by the UK when it comes to the assimilation of water pollutants in its relatively fast-flowing rivers and along its ample coastline. But they also relate to a national administrative style of environmental regulation which, traditionally, emphasised discretionary and pragmatic decision-making based on local environmental quality rather than any more uniform approach.[87] The compromise provided by the Directive under the parallel approach reflected a political bargain between the UK and the other Member States,[88] rather than any attempt to resolve fundamental differences of view about pollution control strategy. Nevertheless, it seems fairly clear that the considerable opposition amongst other Member States to the UK insistence on environmental quality standards was at least as much to do with the informality, flexibility and secrecy with which such standards were used at national level than it was about hostility as such to the use of quality standards.[89]

### 5.4.1C 'Black List' substances and daughter directives

The status of the Dangerous Substances Directive as a 'framework directive' means that it depends in part on further measures, which specify limit values and quality objectives for Black List substances (including organohalogens, organophosphorus and organotin compounds, mercury, cadmium and their compounds, and substances possessing carcinogenic properties), in order to realise its ultimate objectives. A small number of these 'daughter directives' were initially adopted which established parameters for specific substances, namely:

   (a) Directives on limit values and quality objectives for mercury discharges by the chloroalkali electrolysis industry (82/176/EEC) and by other sectors (84/156/EEC);

---

[86] Generally see Renshaw (1980) pp.239-240: 'in the UK at least, the most important [conclusion] is that environmental quality objectives offer the best way through to the achievement of desired environmental standards at least cost'. See here also Boehmer-Christiansen (1990) and Ogus (1994) Ch.8.

[87] Bell and McGillivray (2000) p.190. Jordan and Greenaway (1998) p.686 remark that, in the context of the water quality approach *par excellence* (marine treatment) that 'it is more accurate perhaps to regard [marine treatment] as a set of politically and economically expedient tools, which were only worked up into a broader 'philosophy' in the late 1970s by British officials seeking to justify the status quo to foreign observers'.

[88] The Directive required a unanimous vote in the Council of Ministers to be adopted.

[89] Haigh (1992, updated), 3.9 and 4.8. That the episode did not reveal a 'continental' hostility to water quality standards is evidenced by the adoption of several quality directives at the same period, see 5.5 below.

(b) Directive on limit values and quality objectives for cadmium discharges (83/513/EEC); and

(c) Directive on limit values and quality objectives for discharges of hexachlorocyclohexane ('HCH' or lindane) (84/491/EEC);

Notwithstanding the adoption of these measures, progress in enacting daughter directives was desperately slow. To address the difficulties and speed up the process, the General Application Directive[90] was enacted. This provides for the consolidation of procedures and application rules to avoid repetition in every subsequent daughter directive. The General Application Directive also establishes specific programmes to avoid or eliminate pollution from pollution from significant sources of substances in List II to the Annex of the Dangerous Substances Directive other than waste, and sets specific standards for carbon tetrachloride, pentachlorophenol (PCP) and DDT. Two further directives have been made under the General Application Directive, adding further substances to the Black List control regime:

(a) Directive 88/347/EEC (adding chloroform, hexachlorobenzene, hexachlorobutadiene, and the pesticides aldrin, dieldrin, endrin and isodrin); and

(b) Directive 90/415/EEC (adding 1-2-dichloroethane, trichloroethylene, perchloroethylene and trichlorobenzene).

By way of illustration, the daughter directive on the organohalogen compound HCH (lindane) lays down limit values for plant for the production of HCH which are 2 grams of HCH per tonne of HCH produced and 2 milligrams of HCH per litre discharged. The current limit values for plant for the extraction of lindane (meaning the separation of lindane from a mixture of HCH isomers) are 4 grams of HCH per tonne of HCH treated and 2 milligrams of HCH per litre discharged. The current limit values for plant where the production of HCH and extraction of lindane is carried out are 5 grams of HCH per tonne of HCH produced and 2 milligrams of HCH per litre discharged. These values are subject to detailed provisions.[91] In addition, it is notable that while limit values normally apply to the point of discharge from the industrial plant concerned, an exception is made where discharges are sent to treatment works. In such cases, the point of discharge for the purposes of compliance with limit values is the point where the waste waters leave the treatment plant.[92]

In line with the 'parallel approach', however, the Directive also lays down quality objectives for HCH.[93] Where quality standards are used, as in the UK, the obligation is on the competent authority to determine the area affected. The water quality standards which are provided for, which must

---

[90] Directive 86/280/EEC on limit values and quality objectives for discharges of certain dangerous substances included in List I of the Annex to the Dangerous Substances Directive (76/464/EEC).

[91] Annex I Directive 84/491/EEC.

[92] *Ibid* Art.3(2).

[93] As laid down in Annex II of the Directive.

be measured at a point sufficiently close to the point of discharge, are that the total HCH concentration in different bodies of water should not exceed the following limits:

(a) for inland surface waters affected by a discharge, 100 nanograms per litre;

(b) for estuarial waters and waters of the territorial sea, the total concentration of HCH must not exceed 20 nanograms per litre; and

(c) for water used for the abstraction of drinking water, the HCH content must conform to the requirements of the Drinking Water Abstraction Directive.[94]

In addition, there is a 'baseline' requirement that the total concentrations of HCH in sediments, molluscs, shellfish and fish must not increase significantly with time.

The Directive also lays down time limits, reference methods for measuring the concentration of HCH in discharges and in the aquatic environment (these were not explicitly provided for in the framework directive), establishes a monitoring procedure and makes arrangement for co-operation between Member States where discharges affect the waters of more than one Member State. While the Directive puts the obligation on monitoring the quality of the aquatic environment on the Member States, it is silent as to who is responsible for monitoring the industrial installations covered (which, as noted above, may include effluent treatment works). In particular, there is a lack of guidance as to whether it would be acceptable to allow self-monitoring[95] to be undertaken and, if so, what degree of scrutiny of this (if any) would be required of the national authorities.

Despite the adoption of various 'daughter directives' such as that outlined above, a fundamental difficulty with the Dangerous Substances Directive is that only a handful of Black List substances have actually had specific emission limits or quality standards set for them in such directives.[96] Moreover, enforcement action by the Commission in relation to the daughter directives has, since 1990, 'come to a standstill', which has been attributed to the impact of the post-Maastricht emphasis on subsidiarity.[97] One obvious consequence of this is that enforcement action at national level takes on a particular importance.[98] Here, it might be noted that the UK preference for quality standards rather than emission limit values makes individual enforcement action exceedingly difficult. Rather than establish that a particular discharge exceeds a limit value (e.g. the limit of

---

[94] Directive 75/440/EEC, see 5.5.3 and 17.6 below. This Directive contains a mandatory 'total pesticides' value (which includes HCH).

[95] On self-monitoring generally see 16.11 below.

[96] Proposals to amend the Directive to speed up the adoption of daughter directives (COM(90)9) were withdrawn by the Commission in 1993.

[97] Krämer (2000) p.196, although see Case C-213/97 *Commission v Portugal* [1998] ECR I-3289. On subsidiarity see 4.4.2 above.

[98] See the discussion of Case C-168/95 *Arcaro* [1996] ECR I-4705 at 4.16.2 and 4.16.5 above.

2 milligrams of HCH per litre discharged), claimants at national level would have the more difficult task of establishing that a quality standard (e.g. the 100 nanograms per litre standard for inland surface waters affected by a discharge of HCH) had been breached. Needless to say, this would require much more extensive evidence, in practice severely limiting the possibility of individually-initiated enforcement at national level.[99]

### 5.4.1D 'Grey List' substances

Failing the adoption of daughter directives, the remaining Black List substances, and all Grey List substances (including metals such as zinc, copper, nickel, chromium, lead and their compounds, biocides and their derivatives, and substances such as cyanide and ammonia), are subject to the much less restrictive regime relating to List II substances. This requires general and specific reduction programmes to be established at national level for 99 substances.[100] For many years this provision was generally treated in practice as little more than exhortatory, and the extent to which Member States have either established programmes for List II substances in order to reduce pollution, or fixed quality objectives for them, has been very limited.[101] That said, a number of infringement actions by the Commission have now been decided by the Court of Justice, which has stressed the need for specific, tailored, reduction programmes. As the Court has observed:

> It is settled case-law that what is specific to the programmes in question is the fact that they must have a comprehensive and coherent approach, covering the entire national territory and providing practical and coordinated arrangements for the reduction of pollution caused by any of the substances in List II which are relevant in the particular context of each Member State, in accordance with the quality objectives fixed by those programmes for the waters affected. They differ, therefore, both from general purification programmes and from bundles of ad hoc measures designed to reduce water pollution.[102]

---

[99] Somsen (2000) p.337 and see genrally 4.6 above.

[100] As a matter of practice, List II currently includes 99 substances contained in List I. This is because in 1982, the Commission published a list of 129 potential Black List substances, subsequently revised to 132 substances, comprising mainly pesticides, organic solvents and a small number of heavy metals. This list was agreed by the Council (OJ 1983, C46/17). However, 18 of these substance have had emission limits and quality standards set for them under daughter directives, while a few further 15 substances were included in COM(90)9 (see 5.4.1C above). In practice, this left 99 substances where the onus was on the Member States to devise reduction programmes.

[101] Krämer (2000), p.194 suggests this has not happened anywhere, but see s.83 Water Resources Act 1991 and the Surface Waters (Dangerous Substances) (Classification) Regulations 1997 (SI 1997 No.2560); see 14.8.3 below on these Regulations.

[102] Case C-384/97 *Commission* v *Hellenic Republic* [2000] ECR I-3823, para.40, citing Case C-207/97 *Commission* v *Belgium* [1999] ECR I-275, para.40. On what 'specific' pollution reduction programmes under Art.7 of the Directive might require see Case C-298/95 *Commission* v *Germany* [1996] ECR I-6747, ECJ, paras 22 and 26; Joined Cases C-232, 233/95 *Commission* v *Greece*

*5.4.1E  National implementation and future developments*

Nationally, discharges[103] into the natural water environment are controlled
through the consenting powers contained in Part III of the Water
Resources Act 1991. Discharges of Black List substances to sewer are
controlled under the Trade Effluent (Prescribed Processes and Substances)
Regulations 1989.[104] Processes discharging significant quantities of Black
and Grey List substances will likely be processes subject either to the
integrated pollution control regime under Part I of the Environmental
Protection Act 1990, or to a permit under the Pollution Prevention and
Control Act 1999. See also the Surface Waters (Dangerous Substances)
(Classification) Regulations.[105]

In time, the Dangerous Substances Directive will be repealed as a
consequence of the Integrated Pollution Prevention and Control
Directive[106] and the Water Framework Directive.[107] On adoption of the
Framework Directive at the end of 2000, the Black List under the
Dangerous Substances Directive and the provisions relating to setting limit
values for these substances were repealed and replaced by the list of
priority substances adopted under the Water Framework Directive.[108] From
this date also, the pollution reduction programmes required for Grey List
substances may (but need not) be replaced by Member States applying the
principles for identifying pollution problems and the substances causing
them, establishing quality standards, and adopting the measures laid down
in the Water Framework Directive.[109] The 'good status' objectives under
the Framework Directive, together with the provisions relating to non-
priority substances and priority substances which the Community has yet
to agree, are to be regarded as environmental quality standards for the
purposes of the Integrated Pollution Prevention and Control Directive.[110]
For surface waters, the Water Framework Directive seeks to prevent
deterioration of water quality by stipulating that the environmental
objectives established under the first river basin management plans shall,
as a minimum, give effect to quality standards at least as stringent as those
required to implement the Dangerous Substances Directive, the remaining
provisions of which continue in force until 22 December 2013.

---

[1998] ECR 3343 para.35; Case C-214/96 *Commission* v *Spain* [1998] ECR I-7661; Case C-
384/97 *Commission* v *Hellenic Republic*, 25 May 2000, ECJ, not yet reported, para. 39; Case C-
261/98 *Commission* v *Portugal*, 13 July 2000, paras 28-33.
[103] As this term is understood nationally, see 9.10 below.
[104] SI 1989 No.1156, as amended by SI 1990 No.1629; see 11.10 below.
[105] SI 1992 No.337, SI 1997 No.2560 and SI 1998 No.389, discussed at 14.8.3 below.
[106] Art.20(s) Directive 96/61/EC, see 12.2.3 below.
[107] See 5.7 below.
[108] Art.22(3)(a) Water Framework Directive, i.e. substances listed under Art.16.
[109] *Ibid* Art.22(3)(b).
[110] I.e., for Point 7 Art.2 and Art.10 Directive 96/61/EC, see *ibid* Art.22(4).

### 5.4.2 The Groundwater Directive

Whilst the Dangerous Substances Directive originally applied to a range of waters including groundwater, and aimed for zero pollution from List I substances in groundwater, it was stated that the provisions of the Directive relating to groundwater would cease to be applicable on implementation of a separate directive concerning groundwater.[111] Hence, the 1980 Groundwater Directive superseded the Dangerous Substances Directive in relation to groundwater, by providing a distinct scheme of regulation for groundwater quality, though in many respects its provisions are modelled upon the earlier Directive.

The purpose of the Groundwater Directive is to prevent or limit the direct or indirect introduction into groundwater of dangerous substances identified in List I or List II[112] of the Annex to the Directive. 'Groundwater' is defined as meaning all water below the surface of the ground in the saturation zone and in direct contact with the ground or subsoil.[113] The main obligation upon the Member States is to prevent the introduction of List I substances to groundwater and to limit the introduction of List II substances so as to prevent pollution.[114] This obligation is subject to certain exceptions including the introduction into groundwater of domestic effluents from isolated dwellings outside areas where water is abstracted for human consumption, and discharges which contain List I or List II substances in such small quantities and concentrations that there is no danger of deterioration in the quality of the receiving groundwater.[115] Subject to these exceptions, all direct discharges[116] of List I substances must be prohibited, and any disposal or tipping that might lead to indirect discharge must be subject to prior investigation and prohibition of authorisation where appropriate. For List II substances a general investigation and authorisation procedure must be established for direct discharges, disposal or tipping subject to criteria established by the Directive. Specifically, authorisations may only be issued if all technical precautions for preventing groundwater pollution by List II substances are observed.[117]

In addition to these general provisions, the Directive also regulates artificial enrichment for the purposes of groundwater management, i.e. for drinking water purposes, which is only allowed 'if there is no risk of polluting the groundwater'.[118] It also regulates discharges of leachate from

---

[111] Art.4 Dangerous Substances Directive.

[112] In most respects corresponding to List I and List II of the Dangerous Substances Directive.

[113] Contrast the national definition in s.104(1)(d) Water Resources Act 1991, see 9.4 below.

[114] Art.3 Groundwater Directive. 'Pollution' is similarly defined as under the Dangerous Substances Directive, cited above (Art.1 Groundwater Directive).

[115] *Ibid* Art.2. A further exception concerns matter containing radioactive substances.

[116] 'Discharge' carries the same meaning as under the Dangerous Substances Directive, which suggests that the case law on the meaning of discharge under that Directive will, at the very least, be persuasive, although as noted in certain respects the Groundwater Directive also applies to 'indirect discharges'.

[117] Arts.3-5 Groundwater Directive.

[118] *Ibid* Art.6.

landfills, although, rather curiously, only those in existence at the time the Directive was notified (i.e. as at 20 December 1979). As has been remarked, 'both these provisions ... were, in practice, virtually ignored by Member States and not seriously monitored by the Commission'.[119]

The central observation on the Groundwater Directive is that, while it is built on the same strategy that underlies the Dangerous Substances Directive, the Groundwater Directive is exclusively focused on emission controls. Whilst the Dangerous Substances Directive allows for the alternative of an environmental quality approach to be applied by Member States, there is no equivalent to this in the Groundwater Directive. Within EC water legislation, therefore, it is the purest example of an emission-centred directive. That is, subject to the limited *de minimus* provision that is made, emissions must be controlled regardless of the impact they have on receiving waters. Arguably, this may reflect the greater difficulties involved in monitoring and assessing environmental impacts, and adherence to environmental quality standards, in relation to water which is not readily available for inspection. Alternatively, it may show a need for greater stringency in relation to groundwater protection because of the greater persistency of pollutants in groundwater by comparison with surface waters where replacement and self-purification have a tendency to counteract pollution.

The Council Resolution on Future Groundwater Policy[120] invited the Commission to revise the Groundwater Directive by integrating the protection of groundwater into a general policy for the management of fresh waters. The response to this was a Commission Proposal for an action programme for integrated groundwater protection and management which was endorsed by the European Parliament and Council.[121] The Groundwater Action Programme had as its objectives to ensure protection and use of groundwater through integrated planning and sustainable management aimed at preventing further pollution, maintaining the quality of unpolluted groundwater, where appropriate restoring polluted groundwater and preventing the over-exploitation of groundwater resources. Significant emphasis was placed on the principle of subsidiarity,[122] in requiring, as a priority, that action should be taken at the level of the Member States by establishing and implementing nationally adapted action programmes for sustainable groundwater protection and management. Such national action programmes, however, were to be formulated in accordance with common principles and an overall framework for action established at Community level.

Implementation of the Groundwater Action Programme would have required extensive revision of the Groundwater Directive. However,

---

[119] Krämer (2000) p.190.

[120] Council Resolution of 25 February 1992 on the future Community groundwater policy, OJ 1992, C59/2; also see later Resolution of 28 February 1992, OJ 1995, C49/1.

[121] Proposal for a European Parliament and Council Decision on an action programme for integrated groundwater protection and management, COM(96)315 final, OJ 1996, C355/1.

[122] See 4.4.2 above on subsidiarity.

adoption of the Water Framework Directive[123] entails the eventual repeal of the Groundwater Directive and provisions for the protection of groundwater being placed in the Framework Directive. Accordingly, many of the recommendations in the Groundwater Action Programme are incorporated in legally binding form in the Water Framework Directive.

Implementation of the Groundwater Directive at national level has taken a variety of forms, reflecting the breadth of the obligations in the Directive. Initially this was by administrative circular, and these are still relevant.[124] However, these should be seen alongside the consenting procedures under Part III of the Water Resources Act 1991 and the Waste Management Licensing Regulations 1994[125] concerning waste disposal sites. In relation to pollution from mineral workings, the powers of minerals planning authorities under the Town and Country Planning Act 1990 and the Town and Country Planning (General Permitted Development) Order 1995 are a mechanism for implementation.[126] More recently, recognising the inadequacies of implementation to date, and particularly the difficulties in regulating discharges into groundwater of various agricultural chemicals, the Groundwater Regulations 1998 have been enacted.[127]

### 5.4.3 The Detergent Directives and other product controls

A contrasting approach to the control of contaminating emissions is to be found in the two Detergent Directives. These have as their objective the reduction of river pollution by foaming due to persistent detergents comprising surfactants and additional constituents. Accordingly, the First Detergent Directive[128] requires Member States to prohibit the marketing and use of detergents where the average level of biodegradability of the surfactants contained therein is less that 90% for specified surfactants, and requires that surfactants must not be harmful to human or animal health.[129] The trade-related counterpart of this is that no Member State may, on grounds of biodegradability or toxicity of surfactants, prohibit or restrict or hinder the placing on the market of detergents which comply with the provisions of the Directive.[130] The Second Detergent Directive[131] establishes test methods for determining where the biodegradability requirement for surfactants is complied with and has been amended to allow an alternative method of determination. The underlying approach, in applying product performance standards to substances which are potentially harmful to the aquatic environment, is unique amongst those

---

[123] See 5.7, and see specifically 5.9.17 below on good groundwater status and the early obligation to adopt proposals on good groundwater chemical status.

[124] See Joint Circular 20/90 (Department of Environment) and 34/90 (Welsh Office), 29 October 1990.

[125] SI 1994 No.1056, in particular Reg.15, see 12.2.6 below.

[126] SI 1995 No.418.

[127] SI 1998 No.2746, see 13.6 below.

[128] Directive 73/404/EEC, as amended by Directive 82/242/EEC and Directive 86/94/EEC.

[129] *Ibid*, Art.2.

[130] *Ibid*, Art.3.

[131] Directive 73/405/EEC, as amended by Directive 82/243/EEC.

directives which are usually classified as 'water directives', but is used in relation to other products and substances which are regarded as potentially harmful to the environment in general. National implementation of the Detergents Directives is through the Detergents (Composition) Regulations 1978.[132]

The product control approach to reducing emissions, illustrated in the Detergents Directives, is adopted in a wide range of EC enactments. Measures concerned with the classification, labelling and risk assessment of chemicals are capable of being relevant to the protection of the aquatic environment, though not exclusively concerned with water protection. For example, there are several directives and regulations establishing framework requirements for the classification and labelling of dangerous substances.[133] Similarly measures concerning the evaluation of risks for new and existing chemicals may be important in preventing environmental harm.[134] The information and test results obtained in the evaluation of chemicals for the purposes of this legislation may prompt action in legislation dealing more directly with pollution of the aquatic environment and the protection of aquatic ecosystems.[135] Links may also be drawn with mechanisms for improvement of the environmental features and performance of consumer products generally under the Community eco-labelling scheme.[136] In relation to matters such as the ecological criteria for the award of the Community eco-label to washing machines,[137] dishwashers,[138] laundry detergents[139] and detergents for dishwashers,[140] the impact of such products upon water and the aquatic environment is a matter of particular relevance.

## 5.5 Directives Imposing Environmental Quality Objectives

As explained, the contrasting feature of those directives which impose water quality objectives or standards is their concern with the environmental impacts of pollutants, rather than the control of emissions of particular substances. However, their characterisation as being concerned to impose 'environmental' quality objectives is a generalisation in that each directive reflects a more specific concern with water within a particular use category.

Examples of this kind of approach are to be found in directives concerned with the quality of bathing water, shellfish waters, waters for freshwater fish and, in certain respects, drinking water. Although these directives differ markedly in their individual objectives, and the detailed

---

[132] SI 1978 No.564 as amended by SI 1986 No.560.

[133] For examples see Directive 67/5448/EEC, Regulation 793/93/EEC and Directive 88/379/EEC.

[134] See Directive 93/67/EC and Regulation 1488/94/EC.

[135] See the provisions of the Water Framework Directive, at 5.8.5 below.

[136] Regulation 880/92/EEC.

[137] Commission Decision 96/461/EC, OJ 1996, L191/56.

[138] Commission Decision 98/483/EC, OJ 1998, L216/12.

[139] Commission Decision 95/365/EC, OJ 1995, L217/14.

[140] Commission Decision 1999/427/EC, OJ 1999, L167/38.

requirements which they impose, a number of general characteristics of water use directives may be identified. Because many of the quality standard directives merit full consideration in other chapters, especially those on the quality of surface waters for abstraction and on shellfish and freshwater fish,[141] only the Bathing Water Directive is discussed in detail here. However, this is sufficient to highlight the main features of the environmental quality objective approach and the view of the Court of Justice on the discretion afforded to Member States in implementation. The Bathing Waters Directive is also the only directive discussed in this section which is not to be repealed by the Water Framework Directive.

### 5.5.1 General Characteristics

Typically, environmental quality-centred directives require Member States to designate or identify the waters within their area to which the particular directives apply, though in some instances the criteria which have been provided for this purpose are rather unspecific. A second general characteristic feature, in relation to the waters concerned, is that the directives incorporate Annexes setting out parameters relating to imperative ('I') values, and to guide ('G') values, for water quality. Member States must then establish parameters for the waters concerned which must not be less stringent than the mandatory I values, and must endeavour to respect the stricter G values. Third, the directives incorporate a non-degradation principle which requires that implementation may not directly or indirectly lead to deterioration of the waters at issue. Fourth, the directives enable Member States to derogate from their requirements in exceptional circumstances with communication of the grounds of derogation to the Commission being required. Fifth, the competent authorities in the Member States are made responsible for sampling, analysis and inspection of the quality of water concerned in accordance with the provisions of each directive. Sixth, in some instances a simplified procedure is provided for to allow the directives to be adapted in the light of technical progress. Seventh, the directives make provision for reporting back to the Commission on their operation within the different Member States.

### 5.5.2 The Bathing Water Directive

The Bathing Water Directive[142] is intended to protect the environment and public health,[143] and for that purpose is concerned with the quality of bathing water with the exception of water intended for therapeutic purposes and water used in swimming pools.

---

[141] Thus, Directive 79/923/EEC on shellfish waters and Directive 78/659/EEC on freshwaters for fish are considered at 15.3.1 below, while Directive 75/440/EEC on surface water for abstraction is considered at 17.6 below.

[142] Directive 76/160/EEC.

[143] *Ibid*, preamble.

*5.5.2A   What is bathing water?*

'Bathing water' means all running or still fresh waters, or parts thereof, and sea water in which bathing is explicitly authorised by the competent authorities of each Member State, or bathing is not prohibited and is traditionally practised by a large number of bathers.[144] This definition has proved somewhat problematic to interpret, and was initially construed as allowing a wide discretion to Member States in identifying those waters that fell within its meaning. Later case law of the European Court of Justice, however, narrowed this discretion considerably, requiring an objective approach to be taken under which 'bathing waters' were to be identified according to the presence of things like bathing huts, changing facilities and the presence of lifeguards.[145] Nevertheless, the UK Government has come under scrutiny for, until 1998, not designating any inland bathing waters, and in other respects for a minimalistic approach to transposition.[146]

The question has arisen whether 'bathing waters' is to be read as equating to waters actually used for 'bathing' or 'swimming'. Hence, is the Directive to be limited to waters where some form of swimming is authorised or practised, or whether it has a wider meaning encompassing waters where other recreational uses of water are engaged in? This issue has arisen, in a domestic context, in relation to waters used by surfers, where it has been argued that the human health objective of the directive means that on a purposive reading it should also encompass any recreational use of water where there is contact between people and water of the kind experienced by bathers. That is, a distinction can be drawn between 'bathers' and, for example, those engaged in recreational sailing, where the purpose is to avoid contact with the water. However, in the case of surfing the majority of the time is spent in the water where the amount of contact with the water is indistinguishable from that experienced by swimmers.[147] In *Moase* v *Secretary of State for the Environment, Transport and the Regions*,[148] this line of argument was not directly rejected, although the part of the case relating to the argument that the waters in question should have been designated as 'bathing waters' was dismissed because it was not established that, in the absence of bathing facilities etc, the waters were used by a 'large number' of any type of users. This leaves open the possibility that, in an appropriate case, waters used by surfers, and thus waters tending to be used all year round,[149] might be held to be bathing waters.

---

[144] Art.1 Bathing Water Directive.

[145] See Case C-56/90 *Commission* v *United Kingdom* [1993] ECR I-4109 (the *Blackpool Bathing Water* case), discussed at 4.15.2 above.

[146] See House of Commons Select Committee on the Environment, Transport and Regional Affairs, *Sewage Treatment and Disposal* (1998).

[147] One might speculate what line of argument might be raised in relation to windsurfers.

[148] [2001] Env LR 13, and see now also *Moase and Lomas* v *Environment Agency* [2001] EWHC Admin 231, and see 5.6.2 below.

[149] See also the provisions relating to monitoring, discussed below and at 16.2.2.

### 5.5.2B  Monitoring and other obligations

In relation to all parameters, including those where no I or G values are specified, monitoring requirements, expressed in terms of the minimum sampling frequency and method of analysis and inspection, are imposed. Conformity with the relevant parameters is realised where samples of water taken at the same sampling point, and at the intervals specified in the Annex, show that 95% of samples for the I values conform, or where 90% of samples in all other cases conform, with the exception of the total coliform and faecal coliform parameters where the requirement is 80% compliance.[150] Monitoring is only required during the 'bathing season', which has led to concerns that national interpretations of this term may be unduly restrictive.[151] In some countries, this might mean that one poor quality sample is enough to establish non-compliance, although to avoid this the sampling frequency could simply be increased. For non-compliant samples, the water must not deviate from the parametric values by more than 50%, except for microbiological parameters, pH and dissolved oxygen, and consecutive water samples taken at statistically suitable intervals do not deviate from the relevant parametric values. In relation to deviations from parametric values, these are to be discounted where they are the result of floods, other natural disasters or abnormal weather conditions.[152]

Responsibility for undertaking sampling operations, at the frequency provided for in the Annex to the Directive, is allocated to the competent authorities in the Member States. In accordance with this duty, competent authorities must take samples, commencing two weeks before the start of the bathing season, at those places where the daily average density of bathers is greatest. Samples should preferably be taken 30cm below the surface of the water except for mineral oil samples where surface level samples should be taken. Further requirements require local investigation of the ambient water conditions to be scrupulously undertaken, to be repeated periodically to obtain geographical and topographical data and to determine the volume and nature of all polluting and potentially polluting discharges and their effects upon the bathing area. Where such investigations reveal a discharge of substances likely to lower the quality of bathing water, or where there are other grounds to suspect a decline in water quality, additional sampling must be undertaken.[153]

Modification of the requirements of the Directive is anticipated in that necessary amendments to allow adaptation to technical progress relating to

---

[150] Art.5 Bathing Water Directive.

[151] 'Bathing season' means the period during which a large number of bathers can be expected, in the light of local custom, and any local rules which may exist concerning bathing and weather conditions (*ibid* Art.1(2)). In the UK, this is defined as 15 May to 30 September. For criticisms see House of Commons Select Committee on the Environment, Transport and the Regions, *Sewage Treatment and Disposal* (1998) para.135, which notes that the bathing season in some areas extends until October. There is also the related issue as to whether the Directive extends to waters used for other recreational activities like windsurfing, which may take place all year round.

[152] Art.5 Bathing Waters Directive.

[153] *Ibid* Art.6.

the methods of analysis of samples and the G and I parameters are provided for in accordance with committee procedures.[154] Ongoing monitoring of progress is provided for by way of a requirement that Member States submit an annual report to the Commission on implementation of the Directive, including information about the quality of their bathing waters.[155] From this obligation, which is unique to the water directives,[156] the Commission publishes an annual report on the quality of EC bathing waters.[157] This relates to water quality in the preceding bathing season, though 'real-time' information on bathing water quality may soon be accessible. Although not formally provided for under the Directive, the 'Blue Flag' scheme run by the Foundation for Environmental Education in Europe, a body funded by the Commission, relies in part on compliance with the guideline values in the Directive, as well as other non-water quality criteria relating to standards of facilities.[158]

### 5.5.2C  The obligation to achieve the environmental quality standards

In relation to specific water quality requirements, the Bathing Water Directive requires Member States to achieve for all bathing areas, or for each bathing area, parameters set out in the Appendix to the Directive. These are divided into mandatory I values, and G values which Member States must endeavour to achieve 'as guidelines'.[159] Accordingly, the Annex specifies some 19 physical, chemical and microbiological parameters for the quality of bathing water. Ten of these are mandatory I parameters, and seven G parameters, though it was envisaged that subsequent parameters would later be added to the list. Non-degradation is provided for in the Directive by a requirement that implementation of the measures taken pursuant to the Directive may in no circumstances lead, either directly or indirectly, to deterioration in the quality of bathing water. Also, Member States may at any time establish more stringent values for bathing water than those laid down in the Directive.[160]

Member States were allowed ten years from the date of notification (i.e. by 10 December 1985) to take all necessary measures to implement the Directive. However, in 'exceptional circumstances', Member States may grant derogations from the ten-year time limit providing that justifications for such derogations are based on management plans for the waters concerned and these are communicated to the Commission as soon as possible and not later than six years following the notification of the Directive.[161] Only the UK requested and obtained such derogations. Further provision for derogation from the requirements of the Directive

---

[154] *Ibid* Art.9.

[155] *Ibid* Art.13, as amended by Directive 91/692/EEC, on which see 16.2.2 below.

[156] See discussion of the Reporting Directive (91/692/EEC) at 16.2.5 below.

[157] See the most recent report, 'Quality of bathing water (1999 bathing season)'. In theory the national reports should be available at http://europa.eu.int/water/water-bathing/index_en.html.

[158] European Parliament Written Question No.1117/97 (Diez de Rivera Icaza) OJ 1997, C319/231.

[159] Art.3 Bathing Water Directive.

[160] *Ibid* Art.7.

[161] *Ibid* Art.4.

allows it to be waived, in relation to certain parameters, because of exceptional weather or geographical conditions or when bathing water undergoes natural enrichment in certain substances causing a deviation from the values prescribed in the Annex. However, in no case may these exceptions disregard the essential requirement of public health protection, and where a waiver of this kind takes place the Member State must notify the Commission directly and state the reasons for this and the period of waver anticipated.[162]

The strictness of the duties on Member States contained in the Directive have been illustrated by the judgment of the Court of Justice in the *Blackpool Bathing Water* case, which stressed that the obligations contained in the Directive are obligations of result, rather than to do all that is reasonably practicable.[163] This approach has been reaffirmed in later cases, which have discounted the possibility that the proportionality principle might be used to justify not taking sufficient water quality improvement measures.[164] These cases are in line with the general approach that proportionality is not a relevant factor in the implementation of directives laying down minimum public health standards.

More recent proceedings by the Commission against Spain in relation to alleged non-compliance with the Directive at a number of freshwater bathing waters illustrate a number of other, unsuccessful, arguments concerning the obligation to comply with the limit values in the Directive.[165] In this case, Spain raised four grounds to justify non-compliance:

(a) that an abnormal drought, lasting five years, amounted to 'abnormal weather conditions';
(b) that proposals of the Commission to revise the Directive, bringing it more closely into line with current technical knowledge,[166] as well as (then) proposals for a Water Framework Directive which would provide more of a framework for bathing water quality rather than detailed rules,[167] made the present Directive obsolete;
(c) that the main factor behind poor bathing water quality was urban waste water, which was the subject of the Urban Waste Water Treatment Directive, the provisions of which, and the timetable for compliance in which, should be taken into consideration; and
(d) that many of the bathing areas inspected were no longer used as a result of a change in social habits.

In relation to all but the first justification, the Court of Justice remarked that:

---

[162] Art.8 Bathing Water Directive.

[163] Case C-56/90 *Commission v United Kingdom* [1993] ECR I-4109, see 4.15.2 above.

[164] Case C-92/96 *Commission v Spain* [1998] ECR I-505, para.28; Case C-198/97 *Commission v Germany* [1999] ECR I-3257 para.35

[165] Case C-92/96 *Commission v Spain* [1998] ECR I-505.

[166] See 5.5.2D below.

[167] See now the Water Framework Directive at 5.7 below.

neither the fact that the amendment of existing legislation is envisaged, nor the fact that the Member States are allowed a longer period in which to comply with certain provisions of [the Urban Waste Water Treatment Directive], with which, it is argued, [the Bathing Water Directive] is closely connected, nor the change in social habits said to have resulted in bathers abandoning a large number of bathing areas, forms part of the derogations provided for in the directive, with the result that those considerations cannot usefully be relied upon to justify a failure to fulfil the obligation imposed by the directive on the Member States regarding the quality of bathing water.[168]

The Court did, however, recognise that drought could amount to 'abnormal weather conditions', but dismissed this contention for lack of any specific evidence having been provided by Spain.

The Court of Justice has also considered the extent to which a Member State may plead that it is physically impossible for it to realise its water quality obligations under the Directive, a possibility left open in the *Blackpool* case.[169] In a defence to Commission proceedings under the Directive, Germany argued that five coastal bathing areas in its old Länder had a catchment area extending beyond German territory (into Switzerland) and that, despite the measures implemented by Germany, the waters did not conform to the limit values. This line of argument was rejected on various grounds, including that there are, in effect, various 'exit' mechanisms in the Directive to deal with such circumstances.[170] The assertion that effluent from Switzerland would not have degraded sufficiently by the time it reached German bathing waters needed to be balanced against the fact that Germany had not shown that compliance was physically impossible and that it had failed to engage in collaboration with neighbouring states to address the problem.[171] On this last point, given the lack of shared catchments with other countries[172] (other than in Northern Ireland), and the dispersing effects of tidal currents upon contaminants, trans-boundary contamination is likely to be less of an issue in relation to the UK. Nevertheless, it does serve to indicate that the duty to comply with the limit values in the Directive may require joint action with other countries. Hence, there may be circumstances where, in effect, it is not merely the state of origin of the contamination that may 'pay' for the pollution of bathing waters.

A further point in this context is whether, in the event of breaches of water quality standards, Member States must prohibit bathing in designated bathing waters.[173] In recent infringement proceedings against Belgium,[174]

---

[168] Case C-92/96 *Commission v Spain* [1998] ECR I-505, para. 29.
[169] Case C-56/90 *Commission v United Kingdom* [1993] ECR I-4109, see 4.15.2 above.
[170] For example, bathing could be prohibited at the relevant waters.
[171] Case C-198/97 *Commission v Germany* [1999] ECR I-3257 para.39.
[172] The pollution need not originate from another *Member* State.
[173] This appears to be the practice in Denmark, Luxembourg and Germany, see Legge (2000) p.11.
[174] Case C-307/98 *Commission v Belgium*, [2000] ECR I-3933.

one issue was whether the absence, in legislation, of a prohibition on bathing in bathing waters breaching the mandatory standards was a breach of the Directive. The particular assertion in this case was that the Belgian legislation only required the public health administration of central government to notify the municipal authorities of breaches, leaving it to their discretion what action to take, and that in practice there was little evidence of bathing being prohibited. While acknowledging that the Directive does not expressly require prohibitions upon bathing where water quality is unsatisfactory, the Commission argued that, taken as a whole, bathing had to be prohibited in such areas if the objective not to expose bathers to health risks was to be realised in practice.[175] The Court held that:

> The need to protect public health does not entail any obligation on a Member State to prohibit bathing in a given area unless, because of local conditions, the extent of the deviation from the limit values observed in that area or the nature of the limit values not complied with is such that a danger to public health is involved.[176]

Accordingly, the case against Belgium on this point was rejected. It is worth noting, though, that the Commission did not seek to argue that Belgium had *in fact* not complied with the Directive by not banning bathing in waters exceeding standards. The result, therefore, is that the Member States may be in breach of their obligations by not, in practice, banning bathing where there is a risk to public health; that is, there may be substantive non-compliance without there being formal non-compliance.[177]

Two further points in relation to compliance with the Directive are notable, both of which have been raised recently in the early stages of proceedings involving the UK. First, while the Court of Justice has ruled on non-compliance with the Directive at particular waters (including Blackpool and Southport) the Court has yet to rule on general non-compliance with the Directive. That is, there does not appear to have been a decided case relating to the *average* or 'headline' compliance figures for a Member State, on the basis that these fall short of the mandatory standards in the Directive. From its case law, however, it seems fairly clear that such an action would be well founded,[178] and the Commission is now beginning to bring infringement proceedings against a large number of Member States on this ground. Recently, this has included bringing the UK before the

---

[175] Specifically, the Commission argued for a combined reading of Articles 1(2)(a)and 4(1) of the Directive, interpreted in the light of its public health objective (for which see the first recital in its preamble and the third paragraph of Article 8).

[176] Case C-307/98 *Commission* v *Belgium*, [2000] ECR I-3933, para.62. Reference to 'limit values' here is misleading – as we use the terms, the Directive lays down water quality standards, see 5.3 above.

[177] In the UK, there are no mechanisms formally in place for prohibiting bathing in non-compliant bathing waters.

[178] Mention might also be made here of case C-3/96 *Commission* v *Netherlands* [1999] Env LR 147, where the Commission was successful in bringing proceedings based on an *insufficient* designation of special protection areas under the Wild Birds Directive, as opposed to non-designation of *particular* sites, and see 15.8.1 below on this case.

Court.[179] In 1998 the figure for UK compliance with mandatory standards was 88.7%, although this rose to 91.5% in 1999.[180]

Significantly, the Reasoned Opinion in these proceedings also referred to the fact that there had only been 44.2% compliance with 'guide' standards.[181] What degree of legal obligation a Member State is under to 'endeavour to achieve' these standards as guidelines has never been decided by the Court of Justice. At national level, as the figures for the UK indicate, they appear not to have been treated particularly seriously,[182] but it remains to be seen whether this approach has been contrary to the letter of the law as well as its spirit.

### 5.5.2D  Summary, implementation and revisions

It is important to emphasise the almost complete concentration upon water quality parameters in the Bathing Water Directive. With the minor exception of the duty upon competent authorities to investigate sources of water pollution which impact upon bathing water quality and to undertake additional sampling in such instances,[183] the Directive is not concerned with the origins of substances which cause unsatisfactory water quality. In practice, meeting the requirements of the Directive will involve Member States addressing emission sources to secure improvements where bathing water quality requirements are not met, but this falls outside the scope of the legal requirements imposed by the Directive.

National implementation of the Directive is by the Bathing Waters (Classification) Regulations 1991[184] and the National Rivers Authority (Bathing Waters) Directions 1992. In practice, compliance levels, which as seen above have only recently exceeded 90%,[185] will be achieved by the aggregation of determinations on discharge consents from operations such as sewage treatment works. The apparent failure to implement the mandatory standard on entero-viruses has been judicially noted.[186] Compliance with standards in the Directive will not in itself guarantee the

---

[179] See 'Bathing Water Quality: Commission moves against Spain, the UK and Sweden', RAPID IP/00/871, 27 July 2000.

[180] *www.environment-agency.gov.uk/s-enviro/viewpoints/3compliance/5bathing/3-5.html*

[181] Or, at least, the relevant press release did so, the Reasoned Opinion not being publicly available.

[182] On general difficulties with 'minimisation' obligations and obligations to 'endeavour to achieve' objectives see 4.17 above.

[183] Under Art.6 Bathing Water Directive, see above.

[184] SI 1991 No.1597. On implementation generally see Ward, Buller and Lowe (1995) pp.23-66; Jordan and Greenaway (1998) and Jordan (1999).

[185] There are now 463 designated bathing waters.

[186] *R v National Rivers Authority ex parte Moreton* [1996] Env LR 234. The Government had argued that there was no scientific basis for maintaining the mandatory level, although this was, of course, an irrelevant consideration.

cleanliness of beaches for other purposes, such as statutory nuisance law.[187]

There has been a fair degree of criticism of the Bathing Water Directive, perhaps not surprising given its early adoption and lack of subsequent amendment. The Commission presented a proposal for the revision of the Directive[188] which was intended to simplify, consolidate and modernise the Directive and adapt it to scientific and technical progress. This would have involved simplification of the operation of the Directive by the deletion of redundant parameters whilst maintaining the protection of the environment and public health. In addition, the proposal sought to ensure that Member States take action in cases of deteriorating water quality and to make further provisions for the identification of new bathing waters, whilst allowing time for the waters in question to be brought up to the standards required by the Directive, albeit 'as soon as possible'. This would have marked a significant change from the earlier Directive, in that non-compliance in fact with the quality parameters would no longer be the basis for infringement proceedings by the Commission, as illustrated by the *Blackpool Bathing Water* case.

Specifically, the proposal sought to make technical changes to the parameters which are provided for, to introduce an imperative standard for faecal streptococci; to make the standard for enterovirus more stringent; to test for *E. coli,* rather than faecal coliforms; to withdraw testing for total coliforms and salmonella; and to add a requirement for the absence of sewage solids. To achieve compliance with the Directive, a single criterion for compliance would be imposed for each parameter requiring 95% or more of the samples to meet the imperative standard.

Despite being published, however, these proposals, which have subsequently been revised formally,[189] generated little enthusiasm amongst any of the Member States, and it is clear that fresh proposals, rather than an amendment of the 1994 proposals, will have to be forthcoming. The projected timetable for developments would see a draft directive emerge no sooner than July 2001, following a Communication and conference of stakeholders. Although nothing formal has been published, one possibility is that the Commission may propose a degree of differentiation in standards between different waters in the Community, thus moving away from the uniform quality standards that now apply. Specifically, there may be some differentiation between warmer and colder waters on the basis that faecal coliforms and other parameters are broken down more quickly in the presence of sunlight and thus there may be some scope for the southern Member States to be treated less strictly. Following the judgment

---

[187] See *R v Carrick District Council ex parte Shelley* [1996] Env LR 273, discussed at 8.5.6 below.
[188] *Proposal for a Council Directive concerning the quality of bathing water,* COM(94)36 final, amended by OJ C6/9 (1998). See also House of Lords Select Committee on the European Communities, *Bathing Water* (1994), and *Bathing Water Revisited* (1994).
[189] See COM(97)585.

of the Court of Justice in proceedings against Belgium,[190] it might also be thought desirable for any revised directive to require that bathing be prohibited in non-compliant bathing waters. However, a difficulty here relates to how strict the standards in the revised directive will be. If they are minimum health-related standards then a bathing ban might be justified; if they contain a wide margin of safety, then there is a case for saying that bathing should only be banned where there is actual danger to the public rather than merely a risk to health.[191] Any proposal which emerges will also need to ensure consistency with the Water Framework Directive.[192]

### 5.5.3  Other Environmental Quality Directives

In addition to the Bathing Water Directive, there are other directives which adopt a water quality approach. These are the Directives on Shellfish Waters and on Freshwater Fish Waters, and on Drinking Water Abstraction. These directives, which will be repealed and replaced by the Water Framework Directive, are considered in more detail elsewhere.[193]

### 5.5.4  The Proposed Ecological Quality of Water Directive

Although not a part of the existing body of EC water quality legislation, and now overtaken by the adoption of the Water Framework Directive, the proposed Ecological Quality of Water Directive[194] is usefully discussed alongside other measures concerned with water quality objectives. The reason for this is that it demonstrated a comprehensive concern with water quality issues to the almost complete exclusion of issues relating to emission controls and, therefore, could be seen as a 'high water mark' in the water quality approach.

The proposed Directive required Member States to adopt measures for the control of pollution of surface waters from point sources, sources of diffuse pollution and other anthropogenic factors affecting surface water quality. More specifically, the objectives of the proposed Ecological Quality of Water Directive were to maintain and improve the ecological quality of waters generally, to increase their value as sources of water for drinking, and other purposes, and to increase their amenity value. For these purposes, for each water, or groups of waters, an operational quality target would have been set for 'good ecological quality' such that the water

---

[190] Case C-307/98 *Commission v Belgium*, [2000] ECR I-3933, see above.
[191] An interesting comparison here is with 'alert thresholds' under the Framework Ambient Air Quality Directive (96/62/EC). These stipulate concentrations above which there is a risk to human health from brief exposure, and require the population, and the Commission, to be alerted of such danger. Alert thresholds are therefore an informational and precautionary standard. See also the Revised Drinking Water Quality Directive (98/83/EC) which contains an obligation to notify the population affected if a derogation has been taken out, see 17.7.8 below.
[192] Postscript: see now *Developing a New Bathing Water Directive*, COM(2000)860.
[193] See 15.3.1 and 17.6 below.
[194] COM(93)680 final, OJ 1994, C222/6.

quality was suitable for the needs of the ecosystem, taking into account the need to maintain the capacity of water for self-purification and the satisfaction of specified requirements. However, the specification of 'good ecological quality' was only generally outlined by the proposed Directive and the adoption of specific operational targets by Member States would have had to take account of local conditions. In this sense, the definition of 'good ecological quality' of water would have been left to the Member States, a considerable degree of flexibility by contrast with other water quality directives.

Once these operational quality targets were adopted, the Member States would have been required to establish integrated programmes with the object of meeting those targets, again giving them considerable flexibility in how the quality standards were met. Member States would also have been required to monitor the ecological status of surface waters and, identify sources of pollution and adverse anthropogenic influences. In addition the proposal incorporated requirements for public consultation on the contents of the integrated programmes. The proposal envisaged that a Directive on Ecological Quality of Water would have replaced the Freshwater Fish Waters Directive and the Shellfish Waters Directive.[195]

It is now clear that the Water Framework Directive[196] has superseded the proposals relating to the Ecological Quality of Water and, in essence, all the main elements of the proposal, in essence, appear in the Framework Directive. In addition, the Framework Directive is wider in scope than the Ecological Quality proposal in covering groundwater and dealing with water quantity issues. Nevertheless, the ecological quality approach to water quality formulated in the Ecological Quality proposal remains an important advancement from previous directives in seeking to impose requirements based on the ecological characteristics of water, as opposed to the physical and chemical features which have been provided for in the existing water quality directives.

## 5.6 Directives Regulating Polluting Activities

The more recent EC water directives illustrate a different emphasis from earlier directives, which tended to concentrate upon emission controls and the quality of water for particular uses, and there is a discernible shift towards the regulation of water polluting activities. In part, the background to this new emphasis is to be found in the Community's *Fourth Action Programme on the Environment* which sought a development of policy towards combating fresh water and marine pollution from both specific and diffused sources, and by encouraging the development of improved management practices, specifically, in relation to waste water.[197] Although an early example of the approach of seeking to control polluting activities

---

[195] See 15.3.1 below on the Shellfish Waters Directive and the Freshwater Fish Waters Directive.
[196] See 5.7 below.
[197] See the *Fourth Action Programme* and the continuation of this theme under the *Fifth Action Programme*.

is to be found in the Sewage Sludge Directive,[198] the approach has been developed significantly in two of the more recent water directives to be enacted. These are the Urban Waste Water Treatment Directive[199] and the Nitrates Directive.[200] Although not specifically concerned with water, and so not discussed here, a similar emphasis upon the control of polluting activities is also seen in the Directive on Integrated Pollution Prevention and Control.[201]

In certain respects, these directives do make use of controls upon emissions and the imposition of environmental quality requirements. However, this is done as an adjunct to their main purpose, which is to control installations, processes and activities which carry the greatest potential for water pollution: effluent treatment, agricultural use of nitrates and hazardous industrial installations. This contrast in strategic emphasis distinguishes them from previous directives, where emission controls and environmental quality requirements were imposed without directly targeting problematic activities.

### 5.6.1 The Sewage Sludge Directive

Although the application of sludge may have valuable agronomic benefits if correctly utilised, the primary purposes of the Sewage Sludge Directive[202] is to prevent the heavy metal contamination of land to prevent hazards to human health and the environment, and to protect drinking water and groundwater.[203] Accordingly, the Directive aims to control the use of sewage sludge in agriculture by establishing maximum limit values for concentrations of heavy metals in soil and in sludge which may be applied to land. The heavy metals which must be analysed are cadmium, copper, nickel, lead, zinc, mercury and chromium. Conditions are imposed as to when sludge may be applied to agricultural land, including limit values for specified substances and minimum time limits separating the use of sludge on certain types of agricultural land. It should be noted that the use of sludge in agriculture is not regulated under the Waste Framework Directive.[204]

Specifically, Member States must prohibit the use of sludge where this is necessary to prevent concentrations of heavy metals in the soil being exceeded *either* by limiting the quantities of sludge which may be applied, *or* by limiting the quantities of heavy metals which may be applied to unit

---

[198] Directive 86/278/EEC, see 5.6.1 below.

[199] Directive 91/271/EEC, see 5.6.2 below.

[200] Directive 91/676/EEC, see 5.6.3 and 13.5.4 below.

[201] Directive 96/61/EC, see 12.2.3 below.

[202] Directive 86/278/EEC. There is only one infringement case (against Belgium) relating to the Directive, which sheds no light on its interpretation (see below).

[203] For an example of water pollution incidents following the spreading of sludge see *Southern Water Authority* v *Pegrum and Pegrum* (1989) 153 JP 581 and *R* v *Dovermoss Ltd* [1995] Env LR 258, discussed at 9.6.3 and 9.8 respectively above.

[204] Directive 75/442/EEC as amended, see 12.2.2 below.

areas of land over specified time periods.[205] Sludge must be treated before use,[206] and may not be applied to grassland or forage crops which are to be grazed within a certain period after the application; soil in which fruit and vegetable crops are growing, with the exception of fruit trees; and fruit and vegetable crops which are normally in direct contact with the soil, and normally eaten raw, for a period of ten months before the crops are harvested.[207]

Arguably, the maximum limits presently set by the Directive are not particularly precautionary, although doubtless because of concerns raised by farmers and consumers, many Member States have chosen to set stricter standards, as the Directive expressly allows.[208]

With landfill of sludge likely to be used less in future and eventually to cease,[209] and the ban on the disposal of sludge at sea which came into effect at the end of 1998,[210] the amount of sludge disposed to land in the UK is set almost to double in the ten years to 2005,[211] though a consequence of tightening the controls on the quality of sludge that can be spread on land may be to limit significantly the land area suitable for spreading. This, in turn, may lead to knock-on adverse environmental consequences.[212]

Implementation in the UK is by the Sludge (Use in Agriculture) Regulations 1989,[213] and an accompanying Code of Practice.[214] Certain wastes spread on land used for agriculture are exempt from the Waste Management Licensing Regulations 1994 if the spreading will result in 'benefit to agriculture or ecological improvement'.[215] On precautionary grounds, the Royal Commission on Environmental Pollution has called for an end to the disposal of untreated sewage sludge to agricultural land.[216] The House of Commons Environment, Transport and Regional Affairs Committee has also made a number of recommendations relating to

---

[205] Art.5 Sewage Sludge Directive. For criticism of the UK's choice to regulate the limit values of potentially toxic elements according to their accumulation in the soil see, House of Commons Select Committee on Environment, Transport and Regional Affairs, *Sewage Treatment and Disposal* (1998).

[206] *Ibid* Art.6.

[207] *Ibid* Art.7.

[208] *Ibid* Art.12 ('where conditions so demand'). There is only one instance of enforcement proceedings being brought concerning the Directive generally, see Case C-260/93 *Commission* v *Belgium* [1994] ECR I-1611.

[209] Under the Landfill Directive (1999/31/EC), see 12.2.7 below.

[210] Under Art.14(3) Urban Waste Water Treatment Directive, giving effect to political agreement at the Third North Sea Conference, see 19.19.4B below.

[211] Royal Commission on Environmental Pollution (1996).

[212] Such as greater transportation of sludge, see *ENDS Report* 303 (2000) p.50.

[213] SI 1989 No.1263, as amended by SI 1990 No.880.

[214] Department of the Environment, *Code of Practice for Agricultural Use of Sewage Sludge*, (1989). Both the regulations and the Code of Practice are in the process of revision. However, changes to the Directive are at a less advanced stage, and a proposal is not expected before early 2001. For a general review of developments see 'Sludge – the Final Frontier', *Water Magazine*, 21 June 2000, p.8

[215] Reg.17 and Sch. 3 SI 1994 No.1056, see generally 12.2.6 below.

[216] Royal Commission on Environmental Pollution (1996).

sewage sludge, notably that by 2002, all sewage should be treated to tertiary level at all times and in all places, and all sludge recycled to land should be subjected to stabilisation and pasteurisation, requirements which should be included in the Sludge (Use in Agriculture) Regulations 1989 and not in the accompanying Code of Practice.[217]

### 5.6.2 The Urban Waste Water Treatment Directive

The purpose of the Urban Waste Water Treatment Directive[218] is to prevent the environment from being adversely affected by the disposal of inadequately treated urban waste water.[219] Accordingly, it recognises the need for secondary treatment of such water along with the need for similar treatment for industrial discharges of biodegradable industrial waste water[220] which does not pass through urban waste water treatment plants before being discharged to receiving waters.[221] Hence, the Directive is primarily concerned with the collection, treatment and discharge of urban waste water, and the treatment and discharge of waste water from specified industrial sectors, in order to protect the environment from the adverse effects of these kinds of effluent.[222] Because of its significant cost implications in the UK,[223] (indeed, the Directive may be the most costly environmental directive ever to be implemented) and because of the extent to which consenting procedures for discharge consents and for trade effluent consents must be determined in line with the requirements of the Directive,[224] it is worth discussing its provisions in some depth.

A central duty is that all Member States must ensure that all urban areas, or 'agglomerations',[225] are provided with collecting systems[226] for urban waste water, at the latest by the end of 2000 for those with a 'population

---

[217] *Sewage Treatment and Disposal* (1998).

[218] Directive 91/271/EEC, amended by Commission Directive 98/15/EC.

[219] 'Urban waste water' is defined as domestic waste water or the mixture of domestic waste water with industrial waste water and/or run-off rain water (Art.2(1) Urban Waste Water Treatment Directive).

[220] 'Industrial waste water' means any waste water which is discharged from premises used for carrying on any trade or industry, other than domestic waste water and run-off water (*ibid* Art.2(3)).

[221] *Ibid* Preamble. 'Domestic waste water' means water from residential settlements and services which originates predominantly from the human metabolism and from household activities (*ibid* Art.2(2)).

[222] *Ibid* Art.1.

[223] It is also worth noting that in 1990, just prior to its adoption, the British public was more apprehensive about sewage disposal than any other environmental issue; Norris (1997) p.324, cited in Jordan and Greenaway (1998) p.682.

[224] See, respectively, Chs.10 and 11 below.

[225] 'Agglomeration' means an area where the population and/or economic activities are sufficiently concentrated for urban waste water to be collected and conducted to an urban waste water treatment plant or to a final discharge point (Art.2(4) Urban Waste Water Treatment Directive).

[226] 'Collecting system' means a system of conduits which collects and conducts urban waste water (*ibid* Art.2(5)). Further details concerning the requirements for collecting systems are provided in Annex I to the Directive.

equivalent'[227] of more than 15,000 and the end of 2005 for those with a population equivalent between 2,000 and 15,000. The obligation to provide a waste water collection system arises unless the establishment of a general collecting system is not justified, either because it would produce no environmental benefit or because it would involve excessive cost. In these cases individual, or other appropriate, systems of collection which achieve the same level of collection must be used.[228]

In addition to the obligation to provide urban waste collecting systems, Member States must ensure that water entering these systems is subject to secondary or equivalent treatment by the year 2000 for discharges from areas of a population equivalent of more that 15,000; by 2005 for areas of population equivalents between 10,000 and 15,000; and by 2005 for discharges to freshwater and estuaries for areas of population equivalents between 2,000 and 10,000.[229] 'Secondary treatment' means treatment of urban waste water by a process generally involving biological treatment with a secondary settlement or other process in which the requirements established in Table 1 of Annex I to the Directive, concerning biochemical oxygen demand, chemical oxygen demand and total suspended solids, are respected.[230] Further details about the requirements for discharges for waste water treatment plants are set out in the Annex.

While the requirements for waste water collection systems and treatment works that have been described are of general application, departures from this regime are provided for in areas that are identified as being 'sensitive areas' or 'less sensitive areas'. Member States must identify sensitive areas and ensure that urban waste water discharging into these areas is subject to more stringent treatment;[231] that was to be achieved by the end of 1998 for all discharges from areas of population equivalent greater than 10,000 persons.[232] The criteria for identification of sensitive areas require natural freshwater lakes, other freshwater bodies, and estuaries coastal waters to be identified as such where these are found to be eutrophic or which may become eutrophic[233] if protective action is not taken; where surface waters intended for the abstraction of drinking water could contain more than the concentration of nitrate laid down under the Drinking Water Abstraction

---

[227] 'One population equivalent' means the organic biodegradable load having a five-day biochemical oxygen demand (BOD5) of 60g of oxygen per day (*ibid* Art.2(6)).

[228] *Ibid* Art.3.

[229] *Ibid* Art.4.

[230] *Ibid* Art.2. This contrasts with 'primary treatment' which means treatment of urban waste water by a physical and/or chemical process involving settlement of suspended solids, or other processes in which the BOD5 (five-day biochemical oxygen demand) of the incoming waste water is reduced by at least 20% before discharge and the total suspended solids in the incoming waste water are reduced by at least 50% (*ibid* Art.2(7)).

[231] In accordance with requirements set out in Annex I(B) to the Directive.

[232] *Ibid* Art.5(1) and (2).

[233] 'Eutrophication' means the enrichment of water by nutrients, especially compounds of nitrogen and/or phosphorus, causing an accelerated growth of algae and higher forms of plant life to produce an undesirable disturbance to the balance of organisms present in the water and to the quality of the water concerned (*ibid* Art.2(11), and see 1.3.1–2 above on eutrophication.

Directive[234] if action is not taken; and areas where further treatment is necessary to meet other directives.[235] As an alternative to the requirement for more stringent treatment of waste water being discharged into sensitive areas, requirements for individual wastewater treatment plants may be applied so that the reduction of overall load entering such plants is at least 75% for phosphorus and at least 75% for nitrogen.[236] Some Member States have designated their whole territory as a sensitive area for these purposes.[237]

The counterpart of the provision for sensitive areas is that Member States may identify 'less sensitive areas',[238] where the environment of marine waters (including open bays and estuaries) is not adversely affected as a result of morphology, hydrology or specific hydraulic conditions in the area, for example, because of good water exchange and waters not being subject to eutrophication or oxygen depletion.[239] Hence, urban waste water discharges from agglomerations between 10,000 and 150,000 population equivalents to estuaries situated in less sensitive areas may be subject to less stringent treatment providing that such discharges receive at least primary treatment and comprehensive studies indicate that such discharges will not adversely affect the environment.[240] In relation to smaller agglomerations, for discharges to freshwater and estuaries for less than 2,000 population equivalents and 10,000 population equivalents for discharges into coastal waters, the requirement is that by 31 December 2005 these discharges are to be subject to appropriate treatment.[241] 'Appropriate treatment' for these purposes means treatment of urban waste water by a process generally involving biological treatment with a secondary settlement or other process which meets specified requirements.[242]

Given the extent to which the UK in particular relied upon the designation of less sensitive areas or 'high natural dispersion areas' (HNDAs),[243] a central question is how the boundaries of these areas are to be defined. This issue arose at national level in joined cases which challenged the classification of a number of estuarial waters as coastal for the purposes of the implementing Regulations,[244] thus allowing lower levels of treatment to be applied. In *R v Secretary of State for the Environment, ex parte*

[234] Directive 75/440/EEC, see 17.6 below.

[235] Annex II(A) Urban Waste Water Treatment Directive.

[236] *Ibid* Art.5(4).

[237] Denmark, Luxembourg, the Netherlands, Finland and Sweden. See COM(98)775, *Implementation of Directive 91/271*, p.8.

[238] In the UK implementing Regulations, these are referred to as 'high natural dispersion areas' (HNDAs).

[239] Annex II(B) Urban Waste Water Treatment Directive.

[240] *Ibid* Art.6.

[241] *Ibid* Art.7.

[242] *Ibid* Art.2(9), the specified requirements are set out in Table I of Annex I to the Directive.

[243] Thus preserving some remnants of the 'marine treatment' policy approach; see generally Jordan and Greenaway (1998), p.680. The initial use of HNDAs was perhaps not surprising since they were included in the Directive at the UK's urging.

[244] The Urban Waste Water Treatment (England and Wales) Regulations 1994 (SI 1994 No.2841).

*Kingston upon Hull City Council*[245] the Secretary of State drew the boundaries of the estuary for the Humber and Severn rivers at the Humber and Severn road bridges respectively, thus ensuring less costly levels of treatment for treatment works alongside the rivers. His decision was successfully challenged on the grounds that costs should not have been taken into account, and that the correct way of drawing the boundaries was to carry out a 'genuine and rational assessment' of what actually constituted the estuary.[246]

Exceptions to the obligations imposed by the Directive are provided for in exceptional cases, but only in relation to technical problems for geographically defined population groups. In such cases Member States may request from the Commission a longer period for compliance with the requirement of ensuring that urban waste water entering collection systems is subjected to secondary treatment. Where this is done, however, the request must set out the technical difficulties experienced and propose an action programme with an appropriate timetable for its implementation. In exceptional circumstances, where it can be demonstrated that more advanced treatment will not produce any environmental benefits, discharges into less sensitive areas of waste waters from agglomerations of more than 150,000 population equivalents may be subject to the level of treatment required of discharges to less sensitive areas for smaller agglomerations. However, such exceptions will be subject to the scrutiny of the Commission according to a specified procedure.[247]

Significant emphasis is also placed on the operational aspects of urban waste water treatment through an obligation that treatment plants are to be built to comply with obligations under the Directive. Specifically, plants are to be designed, constructed, operated and maintained to ensure sufficient performance under all normal local climatic conditions, taking into account seasonal variations in the effluent load.[248]

Before the end of 1993 the discharge of industrial waste water into collecting systems had to be made subject to prior regulations and/or specific authorisations by the competent authority.[249] Such regulations had to satisfy stated requirements for pre-treatment of waste water, for example, to protect the health of staff working in treatment plants, to prevent damage to equipment at treatment plants and to ensure that discharges from treatment plants do not adversely effect the environment.[250]

'Competent authorities or appropriate bodies' must ensure that the disposal of waste water from urban waste water treatment plant is subject to prior

---

[245] [1996] Env LR 248. For comment see Blatch (1996) and Sands and Blatch (1998).
[246] Subsequently, the estuaries were redefined as a line between the two furthest points of land on each side of the river. Also on this case see 4.16.3 above.
[247] Art.8 Urban Waste Water Treatment Directive.
[248] *Ibid* Art.10.
[249] *Ibid* Art.11.
[250] *Ibid* Annex I(C).

regulations and/or specific authorisation.[251] For this purpose, regulations or authorisations for discharges from treatment plants must satisfy specified requirements.[252]

By the end of 2000, biodegradable industrial waste water from certain industrial sectors, which does not enter urban waste water plants before discharge to receiving water, must be subject to conditions in regulations or prior authorisation by the competent authority in relation to discharges from plants representing a population equivalent of 4,000 or more.[253] For this purpose some eleven industrial sectors are identified primarily concerned with food and drink manufacture and processing.[254]

Sludge arising from waste water treatment must be reused wherever appropriate. Disposal routes for treated waste water must, as far as possible, minimise the adverse effects on receiving waters,[255] an obligation which is specifically stated to apply to sludge arising from waste treatment. The disposal of sludge is to be subject to regulations or authorisation. However, the scope for Member States to choose the least damaging disposal route is limited by the political agreement reached at the Third International North Sea Conference. This was that, by the end of 1998, the disposal of sludge to surface waters by dumping from ships, or discharge from pipelines, must be phased out, an obligation reaffirmed in the Directive.[256]

Monitoring duties are imposed upon competent authorities, or appropriate bodies, to monitor discharges from urban waste water treatment plants to verify compliance with requirements and procedures under the Directive, and to monitor the amounts and composition of sludges disposed of to surface waters. Also, monitoring is required of waters subject to discharges from treatment plans and direct discharges where it may be anticipated that the receiving environment will be significantly affected. Where sludge is disposed of to surface waters, Member States must monitor this and carry out studies to verify that the discharge or disposal does not adversely affect the environment.[257] Member States must also ensure that every two years the relevant authorities or bodies publish situation reports on the disposal of urban waste water and sludge in their areas.[258] There is a further obligations upon Member States to establish programmes for implementing the Directive.[259]

By way of general commentary on the Urban Waste Water Treatment Directive, the rather eclectic approach that it adopts must be emphasised.

---

[251] *Ibid* Art.12.

[252] Under *ibid* Annex I(B).

[253] *Ibid* Art.13.

[254] *Ibid* Annex III.

[255] For national interpretation of this see *Moase* v *Secretary of State for the Environment, Transport and the Regions* [2001] Env LR 13.

[256] Art.14 Urban Waste Water Treatment Directive, and see 19.19.4(b) below.

[257] *Ibid* Art.15.

[258] *Ibid* Art.16.

[259] *Ibid* Art.17. On this obligation see Case C-236/99 *Commission* v *Belgium*, [2000] ECR I-5657.

The various standards that are provided for in relation to discharges of waste water incorporate a range of emission standards for effluent which falls into the different categories of treatment provided for in the Directive. Also, there are numerous respects in which the Directive is concerned with environmental impacts, in imposing monitoring requirements and duties to take particular actions where environmental quality objectives, particularly in relation to eutrophication, are not met. However, perhaps the most distinctive feature of the Directive, by comparison with previous Community water legislation, is the emphasis placed on operational and infrastructural matters. Hence, the detailed controls which are imposed on operational activities, extending to the design, construction and maintenance of treatment plants, demonstrate an approach which goes beyond emission controls or a requirement to meet environmental quality objectives. Perhaps the greatest innovation provided by the Directive is the direct regulation of the activity of waste water treatment.

National implementation of the Directive is through the Urban Waste Water Treatment (England and Wales) Regulations 1994.[260] In 1994, 33 sensitive areas and 58 high natural dispersion areas were initially identified although, as the Humber and Severn estuary cases discussed above made clear, some of the HNDAs originally designated required their boundaries to be redrawn once taking cost considerations into account was judicially ruled out. Further criticism was directed at the low number of sensitive areas designated,[261] and in 1998 a further 47 sensitive areas were added. More recently, the approach of the UK Government to designating sensitive areas only on grounds of eutrophication has come under criticism from the Commission, and it appears that further designations will be made so that waters meriting special protection under other directives (e.g. the Bathing Water Directive and the Directives on Shellfish Waters and on Freshwater Fish Waters) may also be designated as 'sensitive areas'.[262]

Implementing the Directive has been a major component of the water utility price review settlements in 1994 and in 1999. A result of the latest review is that all discharges to coastal waters will be given at least secondary treatment (i.e. there will be no resort to the use of high natural dispersion areas). Action is also being taken with the aim of improving the performance of 85% of combined sewer overflows, against the Directive's requirement that Member States 'decide on measures to limit pollution from storm water overflows'. Despite these advances there are some concerns that obligations under other directives are being postponed by being categorised as obligations which fall to be given effect to within the longer compliance periods of the Urban Waste Water Treatment Directive.[263]

---

[260] SI 1994 No.2841.

[261] House of Commons Select Committee on Environment, Transport and Regional Affairs, *Sewage Treatment and Disposal* (1998), and *Government Response* (Cm 4023, July 1998).

[262] *ENDS Report* 305 (2000) p.9, and see 15.3.2 below.

[263] E.g. under the Bathing Water Directive, see *ENDS Report 305* (2000) p.9.

### 5.6.3 The Nitrates Directive

Another major illustration of a primarily activity-related approach to water quality protection and improvement is provided by the Nitrates Directive.[264] The Nitrates Directive is founded upon the need to encourage agricultural practices which are environmentally beneficial and, in particular, the reduction at source of fresh water and marine pollution from diffused sources including particular products used in agriculture.[265] Water pollution caused by nitrate, originating from farming practices such as the excessive application of nitrogen fertiliser and the spreading of animal manure, is recognised to be a serious problem in many parts of the Community. Despite a requirement in the Drinking Water Quality Directive[266] that the nitrate content of drinking water should not exceed 50mg/l, this parameter has been exceeded in many parts of the Community, or met otherwise than by reductions in ambient levels of nitrate (e.g. by the blending of supplies or by water treatment). Accordingly, common action at Community level was seen as justified for protecting human health and living resources, including aquatic ecosystems; to safeguard other legitimate uses of water; to prevent further pollution; to require measures to be taken for the storage and application of nitrogen compounds; and concerning certain land management practices.[267]

The essential objectives of the Nitrates Directive are to reduce water pollution caused or induced by nitrate from agricultural sources and to prevent further such pollution.[268] These objectives are tackled by a requirement that waters which are affected, or could be affected, by pollution by nitrogen compounds[269] from agricultural sources must be designated by the Member States. These 'nitrate vulnerable zones' (NVZs) consist of all areas of land which drain into polluted or vulnerable waters and which contribute to, or potentially contribute to any pollution.[270] Specifically, the waters concerned must be identified according to whether they meet one of the following criteria:

(a) whether surface waters contains more that the concentration allowed by the Drinking Water Abstraction Directive;[271]
(b) whether groundwaters contain more than 50mg/l nitrates; or
(c) whether natural freshwater lakes or other bodies, estuaries, coastal waters and marine waters are found to be eutrophic.[272]

---

[264] Directive 91/676/EEC.

[265] See 1.3.1–2 above generally on regulating diffuse contamination.

[266] 80/778/EEC, see 17.7.1 below.

[267] Preamble, Nitrates Directive.

[268] *Ibid* Art.1.

[269] 'Nitrogen compound' means any nitrogen containing substance except for gaseous molecular nitrogen (*ibid* Art.2(c)).

[270] *Ibid* Art.3.

[271] Directive 75/440/EEC, see 17.6 below.

[272] For these purposes, 'eutrophication' means the enrichment of water by nitrogen compounds, causing an accelerated growth of algae and higher forms of plant life to produce an undesirable

In each case waters must also be designated where they *would* fall into any of the above categories if action in accordance with the directive is not taken. In applying these criteria, Member States must also take account of the physical and environmental characteristics of the waters and land, the current understanding of the behaviour of nitrate compounds in the environment, and the current understanding of the impact of actions which must be taken under the Directive.[273] Rather than designate individual NVZs, a Member State may decide to apply the measures in the action programmes, discussed below, across their whole territory, in which case NVZs need not be designated.[274]

Following the designation of nitrate vulnerable zones, Member States must establish action programmes in respect of these zones. These action programmes must take into account available scientific and technical data with reference to nitrogen contributions originating from agricultural and other sources, and environmental conditions in the relevant regions of the Member State concerned. In particular, the measures provided for require rules to be established concerning:

(a) the periods when land application[275] of certain types of fertiliser[276] is to be prohibited;
(b) the capacity of storage vessels for livestock manure,[277] so that it may be contained during the period during which application to land is prohibited (unless it can shown that it will be disposed of in a manner which will not cause harm to the environment); and
(c) for limitations to be imposed upon the land application of fertiliser taking account of the characteristics of the zone concerned, the foreseeable nitrogen requirements of the crops and the alternative nitrogen supply to the crops from other sources.

These measures must ensure that for each farm or livestock unit the amount of livestock, the annual application of manure does not contain an excess of 170kg of nitrogen per hectare, though departures from this limit are allowed for in specified circumstances.[278] Action programmes with

---

[273] *Ibid* Annex I.

disturbance to the balance of organisms present in the water and to the quality of the water concerned (Art.2(1)) and see 1.3.1 above on eutrophication.

[274] This 'whole country' approach has been taken in, e.g., the Netherlands, Denmark, Germany, Austria and Luxembourg, Written Question No. 1566/97 (Maij-Weggen and Sonneveld) OJ 1997, C391/1.

[275] 'Land application' means the addition of materials to land whether by spreading on the surface of the land, injection into the land, placing below the surface of the land or mixing with the surface layers of the land (Art.2(h) Nitrates Directive).

[276] 'Fertiliser' means any substance containing a nitrogen compound or nitrogen compounds utilised on land to enhance growth of vegetation, and may include livestock manure, the residues from fish farms and sewage sludge (*ibid* Art.2(e)).

[277] 'Livestock manure' means waste products excreted by livestock or a mixture of litter and waste products excreted by livestock, even in processed form, and 'livestock' means all animals kept for use or profit (*ibid* Art.2(d) and (g)).

[278] *Ibid* Annex III.

mandatory measures must be implemented in NVZs by the end of 1998, when the codes of good practice under the Directive become mandatory in the NVZs.[279]

In addition to these requirements, Member States must establish a code of good agricultural practice which, although voluntary, must be promoted to farmers through a programme of training and information.[280] Such codes 'should' provide for items such as the periods when land application of fertiliser is inappropriate; the conditions for land application of fertiliser near watercourses; and the capacity of and construction of storage vessels for livestock manures.[281] The wording of the obligation, i.e. the use of 'should' rather than 'shall', suggests that the inclusion of any particular item may not be mandatory. Nevertheless, failure to establish such codes will be a breach of the Directive.[282]

Beyond the specified mandatory measures, and the attachment of a mandatory status to the code of good agricultural practice in nitrate vulnerable zones, Member States must also take such additional measures or reinforcement actions as are considered necessary, in the light of experience, to ensure that the objectives of the Directive are met.[283]

Whilst monitoring programmes are required to assess the effectiveness of action programmes in nitrate vulnerable zones,[284] an initial programme is provided for the purpose of designating and revising the designation of such zones. For that purpose, surface water and groundwater sampling stations must be established for the purpose of monitoring the content of nitrate in waters, and the eutrophic state of other estuarial and coastal water must be periodically reviewed.[285]

Finally, Member States must submit periodic reports to the Commission of specified information relating to the implementation of the Directive, such as the location of waters subject to nitrate pollution and the location of nitrate vulnerable zones, monitoring information, and a summary of action programmes which have been drawn up in response to the requirements of the Directive.[286]

By way of comment, the Directive is notable for the combination of environmental regulatory strategies that it utilises. The Directive may be conceived of as an emission control measure insofar as it limits the application of nitrogen compounds to agricultural land by prescribing an upper limit to the amounts of such applications on a given area. On the other hand, it has the characteristics of an environmental quality measure

---

[279] In support of this interpretation see Case C-274/98 *Commission v Spain*, 13 April 2000, not yet reported. On agricultural codes of practice generally see 13.5.7 below.
[280] Arts 4 and 5(4) Nitrates Directive.
[281] *Ibid* Annex II.
[282] Case C-71/97 *Commission v Spain* [1998] ECR I-5991.
[283] Art.5(5) Nitrates Directive.
[284] *Ibid* Art.5(6).
[285] *Ibid* Art.6.
[286] *Ibid* Art.10 and Annex V.

to the extent that most of its requirements are activated by a finding that water quality is exceeding, or is likely to exceed, specified environmental quality parameters in relation to nitrate contamination. Beyond these features, however, it is the impacts that it provides for in relation to agricultural practice that distinguishes it from other emission control or environmental quality directives. The distinctive purpose of the Directive, therefore, is to impose new kinds of control upon those agricultural activities which have been recognised to be harmful to water and the aquatic environment.

Despite the novel objectives of the Directive, implementation across the Community generally has been poor, and widely criticised,[287] although the UK is probably not the worst offender. Although the Government suggested that the process of designating NVZs had been completed, following further infringement proceedings instigated by the Commission it has now been conceded that this is not the case and that the current extent of designation is insufficient.[288] Implementation of the Directive is under the Protection of Water against Agricultural Nitrate Pollution (England and Wales) Regulations 1996[289] and the Action Programmes for Nitrate Vulnerable Zones (England and Wales) Regulations 1998.[290] In particular, mention might be made of litigation concerning the designation of the first tranche of NVZs, which was, for practical purposes, resolved by the judgment of the European Court of Justice on a reference from the High Court.[291]

## 5.7 The Water Framework Directive

For the future, the topography of European Community water legislation will be dramatically changed by the recent adoption of the Water Framework Directive.[292] Alongside the progressive repeal of a substantial number of the existing directives, the new Directive seeks to establish a consolidated approach to water management across the Community and to introduce several new principles to accomplish this. As will be seen, the schedule for implementation of the Directive is a long-term one. Nonetheless, the impacts of the Directive are sure to become central concerns in water quality protection over the next two decades and beyond. Hence, the following discussion examines, in some detail, the

---

[287] See generally COM(97)473, *The Implementation of Council Directive 91/676/EEC concerning the Protection of Waters against Pollution caused by Nitrates from Agricultural Sources.*

[288] See Case C-69/99 *Commission v UK*, 7 December 2000, not yet reported, where the UK approach to designating only waters intended for human consumption was held to be unlawful.

[289] SI 1996 No.888.

[290] SI 1998 No.1202. See also the Farm Waste Grant (Nitrate Vulnerable Zones) (England and Wales) Scheme 1996 (SI 1996 No.908) which provides grants to assist with compliance.

[291] Case C-293/97 *R v Secretary of State for the Environment and Minister of Agriculture, Fisheries and Food, ex parte Standley* [1999] ECR I-2603, and on implementation of the Directive generally and this case see 13.5.4–6 below.

[292] Directive of the European Parliament and of the Council establishing a framework for Community action in the field of water policy (2000/60/EC).

background to the Directive, its general themes, substantive content and implications for national practice.

### 5.7.1 The Background to the Water Framework Directive

In June 1995 the European Council and the Environment Committee of the European Parliament called for a review of Community water policy and, in response to this, the Commission published a Communication on Water Policy.[293] The Commission Communication noted the need to develop water policy towards greater sustainability, in accordance with the Fifth Environment Action Programme,[294] and that a sustainable water policy should achieve a cost-efficient and effective balance between number of objectives. The main objectives were identified as the following:

(a) the provision of a secure supply of drinking water in sufficient quantity and with sufficient reliability;

(b) the provision of water resources of sufficient quality and quantity to meet economic requirements, such as those of industry and agriculture, to sustain fisheries, transport and power generation activities, and to meet recreational needs;

(c) the quality and quantity of water resources and the physical structure of the aquatic environment should, in all but exceptional cases, be sufficient to protect and sustain the good ecological state and functioning of the aquatic environment, as well as meeting the water needs of wetland and terrestrial ecosystems and habitats; and

(d) water should be managed to prevent or reduce the adverse impact of floods and minimise the impact of droughts.

It was recognised that these objectives are not always mutually compatible and their realisation involved meeting a number of challenges. Pollution, both from point and diffuse sources, along with problems of accidental pollution, acidification and eutrophication, were seen as particular difficulties needing to be addressed more effectively. Water shortages were recognised as a significant problem in parts of the Community where high levels of abstraction for water supply purposes had produced significant impacts upon water flows and groundwater levels and resulted in damage to the aquatic environment. In physical terms, damage to the aquatic environment had also resulted from changes to watercourses and coastal waters and further anthropogenic influences, through economic activities such as fishing, shipping and offshore activities, were also recognised to have adverse impacts upon the habitat potential of the waters concerned.[295]

---

[293] Communication from the Commission to the Council and the European Parliament, *European Community Water Policy*, COM(96)59 final.

[294] *Towards Sustainability*, see 5.2 above.

[295] COM(96)59 final, section 4.

Clearly, realisation of fundamental policy principles, both environmental and political,[296] in the water sector, and particularly the achievement of sustainability, needed some rather fundamental, particularly in view of the age of much of the existing water legislation.[297] At the same time, however, there was considerable political pressure to simplify Community water legislation and to subject it to greater degree of subsidiarity.[298]

Nevertheless, application of new policy objectives to the water sector involved consideration of a number of specific issues in water management, which required the following matters to be addressed.

(a) Previous Community water legislation had been characterised by two extremes of approach: the emission limit value approach and the environmental quality objective approach.[299] The limitations of each approach needed to be recognised and their complementary characteristics incorporated into future legislation.

(b) Whilst a uniformity of approach often characterised previous legislation, increasingly it was recognised that water resource management requires designation of water resources which are worthy of particular protection in terms of their quality or quantity. For example, special protection may be needed for water supply purposes, because of special sensitivity of water resources or because areas of water support rare habitats. Accordingly, the designation of distinct zones for water management is important in order to provide for special protection measures. The counterpart of this targeting approach is that areas which are less sensitive should also be zoned to recognise their distinctive character, providing always that this does not allow abuses of such waters.

(c) Whilst previous Community water legislation has been concerned exclusively with issues of water quality, integrated management of water resources cannot be accomplished without attention to water quantity issues. Excessive abstraction has an impact upon water quality and significant adverse environmental consequences and must be addressed in ensuring sustainable water use.

(d) Water management is not possible without reliable data upon which to base policy decisions, and existing monitoring obligations, under a range of directives, may be in need of rationalisation to draw together the different monitoring requirements and to ensure comparability and comprehensiveness of data across the Community. Linked to this, however, the

---

[296] See generally 5.2–5.6 above.

[297] Most of the existing water directives predate the 1986 Single European Act which formally established Community environmental policy. See also 4.3 above on the contrast between trade-related and environmental directives.

[298] Following the national response to Case C-337/89 *Commission v United Kingdom* [1992] ECR I-6103, see 4.4.2 above on subsidiarity generally.

[299] See 5.4.1 above on the Dangerous Substances Directive (76/464/EEC).

harmonisation of reporting under the Reporting Directive[300] already applies to most Community water legislation.

(e) In relation to transparency, public participation and accountability, the general public should have the right to know the results of environmental monitoring, and should be informed about the policies adopted to protect the environment. Beyond this, the public should have the right to contribute to the environmental decision-making processes.

(f) Greater integration is needed to realise the policy objectives for water and this should be achieved by rationalisation and co-ordination of the different measures sometimes being taken by different authorities to improve a particular water. An integrated approach would allow a greater degree of coherence in the setting and achievement of objectives for water policy.

(g) The only logical unit for the administration or co-ordination of river management is the river basin or catchment area. The establishment of administrative bodies to oversee activities with each river basin will, therefore, be the most effective mechanism for planning water resource measures.[301]

The conclusions which the Commission Communication drew from these observations were that, whilst existing legislation continues to have a positive effect in protecting the environment, much still remains to be done. Specifically, while recognising the limitations of Community competence in relation to water measures, and that some of the existing enactments may be left as free-standing measures, much of the quality objective-related legislation could be drawn together into a framework directive on water resources which would help give greater legislative coherence.

Alongside the need for consolidation as an aid to coherence, the Commission took the view that more effective EC controls are needed in some areas. In particular, the protection of the natural ecological state and function of the aquatic environment, which had been the subject of a proposal for a Directive on the Ecological Quality of Water,[302] should be incorporated into the Framework Directive. In addition, the objectives of some of the existing water legislation might be better realised under the Framework Directive, providing that in repealing certain existing directives the level of environmental protection was not diminished.

Perhaps most compellingly, the Commission proposed that greater integration was required in the practical implementation of EC water legislation. Integration was required between:

---

[300] Directive 91/692/EEC, and see 16.2.5 below on this.
[301] COM(96)59 final, section 7.
[302] See 5.5.4 above.

(a) water quantity and water quality issues;
(b) surface water management and groundwater management;
(c) water use and environmental protection;
(d) control of pollution thorough emission controls and through quality objectives; and
(e) water policy and other policies.[303]

The Commission Communication was considered by the Council, the Parliament, the Economic and Social Committee, the Committee of the Regions and a number of other interested organisations and individuals.[304] Taking account of representations, the Commission prepared a legislative proposal[305] affirming the four main objectives of a sustainable water policy:

(a) the provision of drinking water;
(b) the provision of water for other economic requirements;
(c) the protection of the environment; and
(d) the alleviation of the impact of floods and droughts.

Amongst these objectives, priority was to be given to the protection of the environment, whilst noting that this made a contribution to other objectives. As a framework directive, the object should be to establish a structure within which the four objectives may be better integrated at the national or regional level.

The Commission proposed that the Framework Directive would achieve its objectives in four main ways:

(a) by providing an overall framework within which Community, national and regional authorities may develop integrated and coherent water policies;
(b) by providing a 'safety net' to identify water issues which are not adequate addressed at present and will require action to be taken at the appropriate scale to remedy the situation;
(c) by establishing a sound basis for the collection and analysis of a large amount of information on the state of the aquatic environment and the pressures being placed upon it, thereby providing the essential information base upon which the competent authorities may develop sensible and sustainable policies; and
(d) by requiring transparency based on the publication and dissemination of information and public consultation, and also by the establishment of a network for the exchange of information

---

[303] COM(96)59 final, section 8.
[304] The process included a conference with stakeholders on 28-29 May 1996.
[305] European Commission, *Proposal for a Council Directive establishing a framework for Community action in the field of water policy*, COM(97)49 final, and see House of Lords, Select Committee on the European Communities *Community Water Policy* (1997) for a discussion of the Commission Proposal.

and experience between water professionals throughout the Community.[306]

In particular, the original proposal sought to establish the overall objective of achieving good water status by the following requirements:

(a) river basin management;
(b) an assessment of the characteristics of river basins;
(c) monitoring of the status of the surface water and groundwater of the river basin;
(d) establishing programmes of measures to achieve the objective of good water status;
(e) the summarising of all these matters in a River Basin Management Plan; and
(f) public consultation on that Plan.

Additional requirements were proposed for;

(a) a mechanism to ensure that water use is paid for at full cost recovery prices;
(b) a feedback mechanism to inform national authorities and the Commission of particular problems;
(c) action to combat accidental pollution;
(d) simplified reporting procedures; and
(e) a procedure for the development of co-ordinate strategies for dealing with pollution by individual pollutants or groups of pollutants.[307]

The detailed mechanisms provided for in relation to these matters are considered below.

### 5.7.2 *Modifications of the Proposal*

The original Commission proposal for a Water Framework Directive was modified twice by the Commission prior to deliberations in Council and Parliament. The first modification was to integrate a revision of the Dangerous Substances Directive into the proposed Framework Directive,[308] and a consolidated text was produced to interpolate the amendments consequent upon this.[309] The second amendment was to elaborate technical specifications for the 'good status' requirement for water in Annex V of the proposed Directive.[310] Broadly, however, the objectives and mechanisms envisaged by the proposal were not significantly altered by these changes. Its scope was extended by the first amendment in relation to territorial and other marine waters and in relation to emission controls and environmental quality objectives provided for

---

[306] COM(97)49 final, *Explanatory Memorandum* section 2.3.
[307] *Ibid* section 2.4.
[308] On the Dangerous Substances Directive (76/464/EEC) see 5.4.1 above.
[309] COM(97)49 final, and COM(97)614 final.
[310] COM(98)76 final.

under the Dangerous Substances Directive and its daughter directives.[311] The second amendment provided significantly more detail on the monitoring of surface water and groundwater status than had previously been given.

At the Environment Council meeting in June 1998, the amended proposal for a Water Framework Directive was considered and a considerable degree of consensus reached which, it was thought, would enable the Council to finalise a common understanding once the opinion of the European Parliament was given.[312] However, it appeared that the effective realisation of a political agreement in the Council, without waiting to receive the opinion of Parliament, was not well received by Parliament, which subsequently proposed to introduce a large number of amendments which would have the effect of delaying the progress of the proposal.[313]

At its plenary session in February 1999 the European Parliament approved the proposal for a Water Framework Directive subject to a total of 133 amendments. It was open to the Commission to accept such amendments where they improved the text by removing ambiguity or increasing transparency, but not where, in the opinion of the Commission, they were unworkable or unduly onerous. Accordingly, the Commission initially accepted 88 of the amendments proposed by the Parliament but declined to accept a further 47 proposed amendments mostly directed towards increasing the stringency of the Directive.[314]

Broadly, the key differences between the Council and Parliament lay, first, in the enforceability of the environmental objectives for surface waters and groundwaters, with the Parliament preferring an unqualified general duty to protect such waters and the Council preferring this duty to apply only 'where practicable'. In addition, there were differences in the preferred wording of the obligation to achieve good status for waters, with the Council advocating that actions should be required 'with the aim of achieving' good status whereas the Parliament preferred that actions should be required 'in order to achieve' good status. Underlying these apparently semantic disputes, there were more practical concerns as to the practical impact of the Directive and the stringency and precision of the central obligations to be imposed upon the Member States.

Second, there were differences as to the measures that should be required for the protection of groundwater, with the Parliament arguing that the lack of provision to prevent the input of pollutants into groundwater amounted to a relaxation of existing requirements, under the Groundwater

---

[311] On the Dangerous Substances Directive and its daughter directives see 5.4.1 above.

[312] Council – Environment Press Release, 16 June 1998, *Community Action in the field of Water Policy*.

[313] See 'MEPs Stall Water Directive to get Greater Say' *ENDs Environment Daily* 16 October 1998 and 'EU Water Framework Talks End with No Deal' *ENDs Environment Daily* 3 February 1999. Generally see Tydeman (2000).

[314] COM(1999)271 final, *Amended proposal for a European Parliament and Council Directive establishing a framework for Community action in the field of water policy (COM(97) 49 final)*.

Directive,[315] and proposing that this should be addressed by the incorporation of explicit requirements concerning discharges to groundwater.

Third, there were disputes as to the mechanisms for controlling hazardous substances under the Directive. The Council proposed to prevent discharges of 'significant risk' substances presenting an 'unacceptable risk' to waters but this was thought by the Parliament to be insufficiently precise. The Parliament proposed that the aim should be to prevent all discharges of 'hazardous substances' with these being defined on the basis of 'intrinsic hazard'. Action would be required once a substance was placed on a priority list established at Community level and a target date should be specified for cessation of such discharges. Notably, the Parliament's position was strongly influenced by the water quality strategy established under the OSPAR Convention. This requires the cessation of discharges, emissions and losses of hazardous substances by 2020 and continuous reductions in releases of such substances with the ultimate objective of achieving concentrations in the environment near background levels for naturally occurring substances and close to zero for synthetic substances.[316] The objective of the Parliament was directly to incorporate requirements from the OSPAR Convention into the Directive, where relevant, by following the literal wording of the Convention.

Finally, the Parliament was generally pressing for a reduction in the timetable for implementation of various requirements under the Directive to require these to be met more speedily than proposed by the Council.[317]

The reconciliation of these, and other, differences was the subject of a referral to a Conciliation Committee consisting of equal numbers of members from the Council and Parliament and charged with the task of reaching agreement on a joint text by a qualified majority of the Council representatives and a majority of the Parliament representatives.[318] On 29 June 2000, in the closing hours of the Portugese Presidency, the second round of conciliation negotiations were completed by the agreement of a text of a Parliament and Council Directive establishing a framework for Community action in the field of water policy.[319] Following this, the text was agreed by the Parliament and Council and entered into force on 22 December 2000, the day of publication in the *Official Journal*.[320]

---

[315] On the Groundwater Directive see 5.4.2 above.

[316] On the OSPAR Convention see 18.8 below.

[317] Generally see European Environmental Bureau, Press Release, 27 June 2000, *Water Framework Directive: Council wants to undermine existing law* and *ENDS Report* 305 (2000) p.50.

[318] Under Art.251(4) EC (ex Art.189b(1)).

[319] Under Art.175(1) EC (ex Art.130s(1)).

[320] OJ 2000, L327/1.

## 5.8 General Themes in the Water Framework Directive

The detail of the Water Framework Directive is considered later in this chapter but it is useful here to draw out some general themes concerning pollution; good status; river basin management; emission controls and environmental quality objectives; hazardous substances; and cost recovery pricing for water services.

### 5.8.1 Pollution

The ultimate environmental quality objectives of the Water Framework Directive are the elimination of 'pollution' and the achievement of 'good status' for all waters within its scope. 'Pollution' is defined as the direct or indirect introduction, as a result of human activity, of substances or heat into the air, water or land which may be harmful to human health or the quality of aquatic ecosystems or terrestrial ecosystems directly depending on aquatic ecosystems, which result in damage to material property, or which impair or interfere with amenities and other legitimate uses of the environment.[321]

The implications of this kind of approach to defining 'pollution' have been previously considered[322] and it is necessary only to note here that the consciously anthropocentric formulation that has been chosen has a range of potentially important implications. First, it serves to exclude any amount of water quality variation arising for natural reasons, second, it raises significant issues as to where an 'introduction' actually results from human activity, third, it limits 'pollution' to situations where specified consequences ensue and, finally, that the human-utility rationale may give insufficient weight to ecological damage.

Remarkably, the definition of 'pollution' is not critically important to the achievement of most of the objectives of the Directive. This is because the obligations to which it gives rise are primarily concerned to prevent or restrict specified kinds of discharges or emissions or to achieve defined environmental quality objectives and standards. To a great extent, these obligations are formulated independently of the definition of 'pollution' or make reference to 'pollutants' which are indicatively listed in Annex VIII, though it is recognised that 'pollutant' may encompass other substances liable to cause pollution.[323]

### 5.8.2 Good Status

The other overriding environmental quality objective in the Directive is the achievement of 'good status' for all waters. Hence for surface waters and groundwater it will generally be necessary for Member States to

---

[321] Art.2(33) Water Framework Directive.
[322] See 1.3.3 above on definitions of 'pollution'.
[323] See Art.2(31) Water Framework Directive on the definition of 'pollutant'.

implement measures necessary to achieve good surface water[324] status and good groundwater[325] status by a specified date. In relation to surface water, this means meeting general requirements of 'good ecological status'[326] and 'good chemical status',[327] and in relation to groundwater, status is determined by the poorer of its quantitative status[328] and its chemical status.[329]

Clearly the 'common level of ambition'[330] which 'good status' provides is a central feature of the Directive, but equally clearly it needs to be interpreted in the light of extensive technical guidance. This is provided for under Annex V to the Directive which provides a general outline for technical specification, classification and monitoring of the ecological and chemical status of surface waters, and quantitative and chemical status of groundwaters. A telling observation in the original Commission Proposal was that 'the natural conditions of surface waters and groundwaters vary enormously throughout the Community and, therefore, it is not always possible or desirable to establish identical methods or, for example, parameters of parametric values for use in all circumstances'.[331] Nevertheless, the Commission believed that basic criteria for technical annexes existed which would allow environmental objects to be 'common' to all Member States.[332]

However, the complexity of applying a detailed categorisation system to particular waters is clearly evident given the number of subcategories of waters involved, their ecological variability and the diverse range of parameters which are needed to take account of this. The complexity of the

---

[324] 'Surface water' means inland waters, except groundwater; transitional waters and coastal waters, except in respect of chemical status for which it also includes territorial waters (*ibid* Art.2(1)). 'Transitional waters' are bodies of surface water in the vicinity of river mouths which are partly saline in character as a result of their proximity to coastal waters but which are substantially influenced by freshwater flows (Art.2(6)).

[325] 'Groundwater' means all water which is below the surface of the ground in the saturation zone and in direct contact with the ground or subsoil (*ibid* Art.2(2)).

[326] 'Ecological status' is stated to be an expression of the quality of the structure and functioning of aquatic ecosystems associated with surface waters, classified in accordance with Annex V to the Directive (*ibid* Art.2(21)). 'Good ecological status' is the status of a body of surface water, so classified in accordance with Annex V (Art.2(22)).

[327] 'Good chemical status' for surface waters means the chemical status required to meet the environmental objectives (under *ibid* Art.4(1)(a)), that is, the chemical status achieved by a body of surface water in which concentrations of pollutants do not exceed the environmental quality standards (established in Annex IX under Art.16(7)) and under other relevant Community legislation setting environmental quality standards at Community level (Art.2(24)).

[328] 'Quantitative status' is an expression of the degree to which a body of groundwater is affected by direct of indirect abstractions. 'Good quantitative status' for groundwater is defined by table 2.1.2 of Annex V to the Directive (*ibid* Art.2(28)).

[329] 'Good groundwater chemical status' is defined as the chemical status of a body of groundwater which meets all the conditions set out in table 2.3.2 of Annex V to the Directive (Art.2(25) *ibid*). By contrast, the lack of a quantitative component in the requirements for good status of surface waters has been the subject of criticism (see House of Lords, Select Committee on the European Communities, Eighth Report (1997) *Community Water Policy*, para.51(iii)).

[330] COM(97)49 final, *Explanatory Memorandum* section 3.3.3.

[331] *Ibid.* There were similar difficulties in determining 'good ecological status' in the proposed Ecological Water Quality Directive, discussed at 5.5.4 above.

[332] COM(97)49 final, *Explanatory Memorandum* section 3.3.3.

exercise, however, should not detract from the broader issue of whether the classification system will function adequately in practice and allow consistent and accurate comparisons to be made between the status of different kinds of waters in different parts of the Community. The basic point remains that the ultimate determination of 'good status' will be for the Member States to decide, taking local environmental conditions into account, which raises significant issues in relation to discretion and enforcement.[333]

Difficulties underlying the enforceability of the good status obligation are further compounded by the ambivalent wording of the Directive. Specifically, the Directive requires Member States to protect, enhance and restore all bodies of water 'with the aim'[334] of achieving good status within a stated time period. If good status is an *'aim'* rather than a *requirement* of the Directive then it is arguable that a Member State would not be in breach of the Directive if it actually failed to realise good status in the time allowed. This contrasts with previous directives, where environmentally quality standards actually needed to be met, rather than Member States using their best efforts to meet them, as the United Kingdom has found out to its cost in relation to directives concerned with drinking water and bathing water quality.[335]

Another respect in which achieving good status seems to serve as an aspiration rather than an obligation is because of the range of exceptions which are allowed in relation to the realisation of the good status requirement. As will be seen, these relate to artificial and heavily modified surface waters, phased achievement of objectives, less stringent environmental objectives, temporary deterioration of water status, and new modifications of physical characteristics and sustainable development activities.[336] The cumulative effect of these exceptions may be that there are actually quite extensive bodies of waters to which the good status requirements is not fully applicable.

The upshot of all this is that 'good status' is a far less certain requirement than might be hoped for. Some reassurance is provided by provisions of the Directive stating that it will achieve a level of protection at least equivalent to the various directives that are to be repealed once the relevant provisions of the Water Framework Directive have been implemented.[337] Until their repeal, the retention of the existing directives in the background should provide some guarantee of this. However, the inevitable concern about the Water Framework Directive relates to its enforceability. The absence of precise standards for particular waters, and the ambivalence concerning what 'good status' requires, and when it is

---

[333] Generally see the discussion of direct effect at 4.16.1–3 above.

[334] Generally see Art.4 Water Framework Directive.

[335] See the discussion at 4.15.1 above (concerning drinking water quality) and at 4.15.2 above (concerning bathing water quality). On the uncertain meaning of the similar expression 'endeavour to achieve' see 5.5.2C above concerning guide values in the Bathing Water Directive.

[336] Generally see Art.4 Water Framework Directive.

[337] *Ibid* para.51 Recitals and see also Art.4 and 22(6).

required, will make it more difficult to say with confidence when a Member State is in breach of the Directive than with many provisions of existing directives.

### 5.8.3 River Basin Management

Perhaps because many Member States already organise their national water management in administrative units corresponding to river catchments, a widely supported feature of the Water Framework Directive is its adoption of river basin management.[338] Because watercourses and stillwaters do not respect political or administrative frontiers the only practicable unit for the administration of river management is the river basin, that is, the area of land from which all surface run-off flows through a sequence of streams, rivers and lakes into the sea at a single river mouth or delta. In continental Europe, this practice is increasingly adopted in relation to larger transfrontier rivers insofar as these are subject to international conventions which allow for co-ordination of water policy between the authorities in the different countries involved.[339] Insofar as England and Wales is concerned, there has been a relatively long-standing practice of determining the boundaries of regulatory authorities with responsibility for the aquatic environment by reference to the watersheds of the main rivers.[340]

The use of natural geographic and hydrological areas for the purposes of water management is provided for under the Water Framework Directive as a duty upon Member States to identify individual river basins and to assign these to River Basin Districts. This is to be done by combining small with larger river basins and allocating groundwaters to the nearest or most appropriate District. Appropriate administrative arrangements are to be established including the identification of the competent authority with responsibility for each River Basin District. However, the possibility is allowed for that the competent authority may act as a coordinating body for other competent authorities, in which case the institutional arrangements established to ensure coordination need to be specified.[341]

River basins are the geographical unit upon which several kinds of analysis, review and register are based and for this purpose River Basin Management Plans must be produced.[342] Hence, for each River Basin District the Directive requires:

(a) an analysis to be undertaken of its characteristics;
(b) a review of the impact of human activity upon surface waters and groundwaters; and

---

[338] House of Lords Select Committee on the European Communities, *Community Water Policy*, (1997) para.44.
[339] See COM(96)59 final, section 7.8.
[340] See 2.14 above on the Water Act 1973 and 6.5 below on the regional administration of the Environment Agency.
[341] Art.3 and Annex I Water Framework Directive.
[342] *Ibid* Art.13.

(c) an economic analysis of water use.[343]

Beyond this, registers are to be compiled, on a River Basin District basis, of areas requiring special protection for water abstraction, nature conservation and other purposes.[344] Within each River Basin District, bodies of water used for abstraction for water supply purposes, or intended to be used for that purpose, are to be identified.[345] Monitoring programmes are also to be established giving a coherent and comprehensive overview of water status within each River Basin District.[346] Perhaps most significantly, programmes of measures, directed towards the achievement of the environmental objectives of the Directive, are to be established at the level of River Basin Districts.[347]

Clearly, great emphasis is placed upon river basins as the appropriate unit for water management and River Basin Management Plans will have considerable significance for the future. Such plans will provide an evaluation of the effect of the existing legislation in the district, the extent of its deficiency in meeting environmental objectives and provide the basis for indicating measures designed to meet this deficiency.

The formulation of River Basin Management Plans, and the elements of which they are comprised, are intended to facilitate an informed evaluation of the cost-effectiveness of various improvement measures. River Basin Management Plans also fulfil the important function of providing information and facilitating public involvement in water management. Accordingly, the provision of public information and consultation is required before river basin management plans are established, involving a publication of these in draft along with background documentation on which decisions are based.[348] Greater transparency in the formulation of water management objectives, the imposition of measures and the reporting of standards is thought to be conducive to more effective implementation and enforcement of the legislation.[349]

### 5.8.4 Emission Controls and Environmental Quality Objectives

As previously noted,[350] there has been a long-standing dichotomy of approach to pollution control in Community policy and legislation between those measures seeking to control emissions and those seeking to realise environmental quality objectives. A major innovation of the Water Framework Directive is the appreciation that both approaches have advantages which must be appropriately utilised to reinforce each other in

---

[343] *Ibid* Art.5.

[344] *Ibid* Art.6 and Annex IV.

[345] *Ibid* Art.7.

[346] *Ibid* Art.8.

[347] *Ibid* Art.11.

[348] Art.14 Water Framework Directive.

[349] COM(96)59 final, section 7.6.

[350] See 1.4.5 above on the contrast between emission controls and environmental quality objectives.

a 'combined approach' which, in any particular situation, requires that the more stringent of the two approaches should be applied.[351] Hence, whilst the Directive requires adherence to emission restrictions based upon best available techniques, relevant emission limits and best environmental practices for diffuse impacts, meeting these requirements may not be sufficient. Where a quality objective or standard is established pursuant to the Directive, which requires stricter controls than are imposed by emission restrictions, then the more stringent emission controls must be imposed.

Programmes of measures established to realise the environmental objectives of the Directive specifically require adherence to the combined approach. This is provided for by a reaffirmation of the need for emission controls, as these are provided for, for example, under the best available technology requirement imposed under the Integrated Pollution Prevention and Control Directive,[352] but *also* by requiring environmental quality standards to be met for particular substances where these are provided for under the daughter directives to the Dangerous Substances Directive and under other legislation.[353]

The adoption of the combined approach under the Water Framework Directive is generally regarded as a significant advance upon the parallel approach provided for under the Dangerous Substances Directive. Whilst the parallel approach allowed Member States to opt for either emission controls or environmental quality objectives, the combined approach requires both to be applied and, in practice, this will mean that the more stringent approach will be of critical importance. Nonetheless, fundamental issues of environmental quality management strategy are raised by the characterisation of emission controls and environmental quality objectives as cumulative requirements. If environmental quality is satisfactory, in the sense that an environmental quality objective is actually being met, it is not clear what justification exists for more stringent emission controls being imposed.[354]

### 5.8.5 Hazardous Substances

Beyond the combined application of emission controls and environmental quality objectives and standards, the Water Framework Directive seeks to provide a framework for developing further controls. This involves the formulation of new strategies in relation to 'priority substances' that present an unacceptable risk to the environment. When such substances are identified as a result of risk assessment, and these substances are not the subject of existing measures, proposals will be formulated for controls

---

[351] Art.10 Water Framework Directive.
[352] See 12.3.3 below on this Directive.
[353] See 5.4.3 above on the daughter directives to the Dangerous Substances Directive.
[354] See Howarth (1999).

upon the principal sources of emissions *and also* for environmental quality standards for the environmental media and biota.[355]

Although the Directive seeks to combine the application of both emission controls and environmental quality objectives and standards, beyond this, it seeks to provide a framework for developing further controls. This involves the Community adopting specific measures to protect water quality against contamination by hazardous substances presenting a significant risk in relation to the aquatic environment. For these substances, measures will be aimed at progressively reducing discharges, emissions and losses. For 'priority hazardous substances' the aim will be to cease or phase out discharges, emissions and losses.[356]

An explicit duty is imposed upon the Commission to submit proposals relating to priority substances, identified according to specified criteria, in accordance with a stated timetable, and provision is made for the review of the list of priority substances. In particular, after substances have been included in the first priority list the Commission must submit proposals for emission controls and environmental quality standards within two years. In the absence of agreement at Community level within six years of entry into force of the Directive, Member States must establish environmental quality standards for these substances for all surface waters and controls upon principal discharges.

Some comparisons may be drawn here with the programme of adopting daughter directives under the Dangerous Substances Directive.[357] By common consensus, the programme was subject to regrettable delays and the daughter directives actually enacted amounted to a substantial failure to establish emission limits and environmental quality standards for most of the substances covered by the Directive. The issue which this raises is whether progress will be any better with the adoption of measures concerning priority substances and priority hazardous substances under the Water Framework Directive. On progress with substance-specific controls, only time will tell, but it is notable that the Directive places the burden upon Member States to impose controls upon such substances in the event of a failure to reach agreement at Community level. In practical terms, nationally formulated controls must be better than no controls at all, but the approach which is taken does seem to involve the abandonment of a common approach to the formulation and imposition of controls. Perhaps the prospect of national disparity of approach may be seen as an incentive to ensure that agreement is actually reached at Community level.

### 5.8.6 Cost-Recovery Pricing

Another important innovation in the Water Framework Directive is the introduction of full cost-recovery pricing for water services, for water use

---

[355] Art.21 Water Framework Directive.
[356] *Ibid* Art.16.
[357] See 5.4.1C above on the daughter directives to the Dangerous Substances Directive.

overall and within certain economic sectors, by a specified deadline.
Hence, subject to specified exceptions, the price to be charged to water
consumers will come to represent the true cost of that water both in
economic terms and in terms of the environment resource costs incurred.[358]
The reasoning behind this initiative is to remove subsidies which cause the
full cost of water services not to be reflected in water prices. By analogy
with the polluter pays principle,[359] the Directive requires water users to
meet the environmental costs which water uses impose on society as a
whole by the depletion of a resource beyond its natural state of recharge.
In principle, charging the full economic and environmental cost of water
use allows for a more equitable distribution of the cost burden involved
and also is intended to provide an incentive for more rational and efficient
use of water resources.[360] It is important to note, however, that full cost
charging would relate only to the *use* of water, rather than providing more
generally for an economic approach to the control of water pollution.

Although the theoretical desirability of making water users pay the
genuine costs of water use is widely recognised, the difficulties which
arise in devising workable mechanisms to realise this have been previously
noted.[361] As an issue of principle, the assessment of costs to the aquatic
environment arising from water use is likely to prove as problematic in
relation to the implementation of the Directive as it has in relation to
national initiatives which presuppose the feasibility of placing an
economic value upon the state of the aquatic environment. As a matter of
practicality, the imposition of charges which reflect costs and provide
appropriate incentives presupposes that a satisfactory mechanism, such as
metering, exists for the calculation of such charges to individual
consumers. As will be seen, this may be problematic in the national
context because of the absence of comprehensive metering at least in
relation to domestic consumers.

## 5.9  The Content of the Water Framework Directive

### 5.9.1  Purposes

Turning from the broader policy issues to the more detailed content of the
Water Framework Directive, the overall purpose is stated to be the
establishment of a framework for the protection of Community waters.
Within this overall objective, a number of more particular purposes are
identified.

---

[358] Art.9 Water Framework Directive.

[359] See 4.7.3 above on the polluter pays principle. Hence it has been suggested that the polluter
pays principle should be extended to encompass an 'abstractor pays' principle, see House of Lords,
Select Committee on the European Communities *Community Water Policy*, (1997) para.43.

[360] COM(97)49 final, *Explanatory Memorandum* section 3.7.

[361] See 1.7.9 above on the use of economic instruments in relation to water pollution control and
the discussion of the Environment Agency's duty to have regard to costs and benefits when
exercising its functions at 6.14 below.

(a) in relation to inland surface fresh water, estuaries (termed 'transitional' waters), coastal waters and groundwaters, the purpose of the Directive is to prevent further deterioration and to protect and enhance the status of aquatic ecosystems, and related terrestrial ecosystems;

(b) in relation to the same waters, the Directive seeks to promote sustainable water consumption based on a long-term protection of available water resources;

(c) the Directive strives to provide enhanced protection and improvement of the aquatic environment through specific measures for the progressive reduction of discharges, emissions and losses of priority substances and the cessation or phasing-out of similar introductions of priority hazardous substances;

(d) the Directive aims to ensure the progressive reduction of pollution of groundwater and to prevent its further pollution; and

(e) the Directive seeks to contribute to mitigation of the effects of floods and droughts and thereby to contribute to the provision of a sufficient supply of good quality surface water and groundwater as needed for sustainable, balanced and equitable water use; a significant reduction in groundwater pollution; the protection of territorial and marine waters; and achieving the objectives of relevant international agreements,[362] including those which aim to prevent and eliminate pollution of the marine environment.

(f) additionally, Community action will be directed towards the phasing-out of discharges, emissions and losses of priority hazardous substances, with the ultimate aim of achieving concentrations in the marine environment near background values for naturally occurring substances and close to zero for man-made synthetic substances.[363]

## 5.9.2 River Basin Districts

The centrally important mechanisms for water management under the Water Framework Directive envisage a coordination of administrative arrangements within River Basin Districts. For that purpose, Member States are to identify individual river basins, where necessary by combining the areas of small river basins, and to assign these to River Basin Districts. Groundwaters are to be assigned to the nearest or most appropriate River Basin District and coastal, territorial and other marine waters are to be similarly assigned. Appropriate administrative arrangements are to be established, including the identification of an appropriate competent authority, or authorities, to apply the rules of the Directive applicable within their respective areas. The achievement of the environmental objectives of the Directive, and related programmes of

---

[362] See the discussion of the United Nations Convention on the Law of the Sea at 18.7 below and the OSPAR Convention at 18.8 below.
[363] Art.2 Water Framework Directive.

measures, are to be coordinated for the whole of the relevant River Basin District.[364]

It is explicitly provided that existing national or international bodies may be identified as competent authorities for the purposes of the Directive, but such bodies must be identified within three years of the Directive entering into force. Member States must send the Commission specified information concerning competent authorities, at national and international level, in a format provided by Annex I of the Directive, and changes to this information must be similarly notified to the Commission.[365]

### 5.9.3 *Environmental Objectives*

To make operational the programmes of measures which are to be specified in River Basin Management Plans, Member States must adhere to the following environmental objectives for surface waters:

(a) to implement measures which are necessary to prevent deterioration of the status of all bodies of surface water;

(b) to protect, enhance and restore all bodies of surface water, with the aim of achieving good surface water status by 15 years after the entry into force of the Directive i.e. by December 2015;[366]

(c) to protect and enhance all artificial and heavily modified bodies of water with the aim of achieving good ecological potential and good surface water chemical status by 2015; and

(d) to implement measures, in accordance with the Directive's strategies against pollution of water and groundwater, with the aim of progressively reducing pollution from priority substances and ceasing or phasing out emissions, discharges and losses of priority hazardous substances, without prejudice the requirements of relevant international agreements.

In relation to groundwater, the corresponding requirements are that Member States must adhere to the following matters:

(a) to implement necessary measures to prevent or limit the input of pollutants into groundwater and the deterioration of the status of all bodies of groundwater;

(b) to protect, enhance and restore all bodies of groundwater and ensure a balance between the abstraction and recharge of groundwater, with the aim of achieving good groundwater status by 2015; and

(c) to implement the necessary measures to reverse any significant upward trend in the concentration of any pollutant resulting from the impact of human activity in order progressively to reduce pollution of groundwater.

---

[364] *Ibid* Art.3(1), (2) and (4).
[365] *Ibid* Art.3(6) to (9).
[366] On the implementation schedule see 5.9.21 below.

In respect of protected areas, Member States are to achieve compliance with any standards and objectives by 2015 unless otherwise specified in Community legislation under which a particular protected area has been established.[367]

In respect to surface waters and groundwaters, where more than one environmental objective is stated to be applicable, it might be understood that the various objectives should be applied cumulatively, so that Member States are bound to meet all of them. However, this seems difficult to reconcile with a statement to the effect that the multiple objectives are to be interpreted so that the most stringent of the requirements is applicable.[368] This statement is puzzling in that it may be difficult to ascertain which of the different objectives is actually more stringent, since they envisage different kinds of actions and programmes to be undertaken and comparisons in terms of greater or lesser stringency may be problematic. However, supposing that a single objective can be identified as the most stringent for a particular Member State, the stipulation that the most stringent requirement is to be applicable raises the issue of whether that State is entitled to disregard the other, less stringent, environmental objectives. This seems improbable given various provisions in the Directive that particular actions should not allow the objectives of the Directive to be undermined, but the greatest-stringency stipulation seems to raise uncertainties as to the status of objectives which are of lesser stringency.

### 5.9.4 Exceptions to Environmental Objectives

Despite the apparently broad formulation of the environmental objectives for surface waters, groundwaters and protected areas, the obligation upon Member States to achieve good status and related requirements are not so categorical as they may first appear. As has been noted, in various respects the obligations are formulated as requirements to take specified actions 'with the aim' of achieving good status, rather than an obligation to secure that good status is actually achieved. Moreover, even the need to take requisite actions with the objective of good status in contemplation is subject to five distinct kinds of exception or proviso. Respectively, these relate to:

(a) artificial and heavily modified surface waters;
(b) phased achievement of objectives;
(c) less stringent environmental objectives;
(d) temporary deterioration of water status; and
(e) new modifications of physical characteristics and sustainable development activities.

In respect of bodies of surface water which are to be identified as 'artificial and heavily modified', and made subject to the lesser requirement of

---

[367] *Ibid* Art.4(1).
[368] *Ibid* Art.4(2).

achieving good ecological *potential*, designation is subject to particular requirements. Hence, surface waters may be categorised as 'artificial or heavily modified' when the changes to the hydromorphological characteristics of the water which would be necessary to achieve good ecological status would have significant effects on the wider environment; navigation or recreation; activities involving water storage such as drinking water supply, power generation or irrigation; water regulation, flood protection or land drainage; or 'other equally important sustainable human development activities'. In any of these instances, the beneficial objectives served by the artificial and modified characteristics of the water body cannot, for reasons of technical feasibility or disproportionate costs, reasonably be achieved by other means which are a significantly better environmental option. In essence, designation of artificial and heavily modified waters envisages that the lesser quality status of such waters is needed for some significantly beneficial human purpose or that meeting the general good ecological status requirement for surface waters would not be reasonable for environmental, technical or cost reasons. However, even where artificially and heavily modified waters are identified, their reason for designation must be specifically stated in the appropriate River Basin Management Plan and their status must be reviewed every six years.[369]

The general deadline of achieving good status for surface water, groundwater and protected areas by 2015 is subject to extension for various reasons. Hence, the deadline may be extended for the purposes of phased achievement of environmental objectives providing that there is no further deterioration of the status of the body of water and providing that a number of specified conditions are met. Specifically, this applies where a Member State determines that the necessary improvements in the status of a body of water cannot reasonably be achieved within the normal timescale. This must be because the scale of improvements needed can only be achieved in phases which exceed the timescale for reasons of technical feasibility; completion of the improvements within the timescale would be disproportionately expensive; or natural conditions do not allow the timely improvement of the status of the water. The reason for extension of the deadline must be stated and explained in the relevant River Basin Management Plan. Extensions will be limited to a maximum of two further updates of the Plan except where natural conditions prevent the objectives being achieved within this period. A summary of the measures which are necessary to bring waters progressively to the required status by an extended deadline, and the reasons for any significant delay in making these measures operational, must also be set out in the relevant Management Plan.[370]

Alongside extensions of deadlines, another potentially important exception to the overall requirements to achieve the general environmental objectives for surface waters, groundwaters and protected areas is the facility for less

---

[369] *Ibid* Art.4(3).
[370] *Ibid* Art.4(4).

stringent environmental objectives to be established under certain circumstances. In particular, this applies where waters are so affected by human activity that their natural condition is such that the achievement of these objectives would be unfeasible or disproportionately expensive and all the following conditions are met:

(a) the environmental and socio-economic needs served by the human activity cannot be achieved by other means which are a significantly better environmental option not entailing disproportionate costs;

(b) the Member State ensures that, for surface water, the highest ecological and chemical status possible is achieved, given impacts that could not reasonably have been avoided due to the nature of the human activity or pollution and, for groundwater, the least possible changes to good groundwater status, given impacts that, similarly, could not reasonably have been avoided;

(c) no further deterioration occurs in the affected body of water; and

(d) the establishment of less stringent objectives, and the reasons for these, are specifically mentioned in the appropriate River Basin Management Plan and reviewed every six years.[371]

Another exception to the need to achieve the environmental objectives of the Directive in relation to surface waters, groundwaters and protected areas is created in relation to 'temporary' deterioration in water quality. Accordingly, temporary deterioration of water status will not be in breach of the Directive if it is the result of a natural cause or *force majeure* which is exceptional or could not reasonably have been foreseen. Particular instances of this are identified as extreme floods and prolonged droughts or the results of accidents which could not reasonably have been foreseen. Additionally, however, all the following conditions need to be met for a deterioration in water quality to fall within the 'temporary' exception:

(a) all practicable steps must be taken to prevent further deterioration in water status and to avoid the objectives of the Directive not being met in relation to waters which are not directly affected by the relevant circumstances;

(b) the conditions under which circumstances are exceptional or could not reasonably have been foreseen are stated in the River Basin Management Plan;

(c) the measures to be taken under exceptional circumstances are included in the programme of measures and will not compromise the recovery of the quality of the water once the circumstances are over;

(d) the effects of the circumstances which are exceptional or could not reasonably have been foreseen are reviewed annually and, subject to reasons of technical feasibility, disproportionate expense or natural conditions, all practicable measures are taken to restore the

---

[371] *Ibid* Art.4(5).

water to its status prior to the temporary deterioration as soon as reasonable; and

(e) a summary of the effects of the circumstances and the measures taken are included in the next update of the River Basin Management Plan.[372]

Alongside the other exceptions to the requirements in relation to good status for surface waters, groundwaters and protected areas, potentially wide ranging exceptions are provided for in relation to new modifications to the physical characteristics of surface waters or groundwaters and new sustainable development activities. Hence, it is stated that Member States will not be in breach of the Directive when failure to achieve relevant status or ecological potential requirements is the result of new modifications to the physical characteristics of a surface water body. Similarly, there will be no breach where there are alterations to the levels of bodies of groundwater or where failure to prevent deterioration from high status to good status of a body of surface water is the result of new sustainable human development activities. Again, the availability of this exception is subject to explicit conditions which require the Member State to show that all the following are met:

(a) all practicable steps are taken to mitigate the adverse impact on the status of the body of water;

(b) the reasons for the modifications or alterations are specifically set out and explained in the River Basin Management Plan and reviewed every six years;

(c) the reasons for the modifications or alterations are of overriding public interest and/or the benefits to the environment and to society of achieving the objectives are outweighed by the benefits of the new modifications or alterations to human health, the maintenance of human safety or to sustainable development; and

(d) the beneficial objectives served by the modification or alteration of the water body cannot, for reasons of technical feasibility or disproportionate cost be achieved by other means which are a significantly better environmental option.[373]

The reference to 'disproportionate cost' amongst the grounds justifying a failure to achieve good status raises significant questions as to how this is to be assessed. It would mark a profound shift in EC water law if the quality of water in different regions was allowed to vary according to their capacity to meet the costs of improving water bodies. Nevertheless, without any indication that the reasonableness of costs is to be assessed by a common measure, variability between River Basin Districts seems to be a possibility.

Two general requirements apply where a Member States seeks to apply any of the provisions creating exceptions and provisos to the general requirements of the Directive, that is, relating to artificial or heavily

---

[372] *Ibid* Art.4(6).
[373] *Ibid* Art.4(7).

modified surface waters, phased achievement of objectives, less stringent environmental objectives, temporary deterioration of water status, and new modifications of physical characteristics and sustainable development activities. The first of the general requirements is that the use of an exception must ensure that it does not permanently exclude or compromise the achievement of the objectives of the Directive in other bodies of water within the same River Basin District and that it is consistent with the implementation of other Community environmental legislation. The second requirement is that the application of the new provisions, including the exceptions and provisos, guarantees at least the same level of protection as under existing Community legislation.[374]

These provisions reflect the underlying principle that the implementation of the Directive should achieve a level of protection which is at least equivalent to that provided by previous legislation. Although it is envisaged that several of the earlier water quality directives will eventually be repealed,[375] until such repeals actually take place, it would appear that if a Member State sought to claim an exception to the requirements of the Water Framework Directive which failed to meet a requirement of an earlier directive then this would be contrary to both directives. However, it should be noted that many of the earlier directives contain exemptions for various contingencies, such as where naturally arising conditions prevent water quality requirements being met.[376] The assertion of the principle that the requirements of the Water Framework Directive are at least as strict as previous directives is clearly important. However, following the repeal of the earlier directives, reliance upon the Framework Directive alone may prove more problematic legally insofar as many of the obligations are couched in terms of actions which are required with the 'aim' of achieving relevant good status requirements (rather than actually achieving such requirements). This contrasts with earlier directives which were categorical in requiring actual water quality requirements to be met.[377]

### 5.9.5 Characteristics of River Basin Districts

Given the centrality of the concept of river basins in the system of water management envisaged by the Water Framework Directive, the need for characteristics of river basins to be ascertained and for environmental impacts upon basins to be assessed is provided for as a key obligation under the Directive. Accordingly, a Member State must ensure that for each River Basin District, and any portion of an International River Basin District falling within its territory, an analysis is undertaken of its characteristics, a review of the impact of human activity on the status of surface water and groundwater, and an economic analysis of water use. These analyses and the review must be undertaken in accordance with

---

[374] *Ibid* Art.4(8)-(9).

[375] See 5.9.19 below on the programme for repeal of existing legislation.

[376] See 5.5 above on previous water quality directives.

[377] See discussion of the United Kingdom cases before the European Court of Justice at 4.15 above.

technical specifications which are set out in Annexes II and III to the Directive and must be completed by 2004. The analyses and review must be reviewed and, if necessary updated, at the latest by 2013 and every six years thereafter.[378]

Annex II to the Directive sets out systems for the characterisation of surface water body types; ecoregions and surface water body types; type-specific reference conditions for surface water body types; the identification of anthropogenic pressures on surface waters; and the assessment of impacts. In respect of groundwater, systems are established for initial characterisation of groundwaters; further characterisation; review of the impact of human activity; review of the impact of changes in groundwater levels; and review of the impact of pollution on groundwater quality. Annex III indicates the requirements for the economic analysis of water use and requires sufficient information to be provided to make calculations as to the recovery of costs for water services and to make judgements as to the most cost effective combination of measures in respect of water uses to be included in programmes of measures to be established for River Basin Districts.

### 5.9.6 Registers of Protected Areas

Member States are also to establish a register of all areas within each River Basin District which have been designated as requiring special protection under specific Community legislation for the protection of their surface water and groundwater or for the conservation of habitats and species depending upon water. Registers are to be completed by 2005 and thereafter must be kept under review and up to date.[379]

The registers of protected areas are to include all areas identified as waters used, or to be used, for abstraction for drinking water and also protected areas which are indicated by Annex IV to the Directive as follows:[380]

(a) areas designated for the abstraction of water intended for human consumption;
(b) protected areas for economically significant aquatic species;
(c) recreational waters, including bathing waters under the Bathing Water Directive;[381]
(d) nutrient-sensitive areas including vulnerable zones under the Nitrates Directive;[382]
(e) areas designated as sensitive under the Urban Waste Water Treatment Directive;[383] and

---

[378] Art.5 Water Framework Directive.

[379] *Ibid* Art.6.

[380] Reference to 'including' in the following list highlights the baseline nature of the provisions, and that more extensive area designation is not to be precluded.

[381] See 5.5.2 above on the Bathing Water Directive (76/160/EEC).

[382] See 5.6.3 above on the Nitrates Directive (91/676/EEC).

[383] See 5.6.2 above on the Urban Waste Water Treatment Directive (91/271/EEC).

(f)  areas designated for their conservation importance where water is an important factor in their protection including under the Habitats and Wild Birds Directives.[384]

### 5.9.7  Waters for Drinking Water Abstraction

Within each River Basin District, Member States must identify all significant bodies of water which are used for the abstraction of water intended for human consumption, where these provide more than ten cubic metres as a daily average or serve more than 50 persons, or are waters which may be used for this purpose. In respect of waters to be abstracted for drinking water, specific monitoring obligations are imposed upon Member States for water bodies which provide more than 100 cubic meters of water as a daily average. In relation to each body of water identified for drinking water abstraction, in addition to meeting the environmental objectives of the Directive, Member States are to ensure the establishment of quality standards designed to ensure that, under the anticipated water treatment regime, the resulting water will meet the requirements of the amended Drinking Water Quality Directive.[385] Member States are also to ensure the necessary protection of the identified bodies of water with the aim of avoiding deterioration in the quality in order to reduce the level of purification treatment required in the production of drinking water and safeguard zones may be established for the protection of these zones.[386] The link which is established here, between natural waters and water used for supply purposes, is a significant departure in Community water quality legislation. Previously, water for abstraction for use as drinking water following treatment had to meet the requirements of the Drinking Water Abstraction Directive,[387] but no specific provisions existed concerning measures to be adopted for the protection of supplies to be used for drinking water.

### 5.9.8  Monitoring Requirements

In addition to the requirement upon Member States to monitor significant supplies for drinking water purposes, noted above, extensive requirements are imposed in relation to the general monitoring of surface water status, groundwater status and protected areas. Hence, Member States are to ensure the establishment of programmes for the monitoring of water quality to establish a coherent and comprehensive overview of water status within each River Basin District. In respect of this, monitoring programmes for surface waters are to encompass the volume and level or rate of flow to the extent to which this is relevant for determining ecological and chemical status and ecological potential, and the actual

---

[384] See 15.8 below on the Habitats and Wild Birds Directives (79/409/EEC and 92/43/EEC).

[385] On the Revised Drinking Water Quality Directive (Directive 80/778/EEC amended by Directive 98/83/EC) see 17.7.1 and 17.7.8 below.

[386] Art.7 Water Framework Directive.

[387] See 17.6 below on this Directive.

ecological and chemical status and ecological potential. For groundwaters, monitoring programmes are to cover chemical and quantitative status and, for protected areas, programmes are to be supplemented by matters contained in Community legislation under which individual protected areas have been established. The monitoring programmes are to be in operation by 2006 unless otherwise specified in the legislation concerned.[388]

Although provision is made for technical specifications and standardised methods for analysis and monitoring to be laid down in accordance with procedures set by the Regulatory Committee established under the Directive, the initial requirements for monitoring are set out in Annex V to the Directive. This Annex goes into considerable detail as to the technical specifications of monitoring of surface waters and groundwater, indicating the characteristics which must be satisfied for relevant waters to be categorised of high, good and moderate ecological status, the procedures and parameters for establishing chemical status, the design, frequency and presentation of monitoring and a range of related matters. Applying these requirements to the circumstances of national waters is likely to be a task of some technical complexity but, hopefully, the criteria will provide an appropriate balance between national flexibility and supranational transparency.

### 5.9.9 Cost-Recovery for Water Services

Another significant innovation introduced by the Water Framework Directive is the need for water services pricing to be related to the environmental and resource costs involved. Thus, Member States are bound to take account of the principle of recovery of environmental and resource costs of water services by having regard to the economic analysis of water costs, which must be conducted in accordance with Annex III to the Directive, and also to have regard to the polluter pays principle.[389] Specifically, by 2010, Member States must ensure that water pricing policies provide adequate incentive for water users to use water resources efficiently, thereby contributing to the environmental objectives of the Directive. Water pricing policies must ensure an adequate contribution to the costs of water services by different water uses, disaggregated at least into industry, households and agriculture. The planned steps towards implementation of cost-recovery pricing, and the contribution to be made by various water users, must be reported in the relevant River Basin Management Plan.

However, this general requirement of cost-recovery is subject to Member States having regard to the social, environment and economic effects of the recovery as well as the geographic and climatic conditions of any particular region. Moreover, the cost-recovery obligation is subject to certain qualifications in that it is not to prevent the funding of particular

---

[388] Art.8 Water Framework Directive.
[389] See 4.7.3 above on the polluter pays principle.

preventative or remedial measures which are needed in order to achieve the objectives of the Directive. This seems to allow the possibility of funded action being taken in respect of particular water contamination problems, or actions to address artificial and heavily modified bodies of water, without the cost of these being brought into a cost-recovery calculation. Another qualification allows a Member State to determine that, in accordance with established practice and for a given water use activity, the cost-recovery obligation should not be applied. This may be done providing that it does not compromise the purposes and the achievement of the objectives of the Directive and the reasons for non-application are given in the River Basin Management Plan. The implications of apparently allowing Member States to opt out of cost-recovery in relation to particular water users is far from clear and difficult issues are raised as to the circumstances in which allowing this will significantly undermine the purposes and objectives of the Directive.

### 5.9.10 The Combined Approach

Another central feature of the Water Framework Directive is the adoption of a 'combined approach' for the control of point and diffuse sources of contamination. This requires Member States to ensure the establishment and/or implementation of:

(a) emission controls based on best available techniques; or
(b) relevant emission limit values; or
(c) in the case of diffuse impacts controls including, as appropriate, best environmental practices,

which are established under relevant Community environmental legislation. The relevant measures are:

(a) the Integrated Pollution Prevention and Control Directive;[390]
(b) the Urban Waste Water Treatment Directive;[391]
(c) the Nitrates Directive;[392]
(d) directives adopted under the Water Framework Directive which provide for strategies against pollution of water or groundwater;[393]
(e) daughter directives to the Dangerous Substances Directive;[394] and
(f) any other relevant Community legislation.[395]

---

[390] See 12.3.3 below on this Directive.

[391] See 5.6.2 above on this Directive.

[392] See 5.6.3 above on this Directive.

[393] That is, directives adopted under Art.16 or 17 of the Water Framework Directive.

[394] See 5.4.1C above on the daughter directives to the Dangerous Substances Directive. The relevant daughter directives are listed in Annex IX to the Water Framework Directive.

[395] Although unspecific as to what other Community legislation is relevant here, the context indicates that this must be legislation establishing emission controls or limits, or controls upon diffuse impacts.

The required emission controls, emission limits or controls upon diffuse impacts are to be established by 2012 unless otherwise specified in the relevant legislation.

Notwithstanding the implementation of the required emission controls, emission limits and controls upon diffuse pollution, where a water quality objective or quality standard requires stricter conditions than can be achieved by the required emission controls, then more stringent emission controls must be established. For this purpose, relevant water quality objectives or standards arise from measures adopted under the Water Framework Directive, daughter directives under the Dangerous Substances Directive[396] or any other Community legislation which establishes water quality objectives or standards.[397] In essence a two stage process is envisaged, whereby Member States are first obliged to give full effect to legislation imposing emission controls. However, if this fails to result in specified water quality objectives or standards actually being met, then the second stage is to require the imposition of more stringent emission controls which ensure that the water quality objectives or standards are actually met. Hence, the option of meeting *either* emission controls *or* water quality objectives, which existed under 'parallel approach' followed in the Dangerous Substances Directive, is removed and actually meeting environmental quality objectives will not be a justification or excuse for a Member State failing to impose the required emission controls.

### 5.9.11  Programmes of Measures

Within each River Basin District, or each part of an International River Basin District within its territory, a Member State must establish a programmes of measures to achieve the environmental objectives established under the Water Framework Directive. Programmes of measures are to take account of the analysis of the characteristics of the River Basin District, the review of the impact of human activity on the status of surface waters and groundwater, and the analysis of water use which must be undertaken in relation to the District.[398] However, programmes of measures may be of wider extent than any particular District, in that they may make reference to national legislation and may incorporate measures which are applicable to all Districts falling within a national territory.[399]

Programmes of measures are to include 'basic measures' and, where necessary, 'supplementary measures'. Basic measures, representing the minimum requirements which must be complied with, consist of the following:

---

[396] Listed in Annex IX to the Water Framework Directive.
[397] *Ibid* Art.10.
[398] See *ibid* Art.5, discussed at 5.8.3 above.
[399] *Ibid* Art.11(1).

(a) measures to implement Community legislation for the protection of water including the legislation establishing emission controls (which must be adhered to for the purposes of the combined approach) and other relevant Community water and environmental legislation listed in Part A of Annex VI to the Directive;

(b) measures appropriate to implement cost-recovery charges for water use;[400]

(c) measures to promote efficient and sustainable water use to avoid compromising the achievement of the environmental objectives of the Directive;

(d) measures required to meet the environmental quality standards for water intended for the abstraction of drinking water, including measures to safeguard water quality in order to reduce the level of purification required for the production of drinking water;

(e) controls over the abstraction of fresh surface water and groundwater, including a register of water abstractors and a requirement of prior authorisation for abstraction unless it can be shown that abstraction has no significant impact on water status or water resources;

(f) controls, including a requirement of prior authorisation, for artificial recharge or augmentation of groundwater bodies;

(g) for point source discharges liable to cause pollution, a requirement of prior regulation, such as a prohibition on the entry of pollutants into water, prior authorisation or registration based on general binding rules, laying down emission controls for the pollutants concerned, and including controls facilitating a combined approach[401] and for strategies against pollution of water;[402]

(h) for diffuse sources liable to cause pollution, measures to prevent or control the input of such pollutants such as prior regulation, prior authorisation or registration based on generally binding rules;

(i) for any other significant adverse impacts on the status of water, particular measures to ensure that the hydromorphological conditions of bodies of water are consistent with the achievement of the required ecological status or potential;

(j) a prohibition on the direct discharge of pollutants into groundwater, subject to a range of specified circumstances where injection or re-injection of water and other substances may be permitted;

(k) in accordance with the strategies against water pollution provided for under the Directive, measures to eliminate pollution of surface waters by substances specified under the priority list and progressively to reduce pollution by other substances which would otherwise prevent Member States from achieving the environmental objectives for surface waters; and

---

[400] Under *ibid* Art.9 discussed at 5.8.6 above.
[401] Under *ibid* Art.10 and see 5.8.4 above on the combined approach.
[402] Under *ibid* Art.16 and see 5.9.16 below on strategies for pollution control.

(1)  any measures required to prevent significant losses of pollutants
     from technical installations and to prevent and/or reduce the
     impact of accidental pollution incidents including appropriate
     measures to reduce the risk to aquatic ecosystems.[403]

Alongside the fairly extensive list of measures that are mandatorily
required as basic measures, further 'supplementary measures' are
envisaged where the basic measures are inadequate to achieve the
environmental objectives of the Directive.[404] However, what particular
supplementary measures may be needed in the event of the basic measures
proving insufficient is not clearly specified. Part B of Annex VI to the
Directive provides a 'non-exclusive' list of possible supplementary
measures and it is also stated that further supplementary measures may be
adopted, beyond those on the list, particularly where these are needed to
implement international agreements. Nonetheless, some indication of the
kinds of measures that are envisaged is provided by the list in Annex VI.
This refers to a spectrum of mechanisms ranging from legislative and
administrative measures to voluntary approaches including education,
research, development and demonstration measures and concludes with an
unspecific 'catch-all' category of 'other relevant measures'. Hence, it
appears that the possibilities for supplementary measures are open ended.

The circumstances in which a Member State will be bound to take
measures beyond the basic measures seems to be dependent upon the
outcome of monitoring data concerning the status of relevant waters. Thus,
where monitoring and other data indicate that the environmental objectives
of the Directive are unlikely to be achieved for a particular body of water,
the Member State must ensure that:

(a)  the causes of the possible failure are investigated;
(b)  relevant permits and authorisations are examined and reviewed as
     appropriate;
(c)  monitoring programmes are reviewed and adjusted as appropriate;
     and
(d)  such additional measures as may be necessary in order to achieve
     the objectives are established, including, where appropriate, the
     establishment of stricter environmental quality standards.

Where the environmental objectives are unlikely to be achieved for a
particular water due to circumstances which are naturally caused or *force
majeure*, and these are exceptional and could not reasonably have been
foreseen, a Member State will be entitled to determine that additional
measures are not practicable. However, such a determination will be
subject to the conditions which apply generally to temporary deterioration
of water quality status.[405]

---

[403] *Ibid* Art.11(3).

[404] *Ibid* Art.11(4).

[405] *Ibid* Art.11(5). The requirements concerning temporary deterioration are specified under
Art.4(5) *ibid*.

In implementing basic measures, Member States are placed under a duty not to realise the environmental objectives of the Directive in relation to particular waters at the expense of transferring pollution elsewhere. Hence, appropriate steps must be taken to avoid the pollution of marine waters, and application of basic measures must not lead, directly or indirectly, to increased pollution of surface waters unless the alternative would be to increase pollution of the environment as a whole.[406]

The programmes of measures must be established by 2009 and all the measures made operational by 2012. Programmes of measures must be reviewed and, if necessary, updated by 2015 and every 6 years thereafter. New or revised measures established following revision of a programme must be made operational within three years of the establishment.[407]

### 5.9.12  Issues beyond the Competence of Member States

Where a Member State identifies an issue which has an impact on the management of water but which cannot be resolved by that Member State, it must report the issue to the Commission and to any other Member State concerned and may make recommendations for the resolution of the issue. The Commission will then be bound to respond to any reports or recommendations from Member States within a six month period.[408] It is anticipated that possible reasons for the identification of such issues may be that the source of the problem lies outside a national River Basin District.[409] In such circumstances, it is foreseeable that the issue might only be capable of resolution through negotiation or legislation at Community level.

### 5.9.13  River Basin Management Plans

A basic duty upon a Member State is to ensure that a River Basin Management Plan is produced for each River Basin District within its territory. The specific information which must be contained in River Basin Management Plans is spelt out in some detail in Annex VII to the Directive. Broadly, Plans must provide a general description of the characteristics of the District and maps of the surface waters and groundwaters. A summary of significant pressures and impacts of human activity on waters must be included estimating the impacts of point and diffuse sources of pollution. Maps must indicate monitoring networks and the status of surface waters, groundwaters and protected areas. Summaries must be provided of the economic analysis of water uses and the programme of measures that have been adopted and other measures to

---

[406] *Ibid* Art.11(6). A rather vague reference to something resembling the BPEO, on which see 12.3.2A below.

[407] *Ibid* Art.11(7) and (8).

[408] *Ibid* Art.12.

[409] On the approach of the European Court of Justice to difficulties in meeting standards stemming from outside the Member State see Case C-198/97 *Commission v Germany* [1999] ECR I-3257, discussed at 5.5.2C above.

implement Community water protection legislation. A report of the measures taken to ensure cost-recovery for water use must be incorporated along with summaries of information concerning water abstracted for drinking water, controls upon abstraction and impoundment, controls upon point source discharges and discharges to groundwater. Summaries are also required to be provided of action taken on priority substances, measures to prevent accidental pollution incident and measures which are taken where the environmental objectives of the Directive are unlikely to be achieved. Finally, details must be provided as to public information and consultation measures undertaken and contact points and procedures for obtaining further information, including actual monitoring data, from competent authorities.

River Basin Management Plans must be published by 2009. Plans must be reviewed by 2015 and every six years thereafter.[410]

### 5.9.14 Public Information and Consultation

Another key theme in the Water Framework Directive is the need for plans and programmes of action in relation to water quality to be formulated and undertaken with the maximum degree of public involvement. For this purpose Member States must encourage the active participation of all interested parties in the implementation of the Directive and, more specifically, in the formulation, review and updating of River Basin Management Plans. In particular, Member States must ensure that, for each River Basin District, the following are published and made available for comment by the public and water users:

(a) a timetable and work programme for the production of the plan, including a statement of the consultation measures taken;
(b) an interim overview of significant water management issues identified in the river basin; and
(c) draft copies of the River Basin Management Plan;

Upon request, access must be provided to background documents and information used for the development of the draft River Basin Management Plan. At least six months must be allowed for comment in writing on the documents in order to allow active involvement and consultation. The same requirements will apply in relation to updated River Basin Management Plans.[411]

Some overlap may be noted with other provisions allowing access to environmental information generally,[412] and comparisons may also be drawn with procedures which must be followed in relation to environmental impact assessment.[413] Nonetheless, the public information

---

[410] *Ibid* Art.13(6)-(7).
[411] *Ibid* Art.14.
[412] See 16.14-16.19 below on access to environmental information.
[413] See 14.6 below on environmental impact assessment.

and consultation provisions of the Water Framework Directive show significant innovation by comparison with previous water directives. Whilst the particular duties to publish information and solicit comments on proposals are important, they may be seen as particular aspects of the broader duty upon Member States to encourage active involvement in the implementation of the Directive. Hence, there may be other things that Member States need to do to encourage involvement which go beyond the specified public information and consultation duties.

### 5.9.15 Reporting

Other aspects of information access which are explicitly provided for under the Water Framework Directive concern reporting duties upon Member States. In relation to this, Member States are bound to send copies of River Basin Management Plans, and updates of these, to the Commission and any other Member State concerned within three months of their publication. Similarly, Member States must submit summary reports of analyses of the characteristics of River Basin Districts, reviews of the environmental impact of human activity, economic analyses of water use and monitoring programmes which have been undertaken within three months of their completion. In addition, Member States must, within three years of publication of each River Basin Management Plan or update, submit an interim report describing progress in the implementation of the planned programme of measures.[414]

### 5.9.16 Strategies against Pollution of Water

The 'framework' character of the Directive is evident from the mechanisms which it provides for the adoption of further measures for the control of especially problematic pollutants. However, the particular pollutants at issue, and the measures which must be adopted in relation to them, is a matter of some complexity. Notably, the Directive incorporates three pertinent definitions respectively for 'hazardous substances', 'priority substances' and 'priority hazardous substances'. 'Hazardous substances' means substances or groups of substances that are toxic, persistent and liable to bio-accumulate and other substances or groups of substances which give rise to an equivalent level of concern.[415] 'Priority substances' means substances which are identified and listed under the Directive.[416] 'Priority hazardous substances' means substances which have been identified and for which specified measures have to be taken under the Directive.[417] Different obligations are provided for in relation to these categories of substance.

---

[414] Art.15 Water Framework Directive.
[415] *Ibid* Art.2(29).
[416] *Ibid* Art.2(30), with identification being made under Art.16(2) and the substances listed under Annex X to the Directive.
[417] *Ibid* Art.2(30) with identification made in accordance with Art.16(3) and (6) and measures taken in accordance with Art.16(1) and (8).

A general obligation requires the European Parliament and the Council to adopt specific measures against pollution of water by individual pollutants or groups of pollutants which present a significant risk to, or via, the aquatic environment, including risks to waters used for abstraction for drinking water. For these generally hazardous substances, measures must be aimed at progressively reducing and, for priority hazardous substances, at ceasing or phasing out discharges, emissions and losses.[418] The background to this wording lies in the OSPAR Convention, under which parties are bound to make every endeavour to move towards the target of cessation of discharges, emissions and losses of hazardous substances by 2020. Additionally, parties agreed to achieve continuous reductions in releases of hazardous substances with the ultimate aim of achieving concentrations in the environment near background levels for naturally occurring substances and close to zero for man-made synthetic substances.[419] However, the wording of the Directive requires a progressive (rather than 'continuous') reduction in hazardous substances and only applies the phasing out obligation to 'priority hazardous substances'. The effect of this is to greatly reduce the number of substances in respect of which, and the extent to which, the Directive gives effect to obligations under the Convention. On the other hand, it is notable that although the OSPAR Convention is concerned with the protection of the marine environment, the Water Framework Directive also applies to inland and estuarial waters. Hence, a significant extension of the geographical scope of OSPAR obligations is brought about by the Directive.

The Commission is bound to submit a proposal setting out a list of priority substances from amongst those which present a significant risk to, or via, the aquatic environment. Particular substances are to be prioritised for action on the basis of risk, as identified by specified criteria. The criteria are a risk assessment or a targeted risk-based assessment focusing solely on aquatic ecotoxicology and human toxicity via the aquatic environment conducted in accordance with specified methodological requirements. However, where necessary to meet a deadline imposed upon the Commission, substances may be made priorities for action on the basis of a simplified risk-assessment procedure taking account of evidence of intrinsic hazard, monitoring evidence of widespread contamination and other proven factors which may indicate the possibility of widespread contamination.[420]

The Commission's proposal for priority substances must also identify priority *hazardous* substances. In doing so, the Commission must take account of the selection of substances of concern in relevant Community legislation or relevant international agreements, such as the OSPAR Convention. In preparing its proposal, the Commission must take account of recommendations of various official, expert and advisory bodies, and

---

[418] *Ibid* Art.16(1).

[419] See 18.8 below on the OSPAR Convention.

[420] Art.16(2) Water Framework Directive.

representatives of business organisations. The Commission must also review the adopted list of priority substances by 2004 and every four years thereafter.[421]

The Water Framework Directive echoes the approach taken under the Dangerous Substances Directive of making provision for the enactment of subsequent daughter directives establishing emission limits and environmental quality objectives for particular substances.[422] Hence, for priority substances, the Commission must submit proposals for control incorporating the progressive reduction of discharges, emissions and losses of the substances concerned. In particular, these proposals must encompass the cessation or phasing out of discharges, emissions and losses of the priority *hazardous* substances, including a timetable for doing so. This timetable may not exceed 20 years after the identification of priority hazardous substances. The Commission proposal must identify an appropriate, cost-effective and proportionate level and combination of product and process controls for both point and diffuse sources and take account of Community-wide uniform emission limit values for process controls. In addition, the Commission must submit proposals for quality standards applicable to the concentrations of priority substances in surface water, sediments or biota.[423]

In accordance with these requirements, the Commission must submit proposals at least for emission controls for point sources and environmental quality standards within two years of the inclusion of a substance within the priority list. In contrast to the unsatisfactory progress which was made in establishing daughter directives under the Dangerous Substances Directive, however, the Water Framework Directive places specific obligations upon the Member States to take action in respect of priority substances in the event of a failure to reach agreement at Community level as to the actions needing to be taken in relation to such substances. Accordingly, for substances in the first priority list, in the absence of agreement at Community level, Member States must establish environmental quality standards for these substances for all affected surface waters and controls upon the principal sources of those substances. In relation to the first priority list Member States must establish these standards and controls by 2006. For substances subsequently included in the priority list, Member States must take such action by five years after the date of inclusion in the list.[424]

In formulating proposals for a list of priority substances, the Commission must review the directives listed in Annex IX to the Directive. This Annex lists daughter directives to the Dangerous Substances Directive which establish limit values and quality objectives and states that these are to serve as emission limit values and environmental quality standards for the purposes of the Water Framework Directive. As a result of the review of

---

[421] *Ibid* Art.16(3), (4) and (5).
[422] See 5.4.1C above on the Daughter Directives to the Dangerous Substances Directive.
[423] Art.16(6)-(7) Water Framework Directive.
[424] *Ibid* Art.16(8).

the daughter directives, the Commission must propose a revision of the controls imposed by the Annex for all substances which are included in the priority list of substances. The priority list proposed by the Commission will, on its adoption by the European Parliament and Council become Annex X to the Water Framework Directive.[425]

### 5.9.17 Strategies to Prevent and Control Pollution of Groundwater

Whilst the preceding discussion of strategies against the pollution of water contains the provisions which are the natural successors to the Dangerous Substances Directive, broadly corresponding provisions were needed to ensure the continuation of protection of groundwater quality presently provided by the Groundwater Directive.[426] Although, as has been seen, the environmental objectives of the Water Framework Directive encompass various general obligations upon Member States in relation to the protection of groundwater quality, these are relatively unspecific in respect of the assessment of groundwater chemical status, what protection measures are needed and what must be done to reverse increasing concentrations of pollutants in groundwater. These matters are specifically addressed by the imposition of a duty upon the European Parliament and the Council to adopt specific measures to prevent and control groundwater. These measures are aimed at achieving the objective of good chemical status for groundwater and must be adopted by 2002 on the basis of a proposal presented by the Commission.[427]

In proposing measures for the protection of groundwater quality, the Commission must have regard to the analyses carried out of the characteristics of River Basin Districts and particularly the provisions relating to groundwaters under Annex II to the Directive. The measures must include criteria for assessing good groundwater chemical status[428] and criteria for the identification of significant and sustained upward trends and for the starting points for trend reversals in groundwater pollutant concentrations.[429] Measures for the protection of groundwater must include programmes of basic and supplementary measures for this purpose.[430]

The formula for dealing with priority substances is followed in relation to groundwater protection insofar as, in the absence of criteria for groundwater protection being adopted at Community level, Member States will have to establish appropriate criteria by 2005. Again, the prospect of appropriate criteria needing to be established by each Member State may provide an incentive to reaching an agreement at Community level in the time allowed. However, in respect of groundwater, further provision is

---

[425] *Ibid* Art.16(10)-(11).
[426] See 5.4.2 above on the Groundwater Directive.
[427] Art.17(1) Water Framework Directive.
[428] Under Annex II.2.2 and Annex V.2.3.2 and 2.4.5 *ibid*.
[429] Under Annex V.2.4.4 *ibid*.
[430] *Ibid* Art.17(2)-(3).

made for the possibility of criteria failing to be established at national level. This is provided for by a stipulation that trend reversal in groundwater quality is to take as its starting point a maximum of 75% of the level of the quality standards set out in existing Community legislation applicable to groundwater.[431] Whilst this appears to seeks improvements in groundwater quality beyond those presently provided for, it is not entirely clear what existing quality standards are at issue since the Groundwater Directive is unspecific on environmental quality standards for groundwater and other legislation which may possibly be relevant is less comprehensive in coverage.[432]

### 5.9.18 Administrative Provisions

Alongside the substantive environmental obligations arising under the Water Framework Directive, a number of additional administrative and procedural matters are explicitly provided for:

(a) the Commission must publish a report on the implementation of the Directive by 2012 at the latest and this must provide a review of progress in its implementation and the status of surface water and groundwater in the Community along with various surveys and summaries of particular matters within the Directive;[433]

(b) the Commission must prepare annual indicative plans of measures having an impact on water legislation which it intends to propose in the near future including emerging proposals, control measures and strategies against water pollution which are required under the Directive. The Commission must undertake a general review the Directive by 2019;[434]

(c) provision is made for certain Annexes of the Directive[435] to be adapted to scientific and technical progress;[436]

(d) the Commission will be assisted by a Regulatory Committee which will adopt its own rules of procedure;.[437] and

(e) in respect of implementation, Member States must bring into force the laws, regulations and administrative provision necessary to comply with the Directive by 2003.[438]

---

[431] *Ibid* Art.17(4)-(5).

[432] See, for example, the Nitrates Directive (91/676/EEC) which provides a parameter for nitrate in groundwater, discussed at 5.6.3 above, and the Drinking Water Quality Directive (80/778/EEC as amended) which may provide implicit limits upon permissible pollution of groundwater by pesticides and other substances, discussed at 17.7.1 and 17.7.8 below. Generally see *ENDS Report* 305 (2000) p.50.

[433] Art.18 Water Framework Directive.

[434] *Ibid* Art.19.

[435] Specifically *ibid* Annexes I, III and section 1.3.6 of Annex V.

[436] *Ibid* Art.20.

[437] *Ibid* Art.21.

## 5.9.19 Repeals and Transitional Provisions

The consolidating effect of the Water Framework Directive is such that a large amount of previous Community water quality legislation will be superseded and need to be repealed. However, this is to be done in stages, so that there will be a significant time before the Framework Directive has its full impact and, during this period, it will be in force alongside the earlier legislation. Hence the following measures are to be repealed with effect from 2007:[439]

    (a) the Drinking Water Abstraction Directive;[440]
    (b) the Information Exchange Decision;[441] and
    (c) the Drinking Water Sampling Directive.[442]

The following Directives will be repealed with effect from 2013:[443]

    (a) the Freshwater Fish Waters Directive;[444]
    (b) the Shellfish Waters Directive;[445]
    (c) the Groundwater Directive;[446] and
    (d) the Dangerous Substances Directive.[447]

Other legislative proposals have been reconsidered as a result of the Water Framework Directive, and have been brought within its scope so that plans for separate legislation have become unnecessary. Hence, a proposal for an Ecological Quality of Water Directive[448] has been incorporated and extended within the Framework Directive and a distinct directive on this is no longer needed. Also, a proposal for a Groundwater Action Programme,[449] which would have involved a revision of the Groundwater Directive, is also overtaken by the Framework Directive.

However, it is notable that a significant amount of Community water legislation remains largely unaffected by the Framework Directive and

---

[438] *Ibid* Art.24.
[439] *Ibid* Art.22(1).
[440] See 17.6 below on this Directive.
[441] See 16.2.5 below on this Decision.
[442] See 17.6 below on this Directive.
[443] Art.22(2) Water Framework Directive.
[444] See 15.3.1 below on this Directive.
[445] See 15.3.1 below on this Directive.
[446] See 5.4.2 above on this Directive and see 5.9.17 above.
[447] See 5.4.1 above on this Directive. However, Art.6 of the Dangerous Substances Directive is to be repealed with effect from the entry into force of the Water Framework Directive. Also, the priority list of substances under the Dangerous Substances Directive (under Art.7) is to be replaced by the priority list under the Water Framework Directive (Art.16) and the principles for identification of pollution problems, the establishment of quality standards and the adoption of measures (under Art.7 Dangerous Substances Directive) may be superseded by corresponding measures under the Water Framework Directive (see Art.22(3) Water Framework Directive).
[448] COM(93)680 final, and see 5.5.4 above.
[449] COM(96)315 final, and see 5.4.2 above.

continues to be operative. Key measures falling into this category are the following:

(a) the First Detergent Directive;[450]
(b) the Bathing Water Directive;[451]
(c) the Drinking Water Quality Directive;[452]
(d) the Urban Waste Water Treatment Directive;[453] and
(e) the Nitrates Directive.[454]

The environmental objectives and quality standards established, or to be established, under the Water Framework Directive[455] have implications for other environmental quality legislation with similar concerns. In particular, it is specified that these environmental objectives and standards are to be regarded as environmental quality standards for the purposes of the Integrated Pollution Prevention and Control Directive.[456]

The assurance that implementation of the Water Framework Directive will not result in a deterioration of surface water quality below that required by existing directives is further provided for by an initial requirement to adhere to standards established under the Dangerous Substances Directive. Hence, for bodies of surface water, environmental objectives established under the first River Basin Management Plan must, as a minimum, give effect to quality standards as least as stringent as those required by the Dangerous Substances Directive.[457] However, it may be revealing that this requirement is not applied to subsequent River Basin Management Plans.

### 5.9.20 Penalties

A final significant innovation upon previous water directives is the incorporation of an explicit provision concerning penalties in relation to the Water Framework Directive.[458] This requires Member States to determine penalties applicable to breaches of the national provisions adopted pursuant to the Directive. It is expressly stated that the penalties must be effective, proportionate and dissuasive.[459] No further guidance is offered as to what this might mean in practice and the possibility remains open for Member States to adopt widely different punitive regimes in relation to those causing damage to the water environment.

---

[450] See 5.4.3 above on this Directive.
[451] See 5.5.2 above on this Directive.
[452] See 17.7.1 and 17.7.8 below on this Directive.
[453] See 5.6.2 above on this Directive.
[454] See 5.6.3 above on this Directive.
[455] That is, environmental objectives established in Annex IX of the Water Framework Directive and pursuant to Art.16(7) and by Member States under Annex V for substances not on the priority list under Art.16(8) in respect of which Community standards have not been set.
[456] Art.22(4) Water Framework Directive. That is, environmental quality standards for the purposes of Art.2(7) and Article 10 of the Integrated Pollution Prevention and Control Directive, and on this Directive see 12.3.3 below.
[457] Art.22(6) Water Framework Directive.
[458] See also the discussion of penalties in relation to Community Directives at 4.18.1 above.
[459] Art.22 Water Framework Directive.

### 5.9.21 Implementation Schedule

Clearly, the phased implementation of the Water Framework Directive amounts to a long-term project and it is helpful to set out the main stages and deadlines that must be adhered to.

| | |
|---|---|
| *Entry into force*<br><br>(22 December 2000) | (This is the date of publication in the *Official Journal of the European Communities*); and repeal of Article 6 of the Dangerous Substances Directive in relation to limit values and quality objectives. |
| *Three years after entry into force*<br><br>(22 December 2003) | Member States are to bring into force the laws, regulations and administrative provisions to comply with the Directive. |
| *Three years and six months after entry into force*<br><br>(22 June 2004) | Member States are to provide the Commission with a list of competent authorities. |
| *Four years after entry into force*<br><br>(22 December 2004) | Analyses and reviews of characteristics of River Basin Districts are to be undertaken; and the Commission is to review the adopted list of priority substances. |
| *Five years after entry into force*<br><br>(22 December 2005) | Member States are to establish criteria for groundwater status (if there is no agreement at Community level). |
| *Six years after entry into force*<br><br>(22 December 2006) | Monitoring programmes for surface water status, groundwater status and protected areas must be operational; and Member States are to establish environmental quality standards for surface waters (if no agreement at Community level). |
| *Seven years after entry into force*<br><br>(22 December 2007) | Repeals of Drinking Water Abstraction Directive, Information Exchange Decision and Drinking Water Sampling Directive. |
| *Nine years after entry into force*<br><br>(22 December 2009) | Programmes of measures are to be established; and River Basin Management Plans are to be published. |

| *By 2010* | Cost-recovery requirements for water services must be met. |
| --- | --- |
| *12 years after entry into force* (22 December 2012) | The Commission is to report on implementation, at the latest. |
| *13 years after entry into force* (22 December 2013) | A first review of the initial analyses and reviews of characteristics of River Basin Districts is to be undertaken; requirements for the combined approach are to be met; and further repeals of existing legislation, namely the Freshwater Fish Waters Directive, the Shellfish Waters Directive, the Groundwater Directive and the Dangerous Substances Directive (except for Art.6, already repealed in 2000). |
| *15 years after entry into force* (22 December 2015) | Member States are to have taken actions with the aim of achieving good surface water status, good ecological potential, good groundwater status and requirements for protected areas; initial programmes of measures must be reviewed; and initial River Basin Management Plans are to be reviewed. |
| *19 years after entry into force* (22 December 2019) | The Commission is to review the Directive. |
| *21 years after entry into force* (22 December 2021) | Programmes of measures are to be operational. |

## 5.10 National Implications of the Water Framework Directive

Having considered the background to, and content of, the Water Framework Directive, key issues for water protection in England and Wales are the mechanisms for implementation and the impacts upon national practice.[460] Given the considerable duration over which complete implementation will take place, this involves a long-term evaluation of how existing national measures will need to be modified to give effect to the Directive. Unavoidably, this must be a rather speculative exercise

---

[460] Generally see House of Lords Select Committee on the European Communities *Community Water Policy* (1997) and Foster, Wood and Griffiths (2000).

given the rather broad formulation of some obligations arising under the Directive.[461] Nonetheless, in brief, the following seem to be the key issues to be addressed in the national response to the Directive.

### 5.10.1 Pollution and Good Status

The consciously anthropocentric formulation of the definition of 'pollution' used in the Directive has been noted. Also, it has been observed that national environmental legislation has tended to avoid extensive reliance upon the general idea of 'pollution' because of the uncertainties which surround the concept.[462] Fortunately, if remarkably, the definition of 'pollution' is of limited importance in that most of the obligations under the Directive are actually concerned to prevent specified kinds of discharges or emissions, or to require particular actions to be taken to achieve defined environmental quality objectives and standards. To a great extent, these obligations are formulated independently of the definition of 'pollution'. Hence, a tentative inference for national practice is that the concept of 'pollution' is likely to be of less importance than the substantial obligations to take various kinds of action that are needed to secure the implementation the Directive.

In respect of the overriding environmental quality objective of good status for surface waters, groundwater and protected areas, it will be necessary for all Member States to implement measures with the aim of achieving this status within the 15 year period allowed by the Directive. However, the aspirational nature of the objective, the exceptions to which it is subject and the absence of precise and binding standards for particular waters will make it more difficult to say with confidence when a Member State is in breach of this aspect of the Directive than with existing directives. Nonetheless, binding national legal mechanisms will need to be established to ensure that the actions needed to achieve good status are undertaken. A critical issue in this respect, however, will be the extent to which the United Kingdom seeks to apply the various exceptions and provisos to the good status requirement. For instance, the lesser requirement of achieving good ecological potential applied in relation to 'artificial and heavily modified' waters begs the question as to how these are to be designated and whether canal waters, for example, might be identified for this purpose.

Despite the national tradition of avoiding legislative stipulation of environmental quality objectives and standards,[463] the need for greater use of mandatory standards of this kind, for all waters within the scope of the Directive, seems unavoidable. Similarly, the programmes of measures and other actions needed to realise good status will need to be the subject of legal duties upon relevant bodies. In more practical terms, the issue is

---

[461] See also the discussion of 'progressive' implementation of Community water directives at 2.22 above.

[462] See the discussion of 'pollution' at 1.3.3 above.

[463] See 1.4.4 above on the national approach to environmental quality objectives and standards.

whether the existing facilities for the establishment of statutory water quality objectives, and corresponding obligations upon the Environment Agency to use its powers to realise these,[464] will be sufficient to transpose the obligations arising under the Directive. If so, further secondary legislation will be needed to encompass the full scope of the good status requirement. Also, it seems likely that further specification will be needed to detail the way in which powers of the Agency are to be used for the purpose of imposing programmes of measures and related matters.

### 5.10.2 Competent Authorities and River Basin Management

The requirement of the Directive that water protection should be organised on a river basin catchment basis should not be an especially problematic matter to encompass in national practice. Indeed, there is a longstanding national approach of regional water administration based upon the catchments of the major rivers.[465] In the present national context, the eight regional divisions of the Environment Agency covering England and Wales might, possibly, serve as River Basin Districts, though it is notable that these districts would be much smaller than those which are likely to be established in continental European Member States. Nonetheless, the present regional administrative basis upon which the Agency administers its water functions should serve as a useful starting point, though careful coordination will be needed between water and non-water functions to ensure full compliance with river basin catchment requirements. In addition, coordination would be required with competent authorities with responsibility for Scotland.[466]

The Directive obliges Member States to establish appropriate administrative arrangements, including the designation of competent authorities. In this respect, the Environment Agency appears to be the most likely body to serve as the competent authority for the national implementation of the Directive. Alongside the regulation of water quality, the extensive functions of the Agency,[467] including waste management and the regulation of industrial processes, mean that it will be best placed to adopt the integrated approach to environmental management which is needed. One consequence of this is that catchments may become the geographic basis for *all* the Agency's functions.

Indeed, the Agency has for several years been engaged in a process of establishing informal environmental management plans of various kinds which share many characteristics with the River Basin Management Plans required by the Directive. Most notable amongst these plans are Local Environment Agency Plans[468] (LEAPs) which are characterised as

---

[464] Under ss.82-84 Water Resources Act 1991, and see discussion of these at 14.8 below.

[465] See, in particular, the discussion of the Water Act 1973 at 2.14 above.

[466] Postscript: 11 basins (including one cross-border basin) have been proposed; see *ENDS Report* 315 (2001) p.47.

[467] Generally see Ch.6 below on the Environment Agency.

[468] See 14.9 below on Local Environment Agency Plans.

integrated local plans for identifying, assessing, prioritising and solving local environmental issues related to the Agency's functions. Significantly, LEAPs seek to establish water quality objectives for various lengths of rivers and indicate how environmental regulatory powers relating to both water and land will be used for the purpose of realising water quality objectives. LEAPs, and particularly, the emphasis which is placed upon consultation with the public in formulating such plans, are closely in accordance with the requirements for the content and formulation of River Basin Management Plans.

However, in certain respects LEAPs fall short of the requirements for River Basin Management Plans. LEAPs do not cover several matters which must be incorporated in Management Plans and lack the legal status which is needed for Management Plans. The essentially informal character of LEAPs is perhaps the key point of contrast, in that, in contrast to Management Plans, a failure to meet a commitment indicated in a LEAP has no direct legal consequences. Clearly, if LEAPs were to be developed to meet the requirements of the Directive this would need to be addressed.

There are other respects in which LEAPs would need to be developed to meet the requirements of the Directive. First, the analysis of the characteristics of each river basin district will require the application of a significantly new methodology involving the more precise classification of water types and this appears to raise some significant technical issues.

Second, the Directive requires a review of the impact of human activity upon surface and groundwaters which is much more extensive and detailed than is presently undertaken nationally, at least for the purposes of establishing LEAPs. The general obligation is to collect and maintain information on the type and magnitude of significant anthropogenic pressures upon waters may not be as great an innovation as it first appears, since much of this information is already held by the Environment Agency under diverse legislation concerned with water and environmental quality. Hence, the task is largely an administrative coordination exercise of bringing the relevant information together in a coherent form in accordance with the requirements of the Directive. However, there may be other elements, particularly aspects of land use, where liaison with local planning authorities and other bodies are likely to be required.

Third, the economic analysis of water use requires the collection of sufficient information to make calculations relating to cost-recovery pricing for water services. This is a substantial innovation in the national context. Although the Environment Agency has responsibilities for abstraction licensing from surface and groundwaters, and is possessed of information relating to the quantities of such abstractions, it does not have direct responsibilities for matters relating to water utility functions. These are the concern of water and sewerage undertakers, which are subject to economic regulation which determines the amounts that they may charge for water services.[469] Clearly, a new link will need to be forged between the abstraction data and the information concerning the cost of water services. Information which has previously been used for largely separate purposes will need to be brought together to provide economic analyses of water use and to make determinations of appropriate cost-recovery practice in relation to water services. Also notable is that the six year period allowed for recurrent reviews of the economic analysis of water use under the Directive contrasts with the five year period which has been used nationally for the periodic review of water services.[470]

Fourth, the need for a register of various kinds of protected area within a River Basin District seems a fairly straightforward requirement involving a listing of various matters including the location of Natura 2000 sites.[471] Nature conservation matters are the responsibility of English Nature and the Countryside Council for Wales and information relating to Special Protection Areas and Special Areas of Conservation could readily be provided. What is less clear is the extent to which nationally designated Sites of Special Scientific Interest[472] which are dependent upon water quality would also need to be registered. In principle, however, it would seem unproblematic for the nature conservation councils to provide the necessary information about these sites for inclusion in the register. Again the need for close co-ordination between the Environment Agency and the relevant nature conservation council will be important in collating this information.

Fifth, the register of protected areas requires the inclusion of waters designated for abstraction for drinking water, but further provisions require River Basin Management Plans to identify water for significant drinking water abstraction. Specific monitoring requirements are provided for in relation to waters which provide significant quantities of drinking water. Again, the provision of information as to which waters are abstracted for drinking water supply purposes should not be problematic, in that the necessary information may be gathered from information which is already collected for water supply abstraction licensing purposes. With regard to the monitoring requirements, the monitoring of water to be used for water supply purposes has been provided for under Community and national legislation for some years and monitoring requirements under the Water Framework Directive appear to follow existing requirements.

Sixth, the Directive requires the establishment of monitoring programmes to ensure a coherent and comprehensive overview of water status within each River Basin District. Commentary on the impact of the new requirements is difficult, given the technicality of what is involved. However, it is apparent that substantial national innovation is anticipated

---

[469] See Ch.7 below on the economic regulation of water and sewerage undertakers. There is some uncertainty whether the Environment Agency would become the competent authority in relation to economic analysis of water use, see *ENDS Report* 315 (2001) p.49.

[470] See 7.8 below on price regulation and water quality.

[471] See 15.8 on Natura 2000.

[472] See 15.7.1 below on Sites of Special Scientific Interest.

in relation to ecological monitoring requirements and similarly in relation to groundwater quality monitoring.

A final feature is the need for Member States to specify 'programmes of measures' in relation to each River Basin District, based upon the analyses of the District and in order to achieve the environmental objectives of the Directive. Hence, River Basin Management Plans are intended to secure an important strategic function in identifying the range of basic and supplementary measures that are needed to ensure good status is achieved. The national contrast, which has been previously noted, is that LEAPs do not have a formal status in determining what actions must be taken in relation to a particular catchment and serve only as an informal guide to the way in which the Environment Agency intends to use its powers and to bring a range of stakeholders together. Another national contrast which may be drawn is with the national use of statutory water quality objectives, which do have mandatory status but are not necessarily associated with particular catchment plans. Hence, there is a sense in which River Basin Management Plans will need to combine the role of LEAPs and statutory water quality objectives and introduce a stronger strategic water quality management dimension than presently exists by consolidating the two distinct national approaches.

### 5.10.3  Cost-Recovery Water Pricing

Another key innovation in the Water Framework Directive is the obligation upon Member States to take account of the principle of cost-recovery pricing for water services and environmental and resource costs, in accordance with the polluter pays principle. However, as has been noted, substantial derogations from this obligation are available, where these do not compromise the achievement of the objectives of the Directive. The key issue for the United Kingdom is whether a derogation of some kind is to be sought or, to the extent that it is not, what system of cost-recovery pricing is to be put in place.

As has been noted, the polluter pays principle,[473] reformulated here as the 'water service user pays principle', gives rise to a range of difficult issues in relation to the economic costing of environmental impacts. There seems to be a general view that making polluters pay is a good thing, but rather fundamental problems in identifying who the polluters are, what they should be paying for and how much they should be paying. Because of these difficulties, political endorsements of the use of economic instruments have not always been matched by progress in the formulation and application of such instruments in actual practice. The national approach to economic environmental instruments has been similarly ambivalent, in that the repeated Government support for such instruments has not been matched by corresponding levels of implementation in practice. A pertinent example is the recent Government proposal for economic instruments relating to effluent discharges to the aquatic

---

[473] See 4.7.3 above on the polluter pays principle.

environment[474] which was eventually abandoned by the Government when it became clear that this would not necessarily be a more cost-effective means of achieving improvements in water quality.[475]

A particular difficulty that the United Kingdom may face in implementing cost recovery pricing is that of determining which water consumers are to pay. Although industrial and agricultural water use is normally metered, the remarkable fact is that water supplied for domestic use is not normally metered, since domestic consumers usually pay a standard charge which does not necessarily reflect their actual consumption of water.[476] Potentially, this is a significant problem, since if there is no way of relating charges to actual use by an individual consumer it is difficult to see what incentive that consumer would have for reducing water use. Although metering is required in relation to new properties, and some consumers are taking up the *option* of having their water supply metered and paying according to actual use, the imposition of comprehensive compulsory metering is generally thought to be an extremely costly exercise. Hence, there is presently a difficulty in seeking to impose cost-recovery pricing for domestic use. Analogous points could be made about sewage treatment where, again, costs would have to be related to the amount and nature of the effluent produced and, presently, mechanisms do not exist to relate effluent produced to sewerage charges outside industrial sectors.

---

[474] See the discussion of DETR, *Economic Instruments for Water Pollution* (1997) at 1.7.9 above.
[475] On the Environment Agency's cost/benefit duty see 6.14 below, and see also the periodic review of water service charges at 7.8.3 below.
[476] Although metering of water supply is legally provided for under s.142 Water Industry Act 1991 (giving undertakers the power to charge for water), s.143 (allowing for the establishment of charging schemes), s.148 (which places the cost of installing meters upon the undertaker) and s.149 (allowing for regulations concerning meters). Under the Water Industry Act 1999, consumers may elect to be charged according to volume, while consumers who had previously paid according to rateable value can request to revert to paying on an unmeasured basis (s.144A Water Industry Act 1991). Consumers moving to new premises can be transferred to volume-based payment (s.144B).

# Chapter 6

# THE ENVIRONMENT AGENCY

## 6.1 Introduction

The deliberations leading up to the establishment of the Environment Agency for England and Wales under the Environment Act 1995 have been previously discussed.[1] This discussion noted that consolidation of pollution regulation authorities was needed to achieve greater integration of pollution control in relation to the environment *as a whole*, as contrasted with the previously sectoral approach to the different environmental media. Moreover, it was envisaged that establishing a unified environmental authority would make it easier for regulated bodies to have only one inspectorate to approach (the so-called 'one stop shopping' argument);[2] that this would avoid overlap or duplication of effort which might arise with separate regulatory authorities; and that combining authorities under one management would lead to greater consistency of approach across all pollution types and environmental media.[3]

Accordingly, the main purpose of Chapter I of Part I of the Environment Act 1995 was to consolidate, in a single environmental regulatory authority, the former functions of the National Rivers Authority (in relation to the water environment),[4] the functions previously discharged by Her Majesty's Inspectorate of Pollution (in relation to integrated pollution control),[5] certain functions which were previously the responsibilities of local authorities (in relation to waste management regulation)[6] and some environmental matters that were previously the responsibility of the Department of the Environment. The Environment Agency with

---

[1] See 2.16 and 2.19 above on the background to establishment of the Environment Agency.

[2] See 6.20 below on other regulatory authorities concerned with the aquatic environment.

[3] HM Government, *This Common Inheritance: Britain's Environmental Strategy* (Cm.1200, 1990) Ch.18.

[4] Primarily, under Water Resources Act 1991, and see 2.19 above on the National Rivers Authority.

[5] Primarily, under Part I Environmental Protection Act 1990, see 12.3 below on integrated pollution control.

[6] Primarily, under Part II Environmental Protection Act 1990, see 12.2 below on the regulation of waste management.

responsibility for England and Wales[7] assumed its functions under the 1995 Act on the 'transfer date' of 1 April 1996.[8]

Despite the fundamental administrative reforms that have been brought about under the Environment Act 1995, much of the substantive environmental law which is to be administered by the Agency[9] remains as provided for under previous legislation. In particular, the system of regulation relating to the protection of the aquatic environment, under Part III of the Water Resources Act 1991, remains substantially unchanged by the administrative reorganisation.[10] Perhaps most significantly, Part III of the 1991 Act continues to provide for the specification of water quality objectives, the principal offences in relation to the pollution of controlled waters and for powers to prevent pollution.[11]

The purpose of this chapter is to examine the constitution and functions of the Environment Agency, with particular attention to those matters which are of most relevance to water pollution and water quality. Many of the provisions that are discussed actually have application across the range of functions discharged by the Agency, but they serve to place in an institutional context the range of particular policies, powers and duties relating to water discussed later in the work. It is also convenient in this chapter to take account of general policy issues relating to the Agency, such as its approach towards law enforcement, and the extent to which it provides the 'one stop shop' for environmental regulation that was originally envisaged.

---

[7] In relation to Scotland, Part I of the Environment Act 1995 provides for establishment of the Scottish Environment Protection Agency. In this work, the 'Environment Agency' or the 'Agency' is used to refer to the Environment Agency *for England and Wales*. On coordination of working practice between the Agencies, see DETR and Scottish Executive, *Concordat between the Department of Environment, Transport and the Regions and the Scottish Executive* (1999) (republished [2000] *Journal of Environmental Law* 251).

[8] On the transfer date see Environment Act 1995 (Commencement Order No 5) 1996 (SI 1996 No. 186) and see 6.3 below on the transfer of functions to the Environment Agency. Generally, see House of Commons Environment Committee, *The Government's Proposals for an Environment Agency* (1992); House of Commons Environment Committee, *Environment Bill: Hearings of the Draft Environment Agencies Bill* (1994); Howarth (1992*); Carter and Lowe (1995); Jewell and Steele (1996); Howarth (1996); Gallagher (1996).

[9] Including those functions previously exercised by the National Rivers Authority (under s.2(1) Environment Act 1995) and functions with respect to pollution control (under s.5) and general provisions with respect to water (under s.6).

[10] Although some significant new powers concerning water pollution have been introduced under the Environment Act 1995, which provides for enforcement notices (ss.90A and 90B Water Resources Act 1991, added by Schedule 22 para.142 Environment Act 1995 and see 10.11.1 below) and additional powers in relation to anti-pollution works and operations (ss.161A to 161D Water Resources Act 1991, added by Schedule 22 para.162 Environment Act 1995 and see 13.2 below). Additionally, the 1995 Act provided the vehicle for the introduction of the new regime concerning contaminated land (see 13.7 below) and introduced new provisions concerning abandoned mines (see 9.17.3 below).

[11] See 9.3 below on the principal water pollution offences.

## 6.2  Ministerial Responsibilities for the Environment Agency

The Environment Agency is a non-departmental public body and, as such, its management is given a broad freedom to exercise its responsibilities within an explicit regulatory framework.[12] However, a fairly extensive range of powers and duties relating to the Agency were generally allocated to the responsible Ministers under the Environment Act 1995 and, more specifically in relation to water, under the Water Resources Act 1991. These powers and duties are legislative in some instances, allowing or requiring secondary regulations to be made, administrative, in providing for the appropriate Minister to determine appeals of various kinds, and executive in allowing the Minister to give directions or guidance of various kinds to the Agency. Not least important amongst these are the powers and duties to give general policy guidance to the Agency as to the exercise of its functions discussed later in this chapter.[13] Also of fundamental importance are the provisions for public funding of the Agency considered later in this chapter.[14] As originally allocated, these responsibilities were entrusted to 'the Secretary of State and the Minister'[15] or whichever of these was appropriate in particular contexts. In practice, the responsibilities fell to be exercised by the Secretary of State for the Environment, Transport and the Regions, or the Secretary of State for Wales in relation to Wales, and the Minister of Agriculture, Fisheries and Food. In the terminology adopted by the Agency, its 'principal sponsor' was the Department of the Environment, Transport and the Regions whilst it also had 'important policy links' with the Ministry of Agriculture, Fisheries and Food and the Welsh Office.

However, the constitutional situation with regard to Wales has been altered as a result of the Government of Wales Act 1998 which established the National Assembly for Wales as a body corporate exercising various functions on behalf of the Crown.[16] Amongst the areas in which legislative functions are transferred to the Assembly is that of the environment[17] where, as a result of the devolution of power which is provided for, secondary legislation will now be enacted by the Assembly. Primary legislation will remain the responsibility of the United Kingdom Parliament, though there may be instances of so-called 'Henry VIII' clauses which allow principal enactments to be commenced, varied or

---

[12] Environment Agency, *Annual Report and Accounts* 1998/99 (1999) p.5. The Agency is not to be regarded as the servant or agent of the Crown, or as enjoying any status, immunity or privilege of the Crown; or by virtue of any connection with the Crown, as exempt from any tax, duty, rate, levy or other charge, whether general or local; and the Agency's property is not to be regarded as property of or property held on behalf of the Crown (s.1(5) Environment Act 1995).

[13] Also see 6.7 below on ministerial guidance on sustainable development.

[14] See 6.6 below on funding.

[15] s.56(1) Environment Act 1995.

[16] s.1 Government of Wales Act 1998.

[17] s.22 and Schedule 2 Government of Wales Act 1998 and see Art.2 and Schedule 1 National Assembly for Wales (Transfer of Functions) Order 1999 (SI 1999 No. 672) which transfers functions under the Water Resources Act 1991 with certain exceptions. Generally, see Lee (1999). Also town and country planning matters come within the functions of the Assembly, see Bosworth and Shellens (1999).

revoked under secondary legislation. Also notable is the duty of the Assembly to enact secondary legislation to transpose European Community Directives into national law.[18] The overall effect of these provisions is a major transfer of responsibilities from the Secretary of State for Wales to the Assembly as a secondary water-regulatory body and a new sponsor of the Environment Agency.[19] Hence, insofar as 'Ministerial' powers are under consideration, in relation to the Agency, this is to be understood as a shorthand for the allocation of powers to the Assembly that has been outlined.

Whilst Ministerial powers and duties are discussed in this work primarily in relation to the range of particular contexts in which they arise, it is convenient here to note two features of general relevance, concerning Ministerial directions to the Agency and the Ministerial power to delegate functions and appeals. The first of these allows the appropriate Minster to give the Environment Agency directions of a general or specific character with respect to the carrying out of any of its functions. The appropriate Minister may also give the Agency directions of a general or specific character for the implementation of any obligations of the United Kingdom under the European Community Treaties[20] or any international agreement to which the United Kingdom is a party.[21] Any direction of this kind is to be published in an appropriate form for the purpose of bringing the matters to which it relates to the attention of persons likely to be affected by them. Any power to give a direction in accordance with these provisions is exercisable, except in an emergency, only after consultation with the Agency.[22] The effect of a Ministerial direction made in accordance with these provisions is to bind both the Agency and any body or person making a determination concerning its functions. Hence, in determining any appeal against, or review of, a decision of the Agency or any application transmitted from the Agency, the body making the determination is bound by any Ministerial direction to the same extent as the Agency.[23]

Previously, powers had existed for Ministerial directions to be given to the National Rivers Authority for general or specific purposes,[24] in the interests of national security or to mitigate a civil emergency[25] and for regulations to be made to modify water pollution provisions for the purpose of complying with European Community obligations or

---

[18] ss.29 and 106 Government of Wales Act 1998, and see 4.12 on European Community environmental legislation.

[19] s.147 Government of Wales Act 1998 allows the Environment Agency to report to the Assembly on the exercise of its Welsh functions and to be subject to the financial scrutiny of the Auditor General for Wales (provided for under ss.90-96).

[20] See Ch.4 on European Community obligations generally and see 14.8 for examples of specific directions given in relation to water quality.

[21] See Ch.18 on obligations arising under international law generally.

[22] s.40(1)-(3) and (6) Environment Act 1995.

[23] *Ibid* s.40(5) and (8). Further procedural requirements for the giving of directions are provided for in s.122.

[24] Under s.5 Water Resources Act 1991.

[25] Under *ibid* s.207.

international agreements.[26] Under the transitional provisions of the Environment Act 1995,[27] directions issued under these powers continue to apply to the Agency. A complete list of directions previously issued to the National Rivers Authority was provided in draft Ministerial guidance issued to the Agency.[28]

A second general matter concerning Ministerial powers is that the Environment Act 1995 anticipated the transfer of further functions to the Agency from Ministers, though without any explicit indication as to what functions are appropriate for this purpose. Initial candidates for transfer of control to the Agency were thought to be aspects of chemical control, technical guidance on waste and contaminated land, responsibilities for dumping at sea and radioactive discharges.[29] To accomplish such transfers, provision was made allowing agreements to be made between any Minister and the Environment Agency authorising the Agency, or any of its employees, to exercise on behalf of the Minister, with or without payment, any eligible function[30] of his. An agreement of this kind may not authorise the Agency to exercise a Ministerial power to make regulations, other instruments of a legislative character or a power to fix fees or charges. However, an agreement may provide for any eligible function to be exercisable, wholly or partly, by the Agency either generally or in such cases or areas as may be specified; or either unconditionally or subject to the fulfilment of specified conditions. Where anything is done, or omitted to be done, by the Agency in connection with the exercise or purported exercise of the function concerned it will be treated for all purposes as done by the appropriate Minister in his capacity as such.[31]

Alongside the transfer of functions to the Agency, a further power provided for under the Environment Act 1995 allows the Secretary of State to delegate his functions relating to the determining of certain appeals. Most pertinently, in relation to the protection of the aquatic environment, this relates to appeals which may be made concerning the following matters:

---

[26] Under s.102 Water Resources Act 1991.

[27] s.55 Environment Act 1995.

[28] Draft guidance, that is under s.4 Environment Act 1995. Amongst the items listed, the following are of particular relevance to the protection of the aquatic environment: National Rivers Authority (Bathing Water) Directions 1992 (of 5 May 1992, to give effect to the Bathing Water Directive (76/160/EEC) and Bathing Waters (Classification) Regulations 1991 (SI 1991 No. 1597), and see 5.5.2 below on this Directive); National Rivers Authority (Nitrate Pollution) (Council Directive 91/676/EEC) Directions 1992 (of 27 January 1992, to give effect to the Nitrates Directive (91/676/EEC), and see 5.6.3 below on this Directive); and Directions to the National Rivers Authority under s.5 Water Resources Act 1991 and relating to the Groundwater Directive (80/68/EEC) (and see 5.4.2 below on this Directive).

[29] See *ENDS Report* 238 (1994) p.20. In respect of the Agency's responsibility for contaminated land see 13.7 below and in respect of radioactive discharges see 20.10.1 below.

[30] 'Eligible function' for these purpose means any function of a Minister of the Crown which the Secretary of State, having regard to the functions conferred or imposed upon the Agency under or by virtue of the Environment Act 1995 or any other enactment, considers can be appropriately be exercised by the Agency (or any of its employees) on behalf of that Minister (s.38(10) Environment Act 1995).

[31] s.38(1) to (3) and (5) Environment Act 1995.

(a)   consents concerned with the control of pollution including discharge consents;[32]
(b)   requirements to take precautions against pollution;[33]
(c)   regulations in respect of water protection zones and nitrate sensitive areas;[34]
(d)   against works notices;[35]
(e)   against enforcement notices;[36] or
(f)   exclusion from registers of certain confidential information.[37]

In relation to these, the Secretary of State may appoint any person to exercise on his behalf, with or without payment, any of the specified functions, or refer any specified item to such person as may be appointed for the purpose.[38]

### 6.3  The Transfer of Functions to the Environment Agency

The Environment Act 1995 commences with the pronouncement that there shall be a body corporate to be known as the Environment Agency or, in Welsh, *Asiantaeth yr Amgylchedd,* for the purpose of carrying out the functions transferred or assigned to it by or under the Act.[39] On the transfer date[40] the following functions were transferred to the Agency:

(a)   the former functions of the National Rivers Authority, that is,
    (i)   its functions concerning water resources management;[41]
    (ii)   its functions concerning control of pollution of water resources;[42]
    (iii)   its functions concerning flood defence and land drainage;[43]
    (iv)   its functions concerning land and works powers;[44]
    (v)   its functions relating to fisheries;[45]

---

[32] Under s.91 Water Resources Act 1991, and in relation to appeals under Chapter II of Part III. See 10.9 below on the delegation of this function to the Planning Inspectorate.

[33] Under s.92 Water Resources Act 1991, see 13.3 below on precautionary regulations.

[34] Under *ibid* s.96, and see 13.4 below on water protection zones and 13.5 below on nitrate sensitive areas.

[35] Under *ibid* s.161C, see 13.2.2 below on works notices.

[36] Under *ibid* s.90B, and see 10.11.1 below on enforcement notices.

[37] Under *ibid* s.191B(5), see 16.15 below on information registers.

[38] s.114(1), (2) and (4) and Schedule 20 Environment Act 1995.

[39] *Ibid* s.1(1).

[40] *Ibid* s.56(1) provides that 'the transfer date' means such date as the Secretary of State may by order made by statutory instrument appoint for the purposes of Part I of the Act. See Environment Act 1995 (Commencement Order No 5) 1996 (SI 1996 No. 186) providing for 1 April 1996 as the transfer date for these purposes.

[41] Under or by virtue of Part II Water Resources Act 1991.

[42] Under or by virtue of Part III Water Resources Act 1991.

[43] Under or by virtue of Part IV Water Resources Act 1991, Land Drainage Act 1991, and the functions transferred to the National Rivers Authority by virtue of s.136(8) Water Act 1989 and para.1(3) of Schedule 15 to that Act.

[44] Under or by virtue of Part VII Water Resources Act 1991.

[45] Under or by virtue of Diseases of Fish Act 1937, Sea Fisheries Regulation Act 1966, Salmon and Freshwater Fisheries Act 1975, Part V Water Resources Act 1991 or any other enactment.

(vi)   its functions as a navigation authority, harbour authority or conservancy authority;[46]

(vii)  its functions under Schedule 2 to the Water Resources Act 1991;[47]

(viii) functions assigned to the National Rivers Authority by or under any other enactment, apart from the Environment Act 1995;[48]

(b)   the functions of waste regulation authorities, that is, functions conferred or imposed on them by or under,

    (i)   the Control of Pollution (Amendment) Act 1989, or

    (ii)  Part II of the Environmental Protection Act 1990,

    or assigned to them by or under any enactment apart from the Environment Act 1995;

(c)   the functions of disposal authorities under or by virtue of the waste regulation provisions of the Control of Pollution Act 1974;

(d)   the functions of the Chief Inspector for England and Wales,[49] that is, the functions conferred or imposed on him in relation to integrated pollution control;[50]

(e)   the functions of the Chief Inspector for England and Wales[51] in relation to radioactive substances;[52]

(f)   the functions conferred or imposed on the chief, or any other, inspector by or under the Alkali, &c, Works Regulation Act 1906 so far as these are exercisable in relation to England and Wales;

(g)   the functions of inspectors[53] in relation to improvement notices and prohibition notices under Part I of the Health and Safety at Work etc. Act 1974, so far as they are exercisable in relation to England and Wales;

(h)   specified functions of the Secretary of State.[54]

The functions of the Secretary of State under (h) above are the following:

---

[46] Transferred to the National Rivers Authority by Chapter V of Part III Water Act 1989 or para.23(3) of Schedule 13 to that Act or which were transferred to the Authority by any order or agreement under Schedule 2 Water Resources Act 1991.

[47] Schedule 2 Water Resources Act 1991 is concerned with orders and agreements for transfer of navigation, harbour and conservancy functions.

[48] It is not entirely clear what 'functions' this encompasses, but it may be a reference to the powers to act as a statutory consultee for various purposes including in relation to planning applications under town and country planning legislation. On planning law generally see 14.5 below.

[49] Under s.16(3) Environmental Protection Act 1990.

[50] That is, functions conferred by or under Part I Environmental Protection Act 1990 or assigned to him by or under any other enactment, apart from Environment Act 1995. On integrated pollution control see 12.3 below.

[51] Appointed under s.4(2)(a) Radioactive Substances Act 1993.

[52] That is, the functions conferred or imposed on him by or under Radioactive Substances Act 1993 or assigned to him by or under any other enactment, apart from Environment Act 1995.

[53] Appointed under s.19 Health and Safety at Work etc. Act 1974 by the Secretary of State in his capacity as the enforcing authority responsible in relation to England and Wales for the enforcement of Alkali, &c, Works Regulation Act 1906 and s.5 of the 1974 Act.

[54] s.2(1) Environment Act 1995.

(a)   his functions concerning the power to dispose of radioactive waste, so far as they are exercisable in relation to England and Wales;[55]

(b)   his functions in relation to special category effluent;[56]

(c)   the functions conferred or imposed on him by virtue of his being the authority which is made responsible for the enforcement of the Alkali, &c, Works Regulation Act 1906 and s.5 of the Health and Safety at Work etc. Act 1974, so far as these are exercisable in relation to England and Wales;

(d)   his functions concerning registration of works, so far as these are exercisable in relation to England and Wales;[57]

(e)   his functions under the Sludge (Use in Agriculture) Regulations 1989[58] relating to the provision of information and the testing of soil, so far as these are exercisable in relation to England and Wales;[59]

A notable omission from the list of functions transferred to the Agency is any mention of its role in relation to town and country planning. As will be seen,[60] the Agency is identified as a statutory consultee in relation to various categories of planning application and in relation to the formulation of development plans and these roles are of particular practical importance in anticipating and opposing developments which are capable of being detrimental to the aquatic environment. However, under planning law the Agency is provided with powers, rather than duties, to act in consultation processes. There is, therefore, some ambiguity as to whether this collection of powers is properly categorised as an Agency 'function' or not. Another notable feature is the absence of any mention of the status of the Agency as a competent authority for the purposes of relevant European Community directives. Whilst, as will be seen, the Agency fulfils an important role as the responsible national authority in relation to a number of environmental and water-related directives, its designation as such is not explicitly recognised under the 1995 Act.

A cumulative consequence of the allocation of functions to the Agency was that, from the transfer date, the National Rivers Authority and the London Waste Regulation Authority were abolished.[61] Provision for continuity of exercise of functions of the Agency was made so that the abolition of the National Rivers Authority or the London Waste Regulation Authority, as transferors of functions, did not affect the validity of anything done by these Authorities before the transfer date. Similarly,

---

[55] Under s.30(1) Radioactive Substances Act 1993.

[56] Under Chapter III of Part IV Water Industry Act 1991 other than any function of making regulations or of making orders under s.139 of that Act. See 11.10 below on 'special category effluent'.

[57] Under, or under regulations made by virtue, of s.9 Alkali, &c, Works Regulation Act 1906, other than any functions of his as an appellate authority or any function of making regulations.

[58] See 5.6.1 below on these Regulations.

[59] Specifically, regs.7(1) and 8(2) of and para.2(2)(c) of Schedule 2 to the Sludge (Use in Agriculture) Regulations 1989 (SI 1989 No. 1263).

[60] See 14.5 below on town and country planning.

[61] s.2(3) Environment Act 1995.

anything which, at the transfer date, was in the process of being done in connection with any of the transferred functions could be continued by the Agency. Anything done by a transferor before the transfer date, in the exercise of any of the transferred functions, was to have effect as if done by or in relation to the Agency. More specifically, the transfer provisions are stated to apply in relation to any of the following matters:

(a) any decision, determination, declaration, designation, agreement or instrument made by a transferor;
(b) any regulations or byelaws made by a transferor;
(c) any licence, permission, consent, approval, authorisation, exemption, dispensation or relaxation granted by or to a transferor;
(d) any notice, direction or certificate given by or to a transferor;
(e) any application, request, proposal or objection made by or to a transferor;
(f) any condition or requirement imposed by or on a transferor;
(g) any fee or charge paid by or to a transferor;
(h) any appeal allowed by or in favour of or against a transferor;
(i) any proceedings instituted by or against a transferor.[62]

The above provisions, relating to continuity in the exercise of functions, are stated to be without prejudice to any provision made in the Environment Act 1995 in relation to any particular functions. The Secretary of State may, in relation to any particular functions, exclude, modify or supplement any of the continuity provisions or make such other transitional provisions as he thinks necessary or expedient.[63]

The counterpart of the transfer of functions to the Environment Agency was the transfer of specified property, rights and liabilities to the Agency. Accordingly, from the transfer date the property, rights and liabilities of the National Rivers Authority, and the London Waste Regulation Authority, were transferred to and vested in the Agency. In addition, any property, rights or liabilities which are the subject of a scheme, made for the purpose of transferring property, rights and liabilities by the Secretary of State, or a scheme by a waste regulation authority and approved by the Secretary of State, were transferred to and vested in the Agency by and in accordance with the scheme.[64] For the purposes of transferring property, rights and liabilities to the Agency, the Secretary of State was empowered, before the transfer date, to make a scheme or the transfer to the Agency of such of his property, rights and liabilities, or those of any of the inspectors

---

[62] Environment Act 1995 s.55(1) to (5). Any reference in these provisions to anything done by or in relation to a transferor includes a reference to anything which, by virtue of any enactment, is treated as having been done by or in relation to that transferor. Any reference to a transferor in any document constituting or relating to anything to which the provisions apply is, so far as is required for giving effect to those provisions, to be construed as a reference to the Agency (s.55(5) and (6)).
[63] *Ibid* s.55(7). Similar provision is made in relation to the Minister of Agriculture, Fisheries and Food (under s.55(8)) and, in either case, the power to make an order is to be exercisable by statutory instrument subject to annulment pursuant to a resolution of either House of Parliament (under s.55(9)).
[64] *Ibid* s.3.

or chief inspectors under the Environmental Protection Act 1990 and other legislation[65] as appeared appropriate to be transferred in consequence of the transfer of functions to the Agency.[66]

## 6.4 Organisation and Staffing of the Environment Agency

Whilst it is commonplace to associate the 'Agency' with the large number of employees that constitute its workforce, in legal terms its identity is more narrowly defined as being the members of its Board. Hence, the Agency is statutorily defined as a corporate legal body consisting of not less than eight nor more than fifteen members appointed by the relevant Ministers. Three members of the Agency are appointed by the Minister and the others are appointed by the Secretary of State.[67] In appointing Board members, regard is to be had to the desirability of appointing a person who has experience of, and has shown capacity in, some matter relevant to the functions of the Agency.[68]

In general terms, the Agency's Board has responsibility for approving the Agency's Corporate Plan, budget and Annual Report and Accounts. It has also given particular attention to supporting and advising on the development of a strategic approach to the environment and recently gave detailed consideration to the themes encompassed in the Agency's *Environmental Strategy for the Millennium and Beyond*[69] in advising on the general direction that the strategy should follow over the following two decades. Operationally, the role of the Board is necessarily limited, but it does take direct responsibility for determining major applications for consents or licences which have national significance or which are seriously controversial such as high-profile applications for authorisations relating to nuclear processing and related matters.[70] In the past, the openness with which the Board conducted its deliberations was a matter of

---

[65] As indicated in s.2(1) Environment Act 1995.

[66] See *ibid* s.3(2) and on the transfer of functions of the inspectors or chief inspector see s.2(1)(d) to (h).

[67] That is the Minister of Agriculture, Fisheries and Food and the Secretary of State for the Environment. Under Art.2 and Sch.1 National Assembly for Wales (Transfer of Functions) Order 1999 (SI 1999 No.672), with specified exceptions, all functions of a Minister of the Crown under Environment Act 1995 are, so far as exercisable in relation to Wales, transferred to the Assembly. However, this only encompasses s.1(2)(b) Environment Act 1995, concerning appointments to the Agency previously made by the Secretary of State, where his function is transferred to the Assembly to the extent that it may make such appointments as will ensure that there is at all times one member of the Agency appointed by the Assembly.

[68] s.1(4) Environment Act 1995. More detailed provisions concerning the composition, constitution and procedures of the Agency are provided for under Sch.1 to the 1995 Act which provides for matters such as membership, remuneration, staffing, proceedings, members' interests, minutes and the service of documents by or on the Agency. Details of the present membership of the Board of the Agency may be found on the Agency's websites, www.environment-agency.gov.uk and www.environment-agency.wales.gov.uk.

[69] Environment Agency, *Environmental Strategy for the Millennium and Beyond* (1997). Postscript: now see Environment Agency, *An Environmental Vision: the Environment Agency's Contribution to Sustainable Development* (2001).

[70] Under the Radioactive Substances Act 1993, and see 20.10.12 below for an illustration.

some criticism.[71] However, from October 1999, Board meetings were made open to the public and public access allowed to non-confidential Board papers.[72]

A range of Agency advisory committees are provided for under Part I of the Environment Act 1995. These include an Advisory Committee for Wales, regional and local fisheries advisory committees, regional flood defence committees, and local flood defence committees.[73] However, of greatest relevance to the pollution control functions of the Agency are the eight Regional Environment Protection Advisory Committees (REPACs) which the Agency is bound to consult, and to consider representations from, concerning the carrying out of its functions.[74] Regional committees consist of a chairman appointed by the Secretary of State, and such other members as the Agency may appoint in accordance with the provisions of the approved membership scheme[75] for that region. The other members of the committee must not be members of the Agency, but must be persons who appear to the Agency to have a significant interest in matters likely to be affected by the manner in which the Agency carries out any of its functions in the region of the advisory committee.[76]

When the Environment Agency came into formal existence, on 1 April 1996, it comprised 9,450 staff from some 85 different predecessor bodies possessing a range of functions relating to protection of the aquatic environment, the regulation of industrial processes and the regulation of waste management. Not least problematic was the fact that the predecessor bodies had divided the administration of their activities according to different geographical areas which needed to be harmonised.[77] Necessarily, this required a substantial reorganisation in respect of the geographical scope of activities and the need to harmonise and integrate procedures between bodies which had been previously possessed of significantly different working practices and regulatory culture.[78] In some respects, this process of assimilation of operational practice is still continuing.[79]

The present total Agency staff consists of 9,596 persons, though it is anticipated that, due to the significant additions to the workload, the total

---

[71] See ENDS Report 284 (1998) p.22.

[72] Environment Agency, Annual Report and Accounts 1998/99 (1999) p.12–14.

[73] Under ss.11 and 13 to 19 Environment Act 1995. On sea fisheries committees see 15.2.3 below.

[74] *Ibid* s.12(1). Formerly, provision for regional rivers advisory committees was made under s.7 Water Resources Act 1991. By contrast, REPACs will advise the Agency on all its functions.

[75] 'Approved membership scheme' means a scheme, as in force for the time being, prepared by the Agency and approved, with or without modification, by the Secretary of State under Sch.3 Environment Act 1995 which makes provision with respect to the membership of the advisory committee for a region (s.12(9)).

[76] *Ibid* s.12(2) to (4). For the present composition of regional advisory committees see Environment Agency, *Corporate Plan 2000/01* (1999) p.149.

[77] See DoE, *Options for the Geographical and Managerial Structure of the Proposed Environment Agency* (1994) (The 'Touche Ross' Report).

[78] See ENDS Report 247 (1995) p.3.

[79] See DETR, *Review of Legislation Relating to Integration within the Environment Agency and the Scottish Environment Protection Agency* (1999).

will stabilise at around 10,400 over the next three years. Of the present total, 5,569 are devoted to water management generally, though the majority of these are concerned with flood defence. About 19% (1,836) of the total staff are specifically occupied with the Agency's water quality function, though it is fair to note that other categories of staff are likely to be involved in matters that have important implications for the protection of the aquatic environment such as conservation work and other areas of environmental quality control which indirectly impact upon water quality.[80]

Presently, the Agency has its head office at Bristol and has eight regional centres and 26 area offices, with the regional centres covering areas broadly corresponding to those which were the administered by the former National Rivers Authority and before then the regional water authorities: Anglian, Midlands, North East, North West, Southern, South West, Thames and Wales.[81]

## 6.5 Themes and Strategy

A formidable initial task for the Agency's Board has been that of consolidating a range of distinct functions into a coherent vision of its overarching role. In this respect a recent report of the House of Commons Select Committee on the Environment, Transport and the Regions has been critical of progress, in reporting widespread uncertainty and confusion about the overall aim and priorities of the Agency and suggestions that policies of different sections of the Agency actually conflict with each other. It was concluded that the Agency appears still to lack a 'cogent ethos and strategy' and that this affects both its management and staff in the performance of its functions, and also the way that it is perceived by regulated industries and the general public. The appropriate response to this, it was suggested, was for the Agency Board, as an overriding priority, to produce a new environmental strategy which provides a clear vision of its role and the contribution of its different functions towards that role, and to ensure the widespread dissemination of this information.[82]

The Environment Act 1995 conceived of the Environment Agency as a body that would have a wide range of powers and duties extending across the environmental media allowing it to take an integrated approach to the protection of environmental quality in relation to water, air and land. The paradox within this is that the wider the range of functions and activities undertaken by the Agency the more difficult it is to secure an integrated approach. Recognising a number of 'reasonably discrete areas of work', the Agency has adopted a 'thematic' approach towards its overall

[80] Environment Agency, *Corporate Plan 2000/01* (1999) p.67.

[81] Although previously there had been ten areas relating to the catchments of major rivers, these were reduced to eight by the consolidation of the former Northumbria and Yorkshire regions into the North East region and the consolidation of the former Wessex and South West regions into the South West Region.

[82] House of Commons, Environment, Transport and Regional Affairs Committee, *The Environment Agency* (2000) paras.14 to 18.

responsibilities for the environment. Hence, the following nine 'themes' have been identified:

(a) addressing climate change,
(b) regulating major industries,
(c) improving air quality,
(d) managing waste,
(e) managing water resources,
(f) delivering integrated river-basin management,
(g) conserving land,
(g) managing freshwater fisheries, and
(h) enhancing biodiversity.[83]

The functional division of operations in this manner does not seem to reflect the legally defined functions of the Agency or the headings under which its income and expenditure is recorded, but is seen by the Agency as conducive to a more integrated approach than tackling environmental problems in a piecemeal fashion and a better means of realising overall environmental objectives.

The thematic approach has been used as a basis for the formulation of a series of action plans for the different areas of activity concerned, including the formulation of an action plan specifically for water quality which sets out various aims and objectives pursuant to the achievement of a continuing and overall improvement in the quality of waters through the prevention and control of pollution.[84] The specification of objectives for environmental improvement has been further developed by the formulation of 'performance indicators' for different areas of Agency activity. Hence present performance targets relevant to water quality include the objectives that:

(a) by 2002, net class upgrades in water quality will be achieved in respect of 800km of rivers and, by 2005, compliance with river water quality objectives will be greater than 90%;
(b) by the end of 2005, bathing water quality will be improved so that at least 97% compliance with relevant quality standards is achieved consistently and significant improvements towards guideline standards are realised at major holiday resorts; and
(c) by 2005, a 25% reduction in the number of substantiated water pollution incidents will be achieved compared with a 1997 baseline.[85]

The performance targets so specified are reasonably precise and measurable, so that it should be clear whether they have been met by the stated deadlines. This is greatly preferable to vaguely worded objectives which allow different interpretations as to whether they have been realised

---

[83] See Environment Agency, *Annual Report and Accounts 1998/99* (1999) p.22 and Environment Agency, *An Environmental Strategy for the Millennium and Beyond* (1997).
[84] See Environment Agency, *An Action Plan for Water Quality* (1998).
[85] Environment Agency, *Corporate Plan 2000/01* (1999) p.40.

or not, but equally provides a 'hostage to fortune' should the Agency fail to meet the goals that it has set itself. The failures of the Agency to meet previous performance targets have been the subject of critical commentary and it has been alleged that the Agency has been evasive in reporting areas of poor performance.[86]

### 6.6 Financial Provisions

The formal provisions relating to funding of the Environment Agency allow the appropriate Ministers, after consultation with the Agency and with approval of the Treasury, to determine the financial duties of the Agency.[87] Hence, the appropriate Minister may, with Treasury approval, provide the Agency with grants of such amounts, and on such terms, as thought fit.[88] In addition, the Agency will be entitled to borrow in accordance with specified borrowing powers.[89]

The Agency is bound to keep proper accounts and records and to prepare, in respect of each accounting year, a statement of accounts giving a true and fair view of the income and expenditure of the Agency. The statements of accounts are to comply with any requirement which the appropriate Ministers have, with the consent of the Treasury, notified to the Agency.[90] A copy of the accounts and the report on those accounts by the auditor are to be sent to the appropriate Ministers as soon as reasonably practicable. The Secretary of State must lay a copy of the accounts and the report before each House of Parliament. The Comptroller and Auditor General is entitled to inspect the contents of all accounts and accounting records of the Agency and may report to the House of Commons the results of any inspection carried out.[91]

The Agency's *Annual Report and Accounts 1998/99,* covering the financial year to 31 March 1999, indicates an operating budget of £594 million with an actual expenditure of just over £600 million. Of this, 44% was spent on flood defence (£261.8 million), 32% on the prevention and control of pollution (£193.9 million), 22% on the Agency's other water management functions (£132.6 million), with the remaining 2% expenditure on 'other items'.

The Agency derives its income from three main sources: income raised from charging schemes (37%),[92] levies raised on local authorities to fund flood defence activities (37.5%) and Government grants (25.5%). That part of Agency expenditure financed by Government grant totalled £157.3

---

[86] See *ENDS Report* 284 (1998) p.22 and *ENDS Report* 295 (1999) p.6.

[87] Subject to special duties with respect to flood defence revenue, as provided for under s.118 Water Resources Act 1991.

[88] s.47 Environment Act 1995.

[89] See ss.48–50 Environment Act 1995.

[90] See the *Direction on the annual accounts*, Environment Agency, *Annual Report and Accounts 1998/99* (1999) p.140.

[91] ss.45–46 Environment Act 1995.

[92] See, for example, the scheme of charges relating to discharge consents discussed at 10.7 below.

million, with £102 million being provided by grant-in-aid from the Department of the Environment, Transport and the Regions, and £41 million of this being specifically related to water quality matters. However, it is anticipated that a significant proportion of the income presently provided by the Department and the Ministry of Agriculture, Fisheries and Food will, in future, be provided by the Welsh Assembly.[93] In respect of environmental protection activities, including water quality protection, total income amounted to £193.9 million, consisting of £116.4 million operating receipts, generated from charges and licence fees, and £77.5 million from grants and contributions.

## 6.7 The Principal Aim and Objectives

A significant innovation[94] in the legislation establishing the Environment Agency is the inclusion of a statement of the principal aim of the Agency concerning the contribution that it is to make towards achieving 'sustainable development'.[95] The background to this lies in the broader international context in which the concept of sustainable development has developed into a central norm of environmental law and which is discussed elsewhere in this work and the need for specific legal powers to be exercised strategically.[96]

At a national level, the United Kingdom Government initially published a substantial White Paper, *Sustainable Development: the UK Strategy*,[97] by way of a response to the undertakings in the *Rio Declaration*, and much important discussion has taken place as to the methodology by which sustainable development is to be achieved.[98] More recently, the commitment to realising sustainable development has been reaffirmed in a revised strategy for sustainable development, *A Better Quality of Life: A Strategy for Sustainable Development for the UK*, which identifies national priorities for effective protection of the environment and prudent use of natural resources alongside a range of social and economic objectives which might not have been perceived to have an environmental dimension.[99]

---

[93] Environment Agency, *Corporate Plan 2000/01* (1999) p.63.

[94] Although an example of a precursor of this is to be found in the duty imposed upon Scottish Natural Heritage, under s.1(1) Natural Heritage (Scotland) Act 1991, which requires it to have regard to the desirability of ensuring that anything done in relation to natural heritage 'is undertaken in a manner which is sustainable', however, no further legislative indication was given as to the meaning of 'sustainable' in this context.

[95] For further discussion of sustainable development, in relation to European Community environmental policy, see 4.4.1 above.

[96] On the international background to sustainable development see 18.5.3 below.

[97] HM Government, *Sustainable Development: the UK Strategy* (Cm.2426, 1994).

[98] Generally see House of Lords, *Report from the Select Committee on Sustainable Development* (1995); HM Government, *Government Response to the Lords Select Committee Report on Sustainable Development* (Cm.3018, 1995); and British Government Panel on Sustainable Development, *First Report* (1995) and *Second Report* (1996).

[99] HM Government, *A Better Quality of Life: A Strategy for Sustainable Development for the UK* (Cm.4345, 1999).

Despite the widespread endorsement of sustainable development as an overall environmental goal, however, it is not a concept which admits any precise and generally accepted definition of a kind that is readily incorporated into an Act of Parliament. Perhaps because of this difficulty, the duty of the Environment Agency with regard to sustainable development is curiously provided for under the Environment Act 1995. The principal aim of the Agency, in accordance with the provisions of the 1995 Act or other enactments, and taking into account any likely costs and benefits,[100] in discharging its functions to protect or enhance the environment,[101] taken as a whole,[102] is to make the contribution towards attaining the objective of achieving sustainable development mentioned in Ministerial guidance. For that purpose the Ministers[103] must, from time to time, give guidance to the Agency with respect to objectives which they consider it appropriate for the Agency to pursue in the discharge of its functions.[104] The guidance which is given for these purposes must include guidance with respect to the contribution which, having regard to the Agency's responsibilities and resources, the Ministers consider it appropriate for the Agency to make, by the discharge of its functions, towards attaining the objective of achieving sustainable development. In discharging its functions, the Agency is bound to have regard to guidance given for these purposes.[105]

From the above, it is apparent that the duty upon the Agency with regard to sustainable development is provided for by a rather circuitous mechanism. Rather than simply requiring that the Agency use its powers and duties in the manner most conducive to the achievement of sustainable development, the Agency is to make the contribution towards attaining the objective of achieving sustainable development which the Ministers consider it appropriate for the Agency to make. In essence, it is for the Government, rather than the Agency, to decide what contribution is to be made, thereby emphasising the inherently political element in the contribution towards sustainable development. Moreover, the qualifications upon the Agency's duty with regard to sustainable development, stipulate that it is to be subject to other legislative provisions, to be required only within the scope of discharging its

---

[100] See 6.14 below on assessment of costs and benefits.

[101] 'The environment', for these purposes, is defined as 'all or any of the following media: land, water and air' (s.56(1) Environment Act 1995, and similarly see s.1(2) Environmental Protection Act 1990). Significantly, however, this does not encompass human beings or other living organisms that are dependent upon the environmental media. A consequence of this formulation seems to be that the notion of 'cost' for these purposes would appear to discount any costs to the non-human living constituents of the environmental media.

[102] See the discussion of 'best practicable environmental option' at 12.3.2 below.

[103] 'The Ministers' means the Secretary of State and the Minister of Agriculture, Fisheries and Food (s.56(1) Environment Act 1995) and see the discussion of the Welsh National Assembly at 6.2 above.

[104] See discussion below on ministerial guidance and 6.2 above on ministerial responsibilities generally.

[105] s.4(1) to (4) Environment Act 1995.

functions[106] and only where likely costs and benefits are taken into account.[107]

Guidance to the Agency in relation to sustainable development has been provided for in a memorandum issued by the relevant departments, *The Environment Agency and Sustainable Development*.[108] This states that the Ministers consider it appropriate, as a contribution to the objective of attaining sustainable development, and having regard to its responsibilities, for the Agency to act in accordance with the following principles.

(i)   The Agency needs to *take a holistic approach to the protection and enhancement of the environment*. It should therefore strive through its actions to optimise benefit to the environment as a whole, taking proper account of likely costs and benefits.[109] Where practicable and permissible, it should carry out its various functions – whether relating to the environmental media of air, land or water – so as to take account of the impacts of pollutants from different sources across the different media or within any medium, and the interactions of pollutants from different sources.

(ii)  Because it needs to take a *long term perspective* in considering sustainable development the Agency should seek to take properly into account any longer term implications and effects, particularly those which appear likely to be irreversible, reversible only at high cost over a long timescale or which would raise issue of inter-generational equity.

(iii) Conserving and where practicable enhancing *biodiversity* and protecting the natural heritage is an essential element of sustainable development.[110]

(iv)  In protecting *the global atmosphere*, the Agency should have regard to the Government's commitments under the UN Framework Convention on Climate Change on reducing emissions of greenhouse gases, and under the Montreal Protocol on limiting the use of ozone depleting substances.

(v)   In the areas for which the Agency is responsible there will be considerable scope for reconciling the needs of the environment and those of development by regulated organisations adopting *improved technologies and management techniques* as an integral part of their industrial and commercial investment. The Agency should therefore where possible discharge its regulatory functions

---

[106] See 6.3 above on the functions of the Agency.

[107] 'Costs', for these purposes, is defined to include the likely costs to any person and to the environment (s.56(1) Environment Act 1995). Contrast the duty to have regard to 'likely costs and benefits' (under s.39 and discussed in 6.14 below) which would not be applicable to the pursuit of the principal aim of sustainable development (under s.39(2)).

[108] DoE, MAFF and WO (1996). This should be read alongside DoE, MAFF and WO, *The Environment Agency Management Statement* (1996) and more generally, on sustainable development, HM Government, *Sustainable Development – The UK Strategy* (Cm.2426, 1994) and HM Government, *A Better Quality of Life: A Strategy for Sustainable Development for the UK* (Cm.4345, 1999).

[109] On the Agency's costs and benefits duty see 6.14 below.

[110] See Ch.15 below on biodiversity conservation.

in *partnership with regulated organisations* in ways which maximise the scope for cost-effective investment in such technologies and techniques.

(vi) Achieving sustainable development will involve contributions from many different groups in society – such as local communities working towards Local Agenda 21. How the Agency carries out its functions will affect there wider developments. So it should strive to develop a *close and responsive relationship* with the public, local authorities and other representatives of local communities, regulated organisations and public bodies with environmental responsibilities.

(vii) *High quality information[111] and advice* on the environment is an important element in taking forward strategies for sustainable development.

Alongside the guidance which has been provided for the Agency in relation to sustainable development an 'Explanatory Document' is appended which provides further informal guidance in relation to particular functions of the Agency for the purpose of setting out the Government's main policy objectives. Although this emphasises that the creation of the Agency provides the opportunity for more coherent and integrated protection and enhancement of the environment taken as a whole, specific observations are offered on different functions of the Agency including water protection.

The Government's policy objective for water protection is where possible to prevent deterioration in water quality and to seek to secure improvements in accordance with agreed priorities which reflect the requirements of Community legislation. As regards groundwater, management and protection should aim to prevent pollution of water resources reflecting the requirements of Community legislation. These priorities must acknowledge that society's resources are not unlimited and that choices must be made between environmental and other objectives and between different environmental objectives. This policy objective promotes sustainable development by aiming for high standards of health and environmental protection whilst focusing measures and expenditure where action is most necessary (for example in relation to toxic, persistent and bioaccumulative substances) and the efforts are justified and cost-effective reflecting proper protection of health and safety, the environment, the water consumer and other interest such as agriculture and industry. When carrying out its water protection functions (in conjunction with other powers and duties as necessary) the Agency should seek to fulfil this objective.[112]

---

[111] See 16.14–15 below on provision of information by the Agency.
[112] *Ibid* Ch.6 and 'Guidance material on particular functions' para.6.23.

Despite the guidance on the meaning of sustainable development in relation to the Agency's water protection function and the exercise of its functions generally, the position remains that the concept of sustainable development is formulated at a high level of generality. The legal implication of this is that the Agency will have a wide margin of discretion in its interpretation of how these considerations will apply to detailed day-to-day decisions that need to be made in exercising its functions.

Alongside the Ministerial duty to provide statutory guidance on sustainable development, the Ministers are bound, from time to time, to give guidance to the Agency with respect to objectives which they consider it appropriate for the Agency to pursue in discharging its functions.[113] In relation to this, separate Ministerial guidance has been given from that concerning sustainable development, *The Environment Agency Management Statement*. In respect of objectives, and having regard to the Agency's responsibilities and resources, the Ministers have given guidance that it should do the following:

(i) adopt, across all its functions, an integrated approach to environmental protection and enhancement which considers impacts of substances and activities on all environmental media and on natural resources;

(ii) work with all relevant sectors of society, including regulated organisations, to develop approaches which deliver environmental requirements and goals without imposing excessive costs (in relation to benefits gained) on regulated organisations or society as a whole;

(iii) adopt clear and effective procedures for serving its customers, including by developing single points of contact through which regulated organisations can deal with the Agency;

(iv) operate to high professional standards, based on sound science, information and analysis of the environment and of processes which affect it;

(v) organise its activities in ways which reflect good environmental and management practice and provide value for money for those who pay its charges and taxpayers as a whole;

(vi) provide clear and readily available advice and information on its work; and

(vii) develop a close and responsive relationship with the public, local authorities and other representatives of local communities, regulated organisations and public bodies with environmental responsibilities.[114]

To some extent, these seven principles stating the objectives of the Agency are provided for in law within the Environment Act 1995 and the

---

[113] Under s.4(2) Environment Act 1995.

[114] DoE, MAFF and WO, *The Environment Agency and Sustainable Development* (1996) 'Statutory Guidance Given Pursuant to Section 4(2) of the Environment Act 1995 with Respect to Objectives of the Agency' p.3, see also DoE, MAFF and WO, *The Environment Agency Management Statement* (1996).

associated legislation under which the Agency operates, or are obligations which are, as a matter of practice, inevitable aspects of the efficient and accountable functioning of a public body of the stature of the Agency.

## 6.8  General Functions concerning Pollution Control

The powers given to the Agency in relation to pollution control are to be exercised for explicit purposes.[115] The Agency's pollution control powers[116] are stated to be exercisable for the purpose of preventing or minimising, or remedying or mitigating the effects of, pollution of the environment.[117] The reference to the 'effects' of pollution of the environment may be significant in that such effects may potentially be wide-ranging and could clearly impact upon flora and fauna dependent upon the aquatic environment.[118] Given previous observations on the broad and narrow senses of 'pollution', it must also be noted that 'pollution', in the context of the Agency's general functions, seems to be used in the wider sense encompassing matters of environmental quality generally, rather than merely extremes of environmental contamination.

For the purpose of facilitating the carrying out of its pollution control functions, or of enabling it to form an opinion of the general state of the environment, the Agency is bound to compile information relating to pollution. This duty applies whether the information is acquired by the Agency carrying out observations or is obtained in any other way.[119] The need for the Agency to form an opinion on the state of the environment is closely related to the consultative capacity in which it may be required to act for certain purposes such as providing advice to Ministers. Hence, if required by either of the Ministers to do so, the Agency must carry out assessments, either generally or for specified purposes, of the effect, or likely effect, on the environment of existing or potential levels of pollution

---

[115] This contrasts with the position of the former National Rivers Authority which was not subject to any express duty with regard to the exercise of its pollution control functions, though a duty of this kind was provided for in relation to integrated pollution control, see s.4(2) Environmental Protection Act 1990.

[116] For these purposes, 'pollution control powers' and 'pollution control functions', in relation to the Agency, mean respectively its powers or its functions under or by virtue of the following enactments (a) the Alkali, &c, Works Regulation Act 1906; (b) Part I of the Health and Safety at Work etc. Act 1974; (c) Part I of the Control of Pollution Act 1974; (d) the Control of Pollution (Amendment) Act 1989; (e) Parts I, II and IIA of the 1990 Act (integrated pollution control etc., waste on land and contaminated land); (f) Chapter III of Part IV of the Water Industry Act 1991 (special category effluent); (g) Part III and sections 161 to 161D of the Water Resources Act 1991 (control of pollution of water resources); (h) the Radioactive Substances Act 1993; (j) regulations made by virtue of s.2(2) of the European Communities Act 1972, to the extent that the regulations relate to pollution (s.5(5) Environment Act 1995).

[117] The 'environment', for these purposes, is defined to include all, or any, of the following media, namely the air, water and land as (s.56(1) Environment Act 1995 and s.1(2) Environmental Protection Act 1990). 'Pollution' is not defined for these purposes, but see s.1(3) Environmental Protection Act 1990 and see discussion at 1.3.3 above and 12.3 below.

[118] s.5(1) Environment Act 1995.

[119] *Ibid* s.5(2) Environment Act 1995. For further discussion of the duties upon the Agency to compile and provide environmental information see Ch.16 below. For discussion of the powers of the Agency to acquire information see 6.16 below.

of the environment and report its findings to the Minister. Alternatively, the Agency may be required to prepare and send to the Minister a report identifying the options which the Agency considers to be available for preventing or minimising, or remedying or mitigating the effects of, pollution of the environment, whether generally or in specified circumstances, and the costs and benefits[120] of such options as are identified.[121]

The Agency is placed under a duty to follow developments in technology and techniques for preventing or minimising, or remedying or mitigating the effects of, pollution of the environment.[122] Clearly this is closely related to the research and development obligation imposed upon the Agency. In accordance with the its Research and Development Strategy,[123] the Agency supports a range of projects which are perceived to be conducive to the acquisition of knowledge and techniques that allow an informed response to a range of environmental management issues. The Agency's overall research and development budget for 1999/2000 was £10.7 million.[124]

### 6.9 General Obligations concerning Water Functions

The Agency is subject to a number of general duties with regard to the exercise of its water-related functions. As with the sustainable development duty, these obligations are capable of arising in relation to various functions of the Agency and, in theory, their disregard would expose the Agency to judicial review proceedings. However, in practice, their scope for use as grounds for litigation is likely to be limited because of their generality. Nevertheless, they may be of some importance in influencing the decision-making processes of the Agency in relevant deliberations, such as where an operational objective is capable of being achieved by different means. Other considerations being balanced, general obligations upon the Agency may assume particular importance.

Specifically, in relation to conservation, amenity and recreation, the Agency must, to such extent as it considers desirable, generally promote,

(a) the conservation and enhancement of the natural beauty and amenity of inland and coastal waters and of land associated with such waters;

---

[120] On costs and benefits, see 6.14 below.

[121] s.5(3) Environment Act 1995. For a discussion of other kinds of information that the Agency is required to supply to Ministers see 6.16 below.

[122] *Ibid* s.5(4). For a similar duty imposed, formerly, on Her Majesty's Inspectorate of Pollution and local authorities, see s.4(9) Environmental Protection Act 1990 prior to amendment by Schedule 22 para.46 Environment Act 1995.

[123] Environment Agency, *Research and Development Strategy* (1998).

[124] See www.environment-agency.gov.uk

(b)   the conservation of flora and fauna which are dependent on an aquatic environment;[125] and

(c)   the use of such waters and land for recreational purposes;

and the Agency must, in determining what steps to take in performance of the duty imposed by virtue of (c) take into account the needs of persons who are chronically sick or disabled.[126]

Significantly, the formulation of the conservation, amenity and recreation obligations upon the Agency is stated to be 'to such an extent as it considers desirable' which appears to incorporate a wide degree of discretion exercised within the principal aim and objectives of the Agency, the Ministerial guidance provided in relation to this,[127] and the general environmental and recreational duties imposed upon it.[128] In addition, the duty upon the Agency to have regard to costs and benefits in exercising its functions[129] will need to be balanced against the assessment of what is desirable.

The interrelationship between the Agency and the water supply industry is provided for by way of another broadly formulated duty upon the Agency to take all such action as it may from time to time consider to be necessary or expedient, in accordance with Ministerial directions,[130] for the purpose of conserving, redistributing or otherwise augmenting water resources in England and Wales and securing the proper use of water resources in England and Wales. However, this duty is not to be construed as relieving any water undertaker of the obligation to develop water resources for the purpose of performing any duty[131] imposed upon water undertakers to maintain an efficient and economical system of water supply in its area.[132]

The Agency is bound to maintain, improve and develop salmon fisheries, trout fisheries, freshwater fisheries and eel fisheries.[133]

## 6.10  General Environmental and Recreational Duties

Following previous practices of imposing general environmental and recreational duties upon the former National Rivers Authority[134] and water

---

[125] The duty in relation to flora and fauna contrasts with duties imposed elsewhere in the Environment Act 1995 relation to the environment, meaning the environmental media of air, water and land, see, for example, discussion of s.5 at 6.8 above.

[126] s.6(1) Environment Act 1995. This subsection is stated to be without prejudice to the duties of the Agency under s.7 of the Act concerning general environmental and recreational duties and see 6.10 below on this. On the meaning of 'chronically sick and disabled', see Chronically Sick and Disabled Persons Act 1970.

[127] See s.4 Environment Act 1995 and the discussion of Ministerial guidance at 6.7 above.

[128] See *ibid* s.7 and the discussion of environmental duties at 6.10 below.

[129] *Ibid* s.39 and see 6.14 below on costs and benefits.

[130] Ministerial directions are provided for under s.40 Environment Act 1995, and see 6.2 above.

[131] Under s.37 Water Industry Act 1991.

[132] s.6(2) Environment Act 1995.

[133] s.6(6) Environment Act 1995. On fisheries generally, see Ch.15 below.

[134] Under s.16 Water Resources Act 1991, now repealed.

and sewerage undertakers,[135] the Agency, and the Ministers, are subject to broadly formulated obligations applicable where it, or they, are formulating or considering any proposal.[136] However, the present formulation of this duty differs according to whether the proposals at issue relate to the pollution control functions or other functions of the Agency.[137] Hence, in relation to proposals relating to any of the functions of the Agency *other than its pollution control functions*, it is the duty of each of the Ministers and of the Agency, in formulating or considering any proposals, to exercise any power conferred on him, or it, with respect to the proposals as to *further* the conservation and enhancement[138] of natural beauty and the conservation of flora, fauna and geological or physiographical features of special interest. However, this is to be done only so far as may be consistent with the purposes of any enactment relating to the functions of the Agency; in the case of each of the Ministers, with the objective of achieving sustainable development;[139] in the case of the Agency, with any Ministerial guidance;[140] and in the case of the Secretary of State, with his duties with respect to the water industry.[141]

The general environmental duty upon the Minister and the Agency in relation to functions other than pollution control, to 'further' conservation and other matters, contrasts with that which is applicable in relation to its pollution control functions. In relation to any proposals relating to pollution control functions, the Minister and the Agency is '*to have regard*' to the desirability of conserving and enhancing natural beauty and of conserving flora, fauna and geological or physiographical features of special interest.[142]

The significance of the differently formulated environmental duties in relation to non-pollution control and pollution control functions proved to be one of the more controversial features of the Environment Act 1995.[143] In many practical contexts there may not be much difference between a duty to 'further' and a duty to 'have regard' to conservation and other matters, and the contrast might be regarded as semantic rather than substantial. However, the difference was thought to be necessary because of a perceived conflict between the responsibilities that are imposed upon the Agency to determine discharge consents[144] authorising potentially harmful emissions to the aquatic environment and an over-broadly

---

[135] Under s.3 Water Industry Act 1991.

[136] Significantly, perhaps, the meaning of 'proposal', for these purposes, is not defined and this would seem to imply that the provisions are applicable to a broad range of contexts from the widest matters of policy formulation to the narrowest issues involved in determining particular licence and authorisation applications.

[137] Generally see *ENDS Report* 238 (1994) p.20.

[138] On the meaning of 'conservation and enhancement' see Leeson (1995) p.111.

[139] See 4.4.1 above on sustainable development.

[140] Issued under s.4 Environment Act 1995, and see 6.7 above.

[141] s.7(1)(a) Environment Act 1995. The duties of the Secretary of State with respect to the water industry are provided for under s.2 Water Industry Act 1991.

[142] s.7(1)(b) Environment Act 1995.

[143] See *ENDS Report* 238 (1994) p.20.

[144] On discharge consents generally see Ch.10 below.

formulated general environmental duty. On this contention, there was thought to be an inconsistency between furthering conservation and allowing *any* discharge to be made which might adversely impact upon the environment. Therefore, the lesser duty of 'having regard' to conservation was thought to be a more appropriate form of wording to apply to pollution control contexts.

There has been recent criticism of the Agency's cross-functional role in relation to nature conservation, and particularly of its failure effectively to integrate conservation and biodiversity objectives into its core functions. In some respects, the view has been expressed that the Agency has different primary objectives which cause insufficient account to be taken of the effects of projects and policies upon biodiversity requirements. One solution to these failures to integrate conservation concerns into core functions, advocated by the House of Commons Environment, Transport and Regional Affairs Committee, is that the Agency's most relevant position statements and programmes should undergo a 'biodiversity check', amongst other things, scrutinising whether positive or negative biodiversity consequences are likely to follow.[145]

Alongside nature conservation, there are a number of other broadly social and cultural duties imposed upon the Agency. Hence, in relation to any proposal relating to any of its functions, the Agency is to have regard to, or to take into account,

(a)   the desirability of protecting and conserving buildings, sites and objects of archaeological, architectural, engineering or historic interest;

(b)   any effect which the proposals would have on the beauty or amenity of any rural or urban area or on any such flora, fauna, features, buildings, sites or objects; and

(c)   any effect which the proposals would have on the economic and social well-being of local communities in rural areas.[146]

Again, it may be noted that these duties require the Agency to take cognisance of the specified matters and must be assumed to be purposefully of a weaker character than might otherwise have been provided for.

Subject to the general environmental duties,[147] it is the duty of the Ministers and the Agency, in formulating or considering any proposals relating to any functions of the Agency,

---

[145] House of Commons Environment, Transport and Regional Affairs Committee, *The Environment Agency* (2000) paras.137 to 139.

[146] s.7(1)(c) Environment Act 1995.

[147] That is to say, those duties under s.7(1) Environment Act 1995, described above, are to take priority over the subsequent matters provided for under s.7(2).

(a)  to have regard to the desirability of preserving for the public any freedom of access to areas of woodland, mountains, moor, heath, down, cliff or foreshore and other places of natural beauty;

(b)  to have regard to the desirability of maintaining the availability to the public of any facility for visiting or inspecting any building, site or object of archaeological, architectural, engineering or historic interest; and

(c)  to take into account any effect which the proposals would have on any such freedom of access or on the availability of any such facility.[148]

The general environmental duties apply so as to impose duties on the Agency in relation to,

(a)  any proposals relating to the functions of a water or sewerage undertaker,

(b)  any proposals relating to the management, by the company holding an appointment as such an undertaker, of any land for the time being held by that company for any purpose whatever, whether or not connected with the carrying out of the functions of a water undertaker or sewerage undertaker, and

(c)  any proposal concerning disposals of protected land[149] which falls to be treated[150] as a proposal relating to the functions of a water undertaker or sewerage undertaker,

as they apply in relation to proposals relating to the Agency's own functions, other than its pollution control functions.[151]

In addition to the matters provided for by way of general environmental duties, the Agency is under a general duty to take reasonably practicable steps, which are consistent with the purpose of its functions, for securing that the rights of the Agency to use water or land are exercised so as to ensure that these are made available for recreational purposes. In relation to this, it is the duty of the Agency, in determining what steps to take, to take into account the needs of persons who are chronically sick or disabled. However this is not to be construed as requiring recreational facilities to be made available by the Agency free of charge.[152]

### 6.11 Duties concerning Sites of Special Interest

Following duties which were imposed upon the former National Rivers Authority,[153] the Agency is subject to specific obligations, in addition to the general environmental duties previously described, with regard to sites

---

[148] s.7(2) Environment Act 1995.
[149] Under s.156(7) Water Industry Act 1991.
[150] Under *ibid* s.3.
[151] s.7(3) Environment Act 1995.
[152] *Ibid* s.7(4)–(6).
[153] Under s.17 Water Resources Act 1991.

of special interest.[154] These duties apply where English Nature or the Countryside Council for Wales is of the opinion that any area of land is of special interest by reason of its flora, fauna or geological or physiographical features. Where land may at any time be affected by schemes, works, operations or activities of the Agency, or by an authorisation[155] given by the Agency, the relevant body must be notified that the land is of special interest.[156] Similarly, where a National Park authority or the Broads Authority is of the opinion that any area of land in a National Park or in the Broads is land of particular importance,[157] and may at any time be affected by schemes, works, operations or activities of the Agency or by an authorisation given by the Agency, the National Park authority or Broads Authority is bound to notify the Agency of the fact that the land is such land, and of the reasons why those matters are of particular importance in relation to the land.[158]

Where the Agency has received a notification from a council or authority, as described, with respect to any land, it must consult the notifying body before carrying out or authorising any works, operations or activities which appear to the Agency to be likely to destroy or damage any of the flora, fauna, or geological or physiographical features by reason of which the land is of special interest, or significantly to prejudice anything of particular importance in relation to the notification of that land.[159] This requirement is not to apply in relation to anything done in an emergency[160] where particulars of what is done and of the emergency are notified to the relevant council or authority as soon as practicable after that thing is done.[161]

The environmental duties with respect to sites of special interest have potentially broad application in relation to conservationally sensitive land. The formula that the land may at any time be affected by schemes, works, operations or activities of the Agency or by an authorisation given by it is clearly of wide application and would apply, for example, to a determination of a discharge consent which was capable of having an adverse environmental impact upon such land.

---

[154] Generally see 15.7.1 below on sites of special scientific interest.

[155] 'Authorisation' for these purposes is stated to include any consent or licence (s.8(5) Environment Act 1995) and is, therefore, capable of encompassing various authorisations in relation to the water pollution control function of the Agency.

[156] s.8(1) Environment Act 1995.

[157] That is, of 'particular importance' in relation to the duty upon the Agency to promote the conservation of natural beauty and flora and fauna (under s.6(1) Environment Act 1995) or the general environmental and recreational duties upon the Agency (under s.7, other than s.7(1)(c)(iii)) concerned with the effect which proposals would have on the economic and social well-being of communities in rural areas.

[158] s.8(2) Environment Act 1995.

[159] See also the consultation duties imposed upon persons proposing to conduct 'potentially damaging operations' in relation to sites of special scientific interest, discussed in 15.7.1 below, and the impacts of the European Community Habitats Directive, discussed in 15.8 below.

[160] See 9.17.1 below on the meaning of 'emergency'.

[161] s.8(3) and (4) Environment Act 1995.

The need for consultation in situations of this kind was graphically illustrated, in a drainage context, by *Southern Water Authority* v *Nature Conservancy Council*,[162] where a Site of Special Scientific Interest was seriously damaged by a water authority exercising drainage powers which are now possessed by the Agency.[163] In this case, land on the Isle of Wight had been designated as a Site of Special Scientific Interest. Two farmers, who owned land bordering on a ditch on the site, were anxious to dredge the ditch to alleviate flooding. However, the farmers had been notified that dredging was a potentially damaging operation requiring prior notification to the Nature Conservancy Council. The farmers engaged the former water authority to do the work. The water authority entered onto the farmers' land and carried out the dredging, damaging the ecological value of the site in the process. The water authority was prosecuted for carrying out a potentially damaging operation on the site without notification.[164] On appeal the House of Lords held that although the water authority had been present at the ditch for a month, it was not an 'occupier' of the particular piece of land. This was unaffected by the fact that the water authority, coincidentally, owned land elsewhere on the site and knew of its designation. The circumstances of the case predated the obligations to notify English Nature or the Countryside Council for Wales that have been described, however, were the circumstances to arise today in relation to the drainage function of the Agency, it is hoped that the combination of the duty of the Agency to notify the appropriate council, the general environmental duty upon the Agency and the Code of Practice relating to this would prevent the kind of 'ecological vandalism' that occurred.[165]

### 6.12 Codes of Practice concerning Environmental and Recreational Duties

The general environmental and recreational duties upon the Agency are provided for at a high level of generality and need to be interpreted more specifically to be applied to particular contexts. For this purpose, each of the Ministers has the power to approve any code of practice issued for the purpose of giving practical guidance to the Agency with respect to specified environmental and related duties,[166] and promoting what appear to him to be desirable practices by the Agency with respect to those matters. The Ministers may at any time, by order, approve a modification of such a code or withdraw approval of a code or modification.[167] In

---

[162] [1992] 3 All ER 481 and see 15.7.1 below.

[163] Under the Land Drainage Act 1976.

[164] It is not clear why a prosecution, with no complications about the meaning of 'occupier', was not brought against the farmers.

[165] Postscript: See now the duties that are provided for under the Countryside and Rights of Way Act 2000, discussed in 15.7.4 below.

[166] Specifically, the promotion of water conservation (under s.6(1) Environment Act 1995), general environmental duties (under s.7) and environmental duties with respect to sites of special interest (under s.8).

[167] The Ministers may not make an order in accordance with these powers unless they have first consulted the Agency, the Countryside Commission, English Nature and the Countryside Council for Wales, the Historic Buildings and Monuments Commission for England, the Sports Council

discharging its duties in relation to the specified environmental and related duties, the Agency must have regard to any code of practice, and any modifications of a code of practice, for the time being approved for these purposes.[168]

Under the previous provisions, it was explicitly stated that failure to have regard to such a code of practice would not give rise to any civil or criminal liability upon the part of the former National Rivers Authority.[169] In theory, therefore, the removal of this safeguard in relation to the Agency leaves open the possibility of such liability, though the generality of the provisions in the Code makes this unlikely. By contrast to the position of the Agency, insofar as a code of practice also applies to water and sewerage undertakers, the exclusion of criminal or civil liability is retained and the Ministers are to take into account whether there has been or is likely to be a contravention of the code when considering whether to give directions to undertakers.[170]

The Ministerial powers under the Environment Act 1995 to approve codes of practice have recently been exercised by the approval of the *Code of Practice on Conservation, Access and Recreation*.[171] The *Code of Practice* provides guidance to the Environment Agency, and water and sewerage undertakers,[172] on matters concerning conservation, access and recreation that they should take into consideration when discharging their duties. The general responsibilities of the Agency with regard to sustainable development, the pursuit of an integrated approach to the management of the environment and the need for consultation with relevant bodies are reaffirmed. More specific guidance in relation to conservation of aquatic environments requires, as a general practice, the retention of natural river features such as pools, riffles, sand bars, shingle banks, cliffs, meanders and braided channels and the retention of waterside land features and habitats such as ponds, brackish lagoons, marshes, fens, water meadows, bog, scrub and marginal trees. In respect of effluent and water quality, the Agency is to plan for improvement, particularly to avoid adverse impacts on Sites of Special Scientific Interest[173] and other sites of conservation importance, by the review of discharge consent conditions. Particularly in relation to Special Areas of Conservation and Special Protection Areas,[174] the Agency is to assess the implications for sites of proposed or existing discharges. It is restated that in determining consent conditions, the

---

and the Sports Council for Wales and such other persons as they consider it appropriate to consult. The power of the Ministers to make an order of this kind will be exercisable by statutory instrument subject to the negative resolution procedure. See s.9(3) and (4) Environment Act 1995.

[168] s.9(1) and (2) Environment Act 1995.

[169] s.18 Water Resources Act 1991 (now repealed).

[170] s.5(2) Water Industry Act 1991.

[171] DETR, National Assembly for Wales and MAFF, (2000) approved by Water and Sewerage (Conservation, Access and Recreation) (Code of Practice) Order 2000 (SI 2000 No. 477).

[172] Corresponding duties upon water and sewerage undertakers are provided for under ss.3–5 Water Industry Act 1991, and see 7.6.4–5 below.

[173] See 15.7.1 below on Sites of Special Scientific Interest.

[174] See 15.8 below on Special Areas of Conservation and Special Protection Areas.

Agency will be bound to adhere to its environmental and recreational duties. In most respects the matters dealt with by the *Code of Practice* are stated at a level of some generality and seem unlikely to be decisive of legal obligations but may, nevertheless, be influential in guiding practice on relevant matters.

## 6.13 Incidental Functions

As has previously been emphasised, the functions of the Agency are exhaustively defined by statute and, in certain respects, are subject to powers and duties concerning the manner in which they are to be exercised. However, some flexibility is allowed to the Agency in that it has widely formulated incidental powers clarifying, and in some respects broadening, the activities in which it may engage in relation to certain functions. Accordingly, for relevant purposes,[175] the functions of the Agency are to be taken to include the protection against pollution of:

(a) any waters, whether on the surface or underground, which belong to the Agency or any water undertaker or from which the Agency or any water undertaker is authorised to take water;

(b) without prejudice to (a) above, any reservoir which belongs to or is operated by the Agency or any water undertaker or which the Agency or any water undertaker is proposing to acquire or construct for the purpose of being so operated; and

(c) any underground strata from which the Agency or any water undertaker is for the time being authorised to abstract water in pursuance of a licence under Chapter II of Part II of the Water Resources Act 1991 (concerned with abstraction and impounding).[176]

Further incidental operational functions of the Agency relate to the carrying out of works or the acquisition of land when acting jointly with, or on behalf of, a water or sewerage undertaker, and the provision of water supplies in bulk.[177]

Various miscellaneous, general and supplemental provisions relating to the Agency are provided for allowing the Agency to do anything which, in its opinion, is calculated to facilitate, or is conducive or incidental to, the carrying out of its functions. Without prejudice to the extreme generality of this power, it may, for the purposes of, or in connection with, the carrying out of its functions, acquire and dispose of land and other property and carry out such engineering or building operations as it considers appropriate.

---

[175] 'The relevant purposes' is a reference to the purposes of s.37(1) Environment Act 1995 (concerning incidental general functions of the Agency) as it applies in relation to the Agency and the construction of any other enactment which, by reference to the functions of the Agency, confers any power on or in relation to the Agency (s.10(1) Environment Act 1995).

[176] s.10(2) Environment Act 1995. In relation to the former National Rivers Authority similar incidental functions were provided for under s.3 Water Resources Act 1991.

[177] s.10(3) and (4) Environment Act 1995.

Of particular importance is the statement that the Agency may institute criminal proceedings in England and Wales.[178] Remarkably, no explicit general power is given to the Agency to instigate or participate in civil proceedings, such as those involving the seeking of an injunction to prevent the continuation of pollution. It has been suggested that the power of the Agency to do anything which is conducive or incidental to the carrying out of its functions allows civil proceedings to be brought.[179] This view is supported by a recent High Court decision where the Agency was granted an injunction to prevent unlawful tipping of controlled waste on the basis that the Agency was entitled to seek this remedy in accordance with its incidental powers.[180] Despite the absence of a general facility for the Agency to seek injunctions, this power has been expressly provided for in specific situations, such as where proceedings are undertaken in relation to enforcement notices for contravention of discharge consents[181] or in relation to works notices requiring persons to carry out anti-pollution works and operations where these have not been complied with.[182]

## 6.14  The Costs and Benefits Duty

A significant innovation amongst the duties imposed upon the Environment Agency is the explicit duty upon the Agency to have regard to costs and benefits in exercising its *powers*. This requires that the Agency, in considering whether or not to exercise any power conferred upon it by any enactment, or in deciding upon the manner in which to exercise any such power, must, unless and to the extent that it is unreasonable for it to do so, take into account the likely costs and benefits of the exercise of non-exercise of the power or its exercise in the manner in question.[183] For these purposes, 'costs' is stated to include costs to any person and costs to the environment.[184] However, the cost-benefit duty imposed upon a the Agency does not affect its obligation, nevertheless, to discharge any *duties*, comply with any requirements, or pursue any objectives, imposed upon or given to it otherwise than under this

---

[178] *Ibid* s.37(1). In England and Wales, a person who is authorised by the Agency to prosecute on its behalf in proceedings before a magistrates' court shall be entitled to prosecute in any such proceedings although not a barrister or a solicitor (s.54 Environment Act 1995).

[179] See Viscount Ullswater, Minister of State, Department of the Environment, *Hansard*, HL Vol.562 col.1035, discussed in Tromans (1996) pp.534-35.

[180] See Environment Agency, Press Release, *High Court Injunction Stops Tipping*, 23 March 1999, but contrast the general view that the civil law should not be used to support the operation of the criminal law unless the claimant shows a special interest or the proceedings are brought with the support of the Attorney-General (*Gouriet* v *Union of Post Office Workers and Others* [1978] AC 435).

[181] s.90B(3) Water Resources Act 1991, inserted by para.142 Schedule 22 Environment Act 1995, and see 10.11.1 below in relation to enforcement notices.

[182] s.161D(4) Water Resources Act 1991, as inserted by para.162 of Schedule 22 Environment Act 1995, and see 13.2.2 below in relation to works notices.

[183] s.39(1) Environment Act 1995.

[184] *Ibid* s.56(1).

provision.[185] Significantly, therefore, the obligation to have regard to costs and benefits applies to the powers but not to the duties of the Agency.

Ministerial guidance that has been given to the Agency in relation to its principal aim and objectives[186] emphasises the link between the cost-benefit duty and the recognition that sustainable development involves reconciling the need for economic development with that of protecting and enhancing the environment without compromising the ability of future generations to meet their own needs.[187] Accordingly, the Ministers are of the view that decisions of the Agency should not only ensure that financial and other considerations are taken into account, but that environmental considerations are given a central role unless this is unreasonable.[188]

The application of the cost-benefit duty requires the Agency to take account of all likely costs and benefits. If necessary, this may involve an environmental assessment[189] or environmental appraisal to highlight the options and to reduce the extent of the uncertainty confronting decision makers and generally to improve the quality of the decision making process. In the view of the Ministers, the need to take account of likely costs and benefits does not mean that these need be precisely quantified. It is recognised that many kinds of costs and benefits, particularly in relation to the environment, are inherently difficult to quantify in money terms. On methodology and procedures, it is advised that, when assessing likely costs and benefits, the Agency may consider it appropriate to consider the following matters:

(i)    principles, procedures and techniques – in particular, risk assessment, and economic and policy appraisal – for giving proper consideration to non-market impacts including those on the environment;

(ii)   the precautionary principle;[190]

(iii)  reliance on sound science;

(iv)   the likely impact on the carrying capacity of the environment, and on natural environmental capital;

(v)    the likely longer-term implications and effects, having particular regard to those which appear likely to be irreversible or reversible only at high cost and over a long time-scale. In the Ministers' view, such analyses should take proper account of long-term environmental benefits as well as immediate financial costs;

(vi)   the likely costs and benefits of its actions for society as a whole, including the effects on the welfare of people and business, impacts on the environment and changes in the use of resources

---

[185] *Ibid* s.39(2).

[186] Under s.4 *ibid* and see 6.7 above on the principal aim and objectives of the Agency.

[187] See the discussion of sustainable development at 4.4.1 above and see 4.8 above on the assessment of costs and benefits in European Community environmental policy.

[188] DoE, MAFF and WO, *The Environment Agency and Sustainable Development* (1996) Chapter 5 'Costs and Benefits' para.5.2.

[189] See 14.6 below on environmental impact assessment.

[190] See 4.7.1 above on the precautionary principle.

(labour, capital and natural resources). In doing so the Agency may be guided where appropriate by:

(a)    the views of the Government's Chief Medical Officers, the Health and Safety Executive and Commission and other bodies as to the effects on human health;

(b)    evidence within the UK and internationally about proven and likely impacts on the environment;

(c)    the impacts on the economy and on all affected business sectors and individual companies; and

(d)    the distribution of costs and benefits across the economy. For example, some options open to the Agency may impose particularly heavy costs on particular groups of people of companies or on certain parts of the environment.[191]

Further reinterpretation of these matters has been provided by the Environment Agency in *Sustainable Development: Taking Account of Costs and Benefits*.[192] This policy note seeks to give practical guidance to Agency staff as to how the duty with regard to costs and benefits is to be implemented. It is recognised that the duty does not prescribe any particular technique and that the cost of applying the duty should be proportionate to the benefit to be gained. Hence, in relation to a small-scale licence or consent applications a detailed survey of all related costs and benefits might be more expensive, in terms of diverted Agency resources, than any eventual benefit secured. Similarly, there may be situations where it is not reasonable fully to apply the duty on a case-by-case basis, such as where action needs to be taken urgently in an emergency, or in relation to taking legal action.

In some instances, where an environmental quality objective is a legal requirement which is non-negotiable, the assessment may involve a determination of the least-cost means of achieving that goal. More problematically, however, are those situations where the environmental objective is not predetermined and a range of different kinds of costs need to be weighed into the balance: costs to society as a whole; effects on the welfare of people and businesses; changes in the use of resources such as capital, labour and natural resources; and impacts upon the environment. In relation to environmental and ecological impacts, the assessment of these in terms of monetary valuations is particularly problematic since there are clear difficulties in the quantification of such 'intangible' costs and benefits.

Despite the Ministerial guidance and the Environment Agency's interpretation of this, the practical implications of the cost-benefit duty are difficult to evaluate. Arguably, the financial constraints placed upon any publicly funded body are sufficient incentive to ensure that internal resources are used in the most cost effective manner, and the Agency is no

---

[191] DoE, MAFF and WO, *The Environment Agency and Sustainable Development* (1996) Chapter 5 'Costs and Benefits' para.5.6.
[192] Environment Agency (1999).

exception in this respect. Similarly, where others are required by an environmental regulatory authority, in the exercise of its discretion, to take action which involves a cost, the basis for this has always been informally weighed into the balance against the environmental benefit that will be secured unless overriding legal duties prevail.

The potential difficulty, however, lies in the attempt to formalise this process of balancing costs and benefits. A major problem, in doing so, is that the quantification of any environmental benefit will always be difficult, if not impossible, to assess in terms which correspond with the costs involved in securing it. This is because of the incommensurability between environmental improvement and financial expenditure and the fact that the state of the environment does not have a readily identifiable market value.[193] A fear is that the need to undertake this analysis as a precursor to action by the Agency may give rise to extensive disputes and litigation, either by regulated bodies or environmental pressure groups, on the basis that the analysis has not been properly conducted in a particular case. Given the relatively open-endedness of what is involved, claims of this kind may be difficult either to substantiate or to rebut.

The way in which monetary values can in practice be put on water quality, in relation to the Agency's duty to have regard to costs in benefits in its decision-making, is illustrated by a decision of the Secretary of State in an abstraction licensing appeal.[194] The appeal was brought by Thames Water against the variation of an abstraction licence. The Environment Agency made the variation primarily on the grounds of alleged damage caused to the ecology of the River Kennet, an Area of Outstanding Natural Beauty and a riverine Site of Special Scientific Interest.[195] The central issue was the way in which the Agency had sought to justify its actions on cost and benefits grounds.

All parties agreed that it was appropriate to use contingent valuation (specifically, the benefit transfer method) a valuation method which uses direct survey questions to the public about their willingness to pay for the conservation or preservation of environmental goods. Where they disagreed was on how to calculate benefits, in particular non-use values associated with conservation of the environment as a resource, and *whose* views ought to be taken into account in this process. Stated briefly, the question for the Inspector was whether to accept the Agency's position, based on the average (mean) figure per household across the 3 million households in the Thames area, or to prefer the undertaker's position that only the views of a much lower number of people alleged to be more directly affected should be preferred. On the basis of a 'Public Perception Survey', the company thought that what was at stake was, despite the

---

[193] See the discussion of economic instruments at 1.7.9 above.

[194] See Planning Inspectorate (Appeal WAT/95/22) Water Resources Act 1991 – Section 43, Water Resources Licences Regulations 1965, *Appeal by Thames Water Utilities Limited (Axford Abstraction)* and letter on behalf of the Secretary of State, 13 February 1998 and see *ENDS Report* 278 (1998) p.16 and McGillivray (1998).

[195] On Sites of Special Scientific Interest see 15.7.1 below.

conservation designation, mainly of local interest and that a figure of 100,000 people would be generous.[196] The Inspector largely accepted the argument of the undertaker and the view of the Inspector was endorsed by the Secretary of State.

The decision is notable in that, despite its infancy, a willingness to pay approach was accepted by all the key actors, the Agency, central government and Ofwat, and implicitly also the water companies. Willingness to pay approaches are said to have an advantage over decision-making through the normal political process by allowing the *intensity* of preferences to be taken into account. In this respect this form of cost-benefit analysis is considered to be 'democratic'.[197] However, three points may be made. First, there are many ways in which the value of environmental benefits may be captured, of which individual use or preference is only one. For example, value may be sought through social consensus, on the basis that values are to be reasoned towards rather than stated as preferences.[198] Second, there is empirical evidence to suggest that many participants in contingent valuation studies feel that the process conceals the purposes for which the information is to be used, and does not measure what it purports to measure.[199] In any case, attitudes and political views inevitably colour responses. Third, it would seem that insufficient attention has been paid to the weight to be given to the opinions of different respondents. For example, even a recent study that seeks to move towards a more sophisticated valuation of environmental capital fails to address this inherent problem, referring rather uncritically to terms like 'the community'.[200] This is particularly pertinent to wider water quality issues, since it is difficult to define with any precision the 'beneficiaries' of regulatory action. The danger is that more attention is paid to 'willingness to pay' confrontations than to wider appreciation and discussion of environmental values.

Although the River Kennet Abstraction determination was concerned with water quantity rather than water quality, comparable issues would arise if a discharger were to contest a revision of a discharge consent where the Agency sought to impose greater stringency to secure environmental improvement. The unavoidable problem is that there is no consensus as to the methodology that should be used to assess the value of the environmental improvement so as to gauge whether expenditure on pollution abatement is justified.[201] Whilst it would be hoped that the Agency would not act unreasonably in requiring significant expenditure without good cause, the imposition of a statutory duty with regard to cost-benefit seems unduly burdensome without more explicit and precise guidance as to how that duty is to be discharged.

---

[196] In fact, a figure of only 14,000 'local' residents would probably have been argued for, had it been necessary to do so.

[197] But see O'Neill (1996).

[198] On which see generally Sagoff (1988).

[199] See Burgess, Clark and Harrison (1998).

[200] See CAG Consultants and Land Use Consultants (1997).

[201] Generally, see Hanley (1997) on the valuation of freshwaters.

## 6.15 Charging Schemes

As has been previously noted,[202] a significant proportion of the income of the Agency is raised through charges imposed upon the recipients of the services that it provides. Whilst the implications of this in relation to charges for discharge consents are considered in detail later in this work,[203] it is convenient at this point to consider the general legal basis for charges to be imposed by the Agency.

Provision for *ad hoc* charging by the Agency is made so that, by agreement with any person, it may charge that person a fee in respect of work done, or services or facilities provided, as a result of a request for advice or assistance. This power to charge such 'one-off' fees is without prejudice to the general power of the Agency to make charges subject to any express provisions with respect to charging contained in other provisions of Part I of the Environment Act 1995 or any other enactment [204]

Further provision for incidental charges to be levied is made, so that the Agency has the power to fix and recover charges for services and facilities provided in the course of carrying out its functions.[205] It is not entirely clear what 'services and facilities' this charging power might be applied to, but it would not seem to address the more fundamental issues surrounding the imposition of environmental impact charges, as opposed to charges for administrative cost recovery or charges for services actually provided.

The general power of the Agency to impose charges in relation to environmental licences[206] is provided for by way of a stipulation that there will be charged by and paid to the Agency such charges as may from time to time be prescribed. 'Prescribed', for these purposes, means specified in, or determined under, a charging scheme made by the Agency.[207] The term 'environmental licence' is widely defined to encompass a range of registrations and authorisations. However the most relevant of these, in relation to the protection of the aquatic environment, are:

(a)  an authorisation concerning integrated pollution control;[208]
(b)  a discharge consent or other consent under Chapter II of Part III of the Water Resources Act 1991;[209]
(c)  a consent authorising the deposit of mine or quarry refuse;[210]

---

[202] See 6.6 above on financial provisions relating to the Agency.

[203] See 10.7 below in relation to charges for discharge consents.

[204] s.37(7) and (8) Environment Act 1995. However, this power may not be exercised outside the United Kingdom, except with the consent of the appropriate Minister and this consent may be given subject to conditions (s.37(3) and (4)).

[205] *Ibid* s.43.

[206] Other than licences under Chapter II of Part II of the Water Resources Act 1991, concerning abstraction and impounding, which are similarly provided for under s.41(1)(a) Environment Act 1995.

[207] s.41(1) Environment Act 1995. Previously, charges in connection with the control of pollution were provided for under ss.131 and 132 Water Resources Act 1991.

[208] Under Part I of the Environmental Protection Act 1990 (other than an authorisation granted by a local enforcing authority). These authorisations are discussed at 12.3 below.

[209] As provided for under s.88(1) Water Resources Act 1991, discussed in Ch.10 below.

(d)  a consent concerned with deposits and vegetation in rivers;[211] and

(e)  a registration or authorisation under the Radioactive Substances Act 1993.[212]

In relation to these kinds of environmental licence, charges may be prescribed in respect of the following matters:

(a)  the grant or variation of an environmental licence, or any application for, or for a variation of such a licence;

(b)  the subsistence of an environmental licence;

(c)  the transfer (where permitted) of an environmental licence, or any application for such a transfer;

(d)  the renewal (where permitted) of an environmental licence, or any application for such a renewal;

(e)  the surrender (where permitted) of an environmental licence, or any application for such a surrender; or

(f)  any application for the revocation (where permitted) of an environmental licence.[213]

In relation to the subsistence of an environmental licence, under (b) above, a charging scheme may impose a single charge in respect of the whole of any relevant licensed period; separate charges in respect of different parts of any such period; or both a single charge and separate charges. The 'relevant licensed period' means the period during which an environmental licence is in force or a part of that period. A charging scheme may provide for different charges to be payable in respect of an environmental licence according to a range of factors:

(a)  the description of the environmental licence in question;

(b)  the description of the authorised activity;

(c)  the scale on which the authorised activity is carried on;

(d)  the description or amount of the substance to which the authorised activity relates; and

(e)  the number of different authorised activities carried on by the same person.[214]

A charging scheme is to specify persons who are liable to pay the charge and may provide for a condition that any prescribed charge is paid in accordance with the scheme. If it appears to the Agency that any charges due and payable to it in respect of the subsistence of an environmental licence have not been paid, it may, in accordance with the appropriate

---

[210] Under s.89(4) Water Resources Act 1991, discussed in 9.17.4 below.

[211] Under s.90 *ibid*, discussed in 9.15 below.

[212] The full definition of 'environmental licence' is provided in s.56(1) Environment Act 1995. For further discussion of radioactive contamination of water see Ch.20 below.

[213] s.41(2) Environment Act 1995.

[214] *Ibid* s.41(3) and (4).

procedure,[215] suspend or revoke the licence to the extent that it authorises the carrying on of the authorised activity. A charging scheme may make different provision for different cases, including different provision in relation to different persons, circumstance or localities; provide for the times at which, and the manner in which, the charges prescribed by the scheme are to be paid; revoke or amend any previous charging scheme; and contain any supplemental, incidental, consequential or transitional provisions for the purposes of the scheme.[216]

Before implementation, charging schemes require consultation and Ministerial approval.[217] Specified matters which need to be considered encompass the desirability of ensuring that, in the case of any description of relevant environmental licence, the amounts recovered by the Agency by way of charges under the proposed scheme are amounts which, taking one year with another, need to be recovered by the Agency to meet certain costs and expenses. The cost and expenses are such of those which the Agency incurs in carrying out its functions[218] as the Secretary of State considers it appropriate to attribute to environmental licences of the kind to which the charges relate.[219] That is to say, the amounts recoverable in relation to any particular environmental licence charging scheme should seek to recover the costs to the Agency involved in operating that licensing system.

It may be noted that the aim of charging schemes, as presently provided for, is primarily that of administrative cost recovery. Administrative costs may be related to the greater difficulties involved in monitoring those discharges which have greatest water contamination potential and, to some extent, environmental impact may be reflected in charging schemes as an administrative cost.[220] Although it is seen as desirable that dischargers should make contributions which reflect the environmental impact of their activities, in accordance with the 'polluter pays principle',[221] and to provide an economic incentive for improvement, the legal power to impose such charges is not explicitly provided for. Consequently, imposition of environmental impact or incentive charges would require legislative

---

[215] See Environmental Licences (Suspension and Revocation) Regulations 1996 (SI 1996 No. 508) and see 10.8 below.

[216] Environment Act 1995 s.41(5)–(7).

[217] Final approval of a proposed charging scheme by the Secretary of State requires the consent of the Treasury. Following approval, it is the duty of the Agency to take appropriate steps to bring the attention of persons likely to be affected to the provisions of the charging scheme (s.42(7) and (8) Environment Act 1995).

[218] Also, in relation to environmental licences which are authorisations under s.13(1) of the Radioactive Substances Act 1993, account is to be taken of costs and expenses which the Minister incurs in carrying out functions under that Act and, in appropriate cases, which the Secretary of State incurs. Accordingly, where sums are recovered as charges which may fairly be regarded as expenses incurred by the Secretary of State or the Minister they will be payable to whichever of these is appropriate (s.42(9) Environment Act 1995).

[219] s.42(1)–(3) Environment Act 1995.

[220] See the discussion of economic instruments at 1.7.9 above.

[221] See 4.7.3 above on the polluter pays principle.

amendment to enable this and care would be needed in the design of such a scheme to ensure fairness between dischargers.[222]

## 6.16 Information

The subject of information concerning the aquatic environment, and particularly the public right of access to such information, is considered in detail later in this work.[223] However, it is convenient to note at this point some general duties which apply to the Agency's activities in respect of information provision.

The Agency is bound to furnish the appropriate Minister with all information that he may reasonably require relating to the Agency's property, the carrying out, and proposed carrying out, of its functions and its responsibilities generally. The information required to be furnished is to include information which, although it is not in the possession of the Agency, or would not otherwise come into its possession, is information which it is reasonable to require the Agency to obtain.[224]

As soon as reasonably practicable after the end of each financial year, the Agency must prepare a report on its activities during that year and send a copy of that report to the appropriate Ministers. Each annual report must set out any directions[225] that have been given to the Agency which are identified to the Agency by the appropriate Minister, providing that these are not directions the disclosure of which, in his opinion, would be contrary to the interests of national security. The Secretary of State must lay a copy of each annual report before each House of Parliament and arrange for their publication in an appropriate manner.[226]

More specific information provisions, relating to water pollution functions under the Water Resources Act 1991, are provided for. Thus, the Agency is subject to a duty, so far as requested by the Ministers, to provide advice and assistance in relation to their functions under the 1991 Act. The gathering of information by either the Ministers or the Agency is also provided for, insofar as they may serve on any person a notice requiring that person to furnish reasonably required information within a reasonable time, or at specified times, for the purpose of functions under the 1991 Act. Failure to provide such information without reasonable excuse is an offence which, on summary conviction, is punishable by a fine not

---

[222] See Royal Commission on Environmental Pollution (1992) Ch.8 which proposed the imposition of environmental charges and see House of Commons Environment Committee, *The Environment Agency* (2000) paras.86 and 87. See 1.7.9 above on economic instruments for water pollution.
[223] See Ch.16 below on water quality information.
[224] s.51(1) to (3) Environment Act 1995.
[225] Under s.40 *ibid*, other than Ministerial directions under s.40(1), and see 6.2 above.
[226] *Ibid* s.52(1) to (3).

exceeding £5,000 and, on conviction on indictment, to a fine of unlimited amount and imprisonment for up to two years.[227]

### 6.17 Powers of Entry

Various powers of entry and associated powers are given to staff of the Agency[228] for the purpose of implementing the pollution control provisions of the Environment Act 1995. Thus, any person who appears suitable to the Agency may be authorised in writing to exercise, in accordance with the terms of the authorisation, specified powers of entry for certain purposes. The purposes for which the 'powers of entry' may be exercised are the following:

(a) determining whether any provision of certain pollution control enactments, relating to the pollution control functions of the Agency is being, or has been, complied with;

(b) exercising or performing one or more of the pollution control functions[229] of the Agency; or

(c) determining whether and, if so, how such a function should be exercised or performed.[230]

Authorised persons may be allowed to exercise any of the specified powers of entry for the purpose of enabling the Agency to carry out any assessment or prepare any report which the Agency is required to carry out or prepare.[231] However, this applies only where the relevant Minister has notified the Agency that the assessment or report relates to an incident or possible incident involving, or having the potential to involve, serious pollution of the environment, serious harm to human health or danger to life or health.[232]

The 'powers of entry' of a person authorised by the Agency, referred to above, are specified in the following manner:

---

[227] s.202(1), (2) and (4) Water Resources Act 1991 (as amended by para.172(1) Schedule 22 Environment Act 1995). See also 16.7 below on the use of this power.

[228] The Agency is termed an 'enforcing authority' under s.108(15) Environment Act 1995. Other enforcing authorities are the Secretary of State and local enforcing authorities.

[229] 'Pollution control functions' in relation to the Agency is defined, under s.108(15) Environment Act 1995, to encompass a wide range of statutory functions relating to the protection of the environment. Of these, the most relevant to the protection of the aquatic environment are the functions provided for under Part III and ss.161 to 161D of the Water Resources Act 1991 (on these see 13.2 below).

[230] s.108(1) Environment Act 1995. A general restriction upon the powers of entry is provided for in relation to any premises belonging to or used for the purposes of the United Kingdom Atomic Energy Authority, where entry is subject to s.6(3) Atomic Energy Authority Act 1954 (which restricts entry to such premises where they have been declared to be prohibited places for the purposes of the Official Secrets Act 1911).

[231] The relevant assessments and reports are provided for under ss.5(3) and 33(3) Environment Act 1995.

[232] s.108(2) and (3) Environment Act 1995.

(a) to enter any premises at any reasonable time or, in an emergency, at any time and, if need be, by force;[233]

(b) on entering premises, to take any other authorised person and, if there is reasonable cause to apprehend any serious obstruction, a constable and any required equipment or materials;

(c) to make such examination and investigation as may be necessary;

(d) to direct that entered premises, or anything in them, are to be left undisturbed, for so long as is reasonably necessary for the purpose of any examination or investigation;

(e) to take measurements and photographs and make recordings for the purpose of any examination or investigation;

(f) to take samples,[234] of any articles or substances found in or on any premises and of the air, water or land in, on, or in the vicinity of, the premises;

(g) in the case of any article or substance found in or on any premises which appears to have caused pollution of the environment or harm to human health, to cause it to be dismantled or subjected to any process or test, but not so as to damage or destroy it, unless that is necessary;[235]

(h) in the case of any such article or substance, to take possession of it and detain it for so long as is necessary for all or any of the following purposes:

    (i) to examine it;

    (ii) to ensure that it is not tampered with before examination of it is completed;

    (iii) to ensure that it is available for use as evidence in any proceedings for an offence under the pollution control enactments or in any other proceedings relating to a variation notice, enforcement notice or prohibition notice under those enactments;

(j) to require any person who is able to give any relevant information to any examination or investigation to answer questions and to sign a declaration of the truth of his answers;[236]

(k) to require the production of any records which are required to be kept under the pollution control enactments, or which it is

---

[233] 'Premises' is defined to include any land, vehicle, vessel or mobile plant (s.108(15) Environment Act 1995).

[234] The Secretary of State may by regulations make provision as to the procedure to be followed in connection with the taking of, and the dealing with, samples (s.108(9) *ibid*).

[235] Where an authorised person proposes to exercise this power in the case of an article or substance found on any premises, he must, if so requested by a person who at the time is present on and has responsibilities in relation to those premises, cause anything which is to be done by virtue of that power to be done in the presence of that person (s.108(10) *ibid*). Before exercising this power in the case of any article or substance, an authorised person must consult such persons having duties on the premises where the article or substance is to be dismantled or subjected to the process or test, and such other persons, as appear to him appropriate for the purpose of ascertaining what dangers, if any, there may be in doing anything which he proposes to do or cause to be done under the power (s.108(11) *ibid*).

[236] No answer given by a person in pursuance of these requirement will be admissible in evidence in England and Wales against that person in any proceedings (*ibid* s.108(12)).

necessary to see for the purposes of an examination or investigation, and to inspect and take copies of the records;

(l)   to require any person to afford facilities and assistance with respect to any matters or things within that person's control which are necessary to enable the authorised person to exercise any of the powers of entry and associated powers conferred on him;[237]

(m)   any other power[238] relating to pollution control enactments and functions of the Agency or relating to certain assessments and preparations of reports[239] which is conferred by regulations made by the Secretary of State.[240]

The powers which are conferred in relation to any premises, for the purpose of enabling the Agency to determine whether any provision of its pollution control enactments is being, or has been, complied with, is to include the power, to carry out experimental borings or other works on those premises and to install, keep or maintain monitoring and other apparatus there.[241]

Except in an emergency,[242] in any case where it is proposed to enter any premises used for residential purposes, or to take heavy equipment onto premises, entry may only be effected after the expiration of at least seven days' notice given to a person who appears to be in occupation of the premises. Entry in such circumstances must either be with the consent of a person who is in occupation of those premises or under the authority of a warrant.[243] Other than in an emergency, where an authorised person proposes to enter any premises and entry has been refused and it is reasonably apprehended that the use of force may be necessary, any entry may only be effected under the authority of a warrant.[244] Supplemental provisions are provided concerning the issue of warrants, the manner of exercise of powers, the admissibility in evidence of information obtained, the duty to secure premises and the payment of compensation for loss in pursuance of the exercise of powers.[245]

None of the powers of entry and associated powers, previously described, may be taken to compel the production by any person of a document of

---

[237] That is, powers conferred under s.108 Environment Act 1995.

[238] As specified under s.108(1) *ibid.*

[239] As specified under s.108(2) *ibid.*

[240] *Ibid* s.108(4).

[241] *Ibid* s.108(5).

[242] 'Emergency', for these purposes, is defined to mean a case in which it appears to the authorised person in question that there is an immediate risk of serious pollution of the environment or serious harm to human health, or that circumstances exist which are likely to endanger life or health, and that immediate entry to any premises is necessary to verify the existence of that risk or those circumstances or to ascertain the cause of that risk or those circumstances or to effect a remedy (s.108(15) *ibid*). See also discussion of 'emergency' at 9.17.1 above.

[243] *Ibid* s.108(6) and Schedule 18.

[244] *Ibid* s.108(7).

[245] *Ibid* Schedule 18.

which he would on grounds of legal professional privilege be entitled to withhold production on an order for discovery in an action in the High Court.[246]

Specific powers are provided for in order to allow authorised persons to deal with imminent dangers of serious pollution and related matters. Hence, where an authorised person finds any article or substance on any premises which he has power to enter, and there is reasonable cause to believe that the article or substance is a cause of imminent danger of serious pollution of the environment or serious harm to human health, he may seize it and cause it to be rendered harmless, by destruction or otherwise. As soon as possible after this, the authorised person must prepare and sign a written report giving particulars of the circumstances in which the article or substance was seized and dealt with. A signed copy of the report must be given to a responsible person at the premises where the article or substance was found. Unless that person is the owner of the article or substance, a copy of the report must also be served on the owner.[247]

Specific offences are provided for in relation to the powers of entry, previously described. Hence, it is an offence for a person intentionally to obstruct an authorised person in the exercise or performance of his powers or duties. In addition, it is an offence for a person, without reasonable excuse,

(a) to fail to comply with any requirement imposed under the powers of entry and related powers of authorised Agency personnel;[248]
(b) to fail or refuse to provide facilities or assistance or any information or to permit any inspection reasonably required by an authorised person in the execution of his powers or duties relating to entry and related matters; or
(c) to prevent any other person from appearing before an authorised person, or answering any question to which an authorised person may require an answer.[249]

It is also an offence for a person falsely to pretend to be an authorised person.[250]

A person guilty of an obstruction offence will be liable, in the case of an offence of obstructing an authorised person in the execution of his powers to deal with an imminent danger of serious pollution,[251] on summary conviction, to a fine not exceeding the statutory maximum (presently £5,000) and on conviction on indictment, to an unlimited fine or to

---

[246] s.108(13) Environment Act 1995, and see 16.13 below on self-incrimination in relation to water pollution evidences.
[247] *Ibid* s.109(1) and (2).
[248] As provided for under s.108 *ibid*.
[249] As provided for under s.108(4) *ibid*.
[250] *Ibid* s.110(1) to (3).
[251] Under s.109 *ibid*.

imprisonment for a term not exceeding two years, or to both. In relation to any other offence of obstruction, on summary conviction, the offender will be liable to a fine not exceeding level 5 on the standard scale (presently £5,000). Similarly, in relation to the offences concerning failure to comply with requirements, failure to provide facilities, assistance or information or to permit inspection, preventing of persons appearing before authorised officers and answering questions or pretending to be an authorised officer, a person guilty of these offence will, on summary conviction, be liable to a fine not exceeding level 5 on the standard scale (presently £5,000).[252]

## 6.18 Law Enforcement

As has been noted, the incidental general functions of the Agency allow it to do anything which is conducive to the carrying out of its functions and, explicitly, this includes the institution of legal proceedings.[253] However, the practical use that is made of this power is subject to important strategic considerations. In particular, a balance will need to be drawn between a litigious approach to law enforcement, using prosecution powers relatively frequently, and a more conciliatory approach, for example, by declining to prosecute where a polluter agrees to undertake measures to prevent future pollution incidents.[254]

The merger of National Rivers Authority staff with those from other former environmental regulatory authorities has meant that it is necessary to resolve differences of regulatory culture,[255] and the balance which the Agency draws between litigation and conciliation will only be fully apparent in the years ahead. However, some indication of the Government's initial intentions for the Agency in relation to law enforcement may be drawn from early policy statements. Hence in *The Environment Agency and Sustainable Development*,[256] in summarising the aim and objectives of the Agency, tends to stress a collaborative relationship between the Agency and regulated bodies. Amongst the strategic objectives of the Agency it was stated that it should work with all relevant sectors of society, including regulated organisations, to develop

---

[252] s.110(3) to (5) Environment Act 1995.

[253] *Ibid* s.37(1), and see 6.13 above on incidental functions.

[254] The contrast between these approaches was neatly illustrated by presentations at a Confederation of British Industry conference in 1995 where Ed Gallagher, the then Chief Executive of the Environment Agency, had suggested that the Agency will seek to do 'deals' with companies to reduce their monitoring costs if some of the savings were ploughed back into environmental improvement and, as a consequence, polluters were less likely to be prosecuted by the Agency than by the former National Rivers Authority. By contrast, Brian Glicksman, the head of the division of the Department of the Environment (now DETR) which shadows the Agency, expressed the view that, though the Government was concerned not to impose new burdens on business unless convinced of the benefits, however, he was 'not sure' that the Environment Act 1995 would allow the Agency to do the kind of deals with industry proposed (*ENDS Report* 249 (1995) p.5). It should also be noted that this debate was closely linked with the previous Government's broader policy for the deregulation of industry (*ENDS Report* 252 (1996) p.3).

[255] On the approach towards prosecution of the National Rivers Authority see 2.19 above.

[256] DoE, MAFF and WO (1996) p.3, and see also DoE, MAFF and WO, *The Environment Agency Management Statement* (1996) p.9.

approaches which deliver environmental requirements and goals without imposing excessive costs, in relation to benefits gained, on regulated organisations or society as a whole.[257] In a similar vein, it is noted that there was considerable scope for reconciling the needs of the environment and those of development by regulated organisations adopting improved technologies and management techniques as an integral part of their industrial and commercial investment. The Agency should therefore, where possible, discharge its regulatory functions in partnership with business in ways which maximise the scope for cost-effective investment in such technologies and techniques.[258]

### 6.18.1 The Enforcement and Prosecution Policy

More recent indications as to the circumstances in which the Environment Agency will make use of its prosecution powers, and other enforcement mechanisms available to it, are provided by policy guidance incorporated the Agency's *Enforcement and Prosecution Policy*,[259] setting out the general principles and approach that the Agency will adopt in exercising its powers. However, it is to be noted that this policy is of general application to all matters relating to enforcement, across the range of its functions, and is not restricted to the use of enforcement powers merely in relation to water pollution and water quality matters.

From the outset, the emphasis of the policy is placed upon the preference for prevention rather than cure, with provision of informal advice and information being seen as a means towards cooperation between regulators and regulated which avoids enforcement proceedings. Nonetheless, the policy recognises that where encouragement of good practice is not sufficient, enforcement and prosecution will be required to ensure compliance with the regulatory system. Enforcement mechanisms include a range of powers to secure prevention, remediation and punishment where necessary. Hence, these powers encompass enforcement notices, works notices, prohibition notices, suspension or revocation of environmental licences, variation of licence conditions, injunctions, the conduct of remedial works and the recovery of costs for remedial works carried out by the Agency. Specifically, where a criminal offence has been committed, the Agency has the options of instituting a prosecution, administering a caution or issuing a warning.

In relation to the decision to prosecute for pollution offences,[260] the Agency emphasises its belief in 'firm but fair regulation' and interprets this in terms of four key principles: proportionality, consistency,

---

[257] See DoE, MAFF and WO, *The Environment Agency and Sustainable Development* (1996) para.9(ii) of Statutory Guidance (under s.4 Environment Act 1995).

[258] *Ibid* para.10(v).

[259] Environment Agency (1998) approved by the Board of the Agency and the Environment Minister for DETR.

[260] See the criteria set out in the Code for Crown Prosecutors published by the Crown Office, establishing evidential sufficiency and public interest tests. The Code is provided for under s.10 Prosecution of Offenders Act 1985; generally see Uglow (1995) Ch.10.

transparency and targetting of enforcement action. 'Proportionality' envisages a balance of action to protect the environment against risks and costs so that enforcement action will be proportionate to the risks posed to the environment and the seriousness of any offence. 'Consistency' means taking a similar approach in similar circumstances, though it is recognised that account needs to be taken of many variables such as the scale of impact, the attitude of the offender and previous incidents or breaches. 'Transparency' means informing those that are regulated what is expected of them and making it clear why enforcement action is to be taken or what action is required to avoid enforcement action. 'Targetting' involves the prioritised application of regulatory effort towards those whose activities risk giving rise to the most serious environmental damage, or where risks are least well controlled or offending actions of a deliberate or organised character.

In accordance with the four principles, a decision to prosecute will not be commenced unless the Agency is satisfied that there is sufficient, admissible and reliable evidence that the offence has been committed and that there is a realistic prospect of a conviction being secured. Where the 'sufficiency of evidence' test is satisfied a prosecution will not be undertaken unless it is in the public interest to do so, taking account of the seriousness of the offence and the circumstances of the offender. More specifically, the Agency will consider the following factors in deciding whether to prosecute:

(a)  the environmental effect of the offence;
(b)  the foreseeability of the offence and the circumstances leading to it;
(c)  the intent of the offender, individually and/or corporately;
(d)  the history of offending;
(e)  the attitude of the offender;
(f)  the deterrent effect of a prosecution on the offender and others; and
(g)  the personal circumstances of the offender.

In respect of proceedings against corporate bodies, the Agency will normally prosecute the company concerned. However, where it is shown that the senior officers of the company consented to the offending activity or 'turned a blind eye' to it, the Agency will consider proceedings against Directors or other officers concerned, and may consider seeking disqualification of directors under companies legislation.

Alongside these considerations, it is stated that the Agency will *normally* prosecute in specified circumstances:

(a)  where there are incidents or breaches which have significant consequences for the environment or which have the potential for such consequences;
(b)  where operations are conducted without a relevant licence;

(c)   where there has been excessive or persistent breaches of regulatory requirements;

(d)   where there has been a failure to comply adequately with formal requirements;

(e)   where there has been reckless disregard for management or quality standards;

(f)    where there has been a failure to supply information without reasonable excuse or knowingly or recklessly supplying false or misleading information;

(g)   where there has been obstruction of Agency staff in carrying out their powers; and

(h)   where there has been impersonation of Agency staff, for example, to gain access to premises.

### 6.18.2  The Functional Guidelines

Although the publication of an official statement of the basis upon which legal proceedings by the Agency are likely to be pursued is welcomed as a contribution to openness in decision-making, the generality of expressions such as 'significant consequences for the environment' and 'excessive breaches of regulatory requirements' leaves considerable scope for interpretation. Read in isolation, the policy statement allows few specific conclusions to be drawn as to how the balance between litigious and conciliatory approaches towards environmental law enforcement will be drawn.

However, the enforcement policy statement has subsequently been supplemented by *Guidance for the Enforcement and Prosecution Policy*.[261] The '*Functional Guidelines*' published by the Agency, explain how the enforcement policy will be put into practice and seek to achieve a consistent approach to enforcement across all the Agency's various functions. The Guidelines reaffirm the threefold system of categorising incidents, under a 'Common Incidents Classification Scheme', as having 'major', 'significant' and 'minor' impact. In respect of the first category, prosecution will normally result in relation to the principal water pollution offences.[262] For the second category prosecution or formal caution will be the normal course of action and for the third category a warning will usually be sufficient unless other factors are present such as poor co-operation or repetition of an offence. In respect of the contravention of a condition of a discharge consent, an additional option is the service of an enforcement notice on the offender.[263]

---

[261] Environment Agency (1999) (Version 2, 30 September 1999) and see discussion of water pollution incidents at 9.2 below.

[262] Under s.85 Water Resources Act 1991 and see 9.3 below on the principal water pollution offences.

[263] Under ss.85(6) and 90(1)-(2) *ibid* and see 10.11.1 below on enforcement notices.

## 6.19 Publicising Environmental Performance

Whilst a criminal conviction for an environmental offence serves an immediately punitive purpose in publicly identifying the offender and imposing whatever punishment is appropriate, some reservations may be held as to the overall effectiveness of this process in deterring environmental crime.[264] In part this may be due to the reluctance of the courts to impose sentences which reflect the damage caused by environmental offences, but also because of the perception that environmental convictions are not sufficiently publicised to impact upon the commercial reputations of the offenders. Mechanisms which might enhance the impact of criminal prosecutions, or which publicise the genuine state of environmental performance of a regulated body, are seen as beneficial by the Agency.

A development which added new significance to environmental convictions, was the 1999 Agency initiative of 'naming and shaming' those convicted of environmental pollution offences by their identification on a 'league table' of worst offenders.[265] Despite numerous calls upon the courts to impose more realistic fines for environmental offences, the overall result of the 744 prosecutions that the Agency brought in 1998 was to secure fines totaling just over £2 million. That is, the average fine for an environmental offence was only £2,786[266] and regarded by the Agency as excessively low. Consequently, the compilation of the table of worst offenders was an initial attempt to 'add value' to convictions by maximising the publicity impact.

The pollution 'hall of shame', first presented in 1999, related to all kinds of pollution offence though those convicted of water pollution offences figure prominently. Top of the table was ICI which accumulated fines totaling £382,500 arising from three water pollution convictions. Sewerage undertakers also featured prominently in the fines league table, with Wessex Water Ltd placed fourth, Anglian Water Services Ltd placed sixth, North West Water Ltd placed thirteenth equal, Welsh Water placed fifteenth, and Severn Trent Water Ltd placed sixteenth equal.[267]

An initial impression of the first use of the 'naming and shaming' approach was that it was crude but properly motivated. The media was enthusiastic about bringing the serious offenders into the spotlight, and inviting them to answer difficult questions, but the approach was subject to criticism as to the precision of the information upon which it was based. Also, it tended to direct attention to those large corporate polluters who came before those courts which made greater use of the available sentencing powers, rather

---

[264] See de Prez (2000) on the impacts of convictions for environmental offences and Merrett (1993) on the benefits of satisfactory environmental performance.

[265] See DETR press release *Meacher Welcomes Pollution League Tables,* 20 March 1999 and Environment Agency press release *Environment Agency's Hall of Shame points the finger at guilty polluters,* 22 March 1999. See *www.environment-agency.gov.uk,* for table of 'worst offenders'.

[266] Although see *ENDS Report* 295 (1999) p.49 indicating that the average fine for water companies convicted of water pollution offences is about £4,000.

[267] Generally, see 9.2 below on water pollution incident statistics.

than necessarily showing anything conclusive about the gravity of the offence committed, particularly given diverse range of considerations which may apply in the sentencing of pollution offenders.[268] Hence, a reservation was that the table assumed a degree of comparability in sentencing which may not always be well-founded. Moreover, no account was taken in the league table of the 312 enforcement and prohibition notices issues by the Agency in the same year which, arguably, again serve as an equally significant element in assessing unsatisfactory environmental performance as actual convictions. More generally, it was thought that a more meaningful index could be used to shape opinions as to the genuine state of corporate environmental performances through a more comprehensive environmental performance league table, indicating the best as well as the worst environmental performers.[269]

To some extent, these reservations have been responded to in the more broadly based approach to publicising environmental performance that has recently been placed on the Agency's website. *Spotlight on business environmental business performance – 1999*[270] identifies those companies which have substantially reduced impact upon the environment in addition to companies that have been prosecuted for environmental offences. The 1999 report highlights encouraging reductions in polluting emissions from power stations, metal production and processing, and the chemical and minerals industries. In all, 28 companies, across a wide range of industries, are singled out for achieving significant reductions in environmental pollutants in 1999. Particular note is given to reduced emissions of sulphur dioxide from power stations, reductions in volatile organic compounds from installations operated by Associated Octel, BP Chemicals and Union Carbide and reductions in particulate emissions from the metal production and processing and the minerals sectors.

However, it is reported that the Agency also prosecuted over 500 companies nationally for a range of serious pollution offences that exposed the public and the environment to dangers including asbestos, hazardous wastes, chemical gas clouds and raw sewage. Amongst these, 48 offenders appear either in the league table of offences or the league table of total fines for pollution offences, with water and sewerage undertakers continuing to dominate the league of most frequent offenders, occupying all 5 top places and 7 out of the top 11 rankings for companies most often prosecuted by the Agency in 1999. The most frequent offender was Thames Water Utilities Ltd, placed third place in the ranking for fines after having been prosecuted by the Agency on eight separate occasions in 1999, with total fines of £79,000.

The Agency continues to be disappointed about the overall level of fines imposed on companies convicted of environmental crimes. In 1999 the

---

[268] See 9.19 below on sentencing for water pollution offences.

[269] House of Commons, Environment, Transport and Regional Affairs Committee, *The Environment Agency* (2000) paras.88-94.

[270] Available at www.environment-agency.gov.uk, and see Environment Agency, Press Release, *Environmental Record in North East Improves but Pollution Failures Continue*, 7 August 2000.

average level of fines imposed overall was £3,500, a slight increase over the 1998 average of £2,768. However, in the Agency's view, this small increase in the current average level of fines still does not reflect the long-term environmental damage caused through criminal neglect and it will continue to call on the courts to impose penalties that are real deterrents for future environmental mismanagement.

A relatively sophisticated approach to the dissemination of local information concerning environmental performance is the production by the Agency of a 'pollution inventory' which shows emissions from all processes which are subject to integrated pollution control. Operators of all prescribed industrial processes were made subject to reporting requirements for releases of chemicals into the environment, so that information was required to be provided as to the release of more than 150 substances to water, air or land where these exceeded stated thresholds. The data which was gathered for 1998 was collated and made available on the internet,[271] so that it is possible to search the database by postcode or map to discover the location of sites which are subject to process authorisation and associated releases. Alternatively, the information may be searched by company name, industry sector or pollutant, though data with regard to compliance is not incorporated. The same website allows rivers and bathing waters to be searched by locality to ascertain the results of general quality assessment. Whilst comment has been raised as to the accuracy and completeness of the data which is presently recorded on the inventory, it has been generally welcomed as a meaningful guide to the most harmful emissions.[272] Clearly the extension of this approach to all discharges to controlled waters would be a valuable means of disseminating environmental information and drawing attention to the most significant point sources of water contaminants.[273]

## 6.20 The Agency and Other Regulators

A key justification for the establishment of the Environment Agency from its predecessor bodies lay in the belief that this would allow a greater consistency of approach towards all types of pollution and across all environmental media. Moreover, the amalgamation of functions would avoid overlap and duplication of effort and this would be advantageous to regulated bodies in leaving them with a single regulatory authority to approach.[274] Although the consolidation of regulatory control of water, waste and industrial processes has brought about a significant concentration of regulatory responsibilities within the Agency, the, so-called, 'one stop shopping' view of regulatory integration has not been realised insofar as the regulation of water quality is concerned.

---

[271] See www.environment-agency.gov.uk

[272] See *ENDS Report* 292 (1999) p.24.

[273] Generally, see Ch.16 below on access to water quality information.

[274] See, HM Government, *This Common Inheritance* (Cm.1200, 1990) p.232, and House of Commons Environment Committee, *The Government's Proposals for an Environment Agency* (1992).

Responsibilities with regard to water are actually dispersed between a significant number of different regulatory authorities which must interface with the Agency in relation to the protection of water quality and the aquatic environment. Whilst integration, both of substantive legislation and administrative responsibilities, has been a key theme in the development of environmental law over the last decade, the resistance of water regulation to this trend is remarkable and demonstrates the breadth of concerns to which it gives rise. In essence, multiple regulatory controls are needed because different purposes underlie different branches of legislation and different regulatory objectives, pursued by different regulatory authorities, are required to administer and implement that legislation. A brief scan of key regulatory responsibilities for water quality, which fall outside the remit of the Agency, serves to illustrate the variety of regulatory interests that are involved.

### Water and Sewerage Undertakers

Although primarily the suppliers of water services, water and sewerage undertakers also posses powers in respect of the contamination and misuse of water supplies[275] and in respect of the discharge of domestic and trade effluent to sewers.[276]

### The Director General of Water Services

The Director General serves as the primary economic regulator of water and sewerage undertakers in restricting the prices of these services and regulating permissable levels of environmental expenditure by the undertakers.[277]

### The Drinking Water Inspectorate

Within the Department of the Environment, Transport and the Regions, the Drinking Water Inspectorate has overall responsibility for the monitoring of potable water supplies, advising the Secretary of State as to when legal proceedings should be brought in relation to unsatisfactory drinking water and, in practice, actually bringing such proceedings.[278]

### The Ministry of Agriculture, Fisheries and Food

The Ministry of Agriculture, Fisheries and Food has responsibility for aspects of water quality relating to agriculture, such as the controls imposed upon fertilisers and pesticides,[279] and has ultimate responsibility

---

[275] Generally see Ch.17 below on drinking water quality.
[276] Generally see Ch.11 below on trade effluent controls.
[277] Generally see Ch.7 below on the economic regulation of the water industry.
[278] Generally see 17.5 below on the Drinking Water Inspectorate.
[279] Generally see 13.5 below on the control of nitrate.

for fishery matters[280] and certain marine activities which may relate to water quality.[281]

*Local Authority Environmental Health Departments*

Local authorities have a wide range of responsibilities and regulatory powers concerning public health aspects of water, including powers relating to unsanitary drinking water supplies,[282] bathing water quality[283] and duties relating to statutory nuisances[284] which may be relevant in relation to water.

*Local Planning Authorities*

Local planning authorities have extensive powers and duties in relation to the control of development and the formulation of development plans which may have important implications where projects with potential adverse impacts upon water quality are under consideration or where particular waters need special protection.[285]

*The Statutory Nature Conservation Councils*

English Nature and the Countryside Council for Wales, have responsibility for conservation of species and habitats of wild flora and fauna and important powers to designate land and water and restrict harmful activities where ecological protection is needed.[286]

*Department of the Environment, Transport and the Regions and Department of Trade and Industry*

For matters relating to the marine environment, the lead regulators are the Department of the Environment, Transport and the Regions, in relation to shipping, and the Department of Trade and Industry for offshore installations, including spills from oil installations.[287] There is an independent Maritime and Coastguard Agency which is the regulatory authority for ship safety. There is also the Marine Accident Investigation Branch which has the power to investigate accidents involving or occurring on board any ship within UK territorial waters, and which also reports to the Secretary of State for the Environment, Transport and the Regions.

More detailed consideration is given to the legal responsibilities of these bodies later in this work, but for the present it is sufficient merely to note the range of regulatory authorities involved and the diversity of purposes

---

[280] Generally see Ch.15 below on fisheries and water quality.

[281] Generally see 19.17–20 below on dumping at sea.

[282] Generally see 17.9 below on local authority responsibility for drinking water quality.

[283] Generally see 5.5.2 above on bathing water quality.

[284] Generally see 8.5 below on statutory nuisances.

[285] Generally see Ch.14 below on town and country planning law.

[286] Generally see Ch.15 below on nature conservation and water quality.

[287] Generally see Ch.19 below on the marine environment.

for which water quality regulation is required. In relation to each of the bodies listed, an interface with the responsibilities of the Environment Agency will exist, but it is readily apparent that the Agency is far from having a monopoly upon water quality regulation. Far from the original objective that there should be 'one stop shopping', there is actually an 'arcade' of regulators each trading in a different commodity!

# Chapter 7

# ECONOMIC REGULATION OF WATER SERVICES

## 7.1 Introduction

The economic regulation of water services plays a crucial role in preventing water pollution and securing water quality improvements. Upgrading treatment works, constructing nitrate and pesticide removal plants, treating sludge before it is spread on land; all these require considerable amounts of investment if they are to play their part in improving the quality of the water environment and the use of water for drinking, conservation, recreation and other purposes. Of course, paying for infrastructure improvements was as important before 1989 as it is today, though the underfunding during this period has been cited as one of the driving forces behind privatisation of the water industry that year.[1] In this sense, nothing has changed. What *has* changed is that the process by which water and sewerage undertakers are funded has become more open and more transparent. The process is also one that is now laid down as a matter of law, with a specialist economic regulator, the Director General of Water Services, acting under specific legal duties and at one remove from central government in financing the undertakers.

The principal objective of this chapter is to describe the current regulatory framework under which, from an economic point of view, water and sewerage undertakers are regulated in England and Wales. This involves looking at the functions of central government, the Director General of Water Services ('the Director') and the undertakers, and the duties these bodies must adhere to when exercising their functions, including specific environmental duties. It also requires discussing the nature of competition in the water industry, how this is facilitated, and how prices for water and sewerage services are determined. While later chapters discuss in detail the powers and duties of the undertakers in regulating the discharge of effluent to sewers[2] and in supplying drinking water of a suitable quality,[3] the chapter concludes by considering the general enforcement mechanisms intended to ensure compliance by the undertakers with their water quality functions.

In this chapter, reference to 'the undertakers' is a reference to both the ten combined water and sewerage companies established on privatisation, and the (presently) 15 smaller private water supply companies with a longer heritage and now established under separate legislation. Both are subject to the general provisions relating to undertakers discussed below.

---

[1] See 2.15 above.
[2] See Ch.11 below.
[3] See Ch.17 below.

## 7.2 Outline of the Present Legal Framework

The allocation of responsibility for water quality regulation can be conceived of hierarchically. First, there is the role of central government, both in negotiating quality standards at EC and international level, and setting legal standards nationally. A central role of the water quality regulators, the Environment Agency and the Drinking Water Inspectorate,[4] in protecting the water environment and enforcing drinking water quality standards, is to ensure that centrally determined requirements and standards are met.

Second, the undertakers are themselves made subject to certain legal duties, including environmental duties, concerning their activities.[5] More generally, while the Environment Agency draws up proposals for environmental improvement works (in its 'National Environment Programme'),[6] it is the undertakers who price the works considered necessary to meet water quality standards, and submit these to the Director General of Water Services ('the Director'), the economic regulator that heads up the Office of Water Services ('Ofwat'). The Director must allow the companies sufficient resources to meet their legal obligations while taking consumer interests into account. The first Director's[7] increasing advocacy of consumer interests was, at least during the first price review of the undertakers in 1994, a crucial factor in holding back many water quality improvements.

There are some important limitations to thinking of economic regulation in this 'cascade'-type fashion. Few water quality obligations are formulated as mandatory obligations without any ambiguity as to their scope. To take one example, there is some uncertainty whether or not the obligation to endeavour to meet 'Guide' values for EC water quality directives gives complete freedom to the Member States to decide the duration within which such standards are reached.[8] There is therefore some room for Ministers to give water quality obligations their own interpretation when it comes to advising the Director on the financing of any schemes necessary to realise quality improvements. In reality, therefore, the price-setting process is an iterative one. The undertakers cannot estimate costs, and Ofwat cannot estimate the impacts on consumers bills, without a fair degree of certainty over the obligations with which the undertakers will be faced, and the Government cannot confirm the scope of the investment programme before knowing what it will cost.[9]

While the Director is under a duty to ensure that undertakers meet their legal obligations in relation to water quality, and is given enforcement

---

[4] See Ch.6 and 17.5 below respectively.

[5] See 7.6.4–5 below.

[6] See 7.8.3 below on the National Environment Programme.

[7] Ian (now Sir Ian) Byatt served as Director from 1989. He was replaced by Philip Fletcher on 1 August 2000.

[8] See 5.5.2C below on this for the Bathing Water Directive (76/160/EEC).

[9] House of Commons Select Committee on Environmental Audit, *Water Prices and the Environment* (2000), see 7.8 below.

powers to do so,[10] the Director also plays a key role in relation to competition within the water industry. Establishing the National Rivers Authority (and now the Environment Agency) largely removed the principal 'poacher-gamekeeper' problem that operational matters and regulatory control were vested in the same bodies. But the geographical division and general nature of the water industry has meant that the scope for direct competition between undertakers has been limited. Competition has therefore only been at the margins, and a key role of the Director has so far been to operate a system of 'comparative' competition where relative best practice between undertakers is established and used to set industry-wide requirements.

At present, however, there is the prospect of enhanced competition within the water sector, perhaps by giving undertakers access to their competitors water supply infrastructure (known as 'common carriage').[11] This raises many legal issues, not least concerning liability for the supply of water of sub-standard quality.[12]

The current legal provisions regulating the activities of the water and sewerage undertakers are mainly contained in the Water Industry Act 1991. Parts I and II of the 1991 Act state the functions and enforcement powers of the Director and the Secretary of State,[13] while the legal provisions relating to competition between undertakers are also provided for in the Competition Act 1998, which transferred scrutiny of mergers from the Monopolies and Mergers Commission to the Competition Commission from 1 April 1999. Proposals providing for direct competition between undertakers, and certain changes to the role of the Director, were included in the draft Water Bill, published at the end of 2000.

## 7.3 The Functions of the Secretary of State

Although day to day control of the undertakers is the responsibility of the Director, the Secretary of State made the initial appointments of undertakers on privatisation, and continues to exercise certain important powers and duties over the Director and the industry. References here to the Secretary of State are generally to the Secretary of State for the Environment, Transport and the Regions.[14] In relation to Wales, reference to the Secretary of State should be taken as reference to the National Assembly for Wales.[15]

---

[10] On enforcement see 7.9 below.

[11] Or by allowing new entrants the right to put new sources of water into the network of an existing undertaker. See 7.7.3 below on 'common carriage'.

[12] See 17.7.6–7 on liability issues relating to common carriage.

[13] In Wales, the National Assembly for Wales, see 7.3 below.

[14] Rather than the Secretary of State for Trade and Industry as with other privatised utilities, although the latter has functions in respect of mergers, on which see 7.7.1 below.

[15] And references in this chapter to the Secretary of State (either the Secretary of State for the Environment, Transport and the Regions, or the Secretary of State for Trade and Industry) are references to the Welsh Assembly unless otherwise indicated.

Principally, new appointments of undertakers made by the Director are subject to the terms of a general authorisation by the Secretary of State,[16] who also exercises a right of veto over modifications to an appointment.[17] The Secretary of State may instruct the Director to exercise his functions in specific ways, or make the exercise of such functions subject to his authorisation.[18] The Director must also make Annual Reports to the Secretary of State concerning the exercise of his functions.[19]

The Secretary of State may require the Director, by direction, to have particular regard to specific considerations in exercising both his general review functions and his powers to appoint and regulate undertakers, and in relation to water supply and sewerage services.[20] The Secretary of State is also empowered to prescribe performance standards in respect of an undertaker's general duties relating to water supply[21] and sewerage services.[22]

The Secretary of State also has important enforcement duties.[23] While many of these may be exercised concurrently with the Director, or by the Director acting under the direction of the Secretary of State, the Secretary has sole power to enforce the Act's environmental duties[24] and those relating to the quality of drinking water.[25] The Secretary of State has also certain rights to information from undertakers,[26] and the power to refer a merger to the Competition Commission.[27] The Secretary of State is subject to the general duties in relation to competition and consumers, and in respect of the environment and recreation.[28]

After consultation, the Secretary of State may give undertakers general or specific directions as appear to him requisite or expedient in the interests of national security or for the purpose of mitigating the effects of any civil emergency which may occur (or, in the case of specific directions, has occurred). Such directions override any other duties on the undertaker, and are enforced under Part II of the Water Industry Act 1991.[29]

---

[16] s.6(1)(b) Water Industry Act 1991.
[17] *Ibid* s.13(4).
[18] *Ibid* ss.6, 19(1)(b), 37 and 94.
[19] *Ibid* s.193(1).
[20] Under Parts II-IV and Part VII Water Industry Act 1991, see s. 27(3), discussed at 7.4.3 below.
[21] *Ibid* s.38(2).
[22] *Ibid* s.95(2).
[23] *Ibid* ss.18-22, see 7.9 below.
[24] *Ibid* ss.3(7) and 4(5), discussed at 7.6.4–5 below.
[25] *Ibid* ss.68(5) and 79(6), and see also Reg.34 Water Supply (Water Quality) Regulations 1989 (SI 1989 No. 1147) discussed at 17.6 below.
[26] Bates (1990) para 3.43 s.202 Water Industry Act 1991.
[27] ss.32 and 33 Water Industry Act 1991, see 7.7.1 below.
[28] In *ibid* ss.2 and 3 respectively, and see 7.5 and 7.6.4 below.
[29] *Ibid* s.18, discussed at 7.9 below.

## 7.4  The Director General of Water Services

### 7.4.1  Appointment and Principal Functions

The Director General of Water Services is appointed by the Secretary of State, and has responsibility for the Office of Water Services, a non-ministerial government department. Powers and duties are accorded to the Director, rather than to his office, with the result that regulation can take on something of a 'personalised' character. Directors serve renewable five-year terms, subject to removal by the Secretary of State for incapacity or misbehaviour.[30] The functions of the office of the Director are governed by Part I of the Water Industry Act 1991 which also imposes general duties on the Secretary of State.[31]

The primary duty of the Director is towards the proper carrying out by the undertakers of their key statutory supply and sewerage duties (i.e. ensuring that they are actually carried out fully), and ensuring the sufficient economic wellbeing of the undertakers to allow them to do so. The Director is not directly responsible for determining or enforcing water quality or sewerage standards, although he is consulted on the setting of quality standards. His key role is in the appointment of undertakers and, under Instruments of Appointment (or 'licences'), setting the terms and conditions of such appointments.[32] Crucially, this includes the power to determine the prices undertakers may charge, which will have a direct impact on the levels of investment made by undertakers in improving water quality. In this respect the Director both determines the cost to consumers of improvements in water quality set at Community and national level, as well as the extent to which undertakers may finance projects going beyond minimum required standards.

In this sense, therefore, the office of Director has developed from that of a technocratic economic regulator into, over time, a more multi-dimensional regulatory body.[33] The Director has also played a central role in seeking to influence the climate within which current legal obligations as regards water quality are interpreted, and in certain respects has moved to a role of 'standard-maker', not merely 'standard-taker'.[34] This has occurred within a framework that relegates his environmental duties beneath those owed to the undertakers and to consumers. Nevertheless, it is this combination of economic, social and environmental factors that makes the role of the Director central in relation to sustainable development issues concerning water quality.

---

[30] See *ibid* ss.1(2), (3) and (4).

[31] See also 7.3 above.

[32] See 7.6.3 below on such licences.

[33] See Saunders and Harris (1994) pp.61-67 and Prosser (1994a). Contrast Littlechild (1986).

[34] Kinnersley (1994) pp.176-8. See further Byatt (1996b).

## 7.4.2 Customer Service Committees

The obligation of the Director towards customers is assisted by the establishment, by the Director, of a maximum of 10 Customer Service Committees.[35] The Director assigns each water or sewerage company to a Committee. In practice, the Committee areas shadow the areas of the combined water and sewerage undertakers. Each Committee consists of a chairman[36] and between 10 and 20 members appointed by the Director. Committees must be staffed by members with experience of the sector, the intention being to achieve a balance between business, consumers and local authorities.[37] Although established and appointed by the Director, the Committees are independent of the Director (and of the undertakers) and are subject to their own legal duties.

The duties of the Committees[38] include general duties to keep matters affecting customers, or potential[39] customers, under review, and to consult with and make representations to each company. With the exception of frivolous or vexatious matters, any complaint brought to the Committee by a customer or potential customer, or referred to it by the Director, must be investigated. Complaints relating to any of the following must be referred to the Director:

(a) any condition of the undertaker's appointment or any statutory or other enforceable requirement;[40]

(b) a complaint relating to an undertaker's right to lay pipes, etc;[41] and

(c) complaints which the Committee is unable to resolve following the making of representations to the company.

While the duties of the Committees are broadly formulated, no specific powers of investigation are given. Undertakers must meet their Committee at least annually and at other times as reasonably required by the Committee, and consult with the Committee on their codes of practice concerning matters unrelated to water quality.[42]

Depending on the nature of the complaint, the Director has a duty to consider whether a complaint made directly to him should be referred to the Committee, dealt with by himself or referred by him to the Secretary of State. If the Director deals with the complaint himself, he may take such steps as he considers appropriate.[43] The functions given to the Committees supersede the jurisdiction of the Local Government Ombudsman in

---

[35] s.28 and Schedule 4 Water Industry Act 1991.

[36] Appointed in consultation with the Secretary of State for Trade and Industry (for the nine Committees in England).

[37] See Standing Committee D, col. 511, 1989 (Committee Stage of the Water Bill 1989).

[38] See generally ss.29 and 30 Water Industry Act 1991.

[39] See the definition of 'potential customers' at 7.5 below.

[40] Enforceable under s.18 Water Industry Act 1991, see 7.9.1 below.

[41] Which the Director would be required to investigate under *ibid* s.181.

[42] Model Instrument of Appointment, Condition G.9.

[43] s.30 Water Industry Act 1991.

relation to allegations of maladministration.[44] Customer Service Committees are subject to the provisions of the Public Bodies (Admission to Meetings) Act 1960, which means that meetings must be publicised in advance and, as a rule, be open to the public.

A further key body, established by the Director, is the Ofwat National Customer Council (ONCC), an umbrella organisation for the Customer Service Committees. The chairman and members of the Council are the chairmen of the Committees. The Director attends for part of every meeting. The Director has recommended to the Government that the Council, like the Committees, should become a statutory body. Until such time the Director will have regard to the ONCC's representations as if it were a statutory body.[45]

### 7.4.3 Duty to Review Undertakers' Activities and Obtain Information

The Director is under a duty to keep under review the activities of water and sewerage undertakers generally.[46] Notably, this obligation requires the Director to review operational and regulatory matters not only in England and Wales but, as he considers practicable, to review regulatory best practice in other countries. Generally, however, it appears that utility Directors have made little use of such information, considering it vulnerable to challenge before the Competition Commission or in judicial review.[47] The Director must also collect information regarding the discharge of undertakers' functions.[48] These general review and information-gathering duties are subject to any general direction given by the Secretary of State.[49] The Director also exercises certain powers and duties regarding the giving of information, advice and assistance to the Secretary of State or the Director General of Fair Trading with respect to undertakers' functions or performance.[50]

The Director has wide powers to obtain information from undertakers concerning enforcement orders.[51] This does not restrict the Director's powers to obtain information under conditions of appointment,[52] and the Model Instrument of Appointment contains a number of conditions requiring undertakers to supply such information to the Director as he reasonably requires for the purposes of carrying out his functions under the Act.[53] The ability of the Director to gain sufficient information from the

---

[44] See previously Water Act 1983.

[45] Ofwat Information Note No. 33, January 1996 (revised June 1998).

[46] s.27(1) Water Industry Act 1991.

[47] Kay (1996). It might also be said that the arrangements for the economic regulation of the water sector in England and Wales are fairly *sui generis*, which might make formal international comparisons less valuable.

[48] s.27(2) Water Industry Act 1991.

[49] *Ibid* s.27(3).

[50] *Ibid* s.27(4).

[51] *Ibid* s.203. On enforcement orders see 7.9.1 below.

[52] *Ibid* s.203(7).

[53] Condition M.

undertakers is a key factor in effective economic regulation, but is inherently limited.[54]

### 7.4.4 Registers and Information Dissemination

The Director must maintain a register containing certain information relating to matters that fall within his jurisdiction. This includes details of any appointment; any variation, modification, transfer or termination of an appointment; and any directions, consents or determinations given or made under an appointment. Records relating to any enforcement action taken against an undertaker, including any undertakings given to and accepted by the Secretary of State, must also be entered. The register must be available for public inspection[55] and charges can be made for copies of information drawn from the register.[56] The Director also has a proactive power to publish such information and advice as he considers it would be useful for customers to have.[57]

The Director must submit an annual report to the Secretary of State. This must include a general survey of developments during the year, and any directions given to him by the Secretary of State concerning matters to keep under review. The Report may contain, for example, information on the extent to which undertakers are in compliance with the terms of their discharge consents.[58] The Report is laid before Parliament. The Director may publish other reports as he sees fit.[59]

### 7.4.5 Dispute Resolution Functions

The Director exercises a number of dispute resolution functions. Of particular note is his duty to determine disputes concerning the discharge of trade effluent, other than 'special category effluent', to sewers.[60] The Director will also resolve disputes over standards of performance as regards water supply or sewerage services. Broadly, the Director has a fairly wide power to adopt such practices and procedures as he considers appropriate.[61] He cannot determine disputes that are, or have been, the subject of court proceedings. Reasons must be given for any decision, and his determinations are final. Insofar as the Director's determination includes provision as to costs and expenses, in relation to which he must

---

[54] Ogus (1994) p.306.

[55] See Director-General of Water Services' Register (Inspection and Charges) Order 1989 (SI 1989 No. 1154).

[56] See generally s.195 Water Industry Act 1991.

[57] *Ibid* s.201(2).

[58] On undertakers' compliance with consents see 10.11 below.

[59] See generally s.193 Water Industry Act 1991. The Annual Report is available at www.open.gov.uk/ofwat/index.htm

[60] *Ibid* s.123. On special category effluent see 11.10 below.

[61] Subject to the requirements of natural justice, and rights to a fair hearing derived from the European Convention on Human Rights (see Art.6).

have regard to the conduct of the parties and their ability to pay, it is enforceable as if it were a county court judgment.[62]

### 7.4.6 Competition Functions

The Water Industry Act 1991 places responsibility for competition within the industry largely upon the Director. In particular, the Director General of Fair Trading may delegate his powers under Part III of the Fair Trading Act 1973 to the Director as regards matters that may prejudice the interests of water or sewerage customers.[63] Consumer interests may extend to health, safety and other matters. The Director may therefore be put under a duty to use his best endeavours to obtain a written assurance from the undertaker concerned to refrain from the practice identified, and is empowered to obtain a court order if the assurance is subsequently broken.

The Director has concurrent jurisdiction with the Director General of Fair Trading as regards certain provisions of the Fair Trading Act 1973,[64] and as regards the functions of the latter under the provisions of Part I of the Competition Act 1998,[65] so far as they relate to:

(a) actual or potential monopoly situations in relation to commercial activities connected with the supply of water or the provision of sewerage services;

(b) agreements, decisions or concerted practices which may affect trade within the UK and have as their object or effect preventing, restricting or distorting competition within the UK;[66] or

(c) conduct on the part of one or more undertakings which amounts to the abuse of a dominant position in a market, if it may affect trade within the UK,[67] which relate to commercial activities connected with the supply of water or securing a supply of water or with the provision or securing of sewerage services.[68]

There are general duties of consultation between the two Directors.[69]

### 7.4.7 General Accountability Issues

While specific issues about access to information and public participation in the process of regulating the undertakers are considered in various

---

[62] See Water Industry Act 1991 s.30A, added by the Competition and Service (Utilities) Act 1992. These may be the subject of regulations made under s.213.

[63] *Ibid* s.31.

[64] ss.44, 50, 52, 53, 86 and 88 Fair Trading Act 1973 and see Office of Fair Trading *et al* (2000). The Competition Act 1998: Concurrent Application to Regulated Industries. OFT 405 (January 2001).

[65] Other than s.38(1)–(6) and 51.

[66] See further s.2 Competition Act 1998.

[67] See further *ibid* s.18.

[68] *Ibid* s.31(2), as amended by s.7(2) and para.8 Sch.2 Deregulation and Contracting Out Act 1994 and s.31(3) Water Industry Act 1991 as replaced by para.5 Sch.10 Competition Act 1998.

[69] See the Competition Act 1998 (Concurrency) Regulations 2000 (SI 2000 No.260).

places in this chapter, it is convenient here to reflect on wider issues of accountability. In particular, it should be stressed that the powers of the Secretary of State over the Director stop short of accepting general political accountability for his actions. This is to 'insulate' the Minister from the Director's more difficult decisions, but arises also in part from a wish to promote the technocratic, economistic role of the Director as, in a sense, 'above politics'. This presents various difficulties. First, the Director now takes certain decisions on which the Minister was previously answerable to Parliament and to the public. At best, the Director may have to answer questions before a Parliamentary Select Committee. As has been remarked, the establishment of 'non-ministerial departments' such as the Office of Water Services, created agents of the state 'responsibility to it only in some metaphysical sense'.[70] Second, it is clear that the split between Minister and Director is not a straightforward one between policy and operational matters.

## 7.5 General Duties on the Secretary of State and the Director

In carrying out their functions under the Water Industry Act 1991, both the Secretary of State and the Director must have regard to two primary and several secondary duties.[71] Of the two primary duties, priority is given to ensuring that the functions of the undertakers are properly carried out in relation to every area of England and Wales. In practice, this relates to the three principal duties on undertakers under the Water Industry Act of:

(a)  supplying water;[72]
(b)  delivering drinking water of a minimum quality;[73] and
(c)  providing a general system of sewerage,[74]

as well as any other functions.[75] Without prejudice to securing these general duties, the Director and Secretary of State are bound by a further primary duty of ensuring the financial viability of the companies by ensuring that undertakers are able, in particular by securing reasonable returns on their capital, to finance the proper carrying out of these functions.

The secondary duties require the Director and the Secretary of State to exercise and perform their powers and duties so as to do various things, which are quoted from the 1991 Act in full:

---

[70] Jenkins (1995) p.40.

[71] s.2 Water Industry Act 1991. The interpretation of s.2 was considered in *R v Director General of Water Services ex parte Lancashire County Council and others* [1999] Env LR 114, see 7.9.1 below on enforcement.

[72] *Ibid* s.37.

[73] *Ibid* s.68.

[74] *Ibid* s.94.

[75] In relation to the definition of undertakers' 'functions', see 7.6.2 below.

(a) ensure that the interests of customers[76] or potential customers[77] are protected as respects the fixing and recovery of water and drainage charges, in particular:

    (i) by protecting the interests of such customers in rural areas; and

    (ii) by ensuring that there is no undue preference or discrimination in the fixing of such charges;

(b) ensure that the interests of such customers are also protected as respects the other terms on which any services are provided by the undertaker and the quality of those services;[78]

(bb) ensure that the interests of such customers are also protected as respects any of the undertaker's 'non-core' functions, or as respects any activities of a subsidiary or holding company of the undertaker, in particular by ensuring that:

    (i) transactions are carried out at arm's length; and

    (ii) proper accounts are maintained by the undertaker in respect of its activities as such;[79]

(c) ensure the interests of customers on the disposal of any of the undertakers protected land or of any interest or right in or over any of that land;

(d) promote economy and efficiency on the part of undertakers in carrying out their core functions; and

(e) facilitate[80] effective competition, with respect to such matters as he considers appropriate, between current or future undertakers.

These duties are of central importance in prescribing both the obligations on the Director and the general criteria on which the Director is to judge the performance of the undertakers. They form the basic criteria used to determine the reasonableness or legality of any action of the Director in judicial review proceedings. Although not directly applicable to the undertakers, it may still be said that 'it is . . . difficult to over-emphasise the importance of these . . . duties in establishing the foundation or underlying principles against which the performance of the industry is to be measured'.[81]

Nevertheless, and despite a widely acknowledged improvement in the availability of information, the Director's decision-making processes continue to lack transparency. Even with the changes made under the Competition and Service (Utilities) Act 1992, the Director is not subject to a general duty to give reasons for decisions,[82] and the manner in which economic, social and environmental duties are balanced is not always

---

[76] On some problems with understanding who 'the customer' is see 7.8.5 below.

[77] 'Potential customers' is defined narrowly in s.219(1) Water Industry Act 1991 to mean any person who might become a customer of an undertaker on application. The duty does not therefore extend more generally to future generations; see further 4.4.1 above.

[78] With particular regard to the needs of the disabled and those of pensionable age.

[79] Subsection (bb) added by s.50 Competition and Service (Utilities) Act 1992.

[80] Deliberately, not 'promote', as with other utility regulator's duties.

[81] Leeson (1995) p.110.

[82] Such a duty is proposed in the draft Water Bill, see 7.10.2 below.

clear. However, the shifting nature of the regulated area inevitably creates a tension between securing the performance of core functions, protecting the interests of all consumers and adhering to environmental and conservation duties.[83]

The Competition Act 1998 disapplies the general duties in relation to anything done by the Director in the exercise of certain functions assigned to him, referred to as 'Competition Act functions'.[84] However, while Competition Act duties are prioritised in this way, in order to give effect to obligations in EC law the Director may still, when exercising any Competition Act function, have regard to any matter in respect of which a general duty is imposed if it is a matter to which the Director General of Fair Trading could have regard when exercising that function.[85]

As a final point here, both the Director and the Secretary of State are also subject to certain environmental and conservation duties. However, it is notable that guidance which has been issued by the Secretary of State on conservation issues is given only to the Environment Agency and to the water and sewerage undertakers but does not extend to the Director.[86]

## 7.6 Water and Sewerage Undertakers

As with the Director, the functions of the water and sewerage undertakers are prescribed by statute, though they may go beyond these 'core' functions and engage in non-core activities as they see fit. As far as their functions are concerned, these are subject to what, in effect, are licence conditions, and to general and specific environmental duties and guidance on these. It is also worth noting here some issues relating to provisions governing the way in which undertakers deal with their customers.

### 7.6.1 'Undertakers' and their legal status

In the Water Industry Act 1991, 'relevant undertaker' is defined as meaning a water undertaker or sewerage undertaker[87] although these terms are not defined further.[88] As noted above, 'undertakers' in this chapter, and this book more generally, refers both to the 10 water and sewerage undertakers established on privatisation, and the (now) 15 statutory water supply companies established either under local Acts in the nineteenth century (or by mergers and acquisitions since 1994, but retaining their distinct status) and which have always been in private ownership.[89] Water

---

[83] On environmental and conservation duties see 7.6.4–5 below.

[84] By s.31(3) Water Industry Act 1991 as amended.

[85] para.5 Sch.10 Competition Act 1998. On the Competition Act see 7.7.3 below.

[86] See 7.6.4 below.

[87] s.219(1) Water Industry Act 1991.

[88] However, they should be interpreted in accordance with *ibid* s.6.

[89] See the Statutory Water Companies Act 1991, the principal purpose of which is to allow for the conversion of such companies to companies registered under the Companies Act 1985.

undertakers must be limited companies or statutory water companies. Sewerage undertakers must be limited companies.[90]

Compared to other utility privatisations, the case of water was relatively unique, with shares in holding companies, rather than the successor companies, being offered for sale.[91] While the holding companies are public companies,[92] the successor companies are private companies whose status is set out in their memoranda. Although it is the successor companies to whom the water and sewerage functions of each water authority were transferred,[93] and that are subject to the general regulatory regime of the Director, provision was therefore made for the privatised undertakers to engage in non-core activities beyond their utility functions. These non-core activities are generally subject only to normal commercial constraints.

Until 1994, the Secretary of State for the Environment (and the Secretary of State for Wales in the case of Welsh Water) held a special share in the water and sewerage holding companies, termed the 'golden share'. The golden share enabled the Secretary of State to have ultimate control of the ownership of each company. The special shares were redeemed at par on 31 December 1994, exposing the holding companies to the potential for mergers and takeovers as for any other quoted company. This has led both to inter- and intra-industry takeovers, for example the 'merger' between York Waterworks Company Ltd and Yorkshire Water Services Ltd, or the merger of Swalec and Welsh Water (Dŵr Cymru) to form Hyder plc.[94]

Under the Statutory Water Companies Act 1991, the statutory water companies may convert to public or private limited companies. The 1991 Act also grants any water supply-only company the general powers to ensure that any company appointed as an undertaker has the necessary powers to fulfil its functions.[95] This general power allows these companies to do anything, within their area or outside, which they consider is calculated to facilitate, or is conducive or incidental to, carrying out their functions as a water undertaker. While these provisions confer on a company the *capacity* to carry out works, *power* to do so is granted under Part IV of the Water Industry Act 1991.

### 7.6.2 Undertakers' Functions

For the purposes of the Water Industry Act 1991, 'functions', in relation to a relevant undertaker, is defined as meaning the functions of the undertaker under or by virtue of any enactment.[96] However, 'functions'

---

[90] s.6(5) Water Industry Act 1991.

[91] See Water Reorganisation (Holding Companies of Successor Companies) Order 1989 (SI 1989 No. 1531).

[92] Within the meaning of s.1(3) Companies Act 1985.

[93] See Water Authorities (Successor Companies) Order 1989 (SI 1989 No. 1465).

[94] Although with Welsh Water continuing to have a separate listing for regulatory purposes.

[95] s.1 Statutory Water Companies Act 1991.

[96] s.219 Water Industry Act 1991.

must be construed subject to further provisions that define the scope of the undertaker's functions in relation to the conferring of any power on or in relation to that undertaker, albeit in a rather circuitous way.[97] Thus, it includes the power to join with or act on behalf of the Environment Agency and/or another undertaker for the purpose of carrying out certain works or acquiring certain land, if related to the undertaker's functions.

The functions of undertakers are further defined as including, amongst other things, the protection against pollution of:

(a) surface or underground waters which belong to the Agency or any water undertaker or from which the Agency or the undertaker is authorised to take water;
(b) Agency or undertakers' reservoirs; and
(c) groundwater from which the Agency or any water undertaker is authorised to abstract.[98]

Undertakers' functions also include doing anything in pursuance of a water resource management order.[99] An indication of the uncertainty surrounding the scope of undertakers' functions as regards water quality may be seen in the seeking, by the Director, of guidance from the Secretary of State as to his functions in this area.[100] Nevertheless, in practice it appears that the previous Director at least would have appeared to have appreciated the discretionary space provided by a relative lack of precision in defining what are known as the 'core' functions of undertakers.[101]

The companies may also engage in 'non-core' business in relation to which they are not generally subject to regulatory controls beyond those relating to any private or public company. A significant legal issue is whether, outside of land disposals that are specifically provided for, these utility 'functions' are defined sufficiently strictly and precisely to avoid their misuse in the interests of non-utility business.[102] The Water Industry Act 1991 itself gives little guidance. An example of where issues of this kind may arise is that if a commercial company with large volumes of effluent discharges directly to sewer, this will be core business for the undertaker. If instead, however, the company asks the undertaker to operate treatment works on site, this will be non-core, and therefore 'unregulated', business.[103] Although this might not present any immediate water quality issues, the fact remains that in the latter case the undertaker

---

[97] s.217 Water Industry Act 1991.
[98] *Ibid* s.217(3).
[99] Under s.20 Water Resources Act 1991.
[100] See Byatt (1996a) p.35.
[101] *Ibid.*
[102] See ss.217 and 219 Water Industry Act 1991 and see further Macrory (1990) pp. 80-1.
[103] Kinnersley (1994) p.64.

will not be subject to environmental and conservation duties, whereas in the former case it would be.[104]

### 7.6.3 Appointment of Undertakers and Instruments of Appointment

Responsibility for appointing undertakers and varying the terms of their appointments rests principally with the Director. Chapter I of Part II of the Water Industry Act 1991 lays down the legal framework for the appointment of undertakers, including provisions as to the making of conditions of appointment and their modification.[105] Such conditions are contained in the Instruments of Appointments which must be served on the company and which describe the area for which they are made. The areas served by water and sewerage undertakers need not be co-extensive.[106] In practice, the conditions of the Instrument of Appointment determine the powers and duties of undertakers. There is a Model Instrument of Appointment, which provides a good guide to the terms under which any undertaker operates.[107] The conditions of each undertaker's appointment are contained in the Director's register.[108]

It is through the Instrument of Appointment that flesh is added to the bare legislative bones contained in the Water Industry Act 1991. The crucial price limit and the provisions for its review, for example, are wholly provided for this way.[109] In many cases, however, the conditions contained in the Instrument of Appointment have the effect of changing what appear, on the face of the 1991 Act, to be discretionary legislative powers into mandatory obligations. This is the case, for example, with trade effluent charges schemes, where the discretionary power in the Act for undertakers to operate charges schemes is effectively translated into a duty to do so by their Instruments of Appointment.[110]

The appointments, initially granted by the Secretary of State, are subject to amendment by agreement between the Director and the undertaker,[111] with a reference by the Director to the Competition Commission if agreement cannot be reached.[112] The Secretary of State may also modify the

---

[104] But see now the imposition of general conservation duties on statutory undertakers in relation to all of their functions; see s.28G–I Countryside and Rights of Way Act 2000, and see 7.6.5 and 15.7.4 below.

[105] ss.6-17 Water Industry Act 1991.

[106] In practice the areas are not co-extensive as they are based on the areas of the former water authorities for water supply and sewerage functions.

[107] For the initial appointments see *Instrument of Appointment of the Water Undertakers* (1989) and *Instrument of Appointment of the Water and Sewerage Undertakers* (1989). For a summary see Ofwat Information Note No. 23, undated, and see also Merry and Venters (1991). Current versions of individual appointments may be obtained from Ofwat.

[108] Under s.195 Water Industry Act 1991.

[109] See 7.8.1 below.

[110] On trade effluent charging see 11.6 below.

[111] s.13 Water Industry Act 1991.

[112] *Ibid* s.14.

conditions of an undertaker's appointment under general powers relating to monopolies and mergers.[113]

With respect to both appointments and variations, certain procedures must be followed. These require notification of any such proposals, by the Secretary of State or the Director, to the existing appointee, local authorities and, through appropriate publicisation, to persons likely to be affected. Opportunity must be given for representations or objections to be made within 28 days.[114]

By contrast with the position elsewhere, however, the legislative framework for licensing undertakers and varying the terms of their appointments tends to promote negotiation rather than open decision-making.[115] For example, the amendment of licence conditions by agreement will be undertaken solely through negotiation between the Director and the undertaker, subject only to notification of the deal that has been struck and 28 days' notice within which representations or objections may be made. Moreover, the complexity of a reference to the Competition Commission, and the fact that referral opens up the whole licence to scrutiny, appears in practice to put considerable pressure on the parties to secure amendments through agreement, and thus out of public view.[116] This was again borne out following the 1999 price review, when despite much disquiet amongst undertakers generally only two sought such a reference. It is clear that the inability to appeal against specific aspects of a licence determination, the cost of doing so and the uncertainties involved (which tends to generate a negative response from the City) all contribute towards a lack of requests for redetermination.[117]

This emphasis on negotiation might be seen as encouraging the form of consensual approach to decision-making said to be a hallmark of the 'British approach' to environmental regulation,[118] though clearly experience in environmental regulation cannot simply be transposed into the very different arena of utility regulation. More particularly, however, the scope to review the Director's decisions was deliberately confined because of concerns, raised during privatisation, to avoid what was seen as the unduly legalistic nature of United States utility regulation, stemming from obligations under 'notice and comment' provisions.[119] It is also arguable that the breadth of the Director's discretionary powers, to say nothing of matters of cost etc., militate strongly against the use of judicial review of the Director's determinations. In sum, trans-Atlantic insights

---

[113] *Ibid* s.17, as amended by Sch.5 Competition Act 1998.

[114] s.8(2)-(4) Water Industry Act 1991.

[115] By contrast, e.g., with the comparative position in the US where formal, adjudicative hearings are held. 'The operation of the price cap has been too dependent on negotiations between the regulators and the firms, with outcomes tending to reflect pragmatic compromises rather than public interest goals' (Ogus (1994) p.341).

[116] Prosser (1994a) p.257.

[117] On the 1999 price review see 7.8.3 below.

[118] See generally Bell and McGillivray (2000) Ch.7. As this approach has been manifested in enforcement practice see 6.18 above.

[119] Under s.533 Administrative Procedure Act 1946.

always need to be tempered by cultural[120] and institutional[121] considerations. In addition, there are indications that, across the utilities generally, the undertakers have themselves sought a greater role for the Competition Commission and for judicial scrutiny, believing this will strengthen their bargaining position against the regulators.[122]

### 7.6.4 *Environmental Duties of Undertakers, the Secretary of State and the Director*

As with the Environment Agency, general environmental and conservation duties are imposed on the Secretary of State, the Minister of Agriculture, Fisheries and Food,[123] the Director and every undertaker.[124] These duties should be read alongside the specific duties towards customers, and to the health and competitiveness of the water industry, considered above.[125] The general environmental and conservation duties are, in formulating or considering any proposals relating to any functions of an undertaker:

(a) consistent with the purposes of any enactment relating to the functions of the undertaker, and in the case of the Secretary of State and the Director, with their consumer and competitiveness duties, to exercise such powers so as to further the conservation and enhancement[126] of natural beauty and the conservation of flora, fauna and geological or physiographical features of special interest;

(b) a requirement to have regard to the desirability of protecting and conserving buildings, sites and objects of archaeological, architectural or historic interest; and

(c) a requirement to take into account any effect which the proposals would have on the beauty or amenity of any rural or urban area or on any such flora, fauna, features, buildings, sites or objects.[127]

These duties must be exercised having regard to:

(a) the desirability of preserving for the public any freedom of access to areas of woodland, mountains, moor, heath, down, cliff or foreshore and other places of natural beauty;

(b) the desirability of maintaining the availability to the public of any facility for visiting or inspecting any building, site or object of archaeological, architectural or historic interest; and

---

[120] Price (1994).

[121] Graham and Prosser (1991).

[122] Kay (1996) pp.151-2. For Kay, however, the only legal relationship worthy of comment is that between company and regulator.

[123] In Wales, the National Assembly. The involvement of Agriculture Departments is likely to be limited in practice to land drainage and flood defence matters.

[124] s.3 Water Industry Act 1991. For the equivalent duties on the Agency see 6.10 above.

[125] Under *ibid* s.2, see 7.5 above.

[126] On the meaning of 'conservation and enhancement' see Leeson (1995) p.111.

[127] s.3(2) Water Industry Act 1991.

(c)  taking into account any effect on any such freedom of access or on the availability of any such facility.[128]

Further duties relate to securing, where practicable, that navigation rights are exercised so that the water or land in question is made available, in the best manner, for recreational purposes, and taking into account the needs of persons who are chronically sick or disabled.[129] The prospect of general nature conservation duties being placed on all public bodies, thus including the Secretary of State and the Director, is considered in the following sub-section.

It is notable that, in relation to conservation, access and recreation matters, a code of practice is provided for in relation to the Agency and the undertakers but not in relation to the Director.[130]

### 7.6.5 Specific Environmental Duties on Undertakers

With the exception of any land management,[131] the general environmental duties described above extend only to the 'core' activities of undertakers.[132] By contrast, undertakers have further duties in relation to land of special scientific interest[133] and to land in National Parks or the Broads that extend to their non-core activities.[134] Where such land may at any time be affected by their schemes, works, operations or activities, the appropriate conservation or countryside organisation must notify the undertaker, which in turn must consult the notifying body before carrying out any potentially damaging works, operations or activities. Importantly, the undertaker must be notified not merely of the status of the land but also of the nature of the damaging works etc for which consultation is required. In the case of National Parks and the Broads, the undertaker must also be supplied with reasons for the relevant authority's decision.

An illustration of the importance of such duties can be seen from the facts in *Southern Water Authority* v *Nature Conservancy Council*,[135] a case discussed in the previous chapter.[136] The judgment in this case gave a narrow interpretation to the meaning of 'occupier' for the purposes of the safeguarding provisions relating to sites of special scientific interest.[137] In holding that those whose connection with land is transient cannot be occupiers for the purpose of nature conservation law, it is clear that

---

[128] *Ibid* s.3(3). There is an obvious similarity between these duties and the general environmental duties imposed upon the Environment Agency, discussed at 6.10 above.

[129] s.3(5) and 3(6) Water Industry Act 1991.

[130] See further 7.6.5 below.

[131] s.3(9) Water Industry Act 1991.

[132] On the distinction between 'core' and 'non-core' activities see 7.6.2 above.

[133] Notably, not necessarily those notified as sites of special scientific interest under s.28 Wildlife and Countryside Act 1981, although nature conservation agency guidance requires details of all SSSIs to be sent to undertakers, see 15.7.1 below. Contrast s.156(8) Water Industry Act 1991.

[134] s.4 Water Industry Act 1991.

[135] [1992] 3 All ER 481.

[136] See 6.11 above.

[137] Contained in s.28 Wildlife and Countryside Act 1981 and see 15.7.1 below.

undertakers carrying out works will often fall outside the bounds of conservation law. The decision therefore emphasises the importance of prior consultation mechanisms of the kind contained in the specific environmental duties on undertakers mentioned above. However, the duty is phrased as requiring undertakers to consult with the notifying body where works, operations and activities appear *to the undertaker* to be 'likely' to damage the site or prejudice its importance.[138] It is notable, also, that this section neither requires of undertakers a general duty of care towards the environment, nor requires anything more than mere consultation.

Proposals currently contained in the Countryside and Rights of Way Bill would alter this position significantly. The Bill places a general conservation duty on public bodies, including water and sewerage undertakers. This duty is to take reasonable steps, consistent with the proper exercise of their functions, to further the conservation and enhancement of the flora, fauna or geological or physiographical features by reason of which the site is of special scientific interest. The proposals also envisage undertakers and other public bodies being required to notify the relevant nature conservation agency before carrying out any potentially damaging works, including works outside SSSIs which might damage a site. Correspondingly, the conservation agencies would be empowered to refuse to grant an authorisation, or to impose conditions on any such grant. However, there is scope for undertakers to carry out works if they follow any advice offered by the conservation agency and cause as little damage as is reasonably practicable in all the circumstances to the flora, fauna or geological or physiographical features by reason of which the site is of special interest. Similar provisions apply to activities which must be consented to by public bodies, including undertakers, and thus might conceivably apply to trade effluent consents. Failure to comply with these provisions would give rise to an offence and, on summary conviction, to a fine not exceeding £20,000 or on conviction on indictment to a fine.[139]

At present, undertakers' environmental, recreational and conservation duties are enforceable by the Secretary of State,[140] who also has the power to approve a code of practice giving practical guidance on the environmental duties and encouraging 'desirable' (not necessarily 'best') practices by undertakers.[141] For example, there is a Code of Practice which advises undertakers to consult with the statutory nature conservation agencies in respect of any works or operations within or outside an SSSI which are likely to affect it.[142] Contravention of such a code does not in itself give rise to any criminal or civil liability.

---

[138] See further Last (1997). On the meaning of 'likely' see 15.7.1 below.

[139] See now the Countryside and Rights of Way Act 2000, s.75 and Sch.9.

[140] Under s.18 Water Industry Act 1991, see 7.9.1 below.

[141] *Ibid* s.5. See the Water and Sewerage (Conservation, Access and Recreation)(Code of Practice) Order 2000 (SI 2000 No. 477), discussed in more detail at 6.12 above.

[142] DETR, *Code of Practice on Conservation Access and Recreation: Guidance for the Environment Agency and Water and Sewerage Undertakers* (2000) para.6.5.

It is notable, however, that the power to issue a Code of Practice does not extend to issuing guidance to the *Director* on his contribution towards environmental and other objectives. Thus, there is something of a contradiction. For example, while the undertakers are subject to conservation obligations in relation to particular SSSIs that might be affected by their operations, the Director is not at present subject to any comparable obligation when it comes to setting the price limits that will, in practice, play at least as significant a role in relation to conserving SSSIs. It is arguable that insufficient weight was given to environmental improvements in the 1994 price review, which might be attributable in part to the absence of robust guidance to the Director on the exercise of his environmental responsibilities.[143]

### 7.6.6 The Guaranteed Standards Scheme

The Water Supply and Sewerage Services (Customer Service Standards) Regulations 1989 (commonly referred to as the 'Guaranteed Standards Scheme')[144] provides for certain standards of service to be maintained by the undertakers, and payment to customers in certain situations where these are not met.[145] Remedies obtained under the Scheme are without prejudice to any civil claims.[146] The Scheme can only be altered by the Secretary of State on the written recommendation of the Director.[147] It is notable that the Scheme stipulates standards for such things as the making of appointments, responding to account queries and responding to complaints, and in relation to water resource matters such as interruptions to supply, low flows and flooding from sewers. The Scheme does not directly address water quality issues, though supplying sub-standard drinking water might lead to an interruption in supply for which compensation is payable.[148] Many undertakers have compensation schemes which go beyond these minimum standards.[149]

### 7.6.7 The Legal Relationship between Undertakers and their Customers

A final issue concerning water and sewerage undertakers relates to the relationship between undertakers and their customers. There is a tendency, in the economic literature at least, to conceive of price regulation as a 'contract' between the utility provider, on the one hand, and customers (represented by the regulator) on the other.[150] Some have even argued for

---

[143] See 7.8.3 below on the price review process and see further the reform proposals discussed at 7.10.2 below.

[144] SI 1989 No. 1159, as amended.

[145] See Ofwat Information Note No. 4 (1991, revised 1998), available at www.open.gov.uk/ofwat/info4.htm

[146] On civil claims see generally Ch.3 above, and specifically on claims relating to drinking water see 17.11 below.

[147] ss.39 and 96 Water Industry Act 1991.

[148] See, for example, the Worcester Drinking Water Incident, at 1.6.3 above.

[149] On compensation for sub-standard drinking water quality see 17.11 below.

[150] See, e.g., Helm and Rajah (1994) p.75, and references cited there at n.2.

the existence of contracts proper between water undertakers and customers.[151] The more traditional view, however, is to see the relationship as statutory, the respective rights and duties of the parties being contained in the water industry legislation.[152]

## 7.7 Competition in the Water Industry

A brief overview of the limited extent of competition within the water industry, and prospects for much greater competition, is useful in further understanding the role of the Director and introducing issues concerning 'common carriage' and some of the implications this may have for water quality.

### 7.7.1 The Nature of Competition in the Water Industry

A common feature of the utility privatisations of the 1980s was the extent to which price regulation[153] was intended only as a temporary substitute for competition, being considered necessary only to 'hold the fort'[154] before full competition would lead to the role of the Directors withering away. Certain features of the water industry, however, have meant that, by comparison with other privatised utilities, the emphasis has so far remained on regulation rather than competition. These features include the absence of any national water or sewer network, high capital costs of infrastructure and high transportation costs,[155] and the public obligations associated with the supply of such essential (and almost universal) services as water supply and sewage treatment.

It is notable, therefore, that the duty on the Director is to 'facilitate' rather than 'promote' competition in the water industry.[156] And by contrast with other regulators who have taken a bullish attitude to securing competition, most notably in relation to gas supply, the Director has until recently tended not to see promoting competition as a primary concern. The importance of this is that the concern of Government in the 1980s was to promote competition not merely for its own sake but because of concerns over the possibility of 'regulatory capture'. By regulatory capture, what is meant is the prospect of an unduly close relationship developing between the regulator and the regulated such that the public interest focus of the regulator is undermined. In this sense there was an incentive, of sorts, to avoid building a detailed regulatory structure and to push the regulators into promoting competition, thus making the Directors the champions of consumer interests at the expense of developing excessively close relationships with the companies. By comparison with other utilities,

---

[151] Kaye (1996a) and (1996b).

[152] *Norweb plc* v *Dixon* [1995] 1 WLR 636. See also Stiff (1996). This has implications for civil claims in relation to sub-standard water, on which see (on drinking water) 17.11 below.

[153] On price regulation see 7.8 below.

[154] Beesley and Littlechild (1986) p.42.

[155] For a critique of these objections, see Robinson (1997).

[156] s.2 Water Industry Act 1991, see 7.5 above.

however, water is something of a special case. In any event, public interest regulation is required in the water sector, not least for reasons of health and environmental protection. Given this background, it might be thought remarkable that more attention was not paid to putting in place effective institutional and procedural provisions which recognised that regulation would persist into the long-term.

Where provision is made for competition in the water industry it is generally competition *ex-ante*, that is, competition *for* the market rather than *in* the market.[157] However, all 10 of the successor companies to the water authorities were first appointed as undertakers and given lengthy initial licence periods.[158] Inset appointments, mechanisms under which the Director can appoint a new undertaker to operate within the jurisdiction of an existing company, but only in relation to a specific site, provide the possibility of competition. So far, however, they have been little used, arguably because of the advantages enjoyed by the existing undertaker.[159]

The manner in which the Director obtains market-type information for the purposes of facilitating regulation is through 'comparative' (or 'yardstick') competition. This is intended to allow the Director to identify best practice by comparing the performance of undertakers, and use the standards of the best when setting prices or otherwise acting in a regulatory capacity. In a sense, therefore, yardstick competition is the economic regulatory counterpart to identifying 'best available techniques' in the environmental field in that it allows performance standards to be set on the basis of what is actually achievable.[160]

Comparative competition is protected through the provisions relating to mergers.[161] These require the Secretary of State to make a merger reference to the Competition Commission in respect of any actual or prospective merger of two or more water enterprises, subject to a threshold test excluding mergers where the assets of the target company do not exceed £30 million or the person making the take-over owns no other water enterprises with assets less than £30 million. These thresholds may be revised by regulations. Notably, the threshold refers to 'assets', and so take-overs of undertakers where the sum involved exceeds £30 million may nevertheless not be referred, so long as the value of the undertakers *assets* do not exceed this figure.[162]

Mergers are subject to the general provisions of the Fair Trading Act 1973. Specifically, however, the Competition Commission is under a duty to

---

[157] Littlechild (1986), Ch.5 saw the *threat* of takeover as of considerable importance, although needing to be limited in the interests of comparative competition. There is little to suggest that such competition is a credible 'regulatory' mechanism, see Kay (1996).

[158] Licenses were issued for 25 years, and not to be reviewed within 15 years. Arguably, these terms are barriers to entry and anti-competitive.

[159] See 7.7.2 below on inset appointments.

[160] On best available techniques and similar standards see 12.3 below.

[161] Set out in ss.32-35 Water Industry Act 1991.

[162] As with the successful bid in 1999 by Yorkshire Water for York Waterworks Co., which valued the latter at £33.8 million but which was not referred.

'have regard to the desirability of giving effect to the principle that the Director's ability, in carrying out his functions by virtue of this Act, to make comparisons between different water enterprises should not be prejudiced'.[163] This gives the Commission a wide discretion that depends on a subjective understanding not just of what the public interest demands but also of what constitutes effective comparative competition.[164]

As the first Director pointed out, a reduction in numbers of undertakers inevitably damages the capacity to identify best practice in the industry.[165] Nevertheless, these concerns have not stopped the reduction in the number of water supply only companies from 29 in 1989 to 15 at present (and it should be noted that 4 of the statutory water companies are under the control of the same parent company).[166] Guidance suggests that only the prospect of 'substantial price reductions which have the effect of pushing [a] newly merged company to the forefront of efficiency in the industry' will be sufficient to satisfy competition concerns and compensate for the loss of an independent comparator.[167] Mergers and acquisitions, therefore, may pose a significant threat to the Director's ability to determine prices efficiently and effectively, and there are examples where the Director has blocked mergers or acquisitions where this might have inhibited competition comparisons.[168] Comparative competition concerns, however, do not arise in the same way when undertakers are taken over by firms from outside England and Wales, at least where only one water company is taken over.[169]

The creation of 'super utilities' combining water and other utility functions, such as with United Utilities plc and Hyder plc, leads to different competition considerations. The purpose of the provisions[170] is to deal with intra-industry consolidations. A reference to the Competition Commission is not therefore required under the Water Industry Act 1991 and may only be made by the Secretary of State for Trade and Industry on the recommendation of the Director General of Fair Trading acting under his residual powers in the Fair Trading Act 1973. These give the Secretary of State for Trade and Industry power to refer the bid to the Competition

---

[163] s.34(3) Water Industry Act 1991, as substituted by s.39(1) Competition and Service (Utilities) Act 1992. The Act originally made explicit reference to the number of independent undertakers.

[164] Graham (1990), citing Vickers and Yarrow (1988), pp.115-9, 415-9.

[165] See, e.g., Cm 1125, Cm 1126, para 4.14 in both, discussed in Graham (1991).

[166] That is, as at 13 June 2000 Folkestone and Dover Water Services Ltd, North Surrey Water Ltd, Tendring Hundred Water Services Ltd and Three Valleys Water plc are all part of the General Utilities group.

[167] *Lyonnaise des Eaux SA and Northumbrian Water Group plc*, Monopolies and Mergers Report, Cm 2936 (1995) [1995] *Water Law* 120. For the view of the Director on future referrals see Ofwat press notice 33/95, 7 November 1995, cited in [1996] *Water Law* 20.

[168] For example, blocking moves by Severn Trent Water and Wessex Water to take over South West Water.

[169] For example, Lyonnaise des Eaux's acquisition of Northumbrian Water, see above in this section, or Scottish Power's acquisition of Southern Water. The Suez Lyonnaise des Eaux Group now control both Northumbrian Water and Essex and Suffolk Water. The Director has now issued a combined licence for these undertakers, although he has sought to retain comparative competition by continued use of ring fencing arrangements for each licence.

[170] Under s.32 Water Industry Act 1991.

Commission if the target's assets exceed £70 million.[171] Such mergers will, however, result in amendment to the undertaker's appointment, and may result in a voluntary re-determination of the company's price charging factor.[172] If the water undertaker simply becomes a subsidiary of the new group, comparative competition may still be possible, but share price information (that is, information about the way investors view the company) may be lost unless a separate listing is undertaken. This may not always be insisted upon.[173]

### 7.7.2 Inset Appointments

Although, on privatisation, little scope for competition between undertakers was envisaged, limited provision was made allowing the Director to appoint a new undertaker to operate within the jurisdiction of an existing company, but only in relation to a specific site.[174] Originally confined to 'greenfield' sites, the power now extends to making such appointments where:

(a) the existing undertaker consents;
(b) the appointment or variation relates only to sites not connected to the existing undertaker's main or sewer ('greenfield' insets);
(c) provision is made as part of the undertaker's instrument of appointment; or
(d) the premises receive water or sewerage services from an undertaker provided the supply was 250 megalitres a year or more,[175] and the customer consents in writing to the appointment or variation ('large user insets').

Inset appointments may be given to any company that satisfies the Director of its competence and financial viability,[176] and large customers can effectively become their own suppliers by setting up affiliated companies to be the appointee. They are not therefore restricted to existing undertakers. The first inset appointment under which a commercial customer changed supplier came into force in May 1997, allowing Anglian Water to supply a large user (Buxted Chickens) previously supplied by Essex and Suffolk Water. In May 1999 Albion Water (Shotton) Ltd replaced Dŵr Cymru (Welsh Water) as water supplier to a large user in North Wales and became the first new licensed water supplier since

---

[171] See s.64 Fair Trading Act 1973 and the Merger References (Increase in Value of Assets) Order 1994 (SI 1994 No. 72).

[172] On these factors, known as 'K factors', see 7.8.1 below.

[173] See, e.g., the merger of Welsh Water and the electricity utility Swalec to form Hyder, [1996] *Water Law* 103 at 104, but see Ofwat news release 39/95, 'Water regulator calls for separate listing for merged business', 13 December 1995.

[174] See now s.7 Water Industry Act 1991, as amended by s.40 Competition and Service (Utilities) Act 1992, and www.open.gov.uk/ofwat/inset_appointments.htm

[175] Only around 500 customers in England and Wales use this volume of water. But see 7.10.1 below on recent changes.

[176] Ofwat, *Inset Appointments: Guidance for Applicants*, at www.open.gov.uk/ofwat/inset_appointments.htm

privatisation.[177] Beyond this, competition via inset appointments has been limited, although a number of further appointments may soon be made as the process becomes less time-consuming and as competition within the water industry is promoted.[178]

### 7.7.3 EC Competition Law and the Competition Act 1998

Because competition generally arises only for shares, not the commodity of water itself, the water industry in the European Community has largely escaped the pressures on other sectors for utility regulation developments at EC level. These developments may be characterised as inaction, followed by pressures towards economic liberalisation in the 1980s, followed by more co-operative, co-ordinative processes such as trans-European networks,[179] which does not apply to water.[180] Moves to create harmonised public service obligations appear to have stalled indefinitely. In particular, the nature of the water sector has meant that many of the general provisions of EC competition law, which are intended to prohibit anti-competitive practices,[181] have not had a direct impact. Nor have the provisions of the EC Treaty which relate specifically to public and quasi-public undertakings[182] affected matters greatly. Where Community law has so far had an impact has been as regards merger control,[183] although as the following section describes, the impact of general principles of EC competition law are now being felt more keenly.

The prospect for greatly enhanced competition amongst water and sewerage undertakers has, however, recently been raised with the coming into force, on 1 March 2000, of the Competition Act 1998. The Act is intended to bring national law into line with EC competition law,[184] and strengthens the legal powers available to prevent the abuse of a dominant position and other anti-competitive behaviour. In relation to the water industry,[185] the Competition Act 1998 gives concurrent regulatory powers to the Director General of Fair Trading and the Director, although in

---

[177] *Market Competition in the Water and Sewerage Industry*, Ofwat Information Note 10 (revised 2000).

[178] See Ofwat, *The Current State of Competition* (2000). In practice, most undertakers have responded to the threat of inset appointments by offering large user tariff reductions; see 7.8.5 below. On competition proposals see 7.10.1 below.

[179] Under Art.154 EC (ex Art.129b).

[180] For an overview see Scott (1995) and Prosser and Moran (1994).

[181] See Arts.81 and 82 EC (ex Arts.85 and 86).

[182] Art.86 EC (ex Art.90).

[183] Notably, Regulation 4064/89/EEC (the Merger Control Regulation). See, e.g., "Legitimate interest' exception in Merger Regulation allows UK Government to refer Lyonnaise des Eaux's take over bid for Northumbria Water to MMC' and see 7.7.1 above. See generally Freeman and Whish (1991, updated) paras 15.01-15.45.

[184] In particular, Arts.81 and 82 EC (ex Arts.85 and 86).

[185] See further Ofwat, *Competition Act 1998: Application in the Water and Sewerage Sector* (January 2000), at www.open.gov.uk/ofwat/competition_act_guidelines.htm

practice it is envisaged that the Director will have primary responsibility.[186] As a matter of EC law, 'dominance' has been defined as:

> a position of economic strength enjoyed by an undertaking which enables it to prevent effective competition being maintained on the relevant market by affording it the power to behave to an appreciable extent independently of its competitors, customers and ultimately of consumers.

Dominance is generally presumed if an undertaking has a market share persistently above 50%.[187] In particular, the Competition Act 1998 opens the scope for what is known as 'common carriage', that is, effectively establishing something resembling a national 'water grid' through the shared use of assets by undertakers. Whether the Competition Act 1998 alone will provide a sufficient basis for competition within the water industry, however, must be doubted, and specific proposals for reform have been put forward by Government. For this reason, common carriage is discussed in more detail below in relation to these reform proposals. [188]

In addition to parties to agreements over which the Director has made a decision having a right of appeal,[189] the 1998 Act provides for third party appeal rights for those who have sufficient interest in the decision made by the Director. Third parties who consider that they have suffered a loss as a result of any unlawful agreement or conduct may also have an action for damages.[190]

## 7.8 Price Regulation and Water Quality

Perhaps the most contentious aspect of water privatisation has been the process under which undertakers charge for the services they deliver. Particular concerns have been raised about the manner in which this process has balanced affordability to, and fairness between, consumers; profitability to companies; and environmental considerations. Concerned as it is with economic, social and environmental factors, water and sewerage pricing can be seen as something of a litmus test for the achievement of sustainable development. The following sections consider the process by which, in the absence of direct competition, prices are determined. In particular, attention is given to how the regulatory system sets the general context for more specific decisions about improving water quality to be taken at local level, for example when decisions are taken about the level of investment in facilities at a sewerage treatment works.

---

[186] On the relationship between the duties of the Director under the Competition Act 1998 and Part I of the Water Industry Act 1991 see 7.5 above.

[187] Case C62/86 *AKZO Chemie BV* v *Commission* [1991] ECR I-3359, para. 60.

[188] These are discussed at 7.10.1 below.

[189] Appeals are heard by the Appeals Tribunal of the Competition Commission.

[190] The Competition Act 1998 is unclear, but various actions are possible, and discussed in MacCulloch (2000).

## 7.8.1 Price Regulation: the Principles

Legal responsibility for determining prices for water and sewerage services rests ultimately with the Director, guided by his general competition duties, his duties towards customers and to the undertakers, and his specific environmental and conservation duties.[191] The Director sets price limits intended to allow the undertakers to finance their functions and, in principle, to encouraging greater efficiency. The Director does not, however, control profits or dividends, nor approve tariffs, but checks that they are in line with the company's charging limit by requiring undertakers to produce an annual Principal Statement.

The Director is empowered to limit the annual price increase to reflect what each undertaker needs to charge to finance the provision of core services to customers.[192] This is done under 'local tariff reduction', better known as the 'RPI - X' model, where RPI is the retail price index (indicating inflation) and X is an annual adjustment factor set for each regulated company as being the regulator's assessment of the company's cost-efficiency potential. In the case of water, 'RPI + K' is used. 'K' is used partly for distinctiveness, but partly also to reflect the unique case of the water sector as requiring considerable infrastructure investment, since privatisation, to take account of the costs involved in meeting quality obligations and making up for past underinvestment. 'K' thus comprises 'Q', the amount needed to meet quality improvements, minus 'X', a figure for efficiency savings.

Price review periods are generally referred to as 'AMPs', by reference to the Asset Management Plans authorised by the Director. On privatisation in 1989, the first determination of K, 'AMP1', allowed costs to consumers to rise by around 5% above inflation. A major review of price limits must take place after ten years, or after five years if the company or the Director chooses. Undertakers licences have now been modified to allow for an automatic review of prices at five-yearly intervals. Certain adjustments can be made between reviews for a limited number of reasons ('interim determinations').[193] Companies have the right to ask the Director to refer the determination to the Competition Commission.[194] Price limits were revised in 1994 and took effect on 1 April 1995. These limits, 'AMP2', lowered K significantly.[195] In November 1999 the Director announced new

---

[191] See 7.5 and 7.6.4 above.

[192] The framework for charging is set out in s.142(1) Water Industry Act 1991, but the flesh is provided by Condition B of the Model Instrument of Appointment, on which see Merry and Venters (1991). s.142(1) is amended by s.3 Water Industry Act 1999, with effect from 1 April 2000.

[193] For Ofwat policy on what will be regarded as a 'Relevant Change of Circumstances' justifying an interim determination, and what will be regarded as trivial and an expense which must be absorbed within existing determinations, see Ofwat, *Final Determinations: Future water and sewerage charges 2000-05* (1999), Annex E.

[194] See the Water Appointments (Monopolies and Mergers Commission) Regulations 1989 (SI 1989 No.1162), which provide for notification to affected persons, and see Ofwat, *The Role of the Competition Commission in the Price Review*, Ofwat Information Note 44 (1999).

[195] Over the country as a whole, these provided for average increases in water and sewerage prices of around 1.4% in real terms for each year of the first quinquennium (1995-2000) and for average

price limits, 'AMP3', to operate from April 2000 for five years.[196] It is notable that RPI+K has no formal legislative status. K can be positive, negative or zero. Determining 'K' is clearly of central importance to economic regulation and securing funding for water quality improvements.

Although not explicitly designed as a system by which costs incurred by the undertakers are directly passed on to their customers (a 'cost-pass-through' system),[197] concerns were nevertheless expressed that the system, at least in the early price determinations, encouraged capital investment.[198] This is because of the extent to which rate of return regulation, albeit forward looking, is provided for, since a primary duty of the Director is 'to secure that companies . . . are able (in particular, by securing reasonable returns on their capital) to finance the proper carrying out of [their] functions'.[199] While securing financial viability is a common duty of privatised utility regulators, the bracketed condition is unique to the water regulator, allowing operating costs to be 'passed through' the system, with an efficiency discount, plus a return on capital invested. Over the long term, therefore, the share price will be directly proportional to the amount of capital employed. As one leading commentator summarised the situation: 'The industry will always be pressing to persuade the Regulator of the virtue of future capital projects and the Regulator will always be doing his best to prevent unjustified ones'.[200] It is arguable whether this approach is compatible in practice with the principles that water contamination should be prevented and rectified at source.[201] However, the tendency will always be to allow a rate of return that is slightly too high. The Director is, however, aware of this tendency in the system, especially as regards quality-related investments.[202]

## 7.8.2 *Price Regulation and Water Quality Considerations*

Mandatory, and sometimes discretionary, quality standards are determined by central government, either nationally or, more usually, at EC level. In the case of environmental quality standards, these are notified to the Environment Agency, which may be placed under a legal obligation to

---

increases of 0.4% in real terms for each year of the second quinquennium (2000-05), see [1994] *Water Law* 156.

[196] See Ofwat, *Final Determinations: Future Water and Sewerage Charges 2000-05* (November 1999).

[197] However, Agency-directed action can be paid for by the undertakers and costs passed on. See ss.142(1) and 217 Water Industry Act 1991.

[198] Glaister (1996) pp.35-37. On the technical domination of water policy-making see Parker and Penning-Rowsell (1980) p.48; Rhodes (1988) pp.78-79 and Maloney and Richardson (1995) pp.10-15.

[199] s.2 Water Industry Act 1991, see 7.5 above.

[200] Glaister (1996) pp.36-37. In addition, any additional capital investment would strengthen cash flows through higher depreciation provisions and the balance sheet enhancement would likely contribute to a stronger share price. See also Prosser (1994a).

[201] On these principles see 4.7.2 above.

[202] See Byatt (1996a).

achieve them.[203] Even if this is not the case, these standards will be used by the Agency in determining the conditions of discharge consents held by the undertakers.[204] The Agency will be likely to be involved with the undertaker in designing appropriate engineering solutions, the process being iterative.[205] Once designed to the Agency's satisfaction, the solutions are costed by the undertakers and submitted to the Director, who decides on the 'Q' element of K accordingly.

Where the undertaker considers it necessary or desirable to spend more than is required to meet mandatory standards, the undertaker will need to select from a prioritised list of schemes drawn up by the Agency and approved by the Secretary of State. The Director then decides on the amount of money that can be authorised out of 'K' to allow the schemes to go ahead. Thus, the Director has no direct role in determining mandatory quality standards, but has some say as regards discretionary spending insofar as expenditure on environmental improvements may be prioritised ahead of non-environmental expenditure.

A central issue, though, is that water quality obligations do not always divide neatly into the mandatory and discretionary. Many provisions of EC water directives, for example, are couched in ambiguous or imprecise language, and there is room for differences of opinion about what is required. For example, the Urban Waste Water Treatment Directive requires Member States to take action to limit pollution from storm water overflows.[206] This requires measures to be undertaken to improve unsatisfactory intermittent discharges, although no specific requirements are imposed, nor is a timetable laid down for completing such action. Although the Environment Agency may take a view as to how binding these and other obligations are, the decision ultimately rests with Ministers in their advice to the Director, which will be influenced by how much such works will cost.

There are also other considerations. For example, there has been an obligation to meet the mandatory standards under the Bathing Water Directive since 10 December 1985, subject to exceptional circumstances. But neither the 1989 nor 1994 price review settlements aimed at ensuring sufficient compliance with these standards. Only towards the end of AMP3 is this envisaged. There is also the issue as to which beaches will *not* be brought up to compliance within this period, the implication being that these will be chosen on the basis of costs and benefits. Again, the implication is that the 'cascade' model of regulation, outlined previously,[207] has its practical limitations.

---

[203] See 14.8.10 below.

[204] On discharge consents generally see Ch.10 below.

[205] See *R v National Rivers Authority ex parte Moreton* [1996] Env LR 234 at 241, discussed at 10.6.4 below.

[206] Art.3(2) and Annex I(A) Urban Waste Water Treatment Directive (91/271/EEC) and see 5.6.2 above.

[207] See 7.2 above.

A difficulty with these arrangements for improving water quality is that environmental improvements should not necessarily require higher customer bills, or even higher costs generally.[208] The best environmental option is not necessarily the most capital-intensive. However, the price formula may encourage undertakers to adopt more capital-intensive solutions, that is, to substitute between operating and capital expenditure, all other things being equal. Thus:

> one can use more chemicals in water purification or one can build larger storage reservoirs to give water more time. One can pump or purify difficult local water or one can build long-distance pipes to remote sources.[209]

Or if the objective is to achieve compliance with coastal water quality standards, the solution might either be a long sea outfall or a treatment works using ultraviolet disinfection.[210]

The central issue is that over-investment in capital projects may not be a problem for shareholders, or even for the environment directly, but may be for consumers and society more generally.[211] A good example is seen in measures to comply with various parameters in the Drinking Water Quality Directive.[212] In the 1994 periodic review, the Director allowed the water undertakers to spend £3.9 billion to bring quality up to required standards, including money to build over 120 pesticide removal plants, 30 nitrate removal plants and 70 cryptosporidium removal plants, together with various capital-intensive measures to reduce lead levels.[213] Yet in relation to some of these improvements, the undertakers might have taken other action. One frequently used method to meet standards is to blend more and less contaminated waters from different sources. Another method, pertinent here, is for the undertakers themselves to instigate voluntary self-regulatory pollution prevention strategies. Good examples are the various means used successfully by Severn Trent Water to persuade pesticide users to switch to the use of less harmful substances in a bid to reduce pesticide levels in water for supply.[214] This example also shows the extent to which capital-intensive solutions may differ from what effective pollution prevention, and perhaps the polluter pays principle, require. Although most capital-intensive plants will require planning permission, there is a clear

---

[208] On the 'more from less' approach (an aspect of 'ecological modernisation') see Weale (1992) Ch.3 and Hajer (1995).

[209] Glaister (1996) p.39.

[210] The last-mentioned is a counter-example to his hypothesis, given by Glaister himself; the National Rivers Authority wanted the outfall (cost: £22 million), while the undertaker wanted the ultraviolet disinfection (cost: £15 million).

[211] Similar points may be made as regards water supply: that there may be no incentives for companies to reduce demand, although see Part IIIA Water Industry Act 1991.

[212] Directive 80/778/EEC as amended, see 17.7.1 and 17.7.8 below.

[213] Ofwat, *Future Charges for Water and Sewerage Services: the Outcome of the Periodic Review* (1994). A further £7.3 billion capital programme was allowed in relation to sewerage improvements, £6.8 billion to meet the requirements of EC quality legislation.

[214] The 'Spray Safe' Campaign, discussed in Matthews and Pickering (1997).

sense in which it is the decision on economic financing which is the central practical consideration.[215]

The argument that capital-intensive solutions may not always be environmentally preferable, however, has its limitations. For example, there is no evidence to suggest that the price formula led the undertakers to lobby for costly specification standards of the kind contained in the Urban Waste Water Treatment Directive.[216] Indeed, the evidence points in the opposite direction: in 1990 the industry was still advocating the disposal of raw sewage at sea. Moreover, it was at Britain's urging that Member States agreed that discharges to coastal waters would generally require only basic primary treatment.[217]

### 7.8.3 The Price Review: Stakeholders and Process

The price review is a process bringing together the economic and environmental regulators, the undertakers and consumers, but for which almost no formal provision is made in law. The 1999 price review, preceded by three years of negotiation, illustrates both the process and the development of practice.[218]

The 1999 review was preceded by lengthy dialogue between the Secretary of State, Ofwat, the Environment Agency, the Drinking Water Inspectorate and the undertakers.[219] This can be seen as a two stage process, first, involving the initial estimation of likely environmental obligations and other factors, including market research into customers preferences and priorities.[220] The second stage[221] involved establishing with greater certainty what these obligations would be. In particular, once the draft price determinations were issued in July 1999, final representations from all stakeholders was invited, and meetings held by Ofwat with all the undertakers, customer representatives, environmental groups and analysts. However, the process is inherently problematic, since the extent to which the improvements granted funding (the National Environment Programme) can be required of undertakers cannot be determined until its cost is known, and Ministers cannot confirm the scope of the programme without knowing its cost.[222]

---

[215] On planning law and planning policy concerning development needed by undertakers to carry out their core functions see 14.2–5 below.

[216] See 5.6.2 above on this Directive.

[217] See Jordan and Greenaway (1998) pp.680 and 690.

[218] The process is outlined in *The 1999 Periodic Review*, Ofwat Information Note No.38 (revised, 1999). For reflections on the process see House of Commons Select Committee on Environmental Audit, *Water Prices and the Environment* (2000) ('*Water Prices and the Environment*').

[219] See Ofwat, *Setting the Quality Framework* (1998); Environment Agency, *A Price Worth Paying* (1998); Ofwat, *Prospects for Prices* (1998); DETR, *Raising the Quality* (1998). See generally *ENDS Report* 280 (1998) pp.40-41 and *ENDS Report* 284 (1998) p.43.

[220] See 7.8.4 below.

[221] Beginning with DETR, *Raising the Quality* (1998).

[222] See 7.8.2 above.

Key issues in the 1999 review were the impact of sewage effluent and over-abstraction on SSSIs, and coastal sewage discharges. Following discussion on the draft determinations, 63 sewage treatment plant improvement schemes were removed from the companies' business plans.[223] Other schemes were deferred to allow for a significant price reduction in the first year of the new price controls. This 'back-end loading' of obligations onto the undertakers (and 'front-end' price cuts) raises issues about the commitment with which the UK is endeavouring to meet many of Community obligations, for example whether it can be said to be 'endeavouring to achieve' guideline standards.[224] In some respects, this mirrored the 1994 review, where the Director had advocated a minimal interpretation of EC environmental obligations, or at least their staggered implementation, in line with what customers were thought to be willing to pay.[225] Although the excesses of the Director never prevailed, undertakers' did abandon existing obligations going beyond mandatory EC requirements, significantly reducing the scale of investment planned for.[226]

The final outcome of the 1999 review was the most substantial water quality investment programme so far, involving more than 6,000 projects at a total estimated cost of £5.3 billion.[227] In particular, all discharges to coastal waters deemed 'significant' for the purposes of the Urban Waste Water Treatment Directive are to have at least secondary treatment,[228] the pace of improving the performance of combined sewer overflows is to be accelerated,[229] and work will be undertaken to ensure greater levels of compliance both with mandatory and guide values for EC water quality directives.[230] The 1999 review also saw a phase out of the spreading of untreated sewage sludge to land as a precautionary measure, a good illustration of the way that the review process is central when action beyond clear mandatory requirements is sought.[231] The outcome was warmly received by the Environment Agency and by other environmental

---

[223] Pending a re-assessment of the most cost-effective means of achieving objectives, see Environment Agency, *Achieving the Quality* (2000) p.16. On the removal of these schemes see *Water Prices and the Environment*, Ofwat evidence.

[224] For example, under the Bathing Water Directive (76/160/EEC) and see 5.5.2C above. As the national courts presently construe such obligations, however, this approach is probably immune to challenge in judicial review (see 4.17 above) though the European Court of Justice may take a different view.

[225] Ofwat, *The Cost of Quality* (1992) and, especially, Ofwat, *Paying for Quality: The Political Perspective* (1993) and see Byatt (1996b). Byatt notes that the impact of the judicial review of the boundaries of the Humber and Severn estuaries, arguably the kind of 'minimal' interpretation preferred, was additional expenditure of between £115-£150 million. See *R v Secretary of State for the Environment, ex parte Kingston upon Hull City Council* [1996] Env LR 248, and see 5.6.2 above.

[226] See Helm and Rajah (1994) p.86.

[227] On the final determinations see Ofwat, *Final Determinations – Water and Sewerage Charges 2000-2005* (1999).

[228] On 'secondary treatment' see 1.6.1 above. On the Directive see 5.6.2 above.

[229] And see 1.6.1 above on the legacy of poorly performing sewage treatment works.

[230] On the EC water quality directives see 5.5 above.

[231] See also Government Response (Cm.4023) to House of Commons Select Committee on the Environment, Transport and the Regions, *Sewage Treatment and Disposal* (1998), para.33.

regulators,[232] although the Environment Audit Committee was critical of 'roller coaster pricing' and the impact this might have on public attitudes to water quality and conservation.[233]

Some general observations may be made about the latest determinations. First, while there was considerable unease about the impact of the price cuts on share prices, only two undertakers exercised the right to ask the Director to refer their determinations to the Competition Commission, emphasising the extent to which the price determinations are, in practice, immune from challenge.[234] Second, there is the prospect of interim determinations, for example in relation to reducing exposure to lead, and £700 million has been factored into the initial determinations to cushion against new obligations between 2000 and 2005.[235] Third, some doubts have been raised as to whether water consumers are bearing a disproportionate cost of improved water quality since only a proportion of the current shortfall in meeting river quality objectives can be attributed to the impact of undertakers' discharges. Finally, annual reports on progress of the National Environment Programme are to be published by the Environment Agency, which should go some way to publicising the cost of water quality throughout the period of the price review.

A final observation is that restrictive price limits may encourage questionable behaviour at the margins, such as greater risk taking, less environmental precautions or even regulatory non-compliance.[236] The scope for companies to engage in discretionary environmental improvements may also be reduced quite significantly. However, because of greater openness, it is probably now more difficult for industry 'hardship' to be relieved through changes in enforcement behaviour.[237]

## 7.8.4 Willingness to Pay for Water Quality

The 1994 price review brought customers' willingness to pay for environmental quality improvements firmly onto the agenda, where it remains. As was remarked, 'river quality began to look like a luxury item, to be determined solely by drinking water customers' willingness to pay'.[238] During the first price review there was considerable disagreement

---

[232] For complete details on the programmes eventually agreed (the 'National Environment Programme') see Environment Agency, *Achieving the Quality* (2000) and the Annex thereto.

[233] *Water Prices and the Environment*, para.128.

[234] See 7.8.1 above. Appeals were lodged on behalf of Sutton and East Surrey Water and Mid Kent Water. These were decided in August 2000, but for commercial confidentiality reasons the full decisions were not available until September 2000. See Ofwat press release, 'Ofwat Announces Competition Commission Decisions Following Companies' Appeals Against Price Limits', 8 August 2000.

[235] At the time of the determinations, the exact nature of the obligation to reduce exposure to lead was not clear, see 17.7.8 below. A consequence of the 1994 review was a policy decision to avoid the need for interim determinations on environmental grounds by synchronising major changes to environmental policy with the price review.

[236] [1994] *Water Law* 153 at 159.

[237] On enforcement policy and practice generally see 6.18 above.

[238] Wilkinson (1994) p.156.

between Ofwat and the National Rivers Authority, each accusing the other of overplaying costs or benefits. In the final outcome, the £919 million investment programme put forward by the Authority was pared down by Ofwat to £522 million. This should be seen within a wider context of attacks on business regulation, which have focused on costs to business rather than benefits to those served by those firms or wider public benefits.[239]

The latest price review also illustrated issues relating to willingness to pay for water quality and the role of customer surveying in this.[240] While emphasising that 'listening to customers' might be seen as a good thing, the difficulty remains that 'the customer' is something of a problematic concept. That is, there is no such thing as 'the customer', but different customers, often with very different concerns and interests. Also, it is a matter of dispute whether those aspects of an individual's behaviour relating to his or her consumption of goods and services can be neatly separated from other concerns.[241] Nevertheless, what may emerge is something of a 'battle of the surveys' between the various stakeholders, each keen to elucidate what 'customers' want in terms of water quality and the costs involved.[242] That said, it should be emphasised that only around 10% of the latest price review related to matters in which the Agency's duty to take costs and benefits into account applied. The rest of the National Environment Programme related to mandatory EC obligations or the protection of SSSIs (70%) and to the implications of Government policy decisions concerning the disposal of sewage sludge to land (20%).

### 7.8.5 Equity Considerations

Questions about willingness to pay for improved water quality lead to complex, often ethical, questions concerning who should pay for water quality and the extent to which water of any particular quality is a right or a preference.[243] The present context is that privatisation has shifted the burden of paying for water quality improvements from taxpayers generally to water charge payers. Although rateable values are still generally used for unmetered water charging, this should not hide the regressive nature of water charges.[244] Largely because of the Bathing Water and Urban Waste Water Treatment Directives,[245] water charges fall disproportionately on those living in regions with unsatisfactory bathing beaches and long

---

[239] This may be seen in the context of the Major Administration's Deregulation Initiative as regards social regulation. See, e.g., Deregulation Initiative, *Thinking About Regulating: A Guide to Good Regulation* (1993), a precursor to the Deregulation and Contracting Out Act 1994.

[240] See Environment Agency, *A Price Worth Paying* (1998) and Ofwat, *Prospects for Prices* (1998). Also on methodologies relating to willingness to pay see 6.14 above.

[241] See generally Sagoff (1988).

[242] See House of Commons Select Committee on Environmental Audit, *Water Prices and the Environment* (2000) paras.43–52.

[243] See also the issue as to whether costs are borne by present or future generations, noted at 7.5 above.

[244] On which see generally the Water Industry Act 1999.

[245] See 5.5.2 and 5.6.2 above.

coastlines. Such areas are disproportionately populated by the retired, or are simply relatively underpopulated. The classic example is the South West Water area, which has one third of the English coastline but only 3% of its population, a disproportionate number being on low incomes and who have to bear the cost of major water infrastructure improvement projects.

While allowance can be made for regional variations in the individual appointments, the Director is subject to duties prohibiting 'undue preference or discrimination'.[246] These, however, are traditionally weak legal concepts,[247] and it is debatable whether they would be sufficient to ground a legal challenge to significantly higher bills in, say, the South West. A challenge to the basis of charging water and sewerage charge payers, rather than the public generally, would be unlikely to succeed.

The extent to which water quality should be considered a right or as a privilege, and the implications, is a more difficult question that cannot be addressed here.[248] At a general level, however, a distinction might be made between water used for essential human uses (drinking, washing, etc.) and conservation functions, and water used for the production of non-essential goods or services. However, the notion that water should be charged according to the costs involved (individual cost attribution) can already be seen. For example, charges to large users have already come down because of the threat of inset appointments.[249] This trend would seem to conflict with the legislative prohibition against 'undue discrimination' as well as general principles such as the right of access to the service and non-discrimination in its provision[250] that underpin universal service in the water industry. Although not as manifest as in other utilities, distributional objectives may be subsumed to efficiency goals and competition.[251]

Those for whom basic water provision is as essential provision may end up facing higher bills than those who, solely for reasons of scale and economics, see their bills reduced. In any event, the principle that consumers should pay different prices and different percentages of disposable income for basic water and sanitation services is an essential feature of comparative competition amongst the undertakers. Moreover, as at least domestic customers have little means of affecting the effluent load from their premises, it is not clear why quality improvements, enjoyed by all, should be paid by water customers as opposed to the public purse.

The current price review suggests that the pressures on water and sewerage charge payers in certain regions, especially the South West, persists.

---

[246] s.2 Water Industry Act 1991, discussed at 7.5 above.

[247] *London Electricity Board* v *Springate* [1969] 3 All ER 289.

[248] In those jurisdictions where ambient water quality is protected as a matter of specific constitutional right, it is rare for constitutional provisions to be set other than at a high level of generality. See generally Boyle and Anderson (1996).

[249] On inset appointments see 7.7.2 above.

[250] See further Craig (1991) and Prosser (1994b).

[251] See also Price (1997).

Recent guidance issued by the Secretary of State indicates a desire to avoid unacceptable impacts on water prices in different parts of England and Wales, but notes that the ability to do so is hampered by existing EC obligations.[252] Nevertheless, the decision of Ministers was to limit the size of the National Environment Programme to achieve river quality objectives in the South West water area.[253]

## 7.9  Enforcing Undertakers' Obligations

The Water Industry Act 1991 provides a distinctive and often contentious mechanism for enforcing obligations owed by water and sewerage undertakers. Enforcement action by the Director and the Secretary of State *against* undertakers relates to their obligations to carry out their core functions, as opposed to other obligations owed by undertakers such as supplying water that is fit for human consumption where enforcement is through the usual channels of criminal prosecution and where there may also be individual 'enforcement' remedies.[254] Enforcement in this context should also be distinguished from enforcement *by* undertakers, for example the powers of undertakers to enforce the terms of trade effluent consents or enforce trade effluent agreements.[255]

Drafted in consultation with the European Commission in order to comply with obligations under EC law, the enforcement provisions in the 1991 Act have been criticised in some quarters for their apparently conciliatory approach to compliance. More pertinently, perhaps, the European Court of Justice has recently held certain of the national enforcement provisions to be in violation of Community law,[256] although the eventual ramifications of this decision remain uncertain.

### 7.9.1  Enforcement Orders

Enforcement action against water and sewerage undertakers may be taken either through the issuing of enforcement orders by the Secretary of State or the Director,[257] or by the imposition of a special administration order through proceedings in the High Court.[258] There is no general right to prosecute for breaches of undertakers' duties.

---

[252] DETR, *Raising the Quality* (1998).

[253] On the National Environment Programme see 7.8.3 above.

[254] On the offence of supplying water 'unfit for human consumption' see 17.7.7 below. On individual enforcement for sub-standard water quality see 3.11–12 and 17.11 below.

[255] See 11.11 below on these powers.

[256] Case C-340/96 *Commission* v *United Kingdom* [1999] ECR I-2023.

[257] Under s.18 Water Industry Act 1991.

[258] *Ibid* s.23.

## 7.9.1A The availability of enforcement orders

Enforcement orders, and more generally the machinery in this part of the Act, are used in a range of situations, including:

(a) Any duty or requirement imposed under Parts IV to VII of the Water Supply (Water Quality) Regulations 1989 on a water undertaker (i.e. duties to supply wholesome water and to comply with specification standards).[259]

(b) The duty on sewerage undertakers to provide a public sewer for the drainage, for domestic sewerage purposes, of premises in a particular locality in its area if certain conditions are satisfied.[260]

(c) The duty on undertakers to supply, through some other means, water for domestic purposes where there is a danger to life or health and it is practicable at reasonable costs for the undertaker to do so.[261]

(d) The duty on undertakers to enforce their own water supply byelaws.[262]

(e) The duty on undertakers to provide annual data on drinking water quality.[263]

Enforcement orders may be issued where the Director or Secretary of State is satisfied that the undertaker:

(a) is contravening any condition of its appointment (in relation to which he is the enforcement authority);

(b) is contravening any statutory or other requirement which is enforceable under this provision and in relation to which he is the enforcement authority; or

(c) has contravened any such condition or requirement and is likely to do so again.

If any of these apply, a final enforcement order must be made, making such provision as is requisite for the purpose of securing compliance with that condition or requirement. Alternatively, a provisional enforcement order may be made. The criteria for deciding which form of order to issue is whether there will be any consequential loss or damage arising from the decision which could be avoided by using the procedurally less time-consuming provisional order. Provisional orders take immediate effect but have a maximum duration of three months unless confirmed.

## 7.9.1B Procedural requirements and challenges to orders

Final enforcement orders must satisfy specified procedural requirements.[264] These require reasons to be given for their making, and

---

[259] See 17.7.2 below.

[260] s.101A Water Industry Act 1991, see 11.3.2A below.

[261] s.79 Water Industry Act 1991 see 7.9.1 below.

[262] See 7.10.3 below.

[263] Under the Water Undertakers (Information) Direction 1998, see 17.7.5 and 17.12 below.

the specific measures required of the undertaker. There must also be notification to the undertaker and, where appropriate, the Director, and appropriate publication to bring the matter to the attention of persons likely to be affected by the order. At least 28 days notice for representations or objections must be allowed. The 1991 Act then gives the undertaker, and only the undertaker, a second opportunity to make representations or objections before the order is finally made. When the order is eventually made, its terms must be notified to the undertaker and, through publication, to others likely to be affected. Provision is also made for the modification and revocation of orders. Details of final enforcement orders, provisional enforcement orders (either made or confirmed) and any revocation of such orders must be entered on the Director's register.[265] The Director or the Secretary of State may, by notice, require information from undertakers where the undertaker may be contravening, or may have contravened, appointment conditions or any statutory or other requirement enforceable through the use of enforcement orders.

A company aggrieved by an enforcement order may challenge its validity on two grounds, either:

(a) that its making or confirmation was not within the powers in the Water Industry Act 1991 to make enforcement orders; or
(b) that any of the procedural requirements mentioned above have not been complied with in relation to it.[266]

Application must be made to the High Court within forty-two days from the date of service on the undertaker of a copy of the order. The High Court may, if satisfied that the making or confirmation of the order was not within those powers or that the interests of the company have been substantially prejudiced by a failure to comply with those requirements, quash the order or any of its provisions. It would seem easier to challenge the making of a final order as being outwith the powers of the Act since, by contrast with provisional orders, the power does not depend on the subjective judgement of the person making the order. Except as provided for above, the validity of an enforcement order shall not be questioned in any legal proceedings whatsoever.[267]

When making regulations, the Secretary of State may give enforcement order functions either to himself or the Director or both. Enforcement by the Director may be made subject to the Secretary of State's consent or authorisation.[268]

---

[264] s.20 Water Industry Act 1991.
[265] *Ibid* s.195(2)(c).
[266] *Ibid* s.21(1).
[267] *Ibid* ss.21(2) and (3).
[268] *Ibid* s.213(2)(a) and (b).

## 7.9.1C  *The contents of enforcement orders*

An enforcement order:

(a) must require the company to which it relates (according to the circumstances of the case) to do, or not to do, such things as are specified in the order or are of a description so specified;

(b) must take effect at such time, being the earliest practicable time, as is determined by or under the order; and

(c) may be revoked at any time by the enforcement authority who made it.[269]

The enforcement authority in relation to the conditions of an undertaker's appointment is the Director. By contrast, the enforcement authority in relation to each of the statutory and other requirements subject to enforcement provisions is the Secretary of State, the Director, or either of them, according to whatever provision is made by the enactment or subordinate legislation by which the requirement is made so enforceable.

## 7.9.1D  *Sanctions for non-compliance*

There are three possible sanctions for non-compliance with an enforcement order. First, the duty to comply with an enforcement order is owed to any person who may be affected by a contravention of the order, and any breach of the duty that causes that person to sustain loss or damage will be actionable.[270] In such cases, however, the undertaker may rely on a due diligence defence.[271] Second, and without prejudice to individual rights to bring civil proceedings, the Secretary of State or Director, as appropriate, may seek an injunction or any other appropriate relief.[272] Third, a breach of any final or confirmed provisional order, so long as it is not the subject of an appeal by the undertaker to the High Court, may be considered sufficiently serious for the Court to grant a special administration order.[273]

Unless otherwise provided for, the only remedies for contravening appointment conditions or statutory or other requirements enforceable under these provisions, apart from enforcement orders, are those for which express alternative provision is made. The 1991 Act therefore seeks to oust the scope for individual rights of action in relation to undertakers' obligations. Although this does not preclude judicial review of the actions of the Secretary of State,[274] the enforcement of disputes under the Act

---

[269] *Ibid* s.18(5).

[270] *Ibid* s.22(1) and (2).

[271] *Ibid* s.22(3).

[272] *Ibid* ss.22(4) and (5).

[273] *Ibid* s.24(2)(b). Detailed provisions seek to ensure the continuation of the undertakers business in the interests of ensuring that essential services are maintained. See generally ss.23, 25 and 26 Water Industry Act 1991.

[274] See, e.g., *R* v *Secretary of State for the Environment ex parte Friends of the Earth* [1996] Env LR 198, discussed at 7.9.3 below.

between undertakers and individuals will always be mediated through the Director or Secretary of State under the enforcement provisions.

### 7.9.1E  Exceptions to making enforcement orders

Despite the provisions described above, the making of enforcement orders is tempered by four exceptions to the above.[275] If any of these pertain, the Director or Secretary of State must:

   (i)  serve on the undertaker notice that he is so satisfied;
   (ii) publish a copy of the notice in a manner considered appropriate for bringing the matters to which the notice relates to the attention of persons likely to be affected by them; and
   (iii) in relation to accepting an undertaking, serve a copy of the notice and of the undertaking given for the purposes of that paragraph on the Director.[276]

The first exception to the making of an enforcement order arises where the contravention, or apprehended contravention, is of a trivial nature. Although no guidance is given in the legislation on the meaning of 'trivial', during the passage of the Water Bill in 1989 the Minister remarked that it was unlikely that circumstances giving rise to danger to health would be regarded as trivial.[277] At the other end of this spectrum, the second exception is where the duties imposed on the Director or Secretary of State preclude the making or, as the case may be, the confirmation of the order. The general financial, customer and environmental duties[278] may therefore override the duty to make an enforcement order. Third, the Director need not make an order if he is satisfied that the best way to proceed is under the Competition Act 1998.[279]

### 7.9.2  Undertakings

Of greatest practical importance in relation to compliance is a fourth exception to the duty to make an enforcement order. This arises where the undertaker has given, and is complying with, an undertaking to take all such steps as appears appropriate, to the Director or Secretary of State, for securing or facilitating compliance with the condition or requirement in question. In practice, undertakings are the principal enforcement

---

[275] See s.19 Water Industry Act 1991. There is evidence of the Director threatening the use of an enforcement order to secure compliance, although the Act makes no provision for this. See Kinnersley (1994) p.172.
[276] s.19(3) Water Industry Act 1991. Subject to national security considerations (s.19(4)).
[277] Michael Howard, Standing Committee D, Col.923, February 9, 1989. This provision was considered briefly in *R v Director General of Water Services ex parte Lancashire County Council and others* [1999] Env LR 114.
[278] In Part I Water Industry Act 1991, see 7.5 and 7.6.4–5 above.
[279] *Ibid* s.19(1A), added by para.5 Sch.10 Competition Act 1998, that is, by initiating enforcement action for anti-competitive behaviour.

mechanism used, and enforcement orders are resorted to only in the event of breach of an undertaking.[280]

Although the terms of undertakings may not differ greatly from those that might be imposed under an enforcement order, their perceived advantage lies in the onus placed on the undertaker to draft the undertaking. In this sense there is an element of self-regulation to undertakings. It is arguable that the comparative informational advantage enjoyed by the undertaker over the Director or Secretary of State as to what may practicably be achieved within any specified time period will result in the drafting of undertakings relatively favourable to the undertaker. A principal objective behind the giving of undertakings is to enable economic considerations to be taken into account in relation to compliance, specifically with water quality standards. Undertakings must be placed on the public register.[281] Failure to comply with an undertaking will result in enforcement order action.[282]

What at first appears to be a relatively exceptional instance of the enforcing body not having discretion to bring proceedings is therefore, on closer inspection, a largely discretionary and in some respects self-regulatory system of supervision. This is all the more remarkable given the background to the provisions. This can be traced back to privatisation, and the aftermath of the Government's retreat on full transfer of the water authorities into the private sector following legal opinion, and the threat of judicial review, on the legality of the privatised authorities as 'competent authorities' for certain EC water directives.[283] A notable consequence of these concerns was the Government's decision to consult with the Commission over certain aspects of its privatisation legislation relating to the enforcement of drinking water standards, 'probably the first occasion since Britain's accession to the Community that a UK government had entered into direct negotiations with the Commission on the proposed details of a major item of its domestic legislation'.[284] These discussions led directly to the more stringent measures in relation to water company compliance, outlined above, in place of rather weaker agreements entered into either with the Secretary of State or the Director that the Water Bill originally contained. As events have transpired, however, the resulting provisions, now contained in the 1991 Act, still failed to comply with EC obligations.

---

[280] In 1997, for example, 71 undertakings were entered into, while just one enforcement order was made.
[281] s.195(2)(d) Water Industry Act 1991.
[282] *Ibid* s.19(2).
[283] See 2.16 above on this episode.
[284] Haigh (1992) paras 4.4-4.6.

## 7.9.3 The 'Drinking Water Litigation'

In October 1989 the Commission began infraction proceedings[285] against the UK Government for failure to comply with the Drinking Water Quality Directive.[286] In November 1992, the Court of Justice upheld the Commission's action, which included a complaint concerned with failing to comply with the maximum admissible concentrations for nitrate in 28 supply zones in England.[287] The ruling was important for its finding in relation to practical compliance, an area until then which the Court had not fully explored.[288] The Court of Justice held practical compliance to be a strict obligation, subject only to those derogations allowed in the Directive which the Government was, in any case, time-barred against relying upon.[289]

Subsequently, the environmental pressure group Friends of the Earth brought a judicial review action regarding the decision of the Secretary of State to accept undertakings from the water undertakers concerned (Thames and Anglian), rather than bring enforcement action.[290] Despite the earlier ruling of the Court of Justice on the *primary* obligations under the Directive, however, the Court of Appeal held that the *secondary* duty, to comply with the judgment of the Court of Justice, was not strict but could be qualified by practical considerations. The Court of Appeal was not persuaded that the Government's obligations extended further than securing the agreement of the water undertakers to the undertakings entered into, for example by expediting or overriding planning legislation in order to allow pesticide removal works to be built more quickly. However, less drastic measures might have been contemplated, for example the designation of water protection zones[291] or other, perhaps fiscal, measures for reducing nitrate levels to prescribed maxima in supplies.[292] The Court accepted that meeting EC requirements remained the Government's policy objective and that it would ultimately comply with the obligations of the Directive. Especially at first instance, there was insufficient evidence to support the argument that compliance could be achieved more swiftly by other means than provided for through undertakings.[293] While speedier implementation was essentially a matter of political will, the decision essentially left the compliance timetable under the control of the Secretary of State, although as noted previously the undertakers have a considerable input in determining the conditions of undertakings.[294]

---

[285] Under Art.169 EEC Treaty (now Art.226 EC), see 4.13.1 above.

[286] Directive 80/778/EEC as amended, see 17.7.1 below. On the 'Drinking Water Litigation' see also 4.15.1 above.

[287] Case C-337/89 *Commission* v *United Kingdom* [1992] ECR I-6103.

[288] Somsen (1993) p.62.

[289] Arts.9, 10 and 20 Drinking Water Quality Directive.

[290] *R* v *Secretary of State for the Environment ex parte Friends of the Earth* [1996] Env LR 198.

[291] Under s.93 Water Resources Act 1991, see 13.4 below.

[292] See [1993] *Water Law* 79, and further comment by Hilson (1995) p.1467.

[293] Hilson, *Ibid* at p.1466.

[294] See 7.9.2 above.

More recently, the Commission brought further proceedings against the UK, arguing that continued breach of the Drinking Water Quality Directive is attributable to accepting undertakings.[295] In terms similar to the judgment in the *Friends of the Earth* litigation, the UK conceded a breach of the primary obligation to comply but not the secondary obligation to remedy as swiftly as possible which, it argued, is guaranteed through undertakings. In the Advocate General's opinion, however, undertakings did not provide an effective mechanism to achieve the results required by the Directive. In particular, he considered it important that companies giving undertakings are not obliged to achieve particular results, only to undertake certain works, and may ask for either more time or modifications to the technical specifications of works to be carried out. Regardless of the factual breach, therefore, there had been defective transposition. Frequent resort to undertakings simply deferred the deadline for compliance: 'there is an indissoluble link between the system of undertakings, which necessarily involves, each time it is applied, a deferral of the deadline for complying with the wholesomeness standards, and the fact that those standards are not always met'.[296] That the Government had consulted the Commission on the enforcement provisions of the Act was, following settled Community case law, irrelevant.[297]

In its judgment, the Court of Justice upheld the approach taken by the Advocate General. In particular, the Court held that while enforcement orders were an acceptable means to ensure compliance with the Directive, undertakings were unlawful because of the latitude given to the Secretary of State in agreeing them with the undertakers, especially in relation to the time allowed to comply with the Directive's standards.[298] As an interpretation of EC law, this decision is unsurprising, since the Water Industry Act 1991, under which the undertakings are made, does not itself specify the matters to be covered in the compliance programme. Nevertheless, the judgment did leave the situation at something of an impasse, although in addition to those changes to national law that were made, discussed below, the position is affected by significant revisions to the Drinking Water Quality Directive. These give Member States greater flexibility to derogate from standards where there is no danger to health and the supply of water cannot otherwise be maintained.[299]

A further argument of the Commission was that undertakings 'would seem' to preclude reliance by individuals on the rights conferred by the Directive in proceedings against water companies before the national courts.[300] Although this point was not made timeously, and was not considered in the judgment of the Court of Justice, the Advocate General's opinion nevertheless gives a helpful analysis of how the issue might be

---

[295] Case C-340/96 *Commission* v *United Kingdom* [1999] ECR I-2023.

[296] Opinion of A-G Mischo at para.56.

[297] See, e.g., Case C-415/93 *Union Royale Belge des Sociétés de Football Association and Others* v *Bosman and Others* [1995] ECR I-4921, para. 136.

[298] Case C-340/96 *Commission* v *United Kingdom* [1999] ECR I-2023.

[299] Directive 98/83/EC, in effect from December 2000, see 17.7.8 below.

[300] See 4.16.3 above.

approached. In essence, the Advocate General found that the right to bring a judicial review of the Secretary of State's decision to accept an undertaking would, if successful, annul the undertaking, giving immediate effect to the quality objectives in the Act and obliging the Secretary of State to make an enforcement order against the undertaker. This was considered sufficient to protect individual rights guaranteed under the Directive. In dismissing this part of the proceedings, the Court of Justice merely recounted previous case law establishing that, where a directive is intended to create rights for individuals, Member States must lay down the provisions necessary to ensure that the persons entitled to exercise those rights enjoy judicial protection.[301]

A further consideration is the possibility of further action by the Commission, under which the Member State may be set a timetable for compliance with its legal obligations, backed by possible financial penalties.[302] So far, no action on these lines has been instigated, and in the circumstances it is unlikely whether the Commission would take such proceedings given the extent to which, as the next section describes, measures towards compliance are being taken at national level.

### 7.9.4 The Undertakings Regulations

Regulations have been made which seek to give practical and legal effect to the judgment of the Court of Justice. The Drinking Water (Undertakings) (England and Wales) Regulations 2000[303] require all undertakings to be formally renegotiated so that any relaxations from mandatory EC standards are agreed to only for the minimum length of time and only if no reasonable alternatives exist. The Regulations are limited in their application to undertakings accepted in relation to drinking water, and do not alter the enforcement regime in the Water Industry Act 1991 beyond this. The Regulations contain a number of novel features and are worth considering in some depth.

In particular, the Regulations require that undertakers must apply in writing to the relevant enforcement authority[304] setting out:

   (a) the terms of the proposed undertaking;
   (b) details of relevant investigations into the contravention and its cause;
   (c) reasons for the remedial steps proposed, details of any alternative remedial steps considered and the reason for preferring those proposed;

---

[301] See, e.g., Case C-58/89 *Commission* v *Germany* [1991] ECR I-4983.

[302] Under Art.228 EC (ex Art.171).

[303] SI 2000 No. 1297. The Regulations also amend s.19(1) Water Industry Act 1991 so that the exceptions to the making of enforcement orders are all made subject to the Regulations.

[304] The Secretary of State or the National Assembly for Wales.

(d) details of any alternative means for maintaining supplies to the population affected and, if so, what they are and the reason for not using them;

(e) an estimate of the maximum deviation from the 'wholesomeness' standards[305] in relation to each relevant parameter which is likely to occur while remedial steps are being taken and an explanation of the basis of that estimate;

(f) an explanation of the measures proposed for monitoring the quality of water supplied in relation to each relevant parameter, and for preventing any danger to public health arising, while remedial steps are being taken; and

(g) all other information the company relies on.[306]

In addition, any undertaking entered into must specify:

(a) the nature of the contravention and its cause or suspected cause;

(b) the water supply zone affected and the size of the population supplied;

(c) the remedial steps which are to be taken and the date by which each step is to be completed;

(d) the maximum deviation from the wholesomeness requirements in relation to each relevant parameter which the company undertakes to ensure is not exceeded while remedial steps are being taken; and

(e) the measures which are to be taken to monitor those parameters, and to prevent any danger to public health arising, during that period.[307]

Finally, the relevant enforcement authority must be satisfied that:

(a) the specified remedial steps are being and will be taken as quickly as possible and that the dates specified in the undertaking are consistent with this;

(b) there is no potential danger to human health;

(c) there are no reasonable alternative means for maintaining supplies to the population affected by the contravention; and

(d) the specified remedial steps are the most appropriate in the circumstances of the case for remedying the contravention as quickly as possible.[308]

It is further provided that undertakings cannot be relied upon as a means of ensuring that the contravention is remedied if the enforcing authority ceases to be satisfied about these matters.

---

[305] As laid down in s.68 Water Industry Act 1991, and see 17.7.3 below.

[306] Reg.3 Drinking Water (Undertakings) (England and Wales) Regulations 2000 (SI 2000 No. 1297).

[307] *Ibid* Reg.4.

[308] *Ibid* Reg.5.

The relevant enforcement authority must, no later than 31 July 2000, review all existing undertakings, and following the review can only rely on an undertaking if its terms comply with the requirements noted above, or if it is satisfied at all times about those matters specified above.[309] Practical guidance on how it will interpret the Regulations has been given by the Drinking Water Inspectorate, which set out the conditions which will trigger consideration of an undertaking and the timescales involved.[310]

The Regulations may, in practice, be sufficient to satisfy the Commission in relation to the specific issue as to the legality of undertakings. However, they cannot be relied upon to avoid liability for breach of water quality standards. It is clear from the case law of the Court of Justice that the obligation to meet mandatory standards is a strict one which must be met in practice.[311] Thus, the Regulations serve at best to protect the system of undertakings from further challenge by the Commission, and cannot by themselves prevent the Commission taking further infringement proceedings against the UK for breach of drinking water quality standards. The extent to which the enforcement provisions of the Water Industry Act 1991 may be questioned in relation to EC obligations, however, should not detract from their application to purely national matters.

Nevertheless, the Regulations are some of the most procedurally demanding in the field of water quality. Although it is too early to assess their practical impact, it is clear that they impose stringent conditions on the acceptance of undertakings, requiring a level of justification and reasoned decision-making which, regrettably, is seldom found in environmental law. On paper at least, the contrast between the Undertakings Regulations and the more pragmatic and informal approach that has traditionally characterised decision-making in water quality regulation could not be more stark.

## 7.9.5  Individual Enforcement

As noted above, the Water Industry Act 1991 seeks to provide for an exclusive mechanism for those matters that fall within its provisions relating to enforcement orders and undertakings. Nevertheless, it is worth noting here briefly some of the possible ways in which undertakers' obligations might be enforced through individually initiated action.

While only the Director of Public Prosecutions or the Secretary of State (in practice, the DWI) may prosecute in relation to water unfit for human consumption,[312] a private prosecution might be brought by an individual against a water undertaker for causing the pollution of controlled waters.[313]

---

[309] *Ibid* Reg.7.

[310] DWI Information Letter No. 15/2000, *Implementation of the Drinking Water (Undertakings) (England and Wales) Regulations 2000* (2000), at www.dwi.detr.gov.uk/azindex.htm

[311] On the very limited scope for less stringent standards see 4.11.4 above.

[312] On water which is 'unfit for human consumption' see 17.7.7 below.

[313] See 9.3–6 above.

Also, it may be possible to bring a civil action for damages, under a number of possible heads of claim, for supplying water that causes illness or otherwise causes damage to assets.[314] In addition, an individual may enjoy rights to be compensated under EC law that may be enforced either against an undertaker or the Government. An action against the State or an emanation of the State may be possible under the direct effect doctrine, and there is considerable authority to suggest that water undertakers will be considered to the public bodies, at least as far as their core functions are concerned.[315]

The possibility also arises of an action, under the doctrine of state liability or *Francovich* liability,[316] for any loss following improper implementation of a directive or Treaty obligation. It is now fairly clear that where human health is an objective of the directive (usually ascertained from the preamble), the directive may confer rights on individuals.[317] This approach has been taken in relation to the Drinking Water Abstraction Directive[318] and has been implicitly accepted by Advocate General Mischo as regards the Drinking Water Quality Directive.[319] It has also been accepted in relation to *economic* rights that may be conferred on individuals under water directives.[320] However, proving causation may be a problem.[321]

## 7.10  Economic Regulation: Proposals for Reform

Calls for greater direct competition within the water industry and for reform of the role of the Director General of Water Services are the subject of ongoing proposals.

### 7.10.1  Competition in the Water Industry

The need to comply with EC competition law has acted as a spur towards greater direct competition in the water industry, though moving beyond comparative competition has always been a long-term policy objective.[322] Specific proposals for reform were published by Government in April 2000.[323] Beyond recommending reductions in the thresholds for inset

---

[314] See 17.11 below on civil liability for substandard drinking water quality.

[315] See 4.16.1 above.

[316] See 4.16.6 above.

[317] See generally Hilson (1997).

[318] Case C-58/89 *Commission* v *Germany* [1991] ECR I-4983, para 14.

[319] In Case C-340/96 *Commission* v *United Kingdom* [1999] ECR I-2023.

[320] *Bowden* v *South West Water Services Ltd and others* [1999] Env LR 438, and see 3.12 above.

[321] See, e.g., Elworthy and Holder (1996).

[322] See 7.7.1 above.

[323] DETR, *Competition in the Water Industry in England and Wales* (2000). On competition see also Ofwat, *The Current State of Market Competition* (2000) and for earlier proposals see Ofwat, *The Regulation of Common Carriage Agreements in England and Wales: A Consultation Paper* (1996). For a brief yet perceptive overview of current issues see Sage (2000).

appointments,[324] and for the provision of time-limited inset appointments, the proposals raise the prospect of establishing 'common carriage' in both the drinking water and sewerage service sectors.

Common carriage envisages allowing access to and distribution from an undertaker's supplies on fair terms, in a way not entirely dissimilar to the way in which gas and electricity companies have access to rival supply networks. Common carriage therefore describes the shared use of the supply pipes and other infrastructure of an existing statutory undertaker by a third party in order to enable that third party to provide services in the statutory undertaker's area. This shared use could be by some division of the vertical integration of the water industry, for example through restructuring or through franchising, although some more evolutionary approach is more likely under which the infrastructure would continue to be owned by the statutory undertaker. Both treated and untreated water and sewage could potentially be subject to common carriage arrangements. Common carriage might even lead to a national 'water grid', though for practical reasons this is unlikely to emerge in the short to medium term.[325]

Common carriage has been under consideration for some time,[326] but has generally been met with little commercial enthusiasm, or by concerns about compromising drinking and ecological water quality. Mixing water from different catchments might lead to unwanted ecological changes, for example the introduction of alien species, the spread of fish disease, changes in water quality and river ecosystems and even increasing flood risk.[327] Legal issues here include whether an undertaker transferring water between river systems might be liable for breach of wildlife protection or fish disease legislation, including the water pollution offence arising under fisheries legislation.[328] In practice, it might be difficult to screen out undesirable substances in such bulk transfers; it might be practically impossible to prevent the movement between catchments of crayfish plague, which has done much to destroy populations of native crayfish.[329] Variability in drinking water quality between regions and supply zones has also led to concerns,[330] principally whether the mixing of sources might breach mandatory standards for drinking water quality.[331] However, there

---

[324] To 100 megalitres/year, from 250 megalitres/year. See now the Water and Sewerage Undertakers (Inset Appointments) Regulations 2000 (SI 2000 No.1842) (a similar reduction is planned for Wales).

[325] Some regional water grids already exist.

[326] DoE, *Water: Increasing Customer Choice* (1996) see [1996] *Water Law* 101; DETR, *Water Charging in England and Wales – A New Approach*, Consultation Paper (1998).

[327] See, e.g., The Environmental Threats of the Kielder Transfer Scheme, Friends of the Earth Briefing Sheet, July 1996. Bulk transfers of raw or treated water have been taking place since the early 20th century, and criticism of common carriage by the voluntary conservation sector has tended to focus on pressure for increased abstraction from supplies, see 'Wildlife Trusts warn on competition', Water Magazine, 3 March 2000, p.7.

[328] Under s.4 Salmon and Freshwater Fisheries Act 1975, see 15.4.1 below.

[329] Long-distance aqueducts are subject to environmental impact assessment, on which see 14.6 below.

[330] 'Competition law "poses threat" to water quality', *Financial Times*, 13 January 2000.

[331] The liability issues are considered at 17.7.6 below.

are other concerns, for example co-operation between undertakers in emergency situations, and differences in fluoridation arrangements.[332]

There are still concerns about these issues, especially liability issues. But a result of the Competition Act 1998 has been that undertakers and the Director now present common carriage as a management issue, with less emphasis on possible adverse ecological and public health effects.[333] This might be because the present proposals indicate that it will continue to be permissible for an existing undertaker to refuse access by a competitor to its infrastructure if this is done to protect water quality standards. This poses a number of problems, however, not least because most of the existing water undertakers are, in some respects, themselves breaching drinking water quality (or sewage effluent quality) standards.[334] One issue this raises, for example, is whether an undertaker could refuse access to its network because a new entrant would lower the quality of its water, but not so as to breach any mandatory standards (i.e. whether there would be a 'no deterioration' provision).

Issues relating to the relationship between undertakers are also evident in general requirements that might be imposed on new suppliers. As noted above,[335] the present position is that inset appointees need only satisfy the Director of their competence and financial viability. The scope for common carriage has led to proposals that new entrants might be 'licensed' on the same basis as, and be subject to the same general and environmental obligations as, the statutory undertakers, or be required to show that they were 'fit and proper' to be involved in common carriage.[336] Alternatively, incumbent undertakers when opening up their networks could deal this with through contractual requirements. For example, an incumbent might require that anyone adding water to, or taking water from, its network was of sufficient technical expertise and had sufficient financial backing to compensate for any losses incurred. Any such contractual arrangements, however, would have to be entered into 'in the shadow' of oversight by the Director that any such requirements were not unduly strict to the point where they were anti-competitive or amounted to an abuse of a dominant position.[337]

---

[332] See 17.8 below on water fluoridation.

[333] In advance of the present proposals, but in light of the Competition Act 1998, Ofwat required undertakers to draw up access codes by 31 August 2000, and also offered other views on competition, see MD162 (12 April 2000), available at *www.open.gov.uk/ofwat*

[334] See Ofwat, *Levels of service of the water industry in England and Wales: 1999-2000 report* (2000).

[335] See 7.7.2.

[336] DETR, *Competition in the Water Industry in England and Wales* (2000) paras 7.15 and 9.6. The 'fit and proper person' approach is taken to waste management licensing, see 12.2.6 below.

[337] Ofwat, *Competition Act 1998 – Application in the Water and Sewerage Sectors* (2000), available at *www.open.gov.uk/ofwat/competition_act_guidelines.htm*

## 7.10.2 Reforming the Role of the Director

Here, concerns have been raised about the lack of openness throughout much of the regulatory process, and the impact of this on the credibility and legitimacy of economic regulation.[338] Precisely *because* the Director is necessarily more than an economic technocrat, questions of legitimacy, and thus the legitimacy of the sector, have been raised.[339] For some, a narrow confining of the Director's discretion to economic considerations is required;[340] others call for broadening the Director's environmental and social remit, and checking his discretion by greater Parliamentary oversight.[341] While rejecting the latter, Government proposals to subject the Director to a legal duty to have regard to statutory guidance from the Secretary of State on social and environmental objectives emerged in 1998.[342] Through something of a tortuous route, amendments to the Director's duties, and other changes to the institutional arrangements for economic regulation, are now contained in a draft Water Bill.[343]

The salient features of the draft Bill in relation to economic regulation are:

(a) the appointment by the Minister (or National Assembly) of a 'Water Advisory Panel' to 'advise the Director in the exercise of his functions' (what this will entail is unclear);

(b) a new 'consumer objective' linked to a move from 'facilitating' to 'promoting effective competition';

(c) a partial balancing of this consumer duty with a duty on the Director to 'have regard to' Ministerial guidance on social and environmental duties, but consumer and economic interests are clearly prioritised;

(d) empowering the Minister to set service standards for water supply or sewerage services directly, without following a proposal from the Director;

(e) requiring the Director to give reasons for decisions;

(f) a 'Consumer Council for Water' to replace the ONCC, and to be external to Ofwat, with Ministerial appointees; and

(g) a power for the Director or Minister to impose financial penalties on undertakers, up to 10 per cent of their annual turnover, for breaching licence conditions or failing to achieve performance standards (hence going beyond an 'enforcement notice' approach).

Whether these developments will resolve long-standing tensions between economic and environmental regulation of water and sewerage undertakers remains to be seen. On publication, central provisions concerning competition and the use of economic instruments in abstraction licensing

---

[338] Stelzer (1996). See also Kay (1996).

[339] For an overview, see Graham (1995) pp.73-79.

[340] Contrast Foster (1992) p.7.

[341] See, e.g., Souter (1994) p.82. On confining, structuring and checking discretion generally see Davis (1969).

[342] Department of Trade and Industry, *A Fair Deal for Consumers: Modernising the Framework for Utility Regulation* (1998)

[343] DETR, *Water Bill: Consultation on Draft Legislation* (2000).

were excluded, making any assessment of future changes to competition in the water industry, and to economic regulation, particularly difficult. One feature of the draft Bill, however, is that no sustainable development duty upon the Director is proposed. Even if such a duty emerges, however, as has been observed: 'the debate over the accountability of the regulators is just one facet of a bigger problem and it is doubtful whether it can be tackled in isolation'.[344]

---

[344] Graham (1995) p.77.

# Chapter 8

# LOCAL AUTHORITY RESPONSIBILITIES

## 8.1 Introduction

The early regulatory control of water pollution evolved both from controls aimed at improving public health conditions, and to combat the consequent effects of public health legislation.[1] In requiring sewerage infrastructure, the latter had tended to increase the amount of waste and effluent discharged to rivers in the interests of urban sanitation. This was clearly envisaged by Edwin Chadwick, whose 'Sanitary Report' of 1842 remarked, on the impact of water carriage system on rivers, that:

> The chief objection to the extension of this system is the pollution of the water of the river into which the sewers are discharged. Admitting the expediency of avoiding the pollution, it is nevertheless proved to be an evil of almost inappreciable magnitude in comparison with the ill health occasioned by the constant retention of several hundred thousand accumulations of pollution in the most densely peopled districts.[2]

Or, as Lord Macnaghten later observed:

> Ever since the attention of the legislature was first directed to the very difficult subject of the disposal of sewage, it has always been considered, at any rate up to very recent times, that the most proper mode of getting rid of town sewage was to pour it into a tidal or public river.[3]

Today, the control of much gross pollution of water, and thus the greatly reduced extent to which the water environment acts as a carrier of disease, means that the public health dimension to water pollution control is beginning to receive somewhat less attention when compared to the pursuit of improved ecological quality. With some notable exceptions, such as campaigns to improve the quality of coastal waters to prevent sewage-related viral infections,[4] matters of water quality and public health are now largely confined to the quality of potable supplies.[5] One consequence of this is the frequent focus in this book on the functions exercised by the Environment Agency in relation to natural water quality or controlled

---

[1] See generally Ch.2 above.

[2] Chadwick, *Report on the Sanitary Condition of the Labouring Population of Great Britain* (1842) p.120. The text is contained in Flinn (1965).

[3] *Somersetshire Drainage Commissioners* v *Corporation of Bridgwater* (1899) *Law Times* 729 at 731. On the 'flush and forget' approach, see Kinnersley (1988) p.166.

[4] Most notably, through organisations such as Surfers Against Sewage, on which see *R* v *Carrick District Council ex parte Shelley and Another* [1996] Env LR 273, discussed at 8.5.3 below.

[5] On drinking water quality see Ch.17 below.

waters.[6] Nevertheless, local authorities, often exercising public health responsibilities in their areas, retain certain functions impinging not merely on drinking water quality but also on the quality of water in the natural environment.

Given that public health imperatives are generally at issue, most of the water-related functions of local authorities are now cast as legal duties, though a brief look at the historical evolution of controls in this area reveals the permissive nature of much early public health law. Following an introduction to the constitution and general powers and duties of local authorities, a range of the more important functions entrusted to local government which now bear upon water quality are considered. Many of these are discussed in other chapters of this work, in particular the responsibilities of local authorities:

    (a)  to prevent or regulate polluting discharges through town and country planning law;[7]

    (b)  to regulate drinking water quality, especially private water supplies;[8]

    (c)  to prevent the pollution of water from contaminated land;[9]

    (d)  to regulate, in an integrated way, certain industrial processes;[10] and

    (e)  to act as the 'competent authority' for a number of Community directives relating to water quality.[11]

The focus of much of this chapter, therefore, is the law relating to the control of statutory nuisances which, as with the private law actions discussed elsewhere,[12] serves as both a potentially useful mechanism for the protection of individual interests which might be affected by water pollution, and as a tool capable of being utilised, strategically, to protect water quality in the wider interest. Although there is some scope for abatement action to be initiated by individual action, local authorities are placed under a general duty to monitor their areas for certain prescribed nuisances, and the obligation to do so may act as an alternative mechanism for addressing problems of water quality. Like many of the other public health functions of local authorities, the origins of statutory nuisance law lie in controlling circumstances that may adversely affect public health. Most of this chapter is therefore concerned with abating situations where certain kinds of nuisance are at issue, particularly where these have a

---

[6] Of course, many of the Agency's powers and duties can be traced back to those exercised by local authorities, and later water authorities, before privatisation of the water industry in 1989, see Ch.2 above.

[7] On town and planning law see Ch.14 below.

[8] On drinking water quality see Ch.17 below, especially 17.9.1 on private water supplies.

[9] On contaminated land see 13.7 below.

[10] On the regulation of Part 2(A) process under the pollution prevention and control regime see 12.3.6 below.

[11] These include the Habitats Directive (see 8.3.2 below), the Bathing Water Directive (see 5.5.2 above) and the Directive on the sale and marketing of pesticides (see 12.4.7 below).

[12] See Ch.3 above on the civil law.

public health aspect, rather than with regulating the entry or discharge of polluting or contaminating matter into the environment as such.

## 8.2 The Development of Public Health Responsibilities

Public health law emerged in the mid-nineteenth century, prompted by the appreciation of the connection between environmental conditions and human health and thus the contribution that improved public health conditions could make to the reduction both of poverty and disease.[13] Local authorities, or local boards of health, were given a range of powers, including the power to remove nuisances and levy rates to construct drains and sewers.[14] While in the early days their establishment was generally unsuccessful, successive reforms to the law relating to the removal of nuisances, and to the institutional structure to provide for public health improvements, saw considerable improvement.[15] Local authorities also took increasing control of the provision of water supplies in their areas from private companies. In addition, the consolidating Public Health Act 1875 required local authorities, for the first time, to inspect their areas for prescribed statutory nuisances, marking an important move away from what had hitherto been a generally permissive regime.[16] As regards those things categorised as statutory nuisances, this owed much to the 'miasm' or 'foul odour' theory[17] rather than the later establishment of the contagious spread of pathogenic micro-organisms, generally through water, as the cause of the spread of diseases such as cholera.[18] These early influences may still be seen in the categorisation of various states of affairs as statutory nuisances.[19] Nevertheless, both the contagion and miasmatic theories of public health pointed to the need to improve the quality of water supplies.

Since the 19th century, local authorities have retained primary responsibility for matters of public health within their areas, although there has been a gradual removal of most of their functions relating to environmental water quality. As from the Rivers Pollution Prevention Act 1876,[20] which made local authority control subject to oversight by local government boards, responsibility for water pollution control generally has passed from local authorities to catchment boards and then to catchment-based water authorities before passing, on privatisation of the water

---

[13] And, it should be said, social unrest, see Briggs (1963) p.108. Generally the legislation can be traced back to the Cholera Act 1832.

[14] Public Health Act 1848, see 2.4 above.

[15] See the Nuisance Removal Acts of 1855, 1860 and 1863 and the Local Government Act 1871 and on the public health background to modern water pollution and water quality law see generally 2.4 above.

[16] Although the Sanitary Act 1866 had empowered central Government to compel action rather than merely advise local authorities. On statutory nuisance see 8.5 below.

[17] Chadwick, *Report on the Sanitary Condition of the Labouring Population of Great Britain* (1842), reproduced in Flinn (1965).

[18] See generally McManus (1994) p.3.

[19] Discussed in detail at 8.5 below.

[20] See 2.6 above.

industry in 1989, to the National Rivers Authority and now to the Environment Agency.[21] Thus, from the time that water pollution control expanded beyond the removal of nuisances, it has generally been the responsibility of specialist bodies. It is also worth noting that a number of public health functions previously exercised by local authorities are now vested in the private water and sewerage undertakers, in particular most operational functions such as water supply and functions relating to sewerage.[22]

A further trend of note is the transmission of controls, over the more complex or polluting industrial processes or sites, from local authorities to specialist regulators. Thus the Alkali Inspectorate, established under the Alkali Act 1863, assumed responsibility in the main for atmospheric emissions primarily from the caustic soda industry, while local authorities remained responsible for other atmospheric emissions. This trend continues to the present, the Environment Agency being responsible for the regulation of certain prescribed processes while, for example, local authorities regulate less polluting industrial emissions and emissions to air.[23] The same approach can be seen with contaminated land, where the Agency has responsibility for the most contaminating 'special sites' while local authorities have responsibility for other contaminated sites.[24]

## 8.3  Local Government

Appreciating the role played by local authorities in relation to water quality issues involves a general overview of local government structures and decision-making in local government, as well as a look at the impact of recent reforms. It is also useful to look briefly here at the role played by local authorities in acting as a point of contact between other regulators and the public.

### 8.3.1  The Structure of Local Government

The structure of local government in England and Wales is somewhat convoluted. Most parts of the country are divided into county councils, with these regions being further divided into district councils (depending on the area, these may be called 'City' councils). In these areas, therefore, there is two-tier local government, with the county council responsible for more strategic matters such as waste planning, and the district council responsible for more day-to-day matters such as contaminated land, decisions on most planning applications and matters of public health.

In the metropolitan areas, however, county and district matters are the responsibility of one authority. Outside of London (in Greater Manchester,

---

[21] On the Environment Agency generally see Ch.6 above.

[22] See generally Ch.7 above, and see Chs. 11 and 17 below on trade effluent and drinking water respectively.

[23] On integrated pollution control and integrated pollution prevention and control see 12.3 below.

[24] On contaminated land see 8.3.5 below and 13.7 below.

Merseyside, South Yorkshire, West Yorkshire, the West Midlands and Tyne and Wear) these are metropolitan district councils. In London, the administrative units are the 33 London borough councils, including the City of London. In these areas, therefore, public health will be a responsibility of the metropolitan district councils or London borough councils.[25]

Since the mid-1990s, however, there has been a movement towards creating further unitary authorities outside of the metropolitan areas. This began in Wales, where the two-tier split was removed in 1996 by the creation of 22 unitary councils: 11 county councils and 11 county borough councils.[26] In England, the movement towards unification has been more cautious, but there are now 25 unitary authorities. In essence, the unitary authorities follow the approach in the metropolitan district councils and London boroughs, and have responsibility for the functions assigned both to county and district councils.

Below the level of county and district councils and unitary authorities, referred to as 'principal authorities', there is a further level of local government involving parish councils or, in Wales, community councils. These authorities have only minor functions in relation to water quality such as preventing ponds, pools, etc. from being a risk to human health.[27]

Reference to 'local authorities' below is therefore generally to the relevant district council, metropolitan district council, Welsh county or county borough council or English unitary authority, since public health functions are generally a matter for the lower tier of the principal local authorities. It should also be noted that, in customs ports, 'port health authorities' may be constituted.[28] These may have assigned to them local government-type functions in their designated areas, and may, for example, bring proceedings for statutory nuisance in their districts.[29]

Finally, it is worth recalling that the geographic extent of a local authority area may not take in the whole of a river catchment, and in the case of the larger rivers will almost certainly not do so. For this reason the powers of local authorities to affect activities outside their areas may be important.

The seaward boundary of a local authority may be fixed by local Act, but in general the boundary is determined according to the low water mark of median tides. Unless stated otherwise, therefore, this is the limit of a local

---

[25] The Greater London Authority has an environmental and sustainable development remit, but is generally prevented from exercising functions in relation to health (see ss.30 and 31 Greater London Authority Act 1999).
[26] Under the Local Government (Wales) Act 1994. The difference in names is of no legal effect.
[27] See, e.g., s.260 Public Health Act 1936, discussed at 8.4.4 below.
[28] By an order under s.2 Public Health (Control of Disease) Act 1984.
[29] s.79(8) Environmental Protection Act 1990, and see 8.5 below on statutory nuisance.

authority's jurisdiction.[30] However, there is the power to review seaward boundaries.[31]

### 8.3.2 Decision-Making in Local Government

Unlike regulatory agencies such as the Environment Agency, local authorities are elected bodies. In theory it is the elected members who take decisions, usually through the appropriate committee. Since the Local Government Act 1972, it has been possible for a local authority to delegate most of its powers, either to committees of councillors or to individual officers. In practice, most decisions are delegated to officers and endorsed by councillors. Members of the public may attend meetings of the council or any of its committees or sub-committees, and have reasonable access to agendas, minutes and background reports.[32]

It is worth emphasising that, as with the regulatory agencies, local authorities are limited in what they can achieve because of financial restrictions imposed by central government. The likelihood is that this restriction compromises the ability of local authorities adequately to carry out many of the functions entrusted to them.

### 8.3.3 Local Government Reform

Under the Local Government Act 2000, local authorities may do anything they consider likely to achieve the promotion or improvement of the economic, social and environmental well-being of their areas.[33] In doing so, however, local authorities must have regard to strategies (termed 'community strategies') which they must prepare for promoting or improving the economic, social and environmental well-being of their area and contributing to the achievement of sustainable development in the United Kingdom.[34] These strategies must be introduced following consultation and the seeking of public participation. Thus, while promoting well-being is defined as a power, the exercise of this power is set within a wider context where local authorities are obliged to prepare what are, in effect, local sustainable development strategies.[35] The 'well-being' provisions extend to doing anything outside a local authorities area if this is considered likely to achieve any one or more of the well-being objectives, but would be limited by any express statutory prohibition, restriction or limitation on the exercise of such powers. The exercise of the

---

[30] For statutory nuisance the limit is the territorial limit i.e. 12 nautical miles (s.79(11) Environmental Protection Act 1990).

[31] s.14(3)(a) Local Government Act 1992; s.71 Local Government Act 1972.

[32] See generally the Public Bodies (Admission to Meetings) Act 1960, s.100 Local Government Act 1972, the Local Government (Access to Information) Act 1985 and Ch.16 below.

[33] s.2(1) Local Government Act 2000.

[34] *Ibid* s.2(3) and 4.

[35] The DETR White Paper *Modern Local Government: In Touch with the People* (Cm 4014, 1998) recommended that the specific well-being provisions be cast as duties rather than a power; see paras. 8.8-8.11. During passage of the Bill, a power to prepare community strategies became a duty to do so.

well-being power, and the preparation of community strategies, are both subject to guidance from the Secretary of State.[36]

New powers to promote environmental well-being might not impact on the exercise of public health controls where these are formulated as legal duties. However, local authorities might use them, for example, in promoting the aesthetic character of the local water environment or furthering their role in the exchange of information and ideas about local water quality.

It is also worth mentioning that the Local Government Act 2000 paves the way for a radical shift from the present responsibilities of elected councillors to requiring that some form of executive administration is put into place. This might be through a directly elected mayors, but other possible executive arrangements are also provided for.[37] One consequence of this may be a greater involvement in day-to-day decision-making by cabinet executives, although in technical areas such as public health it is unlikely that change will be significant and most decisions are likely in practice to be determined by technically qualified officers.

### 8.3.4 Information Exchange and Local Agenda 21

The responsibilities of local authorities in their areas mean that they are involved in a range of decision-making processes. This may be as a body to whom information or matters to be determined are notified, i.e., as a statutory consultee, and as a conduit to the general public for certain environmental information.

Thus, local authorities must be notified of:

(a) applications for a discharge consent, unless this is waived;[38]
(b) proposed water protection zone orders;[39]
(c) proposals to make a nitrate sensitive areas order within their area;[40]
(d) proposals by a district health authority to fluoridate the public water supply in its area;[41] and
(e) the notification of sites of special scientific interest.[42]

However, there is no requirement to notify local authorities of applications for trade effluent consents or consents to discharge special category waste to sewers. A sewerage map of the local area must be given to local authorities by sewerage undertakers and made available for inspection by

---

[36] Or, in Wales, the National Assembly.
[37] ss.11 and 14-16 Local Government Act 2000.
[38] See 10.5.3 below.
[39] See 13.4 below.
[40] See 13.5.1 below.
[41] See 17.8 below.
[42] See 18.7.1 below.

the local authority,[43] although concerns have been raised about the extent to which undertakers may prevent the release of such information on the grounds of commercial confidentiality.[44]

A further role for local authorities is in relation to implementing Local Agenda 21, the local response to Agenda 21, the global action plan for sustainable development signed at the Rio 'Earth Summit' in 1992. A central emphasis of Agenda 21, and thus of Local Agenda 21, is to secure greater local involvement and public participation in environmental policy-making and decision-making, which involves both a greater role for individuals and for local government. Local Agenda 21, however, is a creature of policy and not law; Agenda 21 matters are dealt with through the Local Government Management Board which has a general remit to give education, support and guidance on enhancing participatory environmental democracy. While experience at national level has been mixed, Local Agenda 21 tends to involve local involvement in assessing the state of the local environment and environmental monitoring, awareness raising, consultation processes, strategic visioning processes, as well as integrating environmental considerations into other sectors of local government of the kind considered above.[45]

Some limitations of Local Agenda 21 in practice have been noted. These include a certain lack of willing for sustainability issues at local level to go beyond the usual core areas of local government,[46] and within these areas for Local Agenda 21 to have relatively little impact on what might be termed the 'technocentric' areas such as health, environmental health and buildings control. Integrating sustainability concerns generally into areas like health has been sluggish.[47] Thus, the impact of Local Agenda 21 on the topics covered in this chapter might be relatively slight. However, Local Agenda 21 may be playing a wider role in changing the way in which decision-making is undertaken at local level, and this may have a significant impact on the role of local government through its 'information exchange' function identified above.

## 8.4 Local Authority Functions and General Powers and Duties

Local government in England and Wales is entirely the creation of statute. Thus, a local authority may only carry out those functions that are expressly conferred on it in legislation. Exceeding this may expose an authority to an action in judicial review for having acted beyond its legal powers. In this respect, therefore, local authorities are similar to other regulatory bodies such as the Environment Agency, whose functions, and the way in which these are exercised, are circumscribed by statute.

---

[43] s.200 Water Industry Act 1991.

[44] House of Commons Select Committee on the Environment, Transport and the Regions, *Sewage Treatment and Disposal* (1998) paras 236 and 242.

[45] See 8.3 for a range of relevant local authority responsibilities.

[46] A criticism of Audit Commission 1997.

[47] Tuxworth and Thomas (1996). See generally Voisey (1998).

It is, however, difficult to give a comprehensive list of local authorities' functions. Unlike the Environment Agency, whose functions are exhaustively provided for in Part I of the Environment Act 1995, there is no similarly comprehensive statute in relation to local government. It is therefore necessary to give a brief overview of relevant local authority functions and where these are contained, and also to look at the interface between local authorities and the Environment Agency in relation to public health controls.

### 8.4.1 Town and Country Planning

A key function of local government in relation to water quality is town and country planning. Planning law remains a pre-eminent means of preventing water quality problems, both through strategic decisions about future development and through carefully imposed siting and design requirements on new structures.[48]

### 8.4.2 Nature Conservation

Through their role as local planning authorities, local authorities can further the conservation of the aquatic environment by adopting appropriate development plan policies and taking aquatic conservation fully into account when determining planning applications, and imposing planning conditions or agreeing planning obligations. In addition, local authorities have the power to provide for, or otherwise secure the provision of, local nature reserves in their area. Local nature reserves have the same protective controls as apply to national nature reserves, with the local authority being the main regulatory body. Notably, local authorities must consult with English Nature or the Countryside Council for Wales before designating a local nature reserve.[49] All principal local authorities are 'relevant authorities' for the purposes of implementing the EC Habitats Directive in relation to marine conservation.[50]

### 8.4.3 Drinking Water Quality

The functions of local authorities relating to drinking water quality, especially private water supplies, reflect a pragmatic approach to regulation. The small, centralised, Drinking Water Inspectorate[51] has primary responsibility for the quality of water supplied by water undertakers and statutory water supply companies, and relies heavily on undertakers monitoring the quality of their supplies. On the other hand, local authorities must keep themselves informed about the wholesomeness of supplies in their area. In relation to private water supplies, they may

---

[48] On planning law generally see Ch.14 below.

[49] On local nature reserves generally see 15.7.3 below.

[50] Directive 92/43/EEC and Reg.6 Conservation (Natural Habitats etc.) Regulations 1994, see 15.8 below.

[51] Located in the DETR, see 17.5 below.

serve notices on the owners or occupiers of premises served by such supplies, as well as on the owner or occupier of the source of supply, if there is a danger of the water not being wholesome.[52]

### 8.4.4 Statutory Nuisance Control and Other Public Health Functions

Some functions of local authorities are residual in nature, such as the duties of local authorities to abate statutory nuisances, discussed in detail below. In addition, local authorities have a range of further functions which relate to ensuring public health in their areas and preventing the spread of disease or other risks.

Thus, local authorities, or parish or community councils, may deal with any pond, pool, ditch, gutter or place containing or used for the collection of any drainage, filth, stagnant water or matter likely to be prejudicial to health by draining, cleansing or covering it, or otherwise preventing it from being prejudicial to health. This can be by works undertaken directly or by another person from expenses contributed by the local authority. However, any such action must not interfere with any private right or with any public drainage, sewerage or sewage disposal works.[53] Further powers are given to magistrates' courts to order the cleaning of ditches forming the boundary between local authority areas where these are so foul and offensive as injuriously to affect the complainant's area.[54] Also, if a local authority considers that certain features of a building, such as a cesspool, private sewer, drain, soil pipe or rainwater pipe is in such a condition as to be prejudicial to health or a nuisance, then it must serve a notice on the owner or occupier of the building requiring such work as may be necessary to be undertaken.[55]

Also outside of statutory nuisance law, local authorities have notice-serving powers where a nuisance emanates from a house or any appurtenance thereof and causes contamination of water which is prejudicial to health or a nuisance. Alongside the possibility of serving a housing repairs notice,[56] a local authority may serve a defective premises notice which may either require the owner or occupier to carry out work to abate the nuisance or empower the local authority to abate the nuisance at the owner or occupier's expense.[57] These powers are a recognition of the particular need for safe drinking water and the control of disease, and are only available where obtaining an abatement order through the usual statutory nuisance provisions of Part III of the Environmental Protection Act 1990[58] would lead to an unreasonable delay in dealing with the nuisance.

---

[52] On drinking water generally see Ch.17 below.
[53] See generally s.260(1) Public Health Act 1936.
[54] *Ibid* s.261.
[55] s.59(1) Building Act 1984.
[56] s.130 Housing Act 1985.
[57] s.76(1) Building Act 1984, as amended by para.24 Sch.15 Environmental Protection Act 1990.
[58] On which see 8.5 below.

## 8.4.5 Contaminated Land

Local authorities have regulatory responsibility for those areas of contaminated land not falling within the category of 'special sites' regulated by the Environment Agency. While there may be a public health dimension to contaminated land law, this tends to merge with other objectives such as urban regeneration and wider environmental conservation.[59]

## 8.4.6 Integrated Pollution Prevention and Control

Under the Pollution Prevention and Control (England and Wales) Regulations 2000[60] which implement the EC Directive in this area, lower-tier local authorities are responsible for the regulation of 'Part A(2)' installations in an integrated way, and must do so in a way that achieves a high level of protection for the environment taken as a whole by preventing or, where this is not possible, reducing emissions to air, water and land.[61] As noted elsewhere, where a local authority determines a permit for such an installation, it must, as a minimum, impose any conditions which, as a matter of its discretion, the Environment Agency requires concerning emission limit values or any other matter in order to prevent harm to human health or the quality of the environment.[62] This may a unique instance where local authorities are bound to follow the directions of the Environment Agency in relation to matters of public health.

## 8.4.7 Land Drainage

Local authorities also have functions in relation to land drainage and flood defence which may impact on water quality, for example, through sediment disturbance. These are beyond the scope of this book,[63] but it is worth noting that, in relation to carrying out drainage schemes for small areas within its area and on 'ordinary watercourses',[64] a local authority may maintain any existing watercourse or drainage work, improve any existing work or construct new works.[65] Unless carried out in an emergency, however, any work beyond this must have the consent of the Environment Agency. Local authorities must take account of

---

[59] On contaminated land generally see 13.7 below.

[60] Reg.8(3) Pollution Prevention and Control (England and Wales) Regulations 2000 (SI 2000 No.1973) Implementing Directive 96/61/EC.

[61] See generally 12.3.6 below.

[62] Reg.13 Pollution Prevention and Control (England and Wales) Regulations 2000.

[63] See Bates (1990–updated) Chs.13 and 14 and Institution of Civil Engineers (1996). On civil law controls a valuable source remains Hobday (1952).

[64] The Environment Agency is primarily responsible for flood defence on 'main rivers' under Part IV Water Resources Act 1991 (and see s.193 on main river maps) but local authorities have drainage powers in relation to 'ordinary watercourses', that is, those which are not designated as main rivers, under the Land Drainage Act 1991.

[65] s.14 Land Drainage Act 1991.

environmental considerations when carrying out drainage works.[66] In undertaking works, the disposal of spoil created by drainage works covering small areas or carried out in order to prevent flooding may be deposited on the banks of a river or a strip of land next to a river, though not if this would amount to a statutory nuisance.[67] Also, a local authority may by notice require the flow of an ordinary watercourse in its area to be maintained where the flow is impeded either by the condition of the waters or by an obstruction, for example a mill or sluice gate.[68] Conceivably, such powers might be used where a localised water quality problem arises due to the stagnation of water because of disruption to its flow, and might therefore be used where resort to statutory nuisance law might be uncertain. There are also powers for the Agricultural Land Tribunal to order the clearance of ditches, but only to prevent injury to land or to enable improvement to land drainage, and not to avoid or rectify pollution of a watercourse.[69]

Under public health legislation local authorities also have certain powers to control culverting and watercourses for purposes similar to land drainage. However, the Environment Agency must normally be consulted if any stream, watercourse, ditch or culvert is under the jurisdiction of that body. The owner or occupier of any land within a local authority area to which that legislation applies must repair, maintain and cleanse any culvert in, on or under that land. If it appears to the local authority that any person has failed to fulfil these obligations the authority may by notice require the execution of necessary works of repair, maintenance or cleansing.[70] It is important to note here, though, that 'cleanse' is to be understood as relating to the removal of sediment, rather than as a more general water quality provision.

### 8.4.8  Highway Drainage

Other than for trunk roads, local authorities are the highways authority for their areas and therefore have certain responsibilities in relation to the drainage of highways and dealing with any water quality problem which may arise from contaminated highway runoff.[71]

### 8.4.9  Operational Matters

Although not a matter of regulatory responsibility, local authorities continue to carry out activities relating to sewerage following privatisation. Under agency arrangements, local authorities[72] may undertake sewage

---

[66] *Ibid* s.61B, added by the Land Drainage Act 1994.

[67] *Ibid* s.15(3).

[68] *Ibid* ss.23-25.

[69] s.28 Land Drainage Act 1991.

[70] See generally ss.262-266 Public Health Act 1936.

[71] On highway drains see 1.6.5 above.

[72] Defined here as including the Commission for the New Towns and a development corporation; see s.97 Water Industry Act 1991.

collection, although it will be the sewerage undertaker that retains regulatory responsibility for trade effluent regulation and for sewage treatment and disposal operations.[73] Agency arrangements do, however, impinge on regulatory controls, insofar as an agreement may provide the local authority with access to a sewer in order to carry out public health functions.[74]

### 8.4.10 Local Authorities and the Environment Agency

Alongside a general overview of local authority functions concerning public health and environmental protection, it is useful to consider the extent to which the Environment Agency acts as a public health regulator. This role has been variously described as 'limited and somewhat confused' and 'ambiguous'.[75] There are several reasons for this. For example, where environmental regulatory decisions have health implications, there are generally statutory consultation mechanisms that provide the Agency with a sufficient public health input into decision-making.[76] However, the Agency is the competent authority for a range of EC water directives that include a human health component,[77] and therefore responsible for ensuring practical compliance with such directives. The matter is further complicated by the fact that, for the purposes of integrated pollution control and integrated pollution prevention and control, the concept of 'harm' includes harm to humans.[78] However, the Water Resources Act 1991 does not refer to 'harm', referring instead to 'pollution' and to 'polluting' substances.[79] Although it is clear that conditions relating to public health are in practice placed on discharge consents,[80] the ambiguity of the Agency's responsibilities for public health might be regarded as unsatisfactory and in need of clarification.

By way of example of the division of responsibility between local authorities and the Environment Agency, the Agency consents the discharge of sewage effluent and regulates the quality of the waters into which the effluent is discharged, including the quality of bathing water.[81] However, the Agency view is that 'beach management' is the responsibility of local authority environmental health departments and does not fall within the Agency's duties in monitoring compliance with the EC Bathing Water Directive. On this view, only local authorities have

---

[73] On sewage treatment see Ch.11 below.

[74] House of Commons Select Committee on the Environment, Transport and the Regions, *Sewage Treatment and Disposal* (1998), para. 223.

[75] *Ibid* paras.231 and 232.

[76] See 8.3.4 above.

[77] E.g., the Urban Waste Water Treatment Directive and the Shellfish Waters Directive, on which see respectively 5.6.2 above and 15.3 below.

[78] See s.1(4) Environmental Protection Act and s.1(3) Pollution Prevention and Control Act 1999; see further 12.3.4 below.

[79] See 9.8 below on 'poisonous, noxious or polluting matter'.

[80] See 10.6 below.

[81] Under the Bathing Water Directive, discussed at 5.5.2 above.

responsibility for sewage effluent washed up on their beaches[82] which may explain why an effluent discharge may be consented which nevertheless leads to serious sewage pollution of beaches.[83] The House of Commons Select Committee on the Environment, Transport and the Regions has described this state of affairs as:

> Either . . . an example of a minimalistic and legalistic approach to the duties of an Environment Agency, or . . . an example of the gaps in public protection that open up because the system of control and management is a ramshackle Heath Robinson affair. In either case, we do not find it reassuring . . . We are deeply concerned that no public body interprets its responsibilities as actively, and solely, campaigning for health and environmental protection.[84]

## 8.5 Statutory Nuisance

Of particular importance in relation to public health are the duties of local authorities to control 'statutory nuisances'.[85] As discussed elsewhere, actions in public or private nuisance at common law, or by protecting riparian rights, may be relied on in relation to certain incidents of water pollution.[86] However, Part III of the Environmental Protection Act 1990 provides a more expedient means of dealing with various defined categories of nuisances largely derived from the Public Health Act 1936 and earlier public health statutes.[87]

The 1990 Act lays down procedures for the removal of statutory nuisances. The local authority is required to inspect its area periodically for statutory nuisances, and must investigate any specific complaints made to it. By contrast to the civil law of nuisance, however, statutory nuisance law revolves around the service of notices to abate the nuisance backed up by specific criminal offences in the event of non-compliance with such notices. Although the duty to serve abatement notices falls, for the most part, on the local authority, it is possible for individuals to instigate proceedings in the magistrates' court requiring the local authority to take abatement action.

---

[82] For example, under statutory nuisance, on which see 8.5 below.

[83] As in *R v Carrick District Council ex parte Shelley* [1996] Env LR 273, discussed at 8.5.7A below.

[84] House of Commons Select Committee on the Environment, Transport and the Regions, Second Report, *Sewage Treatment and Disposal* (1998), paras. 236 and 242. On the need to better integrate environment and public health see Chartered Institute of Environmental Health (1997).

[85] On which see further Bell and McGillivray (2000) Ch.15.

[86] See Ch.3 above.

[87] Traceable back to the Nuisances Removal and Diseases Prevention Acts 1848 and 1849, consolidated in the Nuisance Removal Act 1855, and see later the Public Health Acts of 1936 and 1961 and the Control of Pollution Act 1974. On whether statutory nuisance retains an essentially public health character see 8.5.5 below.

### 8.5.1  The Meaning of 'Statutory Nuisance'

Unlike the open-ended nature of those activities that may amount to a public or private nuisance, the 1990 Act identifies a restricted range of activities which may amount to a statutory nuisance. This narrow compass generally reflects the public health heritage of the provisions, the most relevant to water pollution control being:

(a) premises in such a state as to be prejudicial to health or a nuisance;

(b) any accumulation or deposit which is prejudicial to health or a nuisance;

(c) any other matter declared by any enactment to be a statutory nuisance.[88]

### 8.5.2  'Premises'

For the purposes of the above categories, 'premises' includes land and any vessel except vessels powered by steam reciprocating machinery,[89] and references to the occupier is taken to include the master of such vessels.[90] Thus, it has been suggested that a houseboat would, because of the degree of permanency, be 'premises'.[91] On the other hand, the courts have been reluctant to characterise sewers as 'premises', although this may reflect a previous policy objective not to extend the scope of statutory nuisance provisions to public infrastructure works, an approach which may no longer be followed.[92] If the concern was not to categorise minor works as 'premises', it is debatable whether the same approach should, in any event, be taken in relation to sewage treatment and disposal plants.[93] Nevertheless, the approach taken in the older authorities has been followed in a recent case concerning a public sewer.[94] The case is notable because arguments that the law on statutory nuisance is now contained in an environmental statute were dismissed,[95] and old authority relied upon.

Land, or water, in its 'natural' state is unlikely to amount to 'premises', so any nuisance caused simply by a natural build-up of stagnant water is unlikely to be a statutory nuisance where the category of nuisance must involve premises.[96]

---

[88] s.79 Environmental Protection Act 1990.

[89] *Ibid* s.79(7) and (12). See also ships as 'premises', discussed at 8.5.3 below.

[90] *Ibid* s.79(11)(a).

[91] Hawke (1995), p.418, citing *West Mercia Urban District Council v Frazer* [1950] 2 KB 119, and see also 9.17.2 below on water pollution offences relating to vessels.

[92] See *Fulham Vestry v London County Council* [1897] 2 QB 76, concerning the Public Health (London) Act 1891 which referred to 'watercourses or drains'.

[93] *Fulham Vestry v London County Council* [1897] 2 QB 76, but compare *R v Parlby* (1889) 22 QBD 520 and see Hawke (1995) p.90.

[94] *East Riding of Yorkshire Council v Yorkshire Water Services Ltd*, [2001] Env LR 7.

[95] See further 8.5.5 below.

[96] For possible remedies under statutory nuisance law in this situation see 8.5.4 below.

### 8.5.3 'Accumulation or Deposit' and Contaminated Land

The relevance, in a water context, of the category of statutory nuisance relating to any 'accumulation or deposit' is illustrated in two cases. In *R v Carrick District Council ex parte Shelley*[97] it was held that sewage-related materials such as sanitary towels and condoms which were washed ashore on to Porthtowan beach constituted an accumulation or deposit within the meaning of the Act. And in *Margate Pier & Harbour Co v Margate Town Council*[98] an accumulation of seaweed constituting a nuisance in the harbour, which was the responsibility of the Harbour Company, was held to be an accumulation within the meaning of the Act. Lush J said:

> I have no doubt, whatever, that it is the duty of the appellants to prevent the accumulation of seaweed so that it shall not become a nuisance, and that, whether produced by natural or artificial causes, they are bound to remove all matter in the harbour which is a nuisance or injurious to health.

This decision makes clear that the mere presence of seaweed in the harbour, by natural accumulation, is capable of constituting a statutory nuisance. On this basis, there can be an accumulation or deposit in water rather than on land.[99] It is an unresolved point whether, by virtue of its responsibilities to abate nuisances, a local authority can be said to be the party by whose 'act, default or sufferance' a nuisance arises from an accumulation or deposit in a watercourse, harbour or estuary.[100]

The application of the category of statutory nuisance relating to accumulations and deposits, however, is restricted by amendments to the law under which land no longer constitutes a statutory nuisance to the extent that it consists of, or is caused by, land being in a 'contaminated state'.[101] However, under the detailed rules which now govern historically contaminated land,[102] land is to be judged as 'contaminated' by reference to there being 'significant harm' whilst all harm, whether significant or not, is excluded from statutory nuisance where it results from the contaminated state of land.[103] The result is that there is a gap between the two regimes which will mean that land which is giving rise to harm which is not 'significant' under the terms of the new contaminated land provisions cannot be cleaned up by way of an abatement notice under the statutory nuisance provisions of the Environmental Protection Act 1990.

Most likely, this is a deliberate attempt to deal with concerns that the alternative would be for serious contamination to be dealt with under the

---

[97] [1996] Env LR 273 and see 8.5.7A below.

[98] (1869) 33 JP 437.

[99] Water will not generally be 'premises' for Part III of the Act, see 8.5.2 above.

[100] On 'act, default or sufferance' see 8.5.8 below.

[101] s.79(1A) Environmental Protection Act 1990, added by para.89 Sch.22 Environment Act 1995, in force 1 April 2000.

[102] Contained in Part IIA Environmental Protection Act 1990, and see generally 13.7 below.

[103] *Ibid* s.79(1B), which also provides that any actual or likely pollution of controlled waters will give rise to 'harm'.

new regime concerning contaminated land whilst less serious contamination would, in theory at least,[104] be subject to what are, in several respects, more stringent requirements of statutory nuisance law. Whether this gap is desirable is another matter. However, the central issue for present purposes is that there is no regulatory 'gap' in relation to land which is contaminated because it is in a condition such that pollution of controlled waters is being, or is likely to be, caused. If this is the case, then no statutory nuisance arises and either the new contaminated land regime, or other water pollution prevention provisions, must be used.[105]

It should be noted that the statutory nuisance regime continues to apply to land contamination in any case where an abatement notice,[106] or an abatement order made by the court,[107] has already been issued and is still in force. This is to ensure that any enforcement action taken under the statutory nuisance regime continues and is not interrupted by the implementation of the new regime for contaminated land.

### 8.5.4 'Any Other Matter Declared to be a Statutory Nuisance'

The category of statutory nuisance relating to 'any other matter declared by any enactment to be a statutory nuisance' is particularly pertinent to water quality. Amongst the provisions that the category encompasses are provisions relating to wells, tanks, cisterns or water-butts which are so placed, constructed or kept as to be prejudicial to health.[108] It is notable that this provision relates only to matters prejudicial to health and not other categories of nuisance. Given the context of quality standards for private drinking water supplies, and their monitoring by local authorities,[109] this provision is probably obsolete, at least in relation to dedicated private supplies. However, it might be relied upon if there was contamination of a well, tank etc. used for storing water other than for drinking, and which became contaminated or infested in a way that was prejudicial to health. This might be the case, for example, with a mosquito infestation of a non-drinking water tank, where a local authority might want to act.

In addition, two further states relating to the quality of water other than water for drinking are brought within the meaning of statutory nuisance via this category. It should be noted that the effect of these, together with the other categories of statutory nuisance, is that the vast majority of discharges of effluent will not fall within the statutory nuisance regime.

The first state of water categorised as a statutory nuisance is where any pond, pool, ditch, gutter or watercourse is so foul or in such a state as to be

---

[104] Local authorities have shown a distinct reluctance to use statutory nuisance law to deal with the problem of historically contaminated land, which may in part be attributable to uncertainties with the legislation, and see also 13.7.2 below.

[105] See generally Ch.13 below.

[106] Under s 80(1) Environmental Protection Act 1990, see 8.5.7 below.

[107] Under *ibid* s.82(2)(a), see 8.5.12 below.

[108] s.141 Public Health Act 1936.

[109] See 17.9 below.

prejudicial to health or a nuisance.[110] The meaning of this provision was considered in *R* v *Falmouth and Truro Port Health Authority ex parte South West Water Ltd,*[111] a case relating to an outfall through which, under a consent granted by the Environment Agency, sewage was discharged into a part of the estuary of the River Fal known as the 'Carrick Roads'. Following complaints, the port health authority issued an abatement notice[112] on the grounds that the estuary, being a 'watercourse' was, as a result of the discharge of sewage, prejudicial to health or a nuisance. However, the Court of Appeal upheld the view taken by Harrison J in the High Court that the legislative history of the sub-section suggested that only a more limited body of water was envisaged. The meaning to be given to 'watercourse' in this context was, therefore, narrower than its common law meaning[113] and, accordingly, the abatement notice that had been served was invalid.

For Hale LJ, with whose detailed analysis the other judges agreed, extending 'watercourse' to include open sea could not be done even with 'linguistic contortions'. Moreover, it was relevant that health hazards arising from the state of estuarial and coastal waters could be regulated by consents granted by the Environment Agency. Notably, however, the Court of Appeal took a slightly broader approach than the High Court, which had adopted a *euisdem generis* approach to the construction of this part of the sub-section and had therefore held that 'watercourse' here must mean something much more limited than a river or an estuary. This approach was rejected by the Court of Appeal, not least because it had to be assumed that 'watercourse' had the same meaning in both parts of the provision in question, and the other provision clearly included navigable waters.[114] Looking to the historical development of water pollution law, however, required a distinction between bodies of water into which human waste might collect or be deposited and cause a health hazard, and other bodies of water into which, as a matter of law and policy, discharges of effluent were to be directed.[115] It was therefore relevant that discharges to estuaries such as the Carrick Roads were not controlled until the Clean Rivers (Estuaries and Tidal Waters) Act 1960. Therefore, when the 1936 Act was passed it could be assumed that the disposal of effluent into estuarial waters was a legislative objective which would have been frustrated if, under statutory nuisance law, local authorities were required to abate the consequent pollution.

It should also be pointed out that the provision is specifically directed to the condition of water, and is concerned with whether water is in such a state as to *be* a nuisance and not merely to *cause* a nuisance. In this respect the provision may be of application in relation to states of water which are

---

[110] s.259(1)(a) Public Health Act 1936.

[111] [1999] Env LR 833 (High Court); [2000] 3 All ER 306 (Court of Appeal).

[112] On abatement notices see 8.5.7 below.

[113] See 3.4.1 above.

[114] That is, s.259(1)(a) and (b) Public Health Act 1936, the latter being discussed below.

[115] See *Somersetshire Drainage Commissioners* v *Corporation of Bridgwater* (1899) *Law Times* 729, and see 8.1 above.

caused other than by entries or discharges which might be controlled under Part III of the Water Resources Act 1991[116] and may therefore be of considerable practical use. Specifically, it is not necessary for any pond, pool, ditch, gutter or watercourse to be polluted for it to be a statutory nuisance, since the provision is capable of including water which has deteriorated in quality to the point where it has become a breeding ground for pests or vermin or waters which, for example, have become a risk to health or a nuisance through stagnation or the accumulation of rotting vegetation. Thus, in *Upper District Committee of the County of Renfrew* v *Woddrop's Trustees*[117] there was a statutory nuisance where the defendant's waters had become so overgrown with vegetation and silted up that water flowed onto neighbouring land, where it stagnated and became a breeding ground for mosquitoes which affected a residential area nearby. Nevertheless, the satisfaction of public health concerns may not satisfy wider environmental quality objectives, while conversely it remains similarly problematic to assume that environmental quality regulation will be sufficient to serve the purposes of public health control.

The second type of statutory nuisance specifically concerned with the state of water (other than for drinking) concerns any part of a watercourse, not being a part ordinarily navigated by vessels employed in the carriage of goods by water, which is so choked or silted up as to obstruct or impede the proper flow of water and thereby to cause a nuisance, or give rise to conditions prejudicial to health.[118] In this situation no liability is to be imposed on any person other than the person by whose act or default the nuisance arises or continues.[119] It is notable that the waters concerned in this category are limited to 'watercourses' and, moreover, parts of watercourses which are not ordinarily navigated.[120] Following the *Falmouth* case, it is likely that the interpretation of 'watercourse' in this provision will begin from a presumption that the meaning is the same as that in the first mentioned provision of the 1936 Act,[121] despite their different legislative pedigrees.[122]

### 8.5.5 'Prejudicial to Health or a Nuisance'

Central to all the categories of statutory nuisance is the phrase 'prejudicial to health or a nuisance'. These terms are to be read disjunctively, so that a state of affairs need not be both prejudicial to health and a nuisance.[123]

---

[116] On discharge consents generally see Ch.10 below.

[117] 1927 SLT (Sh Ct) 69. The provision at issue was s.16(2) Public Health (Scotland) Act 1897, which in material respects is analogous to s.259(1)(a) Public Health Act 1936.

[118] s.259(1)(b) Public Health Act 1936.

[119] *Ibid* s.259(1). On 'act' and 'default' see further 8.5.8 below.

[120] The common law may provide a remedy where there is obstruction of a right of navigation, see *Tate and Lyle Ltd* v *Greater London Council* [1983] 1 All ER 1159 at 1165, in respect of riparian rights of navigation; see public nuisance at 3.17 above and Ch.3 generally on the common law.

[121] I.e s.259(1)(a) Public Health Act 1936.

[122] The origins of s.259(1)(b) of the 1936 Act are in s.54(1) Public Health Act 1925.

[123] *Betts* v *Penge Urban District Council* [1942] 2 KB 154.

'Prejudicial to health' is defined as meaning 'injurious, or likely to cause injury, to health'.[124] This has been interpreted by the courts as requiring a threat of disease, vermin or the like.[125] This approach to the interpretation of injury to health continues even under the Environmental Protection Act 1990, despite the difficulty in conceiving of the 1990 Act as a continuation of the pre-existing public health controls and, for example, its inclusion of noise controls[126] which, though certainly associated with health, have little relationship with the spread of disease.[127] Whether a matter is prejudicial to health is to be judged objectively rather than with regard to a complainant's individual health requirements.[128]

The term 'nuisance' was originally construed narrowly, limiting its application in line with the public health origins of statutory nuisance,[129] and there have been some relatively recent decisions which appear aimed at limiting the operation of the nuisance limb to matters impinging upon the personal comfort of the person aggrieved and not extending to cover all property-based losses.[130] However, the more usual approach is for the statutory meaning of 'nuisance' to be equated with the common law meaning of the term.[131] Moreover, although there is no direct authority on the point, the 're-statement'[132] of the law of statutory nuisance within the Environmental Protection Act 1990 might mean that 'nuisance' must at least be given its ordinary common law meaning. This is because the overall purpose of the 1990 Act is unquestionably environmental protection and is not limited to public health matters.[133] Indeed, there are instances where statutory nuisance goes beyond the normal rules for a common law nuisance, for example by not requiring an interference with the enjoyment of neighbouring property.[134] Nevertheless, statutory nuisance remains limited in its protection of the unowned environment. It remains to be seen whether any power or duty on local authorities to promote the environmental well-being of their areas will affect the interpretation of the statutory nuisance provisions of the 1990 Act.[135]

---

[124] s.79(7) Environmental Protection Act 1990.

[125] *Coventry City Council v Cartwright* [1975] 1 WLR 845.

[126] See, for example, s.79(1)(g) and (ga) Environmental Protection Act 1990.

[127] *R v Bristol City Council ex parte Everett* [1999] Env LR 587 and comment by Malcolm (1999).

[128] *Cunningham v Birmingham City Council* [1998] Env LR 1; *O'Toole v Knowsley Metropolitan Borough Council* [1999] EHLR 420.

[129] *Great Western Railway v Bishop* (1872) LR 7 QB 550.

[130] *Wivenhoe Port v Colchester Borough Council* [1985] JPL 175.

[131] *National Coal Board v Neath Borough Council* [1976] 2 All ER 478, also referred to as *National Coal Board v Thorne* [1976] 1 WLR 543. For a discussion of nuisance at common law see 3.7 above.

[132] See the Long Title to the Environmental Protection Act 1990.

[133] See, e.g., Burnett-Hall (1995) para.23-004; and the view of Carnwath J in *R v Carrick District Council ex parte Shelley* [1996] Env LR 273, discussed by Purdue (1997).

[134] See *Network Housing Association Ltd v Westminster City Council* [1995] 93 LGR 280 and especially *Carr v London Borough of Hackney* [1995] Env LR 372.

[135] See the Local Government Act 2000, discussed at 8.3.3 above.

### 8.5.6  The Duty to Inspect for Statutory Nuisances

Every local authority[136] must inspect its area from time to time in order to detect any statutory nuisances that should be dealt with under Part III of the 1990 Act.[137] Where the area of a local authority includes part of the seashore, the area to be inspected includes the territorial sea lying seawards of that part of the shore.[138] No guidance, statutory or otherwise, is given on how frequently such inspections should be undertaken, giving local authorities a considerable measure of discretion in complying with this general obligation. However, where a complaint of a statutory nuisance is made by any individual living in the area, the authority must take reasonably practicable steps to investigate.[139] Such inspections will be carried out by an environmental health officer who must decide if a statutory nuisance is occurring or is likely to occur or recur.[140]

The duty of inspection is, in principle, amenable to judicial review. However, persons aggrieved by the failure of a local authority to act in such situations may persuade the Secretary of State to use the default powers available to him. Under these, the Secretary of State[141] may make an order against the authority to inspect its area and, ultimately, transfer to himself the inspection duty, with any necessary inspection being carried out at the local authority's expense.[142] These administrative powers may be sufficient to oust any judicial challenges for non-inspection.[143]

### 8.5.7  Abatement Notices

### 8.5.7A  The mandatory nature of the duty to serve abatement notices

Once a local authority is satisfied that a statutory nuisance exists, or is likely to occur or recur, within its area it is under a duty to serve an abatement notice.[144]

The exact nature of a local authority's duty to serve an abatement notice was considered in *R v Carrick District Council ex parte Shelley*.[145] The consented discharge of unscreened sewage resulted in debris being washed up on Porthtowan beach and deposited in significant quantities.[146] In 1992 the National Rivers Authority had sought to impose a condition on the consents requiring screening but the sewerage undertaker, South West

---

[136] And, where relevant, every port health authority, see 8.3.1 above.

[137] s.79(1) Environmental Protection Act 1990.

[138] *Ibid* s.79(11). The territorial sea extends to 12 nautical miles from the baselines, see 18.7.1 below. Contrast the general jurisdiction of local authorities, noted at 8.3.1 above.

[139] *Ibid.*

[140] *Ibid,* s.80(1), and see *Southwark Borough Council* v *Simpson* [1999] Env LR 553.

[141] In Wales, the National Assembly.

[142] para.4 Sch.3 Environmental Protection Act 1990.

[143] *Passmore* v *Oswaldtwistle Urban District Council* [1898] AC 387.

[144] s.80(1) Environmental Protection Act 1990. On further notice serving powers see 8.4.4 above on housing repairs notices and defective premises notices.

[145] [1996] Env LR 273.

[146] For further details on discharge consents see Ch. 10.

Water, had appealed against this requirement to the Secretary of State. At the time the case was heard in 1996 the appeal had not yet been determined.[147] Because of this delay and complaints it had received, the District Council considered the possibility of taking abatement action against the sewerage undertaker. However, it resolved instead to do nothing but request the Secretary of State to determine the appeal urgently and reject it. The applicants in the case were local residents who, backed by the environmental interest group Surfers Against Sewage, argued that, having identified a statutory nuisance, the Council was legally bound[148] to serve notice on the person responsible for the nuisance and commence abatement proceedings.

The application for judicial review succeeded. Carnwath J found, firstly, that the overlapping jurisdictions of local authorities and the Environment Agency in this context presented no valid reason for inaction by the local authority and, secondly, that the Council was not entitled to consider the 'appropriateness' of issuing an abatement notice. The only material issues were whether there was, in fact, an accumulation or deposit which constituted a statutory nuisance, and the person responsible for it. Notably, the responsibility of the sewerage undertaker was not precluded by the deposits depending upon the 'vagaries of the tide'.[149]

The *ex parte Shelley* case indicates the mandatory nature of a local authority's duty, once a statutory nuisance is discovered, to take steps to abate the nuisance by the service of an abatement notice on the person responsible. This appears to be the case even if a defence can be made out.[150] The case also highlights the absence within the Act of provisions for overlapping regulatory responsibilities between statutory nuisance law and Part III of the Water Resources Act 1991 dealing with discharge consents. A possible approach might be to require the consent of the Secretary of State before proceedings for statutory nuisance are brought, as is provided for concerning the relationship between statutory nuisance law and Part I of the 1990 Act dealing both with integrated pollution control and local air pollution control.[151] In practice, however, overlaps with water pollution control are uncommon and do not appear to pose a serious practical problem. Finally, it is worth noting that, following the decision in *ex parte Shelley*, the local authority found that there was a statutory nuisance and served an abatement notice on the sewerage undertaker requiring screening, which was complied with within the time allowed.[152] Significantly, before the local authority original resolution, its

---

[147] It is not clear whether in fact the new condition was suspended or not. If not, then a private prosecution for breach of the discharge consent might have been brought (Purdue (1997) p.117). On the legal impact of the variation of conditions see 10.8 above.

[148] Under s.80(1) Environmental Protection Act 1990.

[149] On which, contrast trespass law, see 3.7.2 above.

[150] On defences, see 8.5.10 below.

[151] See s.79(10) Environmental Protection Act 1990.

[152] Carnwath (1999) pp.8-9. 'Abatement' is, however, a less onerous obligation than, for example, restoration of land or water, restricting the utility of statutory nuisance for non-transitory water quality problems.

environmental health officer had originally taken the view that no statutory nuisance existed. If this had been endorsed, then this would have been an unchallengeable matter of fact, not law, leaving the applicants without redress.

### 8.5.7B  The wording of abatement notices and the process of their being served

An abatement notice must impose any or all of the following requirements:

(a) requiring the abatement of the nuisance or prohibiting or restricting its occurrence or recurrence; and/or
(b) requiring the execution of such works, and the taking of such other steps, as may be necessary for any of those purposes.

The abatement notice must specify the time or times within which its requirements must be complied with. Depending on the nature of the nuisance or prejudice to health, the local authority may require merely that a statutory nuisance is abated. [153] This might be the case, for example, where the statutory nuisance arises from a stagnant pool of water posing a threat of a spread of disease. However, where specific works are stipulated, the defendant should be provided with a sufficiently clear explanation from the authority of what is required.[154] This is because of the criminal sanctions that follow if the notice is breached, and is the case even where the notice is served on a body with statutory duties, such as a sewerage undertaker.[155] Once issued, an abatement notice takes effect in perpetuity.[156]

In *R v Falmouth and Truro Port Health Authority ex parte South West Water Ltd,*[157] however, the Court of Appeal overruled a line of authority which had held that if the only way in which a nuisance can be abated is by works or particular actions (as e.g. if the abatement notice required the cessation of a discharge from a sewage treatment works) then the notice must specify them. For example, in *Kirklees Metropolitan Council v Field & Others,*[158] concerning a rock-face and wall which were in imminent danger of collapsing on to a row of cottages, the Court of Appeal held that by not specifying the necessary works the abatement notice was invalid. In contrast to cases where the nuisance could be abated by some activity being stopped, in *Kirklees* it was obvious that major works of a positive

---

[153] *R v Wheatley* (1885) 16 QBD 34 and *Sterling Homes v Birmingham City Council* [1996] Env LR 121.

[154] See for example *R v Horrocks* (1900) 69 LJ QB 688, *Kirklees Metropolitan Council v Field* [1998] Env LR 337. See also the discussion in the High Court in *R v Falmouth and Truro Port Health Authority ex parte South West Water Ltd* [1999] Env LR 833 (subsequently overruled, see below).

[155] *R v Falmouth and Truro Port Health Authority ex parte South West Water Ltd* [1999] Env LR 833.

[156] *Wellingborough District Council v Gordon* [1991] JPL 874 and *Aitken v South Hams District Council* [1994] 3 All ER 400.

[157] [2000] 3 All ER 306, discussed at 8.5.4 above.

[158] [1998] Env LR 337.

nature were necessary, and the Court held that these should have been specified. The same approach was originally taken in the *Falmouth* case, where the High Court held that the abatement notice had to stipulate what the sewerage undertaker should do to abate the nuisance because the problem could not be abated simply by turning off the effluent pumps. In the Court of Appeal, however, the *Kirklees* case was overruled and it was held that local authorities could not as a rule be obliged to specify works where work was needed. Instead, as where works did not need to be undertaken, the recipient of the notice should be free to choose a preferred course of action, so long as in doing so they would comply with the abatement notice. This was because the provision in question relates to 'all or any' of the requirements being complied with.

The Court of Appeal did indicate, however, that there might be extreme cases where this general principle might not be appropriate. The recipient will, of course, always be best placed to choose the method of abatement on grounds of cost and convenience. However, it is at least arguable that where works require considerable technical expertise, then it might be a relevant factor whether the recipient can reasonably be expected to have knowledge of this, or know where to obtain it. In situations like that in *Kirklees*, therefore, knowledge of what was needed to abate the nuisance might be seen as beyond the capacity of the residents of the cottages, and therefore something on which they should properly be advised by the local authority. Thus, it might still be appropriate to distinguish between cases according to the relative degree of awareness and technical expertise as between the local authority and the recipient of the abatement notice. On this approach, however, it would probably be difficult for water or sewerage undertakers ever to demonstrate that a local authority held such technical superiority that it ought to specify the works to be undertaken.

This leads to a further, related, consideration, namely whether there can ever be a requirement on local authorities to consult with parties before abatement notices are served. In some situations, for example, serving an abatement notice might be thought too blunt an instrument to resolve a situation which may have many underlying causes and involve other public bodies exercising their functions. This is well illustrated by the *Falmouth and Truro Port Health Authority* decision, where the undertaker was acting under a discharge consent, and was also subject to a range of statutory duties concerning the environment and the adequate provision of sewerage services in its area. The wider problem was not one that could be resolved simply by turning the effluent pumps off and might have been thought a situation better resolved by co-operation rather than criminal enforcement. Nevertheless, the Court of Appeal refused to find that the enforcing authority needed to consult on possible abatement action. This might have been desirable as a matter of policy, but the Court of Appeal overruled the decision of the lower court that this might be required as a matter of legal fairness, a further decision emphasising the extent of the powers that local authorities have to abate statutory nuisances. This appears to be the case even if there is some expectation of being consulted, since the statutory nuisance regime is intended to allow for a swift response to abating situations which might have potentially damaging consequences for public health.[159]

### 8.5.7C Appeals

The person served with an abatement notice must be notified of their right of appeal against the notice.[160] Any appeal must be made within 21 days of service of the notice and must be based upon one of the grounds of appeal provided for in the Statutory Nuisance (Appeals) Regulations 1995.[161] An appeal will suspend the abatement notice, unless the nuisance is claimed to be prejudicial to health or the expense of abating the nuisance during the period of an appeal would be disproportionate to any public benefit. On appeal, the court may quash the notice, vary it in favour of the applicant or dismiss the appeal.[162] Thus the court can itself impose abatement requirements without having to refer the case back to the local authority.

### 8.5.8 The 'Person Responsible'

Ordinarily an abatement notice must be served on the 'person responsible', defined as meaning 'the person to whose act, default or sufferance the nuisance is attributable'.[163] Hence, it is the wrongdoer who, in the first place, is liable to rectify the situation giving rise to the complaint. It has been held that, for these purposes, an 'act' includes the giving of an order to another person as a consequence of which the nuisance arises.[164] 'Default' suggests the breach of some obligation such as the failure to keep premises in a satisfactory state of repair,[165] while 'sufferance' implies that a person has permitted a nuisance to arise or continue, so that an occupier of land 'continues' a nuisance if with knowledge of its existence, which may be presumed in some cases,[166] that person fails to take reasonably prompt and efficient steps to bring it to an end.[167] A person may fall within this definition even if their actions constitute a failure to abate a nuisance on their land caused by the activity or default of another, regardless of whether they are any other legal or contractual duties to remediate this nuisance. Thus a defendant has been held liable to abate a nuisance which occurred due to flooding after the breaching of a flood bank which they were under no duty to repair.[168]

---

[159] Hence, the principle that, in defined situations, there can be a legitimate expectation of being consulted before a public law decision is reached did not apply.
[160] Under s.80(3) Environmental Protection Act 1990.
[161] SI 1995 No.2644.
[162] Reg.2(5) Statutory Nuisance (Appeals) Regulations 1995.
[163] ss.80(2)(a) and 79(7) Environmental Protection Act 1990.
[164] *R v Mead ex parte Gates* (1895) 59 JP 150.
[165] *Nathan v Rouse* [1905] 1 KB 527.
[166] *Leanse v Egerton* [1943] KB 323.
[167] *Sedleigh-Denfield v O'Callaghan* [1940] 3 All ER 349.
[168] *Clayton v Sale Urban District Council* [1926] 1 KB 415.

Liability under statutory nuisance is not therefore dependent upon any duty to prevent the nuisance before it occurs and may arise after such events have taken place. However, the courts have looked to see whether there has been some failure to meet acceptable standards, e.g. in relation to noise nuisances, sound insulation standards at the time of construction.[169] This seems to be motivated by policy concerns, especially about resources (which in theory would be irrelevant in a common law nuisance claim) but it might have a bearing on whether compliance with a discharge consent or pollution prevention and control permit would be a relevant consideration.

More than one person may be responsible for a statutory nuisance. However, there is a practical limitation in that an abatement notice will only be upheld against a person who has the capacity to abate the nuisance. The best illustration of this is the limitation on an owner or occupier to abate a nuisance arising outside their land. Thus in *R v Cumberland Justices ex parte Trimble*[170] the occupier of a brewery discharged offensive liquid into drains on his premises which emptied on to a field occupied by another person and caused a large pool to accumulate which was injurious to health and a nuisance. It was held that in such circumstances there was no power to order the occupier of the brewery to abate the nuisance outside his land. The capacity to abate a nuisance on another's land is not restricted to situations where there is no power to enter other land, since there may be other limitations on serving an abatement notice if that person has no capacity to lawfully abate the nuisance once on the land (e.g. because the person has no power to handle any waste, or no power to remove a nuisance without being exposed to criminal liabilities). In practice, other powers are available to deal with these types of situations.[171]

In the case of statutory nuisance arising from obstructions to the flow of a stream, it is notable that only the person whose act or default causes the nuisance may be liable. As riparian owners have no duty to maintain the flow of a watercourse, they cannot therefore be guilty of 'default' here if they had merely failed to clean a natural obstruction,[172] though if the obstruction was caused other than 'naturally' there may be default.[173]

Where the person responsible cannot be found, or the nuisance has not yet occurred, the abatement notice must be served on the owner or occupier of the premises, though only if the premises are the source of the nuisance.[174]

---

[169] *Salford City Council v McNally* [1976] AC 379; *London Borough of Haringey v Jowett* [1999] NPC 52.

[170] (1877) 41 JP 454 T. See also *Scarborough Corporation v Scarborough Sanitary Authority* (1876) 1 Ex D 344.

[171] s.161 Water Resources Act 1991 see 13.2.1 below.

[172] *Neath Rural District Council v Williams* [1950] 2 All ER 625.

[173] *Sedleigh-Denfield v O'Callaghan* [1940] AC 880, and see now *Bybrook Barn Garden Centre Ltd and others v Kent County Council* [2001] Env LR 30.

[174] s.80(2)(c) Environmental Protection Act 1990. It has been suggested that the interpretation of 'occupier' in *Southern Water Authority v Nature Conservancy Council* [1992] 3 All ER 481 at 487, discussed at 6.11 above, might be followed in this context; see Burnett-Hall (1995) para.23-038.

Where more than one person is responsible for the nuisance the authority must serve abatement notices against all persons but the fact that each individual's actions would not amount independently to a nuisance is not a valid defence.[175]

### 8.5.9 'Reasonable Excuse'

The offence of non-compliance with an abatement notice only occurs if an abatement order is breached without 'reasonable excuse'. Thus, whether there has been a reasonable excuse is not strictly a defence but rather a component part of the offence itself.[176] If the defendant puts forward an excuse, the burden is therefore on the local authority to show, on the criminal standard, that it is not reasonable.[177] 'Reasonable excuse' is to be read as an objective test and so, for example, a defendant running out of funds part way through a mitigation programme did not provide a reasonable excuse for a breach of an abatement order.[178] Reasonable excuse may be made out where matters are beyond the control of the defendant, although, as noted above, material being deposited because of the actions of the tides is immaterial.[179] 'Reasonable excuse' is not intended to be an opportunity to challenge the terms of the abatement notice.[180]

### 8.5.10 'Best Practicable Means' as a Defence

Where nuisances arise on industrial, trade or business premises, there is a defence of proving that the 'best practicable means' have been used to prevent or counteract the nuisance complained of.[181] There is no direct authority on whether a water or sewerage undertaker operates from 'industrial, trade or business' premises, but the better view is that they do, since the courts have not restricted 'business' to purely contractual arrangements.[182] However, the defence is not available in relation to activities which are a statutory nuisance because they are declared to be so in other enactments,[183] and so cannot be used in relation to an abatement notice served in respect of foul ponds, pools etc. or obstructed non-navigable watercourses.[184]

---

[175] Ibid s.81(1).

[176] Contrast the offence of polluting controlled waters under s.85 Water Resources Act 1991, discussed in Ch.9 below.

[177] Polychronakis v Richards and Jerrom Ltd [1998] Env LR 346.

[178] Saddleworth Urban Development Corporation v Aggregate and Sand (1970) 114 SJ 931.

[179] See R v Carrick District Council ex parte Shelley and Another [1996] Env LR 273, above at 8.5.5.

[180] AMEC Building Ltd v London Borough of Camden [1997] Env LR 330.

[181] s.80(7)Environmental Protection Act 1990.

[182] Tromans, Grant and Nash (1996), updated.

[183] s.79(1)(h) Environmental Protection Act 1990.

[184] Under s.259(1) Public Health Act 1936, see 8.5.4 above.

'Best practicable means' is determined by various considerations[185] and must be proven by the defendant on the balance of probabilities, the burden of proof being on the defendant. What is 'practicable' will depend upon the locality, current technical abilities and financial implications. 'Means' may include the 'design, installation, maintenance and manner and periods of operation of plant and machinery and the design, construction and maintenance of buildings and structures'.[186] However, reduced profitability is not itself enough to show impracticability and it is for the defendant to satisfy the court of the magnitude of loss where impracticability is claimed on this ground.[187] It must be doubted, assuming the defence was available, whether a water or sewerage undertaker could rely on the absence of allowable expenditure in the price determination to abate nuisances.[188]

It is worth noting that compliance with an environmental license as such is not a defence to abatement proceedings. Thus compliance with, for example, a discharge consent, integrated pollution control authorisation or integrated pollution prevention and control permit will not absolve any person served with an abatement notice or order. The principal reason for this is because such licences may not relate sufficiently to matters of public health.[189] However, compliance may go towards establishing that the best practicable means were used, and may also go to the question of whether the person is 'responsible'.[190]

### 8.5.11 Sentencing Powers for Contravening an Abatement Notice

It is a criminal offence to contravene or fail to comply with an abatement notice without reasonable excuse.[191] If the person responsible has failed to do so the local authority may abate the nuisance itself and recover its costs.[192] Should the authority choose to abate the nuisance this does not preclude it from also pursuing an action for non-compliance with the original abatement notice.[193] On summary conviction the maximum penalty is a fine not exceeding level 5 on the standard scale, currently £5000, plus a maximum of a further £500 for each day that the nuisance continues.[194] In relation to industrial, trade or business premises the maximum fine is £20,000 although there is no provision for additional fines for continuing breaches.[195] The criminal nature of this part of the Act

---

[185] s.79(9) Environmental Protection Act 1990.

[186] *Ibid* s.79(9)(b).

[187] *Wivenhoe Port* v *Colchester Borough Council* [1985] JPL 175.

[188] On the funding of undertakers see 7.8 above.

[189] On which see 8.4.10 above on the Environment Agency and local authorities.

[190] See 8.5.10 and 8.5.8 above respectively.

[191] s.80(4) Environmental Protection Act 1990.

[192] *Ibid* s.81(3) and (4).

[193] s.81(3) Environmental Protection Act 1990.

[194] *Ibid* s.80(5).

[195] *Ibid* s.80(6), and contrast actions brought by individuals, at 8.5.12 below.

means that the court can also make a compensation order under the Powers of Criminal Courts Act 1973.[196]

### 8.5.12  Action by Individuals

Although the provisions described above revolve around duties on local authorities, it is also possible for a magistrates' court to act on a complaint made by any person aggrieved by the existence of a statutory nuisance.[197] While the court has a discretion to act,[198] if it is satisfied that the alleged nuisance exists, or that an abated nuisance is likely to recur, it must make an order requiring the nuisance to be abated and, if necessary, requiring any works to be undertaken.[199] One disadvantage compared to abatement notices served by local authorities, therefore, is that individuals cannot rely on this provision to prevent statutory nuisances from first occurring. Such abatement orders need not follow any practice adopted by the local authority in the area, although where works are required to be undertaken the order will have to specify the nature of them.[200] Analogous provisions relate to the identification of the person responsible, offences, defences and notification periods as apply to abatement notices served by local authorities.[201] In addition, however, the court has the power to impose on the defendant a fine.[202] Unlike abatement notices, no distinction is made between commercial and other premises in relation to penalties for non-compliance, and the maximum penalty is a fine not exceeding level 5 on the standard scale, currently £5000, plus daily fines of up to £500. The court may also make a compensation order.[203]

The provision for individually-initiated statutory nuisance actions may usefully be relied upon where it is considered that a local authority has failed to act, and in practice is particularly valuable where it is the local authority itself which is alleged to be responsible for a statutory nuisance. In relation to accumulations or deposits,[204] abatement orders can be sought where, to avoid duplication of controls with integrated pollution control, local authorities may not bring proceedings.[205] For practical reasons, however, such as placing on the local authority the burden of bringing

---

[196] s.35 Powers of Criminal Courts Act 1973 and *Herbert* v *Lambeth London Borough Council* (1991) 156 JP 389. And see 9.21 below on Powers of the Criminal Courts Act 1973.

[197] s.82(1) Environmental Protection Act 1990.

[198] It is uncertain whether this power not to entertain proceedings would withstand a challenge under the European Convention on Human Rights or the Human Rights Act 1998.

[199] The scope of the duty is therefore analogous to that provided for in relation to abatement notices, although it does not extend to nuisances which are likely to occur, see 8.5.7A above.

[200] See 8.5.7B above on specifying works in abatement notices.

[201] See generally s.82 Environmental Protection Act 1990.

[202] *Ibid* s.82(2).

[203] Under s.35 Powers of Criminal Courts Act 1973, and see *Botross* v *Hammersmith and Fulham London Borough Council* [1995] Env LR 217 and *Davenport* v *Walsall Metropolitan Borough Council* [1997] Env LR 24.

[204] Specifically, s.79(1)(b), (d) and (e) Environmental Protection Act 1990.

[205] On the overlap between Parts I and III of the Environmental Protection Act 1990 see 8.4.10 above.

abatement proceedings,[206] it may be that individuals may seek a judicial review of any decision not to serve an abatement notice, and this has not been precluded.[207] It is also possible that, on an individual complaint, the Local Government Ombudsman may make a finding of maladministration if a local authority fails to act against a statutory nuisance, which may lead to the aggrieved party receiving an award of compensation from the authority.

### 8.5.13 Injunctions and Proceedings in the High Court

Where proceeding under the above provisions would not reflect the gravity or urgency of the case in question the local authority may seek an injunction in the High Court.[208] The use of this procedure has been approved as a means of stopping a nuisance during the time between the issuing of an abatement notice (and subsequent non-compliance) and prosecution for contravention of the notice before the magistrates' court.[209] Injunctions are, however, a discretionary and equitable remedy and will not be granted lightly. The action complained of must be of sufficient gravity and/or duration to justify an injunction.[210]

---

[206] Given the amount and detail of evidence that may be required, this may be significant.

[207] See *R v Carrick District Council ex parte Shelley and Another* [1996] Env LR 273.

[208] s.81(5) Environmental Protection Act 1990 and see 3.16 above on injunctions in civil law.

[209] (1987) 35 BLR 34.

[210] *Goldsmid v Tunbridge Wells Improvement Commission* (1866) LR 1 Ch App 349.

# Chapter 9

# THE POLLUTION OF CONTROLLED WATERS

## 9.1 Introduction

By international comparisons, the regulation of water pollution in England and Wales has a relatively long history.[1] Criminal offences relating to the entry of polluting matter and the discharge of effluent into water may be traced back at least as far as the Rivers Pollution Prevention Act 1876.[2] Whilst these offences have been applied to an increasing range of receiving waters with successive legislation, the basic formulation of the offences demonstrates remarkable durability. For that reason, much of the case law under earlier enactments remains of relevance to the interpretation of the present law which is provided for under Chapter II of Part III, and particularly s.85, of the Water Resources Act 1991. Although the contamination of various kinds of water as a result of particular activities or by particular contaminants is separately regulated under a wide range of legislation which is discussed elsewhere,[3] for practical purposes the 'principal' offences concerning the pollution of 'controlled waters' are of greatest general relevance. It is these offences which are most appropriately applied to the regulation of those industrial activities which have the capacity to cause the most direct and damaging impact upon the aquatic environment.

Despite their practical importance, however, the limitations in the scope of the principal offences concerning water pollution must be noted from the outset. Historically, the offences relating to water pollution have been formulated with a particular kind of event in contemplation, that is, typically, the discrete release or escape of a seriously polluting substance in a pollution 'incident' which, over a relatively short period of time, brings about a dramatic deterioration in water quality and consequent damage to the ecosystem of the receiving waters. Typically, such an incident may affect the quality of the receiving waters for only a relatively brief period. However, in passing down a watercourse, the polluting matter may inflict an immense amount of ecological damage, most visibly in terms of fish mortality, but also largely imperceptible harm to the whole range of flora and fauna dependent upon the aquatic ecosystem. Whilst the

---

[1] See Ch.2 above on the history of water pollution legislation.

[2] Criminal offences relating to causing or knowingly permitting polluting matter into any stream under the Rivers Pollution Prevention Act 1876 were substantially re-enacted into the Rivers (Prevention of Pollution) Act 1951 (see s.2(1) in particular). Essentially, the same offences were subsequently re-enacted as ss.31(1) and 32(1) of the Control of Pollution Act 1974, s.107(1) and (3) of the Water Act 1989, and are now provided for under s.85 of the Water Resources Act 1991. For further discussion of this progression see Ch.2 above.

[3] See, for example, s.68 Public Health Act 1875 (concerning the manufacture of gas); s.4 Salmon and Freshwater Fisheries Act 1975 (concerning fishery protection offences); and, Part I of the Environmental Protection Act 1990 (concerning prescribed process authorisations). See 15.4.1 and 12.3 below on these.

physical and chemical water quality of the watercourse may return to its former state after a relatively short period, the ecological damage will require a much longer time for recovery.

Although discrete pollution incidents of this kind are a regrettably common occurrence,[4] it would be a misconception to suppose that they constitute the sole reason for the unsatisfactory state of many waters. The reason for much of the problem of unsatisfactory water quality is to be found in the cumulative effects of continuing discharges of sewage and trade effluent of poor quality, frequently under the authority of a discharge consent,[5] and surface water run-off. In addition, contaminants may enter water from other environmental media, as where there is percolation of substances into water from land on, or under, which they have been placed[6] or where atmospheric contaminants are deposited in water. Many of the problems generated by transmission of such 'diffuse' pollutants are discussed elsewhere in this work[7] but, for the present, the practical limitation must be noted. It is to be emphasised that there are many factors contributing to poor water quality which fall outside the scope of the principal water pollution offences.

The purpose of this chapter is, after an initial discussion of the extent of water pollution incidents and their legal consequences, to examine the principal water pollution offences, outlining the key elements of the offences and the defences to these. Discussion is provided of various difficulties which have arisen in proceedings for the principal offences in the courts and particularly, in the later sections, the issue of sentencing in relation to the offences.

## 9.2 Water Pollution Incidents

Despite the limitations of the principal water pollution offences, some insight is to gained by considering the kinds of incident which, potentially, may give rise to criminal proceedings. In respect of water pollution incidents, a degree of objectivity as to the extent of the problem, and the most seriously offending activities, is provided by annual reports issued by the Environment Agency as to the numbers of such incidents and the activities and substances involved. According to the report on *Water Pollution Incidents 1998*,[8] the Agency responded to 28,670 reports of water pollution during 1998 and, of these, 17,863 were substantiated on investigation. These figures represented decrease of 7% in reported incidents, and 9% in substantiated incidents, over the previous year and a significant fall in the number of incidents classified as 'major' from 194 to 128. 'Major' or 'Category 1' incidents are identified where one or more of the following factors are present:

---

[4] See pollution incident statistics discussed at 9.2 below.

[5] See Ch.10 below on discharge consents.

[6] See 13.7 below on contaminated land and 13.5 below on agricultural pollution.

[7] Generally see Ch.13 below on preventative approaches to water quality.

[8] Environment Agency, *Water Pollution Incidents in England and Wales 1998* (1999).

(a) potential or actual persistent effect on water quality or aquatic life;
(b) closure of potable water, industrial or agricultural abstraction is necessary;
(c) extensive fish kill;
(d) excessive breaches of consent conditions;
(e) instigation of extensive remedial measures;
(f) significant adverse effect on amenity value; or
(g) significant adverse effect on a site of conservation importance.[9]

The distribution of substantiated incidents according to source was as follows:

Sewage and Water Industry: 24% (4,253 incidents)
Industry: 20% (3,600)
Agriculture: 11% (2,050)
Transport: 10% (1,727)
Domestic/Residential: 7% (1,256)
Other: 28% (4,977).

In relation to major incidents the distribution was:

Industry: 33% (42 incidents)
Agriculture: 17% (22)
Sewage and Water Industry: 13% (17)
Transport: 11% (14)
Domestic/Residential: 1% (1)
Other: 25% (32).

Categorised according to the pollutants involved, the distribution of substantiated incidents was:

Oil: 30% (5,308 incidents)
Sewage: 24% (4,347)
Organic Wastes: 11% (2,026)
Chemical: 8% (1,405)
Silt: 7% (1,177)
Other: 20% (3,600).

In relation to the pollutants involved in major incidents the distribution was:

Oil: 31% (40 incidents)
Chemical: 21% (27)
Organic Wastes: 14% (18)
Sewage: 9% (12)
Silt: 1% (1)
Other: 23% (30).

---

[9] *Ibid* Appendix A. See also Environment Agency, *Guidance for the Enforcement and Prosecution Policy* (1999) ('*The Functional Guidelines*', Version 2, 30 September 1999) para.2.5.2-4.

The legal consequences of the incidents recorded in 1998 were that 92 prosecutions were brought, with convictions being secured in 90 cases (94%), though a further 95 cases were still to go before the courts after the end of 1998. However, it may be noted that, even if all the pending cases resulted in convictions, the outcome would be that only about 1% of substantiated incidents resulted in conviction, though clearly the percentage of the most serious incidents would be much higher. Alongside court proceedings, the Agency issued 73 formal cautions, where polluters admitted guilt, with a further 9 outstanding.

Although the Agency's documentation of pollution incidents provides a valuable objective record of the most damaging events which take place in relation to the aquatic environment, it is evident that this record does not represent the whole picture. The numbers given do not include instances of breaches of discharge consents, unless severe pollution is caused, even where contraventions of consents result in legal proceedings.[10] Beyond that, the statistics on pollution give no indication as to the extent or duration of poor water quality especially where this is not directly attributable to identified incidents. Although the general state of the aquatic environment is more meaningfully described in periodic reports on general water quality,[11] the relationship between poor water quality and particular offending activities is less clearly documented.

In relation to the actual use of legal proceedings, cross reference must be made to the law enforcement policy of the Environment Agency with regard to water pollution prosecution.[12] The disparity between the apparent breadth of what is proscribed under the principal offences concerning water pollution and the kinds of incident which actually become the subject of legal proceedings is considerable. Consequently, for a practical appreciation of the law in action, the discussion which follows must be read alongside important policy principles which determine when a prosecution actually will be undertaken, alongside the circumstances where some lesser kind of enforcement action will be pursued.

### 9.3 The Principal Offences concerning Water Pollution

The principal offences concerning water pollution are stated in s.85 Water Resources Act 1991, which reads as follows.

s.85 (1) A person contravenes this section if he causes or knowingly permits any poisonous, noxious or polluting matter or any solid waste matter to enter any controlled waters.

(2) A person contravenes this section if he causes or knowingly permits any matter, other than trade effluent or sewage effluent, to enter controlled waters by being discharged from a drain or

---

[10] *Ibid* para.7.1. For discussion of the statistics on breaches of discharge consents see 10.11 below.

[11] See 14.8 below on general quality assessment.

[12] See 6.18 above on the Environment Agency's law enforcement policy.

sewer in contravention of a prohibition imposed under s.86 below.

(3) A person contravenes this section if he causes or knowingly permits any trade effluent or sewage effluent to be discharged –

    (a)    into any controlled waters; or

    (b)    from land in England and Wales, through a pipe, into the sea outside the seaward limits of controlled waters.

(4) A person contravenes this section if he causes or knowingly permits any trade effluent or sewage effluent to be discharged, in contravention of a prohibition imposed under s.86, from a building or from any fixed plant –

    (a)    on to or into any land; or

    (b)    into any waters of a lake or pond which are not inland freshwaters.

(5) A person contravenes this section if he causes or knowingly permits any matter whatever to enter any inland freshwater so as to tend, (either directly or in combination with other matter which he or another person causes or permits to enter those waters) to impede the proper flow of the waters in a manner leading, or likely to lead, to a substantial aggravation of –

    (a)    pollution due to other causes; or

    (b)    the consequences of such pollution.

(6) Subject to the following provisions of this Chapter, a person who contravenes this section or the conditions of any consent given under this Chapter for the purpose of this section shall be guilty of an offence and liable –

    (a)    on summary conviction, to imprisonment for a term not exceeding three months or to a fine not exceeding £20,000 or to both;

    (b)    on conviction on indictment, to imprisonment for a term not exceeding two years or to a fine or to both.

It will be noted that this section contemplates five distinct offences and, implicitly, a sixth in relation to contraventions of the conditions of discharge and other consents under Chapter II of Part III of the Water Resources Act 1991.[13] Broadly, these offences are concerned, first, with the entry of polluting matter (s.85(1));[14] second, the contravention of a prohibition other than in relation to trade or sewage effluent (s.85(2));[15] third, the discharge of trade or sewage effluent (s.85(3));[16] fourth, the contravention of a prohibition in relation to trade or sewage effluent (s.85(4));[17] fifth, impeding the flow of waters leading to pollution (s.85(5));[18] and, finally, the contravention of a consent (s.85(6)).[19] Of these, the first, third and perhaps the last give rise to legal proceedings

---

[13] See Ch.10 on discharge consents.

[14] See 9.8 below.

[15] See 9.11 below.

[16] See 9.9 below.

[17] See 9.11 below.

[18] See 9.12 below.

[19] See 9.13 below.

most frequently in practice. Discharge consents are considered later in this work,[20] and it is convenient initially to consider the offences relating to the entry of polluting matter and the discharge of effluent and to return to the other matters later in this chapter.

Whilst the offences relating to the entry of polluting matter and the discharge of effluent each have their own distinctive features, certain key concepts need to be defined and contrasted from the outset: first, the nature of 'controlled waters'; second, the meaning of 'cause or knowingly permit'; third, the meaning of 'poisonous, noxious or polluting'; fourth, the meaning of 'trade or sewage effluent'; and, finally, the meanings of 'entry' and 'discharge'.

## 9.4  The Definition of 'Controlled Waters'

With some qualifications,[21] the principal water pollution offences provided for under s.85 of the Water Resources Act 1991 arise only in relation to entries and discharges to 'controlled waters'.[22] 'Controlled waters' fall into four sub-categories: 'relevant territorial waters'; 'coastal waters'; 'inland freshwaters' and 'groundwaters'.[23] The meanings of these expressions are described in the following paragraphs.

'Relevant territorial waters' means waters which extend seaward for three international nautical miles[24] from the baselines from which the breadth of the territorial sea adjacent to England and Wales is measured.[25] This definition is subject to the power of the Secretary of State to provide by order that any particular area of territorial sea adjacent to England and Wales is to be treated as if it were an area of relevant territorial waters.[26] The extent of the territorial sea is largely determined by international law and, specifically, the United Nations Convention on the Law of the Sea[27] which allows a coastal state establish the breadth of its territorial sea up to a limit not exceeding 12 nautical miles.[28] The mechanism by which this is provided for in national law is the Territorial Sea Act 1987, which allows for baselines to be established by Order in Council so that, in any legal

---

[20] See Ch.10 below on discharge consents.

[21] For example, s.85(3) may apply in relation to discharges into waters beyond the seaward limits of controlled waters, and s.85(4) may apply in relation to discharges of effluent on to land or into certain stillwaters which are not controlled waters.

[22] Note that the expression 'controlled waters' is used in a different sense in relation to 'United Kingdom controlled waters' (designated under s.1(7) Continental Shelf Act 1964) where, for example, the deposit of waste at sea is at issue, see 18.10.2 and 19.20.1 below.

[23] Defined by s.104 Water Resources Act 1991.

[24] 'International nautical mile' means a distance of 1,852 metres (s.104(3) Water Resources Act 1991).

[25] s.104(1)(a) and (3) Water Resources Act 1991.

[26] *Ibid* s.104(4)(a).

[27] Generally see 18.7 below on this Convention.

[28] Art.2 Law of the Sea Convention (1992).

proceedings, a certificate issued by, or under the authority of, the Secretary of State will be conclusive evidence of any baseline.[29]

It is curious that the national interpretation of 'relevant territorial waters', as extending to three nautical miles, is less than the international limit of 12 nautical miles. To some extent, this may be historically explained in that three miles was traditionally regarded as the distance over which sovereignty could be defended, since this was assumed to be the maximum trajectory of a cannon-shot from the shore.[30] Whatever its historical basis, however, the restriction to three nautical miles had been regarded as relatively unproblematic, until recently, because the principal offences have normally been applied to land-based sources of water contamination, with other legislation dealing with marine discharges from ships and other non-land based activities.[31] The issue of the appropriateness of applying the principal offences to pollution incidents arising from shipping casualties within the three mile limit has, however, recently become the subject of criticism and scrutiny.[32] Nonetheless, it is notable that an offence may be committed outside the seaward limits of controlled waters where effluent is discharged from land, through a pipe, into the sea outside the three nautical mile limit.[33] By this means, the control of land-based marine pollution is fairly comprehensively provided for.

'Coastal waters' means waters which are within the area which extends landward from the baselines of the territorial sea as far as the limit of the highest tide or, in the case of the waters of any relevant river of watercourse, as far as the freshwater limit of the river or watercourse, together with the waters of any enclosed dock which adjoins waters within that area.[34] Within this definition 'watercourse' is stated to includes all rivers, streams, ditches, drains, cuts, culverts, dykes, sluices, sewers and passages through which water flows except mains and other pipes which belong to the Agency or a water undertaker or are used by a water undertaker or any other person for the purpose only of providing a supply of water to any premises.[35] 'Relevant river or watercourse' means any river or watercourse, including an underground river and an artificial river or watercourse, which is neither a public sewer nor a sewer or drain which drains into a public sewer.[36] 'Freshwater limit', in relation to any river or watercourse, means the place for the time being shown as the freshwater limit of that river or watercourse in the latest map deposited by the

---

[29] s.1(1) and (3) Territorial Sea Act 1987. For further discussion of the territorial sea, see Howarth (1992) pp.26–32.

[30] See *Gann* v *Free Fishers of Whitstable* (1865) 1 HL Cas 192, per Lord Chelmsford at p.218, and generally see Marston (1981).

[31] See Ch.19 below on controls on shipping and dumping of waste at sea.

[32] See the discussion of discharges from vessels at 9.17.2 below.

[33] Under s.85(3)(b) Water Resources Act 1991.

[34] *Ibid* s.104(1)(b).

[35] *Ibid* s.221(1), as amended. In relation to the meaning of 'watercourse' in respect of statutory nuisances, under Part III Environmental Protection Act 1990, contrast *R* v *Falmouth and Truro Port Health Authority, ex parte South West Water Ltd* [2000] 3 All ER 306 and see 8.5.4 above.

[36] *Ibid* s.104(3).

Secretary of State with the Agency for that purpose.[37] The Secretary of State may order that a watercourse of a specified description is to be treated for these purposes as if it were not a relevant river or watercourse.[38]

'Inland freshwaters' means the waters of any relevant lake or pond or of so much of any relevant river or watercourse as is above the freshwater limit.[39] Within this definition 'lake or pond' is stated to include a reservoir of any description. 'Relevant lake or pond' means any lake or pond which, whether natural or artificial or above or below ground, discharges into a relevant river or watercourse or into another lake or pond which is itself a relevant lake or pond.[40] The Secretary of State may provide by order that any lake or pond which does not discharge into a relevant river or watercourse or into a relevant lake or pond is to be treated as a relevant lake or pond, or to be treated as if it were not a relevant lake or pond as the case may be.[41]

'Ground waters' are defined as any waters which are contained in underground strata.[42] 'Underground strata' means strata subjacent to the surface of any land.[43] Notably, this definition is a broad one which extends to encompass *all* underground water and not merely water within the saturated zone below the water table. A contrast may be drawn here with the European Community Groundwater Directive which defines 'groundwater' as all water which is below the surface of the ground *in the saturation zone* and in direct contact with the ground or subsoil.[44]

Clearly, the overall effect of the definition of 'controlled waters', as detailed within the four sub-categories, is that near-comprehensive provision is made for the application of the principal water pollution offences to almost all kinds of fresh and saline waters that may commonly be affected by water contamination. However, the meaning of the concept is also defined by the kinds of water that it *excludes*. In that respect, the following exceptions may be noted.

First, the definition of 'controlled waters' does not encompass waters which are contained within a public sewer or a sewer or drain which drains

---

[37] ss.104(3) and 192 Water Resources Act 1991.

[38] *Ibid* s.104(4)(d).

[39] *Ibid* s.104(1)(c).

[40] *Ibid* s.104(3).

[41] *Ibid* s.104(4)(b) and (c). See Controlled Waters (Lakes and Ponds) Order 1989 (SI 1989 No.1149) which brings certain reservoirs which do not discharge into relevant waters within the meaning of 'relevant lake or pond'. See Reg.7(2) Surface Waters (Abstraction for Drinking Water) (Classification) Regulations 1996 (SI 1996 No.3001) which states that all waters within the scope of the Regulations are to be 'inland freshwaters' for the purposes of the definition of 'controlled waters'. See also Reg.6(2) Surface Waters (Fishlife) (Classification) Regulations 1997 (SI 1997 No.1331) and Reg.6(2) Surface Waters (Shellfish) (Classification) Regulations 1997 (SI 1997 No.1332) which state that all waters within the scope of these Regulations are 'inland freshwaters'. Generally see 14.8 below for discussion of the water classification regulations.

[42] s.104(1)(d) Water Resources Act 1991.

[43] *Ibid* s.221(1).

[44] See Art.1(2)(a) Groundwater Directive (80/68/EEC) discussed at 5.4.2 below. See also Groundwater Regulations (SI 1998 No.2746) discussed at 13.6 below.

into a public sewer, thereby excluding waters which are comprised of domestic or trade effluent.[45] The reason for excluding such waters is that the discharge of domestic and trade effluent to sewers is separately provided for under Part IV of the Water Industry Act 1991.[46]

Second, water which is distributed to provide a potable supply will not be 'controlled water', since the definition of 'watercourse' explicitly excludes mains or other pipes which are used by a water undertaker or any other person for the purpose only of providing a supply of water to any premises.[47] Again, the reason for this exclusion is that the quality of drinking water is separately regulated, primarily, under Part III of the Water Industry Act 1991.[48]

Third, 'enclosed' stillwaters which do not discharge to other waters will not be 'controlled waters', though certain discharges of effluent into such waters may be the subject of an offence if they are the subject of a prohibition.[49] Of relevance here is the definition of 'discrete waters': inland waters so far as they comprise (a) a lake, pond or reservoir which does not discharge to any other inland waters; or (b) one of a group of two or more lakes, ponds or reservoirs (whether near to or distant from each other) and of watercourses or mains connecting them, where none of the inland waters in the group discharges to any inland waters outside the group.[50] Some interesting practical questions may arise as to whether pollution of such waters might lead to the pollution of groundwater, which would be within the definition of 'controlled waters' but, in principle, ponds and other kind of enclosed water are not within the definition of 'controlled waters'.

The question of whether an allegedly enclosed water, which had been polluted by leachate effluent from a landfill site, was a controlled water arose in *Environment Agency* v *Brock plc*.[51] Here the defendant had allowed the leachate to enter a ditch after a seal on a pipe had burst, but it was contended that the ditch, which was man-made rather than natural, was not a 'controlled water'. This view was rejected by the Court which noted the explicit reference to 'ditches' within the meaning of 'watercourse'. It was concluded that if water flowed thorough the ditch to connect with another watercourse it would be within the meaning of 'controlled waters'. On the facts of the case, it was clear that the ditch allowed water to run into a nearby brook and, therefore, it fulfilled all the requirements for being a controlled water.

Fourth, as has been noted, the definition of 'controlled waters' excludes the sea beyond the three nautical mile limit which is used to define

---

[45] s.104(3) Water Resources Act 1991.
[46] See Ch.11 below on the discharge of effluent to sewers.
[47] s.221(1) Water Resources Act 1991.
[48] See Ch.17 below on drinking water quality.
[49] s.85(4) Water Resources Act 1991.
[50] *Ibid* s.221(1).
[51] [1998] Env LR 607.

relevant territorial waters, though an offence is specifically provided for in relation to the discharge of trade or sewage effluent through a pipe outside the seaward limits of controlled waters.[52] However, the main categories of marine contamination are extensively provided for in other legislation.[53]

Finally, the placing or discharge of polluting matter or effluent on to land will not normally constitute an entry or discharge into controlled waters.[54] This is subject to specific provision which is made for an offence involving discharge of effluent on to or into land in contravention of a specific prohibition.[55] Also, it is notable that, for the purposes of the definition of 'controlled waters', any reference to waters of any lake or pond or of any river or watercourse includes a reference to the bottom, channel or bed of any lake, pond, river or, as the case may be, watercourse which is for the time being dry.[56] It is curious that, despite the absence of water, an emission or discharge of polluting matter or effluent onto the bed of a dried up watercourse or stillwater will, nevertheless, amount to an entry or discharge into 'controlled waters'. Nonetheless, this possibility is statutorily provided for.

Although the question of whether the waters into which an entry or discharge takes place are 'controlled waters' has not been subject to frequent judicial consideration, one decision which sheds some light on the matter is *R v Dovermoss Ltd.*[57] Here, the defendant was alleged to have put animal slurry on a field alongside a stream. Due to an obstruction of the stream, water subsequently flowed over the field where the slurry had been spread, and this resulted in the contamination of subterranean water used for supply purposes. It was argued that since the stream had departed from its normal course, the polluting matter did not enter a controlled water. However, this contention was rejected by the Court in noting that the definition of controlled waters referred to 'waters of any . . . watercourse'[58] not waters *in* any watercourse. Accordingly, it was concluded that there had been an entry of polluting matter into controlled waters, albeit waters that had departed from their normal course of flow and despite the slurry having been spread on what was previously adjoining land. More generally, it must be inferred from this ruling that a distinction is to be drawn between the 'watercourse', comprising the channel in which water normally flows, and the 'controlled water' which may, or may not, be contained in that channel at any particular time.

---

[52] s.85(4)(b) Water Resources Act 1991.

[53] See Chs.18–20 below on marine pollution. However, the Water Resources Act 1991 may be contrasted with marine pollution legislation in that, whilst the latter is generally substance-specific, the 1991 Act applies to almost all kinds of pollutants.

[54] Although this activity is likely to be regulated under waste management law, see Part II Environmental Protection Act 1990, concerned with 'Waste on Land' and see 12.2 below.

[55] s.85(4) Water Resources Act 1991, and see 9.11 below on prohibitions.

[56] s.104(2) Water Resources Act 1991.

[57] [1995] Env LR 258.

[58] s.104(1)(c) Water Resources Act 1991.

## 9.5 Causing or Knowingly Permitting

Other than in relation to contraventions of a discharge consent, all the principal offences concerning water pollution arise where a person 'causes or knowingly permits' the entry or discharge of polluting matter or effluent into controlled waters.[59] The phrase 'causes or knowingly permits' is a statutory formula which has been used in a range of different contexts, and has been the subject of consideration by the courts on many occasions. The phrase has, in the past, generally been thought to contemplate two separate offences: first, causing certain polluting matter to enter a specified waters; and, second, knowingly permitting certain polluting matter to enter specified waters.[60] From the outset, the meanings of the two phrases must be distinguished. Hence it has been stated that,

> To cause . . . involves some express or positive mandate from the person 'causing' to the other person, or some authority from the former to the latter, arising in the circumstances of the case. To 'permit' is a looser and vaguer term. It may denote an express permission, general or particular, as distinguished from a mandate . . . . However, the word also includes cases in which permission is merely inferred.[61]

In a similar vein, it has been observed that,

> the subsection[62] evidently contemplates two things – *causing*, which must involve some active operation or chain of operations involving as the result the pollution of the stream; knowingly permitting, which involves a failure to prevent the pollution, which failure, however, must be accompanied by knowledge.[63]

It is apparent, therefore, that to 'cause' an occurrence entails some degree of dominance or control in bringing that state of affairs about, whereas to 'permit' such a state of affairs implies the possession of some influence over it which is not exercised in such a way as to prevent or forbid it taking place. This difference between causing and knowingly permitting an event, frequently corresponding to a distinction between acts and omissions to act, has been redrawn along similar lines on several occasions and remains of importance.

Previously it has been thought that the distinction between 'causing', as a positive activity which results in pollution, and 'knowingly permitting',

---

[59] General reading on the offence of causing or knowingly permitting polluting matter to enter waters includes: Bentil (1986); Howarth (1993); Wilkinson (1993); and Bell and McGillivray (2000) pp.587-94.

[60] See *Alphacell Ltd* v *Woodward* [1972] 2 All ER 475, per Lord Wilberforce at p.479; and *Price* v *Cromack* [1975] 2 All ER 113, per Lord Widgery CJ at p.117.

[61] *McLeod* v *Buchanan* [1940] 2 All ER 179, per Lord Wright at p.187, and see Hobday (1952) pp.208-10.

[62] s.2(1) Rivers (Prevention of Pollution) Act 1951, see now s.85(1) Water Resources Act 1991.

[63] See *Alphacell Ltd* v *Woodward* [1972] 2 All ER 475, per Lord Wilberforce at p.479, and see also *Kirkheaton District Local Board* v *Ainley Sons and Co* [1892] 2 QB 274, at p.283 per Bowen LJ.

involving a failure to prevent pollution accompanied by knowledge, is that two distinct criminal offences are created. As a consequence of this, a charge of causing *or* knowingly permitting water pollution was thought to be invalid on grounds of duplicity.[64] For this reason, the general practice of prosecutors has been to avoid the disjunctive formulation of causing *or* knowingly permitting, and to bring charges for one or the other, or perhaps both, of these. There are examples of charges being brought for 'causing' where prosecutions have failed because when it became clear that the appropriate charge should have been 'knowingly permitting', and *vice versa*.[65]

Despite the traditional orthodoxy, that causing and knowingly permitting constitute two different offences, there are indications that the matter may not be so self-evident. *R v Leighton and Town and Country Refuse Collections Ltd*[66] involved proceedings for waste management offences[67] in contravention of licensing conditions where it was alleged that the particulars of the offences charged were bad for duplicity. Specifically, it was argued that a charge for 'depositing', 'causing' or 'knowingly permitting' the relevant activities was improper because it alleged three different offences which should have been charged separately.

After reviewing the relevant authorities,[68] it was concluded that,

> the effect of those authorities . . . is that where such a statutory formula is employed . . . causing and permitting the contravention are different acts requiring different proof. They are not authorities for the proposition that wherever those two acts appear in the alternative in an offence creating provision they should be treated on indictment as creating different offences which should be separately charged.[69]

The Court took the view that, whether a statute creates one offence which may be committed in different ways or more than one offence, is a matter of construction of the statutory formula in each case. Accordingly, a single offence was created by the prohibition that a person should not deposit controlled waste, or knowingly cause or knowingly permit controlled waste to be deposited, otherwise than in accordance with a waste management licence.[70] It followed that it was, in principle, permissible for the prosecution to charge the accused with a single offence stating the various modes of committing the offence in the alternative. That is, it was

---

[64] Generally see *Edwards v Jones* [1947] KB 659, *R v Thomas* [1950] 1 KB 26 and s.18 Interpretation Act 1978 which precludes multiple punishments for the same offence.

[65] See *Price v Cromack* [1975] 2 All ER 113; *Wychavon District Council v National Rivers Authority* [1993] 2 All ER 440; and *Bruton and the National Rivers Authority v Clarke* (1993) unreported, 23 July 1993, Cambridge County Court, discussed at 13.2.4 below and see Carty (1995).

[66] [1997] Env LR 411.

[67] Contrary to s.3 Control of Pollution Act 1974 and s.33 Environmental Protection Act 1990.

[68] Including *Price v Cromack* [1975] 2 All ER 113.

[69] [1997] Env LR 411 per Lord Justice Auld at p.416.

[70] Under s.33(1)(a) Environmental Protection Act 1990.

not necessary separately to charge each alternative manner of committing the offence as a different count.

Whilst the proceedings in this case were concerned with a waste management rather than a water pollution offence, the reasoning would seem to be similarly applicable to a charge of 'causing *or* knowingly permitting' a principal water pollution offence. If so, such a charge would not, as previously thought, be void for duplicity. However, it is apparent that the facts which would need to be established for a conviction to succeed would have to satisfy the Court that the accused had actually 'caused' or 'knowingly permitted' the offending entry or discharge, and there remain important factual differences between these despite it being established that they are alternative ways of committing the same offence.

There is no difficulty in charging an offender with more than one distinct offence arising from the same pollution incident. Not uncommonly, a person is charged with one of the principal water pollution offences and the fishery protection offence relating to putting liquid matter into water containing fish.[71] Another possibility is that the defendant may be charged with more than one of the principal offences. In a recent decision,[72] Welsh Water plc caused a major pollution incident by its failure to divert sewage away from a river when undertaking maintenance at a sewage treatment works. As a result of the incident, the sewerage undertaker was found guilty of three distinct offences: causing the entry of polluting matter, causing the discharge of sewage effluent and causing the receiving waters to be toxic to fish.[73]

## 9.6 Causing

Amongst the considerable amount of litigation to which the principal water pollution offences have given rise, perhaps the most frequently recurring issue is that of what must be shown to conclude that a defendant has 'caused' the entry of polluting matter.

### 9.6.1 The Alphacell Case

A leading authority on the meaning of 'causing' the entry of polluting matter is the House of Lords decision in *Alphacell Ltd* v *Woodward*.[74] In this case the appellant, Alphacell, was engaged in paper making at a riverside site. The water used to wash raw materials was piped into settling tanks. The tanks were equipped with a pump which automatically switched on when the water reached a certain level, to prevent any overflow into the river. Although the tanks were periodically inspected, and protected by a

---

[71] Under s.4 Salmon and Freshwater Fisheries Act 1975 and see the discussion at 15.4.1 below.

[72] See *ENDS Report* 305 (2000) p.55.

[73] That is, offences under s.85(1) and s.85(3) Water Resources Act 1991 and s.4 Salmon and Freshwater Fisheries Act 1975.

[74] [1972] 2 All ER 475, similarly, in Scots law, see *Lockhart* v *National Coal Board* 1981 SLT 161.

rose which was intended to act as a filter to prevent the entry of foreign matter, the pump failed to operate through becoming obstructed by a quantity of brambles, ferns and leaves. As a result of this, contaminated effluent from the tanks overflowed into the river and the appellants were convicted of causing polluting matter to enter a river.[75] It was not found that the appellants had any knowledge that effluent was flowing into the river or that they were negligent in failing to see that the pumps were operating properly. The appellants appealed to the House of Lords on the ground that the conviction should be set aside in the absence of knowledge or negligence on their part. In effect, the contention was that the offence of causing pollution required it to be shown that there had been recklessness, negligence or an intention to pollute.

The House of Lords unanimously dismissed the appeal on the ground that the offence did not require the prosecution to establish that the accused had knowingly, intentionally or negligently caused the polluted water to enter the river. The reasoning of Lord Wilberforce was specifically directed to the meaning of 'cause' in the provisions to be construed:

> In my opinion, 'causing' here must be given a common sense meaning and I deprecate the introduction of any refinements, such as *causa causans*, effective cause or *novus actus*. There may be difficulties where acts of third persons or natural forces are concerned but I find the present case comparatively simple. The appellants abstract water, pass it through their works where it becomes polluted, conduct it to a settling tank communicating directly with the stream, into which the polluted water will inevitably overflow if the level rises over the overflow point. They plan, however, to recycle the water by pumping it back from the settling tank into their works; if the pumps work properly this will happen and the level in the tank will remain below the overflow point. It did not happen on the relevant occasion due to some failure in the pumps.

> In my opinion, this is a clear case of causing the polluted water to enter the stream. The whole complex operation which might lead to this result was an operation deliberately conducted by the appellants and I fail to see how a defect in one stage of it, even if we must assume that this happened without their negligence, can enable them to say they did not cause the pollution. In my opinion, complication of this case by infusion of the concept of *mens rea*, and it exceptions, is unnecessary and undesirable.[76]

Other speeches followed this reasoning and emphasised the difficulties that would arise if the offence were to be construed as requiring intention. As Lord Salmon made the point,

---

[75] Contrary to s.2(1) Rivers (Prevention of Pollution) Act 1951, which provided for the offence of causing or knowingly permitting any poisonous, noxious or polluting matter to enter a stream, corresponding to s.85(1) Water Resources Act 1991.

[76] [1972] 2 All ER 475, at p.479.

If this appeal succeeded and it were held to be the law that no conviction could be obtained under the 1951 Act unless the prosecution could discharge the often impossible onus of proving that the pollution was caused intentionally or negligently, a great deal of pollution would go unpunished and undeterred to the relief of many riparian factory owners. As a result, many rivers which are now filthy would become filthier still and many rivers which are now clean would lose their cleanliness. The legislature would no doubt recognise that as a matter of public policy this would be most unfortunate. Hence s.2(1)(a) which encourages riparian factory owners not to take reasonable steps to prevent pollution but to do everything possible to ensure that they do not cause it.[77]

Hence, it was concluded that the offence of causing the entry of polluting matter was an 'absolute' offence, or an offence of 'strict liability',[78] in relation to which no intention to pollute or negligence needed to be shown. The only relevant consideration is whether the defendant actually caused the entry of polluting matter and this is a question to be determined by looking at the facts alongside the ordinary meaning of the word 'cause'.

It follows that the interpretation of 'causes' within the present legislation will be similarly construed in such a way as to make it unnecessary for the prosecution to show that the accused acted knowingly, intentionally or negligently with regard to the entry of the polluting matter or effluent. If the other elements of the offence are present, the fact that the accused 'caused' the pollution will be sufficient to establish guilt.

The irrelevance of knowledge, intention or negligence to the issue of causation has been reaffirmed in a number of subsequent cases, and a good example is to be found in the decision in *Wrothwell Ltd* v *Yorkshire Water Authority*.[79] In this case a director of the defendant company deliberately poured 12 gallons of a concentrated herbicide, known to be toxic to fish life, into a drain. The expectation of the director was that the liquid would pass through the drain into the public sewer system and would ultimately reach the public sewage works where it would be treated before final discharge. It turned out, however, that the drain was not connected to the public sewer, but to a system of pipes through which the herbicide was discharged into a nearby stream bringing about extensive fish mortality. The director appealed against a conviction[80] of causing poisonous matter to enter a stream, arguing that since the actual result of his act had been so different from its expected result, the entry of the poison into the stream could not be said to have been 'caused' by his act. It was held on appeal,

---

[77] [1972] 2 All ER 475, at p.491.

[78] Although the speeches in the *Alphacell* case frequently refer to the offence as 'absolute' it is thought preferable to use the term 'strict liability' since it has been pointed out that though intention is not required the offence does not preclude the possibility of other defences being available, see Smith (1999) p.112. Hence, crimes which do not require intention, recklessness or even negligence as to one or more elements in the *actus reus* are offences of 'strict liability' (see *ibid* p.97).

[79] [1984] Crim LR 43.

[80] Under s.2 of the Rivers (Prevention of Pollution) Act 1951.

however, that following *Alphacell Ltd* v *Woodward*, 'cause' is a word in everyday usage on which justices needed only to apply their common sense as to its meaning. The court declined to overturn the finding that, despite his ignorance of the consequence of his actions, the director had 'caused' the liquid to enter the stream.

Another useful illustration of the impact of strict liability arose in *CPC (UK) Ltd* v *National Rivers Authority*[81] where a company was convicted of causing polluting matter to enter controlled waters following an accidental spillage of cleaning fluid used in its production process. The fluid was carried from storage tanks through plastic piping which ran outside a building at roof level. On investigation it was discovered that the piping had fractured and fluid had leaked onto a roof, from where it had fallen to the ground, and entered a storm drain from which it was discharged into a nearby river. It transpired that the cause of the fracture in the pipe was a defect in the piping, present at the time it was installed, which arose because of the failure properly to apply adhesive to two adjoining sections of the pipe. The work had been conducted by reputable sub-contractors in the field about nine months before the appellants acquired the factory. At the time the factory was purchased by the appellants, a full survey was conducted but this failed to detect the latent fault. Despite the appellant's argument that the entry of fluid into the river was entirely caused by the previous owner's sub-contractors, the Court found the appellants guilty of the offence. The latent character of the defect was irrelevant, since no knowledge or foreseeability needed to be proved, and it was equally irrelevant that a third party, along with the appellant, might also have been held to have 'caused' the entry. Again, the decision emphasises that 'cause' does not imply any necessary moral blameworthiness since, as the facts have shown, it would be difficult to conceive of anything further that the appellants could reasonably have done to have prevented the incident. Blameworthiness is a matter which may justifiably be taken into account when sentencing is being considered, but not in relation to the issue of guilt.[82]

### 9.6.2 *The Empress Cars Case*

Despite Lord Wilberforce's forthright affirmation in the *Alphacell* case that 'cause' should be given a common sense meaning in the context of water pollution offences, a considerable number of subsequent cases came before the courts in which parties were found not to have 'caused' the entry of polluting matter into controlled waters. The situations which proved most problematic arose where more than one person was involved in a collaborative activity which resulted in water pollution, where it was alleged that a water pollution incident was wholly the consequence of an act of a third party or where an incident was alleged to be the result of natural causes.

---

[81] [1995] Env LR 131.
[82] See 9.19 below on sentencing water pollution offences.

The House of Lords has recently returned to consider the meaning of 'cause' in the water pollution context in *Environment Agency (formerly National Rivers Authority) v Empress Car Co (Abertillery) Ltd*.[83] The facts at issue concerned the entry of oil into controlled waters as a result of the alleged vandalism of a storage tank. The owners of the tank had overridden the protection provided by a containment bund around the oil storage tank by fitting an extension pipe from the tank connecting with a barrel placed outside the bund. An unknown person had opened the tap and allowed the entire contents of the tank to run into the drum and overflow across a yard into a storm drain and from there into a nearby river. On appeal, the company claimed that the act of the stranger in turning on the tap meant that it should have been acquitted of the charge of causing the entry of the polluting matter, since this had been caused wholly by the act of the stranger and there had been no positive act on the part of the company which amounted to 'causing' the entry. Accordingly, the following question was put to the House of Lords for consideration:

> Whether a person can be convicted of an offence under s.85(1) of the Water Resources Act 1991 of causing polluting matter to enter controlled waters if it is proved that:– (a) he held the polluting matter and contained it in such a way as it would not escape but for the positive act by himself or another; and (b) he failed to take reasonable precautions to prevent such an escape occurring as a result of an action by a third party; and it is not proved that he took any other actions which resulted in the pollution.

The House of Lords ruled that a person may be held to have caused the entry of polluting matter if that person did something, with or without the occurrence of other facts, which produced a situation in which the polluting matter could escape, even though this was not the immediate or only cause of the pollution. On the facts of the case it was concluded that there was ample evidence to allow a finding that the company had caused the entry of the polluting matter.

In summary of the main judgment, by Lord Hoffmann, the following points were made.

(1) Justices dealing with prosecutions for 'causing' pollution under s.85(1) should first require the prosecution to identify what it says the defendant did to cause the pollution. If the defendant cannot be said to have done anything at all, the prosecution must fail: the defendant may have 'knowingly permitted' pollution but cannot have caused it.

(2) The prosecution need not prove that the defendant did something which was the immediate cause of the pollution: maintaining tanks, lagoons or sewage systems full of noxious liquid is doing something, even if the immediate cause of the pollution was lack of maintenance, a natural event or the act of a third party.

---

[83] [1998] 1 All ER 481, formerly *Empress Car Co (Abertillery) Ltd v National Rivers Authority*, and see Parpworth (1998); MacDonald (1998); Ryan (1998); and Stanley (1999).

(3) When the prosecution has identified something which the defendant did, the justices must decide whether it caused the pollution. They should not be diverted by questions like 'What was the cause of the pollution?' or 'Did something else cause the pollution?' because to say that something else caused the pollution (like brambles clogging the pumps or vandalism by third parties) is not inconsistent with the defendant having caused it as well.

(4) If the defendant did something which produced a situation in which the polluting matter could escape but a necessary condition of the actual escape which happened was also the act of a third party or a natural event, the justices should consider whether that act or event should be regarded as a normal fact of life or something extraordinary. If it was in the general run of things a matter of ordinary occurrence, it will not negative the causal effect of the defendant's acts, even if it was not foreseeable that it would happen to that particular defendant or take that particular form. If it can be regarded as something extraordinary, it will be open to the justices to hold that the defendant did not cause the pollution.

(5) The distinction between ordinary and extraordinary is one of fact and degree to which the justices must apply their common sense and knowledge of what happens in the area.[84]

A number of observations are warranted on these five points.

In respect of the first point made by Lord Hoffmann, that the defendant must have done something to cause the entry of the polluting matter, the significance of this lies in the line of thinking that it overturns. Previously, it had been accepted that a defendant could not be found to have caused the offending entry without a 'positive act' being shown. Following this reasoning, a defendant who failed to maintain effluent lagoons upon his land was found not guilty of causing an entry of effluent into controlled waters because there was no 'positive act' on his part and his omission to act was held not to amount to causing the entry.[85] In another case,[86] a local authority which maintained sewers, as agent for a sewerage undertaker, failed to take sufficiently swift action to remove a blockage of the sewers for which it was responsible and effluent flowed through a stormwater drainage system and into a river. Again, the finding was that there had been no 'positive act' on the part of the defendant, as opposed to a failure to act, which could amount to it causing the entry of the effluent. In Lord Hoffmann's view these decisions took far too restrictive a view of the requirement that the defendant must have done something. The maintaining of the lagoons, in the first case, and the responsibilities in respect of the operation of the sewage system, in the second, was sufficient to count as 'doing something' for the purpose of showing that the defendants had caused the respective incidents. Whilst previously reservations had been expressed in the suggestion that the two cases

---

[84] [1998] 1 All ER 481, per Lord Hoffman at p.492.

[85] *Price v Cromack* [1975] 2 All ER 113.

[86] *Wychavon District Council v National Rivers Authority* [1993] 2 All ER 440.

should be regarded as 'turning on their own facts',[87] a better view was that a positive act as the immediate cause of the offending entry was a 'further requirement' which should not have been added to the essential requirement that the defendant has done something which has caused the entry.[88]

Lord Hoffmann's second point was that maintaining an operation was sufficient to establish that the defendant was 'doing something' even if the immediate cause of the offending entry was a lack of maintenance, a natural event or the act of a third party. The implication of this is that a particular event may have a number of different causes and common sense answers to enquiries as to what caused an event will have different answers depending upon the rule by which responsibility is to be attributed. 'Causation' is capable of meaning different things for the purposes of establishing moral blameworthiness, civil liability in negligence or criminal culpability for water pollution. For the purpose of enquiry into criminal guilt it is critical to determine whether an individual can be said to have 'caused' an event in the appropriate sense.

Moreover, the inference that one person has caused a pollution incident is not inconsistent with a conclusion that others have also caused the same incident. Hence, in *National Rivers Authority* v *Yorkshire Water Services Ltd*[89] the defendant, a sewerage undertaker, established a system of sewerage treatment which involved the eventual discharge of treated effluent into a river. As a result of an unlawful discharge into a sewer, polluting matter passed from the treatment works and resulted in the pollution of the river. The ruling was that the undertaker, having established a system for gathering and treating effluent, had caused the entry of the polluting matter into the river. However, this did not preclude the possibility that the person who had been responsible for the 'immediate' cause of the incident, the unlawful discharge to the sewer, might also have been found to have caused the entry into controlled waters if that person had been identified.[90]

Similar observations may be made in relation to Lord Hoffmann's third point. It must be determined whether the defendant's actions caused the polluting entry or discharge, and the existence of multiple causes of a pollution incident is not relevant. The question to be addressed is whether the defendant's actions caused the incident, not whether there were other causes which could be identified and which might also be the subject of criminal proceedings. This issue was considered, in relation to the operation of sewerage systems, in *Attorney-General's Reference (No 1 of 1994)*.[91] This Reference affirmed that where a party has taken on the

---

[87] See *National Rivers Authority* v *Yorkshire Water Services Ltd* [1995] 1 All ER 225, per Lord Mackay of Clashfern at p.232.

[88] See *Attorney-General's Reference (No 1 of 1994)* [1995] 2 All ER 1007 per Lord Taylor of Gosforth CJ at p.1018.

[89] [1995] 1 All ER 225, and see 9.14.3 below.

[90] See also the discussion of the Worcester Drinking Water Incident at 1.6.3 above.

[91] *Attorney-General's Reference (No 1 of 1994)* [1995] 2 All ER 1007.

responsibility of running a sewerage system and failed to maintain the system properly, that was sufficient to justify a finding that the party was guilty of causing pollution of controlled waters.[92] Specifically, it was stated that the offence of causing pollution could be committed by more than one person where separate acts contributed to polluting matter entering controlled waters.

Lord Hoffmann's fourth point directly addressed situations where the act of a third party or a natural event was involved and proposed that, in such situations, the defendant's liability should depend upon whether the act or event was to be regarded as an ordinary or extraordinary occurrence. The critical issue here is to ascertain whether an intervening cause is of such significance that the conduct of the defendants ceases to be regarded as the cause of an incident and constitutes merely the surrounding circumstances. One example given by Lord Hoffmann[93] is of a situation where polluting matter enters controlled waters as a result of a containment lagoon being breached by a bomb being planted by terrorists, where it would be difficult to conclude that the owner of the lagoon had caused the offending entry. This would fall into the category of 'extraordinary events' as would certain extreme natural events.[94]

However, the practical difficulty must lie in drawing a line between 'ordinary' and 'extraordinary' events: characterised as a common sense distinction between acts and events, which though not necessarily foreseeable in a particular case, are in the generality a normal and familiar fact of life and those which are abnormal and extraordinary.[95] In the circumstances of the *Empress Car* case it was noted that there had been a history of local opposition to the business conducted by the company and the incident coincided with a public inquiry concerning a disputed footpath held on the following day. It may, therefore, have been contemplated that the threat of vandalism of the premises was particularly acute. However, in another case where water pollution originated from the vandalism of an oil tank the Court found that such vandalism was not reasonably foreseeable since it was out of all proportion to previous, more minor, incidents.[96] Whilst Lord Hoffman accepted that foreseeability was a factor to be considered in determining whether an incident fell into the 'ordinary' category, he resisted any assimilation between 'ordinariness' and 'foreseeability'.[97] He offered the opinion that the defendants in previous cases concerning vandalisation of oil tanks on their premises[98] should have been convicted of water pollution offences despite the apparent lack of foreseeability of the specific events which occurred. The inference,

---

[92] See 9.14.2 below sewerage undertaker's responsibilities.

[93] [1998] 1 All ER 481, per Lord Hoffman at p.490.

[94] See the discussion of 'acts of God' at 9.6.3 below.

[95] [1998] 1 All ER 481, per Lord Hoffman at p.491.

[96] See *National Rivers Authority* v *Wright Engineering Co Ltd* [1994] 4 All ER 281.

[97] See also [1998] 1 All ER 481, per Lord Clyde at p.494.

[98] *Impress (Worcester) Ltd* v *Rees* [1971] 2 All ER 357, and *National Rivers Authority* v *Wright Engineering Co Ltd* [1994] 4 All ER 281.

therefore, is that vandalism falls into the 'ordinary' category whether or not particular acts of vandalism are foreseeable.

Notwithstanding the rather gloomy conclusion that vandalism, at least in the area in which the facts arose, is a fact of 'ordinary' everyday life, Lord Hoffmann recognised, in his final point, that the distinction between ordinary and extraordinary events is one of fact and degree to which the justices must apply their common sense and knowledge of what happens in the area. Whilst the kind of vandalism which occurred in the facts of the case might be regarded as 'ordinary', given the circumstances of local hostility, it might be speculated whether a determined vandal, armed perhaps with metal cutting equipment to pierce a locked oil tank, would be considered 'extraordinary'. The implication of the final point is that, despite the extensive guidance offered, the question of causation remains a factual matter on which lower courts possess the capacity to reach differing views of the facts in the situations which confront them.[99]

### 9.6.3 Causation and Control

The *Empress Cars* case is of considerable importance in reaffirming the strict liability approach to causation, established in the *Alphacell* case, in relation to the water pollution offences. Persons who keep oil, or any other kind of polluting matter, on their land will be under a strict duty to prevent its escape into controlled waters, and the involvement of a third party or a natural event may not necessarily serve as a defence to a charge of causing the entry of polluting matter. In practical terms, the decision will be to make it much more difficult for defendants to escape prosecution by attributing the blame to a third party. Nonetheless, there remain a number of potentially problematic issues which were not directly addressed in the *Empress Cars* decision which are deserving of comment.

Most notable is the issue of the extent to which causation implies control. Previously, it had been stated that '"causes" in criminal provisions assumes some degree of dominance or control or some express or positive mandate from the person "causing"'.[100] In both the *Empress Cars* and *Alphacell* decisions this issue was not directly under consideration because the defendants were the owners of the respective premises and, therefore, assumed to have general control over the activities taking place within them. However, there are diverse situations where, for various reasons, the element of control may be lacking. These may arise because another person is actually in exclusive control of the operation which causes the pollution incident, or because the events take place outside the premises of the defendant or for other reasons.

---

[99] See *Environment Agency* v *Brock plc* [1998] Env LR 607 where it was found that a leakage in pipes was an 'ordinary' fact of life.
[100] *McLeod* v *Buchanan* [1940] 2 All ER 179, per Lord Wright at p.187.

One pertinent illustration, cited with apparent approval in *Alphacell*, was *Moses* v *Midland Railway Co*[101] where a court was obliged to consider whether a railway company had 'caused' creosote to enter a stream resulting in the death of fish.[102] The circumstances were that the railway company transported a tank wagon belonging to a private owner as part of a train. At the beginning of the journey the wagon was subjected to a careful examination but this failed to reveal a latent defect in one of the taps on the tank. Due to the defect, polluting creosote leaked from the tank until the leak was discovered and remedied. By then, however, creosote had found its way into a tributary of a salmon river and caused fish mortality. It was found that since the wagon was not owned by the railway company: 'they were in no way responsible for its design or maintenance; they exercised no control over the defective tap; and they had no knowledge or means of knowledge of the latent defect which caused the leak'.[103] The 'inevitable'[104] conclusion was that the railway company had not 'caused' the contaminating matter to flow into the river.

Another illustration of the need for control if causation is to be established arises where the offending entry or discharge arises from an activity which involves collaboration between more than one party. An example of this situation is to be found in *Welsh Water Authority* v *Williams Motors (Cwmdu) Ltd*[105] where pollution of a canal arose after a spillage from an oil delivery tanker during refilling operations at a garage. In response to proceedings against the owner of the garage for having caused the entry of the oil, it was contended that liability would only arise if the garage owner's activities had been the causative factor, but, on the facts, they were held not to be. The Court implicitly accepted that the spillage which arose from the actions of the driver of the delivery tanker whilst on the defendant's land, was insufficient to show liability on the part of the garage owner. Although the tanker driver was not charged with any offence, the implication of this decision must be that, the owner of the garage had no control over the operation which gave rise to the incident.

Although it is evident from the *Empress Cars* decision that the extent of a landowner's 'control' over activities taking place on his or her premises has been greatly extended, even to the extent of encompassing responsibility for unlawful acts of vandalism, there remains a difficulty in relation to collaborative activities. This is that there must come a point where an activity falls wholly outside the landowner's control and at which, applying a common sense test of causation, it becomes impossible to attribute the cause of pollution incident to him. Whether that point had been reached in the facts of the *Williams Motors* case is uncertain. If the garage owner had 'done nothing' in respect of the supervision of the oil

---

[101] (1915) 113 LT 451, and see *Alphacell Ltd* v *Woodward* [1972] 2 All ER 475, per Lord Wilberforce at p.479, per Lord Pearson at p.486 and per Lord Salmon at p.490.

[102] Contrary to s.5 of the Salmon Fisheries Act 1861, now see s.4(1) Salmon and Freshwater Fisheries Act 1975 discussed at 15.4.1 below.

[103] See *Alphacell Ltd* v *Woodward* [1972] 2 All ER 475, per Lord Salmon at p.490.

[104] [1972] 2 All ER 475, per Lord Wilberforce at p.479.

[105] (1988) *The Times*, 5 December 1988.

delivery then the first of Lord Hoffmann's points would not be satisfied. On the other hand, if the activity of operating a garage, and all the particular activities that this entails, satisfies the 'doing something' test he would be liable, though this would not exclude the possibility of liability on the part of the tanker driver. Even then, it might be asked whether the degree of incompetence apparently shown by the tanker driver could be categorised as 'extraordinary'.

Another aspect of causation which was not directly addressed in the *Empress Cars* case was the extremity of a natural event which will be required for it to be categorised as 'extraordinary' such that it would provide a defence to a water pollution prosecution. Previously, it had been suggested that an 'act of God'[106] may be held to break the chain of causation and amount to a distinct cause of an incident of pollution. Hence, in relation to the facts of the *Alphacell* case it was suggested that the destruction of the pumps by lightning or the flooding of the tank by a storm of altogether unexampled severity and duration might have relieved the defendant of liability.[107] However, the circumstances in which an event will amount to an act of God seem to be narrowly defined and relate only to those events which happen independently of human intervention, due to natural causes such as extreme storms or earthquakes, against which no reasonable amount of human prudence can be expected to provide.

Whilst their appears to be little authority on the meaning of 'act of God' as a defence to criminal proceedings the phrase has been used more commonly in civil proceedings where liability is sought to be avoided on the ground of extreme weather conditions. Hence, in *Nichols* v *Marsland*[108] the defence was allowed against liability for flood damage caused by heavy rainfall where this was greater and more violent than any within the memory of witnesses. However, this was questioned in *Greenock Corporation* v *Caledonian Railway*[109] where it was doubted whether an unprecedented amount of rainfall would be sufficient to amount to an act of God. Remarkably, given the observations in the *Alphacell* case, the defence was not accepted in one instance where it was alleged that a chemical leak had been caused by a lightning strike which caused a power surge and fractured a supply pipe containing the chemical, though, as a magistrates' court decision, this is not authoritative.[110]

An illuminating, though unsuccessful, attempt to plead the defence of act of God in criminal proceedings is to be found in *Southern Water Authority*

---

[106] An 'act of God' has been defined as 'circumstances which no human foresight can provide against, and of which human prudence is not bound to recognise the possibility', per Lord Westbury in *Tennent* v *Earl of Glasgow* (1864) 2 Macph 22 at p.26 to 7 and approved by the House of Lords in *Greenock Corporation* v *Caledonian Railway Co* [1917] AC 556.

[107] *Alphacell Ltd* v *Woodward* [1972] 2 All ER 475, per Lord Pearson at p.488; Lord Cross at p.489; and Lord Salmon at p.490. Similarly see Schiemann LJ in the Divisional Court in *Empress Car Company (Abertillery) Ltd* v *National Rivers Authority* [1997] Env LR 227, at p.229.

[108] (1876) 2 Ex D 1.

[109] [1917] AC 556, and see Barrett (1992).

[110] *National Rivers Authority* v *South West Water* (1993) unreported but see *ENDS Report* 224 (1993) p.46.

v *Pegrum and Pegrum*.[111] Here, the defendants were pig farmers, who managed slurry produced by the pigs by transferring it into a lagoon[112] from which it was normally emptied four or five times a year by contractors and spread on fields as manure. Rainwater which fell on farm buildings normally discharged into an underground drain, but the drain had become blocked allowing water to escape and flow into the lagoon. A crack had developed in the top of the lagoon and, after a period of four days during which the rainfall had been three times the average, the slurry flowed out through the crack, resulting in pollution of a nearby stream. The defendants were unaware that the rainwater had found its way into the lagoon, but they admitted that the lagoon was not regularly inspected, and that polluting matter had escaped from the lagoon the previous year. They were charged with causing polluting matter to enter a controlled water.[113]

Before the magistrates, the defendants were acquitted on the ground that, in order for them to be guilty of 'causing' pollution there had to be an unbroken chain of causation leading to the pollution of the stream. On the facts, the chain had been broken by an act of God, in the form of an exceptional ingress of rainwater, which was sufficiently strong as to be the sole cause of the pollution. On appeal, the High Court ruled that the case should be returned to the magistrates with a direction to convict. The farmers had in fact 'caused' the pollution, and the rainfall was not so exceptional as to amount to an act of God. A landowner who chooses to keep on his land matter capable of polluting is liable for the breakdown of a system for dealing with that matter if it is within his control and utilised for his purposes. The fact that the drain had become blocked was irrelevant, even if the blockage was not caused by the negligence of the farmers.[114] It was accepted that a heavy fall of rain could, in some circumstances, provide an act of God defence against a pollution offence, but the rainfall which had preceded the incident, though heavy, was not exceptional, and the main reason for the overflow was the blocked drain which could not be an act of God. In deciding whether an intervening factor, such as an alleged act of God, could serve as a defence, the crucial question was whether this was an activity outside the defendant's control and of such a powerful nature that the accused person's conduct was not a cause at all but was merely a part of the surrounding circumstances. In the situation that had arisen it was clear that this was not the case.

Alternatively, a wider scope for the effect of natural forces may be drawn from the outcome in *R v British Coal Corporation*[115] where the defendant decommissioned a mine and ceased pumping to remove water. Contrary to expectations, the rising water flowed through an old seam, where it became contaminated, and was discharged into a river. In respect of a

---

[111] (1989) 153 JP 581.

[112] On the containment of agricultural waste, generally see Control of Pollution (Silage, Slurry and Agricultural Fuel Oil) Regulations 1991 (SI 1991 No.324, as amended) and 13.3 below on precautionary regulations.

[113] Contrary to s.31(1) Control of Pollution Act 1974, see now s.85(1) Water Resources Act 1991.

[114] Citing *Alphacell Ltd v Woodward* [1972] 2 All ER 475 as authority for this.

[115] *ENDS Report* 227 (1993) p.42; (1994) *Water Law* 48 and see 9.17.3 below.

charge of causing polluting matter to enter the river, the defendant was held not guilty, amongst other reasons, because the discontinuation of pumping was found not to have directly caused the pollution. This was found to be the consequence of the naturally rising water level, ultimately due to rainfall, which was outside the control of the defendant. However, it must be noted that this decision predates the *Empress Cars* case and whether ordinary rainfall would now be regarded as falling into the category of 'extraordinary' events seems unlikely.

It may be concluded, therefore, that an 'act of God' defence is not likely to be successful in anything but the most extreme circumstances. However, the possibility remains that extreme weather or other natural conditions might be sufficient to place a pollution incident in the 'extraordinary' category, but what is required to establish this remains a matter of speculation.

### 9.6.4 General Implications of Strict Liability

It is evident from the leading cases that the offences involving the causing of an entry or discharge of polluting matter or effluent into controlled waters are the subject of strict liability.[116] The basic principle is that causing water pollution does not necessarily entail intention, recklessness, negligence, or any other kind of fault or blameworthiness to be established against the accused. Hence, it has been suggested that water pollution offences are 'prototypes of offences which are not criminal in any real sense, but are acts which in the public interest are prohibited under a penalty'.[117] It follows that a conviction of causing water pollution does not, or perhaps should not, carry the same moral stigma as other kinds of criminal offence.[118]

Nevertheless, the use of strict liability in environmental and regulatory offences is widespread.[119] From the pollution regulator's perspective it has the advantage that there is no need to discharge the often 'impossible' onus of proving that pollution was caused intentionally or negligently.[120] This seems to reflect the practical reality that, outside vandalism, relatively few instances arise where a person sets out purposefully to cause pollution, but rather that it is most commonly an unintended incidental consequence of various kinds of industrial and commercial activities. Consequently, requiring an intention to cause water pollution to be shown would have the consequence that few, if any convictions, for water pollution would ever be secured.

---

[116] Generally see Padfield (1995).

[117] *Alphacell Ltd* v *Woodward* [1972] 2 All ER 475 per Viscount Dilhorne at p.483 and per Lord Salmon at p.490-91. Contrast the view of Morland J that strict liability does not offend 'the concept of a just and fair legal system having regard to the magnitude of environmental pollution even though no due diligence defence was provided for' in *National Rivers Authority* v *Alfred McAlpine Homes East Ltd* [1994] Env LR198, at p.212.

[118] Generally see de Prez (2000a).

[119] Generally see Leigh (1982).

[120] *Alphacell Ltd* v *Woodward* [1972] 2 All ER 475 per Lord Salmon at p.491.

On the other hand, standard criticisms of strict liability are equally directed towards the offences of causing water pollution.[121] Because an intention to cause water pollution does not need to be established, there can be situations where a person who is exemplary in taking all reasonable precautions to protect environment is nonetheless found to be guilty of causing pollution.[122] Taking every precaution to avoid pollution, and to adhere to the highest standards of practice in the relevant industry, still provides no guarantee against an unforeseeable, if not 'extraordinary', contingency which gives rise to a pollution incident.[123] In such circumstances, a criminal conviction seems to be a harsh consequence, and may even serve as a disincentive to improvements in environmental performance, since no degree of improvement will ever provide and absolute guarantee against criminal liability. Although there may be other good reasons for improvement in environmental performance, such as reductions in the cost of anti-pollution insurance or improvement in environmental reputation, the possibility of non-intentional criminal liability can never be excluded. In short, strict liability fails to distinguish between different levels of moral culpability, though these matters may feature in the decision to prosecute[124] and in relation to the sentence which is imposed where a conviction is secured.[125] For example, in *CPC (UK) Ltd v National Rivers Authority*,[126] the defendant was found guilty of water pollution offences but given an absolute discharge in recognition of the fact that everything that reasonably could have been done to prevent pollution.

An alternative to strict liability in the water pollution context would be to allow for a due diligence defence whereby an offence would not be committed where the accused could show that due diligence had been exercised to avoid the entry or discharge of polluting matter or effluent into controlled waters.[127] A defence of this kind is provided for in relation to certain discharges made by sewerage undertakers[128] and, more comprehensively, in relation to waste management offences, where no offence concerning the deposit of waste is committed where the person charged is able to prove 'that he took all reasonable precautions and exercised all due diligence to avoid the commission of the offence'.[129]

---

[121] See Smith (1999) p.113 and MacDonald (1998).

[122] See, for example, *CPC (UK) Ltd v National Rivers Authority* [1995] Env LR 131, discussed at 9.6.1 above.

[123] See *ENDS Report* 265 (1997) p.43.

[124] See Environment Agency, *Enforcement and Prosecution Policy* (1998), discussed at 6.18.1 above.

[125] See 9.19 below on sentencing issues.

[126] [1995] Env LR 131 discussed at 9.6.1 above.

[127] On due diligence, generally see *Tesco Stores Ltd v Natrass* [1972] AC 153. See also, in the criminal context, Law Commission, proposed *Codification of the Criminal Law* (1989) clause 20(i) of which proposes that recklessness should be required in respect of any criminal offence unless otherwise provided for. See also the provision which is made for due diligence in relation to oil pollution offences, discussed in 12.4.9, 19.6.1 and Ch.19 generally.

[128] That is, where a sewerage undertaker could not reasonably have been expected to prevent certain discharges (under s.87(2)(c) Water Resources Act 1991) see 9.14 below.

[129] s.33(7) Environmental Protection Act 1990.

Also, due diligence is provided for as a defence in relation to water pollution offences in other jurisdictions.[130] However, a recent parliamentary proposal to introduce a defence of this kind in relation to water pollution offences was not successful.[131]

Perhaps because of this rather undiscriminating approach, there is some evidence that convictions for strict liability offences have, in the past, been treated dismissively by offenders as relatively inconsequential matters which should not be dwelt upon excessively or require significant changes to operational practice.[132] In the case of water pollution, it may be speculated that this perfunctory attitude is less prevalent than in other areas because of the increasing stigma that is attached to environmental crime and the objective of many company's to enhance their 'green' reputation.[133] Nevertheless, the past tendency to regard strict liability regulatory infringements as not 'genuinely' criminal offences is an unavoidable consequence of the formulation that has been adopted.

It has been suggested that securing convictions for strict liability offences has the relative simplicity that there is no need for a court to enquire into the motives of the offender or the surrounding circumstances insofar as they might indicate the degree of culpability associated with a particular pollution incident. However, this simplicity is illusory in the sense that many of the factors which, in relation to non-strict liability offences, would be considered for the purpose of establishing the intention to commit the wrongful act, and so the guilt of the accused, are deferred for consideration in relation to mitigation and sentencing.[134] As a consequence, the overall complexity and length of a trial for a water pollution offence may not be reduced as a consequence of the strict liability offence. It is merely that the balance between the issues which relate to the substantive finding of guilt and those which are relevant to the determination of sentence are shifted from the former to the latter.

Another contentious aspect of strict liability offences is that they frequently leave a very wide margin of discretion to regulatory authorities. The considerable discrepancy between the large numbers of pollution incidents and the relatively small number which actually lead to convictions is remarkable.[135] In theory, almost all the evidentially

---

[130] See Parpworth (1997) considering s.16 Clean Waters Act 1970 of New South Wales and allowing for a defence of due diligence, and see MacDonald (1998).

[131] See *Hansard, Parliamentary Debates, House of Lords*, Vol.561 Col.611 (14 February 1995) where it was proposed that s.85 Water Resources Act 1991 should be amended by the addition of the following words, 'it shall be a defence for a person charged with an offence under this section to prove that he took all reasonable precautions and exercised all due diligence to avoid commission of the offence'. A similar amendment was proposed in relation to s.4 Salmon and Freshwater Fisheries Act 1975, see 15.4.1 below on this.

[132] In relation to strict liability trading standards offences, see Croall (1988).

[133] In relation to this, see the discussion of publicisation of environmental performance, including pollution convictions, at 6.19 above.

[134] See, for example, the discussion of *R v Yorkshire Water Services Ltd* [1994] *Water Law* 175 and *The Times* 19th July 1994 discussed at 9.19.4 below.

[135] See 9.2 above for statistics on water pollution incidents.

substantiated water pollution incidents could result in convictions because of the operation of strict liability. The fact that they do not is a result of the enforcement and prosecution policy of the Agency which seeks to limit the use of criminal proceedings to situations where it is in the public interest to prosecute and a range of other criteria are satisfied.[136] Whilst no criticism is intended of the application of an enforcement policy to limit the pursuit of criminal proceedings to those situations where they are most usefully pursued, the unavoidable fact is that strict liability entrusts a regulatory authority with extremely broad discretion in the exercise of its prosecution powers and these powers are only narrowed by non-legislative restraint. The constitutional question to which this gives rise is whether this is an abdication of legislative responsibility in failing to specify in law the circumstances in which a broadly-formulated discretion to prosecute should actually be applied in practice.

## 9.7 Knowingly Permitting

The second limb of liability in respect of the principal water pollution offences,[137] is that they are all capable of commission where the accused 'knowingly permits' a proscribed activity. As has been noted, 'knowingly permitting' has been said to involve a failure to prevent pollution which must be accompanied by knowledge.[138] Hence, permitting pollution in this context involves an express or implied element of authority or responsibility over the situation giving rise to a pollution incident. This may not be present where a person lacks control over the circumstances giving rise to the incident, or simply fails to act to prevent polluting matter entering a watercourse where it is within his power to do so but he is under no duty to do so. Thus, in *High Wycombe Corporation* v *Thames Conservators,*[139] it was held that the defendants were not guilty of 'wilfully suffering' offensive matter to pass into a river by omission to do something which might have mitigated the evil. It was commented: 'If you permit a thing, not under compulsion, you do it wilfully'.[140]

A further aspect of 'knowingly permitting' the entry of polluting matter is the requirement of knowledge on the part of the accused. Thus in *Impress (Worcester) Ltd* v *Rees*[141] it was observed that the justices had dismissed, on a submission of no case to answer, an information alleging that the appellant had committed an offence of knowingly permitting pollution. The fact that the pollution at issue had been caused by an unknown trespasser, who had entered premises at night and opened an outlet on a fuel storage, was sufficient to place the circumstances outside of the

---

[136] See the discussion of Environment Agency, *Enforcement and Prosecution Policy* (1998) at 6.18 above.

[137] Under s.85 of the Water Resources Act 1991, see 9.3 above.

[138] *Alphacell Ltd* v *Woodward* [1972] 2 All ER 475 per Lord Wilberforce at p.479; and see *Ex parte Austin* (1880) 45 JP 302.

[139] (1898) 78 LT 463.

[140] *Ibid* p.465.

[141] [1971] 2 All ER 357 at p.358, though see the discussion of *Empress Car Co (Abertillery) Ltd* v *National Rivers Authority* [1998] 1 All E R 481 at 9.6.2 above.

knowledge of the owners of the tank. By contrast, in *Price* v *Cromack*[142] there was a strong hint in the judgment of Ashworth J that the behaviour of the defendant in allowing effluent to escape from storage lagoons would have supported a conviction for 'knowingly permitting' pollution. This, however, was not an offence with which the accused had been charged.[143] Whilst it has been noted that 'causing' and 'knowingly permitting' water pollution may no longer be regarded as separate offences,[144] these examples serve to emphasise the importance of prosecutions being supported by appropriate evidence depending upon which of the two is pursued.

Two significant practical issues that arise in relation to proceedings for 'knowingly permitting' water pollution relate to the problems of 'wilful ignorance' and delay in taking action to rectify a polluting emission. In respect of the former, it is apparent that courts will be unwilling to accept a 'turning a blind eye' defence where it is apparent from the circumstances that the defendant should reasonably have known about offending activities.[145]

The problem of delay, in relation to 'knowingly permitting', arises in relation to situations where a person is informed, or becomes aware, of an offending entry of polluting matter, or the discharge of effluent, but fails to take immediate or sufficiently swift action to rectify the situation. Essentially, the question which arises is as to the point where delay amounts to 'knowingly permitting'. This question was considered in *Schulmans Incorporated* v *National Rivers Authority*,[146] where an oil spillage occurred from a tank on the premises of the defendant, Schulmans Incorporated. The oil flowed into the drainage system on the premises and drained into a nearby controlled watercourse. It was not established at precisely what time the defendant became aware of the spillage, though it must have been at 7.30pm at the latest. The defendant arranged to have the drain cleared the following day, by which time the watercourse had become further contaminated by the oil. As a consequence of this delay, the defendant was prosecuted by the National Rivers Authority for knowingly permitting 'poisonous' matter to enter controlled waters,[147] and for knowingly permitting liquid matter injurious to fish 'to be put' into

---

[142] [1975] 2 All ER 113 at p.119.

[143] See also *Yorkshire West Riding Council* v *Homfirth Urban Sanitary Authority* [1894] 2 QB 842 at p.847, where it was said by Lindley LJ that, 'Prima facie I take it that the owner of a sewer which discharges itself into a river knowingly permits that discharge'.

[144] See 9.5 above.

[145] See *Kent County Council* v *Beaney* [1993] Env LR 225 where the Court found that there was ample evidence that the defendant knew, and therefore 'knowingly permitted, deposits of waste at his premises contrary to s.3(2) Control of Pollution Act 1974 (and now see s.33(1) Environmental Protection Act 1990). Similarly, see *Westminster City Council* v *Croyalgrange* [1986] 1 WLR 674 where wilful blindness to the obvious or failing to make enquiries to confirm suspicions was held to constitute knowledge. Similarly, see *R* v *Shorrock* [1993] 3 All ER 917 where similar reasoning was applied in relation to a public nuisance.

[146] (1991) unreported but see [1992] *Water Law* 72 and [1992] 1 Env LR D2.

[147] Under s.107(1)(a) Water Act 1989, now s.85(1) Water Resources Act 1991.

waters containing fish.[148] On appeal, the defendants argued that they had acted to have the drain cleared as soon as reasonably possible after becoming aware of the spillage, and had not therefore 'knowingly permitted' the water pollution. It was held that there was insufficient evidence to show that the defendants had 'permitted' the escape of the oil into the watercourse.

In reaching this conclusion, the Court observed that the manner in which the charges had been framed was 'wholly unsatisfactorily' in several respects. First, the basis for a prosecution would have been clearer if the charge had been for knowingly permitting 'polluting' matter to enter controlled waters, rather than the charge relating to 'poisonous' matter which had been brought,[149] and, on the second count, with permitting liquid matter 'to flow', rather than permitting liquid matter 'to be put' as the charge had been formulated.[150] Beyond that, in relation to the second offence, there was an absence of evidence to suggest that the concentration of fuel oil was such as would prove poisonous to fish, nor was there any evidence that the waters had, in fact, contained fish.

More specifically, in relation to the matter of 'knowingly permitting', it was stated that, for the prosecution to succeed, a sequence of factual questions had to be answered: first, that the defendants' manager had known, before the discharge had reached the controlled water, that the spillage of oil had occurred, that the drainage system discharged into a controlled water and that unless the drain was cleared, the oil would enter the controlled water; second, that the oil was draining into the water at a time when the defendants could be aware of it; third, that if the defendants could have been aware of the pollution during that period, they either knew of it or 'turned a blind eye' to it; and, finally, that they could have arranged for the cleaning of the drain on the day the discharge commenced but failed to do so.

On the facts which were actually established to the satisfaction of the Court, it was not found that the defendant had 'knowingly permitted' the matters which were alleged to constitute the offence. In particular, it was stated that 'the essential reason why neither conviction can be upheld, is that there was no evidence that [the defendants] could have prevented the escape of fuel oil sooner than they did'.

## 9.8 Poisonous, Noxious or Polluting Matter

The first, and perhaps most commonly prosecuted, of the principal offences concerning water pollution arises where a person causes or knowingly permits any poisonous, noxious or polluting matter or any solid waste matter to enter controlled waters.[151] Alongside the issues which have

---

[148] Under s.4(1) Salmon and Freshwater Fisheries Act 1975, and see 15.4.1 below on this.

[149] See 9.8 below on the meanings of these expressions.

[150] See 15.4.1 below on fishery offences.

[151] Under s.85(1) Water Resources Act 1991 and generally see Howarth (1993).

already been discussed, a particular difficulty in relation to this offence relates to the precise meaning of the phrase 'poisonous, noxious or polluting matter'. The phrase was first enacted into law under the Rivers Pollution Prevention Act 1876 which created an offence where any person caused to fall or flow or knowingly permitted to fall or flow or to be carried into any stream any poisonous, noxious, or polluting liquid proceeding from any factory or manufacturing process.[152] The meaning of 'poisonous, noxious or polluting', however, has never been statutorily defined but nevertheless was re-enacted into subsequent statutes, and its meaning has, therefore, to be discerned from the body of case law concerning its interpretation.

The difficulties in interpreting 'poisonous, noxious or polluting' have been recognised by several commentators. Hence, as it has been critically observed:

> the first and most obvious comment is that . . . [the Rivers Pollution Prevention Act 1876] does not define pollution. It is surely extraordinary that a statute, the ultimate consequences of which are penal, nowhere gives notice to those whom it may concern of the offence they are to avoid. Nor does it afford assistance to the judges who have to decide the cases under the Act.[153]

Further, it has been suggested that, 'the words "poisonous, noxious or polluting matter" are . . . emotive rather than scientific and must be approached with great caution'.[154]

However, the same commentators went on to offer the following suggestions as to the meanings of the words used:

> 'Poisonous' has a fairly definite meaning, though the same substances do not necessarily poison man, fish, aquatic flora and other aquatic fauna. But the poisonous character of an effluent must be affected by the amount of the poison and the volume of the dilutant. 'Polluting' presumably means that which pollutes or is capable of polluting and again must be interpreted in the context. A discharge of a very good effluent may well be incapable of polluting a large clean river, while the discharge of an effluent of the same size and quality into a brook near the top of a watershed may be capable of polluting, and may in fact pollute, the brook into which it is discharged to the extent of creating even a public nuisance, 'Noxious' in its dictionary meaning means no more than 'hurtful', or 'injurious' and appears to add nothing to the other adjectives. Thus there seems to be a good deal of scope for argument whether a given

---

[152] Rivers Pollution Prevention Act 1876 s.4.
[153] Taylor (1928) p.82.
[154] Newsom and Sherratt (1972) p.29.

discharge, taken by itself, is within the words of this part of the subsection.[155]

The suggestion that the words 'poisonous', 'noxious' and 'polluting' should be taken to have separate meanings was shared by the authors of *Lumley's Public Health Law* in expressing the view that: ' "poisonous" implies destruction of life, human or animal; "noxious" is lower in degree, and signifies some injury; "polluting" will include both the other qualities and also what is foul and offensive to the sense'.[156]

Arguably, it would have been superfluous for the draftsman to have used three distinct words if they did not have distinct meanings. However, the commentators referred to suppose that the differences between the three terms are simply the degrees of harmfulness, with 'poisonous' the most harmful of the three. This is a plausible construction from dictionary definitions, but it has been observed judicially that dictionary definitions are 'too vague for practical purposes' when seeking to define water pollution.[157]

Moreover, the 'degree of harm' approach to the interpretation of 'poisonous, noxious or polluting' contrasts with other legal contexts in which the expressions are used. The expressions 'poison' and 'noxious' have been afforded frequent consideration by the courts in the context of the Offences Against the Person Act 1861.[158] In *R v Cramp*[159] the accused was charged with administering a 'noxious thing', specifically oil of juniper, with attempt to procure a miscarriage. Field J said that, 'if the thing administered is a recognised poison the offence may be committed, though the quantity given is so small as to be incapable of doing harm', thereby placing a clear emphasis upon the intrinsic nature of the substance rather than the effect which it has when administered. However, he continued, 'what was the thing administered in the present case? So much oil of juniper. Was this proved to be noxious? It was, consequently it was a "noxious thing"'.[160] Hence, the defining characteristic of a 'noxious' thing is the effect of the substance in the quantity and manner in which it was administered, as opposed to a 'poison' which is deemed to be harmful irrespective of its actual effect:[161] 'there must be a distinction between a

---

[155] *Ibid* note 2 p.30, referring to former s.11(3) Rivers (Prevention of Pollution) Act 1951, as amended.

[156] Simes and Scholefield (1954) p.5158 note e.

[157] Per Cox J in *Cook v South West Water plc*, Exeter Crown Court, 15 April 1992, unreported, see [1992] *Water Law* 103 and see discussion at 3.18.5 above.

[158] In particular, see cases which have arisen under ss.23 and 58 Offences against the Person Act 1861. Section 23 concerns the unlawful and malicious administration of *any poison or other destructive or noxious thing*, so as thereby to endanger life or to inflict grievous bodily harm (emphasis added). Section 58 concerns the unlawful administration of *poison or other noxious thing* with intent to procure the miscarriage of any woman (emphasis added).

[159] (1880) 5 QBD 307.

[160] *Ibid* at pp.309-10.

[161] See also comments of Smith on *R v Marlow* [1965] Crim LR 35.

thing only noxious when given in excess, and a thing which is a recognised poison, and is known to be a thing noxious and pernicious in effect'.[162]

The contrast between 'poisons', as substances deemed to be harmful, and 'noxious' substances, which are determined by the effect in the circumstances at issue, has some counterparts in water pollution case law. Here, the contrast is between the nature of the offending emission and the effect that it has upon the receiving aquatic environment. In *R v Justices of Antrim*[163] mill owners were prosecuted for having caused 'deleterious or poisonous liquid' to flow from their works.[164] It was held that the time at which the character of the matter was to be ascertained was the instant it entered the river, and that the subsequent effect of the action of the river upon it was immaterial. Gibson J, speaking for the majority, said of the offence that it:

> forbids the doing of the specified act without reference to the intent of the offender, or the consequences of the act done. It applies to all rivers, large and small, irrespective of the volume of water they discharge. The object was no doubt to protect fish and river animals, but the section excludes from the Magistrates' consideration any question of the results of the prohibited act, which in case of several contributory riparian wrongdoers might involve a perplexing and uncertain enquiry. If the act would be criminal in fair weather when a river was low, it does not become innocent because rainfall causes a flood. To throw in lime or spurge is made absolutely unlawful, irrespective of effect.[165]

Clearly, the view being expressed here is that it is the intrinsic nature of the substance, rather than its effect upon the aquatic environment, in determining whether matter is a 'deleterious or poisonous' liquid.

In relation to the meaning of 'noxious' there are indications that this phrase should be interpreted in relation to the actual environmental impact of the substance rather than its intrinsically harmful nature. Thus, in *Attorney-General v Birmingham, Tame and Rea District Drainage Board*,[166] the drainage board was charged with having conveyed into a stream water 'not freed from ... noxious matter'.[167] It was stated 'it is impossible to conclude that there has been an offence against the prohibition unless that special purity and quality [of the watercourse] have been shewn to be deteriorated', and 'in judging the effect of their operations one must regard this stream as a whole, and that if, regarded as

---

[162] *R v Hennah* (1877) 13 Cox CC 547 per Cockburn CJ at p.549, and see also *R v Marcus* [1981] 1 WLR 774.
[163] (1906) 2 IR 298.
[164] Under s.80 5 & 6 Vict c106 (Ireland).
[165] (1906) 2 IR 298, at p.319.
[166] [1908] 2 Ch 551.
[167] Under s.17 Public Health Act 1875.

a whole, the water in the stream or watercourse has not been deteriorated, no offence has been or can be established'.[168]

A tentative inference which might be drawn from these cases is that 'poisonous' relates to the quality of an emission, whereas 'noxious' relates to the impact upon the receiving aquatic environment.[169] This might be a convenient way of distinguishing the two expressions, but it is far from clear that it is followed in other cases where, for the most part, any attempt clearly to distinguish between the meanings of 'poisonous', 'noxious' and 'polluting' seems to have been avoided.

Recent cases concerned with the interpretation of 'polluting' substances seem to demonstrate a rather different approach. The question as to what is a 'polluting' discharge was considered in *National Rivers Authority* v *Egger (UK) Ltd.*[170] Here, discharged effluent was found to have caused a highly turbid plume some 5 metres wide and 100 metres in extent from the defendants' premises. A sample of the discharge contained an excessive concentration of suspended solids and had a high biochemical oxygen demand indicating the seriously deoxygenating capacity of the effluent. The source of the discharge was contaminated surface water from the defendants' formaldehyde resin plant which was being pumped from a sump into the surface water sewer on the site without authorisation. The Company was found guilty of the offence of causing poisonous, noxious or polluting matter to enter controlled waters.[171] Significantly, it was conceded by the prosecution that the case did not concern poisonous or noxious matter, and that it was solely concerned with the meaning of 'polluting matter'. Accordingly, Bryant J offered some observations as to the meaning of the word 'polluting' in the context at issue. He took the view that the water pollution offence is primarily concerned with the nature of the material being discharged into the controlled water rather than the actual impact on the water itself:

> one looks at the nature of the discharge and one says, 'is that discharge capable of causing harm to a river, in the sense of causing damage to uses to which a river might be put?'. . . One looks at that test in relation, it seems to me, to a natural, unpolluted river, and if the discharge is capable of causing such harm, then the offence is made out; the material amounts to polluting matter. It is, in my view, wholly unnecessary to prove that damage was, in fact, caused.

Conceding the possibility of error in his analysis, Bryant J suggested in the alternative that, having regard to the state of the receiving water in the vicinity of the discharge, there was actual evidence of harm. In particular, the visible effects of the discharge for 100 metres downstream was sufficient to satisfy the definition of 'polluting matter', despite the fact that

---

[168] [1908] 2 Ch 551 per Kekewich J at p.556.

[169] See the discussion of emission and ambient standards at 1.4.5 above.

[170] Unreported, Newcastle Upon Tyne Crown Court, 17 June 1992, but see Howarth (1993) at p.184.

[171] Under s.107(1)(a) Water Act 1989, corresponding to s.85(1)(a) Water Resources Act 1991.

these effects had substantially disappeared within a distance of 150 metres. However, it is apparent from the judgment that the preferred basis for the decision lies with the identification of the matter having the *capacity* to cause harm to a hypothetical unpolluted river rather than any harm actually being caused.

This approach seems to have been preferred in the subsequent case of *R v Dovermoss Ltd*[172] where spring water used for water supply purposes was found to be contaminated with excess ammonia. The source of contamination was traced to two fields near to the source of supply on which animal slurry had been spread. Heavy rain resulted in the slurry being transmitted into the ground near to the spring and contaminating the water supply. One of the issues raised by these facts was the question whether the slurry concerned was actually 'polluting matter'. It was argued on behalf of the defendant that the prosecution had not proved any actual harm had been done to the receiving waters, and it was noted that the ammonia levels did not exceed maximum concentrations permitted under regulations which define acceptable quality for drinking water.[173] A key question was whether the existence of 'polluting matter' is determined by the intrinsic nature of the substance or the effect which it has when it enters the particular controlled waters. The Court held that it was unnecessary for the prosecution to prove that the substance had actually caused harm, it was sufficient that there was a likelihood or capability of causing harm to animal or plant life or those who use water, and this had been sufficiently established on the facts.

The overall conclusion must be that the precise meanings of the expressions 'poisonous', 'noxious' and 'polluting' may still be a matter of uncertainty. However, this difficulty has not prevented the words being fairly widely and contextually construed. In response to the question, 'poisonous, noxious or polluting' to whom, or to what? the answer has been offered that the formula 'is wide enough to include matter that is harmful to fauna, or possibly to flora, even if it is harmless to human beings'.[174] This view has certainly been endorsed by lower courts dealing with diverse water pollution cases, where numerous instances of food substances, such as milk and fruit juice, which would not normally be regarded as 'poisonous, noxious or polluting' to human beings, have been found to have a damaging effect upon the aquatic environment and held to come within the meaning of the phrase.[175]

---

[172] [1995] Env LR 258, and see the discussion at 9.4 above.

[173] Water Supply (Water Quality) Regulations 1989 (SI 1989 No.1147) and see 17.7.2 below.

[174] Garner (1975) p.17, see also Macrory (1985) p.22.

[175] See, *Severn-Trent River Authority* v *Express Foods Group Ltd* [1989] Crim LR 226 (milk processing waste), and *National Rivers Authority* v *Appletise Bottling; Northumbrian Water* v *Appletise Bottling* [1991] 3 LMELR 132. See also *ENDS Report* 232 (1994) p.3 and *ENDS Report* 246 (1995) p.43.

## 9.9  Trade and Sewage Effluent

Another of the most commonly charged of the principal offences concerning water pollution arises where a person causes or knowingly permits the discharge or trade or sewage effluent into controlled waters, or from land through a pipe into the sea outside the seaward limits of controlled waters.[176] In relation to this offence, the definitions of some key expressions are defined in the following manner. 'Effluent' means any liquid, including particles of matter and other substances in suspension in the liquid. 'Substance' includes micro-organisms and any natural or artificial substance or other matter, whether it is in solid or liquid form or in the form of a gas or vapour. 'Sewage effluent' is stated to *include* any effluent from the sewage disposal or sewerage works of a sewerage undertaker but does not include surface water, and 'surface water' includes water from roofs. The difficulty here is whether the use of the word 'includes' in the definition excludes other kinds of effluent such as sewage from vessels.[177] Similarly, 'trade effluent' *includes* any effluent which is discharged from premises used for carrying on any trade or industry, other than surface water and domestic sewage. For the purposes of this definition any premises wholly or mainly used (whether for profit or not) for agricultural purpose or for the purposes of fish farming or for scientific research or experiment are to be deemed to be premises used for carrying on a trade.[178]

Some aspects of these definitions require comment. First, the meanings of 'poisonous, noxious or polluting matter' and 'trade effluent or sewage effluent' are not mutually exclusive. That is, certain kinds of polluting emission are capable of being categorised as either of these and proceedings pursued accordingly if the other components of the relevant offence are present.[179] Second, the apparently 'activity-specific' character of the definitions of 'sewage effluent' and 'trade effluent' should be noted. The categorisation of effluent appears to be independent of its nature or quality and wholly determined by the kind of activity conducted at the premises from which it originates. Hence, in another legal context, it was argued in *Thames Water Authority* v *Blue and White Launderettes Ltd*[180] that effluent which was discharged from washing machines should not be classified as 'trade effluent' since it was indistinguishable in character from domestic waste water. However, it was held that the definition of 'trade premises' related to the purpose of the activity producing the effluent rather than the nature of the discharge. The effluent at issue, originating from commercial premises was, therefore, properly classified as trade effluent. Third, depending on how the use of 'includes' in the definitions of trade and sewage effluent is construed, it may follow that certain other kinds of 'effluent' may be excluded such as waste water

---

[176] s.85(3) Water Resources Act 1991.

[177] On effluent from vessels see 9.17.2 below.

[178] s.221(1) Water Resources Act 1991.

[179] See the discussion of *National Rivers Authority* v *Yorkshire Water Services Ltd* [1995] 1 All ER 225 at 9.14.3 below.

[180] [1980] WLR 700.

originating from domestic premises which does not appear to fall into either of the categories. Finally, a contrast between sewage and trade effluent should be noted, in that 'sewage effluent' is characterised as including effluent from a sewage disposal works whereas 'trade effluent' includes effluent from trade premises. The implication of this is that the classification of trade effluent is made, normally, at the point of discharge to sewer and before the effluent reaches a sewage treatment works, whereas other wastewater discharged to sewer does not become 'sewage effluent' until after it leaves a sewage treatment works. Again, however, the difficulty is whether characterisations of trade and sewage effluent, as *including* effluent of a particular origin, *excludes* similar effluent from elsewhere. Discharges to trade effluent to sewers are regulated under Part IV Water Industry Act 1991.[181]

### 9.10  Entry and Discharge

A potentially significant contrast is to be noted between the formulation of the first principle offence,[182] concerning poisonous, noxious or polluting matter, and the third offence,[183] relating to trade or sewage effluent. This is that the first offence concerns the 'entry' of polluting matter, whilst the third concerns the 'discharge' of effluent. The reason for the distinct forms of wording which have been used is not clear, and its significance has not been judicially considered,[184] but it seems to suggest a distinction between two kinds of emission into the aquatic environment. One tentative interpretation is that 'discharge' refers to a purposeful and perhaps ongoing emission, whereas 'entry' is more appropriately applied to situations where the emission is non-purposeful and isolated in character.

Notwithstanding the use of the contrasting terminology of 'entry' and 'discharge' the common feature of the first and third of the principal offences concerning water pollution is that an emission, of either kind, into controlled waters must be shown. Moreover, it is the entry of discharge which constitutes the offence, rather than the effect which it has on the receiving waters. This point is neatly illustrated by *National Rivers Authority v Biffa Waste Services Ltd*[185] which arose after vehicles were driven along a river bed causing mud and silt to be disturbed and transmitted downstream, allegedly resulting in damage to fish and plant life. On an appeal against an acquittal for causing the entry of polluting matter, it was held that the accused had not caused anything to enter the watercourse which was not already there. Whether pollution of controlled waters had occurred was disputed but, even supposing that it had, it is evident that the element of 'entry' of polluting matter is vital to the success of a prosecution. It follows, therefore, that there can be situations where

---

[181] See Ch.11 below on trade effluent discharges.

[182] Under s.85(1) Water Resources Act 1991.

[183] Under *ibid* s.85(3).

[184] Although see *Smeaton v Ilford Corporation* (1954) 1 Ch D 923, where Upjohn J considers the contrast between 'discharge' and 'escape' in a civil law context, at p.927.

[185] [1996] Env LR 227.

water pollution arises without any relevant 'entry' or 'discharge' and that no water pollution offence will be committed in such circumstances.[186]

Another practical problem arising in relation to the need to show an entry or discharge arises where diffuse kinds of water contaminant are at issue. The application of fertiliser or pesticides to agricultural land,[187] for example, enables contaminants to pass gradually into watercourses and groundwater by surface water run off or through percolation through soil. Whilst it is possible to identify a significant deterioration in the quality of the receiving waters as a result of this, it is almost impossible to identify any particular entry or discharge as the cause of the deterioration. Contaminants are likely to have entered the water by diverse routes from many different points of origin and applications of substances to land which may have taken place over a considerable period of time. Because of the nature of transmission of diffuse pollutants, and the absence of any distinct point of entry or discharge, the principal water pollution offences are of limited relevance to this kind of water quality problem.[188]

The national characterisation of 'discharges' as point sources of entry of effluent passing from pipes into controlled waters may, however, be contrasted with a wider interpretation of 'discharge' as the expression is used in European Community water law. In Community law, the need for a prior authorisation arises in relation to the discharge of specified substances which fall within the scope of the Dangerous Substances Directive.[189] A critical question was raised by a recent case, referred to the European Court of Justice by the Netherlands, concerned the precise scope of the term 'discharge' for these purposes.

In *Nederhoff*[190] the Dutch competent authority refused to grant authorisation, under national legislation enacted to give effect to the Dangerous Substances Directive, for the placing of fence posts treated with creosote, (containing a List I substance under the Directive) in a watercourse to support its banks. This decision was contested on the ground that the placing of the posts in the watercourse did not amount to a 'discharge' within the meaning of the Directive. However, the European Court ruled that the concept of a 'discharge' must be understood as referring to any act by which a dangerous substance under the Directive is directly or indirectly introduced into waters. Accordingly, the placing of the posts in the watercourse constituted a 'discharge' which was required to be authorised under the Directive.

---

[186] Although see s.90(1) Water Resources Act 1991, concerned with the removal of deposits from bed of inland freshwaters, is potentially relevant to situations of this kind, see 9.15 below.

[187] See 13.5 below on nitrate contamination of water.

[188] Generally, see Ch.13 on preventative approaches to water quality protection.

[189] Directive 76/464/EEC and see 5.4.1 above on this Directive.

[190] Case C-232/97 L *Nederhoff and Zonen* v *Dijkgraaf en Hoogheemraden van het Hoogheemraadschap Rijnland* [1999] ECR I-6385. See also Case C-231/97 *AML Van Rooij* v *Dagelijks Bestuur van het Waterschap de Dommel* ex parte Gebr van Aarle BV [1999] ECR I-6355. See also 5.4.1 above.

*Nederhoff* raises some quite significant issues when considered from a United Kingdom perspective, since it is not altogether clear how activities of the kind at issue would be dealt with under national law. The placing of creosote-treated fence posts in controlled waters might constitute an entry of a polluting matter which would require a discharge consent if it was not to constitute an offence. If this is correct, it is apparent that some rethinking of the scope of the 'discharge' consent system is necessary to ensure compliance with Community obligations in relation to dangerous substances entering waters by indirect means.

### 9.11 Prohibitions of Certain Discharges

The second and fourth of the principal offences concerning water pollution arise in relation to the contravention of prohibitions. Respectively, these relate to causing or knowingly permitting any matter, other than trade or sewage effluent, to enter controlled waters by being discharged from a drain or sewer;[191] and causing or knowingly permitting trade or sewage effluent to be discharged from a building or from fixed plant on to any land or into the water of a lake or pond which are not inland freshwaters.[192] In each case, the reference to contravention[193] of a prohibition refers to the power of the Environment Agency to prohibit certain discharges by notice or regulations by giving a person notice prohibiting him from making or continuing a discharge, or from making or continuing a discharge unless specified conditions are observed.[194] Similarly, a discharge will be in contravention of a prohibition if it contains any prescribed substance or a prescribed concentration or such a substance, or derives from a prescribed process or a process involving the use of prescribed substances exceeding specified amounts.[195]

A curious feature of prohibition notices is that, insofar as an offence is committed by contravention of a prohibition by permitting trade or sewage effluent to be discharged on to any land or into the waters of any lake or pond which are not freshwaters, this offence is only committed where the effluent is discharged from a building or from fixed plant.[196] It is not clear why the offence should be restricted to discharges from buildings or fixed plant since there may be many mobile sources of polluting effluent which might be equally damaging to the environment and equally deserving of control by the use of prohibitions.

One notable consequence of a discharge becoming the subject of a prohibition notice is that it may subsequently be possible for the Agency to impose a discharge consent on the discharge, even in circumstances where

---

[191] s.85(2) Water Resources Act 1991.
[192] *Ibid* s.85(4).
[193] Which is stated to include 'a failure to comply', *ibid* s.221(1).
[194] s.86(1) Water Resources Act 1991.
[195] *Ibid* s.86(2). See Environmental Protection (Prescribed Processes and Substances) Regulations 1991 (SI 1991 No.472) as amended.
[196] s.85(4) Water Resources Act 1991.

this would not normally be required.[197] Hence, if a person has caused or permitted effluent or other matter to be discharged in contravention of any prohibition, and a similar contravention is likely, the Agency may serve a consent upon the discharge subject to appropriate conditions.[198] This may be done even in circumstances where a discharge consent would not normally be required, for example, in relation to highway drains.[199] The effect of this would be that, if the discharge contravened the conditions of the imposed discharge consent, a separate principal water pollution offence, concerning contravention of the conditions of a consent, would be committed.[200]

Other matters concerning prohibition notices which may usefully be noted here are the comparisons and contrasts between such notices and various other powers which may be exercised by the Agency.[201] Specifically, interrelationships must be noted here between prohibition notices and the following: anti-pollution works and operations powers;[202] anti-pollution works notices;[203] and powers to impose consents without application.[204]

First, in respect of the powers of the Agency to conduct anti-pollution works, an initial contrast between these and prohibition notices may be drawn in respect of their respective scope. Offences in relation to the contravention of prohibition notices arise in relation to the discharge of effluent in four fairly distinct situations: from drains, from sewers, onto or into land and into discrete waters. By contrast, the anti-pollution works powers arise in any situation where polluting matter is likely to enter, or to be present in, or to have been present in controlled waters, though the powers must not be exercised to impede or prevent the making of any discharge in pursuance of a discharge consent.[205] Another contrast between prohibition notices and anti-pollution works powers concerns their respective purposes. Prohibition notices serve to control a continuing activity which, though otherwise lawful, may give rise to a water quality problem and these notices are potentially punitive in the sense that criminal proceedings may follow if the notice is contravened. By contrast, the anti-pollution works powers are primarily remedial in purpose in allowing the Agency to take action to prevent or remedy pollution or to restore the aquatic environment to its state before a pollution incident and to recover reasonably costs incurred in so doing.

---

[197] For example, in relation to highway drains which are normally subject to a special defence under s.89(5) Water Resources Act 1991, and see 9.17.5 below on this. See Ch.10 on discharge consents generally.

[198] para.6 Sch.10 Water Resources Act 1991, as inserted by para.183 Sch.22 Environment Act 1995.

[199] See 9.17.5 below on highway drains.

[200] Under s.85(6) Water Resources Act 1991, and see 9.11 below on this.

[201] See the discussion of the Groundwater Regulations 1998 (SI 1998 No.2746) at 13.6 below.

[202] Under s.161 Water Resources Act 1991, and see 13.2 below on anti-pollution works and operations.

[203] Under *ibid* s.161A-D, and see 13.2.2 below on works notices.

[204] Under *ibid* para.6 Sch.10, as amended.

[205] Under *ibid* s.161(2).

The second contrast is between prohibitions and anti-pollution works notices. A works notices may be served where polluting matter is likely to enter controlled waters or to be, or to have been, present in such waters. The notice will require the person upon whom it is served to carry out specified works or operations for the purpose of preventing the matter entering the waters, removing the matter from the waters or remedying the pollution, or restoring the waters to their former state. Again, a contrast may be drawn between prohibition notices and works notices in terms of their respective scope, with works notices being of broader application and serving a primarily remedial, rather than punitive, purpose though backed up by a criminal offence where there is failure to comply with a works notice.

The third contrast is between prohibition notices and the power of the Agency to impose discharge consents without application. In respect of this, as has been noted, a consequence of a discharge becoming the subject of a prohibition notice is that it becomes possible for the Agency to impose a discharge consent on the discharge. This may be done where a person has caused or permitted effluent or other matter to be discharged in contravention of any prohibition and a similar contravention is likely. Where a discharge consent is imposed in this situation, the Agency may incorporate into it such conditions as it may think fit and must publicise the consent and consider representations in such a manner as is prescribed.[206] Whilst the power of the Agency to impose a discharge consent is broader in scope than the power to serve a prohibition notice, the practical import of the two mechanisms is capable of being the same. This is particularly so, since the prohibition notice is capable of being made subject to conditions[207] which could be identical to those incorporated into an imposed discharge consent. Procedural contrasts may be drawn in terms of matters such as advertisements and consultation,[208] and possibly also in relation to matters such as variation, appeals and charges. Most remarkably, no provision appears to be made for the revocation or withdrawal of a prohibition notice before the expiry of its duration. However, the substantial effect of using the two distinct mechanisms is capable of being indistinguishable in practice where the conditions upon a prohibition notice are the same as those in an imposed consent.

## 9.12 Impeding the Flow of Waters

The fifth of the principal offences concerning water pollution is committed where a person causes or knowingly permits any matter whatever to enter

---

[206] para.6 Sch.10 Water Resources Act 1991, as amended, and Control of Pollution (Applications, Appeals and Registers) Regulations 1996 (SI 1996 No. 2971) and see 10.5.1 below on imposed consents.

[207] Under s.86(1)(b) Water Resources Act 1991.

[208] Advertisement and consultation requirements apply retrospectively in relation to imposed consents see Sch.1 Control of Pollution (Applications, Appeals and Registers) Regulations 1996 (SI 1996 No.2971) and see 10.5 and 10.5.1 below.

any inland freshwater so as to tend, either directly or in combination with other matter which he or another person causes or permits to enter those waters, to impede the proper flow of the waters in a manner leading, or likely to lead, to a substantial aggravation of pollution due to other causes or the consequences of such pollution.[209] It appears that this offence is not commonly the subject of proceedings, perhaps because of the rather restricted circumstances in which it would seem to be applicable and the evidential difficulties to which it gives rise. Its scope is limited, first, to inland freshwaters,[210] and, second, to flowing waters. Beyond that, the offence conceives of pollution resulting from the impediment to flow and substantial aggravation of pollution due to other causes, rather than pollution which results directly from the matter that is placed in the waters. This begs the questions, first, as to why the 'other causes', which are probably the real root of the problem, are not tackled directly by legal action; and, second, what sort of evidence is needed to establish that there has been, or is likely to be, 'substantial aggravation' of pollution resulting from other causes due to the impediment to flow. It must be concluded that the rationale of the offence is far from clearly indicated by the statutory wording that has been used. Conceivably, the purpose of the offence might be to provide an alternative means of controlling undesirable impediments to water flow, but this seems unlikely since restrictions upon impoundment and the placing of structures in watercourses are comprehensively provided for elsewhere.[211]

## 9.13 Contravention of Conditions of a Consent

The last of the principal offences concerning water pollution, relates to the contravention of the conditions of any consent given under Chapter II of Part III of the Act in relation to the principal offences. Hence, it is stated that, subject to the following provisions of the Chapter, a person who contravenes the conditions of any consent given for the purpose of s.85 will be guilty of an offence. In theory, this is capable of encompassing various kinds of consent such as those provided for in relation to the deposit of mine or quarry waste,[212] but, in practice, it is most likely to involve an infringement of a discharge consent.[213] Accordingly, contravention of a discharge consent is made an offence which is punishable to the same extent as the other principal offences.[214]

However, the manner in which contravention of the conditions of a discharge consent is made unlawful demonstrates some peculiarity. In particular, whilst the other principal offences are each made subject to the

---

[209] s.85(5) Water Resources Act 1991.

[210] See the definition of 'inland freshwaters' at 9.4 above.

[211] See, for example, s.25 Water Resources Act 1991, concerned with restrictions upon impounding, and Land Drainage Acts 1991 and 1994.

[212] Under s.89(4) Water Resources Act 1991, and see 9.17.4 above on consents relating to the removal of sediment or allowing vegetation to fall into waters (under s.90) and see 9.15 below.

[213] Under s.88(1)(a) and (2) and Sch.10 *ibid*, as amended. On discharge consents generally see Ch.10 below.

[214] On punishments generally see 9.19.2 below.

formula 'causes or knowingly permits',[215] these words do not appear to apply in relation to the contravention of consents and this omission seems to admit differing interpretations. On the one hand, the omission might mean that contravention of a consent is intended to be an offence, regardless of whether causation or anything of that kind is established, properly termed an 'absolute' offence.[216] On the other hand, the omission to specify the required state of mind of the accused means that the ordinary presumption applies and that an intention to commit the offence must be shown.[217]

The former line of argument, to the effect that a strict liability offence is involved, is to be found in commentary on *National Rivers Authority* v *Welsh Development Agency*.[218] In this case, the National Rivers Authority conceded that if the defendant had not caused the discharge, it could not be found guilty of breaching a condition in its consent. However, it was suggested that had the Authority not discontinued these proceedings it might have been possible for the defendant to have been found guilty of the contravention of the consent despite the absence of evidence of causation. In effect, the liability for contravention of a discharge consent may be stricter than that applicable to the other principal offences and is an absolute offence, rather than an offence of strict liability.

A similar line of reasoning was illustrated in *Taylor Woodrow Property Management Ltd* v *National Rivers Authority*,[219] where the defendant had obtained a discharge consent to allow discharge effluent from an industrial estate. The defendant held rights over the drains on the estate and granted rights for surface drainage in relation to individual units on the estate, whilst retaining control over the eventual discharge point. The discharge consent contained conditions including a prohibition over any discharge which contained traces of oil or grease. When a discharge was made which contained oil, the defendant was convicted of contravening the condition of the consent. It was reasoned that there was no need for it to be shown that the defendant caused or knowingly permitted the breach of the condition. The fact that the defendant took the benefit of the condition was sufficient for it to be bound by it and the offence was committed.

Despite reasoning endorsed in the *Taylor Woodrow* case, the courts are generally reluctant to interpret any statutory offence as incorporating strict liability unless there is clear wording to indicate that this is what is intended, and are even more unwilling to generate absolute offences. For that reason, it is thought that the above interpretation is unsatisfactory. Alternatively, the second argument, that the failure to use the words 'cause or knowingly permit' in relation to the contravention of conditions in a discharge consent, means that an appropriate *mens rea* or intention must be shown. This inference is almost equally unsatisfactory, because it means

---

[215] See 9.5 above on 'causes or knowingly permits'.
[216] See Smith (1999) p.112.
[217] See *ibid* p.104.
[218] [1993] Env LR 407, and see discussion in [1993] *Water Law* 52.
[219] [1995] Env LR 52.

that no offence of this kind will ever be committed unless intention is established on the part of the discharger. As has already been noted, if an intention to pollute had to be shown in relation to every offence of water pollution, then a great deal of water pollution would go unpunished.[220] The overall conclusion has to be that the statutory wording on this point is unsatisfactory and in need of clarification.

Another matter deserving comment in relation to the offence of contravening the conditions of a consent, is the use of the plural, 'conditions', rather than the singular. As a general principle of statutory interpretation, the plural would be construed to encompass the singular[221] so that, in this context, an offence will be committed if a single condition of a discharge consent was breached to the same extent as it would if the breach was of multiple conditions of the consent. Hence, the wording serves to clarify the point that only one offence is committed, in any single incident, however many individual conditions of a consent are breached. In effect this confirms the judicial interpretation of the previous law.[222]

In *Severn-Trent Water Authority* v *Express Foods Group Ltd*[223] the defendant operated a milk factory which was permitted to discharge trade effluent into an adjacent river by virtue of a discharge consent,[224] which was subject to several conditions. It was alleged that the defendant had made a number of unlawful discharges of milk processing waste into the river and, in relation to each discharge, there were a number of separate charges entered for the contravention of different conditions of the consent. The defendants pleaded guilty to one charge in respect of each discharge, but contested the others, arguing that only one offence was committed regardless of whether a single or multiple conditions were breached. It was held that the offence lay in the discharge of trade effluent contrary to the discharge consent. Accordingly, where a single offending discharge occurred, in which several conditions of a consent were breached, there could be only a single conviction, regardless of the number of distinct conditions contravened.

Clearly, the number of conditions of a consent which have been breached may serve as an indication of the seriousness of a particular incident, and should, therefore, be a significant consideration in sentencing,[225] but not a determinant of the number of offences that have been committed. It is also notable that the *Severn-Trent* ruling does not exclude the possibility that separate breaches of the same, or different, consent conditions at different times will, nevertheless, be punishable as separate offences.

---

[220] See the discussion of *Alphacell Ltd* v *Woodward* [1972] 2 All ER 475 at 9.6.1 above.

[221] s.6 Interpretation Act 1978.

[222] Contrast s.32(1) Control of Pollution Act 1974, which allowed for a defence where a 'discharge is made with the consent . . . of the water authority', and s.107(6) Water Act 1989, which established the present offence.

[223] (1989) 153 JP 126.

[224] Under ss.32(1) and 34 Control of Pollution Act 1974, now provided for under s.85(3) and Sch.10 Water Resources Act 1991.

[225] See 9.19 below on sentencing.

A final observation on the offence of contravening the conditions of a consent, is to note that discharge consents may incorporate various kinds of condition, not all of which need relate directly to the quality of the effluent that is discharged. Conditions in discharge consents are considered later in this work,[226] but it may be noted here that various kinds of conditions are provided for in relation to matters such as effluent monitoring, the keeping of records and the making of returns.[227] As a consequence of the offence arising in relation to *any* condition of a consent, a range of activities which need not necessarily involve any damage to the aquatic environment are, in principle, as heavily punishable as those offences that clearly do involve such harm.

## 9.14 Discharges into and from Public Sewers

Although, for the most part, the principal water pollution offences are formulated in general terms so as to avoid reference to individual substances or pollutants of particular origin, an exception to this is the relatively specific coverage of sewage effluent treatment and its associated obligations. As has been noted, the problem of poor water quality attributable to unsatisfactory sewage treatment is a significant one, as are the large number of pollution incidents relating to discharges from sewage treatment works.[228] In legal terms, however, the regulation of sewage treatment is complicated in that it spans the interface between two systems of control relating respectively to the protection of controlled waters and the operation of the sewerage system.

### 9.14 1 Trade Effluent Discharges to Sewers

The discharge of trade effluent into sewers vested in sewerage undertakers is subject to a distinct system of trade effluent consents and agreements, under Part IV of the Water Industry Act 1991, the breach of which, on the part of an industrial discharger, will amount to a criminal offence.[229] Insofar as a discharge to a sewer has no impact upon controlled waters, it will not involve a commission of any of the principal offences of water pollution that have been described.[230] However, there may be situations where a discharge of trade effluent which is made to a sewer passes through the sewer, and sewage treatment works, to be discharged into controlled waters and pollution of those waters results as a consequence. In such situations the two questions which arise are as to the respective criminal liability of the sewerage undertaker, from whose works the effluent has been discharged to controlled waters, and the industrial discharger responsible for the original discharge to the sewer. Basically,

---

[226] See Ch.10 below on discharge consents.

[227] Under para.3(4) Sch.10 Water Resources Act 1991, as amended.

[228] See 1.6.1 above on sewage and water quality and 9.2 above on water pollution incidents.

[229] See Ch.11 below on trade effluent consents.

[230] As previously noted, the definition of 'controlled waters' excludes public sewers or drains which drain into public sewers, see s.104(2) Water Resources Act 1991, and the discussion at 9.4 above.

the position is that the undertaker will not be liable where the pollution of controlled waters arises without fault on its part, whereas the industrial discharger will only be liable where the discharge to the sewer was made unlawfully.

For the purposes of the principal water pollution offences concerned with sewage effluent,[231] where any sewage effluent is discharged from any sewer[232] or works vested in a sewerage undertaker, and the undertaker did not cause or knowingly permit the discharge but was bound, either unconditionally or subject to conditions which were observed, to receive into the sewer or works matter included in the discharge, the undertaker will be deemed to have caused the discharge.[233] That is, a sewerage undertaker is bound to treat all trade effluent which is lawfully discharged to sewers and will have no defence where a failure to do so results in a breach of a sewage works' discharge consent. A slight modification of this duty arises where there is an agreement between sewerage undertakers that effluent which is discharged into a sewer by one sewerage undertaker is to be received and discharged into controlled waters by another. In that case the undertaker discharging to the sewer will be similarly deemed liable in relation to matter which it was bound to receive.[234]

The legal position of a sewerage undertaker in relation to lawful discharges to sewer contrasts with situations where the discharge to sewer is made unlawfully. Here it is provided that a sewerage undertaker will not be guilty of any of the principal water pollution offences by reason only of the fact that a discharge from a sewer or works vested in the undertaker contravenes conditions of a consent relating to the discharge if three requirements are satisfied. These are:

   (a) the contravention is attributable to a discharge which another person caused or permitted to be made into the sewer or works;
   (b) the undertaker was not bound to receive the discharge into the sewer or works or was bound to receive it there subject to conditions which were not observed; and
   (c) the undertaker could not reasonably have been expected to prevent the discharge into the sewer or works.[235]

On point (c), some contentious practical questions are raised as to the extent of the duty of a sewerage undertaker to do all that is reasonable to prevent an unlawful discharge. It might be enquired, for example, whether a failure by a sewerage undertaker to take enforcement proceedings[236] in relation to an intermittently offending discharger of trade effluent to sewer

---

[231] That is ss.85(3) and (4) Water Resources Act 1991, see 9.3 above.

[232] On discharges from sewers directly into controlled waters see *British Waterways Board* v *Severn Trent Water Ltd* [2001] EWCA Civ 276, Court of Appeal, 2 March 2001.

[233] s.87(1A) Water Resources Act 1991, as added by s.46(1) Competition and Service (Utilities) Act 1992.

[234] s.87(1B)-(1C) Water Resources Act 1991, as added by s.46(1) Competition and Service (Utilities) Act 1992.

[235] s.87(2) Water Resources Act 1991.

[236] Under s.111 or 118 Water Industry Act 1991, and see 11.11.3 below.

would amount to a failure to take 'reasonable' action to prevent a discharge ultimately resulting in an unlawful discharge into controlled waters. More generally, the apparent limitation of this defence to situations where an undertaker 'contravenes the conditions of a discharge consent' has been broadly construed to allow the defence to be used in a situation where the charge against the undertaker is brought as another principal water pollution offence.[237]

### 9.14.2 Effluent entering Controlled Waters

The position of the industrial discharger to sewer, where pollution of controlled waters from a sewage treatment works arises, is basically dependent upon whether the discharge to sewer was made lawfully. Hence, an industrial discharger will not be guilty of any of the principal water pollution offences in respect of a discharge which he caused or permitted to be made into a sewer or works vested in a sewerage undertaker if the undertaker was bound to receive the discharge there either unconditionally or subject to conditions which were observed.[238] It follows that, in these circumstances, a trade effluent consent or agreement will provide not only a defence to the trade effluent offences under the Water Industry Act 1991,[239] but also a defence to the principal offences of polluting controlled waters under the Water Resources Act 1991. The converse of this is also true, in that an unlawful discharge of trade effluent to a sewer which also leads to a polluting discharge into controlled waters is capable of constituting an offence under both Acts.

An example of a pollution incident giving rise to multiple convictions is to be found in *National Rivers Authority* v *Hickson & Welch Ltd*[240] where there was a spillage of a large quantity of nitrotoluene at the defendant's industrial premises. The chemical passed into the sewerage system at the premises and was transmitted by sewers to a sewerage treatment works, operated by a sewerage undertaker, Yorkshire Water Services Ltd, resulting in the contamination of settlement tanks. The contamination severely reduced the capacity of the sewage treatment works to deal with effluent and, as a consequence of this, discharges to controlled waters breached the discharge consent for the treatment works.[241] As a result, distinct legal proceedings were pursued by the sewerage undertaker and

---

[237] See the discussion of *National Rivers Authority* v *Yorkshire Water Services Ltd* [1995] 1 All ER 225 at 9.14.3 below.

[238] s.87(3) Water Resources Act 1991.

[239] See 11.11 below on trade effluent offences.

[240] Unreported (1996) but see *ENDS Report* 252 (1996) p.46 and *ENDS Report* 253 (1996) p.50. For another example of 'double' prosecutions see *National Rivers Authority* v *Premier Plating Ltd*, unreported but see *ENDS Report* 251 (1995) p.42. Also see *National Rivers Authority* v *Appletise Bottling; Northumbrian Water* v *Appletise Bottling* [1991] 3 LMELR 132, where a spillage of concentrated apple juice at the defendant's premises passed into a sewer and was transmitted into controlled waters. The defendant was convicted under s.107(1)(a) Water Act 1989 (corresponding to s.85(1) Water Resources Act 1995) for the entry of polluting matter into controlled waters and under s.27 Public Health Act 1936 (corresponding to s.111 Water Industry Act 1991) for the unconsented discharge to the sewer.

[241] See *ENDS Report* 230 (1994) p.9.

the Environment Agency. The undertaker brought proceedings against the defendant for the discharge of matter into a public sewer likely to affect prejudicially the treatment and disposal of its contents,[242] and this resulted in a conviction and a fine of £35,000. The Agency brought proceedings against the defendant for the offence of causing polluting matter to enter controlled waters,[243] and this resulted in a conviction and a fine of £2,500.

### 9.14.3  The Yorkshire Water Case

An authoritative and extensive discussion of the legal position with regard to discharges from sewage treatment works is provided in the House of Lords decision in *National Rivers Authority* v *Yorkshire Water Services Ltd.*[244] The situation which gave rise to the proceedings was that a sewerage undertaker was authorised to discharge treated sewage effluent from its treatment works into controlled waters subject to a discharge consent which imposed various conditions including a stipulation as to the composition of the effluent discharged. The undertaker granted various consents to industrial customers allowing them to discharge effluent into its sewers subject to particular conditions including a prohibition upon the discharge of a specified substance, iso-octanol, which was recognised to be harmful to fish life. During the night an unknown industrial discharger made a discharge of iso-octanol into a sewer from where it passed through the undertaker's treatment works and was discharged into controlled waters. Once the unlawful discharge had been made into the sewer it was inevitable, because of the gravitational flow of the effluent, that the substance would enter the controlled waters.

The sewerage undertaker was proceeded against by the National Rivers Authority for the offence of causing poisonous, noxious or polluting matter to enter controlled waters.[245] Significantly, it must be noted, the charge was *not* brought for the offence of contravening a condition of discharge consent.[246] In the appeal to the House of Lords, two main points were at issue: first, whether the sewerage undertaker had 'caused' the entry of the polluting matter into controlled waters; and, second, whether the special defence for sewerage undertakers,[247] was applicable in relation to the offence of causing the entry of polluting matter, as opposed to contravening the conditions of a discharge consent.

With regard to the question of causation, following *Alphacell Ltd* v *Woodward*,[248] it was held that, though the undertaker was not responsible for the presence of the iso-octanol in the effluent discharged into the controlled waters, by establishing and operating a system for gathering

---

[242] Under s.111(1)(a) Water Industry Act 1991.

[243] Under s.85(1) Water Resources Act 1991.

[244] [1995] 1 All ER 225.

[245] Under s.107(1)(a) Water Act 1989, corresponding to s.85(1) Water Resources Act 1991.

[246] Under s.107(6) Water Act 1989, corresponding to s.85(6) Water Resources Act 1991.

[247] Under s.108(7) Water Act 1989, corresponding to s.87(2) Water Resources At 1991.

[248] [1972] 2 All ER 475, and see discussion at 9.6.1 above.

effluent into its sewers and treatment works, it had caused the poisonous, noxious or polluting matter to enter controlled waters. Accordingly, it would have been guilty of the offence of causing the entry of polluting matter into controlled waters but for the outcome on the second point.

With regard to the special defence for sewerage undertakers, it was held that, despite the formulation of the charge in terms of causing the entry of polluting matter into controlled waters, the undertaker was entitled to rely on this defence. Since the entry of the substance into controlled waters was attributable to a discharge which another person made into the sewer, which the undertaker was not bound to receive and could not reasonably have been expected to prevent entering the sewer or treatment works, the defence was established. Most significantly, the defence was not limited to a situation where an undertaker contravened a condition of a discharge consent, and was equally available where the charge was formulated in terms of causing the entry of polluting matter.

Following the *Yorkshire Water Services* case, further consideration has been given as to causality in relation to the operation of sewerage systems in *Attorney-General's Reference (No 1 of 1994)*.[249] This Reference confirmed that where a party has taken on the responsibility of running a sewerage system and failed to maintain the system properly, that was sufficient to justify a finding that the party was guilty of causing pollution of controlled waters. Specifically, it was affirmed that the offence of causing pollution could be committed by more than one person where separate acts contributed to polluting matter entering controlled waters. Where a sewerage undertaker defectively conducts the business of receiving sewage for treatment, so that controlled waters are polluted, this would comprise a chain of operations sufficient to be a 'cause' of a the water pollution offence. Likewise, the failure to maintain a sewerage system in proper order may be sufficient to justify a finding that the undertaker caused pollution of controlled waters.

### 9.15 Unauthorised Deposits and Vegetation in Rivers

Alongside the principal offences of water pollution, miscellaneous offences relating to disturbances of watercourses and the clearing of vegetation are also provided for under Chapter II of Part III of the Water Resources Act 1991. The first of these is that a person will be guilty of an offence if, without the consent of the Agency, he removes from any part of the bottom, channel or bed of any inland freshwaters a deposit accumulated by reason of any dam, weir or sluice holding back the waters, and does so causing the deposit to be carried away in suspension in the waters.[250] This offence is specifically stated not to apply to anything done in the exercise of any power conferred under or by any enactment relating to land drainage, flood prevention or navigation.[251] It is evident, however,

---

[249] *Attorney-General's Reference (No.1 of 1994)* [1995] 2 All ER 1007.
[250] s.90(1) Water Resources Act 1991.
[251] *Ibid* s.90(4), and see, for example, powers available under Land Drainage Act 1991.

that the offence is of quite narrow compass in that it is only capable of arising in relation to fairly specifically defined activities involving the removal of sediment or debris behind water impounding structures. Where such works are undertaken it will be open to the undertaker to obtain a consent for the activities from the Agency incorporating appropriate conditions,[252] and, providing the work is undertaken in accordance with the consent, no offence will be committed. Explicit provision has recently been made in relation to the procedure for applying for consents for this purpose,[253] requiring applications to be made on a form provided by the Agency, to be advertised in accordance with regulations and providing for related matters.[254]

The second offence arises where a person, without the consent of the Agency, causes or permits a substantial amount of vegetation to be cut or uprooted in any inland freshwaters, or to be cut or uprooted so near to any such waters that it falls into them, and fails to take all reasonable steps to remove the vegetation from those waters.[255] Again, this relates to rather specific kind of operation, and consent may be given by the Agency subject to appropriate conditions.[256] Significantly, the offences relating to disturbances of watercourses and the clearing of vegetation are less severely punishable than the principal water pollution offences, and a person found guilty of either of these offences will be liable, on summary conviction, to a fine not exceeding level 4 on the standard scale, presently £2,500.[257]

However, another possibility is that a person actually obtains a consent for deposit removal or vegetation cutting operations and then proceeds to act in breach of any conditions to which the consent is subject. Strangely, such a breach of condition of the consent would seem to fall within the principal water pollution offence arising in relation to contravention of the conditions of a consent.[258] Since, alongside discharge consents, the prohibition upon contravention of consent conditions applies to *any* consent granted for the purpose of Chapter II of Part III of the Water Resources Act 1991, that is, including deposit removal or vegetation cutting consents. The anomalous consequence of this is appears to be that breach of these consents is more severely punishable than the offences which would be committed if no such consents were obtained.

Another significant recent innovation, under the Environment Act 1995, is the provision for 'enforcement notices'[259] in relation to the contravention of 'relevant consents', which encompass consents granted in relation to the

---

[252] Under s.90(5) Water Resources Act 1991.

[253] The same procedure is applicable in relation to consents relating to the offence concerning vegetation in rivers, under s.90(2) Water Resources Act 1991, and in relation to consents for the deposit of mine or quarry refuse, under s.89(1) and (4), and see 9.15 and 9.17.4 below.

[254] s.90A Water Resources Act 1991, inserted by para.142 Sch.22 Environment Act 1995.

[255] *Ibid* s.90(2).

[256] *Ibid* s.90(5).

[257] *Ibid* s.90(3), and contrast the punishments of the principal offences discussed in 9.19.2 below.

[258] Under *ibid* s.85(6), and see the discussion of this at 9.13 above.

[259] See 10.11.1 below on enforcement notices.

above offences.[260] Hence, if the Agency is of the opinion that the holder of any consent is contravening condition of a consent, or is likely to contravene any such condition, it may serve on him an enforcement notice which specifies the matter constituting the contravention, the steps which must be taken to remedy it and the period within such steps must be taken.[261] Failure to comply with a requirement of an enforcement notice will be an offence which is punishable to the same extent as the principal water pollution offences,[262] and where proceedings of this kind would be an ineffectual remedy the Agency may bring proceedings in the High Court for the purpose of securing compliance.[263] The application of enforcement notices in relation to the contravention of discharge consents is considered elsewhere in this work,[264] but it may be observed here that it is remarkable that the use of enforcement notices in relation to the relatively less serious offences considered in this section should be backed by the same levels of sanction as apply to discharge consents.

## 9.16 Authorised Discharges

The principal water pollution offences are subject to two kinds of statutory defence. The first of these relates to a number of activities which may be authorised under diverse environmental legislation, and the second provides defences in a range of specific situations or for particular kinds of substance.

In relation to authorised discharges, a person will not be guilty of any principal water pollution offence in respect of the entry of matter into any waters or any discharge if the entry occurs or the discharge is made under and in accordance with, or as a result of any act or omission under and in accordance with any one of seven kinds of authorisation.[265] These are listed as follows:

(a) a consent provided under Chapter II of Part III of the Water Resources Act 1991;[266]
(b) an authorisation for a prescribed process designated for central control granted under Part I of the Environmental Protection Act 1990;[267]

---

[260] s.90B Water Resources Act 1991, inserted by para.142 Sch.22 Environment Act 1995, and see Payne (1997).

[261] s.90B(2) Water Resources Act 1991, as amended.

[262] s.90B(3) Water Resources Act 1991, as amended, and on the penalties for the principal water pollution offences see s.85(6) and the discussion of this at 9.19.2 below.

[263] *Ibid* s.90B(4), as amended.

[264] See 10.11.1 below.

[265] s.88(1) Water Resources Act 1991.

[266] Primarily relating to discharge consents, discussed at Ch.10 below, though also encompassing consents for the purposes of s.90 Water Resources Act 1991, see 9.15 above.

[267] See 12.3 below on licences for prescribed processes. Note that an amendment is made under Reg.39 and Schedule 10 of the Pollution Prevention and Control (England and Wales) Regulations 2000 (SI 2000 No.1973) to include permits granted under the Pollution Prevention and Control Act 1999, and see 12.3-6 below.

(c) a waste management licence[268] or a disposal licence;[269]

(d) a licence granted under Part II of the Food and Environment Protection Act 1985;[270]

(e) s.163 of the Water Resources Act 1991 or s.165 of the Water Industry Act 1991;[271]

(f) any local statutory provision or statutory order which expressly confers power to discharge effluent into water; or

(g) any prescribed enactment.[272]

The first of these, concerned with discharge consents, is most commonly encountered in practice, and the legal regime surrounding discharge consents[273] is considered in detail in Chapter 10 below alongside other kinds of environmental licence which may be relevant for the purpose of providing a defence to a principal water pollution offence.

### 9.17 Miscellaneous Defences

Apart from the authorised discharges, five other defences are explicitly provided for in relation to the principal water pollution offences under miscellaneous circumstances.[274]

### 9.17.1 Emergencies

The first of miscellaneous defences provides that a person will not be guilty of any of the principal offences in respect of an entry of any matter into any waters or any discharge in certain specified circumstances relating to emergencies. These circumstances are as follows:

(a) the entry or discharge is made in an emergency to avoid danger to life or health;

(b) all reasonably practicable steps are taken to minimise the extent of the entry or discharge and its polluting effects; and

(c) particulars of the entry or discharge are furnished to the Agency as soon as reasonably practicable.[275]

The meaning of 'emergency' is not defined for these purposes, but it has been suggested, in another environmental context, that it should be understood as meaning 'a state of things unexpectedly arising and urgently demanding immediate attention' and that the onus of establishing that, on

---

[268] Granted under Part II of the Environmental Protection Act 1990, see 12.2.6 below.

[269] Issued under Part I of the Control of Pollution Act 1974. However, a disposal licence will not serve to authorise any discharge of trade or sewage effluent, under s.85(2)-(4) Water Resources Act 1991, or any act or omission which results in such an entry or discharge (s.88(3) Water Resources Act 1991).

[270] Authorising the deposit of waste at sea, and see 19.20.1 below.

[271] Concerned with discharges for works purposes.

[272] s.88(1) Water Resources Act 1991.

[273] Provided for under Sch.10 Water Resources Act 1991 and subject to s.91 on appeals (s.88(2)).

[274] s.89 Water Resources Act 1991.

[275] s.89(1) Water Resources Act 1991.

the balance of probabilities, this exists rests upon the defence.[276] It is unlikely, therefore, that a person who is actively responsible for circumstances which are claimed to constitute an emergency could claim the benefit of this defence.[277] It may be significant that although action may be taken in an emergency 'to avoid danger to life or health' there is no indication that action may be taken to avoid harm to the environment. However, the wording might be construed to encompass harm to the living constituents of the water environment.[278]

### 9.17.2 Discharges from Vessels

The second miscellaneous defence to the principal offences of water pollution[279] is that a person will not be guilty of these offences by reason of causing or permitting any discharge of trade or sewage effluent from a vessel.[280] This defence seems obscure given the generally activity-specific definitions of trade and sewage effluent.[281] If, for most purposes, these effluents are defined as *including* effluents originating from trade premises or sewage treatment works, then a discharge from a vessel would not normally constitute effluent of this kind. The only explanations for the defence would seem to be that there are unlikely circumstances where a vessel is capable of constituting trade premises, perhaps where a processing operation of some kind is conducted on board, or as a sewage treatment works or that the definitions of trade or sewage effluent must, despite their wording, be construed broadly to include effluent from vessels.

The extent of the defence concerning trade or sewage effluent discharges from vessels is to be noted though: it will not provide a defence in relation to a charge of causing or knowingly permitting the entry of polluting matter, though if the actual offending 'polluting matter' at issue in a particular case was, in fact, effluent it might be argued that the defence should be broadly construed.[282] In relation to pollution from vessels generally, it may be noted that the byelaw-making powers of the Agency, allowing it to make byelaws for 'purposes connected with the carrying out of its functions', encompass the making of byelaws requiring the provision

---

[276] *Waste Incineration Services Ltd* v *Dudley Metropolitan Borough Council* [1992] Env LR 29.

[277] Generally, see *Perka* v *The Queen* [1985] 13 DLR (4th) 1.

[278] Although contrast the discussion of s.139(3) Merchant Shipping Act 1995 at 19.11.1D below.

[279] Although, the application of prohibitions, under s.85(2) and (4) Water Resources Act 1991, to vessels is excluded by s.86(3), and, in practice, the offence of causing or knowingly permitting the entry of polluting matter, under s.85(1), is the only principal water pollution offence likely to be committed in relation to a vessel.

[280] s.89(2) Water Resources Act 1991. For these purposes 'vessel' is defined to include a hovercraft within the meaning of the Hovercraft Act 1968 (s.221(1) Water Resources Act 1991). See Ch.19 below on the Merchant Shipping Act 1995 and discharges from ships generally.

[281] See 9.9 above on trade and sewage effluent.

[282] See, by analogy, the discussion of the special defence for sewerage undertakers in *National Rivers Authority* v *Yorkshire Water Services Ltd* [1995] 1 All ER 225 discussed at 9.14.3 above.

of sanitary appliances on vessels for the purpose of preventing pollution of controlled waters.[283]

Reference may also be made to the discussion of the *Sea Empress* case,[284] which involved a massive emission of oil into controlled waters from a tanker that had been grounded and gave rise to an important Court of Appeal ruling as to sentencing practice in respect of water pollution offences. A postscript to the ruling concerns the future of the water pollution offences in relation to coastal waters where discharges from vessels are involved. Following the report by Lord Donaldson, *Review of Salvage and Intervention and their Command and Control,*[285] it was announced that a review would be undertaken of the system of prosecutions for offences relating to the entry into the sea of polluting matter following shipping casualties. The review, which is ongoing at the time of writing, is considering whether the system for prosecution of such offences reflects the public interest of having appropriate sanctions available under the criminal law in cases of marine casualties without discouraging appropriate prevention, salvage and clean up operations. Amongst other things, the review focuses upon the offences under Part III of the Water Resources Act 1991 and the final outcome in the *Sea Empress* case.[286]

What lies behind the initiation of the review are observations in the Donaldson report that there are some significant inconsistencies between the 1991 Act and relevant provisions under the Merchant Shipping Act 1995 concerning the actions that salvors or harbour masters may be obliged to take in relation to shipping casualties. One example is the possible need to jettison oil to increase the buoyancy of a grounded vessel and to prevent her breaking up. The action of discharging the oil might constitute a water pollution offence under the 1991 Act, but might also be environmentally beneficial if it prevented a greater quantity of oil being discharged. Moreover, the possibility of a direction being given under the 1995 Act to require a discharge of oil from a foundering vessel[287] would mean that a salvor would be put in an impossible situation since he would be committing an offence if he disobeyed the direction and would be committing an offence if he obeyed it.

One passage from the Donaldson Report is particularly pertinent:

---

[283] s.210 Water Resources Act 1991, and specifically powers under Sch.25 paras.2(4)(c), 3(3)(c) and 4(1)(b). For these purposes, 'sanitary appliances' means any appliance which, not being a sink, bath or shower bath, is designed to permit polluting matter to pass into the water where the vessel is situation and is prescribed for those purposes (Para.4 Sch.25 Water Resources Act 1991).

[284] *Environment Agency v Milford Haven Port Authority and Andrews (The Sea Empress)* [1999] 1 Lloyd's Rep 673, High Court and *R v Milford Haven Port Authority*, [2000] Env LR 632 Court of Appeal, discussed at 9.19.3 below.

[285] Donaldson (1999) and see 19.11.1 below on the *Donaldson Report*.

[286] See DETR Press Release No.1220, *Hill announces terms for sea pollution review*, 16 December 1999.

[287] Under s.139 Merchant Shipping Act 1995 and see 19.11.1D below on this.

In studying this problem it has occurred to us to wonder whether the legislative purpose behind the Water Resources Act was ever that its provisions should apply to pollution from a maritime source, a situation which is amply covered by the internationally recognised MARPOL standards and legislation.[288] Is it not more likely that the Act was intended to apply exclusively to pollution from a land based source which affected controlled waters, e.g. sewage outfalls or the escape of a land based pollutant which ended up on controlled waters?[289]

The possibility of amendment of the law to remove oil pollution from shipping casualties from the ambit of the Water Resources Act 1991 is certainly a matter under consideration in the review.

### 9.17.3 Water from Abandoned Mines

#### 9.17.3A The Abandoned Mines Defence

Although it has recently been the subject of significant amendment, the third miscellaneous defence is that a person will not be guilty of a principal water pollution offence by reason only of permitting water from an abandoned mine[290] or part of an abandoned mine to enter controlled waters.[291] Logically, it is most likely that this defence would be used in relation to proceedings under a charge of knowingly *permitting* poisonous, noxious or polluting matter to enter controlled waters.[292] This is because it is unlikely that an abandoned mine, as opposed to an operational mine, would constitute 'trade' premises, and consequently effluent originating from it would, therefore, be unlikely to fall within the definition of 'trade effluent' for the purposes of the offence concerned with the discharge of such effluent.[293] Significantly, the defence is limited to 'permitting' the entry of water from mines to enter controlled waters. It would not, therefore, be available in relation to a charge of 'causing'[294] the entry of minewater, or where a charge was brought for discharging such water from a drain or sewer in contravention of a prohibition.[295] Whether 'abandonment' is sufficient to amount to 'causing' for the purpose of the principal water pollution offences has, in the past, been a debatable point. However, it is arguable that the recent decision in the *Empress Cars*

---

[288] See Ch.19 below on international legislation concerning oil pollution.

[289] Donaldson (1999) para.3.47.

[290] As defined under the Mines and Quarries Act 1954, s.89(6) Water Resources Act 1991 and see [1996] *Water Law* 43.

[291] s.89(3) Water Resources Act 1991. Provision for exemption from water pollution controls in relation to mine water has a long history and the defence may be traced back, through s.31(2) Control of Pollution Act 1974 and s.2(4) Rivers (Prevention of Pollution) Act 1951, to s.5 Rivers Pollution Prevention Act 1876. Generally, on water quality impacts of mining activities, see 1.6.6 above.

[292] Under s.85(1) Water Resources Act 1991, and see 9.7 above.

[293] See the discussion of trade effluent at 9.9 above.

[294] See 9.6 above on the meaning of 'causing'.

[295] Under s.85(2) Water Resources Act 1991, and see 9.11 above on contravention of prohibitions.

case[296] has interpreted the need to show causation as a broad, 'doing something', test and, on that basis, it seems probable that 'abandonment' will fall within the meaning of 'cause'.

The complexities involved in bringing proceedings in relation to water pollution originating from mining activities are well-illustrated by *R v British Coal Corporation*.[297] The facts were that the defendant operated a deep mine in the vicinity of old mine workings for which it was not responsible. During the deep mining operations, water had been pumped out of the mine so that the water level remained beneath the level of the deep mine and the old workings. It was envisaged that, on the decommissioning of the deep mine, pumping would cease and this would bring about a gradual elevation of the water level. The rising water, which was not significantly contaminated, was expected to rise up a mine shaft to be discharged via a duct into a nearby river. Contrary to these expectations, the rising water table did not follow this course, but flowed through a seam in the old mine workings, where it became contaminated with iron, and was discharged into the river and had an adverse affect on aquatic life.

In proceedings brought by the National Rivers Authority and, privately, by the Anglers' Co-operative Association,[298] the defendant was charged with 'causing polluting matter to enter a controlled water',[299] and 'knowingly permitting liquid matter injurious to fish, or the food or spawning grounds of fish, to enter waters containing fish'.[300] British Coal was found not guilty on both counts. In relation to the first charge, it was found that it had not 'caused' the pollution by switching off the pumps because some positive act was required for causation to be established and, though the discontinuation of pumping was a positive act, it had not directly caused the pollution. This was found to be the result of the naturally rising water level, ultimately due to rainfall, which was outside the control of the defendant. Given the subsequent discussion in the *Empress Cars* case, and the explicit disapproval of the need for any 'positive act' for causation to be established,[301] the reasoning on this point must now be of doubtful authority. However, it is less clear whether the defence that the entry took place for reasons beyond the control of the defendant remains valid or not.[302] In relation to the second charge, of 'knowingly permitting' the entry of matter injurious to fish, the Court held that there was no evidence to establish that the defendant knew that the water would become contaminated by the old workings or that it would take the course that it did.

---

[296] [1998] 1 All ER 481 and see discussion at 9.6.2 above.

[297] *ENDS Report* 227 (1993) p.42 and (1994) *Water Law* 48.

[298] See 3.19 above on the Anglers' Co-operative Association, now the Anglers' Conservation Association.

[299] Under s.85(1) and (6) Water Resources Act 1991.

[300] Under s.4(1) Salmon and Freshwater Fisheries Act 1995, and see 15.4.1 below on this.

[301] See 9.6.2 above on disapproval of the need for a 'positive act' to be shown.

[302] See the discussion of 'acts of God' at 9.6.3 above.

Despite the outcome in the *British Coal* case, two points of significant procedural interest are illustrated. The first is that, by bringing the first charge as that of 'causing' the entry of polluting matter, the defendant was prevented from using the abandoned mines defence,[303] since this is only available where the accused has been charged with knowingly 'permitting' water from an abandoned mine to enter controlled waters. The second point is that, though the abandoned mines defence applies in relation to the principal offences concerning water pollution,[304] it does not apply in relation to any other offence. Accordingly, in relation to the charge under the fishery offence, the abandoned mines defence was, again, unavailable.

It may be noted also, that the *British Coal* case contrasts markedly with the reasoning adopted in the earlier Scots decision in *Lockhart v National Coal Board*[305] where the facts showed many points of similarity and the offence being charged was essentially the same.[306] Here, closely following the reasoning expounded in the *Alphacell* case,[307] the Court accepted the following argument of the Lord Advocate.

> When the mine closed in 1977 all working by the respondent, including pumping, ceased, as a result of which the mine began to fill with water coming from the surface and this brought the oxidised pyrite product into a rich contaminated solution. In the absence of pumping the level of water containing the contaminated solution continued to rise until it broke the ground surface whereby the contaminated solution found its way into the streams. This was all part of a continuous chain of events deliberately carried out by the respondent which resulted in and caused the contamination of the streams as libelled. The respondent has set up a system under which pollution of the water was bound to occur and the polluted water was bound to overflow into the streams unless there were pumps of sufficient capacity to prevent this occurring. When there were no pumps the result was inevitable. On a common sense approach this was a simple and straightforward case of 'causing'.[308]

In retrospect, it is arguable that this line of reasoning is even more compelling, when viewed in the light of the subsequent decision in the *Empress Cars* case.

---

[303] Under s.89(3) Water Resources Act 1991.

[304] Under *ibid* s.85.

[305] 1981 SLT 161.

[306] s.22 Rivers (Prevention of Pollution) (Scotland) Act 1951, corresponding to s.85(1) Water Resources Act 1991, though no fishery offence was charged.

[307] [1972] 2 All ER 475 and see discussion at 9.6.1 above.

[308] 1981 SLT 161 at p.171.

*9.17.3B  Abandonment of Mines*

Whilst the provisions made for exempting contaminated water from abandoned mines under previous legislation[309] may not have been especially problematic during times when there existed a relatively small number of abandoned mines, it is clear that this situation has changed dramatically over recent years.[310] Hence, in a 1994 report, the National Rivers Authority observed,

> the scale of the problem of land-abandoned mines has yet to be fully evaluated in England and Wales, primarily because any of the effects are most acute in streams and upper reaches which are not routinely monitored, and are thus un-classified. Nevertheless, some attempt has been made to characterise the some 200km of waters affected by abandoned coal mines, and . . . some 400km of waters are affected by abandoned metal mines, primarily in the South West of England and Wales, the best known being the Wheal Jane mine.[311]

Since the publication of this report, the number of mines that have been abandoned has greatly increased, with the continuing decline in the coal industry, thereby adding significantly to the extent of the problems posed for the aquatic environment.[312] The legislative response to this, under the Environment Act 1995, has been to remove the abandoned mines defence in relation to any mine, or part of a mine, which becomes abandoned after 31 December 1999.[313] Whilst it would have been possible to remove the defence under the 1995 Act with immediate effect, it is significant that over four years has been allowed for in giving effect to this change in the law. This has had the consequence that it has been possible for a significant number of mines to be closed during the intervening period, thereby enabling mine operators to take the benefit of a defence which it is recognised is, in principle, unjustified. Controversially, the explanation for the delay lay in the desire to avoid an increase in public expenditure at a time when the coal industry was being privatised under the Coal Industry Act 1994.[314]

Further provisions on abandoned mines have been introduced, under the Environment Act 1995, to interpolate a new chapter, Chapter IIA of Part

---

[309] See s.31(2) Control of Pollution Act 1974, which repealed s.2(4) Rivers (Prevention of Pollution) Act 1951 and s.1(2) Rivers (Prevention of Pollution) Act 1961. Previously, see s.5 Rivers Pollution Prevention Act 1876.

[310] Generally, see House of Commons, Welsh Affairs Select Committee *Water Pollution From Abandoned Coal Mines* (1992); Royal Commission on Environmental Pollution (1992) paras.7.69 to 7.73; Ball (1992); Jones (1996); and *ENDS Report* 271 (1997) p.24.

[311] National Rivers Authority, *Abandoned Mines and the Water Environment* (1994) p.1.

[312] See *ENDS Report* 271 (1997) p.24 and see also the discussion of contaminated land at 13.7 below.

[313] s.89(3A) Water Resources Act 1991, as added. In relation to a mine, or a part of a mine, that has been abandoned on two or more occasions, if a later abandonment falls on or after 31 December 1999, then abandonment will be deemed to have taken place after that date (s.98(3B)). See Jones (1995).

[314] Lane and Peto (1995) p.167, and generally see Jones (1994) and (1996).

III, in the Water Resources Act 1991.[315] The purpose of the new Chapter is to provide an explicit definition of 'abandonment' in relation to mines, for the purpose of ensuring that the Environment Agency is given adequate notice of any abandonment which may result in water pollution and to enable consideration to be given to any preventative measures that are needed. Accordingly, the definition of 'abandonment' is stated to include:

(a) the discontinuance of operations for the removal of water from the mine;

(b) the cessation of the working of any seam, vein or vein system;

(c) the cessation of use of any shaft or outlet;

(d) in the case of a mine in which activities other than mining activities are carried on (i) the discontinuance of some of all of those other activities; and (ii) any substantial change in the operations for the removal of water from the mine.

However, this definition does not include any disclaimer by an official receiver[316] acting in a compulsory capacity.[317]

As specified under the definition of 'abandonment', an operator of any mine must give a minimum of six months' notice of any proposed 'abandonment' to the Environment Agency.[318] This notice must contain prescribed information, which may include information as to the operator's opinion as to any consequence of the abandonment.[319] Failure to provide such information amounts to an offence which is punishable, on summary conviction, by a fine not exceeding the statutory maximum, presently £5,000, or on indictment, an unlimited fine.[320] However, no offence will be committed where abandonment happens in an emergency[321] in order to avoid danger to life of health; and notice of the abandonment is given as soon as reasonably practicable after the abandonment.[322] The Mines (Notice of Abandonment) Regulations 1998[323] prescribe the information that must be contained in a notice of proposed or actual abandonment and indicate particulars which a mine operator is required to publish in a local newspaper in relation to a notice of abandonment.[324]

---

[315] s.58 Environment Act 1995.

[316] Under ss.178 or 315 Insolvency Act 1986.

[317] s.91A(1) Water Resources Act 1991, as inserted by s.58 Environment Act 1995.

[318] s.91B(1) Water Resources Act 1991. The Agency is under a duty to inform the local authority in whose area the land is situated of the proposed abandonment if it considers that, in consequence of the abandonment, the land has or is likely to become contaminated land under Part IIA Environmental Protection Act 1990, s.91B(7) Water Resources Act 1991. Generally see 13.7 below on contaminated land.

[319] s.91B(2) Water Resources Act 1991.

[320] *Ibid* s.91B(3) Water Resources Act 1991

[321] See 9.17.1 above on 'emergency'.

[322] s.91B(4) Water Resources Act 1991.

[323] SI 1998 No.892.

[324] Postscript: clause 55 of a draft Water Bill proposes to extend the powers of the Coal Authority, under the Coal Industry Act 1994, to allow it to prevent or deal with water emanating from any coal mine onto any land or into any controlled waters; to enter land to drill boreholes and install monitoring or other equipment, in order to investigate and deal with water from coal mines that

It may be noted that the issue of water from abandoned mines is also addressed within the regime provided for in relation to the remediation of contaminated land.[325] Basically, the emission of water from abandoned mines is excluded from the scope of the contaminated land regime by a stipulation that no remediation will be required in respect of the entry of such water into controlled waters if such remediation could not have been required otherwise than in relation to pollution of controlled waters.[326]

*9.17.3C  European Community Law and Abandoned Mines*

Whilst the recently introduced controls upon water contamination from abandoned mines are to be welcomed, discharges from old mines continue to be environmentally and legally problematic. Not least, this is because of the need comprehensively to implement European Community obligations in respect of discharges and water quality. Water from mines is capable of containing a range of contaminants including heavy metals such as mercury and cadmium. These substances, and others potentially originating from mining activities, are covered by the Dangerous Substances Directive and national regulations implementing this Directive.[327] Whilst implementation of the Directive is possible by the control of discharges which fall within its scope by means of discharge consents and other environmental licences, clearly there is a problem if a particular discharge or emission does not come within the regulatory controls which are provided for.[328] This appears to be the case with respect to contaminated water originating from abandoned mines. If no criminal offence is committed by allowing such water to enter the aquatic environment, it is not necessary for the responsible person to obtain a discharge consent.

The Community law implications of this state of affairs are considerable. If the continuing lack of a legal means to control activities which are contrary to relevant Directives is a correct analysis of the present situation, it is argued that that the exemptions which are available to those responsible for abandoned mines are an unlawful derogation from Community law. Moreover, the effect of this would be that individuals suffering loss or damage as a result would be able to claim damages against the UK Government, due to the failure fully to transpose directives

---

seriously threatens the environment or human health; and compulsorily to buy land in England and Wales to prevent or treat water pollution from coal mines. See DETR, *Water Bill: Consultation on Draft Legislation* (2001).

[325] Under Part IIA Environmental Protection Act 1990, as amended, and see 13.7 below.

[326] s.78J(3) Environmental Protection Act 1990, as amended.

[327] See 5.4.1 above and 14.8.3 below on the Dangerous Substances Directive (76/464/EEC) and the Surface Waters (Dangerous Substances) Regulations 1989 (SI 1989 No.2286). The relevant substances may also be provided for in other Community water directives.

[328] See National Rivers Authority, *Abandoned Mines and the Water Environment* (1994) p.7.

into national law, at least to the extent that the relevant directives conferred rights on them.[329]

### 9.17.4 Deposits of Mine or Quarry Refuse

The fourth miscellaneous defence is that a person will not, otherwise than in respect of the entry of any poisonous, noxious or polluting matter into any controlled waters, be guilty of a principal offence by depositing the solid refuse of a mine or quarry[330] on any land so that it falls or is carried into inland freshwater if three conditions are satisfied. These are that:

(a) the deposit of refuse is made with the consent of the Environment Agency;
(b) no other site for the deposit is reasonably practicable; and
(c) all reasonably practicable steps are taken to prevent the refuse from entering those inland freshwaters.[331]

Explicit provision has been made in relation to the procedure for applying for consents for this purpose,[332] requiring applications to be made on a form provided by the Agency, and to be advertised in accordance with regulations.[333] Another significant recent innovation is the provision for 'enforcement notices' in relation to the contravention of 'relevant consents', which encompass consents granted in relation to the above defence.[334] The power to serve such notices allows the Agency to specify any matter which appears to constitute a contravention, the steps which must be taken to remedy it and the period within such steps must be taken, and penalties are provided for in relation to the failure to comply with a notice of this kind.[335]

Many of observations previously made in relation to the defence concerning water from abandoned mines are also relevant to this exemption, as are the concerns that the defence may give rise to contravention of Community water directives without a legal mechanism for control of water quality problems arising from mine and quarry waste.

---

[329] Under a '*Francovich*' action, discussed at 4.16.6 above, and generally see Williams (1998) and (1999).

[330] For the purposes of these provisions 'mine' and 'quarry' are to have the same meaning as in the Mines and Quarries Act 1954. See also, Anon (1996).

[331] s.89(4) Water Resources Act 1991.

[332] The same procedure is applicable in relation to consents relating to offences concerning deposits and vegetation in rivers, under s.90 Water Resources Act 1991, see 9.15 above.

[333] s.90A Water Resources Act 1991, inserted by para.142 Sch.22 Environment Act 1995.

[334] s.90B Water Resources Act, inserted by para.142 Sch.22 Environment Act 1995, and see Payne (1997).

[335] s.90B(2) to (4) Water Resources Act 1991, as amended, and see the discussion of enforcement notices in relation to s.90 at 10.11.1 below and in relation to discharge consents at Ch.10 below.

## 9.17.5 Highway Drains

As previously noted,[336] road transport constitutes a significant cause of pollution incidents and may be an important contributory factor in relation to more general water quality problems. Whilst major water pollution incidents tend to arise from road traffic accidents and spillages of contaminating substances, there is also an increasing awareness that surface water run off from ordinary road use contains quantities of substances which are harmful to the aquatic environment.[337] Commonly, the route by which such spillages and run off enter controlled waters is through road drainage systems. A final miscellaneous defence arises in relation to highway drains.

Where a highway authority, or other person, is entitled to keep open a drain[338] they will not be guilty of a principal water pollution offence by causing or permitting any discharge to be made from the drain unless the discharge is made in contravention of a prohibition.[339] This defence arises from the general power of highway authorities to construct or lay drains in highways and adjoining land for the purpose of securing adequate drainage. Similarly, highway authorities may erect barriers in a highway, or on adjoining land, to divert surface water into or through drains, and scour, cleanse and keep open all such drains.[340] Where a drain is constructed in this manner, the water may be discharged directly, or through an existing drain, into any natural or artificial inland or tidal waters.[341]

Significantly, the defence for highway drains is only available to the appropriate highway authority, or any other person entitled to keep open the highway drain. Consequently, it would not be available to any other person who made use of a highway drain for the purpose of disposing of polluting matter.[342] Hence, for example, if a person with no rights in respect of a highway drain was to use it for disposing of waste oil, resulting in surface or groundwater pollution, the defence relating to highway drains would not be available. Also, it may be noted, the defence only relates to criminal offences concerning water pollution and has no relevance to civil proceedings for water pollution.[343] Thus in one instance a highway authority was found to be civilly liable in respect of water,

---

[336] See 1.6.5 above on road transport generally and 9.2 above on water pollution incident statistics.

[337] Generally, see Luker and Montague (1994).

[338] Under s.100 Highways Act 1980.

[339] s.89(5) Water Resources Act 1991.

[340] s.100(1) Highways Act 1980.

[341] ss.100(2) and 299(1) Highways Act 1980.

[342] See, for example, *National Rivers Authority* v *Tarmac Construction Ltd* [1993] *Environmental Law Brief* 19.

[343] s.100 Water Resources Act 1991, and see discussion of this at 3.18 5 above.

fouled with tar from the surface of the road, which entered a watercourse.[344]

Another notable qualification upon the extent of the defence for highway drains is that it will not be available where the discharge is made in contravention of a prohibition. As has been noted,[345] prohibition notices may be imposed where the Agency requires particular discharges to be subject to special controls and failure to adhere to such notices will involve the commission of a principal water pollution offence. Beyond that, where a prohibition notice is imposed and effluent is discharged in contravention of it, and a similar contravention is likely, the Agency may impose a discharge consent upon the person who caused or permitted the contravention of the prohibition.[346] Thereafter, breach of the discharge consent will constitute a principal water pollution offence.[347] Hence, although highway drains are not generally subject to discharge consents, because of the special defence which relates to them, there can be situations where the discharge consent system may be used in relation to problematic highway drains.[348]

A potentially problematic issue in relation to highway drains is that highway authorities and sewerage undertakers are empowered to enter into reciprocal agreements concerning the use of highway drains and sewers. Such agreements may allow a highway drain to be used by an undertaker for the purpose of conveying surface water from premises or streets. Alternatively, a sewer vested in the undertaker may be used by the highway authority for conveying surface water from roads. Neither party to such a proposed agreement may unreasonably refuse to enter into an agreement or unreasonably insist upon terms unacceptable to the other party.[349] However, the shared use of surface water sewers or highway drains may give rise to difficulties in respect of the determination of the responsibilities of the bodies concerned. Whilst a prohibition notice may be served upon the person responsible for the highway drain,[350] where its use is shared between a highway authority and a sewerage undertaker, the capacity of the authority to control the discharge from the drain may, in practice, be limited by the reciprocal agreement with the sewerage undertaker.

---

[344] *Dell v Chesham Urban District Council* [1921] 3 KB 427, though this outcome may be contrasted with another decision in which a highway authority was found not to be civilly liable where water carrying sand and silt entered a watercourse where this was found not to have any significant effect on the quality of the receiving waters (*Durrant v Branksome Urban District Council* [1897] 2 Ch 291).

[345] See the discussion of s.86 Water Resources Act 1991, concerning prohibition notices, at 9.11 above.

[346] para.6 Sch.10 Water Resources Act 1991, as inserted by para.183 Sch.22 Environment Act 1995.

[347] s.85(6) Water Resources Act 1991, and see discussion at 9.3 above.

[348] See also Ch.14 below on the use of town and country planning law for the purpose of preventing water contamination.

[349] s.115(1) and (4) Water Industry Act 1991.

[350] See s.264 Highways Act 1980, on ownership of highway drains.

## 9.18 Crown Exemption

A peculiarity concerning the application of the principal water pollution offences concerns the position of the Crown as this has been provided for under the Environment Act 1995, which is stated to be binding upon the Crown. This states that no contravention of any provision of the 1995 Act will make the Crown criminally liable, but the High Court may, on the application of the Agency, declare unlawful any act or omission of the Crown which constitutes such a contravention. Hence, the normal consequences of criminal liability are displaced by a declaratory mechanism which would not appear to give rise to any particular sanction. However, this exclusion of criminal liability of the Crown under the 1995 Act does not apply to persons in the public service of the Crown and the Act will apply to such persons as it applies to other persons.[351]

Further provision is made under the Environment Act 1995 for the purpose of ensuring consistency in the application of various enactments to the Crown.[352] Most relevantly, a new provision concerning Crown application is substituted in the Water Resources Act 1991. This provides that the 1991 Act binds the Crown subject to stated exceptions. However, it is provided that certain powers, including the power to carry out works to secure that waterworks water is not polluted, will only be exercisable in relation to land in which there is a Crown or Duchy interest with the consent of the appropriate authority.[353]

## 9.19 Enforcement and Sentencing

### 9.19.1 Private and Public Enforcement

As has been previously noted, the incidental general functions of the Environment Agency allow it to do anything which is conducive to the carrying out of its functions and, explicitly, this includes the institution of legal proceedings.[354] Notably, though, the Agency does not have a monopoly upon the power to prosecute for the principal water pollution offences.[355] In theory, nothing prevents individuals or environmental pressure groups from bringing private legal proceedings for these offences. In practice, however, relatively little use has been made of private criminal proceedings.

Some exceptional examples of private proceedings exist in two prosecutions brought or supported by the Anglers' Co-operative

---

[351] s.115(1), (3) and (4) Environment Act 1995.

[352] See s.116 and Sch.21 Environment Act 1995.

[353] s.222 Water Resources Act 1991, as substituted by para.2(4) Sch.21 Environment Act 1995. 'The appropriate authority' for these purposes is the Crown Estate Commissioners, the appropriate government department, the Chancellor of the Duchy of Lancaster or the Duke of Cornwall (s.293(2) Town and Country Planning Act 1990).

[354] s.37(1) Environment Act 1995, and see 6.18.1 above on the Agency's law enforcement policy.

[355] Contrast the position where an offence involving the contravention of a trade effluent consent is committed, see 11.11.1 below.

Association.[356] The first of these was a successful prosecution brought against Thames Water Authority in respect of unsatisfactory discharges from its Aylesbury sewage treatment works.[357] The second was the unsuccessful proceedings against British Coal.[358] Successful private proceedings were brought by Greenpeace against Allbright and Wilson,[359] but proceedings by Greenpeace against ICI were unsuccessful and resulted in a substantial award of costs against the organisation.[360]

Hence, whilst private prosecutions are threatened from time to time, the actual use of such proceedings is relatively uncommon. Amongst other things, this may reflect the fact that a person other than the Agency seeking to pursue private proceedings against an alleged polluter would find themselves placed at a disadvantage, in gathering the evidence necessary to support a prosecution, since Agency officers have extensive powers in relation to water quality monitoring[361] and entry onto premises[362] which would not be possessed by an individual.[363] On the other hand the threat of a private prosecution may be important in galvanising an otherwise reluctant enforcement authority into action.

By far the greatest use of the criminal proceedings for the principal water pollution offences is made by the Environment Agency. The policy basis upon which such proceedings are pursued, in accordance with the Agency's *Enforcement and Prosecution Policy*,[364] has been discussed previously, alongside the various mechanisms that have been recently used to draw attention to those found guilty of pollution offences and the publicisation of environmental performances by industrial dischargers generally.[365] Hence, the following discussion involves a more legalistic view of the consequences of successful legal proceedings and, specifically, the penalties that courts impose in relation to convicted offenders.

---

[356] Now renamed the Anglers' Conservation Association and see 3.19 above on the role of this Association.

[357] *DA Wales v Thames Water Authority* (unreported, Aylesbury Magistrates' Court, May 1987); see (1987) Vol.1 No.3 *Environmental Law* p.3, and see Jackson (1988) and Turner (1988).

[358] *R v British Coal Corporation* (1993) unreported but see *ENDS Report* 227 (1993) p.42 and (1994) *Water Law* 48, and see discussion at 9.17.3 above.

[359] See *Greenpeace (Burton) v Allbright and Wilson*, unreported but see [1992] *Water Law* 18, [1991] *Land Management and Environmental Law Reporter* 170 and [1992] *Land Management and Environmental Law Reporter* 56, and see Mumma (1993).

[360] See *ENDS Report* 234 (1994) p.47 and see *The Times* 25 May 1994. See also *R v National Rivers Authority ex parte Greenpeace* [1992] 4 *Land Management and Environmental Law Reporter* 56 on judicial review of environmental enforcement policy.

[361] See Ch.16 below on water quality monitoring.

[362] See 6.17 above on powers of entry.

[363] Generally see Jenn (1993).

[364] See the discussion of the Agency's enforcement policy at 6.18.1 above.

[365] See 6.19 above on publicisation of water pollution convictions.

*9.19.2 Penalties*

Although lower penalties are provided for in relation to lesser offences,[366] the penalties provided for in relation to the principal water pollution offences, and the contravention of any consent given under Chapter II of Part III of the Water Resources' Act 1991,[367] are that a person will be liable, on summary conviction,[368] to imprisonment for a term not exceeding three months, or to a fine not exceeding £20,000 or to both and, on conviction on indictment, to imprisonment for a term not exceeding two years or to a fine or to both.[369] Because the power to impose a fine on indictment is not subject to any specified upper limit, general sentencing principles, discussed later in this section, will apply in determining what level of fine is appropriate in a particular case.

An initial observation concerns the relatively rare use of custodial sentences in relation to water pollution offences, and in relation to environmental offences generally. To date, there is only one instance of a custodial sentence being imposed for a water pollution offence. This occurred in *Environment Agency* v *John Barker*.[370] Here the defendant pleaded guilty to the offence of causing the entry of polluting matter into controlled waters where oil escaped from an unbunded oil tank at his farm and passed into a nearby stream. The Agency had requested, on several previous occasions, that the tank should have been bunded. The defendant received a two month custodial sentence, to run concurrently with other sentences arising from food hygiene and food safety offences. Although a lower court decision, the fact that a custodial sentence was imposed is remarkable but constitutes only slender evidence of a movement towards the greater use of water pollution penalties in the future.

The norm, however, is that a fine is imposed in the event of a conviction for a water pollution offence. Hence, the Agency's statistics for 1998-99 show that for 258 successful water quality prosecutions concluded during that year a total of £4,838,545 in fines were imposed.[371] However, the total includes one, extremely atypical, fine of £4m imposed, at first instance, in relation to the *Sea Empress* case.[372] Taking that fine out of the calculation, the average fine for the other 257 convictions is £3,263. Whilst, the

---

[366] See the discussion of s.90 Water Resources Act 1991, concerned with offences relating to deposits and vegetation in rivers.

[367] See 9.13 above on contravention of conditions of a consent, and Ch.10 below on discharge consents generally.

[368] In respect of proceedings in magistrates' courts a court may try any summary offence if the information is laid not more than twelve months after the commission of the offence (s.101 Water Resources Act 1991). This contrasts with the usual time limit of six months for the laying of informations in respect of summary proceedings (see s.127 Magistrates' Courts Act 1980).

[369] s.85(6) Water Resources Act 1991.

[370] Unreported, Accrington Magistrates' Court, 20 October 1997, but see *ENDS Report* 273 (1997) p.45; [1997] *Water Law* 189 and Environment Agency, *Water Pollution Incidents in England and Wales 1997* (1998) para.7.7.2.

[371] Environment Agency, *Annual Report and Accounts 1998/99* (1999) p.164.

[372] *Environment Agency* v *Milford Haven Port Authority and Andrews (The Sea Empress)* [1999] 1 Lloyd's Rep 673, though the High Court penalty was substantially reduced by the Court of Appeal, see the discussion at 9.19.3 below.

average levels of fines for offences committed by water and sewerage undertakers have been calculated to be slightly above this, at around £4,000, average levels of such fines having been at roughly the same level for the last five years. Fines at these levels are regarded by the Agency as excessively low and this view has been recently endorsed by the House of Commons Environment, Transport and Regional Affairs Committee which expressed concern that efforts of the Agency were being undermined by the failure of courts, in the vast majority of cases, to treat environmental cases with the seriousness they deserve.[373]

### 9.19.3 Sentencing Serious Offences

At the upper extreme, there are a few examples of severe penalties being imposed on water pollution offenders.[374] A rather atypical instance of a high fine being imposed upon a corporate offender arose in *National Rivers Authority* v *Shell UK*[375] where the defendant pleaded guilty to a serious pollution incident involving the escape of about 30,000 gallons of crude oil into the Mersey estuary as a result of the fracture of an oil pipeline. In sentencing the defendants, Mr Justice Mars-Jones observed that the incident was a consequence of human error and a failure of the defendants to discharge the high duty of care which they owed to the community. He imposed a fine of £1m, commenting that the defendants had, otherwise, an outstanding local record in the field of conservation and were it not for that fact the penalty which he would impose would have been 'substantially greater'. It was also noted that, at the time of the hearing, the defendants had already paid some £1.4m towards the cleaning up operation and it has been suggested that the total clean-up operation cost in the region of £6m.[376] The *Shell* case was, until recently, by a sizeable margin, the most severely punished water pollution offence on record.

Most recently, the scope for imposition of high levels of fines in relation to water pollution offences has been illustrated by the highest fine ever awarded in a water pollution case being imposed upon the Milford Haven Port Authority in proceedings brought by the Environment Agency[377] in respect of the Port Authority causing polluting matter to enter controlled waters (though the amount of the fine was reduced on appeal). The

---

[373] Speaking at the Environment Agency's Annual General meeting, the Agency's Chief Executive Ed Gallagher said 'these fines of a few thousand pounds are no deterrent to multi million pound companies – we want fines that reflect the seriousness of the crime' (see Environment Agency, *Water Pollution In England and Wales 1998* (1999) p.3). See also House of Commons Environment, Transport and Regional Affairs Committee (2000) para.95 which concluded, 'If companies are to take their environmental responsibilities seriously, public disapproval through league tables of environmental performance must be backed by serious penalties for significant breaches of environmental law'.

[374] See the discussion of the Environment Agency's approach to publicisation of environmental performance at 6.19 above.

[375] [1990] *Water Law* 40.

[376] See Merrett (1993).

[377] *Environment Agency* v *Milford Haven Port Authority and Andrews (The Sea Empress)* [1999] 1 Lloyd's Rep 673 and see *ENDS Report* 288 (1999) p.50.

incident at issue arose from the grounding of the *Sea Empress* oil tanker at the entrance to the Milford Haven waterway, allowing about 72,000 tonnes of crude oil to be released, along with fuel oil. This resulted in oil being deposited over 200 km of coastline in the Pembrokeshire Coast National Park and necessitated an extensive clean up operation, involving more than 50 vessels, 19 aircraft and 25 organisations providing 250 personnel at sea and 950 on shore. The cost of this operation was estimated to be greater than £60m, though the total environmental and amenity cost of the incident, and its financial impact upon tourism and commercial fisheries, was estimated to be much greater that this. The incident was attributed to negligent navigation by the pilot who was provided by the Port Authority under a system of compulsory pilotage. Although the pilot was the holder of a master's certificate of competency, his experience of piloting vessels of the tonnage of the *Sea Empress* was found to be 'sketchy' in that he had never previously been called upon to supervise the entry of a vessel of this size under the tidal conditions that prevailed.

Although the Port Authority had pleaded guilty to the offence of causing the entry of polluting matter into controlled waters, it was noted that there was no difficulty in concluding that the Authority did something which caused the pollution in that it operated the port and trained and supervised the pilot provided for the vessel. The grounding, whilst attributable to negligent navigation by the pilot, was a normal fact of life and not something extraordinary. Moreover, although the loss of oil may have been partially attributable to bad weather and the uncertainties of the salvage operation, these were normal rather than extraordinary incidents of life in the circumstances which had arisen. Therefore, explicitly applying the principles established in the *Empress Cars* case[378] the Authority's plea of guilt had to be accepted on the basis of strict liability and without any admission of fault.

However, the decision is of greatest importance in relation to the approach to sentencing that is illustrated. In this respect it was noted that Milford Haven and the coast surrounding the Cleddau Estuary was of considerable environmental importance, incorporating several areas designated for their conservation importance, and the casualty posed a grave threat to that environment and its amenities. Given the background to the incident, and its impact, a substantial penalty was necessitated. The Crown Court held that the Port Authority should be fined a total of £4m and ordered to pay costs of £825,000 to the Environment Agency.

In determining this penalty, the Crown Court took account of the following factors. First, it was recognised that the defendant had entered a guilty plea and that some credit should be given for this. However, it was also stated that such credit should be modest because the plea had only been entered at a late stage after costs incurred in preparing for a jury trial had already been incurred. Second, the defendant's agreement, in any event, to pay the

---

[378] *Environment Agency (formerly National Rivers Authority)* v *Empress Car Co (Abertillery) Ltd* [1998] 1 All ER 481, and see 9.6.2 above for discussion of this.

prosecution costs was noted, though again it was recognised that the effect of this in mitigating the fine was limited since it merely recognised that the prosecution had been made to incur wholly unnecessary expenditure which could have been avoided if a guilty plea had been promptly entered. Third, it was argued by the defendant that its status as a public trust for public benefit should limit the extent of any financial penalty. However, the judge rejected this as irrelevant to the standards of efficiency and care that were required in matters of safety. Fourth, following the incident the defendant undertook an elaborate safety assessment and put in place improvements in practice which it claimed had cost £1.3m. Whilst this was thought to be a proper course of action, the view was taken that this would have been called for in any event and so could not be considered as a strong mitigating factor. Finally, in respect of the means of the Authority to meet any fine which might be imposed, an examination of its audited accounts revealed a sound business with a substantial holding in unencumbered fixed assets and borrowing powers up to £30m. It was noted that the Authority did not have the vast resources of a major oil or manufacturing company and, for that reason, a significantly lower fine would be imposed than upon such a company. Also, the remote risk of imposing such a large fine that the viability of the Authority would be jeopardised was also noted.

In the *Sea Empress* decision in the Crown Court considerable reliance was placed upon the Court of Appeal decision in *R v F Howe and Son (Engineers) Ltd*[379] concerning the approach to penalties by way of fines in relation to a health and safety offence.[380] This appeal arose out of prosecutions following from a fatal accident when an employee of the defendants was electrocuted and fines totalling £48,000 were imposed along with an order for costs.

In the Court of Appeal, in the *Howe* case, the previous good record of the company was accepted as a mitigating factor to the extent that there had been no previous convictions, or warnings for health and safety lapses. The plea of guilty was also accepted as a mitigating factor. The Court did not accept that the size of the company and its lack of ability to provide specialist safety staff mitigated the offences, but did accept that the means of the company was a very material factor to the amount of the fine. In respect of the level of fines generally imposed for offences of this kind, the view was taken that these were generally too low and should not be used as a yardstick for determining the level of fine in the present case. Finally, it was accepted that the offence did not involve any deliberate flouting of legal requirements for reasons of economy and account was taken of the appellants' attitude in respect of the expenditure on rewiring.

---

[379] *R v F Howe and Son (Engineers) Ltd* [1999] 2 Cr App R(S) 37 and see *ENDS Report* 288 (1999) p.51.
[380] Arising under s.2(1) Health and Safety at Work Act 1974, Electricity at Work Regulations 1989 (SI 1989 No.635) and Management of Health and Safety at Work Regulations 1992 (SI 1992 No.2051). Although health and safety legislation does not impose an absolute requirement to ensure safety of employees at work, this must be ensured so far as is reasonably practicable.

Alongside these matters, the Court of Appeal took general account of the fact that the average fine in magistrates' courts for offences of this kind was less than one third of the maximum fine available and that disquiet had been expressed that levels of fine were generally too low. In general terms, it was thought that in sentencing it was important to ascertain how far an offence fell below the appropriate standard, whether death or serious injury was present as an aggravating factor and whether a deliberate breach of legal requirements was attributable to cost cutting with a view to profit. The size of a company and its financial strength should not reduce the standard of care which is required in matters of health and safety but should be reflected in the means of the offender to pay any fine which is imposed.[381] On this point, the company's accounts revealed a net profit for the previous year of about £27,000 and it was recognised that any fine of significance was likely to be felt by the management of the company and its shareholders. Because this was regarded as a small company with limited resources, it was concluded that inadequate weight had been given to the financial position of the appellant and the fine of £48,000 was reduced to £15,000, though the order for costs was upheld.

The reasoning in the *Howe* case was broadly affirmed to be relevant to sentencing in environmental convictions in the Court of Appeal decision in the *Sea Empress* case.[382] Reconsidering the circumstances of the Port Authority alongside the relevant criteria, and drawing comparisons from other environmental and health and safety decisions where severe penalties had been imposed, the Court of Appeal took the view that the Crown Court had failed to give sufficient weight to certain factors. Specifically, full credit had not been given to the plea of guilty offered by the Port Authority and there had been a failure adequately to consider the impact of the £4m fine upon the Authority's capacity to perform its public functions. In addition, it appeared that the trial judge had taken too optimistic a view of the Authority's financial position and prospects, and had not given sufficient consideration to the harm to its business and the economy of the area that would arise as a consequence of the fine. On that basis, the Court of Appeal took the view that the penalty was excessive and reduced the amount of the fine from £4m to £750,000.

Understandably, this decision was greeted by the Environment Agency with dismay, but in some respects it may have served to clarify the basis of sentencing decisions in environmental cases.[383] What it seems to show is that, in future, courts will undertake careful scrutiny of the financial means of offenders in determining levels of fines. The status of offenders as public and statutory bodies will be an important consideration, but it remains apparent that a major commercial organisation which commits an environmental offence, even where strict liability is involved, may anticipate receiving a substantial fine.

---

[381] See s.18(3) Criminal Justice Act 1991.

[382] *R* v *Milford Haven Port Authority*, [2000] Env LR 632 Court of Appeal. See also the discussion of sentencing guidelines for environmental offences at 9.19.5 below.

[383] See Environment Agency, Press Release 16 March 2000, *Environment Agency Dismayed at 'Sea Empress' Fine Reduction* and see *ENDS Report* (2000) p.46.

### 9.19.4 Culpability and Mitigation

The existence of strict liability in relation to the principal water pollution offences has the consequence that offences may be committed in circumstances where defendants are morally blameless and even where every possible measure has been taken to avoid committing an offence.[384] Although blamelessness does not serve as a defence, it may be of considerable importance where the sentence is being determined.[385]

An illuminating Court of Appeal decision indicates that it is necessary to 'look behind' a conviction for such an offence to ascertain the degree of culpability involved in determining the appropriate sentence. In *R v Yorkshire Water Services Ltd*[386] the appellant had pleaded guilty to two offences of causing sewage effluent to enter controlled waters[387] in the Crown Court and was fined £50,000 under the first count and £25,000 under the other. The circumstances giving rise to the conviction were that a blocked sewer had enabled untreated sewage to pass onto a beach crowded with holidaymakers. Although the appellant, as the sewerage undertakers, had overall responsibility for the sewerage system, the 'hands on' maintenance duties were to be discharged by Scarborough Borough Council under an agency agreement.[388] Nevertheless, no action could be taken against the council for its 'passive inactivity' in failing to act to remedy the blocked sewer.[389] Therefore, the proceedings were brought against Yorkshire Water Services Ltd alone on the basis that the sewerage undertaker was deemed to have caused the discharge.[390] In mitigation, the appellant had argued that it was morally blameless for the incidents, but the trial judge stated that he was not prepared to accept this plea. On appeal, it was held that the trial judge was not entitled to form his own view of the blameworthiness of the appellant and had erred in his approach to the sentencing exercise. The sentence should reflect the seriousness of the incidents, but must also reflect the fact that the appellant was deemed to have caused the discharges. Accordingly, the levels of fines should have been substantially lower than those imposed, and fines of £10,000 and £5,000 were substituted for those imposed by the lower court.

A more extreme example is *CPC (UK) Ltd v National Rivers Authority*,[391] where it was accepted that there was nothing more that the defendant could have done to have prevented a polluting entry. Here the defendant was found guilty of the strict liability offence, but the sentence was an absolute discharge though coupled with an order to pay the prosecution's costs.

---

[384] See discussion of strict liability at 9.6.4 above.

[385] On mitigation pleas in relation to environmental offences generally see de Prez (2000b).

[386] [1995] Env LR 229.

[387] Contrary to s.107(1)(c) Water Act 1989, the counterpart of s.85(3) Water Resources Act 1991.

[388] See 11.3.1 below on agency agreements.

[389] Following the ruling in *Wychavon District Council v National Rivers Authority* [1993] 2 All ER 440, but now see 9.6.2 above on this.

[390] Under s.107(5) Water Act 1989, and now s.87(1) Water Resources Act 1991, see 9.14.2 above on this.

[391] [1995] Env LR 131 discussed at 9.6.1 above.

## 9.19.5  The Sentencing Advisory Panel Report

The issue of sentencing for environmental offences, including the principal water pollution offences, was the subject of the first use by the Home Secretary of powers of referral to the Sentencing Advisory Panel.[392] This referral was made with a view to the matter being considered in the Court of Appeal hearing in the *Sea Empress* case. A consultation paper[393] issued by the Panel expressed the view that it would be desirable for the Court of Appeal to issue sentencing guidelines for environmental offences. The Panel proposed that, for non-corporate persons, the starting point for sentencing should be a fine, because the offences are non-violent and carry no immediate physical threat to the person and because the offences are generally committed in situations where the defendant has failed to devote proper resources to preventing a breach of the law. Fines should take account of the seriousness of the offence and the financial circumstances of the individual defendant but should also reflect how far below the relevant statutory environmental standard the defendant's behaviour actually falls. Assessment of seriousness requires that the court should consider the culpability of the defendant in bringing about, or risking, the relevant environmental harm and this must be balanced against the extent of the damage which has actually occurred or has been risked.

Hence, if the defendant's culpability was low, there was little or no actual environmental damage or there is strong personal mitigation in a case, an appropriate sentence might be a discharge rather than a fine. At the other extreme, a custodial sentence was thought to be justified only where the pollutant was noxious, widespread or pervasive and the offence is shown to have involved a deliberate breach of the law, or the defendant has acted from a financial motive, for example, to avoid payment for the appropriate licence or by neglecting to put in place the appropriate preventative measures.

In the Court of Appeal hearing in the *Sea Empress* case the Court gave consideration to whether any guidelines should be framed. However, it was concluded that the Court could not usefully do more than draw attention to the factors relevant to sentencing and the guidelines offered by the Sentencing Advisory Panel were not adopted. It appears, therefore, that the work of the Panel, in accordance with its first direction from the Home Secretary, has come to nothing in this instance. Nonetheless, it is thought that many of the factors identified by the Advisory Panel will remain important determinants of the levels of sentence imposed upon those convicted of water pollution offences.[394]

---

[392] Under s.81(3) Crime and Disorder Act 1998.

[393] Sentencing Advisory Panel (1999).

[394] For general discussion see Davies (2000). House of Commons Environment, Transport and Regional Affairs Committee, The Environment Agency (2000) paras.96 to 98 and see discussion of the Environment Agency'' approach to publicising environmental performance at 6.19 above.

## 9.20 Corporate and Concurrent Liability

As a general principle, proceedings for the principal offences of water pollution, and other offences under the Water Resources Act 1991, can be brought against an individual as well as the corporate body concerned. Most frequently, however, proceedings are brought against companies rather than individuals. Nonetheless, where a body corporate is guilty of an offence under the Act and that offence is proved to have been committed with the consent or connivance of, or to be attributable to any neglect on the part of, any director, manager, secretary or other similar officer of the body corporate, or any person who was purporting to act in any such capacity, then he, as well as a body corporate, will be guilty of that offence, and will be liable to be proceeded against and punished accordingly.[395] Where the affairs of a corporate body are managed by its members, then this provision is to apply in relation to the acts and defaults of a member in connection with his functions of management as if he were a director of the corporate body.[396]

The operation of a similarly worded provision,[397] applicable to corporate liability for waste management activities, was illustrated in *R v Leighton and Town and Country Refuse Collections Ltd*[398] where a charge is brought for consent, connivance or neglect. On the facts of the case, it was found that the conviction of both the company concerned and its managing director, who held a 99% shareholding, was established on the basis of overwhelming evidence that the director was the 'moving spirit' in the company and took a central role in the commission of the offences. In respect of the charge that the director was guilty of 'neglect', the Court approved a passage from the Judge's direction to the jury in respect of what needed to be shown for this to be established:

> . . . the prosecution have to satisfy you [the jury] . . . that he [the managing director] failed to perform a duty of which he either knew or ought to have known, in other words, he neglected to bother about the fact that it was obvious what was going on, tipping on the landfill site, and failed to perform his duty, which was to stop it happening because it was in breach of the licence. He certainly should have known it was in breach of the licence, that is the effect of it. You would have to then decide if what happened . . . was attributable to his neglect.[399]

By the time the proceedings were brought the company had gone into voluntary liquidation, with no assets of any substance, and was given an absolute discharge. However, on appeal against the sentence of the lower court, account was taken of the personal circumstances of the managing

---

[395] s.217(1) Water Resources Act 1991. See *Attorney General's Reference (No.1 of 1995)* [1996] 4 All ER 21 on the interpretation of 'consent' in a similarly worded provision (s.96(1) Banking Act 1987).

[396] *Ibid* s.217(2) and on the meaning of 'manager' see *R v Boal* [1992] 3 All ER 177.

[397] s.157(1) Environmental Protection Act 1990.

[398] [1997] Env LR 411.

[399] *Ibid* at p.422.

director and, whilst accepting that the offences were serious, a total fine of £14,000 was reduced to £1,400 to take account of the means of the offender to pay and the fact that he was suffering from ill health.

Alongside corporate liability, concurrent liability is provided for in relation to the principal water pollution offences under the Water Resources Act 1991. Hence, where the commission by any person of an offence under the water pollution provisions of the Act is due to the act or default of some other person, that other person may be charged with and convicted of the offence whether of not proceedings for the offence are taken against the first-mentioned person.[400] Although rather convolutedly worded, the purpose of this provision is to allow for situations where a person who caused a polluting entry was 'acting under orders' from another and situations of that kind. Hence, this power might be used to bring proceedings against a particular employee of a company for a water pollution offence, even in circumstances where no proceedings were pursued against the individual who actually caused the polluting entry or the corporate body.

As between employer and employee, an issue which arises is as to the circumstances in which a company should be liable for a water pollution offence where the acts under consideration are those of an employee rather than those of the company. Essentially, this was the issue considered in *National Rivers Authority* v *Alfred McAlpine Homes East Ltd.*[401] The company in this case was engaged in building houses at a construction site when it was found that a stream which ran through the site had become contaminated by cement being washed into the stream. The company's site agent and manager both accepted responsibility for the pollution but, subsequently, the company claimed that these persons were not of sufficiently high standing in the company to enable their acts to be characterised as acts of the company. However, it was found that where a company, by some active operation or chain of operations carried out under its essential control, caused the pollution of a controlled water the company would be guilty of the offence. Accordingly, criminal liability would result from the acts or omissions of employees whilst acting with the scope of their employment regardless of whether they could be said to be exercising the controlling mind and will of the company. Conceivably, there may be situations where an employee acts in a manner which is completely outside the scope of his or her employment,[402] but the situation which arose did not fall into that category. Hence, normally, a company will be vicariously liable for the acts of its employees, within the scope of their employment, in relation to water pollution offences.

---

[400] s.217(3) Water Resources Act 1991.

[401] [1994] 4 All ER 286.

[402] Such situations would have to fall within the scope of 'extraordinary' occurrences as indicated in *Environment Agency (formerly National Rivers Authority)* v *Empress Car Co (Abertillery) Ltd* [1998] 1 All ER 481 and see 9.6.2 above on this.

## 9.21 Civil Liability and Criminal Proceedings

Although Part III of the Water Resources Act 1991 is the principal enactment concerning criminal liability for the pollution of controlled waters, it operates independently of the civil law on water quality.[403] Accordingly, as has been noted,[404] nothing in Part III of the Act confers, or derogates from, a right of action in civil proceedings or affects any restriction imposed under any other enactment.[405]

The practical implication of this separation between the civil and regulatory law is that, amongst other things, the availability of civil remedies for water contamination will be independently determined and not dependent upon whether a criminal prosecution succeeds or fails. Because of the lower burden of proof required, civil proceedings may sometimes be successful in a situation where a criminal prosecution would fail. Conversely, for example, because of the difficulties which may be encountered in showing that the defendant's pollution of watercourse was the cause of the claimant's loss, civil proceedings for compensation may fail where a criminal prosecution is successful. However, another interrelationship between the compensatory and punitive functions of criminal proceedings is usefully considered here in respect of the power of criminal courts to make a compensation order against a person convicted of a water pollution offence.

The Powers of the Criminal Courts Act 1973 provides that a court before which a person is convicted of a criminal offence, instead of or in addition to dealing with that person in any other way, may make an order requiring payment of compensation for any loss or damage resulting from an offence.[406] Compensation orders are to be of such amount as the court considers appropriate, having regard to the evidence and to any representations made,[407] though the maximum amount which a magistrates' court may order by way of compensation is £5,000 for each offence of which the offender is convicted.[408] In the circumstances of a water pollution incident, compensation might be ordered for, amongst other things, the cost of restocking a fishery where this is a loss which results from an offence involving the pollution of water. The recipient of such an award might be either the owner of the fishery damaged by pollution, or the Environment Agency where it has incurred restocking costs as a consequence of its general responsibility for fisheries.[409]

---

[403] On the civil law generally, see Ch.3 above.

[404] See 3.18.5 above discussing s.100 Water Resources Act 1991.

[405] s.100 Water Resources Act 1991.

[406] s.35(1) Powers of the Criminal Courts Act 1973, as amended by s.67 Criminal Justice Act 1982, and see *R* v *Daly* [1974] 1 All ER 290 and *R* v *Miller* [1976] Crim LR 694 for a discussion of the principles to be followed in making a compensation order.

[407] s.35(1A) Powers of the Criminal Courts Act 1973, as amended.

[408] s.40 Magistrates' Court Act 1980.

[409] Under s.114 Water Resources Act 1991 and Salmon and Freshwater Fisheries Act 1975 and see Bathers (1986) p.47.

However, where the basis for making a compensation order is contentious, or the extent of the loss which has been suffered is unclear, the court must hear sufficient evidence to determine the amount of the compensation order and cannot act upon the representations of the parties alone.[410] Hence, there may be situations where it is preferable for the Agency to pursue civil proceedings to recover its reasonable expenses arising from a pollution incident in accordance with its cost-recovery powers in relation to anti-pollution works and operations.[411] The interrelationship between compensation orders in criminal proceedings and subsequent awards of damages in civil litigation relating to the same loss is provided for by way of a stipulation that an award of civil damages may only be recovered to the extent that it exceeds a compensation order, and any part of the compensation order which has not been paid.[412] In essence, therefore, double-recovery of compensation is precluded.

Although statistical evidence suggests that compensation orders are rarely used in relation to water pollution offences, it has been suggested that courts should always consider making a compensation order and should give reasons if it decides not to do so.[413]

---

[410] *R v Horsham Justices ex parte Richards* [1985] 2 All ER 1114. For a discussion of the discretion allowed to magistrates to determine whether a compensation order should be made, in the context of a statutory nuisance conviction, see, *Davenport v Walsall Metropolitan Borough Council* [1997] Env LR 24.
[411] See s.161 Water Resources Act 1991 and see 13.2 below on anti-pollution works and operations.
[412] s.38 Powers of the Criminal Courts Act 1973, as substituted by s.105 Criminal Justice Act 1988.
[413] Sentencing Advisory Panel (1999) para.5.2.

# Chapter 10

# DISCHARGE CONSENTS

## 10.1 Introduction

In the previous chapter, the pollution of controlled waters and the principal offences in relation to water pollution were considered. As was noted, there are a range of situations that lead to offences where polluting matter is caused or knowingly permitted to enter, or trade or sewage effluent is discharged into, controlled waters. By contrast with other environmental regulatory offences, where liability may be avoided by showing that the 'best available techniques' were used, or that all reasonable precautions were taken, liability for water pollution offences is generally strict. Generally, criminal liability can be avoided only if a discharge is made under specified kinds of authorisations. Of these authorisations,[1] the most important for practical purposes are authorisations and permits for integrated pollution control and the pollution prevention and control regime, and a consent given under Chapter II of Part III of the Water Resources Act 1991, termed a 'discharge consent'. The former are covered later in this work, and the focus of this chapter is therefore on consents to discharge trade or sewage effluent into controlled waters, the most widely used means of authorising discharges of liquid effluent and a key mechanism in giving practical effect to a wide range of objectives and duties relating to reducing emissions and to water quality.

By their nature, however, the utility of consents is limited to those discharges to controlled waters arising from relatively discrete and easily identifiable sources, typically effluent pipes.[2] In contrast, their use as a prior approval and continuing control mechanism for regulating non-point source discharges (e.g. agricultural run-off) is severely limited,[3] and other preventive mechanisms will generally be of greater value in achieving water quality improvements.[4] Nor, it goes without saying, are consents of any relevance in combating the entry of things like litter, or tackling the consequences of fly dumping, which may be perceived as a greater problem than pollution and contamination.[5] However, where surface run-

---

[1] For a full list see 9.16 above.

[2] See 1.7.2 above.

[3] And see ministerial interpretation on the use of consents as quasi-planning tools at 14.10 below.

[4] See Ch.13 below. The European Court of Justice has held that 'discharge' for the purposes of the Dangerous Substances Directive 76/464/EEC should be given a broad interpretation so as to include non-point sources such as the leaching of creosote from wooden posts placed in watercourses, and the effects of the precipitation of steam containing listed substances (see 5.4.1A above). These judgments, while requiring some form of licensing system for such indirect discharges under this and (probably also) related EC water legislation does not necessarily mean that domestic courts would give the same meaning to 'discharge' in the context of the Water Resources Act 1991.

[5] Tunstall et al (1997) p.46.

off is collected and discharged to water by a pipe it may be the subject of control.

This chapter considers the statutory regime relating to discharge consents. It describes the procedures involved in obtaining a discharge consent, the powers and duties of the Environment Agency when determining applications for consents (or modifying or revoking consents), and the powers of the Agency to ensure compliance with their terms. It does not, though, look in any detail at the relationship between the system of discharge consents and that of trade effluent consents, since this is considered in the following chapter.[6]

## 10.2 Background

Discharge consents were first provided for under the Rivers (Prevention of Pollution) Act 1951, under which the central offence – of using a stream for the disposal of trade or sewage effluent from a new or altered outlet – was permitted where the consent of the appropriate river board had been obtained.[7] Under the Clean Rivers (Estuaries and Tidal Waters) Act 1960, consenting powers under the 1951 Act were extended to cover new outlets and new discharges of trade or sewage effluent into tidal waters or parts of the sea within certain seaward limits.[8] The Rivers (Prevention of Pollution) Act 1961 extended the consenting regime generally to include discharges which had been in existence before 1951, but which the non-retrospective 1951 Act had not regulated. Simultaneously, the 1961 Act removed the defence, available under the 1951 Act, that it was not reasonably practicable to dispose of the effluent in any other way.[9] The consenting regime was further expanded in scope under the Control of Pollution Act 1974, which extended the practical requirement for discharge consents to discharges to all underground, tidal and coastal waters.[10]

Since the coming into force of the relevant provisions of the 1974 Act, the need for discharges to be made in accordance with[11] the terms of a discharge consent has, for most practical purposes, been a mandatory requirement for anyone discharging effluent or polluting matter and wishing to avoid criminal liability for any of the principal water pollution offences. Consents have become the key administrative tool for regulating water quality at the level of the individual discharger, albeit within the wider context of quality objectives set either as a matter of national policy or in order to comply with EC obligations. Consenting practice will also be the main means by which international obligations are given effect. The consenting process allows for a degree of administrative 'fine-tuning' that

---

[6] See 11.12 below, and see also 9.14 above.
[7] s.7(1) Rivers (Prevention of Pollution) Act 1951. See more generally 2.10 above.
[8] s.1(1) and Sch.1 Clean Rivers (Estuaries and Tidal Waters) Act 1960.
[9] s.8(3) Rivers (Prevention of Pollution) Act 1951.
[10] Part II, Control of Pollution Act 1974.
[11] Note the extension in 1989 to include all discharges made *under and* in accordance with a consent, and see 10.6.5 below.

the blanket criminal offences of the kind originally provided for, at least notionally, under the Rivers Pollution Prevention Act 1876 is unable to deliver.[12]

## 10.3 Outline of the Present Legal and Policy Framework

Discharge consents are granted by the Environment Agency. By contrast to some other environmental licensing regimes,[13] the regime involves a slightly higher degree of public involvement, though in broad terms the decision-making process is largely technocratic. Formally, the Agency has considerable freedom when determining consents which, in part, is a reflection of the extent to which consents are relatively unsophisticated control mechanisms dating back half a century. For example there is no requirement that the discharger uses the 'best available techniques',[14] nor that discharging the polluting substances to water is the best practicable environmental option.[15] Nor must a discharger be a 'fit and proper person' and be sufficiently in funds to pay for any restoration works or other costs in the event of damage.

In many instances, however, the Agency is constrained in its decision-making by the need to secure compliance with statutory water quality standards derived from EC law[16] and to comply with international obligations.[17] Beyond these, however, there is no wider legal strategic background against which determinations must be made, for example in the way that decisions on applications for planning permission must generally be made in accordance with development plans.[18] The Agency must, however, have regard to its sustainable development, environmental and conservation duties and to its duty to consider the costs and benefits of acting.[19] Consent determinations may be appealed against, though the right of appeal does not extend to third parties that might be affected, illustrating the limits to public involvement. Formally, appeals are to the Secretary of State (or, in Wales, to the National Assembly),[20] though in practice decision-making is generally delegated to the Planning Inspectorate. There is no further appeal beyond the Secretary of State, although consents are amenable to judicial review.

Consents presently take one of three general forms:

---

[12] On the Rivers Pollution Prevention Act 1876 see 2.6 above.

[13] For example, waste management licensing, see 12.2.6 below.

[14] On best available techniques see the discussion of integrated pollution prevention and control at 12.3.3 below.

[15] Compare, e.g. integrated pollution control under Part I of the Environmental Protection Act 1990, at 12.3.2 below.

[16] See 14.8 below on EC-based statutory water quality objectives.

[17] Such as those deriving from the 1992 OSPAR Convention, see 18.8 below.

[18] See 14.3 below.

[19] On the Environment Agency's general duties see 6.9–6.12 and 6.14 above.

[20] And references in this chapter to the former should be taken to include the latter unless otherwise indicated.

(a) those that set *absolute numeric* limits (e.g. a maximum daily limit for a discharged substance);

(b) those setting *percentile* limits (i.e. requiring compliance with a limit, but only on a stated percentage of occasions, typically compliance in excess of the 95th percentile); and

(c) those that set *descriptive* limits (e.g. that the discharge must not be injurious to fish).

Percentile consents have tended to be used where the discharger does not have complete control over the quality of the effluent, as with discharges by sewerage undertakers. Descriptively formulated consents have tended to be used for the majority of relatively minor, or infrequent, discharges that make up the approximately 89,400 consents currently in force, the majority of which apply to sewage disposal.[21] In many cases, a combination of numeric and non-numeric approaches may be used. In prospect is the likelihood of a move towards consents based on the toxicity of the discharge to the receiving environment (measured, e.g. by the impact of the discharge on the aquatic ecology).[22]

The legal provisions relating to discharge consents are contained in Chapter II of Part III of the Water Resources Act 1991. Further detailed provisions relating to consents are set out in Schedule 10 to the 1991 Act, as substituted by the Environment Act 1995,[23] and in the Control of Pollution (Applications, Appeals and Registers) Regulations 1996.[24] In many respects the provisions contained in the revised Schedule 10 are modelled on the corresponding provisions for authorisations in Schedule 1 to the Environmental Protection Act 1990,[25] and provide for a greater degree of delegation of the detailed requirements to Regulations and Directions. The 1996 Regulations also aim to provide a considerable degree of uniformity between the administrative procedures in relation to discharge consents and authorisations for prescribed processed under Part I of the Environmental Protection Act 1990. As at the time of writing, the Government is engaged in consultations over revisions to the 1996 Regulations, and comment on suggested or likely changes to the Regulations is offered. Consents granted before the Water Resources Act 1991 came into force are translated into valid consents for the purposes of the 1991 Act.[26] Consents granted by the National Rivers Authority continue as if granted by the Agency.[27]

---

[21] DETR, *Digest of Environmental Statistics* (2001), para.3.38. Around 6,000 consents are for sewerage undertakers' treatment works. The largest number of consents are for private sewage treatment works.

[22] See 10.12.2 below.

[23] para.183 Sch.22 Water Resources Act 1991.

[24] SI 1996 No.2971. Applications and appeals made before 31 December 1996 continue to be dealt with under the previous version of the Schedule and relevant earlier Regulations; see Art.4 The Environment Act 1995 (Commencement No.8 and Saving Provisions) Order SI 1996 No.2909).

[25] See 12.3.2 below.

[26] s.2 and para.1(1) Sch.2 Water Consolidation (Consequential Provisions) Act 1991.

[27] s.55 Environment Act 1995.

## 10.3.1 The Legal Effect of Complying with Consents

Acting under and in accordance with a discharge consent gives a defence to the principal water pollution offences under s.85 Water Resources Act 1991.[28] Compliance will also provide a defence to charges brought under other enactments relating to the pollution of fisheries and to public health.[29]

In contrast, compliance with a consent will not provide a direct defence to civil proceedings, since nothing in Part III of the 1991 Act derogates from any right of action or other remedy (whether civil or criminal) in proceedings instituted otherwise than under Part III. Acting in accordance with the conditions of a discharge consent, therefore, will not necessarily avoid civil liability for the unlawful interference with a riparian or other common law right.[30] Nor, it is submitted, should the existence of a consent be relevant in determining whether a common law nuisance exists, for example by changing the nature of the locality.[31] Although the courts appear prepared to recognise that the impact of regulatory decisions such as planning permissions may alter locality for the purposes of private and public nuisance, there are considerable difficulties to be overcome in showing that a pollution licence has altered the character of the neighbourhood. In particular, private interests are accorded less weight in water quality decisions than in planning decisions, and the locality test has little relevance to cases involving interference with riparian rights, where the harm is characterised as physical.[32]

## 10.4 Exemption Orders

Before turning to the discharge consent regime, it is convenient to consider another mechanism apart from environmental licenses and discharge consents under which it may occasionally be found that a person is not guilty of a principal water pollution offence. Put differently, the combination of the principal water pollution offences and the environmental licensing systems, which provide defences to these offences, does not provide for a comprehensive legal regime for the control of all emissions and discharges into controlled waters. This is because of the existence of certain exemption orders which, for historical reasons, have the effect of placing particular kinds of discharge outside the controls which would otherwise operate.[33]

---

[28] s.88(1)(a) Water Resources Act 1991 and para.30 Sch.1 Water Consolidation (Consequential Provisions) Act 1991.

[29] See s.4 Salmon and Freshwater Fisheries Act 1975, discussed at 15.4.1 below and s.68 Public Health Act 1875, discussed at 12.4.3 below.

[30] See the discussion of s.100(b) Water Resources Act 1991 and of the County Court decisions in *Cook v South West Water* [1992] *Water Law* 103 and *Hughes v Dŵr Cymru Cyfyngedig* [1995] *Water Law* 40, at 9.21 above.

[31] See 3.8.4 above on nuisance and locality.

[32] Ball (1995) p.295, and *Nicholls v Ely Beet Sugar Factory Ltd* [1936] Ch 343 and see 3.3 above.

[33] Similarly, see the exempt status of certain discharges from previously abandoned mines discussed at 9.17.3 above.

The background to this lies in the Control of Pollution Act 1974, which allowed the Secretary of State to make orders to exempt certain discharges from the effect of the main prohibition upon the discharge of trade or sewage effluent.[34] Such orders could be made in relation to discharges which were of a kind which would not have been required to be subject to a discharge consent under the previous legislation.[35] Although exemption orders were intended as a transitional and temporary concession, because of savings provisions in the Water Act 1989 and the Water Resources Act 1991,[36] these orders have continued to operate.

Initially exemptions were provided for under the Control of Pollution (Exemption of Certain Discharges from Control) Order 1983,[37] though this has been amended by Variation Orders of 1986 and 1987.[38] The 1986 Order withdrew many of the original exemptions by the substitution of a more limited schedule. The 1987 Order harmonised the position of the former water authorities to that of other dischargers, so that any discharge which had been subject to an application for consent made before 15 October 1987 could lawfully be continued, pending the eventual determination of the application.

The cumulative effect of the three orders is, therefore, that various kinds of discharge which commenced before 4 July 1984 are deemed to have a discharge consent, without such a consent actually having been determined, until such time as a consent is determined. The categories involved relate to discharges:

    (a) of trade or sewage effluent from a building or from plant into any lake, lock or pond which does not discharge into a stream;[39]
    (b) of matter other than trade or sewage effluent into any controlled waters from a sewer or drain; and
    (c) of any trade or sewage effluent from a building or from plant on to or into any land.[40]

However, this list of situations where deemed consents are given, is qualified so that none of the exemptions is allowed to operate to contravene relevant European Community water quality directives.[41]

Whilst it would appear that the exemptions are of limited extent or practical importance, it is remarkable that measures, which were originally

---

[34] s.32(1) and (3) Control of Pollution Act 1974, and see Burton (1987).

[35] Rivers (Prevention of Pollution) Acts 1951 and 1961, and see 2.10 above on these Acts. Similarly, 'deemed consents' had been provided for under s.2 of the 1961 Act where a discharger had applied for a consent which had not been determined by the consenting authority.

[36] See para.22 Sch.26 Water Act 1989 and para.3 Sch.13 Water Resources Act 1991.

[37] SI 1983 No.1182.

[38] SI 1986 No.1623 and SI 1987 No.1782.

[39] Similarly, see the definition of 'controlled waters' at 9.4 above which excludes certain discrete waters.

[40] See Schedule to Control of Pollution (Exemption of Certain Discharges From Control) Order 1983 (SI 1983 No.1182) as amended by SI 1986 No.1623.

[41] See Ch.5 above on European Community water quality directives.

intended as transitional and temporary, have not yet been brought within the general procedures concerned for the determination and review of discharge consents. Nonetheless, there is no evidence that the exemption orders give rise to any significant water quality problems, and their continued existence seems to be due to their relative insignificance and, perhaps, legislative oversight.

## 10.5 Applying for consents

Applications for discharge consents must be made to the Agency on a form provided for the purpose. The application must, either on this form, or together with it, provide the Agency with such information as it may reasonably require, and such information as may be prescribed by the Secretary of State. The Agency may also ask for any additional information of any description needed for it to determine the application. Although failure to provide the required information will not invalidate the application, the Agency may refuse to proceed with the application, or refuse to proceed with it until such information is provided.[42] In practice, there will often be considerable discussion and negotiation between the discharger and the Agency prior to submission of the application for consent. The Agency may issue a letter of intent outlining the requirements that are likely to be imposed in order that design of the process or discharge can proceed.

The general requirement in relation to all applications for a consent is that they must be advertised by or on behalf of the applicant in a manner required by the Secretary of State by regulations. This is a departure introduced in the Environment Act 1995, before which the obligation in Schedule 10 to the Water Resources Act 1991 was on the National Rivers Authority to publicise the application, subject to provisions allowing it to recover any associated expenses.

Applications for a new consent, or a variation to a consent, must be advertised through a single round of advertising in a local[43] newspaper, along with an advertisement in the *London Gazette*.[44] The notices must:

(a) give the name of the applicant;
(b) specify the location of the activities to be consented;
(c) describe briefly the nature of the proposed activities;
(d) state where the registers containing information about the application may be inspected, the times when they are open for inspection, and that they may be inspected free of charge; and
(e) explain that any person may make representations in writing to the Agency, specify when the period allowed for making

---

[42] Sch.10 Water Resources Act 1991; see also the general offence of making false statements in s.206, discussed at 16.7 below.

[43] 'Local' both to the place of discharge and the place of impact.

[44] Specific provisions in relation to advertising are found in the Control of Pollution (Applications, Appeals and Registers) Regulations 1996 (SI 1996 No. 2971).

representations ends and give the address of the Agency to which
representations are to be sent.[45]

These provisions do not require the disclosure of any information that is
excluded from being in a register because it affects national security or is
considered confidential.[46] As a general rule, applications must be
advertised within the period of 28 days beginning 14 days after the
application is received by the Agency, though specific provisions relate to
situations where publicity requirements may be waived or further
information is sought by the Agency.[47]

The Secretary of State may, by regulations, prescribe the situations where
the Agency may dispense with these publicity requirements.[48] These are
set out in the 1996 Regulations, which provide two continuing[49] grounds
for exemption: first, where the application contains information which
would affect matters of national security;[50] and second, where the Agency
considers that the discharge is unlikely to have an 'appreciable effect' on
the receiving waters. These should be contrasted with the exemption of
certain *information* from applications. Thus, legitimate grounds relating to
commercial confidentiality may serve to exclude some information from
the publicity notice, but may not serve as the basis for the complete
exemption of the application from publicity as national security
considerations do. In practice, it is the operation of the second of these two
exemptions, concerning the appreciable effect of the discharge, which has
proved most contentious.

### 10.5.1  Consents Without Applications

There are some circumstances where the Agency may grant consents
without applications having first been made. Provision for this is intended
to cover those situations where discharges are already occurring which
require authorisation, but no consent has been applied for. The power
allows the Agency to attach conditions to a discharge as a means of
regulating and controlling the discharge. Consents without application,
however, may not relate to any discharge which occurred before the
consent is granted, and therefore cannot provide retrospective legal
protection in relation to any offence committed before the consent is
granted. There are obvious similarities between granting consents without

---

[45] *Ibid* Reg.2(3).

[46] *Ibid* Reg.2(4) and see ss.191A and 191B Water Resources Act 1991. And see Ch.16 below on
national security and commercial confidentiality considerations.

[47] *Ibid* Reg.3.

[48] para.1(2) Sch.10 Water Resources Act 1991.

[49] A third exemption related only to applications made before 1 April 1997, and was in effect a
transitional provision.

[50] s.191A Water Resources Act 1991 and Reg.4(a) Control of Pollution (Applications, Appeals
and Registers) Regulations 1996 (SI 1996 No.2971).

application and other mechanisms designed to curb problematic discharges, such as works notices and enforcement notices.[51]

The power to grant consents without application applies where a person has caused or permitted effluent or other matter to be discharged in contravention of the obligation not to discharge trade or sewerage effluent into any controlled waters or from land through a pipe into the sea beyond the seaward limits of controlled waters[52]; or in contravention of a prohibition notice;[53] and where a similar contravention by that person is likely. As with applications generally, consent may be granted subject to any appropriate conditions. In relation to publicity and consultation, broadly analogous provisions to those in relation to the normal application procedures are provided for.[54]

### 10.5.2 'No Appreciable Effect'

Although 'no appreciable effect' is not defined or explained in legislation, in practice the Agency appears to rely on practices described in its *Discharge Consents Manual*, originally prepared by the National Rivers Authority and now periodically updated by the Agency. This identifies the criteria to be applied in such determinations, broadly, as those set out in previous ministerial advice issued in 1984.[55] The advice suggests that the exemption from publicity will be available where three criteria are met:

(a) where the discharge does not affect an area of amenity or environmental significance (a beach, marine nature reserve, shellfishery, fish spawning area or site of special scientific interest);

(b) where the discharge does not result in a major change in the flow of receiving waters (e.g. a discharge volume greater than 10% of low river flow would normally constitute a major change); and

(c) where the discharge does not (i) result in a change to water quality which damages existing or future uses of the waters (whether or not these result in a change in water quality classification), or (ii) alter by 10% or more the concentration in the receiving waters of any substance which is important for the quality of the water and the well-being of its flora and fauna (e.g. dissolved oxygen, biochemical oxygen demand, suspended solids, ammonia, nitrates, phosphates and dissolved metals).

In practice, the application of these criteria has been contentious. For example, the emphasis on an alteration of less than 10% to the quality of the receiving waters may seem unduly relativistic to the existing state of

---

[51] See 13.2.2 below and 10.11.1 below respectively.

[52] s.85(3) Water Resources Act 1991.

[53] Under *ibid* s.86.

[54] *Ibid* para.6 Sch.10 and Reg.7 and Sch.1 Control of Pollution (Applications, Appeals and Registers) Regulations 1996.

[55] DoE, Departmental Circular No. 17/84, *Water and the Environment*, Annex 3 para.3.

the receiving waters, since what is an 'appreciable effect' may vary greatly between different controlled waters. Effects may also vary significantly over time where a particular watercourse changes in quality in the short or long term. Conversely, a very small discharge of a contaminant into water of high purity may bring about an increase of over 10% in the presence of a particular parameter but have an insignificant effect upon the overall water quality.[56] Such concerns prompt the question whether more explicit and non-relativistic criteria, perhaps set out in legislation rather than ministerial circular, would be more appropriate. While relativistic criteria fit well within the traditional, discretionary, approach to pollution control in the UK, it is questionable whether they pay sufficient regard to the need to take measures to prevent incremental deterioration in water quality.

More categorical criteria are especially important now that the *Discharge Consents Manual* no longer qualifies the 10% water quality deterioration threshold by reference to the impact of the discharge for which consent is sought 'taken together with previously consented discharges'. The guidance therefore indicates that any discharge resulting in water quality changes damaging to existing or future uses of the waters, regardless of any change in water quality classification, will lead to an appreciable effect. However, the impression is conveyed that water quality deterioration by encroachment is possible without the safeguards provided by public advertisement.[57]

Perhaps more pertinently, figures published by the National Rivers Authority indicated that, 'in practice, relatively few consent applications are advertised, as the majority of applications are for small discharges which are considered to exert "no appreciable effect"'.[58] The legal exception is in reality the practical norm, and it is suggested that 'it is objectionable that the operation of such an important publicity procedure rests on a rather restrictive interpretation given in a Departmental Circular'.[59]

### 10.5.3 Consultation

For all applications, the Agency is under a general duty to notify, and give a copy of the application to, specified consultees and any persons whom the Secretary of State directs to be consulted on any particular application. Those bodies that must be consulted, generally within 14 days of receipt of the application by the Agency, are:

(a) every local authority or water undertaker in the relevant area;

---

[56] Eastwood and Ord (1986) and Matthews (1987).

[57] Or consultation; see para.2(2) Sch.10 Water Resources Act 1991.

[58] National Rivers Authority, *Discharge Consents and Compliance* (1994) p.28. Informal estimates put the number of applications actually publicised at around 10 per cent.

[59] Bell and McGillivray (2000) p.577. The draft Regulations do not envisage any change to the exemption in relation to 'no appreciable effect', nor do they provide any further guidance on the meaning of the phrase.

(b) in the case of discharges to coastal waters, relevant territorial waters or waters outside the seaward limits of relevant territorial waters, each of the Ministers;[60]

(c) harbour authorities; and

(d) local sea fisheries committees.[61]

In relation to consultees, the period allowed for making representations is six weeks beginning with the date on which notice of the application was given. In relation to any other person, the period is six weeks from the last date the application was advertised.[62]

As with provisions in relation to advertisement, however, the duty to consult is considerably restricted by exceptions. In relation to excluded information,[63] consultation with local planning authorities, water undertakers, harbour authorities and sea fisheries committees is not required, nor is consultation required in relation to discharges with 'no appreciable effect' as outlined above.[64]

### 10.5.4 Directions to Delay Considering Applications

Under the Water Resources Act 1991, the Secretary of State may give the Agency a direction with respect to any particular application for consent (or class of applications for consent) requiring the Agency not to determine or not to proceed with the application or applications until the expiry of a period specified in the direction, or until directed by the Secretary of State that it may do so.[65] Such directions need not be given for any particular purpose, but conceivably might be used to allow for a greater period of time for representations to be made to the Agency, or perhaps to ensure that a discharge consent is not determined before another, more strategic, decision is made (e.g. on a planning application). This specific power to make directions should now be seen alongside the more general power for the Secretary of State to make directions to the Agency.[66]

### 10.5.5 References to the Secretary of State

Although applications for discharge consents are normally determined by the Agency, in certain circumstances applications may be 'called-in' by the Secretary of State for his own determination. This power may be exercised either following the making of representations or objections, or otherwise

---

[60] In Wales, the National Assembly.

[61] Reg.5(1) and (2) Control of Pollution (Applications, Appeals and Registers) Regulations 1996.

[62] *Ibid* Reg.5(4); reduced to 5 weeks in relation to the Channel Tunnel Rail Link; see Control of Pollution (Channel Tunnel Rail Link) Regulations 1998 (SI 1998 No.1649).

[63] Under ss.191A and 191B Water Resources Act 1991.

[64] The requirement imposed on the National Rivers Authority in Sch.10 Water Resources Act 1991, when minded to grant a consent, to notify anyone who had made representations or objections that they could, within 21 days, request the Secretary of State to 'call-in' the application, does not apply to the Environment Agency.

[65] *Ibid* para.4 Sch.10.

[66] Under s.40 Environment Act 1995, and see 6.2 above.

following a direction in relation to a particular application or class of applications. Where such a direction is given to the Agency, the Agency must comply with the direction and inform every applicant to whose application the direction relates of the transmission of his application to the Secretary of State.[67] There is no duty to consult the Agency before an application is called in.[68]

In the event of an application for a consent being called-in, the application may be the subject of an inquiry. Any time after the application is transmitted and before it is determined, the Secretary of State may cause a local inquiry to be held or afford the applicant and the Agency the chance of appearing at, and being heard by, a hearing before an appointed person. Aside from the applicant and the Agency, no other party now has the right to appear before, or be heard at, the inquiry or hearing, not even any person who had previously made a timely representation or objection.[69] If requested to do so by the applicant or the Agency, an inquiry or hearing must be held.[70] Such requests must be made in writing to the Secretary of State within 28 days of the applicant being informed by the Agency of the call-in.[71]

Any representations made to the Agency in relation to called-in applications must be referred by the Agency to the Secretary of State and will be considered alongside any representations made by the Agency.[72] The Secretary of State, having determined the application, providing it is properly made, must direct the Agency to give or refuse consent or give consents subject to conditions, and the Agency must comply with this direction.[73] It should be noted that the power of the Secretary of State to call in applications is rarely exercised.[74]

### 10.5.6 Discharge Consents and Powers of the Agency to Discharge Water

Special provision has always been necessary in relation to discharges made by the principal regulatory bodies. Before privatisation, the combination of operational and regulatory functions in the water authorities, especially in relation to sewage treatment works, gave a particular impetus to applications for consents from water authority premises to be determined other than by the water authorities themselves.[75] Following privatisation,[76]

---

[67] Notably, the discretion not to publicise where there is considered to be 'no appreciable effect' (see 10.5.2 above) does not apply to appeals.

[68] *R v Secretary of State for the Environment, ex parte Southwark London Borough Council* (1987) 54 P & CR 226.

[69] But a refusal to hear such views would be unlikely in practice, not least because of the effect of Art.6 European Convention on Human Rights.

[70] paras 5(4) and (5) Sch.10 Water Resources Act 1991.

[71] Reg.6(3) Control of Pollution (Applications, Appeals and Registers) Regulations 1996.

[72] *Ibid*, Reg.6(2) and para.5(3) Sch.10 Water Resources Act 1991.

[73] para.5(6) Sch.10 Water Resources Act 1991.

[74] Bell and McGillivray (2000) p.582.

[75] Although this did not, of course, mean that compliance and enforcement responsibilities were also separated.

[76] On water privatisation see 2.16 above.

and the transfer of most of the water utility functions of the water authorities into the private sector, this has become less problematic. Nevertheless, some means of avoiding the same body both discharging and determining its own consent to discharge is clearly needed in the interests of impartiality. In practice, however, the need for a consent will usually be restricted to those situations where the Agency is required to discharge in the course of carrying out works.

In order to avoid committing an offence, a consent will be required for any discharge made by the Agency, and hence a separate means of considering the granting, variation and revocation of consents held by the Agency is necessary.[77] These provisions are generally analogous to those contained in Schedule 10 to the Water Resources Act 1991, considered above. The key differences are that:

(a) all matters are considered and determined by the Secretary of State;

(b) that the 'no appreciable effect' exemption from publicity does not apply; and

(c) that there is no protected four year period within which consents cannot generally be varied or revoked.

Consents held by the Agency may be transferred to another person, in which case they are deemed to have been granted under the normal procedures.

Where the Agency is carrying out, or is about to carry out, the construction, alteration, repair, cleaning, or examination of any reservoir, well, borehole or other work belonging to the Authority, or it is exercising or about to exercise specified powers,[78] it may cause water in any relevant pipe,[79] or the other waters mentioned, to be discharged into any available watercourse. However, this power will not authorise any discharge which damages or injuriously affects the works or property of any railway company[80] or navigation authority or which floods or damages any highway. If the Agency fails to take all necessary steps to secure that any water discharged by it in accordance with this power is as free as may be reasonably practicable from mud and silt, solid, polluting, or injurious substances, and any substances prejudicial to fish or spawn, or spawning beds or food of fish, it will be guilty of an offence. Liability, on summary

---

[77] See s.99 Water Resources Act 1991and Reg.14 Control of Pollution (Applications, Appeals and Registers) Regulations 1996, which provides that Sch.2 to the 1996 Regulations applies to consents for discharges by the Agency in place of the general provisions contained in Sch.10 to the 1991 Act.

[78] The specified powers concerned relate to laying pieces of pipes in streets (s.159), laying of pipes on other land (s.160), and the power to carry out works in a street or on other land to deal with foul water and pollution (ss.162(2) and (3) and 163(1)(b) Water Resources Act 1991).

[79] 'Relevant pipe' means a resource main or discharge pipe, *ibid* s.159(5).

[80] 'Railway company' means the British Railways Board, London Regional Transport or any other person authorised by any other enactment, or by any rule or regulation made under any enactment, to construct, work or carry on a railway, *ibid* s.163(4).

conviction, is to a fine not exceeding level 3 on the standard scale, currently £1000.[81]

A limitation upon the power of the Agency to discharge for works purposes is that, except in an emergency,[82] no discharge through any pipe the diameter of which exceeds 229 millimetres may be made except with a prescribed consent. Application for a consent of this kind involves an application being made by the Agency to the Secretary of State and served upon specified persons who may be affected by the proposed discharge. The consent may relate to a particular discharge, or to discharges of a particular description, and be made subject to reasonable conditions, but consent may not be unreasonably withheld. If the Agency contravenes, without reasonable excuse, any condition of the consent, it will be guilty of an offence and liable, on summary conviction, to a fine not exceeding level 3 on the standard scale, currently £1000.[83]

## 10.6 Consent Conditions

If the requirements relating to applications are complied with, the Agency must consider whether to give the consent applied for, either unconditionally or subject to conditions, or to refuse it. In doing so the Agency must consider any representations made by a consultee, or any other person, within the period allowed.[84] A consent will be deemed to have been refused if it is not given within four months beginning with the day on which the application is received or within a longer period agreed in writing between the Agency and the applicant. However, if the applicant has failed to supplement the application with information required by the Agency, the Agency may delay the determination for a reasonable period after the information is provided.[85] In practice there is evidence to suggest that the time taken to determine applications may be close to, if not more than, this four month period.[86]

The conditions subject to which a consent may be given are 'such conditions as the Agency may think fit'. In particular, it is explicitly stated that conditions may be included as to the following matters:

(a) the places at which the discharges may be made[87] and the design and construction of any outlets for the discharges;

---

[81] s.163 Water Resources Act 1991.

[82] On discharging in emergencies see 9.17.1 above.

[83] s.164 Water Resources Act 1991.

[84] *Ibid* para.2(3) and (5) Sch.10.

[85] *Ibid* para.3(1) to (3) Sch.10.

[86] House of Commons Select Committee on the Environment, Transport and the Regions, *Sewage Treatment and Disposal* (1998) para.234.

[87] The Agency must ensure that the point of discharge of urban waste water is chosen, as far as possible, so as to minimize the effects on receiving waters, para.5 Sch.3 Urban Waste Water Treatment (England and Wales) Regulations 1994 (SI 1994 No.2841).

(b) the nature, origin, composition, temperature, volume and rate of the discharges and the periods during which the discharges may be made;

(c) the steps to be taken, in relation to the discharges or by way of subjecting any substance likely to affect the description of matter discharged to treatment or any other process, for minimising the polluting effects of the discharges on any controlled waters;[88]

(d) the provision of facilities for taking samples of the matter discharged and the provision, maintenance and use of manholes, inspection chambers, observation wells and boreholes in connection with the discharges;

(e) the provision, maintenance and testing of meters for measuring or recording the volume and rate of the discharges and apparatus for determining the nature, composition and temperature of the discharges;

(f) the keeping of records of the nature, origin, composition, temperature, volume and rate of the discharges and records of readings of meters and other recording apparatus provided in accordance with the consent; and

(g) the making of returns and the giving of other information to the Agency about the nature, origin, composition, temperature, volume and rate of the discharges.

A consent may be given subject to different conditions in respect of different periods.[89]

As can be seen from the wide range of matters for which conditions can be imposed, the Agency has considerable powers to require dischargers to keep records and make returns about the state of the discharge. While dischargers may be best placed to collect this information, there is clearly a reduction in the administrative burden on the Agency in requiring this.[90] The courts have confirmed that the Agency may impose positive obligations, and that failure to perform a positive act may amount to an offence.[91]

### 10.6.1 Consent Conditions: Law and Policy

The use of a non-exhaustive list of possible consent conditions raises questions about the extent of conditions that may validly be imposed. In certain respects, the exercise of discretion by the Agency in imposing conditions is confined by requirements in relation to water quality objectives,[92] and obligations under EC and, to an extent, international law.

---

[88] This provision was not contained in the Control of Pollution Act 1974, leading to uncertainty as to whether the water authorities could insist on any particular form of treatment, see *Re Cutts*, Court of Appeal, 31 January 1991, unreported.

[89] para.3(4) Sch.10 Water Resources Act 1991.

[90] On (e) to (g), see further the discussion of self-monitoring at 16.8 below.

[91] Under s.85(6) Water Resources Act 1991, discussed at 9.13 above.

[92] Especially under s.84 Water Resources Act 1991, discussed at 14.8 below.

The latter may be either in respect of the pollutants a particular discharge contains, or the receiving waters into which it is to be discharged, and generally have legal rather than purely administrative effect. Increasing reliance on river catchment modelling is also made, to assess the cumulative impact of effluent discharges on a catchment basis rather than assessing discharges individually.[93]

The Agency's discretion is also confined by its environmental and other duties under the Environment Act 1995. These include the Agency's sustainable development duty and its obligation to promote conservation, as well as its duty, discussed further below, to have regard to costs and benefits where it exercises any power.[94] However, the Agency is also under a duty to have particular regard to the duties imposed on water or sewerage undertakers under Parts II to IV of the Water Industry Act 1991, as well as a duty, in relation to its pollution control functions only, to have regard to the desirability of conserving and enhancing features of the natural environment.[95]

Further, while the legislative framework gives a degree of discretion to the Agency in determining consents, there are pressures from various quarters for these powers and duties to be exercised in a more consistent manner.[96] Indeed, a rationale behind the creation of a *National* Rivers Authority was greater national consistency in decision-making, and one of the first steps of the Authority was the publication of guidance intended to facilitate this policy objective.[97] Working towards greater consistency in decision-making remains a key objective of the Environment Agency, although in relation to consents this must be balanced against the need to meet ambient water quality standards and differing assimilative capacities. There are clear tensions when pursuing the incompatible objectives of consistency, respect for ambient standards and the balancing of costs and benefits.

Because of the emphasis on ambient water quality, and increasingly on water quality objectives and standards, there is less emphasis in setting consents on process or specification-based techniques such as the requirement to use the 'best available techniques' which is central to the pollution prevention and control regime.[98] In comparison to a regime such as that governing discharges to water from prescribed processes, therefore,

---

[93] National Rivers Authority, *Discharge Consents and Compliance* (1994) p.32. On the setting of consents generally see also Warn (1994) and Waite and Crawshaw (1996).
[94] ss.4, 6 and 39 Environment Act 1995, and see 6.9–6.12 and 6.14 above.
[95] s.15 Water Resources Act 1991 and s.7(1)(b) Environment Act 1995. On the significance of the difference in wording in relation to the pollution control duty see 6.10 above.
[96] In this context note the views of the House of Commons Select Committee on the Environment, Transport and the Regions, *The Environment Agency* (2000) para.76, that 'Inconsistencies in policy and practice between the different regions of the Agency should be limited to those areas where they are a result of a genuine need for local differences in approach (such as to reflect the different ecological nature of river catchments in different areas of the country, or to take account of regional sustainable development strategies) rather than a lack of clarity of policy or a failure effectively to communicate national policy and standard working practices to local staff'.
[97] National Rivers Authority, *Discharge Consents and Compliance Policy* (1990).
[98] See 12.3.3 below.

the Agency has greater discretion in relation to how environmental standards are to be met, and may have a choice of approaches to choose from.[99] In doing so, however, Agency practice has been to be guided by the following considerations:

    (a) that water is a resource on which a range of users may make legitimate demands;

    (b) that receiving waters have a capacity to absorb and assimilate limited quantities of effluent without significant deterioration in water quality; and

    (c) that the costs of regulation to dischargers is a relevant consideration in practice.[100]

This view is now reinforced by the general duty of the Agency to have regard to costs and benefits in exercising its powers. As noted elsewhere, however, this duty does not detract from obligations on the Agency to meet quality standards imposed nationally or under EC obligations.[101] As outlined above, the choice of consenting approaches has usually been between consents using numeric limits (including consents using '95-percentiles' and 'look-up tables', termed 'percentile consents' below) and non-numeric or descriptive consents.

### 10.6.1A Numeric consents

For most industrial discharges it is customary for numeric limits to be imposed on a range of key parameters. Typically, these will relate to biochemical oxygen demand, pH, temperature, suspended solids and toxic or dangerous substances.[102] They may be formulated either as absolute maximum quantities of the parameter in the discharge, or as relative requirements. For example, a requirement concerning the temperature of water immediately downstream from an outlet will be framed in relation to the increase in temperature attributable to the discharge (that is, the difference in temperature between ambient and outflow temperatures) rather than to the ambient water temperature. This avoids imposing conditions which would be unreasonable if subject to the vagaries of unseasonably high temperatures. It is also possible for other quality parameters to be imposed according to the relative impact on the receiving water rather than on the composition of the discharge or merely its effect below the point of discharge, and consents may stipulate that the difference between inflow and outflow quality should not exceed stated amounts.[103] There are approximately 30,000 numeric limited consents in

---

[99] The Agency has a general duty to 'follow developments in technology and techniques for preventing or minimising, or remedying or mitigating the effects of, pollution of the environment' (s.5(4) Environment Act 1995).

[100] Waite and Crawshaw (1996) p.195.

[101] s.39 Environment Act 1995 and see 6.14 above.

[102] E.g., List I and II compounds mentioned in the Dangerous Substances Directive, discussed at 5.4.1 above.

[103] For an illustration see Howarth (1990) p.141.

England and Wales, of which 10,000 are routinely monitored by the Agency.[104]

### 10.6.1B  *Percentile consents*

A variant on the numeric consent, frequently used for common contaminants in consents held by sewerage undertakers,[105] is the 95-percentile formulation, whereby a statistically insignificant number of breaches are permitted over a 12 month period. In practice, consents with percentile limits are always used together with statistical compliance tables, or 'look-up' tables, relating the number of samples of effluent taken in a year to the maximum permitted number of samples in which the key determinants in the discharge consent are allowed to breach their limit values. The 95-percentile formulation, therefore, provides a mechanism by which it is ascertained whether any breach or the consent is due to chance or can be considered statistically significant.

### The Look-up Table

| *Number of Samples* | *Permitted Number of Failed Samples* |
|:---:|:---:|
| 4-7 | 1 |
| 8-16 | 2 |
| 17-28 | 3 |
| 29-40 | 4 |
| 41-53 | 5 |
|  | etc |

(Source: Environment Agency, *Discharge Consents, Monitoring, Compliance and Pollution Load* (1997), p.iii.)

The use of a statistical measure for compliance is regarded as a recognition of the inherent variability of effluent quality, especially where biological treatment methods are used, and has been seen as 'the best compromise which could be made between the conflicting realities of the legal and the real worlds'.[106] Although based upon the need for statistically certain non-compliance, the statistical compliance table incorporates adjustments to take account of statistical errors in sampling. Thus in the case of discharges from sewage works, breach of discharge consent amounts to failure to keep the number of samples which do not meet the specified quality parameters below the permitted number of 'fails' corresponding to the total number of samples which have been taken during the year.[107] It

---

[104] See www.environment-agency.gov.uk:80/s-enviro/stresses/4use-rel-dis/3aquatic-dis/4-3.html

[105] Percentile consents are only used for sewerage undertakers.

[106] Young (1979) p.200; see also Hammerton (1987) p.339 and Matthews (1987) p.143.

[107] The same approach has never been adopted in relation to discharge consents relating to premises other than sewage works.

follows that a single failure to meet single discharge quality requirements, or even a number of such failures, will not necessarily amount to a breach of the discharge consent where the annual number of failures remains less than that permitted according to the compliance table.

The 95-percentile requirement is usually subject to certain limitations and conditions. First, the sampling period is usually any twelve month period chosen at the Agency's discretion. Second, recognising the damage to the aquatic environment that can be done even by very occasional pollution incidents, percentile limits are now usually subject to absolute limits or 'upper tiers' above which an offence is committed even within the percentile limit.[108] However, Government guidance stipulates that absolute limits should not be applied to sewage works with a population equivalent of 2,000 or greater, and should only be introduced for smaller treatment works as required to implement the Urban Waste Water Treatment Directive.[109] In the absence of an upper tier in percentile consents, limits may be exceeded with impunity in a determined proportion of instances, with the only enforcement mechanism against the discharger being through some form of a descriptive condition as described below.

### 10.6.1C Descriptive consents

Descriptive consents specify, in general terms, which impacts on the receiving environment are not permitted. Previously, many consents stipulated that the discharge or effluent, either on its own or in combination with other matter, should at no time contain any matter which will cause the receiving waters to be poisonous or injurious to fish, the spawn of fish, or the food of fish.[110] An additional requirement might have been that such matter would not cause damage to the ecology of the receiving waters, and that the treated effluent did not have any other adverse environmental impact, a condition generally referred to as the 'fish' or 'fish kill' condition.[111]

Following a substantial number of appeals against the fish kill condition brought by sewerage undertakers (known as the 'Kinnersley appeals' because the condition was promoted in the 'Kinnersley Report'),[112] policy has been to use instead a 'works operation condition'. This condition requires sewage treatment works to be operated, as far as reasonably

---

[108] Absolute limits were relaxed for wholly discreditable reasons in what has been described as 'a sort of environmental betrayal' committed in the run up to water privatisation in 1989: Kinnersley (1994) p.149.

[109] See National Rivers Authority, *Discharge Consents and Compliance* (1994). On the Urban Waste Water Treatment Directive see 5.6.2 above.

[110] See further s.4 Salmon and Freshwater Fisheries Act 1975, discussed at 15.4.1 below.

[111] For limited judicial comment on a variant of this condition, see *National Rivers Authority v Egger (UK) Ltd* [1992] *Water Law* 169. See also the discussion of new and unforeseen contaminants at 10.6.5 below.

[112] National Rivers Authority, *Discharge Consents and Compliance Policy* (1990) (the 'Kinnersley Report'), named after the Chair of the responsible group of the Authority which drafted the Report.

practicable, so as to minimise the polluting impact of the effluent discharged. For the Secretary of State:

> This allows a balance to be struck between the ability of the discharger to comply with the consent and the ability of the regulator to enforce the condition reflecting both the unpredictability of events and the inability of the discharger to exercise complete control over all aspects of the discharge . . . [and] acknowledges that the cost-effectiveness of action by the discharger ought to be a relevant consideration.[113]

It is evident that this condition, which in time will be incorporated into a large number of consents held by sewerage undertakers, is a clear move towards the specific use of process standard techniques in water pollution control regulation, echoing the requirement to use the 'best practicable means' found in earlier legislation but consciously avoided in water pollution legislation in recent years.

Many non-numeric consented discharges are only authorised to operate under specific weather conditions, e.g. under storm conditions. There are currently around 50,000 discharges controlled by descriptive consents, mostly consents to discharge sewage effluent.[114]

To date, descriptive consents have only used biological indicators, such as injuriousness to fish or other aquatic fauna and flora. Descriptive consents have not been used for other subjective features such as colour or smell or debris.

### 10.6.2  Consenting Policy in Practice

As discussed above, the practice in relation to numeric and percentile consents has been to take a chemical or substance-specific approach, focusing on those parameters or substances known to cause most damage to the aquatic environment. By contrast, descriptive consents are less concerned about the specific composition of the effluent, and focus instead on the impacts of the discharge on the receiving water, although usually this is through somewhat vague and imprecise standards relating to the impact of the discharge on fish or their food. For more significant discharges, therefore, there is an emphasis on identifying the polluting effects of individual substances. While this may be an adequate response to many discharges, however, concerns have been raised that it fails to take sufficient account of interactive effects in the receiving waters or more generally the synergistic or 'cocktail' effect of different pollutants. That is, the overall toxicity of the discharge cannot be predicted by taking a substance-specific approach. A substance-specific approach is also problematic when regard is had to the exponential number of new

---

[113] Letter to Ed Gallagher, Chief Executive, Environment Agency, dated 22 December 1997. See further Payne (1998).

[114] See www.environment-agency.gov.uk:80/s-enviro/stresses/4use-rel-dis/3aquatic-dis/4-3.html

chemical substances that come onto the market annually, and to the present limitations on identifying the adverse environmental effects of an ever increasing range of substances.

By contrast, it has been suggested for some time that a more effective approach would be to assess the polluting impact of chemical and other substances according to their ecotoxicological effect, that is, the combined effect of effluent discharge on test organisms of the kind found in controlled waters.[115] The prospect for such 'direct toxicity assessment', and the implications this would have for discharge consenting law and policy, is considered in more depth at the end of this chapter.[116]

In practice, a number of consents employ some combination of numeric standards for the discharge, and standards relating to the relative impact of the discharge on the receiving waters, i.e. a combination of numeric and non-numeric approaches. This raises the issue as to the extent to which the general descriptive conditions may be breached even where there is compliance with the numeric parameters. The recent determinations on the 'Kinnersley' appeals, and the new 'works operation condition', makes it clear that compliance with the descriptive condition will not prevent an unlawful breach of a specific, numeric, provision of the consent.[117]

The scope for more prescriptive conditions is unclear. As a matter of law, specified treatment processes may be stipulated, and in some cases conditions to this effect have been used. In a number of related appeals concerning storm and emergency overflows from sewage works, for example, the Secretary of State imposed conditions concerning the circumstances under which the overflow should operate, rather than imposing conditions governing the quality of the effluent.[118] Elsewhere, conditions requiring ultraviolet disinfection have been imposed.[119] But as a matter of policy, the freedom for dischargers to find the most effective means to comply with standards has been greatly cherished. It must therefore be doubted whether, outside of those discharges subject to integrated pollution control or pollution prevention and control,[120] such prescriptively formulated conditions will be imposed more widely.[121]

---

[115] See National Rivers Authority, *Discharge Consents and Compliance Policy* (1990).

[116] See 10.12.2 and see also 1.3.8 above.

[117] See 10.6.1C above.

[118] See McGillivray (1995a) p.73.

[119] It is perhaps significant that in *R* v *National Rivers Authority ex parte Moreton* [1996] Env LR 234 the respondents to the challenge to the decision of the NRA not to require ultraviolet disinfection of sewage effluent did not seek to argue that such a condition would have been unlawful (the respondents were successful on other grounds; see 10.6.4 below).

[120] See 12.3 below.

[121] See also 13.2.2 on works notices, which show similar difficulties of the Agency directing industrialists on the conduct of their operations.

### 10.6.3  Material Considerations in Consenting

When a consent is determined by the Agency, a range of factors will be taken into account. Some of these must be considered and guide the Agency in a strong sense, since they follow from mandatory, statutory standards, generally to comply with European Community water quality objectives. Others are discretionary, in the sense that the Agency must have regard to them only as a matter of the lawful exercise of administrative functions. In this weaker sense, the weight that is given to them will be a matter for the Agency and unlikely to be overturned by the courts unless their reasonableness can be challenged.

### 10.6.3A  EC and international law considerations

The need to comply with EC directives acts as the major constraint on Agency discretion in determining discharge consents. As described in more detail elsewhere, for example, the Agency is under a duty to take steps to eliminate pollution by 'Black List' substances, insofar as these are the subject of 'daughter' directives to the Dangerous Substances Directive. However, the approach adopted by the UK is to do so by resort to water quality objectives and standards rather than emission limit standards. Similarly, for 'Grey List' substances the Agency must act within the context of general and specific pollution reduction programmes.[122] Of course, processes discharging substances listed in the Dangerous Substances Directive will often be regulated under integrated pollution control or integrated pollution prevention and control. But a more general issue is that standards contained in EC law relating to specific substances may, within the context of the relevant water quality standards, act as a significant fetter on the discretion of the Agency in relation to determining discharge consent applications.

The Agency is also under an obligation to ensure that discharges are consented so that any other mandatory standards in EC water legislation are complied with.[123] As described elsewhere, therefore, the Agency must act so as to ensure compliance with the mandatory water quality standards in the following Directives:

(a)  the Drinking Water Abstraction Directive;
(b)  the Bathing Water Directive;
(c)  the Freshwater Fish Waters Directive;
(d)  the Shellfish Waters Directive;
(e)  the Groundwater Directive;
(f)  the Urban Waste Water Treatment Directive.[124]

More generally, the Agency may be under a duty to comply with more generally worded objectives of EC law. Thus, where appropriate, the

---

[122] On the Dangerous Substances Directive see 5.4.1 above.
[123] s.84(1) Water Resources Act 1991 and see 14.8.1 below.
[124] See 14.8 below generally on statutory water quality objectives.

Agency must exercise its functions in accordance with the relevant objectives of waste management law that give effect to the Waste Framework Directive.[125] However, it is worth recalling that the general principles of EC environmental law, such as the principles that pollution should be prevented and rectified at source, and the precautionary principle, do not directly bind national authorities. Thus, a consent cannot be challenged for failing to give effect generally to these principles.[126]

Beyond environmental quality law, special provisions made for sites safeguarded under EC conservation law also bind the Agency. Under the Conservation (Natural Habitats etc.) Regulations 1994, the Agency must assess the effects of any proposed discharge on a 'European site' in the light of that site's conservation objectives.[127] If the Agency considers that any adverse effects of the discharge on the relevant nature conservation interests could be mitigated by conditions then it may only grant consent subject to such conditions. Otherwise, if the discharge will have an adverse effect, consent should be refused unless the project concerned must be carried out for reasons of overriding public interest.[128]

Beyond EC law, requirements under international law may also confine the discretion of the Agency. Most important here, perhaps, are the various obligations under the 1992 'OSPAR' Convention, which in general takes a preventive and precautionary approach to the control of discharges to the water environment of the North Sea and North East Atlantic. For example, agreement reached under the OSPAR Convention places considerable restrictions on the extent to which radioactive discharges to the marine environment may be authorised.[129] International standards for protecting against dangers to human health from radiation also play a central factor in relation to discharges more generally. For example, consents to discharge radiation to water from inland facilities such as hospitals or defence establishments are governed by the need to comply with international radiological protection standards.[130]

### 10.6.3B National law considerations

Subject to those specific restrictions or obligations imposed by EC or international law outlined above, the Environment Agency clearly has very broadly formulated powers to impose conditions on consents. However, the power to do so is an administrative law power and therefore subject to the general obligations on public law bodies to act reasonably within their powers and according to procedural requirements.[131] For example, the

---

[125] Sch.4 Waste Management Licensing Regulations 1994 (SI 1994 No.1056), see 12.2.6 below.
[126] See 4.7 above.
[127] Regs.85 and 48 Conservation (Natural Habitats etc.) Regulations 1994 (SI 1994 No.2716). On the definition of 'European site' see Reg.10. On EC conservation law generally see 15.8 below.
[128] *Ibid* Reg.48(5).
[129] See 20.6.3 below. On the OSPAR Convention generally see 18.8 below.
[130] See 20.6.1 below. These standards have, in fact, been given effect to in Directives under the Euratom Treaty.
[131] See generally Craig (1999).

National Rivers Authority refused an application for a consent for a fish farm on the River Derwent because the proposal was likely to have caused local eutrophication to the only large oligotrophic river in England, for which it was designated as a site of special scientific interest.[132] The Authority took the view that no reasonable limits could have been imposed on nutrient loading in such circumstances.[133]

Although the matter has never been directly tested judicially, it has been suggested that the power to impose conditions on consents should be exercised according to criteria similar to those elaborated by the courts in relation to conditions on the grant of planning permission.[134] Thus, it has been suggested that the criteria for the validity of planning conditions set out in the leading case of *Newbury Borough Council* v *Secretary of State for the Environment*[135] would be applied.[136] On this view, consent conditions will be valid only to the extent that:

(a)  they fairly and reasonably relate to the purposes of Part III of the Water Resources Act 1991 (and not for any ulterior motive);
(b)  they relate to the discharge for which consent is applied for; and
(c)  they are otherwise reasonable and sufficiently certain.[137]

The fact that the Control of Pollution Act 1974 provided that discharge consent conditions should be 'such *reasonable* conditions as the [water] authority sees fit' is of little assistance. The omission of 'reasonable' in the present formulation contained in Schedule 10 to the Water Resources Act 1991 neither adds not detracts from the previous position. Were the Agency to impose conditions violating these general principles, an appeal or judicial review application would be available. A number of cases illustrate the general approach of the courts.

In *R* v *Ettrick Trout Company Ltd and William Baxter*[138] the appellants argued that a condition which related to the volume of effluent which could be discharged was invalid because it had not been imposed for a purpose relevant to Part III of the Water Resources Act 1991. It was argued that the restriction on the volume of water discharged was imposed for the ulterior purpose of limiting the volume of water *abstracted* and therefore unlawful. However, the Court of Appeal held that such a

---

[132] On eutrophication see 1.3.1–2 above. On SSSIs see 15.7.1 below.
[133] Howarth and McGillivray (1994) para.6.3.2.
[134] Under s.70(1) Town and Country Planning Act 1990, discussed at 14.4 below.
[135] [1980] 1 All ER 731, and see 14.5.5A below.
[136] Bates (1990, updated), para.10.122.
[137] It should be noted that Circular 11/95 provides for a slightly wider range of requirements for planning conditions, but these must be seen as of restricted application to planning conditions and only have legal materiality because of judicial decisions providing that the content of government planning circulars may be 'material considerations' for decision-makers in planning law: see generally *Carpets of Worth Ltd* v *Wyre Forest District Council* (1991) 62 P & CR 334. See also *R* v *Wakefield Metropolitan District Council ex parte Pearl Assurance plc* [1997] JPL B130. On the important distinction between whether something is a material consideration, and the weight to be attached to it, see *Tesco Stores Ltd* v *Secretary of State for the Environment* [1995] 1 WLR 759.
[138] [1994] Env LR 165; [1994] *Water Law* 50.

collateral challenge to a charge for breach of consent conditions was an attempt to bypass procedural provisions of administrative law,[139] and statutory appellate procedures, and was an abuse of process.[140] The Court did not, however, go as far as to say that any such collateral challenge would be unlawful, and a challenge to a blatantly irrational consent condition might succeed.[141] A subsequent judicial review application, however, was dismissed.[142]

In a similar vein, the *Scrayingham Sewer Appeal*, discussed in more detail elsewhere,[143] illustrates some of the issues concerning the relationship between the discharge consent system and the system of town and country planning and hence wider land-use controls. While this was only an administrative appeal, it does illustrate the extent to which imposing conditions on discharge consents might be better classified as land use planning controls, though in the appeal itself it was decided that the consent system was not being used for an ulterior motive.

Similarly, it might be questioned whether the Environment Agency would have the legal authority to impose a condition requiring ultra-violet disinfection on a discharge from a crayfish farm. Such a condition might be imposed in the interests of preventing the spread of crayfish plague (a matter of fish health) rather than in the interests of the quality of the water environment. As has been discussed elsewhere, the extent to which the Agency's functions may be exercised in the interests of human health is a matter of debate.[144]

The difficulty with all of these examples, however, is drawing anything resembling a neat boundary around the discharge consent system. Moreover, the nature of regulatory systems is that they change to reflect changes in accepted policy objectives.[145] Perhaps the most likely approach, which would fit in well with the generally pragmatic and discretionary approach taken in national environmental regulation, will be that factors such as town and country planning controls, or water resource controls, will be material considerations in relation to determining discharge consents.[146] Similarly, the consenting system will be a material consideration in other regimes which impact on water quality. As the

---

[139] Rules of the Supreme Court Order 53, now part of the new code of civil procedure created by the Civil Procedure Rules 1998.
[140] See now also *Clark* v *University of Lincolnshire and Humberside* [2000] 3 All ER 752, and see 10.9 below.
[141] See Thornton and Beckwith (1997) p.211. A crucial issue in *Ettrick Trout* was that the alleged invalidity was not apparent on the face of the consent.
[142] *Ettrick Trout Co Ltd* v *Secretary of State for the Environment* [1995] Env LR 269. On collateral challenges see also 10.9 below.
[143] See 14.10 below.
[144] See 8.4.10 above.
[145] See, e.g., the widening concept of 'planning', both in terms of a broader concept of town and country planning (see Bell and McGillivray (2000) p.297), and of 'environmental planning' more generally on which see 14.10 below
[146] On this approach see *Gateshead Metropolitan Borough Council* v *Secretary of State for the Environment* [1995] Env LR 37 and DoE, *Planning Policy Guidance Note 23* (1994).

following section demonstrates, the courts are reluctant to intervene to overturn a decision-makers assessment of the weight to be given to a legal or policy consideration.

### 10.6.4 The Reviewability of Determinations

Although the mechanisms for dischargers to appeal any conditions imposed in discharge consents, and similarly any decision not to issue a consent, are considered later in this chapter, [147] it is useful here to look at the important practical question of how much discretion the Agency has when determining applications for consents. That is, while the previous sections have looked at the range of international, EC and national factors that may be 'material considerations' in the consenting process, this section looks at the extent to which any decision by the Agency might be reviewed by the courts, and on what grounds. Because the Water Resources Act 1991 makes no specific provision for points of law to be referred to the courts, such challenges must be made by way of the normal procedures for applications for judicial review. Because third parties have no right to appeal against determinations to the Secretary of State, however, decisions by the Environment Agency can be taken directly to judicial review by third parties. However, dischargers aggrieved by adverse decisions of the Agency will usually have to exhaust any appeal rights before a judicial review will be entertained.[148]

Two cases illustrate the approach of the courts in judicial review proceedings relating to the criteria which the Agency must, or may, take into account in determining discharge consent applications. First, the decision in *R v National Rivers Authority ex parte Moreton*[149] is instructive. The applicant regularly swam in the sea off Tenby, and brought judicial review proceedings challenging the terms on which the National Rivers Authority had granted a consent to the sewerage undertaker for the area (Welsh Water) to discharge from a new long-sea outfall near to where she swam. The applicant's case was based on what was seen as an impermissible failure on the party of the Authority not to require ultra violet disinfection of the effluent before it was discharged. In particular, it was claimed that the Authority had wrongly taken into account, or considered as a restriction, the investment budget of Welsh Water, as determined through the price review process;[150] and that the Authority had unlawfully failed to have regard to mandatory obligations under the Bathing Water Directive[151] and the Urban Waste Water Treatment Directive.[152]

---

[147] See 10.9 below.
[148] *Ibid.*
[149] [1996] Env LR 234.
[150] On the price review process see 7.8 above.
[151] Directive 76/160/EEC, and see 5.5.2 above.
[152] Directive 91/271/EEC, and see 5.6.2 above.

On the first issue, relating to the investment budget of the sewerage undertaker, it was noted that investment budgets had been published indicating the funds available to the undertaker in relation to environmental improvements. In relation to the first budget, it was noted that amounts allocated for basic investments would not have been sufficient to deal with existing problems (in any event, the date for compliance with the Bathing Water Directive was 1985). A further budget for discretionary schemes had allocated funds to projects which were regarded by the undertaker as more pressing than the particular outfall which was the subject of the complaint. The applicant contended that the Authority had wrongly taken these budgets into account and thereby fettered its discretion in determining the application and had failed to consider the application on its merits.

On the second challenge, concerning the implementation of the Bathing Water Directive, it was alleged that the Authority had failed to have regard to the imperative ('I') standard under the Directive. Specifically, it had failed to adhere to a duty under national legislation[153] to ensure that standards for bathing water were achieved so far as it was practicable to do so. With regard to the third challenge, it was alleged that the Authority had misunderstood the requirements of the Urban Waste Water Treatment Directive. Although the Directive allows less stringent treatment for waters identified as 'less sensitive',[154] this is with the proviso that discharges receive primary treatment and that such discharges do not adversely affect the receiving environment. It was alleged that the Authority had neglected to consider the proviso and had thereby misdirected itself.

In dismissing the application it was held that the Authority had not improperly fettered its discretion in considering what conditions to impose upon the discharge consent since the Authority's decision had not been pre-determined by the statements regarding the undertaker's investment budgets. The Authority had no interest in the resource implications of the engineering solutions needed to meet the mandatory environmental standards and had concerned itself merely with the question of whether the standards would be met. In relation to complying with the Bathing Water Directive, it was found that there was no evidence that the Authority had failed to comply with the imperative standard required by the Directive, although it was observed by the judge that 'it would appear that they [i.e. the UK Government, not the Authority] are not implementing the mandatory virus standard as required by the Directive'.[155] In respect of the failure of the Authority to consider the proviso in relation to the Urban

---

[153] Under the Bathing Waters (Classification) Regulations 1991 (SI 1991 No.1597) and the National Rivers Authority (Bathing Waters) Directions 1992. See also 5.5.2 above and 14.8.4 below.

[154] Under Art.6 and see the discussion of *R* v *Secretary of State for the Environment ex parte Kingston upon Hull City Council* [1996] Env LR 248 at 4.16.3 above.

[155] Subsequent revisions to the (now) Agency's policy on discharges were published in July 1997. These note that previous guidance had focused on the achievement of the mandatory standards in relation to faecal coliforms and total coliforms and was not specifically addressed the achievement of the enterovirus standard. However, it added that 'substantial reductions in enteroviruses could be assumed as a consequence of achieving the mandatory bacterial standard.'

Waste Water Treatment Directive, the failure to *mention* it did not mean that it had misunderstood the Directive. By the end of 2000, the date by when the relevant standards in the Directive had to be complied with, the sewage treatment scheme for the discharge would include both primary and secondary treatment as required by the Directive.

Although, clearly, the applicant was unsuccessful on all three grounds, the decision is nevertheless an important one in considering the criteria and procedures that must be applied in the determination of discharge consents by the Agency. Essentially, the applicant failed to establish the key points of fact which would have substantiated the allegations. Nevertheless, the judgment implicitly affirms that having improper regard to financial considerations or failing to adhere to requirements under Community water quality directives by the Agency may constitute a valid ground for judicial review of a discharge consent determination.

Although the *Moreton* case can be seen as providing a ground for a range of possible challenges to discharge consent determinations, a major difficulty for anyone seeking to challenge a decision by the Agency remains establishing that, in fact, the Agency has acted unlawfully. The issue is particularly problematic when it is alleged that a water quality standards has been breached, since compliance or non-compliance with these standards will generally depend on a number of licensing decisions, possibly including action over activities which are not consented. Even where such standards are mandatory, therefore, there may be a considerable practical and evidential burden on any applicant to show that the Agency has acted unlawfully. Finally, *Moreton* also suggests that the courts are likely to accept the views of the Agency that, where compliance by a future date is required, measures adopted by the Agency to meet their standards will in fact do so.

Although mandatory standards present some difficulties, further issues arise in relation to other types of obligation, particularly under EC law. Some of these are illustrated in the recent decision in *Moase and another* v *Secretary of State for the Environment, Transport and the Regions and South West Water Ltd.*[156] In *Moase*, the applicants challenged a decision of the Secretary of State to confirm a compulsory purchase order sought by the water undertaker in order to construct a sewage disposal system with a short-sea outfall.[157] At the hearing before the Inspector, the applicants had argued in favour of a much longer outfall, on the basis that this was required to comply with mandatory standards in the Bathing Water Directive and the Urban Waste Water Treatment Directive. In supporting the water undertaker's proposals, the Inspector had been guided by the fact that the Environment Agency had issued a discharge consent in 1996 for the treatment works which would be built on the compulsorily purchased land. The Secretary of State accepted the recommendations of the Inspector and confirmed the compulsory purchase order. In the High Court

---

[156] [2000] Env LR 266 (HC); [2001] Env LR 13 (CA).
[157] Under s.23(1) Acquisition of Land Act 1981.

it was held that the Secretary of State could rely on the discharge consent issued by the Agency as evidence that there would be compliance with mandatory water quality standards. The Court of Appeal subsequently upheld this decision.

Specifically, Owen J in the High Court made two central findings. First, unless it could be shown that there would be an 'irremediable breach of European law', the power of the Secretary of State to vary or revoke a consent in order to give effect to an EC obligation[158] did not mean that the Minister had a duty under the European Community Treaty to exercise these reserve powers to ensure the revocation of the consent if the Agency had not done so. The judge took a more pragmatic approach, finding that the bacterial nature of the effluent made it impossible to say that enterovirus standards under the Bathing Water Directive would never be breached. Rather than this requiring, as a matter of EC law, the imposition of stricter standards or an alternative means of treatment, the Agency and the water undertaker would be required to take remedial action, regardless of cost, in the event of future breaches. As he put it, while the challenge was, in certain respects, considerably out of time,

> that, however, does not mean that there is no continuing obligation on the Water Company and the Environment Agency. Their task is to ensure compliance with the Directives. It is worth re-stating that mandatory requirements must be met.

A similar approach can be seen in relation to a second challenge relating to duties in the Urban Waste Water Treatment Directive to minimize adverse environmental effects from discharges 'as far as possible' by the appropriate location of the point of discharge.[159] Again, the judge held that 'if there were to be seen a flagrant breach of the obligations', which he held that there was not, this would have to be considered by the Agency and the Secretary of State. He was satisfied that the Agency had determined the discharge consent correctly, and there were no grounds, either in national law or as a matter of EC law, which required him to overturn the compulsory purchase order on the grounds that granting it would inevitably lead to a breach of mandatory water quality standards or other obligations in the Directive or its implementing legislation.

The *Moase* case nicely illustrates some of the practical problems of challenging official decisions in relation to water quality. As can be seen, the Agency issued the consent some time before decisions about the siting of the works were eventually confirmed, which may have made difficult a judicial review of the terms of the discharge consent itself.[160]

---

[158] In para.7(4)(a) Sch.10 Water Resources Act 1991.

[159] Art.12(1) and Annex I(B)(5).

[160] A further possibility would be asking the Agency to modify or revoke the consent given, and then challenging the failure to do so.

More particularly, even where mandatory EC requirements were involved, it is clear that the Court were reluctant to scrutinise the decision-making processes of the Inspector, other than to satisfy itself that he had had regard to all the material considerations which were before him and that his decision was not perverse. The Court was particularly scathing in its criticism of the applicants' attempts to rely on material which, although it might have been relevant, had not been before the Inspector. Therefore, even if it had not found against the applicants on the substance of the point raised in relation to selecting a point of discharge which minimised pollution, this would have been ruled out of contention because it had not been raised before the Inspector, who was in a position to consider the totality of submissions made on this issue. As the Court of Appeal put it in relation to the challenge relating to failure to meet the enterovirus standards:

> We accept that if the objectors had before the Inspector established that the [Agency] was not enforcing compliance with the mandatory requirements and either was intent on so failing or was bound to fail in the context of the scheme . . . that would have been a highly material fact for the Inspector to consider when deciding whether a [compulsory purchase order] should be confirmed . . . [However] the Inspector was entitled to assume, as he did, that the [Agency's] policy and the setting of the terms of the consent were to produce compliance with the mandatory requirements until the contrary was established [by the objectors].

Finally, it is worth noting that Owen J held that since the remedy sought was discretionary, he would in any case have found against the appellants because there was an urgent need for the sewage treatment works and 'there having been no identification of a more environmentally favourable position the greater good of the local community must require the existing scheme to be put into operation'. This final point is particularly telling, since it highlights that there may be situations where practical realities outweigh what might appear to be strict legal obligations, especially where discretionary remedies such as those available in judicial review proceedings are being sought.

## 10.6.5 New and Unforeseen Contaminants

A general difficulty with the system of discharge consents is the position of new and unforeseen substances introduced into a discharge after the consent has been granted. New contaminants may appear in the discharge because of advances in the development and production of new chemical or other products or changes in the industrial process giving rise to the effluent.[161] Alternatively, substances already in the discharge may subsequently be found to be damaging to water quality, for example through advances in understanding of its effect on the aquatic environment. More simply, a further possibility is that the discharger

---

[161] See Royal Commission on Environmental Pollution (1972) paras 11-18.

introduces existing substances, already known to be environmentally harmful, into the discharge after the consent has been obtained. This may occur intentionally, or it may be something over which the discharger in practice has little power to control, for example in relation to storm and emergency overflows at sewage treatment works. Although consent conditions may stipulate the nature and composition of an authorised discharge on the basis of the information provided by the discharger at the time of application for a consent, no clear provision is made for new contaminants discharged after consent has been given. The critical legal question is whether these may be said to be discharged 'under and in accordance with' the consent.[162]

Although any consent must be interpreted according to its specific provisions, the general issue raised is whether consents are inclusive or exclusive of the consented parameters or activities referred to. It had been suggested that a consent should only permit the discharge of matter in respect of which it is originally granted.[163] Conversely, it was arguable that a discharge consent might serve as a defence to a prosecution for the discharge of effluent even where the discharge contained a polluting substance not explicitly provided for under the consent.[164] This uncertainty could be explained in part because of competing presumptions. On the one hand, because it relates to a criminal offence, any ambiguity ought to be construed in favour of the accused. On the other hand, because the provision authorise what would otherwise be an unlawful activity, its provisions should be construed narrowly as a matter of policy. In practice, it seems that successful prosecutions were taken in relation to parameters not mentioned in the consent.[165]

However, during the passage of the Environment Bill, Lord Crickhowell, speaking for the National Rivers Authority, took the view that the effect of the judgment in the *Yorkshire Water*[166] case was that

> the holder of a discharge consent will have a defence as regards pollution caused by the discharge of matter or substances which are not controlled or regulated by the consent *purely because the consent exists* . . . . I cannot believe that that is the intention of Parliament.[167]

---

[162] s.88(1)(a) Water Resources Act 1991.

[163] House of Commons Environment Committee, *Pollution of Rivers and Estuaries* (1987), para.102. In response, the Government took the view that: 'existing legislation already meets the Committee's underlying concern. Where a discharger adds to his discharge a new pollutant not covered by the consent, which materially adds to the noxious quality of the effluent, he will be guilty of an offence unless he seeks a review of his consent' (*Observations by the Government on the Third Report of the [Environment] Committee in Session 1986-87*, para 4.4).

[164] See Howarth (1988) p.154. The Water Act 1989 changed the wording of the relevant provision to 'under and in accordance with', apparently to solve this problem. See National Rivers Authority, *Discharge Consents and Compliance Policy* (1990).

[165] See National Rivers Authority, *Briefing Paper*, May 1995, cited in McGillivray (1995b) p.101.

[166] *National Rivers Authority* v *Yorkshire Water Services Ltd* [1995] 1 AC 444, and see 9.14.3 above.

[167] *Hansard*, HL, Vol. 1626 Col. 244, 7 March 1995, emphasis added.

However, amendments tabled to make explicit legislative provision for the view that consents are exclusive did not find their way into the Environment Act 1995, the Government view being that any problems or uncertainties were best resolved through variation of individual consents.[168] Perhaps for the avoidance of doubt, the National Rivers Authority recommended that consents be worded so as to be clear that they should not be taken as providing a defence against a charge of pollution in respect of any poisonous, noxious or polluting constituents not specified in it.[169] Following appeals by sewerage undertakers, referred to above,[170] a 'reasonable practicability' test is now incorporated to the rubric of many discharge consents although, curiously, not in relation to storm and emergency overflows.[171]

While the reason for the absence of any 'exclusionary clause' in a descriptive consent is readily apparent, the rationale for its inclusion in a numeric consent is less clear, and it added little to the 'fish kill' condition as this was worded in the model consent conditions. It may, however, cover 'noxious' constituents which are neither poisonous not polluting,[172] or substances which may be unpleasant or unsightly but which do not render the watercourse less habitable for fish.

In the 'Kinnersley' appeal determinations noted above, the Secretary of State held that a requirement that any component of a discharge which was not subject to the specific conditions of the consent should not be polluting, the so-called 'Kinnersley rubric', 'placed a duty on dischargers which cannot in practice be satisfied' and therefore was unreasonable.[173] In its place is to be substituted a 'substantial change condition' making it a condition that any change in the composition of the effluent does not cause a 'significant increase in the polluting effects of the discharge on controlled waters as a result of a new or altered discharge of trade effluent'. The condition, however, is only to be applied to sewage treatment works, making it unclear what the policy position is concerning other discharges. A further condition relating to unauthorised discharges also applies to sewage treatment works, providing that discharges from works are 'not to contain poisonous, noxious or polluting matter or solid waste matter which is attributable to any unauthorised discharge into the works'. This provision, however, does not prevent reliance on the defence

---

[168] See *Hansard*, HL, Vol. 1626 Col. 246, 7 March 1995 per Viscount Ullswater. The 'Kinnersley Report' (National Rivers Authority, *Discharge Consents and Compliance Policy* 1990) had also advocated change to consenting policy and to the wording of existing consents as the best means to secure the general interpretation of the legislation.

[169] An 'exclusionary clause', sometimes referred to as a 'Kinnersley rubric' following the 'Kinnersley Report' (*ibid*).

[170] See 10.6.1C above.

[171] On whether a common test of 'reasonable practicability' might have been used, and the impact that the duty to have particular regard to the duties of water and sewerage undertakers might have in such determinations, see McGillivray (1995a) pp.74-75. On the background, see McFarlane (1993).

[172] On the meaning of these terms, see now *R v Dovermoss Ltd* [1995] Env LR 258, discussed at 9.8 above.

[173] See 10.6.1C above.

given to sewerage undertakers in respect of pollution incidents attributable to substances entering their works which they were not obliged to receive.[174]

## 10.7 Discharge Consent Charges

General provisions relating to charging schemes, including the procedures that apply where charges have not been paid in time, have been considered elsewhere.[175] Under powers first introduced in the Water Act 1989[176] and effective from July 1991, a range of distinct charges may be levied for discharge consents and other consents relating to the control of pollution,[177] or consents granted without application, or consents for the time being in force. At the outset it should be noted that the charging powers now contained in the Water Resources Act 1991, and elaborated in the *Environment Agency Applications and Discharges to Controlled Waters Charging Scheme*,[178] are designed only to recover the costs associated with discharges. Although charges will be determined by a variety of factors including the nature and volume of the effluent, the charge is not intended to cover the full costs of water quality monitoring or to compensate or fund remediation of any environmental damage caused by the consented discharge. In this sense discharge consent charges are administrative cost-recovery charges and do not effectively implement the polluter pays principle.[179]

Under the specific scheme for discharge consent charging, two charges are set out for applications, a standard charge and a reduced charge for minor discharges such as surface water not containing trade effluent. The annual charge is based on three variables, a Volume Factor, a Contents Factor and a Receiving Water Factor, all of which are subdivided into bands, which is then multiplied by a standard Financial Factor. To illustrate present levels of charges, a consent allowing a discharge of 8,000 cubic metres per day of organic trade effluent to a river is calculated by multiplying figures of 3 for volume, 3 for content, 1 for receiving water, giving a total of 9 chargeable units, and multiplying this by the financial factor which for 2000/01 is £498, to give an annual charge of £4,482. In limited situations no charge for discharging is made. This applies to discharges of sewage effluent where the maximum daily volume of discharge permitted by the consent is 5 cubic metres or less.

Where a consent authorises the discharge of more than one effluent then a charge will be made for each effluent discharged whether or not they are

---

[174] Under s.87(2) Water Resources Act 1991, discussed in more detail at 9.14 above.

[175] See 6.15 above.

[176] Powers contained in s.52 Control of Pollution Act 1974 were never introduced.

[177] Under Part III Water Resources Act 1991. That is, consents under ss.88(1)(a), 89(4)(a) or 90.

[178] Produced annually by the Agency, and made under ss.41-42 Environment Act 1995. The provisions of the Scheme are contained in the leaflet *Annual Charges: Discharges to Controlled Waters 2000-1,* available from the Environment Agency.

[179] Charges for *applications* were first introduced in October 1990. On the polluter pays principle see 4.7.3 above.

discharged together or from one or more outlets. However, only one charge will be made in these circumstances if the monitoring requirements for both effluents are the same, unless they are discharged into more than one watercourse. The annual charge is due on 1 April in each year or otherwise on demand in respect of the year in which it is issued. Specific provision is made for the variation, revocation and transfer of consents.

The amounts of the variable heads of charge, and of the financial factor of the annual charge, are determined annually by the Environment Agency with the approval of the Secretary of State. It is notable that, at least since 1996/97, application charges have risen by the same level as the Financial Factor, emphasising the restrictions on using the discharge consent charging scheme to provide incentives for reducing the volume of effluent discharged. In line with recent moves to reduce government grant-in-aid, however, both application charges and the financial factor have increased beyond the rate of inflation, while the respective financing of the consenting regime provided by central government grant-in-aid has fallen sharply in recent years.[180] This may go some way towards more complete cost-recovery charging, but it has been justified on the grounds of complying with obligations under EC Directives (for example, the Habitats Directive[181]) and the review of consents under the latest price review process (the 'AMP3' process).[182] What is clear is the greater transparency in the process of determining annual increases to charges.

At the time of writing, the Government continues to consider the feasibility of introducing a charge to cover the full environmental costs of discharges to controlled waters through the use of economic instruments.[183] This follows on from support from the Royal Commission on Environmental Pollution for full cost recovery charges.[184] The introduction of such a scheme would, however, require changes to primary legislation, it being notable that the Environment Act 1995 did not provide for recovery beyond that of administrative costs.[185] As discussed elsewhere, provisions in the Water Framework Directive require by 2010 adequately incentivised pricing for discharges to water to meet the objectives of the Directive.[186]

## 10.8 Varying and Revoking Consents

If the objective of water quality regulation is progressively to achieve improvements to quality, some means of keeping discharge consents under periodic review is needed. To this end, the Agency may from time to time review any consent, granted with or without application, and any

---

[180] From 50% in 1999-2000 to 22% in 2000-2001.

[181] See 15.8 below. On Water Directives generally see Ch.5 above.

[182] On asset management plans (AMPs) see 7.8 above.

[183] See DETR, Welsh Office, DoE (Northern Ireland) and Scottish Office, *Economic Instruments for Water Pollution* (1997) see 1.7.9 above.

[184] Royal Commission on Environmental Pollution (1992).

[185] s.41 Environment Act 1995, and see 6.15 above.

[186] See further 5.9.9 above.

conditions to which the consent is subject. It should be noted that what is now a power to review consents was, until the de-regulatory changes brought about by the Environment Act 1995, a *duty* to review. Subject to certain restrictions upon the power of the Agency to review consents[187] the Agency may revoke a consent, modify the conditions of a consent or make an unconditional consent subject to conditions. If, when reviewing a consent, it appears to the Agency that no discharge has been made in pursuance of the consent during the preceding twelve months, the Agency may revoke it by a notice served on the holder.[188] Consents may be suspended or revoked if, after service of a notice, charges remain due.[189]

Subject to any restrictions imposed,[190] the Secretary of State may at any time direct the Agency to revoke a consent, modify the conditions of a consent or make an unconditional consent subject to conditions. The purposes for which this may be done are:

(a) to enable the Government to give effect to any Community obligation or international agreement to which the UK is a party;
(b) to protect public health or flora and fauna dependent on an aquatic environment; or
(c) in consequence of any representations or objections made or otherwise.[191]

The Agency is liable to pay compensation to any person in respect of any loss or damage sustained by that person as a result of the Agency's compliance with a direction given in relation to any consent varied or revoked for the protection of public health or of flora and fauna dependent on an aquatic environment. The liability to compensate arises if the revocation or modification takes effect during a period when one of the stated restrictions on the Agency's power to review consents applies, so that the review could not otherwise have been made. However, if the direction was given as a result of a change of circumstances which could not reasonably have been foreseen at the beginning of the period to which the restriction relates, or as a result of material information about the discharge which was not reasonably available to the Agency at the beginning of that period, the Agency will not be liable to compensate under this provision. That is to say, the obligation to compensate provided for here is a restricted one, limited to those situations both where compensation would generally be payable, and where it can be shown that the variation or revocation was in effect unreasonable in the light of specific information or knowledge. For the purposes of the Agency's liability to pay compensation, information is material in relation to a consent if it relates to any discharge made, or to be made by virtue of the

---

[187] See para.8 Sch.10 Water Resources Act 1991, discussed in 10.8.2 below.
[188] *Ibid* para.7(3) Sch.10.
[189] The Environmental Licences (Suspension and Revocation) Regulations 1996 (SI 1996 No.508).
[190] By *ibid* para.8 Sch.10, see 10.8.2 below.
[191] *Ibid* para.7(4) Sch.10.

consent, to the interaction of any such discharge with any other discharge, or to the combined effect of the matter discharged and any other matter.[192]

An instructive decision illustrating the operation of the consent variation provisions under previous legislation is *Trent River Authority* v *Drabble and Sons Ltd*,[193] where the dischargers were granted a consent on 13 October 1966 subject to certain conditions as to water quality and quantity which were stated to operate from 1 April 1968. It was also provided that the conditions of the consent would not be altered before the expiration of two years from the date on which they were granted without the written consent of the dischargers.[194] On 30 September 1968 an information was preferred against the dischargers for failing to meet the conditions which were stated in the consent to become applicable from 1 April 1968. In reply the dischargers pleaded that these conditions were invalid, since the consents which had been given actually amounted to two consents (one operating up to the end of March 1968 and the other operating thereafter), and the latter consent contravened the requirement that the consent should not be altered within the two year period. The court held that the legislation did not prevent one consent containing conditions which varied the required state of the discharge from time to time, and that this was such a consent in which the imposition of more stringent conditions after a date within the two year period did not invalidate those conditions.[195]

A final point worth noting is that the provisions of the Water Resources Act 1991 authorising the Agency to undertake anti-pollution works, or requiring those who have caused or knowingly permitted water pollution to undertake such works,[196] cannot be used where this would interfere with a discharge consent. The powers of the Agency to vary or revoke the consent, or enforce the conditions of the consent, must be used instead.

### 10.8.1  General Review of Consents

The Secretary of State has a general power to direct the Agency to review consents issued with or without application, or any description of such consents, and the conditions, if any, to which those consents are subject. Directions must specify the purpose for which, and may specify the manner in which, such a review is to be conducted. After carrying out a review the Agency must submit to the Secretary of State its proposals, if any, for the modification of the conditions of any consent reviewed pursuant to the direction, or in the case of any unconditional consent reviewed pursuant to the direction, subjecting such consents to conditions. On receipt of such proposals, the Secretary of State may direct the Agency to modify consent conditions, or make unconditional consents conditional,

---

[192] *Ibid* paras. 7(5) and (6) Sch.10.

[193] [1970] 1 All ER 22.

[194] Under s.5(2) and Sch.1 Rivers (Prevention of Pollution) Act 1961.

[195] See para.3(4) Sch.10 Water Resources Act 1991.

[196] *Ibid* ss.161 and s.161A-D respectively.

so long as this is consistent with the Agency's original proposals or as these have been appropriately modified by the Secretary of State.[197]

A review must be made of a consent for a discharge that has implications for a 'European site' of nature conservation importance as soon as reasonably practicable after the date the site is notified.[198] If the review concludes that the discharge does have an adverse effect on the site's integrity the Agency may vary the consent if this will meet the site's needs. Otherwise the consent must be revoked.[199] The review procedure used is that under Schedule 10 to the Water Resources Act 1991. However, if on review the Agency considers that other action that it, or another competent authority, has taken or will take would deal with any adverse effect, it may affirm the consent. Further, if the object to be attained can be secured in a number of ways the Agency and other relevant authorities should choose the way least onerous to those affected.[200]

### 10.8.2 Restrictions on Varying and Revoking Consents

In the interests of commercial certainty, provision is made to restrict the revocation or variation of a consent within a stated period. Every consent must specify a period during which no notice of revocation of consent is to be imposed, or alteration or imposition of conditions imposed without the written agreement of the discharger. The period during which a discharge consent cannot be revoked or varied (without written agreement as appropriate) is not to be less than four years from the date on which the consent takes effect. In order further to provide for commercial certainty, each review notice is also subject to a four year minimum period, beginning when the notice is served, during which further revocation or variation is not permitted without the agreement of the consent holder. Consents granted without application,[201] however, may be varied or revoked within three months of the beginning of the period prescribed for the making of representations and objections with respect to the consent. This can be done where the Agency or the Secretary of State considers, in consequence of any representations or objections received within this period, that it is appropriate for the notice to be served.[202]

Within the restricted periods, consents may always be varied where the consent holder requests this.[203] Otherwise, no provision exists for revocation or variation within the protected four year periods unless it falls within one of the exceptions noted above, for example to give effect to the EC Habitats Directive, or compensation is payable.[204]

---

[197] *Ibid* para.9 Sch.10.
[198] On the meaning of 'European sites' see 15.8, and see generally 15.8.3 below.
[199] Regs. 85, 50 and 51 Conservation (Natural Habitats etc.) Regulations 1994 (SI 1994 No.2716).
[200] Reg. 51(3) Conservation (Natural Habitats etc.) Regulations 1994.
[201] See 10.5 above.
[202] See para.8(4) Sch.10 Water Resources Act 1991.
[203] Paras.8(5) and 10 Sch.10 Water Resources Act 1991.
[204] See 10.8.1 above and 15.8.3 below.

## 10.8.3  Contamination Rationing

Subject to the important restrictions outlined above, the ability of the Agency and the Secretary of State to revoke consents, or vary their terms, is considerable, with compensation payable only in very limited circumstances. While the consenting regime provides much scope for regulating, for example, the discharge of substances subsequently discovered to be harmful, therefore, the administrative burden involved in consent reviews should not be underestimated, nor should the trend to lengthen the time periods within which consents may be revoked or varied be regarded lightly. Moreover, unlike abstraction licences,[205] there is little protection for existing dischargers against conflicting discharges by other, or prospective, consent holders. Other than stressing the wider context of water quality objectives and EC obligations, and increased practical reliance on catchment modelling, the Agency's internal guidance on consents gives little indication of how competing use-claims are to be reconciled. In theory, therefore, the Agency may reduce emissions from existing dischargers in order to accommodate contaminating matter from a new discharger while continuing to meet the relevant water quality objective.[206] This approach is in line with the general policy of retaining a considerable degree of flexibility in water quality regulation, but raises issues as to the criteria by which the Agency 'rations' the use of the assimilative capacity of controlled watercourses.[207]

The discretionary nature of the Agency's powers to vary or revoke consents means that there is no automatic obligation to revoke the consents of those who significantly or persistently breach consent conditions. This is consistent with most other areas of environmental regulation where decisions to remove authorisation rights, with their far-reaching economic and social consequences, are rarely taken as part of the administrative process. The only effective means available to prevent further breaches by persistent violators is through the criminal process, or through the use of enforcement notices.[208]

It should also be noted that the power of the Agency to review or revoke consents makes it difficult for individuals or groups themselves to use the consenting system to improve water quality. That is, although consents can have property-like characteristics, there are significant obstacles to obtaining or keeping consents without intending to make use of the right to

---

[205] s.39 Water Resources Act 1991.

[206] Thornton and Beckwith (1997) p.211. A contrast is with s.306 Clean Water Act 1972 (US), which sets 'New Source Performance Standards' that generally require a greater degree of effluent reduction, while s.306 also directs the US Environmental Protection Agency to 'consider' zero discharge standards for new discharges. However, New Source Performance Standards are exempt from review for 10 years.

[207] Conceivably there may a human rights dimension via Art 14 of the Convention which prohibits discrimination, but this is improbable (in relation to Article 1 Protocol 1 and the protection of property) since holding a consent is unlikely to be seen as amounting to protected 'possessions'. More realistic is a claim under Article 6 on the basis of the *process* by which such a determination has been made.

[208] On enforcement notices see 10.11.1 below.

discharge (in the way that an individual or organisation might acquire land to leave it in a 'wild' state in the interests of conservation). First, it is unlikely that the Agency would grant a consent in such circumstances. Second, a charge would be levied for the consent which, as discussed below, is related to the consented volume of water rather than the actual volume of water discharged. Third, if the consent were acquired from an existing discharger, the Agency would be able to review the consent within, at a maximum, four years, and would be able to revoke it without compensation.

### 10.8.4 Human Rights Issues

With the incorporation of the European Convention on Human Rights into national law by the Human Rights Act 1998, the extent to which possession of a discharge consent (or, for that matter, any other environmental 'licence' discussed in this book) is protected as a matter of human rights law is of ever greater importance. In particular, the Convention provides a measure of protection for the 'peaceful enjoyment of possessions':

> Every natural or legal person is entitled to the peaceful enjoyment of his possessions. No one shall be deprived of his possessions except in the public interest and subject to the conditions provided for by law and by the general principles of international law.

However, this is qualified with the limitation that:

> The preceding provisions shall not, however, in any way impair the right of a State to enforce such laws as it deems necessary to control the use of property in accordance with the general interest.[209]

The European Court of Human Rights has held that licences are capable of constituting a 'possession' in this context, to the extent that they have an economic value or are of a pecuniary nature.[210] However, they must be 'sufficiently established', meaning that a prospective intention to hold, for example, a discharge consent will not be protected by this provision of human rights law.[211]

The approach of the European Court of Human Rights to the right to enjoy possessions peacefully has been that states have a wide 'margin of appreciation' in determining the extent to which restrictions may be imposed in 'the public interest' or 'the general interest'.[212] The action of the state must also be proportional to the objectives to be achieved, so that, for example, revoking a discharge consent when environmental improvements could have been achieved by less restrictive measures may

---

[209] First Protocol, Article 1, European Convention on Human Rights.

[210] Consents have certain 'property-type' features, see 10.10 below.

[211] *National Provincial Building Society* v *United Kingdom* (1997) 25 EHRR 127.

[212] See e.g. *James* v *United Kingdom* (1986) 8 EHRR 123, para.46.

amount to a breach of the protection for property rights.[213] Further, the Court has distinguished between deprivation of possessions and controls on their use. While the former normally carries with it a right to be compensated, the latter 'does not, as a rule, contain any right to compensation'.[214] However, the Court has tended to characterise the revocation of a licence not as a deprivation of a possession but rather as a control on the use of the underlying property or economic asset.[215] Only where the revocation takes away 'all meaningful use' of the underlying property will it tend to be characterised as a deprivation. In summary, therefore, varying or revoking consents, so long as this done in a proportional manner, is unlikely to be seen as a breach of the protection afforded by the European Convention on Human Rights. Also, current practice suggests that few consents will be revoked or varied to the extent that they deprive consent holders of all meaningful use of their business assets.

## 10.9 Appeals

In a range of situations there is a right of appeal to the Secretary of State from Agency determinations of discharge consents,[216] though naturally no appeal lies from a decision of the Agency made in pursuance of a direction of the Secretary of State. Appeals may be taken where the Agency has:

(a) refused a consent application;
(b) given a consent subject to conditions;
(c) revoked or modified a consent or made an unconditional consent conditional;
(d) specified a period during which variation or revocation or variation of a consent is not to take place;
(e) refused a consent for any deposit of solid refuse of a mine or quarry;[217] or
(f) refused or imposed conditions on a consent in relation to deposits and vegetation in rivers.[218]

Under provisions introduced in the Environment Act 1995, appeals may also now be brought in relation to a refusal to vary a consent or, in allowing any such variation, making the consent subject to conditions, and against the service of an enforcement notice.[219] Appeals may be brought either by the person applying for the consent, or the person whose conduct would be authorised by the consent. There is therefore no right of appeal for any third party who may be adversely affected by the granting of a

---

[213] See, in the context of restrictions imposed for fish health reasons, *Booker Aquaculture v Secretary of State for Scotland* [2000] UKHRR 1 referred to the European Court of Justice.

[214] *Baner v Sweden* 60DR 128 (1989), para.6.

[215] *Fredin v Sweden* A/192 (1991) 13 EHRR 784.

[216] See generally s.91 Water Resources Act 1991, as significantly amended by para.143 Sch.22 Environment Act 1995.

[217] See s.89(4)(a) Water Resources Act 1991.

[218] *Ibid* s.90.

[219] *Ibid* s.91(1)(g) and (h).

consent (for example, a downstream proprietor), though any such person would doubtless have sufficient standing to bring an action for judicial review.[220] Increasingly, third parties whose interests are not immediately affected, or more likely representative pressure groups, would also be given permission to raise a challenge in judicial review.[221]

The procedural requirements in relation to appeals are set out in detail in the Control of Pollution (Applications, Appeals and Registers) Regulations 1996.[222] Appeals must generally be brought within 3 months of the original notification, though other periods may apply. Detailed provisions relate to notification of interested parties.[223] In particular appeals may be conducted either by written representations, or by way of a hearing. Appellants may choose either procedure, though the Secretary of State has the power to insist that any appeal is conducted, or continued, through a hearing. If a hearing is to be held, notice must be publicised in the relevant locality and brought to the attention of those who have made relevant representations or objections. The appellant, the Agency and any person required to be notified of the appeal are entitled to be heard at a hearing, but permission to grant other parties the right to be heard at a hearing must not be withheld unreasonably. According to the views of the person hearing the appeal, the hearing may be conducted, in whole or in part, in private. Otherwise the procedures for hearing appeals are informal, though the Secretary of State has issued guidance which refers to the need for openness, fairness and impartiality and to the fact that appeals will normally be open to the public.[224]

Unless the Secretary of State has delegated authority to determine the appeal,[225] the person appointed to hear the appeal must provide the Secretary of State with a written report including his conclusions and his recommendations or his reasons for not making any recommendations. This report must be provided to the appellant at the same time as the appellant is notified of the Secretary of State's determination.

Since 1 January 1997 the hearing of discharge consent appeals has generally been transferred to the Planning Inspectorate.[226] However, the Secretary of State has retained a power to recover jurisdiction and determine personally. In these cases, an Inspector carries out a hearing in

---

[220] See further *Zander* v *Sweden* (1994) 18 EHRR 175 and comment at [1996] *Water Law* 8-9. It may also be that under its general public law duty to act fairly a court may be prepared to hold that the Agency has not acted fairly in respect of a particular application; see Bates (1990-updated) para.10.116.

[221] See Bell and McGillivray (2000) p.76.

[222] See s.91(2B), (2C) and (2K) Water Resources Act 1991 and Regs 8-13 Control of Pollution (Applications, Appeals and Registers) Regulations 1996. The same provisions also apply to appeals in relation to access to public registers, discussed at 16.15.3 below.

[223] Notably, the discretion not to publicise where there is considered to be 'no appreciable effect', discussed at 10.5.2 above, does not apply to appeals.

[224] *Discharge Consents – Code of Practice for Hearings*, available at www.planning-inspectorate.gov.uk

[225] See s.91(2A) Water Resources Act 1991 and s.114 Environment Act 1995.

[226] In Wales, to the National Assembly.

the manner described above, but then prepares a case report which is forwarded to the Secretary of State, together with a recommendation for action. Although each appeal is looked at on an individual basis, the kinds of appeals that might be decided by the Secretary of State are stated in guidance[227] to include:

  (a) cases involving sites of major importance and/or having more than local or significance;
  (b) cases raising more than local or regional issues;
  (c) cases which raise significant legal difficulties;
  (d) cases which can only be decided in conjunction with other cases over which Inspectors have no jurisdiction; and
  (e) cases which raise major new policy issues of discharge consenting control with precedent implications.[228]

Exceptionally, there may also be other cases which merit recovery because of the particular circumstances. For example, the guidance suggests that some cases involving commercial confidentiality might need to be recovered.

Moreover, in practice:

> The principles on which the appeal will be decided are that the appellant has satisfied the decision maker that her discharge or activities will not lead to a significant lowering of water quality and that the Agency has acted unreasonably. An appeal will be considered on its merits and not look at alternative methods of effluent disposal.[229]

On appeal, the Secretary of State (or the Planning Inspector) may:

  (a) affirm the original decision;
  (b) direct the Agency to grant or vary the consent;
  (c) quash any condition of the consent;
  (d) quash a decision to revoke a consent; or
  (e) modify any provisions specifying periods within which consents may not be varied or revoked.

Where appropriate, the Secretary of State may direct the Agency to impose conditions to which the consent is to be subject.[230] If he affirms the consent, he may do so either in its original form or with any modifications considered appropriate.[231] It is to be noted that, unlike previous legislation,

---

[227] *Discharge and Other Consents – appeal procedure guide*, available at www.planning-inspectorate.gov.uk
[228] For example, the 'Kinnersley Rubric' and 'injurious to fish' conditions, see 10.6.1C above.
[229] See Bates (1990-updated) para.10.136.
[230] s.91(2D) Water Resources Act 1991.
[231] *Ibid* s.91(2E).

the Water Resources Act 1991 contains no presumptions as to whether consent has been reasonably withheld.[232]

An appeal against revoking or modifying a consent, or attaching conditions to an unconditional consent, has the effect of suspending the Agency's decision until the appeal is determined or withdrawn.[233] However, this provision will not apply where the notice effecting the revocation, modification or provision in question includes a statement from the Agency that it is necessary for the purpose of preventing or, where that is not practicable, minimising either the entry into controlled waters of any poisonous, noxious or polluting matter or any solid waste matter, or harm to human health. In such cases, the revocation or modification has immediate effect and remains effective during the course of the appeal.[234] If such a decision is subsequently challenged by the holder or former holder of the consent, and the Secretary of State determines that the Agency acted unreasonably in insisting on such a course of action, then the revocation or modification is suspended should the appeal still be pending. In such cases, the consent holder, or former holder, is also entitled to compensation for any consequential losses incurred, any dispute as to compensation being determined by arbitration.[235]

It is notable that the existence of appeal rights affects the extent to which aggrieved parties can take judicial review proceedings against the Agency. The courts have established two relevant tests. First, if the statutory appeal process would afford an adequate alternative remedy, then any application for permission to seek a judicial review will be refused. The adequacy of the statutory right of appeal as an alternative remedy is dependent upon a number of factors, including:

(a) comparative speed, expense and finality of the alternative procedure;
(b) the need and scope for fact finding;
(c) the desirability of an authoritative ruling on any point of law arising; and
(d) the apparent strength of the applicants challenge.[236]

In this context, the lack of speed with some discharge consent appeals are decided might be noted, though here it probably better to classify such appeals as being in abeyance pending resolution of policy issues by central government.[237] (Indeed, the fact that these have remained as appeals rather than being taken as judicial review proceedings is telling). Secondly,

---

[232] s.39(7) Control of Pollution Act 1974, on which see Howarth (1988) p.166.

[233] s.91(2F) Water Resources Act 1991. This may be contrasted with enforcement notices, which remain in force pending the outcome of an appeal (s.91(2J)).

[234] *Ibid* s.91(2G).

[235] *Ibid* s.91(2H).

[236] See *R v Environment Agency ex parte Petrus Oils Ltd* [1999] Env LR 732; *R v Falmouth and Truro Port Health Authority ex parte South West Water Ltd* [2000] NPC 36.

[237] See below.

where there has been a failure to comply with any statutory obligation, and criminal proceedings are brought, the courts have tended to dismiss such collateral or incidental challenges as being an abuse of process where the decision which is being challenged was made many years before and the period for statutory challenge has passed.[238]

Some general observations about the appeals system might be made. First, by comparison with other administrative law appeal mechanisms such as appeals in planning law, appeals in relation to discharge consents are brought relatively infrequently.[239] This may be, as has been suggested, either because there is little perceived difference in policy between the Agency (and also formerly the National Rivers Authority) and the Secretary of State, or because the long delays before appeals are decided has meant that an understanding of the principles to be applied on appeal is only building up slowly.[240] However, the time taken to determine appeals has been somewhat protracted. In a significant number of cases, appeals may go back several years.[241] This draws criticism both from industry and from environmentalists. For the former, in particular the water and sewerage undertakers, delays complicate decisions about future investment. In contrast, the latter complain that while appeals are pending, effluent generally continues to be discharged at levels the Agency has already decided is of an inadequate standard.[242] Where appeals are actively under consideration, as opposed to being held in abeyance, the majority are decided by written representations and a site visit, generally taking around 15 weeks from receipt to the issue of the decision.[243]

## 10.10 Transferring and Surrendering Consents

The nature of the right granted under a discharge consent is no longer personal to the individual named in the consent and, therefore, may now be transferred between owners and occupiers without the need for any fresh determination by the Agency.[244] Consents may therefore be contrasted

---

[238] See e.g. *R v Ettrick Trout Company Ltd* [1994] Env LR 165. See Bell and McGillivray (2000) p.80.

[239] Fifty nine appeals were lodged in both 1998/99 and 1999/2000. Planning Inspectorate, personal communication, 12 May 2000.

[240] Bell and McGillivray (2000) p.582.

[241] As at 12 May 2000, some appeals dated back to 1994. Planning Inspectorate, personal communication. These appeals are effectively in abeyance pending national discussions about matters including the Urban Waste Water Treatment (England and Wales) Regulations 1994 (SI 1994 No.1056) (see 12.2.6), List II substances under the Dangerous Substances Directive (see 5.4.1 above) and trade effluent. Most appeals in abeyance are eventually withdrawn once these negotiations have been concluded and agreed. For example, in 1998/99, 4 appeals were decided but 140 were withdrawn. This was probably attributable to the reaching of a determination in relation to consents for sewage treatment works and unforeseen pollutants, on which see 10.6.1C above.

[242] House of Commons Select Committee on the Environment, Transport and the Regions, *Sewage Treatment and Disposal* (1998) para.235.

[243] Planning Inspectorate, personal communication, 12 May 2000.

[244] Para.11(1) Sch.10 Water Resources Act 1991, amended by para.83 Sch.22 Environment Act 1995.

with other regulatory licences where there is either a personal element to the standard imposed,[245] or where there are specific provisions relating to the suitability of the licence-holder.[246]

On the other hand, provisions in the Environment Act 1995 required discharge consent holders to notify the Environment Agency if the consent had been transferred to the holder by another person.[247] The 'registration'-type provision was intended to ensure that the Agency was appraised of the identity of the current holder of the consent, which was thought to be important because of the change to the law that formally allowed consents to be transferred. However, transitional arrangements were also made under this provision, allowing current licence holders to continue discharging under the consent until 1 October 1996 even where they were not named on the consent. Because such a high proportion of existing consent holders failed to 're-register', provision was made for a simplified scheme for reinstating such consents, until March 1997, on payment of a modest administrative fee. This scheme protected existing licence holders not only from payment of a new licence fee, but also in practice made it less likely that the conditions of consents would be varied on re-application. Since March 1997, existing consent holders who have failed to register consents in their own names are technically subject to prosecution, but the lack of proceedings taken in relation to such situations might suggest that there is no significant practical problem.[248]

Specific provisions are made concerning the transferability of consents.[249] On the death of the consent holder the consent is regarded as non-disclaimable property forming part of the deceased's personal estate, and accordingly vests in the deceased's personal representatives. If a bankruptcy order is made against a consent holder the consent is regarded as property forming part of the bankrupt's estate,[250] and vests in the trustee in bankruptcy.

Where consents are transferred, the new holder is subject to the same conditions as the previous holder. The Agency must be notified of any transfer. In the case of transfers on death or bankruptcy the Agency must be notified within 15 months; failure to do so renders the consent of no effect, i.e. it ceases to become a defence to criminal proceedings for causing or knowingly permitting water pollution. Otherwise, the transferor must notify the Agency within 21 days. In all cases of failure to notify, the person responsible is guilty of an offence and liable, on summary

---

[245] E.g. an authorisation to conduct a prescribed process under Part I Environmental Protection Act 1990, see 12.3.2 below.

[246] E.g., the obligation for the holder of a waste management licence to be a 'fit and proper person', see 12.2.6 below.

[247] Para.21 Sch.23 Environment Act 1995. Similar provisions apply to IPC authorisations, see 12.3.2 below.

[248] It is possible that the Agency overestimated the number of consents still being relied on; estimates at the time referred to 110,000 extant consents, but see the figure referred to in 10.3 above.

[249] para.11 Sch.10 Water Resources Act 1991.

[250] For the purposes of any of the Second Group of Parts of the Insolvency Act 1986.

conviction, to a fine not exceeding the statutory maximum, currently £5000. On conviction on indictment, the maximum penalties are an unlimited fine or imprisonment for a term not exceeding two years (or both).

While consents can be transferred, they cannot legally be surrendered or disclaimed.[251] In this respect, therefore discharge consents resemble waste management licences, in that continuing obligations can be imposed on consent holders which, in the interests of the environment, cannot be avoided by renunciation.[252] Such conditions might relate to plant or equipment on the consented premises, regardless of whether the discharge is in fact continuing, for example in relation to the maintenance of monitoring equipment and/or conditions over start up or shut down. This can be inferred from the fact that consents have effect to the extent that they 'permit the making of any discharges' which, it has been suggested, implies that the consent remains in force to the extent that they create any other obligations.[253] In practice, however, it is common for consent documents simply to be sent back to the Agency. The charging system for consents, being based on the volume of effluent consented rather than actually discharged, gives a strong incentive for dischargers to disclaim consents in the absence of continuing obligations.

## 10.11  Compliance and Enforcement

The principal water pollution offences are formulated in relation to offences of causing or knowingly permitting water pollution in defined circumstances, subject to avoiding criminal liability by acting under and in accordance with the terms of a consent or other authorisation.[254] Thus the principal means of ensuring compliance with conditions contained in consents will be through the desire of consent holders to avoid prosecution for a substantive water pollution offence.

The offence relating to contravention of the conditions of a consent must be seen as a strict liability offence. Also, breaching more than one condition of a consent may give rise to more than one offence, and contravening consent conditions can relate either to a breach which leads to an actual water pollution incident, or to breaching a procedural requirement such as a requirement to conduct self-monitoring. All these issues are covered in more detail elsewhere.[255] This section concentrates on actual levels of compliance with consent conditions and enforcement practice.

---

[251] para.11(4) Sch.10 Water Resources Act 1991.
[252] On waste management licensing see 12.2.6 below.
[253] Waite and Jewell (1997), para 17.82, citing para 11(6)-(8), Sch 10 Water Resources Act 1991. On the lawful scope for conditions see 10.6 above.
[254] See 9.16 and 10.1 above.
[255] See Ch.9 above.

The latest published figures indicate considerable non-compliance with consent conditions, especially for sewage treatment works not operated by undertakers and for industrial discharges. The following figures relate only to works with numeric consents and which were tested for compliance in the period.

### Sewage and Trade Discharges: Compliance with Numeric Consents 1999

| *Region* | *Sewage treatment works (undertakers) (%)* | *Trade discharges (%)* | *Sewage treatment works (non-undertakers) (%)* |
|---|---|---|---|
| Anglian | 98 | 74 | 55 |
| Midlands | 99 | 86 | 65 |
| North East | 98 | 70 | 66 |
| North West | 96 | 86 | 65 |
| Southern | 97 | 60 | 64 |
| South West | 91 | 61 | 55 |
| Thames | 98 | 84 | 69 |
| Wales | 96 | 64* | 40* |

Source: DETR, *Digest of Environmental Statistics* (2001), Table 3.16[256]

* Figures for 1998

Prosecutions will normally be pursued where operations are carried out without a consent where this is required. However, where there is no resulting environmental impact, or the impact is judged to be minor (i.e. category 3), and where an application is submitted within a short timescale, a warning will usually be given. In certain circumstances, e.g., poor co-operation, then firmer action will be more appropriate.[257]

Where there is breach of a discharge consent and this gives rise to Category 1 impact (i.e. major impact), then in principle prosecution should normally result. Where impact or potential impact is Category 2 (i.e. significant) then the normal course of action will be prosecution or formal caution (the choice depending on the weight of other factors such as co-

---

[256] The Digest also provides comparative statistics since 1991 (1993 for treatment works operated other than by undertakers). For figures before 1991 see Ministry of Housing and Local Government and Welsh Office, *Taken for Granted: Report of the Working Party on Sewage Disposal* (1970) (the 'Jeger Report'), which found at least 60 per cent non-compliance at treatment works (para.50), and House of Commons Environment Committee, *Pollution of Rivers and Estuaries* (1987), which also recorded widespread non-compliance (para.26 and Appendix 43). For public registers of consents and breaches of conditions, and access to information about breaches more generally, see Ch.16 below.

[257] Environment Agency, *Functional Guidelines* paras 5.2.5-5.2.6.

operation of the offender, post-remedial works, and history of offending). Prosecution will normally be pursued where a previous warning or formal caution has been given.

Where a consent or authorisation condition has been breached and has resulted in no or Category 3 impact or potential impact, a warning will usually be given unless circumstances dictate otherwise (e.g. if there has been repetition of the offence, the operator is uncooperative or the breach was deliberate). Prosecution will normally be pursued in respect of those type of breaches where the operator has shown a history of non-compliance sufficient to call into question the effective management of the site/operations or to prevent effective regulation by the Agency.[258]

Only where breach of a consent gives rise to a water pollution 'incident' is information contained in the annual enforcement statistics produced by the Agency.[259] Otherwise, breaches of consent conditions will go unrecorded in this headline data.

Figures for the period 1 April 1999 to 31 March 2000 indicate that 14 separate cases relating to breach of conditions came before the courts, concerning 12 separate defendants.[260] The total amount of fines for this period was £102,000, which related to 23 separate charges for the offence under s.85(6), thus averaging at £4,435 per charge,[261] which is as least as stringent as average fine levels for substantive offences.[262] One important observation on any figures relating to charging for breaches of any water pollution offences, however, is that practice across the regions of the Environment Agency may not be consistent, i.e. in the case of offences for contravening the conditions of a discharge consent prosecutors may bring differing numbers of charges in relation to the same violations.

### 10.11.1  Enforcement Notices

As can be seen from the *Taylor Woodrow* case,[263] the nature of liability for breach of consent conditions is strict. But until recently no preventive powers were available to the regulator to avert breaches of conditions in situations where 'accidents were waiting to happen'. As from 1 January 1997, this is now provided for.[264] This gives the Agency the power to serve an enforcement notice on the holder of a discharge consent – and

---

[258] *Ibid* paras 5.2.7-5.2.8

[259] See Environment Agency, *Water Pollution Incidents in England and Wales 1998*, Environment Agency (1999), updated annually.

[260] 11 companies and one individual. One company was prosecuted on three separate occasions.

[261] Comparable figures for 1998/99 are: 20 defendants, 26 charges, total fines £49,995. For 1997/98 (for 7 out of the 8 regions of the Agency): 21 defendants, 31 charges, £129,050 total fines. Information supplied by the Environment Agency.

[262] Compare the figures given at 9.19.2 above.

[263] *Taylor Woodrow Property Management Ltd* v *National Rivers Authority* [1995] Env LR 52.

[264] s.90B Water Resources Act 1991, added by the Environment Act 1995.

other consents[265] – where it is of the opinion that the holder is currently contravening a consent condition or is likely to do so. Enforcement notices are considered in more detail elsewhere, and are not considered further here.[266]

## 10.12 Future Directions

While the preceding sections have discussed the present position in relating to discharge consenting law and policy, two possible future developments are worth commenting on briefly.

### 10.12.1 General Binding Rules

As discussed above, the traditional approach to granting discharge consents has been to consider applications on a case-by-case basis, taking local environmental and other factors into account to the extent that this is permissible within wider constraints such as mandatory water quality standards under EC law. In sight, however, is the prospect that 'general binding rules' may be used, that is, the possibility of determining applications by the use of general conditions for some or all of the conditions of consents rather than consents being individually tailored.[267] The possibility of using general binding rules to set all, or some, permit conditions is provided for in relation to the new pollution prevention and control regime,[268] and their more general adoption, including their use in relation to discharge consents, is under consideration by the Agency.

General binding rules raise various issues. One is the extent to which local and regional differences might still be taken into account, which would be in line with certain general developments in EC law.[269] Linked with this is the decision-making process by which it would be decided that general, rather than specific, conditions will be applied. Finally, experience in relation to pollution prevention and control suggests that there is the prospect that exceptions to general binding rules might be made, meaning that they might not always be either binding or general.[270]

### 10.12.2 Toxicity Based Consents

The other likely future development worth mentioning here is the prospect of the Environment Agency developing a measure of pollution termed 'direct toxicity assessment', aimed at controlling dangerous substances (heavy metals, chlorinated solvents, pesticides and other organic

---

[265] To deposit mine refuse under s.89(4) and consents relating to the removal of river bed material or depositing vegetation in water under s.90; see s.90B(6) Water Resources Act 1991.

[266] See 12.3.2 below.

[267] At present, reference is made to the Environment Agency's *Discharge Consents Manual*, but these are *model* conditions.

[268] Art.9 Integrated Pollution Prevention and Control Directive (96/61/EC).

[269] See generally Ch.5 above.

[270] See Bell and McGillivray (2000) p.395.

substances).[271] Some general issues concerning the advantages and limitations of toxicity as a yardstick for regulating discharges have been discussed in detail elsewhere.[272] As noted there, this form of assessment does not measure individual substances in effluents, but rather seeks to control the impact of effluents as a whole by reference to their overall toxicological impact on the aquatic environment. There is little doubt that such conditions are within the broad powers of the Agency to impose.[273]

The use of direct toxicity assessment to control certain discharges was welcomed in the National Rivers Authority's '*Kinnersley Report*' in 1990.[274] However, it was recognised that this form of assessment raised significant questions as to its general applicability, feasibility, specificity and cost and, for those reasons, that these were matters which should be pursued through research and development programmes with a view to the gradual introduction of consents containing such conditions.[275] Some of the specific legal issues which arise with direct toxicity assessment are the following:

(a) whether breaching a toxicity requirement in a consent would amount to an offence in the same way as when the conditions of a traditional discharge consent are breached, or whether breach would only be the trigger for some form of remedial action? This corrective action might be specified in the consent, or it might be provided for wholly outside the consent, in an agreement with the discharger. There are indications that the lack of *enforceability* of direct toxicity terms may mean that breach of a condition would not lead to a criminal offence.

(b) How direct toxicity assessment might be used when there are controls on individually identified chemical parameters under mandatory EC legislation, most notably under the Dangerous Substances Directive and, in future, the Water Framework Directive.[276]

(c) How toxicity assessment might be judged alongside the contrasting policy approach, taken most notably under the OSPAR Convention and also the Water Framework Directive, of seeking to reduce chemical emissions to zero on a substance by substance basis.[277] Clearly this approach is in tension with the approach under toxicity assessment, which tries to control the totality of chemical emissions, the implication being that this is feasible (the implication underpinning the OSPAR and Water Framework Directive regimes being that controlling certain chemical

---

[271] See, e.g., Waite and Crawshaw (1996) pp.200-202.

[272] See 1.3.7–8 above.

[273] See 10.6 above on consent conditions.

[274] National Rivers Authority, *Discharge Consents and Compliance Policy* (1990), and see 1.3.8 above.

[275] National Rivers Authority, *Discharge Consent and Compliance Policy: the NRA's Reponse to the Public Consultation* (1991) p.7.

[276] On these Directives see 5.4.1 and 5.7–10 above.

[277] See 5.19.6 above.

emissions and discharges is either too complex or too unacceptable).

(d) The impact that the current trade effluent consent regime would have on the enforceability of direct toxicity assessment

More recently, the Environment Agency has undertaken consultation as the introduction of toxicity-based criteria for control of wastewater discharges,[278] recognising that direct toxicity assessment provides a more meaningful and easily understood measure of 'poisonous matter' and the likely risk of environmental damage which could be caused by the release of complex mixtures of toxic substances. In particular, it is seen as a better regulatory tool to control discharges which have an impact on the environment which is 'greater than the sum of its parts' (i.e. have some form of synergistic or 'cocktail' effect). The proposal, therefore, is that present use of substance-specific controls should be supplemented by direct toxicity assessment to reduce toxicity at source via appropriately formulated conditions in discharge consents along with a programme of biological assessment to establish the ecological status of particular receiving waters.

Because of the adverse response from industry to the Agency's direct toxicity proposals, the present state of affairs is that the Agency opted to introduce a 'demonstration programme' in conjunction with the water industry and a number of large industrial organisations (the project was completed in mid 2000) to build up confidence and expertise in the use of direct toxicity assessment before seeking to apply it as a regulatory requirement in individual discharge consents.[279] Nonetheless, the evidence of technically successful use of toxicity assessment in the United States,[280] and the potential advantages that it holds in measuring environmental impacts and regulating the growing number of toxic substances being placed on the market, indicate that it may eventually supercede substance-specific approaches to discharges. In doing so, it might also replace the various, and in many respects more vague, notion of 'pollution'.[281]

---

[278] Environment Agency *The Application of Toxity-Based Criteria for the Regulatory Control of Wastewater Discharges* (1996).

[279] Environment Agency *The Application of Toxity-Based Criteria for the Regulatory Control of Wastewater Discharges: Response Compendium* (1997) and see *ENDS Report* 277 (1997) p.11. The Environment Agency has also produced a series of 'update' papers on the progress of the direct toxicity assessment demonstration programme.

[280] See Environment Agency, *ibid*, p.36.

[281] See 1.3.3–6 above on legal understandings of 'pollution'.

# Chapter 11

# DISCHARGES OF EFFLUENT TO SEWERS

## 11.1 Introduction

Although not involving direct discharges into the aquatic environment, controlling the disposal of trade effluent into sewers forms a key part of water quality regulation as a whole. Indeed, it is probably true to say that the greater part of liquid discharges from industry are not discharged directly to rivers or other watercourses, but (with or without some form of pre-treatment) are discharged instead to sewers.

As far as the legal significance of trade effluent discharges is concerned, sewerage undertakers are both deemed to be criminally responsible for pollution caused by discharges of effluent that they consent to enter their sewers and, conversely, immune from conviction for causing or knowingly permitting pollution by trade effluent if they were not bound to receive it into their sewerage system.[1] So the extent to which an undertaker consents to receive industrial effluent is central to the scope of the principal water pollution offences, and also impacts on the setting of discharge consents for undertakers' treatment works. Sewers also inhabit a unique regulatory space where they are both deemed to be a part of the natural environment, but where any sewage treatment can be taken into account in determining the need for control.[2] The institutional arrangements for controlling discharges to sewers are also quite distinct, the main regulator being the private sewerage undertakers acting under the overall control of Ofwat, with the Environment Agency having only a limited role in controlling discharges of the most toxic substances and discharges from the most hazardous processes. For all these reasons, the legal regime governing discharges to sewers merits separate consideration.

This chapter outlines the basic legal framework relating to discharges to sewers.[3] This involves, first, indicating the general powers and duties of sewerage undertakers to provide sewerage systems in their areas, both for domestic and trade effluent, and the general prohibitions designed to protect the sewerage system from damage caused by the discharge of certain substances and the undertaking of certain activities. Thereafter the system of trade effluent consents and agreements (including special provisions concerning the most toxic substances and most dangerous

---

[1] See 9.14 above.

[2] See e.g. s.1(11)(c) Environmental Protection Act 1990 and 11.10 below.

[3] For general discussions of sewage effluent treatment see Klein (1957) Ch.4; Klein (1962) Ch.4; Rhoades (1992) and Mason (1996) Ch.3. Specifically on its regulation see Department of the Environment, *Taken for Granted: Report of the Working Party on Sewage Disposal* (1970); House of Commons Environment Committee, Pollution of Rivers and Estuaries, Third Report (1987) Chs.3 and 5; Royal Commission on Environmental Pollution (1992) pp.83–101; House of Commons Select Committee on Environment, Transport and Regional Affairs, *Sewage Treatment and Disposal* (1998).

processes) is discussed. As with the previous chapter on discharge consents, the procedural requirements which govern the application for, determination and revision of such consents, and any charges which may be payable, are discussed. Also noted are the comparatively restricted provisions for public involvement in this area, which again highlights some of the limitations with conceiving of the sewers as entirely a part of the natural water environment.

Because of the uniqueness of the legal provisions relating to trade effluent discharges, and the general right of householders to discharge domestic effluent to sewers, the focus of the discussion is on trade effluent consents and agreements rather than sewage discharges more generally. Hence no detailed consideration is given of the licensing of effluent treatment plants under the Waste Management Licensing Regulations 1994,[4] or charges levied for domestic effluent.

## 11.2 Background and Policy

The early origins of the law relating to the discharge of sewage and trade effluent to sewers lie in an emphasis on the swift removal of sewage effluent, in the interests of public health, though it was not until the Public Health Act 1875 that there was a general right to connect to public sewers.[5] At a relatively early stage, however, the need to secure this public health objective whilst, at the same time, providing a measure of protection for the aquatic environment was recognised. Thus, the 1861 amendments to the Local Government Act 1858 restricted the powers of local boards in constructing or using sewers for carrying effluent into any natural watercourse without some form of purification.[6] This was strengthened under the Rivers Pollution Prevention Act 1893, which in effect made sanitary authorities strictly liable for failing to treat discharged sewage effluent adequately by deeming them responsible for permitting unsatisfactory discharges into watercourses. However, in the interests of protecting the sewer system and employees of the sanitary authorities, provisions first contained in the Public Health Acts Amendment Act 1890, and later extended by the Public Health Act 1925, prohibited the discharge of certain hazardous substances into the sewer network.

The first statute dealing specifically with industrial discharges to sewers was the Public Health (Drainage of Trade Premises) Act 1937, which required the owner or occupier of trade premises seeking to discharge to sewers to serve the local authority with a 'trade effluent notice', in effect an application for permission to discharge to the sewer system. Consents were issued by the local authority, subject to an appeal to the Minister. The 1937 Act also introduced trade effluent agreements, intended to allow local authorities to construct works to collect and treat effluent at the expense of dischargers.

---

[4] See 12.2.6 below.
[5] See generally Ch.2 above.
[6] See further 2.4 above.

Following the 1937 Act, therefore, separate provisions regulated trade and other effluent discharged to sewers, a distinction that continues to the present. While sewerage undertakers have a general duty to provide for the removal, via the sewer system, of both domestic and trade effluent, sewerage undertakers must simply accept into public sewers all domestic sewage, subject to prohibitions upon the discharges of certain substances discussed below. This is justified on the grounds that domestic sewage is of a predictable composition and its removal is required in the interests of public health, whereas trade effluent may contain a wide range of polluting and contaminating substances whose entry into the sewer system demands closer regulation.

On privatisation in 1989,[7] the control of discharges of trade and other effluent to sewers passed to the newly constituted sewerage undertakers, it being considered that the sewer network was sufficiently separate from controlled waters that control by the National Rivers Authority was not necessary. A further consideration was that transferring controls over the discharge of trade effluent to sewerage undertakers would help the undertakers impose conditions on trade effluent consents sufficient to ensure that the undertakers could meet the conditions on their discharge consents for sewage treatment works discharging into controlled waters. A further compelling argument for sewerage undertakers to have responsibility for discharges to the sewer network was the necessity for undertakers to have control over effluent discharged to sewer for health and safety reasons (i.e. to protect their employees) and to prevent damage to treatment works and sewerage system.[8]

## 11.3 Outline and Setting the Scene

### 11.3.1 An Outline of the Present Legal Framework

Trade effluent discharges to sewers are regulated principally under Chapter III of Part IV of the Water Industry Act 1991. This regime has a number of procedural similarities with the regulation of discharges to watercourses under Part III of the Water Resources Act 1991 discussed in the previous chapter, though the regulation of the distinct discharges is of a very different character. This is not least because the control of discharges to sewers is largely the responsibility of private sewerage undertakers rather than a public regulatory agency.[9] Thus, for example, appeals in relation to trade effluent consent conditions are directed to the Director General of Water Services, primarily an economic regulator, rather than to the Secretary of State. The role of the Environment Agency is restricted to the most hazardous discharges.

---

[7] On water privatisation more generally see 2.16 above.

[8] On various general prohibitions on discharges designed to protect worker safety and the sewerage infrastructure see 11.3.5 below.

[9] Though the Environment Agency has responsibility for the discharge of 'special category effluent' to sewers, see 11.10 below.

Further important differences also exist in relation to the relative lack of openness and rights of public participation in the trade effluent consent system. These are justified on the grounds that what is being regulated are not direct discharges to the natural environment but discharges to sewers owned and operated by private sewerage undertakers, sometimes made under contractual agreements but always of a commercial nature involving charges for effluent treatment. In addition, unlike discharges to controlled waters, there are health and safety concerns with the entry of potentially hazardous substances to the confined environment of the sewerage network. Consequently, there is a unique system of control, probably the only example in the UK of a private commercial body exercising public regulatory functions with regard to environmental protection.

The extent to which sewerage undertakers must receive discharges to their sewers or treatment works is recognised in the exemption from liability under any of the principal water pollution offences under the Water Resources Act 1991 if the undertaker was bound to receive the discharge. The counterpart of this is that a sewerage undertaker will not be guilty of an offence in relation to contravening a discharge consent due to a discharge by another person into a sewer or works of the undertaker which the undertaker was not bound to receive and could not reasonably have been expected to prevent.[10] The 1991 Act therefore seeks to regulate the relationship between sewerage undertakers and dischargers to sewer by giving dischargers immunity from prosecution if they adhere to the terms of the trade effluent consents issued to them by the undertaker. In return for this, the undertaker avoids criminal liability by discharging only effluent which it has agreed to accept from industrial dischargers, after treatment, or that which it could not reasonably prevent from entering the sewer or treatment works.[11] Whether a discharge to sewer is lawfully made will therefore have important consequences for the potential criminal liabilities of both trade effluent dischargers and undertakers.[12]

In practice, local authorities acting under agency agreements with the sewerage undertaker for the area often undertake regulation of the sewerage system.[13] Such arrangements date back to the Water Act 1973 and the transfer from local authorities to water authorities of primary responsibility for providing sewerage services. However, the power to

---

[10] ss.87(2) and (3) Water Resources Act 1991 and see 9.14 above. A discharger to sewer may be criminally liable both in proceedings brought under the Water Resources Act 1991 for water pollution, and in proceedings brought under the Water Industry Act 1991 for an unlawful discharge to sewer. See, e.g., 'Double whammy for environmentally accredited company' [1997] *Water Law* 128. Also *National Rivers Authority* v *Hickson and Welch Ltd*, unreported (1996), discussed at 9.14.2 above and *National Rivers Authority* v *Appletise Bottling; Northumbrian Water* v *Appletise Bottling* [1991] 3 LMELR 132.

[11] As, for example, was the situation in *National Rivers Authority* v *Yorkshire Water Services Ltd* [1995] 1 AC 444 and see 9.14.3 above.

[12] See 11.12 below, but covered in more detail at 9.14 above.

[13] Power for such arrangements is given in s.97 Water Industry Act 1991. In relation to sewerage functions, the power to delegate extends to all sewerage undertakers' functions with the exception of sewage disposal: see s.6(2). For an illustration of these arrangements see *Wychavon District Council* v *National Rivers Authority* [1993] 1 WLR 125, discussed at 9.6.2 above.

delegate functions to a local authority does not absolve the undertaker of responsibility for any failure or inadequacy of performance. The point is well illustrated by *R* v *Yorkshire Water Services Ltd*[14] where, in an appeal against sentence, the Court made it plain that responsibility for the exercise of functions by the undertaker remained, even where day-to-day responsibility for operating the sewage system had been delegated to the local authority.

Transitional provisions relate to discharges made before the coming into force of the Water Act 1989.[15] These provisions now apply to a small number of discharges of trade effluent into public sewers made under agreements under s.7(4) of the Public Health (Drainage of Trade Premises) Act 1937. Such 'deemed' consents may be replaced by the undertaker with actual consents, subject to a right of appeal.

### 11.3.2 The Provision of Sewerage and Trade Effluent Services

Public sewers, the focus here, are to be distinguished from both drains and watercourses. A 'drain' is a passage for liquids from a single building while a 'sewer' is a system of drainage to deal with liquids from buildings or yards.[16] The distinction between a sewer and a watercourse is more complicated,[17] but a starting point is the statutory map of public sewers which undertakers must keep.[18] If a conduit is not shown on the statutory map, the burden of proof should be regarded as lying on the person seeking to assert that it is a public sewer.[19] Discharges to drains are not governed separately and fall, eventually, within the general scope of discharges to controlled waters, discussed previously. The upkeep of drains, as with private sewers, is the responsibility of the owner of the premises. By contrast, discharges to public sewers are subject to separate legal controls underpinned by the general duty on sewerage undertakers to provide and maintain an effective system of public sewers.[20]

### 11.3.2A The requisitioning duty

Sewerage undertakers must provide public sewers for the drainage of premises for domestic purposes where this is requested by notice.[21] This requisitioning duty applies to any premises containing buildings or in relation to which there are proposals for building, so long as certain financial conditions are satisfied.[22] Where these requirements are met, the

---

[14] See *R* v *Yorkshire Water Services Ltd* [1994] *Water Law* 175 and *The Times*, 19 July 1994. And see discussion in 9.6.4 above.

[15] Provided for under s.140 and Sch.8 Water Industry Act 1991.

[16] *Ibid* s.219(1).

[17] See, e.g. Institute of Civil Engineers (1996) ch.7 and Garner and Bailey (1995).

[18] s.199 Water Industry Act 1991.

[19] Institution of Civil Engineers (1996) p.45.

[20] s.94 Water Industry Act 1991, extended by s.101A(4) and (5), discussed at 11.3.2A below.

[21] *Ibid* s.98.

[22] The financial conditions are specified in *ibid* s.99.

undertaker must make sewerage provision within six months of the notice, otherwise, subject to agreement, it is in default.[23] The duty is owed to owners and occupiers of premises and to the local authority, and to specified development agencies, and extends to the drainage of domestic effluent from non-domestic premises. 'Domestic purposes' is defined to mean the domestic sewerage purposes specified in relation to the premises mentioned above. For the purposes of Chapter II of Part IV of the Water Industry Act 1991 generally 'domestic sewerage purposes' means

(a) the removal from buildings and associated land of the contents of lavatories;

(b) the removal, from buildings and such land, of water which has been used for cooking and washing; and

(c) the removal, from buildings and such land, of surface water.

However, it excludes water used for the business of a laundry, or for the preparation of food or drink for consumption otherwise than on the premises.[24]

Additions inserted under the Environment Act 1995 seek to address problems arising from inadequate, or potentially inadequate, sewage provision in rural areas.[25] Although not restricted to rural areas, and without prejudice to the general requisitioning duty noted above, sewerage undertakers must now provide a public sewer for the drainage, for domestic sewerage purposes, of premises in a particular locality in its area if certain conditions are satisfied. These are:

(a) that the premises had on them certain buildings erected before, or substantially completed by, 20 June 1995;

(b) that these buildings are supported by drains or sewers used for domestic sewerage purposes which, neither directly or indirectly, connect with a public sewer; and

(c) the drainage system in place is giving, or likely to give, rise to such adverse effects to the environment or amenity that it is appropriate, having regard to any guidance issued by the Secretary of State[26] and all other relevant considerations,[27] to provide a public sewer.[28]

Appeals may be made to the Environment Agency for final determination, raising a potential conflict of interest, since the Agency may both generate pressure on the discharger to connect to sewer (or face charges under the

---

[23] *Ibid* s.101.

[24] See 11.3.3 below on the definition of 'trade premises'.

[25] See DoE, *Review of Rural Water Supply and Sewerage* (1994) and see discussion of the *Scrayingham Sewer Appeal* at 14.10 below.

[26] s.101A(4) and (5) Water Industry Act 1991, and see DoE and WO, *Guidance on the Provision of a Public Sewer under Section 101A of the WIA 1991* (1996). For a review see *Water Profile*, 18 June 1999, pp.2-3.

[27] For example, those mentioned in s.101A(3) Water Industry Act 1991.

[28] *Ibid* s.101A, inserted by para.103 Sch.22 Environment Act 1995. The duty is enforceable under s.18 Water Industry Act 1991, on which see further 7.9 above.

principal water pollution offences) while also determining disputes between the discharger and the undertaker about the right to connect.[29]

## 11.3.2B The communication duty

Sewerage undertakers have a general duty to allow owners and occupiers of domestic premises to connect to public sewers, provided appropriate notice is given.[30] Undertakers are given limited powers of refusal, and in particular have 21 days to refuse to permit the connection if it appears that the mode of construction or condition of the drain or sewer is such that the making of the communication would be prejudicial to the undertaker's sewerage system.[31] In general, the duty on sewerage undertakers is 'to permit occupiers of premises to make connections to the sewer and to discharge their sewer therein . . . they have no power to prevent ingress of sewage into the sewer'.[32] The strictness of the duty involved is such that an undertaker cannot decline to connect a sewer, notwithstanding that allowing further discharge may have the effect of overloading a sewage system. This principle would seem to extend to a situation where the sewer is already overloaded, with obvious consequences.[33]

A sewerage undertaker may, through its consultative role in the planning system,[34] seek to prevent or restrict new development in areas where pressure on the sewerage system would arise. Although the adequacy of sewerage provision will be a material consideration in determining any planning application,[35] such objections must be supported by specific evidence of the inadequacy of the existing system and explain why the capacity of the service could not be increased to cater for the new development.[36] Once planning permission is granted, however, the undertaker must accommodate any additional effluent that the new development generates.[37] A sewerage undertaker may, however, direct a

---

[29] While there is no evidence that such conflicts have arisen, it is understood that the Agency is establishing 'Chinese Walls' between its roles of environmental regulator and arbiter in disputes concerning the right to connect.

[30] s.106 Water Industry Act 1991.

[31] *Ibid* s.106(3) and (4). On further procedural matters, see *ibid* s.106(5) to (8). More general restrictions on the matter that may be discharged to sewer are discussed below at 11.3.5.

[32] *Smeaton* v *Ilford Corporation* [1954] 1 All ER 923 at 928-929 per Upjohn J, see below.

[33] *Tayside Regional Council* v *Secretary of State for Scotland* 1996 SLT 473, concerning near identical provisions to s.106 Water Industry Act 1991 contained in s.12 Sewerage (Scotland) Act 1968. For an example of the consequences of overloading see *Pride of Derby and Derbyshire Angling Association* v *British Celanese Ltd* [1953] Ch 149, discussed at 3.12.4 above.

[34] See 14.5.3–4 below.

[35] See para.17 Annex 3 PPG 23 *Planning and Pollution Control* (1994).

[36] Bates (1990, updated) para 9.69; and on planning and sewage treatment infrastructure see 14.5.3–4 below.

[37] In practice, it is likely that *Grampian*-type conditions will be imposed on new development preventing work commencing, or the development being connected to the sewer system, until the necessary sewerage infrastructure is in place. On the legality of such conditions see *W E Black Ltd* v *Secretary of State for the Environment* [1997] Env LR 1, discussed at 14.5.5A below. The cost to sewerage undertakers of providing new sewerage infrastructure is likely to be the subject to a planning agreement, made under s.106 Town and Country Planning Act 1990, entered into

local planning authority to reject plans for a new building or extension where it is to be erected over a particular sewer or drain.[38] Connections to sewers that fall outwith the statutory rights of connection[39] will amount to a trespass, for which the normal remedy awarded is damages.[40]

As noted above,[41] it will be no defence to a civil action for nuisance caused by overloading of the sewage system that the additional development could not be foreseen and sufficiently accommodated, although it will be a defence to a charge of creating a nuisance that the sewerage undertaker was bound to provide sewers and to permit sewage to be discharged into them,[42] and did not therefore do any act which could be said to have caused, continued or adopted a nuisance. Thus, in *Smeaton v Ilford Corporation*,[43] where the claimant brought an action for damages and an injunction against a sanitary authority with responsibility for a sewer which, without any negligence on their part, had become overloaded and occasionally overflowed on to the claimant's land, it was held that the communication, combined with the absence of negligence, meant that the defendants had not created the nuisance within the meaning of the requisitioning and communication duty as it was then provided for and were therefore not liable in nuisance.[44]

### 11.3.3 'Trade Effluent' and 'Trade Premises'

A key distinction is between the discharge of domestic effluent and non-domestic effluent to sewers.[45] The provisions governing discharges of trade effluent to sewers are contained in Chapter III of Part IV of the Water Industry Act 1991. These provisions determine whether trade effluent is of a kind which a sewerage undertaker is bound to receive into a treatment works. Sewerage undertakers have specific forward planning duties in relation to discharges of trade effluent.[46]

For the purposes of controls upon the discharge of trade effluent into public sewers, 'trade effluent' is defined as meaning any liquid, either with or without particles of matter in suspension in it, which is wholly or partly produced in the course of any trade or industry carried on at trade premises; and in relation to any trade premises, means any such liquid which is so produced in the course of any trade or industry carried on at

---

between the developer and the local planning authority (on planning agreements see 14.5.5B below).

[38] s.18 Building Act 1984, as amended.

[39] Under s.106 Water Industry Act 1991.

[40] *Cook v Minion* (1978) 37 P & CR 58.

[41] See 3.8.3 above.

[42] Under s.106 Water Industry Act 1991.

[43] See above and see also 3.13.4 above.

[44] See previously s.31 Public Health Act 1936. See also *Stretton's Derby Brewery Co v Derby Corporation* [1894] 1 Ch 431.

[45] On the meaning of 'effluent' see 9.9 above.

[46] s.94(2) Water Industry Act 1991.

those premises, excluding domestic sewage.[47] 'Trade premises' is defined as any premises used or intended to be used for the carrying on of any trade or industry. This includes any land or premises used or intended for use in whole or in part for agricultural or horticultural purposes or for the purposes of fish farming, or for scientific research or experiment, whether for profit or not.[48] It follows, therefore, that although sewage of a domestic character[49] may emanate from trade premises, it will be subject to a separate system of control from that governing the discharge of trade effluent into public sewers from the same premises. Substances contained in process water, for example will not be 'produced' in the course of trade at the trade premises and will therefore not be trade effluent requiring consent.[50] That trade effluent must be 'produced' also suggests that it does not include surface water run off.

Neither 'trade' nor 'premises', however, are defined for the purposes of the definition of 'trade premises'. The issue was raised in *Thames Water Authority* v *Blue and White Launderettes Ltd*,[51] a case concerning whether, for fiscal purposes, effluent discharged from washing machines should be classified as trade effluent since it was indistinguishable in character from domestic waste water. It was held that the definition of 'trade premises' related to the purpose of the activity producing the effluent rather than the nature of the discharge, and consequently the laundrette was discharging trade effluent within the definition.[52]

### 11.3.4 Restrictions on Discharging Domestic Waste

Although the owner or occupier of any premises or the owner of any private sewer is entitled, subject to certain exceptions, to have their drains or sewer made to communicate with the public sewers of any sewerage undertaker, the permitted use of this facility is limited to the right to discharge foul water or surface water from the premises or that private sewer. In particular:

(a) the right of connection does not entitle any person directly or indirectly to discharge into a public sewer any liquid from a factory, other than domestic sewage, surface or storm water, or any liquid from a manufacturing process; or any liquid or other matter the discharge of which into public sewers is prohibited under any enactment;

(b) where there are separate sewers for foul water and for surface water, foul water must not be discharged into the surface water sewer, or, except with the consent of the sewerage undertaker,

---

[47] *Ibid* s.141.

[48] *Ibid* s.141(1) and (2).

[49] On 'domestic sewerage purposes' see 11.3.2A above.

[50] *R* v *Rechem International Ltd*, Court of Appeal, 11 November 1994, unreported.

[51] [1980] WLR 700.

[52] See now s.117(1) Water Industry Act 1991, which specifically provides that water used for the business of a laundry or for the business of preparing food or drink for consumption otherwise than on the premises will not amount to 'domestic sewage', and see 11.3.2A above.

surface water may not be discharged into the foul water sewer; and

(c) a person's drains or sewers may not be made to connect directly with a storm water overflow sewer.[53]

These criteria are exhaustive, and therefore limit the general right to discharge into the sewer system without restriction to domestic waste and run-off water. Liquid discharges from a 'factory' or 'manufacturing process' are subject to the trade effluent consent regime, discussed below.[54]

### 11.3.5 Prohibitions on Certain Discharges to Sewers

In the interests of protecting the sewerage infrastructure and human health, the Water Industry Act 1991 also makes it unlawful for certain matter to be passed into sewers which may cause damage to the sewer system or to public health or give rise to nuisances. Thus, it is an offence for a person to throw, empty or turn, or suffer or permit to be thrown or emptied or to pass specified matter and substances, into any public sewer, or into any drain or sewer communicating with a public sewer. In particular the offence arises in respect of:

(a) any matter likely[55] to injure the sewer or drain, or interfere with the free flow of its contents or to affect prejudicially the treatment and disposal of its contents;[56]

(b) any chemical refuse or waste steam, or any liquid of a temperature higher than one hundred and ten degrees Fahrenheit which is a prohibited substance; or

(c) any petroleum spirit or carbide of calcium.[57]

For these purposes 'petroleum spirit' is defined to include crude petroleum, oil made from petroleum, or from coal, shale, peat or other bituminous substances, or any product of petroleum or mixture containing petroleum which produces an inflammable vapour under specified conditions.[58] The reference to a 'prohibited substance' in relation to chemical refuse, waste stream or heated liquids means that the substance, either alone or in combination with the contents of the sewer or drain in question, is dangerous, the cause of a nuisance or injurious or likely to cause injury to health. The offence would seem to extend to any substance

---

[53] s.106(1) and (2) Water Industry Act 1991.

[54] On the distinction between 'domestic' and 'trade premises' see 11.3.3 above.

[55] The onus of proof being on the undertaker.

[56] On the meaning of 'affect prejudicially' see *Liverpool Corporation* v *Coghill and Son Ltd* [1918] 1 Ch 307, that the discharges of liquid containing borax injuriously affected the claimants' sewage farm and crops thereon.

[57] s.111(1) Water Industry Act 1991.

[58] s.111(5) Water Industry Act 1991.

that prevents sewage sludge or effluent from being disposed of in accordance, after treatment, with Regulations.[59]

Contravention of any of these provisions gives rise, on summary conviction, to liability to a fine not exceeding the statutory maximum, currently £5,000, and to a further fine not exceeding £50 for each day on which the offence continues after conviction. Daily fines may only be imposed following expiry of any 'compliance' period set by the court.[60] On conviction on indictment the maximum penalty is a term of imprisonment not exceeding two years or a fine or both.[61] An injunction may be granted where the offence continues because the offender considers it in their economic interests to continue the prohibited discharge.[62]

### 11.4 Applying for Trade Effluent Consents

The normal way that a trade effluent consent is obtained is by the owner or occupier of the premises serving a 'trade effluent notice' on the sewerage undertaker. The notice must state the nature or composition of the effluent to be discharged, the maximum quantity proposed to be discharged on any one day, and the highest proposed rate of discharge.[63] Undertakers are given two months within which to determine the application, after which time the applicant may appeal against the non-determination.[64] Alternatively, the discharger may seek to enter into an agreement with the sewerage undertaker.[65] Distinct provisions relate to special category effluent.[66]

Rights enabling public participation in the regulation of discharges to sewer are comparatively limited. There is no explicit right for a member of the public to be informed of an application for a trade effluent consent and no right to participate in the decision whether to grant one, or in any appeal.[67] It may be of some consolation that all consents, variations, agreements and directions by the sewerage undertaker or the Director, and any notification from the Agency to the undertaker in relation to special category effluent, must be placed on a public register.[68] However, this right is limited, since the information contained in the register is significantly less comprehensive than the information provided for under corresponding provisions relating to discharge consents.[69] Notably, there is no public right to information on monitoring or action taken. Indeed, it is a

---

[59] Bates (1990, updated), para 9.104.

[60] s.111(4) Water Industry Act 1991.

[61] *Ibid* s.111(1)-(4).

[62] *Attorney-General* v *Sharp* [1931] 1 Ch 121.

[63] s.119(2) Water Industry Act 1991.

[64] *Ibid* s.122(1)(b).

[65] *Ibid* s.129, discussed at 11.8 below.

[66] See 11.10 below.

[67] But see s.215 Water Industry Act 1991 which provides for the possibility of a local inquiry.

[68] s.196 Water Industry Act 1991.

[69] See 16.5 below on discharge consents and registers.

criminal offence for an employee of the sewerage undertaker to disclose information furnished under the Act[70] unless for purposes such as civil or criminal proceedings or in response to a request for information.[71] Although the Agency has certain powers, by notice, to acquire information for the purpose of its function in relation to special category effluent,[72] no comparable power is given to undertakers as regards their functions.[73]

It may be that the restrictions on access to information on trade effluent consents and special category effluent are mitigated by the impact of the Environmental Information Regulations 1992.[74] Thus it might be possible to use the 1992 Regulations to be informed of applications for trade effluent consent. However, the obvious practical difficulty of using access to information rights is that the time period for determining consent applications is the same as that for dealing with an access to information request. There is also the practical difficulty of knowing when an application had been submitted.

## 11.5  Trade Effluent Consents and their Conditions

The occupier of any trade premises in the area of a sewerage undertaker may discharge any trade effluent proceeding from those premises into the undertaker's public sewers if this is done with the undertaker's consent.[75] This provision applies so long as the discharge is via a drain or sewer, and is subject to certain of the general restrictions noted above. The same procedures as those which apply when seeking to have drains or sewers communicate with a public sewer apply to communication with a sewer for trade effluent disposal.[76] Failure to discharge under any necessary consent or under an appropriate agreement as is necessary for the purposes of Chapter III of Part IV of the Water Industry Act 1991 renders the occupier of the premises guilty of an offence and liable on summary conviction to a fine not exceeding the statutory maximum, currently £5000, and on conviction on indictment to a fine.

The requirement that trade effluent is discharged into public sewers in accordance with a consent granted by a sewerage undertaker is underpinned by a broadly analogous system of authorising discharges to that which operates in relation to dischargers to controlled waters described in the previous chapter, although with some important differences. Most notably, the regulatory role is entrusted to a private commercial undertaking, albeit one with certain public duties. This has led to concerns that the undertaker may not, or may not be seen to, act impartially in relation to what may be competitor or connected

---

[70] s.206 Water Industry Act 1991.

[71] Made by the Environment Agency pursuant to s.203 Water Resources Act 1991, see 16.14.2 below.

[72] s.135A Water Industry Act 1991, see 11.10 below.

[73] Contrast s.202(2) Water Resources Act 1991, see 16.7 below.

[74] On the status of sewerage undertakers as public bodies see 16.17.1 below.

[75] Under s.118 Water Industry Act 1991.

[76] *Ibid* s.118(4).

organisations, or may focus unduly on its commercial rather than regulatory aspects. In turn this has led some to call for a role for the Environment Agency in the issuing of *all* trade effluent consents, or at least a greater proportion of consents than those regulated under integrated pollution control or integrated pollution prevention and control[77] or which involve 'special category effluent' where the need for an environmental regulatory role at the point of discharge to sewer has been accepted in order to give effect to obligations under the EC Dangerous Substances Directive.[78]

### 11.5.1 Trade Effluent Consent Conditions

Consent for a discharge of trade effluent into a public sewer may be given either unconditionally or subject to such conditions as the sewerage undertaker thinks fit to impose with respect to a range of specified considerations. These general considerations are:

(a) the sewer or sewers into which the trade effluent may be discharged;
(b) the nature or composition of that effluent;
(c) its maximum daily quantity; and
(d) the highest rate of discharge.[79]

Conditions with respect to all or any of the following matters may also be attached to a trade effluent consent:

(a) the times during which the trade effluent may be discharged;
(b) the exclusion of all condensing water;
(c) the elimination or diminution of any substances in the effluent which the undertaker is satisfied would, either alone or in combination with any matter with which it is likely to come into contact while passing through any sewers, damage the sewers or make treatment or disposal especially difficult or expensive or, where the effluent may end up, via a sewer outfall, in a harbour or tidal water, lead to injury or obstruction to the navigation on, or the use of, the harbour or tidal water;[80]
(d) the temperature, and acidity or alkalinity, at the time of discharge;
(e) payment by the occupier for the reception and disposal of the effluent;[81]
(f) the provision and maintenance of an access point for the taking of samples;

---

[77] See 12.3 below on integrated controls.
[78] See, e.g. the submission of the Environment Agency to the House of Commons Environment, Transport and Regional Affairs Committee, *Sewage Treatment and Disposal* (1998). On 'special category effluent' see 11.10 below.
[79] s.121(1) Water Industry Act 1991.
[80] 'Harbour' and 'tidal water' have the definition given to them by ss.313 and 255 Merchant Shipping Act 1995.
[81] See discussion of trade effluent agreements at 11.8 below. The power here is in addition to the power under s.142 Water Industry Act 1991.

(g) the provision, testing and maintenance of meters for measuring the volume and rate of the discharge;

(h) the provision, testing and maintenance of apparatus for determining the nature and composition of the trade effluent;

(i) the keeping of records of the volume, rate of discharge, nature and composition of any trade effluent being discharged, including records of the readings of meters and other apparatus; and

(j) the making of returns and the giving of other information to the sewerage undertaker concerning those matters mentioned in (i) above.[82]

Specifically, a trade effluent consent may make it lawful to infringe any of the specific prohibitions on discharges mentioned above.[83] Only the discharge of petroleum spirit or calcium carbides cannot in principle be consented, because of the inherent danger associated with their presence in the sewage system.

Although it has been suggested that the list of conditions that may be attached to a trade effluent consent is not intended to be an exhaustive list,[84] the contrary view may be preferable. In particular, the wording of s.121 Water Industry Act 1991, listing the potential conditions, may be contrasted with that under Schedule 10 to the Water Resources Act 1991 which gives the Agency the power to impose such conditions in discharge consents as it may think fit, but which provides for a list of matters on which conditions may, *in particular*, be included.[85] By contrast, the comparable provision in relation to trade effluent consents gives less discretion to sewerage undertakers and focuses upon the constituents in the effluent. In any event, it is at least arguable that the provision relating to trade effluent consents should be construed more restrictively, since the implications of the distinction should have been in the minds of the draftsman when the water legislation was consolidated in 1991.[86]

The restrictive interpretation of the scope for imposing trade effluent conditions seems to be borne out in practice where, for example, specification standards requiring the fitting of specified treatment plant are not generally imposed. Rather, the usual practice is to specify the effluent standards that must be met and to leave it to the discharger to determine how to meet those standards, albeit often with advice from the sewerage undertaker.[87] A major reason behind the preference of undertakers to avoid imposing prescriptive conditions is that such standards cannot, in themselves, ensure that unsatisfactory levels of substances are excluded from sewers, or therefore ensure that the undertakers own discharges to controlled waters remain within consented levels.

---

[82] s.121 Water Industry Act 1991.

[83] *Ibid* s.106(2)(a) and (b) and s.111(1)(a) or (b), see 11.3.5 above.

[84] Tromans, Nash and Poustie (1996, updated), D23-101.

[85] Discharge consents may stipulate specific treatment plant such as ultra violet disinfection.

[86] On the consolidation of water legislation in 1991 see 2.20 above.

[87] See also 11.5.2 below.

Whether the wording of the above list of consent conditions in relation to the 'nature or composition of the trade effluent'[88] restricts conditions to being 'constituent-based' rather than allowing for restrictions based on the impact on receiving sewer waters is a matter of doubt. On one line of argument, the impact of a pollutant, or combination of pollutants, upon its receiving medium is an intrinsic characteristic of the 'nature' of the substance concerned. Alternatively, the impact is conceived of in terms of the relationship between the pollutant and the sewerage system, or particular features of the system, upon which it impacts (rather than an intrinsic feature of pollutants themselves).[89] The problem has arisen in relation to setting conditions for colour,[90] and arises more generally with synergistic polluting effects and with the legal status of trade effluent consent conditions that might enable direct toxicity assessment requirements to be imposed.[91]

Regardless of the correct interpretation of the power of undertakers to impose conditions in trade effluent consents, there is still a fairly widespread belief in many quarters that most effluent is better and more efficiently treated at the sewage works than at the point of production, making the imposition of such specific conditions unlikely. On the other hand, there are pressures towards greater treatment at source, inspired, for example, by provisions governing integrated pollution prevention and control[92] and by general pressures to improve environmental business performance.

## 11.5.2 Determining Consents

As with discharge consents, the extent to which undertakers are free to impose appropriate conditions on trade effluent consents is constrained by provisions deriving from EC law. Thus, conditions must be imposed in trade effluent consents to meet the requirements of the Urban Waste Water Treatment Directive and consents which conflict with this requirement will be invalid and unenforceable.[93] On the other hand, it must be questioned whether any condition of a consent which, as has been known, requires 'compliance with the Urban Waste Water Treatment Directive' or its

---

[88] s.121(1)(b) Water Industry Act 1991.

[89] See, e.g., the opposing views expressed in *Milnes v Huddersfield Corporation* (1886) 11 App Cas 511 discussed at 17.2.2 below.

[90] See WRc (1998) p.26.

[91] On direct toxicity assessment see 1.3.8 and 10.12.2 above. There is a concern amongst sewage undertakers that difficulties might arise if the Environment Agency were to introduce direct toxicity conditions into trade effluent consents whilst still themselves being subject to standards discharge consent conditions for their own discharges to water (see Environment Agency *The Application of Toxicity-Based Criteria for the Regulatory Control of Wastewater Discharges: Response Compendium* (1997). It is questionable also whether the provisions of the Urban Waste Water Treatment (England and Wales) Regulations 1994 (SI 1994 No.2841) are sufficiently comprehensive to facilitate such assessment, see WRc (1998) p.25.

[92] See 12.3.3–6 below. In this context the prevention and rectification at source principles of Community law might be noted, on which see further 4.7.2 above.

[93] See Sch.4 Urban Waste Water Treatment (England and Wales) Regulations 1994 (SI 1994 No.2841).

implementing regulations will be lawful. Not least, this is because of the vagueness of many of the stipulations in the Directive which have to be given effect *through* national licensing decisions. In 1996 the Government took the view that the Urban Waste Water Treatment Directive provided a sufficiently specific control regime to justify non-application of the Waste Framework Directive[94] to discharges to sewer, and also that the relevant provisions of the Water Industry Act 1991 provided an effective means of pursuing the aims of the Waste Framework Directive as regards discharges to sewer.[95] In addition, sewerage undertakers are statutory undertakers, and therefore 'competent authorities', for the purposes of the Conservation (Natural Habitats etc.) Regulations 1994, and thus subject to general obligations to assess the implications of their consenting decisions on European sites.[96] Undertakers are also 'relevant authorities' in relation to marine areas and European marine sites under the 1994 Regulations.[97]

As discussed above, trade effluent discharges may be thought of as discharges into something more closely resembling the 'built environment' (the sewer system) rather than into the natural aquatic environment.[98] Because they are not direct discharges to controlled waters, a range of factors are justifiably taken into account when determining trade effluent consents, of which eventual environmental impact is only one consideration. In particular, trade effluent quality will have only an indirect effect upon water quality objectives for the receiving waters into which the effluent eventually passes after treatment at a sewage works.

The range of factors actually taken into account in determining trade effluent consents may be gleaned from a publication of the Water Authorities Association from September 1986 entitled *Trade Effluent Discharged to the Sewer*. This notes that the system of trade effluent control seeks to:

(a) protect the sewerage system and the personnel who work in it;
(b) protect the sewage works and their efficient operation (for example, most sewage works operate by a biological process and care has to be taken not to neutralise that process);
(c) protect the environment generally from the residues of the sewage treatment process or from direct discharges from parts of the system such as storm drains; and
(d) ensure that dischargers pay a reasonable charge for the costs of the treatment.

In addition, the booklet stresses the importance of current information on discharges to be kept, so that dischargers can know how to improve their trade effluent control and sewerage undertakers can plan for future sewerage provision and operate the treatment process efficiently.

---

[94] Directive 75/442/EEC as amended, discussed at 12.2.2 below.
[95] HC Written Answers, 23 July 1996, Cols 316-7, discussed in *ENDS Report* 258 (1996) p.27.
[96] SI 1994 No.1056, see 15.8.3 below.
[97] See 15.8.3 below on 'relevant authorities' for marine conservation.
[98] On the 'quasi-environmental' status of sewers see 11.1 above and 11.10 below.

With these factors in mind, consents are generally set by reference to the receiving capabilities of the sewer and sewage works. If the works are already overburdened, the consent may be refused or made subject to strict limits, whereas if there is spare capacity at the works, the limits will be more generous. Certain pollutants, such as heavy metals or persistent chemicals, may be unsuitable for sewage treatment and may be banned from the discharge. The discharger may then have to pre-treat the effluent to remove these constituents, or find an alternative method of disposal. In addition, the sewerage undertaker's own potential liability for discharges from the works will be taken into account.[99] It should be pointed out that an impact of the Urban Waste Water Treatment Directive is that the increased cost of treating effluent to the higher standards required is being reflected in much higher trade effluent charges.[100] As a result, many more firms are likely to do more pre-treatment work at their sites to lower their costs, rather than leave this to the undertaker. In practice, very small discharges of an innocuous nature may simply be acknowledged by the undertaker without the formality of issuing a trade effluent consent and charging for the discharge.

Some guidance on the setting of conditions may also be found in advice from the Director General of Water Services on trade effluent appeals.[101] If a disputed condition is justified on its merits, the Director will determine whether the discharger's long-term costs of complying with the standard is less than those reasonably estimated by the sewerage undertaker to treat the discharge to the same environmental standard at its works. If they are, the Director will normally dismiss the discharger's appeal. But if the discharger's costs are more than those of the undertaker, then the Director will normally uphold the appeal. If necessary, the Director will investigate how the sewerage undertaker's costs can be properly recovered, as far as practicable from dischargers to the works concerned.

### 11.5.3 General Binding Rules

As in other areas,[102] there is scope to substitute case-by-case determinations of trade effluent consents by the use of some form of general binding rule. The use of general binding rules, coupled with a registration scheme, is specifically allowable in order to implement the Water Framework Directive.[103]

To date, there do not appear to be any examples of general binding rules being used as between, say, an industrial sector and a sewerage undertaker or undertakers. There is, however, an agreement entered into between the photo-processing industry and undertakers which aims to provide some

---

[99] See 11.12 below.

[100] On trade effluent charges see 11.6 below.

[101] See Ofwat Information Note No. 21 (1993).

[102] See Art.9(8) Integrated Pollution Prevention and Control Directive, and see also the prospect for such rules in relation to discharge consents, discussed at 10.12.1 above.

[103] See 5.9.11 above.

general, non-binding, starting points for dealing with discharges of substances like mercury and silver which are discharged to sewers from this sector.[104]

General binding rules may have the advantage of lowering administrative costs on each side. But even then this may be limited, since a site visit and other contact between the parties on the ground will still be needed to explain the regulatory requirements. Hence, all that may be saved may be the limited time drafting the consent.

## 11.6 Charges

Discharges to sewer may (and in general practice will) be subject to charges imposed as a condition of a consent[105] or under contract through a trade effluent agreement.[106] More usually, however, charges will be payable under a 'charges scheme'.[107] Sewerage undertakers may apply a charges scheme where a notice containing an application for a consent is served on the undertaker, or where a trade effluent consent is given by the undertaker, or where a discharge is made in pursuance of such a consent (generally, referred to here as a 'trade effluent charge'). Although framed as a discretionary power, Condition D of the Model Instrument of Appointment requires undertakers to have in force at all times a charges scheme for sewerage services. This must be made available on request. Despite the wording of the legislation, the discretionary power to fix charges is circumscribed by Condition B of the Model Instrument of Appointment which provides for the RPI − X formula that sets overall charging limits on undertakers.[108]

In practice, the individual elements of charging schemes are increased annually in agreement with Ofwat. The Water Industry Act 1999 placed specific statutory controls on this arrangement. Thus, a charges scheme cannot take effect unless it has been approved by the Director. In giving his approval, the Director must have regard to any guidance issued by the Secretary of State,[109] and arrangement must be made for any such guidance to be published in an appropriate manner. These amendments, however, made it clear that the Director is not to exercise his power to approve charges schemes for the purpose of limiting the total revenues of relevant undertakers from charges fixed by or in accordance with charges schemes.[110] Guidance was published in February 2000, covering charges

---

[104] WRc (1998) p.67.

[105] s.121(2)(e) Water Industry Act 1991.

[106] Such agreements may override any charges scheme or consent condition regarding charging, see *Nottingham Corporation* v *Bulwell Finishing Company Ltd.* (1970) 68 LGR 128.

[107] Made under s.143 Water Industry Act 1991, as amended by ss.3 and 4 Water Industry Act 1999.

[108] On Model Instruments of Appointment and RPI - X see 7.6.3 and 7.8 above.

[109] Or, in Wales, the National Assembly, discussed below.

[110] s.143(6)-(9) Water Industry Act 1991, added by s.4(1) and (3) Water Industry Act 1999. The Guidance must be entered on the register kept by the Director under s.195 Water Industry Act 1991 (para.4 Sch.3 Water Industry Act 1999).

schemes of undertakers operating wholly or mainly in England. Although this guidance concentrated on social justice issues, specific reference is made to non-household users, in particular that different users should be charged according to the actual use which they make of the sewerage system, thus differentiating between industrial users and, for example, places of worship.[111] The National Assembly of Wales has indicated that it is considering issuing guidance in respect of companies in Wales (including the sewerage undertaker Dŵr Cymru (Welsh Water)), but the timing of this is, at the time of writing, unknown.

The person liable to pay a trade effluent charge is the person who serves the notice, the person to whom the consent is given or, as the case may be, any person who makes a discharge in pursuance of the consent which, in accordance with the scheme, the charge relates. However, subject to any contrary agreement, the person liable will usually be the occupier of the premises.[112] A scheme of trade effluent charges may impose either a single charge in respect of the whole period for which the consent is in force, a separate charge in respect of different parts of that period, or both a single charge and separate charges.[113]

A charges scheme may make different provision for different cases, including different provision in relation to different circumstances or localities, and may contain supplemental, consequential and transitional provision for the purposes of the scheme. This broad discretion, however, is confined by Condition E of the Model Instrument of Appointment which requires that no undue preference or discrimination is shown in respect of any class of customers. This is a slightly different approach from previous guidance, which emphasised that costs could be averaged across a region and need not reflect costs incurred at any particular treatment works.[114] The general duties of the Director and of the Secretary of State also make specific reference to protecting the interests of customers and potential customers in rural areas.[115] Under a provision added by the Environment Act 1995, the costs of an undertaker providing a sewer to existing premises, in the interests of amenity or environmental protection, must be borne by the undertaker's customers generally.[116]

Although charges are generally imposed via a general charges scheme, conditions concerning payment from the occupier to the undertaker may also be attached to a consent. Such charges may be for the reception of the trade effluent into the sewer and for its disposal, regard being had to the nature and composition and to the volume and rate of discharge of the trade effluent discharged, to any additional expense incurred or likely to be incurred by a sewerage undertaker in connection with the reception or

---

[111] DETR, *Water Industry Act 1999: Delivering the Government's Objectives* (2000) paras 2.41-2.46.
[112] s.144(1) Water Industry Act 1991.
[113] *Ibid* s.143(1)-(3).
[114] Water Authorities Association (1986).
[115] See s.2(3)(a) Water Industry Act 1991, see 7.5 above.
[116] *Ibid* s.143(3A). See the duty in s.101A(1) *ibid*, discussed at 11.3.2A above.

disposal of the trade effluent, and to any revenue likely to be derived by the undertaker from the trade effluent.[117]

As a matter of practice, and subject to Ofwat oversight as noted above, undertakers currently use a similar formula based on the so-called 'Mogden Formula', in which charges are calculated according to the volume of the effluent and its strength as measured by the chemical oxygen demand[118] and the solids content.[119] No extra charges are currently levied in relation to metals or other hazardous items; for these, the only control mechanism is any relevant consent condition rather than the indirect effect of charges. Undertakers are, of course, also subject to charges imposed by the Environment Agency, which may have a knock-on effect in minimising discharge of polluting matter to sewers. As presently provided for, however, these are only cost-recovery charges and do not reflect the full environmental cost of discharges.[120] For example, there are concerns from some customers, discharging weak effluent, about the practice of some undertakers to increase their standard charges for receiving and conveying effluent while decreasing the charge for biological treatment and the treatment and disposal of sludge. It is debatable whether this approach gives the proper incentive from an environmental point of view. At the time of writing, Government has asked for views on the adequacy of the Mogden formula as a basis for charging for trade effluent discharges, as part of its wider consultation on water industry competition.[121] Aside from competitive pressures, any move towards some form of effluent control based on direct toxicity assessment would probably also require changes to the way in which trade effluent charges were calculated.

Charges schemes do not affect the rights of sewerage undertakers to enter into agreements with trade effluent dischargers for which charges may be payable, or any other agreement an undertaker may wish to enter into.[122]

Undertakers may not make initial connection charges for domestic sewerage services unless the premises in question have not previously been connected to a sewer.[123] This provision enables the additional

---

[117] s.121(2)(e) and (4) Water Industry Act 1991.

[118] Chemical Oxygen Demand (COD) is considered a statistically more reliable means of measurement than Biological Oxygen Demand measured over 5 days (BOD5), allowing for more accurate data giving the relative strength of the effluent when compared to the average across the undertaker's area. However, measurements based on BOD5 may be used where the difference between COD and BOD5 measurements are deemed unduly to prejudice the discharger. See *R v Secretary of State for the Environment and another ex parte Woolcombers (Holdings) plc*, QBD, 28 July 1989, unreported.

[119] A detailed description of the Mogden formula is given in para. 1.5.2 of DETR, *Economic Instruments for Water Pollution Discharges* (1999).

[120] Somewhat loosely, DETR, *Competition in the Water Industry in England and Wales: Consultation Paper* (April 2000), para. 5.22, describes the formula as being in accordance with the polluter pays principle.

[121] DETR, *Competition in the Water Industry in England and Wales: Consultation Paper* (April 2000), Q6.

[122] s.143(4) and (5) Water Industry Act 1991. On trade effluent agreements see 11.8 below.

[123] *Ibid* s.146(1) and (2).

infrastructure costs of new domestic sewage services to be borne by the developer, rather than by existing customers as was previously the case. A maximum charge for new domestic connections is set by Condition D of the Model Instrument of Appointment. Implicitly, therefore, connection charges may be levied for initial connections required for the disposal of trade effluent. Highway authorities may not be charged for the drainage of any highway or the disposal of the contents of any drain or sewer used for draining any highway.[124]

The Director may fix maximum charges which a person who is not a relevant undertaker may recover from another such person in respect of water supplies or sewerage services provided to that other person with the help of services provided by a relevant undertaker.[125]

There are obvious implications of the Director's policy on setting effluent consent conditions on trade effluent charging policy. If a sewerage company has adopted regional averaging of charges, trade effluent charges are likely to exceed costs at some works and to fall short at others. In these circumstances it would not be reasonable for a company to refuse or limit a discharge solely because costs incurred at a particular works exceeded the corresponding income from charges. However, if there is a significant mismatch between trade effluent charges and costs which seems to amount to undue preference or discrimination, the Director would generally expect this to be remedied by changes to the Charges Scheme. Charges should not differentiate between new and existing discharges in respect of the standard characteristics adopted in Charges Schemes, but they might reflect differences in costs at various locations.

## 11.7  Varying, Transferring and Surrendering Consents

### 11.7.1  Varying Consents

Once a consent has been granted subject to conditions, an undertaker may unilaterally, from time to time, give directions varying conditions attached to the consent. In this context, variation includes the addition or annulment of a condition and the attachment of a condition to a consent to which no condition was previously attached. Where the undertaker proposes to vary the conditions of a consent, the owner and occupier must be given at least two months notice, unless the condition relates to trade effluent charges,[126] and be given notification of appeal rights.[127]

Consent conditions may not generally be varied within two years of the grant of the consent or the last variation of conditions,[128] although there are three exceptions to this. The first is where the owner and occupier of

---

[124] *Ibid* s.146(4), and see 1.6.5 above and 9.17.5 on highway drainage.
[125] *Ibid* s.150.
[126] s.126(3) Water Industry Act 1991.
[127] *Ibid*, s.124. For appeal rights see *ibid* s.126 and 11.9 below.
[128] *Ibid* s.124(2).

the trade premises in question consents to the variation, though such an agreed variation may not affect the time at which any subsequent direction may be given.[129] The second exception is where, without agreement, the undertaker considers it necessary to make the variation in order to provide proper protection for people likely to be affected by the discharges otherwise lawfully made. In this situation, the undertaker must pay compensation to the owner and occupier. As with discharge consents, however, compensation can be avoided if variation is deemed necessary because of a change of circumstances within the two year period, if this change could not reasonably have been foreseen at the beginning of that period, *and* if the reason for variation is for some reason other than as a consequence of consents given after the beginning of the period. In such cases, the undertaker must give notice of the reasons for its opinion to the owner and occupier of the premises in question. The third exception is where variation is necessary to comply with the provisions implementing the Urban Waste Water Treatment Directive.[130] In such situations, the only instance where a consent or agreement may be varied within the time limit on environmental grounds, compensation is not payable. Otherwise, there is a right to compensation for losses incurred because of a variation within the two year period. The Secretary of State may make Regulations governing such compensation payments.[131]

It is to be noted that while the Water Industry Act 1991 makes express provision for the *variation* of consent conditions, no provision is made for the *revocation* (or *suspension*) of trade effluent consents or their conditions. By comparison, the discharge consent regime refers explicitly to the powers of the Agency to revoke discharge consents, in particular where no discharge has actually been made during the preceding 12 months.[132] It may be argued, therefore, that there is no power to revoke trade effluent consents, or their conditions, under the 1991 Act, the only remedy being an injunction in civil proceedings.[133] While this interpretation may follow from the nature of the connection duty, it appears unduly to restrict the ability of undertakers to exercise control over unsatisfactory trade effluent discharges in the interests of meeting their own discharge consents and wider environmental obligations. It may also inhibit the Agency from tightening undertakers' discharge consents as much as is desirable because of what it believes may be ongoing demands on the sewer system.

---

[129] s.124(4) Water Industry Act 1991.

[130] Directive 91/271/EEC, discussed at 5.6.2 above. See Reg.7(6) Urban Waste Water Treatment (England and Wales) Regulations 1994 (SI 1994 No.2841).

[131] s.125 Water Resources Act 1991. No such Regulations have been made under s.125(5).

[132] *Ibid*, para.12 Sch.10, discussed at 10.8 above.

[133] See WRc (1998) p.95. Whether an injunction would be granted if the discharger was paying charges and otherwise complying with conditions might be queried.

## 11.7.2 Transferring and Surrendering Consents

Unlike the equivalent provisions relating to discharge consents,[134] the Water Industry Act 1991 makes no express provision for the transfer and surrender of trade effluent consents. The preferable view, however, seems to be that trade effluent consents are not personal to the discharger but relate instead to the point of discharge. On this basis, trade effluent consents may be transferred between occupiers of the same premises without the authorisation of the undertaker. This, it has been suggested, is supported by the fact that the details which must be submitted in support of an application relate to the nature, quality and quantity of the effluent rather than to the identity of the discharger, and also because the offence of discharging trade effluent without a consent, or in breach of its terms, is committed by the occupier of the property concerned.[135] It is also notable here that most trade effluent consents include a provision that the undertaker must be notified of any change in the constituents of the effluent. Also, the silence in the 1991 Act as to transfer and surrender of consents suggests that undertakers may impose conditions in consents prohibiting the transfer of consents without prior approval. Although some sewerage undertakers appear to take a contrary view, the fact that the matter has never come before the courts might suggest that the current ambiguities in relation to the transfer of consents is not of great significance. Nevertheless, there are clear practical implications in relation to the transferability of consents. For example, if a sewerage system is overloaded, then if the transfer of a consent requires the approval of the undertaker then the opportunity may be taken to vary the terms of the consent. Alternatively, the chance might be taken to force the undertaker to enter into a trade effluent agreement with the cost implications this may involve.[136]

The 1991 Act is similarly silent on whether trade effluent consents can be surrendered. In practice, it seems that the usual approach is simply for the occupier of the premises to hand the documents relating to the consent back to the undertaker. In the absence of any continuing obligations on the discharger in the consent, which is unlikely, the only situation where the undertaker is likely to refuse to accept the relinquishing of a consent is, perhaps, if trade effluent charges are outstanding.[137]

## 11.8 Trade Effluent Agreements

Alongside the power for sewerage undertakers to grant trade effluent consents, the Water Industry Act 1991 also provides for trade effluent agreements to be made between the owner or occupier of trade premises and the sewerage undertaker for the area. Agreements may authorise such discharges as, apart from the agreement, would require a trade effluent

---

[134] See 10.10 above.

[135] Waite and Jewell (1997) para.17.120.

[136] On trade effluent agreements see 11.8 below.

[137] On trade effluent charges see 11.6 above.

consent. Such agreements may cover the reception and disposal by the undertaker of any trade effluent[138] produced on the owner or occupier's premises, or the removal and disposal of substances produced in the course of treating any trade effluent on or in connection with those premises. In particular, agreements may provide for the construction or extension by the sewerage undertaker of such works as may be required for receiving or disposing of trade effluent, and for the repayment by the owner or occupier of the whole or part of the expenses incurred by the undertaker under the agreement.[139]

Typically, agreements will be entered into where the discharger agrees to pay for works necessary to treat its effluent, for example, where an extension to a treatment works is required,[140] and this may result in the discharger paying reduced charges for effluent treatment. Planning permission for new development may be made conditional on such an agreement being entered into.[141] Agreements are contracts between undertakers and dischargers, and are neither subject to rights of appeal to the Director General of Water Services nor enforceable under the Water Industry Act 1991. Agreements do not operate as a consent or authorisation in so far as they conflict with the requirements of the Urban Waste Water Treatment (England and Wales) Regulations 1994.[142] Agreements relating to 'special category effluent' must be referred to the Environment Agency.[143] Because of their contractual nature, agreements cannot be transferred from one discharger to another unless, for some reason, this has been expressly provided for.

There is no specific provision in the Act for breach of a trade effluent agreement to give rise to a criminal offence. However, it is an offence to discharge trade effluent 'without such consent or other authorisation as is necessary for the purposes of [Chapter III of Part IV of the Water Industry Act 1991]'.[144] 'Other authorisation' in this context is clearly intended to cover trade effluent agreements. However, a distinction should be made between trade effluent agreements insofar as they 'authorise' discharges to sewers which would otherwise be unlawful, and terms of agreements which are non-regulatory. In the former case, it will usually be stipulated that breaching the agreement will amount to the withdrawal of consent by the undertaker to discharge, so breach of an agreement could give rise to a criminal offence if effluent is subsequently discharged without consent.[145] In the latter situation, however, the agreement is not an authorisation but

---

[138] On the meaning of 'trade effluent' in this context see *Nottingham Corporation v Bulwell Finishing Company Ltd* (1970) 68 LGR 128.

[139] s.129 Water Industry Act 1991.

[140] To be contrasted with undertakers, for example, advising on schemes for industry to reduce its discharges at source, as is increasingly common, which falls outwith the provisions on trade effluent agreement, see 'Effluent cash shock', 5(4) *Environment Times*, Summer 1999, 40-47.

[141] On such planning conditions see 14.5.5A below.

[142] SI 1994 No.2841, Reg.7.

[143] s.130 Water Industry Act 1991. See 11.10 below.

[144] *Ibid* s.118(5).

[145] On why agreements are defences but not consents see Law Commission (1991) pp.4–5.

simply a contract between two parties and enforceable through the ordinary law of contract.

## 11.9 Appeals

Any person aggrieved[146] by a refusal of an undertaker to give a consent properly applied for, deemed refusal through failure to give such a consent within the two month notice period,[147] or by any condition attached to a consent, may appeal to the Director General of Water Services.[148] In effect, appeals are complete re-hearings of the original determination, and the Director may give the necessary consent, either unconditionally or subject to such conditions as he thinks fit, in accordance with the stated criteria.[149] On an appeal in respect of a consent condition, the Director may review all the conditions attached to the consent, whether appealed against or not, and may either substitute for them any other set of conditions, whether more or less favourable to the appellant, or annul any of the conditions. Any direction given by the Director may include provision as to the charges to be made for any period between the giving of the notice by the sewerage undertaker and the determination of the appeal. The Director may also direct that the trade effluent in question may not be discharged until a specific date.[150] The Director, therefore, exercises the power to rehear the initial application or variation, providing a check against an undertaker exercising its powers to any undue commercial advantage or to the disadvantage of specific customers or groups of customers.

Where the conditions of a consent have been varied, the owner or occupier may appeal to the Director within two months, or later with his written permission. If the appeal is brought within the two month period which the sewerage undertaker must give, then unless it relates to charges the direction will not take effect until the appeal is withdrawn or finally disposed of. Not least because of the lengthy periods taken to determine appeals, this may lead to a risk of consequential environmental damage in the intervening period.[151] Persons notified of variations concerning charging may, in accordance with regulations made by the Secretary of State, appeal to the Director against the notice on the ground that compensation should be paid.[152] In appeals concerning compensation for variation within time limits, the Director may effectively overrule any

---

[146] 'Aggrieved' is not defined in the Water Industry Act 1991. Guidance may be obtained from judicial interpretation of the term in other contexts, e.g. s.288 Town and Country Planning Act 1990. See Moore (2000), p.363. More generally see Leeson (1995), pp.26-29.

[147] Prior to the Water Act 1989 failure to determine an application for consent automatically resulted in the granting of the consent applied for.

[148] On the role of the Director General of Water Services more generally see Ch.7 above.

[149] Listed in s.121 Water Industry Act, see 11.5.1 above.

[150] *Ibid* s.122.

[151] Contrast s.91(2G) Water Resources Act 1991, discussed at 10.9 above.

[152] s.126 Water Industry Act 1991.

view the undertaker has formed about the circumstances giving rise to the review being unforeseeable.[153]

Importantly, there is no right of appeal to the Director in relation to trade effluent charges unless no provision is in force for a trade effluent charging scheme.[154] In such cases, the Act lays down the criteria the Director must have regard to in setting an appropriate charge.[155]

The Director has issued guidelines as to the basis on which trade effluent appeals will be determined.[156] These emphasise the need for full statements of case by both parties, and for prior negotiation. Specifically, any conditions imposed by the undertaker other than to satisfy discharge consent conditions imposed by the Environment Agency to meet environmental quality obligations must be justified. Appeals may be dealt with by a local inquiry.[157] At any stage in an appeal the Director may, and must if so directed by the High Court, state a question of law as a special case for the decision of the High Court.[158] Directions on appeal have effect as if given by the undertaker.

It must be pointed out that few appeals are formally lodged, and of these the vast majority are, in line with the stated preference for prior negotiation, resolved without a formal decision. Thus, figures from 1 September 1989 to 31 March 2000 indicate that of 111 appeals formally lodged, 93 cases were facilitated without formal resolution, 10 appeals were determined and 8 appeals were outstanding.[159] It is therefore difficult to identify any general policy approach that is taken, far less to identify anything resembling a line of precedent that might be relied upon in future appeals. Appeal determinations are not published, but are available from Ofwat on request.[160]

## 11.10 Special Category Effluent and Prescribed Processes

Additional provisions concerning trade effluent relate to effluent containing certain prescribed substances or coming from certain prescribed processes, known as 'special category effluent'.[161] The need for separate controls on special category effluent is to conform to obligations under the EC Dangerous Substances Directive.[162] This requires a 'competent authority' to be responsible for various obligations to reduce pollution by some of the more hazardous substances. Following privatisation, the

---

[153] *Ibid* s.126(5) and (6).
[154] Under *ibid* s.143, see 11.6 below.
[155] *Ibid* s.135.
[156] Ofwat Information Note No. 21 (May 1993).
[157] s.215 Water Industry Act 1991.
[158] *Ibid* s.135.
[159] Ofwat, personal communication, 22 August 2000.
[160] The bare determinations may not be of any great assistance, since the background papers are not held.
[161] See ss. 120, 123, 127, 130-134 and 138 Water Industry Act 1991.
[162] Directive 76/464/EEC, and see 5.4.1 above.

relevant powers described here, which now rest with the Environment Agency, were exercised by the Secretary of State, the privatised sewerage undertakers not being considered capable of constituting 'competent authorities' for the purpose of the Directive.[163] The dual role of the Agency and the undertakers in relation to special category effluent is not without its difficulties.

'Special category effluent' is defined as effluent containing prescribed substances or which contains such substances in prescribed concentrations, or which derives from prescribed processes or from processes involving the use of prescribed substances or the use of such substances in quantities exceeding prescribed amounts. However, trade effluent which is, or will be, produced by a process subject to integrated pollution control or the pollution prevention and control regime is deemed not to be special category effluent for the purposes of these separate provisions,[164] avoiding a duplication of controls in relation to special category effluent.[165] Nevertheless, a trade effluent consent from the undertaker will still be required for non-special category effluent discharges from any process subject to centralised, integrated, control and there is no restriction on the undertaker imposing more stringent standards in the interests of protecting its staff or the sewerage system. The limitation of the special category effluent regime to trade effluent means that the discharges of 'Red List' substances into sewers other than from 'trade premises'[166] are not subject to the scrutiny of the Environment Agency as competent authority for the Dangerous Substances Directive.

The provisions described in this section regulate the discharge of prescribed substances where these are not regulated by central control, but only insofar as the substances are trade effluent.[167] Currently 24 such substances are listed in Sch.1 to the Trade Effluents (Prescribed Processes and Substances) Regulations 1989,[168] and five processes involving asbestos[169] and chloroform[170] are listed in Sch.2 to the 1989 Regulations. The 24 prescribed substances consist of the 'Red List'[171] and carbon

---

[163] On this restriction see 2.16 above.

[164] s.138(1) and (2) Water Industry Act 1991, as amended by s.6(2) and Sch.3 Pollution Prevention and Control Act 1999 and para.8 Sch 10 Pollution Prevention and Control (England and Wales) Regulations 2000 (SI 2000 No.1973). On integrated controls generally see 12.3 below.

[165] See the distinction made between the 'sewer' and the 'natural' environment, in s.1(11)(c), Environmental Protection Act 1990, discussed below.

[166] On the meaning of 'trade premises' see 11.3.3 above.

[167] s.138 Water Industry Act 1991. In practice, nearly all such discharges will be regulated under integrated pollution control (and, in time, the pollution prevention and control regime), but under s.139 the Secretary of State may extend the provisions of Chapter III of Part IV, suitably modified, to any specified liquid or other matter other than trade effluent.

[168] SI 1989 No.1156, as amended by SI 1990 No.1629, and see also the Trade Effluents (Prescribed Processes and Substances) Regulations 1992 (SI 1992 No.339).

[169] See Directive 87/217/EEC on the prevention and reduction of environmental pollution by asbestos.

[170] See Directive 88/347/EEC, discussed at 5.4.1C above

[171] A list slightly broader than the 'Black List' under the EC Dangerous Substances Directives, and deriving from international agreements on the North Sea (see RCEP (1992) p.206). The impact

tetrachloride, to which has been added certain discharged quantities of trichloroethylene or perchloroethylene.[172] The provisions relating to special category effluent do not apply where any such substances are only present in background concentrations (for example, substances present in process water) or in precipitation falling on the site.[173] However, if the concentrations in the effluent exceed background level, special consent will be required.[174] As can be seen, therefore, the emphasis is on the control of a limited number of substances, and specific polluting *processes* are not greatly regulated under this provision.

The sewerage undertaker must refer all discharges containing any prescribed substances above background concentrations, or involving a prescribed process, to the Environment Agency within two months of receipt of the trade effluent notice.[175] The only exception is where the undertaker refuses to give any consent on the application. Otherwise, the Agency must decide whether the notified discharges should be prohibited and, if not, whether any requirements should be imposed as to the conditions on which they are made. An offence is committed if there is no appropriate reference, and the undertaker may not grant consent or enter into an agreement before the Agency makes a determination on the reference.[176] In addition, a failure to notify may activate the Agency's powers to review the consent or agreement in question, discussed below, even within two years of the previous determination, and allow the Agency to proceed as if the undertaker had in fact referred the matter as required.[177] Analogous notification and enforcement provisions apply in respect of agreements.[178] A practical difficulty is that sewerage undertakers rely on traders to notify them that their discharge contains special category effluent. In many cases, it may be that traders are either unaware of the composition of the effluent, or are unaware that substances within their discharge fall within this category.

Before determining an application, the Agency must provide the sewerage undertaker and the relevant owner or occupier with an opportunity to make representations or objections and consider those which are made and not withdrawn within the time allowed.[179] Notably, there is no procedure for public consultation. Instead, recent amendments have introduced a power

---

of the daugther directives to the Dangerous Substances Directive has been to bring the Red and Black Lists together.

[172] Under SI 1992 No.339, giving effect to Directive 90/415/EEC, made under the General Application Directive.

[173] Reg.2 SI 1989 No.1156.

[174] *Ibid* Regs.3 and 4.

[175] See generally s.120 Water Industry Act 1991 as amended by para.105 Sch.22 Environment Act 1995. Following privatisation, the relevant powers of the Agency were first exercised by the Secretary of State, the undertakers not being considered 'competent authorities' for the purposes of the Dangerous Substances Directive.

[176] s.120(9) and (4) Water Industry Act 1991.

[177] *Ibid* s.120(10).

[178] *Ibid* s.130.

[179] *Ibid* s.132(2).

for the Agency to acquire information for the purpose of discharging its functions, subject to a criminal penalty for failure to comply or to make a false or misleading statement.[180] Reference to the Agency effectively suspends the time period within which an appeal on the application may be made.

The Agency must notify the relevant parties that the discharge or process is prohibited or allowed, or to be made subject to specified conditions. There are no specified restrictions on the exercise of the Agency's power to impose conditions.[181] Process-regulating conditions may therefore be imposed both as regards prescribed processes and prescribed substances, and in practice conditions are set with reference to what the use of the best available techniques not entailing excessive cost (BATNEEC) would deliver.[182] The only restrictions on such conditions would seem to derive from general principles of administrative law. While there is a right of appeal to the Director General of Water Services, the Director can only uphold a refusal if he has before him a copy of the Environment Agency's determination. Otherwise, he (and the undertaker) must give effect to the Agency's determination.[183] In practice, therefore, there is effectively no right of appeal against any direction the Agency may give.[184] The only mechanism for traders, undertakers or third parties to challenge relevant determinations of the Agency is by judicial review. Both the undertaker and the Director must ensure compliance with such directions. Failure to do so is both a criminal offence[185] and entitles the Agency to vary or revoke the consent or agreement in question.[186]

Existing consents[187] and agreements[188] relating to special category effluent are reviewable by the Agency. As with ordinary trade effluent discharges, a review may not normally be made within two years of a previous review. However, review within this period is possible if there has been a contravention of a consent or agreement, to give effect to an international or EC obligation, or to protect public health or aquatic flora and fauna.[189] Compensation for loss or damage is payable in some of these circumstances, unless the review resulted from a change of circumstances unforeseeable at the time of the setting of the consent or the previous

---

[180] s.135A Water Industry Act 1991, added by para.113 Sch.22 Environment Act 1995. On penalties for the making of misleading statements see 16.7 below.

[181] *Ibid* s.132(6), referring to those criteria mentioned in s.121(1) and (2), see 11.5.1 above.

[182] On BATNEEC more generally see 12.3.2A below.

[183] s.133 Water Industry Act 1991.

[184] An anomaly apparently caused on transfer to the Agency of the Secretary of State's powers.

[185] s.133(1)-(3) and (5) Water Industry Act 1991. On summary conviction, a fine not exceeding the statutory maximum, presently £5,000, may be imposed, and on conviction on indictment, a fine.

[186] *Ibid* s.133(6).

[187] *Ibid* s.127.

[188] *Ibid* s.131.

[189] *Ibid* s.131(2) and (3).

review, or was as a result of material information not reasonably available to the Agency at that time.[190]

Any process discharging significant amounts of 'Red List' substances will normally be a prescribed process for the purposes of integrated pollution control under Part I of the Environmental Protection Act 1990 and therefore require an authorisation from the Agency. This is in addition to the trade effluent consent that will also be required. In relation to further processes regulated under the Integrated Pollution Prevention and Control Directive and the Pollution Prevention and Control Act 1999,[191] discharges from these into sewers are also deemed to be releases into water. In both cases, however, some concession is made to the fact that the discharge is not directly into the natural aquatic environment. Thus in the case of integrated pollution control, 'a sewer and its contents shall be disregarded in determining whether there is pollution of the environment',[192] while for the pollution prevention and control regime

> the effect of any waste water treatment plant may be taken into account when determining emission limit values . . . provided that an equivalent level of protection of the environment as a whole is guaranteed and taking such treatment into account does not lead to a higher levels of pollution.[193]

The wording of the latter provision seems to be stronger in that it is not the *existence* of the sewer in itself which prevents the discharge of effluent being a release into the environment, but its *effectiveness*. It is not clear whether this requires proactive investigation on the part of the trade effluent discharger into the effectiveness of the sewage system into which he discharges or, for example, if wilful blindness to a defective sewage system outside his control might be a relevant consideration.

It is unclear how the duty under the Integrated Pollution Prevention and Control Directive to avoid the production of waste[194] is to be given effect to where effluent is discharged to sewer. In both the Directive and its implementing Regulations, 'best available techniques' is defined as including 'the need to prevent or reduce to a minimum the overall impact of the emissions on the environment and the risks to it'.[195] This impact-based approach might suggest a different approach that a waste minimisation-based approach.

---

[190] s.134 Water Industry Act 1991.

[191] On which see 12.3.3–6 below.

[192] s.1(11)(c) Environmental Protection Act 1990.

[193] Reg.12(5) Pollution Prevention and Control (England and Wales) Regulations 2000 (SI 2000 No.1973).

[194] Art.3(c) Directive 96/61/EC.

[195] *Ibid* Annex IV and para.1(10) Sch.2 Pollution Prevention and Control (England and Wales) Regulations 2000 (SI 2000 No.1973).

## 11.11  Offences and Enforcement Practice

### 11.11.1  Offences and Penalties

Discharge of trade effluent from trade premises either without the undertaker's consent or in breach of a consent condition is an offence.[196] Contravention renders the occupier of the premises guilty of an offence and liable, on summary conviction, to a fine not exceeding the statutory maximum, currently £5000, and on conviction on indictment, to a fine.[197] Notably, penalties for trade effluent breaches are significantly lower than those for discharges to controlled waters,[198] with no power of imprisonment being provided for. Further, the offence of breaching a condition may be committed only by the occupier of the premises, and implicitly therefore not by the owner of the premises in whose name the consent may be, or any other third party. However, the offence relates to the contravention of 'a condition' of a consent,[199] and therefore more than one charge may be brought where a single incident gives rise to the breach of more than one condition.[200]

The right to bring a prosecution under Chapter III of Part IV of the Water Industry Act 1991 requires the written consent of the Attorney-General, unless brought by an aggrieved party,[201] a sewerage undertaker or a body whose function it is to enforce the provisions in question.[202] In relation to special category effluent, it is unclear whether the Environment Agency is 'a body whose function it is to enforce the provisions in question', since strictly it has only a 'referral' responsibility, albeit one from which there is no right of appeal. In practice, the Agency has resorted to seeking the consent of the Attorney-General.[203]

### 11.11.2  Civil Liability

In addition to criminal liability, it may be that the discharge of effluent into a public sewer is made in such an unsatisfactory manner that it causes a nuisance to others and may be restrained by an injunction.[204] The Water Industry Act 1991 makes no provision excluding civil liability for discharges to sewer made under and in accordance with a consent or

---

[196] s.118(5) Water Industry Act 1991.

[197] *Ibid* s.121(5). For an indication of fine levels see *Yorkshire Water Services Ltd* v *Hickson & Welch Ltd*, Crown Court, 1995, unreported, discussed at *ENDS Report* 252 (1996) p.46; *Severn Trent Water Ltd* v *Foleshill Plating Ltd*, unreported, 1991 2(10) Environmental *Law Bulletin* 120; *Yorkshire Water Services Ltd* v *Pennine Chemical Services*, Crown Court, unreported, discussed at *ENDS Report* 243 (1995) p.45.

[198] See 9.19.2 above.

[199] Unlike the offence under s.85(6) Water Resources Act 1991 which refers to contravention of 'the conditions of any consent'.

[200] Contrast *Severn-Trent River Authority* v *Express Foods Group Ltd* (1989) 153 JP 126, discussed at 9.13 above.

[201] On the meaning of 'aggrieved' see 11.9 above.

[202] s.211 Water Industry Act 1991.

[203] WRc (1998) p.24.

[204] *Wallace* v *McCartan* (1917) 1 ILR 377(R).

agreement. As noted above, the undertaker may avoid civil liability if it can be shown that nothing was done to cause, continue or adopt the nuisance.[205]

### 11.11.3  Enforcement Practice

Looking at enforcement practice more generally, an obvious point of departure from normal environmental controls is that the privatised sewerage undertakers are charged with policing the behaviour of other, potentially competitor or connected, 'private' organisations. In the past, research indicated a strong conciliatory approach to enforcement, although not without some regional differences.[206] The emphasis was on education and problem-solving, rather than 'policing', as the means to secure compliance, reflecting in part the 'white-collar' nature of the criminal activity involved and the low penalties available. There were also found to be practical difficulties in detecting unlawful entries to sewer.[207] Although empirical studies of effluent regulation were carried out when enforcement was the responsibility of the water authorities, many similarities with the present system of controls remain. Not the least of these is the ongoing relationship between undertaker and trade effluent discharger which, if not actually contractual (as with trade effluent agreements) will involve payment to the undertaker under an essentially commercial transaction.

It is not difficult to see why undertakers still hesitate to rely on the use of the criminal sanction.[208] For example, though there are sufficient powers of entry to the undertakers to take samples,[209] their practical use may be problematic given that the principal relationship is between undertaker and discharger.[210] More generally, figures relating to 1996 indicated that 2 undertakers (Severn Trent and Yorkshire) brought the majority of the 70 prosecutions taken in 1996, the other undertakers showing a marked reluctance to bring proceedings.[211] The average fine level was £1,584.[212] Although the 70 cases were mainly in industrial areas, at least one undertaker with a significant concentration of industry in its catchment (North West) took no prosecutions. The undertaker stated that its use of cautions (two in 1996) was in line with the general trend in the Environment Agency to issue cautions rather than prosecute. It was also

---

[205] See 3.13.4 above.

[206] Richardson, Ogus and Burrows (1983).

[207] A failure to try to find the source of such discharges, or failing to prosecute on so finding, may have the effect of depriving an undertaker of relying on the defence provided in s.87(2)(c) Water Resources Act 1991 in relation to subsequent unlawful discharges, see 9.14 above and 11.12 below.

[208] By contrast with figures for criminal proceedings brought by the Agency for water pollution offences, which are published annually, comparable figures for prosecutions brought by the sewerage undertakers for trade effluent offences are not published on such a regular basis.

[209] s.108 Water Resources Act 1991.

[210] WRc (1998) p.23.

[211] *ENDS Report* 267 (1997) p.42.

[212] The highest reported fine appears to be £35,000, with £40,000 costs, dating from December 1995, relating to offences under ss.118(5), 111(1)(a) and 111(1)(b) Water Industry Act 1991, see *ENDS Report* 252 (1996) p.46.

suggested that the specific circumstances in the North West meant that greater priority was given by the Agency to combined sewer overflows and sewage debris than trade effluent. The implication appears to be that the prosecution policy of the undertaker may, to a significant extent, be shaped by the approach of the Agency. In this context, the introduction of a national prosecution policy by the Agency may have important ramifications.[213] As things stand, however, the figures suggest little has changed since the studies of the early 1980s.

A couple of points of contrast between the enforcement regimes for discharge consents and trade effluent consents should be noted. First, the limited right to prosecute for breaches of trade effluent consent differs markedly from the general right to prosecute for breaches of the principal water pollution offences. To the extent that consents are granted and conditions imposed on environmental grounds, the issue can be seen as one of general public concern rather than a commercial matter solely between the undertaker and the discharger. In this light, the justification for retaining such a 'closed' right to prosecute seems weak. Allowing such prosecutions to be brought 'in the public interest' would serve as an important safeguard for environmental protection by checking under-utilisation of the undertakers' discretion to prosecute.[214] Such a change would, of course, require related changes to the provisions on access to information.[215]

Second, under Chapter III of Part IV of the Water Industry Act 1991 there is nothing comparable to enforcement notices or the right to seek as injunction to ensure compliance with such a notice.[216] While the power, backed by sanction, to demand rectification of a contravention within a time limit might be feasible,[217] the exercise by a private company (the undertaker) of a power to instruct another private company (the discharger) how to conduct its activities will, rightly, be objected to. Were such powers to be introduced, their use ought to be recorded on the public register as evidence of a willingness, or otherwise, for undertakers to make full use of their regulatory powers.[218]

Finally, there is an issue as to whether discharges of special category effluent to sewers are policed as rigorously as is necessary. As discussed above, the Agency decides whether discharges of special category effluent should be permitted, and the conditions under which it may be discharged.[219] However, the Agency plays a negligible role in enforcing the conditions of the relevant trade effluent consents, in practice leaving

---

[213] On the introduction of the Agency's *Enforcement and Prosecution Policy* in 1998 see 6.18.1 above.

[214] WRc (1998) p.22. This report, however, notes that the likelihood of such prosecutions being brought would be small.

[215] See 11.4 above on information and participation.

[216] E.g. under s.90B Water Resources Act 1991 in relation to discharge consents, see 10.11.1 above.

[217] Compare s.111(4) Water Industry Act 1991, discussed at 11.3.4 above.

[218] WRc (1998) p.23.

[219] See 11.10 above.

this to the sewerage undertakers. Yet while the undertakers have commercial reasons to police the discharge of special category effluent to ensure that no unconsented effluent is discharged, the Agency is the competent authority for the purposes of the EC Dangerous Substances Directive and therefore bound to 'take all appropriate steps to ensure that the conditions of the authorisation are fulfilled and if necessary the discharge prohibited'.[220] It is difficult to reconcile the relatively 'hands-off' approach of the Agency in practice with its ostensible responsibilities as the competent authority under the Dangerous Substances Directive.

## 11.12 Trade Effluent Consents and Discharge Consents

### 11.12.1 Undertakers' Discharges of Trade and Sewage Effluent

The extent to which trade effluent dischargers operate within the conditions of consents is central to determining whether undertakers will be liable for committing one of the principal water pollution offences, in particular the offence of discharging trade or sewage effluent into controlled waters.[221] This is because the Water Resources Act 1991 provides that sewerage undertakers are deemed to be criminally responsible for pollution caused by discharges of effluent that they consent to enter their sewers, but balances the strictness of this liability by giving undertakers a defence to prosecution if they were not bound to receive the effluent into their sewerage system.

The strictness of this liability, and by implication some of the central policy issues, is considered in more detail elsewhere.[222]

### 11.12.2 The Relationship between Discharge Consents and Trade Effluent Consents

Both the present and previous chapters have discussed mechanisms intended to deal with the uncertain composition of effluent from sewage works. On the one hand, the strategy of the National Rivers Authority was to provide that discharge consents should not provide a defence against a charge of pollution in respect of any poisonous, noxious or polluting constituents not specified in it, the so-called 'exclusionary clause' or 'Kinnersley rubric'.[223] On the other hand, sewerage undertakers have a statutory defence in relation to any polluting matter discharged from sewage works that they were not bound to accept or which breached trade effluent consent conditions. The relationship between these two systems of regulation is well illustrated following the serious contamination of

---

[220] Art.5(4) Directive 76/464/EEC, see 5.4.1 above.
[221] Under s.85(3) and (4) Water Resources Act 1991.
[222] See 9.14 above on s.87 Water Resources Act 1991.
[223] See 10.6.5 above on new and unforeseen contaminants.

drinking water supplies in Worcestershire in 1994, and discussed in more detail elsewhere.[224]

In the 'Kinnersley' appeal determinations, a condition relating to unauthorised discharges was imposed, under which discharges from works are 'not to contain poisonous, noxious or polluting matter or solid waste matter which is attributable to any unauthorised discharge into the works'. This 'unauthorised discharges condition', however, does not prevent reliance on the defence given to sewerage undertakers in respect of pollution incidents attributable to substances entering their works which they were not obliged to receive.[225] There is, therefore, some scope for sewerage undertakers to avoid criminal liability where water pollution arises from pollutants which, without being discharged under a trade effluent consent, enter treatment works.[226]

---

[224] See 1.6.3 above on the River Wem incident.
[225] Under s.87(2) Water Resources Act 1991, outlined at 11.3.1 above.
[226] See further 9.14 above.

# Chapter 12

# ENVIRONMENTAL QUALITY LEGISLATION

## 12.1 Introduction

Alongside the principal water pollution offences and other mechanisms for the protection of water quality under the Water Resources Act 1991, the regime provided for under the 1991 Act has important interrelationships with other systems of environmental quality regulation. Notably, the principal water pollution offences are subject to defences where an entry or discharge into controlled waters is made under and in accordance with an authorisation provided for under a range of statutory provisions. Although discharge consents under the 1991 Act may be the most practically important of these, other key authorisations arise in respect of activities which are permitted under waste management licences,[1] authorisations for prescribed processes designated in relation to integrated pollution control[2] and permits under the recently introduced pollution prevention and control regime.[3]

The initial purpose of this chapter, therefore, is to examine the way in which water quality concerns are provided for in waste management law and the law relating to industrial process authorisation, both of which are administered by the Environment Agency as the regulatory authority.[4] It is also convenient, in the later sections of the chapter, to incorporate discussion of some rather miscellaneous statutory provisions which encompass water quality protection, but which again fall outside the scope of the Water Resources Act 1991.

## 12.2 Waste Management Law

### 12.2.1 Background and Policy

Necessarily, only a selective account of the regulation of waste management can be given relating the general principles to more specific issues which are most pertinent to water quality concerns.[5] However, some initial observations are needed as to the extent and nature of the waste management problem and its implications for the protection of the aquatic environment.

---

[1] Granted under Part II of the Environmental Protection Act 1990, discussed at 12.2.6 below.

[2] Granted under Part I of the Environmental Protection Act 1990, concerned with integrated pollution control, discussed at 12.3.2 below. See also the licensing system governing dumping at sea, provided for under the Part II of the Food and Environment Protection Act 1985, discussed at 19.20.1 below.

[3] Under the Pollution Prevention and Control Act 1999, discussed at 12.35 below.

[4] See Ch.6 above on the Environment Agency.

[5] Generally, see Bates (1997); Pocklington (1997); and Laurence (1999).

The enormity of the waste management problem is worth emphasising from the outset. Although information regarding the quantity of waste that is produced in England and Wales[6] is generally recognised to be unsatisfactory, the Environment Agency is currently undertaking a national survey of the amounts of industrial and commercial waste arising as a baseline for further surveys. Initial indications are that around 78 million tonnes of industrial commercial waste are produced annually along with 28 million tonnes of municipal waste, a quantity that is growing by 3% annually. Adding to this waste produced from construction and demolition, sewage sludge, agricultural wastes, mining wastes and dredged spoils, it is estimated that the total annual amount of waste amounts to about 400 million tonnes.[7]

The United Kingdom differs from most continental European countries in that, for geographical and historical reasons, waste management is heavily dependent upon landfill activities. Hence, in relation to municipal waste, some 90% of which originates from households, about 83% is presently disposed of to landfill. Whilst about 14% of municipal waste has value recovered from it through recycling, composting or energy from waste schemes, the overall percentage of waste collected for recycling or composting is only about 8%.[8]

Although the dependency upon landfill has a range of adverse environmental consequences, it is particularly notable in the present context that the capacity of landfilled waste to generate a greater amount of liquid effluent, or leachate, than other waste management options is a particular concern in relation to protecting the aquatic environment. Whilst other methods of waste management such as incineration tend to distribute environmental impacts more widely through atmospheric contamination, landfill tends to give rise to localised, and in some instances point source, water contamination and particularly contamination of groundwater.[9] Hence, the containment of leachate from landfill sites probably represents the major potential impact of waste management upon water quality.[10]

The preferred policy approach at European Community level is set out in the Commission's 1989 *Community Strategy for Waste Management*[11] which asserts a hierarchy of principles for waste management involving prevention, recovery and safe disposal, and which has been recently reaffirmed.[12] In accordance with the hierarchy of principles, prevention of waste remains the first priority, followed by recovery, involving recycling

---

[6] For comparative data in relation to the European Community see *Community Strategy for Waste Management* (1996) COM(96) 399 final, para.17.

[7] HM Government, *Waste Strategy 2000 for England and Wales* (Cm.4693, 2000) Part I Ch.1.

[8] DETR, *A Way With Waste: A draft waste strategy for England and Wales* (1999) Part II p.12.

[9] See the discussion of the Groundwater Regulations 1998 (SI 1998 No.2746) at 13.6 below.

[10] Generally, see Royal Commission on Environmental Pollution (1996) Ch.7 and see Laurence (1987).

[11] See European Commission, A *Community Strategy for Waste Management* (SEC) 89 (934 final 1989) endorsed by Council resolution of 7 May 1990 (OJ C 122, 18 May 1990 p.2).

[12] See COM (96) 399 final, affirmed by Council Resolution of 24 February 1997 on a Community Strategy for Waste Management (OJ C 76, 11 March 1997, p.1).

and reuse, and finally by the safe disposal of waste. However, the implementation of this hierarchy should be guided by consideration of the best environmental solution taking into account economic and social costs.

Community policy on waste management has been broadly endorsed nationally by successive governments.[13] The present Government, in its recently published *Waste Strategy 2000 for England and Wales*, accepts that the amount of household, industrial and commercial waste being disposed of to landfill should be significantly reduced. By 2005 the amount of industrial and commercial waste which is landfilled should be reduced to 85% of 1998 levels. For municipal waste, 25% should be recycled or composted by 2005, 30% by 2010 and 33% by 2015.[14]

### 12.2.2 European Community Legislation

In respect of Community legislation, the key measure[15] relating to waste disposal is the Waste Framework Directive,[16] as amended, which sets out general requirements of Member States to implement a Community-wide policy on waste management. The central obligation under the Directive is the requirement to take appropriate steps to encourage the prevention, recycling and processing of waste, the extraction of raw materials and the possibility of energy therefrom and any other process for the re-use of waste. Alongside this, Member States must take necessary measures to ensure that waste is recovered or disposed of without endangering human health and without using processes or methods which could harm the environment, and in particular without risk to water, air, soil and plants and animals, without causing a nuisance through noise or odours, and without adversely affecting the countryside or places of special interest.[17]

Pursuant to the general objectives of the Directive, Member States must take appropriate measures to establish an integrated network of disposal installations, taking account of the best available technology not involving excessive costs. More specific obligations are provided for under the Directive so that establishments or undertakings carrying out disposal operations must obtain a permit from the competent authority responsible for implementation. This permit will cover the types and quantities of waste, technical requirements, security precautions, the disposal site and

---

[13] See HM Government, *Making Waste Work: a strategy for sustainable waste management in England and Wales* (Cm.3040, 1995) p.5.

[14] HM Government, *Waste Strategy 2000 for England and Wales* (Cm.4693, 2000) Part I. Note also the targets for reduction of biodegradable waste disposed of to landfill provided for under the EC Landfill Directive 1999/31/EC at 12.2.7 below.

[15] Although a number of other directives and regulations are of significant importance in relation to particular kinds of waste or particular waste management activities: see, for examples, Directive 75/439/EEC on the Disposal of Waste Oils; Directive 76/403/EEC on the Disposal of PCBs; Directive 91/689/EEC on Hazardous Waste; Regulation EEC/259/93 on the supervision and control of shipments of waste within, into and out of the European Community; and Directive 94/62/EC on packaging and packaging waste. See also the discussion of the Landfill Directive 1999/31/EC at 12.2.7 below.

[16] Directive on Waste 75/442/EEC as amended by 91/156/EEC.

[17] Arts.3 and 4 Waste Framework Directive.

the treatment method. Similarly, authorisation or registration for transporters of waste is provided for.[18]

### 12.2.3 National Regulation

Whilst the control of waste management activities is capable of being achieved by the application of diverse kinds of regulation[19] and civil proceedings,[20] the central regulatory mechanism is Part II of the Environmental Protection Act 1990, concerned with 'Waste on Land', and secondary regulations associated with this.[21] Although Part II of the 1990 Act, as amended, serves as the principal mechanism for the implementation of the Waste Framework Directive and provides for important strategic measures in respect of waste management generally,[22] the emphasis here is placed upon more specific matters which are likely to have implications for the aquatic environment.

### 12.2.4 Waste Management Offences

A key feature of the regime governing waste management is the general prohibition upon unauthorised disposal of waste. This makes it an offence to deposit, knowingly cause or knowingly permit[23] the disposal of waste in or on any land unless a waste management licence authorising the deposit is in force and the deposit is in accordance with the licence. Similarly, it is an offence for a person to treat, keep or dispose of waste, or knowingly cause or knowingly permit waste to be treated, kept or disposed of in or on any land, or by means of any mobile plant, except under and in accordance with a waste management licence. A further offence arises where a person treats, keeps or disposes of waste in a manner likely to cause pollution of the environment or harm to human health.[24]

---

[18] *Ibid* Arts.9 and 12.

[19] For example, waste management activities are controlled as developments of land under the Town and Country Planning Act 1990 (see Ch.14 below on planning law) and the potential should be noted for waste to be statutory nuisance as an accumulation or deposit which is prejudicial to health or a nuisance' under s.79(1)(e) Environmental Protection Act 1990 (see 8.5 above on statutory nuisance).

[20] Waste management activities may give rise to civil liability in nuisance as in *Blackburn* v *ARC Ltd* [1998] Env LR 469 where nuisance was established in relation to smell and litter from a landfill site and damages were assessed on the basis of the diminution in value of the plaintiff's house due to the nuisance.

[21] See, in particular, Waste Management Licensing Regulations 1994 (SI 1994 No.1056) and Waste Management (Amendment etc.) Regulations 1995 (SI 1995 No.288). Part II Environmental Protection Act 1990 will soon be repaced by largely corresponding provisions made in regulations under the Pollution Prevention and Control Act 1999 and progressively applied to existing installations over a period extending to 2007, see 12.3.5 below.

[22] s.44A of Environmental Protection Act 1990 (as added by Environment Act 1995) requires the Secretary of State to prepare a strategy for waste covering the matters required to be covered by the Community Framework Directive on Waste.

[23] Contrast the discussion of cause or knowingly permit at 9.5 above.

[24] s.33(1) Environmental Protection Act 1990. Key judicial rulings on this offence, and its predecessor (s.3 Control of Pollution Act 1974) include *Ashcroft* v *Cambro Waste Products* [1981] 3 All ER 699, *Shanks and McEwan (Teesside) Ltd* v *The Environment Agency* [1997] Env LR 305,

It is apparent from the formulation of the main offences relating to unauthorised disposal of waste that, in most respects, an adverse impact upon the terrestrial environment is envisaged. However, this does not preclude the possibility that contaminating waste which is placed upon land will also have an adverse impact upon water quality especially where a waste offence arises near to a watercourse or other controlled water.[25] Where there is an entry or discharge of waste into water, it would appear that a person might commit both a waste offence and a principal water pollution offence[26] arising from the same activity. Moreover, in relation to the offence of treating waste in a manner likely to cause 'pollution of the environment', the meaning of this phrase encompasses the release or escape into *any* environmental medium of waste, or substances from waste, which are capable of causing harm to man or any other living organism supported by the environment.[27] Again, the implication is that there may be situations where an escape of waste enters controlled waters and that both waste and water pollution offences will be committed.

The are several examples of reported decisions where waste management activities have resulted in pollution of controlled waters. Hence in *Environment Agency* v *Brock plc*[28] the operation of a landfill site gave rise to the entry of leachate into a ditch as a result of a defect in the seal of a pipe through which the leachate was conveyed. The defendant was found to be strictly liable for the entry, and the commission of a principal water pollution offence,[29] without the need for negligence on his part to be shown. Another example of a waste management offence giving rise to a water pollution offence is *Caird Environmental Ltd* v *Keith Valentine*[30] where water seeped into an adjacent landfill site where it was contaminated by leachate before passing into a nearby river and causing pollution. The defendant pleaded guilty of the water pollution offence.[31]

In recent proceedings against Thames Water Utilities,[32] a major incident, involving a combination of untreated sewage and toxic industrial chemicals, arose as a consequence a the malfunctioning of pumps at a sewage treatment works. As a consequence, a large amount of effluent was pumped back up a sewer causing a number of houses to be flooded. The incident led to serious contamination of the properties, which became unfit for habitation and were purchased by the sewerage undertaker. Proceedings were brought both for the principal water pollution offence of

---

*Kent County Council* v *Beaney* [1993] Env LR 225 and *Environment Agency* v *Singer* [1998] Env LR 380.

[25] See 9.4 above on controlled waters under s.104 Water Resources Act 1991.

[26] See 9.3 above on the principal water pollution offences under s.85 Water Resources Act 1991.

[27] s.29(1) Environmental Protection Act 1990.

[28] [1998] Env LR 607 and see 9.4 above for discussion of another aspect of this case.

[29] Under s.85(1) Water Resources Act 1991, and see 9.3 above on this offence.

[30] See [1995] SCCR 714, though the appeal was only in relation to sentence.

[31] In Scotland this is provided for under ss.32(1)(a)(i) and 32(7) Control of Pollution Act 1974 as amended.

[32] See *ENDS Report* 301 (2000) p.50.

causing the entry of polluting matter and also with the waste management offence of disposing of waste in a manner likely to cause harm to human health.[33] Magistrates found the sewerage undertaker guilty on both charges but decided that the case was so serious that it should be referred to the Crown Court for sentencing. Setting a new record for a fine for a waste management offence, the defendants were fined £200,000, along with a fine of £50,000 for the water pollution offence.

Various exceptions and defences to the offences are provided in relation to the unauthorised disposal of waste in respect of household waste from a domestic property and situations prescribed for by regulations made by the Secretary of State.[34] Further defences arise where the accused is able to prove that all reasonable precautions were taken and due diligence exercised to avoid the commission of the offence;[35] that the action was under instructions from an employer and without knowledge or reason to suppose that they constituted an offence; or that the action was done in an emergency, taking reasonably practicable steps to minimise pollution of the environment and harm to human health, and particulars were furnished to the Agency as soon as practicable.[36]

A person who commits any of the offences will be liable on summary conviction to imprisonment for a term not exceeding six months or a fine not exceeding £20,000 or both; and on conviction on indictment, to imprisonment for a term not exceeding two years or a fine or both. Notably, the maximum period of imprisonment is increased to five years in relation to 'special waste'.[37] Whilst the penalties for waste management offences not involving special waste are the same as those for the principal water pollution offences,[38] the greater custodial sentence for an offence involving special waste raises the possibility that a waste offence in this category, which involves water pollution, might be prosecuted as a special waste offence allowing a more severe custodial sentence to be imposed than is provided for in respect of the principal water pollution offences.

## 12.2.5 The Duty of Care

In addition to the principal offences relating to unauthorised deposit of waste and related matters, the 1990 Act represents a significant advancement on previous legislation in imposing a 'duty of care' upon

---

[33] That is, s.85(1) Water Resources Act 1991 and s.33(1)(c) Environmental Protection Act 1990.

[34] See Reg.17 and Sch.3 Waste Management Licensing Regulations 1994 (SI 1994 No.1056).

[35] See the discussion of 'due diligence' in relation to the principal water pollution offences at 9.6.4 above.

[36] s.33(2), (3) and (7) Environmental Protection Act 1990.

[37] *Ibid* s.33(8) and (9), and see s.157 providing for liability for directors and similar officers of corporate bodies (corresponding to s.217 Water Resources Act 1991 and see 9.20 above on this). On 'special waste' see ss.75(9), 62 and 63 and Special Waste Regulations 1996 (SI 1996 No.972), listing the categories of 'special waste' and implementing the EC Hazardous Waste Directive (91/689/EEC).

[38] See the penalties for the principal water pollution offences under s.85(6) Water Resources Act 1991 discussed at 9.19.2 above.

those having possession of waste.[39] Hence, it is the duty of any person who imports, produces, carries, keeps, or disposes of waste or, as a broker, has control of such waste, to take all reasonable measures in the circumstances:

(a) to prevent contravention of the offences relating to unlawful deposit of waste by any other person;
(b) to prevent the escape of the waste; and
(c) to secure that a transfer of waste is only to an authorised person, or for authorised transport purposes, with a written description of the waste which will avoid unlawful deposits by others and ensure compliance with the duty of care.[40]

The requirement that waste may only be transferred to an 'authorised person' means that transfers may only be made to a local authority or a registered carrier or licensed disposer. Hence, any transfer of waste to an unregistered person, perhaps offering to dispose of waste cheaply with 'no questions asked', would amount to a breach of the duty of care. Where waste is transferred from one person to another, it must be accompanied by a full written description so that each person who has possession of it knows enough to deal with it properly and avoid committing an offence relating to unlawful deposit of waste.[41]

It should be noted that the objective of the duty of care is to provide for 'cradle to grave' regulation of waste, from the point of origin to that of final destination, and this is capable of being similarly beneficial to both the terrestrial and the aquatic environment. The aim of the duty is to provide a mechanism to prevent, or identify, unlawful flytipping of waste at times and places where this is not likely to be detected. In the past, watercourses and other controlled waters have proved significant targets for flytipped waste and it is intended the system of waste registration and the duty of care will deter such activities through the enhanced mechanisms which are provided for the detection of offenders.

## 12.2.6 Waste Management Licensing

Alongside the offences of unauthorised deposit of waste, it is an offence for any person to contravene any condition of a waste management licence and this offence is punishable to the same extent as the main waste management offences.[42] The counterpart of this is that, whilst conformity with a waste management licence serves as a defence to a principal water pollution offence,[43] acts which are not 'under and in accordance with' a waste management licence may also amount to water pollution offences

---

[39] Generally, see Royal Commission on Environmental Pollution (1985) and House of Commons Environment Committee, *Toxic Waste* (1989).

[40] s.34(1) Environmental Protection Act 1990.

[41] *Ibid* s.34(2).

[42] s.33(6) and (8) Environmental Protection Act 1990, subject to a greater penalty being provided for where special waste is involved (under s.33(9)).

[43] s.88(1)(c) Water Resources Act 1991, and see 9.16 above on authorised discharges.

where they involve the entry or discharge of polluting matter or effluent into controlled waters. That is, adherence to the conditions of a waste management licence is important in providing a dual defence.

A waste management licence is now granted by the Environment Agency authorising the treatment, keeping or disposal of any specified description of controlled waste in or on specified land or the treatment or disposal of any specified description of controlled waste by means of specified mobile plant.[44] Applications for licences are to be made to the Agency, and may not be granted unless planning permission for the use of the land as a waste management site, or an established use certificate, is in force.[45] Where planning permission exists, the Agency is not to reject an application if the applicant is a 'fit and proper person', or unless rejection is necessary to prevent pollution of the environment or harm to human health.[46] A person is not a 'fit and proper person', for these purposes, if the person has been convicted of a relevant offence; or the management of the activities will not be in the hands of a technically competent person; or the person who holds the licence is not able to make financial provision adequate to discharge the obligations arising from the licence.[47] Hence, the appropriateness of a person to hold a waste management licence is to be ascertained according to matters of technical and financial competence and also antecedence, in respect of the applicant having been convicted of certain 'relevant offences'. With regard to the latter, it is notable that principal water pollution offences, and other offences under the Water Resources Act 1991, are within the categories of relevant offences, so that conviction for such an offence may carry a further sanction in respect of disqualifying a person from obtaining a waste management licence.[48]

More generally, the contrasts between waste management licences and discharge consents may be noted.[49] None of the concerns, relating to technical and financial competence and antecendece, are normally relevant to the determination of discharge consent applications. The waste management licensing regime is, therefore, a much more personalised and and exacting system for ensuring standards of environmental control. By contrast, the discharge consent system rests upon the *assumption* that the discharger will have the expertise, resources and commitment to ensure that consent conditions are adhered to.

---

[44] s.35(1) Environmental Protection Act 1990.

[45] Where it proposes to issue a licence, the Agency must refer the proposal to the appropriate planning authority and the Health and Safety Executive and consider any representations about the proposal which the authority or the Executive makes during the period allowed (s.36(4) Environmental Protection Act 1990).

[46] s.36(1) to (3) Environmental Protection Act 1990 and see Ch.14 below on planning law generally.

[47] *Ibid* s.74(3) and see Waste Management Licensing Regulations 1994 (SI 1994 No.1056).

[48] See Reg.3 Waste Management Licensing Regulations 1994 (SI 1994 No.1056). The relevant offences include s.85 Water Resources Act 1991 (the principal water pollution offences) and see 9.3 above; s.202 (information and assistance required in connection with the control of pollution) and see 16.7 below; and s.206 (making false statements) as amended and see 16.7 below.

[49] See Ch.10 above on discharge consents.

During the currency of a waste management licence, the Agency is subject to a duty in respect of the supervision of licensed activities. This requires ensuring that the licensed activities do not cause pollution of the environment, harm to human health or become seriously detrimental to the amenities of the locality affected by the activities. The Agency must also ensure that the conditions of the licence are complied with. Hence, where it appears that a condition of a licence is not being complied with, or not likely to be complied with, the Agency may serve a notice upon the licence holder. Where a notice of this kind is served, it must specify the matters which constitute non-compliance, the remedial steps that must be taken and the period within which those steps must be taken. In the event of non-compliance with such a notice, powers become available to the Agency, partially or entirely, to revoke the licence or to suspend the licence either completely or in relation to specified activities. These powers of licence suspension and revocation are stated to be without prejudice to the power of the Agency to instigate criminal proceedings for a waste management offence.[50]

### 12.2.7 The Landfill Directive

Major changes in the national regulation of landfill activities are in prospect as a consequence of the recent adoption of the Community Landfill Directive,[51] which seeks to reinforce the provisions of the Framework Directive. The overall objective of the Landfill Directive is to impose stringent operational and technical requirements upon landfill activities to reduce negative effects on the environment and, in particular, the pollution of surface water, groundwater, soil and air, the global environment and resulting risks to human health from the landfilling of waste during the whole life-cycle of landfill sites.[52] A basic obligation under the Directive requires the classification of each landfill site as being suitable for hazardous waste, non-hazardous waste or inert waste.[53] This is particularly important in relation to the UK where previous practice has involved significant amounts of co-disposal of different categories of waste in individual landfill sites.

Pursuant to national implementation strategies, the Directive establishes targets for the reduction of biodegradable waste going to landfills so that, generally, by 2006 biodegradable waste going to landfill must be reduced to 75%, by weight, of the amount of waste produced in 1995. By 2209, the amount must be reduced to 50% of the 1995 total and by 2016 to 35% of that total. However, a deferment to these targets is available to Member States which, in 1995, disposed of more than 80% of their municipal waste

---

[50] s.42 Environmental Protection Act 1990 and see also s.38 on revocation and suspension of licences.

[51] Directive 1999/31/EC on the landfill of waste. Generally, see House of Lords Select Committee on the European Communities, *Sustainable Landfill* (1998); Parpworth (1999); and Forster and Morris (2000).

[52] Art.1 Landfill Directive.

[53] Art.4 Landfill Directive, and see Art.3 for the definitions of 'hazardous', 'non-hazardous' and 'inert' waste.

to landfill. The effect of this upon the United Kingdom is that the dates for achieving the biodegradable waste reduction targets are postponed by a maximum of four years, that is, to 2006, 2013 and 2020 respectively. Another basic obligation is that Member States must take measures to ensure that liquid waste is not accepted at landfills, in this case, by the date by which national implementing measures are to be in force, that is, by 2001.[54]

The new regime for landfill regulation provided for under the Directive is challenging and wide-ranging in its impacts upon national waste management practice, though no national implementing regulations have yet been enacted. [55] There are also a number of specific features which are likely to be most directly relevant to the protection of the aquatic environment from contamination originating from landfill sites. Clearly, the potential for water contamination from landfills is related to the presence of liquid in the waste held in a landfill site and the degree to which leachate can be effectively contained within the site and prevented from entering ground or surface waters. In this respect, the prohibition upon disposal of liquid waste in landfill sites, and the reduction in biodegradable waste, is of considerable significance in securing the 'dry' containment of waste.

The Directive's preference for dry containment is in marked contrast to national thinking, in that, previously, the Department of the Environment had expressed support for a biochemical process engineering approach to landfill strategy, termed the 'flushing bio-reactor' concept. It was contended that accelerated stabilisation of sites would be achieved by the deposit of biodegradable and other kinds of waste where this would be maintained in a 'wet' state through the recirculation of leachate. However, it was also recognised that excess leachate in a site increases pollution risks and, generally, that further research was needed to apply the flusing bio-reactor approach in practice.[56]

Whatever the position with regard to the environmental desirability and technical feasibility of the bio-reactor approach to landfill operations, there is reason to doubt whether the bio-reactor approach to landfill will remain a legal possibility. Alongside the targets for progressive reduction of biodegradable waste to landfill, the recirculation of leachate in landfill sites has become of dubious legality in the light of the new Directive. A pertinent comment on this comes from the House of Lords Select Committee on the European Communities:

---

[54] *Ibid* Art.5.

[55] On implementation generally, see Department of the Environment, Transport and the Regions, *Limiting Landfill: A consultation paper on limiting landfill to meet the EC Landfill Directive's targets for the landfill of biodegradable municipal waste* (1999).

[56] See HM Government, *Making Waste Work: a strategy for sustainable waste management in England and Wales* (Cm.3040, 1995) pp.66-67 and, generally, DoE, Waste Management Paper 26B, *Landfill Design, Construction and Operational Practice* (1995).

[w]hether or not the flushing bioreactor can be said to exist, what is
not in dispute is that the ban on co-disposal would *ipso facto* rule it
out for the future, since under UK law . . . landfill leachate is defined
as a liquid waste and would therefore be banned from recirculation
by the Directive . . .[57]

Insofar as contaminating leachate is capable of originating from generally
'dry' waste, the Directive introduces important measures to prevent the
establishment of landfill sites at inappropriate locations. Hence, a
prohibition is imposed upon the granting of a landfill permit unless all the
requirements of the Directive are complied with.[58] Encompassed within
this requirement are a range of criteria which must be taken into account in
respect of the location of a proposed landfill site. Amongst other things,
the criteria require account to be taken of a range of aquatic features: the
distances from the boundary of the site to waterways and waterbodies, the
existence of groundwater and coastal water, and the risk of flooding.
Specifically, in relation to water control and leachate management for non-
inert waste, appropriate measures must be taken to control water from
entering the landfill site, to prevent surface or groundwater entering waste
and for the collection of contaminated water and leachate, which must be
treated to a standard sufficient for discharge. Generally, landfill sites must
be situated and designed to meet conditions for preventing pollution of
soil, groundwater and surface water and ensuring efficient collection of
leachate. This is to be accomplished by means of a combination of a
geological barrier and bottom liner during the operational phase and by the
addition of a top liner during passive or post-closure phases. For these
purposes, technical criteria are specified for the degree of soil permeability
which is required for a geological barrier to be satisfactory in relation to
the different categories of site.[59]

The strongly preventive theme[60] underlying these rather technical
requirements must be noted, in that they seek to exclude the establishment
of landfill activities in locations where water contamination is possible and
in enhancing controls upon leachate containment generally. Hence, it is to
be hoped that the aquatic environmental protection dimension of the recent
Directive will be significantly beneficial in reducing leachate
contamination of water, following national implementation.

## 12.3  Integrated Pollution Control

### 12.3.1  Introduction and Background

A second main category of environmental licence that may serve as a
defence to a principal water pollution offence under the Water Resources

---

[57] House of Lords Select Committee on the European Communities, *Sustainable Landfill* (1998)
para.87.
[58] Art.8(a)(i) Landfill Directive.
[59] See Annex I Landfill Directive on 'General Requirements for All Classes of Landfills'.
[60] See Ch.13 below on preventing water contamination.

Act 1991 is an authorisation for a prescribed process, subject to the integrated pollution control regime provided for under Part I of the Environmental Protection Act 1990. Hence, no offence under the 1991 Act will be committed where a discharge is made under and in accordance with a prescribed process authorisation.[61] Consequently, it is necessary broadly to outline the nature of integrated pollution control governing prescribed processes and to consider the associated licensing regime insofar as it may relate to discharges to water.

However, the exposition of integrated pollution control is greatly complicated by the transitional stage at which the law is presently placed. The need to implement the Integrated Pollution Prevention and Control Directive[62] has resulted in the recent national enactment of the Pollution Prevention and Control Act 1999 which provides for detailed secondary legislation to transpose the Directive into national law. Whilst the 1999 Act envisages the eventual repeal of Part I of the Environmental Protection Act 1990, this is to be done at a future date. Hence, over a transitional period extending to 2007, the integrated pollution control regime and the new pollution prevention and control regime will operate side by side. Accordingly, it is most convenient first to examine the system of integrated pollution control and then to consider how this has been revised by the new legislation.

The starting point for any discussion of integrated pollution control lies in an appreciation of the strongly sectoral approach to pollution control regulation that was traditionally applied in the UK. Since the origins of environmental quality law,[63] the problems generated by water contamination, atmospheric emissions and contaminating land uses have been placed in different legislative categories and been subject to control by distinct regulatory authorities. Although this may have had the advantage of allowing regulatory specialisms to develop, it may also have served to misrepresent the nature of problems involved in securing satisfactory overall environmental quality. The environmental reality is that contaminants introduced into one environmental medium, such as the atmosphere, have the capacity to transfer to another, such as where contamination of water ensues as a consequence.

Similarly, from a regulatory perspective, the restriction of jurisdictions of regulatory authorities to air quality or water quality has meant that interaction between the environmental media has traditionally been neglected. From the perspective of a regulated industrial activity, the fragmented nature of the regulatory controls may have had the distorting consequence that environmental emissions have been directed away from the more strictly regulated environmental media towards less strictly regulated media, regardless of the overall benefit to the environment.[64] The

---

[61] s.88(1)(b) Water Resources Act 1991.

[62] Directive 96/61/EC and see 12.3.3 below.

[63] Generally, see Ch.2 above on the history of water quality legislation.

[64] Note, for example, the traditional reluctance of regulatory authorities to prosecute in relation to air pollution, see Vogel (1986) pp.87–8.

necessary response to these shortcomings in the regulation of environmental quality has been progressively recognised to be a need for an approach to environmental regulation that involves an integration of regulatory responsibility for the environment as a whole and an increasing assimilation between the regulatory approaches applicable across different sectors of the environment. Hence, in 1976, the Royal Commission on Environmental Pollution stressed the need for a unified inspectorate with responsibility for the most polluting industrial processes which would seek to achieve the best practicable environmental option taking into account the entire pollution for a process and the technical possibilities for dealing with it.[65]

### 12.3.2 Integrated Pollution Control

The belated administrative and legislative response to the Royal Commission's proposal was the establishment of Her Majesty's Inspectorate of Pollution to adopt a cross-media approach to pollution control in relation to the most environmentally hazardous industrial processes.[66] Although, as has been noted,[67] the responsibilities of Her Majesty's Inspectorate of Pollution have now passed to the Environment Agency,[68] the substantive obligations relating to integrated pollution control, provided for under Part I of the Environmental Protection Act 1990 remain, for the present,[69] as the regime for imposing process authorisation requirements upon installations which are subject to integrated pollution control and must be considered in outline.

Part I of the 1990 Act establishes two distinct systems of environmental regulation, integrated pollution control[70] and air pollution control by local authorities, though only the former is considered here. In essence, the mechanisms establishing integrated pollution control have allowed the Secretary of State to introduce regulations governing certain prescribed processes and the release of certain prescribed substances.[71] In broad terms, the Regulations identify six categories of industrial activity which are subject to process authorisation:

    (a) fuel production processes, combustion processes (including power generation) and associated processes;
    (b) metal production and processing;

---

[65] See Royal Commission on Environmental Pollution (1976) and (1988).

[66] See O'Riordan and Weale (1989).

[67] See the discussion of the establishment of the Environment Agency at 2.2.1 above.

[68] Under s.2(1)(d) Environment Act 1995.

[69] Although see the discussion of the Pollution Prevention and Control Act 1999 at 12.3.5 below.

[70] For general reading on integrated pollution control see Purdue (1991); Layfield (1992); Jordan (1993); Turner and Powell (1993); and Mehta and Hawkins (1998).

[71] s.2 Environmental Protection Act 1990 and see Environmental Protection (Prescribed Processes and Substances) Regulations 1991 (SI 1991 No.472, as amended). See also Environmental Protection (Applications, Appeals and Registers) Regulations 1991 (SI 1991 No.507) and Environmental Protection (Authorisation of Processes) (Determination Periods) Order 1991 (SI 1991 No.513).

    (c) mineral industries;

    (d) the chemical industry;

    (e) waste disposal and recycling; and

    (f) certain other industries, including paper and pulp manufacturing, and the treatment and processing of animal or vegetable matter.[72]

### 12.3.2A BATNEEC and BPEO

With regard to process authorisation conditions, these must include an implied general condition that the person carrying on the process must use the best available techniques not entailing excessive cost (termed 'BATNEEC') for preventing or reducing the release of prescribed substances into any environmental medium and for rendering harmless any other substances which might cause harm if released.[73] The burden of showing adherence to BATNEEC is placed upon the operator of a process, though in practice indications of what is required are provided by technical guidance notes issued by the Environment Agency.[74] Moreover, the BATNEEC strategy is to be applied to the environment as a whole, having regard to the best practicable environmental option available (termed 'BPEO').[75] Hence, where a prescribed process is capable of involving the release of substances into more than one environmental medium the duty to minimise contaminating releases, subject to the BATNEEC requirement, must be exercised with regard to the BPEO obligation to have regard to the pollution that may be caused to the environment as a whole.[76]

Further conditions which may be imposed in process authorisations are provided for by a power of the Secretary of State to issue directions to the enforcement authority as to conditions which are, or are not, to be included in all authorisation, in authorisations of any specified description, or in any particular authorisation.[77] More generally, alongside the BATNEEC objective, conditions in authorisations must be included for further specified objectives involving compliance with Community or international environmental obligations and to achieve compliance with environmental quality standards or objectives provided for under 'relevant enactments'. The relevant enactments span a range of provisions allowing for environmental quality standards and objectives to be specified include enactments or instruments made under the Water Resources Act 1991.[78] In

---

[72] See Sch.1 Environmental Protection (Prescribed Processes and Substances) Regulations 1991 (SI 1991 No.472).

[73] s.7(2) and (4) Environmental Protection Act 1990.

[74] See s.25(1) Environmental Protection Act 1990 and Department of the Environment, *Integrated Pollution Control: A Practical Guide* (1996) and HMIP (1996).

[75] s.7(7) Environmental Protection Act 1990. See *ENDS Report* 249 (1995) p.22 and *R v Environment Agency and Redland Aggregates Ltd ex parte Leam* [1999] Env LR 73.

[76] Royal Commission on Environmental Pollution (1988) para.2.1. See also Department of the Environment and Welsh Office (1988) which endorsed many of the recommendations of the Royal Commission on Environmental Pollution. See also, United Kingdom Environmental Law Association (1989). For a critical view of technocentric practice on BPEO see Wilkinson (1999) pp.27–8.

[77] s.7(3) Environmental Protection Act 1990.

[78] *Ibid* s.7(2) and (12).

effect, therefore, process authorisations must incorporate conditions that are necessary for the purpose of achieving water quality objectives[79] where these have been established for relevant receiving waters.

### 12.3.2B Enforcement

Enforcement of the integrated pollution control regime is, in the first instance, by means of an enforcement notice which may be served where the Agency is of the opinion that a person operating a prescribed process under an authorisation is contravening any condition of the authorisation, or is likely to do so. Such a notice must specify, amongst other things, the matter constituting the contravention and the steps that must be taken to remedy it.[80] If the Agency is of the opinion that the conduct of a prescribed process under an authorisation involves 'an imminent risk of serious pollution of the environment' then a prohibition notice may be served specifying the risk involved and the steps which must be taken to remove it. This is a more stringent enforcement mechanism in that the prohibition notice will include a direction that the authorisation will cease to authorise the process until the prohibition notice is withdrawn. Thus, the activity cannot lawfully continue until the necessary steps have been taken to address the identified risk.[81]

Beyond the use of enforcement and prohibition notices, a range of criminal offences underpin the provisions for the implementation of integrated pollution control. Whilst a number of these relate to contravention of information provision requirements, the central offence is that of operating a prescribed process without authorisation or in contravention of conditions to which an authorisation is subject and this offence is punishable to the same extent as the principal water pollution offences.[82] Further powers are explicitly provided for allowing the Agency to seek an injunction where it is of the opinion that criminal proceedings would afford an ineffectual remedy against a person who has failed to comply with an enforcement or prohibition notice.[83] Significantly also, in relation to the more serious offences, a court may, in addition to or instead of imposing any punishment, order the convicted person to take specified steps for remedying any matters which it appears to be in his powers to remedy. A distinct offence is committed by a failure to comply with a court order of this kind.[84]

---

[79] See 1.4 above on water quality objectives.

[80] s.13 Environmental Protection Act 1990.

[81] *Ibid* s.14.

[82] *Ibid* s.23 and see 9.19.2 above on penalties for the principal water pollution offences.

[83] *Ibid* s.24 and see 3.16.5 above in relation to the use of injunctions to support criminal penalties.

[84] *Ibid* ss.26(1) and 23(1).

## 12.3.2C  Coordination and interrelationships

Clearly, process authorisations may be used to control emissions and discharges to all environmental media[85] including discharges to the water environment. In the original provisions of the Environmental Protection Act 1990, coordination between process authorisation, then administered by Her Majesty's Inspectorate of Pollution, and discharges to controlled waters, then regulated by the National Rivers Authority, needed to be explicitly provided for. This was done by way of a requirement that process authorisations should not be granted unless appropriate conditions were imposed concerning the releases of any substance to controlled waters and, amongst other things, the National Rivers Authority certified that such conditions would not prevent the realisation of water quality objectives.[86] With the establishment of the Environment Agency as the regulator for both prescribed process controls and discharges to controlled waters, it became unnecessary for the coordination of the two regulatory regimes to be expressly provided for. Nonetheless, essentially the same issues will remain of internal concern to the Agency, in that process authorisations should not be allowed to impede the realisation of water quality objectives or the satisfactory protection of the aquatic environment generally.

Another key interrelationship is that between integrated pollution control and the discharge of industrial effluent to sewers under trade effluent consents.[87] A discharge made to sewer is treated as a release to water for the purpose of establishing that it will constitute a release into the 'environment', but a sewer and it contents are to be disregarded in determining whether there is pollution of the environment.[88] Hence, process authorisation controls will apply to trade effluent discharges, and conditions may be imposed in such authorisations in respect of specified substances, but a discharge to sewer will not constitute an offence of enironmental pollution.[89]

The counterpart of this is that Chapter III of Part IV of the Water Industry Act 1991, concerned with trade effluent, will not apply in respect of effluent which originates from a process which is subject to the integrated pollution control regime.[90] However, this does not exclude the requirement upon dischargers to obtain a trade effluent consent,[91] for discharges which are the subject of control by sewerage undertakers. Clearly, careful

---

[85] Although, to avoid duplication with waste management regulation (see 12.2 above on this), no condition may be imposed in a process authorisation to regulate the final disposal by deposit on land of controlled waste (s.28(1) Environmental Protection Act 1990).

[86] s.28(3) Environmental Protection Act 1990, now repealed by para.61(2) Sch.24 Environment Act 1995. Generally, see DoE and WO, *Integrated Pollution Control* (1996).

[87] Generally, see Ch.11 above on trade effluent controls.

[88] s.1(11) Environmental Protection Act 1990.

[89] See Trade Effluents (Prescribed Processes and Substances) Regulations 1989, SI 1989 No.1156.

[90] See para.28 Sch.15 Environmental Protection Act 1990, which disapplied Schedule 9 to the Water Act 1989 (which became Chapter III Part IV Water Industry Act 1991) in relation to processes prescribed for the purposes of integrated pollution control.

[91] Under s.118 Water Industry Act 1991 and see 11.5 below on this.

coordination of the two licensing regimes is needed since the concerns of the Agency may differ from those of a sewerage undertaker which is likely to be concerned with the capacity of treatment works satisfactorily to treat effluent and for the health and safety of personnel involved in sewage treatment activities.[92]

### 12.3.3 The Integrated Pollution Prevention and Control Directive

As has been noted, the system of integrated pollution control originally provided for under Part I of the Environmental Protection Act 1990 has had to be fundamentally reconsidered as a consequence of the need to transpose the EC Integrated Pollution Prevention and Control Directive into national law.[93]

The purpose of the Directive is to achieve integrated prevention and control of pollution arising from the activities listed in Annex I by specifying measures to prevent or reduce emissions to air, water and land from these activities. The industries concerned are the following:

(a) energy industries;
(b) production and processing of metals;
(c) mineral industry;
(d) chemical industry;
(e) waste management; and
(f) 'other activities', including paper, textiles, leather production, food processing, disposal of animal carcasses, livestock production and installations with specified consumptions of organic solvents.[94]

Notably, 'installation' is defined under the Directive to mean a stationary technical unit where one of more activities listed in Annex I are carried out, and any other directly associated activities which have a technical connection with the activities carried out on the site which could have an effect on emissions and pollution.[95] This site-specific definition contrasts with the national approach of regulating 'processes' which encompass activities, carried out either in premises or by means of mobile plant, which are capable of causing pollution.[96]

The central obligation is that Member States must ensure that the necessary measures are taken by competent authorities to ensure that installations are operated in such a way that:

(a) all the appropriate preventative measures are taken against pollution, in particular through application of the best available techniques;

---

[92] Generally, see DoE and WO, *Trade Effluent Discharges to Sewers* (1988).
[93] Generally see Emmott and Haigh (1996) and Long (1999).
[94] Art.1 and Annex I Integrated Pollution Prevention and Control Directive.
[95] *Ibid* Art.2(3).
[96] s.1(5) Environmental Protection Act 1990.

(b) no significant pollution is caused;

(c) waste production is avoided; where produced it is recovered or where technically and economically possible it is disposed of while avoiding or reducing any impact on the environment;

(d) energy is used efficiently;

(e) necessary measures are taken to prevent accidents and limit their consequences;[97]

(f) necessary measures are taken upon definitive cessation of activities to avoid any pollution risk and return the site of operation to a satisfactory state.

National competent authorities must take account of these matters when they determine the conditions of any permit issued for a relevant industry[98] and Member States must take all necessary measures to ensure that no new installation is operated without a permit issued in accordance with these provisions. Hence, new installations and installations which undergo a 'significant change' will be subject to the Directive by the date at which Member States were bound to adopt necessary implementing measures, that is, by 30 October 1999.[99] Existing installations, generally comprising installations that were in operation before the Directive came into effect, will become subject to most provisions of the Directive not later than eight years after it is brought into effect, that is, by 30 October 2007.[100]

An integrated approach to issuing permits is provided for, so that Member States must take measures necessary to ensure that the conditions of, and procedure for the grant of, permits are fully coordinated. However, an innovation in respect of the obligation to implement the permitting procedure is the facility for Member States to prescribe requirements for categories of installations as 'general binding rules', rather than specifying them as individual permit conditions, provided that an equivalent high level of environmental protection is ensured.[101]

Permits must include all measures necessary for compliance with the requirements of the Directive and to achieve a high level of protection for the environment as a whole by means of the protection of air, water and land. Specifically, permits must include emission limit values for specified pollutants, listed in Annex III to the Directive, and these limits must have regard to the nature of the emissions and their potential to transfer pollution from one environmental medium to another. Emission limit values must be based upon the 'best available techniques', without prescribing the use of any specific technique or specific technology, but taking into account technical characteristics, geographical location and

---

[97] See Directive 96/82/EC on the Control of Major Accident Hazards, and Control of Major Accident Hazards Regulations 1999 (SI 1999 No.743).

[98] Art.3 Integrated Pollution Prevention and Control Directive.

[99] See *ibid* Art.21 concerning the time allowed for Member States to adopt the necessary implementing provisions.

[100] *Ibid* Arts.2(4), 4 and 5.

[101] *Ibid* Art.9(8) and see 10.12.1 on general binding rules.

local environmental conditions of the installation.[102] Despite this, where an environmental quality standard requires stricter conditions than those achievable by the use of the best available techniques, additional measures must be required in the permit.[103]

National competent authorities must interpret Annex IV of the Directive in determining 'best available techniques'. To assist in this process, exchanges of information between national experts, governmental and non-governmental, is co-ordinated by the European Integrated Pollution Prevention and Control Bureau.[104] The Bureau is presently working on best available techniques reference documents for 30 sectors with the objective that these will be completed by 2003. Although these reference documents are intended to assist national authorities, the final decisions on best available techniques will remain with these authorities because the Directive requires that account must be taken of local matters such as the geographical location of an installation and its environmental conditions.[105]

In respect of the specification of emission limits for certain processes, it is envisaged that the Council will set emission limit values for categories of installation within Annex I of the Directive and polluting substances identified under Annex III. This is to be done where a need for Community action has been identified and on the basis of information provided under the Directive. However, in the absence of a Community emission limit value being determined, relevant emission limit values otherwise provided for under a range of environmental Directives, listed in Annex II, must be applied as minimum emission limits for relevant installations.[106] Hence, for example, in relation to discharges to the aquatic environment emission limits established under the Dangerous Substances Directive[107] will be used for the purpose of the Integrated Pollution Prevention Control Directive until such time as further emission limit values have been established under the latter.

### 12.3.4 Implementation of the Integrated Pollution Prevention and Control Directive

Whilst many of the principles underlying the Integrated Pollution Prevention and Control Directive are reminiscent of existing national provisions relating to integrated pollution control, in certain key respects

---

[102] *Ibid* Art.9.
[103] *Ibid* Art.10 and see Scott (2000).
[104] See European Integrated Pollution Prevention and Control Bureau website, http://eippcb.jrc.es/. The Bureau is established in accordance with Art.16(2) of the Integrated Pollution Prevention and Control Directive which requires the Commission to organise an exchange of information between Member States and the industries concerned as to the best available techniques, associated monitoring and developments.
[105] Art.9 Integrated Pollution Prevention and Control Directive.
[106] *Ibid* Art.18.
[107] See 5.4.1 above on the Dangerous Substances Directive.

the Directive extends significantly beyond the national controls.[108] Not least important in this respect is the definition of 'pollution' which is used in the Directive:

> the direct or indirect introduction as a result of human activity, of substances, vibrations, heat or noise, into the air, water or land which may be harmful to human health or the quality of the environment, result in damage to material property, or impair or interfere with amenities or other legitimate uses of the environment.[109]

By contrast, the corresponding national definition of 'pollution of the environment' refers only to the release of 'substances' which are capable of causing harm, with 'harm' being defined to encompass harm to the health of living organisms or other interference with the ecological systems of which they form part and, in the case of man, including offence caused to any of his senses or harm to his property.[110] Hence, a range of matters are provided for under the Directive which do not feature within the national regime for integrated pollution control.[111]

Perhaps the greatest disparity between the national regime for process authorisation and the requirements of the Directive arose because of the greater range of activities subject to the permitting system provided for under the Directive. Whilst a relatively small number of processes regulated by integrated pollution control fall outside the scope of the Directive, a far greater number of installations come within the Directive though falling outside the national regime. Whilst comparability between 'processes' subject to national regulation and 'installations' which fall within the Directive is not entirely clear, it has been suggested that implementation will involve extending regulation to about 3,000 waste management sites; 1,500 installations currently regulated by combinations of local authority air pollution control, trade effluent consents and consents for discharges to controlled waters; 1,000 intensive pig and poultry units; and 500 food and drink plants.[112]

A further difficulty arising from the expansion of the number of activities needing to be the subject of control relates to the range of regulatory jurisdictions to which the relevant installations were subject. Whilst responsibility for integrated pollution processes lies with the Environment Agency, other installations which fall within the Directive are regulated by local authorities, in respect of atmospheric emissions, and by sewerage undertakers, in respect of trade effluent discharges. Although the Directive does not require the establishment of a single regulatory authority for all permitting activities, co-ordination is required and, in the national context,

---

[108] Generally, see *ENDS Report* 270 (1997) p.21 and *ENDS Report* 273 (1997) p.21.

[109] Art.2(2) Integrated Pollution Prevention and Control Directive and see the discussion of 'pollution' at 1.3.3 above.

[110] s.1(3) and (4) Environmental Protection Act 1990.

[111] Arts.3 and 9(6) Integrated Pollution Prevention and Control Directive.

[112] *ENDS Report* 270 (1997) p.21.

allocation of responsibilities needs to take account of the different expertise possessed by regulatory authorities.

Because of the range and gravity of the issues falling for consideration in respect of the implementation of the integrated pollution permitting and control regime, the matter was the subject of an especially wide and intricate series of consultation exercises.[113] Whilst much of the detail of this may be overlooked for present purposes, some pertinent issues must be noted.

A key issue was the allocation of regulatory responsibility. As has been explained, the installations within the scope of the Directive previously fell to be regulated by different regulators: the Environment Agency in respect of processes subject to integrated pollution control, local authorities in respect of many atmospheric emissions and sewerage undertakers in respect of discharges to sewers. Although various options were considered for the coordination of regulatory responsibility, the preference which emerged was for a division of regulatory responsibility with the Agency responsible for some installations and local authorities responsible for others according to their respective regulatory expertise. Notably, sewerage undertakers were not favoured as regulators though it was recognised that they needed to retain a consenting function in relation to sewer discharges in order to protect their assets and workforces. Nonetheless, the distribution of regulatory responsibility between the Agency and local authorities raised important concerns as to how, for example, a permit determination made by a local authority involving a discharge to water would ensure the satisfactory protection of the aquatic environment. It was recognised that a clear and effective means of coordinating the powers of the respective regulators would be needed in situations of this kind.

### 12.3.5 The Pollution Prevention and Control Act 1999

The legislative outcome of the extensive consultation process on the implementation of the Integrated Pollution Prevention and Control Directive, and the associated issues of national regulation, was the enactment of the Pollution Prevention and Control Act 1999. The mechanism of the Act is legislatively unusual in that the substantive provisions allowing for extensive and detailed reforms are contained in only two sections of the Act. Hence, the first section states that provision may be made for, or in connection with:

(a) implementing the Integrated Pollution Prevention and Control Directive;

---

[113] See DETR, Scottish Office and WO, *UK Implementation of EC Directive 96/61 on Integrated Pollution Control Consultation Paper* (1997); *Second Consultation Paper* (1998), *Third Consultation Paper on the Implementation of the Integrated Pollution Prevention and Control (IPPC) Directive* (January 1999); and *Fourth Consultation Paper on the Implementation of the IPPC Directive* (August 1999).

(b) regulating, otherwise than in pursuance of the Directive, activities which are capable of causing any environmental pollution; and

(c) otherwise preventing or controlling emissions capable of causing any such pollution.

The second section states that the Secretary of State may by regulations make provision for any of the purposes listed in Schedule 1 to the Act in accordance with the objectives indicated in (a) to (c) above. Schedule 1 is relatively more explicit in listing the purposes for which regulations may be made in specifying matters which, for example, include the following:

(a) establishing standards, objectives or requirements in relation to emissions;

(b) determining the authorities by whom functions are to be exercisable;

(c) enabling the Secretary of State to give directions which regulators must comply with, or guidance which regulators are to have regard to, in exercising functions; and

(d) prohibiting persons from operating any installation or plant, or otherwise carrying on any specified activities, except under a permit and in accordance with conditions to which it is subject.[114]

The relevant parts of the Pollution Prevention and Control Act 1999 are, clearly, broadly worded: they merely give the Secretary of State enabling powers to enact secondary legislation to give effect to the new regulatory regime. Hence, it was envisaged that the real substance of the new regime would be provided for in delegated legislation.[115] The 1999 Act incorporates requirements that before making regulations the Secretary of State must consult the Environment Agency, bodies or persons representative of the interests of local government, industry, agriculture and small businesses, and such other bodies or persons as are appropriate. A statutory instrument containing regulations made under the Act must be approved by the affirmative resolution procedure. Moreover, in respect of the first regulations to be made applicable to England, and to Wales, and any regulations creating an offence, increasing a penalty of amending or repealing any provision of primary legislation, the enactment procedure must involve the approval of the regulations by a resolution of each House of Parliament.[116] Accordingly, the rather sparse substantive content of the Act has been supplemented by especially strict provisions for scrutiny of the initial secondary legislation needed, amongst other things, to bring about the eventual repeal of Part I of the Environmental Protection Act 1990.[117]

---

[114] Part I Sch.1 Pollution Prevention and Control Act 1999, with numbers corresponding to the paragraphs in Part I of the Schedule.

[115] See *ENDS Report* 288 (1999) p.28.

[116] s.2(4) to (8) Pollution Prevention and Control Act 1999.

[117] Under Sch.3 Pollution Prevention and Control Act 1999.

### 12.3.6 The Pollution Prevention and Control Regulations 2000

The substance of the new regime is provided for in the Pollution Prevention and Control (England and Wales) Regulations 2000.[118] The Regulations effectively amount to a consolidation and harmonisation of provisions deriving from the Directive and Part I of the 1990 Act and apply to operators of installations and plants encompassed by any of these regimes. Significantly also, the bringing of waste-related activities within the new regime has meant that many of the principles originating in Part II of the 1990 Act, concerned with waste management, concerning 'fit and proper persons' and the restrictions upon surrender of licences,[119] have also been incorporated within the new pollution prevention and control permitting system in relation to relevant installations. This regime will be applicable to all new installations, and those undergoing substantial change, as from the commencement of the Regulations. Existing installations will be phased into the new regime on a broadly sectoral basis over a period extending to 2007.[120]

Detailed coverage of the Regulations is beyond the scope of this work, and in some respects repetitive of matters that have already been discussed. However, some comment may be given on their likely implications in relation to regulated installations which involve discharges of liquid effluent and the provision which is made for the protection of the aquatic environment.

The fundamental prohibition, that no person may operate an installation except under and to the extent authorised by a permit granted by the regulator,[121] takes the discussion back to the issue of regulatory responsibilities for pollution prevention and control permitting. Essentially, this is determined by a categorisation of installations, under Schedule 1 to the Regulations, as Part A(1), A(2) and B installations. Although the categorisation of installations is technically complex, the broad effect is that existing integrated pollution control authorisations will become Part A(1) permits, existing local authority air pollution control authorisations will be reclassified as Part A(1), A(2) or B permits and existing waste management authorisations will become Part A(1) permits.

Regulatory functions in respect of Part A(1) installations will be functions of the Environment Agency, and must be exercised for the purpose of achieving a high level of protection of the environment taken as a whole by, in particular, preventing or, where this is not practicable, reducing emissions into air, water and land from the installation. Subject to specific provisions concerning releases to water, the regulation of Part A(2) installations is a function of local authorities who must exercise these functions similarly. Functions relating to Part B installations will also fall

---

[118] SI 2000 No.1973.

[119] See 12.2.6 above on waste management licensing.

[120] See Regs.9 and 10(1) and Sch.3 Pollution Prevention and Control (England and Wales) Regulations 2000.

[121] *Ibid* Reg.9(1).

to local authorities, but since these only relate to atmospheric emissions functions are to be exercisable only for the purpose of preventing or reducing emissions into the air. By way of exception to this general allocation of regulatory responsibilities, the Secretary of State may direct that functions ordinarily exercisable by a local authority are to be exercised by the Agency.[122]

Permits will be subject to general principles which require appropriate preventative measures to be taken against pollution by application of the best available techniques requirement, subject to a requirement that no significant pollution is caused. Permits for Part A installations must also provide for matters required under the Directive such as avoidance of waste, efficient energy use, measures necessary to prevent accidents and restoration of the site to a satisfactory state upon definitive cessation of activities. More specific requirements are also provided for to require permits to include emission limits values for certain pollutants likely to be emitted from an installation in significant quantities and, in respect of Part A installations, having regard to their potential to transfer pollution from one environmental medium to another.[123] Pertinently, in the case of indirect releases into water, the effect of a water treatment plant may be taken into account when determining the emission limit values for an installation providing that an equivalent level of protection of the environment as a whole is guaranteed taking such treatment into account.[124] Otherwise, permitting requirements in relation to Part A installations impose literally transposed obligations arising under the Directive.

Despite all these stipulations as to permitting requirements, the jurisdictional issue remains that where a Part A(2) installation must have a permit application determined by a local authority this will need to take account of impacts upon the aquatic environment which are more generally matters within the remit of the Environment Agency. To address this, special provision is made in relation to conditions in permits where releases to water are allowed from Part A(2) installations. Where a determination of this kind is being made by a local authority, the Agency may give notice specifying emission limit values or other conditions which it considers are required in relation to releases into water from the installation in order to prevent harm to human health or the quality of the environment. Where a notice of this kind specifies emission limit values, the local authority will be bound to impose those specified by the Agency or such stricter limit values as may be determined by the authority. In relation to conditions other than emission limit values, the authority will similarly be bound to impose the conditions specified by the Agency or more onerous conditions which are considered necessary by the authority.[125] In essence, therefore, the solution that has been provided for

---

[122] *Ibid* Reg.8.
[123] *Ibid* Reg.11.
[124] *Ibid* Reg.12.
[125] *Ibid* Reg.12.

is analogous to the national position, prior to the Environment Act 1995, whereby Her Majesty's Inspectorate of Pollution was obliged to give effect to conditions proposed by the National Rivers Authority in relation to discharges to controlled waters unless more onerous conditions were required.[126] Ultimately, the Agency will retain control over the minimum quality of discharges which are allowed to the aquatic environment.

## 12.4 Miscellaneous Water Quality Legislation

The principal water pollution offences concerning controlled waters, under the Water Resources Act 1991, are clearly of the greatest practical importance in that they give rise to the largest number of criminal proceedings relating to contamination incidents. Contamination of waters other than controlled waters under the 1991 Act and contaminants which are placed outside the regime governed by the 1991 Act, are considered in other parts of this work.[127] However, there are also some diverse provisions which relate to water quality, and in many respects the quality of controlled waters, in miscellaneous statutory contexts. Whilst some of these provisions are of antiquity, or of relatively narrow practical application, they are included here for the sake of completeness of coverage and because they remain capable of being relevant in respect of exceptional kinds of legal proceedings relating to water quality.

### 12.4.1 The Cemeteries Clauses Act 1847

A company which is not a local authority and which provides a cemetery which is authorised by a special Act which incorporates the Cemeteries Clauses Act 1847[128] is subject to a special offence in relation to the fouling of water.[129] Hence, if the company causes or suffers to be brought or to flow into any stream, canal, reservoir, aqueduct, pond or watering place, any offensive matter from the cemetery, whereby the water therein is fouled, the company will be liable to forfeit £50.[130] The Act further provides that the penalty imposed, along with the full costs of the proceedings, may be recovered in a superior court by any person having the right to use the water fouled by the offensive matter during the continuance of the offence or within six months of it having ceased.[131] In addition to the recovery of the specified penalty, any person having the right to use the water fouled by the offensive matter may sue the company for any damage specially sustained by reason of the water being fouled, and if no special damage is alleged, for the sum of £10 for each day during

---

[126] s.28(3) Environmental Protection Act 1990, now repealed.

[127] See Ch.19 below on marine pollution and Ch.20 on radioactive contamination.

[128] See 2.3 above on the Cemeteries Clauses Act 1847 and the 'Clauses Acts' generally.

[129] For these purposes a 'company' means a person who by means of a special Act is authorised to construct a cemetery, and a 'special Act' means an Act which authorises the making of a cemetery in accordance with the Cemeteries Clauses Act 1847 (s.2 Cemeteries Clauses Act 1847).

[130] s.20 Cemeteries Clauses Act 1847. As a pecuniary forfeiture this amount was not affected by the general increase in penalties brought about by the Criminal Justice Act 1982.

[131] *Ibid* s.21.

which such offensive matter is brought or flows after the time when the notice of the offence is served on the company by the person.[132]

### 12.4.2  *The Harbours, Docks and Piers Clauses Act 1847*

Where incorporated into a local harbour Act, the Harbours, Docks and Piers Clauses Act 1847 provides that any person who throws or puts any ballast, earth, ashes, stones, or other thing into a harbour or dock shall for every such offence be liable to a penalty not exceeding £200.[133] This offence is made subject to the proviso that it must not interfere with any land preservation or reclamation works. Thus the offence will not prejudice or prevent any person from adopting any measures which, but for the passing of the Act, that person would be lawfully entitled to adopt. In particular, the offence is stated not to prejudice measures for recovering any land which has been lost from a person, or severed from land belonging to that person, by reason of the overflowing or washing of any navigable river, or for protecting that person's land from further loss or damage by the overflowing or washing of such navigable river.[134]

### 12.4.3  *Gas Manufacture*

Historically, the production of gas by the distillation of coal gave rise to the various toxic by-products which caused significant water quality problems[135] and which may remain problematic in those locations where continuing land contamination has resulted.[136] However, despite the discontinuation of gas production by coal distillation, provided for under the Public Health Act 1875, a special offence concerning gas manufacture, remains in existence where water is polluted by matter produced by a person engaged in the manufacture of gas. The offence is committed where a person engaged in the production of gas causes or suffers to be brought or to flow into specified waters any washing or other substance produced in making or supplying gas, or wilfully does any act connected with the making or supplying of gas by which such waters are fouled.[137] The waters specified are any stream, reservoir, aqueduct, pond or place for water, or into any drain or pipe communicating with it. A person found guilty of this offence is liable, on summary conviction, to a forfeiture of £200 along with a further sum of £20 for every day during which the offence continues. However, a defence to these offences arises where offending emission or discharge is made under and in accordance with the terms of a

---

[132] *Ibid* s.22.

[133] An amount substituted by ss.37 and 46 Criminal Justice Act 1982.

[134] s.73 Harbours, Docks and Piers Clauses Act 1847.

[135] See, for example, *Marquis of Granby* v *Bakewell Urban District Council* (1923) 87 JP 105 discussed at 3.15 above.

[136] See 13.7 below on contaminated land.

[137] s.68 Public Health Act 1875.

discharge consent or other authorisation under Part III of the Water Resources Act 1991.[138]

### 12.4.4 The Pipe-lines Act 1962

The Pipe-lines Act 1962 imposes a general duty on the Secretary of State so that, when exercising his powers, he is to have regard to the need to protect water against pollution, whether on the surface or underground, where such water belongs to any water undertaker or local authority or which they are authorised to take.[139] Duties are also imposed upon the owner of a pipe-line in respect of water pollution prevention so that, in the event of the accidental escape or the ignition of any thing in the line, an owner is bound to ensure arrangements whereby immediate notice of the event is given to certain bodies which now include the Environment Agency. Otherwise, the bodies to be notified include all water undertakers and statutory water supply companies who will or may, in consequence of the happening of the event, have to take steps to prevent or combat pollution of water or flooding. Similarly it is the duty of the owner of the pipe-line to inform all sewage undertakers who will or may have, in consequence of the happening of the event, to take steps to prevent injury to their sewers or sewage disposal works, interference with the free flow of the contents of any of their sewers, or the prejudicial effects upon the treatment and disposal of such contents or to combat the effects of any such event.[140] The failure of an owner to fulfil the obligation to inform the various bodies is an offence which, on summary conviction, carries a maximum fine at level three on the standard scale, presently £1,000.[141]

### 12.4.5 The Animal Health Act 1981

An offence with water contamination implications arises under the Animal Health Act 1981 which provides[142] an offence if, without lawful authority or excuse, a person throws or places, or causes or suffers to be thrown or placed, into any river, stream, canal, navigation or other water, or into the sea within 4.8 kilometres[143] of the shore, the carcase of an animal[144] which has died of disease,[145] or been slaughtered as diseased or suspected of being so. The maximum penalty for this offence is, on summary conviction, a fine not exceeding level five on the standard scale, presently £5,000, and an additional fine at level three on the standard scale, presently £1,000, in respect of every 508kg in weight of the carcase.[146] On

---

[138] See para.1 Sch.1 Water Consolidation (Consequential Provisions) Act 1991 and see Ch.10 above on discharge consents generally.

[139] s.44 Pipe-lines Act 1962.

[140] *Ibid* s.37(1), as amended by para.30 Sch.25 Water Act 1989.

[141] *Ibid* s.37(3), as amended by ss.37, 38 and 46 Criminal Justice Act 1982.

[142] s.35 Animal Health Act 1981.

[143] A distance which may be varied by regulations, see s.95(7)(a) *ibid*.

[144] As defined in ss.87 and 89 *ibid*.

[145] As defined in ss.88 and 89 *ibid*.

[146] *Ibid* s.75(1).

a further conviction for a second or subsequent offence the offender is liable at the court's discretion to imprisonment for a term not exceeding one month in lieu of a fine.[147]

### 12.4.6 Powers to Control Injurious Substances

Provisions now contained in the Environmental Protection Act 1990[148] give the Secretary of State general powers to prohibit or restrict the import, use, supply and storage of any specified substance or article for the purpose of preventing pollution of the environment, including water, or harm to human health or the health of animals or plants. Detailed consultation provisions must be adhered to in the making of such regulations.[149]

This power has been used to provide protection for swans and other aquatic wildlife against lead poisoning caused by ingesting weights used by anglers.[150] The Control of Pollution (Anglers' Lead Weights) Regulations 1986[151] prohibit the supply of lead in the form of a lead weight between 0.06 grams and 28.35 grams for the purpose of weighting fishing lines, and a person supplying split shot shall, unless the contrary is shown, be presumed to supply it for the purpose of weighting fishing lines. The offence is punishable, on summary conviction, by a fine not exceeding the statutory maximum, presently £5,000, and on conviction on indictment to a fine. It is notable that the Regulations were amended in 1993[152] to remove the ban on the import of such weights in the context of the single market. It is at least arguable, however, that such a ban was justifiable as a proportionate means of achieving the particular environmental protection objective at stake.[153]

The power has also been used to combat problems arising from the use of anti-fouling paints containing the substance tributyltin, used to protect boats and to prevent the accumulation of algal growth on aquaculture equipment. Tributyltin was found to have seriously toxic effects upon shellfish and other forms of aquatic life.[154] In addition to controls under Part II of the Food and Environment Protection Act 1985,[155] further regulations under the provisions now contained in the Environmental Protection Act 1990 have been enacted. The Control of Pollution (Anti-fouling Paints and Treatments) Regulations 1987[156] make it unlawful to supply for retail sale, or by way of retail sale, any anti-fouling paint, or (by

---

[147] *Ibid* s.75(4).

[148] See previously s.100 Control of Pollution Act 1974.

[149] s.140 Environmental Protection Act 1990.

[150] Generally see Spillet (1985).

[151] SI 1986 No.1992, as amended by SI 1993 No.49.

[152] Under s.2(2) European Communities Act 1972.

[153] See [1993] *Water Law* 87.

[154] See Howarth (1990) 13.08, and Scottish Wildlife and Countryside Link (1988). See also 19.5 below on the MARPOL Convention.

[155] See 19.20 below on Part II Environment Protection Act 1985.

[156] SI 1987 No.783.

way of wholesale also) anti-fouling treatment, containing a tri-organotin compound. The offence is subject to a defence that the person took all reasonable steps, and exercised all due diligence, to avoid committing the offence. Contravention of the regulations is punishable, on summary conviction, by a fine not exceeding level five on the standard scale, presently £5,000 and, on indictment, to a fine of an unlimited amount.[157]

Most recently, the power to control injurious substances has been used in making the Environmental Protection (Restriction on Use of Lead Shot) (England) Regulations 1999.[158] These Regulations seek to address problems of lead contamination of water and waterside land, and particularly its impact upon birds, by prohibiting the use of lead shot for shooting in three situations:

(a) on or over any area below the high-water mark;
(b) on or over the Sites of Special Scientific Interest[159] included in Schedule 1 to the Regulations; and
(c) for shooting any wild bird included in Schedule 2 to the Regulations.

### 12.4.7 Agricultural Chemicals

Diverse provisions governing the use of agricultural chemicals are considered elsewhere in this work, particularly in relation to nitrate fertilisers and pesticides which constitute 'dangerous substances'.[160] However, more specific controls over pesticides are provided for under Part III of the Food and Environment Protection Act 1985 which has effect for the purpose of securing continuous development of means to protect the health of human beings, creatures and plants; to safeguard the environment; and to secure safe, efficient and humane methods of controlling pests.[161] Pursuant to this, the relevant Ministers may, amongst other things, impose specified prohibitions in relation to pesticides[162] and give approval to pesticides of a description specified in regulations. Regulations enacted in accordance with these powers are the Control of Pesticides Regulations 1986[163] which prohibit the use of any pesticide unless it has been approved under the Regulations and the conditions imposed upon its use are adhered to.[164] Contravention of the Regulations, without reasonable excuse, is an offence[165] which is punishable, on summary conviction, to a fine of an amount not exceeding the statutory maximum, presently £5,000; and on conviction on indictment, to a fine of

---

[157] See Howarth (1990) pp.166-167.

[158] SI 1999 No.2170.

[159] See 15.7.1 below on Sites of Special Scientific Interest.

[160] On control of nitrates see 13.5 below and in relation to 'dangerous substances' see 5.4.1 above.

[161] s.16(1)(a) Food and Environment Protection Act 1985.

[162] 'Pesticide' means any substance, preparation or organism prepared or used for destroying any pest (*ibid* s.16(15)).

[163] SI 1986 No.1510, and see Control of Pesticides (Amendment) Regulations 1997 (SI 1997 No.188). The 1986 Regulations implement the Pesticides Directive (79/117/EEC).

[164] Regs.5 and 6 Control of Pesticides Regulations 1986 (SI 1986 No.1510).

[165] s.16(12) Food and Environment Protection Act 1985.

unlimited amount.[166] Persons using pesticides are required to take all
reasonable precautions to protect the health of human beings, creatures and
plants, to safeguard the environment and to avoid the pollution of surface
water or groundwater in accordance with the conditions subject to which
consent has been given for the use of a pesticide.[167] Provision is also made
for the Ministerial approval of Codes of Practice providing practical
guidance in relation to pesticides and other matters covered by Part III of
the 1985 Act.[168]

### *12.4.8 Litter*

A general offence which is capable of having implications upon water
quality, at least in an aesthetic sense, is that of depositing and leaving
litter. Hence, an offence is committed where a person throws down, drops
or otherwise deposits in, into or from any specified place, and leaves any
thing whatsoever in such circumstances as to cause, contribute to or tend
to lead to the defacement by litter of that place.[169] The 'specified places'
are public open places and other areas of land encompassing, amongst
others, Crown Estate land to which the public have access without
payment.

It follows that the offence is capable of arising where litter is deposited
and left on the foreshore or in watercourses or still waters to which the
public have access. The defences which are provided for are that no
offence is committed where the depositing and leaving of the litter was
authorised by law or done with the consent of the owner, occupier or other
person or authority having control of the place in or into which the litter
was deposited. A person convicted of this offence will be liable to a fine
not exceeding level four on the standard scale, presently £2,500.[170] A
peculiarity of the litter offence is that it is committed in relation to
dropping and leaving 'any thing whatsoever' which leads to the
defacement by 'litter' of the relevant place. However, the term 'litter' is
not statutorily defined and leaves open the possibility that things which
have an adverse impact upon water quality might also fall within the
definition of 'litter'. Whilst it is unlikely that a person who deposits a drum
of toxic chemicals into a watercourse would be prosecuted with a litter
offence, the relatively open-ended nature of the offence seems to make this
a possibility. Conversely, activities that would seem to fall squarely within
the litter offence have been prosecuted as water pollution offences,[171] such
as one instance where a member of the crew of a chartered fishing boat
emptied the bin which had been used to collect the day's waste into an

---

[166] *Ibid* s.21(3).

[167] Para.2 Sch.3 Control of Pesticides Regulations 1986 (SI 1986 No.1510).

[168] s.17 Food and Environment Protection Act 1985.

[169] s.87(1) Environmental Protection Act 1990.

[170] s.87(4) Environmental Protection Act 1990, and in relation to the issuing of fixed penalty
notices in respect of the leaving of litter see s.88.

[171] Under s.85(1) Water Resources Act 1991.

estuary and this offence resulted in a fine of £250 being imposed.[172] In appropriate situations, there may be good reasons to take this approach given the greater penalties that may be imposed.

### 12.4.9 Oil Pollution from Land

The regulation of oil discharges and escapes from ships into the marine environment and other navigable waters, as a matter of international and national law, is considered in detail elsewhere.[173] However, provision for oil discharges arising from onshore activities and from pipe lines is made under the Prevention of Oil Pollution Act 1971. Specifically, an offence is provided for where any oil, or mixture containing oil, is discharged in specified circumstances into relevant waters. The persons who commit the offence are identified in the following way:

(a) if the discharge is from a place on land, the occupier of that place, unless he proves that the discharge was caused by the act of a person who was in that place without the (express or implied) permission of the occupier;[174]

(b) if the discharge is from a place on land, and is caused the act of a person who is in that place without the (express or implied) permission of the occupier, that person; or

(c) if the discharge takes place otherwise and is the result of any operations for the exploration of the sea-bed and subsoil or the exploration of their natural resources, the person carrying on the operations.[175]

Although the effect of the Merchant Shipping Act 1995 is to restrict the scope of the 1971 Act to discharges from land, a 'place on land' is broadly defined to include anything resting on the bed or shore of the sea or other waters in respect of which the offence may arise. It also includes anything afloat, other than a vessel, if it is anchored or attached to the bed or shore of the sea or other relevant waters. The 'occupier' of any such 'place on land' means the owner of that place if there is no actual occupier.[176] For the purposes of the offence, 'discharge' includes an 'escape' of oil, while 'oil' has the same broad definition as under the Merchant Shipping Act 1995, encompassing oils of mineral, vegetable and animal origin.[177] References to a 'mixture' containing oil are to be construed to include any mixture of oil with water or with any other substance.[178]

---

[172] See Environment Agency, *Water Pollution Incidents in England and Wales 1998* (1999) p.35.

[173] Generally see Ch.19 below.

[174] On liability for acts of a trespasser, contrast the discussion *of Environment Agency (formerly National Rivers Authority)* v *Empress Car Co (Abertillery) Ltd* [1998] 1 All ER 481 at 9.6.2 above.

[175] s.2(1)(c)-(e) Prevention of Oil Pollution Act 1971, as amended.

[176] *Ibid* s.2(3).

[177] See 19.5 below. However, the Secretary of State may grant exemptions from the 1971 Act in relation to particular discharges or mixtures containing oil (*ibid* s.23, as amended).

[178] *Ibid* s.29.

The waters in respect of which the offence may arise are stated to encompass the whole of the sea within the seaward limits of the territorial waters of the United Kingdom, and all other waters, including inland waters, which are navigable by sea-going ships.[179] From the reference to 'internal waters' it is clear that the offence may be committed in river estuaries containing either brackish water or freshwater providing that such waters are navigable by sea-going ships.[180]

Clearly, there is an overlap between the oil discharge offence under the 1971 Act and the principal water pollution offences under the Water Resources Act 1991 since particular acts can constitute an offence under either Act.[181] Whilst the 1971 Act is relatively limited in being concerned with oil and mixtures containing oil, the offences under the 1991 Act are more broadly formulated in respect of 'effluent' or 'poisonous, noxious or polluting' matter.[182] Contrasts may also be drawn in relation to the extent of the waters covered by the 1971 and 1991 Acts[183] and in respect of the penalties involved for the different offences. A person found guilty of offence concerning discharges of oil provided for under the 1971 Act will be liable, on summary conviction, to a fine not exceeding £50,000 or on conviction on indictment to a fine,[184] whereas a lesser maximum penalty is provided for in relation to summary conviction for the principal offences under the 1991 Act.[185] Another contrast is that restrictions are imposed upon enforcement of the 1971 Act, so that proceedings may only be brought by, or with the consent of, the Attorney General, by a harbour authority (where the discharge is made into the waters of a harbour) or by the Secretary of State (or a person authorised by him).[186]

The 1971 Act also provides for a separate offence in relation to discharge of oil, or mixtures containing oil, from certain pipe lines or as a result of specified operations. This offence arises where oil is discharged into any part of the sea (including estuaries) from a pipe-line or (otherwise than from a ship) or as a result of any operation for the exploration of the sea-bed and subsoil or the exploitation of their natural resources. In such circumstances, the owner of the pipe-line, or the person carrying on the operation, will commit an offence unless the discharge was from a place in his occupation and it is proved that it was due to the action of a person who was there without express or implied permission. However, in respect

---

[179] *Ibid* s.2(2) and on territorial waters see Territorial Sea Act 1987 discussed at 18.10.1 below.

[180] See *Rankin v De Coster* [1975] 2 All ER 303, discussed in 19.9.1 below, where the discharge of fuel oil into waters within a 'dry dock' was found to constitute an offence.

[181] On the principal offences under s.85 Water Resources Act 1991, see 9.3 above.

[182] See 9.8 above on the meaning of 'poisonous, noxious or polluting'.

[183] See the definition of 'controlled waters' which is relevant for the principal offences under the Water Resources Act 1991, discussed in 9.4 above.

[184] s.2(4) Prevention of Oil Pollution Act 1971.

[185] See 9.19.2 above on penalties for the principal water pollution offences under the Water Resources Act 1991.

[186] s.19(1)-(2) Prevention of Oil Pollution Act 1971, and see 9.19.1 above on enforcement of the principal offences under the Water Resources Act 1991.

of operations, the offence is limited to those activities which take place in 'designated areas'.[187]

Four explicit defences are provided in respect of the offences of discharging oil and concerning pipe-lines and operations. The first of these arises where the occupier of a place on land can prove that neither the escape nor any delay in discovering it was due to any want of reasonable care, and that as soon as practicable after it was discovered all reasonable steps were taken for stopping or reducing it.[188]

The second defence arises where a person is charged with an offence concerning a discharge of oil from land where oil refining operations are conducted. In such circumstances, it is a defence to prove that the oil was contained in an effluent; that it was not reasonably practicable to dispose of the effluent otherwise than by discharging it into a relevant water; and that all reasonably practicable steps had been taken for eliminating oil from the effluent. This defence may not be relied upon, however, if the water into which the mixture was discharged was already fouled by oil unless the court is satisfied that the previous fouling was not caused, or contributed to, by oil discharged from that place.[189]

The third defence, concerning the discharge of oil, arises for the protection of acts undertaken in the exercise of powers relating to the removal of wrecks by harbour, conservancy and lighthouse authorities. Alternatively, the defence is allowed where, for preventing an obstruction or danger to navigation, certain powers are exercised by a harbour authority to dispose of sunk, stranded or abandoned vessels. In such circumstances the authority exercising the power is not to be convicted of the offence unless it is shown that it he failed to take such steps, if any, as were reasonable in the circumstances for preventing, stopping or reducing the discharge.[190]

A fourth defence is provided for in respect of any discharge of oil, or in relation to the offence concerning pipe-lines and operations, which is authorised under a permit granted under regulations under the Pollution Prevention and Control Act 1999.[191]

---

[187] s.3 Prevention of Oil Pollution Act 1971. 'Designated area' means an area for the time being designated under s.1 of the Continental Shelf Act 1964. The penalties for the offence concerning pipe lines and operations are the same as for the offence of discharging oil into United Kingdom waters under s.2.

[188] s.6(1) Prevention of Oil Pollution Act 1971. Contrast, the lack of a 'due diligence' defence in relation to the principal water pollution offences under the Water Resources Act 1991 and see 9.6.4 above.

[189] s.6(2)-(3) Prevention of Oil Pollution Act 1971 and, on the meaning of 'reasonably practicable, see *Marshall v Gotham Co Ltd* [1954] 1 All ER 937. Contrast the position with respect to the principal water pollution offences under the Water Resources Act 1991, where the offences are committed by the 'entry' or 'discharge' of the offending matter and, arguably, the actual environmental impact is not relevant to the commission of the offence, and see 9.8-9 above.

[190] s.7 Prevention of Oil Pollution Act 1971.

[191] *Ibid* s.11A(1), as amended by Schedules 2 and 3 of the Pollution Prevention and Control Act 1999 and see 12.3.5-6 above on integrated pollution prevention and control.

Finally, where oil or a mixture containing oil is found to be escaping or to have escaped into relevant waters from a place on land the occurrence must be reported. This duty is imposed upon the occupier of the place on land from which the oil is discharged or escapes. The occurrence is to be reported to the harbour master, or if there is no harbour master the harbour authority. Failure to make such a report makes a person liable on summary conviction to a fine not exceeding level five on the standard scale, presently £5,000.[192] Powers of inspection are also granted, to persons appointed by the Secretary of State, to report on whether prohibitions and obligations imposed under the 1971 have been complied with, and an offence is created in relation to the intentional obstruction of an inspector exercising powers under the Act.[193]

### 12.4.10 Byelaws Concerning Water Pollution

A water undertaker has the power to make byelaws with respect to any waterway owned or managed by it and any land held or managed with the waterway. Such byelaws may be made for the preservation of order, the prevention of damage to the land or anything on or in the waterway or land and for securing that persons resorting to the waterway or land will so behave themselves as to avoid undue interference with the enjoyment of the waters or land by other persons. In accordance with these provisions, byelaws may be made regulating sailing, boating, bathing, fishing and other forms of recreation and related matters. Pertinently, byelaws may require the provision of sanitary appliances on boats where this is necessary for the prevention of pollution.[194] Similar powers in respect of the making of byelaws are given to the Environment Agency, though, an amendment to the power to make byelaws in respect of its fisheries functions is stated to be exercisable for marine or aquatic environmental purposes.[195]

In respect of the control of navigation, the Agency may require the provision of such sanitary appliances on vessels as may be necessary for the purpose of preventing pollution. Specifically in relation to the control of pollution, further powers allow for the byelaw prohibition or regulation of washing or cleaning in any controlled waters of things of a description specified in the byelaws and for prohibiting or regulating the keeping or use on any controlled waters of specified vessels which are provided with water closets or other sanitary appliances.[196]

---

[192] *Ibid* s.11, as amended.

[193] *Ibid* s.18, as amended.

[194] s.157 and Sch.10 Water Industry Act 1991.

[195] s.210 and Sch.25 Water Resources Act 1991, amended by s.103(3) Environment Act 1995 and see 15.4.1 below.

[196] s.210 and paras.2(4)(c) and 4 Sch.25 Water Resources Act 1991. 'Sanitary appliance', in relation to a vessel, means any appliance which, not being a sink, bath or shower bath, is designed to permit polluting matter to pass into the water where the vessel is situated. The procedure in relation to the making of byelaws is provided for under Sch.26.

## 12.4.11 Local Legislation

Historically, the mechanism by which legal powers and duties were conferred upon companies or public bodies established for water supply purposes was a local Act of Parliament or, perhaps, the local adoption of provisions from the Waterworks Clauses Act 1847.[197] Subsequently, use was made of statutory orders granted by the Secretary of State applying provisions from the 'waterworks code', provided for by the Water Act 1945, to particular localities or authorising major waterworks to be undertaken. Since the Water Act 1989, statutory orders of this kind are no longer needed since the necessary powers were provided to water undertakers generally under this statute and subsequently by the Water Industry Act 1991. In most respects, it is thought that local legislation of this kind would have been primarily concerned with water supply powers and duties. However, in many instances this may have encompassed water quality issues both in relation to water actually supplied to premises and the protection of water resources from contamination. Although many of these local statutes appear to have been repealed, it is thought that quite a number of pre-1989 enactments remain in force and continue to confer powers and duties upon statutory water supply companies and water undertakers which may differ from provisions generally applicable in national legislation.[198]

Whilst the bulk of the local legislation that was enacted related to the powers and duties of water supply companies and bodies, in some exceptional instances more general regulatory provision was made for the protection of the quality of controlled waters. Surviving instances of this are to be found in the Thames Conservancy Acts 1932 to 1972.[199] Originally these Acts had provided for powers and duties to be exercised by the Conservators of the River Thames, but subsequently these passed to the Thames Water Authority,[200] the National Rivers Authority and now rest with the Environment Agency.[201] The contemporary impact of this body of local legislation is that, in respect of the River Thames and its tributaries,[202] the Agency is bound to exercise certain functions concerning these waters in addition to matters provided for under national legislation.

Specifically, in relation to the prevention of pollution, it is the general duty of the Agency to preserve and maintain the flow and purity of water in the

---

[197] See 2.3 above on the Waterworks Clauses Act 1847.

[198] See, for example, Kent Water Act 1955, 4 Eliz.2 Ch.xi, concerning the provision of water supply in Kent and making provision for amalgamation of water undertakings, the transfer of undertakings and for the formation of joint boards.

[199] See also Lee Conservancy Act 1868.

[200] s.2 and Sch.1, and s.34(2) and Sch.6 Water Act 1973 and Art.3(1)(a) Thames Water Authority Constitution Order 1973 (SI 1973 No.1360).

[201] s.120(1) and para.233(1) Sch.22 Environment Act 1995.

[202] The 'River' means the Thames from its rise in Gloucestershire to Teddington Lock. 'Tributary' means any river, stream, watercourse, ditch, cut, dock, canal, channel and water within the Thames catchment area communicating either directly or indirectly with the Thames (s.18 Thames Conservancy Act 1950). Provision is also made for the Agency to take action to prevent, remedy or mitigate the pollution of water in any underground strata (s.14 Thames Conservancy Act 1972).

Thames and its tributaries and to cause the surface of the river and its tributaries within three miles of the river to be, as far as reasonably practicable, 'effectually scavenged of substances liable to putrefaction'.[203] The Agency is also empowered to make byelaws for preventing sewage or any other offensive or injurious matter, whether solid or fluid, passing into the river from any vessel and requiring vessels using the river to be equipped with approved sanitary appliances.[204]

Specific prohibitions arise where a person, without lawful excuse, unloads or puts, or causes of suffers to fall, any gravel, or any substance which has been used as ballast, or any stones, earth, mud, ashes, dirt, refuse, soil or rubbish into the river or any tributary, so as to either directly or in combination with similar acts of the same or other persons to impede the proper flow or be detrimental to the purity of the river or any tributary. Also prohibited is any act where a person wilfully causes or knowingly suffers any oil or tar to flow or pass into the river or any tributary.[205] If a person places gravel, or any of the other substances previously referred to, in a place where it is likely to drain, be blown, pass or be carried by floods or extraordinary tides into the river or any tributary, the Agency may serve notice on that person requiring the removal of the matter and compliance with specified conditions to prevent the matter entering the waters. Failure to comply with such a notice will allow the Agency to bring summary proceedings to compel the defaulter to remove the offending matter subject to a penalty or, ultimately, to allow the Agency to undertake the necessary work itself and recover the cost from the defaulter.[206]

Further prohibitions are imposed in relation to discharges of sewage, offensive or injurious matter, first, where anyone who, without lawful excuse,[207] opens any sewer, drain, pipe or channel by which sewage or any offensive or injurious matter, whether solid or fluid, flows or passes or is likely to flow or pass into the river or a tributary. Secondly, a prohibition applies where a person wilfully causes or knowingly suffers any sewage, offensive or injurious matter to flow or pass into the river or a tributary. Exceptions to these prohibitions are provided for, however, in relation to certain discharges from sewerage undertakers' sewers and certain sewers which have been in longstanding lawful use.[208] Where sewage, offensive or injurious matter has been caused or suffered to flow into the river or a

---

[203] s.120 Thames Conservancy Act 1932.

[204] s.233(1) Thames Conservancy Act 1932 and see Thames Navigation Licensing and General Byelaws 1993.

[205] s.121(1) Thames Conservancy Act 1932. The maximum penalty for this offence is at level three of the standard scale, presently £1,000, along with a daily penalty for each day on which an offence continues after conviction (s.242 and s.5(1)).

[206] s.122 Thames Conservancy Act 1932, and see 13.2.2 above on the corresponding provisions relating to works notices under s.161A Water Resources Act 1991.

[207] It is not apparent whether a discharge made under and in accordance with a discharge consent, granted under s.88(1)(a) Water Resources Act 1991, or other environmental licence, would serve as 'lawful excuse' for these purposes.

[208] s.123 Thames Conservancy Act 1932. These offences are subject to a penalty not exceeding level three on the standard scale, presently £1,000 and a daily penalty for each day on which an offence continues after conviction (see ss.242 and 5(1)).

tributary, the Agency is empowered to give notice to the person responsible requiring discontinuation of the flow within a specified time. A person who fails to comply with a notice of this kind will be liable to a penalty and, following conviction, the Agency, with the sanction of the Court, may stop up the outlet of any sewer, drain, pipe or channel in respect of which the offence was committed at the expense of the offender.[209]

Other offences are provided for in respect of cutting of weeds, grass and other vegetation in the river or any tributary and failure to remove the matter at once so as to prevent it decaying in the water and causing contamination. Similarly it is an offence to throw or sweep any weeds, grass or vegetation into the waters.[210]

---

[209] *Ibid* s.124.

[210] *Ibid* s.129. The penalty for this offence is a fine not exceeding level one on the standard scale, presently £200 (s.242). See the similar offence concerning vegetation in inland freshwaters under s.90(2) Water Resources Act 1991, discussed at 9.15 above, though note that the maximum penalty for this offence is level four on the standard scale, presently £2,500.

# Chapter 13

# PREVENTIVE AND RESTORATIVE APPROACHES

## 13.1 Introduction

'After-the-event' mechanisms to punish polluters for wrongful behaviour have traditionally tended to predominate as a legal strategy for securing satisfactory water quality. Increasingly, however, regulatory law has developed from being a retrospective and punitive mechanism to 'bring polluters to book', to a proactive mechanism for preventing contamination of waters and protecting or restoring the aquatic environment. Perhaps the first inroads into a forward-looking approach to water quality are to be found in the introduction of discharge consents[1] as a means of allowing benign emissions into water whilst preventing the entry of effluent of an excessively unsatisfactory standard. From this first step, however, the preventive approach has expanded in diverse directions.

The preventive theme is clearly evident in the use of town and country planning law[2] to restrict potentially polluting developments, there are also a number of legal mechanisms directed towards preventive and restorative objectives having their origins, for the most part, in the Water Resources Act 1991. Specifically, these concern anti-pollution works and operations powers; precautionary regulations; water protection zones; nitrate sensitive areas; and groundwater protection measures.[3] Each of these has as its objective the prevention of polluting matter entering waters and, in some respects, the restoration of waters where entry has taken place. The shift of emphasis is profoundly important: the focus has changed from the punishment of polluters to the regulation of certain failures to take preventive action regardless of whether any pollution incident has actually occurred.

The restorative theme is more directly illustrated by recently implemented measures intended to secure the remediation of contaminated land. Although, outside the 1991 Act and concerned with a range of adverse environmental quality impacts, the contaminated land regime has important implications for the restoration of water quality and is closely interrelated with provisions of the 1991 Act. For those reasons the new contaminated land regime is appropriately considered here alongside the other mechanisms for protecting and restoring the water environment.

---

[1] See Ch.10 on discharge consents.
[2] Generally see Ch.14 below on planning law.
[3] See also the discussion of abandoned mines at 9.17.3 above.

## 13.2 Anti-Pollution Works and Operations

By themselves, neither a conviction for a water pollution offence nor a successful civil action actually secures any immediate benefit for the aquatic environment. Certainly, money may be paid by the person responsible, either as a fine or in compensation, but the payment of money and the physical and ecological restoration of the damaged environment are far from being the same thing. Moreover, prevention is better than cure and if environmental harm is to be avoided or mitigated, swift anticipatory or remedial practical action is needed to counteract the effects of entry of contaminating matter into waters, and corresponding legal provisions providing for such action are necessary, along with cost-recovery powers in accordance with the polluter pays principle.[4]

### 13.2.1 Anti-Pollution Works Powers

Important operational powers are given to the Environment Agency in relation to actual or apprehended water pollution incidents. These provide that, where it appears to the Agency that any poisonous, noxious or polluting matter[5] or any solid waste matter is likely to enter, or to be or to have been present in, any controlled water,[6] the Agency will, under specified circumstances, be entitled to carry out the following works and operations, and related investigations:[7]

(a)   in a case where matter appears likely to enter any controlled waters, works and operations for the purpose of preventing it from so doing; or

(b)   in a case where the matter appears to be or to have been present in any controlled waters, works and operations for the purpose,
  (i)   of removing or disposing of the matter;
  (ii)  of remedying or mitigating any pollution caused by its presence in the waters; or
  (iii) so far as it is reasonably practicable to do so, of restoring the waters, including any flora and fauna dependent on the aquatic environment of the waters, to their state immediately before the matter became present in the waters.[8]

---

[4] See Environment Agency, *Water Pollution Incidents in England and Wales 1998* (1999) para.7.8, and see 4.7.3 above on the polluter pays principle. On 'clean up' powers and cost recovery following oil pollution incidents arising in relation to shipping see Ch.19 below.

[5] See 9.8 above on the meaning of 'poisonous, noxious or polluting'.

[6] See 9.4 above on the meaning of 'controlled waters'.

[7] The addition of 'related investigations' is provided for under s.161(1A) Water Resources Act 1991 which, along with ss.161A to 161D, were inserted by paras.161 and 162 Sch.22 Environment Act 1995. The likely implication of this amendment is that where the Agency, for example, is obliged to undertake an analysis of water to ascertain what pollutants are present, the capacity to undertake such tests would fall within the works and operations powers.

[8] s.161(1) Water Resources Act 1991.

*13.2.2 Works Notices*

As a result of amendments to the anti-pollution works powers, the specified works and operations may now only be undertaken where the Agency considers it necessary to do so forthwith. Hence, where the action that is required is not urgent, the appropriate course will be for the Agency to issue a 'works notice' against the appropriate person who should undertake works in relation to the situation. However, the anti-pollution works powers may be exercised by the Agency itself if, after reasonable enquiry, no person can be found upon whom to serve a works notice requiring the necessary work to be undertaken.[9] The practical difficulties in determining what is to count as a situation requiring action 'forthwith', or what steps are required by way of 'reasonable enquiry', may be considerable. Nonetheless, unless a situation falls into these categories, the first line of approach will need to be the service of a works notice, rather than the Agency itself conducting the required works or operations. Another limitation upon the power of the Agency to undertake anti-pollution works is that it will not be entitled to impede or prevent the making of any discharge in pursuance of a discharge consent[10] or other consent given under Chapter II of Part III of the Water Resources Act 1991.[11]

Where polluting matter is likely to enter controlled waters or to be, or to have been, present in such waters, the Agency will generally be required to serve a works notice on any person who caused or knowingly permitted the matter to be present at a place from which it was likely to enter the waters, or to be present in the waters.[12] The works notice will require the person upon whom it is served to carry out specified works or operations for the purpose of preventing the matter entering the waters, removing the matter from the waters or remedying the pollution, or restoring the waters to their former state insofar as it is reasonably practicable to do so.[13] The notice must specify the period within which the things specified under the notice must be done.[14]

Further provisions are made to clarify that works notices may require persons to conduct works which they would not otherwise be entitled to conduct, for the granting of permission by other persons for relevant works to be undertaken and for consultation in relation to this, and for the payment of compensation to those other persons by the person upon whom the works notice is served.[15] Provision is also made for appeals to be made to the Secretary of State against works notices allowing him to quash a notice or confirm it with or without modification.[16] However, failure to

---

[9] s.161(1A) Water Resources Act 1991, and see 10.11.1 above on enforcement notices under s.90B Water Resources Act 1991, as amended.

[10] See Ch.10 above on discharge consents.

[11] s.161(2) Water Resources Act 1991.

[12] *Ibid* s.161A(1). See 9.5–7 above on the meaning of 'cause or knowingly permit'.

[13] *Ibid* s.161A(2).

[14] *Ibid* s.161A(3).

[15] *Ibid* s.161B.

[16] *Ibid* s.161C.

comply with a works notice is a criminal offence which is punishable to the same extent as the principal water pollution offences.[17] Additionally, where a person fails to comply with the requirements of a notice the Agency may do what was required to be done under the notice and recover any costs or expenses reasonably incurred. Where the Agency believes that proceedings for the offence of failure to comply with the requirements of a works notice would not afford an effectual remedy against the non-compliance, it may take proceedings in the High Court for the purpose of securing compliance with the notice.[18]

Further indications as to the practical use which will be made of works notices is provided by an Agency policy and guidance note on the use of works notices.[19] This emphasises that a risk-based approach is to be adopted in determining whether a notice should be served and that costs and benefits should be taken into account.[20]

### 13.2.3 The Anti-Pollution Works Regulations 1999

The Secretary of State is empowered to make regulations concerning works notices and for this purpose the Anti-Pollution Works Regulations 1999[21] have been enacted. These Regulations prescribe the contents of works notices, the procedure to be followed in relation to appeals against such notices and the compensation to be paid in relation to rights of entry in relation to anti-pollution works. Hence, amongst other things, in the case of a potential pollution incident, a works notice must describe the nature of the risk to controlled waters, identifying the waters which may be affected and the place from which the matter in question is likely to enter those waters and, in the case of an actual pollution incident, describe the nature and extent of the pollution identifying the waters affected by it. In either case, the notice must specify the works or operations required to be carried out by the person upon whom the notice is served and give the Agency's reasons for requiring those works or operations to be carried out.

Where a situation falls into the urgent category, or otherwise allows the Agency to undertake any anti-pollution works or operations of the kinds described, it may recover the expenses reasonably incurred in doing so from any person who caused or knowingly permitted[22] the matter in question to be present at the place from which it was likely to enter any controlled waters, or caused or knowingly permitted the matter in question to be present in any controlled waters.[23] Whilst the wording of this cost-recovery power follows that of the principal water pollution offences, it is

---

[17] See 9.19.2 above on penalties for the principal water pollution offences.

[18] s.161D Water Resources Act 1991. On the punishments for the principal water pollution offences see 9.19.2 above and on the use of injunctions generally see 3.16.5 above.

[19] Environment Agency, *Environment Agency Policy and Guidance on the Use of Anti-Pollution Works Notices* (1999).

[20] See 6.14 above on the Environment Agency's costs and benefits duty.

[21] SI 1999 No.1006. The Regulations apply to England and Wales.

[22] See 9.5–7 above on the meaning of 'cause or knowingly permit'.

[23] s.161(3) Water Resources Act 1991.

significant that the recovery of expenses reasonably incurred by the Agency is not dependent upon any conviction for a principal water pollution offence having been secured.[24] Cost-recovery, therefore, is independent of any potential criminal prosecution that might arise out of a pollution incident. Neither the exercise of anti-pollution works or operations powers nor the recovery of expenses reasonably incurred will derogate from any right of action or other civil or criminal remedy in proceedings instituted otherwise than in relation to anti-pollution works and operations.[25]

In practice, the exercise of the anti-pollution works powers are of considerable value to the Agency.[26] Whilst the terms 'works and operations' are not statutorily defined, it is apparent that they would encompass a wide range of activities such as the containment of an oil spillage by the installation of a boom or the reoxygenation of water where it has been contaminated by a deoxygenating substance. Although waters have a natural capacity for ecological recovery following a pollution incident, nonetheless anti-pollution works powers may be used effectively to accelerate this process by restocking a water with fish or other aquatic fauna or flora.

However, there are difficulties with the extent of the powers to undertake potentially extensive and costly work on land to prevent the leaching of contaminants into adjoining watercourses. In this respect the powers of the Agency are unsatisfactorily unspecific and there are difficulties concerning the interrelationship between the anti-pollution works powers and the regime which is provided for in relation to the remediation of contaminated land under Part IIA Environmental Protection Act 1990.[27]

The powers of the Agency to undertake anti-pollution works also interrelate with its general powers to undertake works to deal with foul water and pollution. These allow the Agency to construct and maintain drains, sewers, watercourse, catchpits and other works for the purpose of intercepting, treating and disposing of any foul water arising or flowing on land which it owns or over which it has acquired the necessary easements or rights, or otherwise preventing pollution on such land.[28] However, in respect of the undertaking of anti-pollution works or operations, it will not be necessary for an interest in land to be acquired by the Agency since the

---

[24] See *Bruton and the National Rivers Authority* v *Clarke*, unreported 23 July 1993, Cambridge County Court, see [1994] *Water Law* 145 discussed at 13.2.4 below, where, in relation to the incident giving rise to these cost recovery proceedings, a conviction for knowingly permitting the pollution was overturned on appeal though the recovery of costs was allowed despite this, see Carty (1995).

[25] s.161(5) Water Resources Act 1991, and see the discussion of s.100 at 3.18.5 above.

[26] See Environment Agency, *Water Pollution Incidents in England and Wales 1998* (1999) para.7.8.

[27] See the discussion of the contaminated land regime at 13.7 below.

[28] s.162(1) Water Resources Act 1991, and in relation to the compulsory purchase of land by the Agency see s.154.

power of entry for these purposes does not depend upon the acquisition of any interest in land.[29]

### 13.2.4 The Bruton Case

Although the power of the Agency to recover the reasonable expenses of anti-pollution works and operations is frequently used in practice where action is taken by the Agency in the aftermath of a pollution incident, there has only been one instance where the exercise of this power has been explicitly considered by the courts. This arose in the case of *Bruton and the National Rivers Authority* v *Clarke*[30] where a serious pollution incident followed the collapse of a bank supporting a slurry lagoon at the defendant's pig farm allowing effluent to enter an adjoining watercourse. Although the defendant admitted liability for the pollution incident, and the resulting fish mortality arising from it, actions were brought by the first claimant to recover civil damages for loss of amenity to the local angling association, and by the National Rivers Authority to recover costs that it had incurred in restoring the watercourse to its former state.

In respect of the Authority's claim for recovery of clean-up costs, the court reduced an amount claimed in respect of a fish survey (approximately £8,000) on the basis that there was an element of 'dual purpose' involved in that this survey would have been conducted eventually regardless of the incident. However, £5,000 was recoverable for this purpose since the incident had necessitated the survey being conducted earlier than had been planned. In respect of a claim for scientific and technical costs (of £22,000), it was held that these costs had to be shown to have been necessarily incurred under the statutory powers to conduct anti-pollution works and operations and, because this could not be established in all respects, the amount allowed was reduced to £12,000. In respect of fish restocking the amount allowed was approximately £21,000 since additional expenditure (of £30,000) was found to have made no significant contribution to the restoration of the fishery. Overall, the outcome in the case indicates that courts will be cautious of allowing cost recovery for anti-pollution works and operations unless it can be shown conclusively that such costs have been necessarily incurred in accordance with the statutory powers of the Agency in respect of anti-pollution works and operations.

Whilst the *Bruton* case illustrates the extreme end of the cost-recovery powers, the general use of these powers to recover lesser amounts is commonplace. In the latest Environment Agency annual report on water pollution incidents, it is recorded that cost-recovery took place in 3,160

---

[29] See *ibid* s.172, but contrast s.170 relating to entry of premises for works purposes. Generally, in relation to powers of entry see 6.17 above.

[30] (1993) unreported 23 July 1993 Cambridge County Court, see [1994] *Water Law* 145, and see Carty (1995). See also National Rivers Authority, *Water Pollution Incidents in England and Wales 1993* (1994) para.7.5.2.1, and *Water Pollution Incidents in England and Wales 1994* (1995) para.8.5.

instances, allowing the recovery of a total of £1,302,640 consisting of amounts ranging from £18 to £72,033.[31]

### 13.3 Precautionary Regulations

Anticipating and regulating the potential of an installation or activity to give rise to water contamination is capable of being extensively provided for in town and country planning law where detailed conditions may be imposed upon new developments to minimise their polluting potential.[32] However, more specifically in relation to water protection, broadly formulated enabling powers are granted to the Secretary of State to enact regulations to prevent pollution where persons have custody or control of substances which have recognised water polluting potential.

In precise usage, 'precaution' and 'prevention' are distinguished. The need for 'precaution' arises where there is some evidence of environmental harm without conclusive evidence of this needing to be established. By contrast, where the potential for environmental harm is established, 'prevention' (rather than precaution) is required.[33] Following to this differentiation, 'precautionary' regulations might be better termed 'preventive' regulations, given the known potential of the substances concerned to cause pollution. Nonetheless, the legal mechanisms that are provided allow a useful substance-specific approach to the prevention of water pollution and contamination.

The powers to regulate custody or control of polluting substances are provided for under the Water Resources Act 1991, which empowers the Secretary of State to make precautionary regulations for specified purposes. These are, first, for prohibiting a person from having custody or control of any poisonous, noxious or polluting matter unless prescribed works and prescribed precautions and other steps have been taken to prevent or control the entry of the matter into any controlled waters. The second purpose is to require a person who already has custody or control of, or makes use of, poisonous, noxious or polluting matter to carry out works or otherwise to take precautions and other prescribed steps.[34]

As a general matter, precautionary regulations may incorporate provision to confer powers on the Agency to determine the circumstances in which a person is required to carry out works or take precautions or other steps. In addition, regulations may impose requirements and specify the works, precautions or other steps which are required; to provide for appeals to the Secretary of State; and provide that a contravention will be an offence, the

---

[31] Environment Agency, *Water Pollution Incidents in England and Wales 1998* (1999) para.7.8.

[32] See Ch.14 on planning law generally and note the Planning (Hazardous Substances) Act 1990 and Planning (Hazardous Substances) Regulations 1992 (SI 1992 No.656).

[33] See the discussion of the precautionary principle at 4.7.1 above and the discussion of the prevention principle at 4.7.2 above.

[34] s.92(1) Water Resources Act 1991.

maximum penalties for which are not to exceed the penalties specified in relation to the principal water pollution offences.[35]

### 13.3.1 The Control of (Agricultural) Pollution Regulations

An important feature concerning precautionary regulations under the 1991 Act is that they are formulated as an *enabling power* rather than a *mandatory requirement*. That is, there is no duty upon the Secretary of State, only a power to enact particular regulations. To date, there is only one instance in which the power to enact precautionary regulations has been exercised, namely the Control of Pollution (Silage, Slurry and Agricultural Fuel Oil) Regulations 1991[36] which impose containment requirements upon some of the substances which, in the past, have given rise to considerable numbers of agricultural pollution incidents. The background to these Regulations lies in a history of serious problems in respect of agricultural pollution in many rural areas and the increasing recognition that the principal water pollution offences are of limited value in addressing incidents of this kind.[37]

The Agricultural Pollution Regulations make it an offence for any person to have custody or control of any crop that is being made into silage unless it is stored in a silo which conforms with construction specifications set out in Schedule 1 to the Regulations, or is contained in bales which are individually wrapped and sealed within an impermeable membrane and stored at least 10 metres from any watercourse, and not unpacked within 10 metres of any watercourse which silage effluent could enter.[38] The requirements for silage silos require design and construction in accordance with specified requirements or the relevant British Standard; the provision of impermeable effluent drainage channels leading to an effluent tank with a specified capacity; that the facility is situated so that no part of it is within 10 metres of any inland or coastal waters which silage effluent could enter if it were to escape; and designed and constructed so that, with proper maintenance, it will continue to satisfy these requirements for at least 20 years.[39]

In respect of the storage of livestock slurry, otherwise than for temporary containment in a tanker used for transportation purposes, no person is to have custody of slurry unless it is contained in a slurry storage system

---

[35] *Ibid* s.92(2), and see 9.19.2 above on the penalties for the principal water pollution offences.

[36] SI 1991 No.324, as amended by SI 1996 No.2044. Also see Ministry of Agriculture, Fisheries and Food and Welsh Office, *Code of Good Agricultural Practice for the Protection of Water*, alternatively titled *The Water Code Revised 1998* (1998), approved by the Water (Prevention of Pollution) (Code of Practice) Order 1998 (SI 1998 No.3084), which provides a more detailed discussion of agricultural pollution prevention measures relating to slurries (Ch.4), silage effluent (Ch.8) and fuel oil (Ch.10), and see 13.5.7 below on the legal status of the *Code*.

[37] See the discussion of agriculture at 1.6.4 above. On the general problem of agricultural pollution, see Nature Conservancy Council (1991) and Jones (1993).

[38] Reg.3. Control of Pollution (Silage, Slurry and Agricultural Fuel Oil) Regulations 1991.

[39] *Ibid* Sch.1.

satisfying the requirements of the Regulations.[40] This requires that slurry storage tanks, effluent tanks, channels and reception pits must be protected from corrosion in accordance with the code of practice on agricultural buildings and structures, published by the British Standards Institution; the base of the slurry storage tank and the base and walls of any effluent tank, channels and reception pit are impermeable; the slurry storage tank has adequate storage capacity for the likely amount of slurry produced on the premises; no part of the storage tank, effluent tank, channels or reception pit is situated within 10 metres of any inland or coastal waters which slurry could enter if it were to escape; and the storage tank, effluent tank, channels and reception pit are designed and constructed so that, with proper maintenance, they are likely to continue to satisfy these requirements for a period of at least 20 years.[41]

In respect of the storage of fuel oil on farms, the corresponding requirements are that no person may have custody of 1,500 litres or more of fuel oil contained in a storage tank unless it satisfies specified requirements.[42] These require that the storage tank is surrounded by a bund capable of retaining within its area a volume of not less than 110% of the capacity of the tank; constructed so that the bund and the base of the storage area are impermeable and designed and constructed so that, with proper maintenance, they are likely to remain so for at least 20 years; and situated so that no part of the fuel storage area is within 10 metres of any inland or coastal waters into which fuel oil could enter if it were to escape.[43]

The Regulations, which came into force on 1 September 1991, operate prospectively so that certain existing facilities are classified as 'exempt structures' to which the requirements do not apply. Specifically, these are where the structure was constructed or used before 1 March 1991 for making silage, storing slurry or containing fuel oil, or where a contract for construction was entered into before that date and construction completed before 1 September 1991.[44] However, exemption will be lost if, after 1 March 1991, a structure is substantially enlarged or reconstructed or where a notice requiring works to be done has not be complied with.[45] In respect of the latter, where satisfied that there is a significant risk of pollution of controlled waters from an exempt structure, the Agency may require works to be done within a reasonable period of not less than 28 days to reduce the risk of pollution to a minimum.[46]

Criminal penalties are provided for in relation to contravention of the requirements for silos, slurry storage systems and fuel oil storage areas. These provide, on summary conviction, for a fine not exceeding the

---

[40] *Ibid* Reg.4.
[41] *Ibid* Sch.2.
[42] *Ibid* Reg.5.
[43] *Ibid* Sch.3.
[44] *Ibid* Reg.6.
[45] *Ibid* Reg.8.
[46] *Ibid* Reg.9.

statutory maximum, presently £5,000, and, on conviction on indictment, to an unlimited fine.[47] In deciding how to exercise any powers provided for under the Regulations, the Agency must take into account whether there has been or is likely to be any contravention of any code of practice issued for the purpose of giving practical guidance to persons engaged in agriculture and promoting desirable practice for avoiding or minimising pollution, that is, the *Water Code*.[48]

The Agricultural Pollution Regulations were amended in 1996[49] to allow greater flexibility and to enhance the powers of the Agency in certain respects. The main changes allowed the continuation of silage making in field heaps, subject to certain controls and prior notification to the Agency; permitted some flexibility in the siting and size of slurry reception pits, subject to precautions agreed with the Agency; and allowed the Agency to serve a notice requiring improvements where there was a significant risk of pollution from continuing use of a containment facility, irrespective of its date of construction (before this works notices had only been allowed for in relation to 'exempt' facilities constructed before September 1991).[50]

By way of general comment, it is notable that that there has been a significant long-term downward trend in the numbers of agricultural water pollution incidents over recent years, though the proportion of incidents attributable to agriculture has remained as a fairly constant proportion, at about 10%, of the total number of water pollution incidents.[51] This general downward trend may be a consequence of the impact of the preventive Regulations, and it has been suggested that the Regulations appear to have been of considerable value in improving standards.[52] However, critics have suggested that the legislative approach underlying the Regulations is limited in concentrating upon the adequacy of containment facilities. Attention should also be directed towards the eventual disposal of farm wastes. This would be better addressed by imposing requirements upon farmers to prepare, and adhere to, farm waste management plans, to minimise the generation of waste and to reintegrate its use with the farm production cycle, and ensure that waste production does not exceed the available absorption capacity of the available land.[53]

---

[47] *Ibid* Reg.12.

[48] Under s.97 Water Resources Act 1991, and see 13.5.7 below on the Water Code.

[49] SI 1996 No.2044.

[50] See Environment Agency, *Water Pollution Incidents in England and Wales 1997* (1998) para.3.2.3.

[51] See *ibid* para.5.1.3, though a slight upward trend is illustrated in the most recent information (see Environment Agency, *Water Pollution Incidents in England and Wales 1998* (1999) para.5.1.3), and it should be noted that the data referred to does not cover agricultural oil pollution incidents.

[52] National Audit Office (1995) para.3.7.

[53] Lowe, Clark, Seymour and Ward (1992). Similarly, see National Rivers Authority, *The Influence of Agriculture on the Quality of Natural Waters in England and Wales* (1992) para.12.23, where it is recommended that, if feasible, farm waste management plans should be a pre-requisite for grant support for pollution prevention measures. See MAFF, *Code of Good Agricultural Practice for the Protection of Water*, (1998)) which now provides guidance on farm waste management planning (Ch.3) and see 13.5.7 below on the legal status of the *Code*.

## 13.3.2 Further Precautionary Regulations on Oil Storage

Despite the lengthy period during which powers to make regulations for the prevention of pollution have been in existence,[54] and repeated indications that further regulations of this kind were envisaged,[55] no further precautionary regulations have yet followed the agricultural Regulations. This is particularly incongruous in that oil storage tanks are differently regulated at present, depending on whether they happen to be on agricultural or non-agricultural premises, a distinction which would appear to be irrelevant to their polluting potential.

However, it appears that pollution prevention regulations covering oil storage facilities are imminent. Following a Department of the Environment consultation paper in 1996,[56] the Control of Pollution (Oil Storage) (England) Regulations have been published for consultation with the intention that regulations will be enacted during 2000.[57] With certain exceptions, the regulations will apply to anyone who has custody of an above-ground oil store with a capacity of 200 litres or greater used for the storage of any kind of oil. Hence, the regulations will apply to industrial and commercial premises and institutions of a residential or non-residential kind, though exceptions are provided for in relation to single private dwellings, separately regulated oil refining or distribution premises and farms, which will continue to be covered by the existing precautionary regulations.

The basic requirement under the proposed regulations is that oil must be stored in a container which is of sufficient strength and structural integrity to ensure that in normal circumstances it is unlikely to burst or leak. Beyond this, the container must be within a secondary containment system with a capacity of not less than 110% of the container's storage capacity; positioned so as to minimise any risk of damage; constructed so that its base and walls are impermeable to water and oil; with walls which are not penetrated by any pipe or opening used for drainage purposes; and with any fill or draw off pipe adequately sealed to prevent oil escaping from the system. Failure to fulfil these requirements, or other requirements relating to specific methods of oil storage, will be a criminal offence punishable on summary conviction by a fine of up to the statutory maximum, presently £5,000, or by a fine of unlimited amount on conviction on indictment.

It is envisaged that the regulations will become applicable to new facilities six months after they have been laid in Parliament. In relation to existing facilities which involve 'significant risk', because they are less than 10 metres away from any inland freshwaters or coastal waters or less than 50 metres away from a well or borehole, a two year period after enactment of

---

[54] Similar powers were provided for under s.31(4) Control of Pollution Act 1974.

[55] See DoE, *The Water Environment: The Next Steps* (1986) para.5.7, and HM Government, *This Common Inheritance* (Cm.1200, 1990) para.12.18.

[56] DoE, consultation paper, *Proposals to Control Water Pollution from Industrial, Commercial, Institutional and Institutional Residential Oil Storage Facilities* (1996).

[57] DETR, *Proposals for regulations to control pollution from oil stores* (2000). It is not clear whether similar regulations are to be formulated for Wales.

the regulations is generally allowed for compliance. However, the Agency may serve a notice requiring works to be conducted within the two year period where there is a significant risk of pollution of controlled water if steps are not taken immediately. Otherwise, for other existing facilities, which do not represent a 'significant risk' in the sense indicated, a five year period will be allowed for compliance with the regulations.

There are clear similarities between the proposed oil storage regulations and the existing Agricultural Pollution Regulations and it is recognised that an overall objective behind the oil storage regulations is to ensure greater equity between controls impacting upon different sectors of the economy. However, there are several points of contrast between the two sets of regulations and some key respects in which the proposed regulations are stricter than the Agricultural Regulations in relation to oil storage. First, the threshold for compliance, set at 200 litres, is significantly less than the 1,500 litre threshold set for the Agricultural Regulations, so that small tanks, oil drums and mobile bowsers will be covered by the oil storage regulations. Second, the definition of 'oil' which is used, encompassing all kinds of oil, is wider than that used in the Agricultural Regulations which apply only to fuel oil. Perhaps most significantly, the oil storage regulations apply to all existing facilities whereas, by contrast, the Agricultural Regulations generally only apply to facilities constructed after their enactment with existing facilities being classified as 'exempt' unless the Agency served a works notice in respect of containment facilities constituting a significant risk of pollution.

## 13.4  Water Protection Zones

The use of precautionary regulations is generally substance-specific, in the sense of being concerned with the custody or control of specific kinds of contaminating substance. By contrast, the facility for the designation of water protection zones is location-specific in being directed towards the regulation of potentially contaminating activities in designated areas. Accordingly, where a particular area requires especially strict regulation, perhaps because of the vulnerability of the waters that may otherwise be affected, the facility for designation of that area as a water protection zone, and the imposition of consequent restrictions upon activities within the area, may provide effective protection in circumstances where the general regime for water protection under the Water Resources Act 1991 has proved inadequate.

The facility for designating of water protection zones allows the Secretary of State, after consultation with the agriculture Minister,[58] to designate such a zone where it is considered that it is appropriate, with a view to preventing or controlling the entry of any poisonous, noxious or polluting matter into controlled waters, and to prohibit or restrict the carrying on in that area of activities which he considers are likely to result in the

---

[58] See 6.2 above on the role of the National Assembly for Wales.

pollution of any such waters.[59] An order designating an area as a water protection zone may also incorporate various provisions:

(a) conferring a power on the Agency to determine the circumstances in which activities are prohibited or restricted;

(b) applying a prohibition or restriction in respect of activities carried on without the consent of the Agency or in contravention of any consent conditions;

(c) providing that a contravention of a prohibition or restriction, or of a condition of a consent, will be an offence;[60] and

(d) providing for anything falling to be determined by the Agency to be determined in accordance with a procedure specified in the order.[61]

The Secretary of State may not make an order for the creation of a water protection zone except on the application of the Agency, and detailed matters relating to the procedure which must be followed in relation to designation are provided for under Schedule 11 to the Water Resources Act 1991.[62] For the purposes of any water protection zone designation order the Secretary of State may enact regulations with respect to any consents that may be required in relation to the designated zone. Such regulations may concern matters such as applications for consent; conditions of consents; revocation and variation of consents; appeals against consent determinations; the exercise of powers of the Agency; the imposition of charges; and the registration of applications or consents.[63]

## 13.4.1 The River Dee Water Protection Zone

Whilst provisions allowing for the designation of water protection zones have existed for some years,[64] no actual use of these has been made until recently. In 1994 the National Rivers Authority submitted a draft order[65] to designate an area of the River Dee catchment as a water protection zone. In part, the motivation for this initiative lay in a number of serious pollution incidents that had occurred in the River, and had seriously detrimental impacts upon the use of it as a source of water supply.

---

[59] s.93(1) and (2) Water Resources Act 1991, however, the entry of agricultural nitrate is excluded by s.93(3)) since this is otherwise provided for (see 13.5 below on nitrate controls).

[60] The maximum penalties for which may not exceed the penalties for the principal water pollution offences and see 9.19.2 above on this.

[61] s.93(4) Water Resources Act 1991.

[62] Effective under s.93(5) Water Resources Act 1991. This Schedule provides that where the Agency applies for an order, a copy of the draft order must be submitted to the Secretary of State and published stating the general effect, a place where a draft may be inspected, and that any person may object within a 28 day period. Following this, the Secretary of State may make an order in the same terms as the draft, or in a modified form, or he may refuse to make an order and he may hold a public inquiry before making the order.

[63] s.96(1) Water Resources Act 1991, and see s.114 and Sch.20 Environment Act 1995, allowing for the Secretary of State to delegate his functions in determining appeals.

[64] See s.31(5) Control of Pollution Act 1974.

[65] See National Rivers Authority, *Proposed Water Protection Zone (River Dee Catchment) Designation Order 1993* (1993) and explanatory memorandum on this.

Therefore, the proposal was based on the grounds that, first, the Authority was bound to have regard to the obligations upon water undertakers to provide wholesome drinking water[66] and, second, that a significant general environmental benefit would result from precautionary measures to reduce the frequency and magnitude of spillages passing into waters within the catchment.[67] However, objections were made to the proposal from interested parties and the Secretary of State decided that the matter should be considered at a public inquiry. Despite a favourable outcome of the inquiry, and perhaps because the River Dee proposal represented the first use of the statutory powers, legislation giving effect to the proposal has only recently been enacted.

Under the Water Protection Zone (River Dee Catchment) Designation Order 1999,[68] the Secretary of State for the Environment, Transport and the Regions and the Secretary of State for Wales exercised their powers to designate part of the freshwater River Dee catchment as a water protection zone. The boundaries of the designated area are indicated in a definitive map available for inspection at the offices of the Department of the Environment, Transport and the Regions and other locations. As a consequence of the Order, protection zone consent must be obtained from the Environment Agency for the carrying on of a controlled activity,[69] involving the keeping or use of a controlled substance within the Zone.[70] A 'controlled substance', for these purposes, is any substance which is:

(a)   a dangerous substance;
(b)   a fuel, lubricant or industrial spirit or solvent, which is liquid under normal conditions or which is kept as a liquid within the site;
(c)   a medicinal product within the meaning of the Medicines Act 1968;
(d)   a food which is liquid under normal conditions;
(e)   a feeding stuff which is liquid under normal conditions;
(f)   an inorganic fertiliser;
(g)   a cosmetic product within the meaning of the Cosmetic Products (Safety) Regulations 1996; or
(h)   a substance identified by its manufacturer as being toxic, harmful, corrosive or irritant;

of which there is kept or used, or proposed to be kept or used, a 'relevant quantity'.

---

[66] Under s.15 Water Resources Act 1991, and see 6.9 above on this.
[67] See *ENDS Report* 290 (1999) p.11.
[68] SI 1999 No.915.
[69] A 'controlled activity' means the keeping or use of a controlled substance within a catchment control site. A 'catchment control site' means a site used in connection with an industrial process (which encompasses the making of food and the 'adapting for sale' of any article or substance); a site for the research and development of products or processes; as storage or as a distribution centre; or the storage or treatment of water (*Ibid* Art.1).
[70] *Ibid* Art.4.

However, these categories are subject to more detailed specifications in some cases and subject to stipulations as to what the 'relevant quantity' is for particular substances. There are also exclusions for substances which are subject to other controls such as waste and radioactive waste and for fuel used exclusively for the production of heat or power, substances contained in certain pipe-lines, substances present on a site for 24 hours or less and substances which are vapour under normal conditions.[71]

Subject to transitional provisions, it will be a criminal offence to contravene protection zone control, subject to various defences including that the accused took all reasonable precautions and exercised all due diligence to avoid commission of the offence.[72] This offence is subject to the same penalties as are provided for in relation to the principal water pollution offences.[73]

Various procedural matters are provided for in the Water Protection Zone (River Dee Catchment) (Procedural and Other Provisions) Regulations 1999.[74] The Regulations provide for the procedure to be followed in relation to:

(a) applications to the Environment Agency for protection zone consent;

(b) consideration and determination of applications by the Agency;

(c) the reference of applications to, and the making of appeals to, the Secretary of State;

(d) continuation of protection zone consent and variation of protection zone consent conditions;

(e) the revocation of protection zone consents and the alteration and imposition of a conditions;

(f) a consents register; and

(g) charges in connection with applications for protection zone consent.

The designation of the River Dee Water Protection Zone is a significant development in providing the first use of area-specific and risk-based controls over polluting substances in order to protect the aquatic environment. The initial impact of the Zone is clearly only within the area of the catchment which has been designated, and it has been estimated that only 260 sites will actually be subject to the controls.[75] However, it should be kept in mind that the powers allowing water protection zones may be applied to further areas where storage of substances gives rise to a water pollution hazard. Depending upon the success of the first such designation, therefore, further designations of such areas may be anticipated.

---

[71] *Ibid* Art.2.

[72] *Ibid* Art.5.

[73] See 9.19.2 above on the penalties for the principal water pollution offences.

[74] SI 1999 No.916, made under s.96(1) Water Resources Act 1991.

[75] *ENDS Report* 290 (1999) p.11.

A general limitation upon the power to designate a water protection zone is that this power may not be used to designate an area in order to prevent the entry of nitrate into controlled waters as a result of anything done in connection with the agricultural use of land.[76] This is because the power to control agricultural land use in respect of nitrate contamination of controlled waters is separately provided for elsewhere under the Water Resources Act 1991.[77]

## 13.5 Nitrate Sensitive Areas and Nitrate Vulnerable Zones

The application of nitrate fertilisers to agricultural land has brought about considerable increases in agricultural productivity over recent decades. However, agriculture improvement has been achieved at significant cost to the quality of natural waters and water used for drinking water supply.[78] Whilst not generally the direct cause of significant pollution incidents, nitrate from fertiliser or manure passing into controlled waters with surface water run-off, or by gradual percolation through the ground, provides a classic example of a diffuse pollutant requiring an activity-specific preventive approach to water quality protection.[79] This is necessary because of the difficulties in dealing with nitrate contamination from farming activities under the principal water pollution offences:[80] first, because it is far from clear that contamination of controlled waters by nitrate amounts to 'pollution'[81] of those waters and, second, because such contamination is likely to have originated from many sources within the catchment of a watercourse and, perhaps, have been contributed over many years, so it will be far from clear to what extent any particular farmer will have 'caused or knowingly permitted'[82] an entry of nitrate to be made to the detriment of receiving waters.

Nonetheless, control over nitrate is necessary because of the problem of nitrate passing from agricultural land and resulting in the enrichment, or eutrophication, of natural waters[83] and the contamination of waters which are used as a source of drinking water supply. The latter has a strong public health dimension as indicated by World Health Organization

---

[76] s.93(3) Water Resources Act 1991.

[77] Under ss.94 and 95 Water Resources Act 1991, and Sch.12.

[78] For general reading on agricultural nitrate contamination see: Royal Commission on Environmental Pollution (1992) paras.7.130 to 7.134 and (1996) paras.5.42 to 5.55; Department of the Environment, *Nitrate in Water* (1986); House of Commons Environment Committee, *Pollution of Rivers and Estuaries* (1987) para.79, and (1988) para.3.18 to 3.24; House of Lords Select Committee on the European Communities, *Nitrate in Water* (1989); National Rivers Authority, *The Influence of Agriculture on the Quality of Natural Waters in England and Wales* (1992) Ch.7; MAFF, *Solving the Nitrate Problem: progress in research and development* (1993); Howarth (1992); Elworthy (1994); Elworthy and Holder (1996) and Hawke and Kovaleva (1998).

[79] See the discussion of eutrophication at 1.3.1 above.

[80] Under s.85 Water Resources Act 1991, and see 9.3 above.

[81] See 9.8 above on the meaning of 'pollution' in relation to the principal water pollution offences, though contrast the definition of 'pollution' incorporated in the Nitrates Directive (91/676/EEC) Art.2(j) and see 13.5.6 below on this.

[82] See 9.5–7 above on 'cause or knowingly permit'.

[83] See 1.3.1 above for a general discussion of the problem of eutrophication.

*European Standards for Drinking Water*[84] which first suggested that 100mg/l of nitrate should be considered as a safe limit and 50mg/l as a target to be sought, because of an association between levels of nitrates in drinking water and methaemoglobinaemia, or 'blue baby syndrome' and gastric cancer. These standards were influential in the quality parameters for drinking water established by the European Community Drinking Water Quality Directive[85] though some doubts have been expressed as to whether the limits provided for in the Directive are genuinely needed to safeguard health and the view has been put forward that the limits have created unnecessary anxiety in the minds of consumers and have diverted resources and attention from more deserving environmental objectives.[86]

Particular prominence was given to the need to address the problem of nitrate contamination of water which may be used as a source of supply by the decision of the European Court of Justice in *Commission* v *United Kingdom.*[87] In this ruling the United Kingdom was found guilty of failing to comply with the Drinking Water Quality Directive in respect of water supplied to 28 supply zones, supplying water to approximately one million water consumers which exceeded the parameter for nitrate concentration provided for under the Directive.

Because the greater part of nitrate contamination results from agricultural activity, the approach that is needed has to be focussed upon agricultural land use as a means of securing satisfactory water quality. Other mechanisms for the control of entry of nitrate into water, such as discharge consents, are not feasible. Essentially, this is the approach that has been adopted both within initial legislation, providing for the designation of nitrate sensitive areas, further national measures enacted in compliance with the EC Agri-environmental Regulation[88] and in subsequent provisions to implement the Community Nitrates Directive[89] allowing for the creation of nitrate vulnerable zones. Throughout this legislative progression, the continuing theme of controlling agricultural land use for the purpose of water quality improvement is well illustrated.

### 13.5.1 Nitrate Sensitive Areas

The initial, national, approach to the control of nitrate entering water was through the provision for the designation of 'nitrate sensitive areas'[90]

---

[84] Originally indicated by World Health Organization (1970) and (1971).

[85] Directive 80/778/EEC, and see 17.7.1 below on this. Although the Directive sets the respective parameters for drinking water at half the amounts originally suggested by the World Health Organization, though the World Health Organization revised the relevant levels for Europe in 1984 to 45mg/l and 15mg/l to take account of the significance of vegetables in the European diet (World Health Organization (1984)).

[86] Royal Commission on Environmental Pollution (1992) para.7127.

[87] Case C-337/89 [1993] Env LR 299 and see 4.15.1 above on this.

[88] Regulation EEC/2078/92 on agricultural methods compatible with the requirements of protection of the environment and the maintenance of the countryside, and see 13.5.3 below on this.

[89] Directive 91/676/EEC, and see 13.5.4 below on this.

[90] Generally see Elworthy (1994).

though, as will be seen, this has now been largely superseded by the designation of nitrate vulnerable zones.

Statutory powers for designation of nitrate sensitive areas were provided to enable the relevant Minister[91] to take action where appropriate to prevent or control the entry of nitrate into controlled waters as a result of, or of anything done in connection with, the use of any land for agricultural purposes. In these circumstances the Minister could make provision designating that land, together with any other land to which it is appropriate to apply the designation, as a nitrate sensitive area.[92] The specific matters provided for in an order designating a nitrate sensitive area allowed the order to require, prohibit or restrict the carrying on, either on or in relation to any agricultural land in the area, of specified activities; and provide for amounts to be paid to specified or determined persons in respect of the obligations imposed on those persons.[93] Further provisions allowed orders to confer various powers on Ministers:

(a) to determine the circumstances in which the carrying on of any activity is required, prohibited or restricted;

(b) to provide for any requirement to carry on an activity to be subject to Ministerial consent;

(c) to apply a prohibition or restriction in respect of any activities, subject to Ministerial consent; and

(d) to provide that contravention of a requirement, prohibition or restriction shall be a criminal offence subject to the same penalty as the principal water pollution offences.[94]

Where an area was designated as a nitrate sensitive area, the relevant Minister could enter into an agreement for payments to be made to the owner of the freehold interest in any agricultural land in the area or, with the permission of the freehold owner, with any other person having another interest in the land. The terms of such an agreement allowed, in consideration of payments being made by the Minister, that person to accept obligations with respect to the management of the land or other obligations imposed under the agreement. Where an agreement between the Minister and a person having an interest in the land concerned was entered into, the terms of the agreement would bind all persons deriving title from that person.[95]

Some general points concerning designation of nitrate sensitive areas may be noted. First, a contrast with water protection zones is evident in that, within nitrate sensitive areas, particular actions may be required to be

---

[91] The 'relevant Minister' for these purposes is the National Assembly for Wales in relation to an area which is wholly in Wales, and in relation to land which is wholly in England, or partly in England and partly in Wales, means the Minister of Agriculture, Fisheries and Food and the Secretary of State acting jointly (s.94(7) Water Resources Act 1991, and see discussion at 6.2 concerning Wales).

[92] s.94(1) and (2) Water Resources Act 1991.

[93] *Ibid* s.94(3).

[94] *Ibid* s.94(4) and see 9.3 above on the principal water pollution offences.

[95] *Ibid* s.95(1) to (3).

taken, as opposed to prohibitions or restrictions, thereby allowing for more extensive use of positive agricultural land management within the purposes for which the area has been designated. A second contrast with water protection zones is that greater flexibility exists in relation to nitrate sensitive areas, in that such areas may be of voluntary or mandatory status and designated with or without provision for compensatory payments to be made to farmers within the area. An area will be voluntary if there is no legal obligation for a farmer within the area to comply with relevant requirements, prohibitions or restrictions, or to enter into a management agreement, and mandatory where the requirements are formulated as binding legal obligations.

In relation to both voluntary and mandatory areas, management agreements are provided for to allow compensatory provision to be made to farmers entering into such agreements. The payment of compensation for adherence to practices which preclude environmental pollution is difficult to reconcile with the polluter pays principle,[96] but it has been maintained that compensation is actually being paid for actions which go beyond the prevention of pollution.[97] Nonetheless, it is evident that the need for a system which maximised participation by farmers was seen as a valuable feature in the initial introduction of measures to reduce nitrate contamination.

Finally, the kind of management agreement provided for in relation to nitrate sensitive areas had implications not only for a tenant farmer entering into an agreement but also for the freehold owner of the land,[98] assuming that permission for entry into the agreement has been given by the landlord, and any person subsequently acquiring an interest in the land. In important respects, therefore, this kind of management agreement has the character of an interest in land rather than a purely contractual arrangement.[99]

## 13.5.2 The Pilot Nitrate Scheme

The Ministerial powers allowing for the designation of nitrate sensitive areas, as previously provided for under the Water Act 1989,[100] were first exercised in the enactment of the Nitrate Sensitive Areas (Designation) Order 1990.[101] This Order identified ten areas in England, covering a total of about 15,000 hectares, where nitrate concentration in water sources exceeded, or was at risk of exceeding, the limit of 50 mg/l specified in the

---

[96] See 4.7.3 above on the polluter pays principle.

[97] See 13.5.3 below on 'compensation' for preventing pollution.

[98] See para.75 Sch.25 Water Act 1989, which amended the Part II Sch.3 Agricultural Holdings Act 1986 to require that in determining whether there has been a failure by a tenant farmer to adhere to rules of good husbandry, or breach of the terms of conditions of tenancy, compliance with an agreement in a nitrate sensitive area will not constitute a ground for such a finding.

[99] On management agreements generally see Rodgers (1992) p.139.

[100] s.112 Water Act 1989.

[101] SI 1990 No.1013, as amended by SI 1990 No.1187 and SI 1993 No.3198.

European Community Drinking Water Quality Directive.[102] The purpose of these designations was to encourage agricultural practices which would reduce the entry of nitrate into watercourses from agricultural land in order to ascertain the effects of changes in farming practice upon water quality. Essentially, the areas selected were intended to serve as pilot areas which would serve as a means of evaluating the effectiveness of limiting nitrate application to land as a means of improving water quality. The approach provided for in the Order was, therefore, voluntary rather than mandatory and made use of the facility for compensation to be paid under management agreements.[103]

Within the ten areas designated under the 1990 Order, farmers were allowed to enter into voluntary agreements with the Minister of Agriculture, Fisheries and Food, whereby compensation would be paid in return for the adoption of specified farming practices, which involved the application of reduced amounts of nitrate to agricultural land. In return, farmers were entitled to compensation payable in accordance with two distinct schemes of payment provided for under the Order, termed the 'basic' and 'premium' schemes. Payments under these schemes varied according to the different areas designated and the extent of the changes in farming practice to which the recipient of the payment agreed to adhere. In any case, however, management agreements were subject to conditions allowing termination of an agreement and the withholding or recovery of payments where a farmer failed, without reasonable excuse, to comply with the requirements of an agreement.

The Pilot Nitrate Sensitive Areas Scheme was intended as an experimental exercise to ascertain how changes in agricultural practice may affect water quality. Uptake of the scheme was good[104] and, in scientific terms, the initial measures proved to be a success in demonstrating considerable reductions in the amount of nitrate leaching from agricultural land in nine out of the ten pilot areas. Contrary to initial uncertainties as to the time that would be required for reduced applications of nitrate to land to be translated into reduced water concentrations, it was concluded that the Scheme:

> has demonstrated that it is possible to substantially reduce nitrate losses from agricultural land, and that significant reductions can result from changes which preserve the cropping and overall farming system. Cover cropping, avoidance of manure applications in autumn or at very high rates, and the conversion of arable land to low-intensity grassland have proved highly effective, but other measures including more precise adjustment of fertiliser use to crop requirements have played a part. The scientific and practical

---

[102] 80/778/EEC and see 17.7.1 below on this.

[103] Although a Ministerial statement emphasised that 'should these measures not prove effective, the 1989 Water Act provides for compulsory powers as a fallback' (MAFF, News Release 310/89 *Announcement of Candidate Areas for Pilot Nitrate Scheme* 31 July 1989).

[104] 80% of farmers within the areas entered the scheme (MAFF, *Proposals for the Continuation of the Original (Pilot) Nitrate Sensitive Areas* (1995)). Generally see Elworthy (1994).

information gained has contributed to the continued development of nitrate policy in England and Wales.[105]

### 13.5.3  Applying the Agri-environmental Regulation

Further provision concerning nitrate sensitive areas was made in conformity with the EC Regulation on agricultural methods compatible with the requirements of protection of the environment and the maintenance of the countryside,[106] the 'Agri-environmental Regulation'. This Regulation established an aid scheme, part-funded by the Community, normally at 50%, to promote the use of farming practices which reduce the polluting effects of agriculture and uses of agricultural land compatible with the protection and improvement of the environment. Specifically, the scheme allowed for aid to be provided to farmers who undertook substantially to reduce their use of fertilisers and to adopt farming practices compatible with the requirements of protecting the environment and natural resources. Member States were required to implement the scheme, in accordance with their specific needs but, within zonal programmes, to include aid for various matters including fertiliser reduction.

The Nitrate Sensitive Areas Regulations 1994,[107] were introduced to comply with the provisions of the Agri-environmental Regulation. The national Regulations, which apply only to England, designate further nitrate sensitive areas in addition to those originally provided for and allow the Minister of Agriculture, Fisheries and Food to grant aid to farmers in the areas at rates of payment defined under the Regulations. In relation to the 22 areas concerned, totalling about 40,000 hectares, three alternative schemes of aid are provided for: the basic scheme, the premium arable scheme, and the premium grass scheme.

To be eligible for a payment of aid under the Regulations, a farmer, with the consent of the landlord where relevant, in any of the nitrate sensitive areas must give undertakings to the Minister, in relation to the land concerned, for a period of five years. The Minister may make payments where certain 'qualifying conditions' are satisfied: the land concerned is eligible for aid; the farmer makes an application in a specified form; the farmer gives the Minister specified forms of undertaking; the Minister

---

[105] MAFF, *Pilot Nitrate Sensitive Areas Scheme: Report on the First 3 Years* (1993) p.9 and see [1994] *Water Law* 47.

[106] Regulation EEC/2078/92. See also Commission Regulation (EC) No.746/96 of 24 April 1996 laying down detailed rules for the application of Council Regulation (EEC) No 2078/92 which establishes detailed rules for the application of the Agri-environmental Regulation. Article 13 of the Commission Regulation, concerned with the transformation of undertakings, is given effect to nationally by the Nitrate Sensitive Areas (Amendment) (No.2) Regulations 1998 (SI 1998 No.2138). The Agri-environment Regulation has been replaced, as from 1 January 2000, by Chapter VI of the EC Rural Development Regulation (1257/99/EC) under the recent Agenda 2000 settlement. Generally see Hawke and Kovaleva (1998) Ch.5.

[107] SI 1994 No.1729, as amended by SI 1996 No.3105, SI 1998 No.79 and SI 1998 No.2138.

accepts the application; and the farmer submits a claim for aid in an approved form.

The undertakings to be provided by the farmer are that, for a period of five consecutive years commencing on 1 October in the year in which the application is made, certain general requirements will be adhered to. These are that, in any period of 12 months, no application of organic nitrogen fertiliser will be applied in excess of the quantity which would result in the application to the land of 250kg of nitrogen per hectare. Additionally, no organic nitrogen fertiliser will be applied within 50 metres of a spring, well or borehole that supplies water for human consumption or for use in a dairy, or within 10 metres of any watercourse. In addition to these general requirements, further requirements apply depending upon whether the application is made under the basic, premium arable or premium grassland schemes.[108]

Where an application for aid is accepted, the farmer must allow specified persons to take action to monitor compliance with the undertaking or to assess the effectiveness of the undertaking in preventing the entry of nitrate into controlled waters. Specifically, the farmer must permit the Minister, or persons acting on his behalf, accompanied by any persons assisting in monitoring compliance, to enter the land at all reasonable times. These persons are entitled to enter upon the land, take samples from the land, install equipment on the land and examine all records which may be kept in compliance with the undertakings. The farmer concerned is bound to render all reasonable assistance to persons exercising these powers, to produce documents or records for inspection and accompany these persons in making an inspection or identification of the land concerned.[109] Provision is also made for various kinds of misconduct in relation to undertakings entered into under the Regulations allowing the Minster may withhold the whole, or any part, of any aid payable and to recover aid already paid.[110] In addition, a criminal offence arises where any person, for the purposes of obtaining aid under the Regulations, knowingly or recklessly makes a statement which is false in a material particular.[111]

The present situation is that there are 32 designated nitrate sensitive areas in existence, comprising the initial 10 pilot areas and the subsequent 22 areas provided for under the 1994 Regulations, with about 70% of the total area subject to management agreements.[112] The 32 areas are predominantly arable in nature, and are located in various parts of England to represent the catchments of selected groundwater sources of water for public supply. The nitrate sensitive area scheme was closed to new applications in July

---

[108] Reg.7 Nitrate Sensitive Areas Regulations 1994.
[109] *Ibid* Reg.9.
[110] *Ibid* Reg.15.
[111] *Ibid* Reg.16.
[112] MAFF, News Release 19/98, *More Money for Making Meadows: Morley*, 22 January 1998.

1998,[113] but given the five year duration of the agreements entered into, obligations under the scheme will continue until 2003.

Ultimately, the success of the scheme will be assessed according to the reduction of nitrate concentrations in receiving waters, however, it will take some years before the effects of land-use changes in nitrate sensitive areas are reflected in average concentrations of nitrates at groundwater abstraction points because of the time taken for water to reach and mix with the groundwater reserve. Nonetheless, the initial monitoring results demonstrate that the measures are reducing nitrate leaching from the designated areas. In particular, the premium scheme options have proved to be extremely effective in reducing nitrate leaching losses to very low levels, and cover crops (which are required on basic scheme land which would otherwise have been bare over the vulnerable autumn/winter period) are proving effective at mopping-up residual nitrate in the soil before it can be leached into water supplies.[114]

By way of general comment, the payment of compensation or aid to farmers in nitrate sensitive areas raises a significant issue with regard to its compatibility with the polluter pays principle.[115] The payment of money to persons to prevent environmental damage of a kind which should not have been caused in the first place is clearly not compatible with the polluter pays principle, since it amounts to paying polluters not to pollute. On the other hand, the payment of money to secure environmental improvements which go beyond preventing pollution should not be inconsistent with the principle. The key question in relation to compensation under the nitrate sensitive areas scheme is whether the payments are made to 'prevent pollution' or to secure 'environmental improvement'. On this, the view of the previous Government was that 'compensation has been given in nitrate sensitive areas but this is to pay farmers to take voluntary measures which go substantially beyond good agricultural practice: e.g. to change from intensive cropping to extensive grassland'.[116] Nonetheless, the boundary between those matters which are legitimately compensated for and those which are not is a fine one.

---

[113] See MAFF, *Code of Good Practice for the Protection of Water* (1998) para.28s.

[114] House of Commons Agriculture Committee, *Environmentally Sensitive Areas and Other Schemes under the Agri-Environment Regulation* (1997), Memorandum by MAFF at p.20.

[115] See 4.7.3 above on the polluter pays principle.

[116] MAFF, DoE and WO, *Government Response to the Consultation on the Designation of Nitrate Vulnerable Zones in England and Wales* (1995) para.2.11. Alternatively, it has been suggested that the impossibility of attributing environmental benefits to the action of any individual farmer is a main reason why the polluter pays principle could not be applied to nitrate leaching prevention measures under the nitrate sensitive areas scheme (House of Commons Agriculture Committee (1997) para.46).

## 13.5.4  Implementing the Nitrates Directive

The EC Nitrates Directive[117] imposes a central requirement upon all Member States to designate all zones vulnerable to pollution from nitrate compounds according to specified criteria, and to take specified action against further nitrate contamination. Significantly, the requirement under the Directive that certain measures to reduce nitrate contamination must be of a mandatory character has meant that specific restrictions or prohibitions are needed to implement the Directive, and the voluntary scheme provided for in relation to nitrate sensitive areas is, therefore, not sufficient to meet the requirements of the Directive.

Provisions were needed to transpose into national law the provisions of the Nitrates Directive, and accordingly, the Protection of Water Against Agricultural Nitrate Pollution (England and Wales) Regulations 1996[118] have been enacted. These Regulations designate 68 nitrate vulnerable zones, covering about 600,000 hectares and including all the 32 designated nitrate sensitive areas, which are subject to mandatory action programmes with the objectives of reducing water pollution caused or induced by nitrate from agricultural sources and preventing further such pollution. Hence, within these zones, good agricultural practices[119] are mandatorily required.[120] In addition to compliance with good agricultural practices, a detailed list of further requirements is set out in Schedule 4 to the Regulations to give effect to the Directive. These include matters such as the periods when the application of certain kinds of fertiliser is prohibited; the capacity of storage facilities; limitations upon the application of fertiliser; and limitations upon the amount of livestock manure applied to land each year.[121] Following the designation of nitrate vulnerable zones by the Minister, in accordance with criteria corresponding to those in the Directive,[122] obligations are imposed upon the Environment Agency to monitor the quantity of nitrate in surface and groundwaters and to review the eutrophic state of waters.[123]

---

[117] 91/676/EEC and see 13.5.4 below and 5.6.3 above on this. Generally see Elworthy and Holder (1996).

[118] SI 1996 No.888.

[119] In accordance with MAFF, Code of Good Agricultural Practice for the Protection of Water (1998) and see 13.5.7 below on this.

[120] Originally provided in Reg.5 1996 Regulations, but subsequently replaced by Reg.9 SI 1998 No.1202.

[121] The overall purpose of the provisions is to ensure that for each farm or livestock unit, the amount of livestock manure applied to the land annually, including by the animals directly, is not to exceed 170 kg N per hectare, though this amount may be varied during the first four years of an action programme and otherwise where this will not prejudice the achievement of the objectives of an action programme (para.2 Sch.4 1996 Regulations).

[122] Reg.3 and Sch.2 1996 Regulations, and see Annex I Nitrates Directive (91/676/EEC).

[123] Reg.4 1996 Regulations.

*13.5.4A  Action programmes*

The obligation under the Nitrates Directive to establish action programmes in nitrate vulnerable zones[124] is implemented by an obligation being placed on the Minister to establish such programmes as soon as practicable after the establishment of the initial zones and within one year after the subsequent designation of any further zones. The Minister is also responsible for the formulation and implementation of monitoring programmes and the review and revision of such programmes.[125] In determining the provisions of an action programme, the Minister must take into account the available scientific and technical data with respect to nitrogen contributions originating from agricultural and other sources, the environmental conditions in the relevant region, and the effectiveness and cost of additional provisions relative to other possible preventive provisions.[126]

Following the designation of an area of land as a nitrate vulnerable zone, the Farm Waste Grant (Nitrate Vulnerable Zones) (England and Wales) Scheme 1996[127] provides for the making of grants in respect of agricultural businesses which are at least partly situated in such zones in relation to facilities for the handling, storage and disposal of certain farm wastes and the separation of clean and dirty water. Hence, the Minister is empowered to give a grant of up to 25% of the expenditure incurred, up to a maximum of £85,000, where this is incurred for the purposes of an agricultural business for specified purposes including the provision, replacement or improvement of facilities for the handling and storage of manure, slurry and silage effluent. However, such grants will only be made where the Minister is satisfied that the expenditure will result in at least some environmental benefit accruing to the nitrate vulnerable zone concerned.

Further provision for mandatory requirements in relation to action programmes in nitrate vulnerable zones is made by the Action Programme for Nitrate Vulnerable Zones (England and Wales) Regulations 1998.[128] These Regulations require the occupier of any farm, or part of a farm, which is within a nitrate vulnerable zone to ensure that the action programme is implemented in relation to any land comprised in the farm and within the zone.[129] Where this requirement has been contravened, or there has been a contravention which is likely to continue or be repeated, the Environment Agency may serve a notice requiring the contravention to be remedied. A notice of this kind will require the person upon whom it is served to carry out such works, or take precautions or other steps, as the Agency requires, and specify the period within which the requirements must be complied with.[130]

---

[124] Under Art.5 Nitrates Directive.

[125] Reg.6 1996 Regulations.

[126] Reg.7 1996 Regulations.

[127] SI 1996 No.908.

[128] SI 1998 No.1202, implementing Art.5 Nitrates Directive.

[129] Reg.3 1998 Regulations.

[130] Reg.4 1998 Regulations. Provision for appeals against such notices is made in Reg.5.

## 13.5.4B  Access and restrictions

Special provision is made for access to farms in nitrate vulnerable zones for monitoring purposes, so that a farmer within a zone is bound to permit Agency personnel access at all reasonable times where this is necessary to monitor implementation of an action programme or to assess its effectiveness. Specific provision for access is made in relation to the entry upon land, the taking of samples, the installation or maintenance of equipment, and the examination of records. Where access is made for these purposes, the farmer must provide all reasonable assistance, produce documents for inspection and, where requested and reasonable, accompany the person undertaking the inspection.[131] Criminal offences are provided for in relation to the failure to comply with the access provisions, the failure to implement an action programme requirement within the farm and the failure to comply with a notice requiring a contravention of an action programme requirement to be remedied.[132]

More specific details as to the practical requirements under the action programme are set out in the Schedule to the 1998 Regulations. This requires account to be taken of local environmental factors in the application of any nitrogen fertiliser; including soil conditions, type, and slope; climatic conditions, rainfall and irrigation; and land use and agricultural practice. Chemical fertiliser must, generally, not be applied between specified dates and is not to be applied where it is likely that it will directly enter surface water. Nitrogen fertiliser is not to be applied in excess of the crop requirement, and where it is applied to land it must be applied in as accurate and uniform a manner as is practicably possible, and must not be applied if the soil is waterlogged, the land is flooded, the soil has been recently frozen or the land is covered with snow. Organic manure is not to be applied to land where the application would result in specified quantities of total nitrogen being exceeded and is not to be applied to any land less than 10 metres from surface water, or during certain times of the year upon land which has a sandy or shallow soil. The capacity of storage vessels for livestock manure on farms is to meet that required to store manure produced throughout the longest period during which land application of manure is prohibited unless it can be demonstrated that it will be disposed of in a manner which will not cause harm to the environment. Finally, records are required to be made of the quantities of chemical fertiliser, its nitrogen content and time of application; the quantity of organic manure, its nature and the time of application; the type of any crop grown and the date it was sown; the numbers and description of livestock kept on the farm; and the quantity of each type of livestock manure moved off the farm and consignment details. These records must be retained for a period of five years after the latest event recorded.[133]

---

[131] Reg.6 1998 Regulations.
[132] Reg.8 1998 Regulations.
[133] Schedule 1998 Regulations.

## 13.5.4C Contrasts with Nitrate Sensitive Areas

By contrast with the nitrate sensitive areas scheme, it is significant that no payment of compensation will be made where a farm is included within a nitrate vulnerable zone despite the imposition of the more onerous obligations upon farmers within the zone as compared with farmers outside nitrate vulnerable zones. As has been previously noted, the question of compensation for environmentally beneficial activities raises weighty issues with regard to compatibility with the polluter pays principle.[134] In relation to the designation of nitrate vulnerable zones, farmers expressed concern that their farming businesses would be seriously affected by the measures imposed and requested that compensation should be paid because of this. However, the Government response to these claims was that the measures to be imposed,

> are based on good agricultural practice. If farmers have to modify their farming in order to adopt them it is almost certainly the case that they were contributing to current or future heightened nitrate levels in their catchment. Consequently, because the Government upholds the Polluter Pays Principle the question of compensation does not arise.[135]

## 13.5.5 Designating Nitrate Vulnerable Zones

Whilst the Protection of Water Against Agricultural Nitrate Pollution (England and Wales) Regulations 1996 transpose the requirements of the Nitrates Directive into national law by designating 68 nitrate vulnerable zones, the methodology applied in determining the areas to be subject to these designations justifies discussion. Significantly, the Governments of Denmark, the Netherlands, Germany and Austria chose to identify the whole of their territories as nitrate vulnerable zones, whereas the United Kingdom opted to apply the mandatory requirements of the Directive only within designated areas.[136]

The reasoning behind this was that it was considered that a blanket approach, involving the imposition of controls upon the activities of farmers who are not contributing to the problem, was not necessary and it would be more appropriate to target only those areas contributing to nitrate pollution of surface or ground waters.[137] Having resolved that the entire

---

[134] See 4.7.3 above on the polluter pays principle.

[135] MAFF, DoE and WO, *Government Response to the Consultation on the Designation of Nitrate Vulnerable Zones in England and Wales* (1995) para.2.11.

[136] Art.3(2) Nitrates Directive requires Member States to designate as vulnerable zones areas in their territory which drain into waters affected by nitrate pollution and which contribute to that pollution, but Art.3(5) exempts Member States from this obligation if they establish action programmes (under Art.5) throughout their national territory. See 5.6.3 above for further discussion.

[137] MAFF, DoE and WO, *Government Response to the Consultation on the Designation of Nitrate Vulnerable Zones in England and Wales* (1995) p.13, and see Hawke and Kovaleva (1998) p.155. It has been noted, however, that designation of the whole of the national territory as a nitrate sensitive zone does not exempt a Member State from the obligation to determine the extent of

area of the UK was not to be subject to the mandatory requirements applicable to nitrate vulnerable zones, the determination as to which areas these requirements were to be applied to was the subject of extensive consultation[138] and controversy both in relation to the general methodology employed and the application of it to particular locations.

Broadly, the approach applied in determining the boundaries of nitrate vulnerable zones was to analyse data for 1992 for water sampling points used for the Drinking Water Abstraction Directive.[139] Where this showed exceedance of the 50 mg/l limit for nitrate, an upper limit on a watercourse was identified as the first upstream sampling point where 95% compliance with the parameter was shown on the basis of the previous five years' data. A lower limit was identified as the downstream abstraction point at which the 50 mg/l parameter was exceeded. Having determined the upper and lower limits, the nitrate vulnerable zone was identified as all the natural catchment land draining into this water. Where non-natural drainage facilities existed, these were taken into account in defining the land draining to the abstraction point. In relation to groundwater supplies, all boreholes, wells and springs used for public drinking water supply were examined to ascertain whether the 50 mg/l limit was being exceeded, or likely to be exceeded within a specified time. For each groundwater supply where this was found, the groundwater source catchment was identified as the area within which all water flowed to the point of abstraction, with the catchment being defined by all relevant hydrogeological factors. When an area was identified according to these criteria, and it was confirmed that agriculture was the principal factor determining nitrate levels in the water, it was identified as a nitrate vulnerable zone. In each instance, some concession to practicability was allowed for, in that the final boundaries of the nitrate vulnerable zone were based on 'hard features' on the ground, such as roads and field boundaries, providing that such adjustment did not affect the environmental impact of the designation.[140]

In practical terms it might have been more straightforward to have identified individual farm or field areas as the boundaries within which

---

nitrate pollution within its territory (Case C-293/97 *R v Secretary of State for the Environment, Minister of Agriculture, Fisheries and Food, ex parte Standley and others, Metson and others and National Farmers Union (Intervener)* [1999] Env LR 801 para.27).

[138] Consultation documents on the methodology for identifying sensitive areas (Urban Waste Water Treatment Directive) and methodology for designating vulnerable zones (Nitrates Directive) were issued by the MAFF, DoE and WO in March 1992 and March 1993. These were followed by the consultation document *Designation of Vulnerable Zones in England and Wales under the EC Nitrate Directive* (91/676) (May 1994); the *Government Response to the Consultation on the Designation of Nitrate Vulnerable Zones in England and Wales* (May 1995); the *Report of the Independent Review Panel of Nitrate Vulnerable Zones 1995* (October 1995); the consultation document *EC Nitrate Directive (91/676): Proposed Measures to Apply in Nitrate Vulnerable Zones and Draft Regulations Transposing the Directive in England and Wales* (November 1995); and the *Explanation of the Final Decision on Nitrate Vulnerable Zone Designations* (March 1996).

[139] Directive 75/440/EEC and see 17.6 below on this.

[140] MAFF, DoE and WO, *Designation of Vulnerable Zones in England and Wales under the EC Nitrate Directive* (91/676) (1994) paras.3.4-3.5, 3.8-3.10 and 3.13.

controls should be imposed. However, this option was rejected in favour of water catchments, or parts of catchments, for the reason that the identification of sources as fields or farms was not thought feasible given the diffuse nature of the pollutant and the timescale during which it might be present. Similarly, designation on the basis of farm or soil type were rejected for the reasons that farming activities may change over time and that a particular soil type does not prevent nitrate loss, though there may be greater run-off to surface waters on heavy soil and greater percolation into groundwater in light soil. In relation to hydrological factors, the areas to be targeted were thought to be those where nitrate concentrations, in either surface water used for drinking water supply or groundwater, justified mandatory measures. However, there was no ground for designating areas on the basis of eutrophication, since no relevant waters had been identified as eutrophic due to nitrate,[141] and eutrophication due to phosphate, which had been identified in certain waters, was otherwise provided for by the designation of areas under the Urban Waste Water Directive.[142]

An Independent Review Panel was established in 1995 with terms of reference which required it to examine submissions about whether the Government's policy on designating nitrate vulnerable zones had been reasonably and justly executed. The principal role for the Panel was to resolve issues arising from disagreements over the original hydrological boundaries of catchments or subsequent revisions proposed to these, and to assess whether the Government's methodology had been correctly and consistently applied in drawing up the zone boundaries. The Panel made a number of recommendations on both issues of principle and specific zone boundaries,[143] which the Government endorsed in the final decision on designations by excluding two previously proposed areas and making changes to the boundaries of seven proposed zones.[144]

Despite the extensive deliberations which preceded the eventual designation of the initial 68 nitrate vulnerable zones, controversy continued on some issues. In particular, almost all the objections to proposed designations received by the Independent Review Panel relied, to some extent, on the existence of non-agricultural sources of nitrate pollution affecting the areas concerned. These non-agricultural sources included sewage effluent, leakage from sewers and septic tanks, landfill sites, urea used as a de-icer on airfield runways and atmospheric

---

[141] *Ibid* para.3.12. 'Pollution', for the purposes of the Nitrates Directive, is defined exclusively in terms of nitrate pollution: 'the discharge, directly or indirectly, of nitrogen compounds from agricultural sources into the aquatic environment, the results of which are such as to cause hazards to human health, harm to living resources and to aquatic ecosystems, damage to amenities or interference with other legitimate uses of water' (Art.2(j) Nitrates Directive (91/676/EEC).

[142] MAFF, DoE and WO, *Government Response to the Consultation on the Designation of Nitrate Vulnerable Zones in England and Wales* (1995) Section 2. See 5.6.2 above on the Urban Waste Water Treatment Directive.

[143] MAFF, DoE and WO, *Report of the Independent Review Panel of Nitrate Vulnerable Zones 1995* (1995).

[144] MAFF, DoE and WO, *Explanation of the Final Decision on Nitrate Vulnerable Zone Designations* (1996).

deposition of nitrogen.[145] As a matter of principle, objectors claimed that it was improper to designate any area as a nitrate vulnerable zone unless it was affirmatively proved that the waters would fail the 50 mg/l of nitrate test even if all the non-agricultural sources of nitrate were discounted.

The treatment of non-agricultural nitrate sources raises important issues about the burden and standard of proof to be applied. On this, the Independent Review Panel noted a lack of clarity and consistency in the Government's approach, and thought that the matter was better dealt with by reverting back to the wording of the Nitrates Directive. This made it clear that the waters concerned 'could be' affected by nitrate pollution if action programmes were not implemented,[146] and from this the Panel concluded that designation did not require it to be conclusively proved that the waters would fail to meet the 50 mg/l test even if all the non-agricultural sources of nitrate were excluded. To require conclusive proof would be contrary to the spirit and purpose of the Directive[147] and would place an impossible practical burden upon Member States to identify and assess the precise impacts of non-agricultural sources.[148]

### 13.5.6 The Standley Litigation

Despite the establishment of the Independent Review Panel, the dispute about the methodology for dealing with non-agricultural nitrate sources continued in the courts. In *R v Secretary of State for the Environment and the Ministry of Agriculture, Fisheries and Food, ex parte Standley and Others and Metson and Others*[149] two farmers, in different nitrate vulnerable zones, supported by the National Farmers Union, contested the validity of the three-stage approach which had been used in the designation of nitrate vulnerable zones. This involved, first, identifying the waters to which the Directive applied, second, identifying the land comprising the nitrate vulnerable zones which drained into those waters and, third, the assessing whether agriculture was a significant source of nitrate pollution in the identified zones. The applicants claimed that the correct approach was, first, to consider the sources of nitrate pollution and, second, to identify only those waters where the nitrate limit was exceeded by virtue of agricultural inputs alone.

Essentially, therefore, the challenge was that the approach which had been adopted failed to take sufficient account of non-agricultural sources of nitrate in zone designation. It was contended that this failure was contrary

---

[145] MAFF, DoE and WO, *Report of the Independent Review Panel of Nitrate Vulnerable Zones 1995* (1995) para.5.11.

[146] Art.3(1) and Annex I A(1) Nitrates Directive.

[147] The preamble to the Nitrates Directive indicates that it is necessary to protect human health and living resources and aquatic ecosystems and to safeguard other legitimate uses of water, to reduce water pollution caused or induced by nitrates from agricultural sources and to prevent further such pollution.

[148] MAFF, DoE and WO, *Report of the Independent Review Panel of Nitrate Vulnerable Zones 1995* (1995) paras.5.13 to 5.15.

[149] [1997] Env LR 589, and see Elworthy (1998) and (1999).

to Community law principles of legitimate expectation, proportionality and the protection of fundamental property rights. In the alternative, the applicants argued that if they were wrong about the correct approach towards non-agricultural nitrate sources in designating zones, then it was the Nitrates Directive itself that should be the subject of the challenge on the basis that it was unlawful by contravening the polluter pays principle[150] and the proportionality principle.[151]

After a referral by the Queen's Bench Divisional Court,[152] the matter was considered by the European Court[153] in relation to two key questions. First, does the Nitrates Directive require Member States to designate as nitrate vulnerable zones all areas of land which drain into waters affected by nitrate pollution which contribute to pollution

(i)   where those waters contain a concentration of nitrates in excess of 50 mg/l and the Member State is satisfied that the discharge of nitrogen compounds from agricultural sources makes a 'significant contribution' to the overall concentration of nitrates; or

(ii)  only where the discharge of nitrogen compounds from agricultural sources itself accounts for a concentration of 50 mg/l (excluding contributions from other sources); or

(iii) on some other basis and, if so, what basis?

Second, if the first question is answered otherwise than in sense (ii), is the Nitrates Directive invalid in its application to surface freshwaters on the grounds that it infringes the polluter pays principle, and/or the principle of proportionality and/or the fundamental property rights of those owning and/or farming land designated as nitrate vulnerable zones?

On the methodological issue, the Court noted the general obligation upon Member States to identify waters affected by pollution under the Directive,[154] and the criteria to be applied in relation to this,[155] particularly in relation to surface waters used or intended for the abstraction of drinking waters, and noted that waters must be identified when they contain or could contain more than the specified concentration of nitrates if action[156] pursuant to the Directive is not taken. The Court noted that the concept of 'significant contribution' of agricultural nitrates was imprecise, and did not appear in the Directive. This raised concerns of legal certainty and practical difficulties in particular situations in relation to the difficulty

---

[150] See 4.7.3 above on the polluter pays principle.

[151] See 4.4.3 above on the proportionality principle.

[152] Under Art.234 (ex Art.177) of the European Community Treaty. Notably this was the first reference from the high Court on an environmental case. See 4.13.1 above on Art.234 references generally.

[153] Case C-293/97, *R v Secretary of State for the Environment, Minister of Agriculture, Fisheries and Food, ex parte Standley and others, Metson and others and National Farmers Union (Intervener)* [1999] Env LR 801.

[154] Under Art.3(1) Nitrates Directive.

[155] *Ibid* Annex I.

[156] *Ibid* Art.5.

in measuring the respective contributions of nitrate from different sources with a sufficient degree of accuracy. Nonetheless, the Court held that it was not necessary for a Member State to determine precisely what proportion of nitrates were of agricultural origin or whether the cause of pollution was exclusively agricultural.

It was concluded that it would be incompatible with the Directive to restrict the identification of waters affected by pollution to situations where agricultural sources alone gave rise to this since the Directive expressly provides that, in establishing action programmes,[157] the respective nitrogen contributions originating from agricultural and other sources are to be taken into account. Accordingly, the Directive could apply where the discharge of nitrate of agricultural origin makes only a significant but not an exclusive contribution. Community law could not provide precise criteria for establishing where, in each case, the contribution made by agricultural nitrate was 'significant', and it was within the discretion allowed to Member States to determine this matter.

On the second question, as to the validity of the Directive, the Court noted the contention of the applicants that the establishment of action programmes would give rise to disproportionate obligations on the part of farmers as opposed to the producers of other industrial sources of nitrate who would escape a financial burden. Nonetheless, the Court concluded that the principle of proportionality was respected by virtue of the mechanisms for flexible application in the Directive, which require account to be taken of available scientific and technical data,[158] the characteristics of the zone concerned,[159] changes in circumstances demonstrated by monitoring programmes,[160] and conditions within different regions of the community as required under codes of good agricultural practice.[161] Whilst it is for national courts to ensure that the principle of proportionality is applied in practice, the Directive contains sufficient flexibility to enable to the principle to be adhered to.

In relation to compatibility with the polluter pays principle, the Court's interpretation of the Directive was that it did not require farmers to take on the burden of eliminating pollution to which they have not contributed. Account is to be taken of other sources of nitrate when implementing the Directive and, having regard to the circumstances, farmers are not to be subject to costs of eliminating pollution which are unnecessary. Similarly in relation to the principle that environmental damage should be prevented at source,[162] the Directive does not contravene this because it does not require the reduction of agricultural nitrates unnecessarily.

---

[157] Art.5 Nitrates Directive.
[158] *Ibid* Art.5(3).
[159] *Ibid* para.1(3) and para.2(b) Annex III.
[160] *Ibid* Art.5(7).
[161] *Ibid* para.A Annex II.
[162] See 4.7.2 above on the preventive principle.

In respect of the applicants' argument that the Directive represented an infringement of their right to property, the Court reaffirmed its previously asserted view that the right to property is not an absolute right and must be viewed in relation to its social function.[163] Because of this, the exercise of property rights may be restricted for reasons of general interest pursued by the Community and do not constitute a disproportionate and intolerable interference which impairs the substance of the property right guaranteed. Whilst it was accepted that the action programmes provided for under the Directive did restrict the freedom of farmers to spread fertiliser and livestock manure on their land in some circumstances, these restrictions were imposed in pursuance of the general objective of protecting public health and without the substance of the farmers' property rights being impaired. Accordingly, the Directive did not offend against the principle of proportionality in imposing the restrictions that were at issue.

Hence, the overall conclusion reached by the Court was that the approach adopted by the United Kingdom Government towards designation of nitrate vulnerable zones had, in principle, been correct and that the challenges to the validity of the Directive were not well-founded. Presumably, it would be open to the farmers to resurrect the dispute by maintaining that the Community requirements had not been faithfully applied in national law and administrative practice, but it would be a challenging task to show that in any of the nitrate vulnerable zones that were at issue the non-agricultural contribution of nitrates was so great that the agricultural input did not constitute a 'significant contribution'.[164]

### 13.5.7 The Code of Good Agricultural Practice

Various references to 'codes of good agricultural practice' have been made in the discussion of the implementation of the Nitrates Directive and elsewhere. It is convenient to consider here the general background to the code and its present status.

The concept of 'good agricultural practice' and the legal purpose of a Code concerning this has undergone profound changes over the years. Under the Control of Pollution Act 1974 an explicit exception existed to the offence of causing or knowingly permitting pollution[165] where the entry in question was attributable to an act or omission which is in accordance with 'good agricultural practice'.[166] However, the defence relating to good

---

[163] In support of this were cited Case 44/79 *Hauer* v *Land Rheinland-Pfalz* [1979] ECR 3727 para.23, Case 265/87 *Schrader* v *Hauptzollamt Gronau* [1989] ECR 2237 para.15 and Case C-280/93 *Germany* v *Council* [1994] ECR I-4973 para.78.

[164] Postscript: however, in a subsequent case determined by the European Court of Justice (Case C-69/99, *Commission* v *United Kingdom*, unreported, 7 December 2000) it was conceded that the United Kingdom had failed to identify relevant surface freshwaters and groundwaters, where these were *not* intended for human consumption, and had failed to designate vulnerable zones throughout its territory within the time period allowed (contrary to Art.3(1)-(2) Nitrates Directive) and had failed to establish action programmes within the period allowed (contrary to Art.5).

[165] s.31(1) Control of Pollution Act 1974.

[166] *Ibid* s.31(2)(c).

agricultural practice could be curtailed by a notice served by the Secretary of State indicating the request of the water authority for the area concerned with a copy of the application served on the Minister of Agriculture, Fisheries and Food.[167] This procedure was allowed for where a water authority judged that any relevant waters had been, or were likely to be, polluted in consequence of an act or omission which was in accordance with good agricultural practice, or were likely to be polluted if such an act or omission occurred. The effect of serving such a notice was that an act or omission which previously came within the defence of good agricultural practice ceased to do so.

Despite the provision for the curtailment, the good agricultural practice defence was subject to serious criticism, amongst others, by the House of Commons Environment Committee in a 1987 Report.[168] Whilst recognising that the concept of the Code was a good one, the Committee thought that its operation in practice did not withstand close scrutiny and failure to observe it was widespread.[169] Moreover the Committee was unable to conceive of any circumstances where pollution of a stream by a farmer could justifiably be excused on the grounds that 'it accorded with good agricultural practice', since the two were mutually exclusive. In conclusion, it was thought that, in view of the increasing numbers of farm pollution incidents, the special defence provided to farmers under the Code should be repealed and the Code replaced by a new form of code having statutory force. The envisaged effect of this was that it would become an offence for a farmer to fail to follow the proposed new form of code regardless of whether or not the default gave rise to any water pollution incident.

Although the proposals of the Environment Committee were not followed in all respects, the status of the code of good agricultural practice was substantially changed by the Water Act 1989 and the provisions re-enacted into the Water Resources Act 1991. These now provide that, after consulting the Environment Agency, the Ministers[170] may approve any code of practice issued for the purpose of giving practical guidance to persons engaged in agriculture with respect to activities that may affect controlled waters and promoting desirable practices by such persons for avoiding or minimising the pollution of such waters.[171] In accordance with this procedure, the Ministers have, most recently, approved the *Code of*

---

[167] *Ibid* s.51.

[168] House of Commons Environment Committee, *Pollution of Rivers and Estuaries* (1987) para.63 to 78, and see House of Commons Environment Committee *Pollution of Rivers and Estuaries: Observations by the Government* (1988) Part III Section 1.

[169] Although it appeared, from evidence supplied to the Committee by the Ministry of Agriculture, Fisheries and Food, that there was no known case were a farmer had successfully pleaded the defence in legal proceedings and only one case where a farmer had even attempted to plead the defence (House of Commons Environment Committee, *Pollution of Rivers and Estuaries* (1987) para.64).

[170] The Minister of Agriculture, Fisheries and Food and the National Assembly for Wales.

[171] s.97(1) and (3) Water Resources Act 1991.

*Good Agricultural Practice for the Protection of Water*, alternatively titled *The Water Code Revised 1998*.[172]

A contravention of the *Code of Good Agricultural Practice* does not of itself lead to any criminal or civil liability,[173] but the Environment Agency is bound to take into account where there has been or is likely to be any such contravention in determining how it should exercise certain powers. Specifically, the Agency must take into account contravention of the code in determining how to exercise its power to impose a prohibition notice[174] and how to exercise any powers conferred by precautionary regulations.[175]

Beyond the national statutory status of the *Code*, under the Nitrates Directive Member States are required to establish a code of practice which will generally operate on a voluntary basis as a means for providing all waters with a general level of protection against nitrate pollution.[176] By way of fulfilling this Community obligation, the *Code* specifically incorporates a range of guidance relating to the avoidance of nitrate pollution.[177] Although it is to be noted that this guidance is of general voluntary application, it is applicable *in addition to* any mandatory measures that are required in designated nitrate vulnerable zones.

## 13.6 Groundwater Protection

As previously explained,[178] the principal offences relating to the pollution of controlled waters apply to situations where an entry or discharge of polluting matter takes place into groundwaters. Groundwater contamination has particularly serious environmental consequences in that such waters have limited capacity to assimilate or disperse contaminants.[179] Particularly where groundwater is intended to be used for

---

[172] Approved by the Water (Prevention of Pollution) (Code of Practice) Order 1998 (SI 1998 No.3084) and revoking the Water (Prevention of Pollution) (Code of Practice) Order 1991 (SI 1991 No.2285). Other codes relating to agriculture and the environment are the *Code of Good Agricultural Practice for the Protection of Air* (1998); and *Code of Good Agricultural Practice for the Protection of Soil* (1998) (all MAFF); and *Pesticides: Code of Practice for the Safe Use of Pesticides on Farms and Holdings* (1998) MAFF and Health and Safety Commission.

[173] However, adherence to agricultural practice has been held to be relevant in determining whether harm is of a kind which is foreseeable in civil proceedings, see *Savage & Another* v *Fairclough & Others* [2000] Env LR 183 discussed at 3.10.5 above.

[174] Prohibition notices are provided for under s.86(1) Water Resources Act 1991, and see 9.11 above on this.

[175] s.97(2) Water Resources Act 1991. Precautionary regulations are provided for under s.92 Water Resources Act 1991, but the only such regulations presently enacted are the Control of Pollution (Silage, Slurry and Agricultural Fuel Oil) Regulations 1991 (SI 1991 No.324, as amended) see 13.3.1 above.

[176] Annex II Nitrates Directive and see 5.6.3 above and 13.5.4 below on this.

[177] See MAFF, *Code of Good Agricultural Practice for the Protection of Water* (1998) para.23, and ss.3 (Farm Waste Management Planning), 4 (Slurries), 9 (Fertilisers) and 14 (Nitrate and Phosphorus). In particular, para.281 of the *Code* states that paras.284 to 295 meet the obligation to introduce a voluntary code of good agricultural practice under the Nitrates Directive in relation to England and Wales.

[178] See 9.4 above on the definition of 'controlled waters'.

[179] Generally, see Royal Commission on Environmental Pollution (1992) Ch.5.

water supply purposes, contaminants may have an especially damaging and persistent effect upon the quality and potential uses of such waters.[180] Because of these distinctive features, groundwater protection has been a matter of particular concern to the Environment Agency which has undertaken an extensive exercise of mapping areas where groundwater is regarded as especially vulnerable to contamination for the purpose of guiding discharge consent determinations and the exercise of other water protection controls.[181]

Because of its relative vulnerability to persistent contamination, a preventive approach towards groundwater protection is particularly appropriate. To some extent this is already provided for under the range of preventive measures for water quality that have been discussed. Precautionary regulations, water protection zones and the designation of areas for nitrate control purposes may each have beneficial effects in relation to groundwater as well as surface waters. However, groundwater protection from certain contaminants is placed on a distinct legal footing because of the need to implement the EC Groundwater Directive.[182]

The broad purpose of the Groundwater Directive is to prevent or limit the direct or indirect introduction into groundwater of dangerous substances identified in List I or List II of the Annex to the Directive. Hence, the main obligation upon the Member States is to prevent the introduction of List I substances to groundwater and to limit the introduction of List II substances so as to prevent pollution. Subject to the exceptions concerning small quantities and low concentrations, all direct discharges of List I substances must be prohibited, and any disposal or tipping that might lead to indirect discharge must be subject to prior investigation and prohibition or authorisation where appropriate. For List II substances a general investigation and authorisation procedure must be established for direct discharges, with disposal or tipping being subject to criteria established by the Directive. Specifically, authorisations may only be issued if all technical precautions for preventing groundwater pollution by List II substances are observed.

Initially, the national interpretation of the Groundwater Directive was such that its implementation required controls upon various industrial activities which may have involved transmission of relevant substances to groundwater. For this purpose, implementation was originally thought to have been accomplished under Parts I and II of the Environmental Protection Act 1990, concerned with integrated pollution control and the management of waste,[183] and under Part II of the Water Resources Act 1991, concerning water resources, along with secondary legislation under these enactments. However, it was subsequently acknowledged that these

---

[180] See discussion of *Cambridge Water Company* v *Eastern Counties Leather plc* [1994] 1 All ER 53 at 3.10 above.

[181] Environment Agency, *Policy and Practice for the Protection of Groundwater* (1998).

[182] (80/68/EEC) and see 5.4.2 above for further discussion of this Directive.

[183] See 12.3 below on integrated pollution control and 12.2 below on waste management regulation.

provisions would not apply to particular activities involving the disposal of relevant substances which fell outside the existing integrated pollution control, waste and water pollution control regimes. Specifically, the problem areas were identified as the following:

    (a)   industrial processes which manufacture, handle or store List I or List II substances and from which leaks or spillages of such substances may occur;

    (b)   agricultural activities involving the disposal of waste pesticides and pesticide tank washings to land, including the disposal of sheep dip; and

    (c)   other users of listed substances who currently dispose of these to land without a waste management licence and all owners of underground tanks which may hold such substances.[184]

Not least problematic amongst this range of issues was the disposal of waste sheep dip. The content of organophosphates in some sheep dip has given rise to serious public health concerns, as well as being known to be highly damaging to aquatic invertebrates. However, it is also recognised to raise difficulties in respect of control because of the large number of farms from which waste sheep dip is disposed to land and groundwater.

Addressing these matters, the Groundwater Regulations 1998[185] require the prior investigation of the potential effect on groundwater of discharges and the potential effect of activities upon the ground. A new system of authorisations is introduced for the disposal or tipping on land of certain substances which may result in a discharge to groundwater. To ensure the enforcement of these requirements, provision is made for the service of notices by the Environment Agency in respect of activities which could result in the entry of relevant substances into groundwater and for costs relating to matters arising under the Regulations to be recovered by the Agency. It is also intended that the Regulations should reaffirm the need for adherence to approved codes of practice relating to agriculture.[186] Hence, applications will need to be made to the Agency for authorisations for disposal of specified substances, notices may be served by the Agency to prohibit the disposal of substances and contravention of these provisions will amount to a criminal offence under the Water Resources Act 1991.[187]

Hopefully, the Groundwater Regulations mark the final chapter in the exercise of implementing the Groundwater Directive in national law. The possibility always remains that some further activity may be identified which is capable of contravening the Directive, and which will be required

---

[184] DETR, *Consultation on Draft Guidance on the Groundwater Regulations 1998* (1999).
[185] SI 1998 No.2746.
[186] See 13.5.7 above on the *Code of Good Agricultural Practice*.
[187] See Regs.14, 18 and 19 Groundwater Regulations 1998 and see s.85 Water Resources Act 1991, discussed in 9.3 above.

to be controlled under national law, but, for the present, the Government is of the view that the implementation of the Directive is complete.[188]

## 13.7 Contaminated Land and Water Quality

### 13.7.1 The Problem of Contaminated Land Remediation

The precise extent of land contaminated by past industrial activities is difficult to assess, but it has been estimated by the Environment Agency that there are between 5,000 to 20,000 sites which are actually contaminated and over 1,200 sites where groundwater contamination has been found, many of which are associated with various kinds of contaminated land.[189] However, it is widely recognised that no genuinely reliable information is available regarding the extent of contaminated land and estimates have varied widely between 5,000 and 200,000 sites, covering up to 600,000 acres. The wide variation in these estimates is attributable to different assumptions that have been made as to the contaminative potential of land for different kinds of use, risks to the environment posed by contamination and the extent of contamination of each site. What does seem to be generally conceded, however, is that costs of remediation are potentially enormous, with estimates of £20 billion or 'substantially greater' having been suggested, depending upon the standard to which remediation is required.[190]

Where the existence of a contaminated site is established, and it is shown that this is a continuing source of contamination, there are likely to be serious difficulties in establishing either civil or criminal liability or in imposing responsibility for the restoration of the land to a non-contaminating state.[191] As has been described,[192] liability in civil law is likely to depend upon foreseeability of damage and, following the *Cambridge Water* case,[193] it will need to be shown that the defendant should have anticipated the environmental damage which resulted from the activities which caused the land to be contaminated. Since many of the activities which have resulted in land contamination took place many years ago when environmental awareness was considerably lower than today, and that those responsible may no longer exist, there are likely to be

---

[188] DETR, *Consultation on Draft Guidance on the Groundwater Regulations* (1999).

[189] House of Commons Environment Committee, *Contaminated Land* (1996) paras.18 and 19.

[190] See DoE, *Paying for Our Past: the Arrangements for Controlling Contaminated Land and Meeting the Cost of Remedying Damage to the Environment* (1994) paras.2.8-2.12. Although more recent assessments have suggested that the area affected is 360,000 hectares and the costs of remediation around £15.3 billion, *ENDS Report* 305 (2000) p.4.

[191] Although see the discussion of proposals for the establishment of environmental liability at European Community level at 3.20 above.

[192] Generally, see Ch.3 above on civil liability.

[193] [1994] 1 All ER 53 and see 3.10 above.

considerable difficulties in seeking compensation or an order for the removal of the offending contaminants.[194]

In relation to criminal liability for pollution originating from contaminated land, analogous difficulties are likely to arise, particularly where the contamination impacts upon the aquatic environment. Fundamentally, as has been seen,[195] the difficulty is that, traditionally, the principal water pollution offences have conceived of the problem of water pollution in terms of a discrete and identifiable entry of polluting matter into a watercourse normally causing a dramatic and sudden change in water quality and, commonly, with obvious environmental consequences such as the death of large numbers of fish. A situation where poor water quality arises from the gradual but long-term seepage of substances from contaminated land would probably fall outside the scope of the principal water pollution offences, either because of the difficulty in showing that a particular person had 'caused or knowingly permitted'[196] an entry or discharge of polluting matter or because of the need to show the quantities of contaminants involved amounted to an 'entry' of 'poisonous, noxious or polluting'[197] matter. Even if a situation did fall within the scope of the water pollution offences, the underlying environmental problem, of removing the source of contamination from the land, would not be directly resolved by any criminal conviction that might be secured, though in certain circumstances the service of an anti-pollution works notice might provide some scope for environmental improvement.[198] Again, the inference is that a preventative or remedial approach to the problem is required rather than the punitive mechanisms provided by the principal water pollution offences.

Essentially, the task is that of providing for a practicable and consistent means by which the environmental regulatory authorities may compel contaminated land to be remediated, within the scope of a set of rules which appropriately designate land needing to be remediated; indicate the standard to which it should be remediated; and operate equitably between those made responsible for securing remediation and the public purse. Whilst considerable legislative progress has been made in addressing these concerns, key problems remain in the definition of 'contaminated land'; the identification of contaminated land; the nature of the remediation requirements; and the allocation of responsibility for remediation.

---

[194] Conversely, in some respects the civil law may be wider in compass than regulatory requirements concerning contaminated land remediation since remediation requirements are limited to restoring the land to a 'suitable for use' standard (see 13.7.5 below on this) whereas no limitation of this kind will apply where a civil claimant claims 'unreasonable interference with enjoyment' of land in nuisance (see 3.8 above on this). For this reason, perhaps, the fact that remediation has been accomplished to a required statutory standard may not serve as a defence in civil proceedings.

[195] See the discussion of the principal water pollution offences at 9.3 above.

[196] See 9.5–7 above on the meaning of 'cause or knowingly permit'.

[197] See 9.8 above on the meaning of 'poisonous, noxious or polluting'.

[198] Under s.161A Water Resources Act 1991 and see 13.2.2 above.

## 13.7.2 The Legal Response

The problem of how to allocate legal responsibility for the restoration of contaminated land has been a matter of extensive discussion and controversy over recent years.[199] Underlying the debate was a recognition that the previously existing legal mechanisms did not satisfactorily address the problem. Although powers existed to allow anti-pollution works and operations to be undertaken,[200] and might have been interpreted as permitting remedial work on contaminated land where this was a cause of water pollution, it was far from clear how far these powers extended. Consequently, the National Rivers Authority was reluctant to take action in relation to contaminated land remediation where the recovery of potentially enormous costs was not assured. Also, provisions existed requiring waste regulation authorities to inspect their areas to detect land that might cause pollution of the environment and, where required, to do work to avoid pollution[201] but, again, uncertainty surrounded the issue of precisely what remediation activities this would authorise. Local planning authorities also have powers to require specified steps to be taken to remedy the condition of land where it adversely affects the amenity of adjoining areas[202] but, because of uncertainties as to the scope of this power, there was a reluctance to make extensive use of it. Similarly, provisions relating to statutory nuisance,[203] potentially, might have been applied to some kinds of contaminated land but, in practice, have never been used.

An initial attempt to address the issue involved an information strategy requiring the compilation of registers of land which had previously been subject to contaminative uses,[204] but this was generally recognised to be flawed, in providing little incentive for remediation, and eventually abandoned. This was followed by a general review of the legal powers to tackle contaminated land,[205] which led to the enactment of an extensive scheme of controls relating to contaminated land being enacted under the Environment Act 1995 and interpolating a new Part IIA into the Environmental Protection Act 1990.[206] Although the primary legislation was thereby put in place, the implementation of this required an extensive body of secondary legislation to determine the more detailed mechanisms by which it should be put into effect.

---

[199] Generally see, House of Commons Environment Committee, *Toxic Waste* (1989) and House of Commons Environment Committee, *Contaminated Land* (1990).

[200] See 13.2 above on anti-pollution works and operations.

[201] s.61 Environmental Protection Act 1990, repealed by the Environment Act 1995, and see also s.59 Environmental Protection Act 1990, concerned with the removal of unlawfully deposited waste.

[202] s.215 Town and Country Planning Act 1990, and see Ch.14 below on planning generally.

[203] Under Part III Environmental Protection Act 1990, and see 8.5 above on statutory nuisance.

[204] Under s.143 of the Environmental Protection Act 1990, repealed by Environment Act 1995.

[205] See DoE, *Paying for Our Past: the Arrangements for Controlling Contaminated Land and Meeting the Cost of Remedying Damage to the Environment* (1994) and *Framework for Contaminated Land : Outcome of the Government's Policy Review and Conclusions from the Consultation Paper Paying for Our Past* (1994).

[206] Under s.57 Environment Act 1995, which inserts Part IIA (ss.78A-78YC) into the Environmental Protection Act 1990.

Following lengthy consultation,[207] Part IIA of the Environmental Protection Act 1990 was brought into force in England,[208] and regulations[209] have been enacted to give effect to this along with a departmental circular[210] setting out statutory guidance, explaining Government policy and indicating the way in which the new regime is expected to operate in practice. Hence, the actual operation of contaminated land remediation requirements are a rather complex combination of primary and secondary legislation and official guidance which must be interpreted alongside each other in determining the legal consequences in relation to any particular area of contaminated land.

Notwithstanding the secondary legislation and guidance, the new Part IIA of the Environmental Protection Act 1990 is an extensive and intricate piece of legislation, raising profound issues in respect of environmental liability generally. It is not possible to provide comprehensive discussion of the issues that it raises in this work.[211] The selective discussion which follows, therefore, introduces the key provisions of the contaminated land regime for the purpose of explaining their inter-relationship with the regime with regard to the pollution of water and the contrasts between the two regimes. That said, it is remarkable that there should be any disparity between the contaminated land provisions and the statutory mechanisms for water protection given that a primary purpose of the new legislation was to rationalise liability under the two legislative regimes.[212] Nevertheless, there are aspects of the contaminated land regime that contrast with the water protection provisions, and issues may remain as to which legislative regime will be most appropriately applied to a particular problem.

Another interrelationship that should be noted is between the contaminated land regime provided for under Part IIA of the 1990 Act and the town and country planning system.[213] Where a planning application relates to land which is contaminated, there is a duty upon the local planning authority to make provision for the remediation of the land as a condition of any planning permission that is granted. In many instances, therefore,

---

[207] See DoE, WO and Scottish Office, *Consultation on Draft Statutory Guidance on Contaminated Land* (1996) and *Contaminated Land: Draft Regulations and Regulatory Assessment* (1996), and for a discussion of these see House of Commons Environment Committee, *Contaminated Land* (1996) and (1999). Subsequently, see DETR, *Contaminated Land: Implementation of Part IIA of the Environmental Protection Act 1990* (1999).

[208] See Environment Act 1995 (Commencement No.16 and Saving Provision) (England) Order 2000 (SI 2000 No.340). Responsibility for implementing Part IIA in Wales rests with the National Assembly for Wales, see 6.2 above.

[209] Contaminated Land (England) Regulations 2000 (SI 2000 No.227) hereafter 'the Regulations'.

[210] Department of the Environment, Transport and the Regions, Circular 02/2000, *Environmental Protection Act 1990: Part IIA Contaminated Land* (2000), hereafter referred to as 'the Circular'.

[211] For general reading on the law relating to contaminated land see Deanesly, Papanicolaou, and Turner (1993); Lomas and Payne (1993 updated) C.4; Tromans and Turrall-Clarke (2000); Tromans (1996); Lewis (1995); Steele (1995); Rossi (1995); Hughes and Kellett (1996), (1997) and (1999); and Bell and Howarth (1997).

[212] On the need to secure consistency between water pollution legislation and the contaminated land regime see s.78J(2) of the Environmental Protection Act 1990, discussed at 13.7.7 below.

[213] See Ch.14 below on town and country planning generally.

remediation will be secured through the planning system rather than the contaminated land regime. However, there are important differences between the remediation requirements under the two mechanisms and work is presently underway to ensure a harmonised approach.[214]

### 13.7.3 The Meaning of 'Contaminated Land'

'Contaminated land' is defined as any land which appears to the local authority in whose area it is situated to be in such a condition, by reason of substances in, on or under the land, that either

(a) significant harm is being caused or there is a significant possibility of such harm being caused; or

(b) pollution of controlled waters is being, or is likely to be, caused.[215]

For the purposes of the definition of contaminated land, 'harm' means harm to the health of living organisms or other interference with the ecological systems of which they form part and, in the case of man, includes harm to his property.[216]

The question as to whether harm is 'significant' is to be determined by guidance issued by the Secretary of State.[217] On this, the Circular goes into some detail in explaining that the definition of 'contaminated land' is intended to embody the concept of risk assessment involving a combination of the probability or frequency of occurrence of a defined hazard and the magnitude or seriousness of the consequences of this. Hence, before land can be found to be contaminated, a 'pollution linkage' must be found, involving a source of contamination, a receptor and pathway between these.[218] In relation to water, the three elements needing to be established involve a contaminant or polluting substance capable of causing harm or pollution of controlled waters; a target consisting of a living organism or ecological system, property or controlled waters themselves;[219] and a pathway, or means by which the receptor may be exposed to, or affected by, the contaminant. Hence, for the purposes of establishing 'significance' of harm, a diverse list of relationships between

---

[214] See the discussion of the contrasts at 13.7.10 below.

[215] s.78A(2) Environmental Protection Act 1990. See also the discussion of 'cause or knowingly permit' in relation to s.85 Water Resources Act 1991 at 9.5–7 above. Postscript: clause 56 of a draft Water Bill proposes to amend the second limb of the definition of 'contaminated land' (under s.78A(2) of the 1990 Act) so that *significant* pollution of controlled waters is being caused or there is a *significant* possibility of *significant* pollution of controlled waters being caused. See DETR, *Water Bill: Consultation on Draft Legislation* (2001).

[216] s.78A(4) Environmental Protection Act 1990.

[217] *Ibid* s.78A(5) and see Circular Annex 3 Part 3.

[218] See 13.3.3 above on the source-receptor-pathway analysis of pollution.

[219] See Circular Annex 3 para.A19 which indicates that controlled waters alone are capable of constituting a receptor.

receptors and kinds of harm are indicated, along with conditions for there being a significant possibility of significant harm.[220]

'Pollution of controlled waters', for the purposes of the 'contaminated land' definition, means the entry into controlled waters of any poisonous, noxious or polluting matter or any solid waste matter,[221] in effect, largely restating the circumstances provided for in relation to the existing principal water pollution offences.[222] However, a distinction may be drawn in that the water pollution offences are concerned with the previous entry or discharge of a pollutant into waters, whereas the contaminated land liabilities arise because of the *continuing* transmission of contaminants into controlled waters or the likelihood of this. Accordingly, the Circular stipulates that land should not be designated as contaminated where a substance is *already* present in controlled waters, where entry of that substance has ceased and it is not likely that further entry will take place.[223]

It seems to follow from the incorporation of pollution of controlled waters within the definition of contaminated land that a situation where a person causes or knowingly permits the entry of polluting matter from land is capable of falling within both the principal water pollution offences and the contaminated land regime. An example of this kind of situation arose in *R v Dovermoss Ltd*[224] where spring water was found to be contaminated with excess ammonia which was traced to fields near to the source of supply which had been spread with animal slurry. Heavy rain and siltation had resulted in a nearby stream departing from its normal course and flowing across the fields which resulted in the slurry being transmitted into the ground near to the spring and contaminating the water supply. It was found that this situation, where polluting matter had originally been placed on land, amounted to an 'entry' of polluting matter into the waters of the watercourse, despite the departure of the stream from its normal course. Hence, under some circumstances, providing the defendant is shown to have caused or knowingly permitted the relevant entry, the contamination of land can give rise to a water pollution offence.[225]

Another relevant issue in the *Dovermoss* case is whether the slurry involved was actually 'polluting matter'. It was argued that the prosecution had not proved any actual harm had been done to the receiving waters and it was noted that the resulting ammonia levels did not exceed maximum concentrations permitted for drinking water.[226] On this issue, it was found that it was unnecessary for the prosecution to prove that the substance had actually caused harm, it was sufficient that there was a likelihood or

---

[220] See Circular Annex 3 Ch.A Parts 2 and 3.

[221] s.78A(9) Environmental Protection Act 1990.

[222] Under s.85 Water Resources Act 1991.

[223] See Circular Annex 3 Ch.A Part 4.

[224] [1995] Env LR 258, and see 9.4 above.

[225] Although the Court found for the defendant on other grounds.

[226] Under Water Supply (Water Quality) Regulations 1989 (SI 1989 No.1147) and see 17.7.2 below on these Regulations.

capability of causing harm to animal or plant life or those who use water, and this had been sufficiently established on the facts.

The implication of this part of the ruling for the definition of contaminated land is that the capacity to cause the pollution of controlled waters, which may justify the finding that land is contaminated, may be of a relatively minor nature. This point was noted by the House of Commons Environment Committee which observed that the relative breadth of scope of 'pollution' of controlled waters may encompass relatively trivial matters. This was thought to indicate a need to incorporate some further guidance as to the degree or severity of water pollution which activates the contaminated land provisions.[227] Whilst the Government seemed to concede this difficulty, though recognising that primary legislation would be needed fully to address it, it was thought that the stipulation that only reasonable requirements could be imposed in relation to remediation would cover such a situation in practice and that the entry of a trivial amount of a pollutant could not justify the imposition of major remediation expenditure.[228] Similarly, the Circular indicates that where small quantities of a contaminant entering controlled waters might lead to an inference that land is contaminated it is also necessary to consider guidance on what remediation it is reasonable to require and, if no remediation is reasonably required, to provide a remediation declaration to that effect.[229] Nonetheless, the position remains that land is capable of being designated as 'contaminated', with potentially major economic consequences for the owner of the land, despite only relatively trivial impacts of this upon the aquatic environment.

### 13.7.4 The Duty to Identify Contaminated Land

Every local authority must cause its area to be inspected from time to time for the purpose of identifying contaminated land and of enabling the authority to decide whether any such land is land which is required to be designated as a special site.[230] A 'special site', for these purposes, is any

---

[227] House of Commons Environment Committee, *Contaminated Land* (1996) para.50.

[228] House of Commons Environment Committee, *Government Response: Contaminated Land* (1999) paras.28 to 31. Postscript: clause 56 of a draft Water Bill recognises the difficulty that land might be identified as 'contaminated' because of the entry, or likely entry, of only small amounts of polluting matter into controlled waters and proposes to amend the second limb of the definition of 'contaminated land' (under s.78A(2) of the 1990 Act) so that *significant* pollution of controlled waters is being caused or there is a *significant* possibility of *significant* pollution of controlled waters being caused. Clause 56 of the draft Bill also provides the Secretary of State with powers to issue guidance on what degree of pollution of controlled waters is to be regarded as 'significant' and whether the possibility of significant pollution of controlled waters being caused is 'significant'. See DETR, *Water Bill: Consultation on Draft Legislation* (2001).

[229] Circular Annex 2 paras.2.9 and 6.30 to 6.32, and see 13.7.5 below on reasonableness and remediation declarations.

[230] s.78B(1) Environmental Protection Act 1990 and see Circular Annex 3 Ch.B on guidance on the inspection duty. If the Agency considers that any contaminated land is land which is required to be designated as a special site, the Agency may give notice of that fact to the local authority (s.78C(4)). See also Contaminated Land (England) Regulations 2000 Regs.2 and 3 and Circular Annex 4 concerning the designation of special sites.

contaminated land which has been so designated and where this designation has not been terminated.[231] In determining whether land is to be designated as a special site, particular regard is to be had to whether contaminated land is likely to be in such a condition that *serious*[232] harm might be caused or serious pollution of controlled waters would be, or would be likely to be, caused and whether the Environment Agency is likely to have the expertise to deal with the harm or pollution concerned.[233] The implication, therefore, is that only the most seriously contaminated sites will fall into this category and, in relation to such sites, the Agency, rather than the local authority, will act as the enforcing authority.[234]

An aspect of the designation of special sites with special relevance to water is that the Regulations require contaminated land with adverse impacts upon water quality to be designated as a special site in three situations:[235]

(a)  where affected controlled waters are used for drinking water supply purposes and require treatment, or a change in treatment, before use to be regarded as 'wholesome' under water supply legislation;[236]

(b)  where affected controlled waters fail, or are likely to fail, to meet relevant criteria for water quality classification under the Water Resources Act 1991;[237] and

(c)  where controlled waters are affected by a contaminating substance which falls within a list of substances identified in the Regulations or the waters are contained within underground strata which comprise formations of rocks listed in the Regulations.[238]

More broadly, in relation to the general inspection duty of local authorities, the similarly of this duty and that imposed upon authorities with regard to statutory nuisances[239] should be noted. The duty imposed in relation to inspection for statutory nuisances, and taking abatement action,[240] will be similarly construed in relation to the inspection responsibility in relation to potentially contaminated land. That is to say,

---

[231] s.78A(3) Environmental Protection Act 1990.

[232] 'Serious' here is to be contrasted with the term 'significant' which is used in relation to the definition of 'contaminated land' generally, see 13.7.3 above on this definition.

[233] s.78C(8) to (10) Environmental Protection Act 1990.

[234] Under s.78A(9) Environmental Protection Act 1990.

[235] Contaminated Land (England) Regulations 2000 Regs.2(1)(a) and 3.

[236] See Part III Water Industry Act 1991 and discussion of 'wholesome' at 17.7.3 below.

[237] Under s.82 Water Resources Act 1991 and see 14.8.2 below on water quality classification.

[238] For the list of substances and the list of rock formations see paras.1 and 2 Sch.1 respectively of the Regulations.

[239] Under Part III Environmental Protection Act 1990, and see 8.5 above on statutory nuisance. Overlap between the contaminated land provisions and those concerning statutory nuisance is avoided by the stipulation that no matter is to constitute a statutory nuisance to the extent that it consists of, or is caused by, land being in a contaminated state (s.79(1A) and (1B) Environmental Protection Act 1990, as inserted by para.89(3) Sch.22 Environment Act 1995) and see Circular Annex 1 paras.59 to 63.

[240] See *R v Carrick District Council ex parte Shelley and Another* [1996] Env LR 273.

the duty to inspect in respect of statutory nuisances is of a mandatory character, as is the duty to take abatement action where a statutory nuisance is identified. Consequently, a local authority will be left with relatively little discretion in relation to these matters. This is in marked contrast to the general discretion given to environmental enforcement authorities where other kinds of enforcement action are provided for.[241] Nonetheless, the Circular indicates that local authorities should adopt a strategic approach towards the inspection of their areas so as to identify the most pressing and serious problems first and concentrate resources on those areas where contaminated land is most likely to be found.[242]

If a local authority identifies any contaminated land in its area, it must notify

(a)   the Environment Agency;

(b)   the owner of the land;

(c)   any person who appears to the authority to be in occupation of the whole or any part of the land; and

(d)   each person who appears to the authority to be an 'appropriate person' for the purpose of serving a remediation notice.[243]

### 13.7.5  The Duty to Require Remediation

Where land has been designated as a special site, or a local authority has identified other contaminated land in its area, the enforcing authority[244] must serve on every 'appropriate person'[245] a remediation notice specifying what that person is to do by way of remediation and the periods within which he is required to do each of the things specified.[246] 'Remediation' is broadly defined to include a wide range of assessment, operational and monitoring activities. Hence, it encompasses anything done for the purpose of assessing the condition of the contaminated land, controlled waters affected by that land or any adjacent land;[247] the doing of any works, the carrying out of any operations or the taking of any steps for preventing or minimising, or remedying or mitigating the effect of, any significant harm, or any pollution of controlled waters, or restoring land or waters to their former state; or the making of subsequent inspections for the purpose of keeping under review the condition of the land or waters.[248]

---

[241] Generally, see 6.18.1 above on the Environment Agency's enforcement policy.

[242] Circular Annex 2 paras.3.2 and 3.3.

[243] s.78B(3) Environmental Protection Act 1990.

[244] That is, the Environment Agency in relation to special sites and in relation to contaminated land other than a special site the local authority for the area (s.78A(9) Environmental Protection Act 1990).

[245] The meaning of 'appropriate person' is discussed at 13.7.6 below.

[246] s.78E(1) Environmental Protection Act 1990.

[247] Contrast the power of the Environment Agency to conduct 'investigations' under its anti-pollution works powers (under s.161 Water Resources Act 1991) which does not require the service of a remediation notice and see 13.2.1 above.

[248] s.78A(7) Environmental Protection Act 1990.

Although the wording of the requirement to serve a remediation notice seems to indicate a mandatory obligation upon the enforcing authority to take the specified enforcement action, the duty to require remediation is actually subject to various qualifications which significantly restrict its impact. Hence, the enforcing authority may only require things which are 'reasonable' to be done by way of remediation, having regard to the cost which is likely to be involved and the seriousness of the harm, or pollution of controlled waters, in question.[249] This duty to have regard to both the costs and the contamination impact involved raises some significant issues both in relation to the functioning of the contaminated land regime and its relationship with other areas of pollution regulation.

In respect of the need to consider costs when determining remediation requirements, there is a clear link with the obligation upon the Environment Agency to discharges its duties in accordance with its duty to have regard to costs and benefits.[250] This requires the Agency, when considering whether, or how, to exercise any power conferred upon it, unless it is unreasonable for it to do so, to take into account the likely costs and benefits of the exercise of non-exercise of the power.

In accordance with the requirement that remediation measures must be 'reasonable' in terms of costs and benefits, a written statement of costs and benefits should be prepared in order to justify the choice of a particular remediation option.[251] Although there is a clear need for a consistent approach in determining what remediation actions are 'reasonable', concern has been expressed as to the extent to which the assessment of cost and benefits should include the environmental externalities associated with a particular remediation technique.[252] The Circular focuses attention upon the extent of benefits secured, expressed in terms of the reduction or mitigation of harm or pollution, and the timing of expenditure, and the financial costs of associated activities.[253] However, no cost-benefit contrasts are apparently drawn between remediation methods that secure the treatment or neutralisation of environmentally harmful contaminants as opposed to remediation methods which simply involve the removal of contaminants to another location where they may give rise to future problems.

Alongside the requirement that remediation requirements should be 'reasonable', there is a general objective that remediation activities should not be required if they go beyond what is necessary to make the land in question 'suitable for use'. This approach requires remedial action only where contamination poses unacceptable actual or potential risks to health

---

[249] *Ibid* s.78E(4) and see Circular Annex 3 Ch.C Part 5.

[250] Under s.39 Environment Act 1995 and see 6.14 above.

[251] Circular Annex 3 Ch.C para.30. See also Regulations Reg.4(1)(g) which requires the enforcing authority to state reasons for its decisions, as to the things that are required to be done by way of remediation, in a remediation notice.

[252] See DoE, MAFF and WO, *The Environment Agency and Sustainable Development* (1996) Ch.5, and House of Commons Environment Committee, *Contaminated Land* (1996) para.74.

[253] Circular Annex 3 Ch.C paras.29-38.

or the environment and there are appropriate and cost-effective means available to do so, taking into account the actual or intended use of the land.[254] Hence, the Circular states that 'suitable for use' consists of three elements:

(a)    ensuring that land is suitable for its *current* use;

(b)    ensuring that land is made suitable for any *new* use for which planning permission is given; and

(c)    limiting requirements for remediation to work which is necessary to prevent unacceptable risks to human health or the environment in relation to current or intended future uses.[255]

However, the 'suitable for use' approach begs the fundamental question, suitable for use *as what*? Land which is to be used as a market garden will, presumably, be subject to far stricter remediation requirements than land which is to be used as a car park. Moreover, a possibility is that certain sites may require successive remediation, to progressively higher standards, for subsequent uses, and, it has been suggested, that this is an inefficient alternative to requiring remediation to be undertaken to a uniformly high standard 'once and for all'.[256]

Nevertheless, the approach which has been endorsed means that multiple remediation is a genuine possibility in relation to successive land uses. It is also pertinent to note that the legislation does not allow for any 'signing off' mechanism whereby, once remediation is undertaken to a required standard, a guarantee will be given that no further remediation work will be required providing the land use does not change.[257]

### 13.7.6 Determining the Appropriate Person

The obligation to serve a remediation notice on an 'appropriate person' raises the critical question as to who should bear the cost of remediation of contaminated land. In respect of this, three priorities were established in the policy discussions on which the contaminated land legislation was based. The first priority was the need to adhere to the polluter pays principle,[258] so that responsibility for remediation lies with the 'polluter' wherever that person can be found. Second, it was recognised that a landowner of a property is ultimately responsible for its condition and, where the polluter cannot be found, the landowner should be responsible for remediation. However, it was recognised that the landowner-responsibility principle may not justify the imposition of responsibility for restoring off-site damage, which may have occurred prior to a present owner's acquisition of the land, and that there may be situations where

---

[254] DoE and WO, *Framework for Contaminated Land: Outcome of the Government's Policy Review and Conclusions from the Consultation Paper Paying for Our Past* (1994) para.2.3.

[255] Circular Annex 1 para.10.

[256] Contrast House of Commons Environment Committee, *Contaminated Land* (1996) para.70 and *Government Response: Contaminated Land* (1999) para.14.

[257] House of Commons Environment Committee, *Contaminated Land* (1996) paras.27-30.

[258] See 4.7.3 above on the polluter pays principle.

special hardship may arise which will need to be taken into account. Third, where neither of the previous principles can be applied, it may be necessary for the burden of contaminated land restoration to be met at public expense. The objective was that the situations where so-called 'orphan sites' will have to be remediated at public expense should be kept to a minimum. Nonetheless, this was regarded as a better alternative than requiring such sites to be remediated on the basis of 'deep pocket' liability regardless of the responsibility an individual may have had for the contamination.[259]

The legislation which seeks to give effect to this policy on allocating responsibility for contaminated land remediation provides that, in the first place, the 'appropriate person', for the purpose of serving a remediation notice, is any person who caused or knowingly permitted the substances by reason of which the land is contaminated to be in, on or under that land.[260] Second, if no person has been found who is an appropriate person to bear responsibility for remediation under the first test, the appropriate person is the owner or occupier for the time being of the contaminated land.[261] In the terminology of the Circular, a person who meets the first test is referred to as a 'Class A person' and a person who comes within the second test is referred to as a 'Class B person'.[262] The meaning of 'Class A person' is further defined in the Circular by a series of exclusionary and apportionment tests which may serve to discount persons from Class A, for example, because they have provided financial assistance, insurance cover or legal, engineering, scientific or technical advice.[263]

The wording that has been used to allocate liability to Class A or B persons in the primary legislation raises several questions as to whether it satisfactorily gives effect to the policy objectives. A key issue is whether the intention to distinguish between polluters and non-polluting landowners or occupiers is satisfactorily achieved by the wording that has been used. The phrase 'cause or knowingly permit', which has been adopted to determine who is a Class A appropriate person, is the same as that used in relation to the principal water pollution offences.[264] However, the wording which has been used in the contaminated land legislation carries with it an extensive and authoritative body of case law indicating where a person will be found to have 'caused' or, alternatively, 'knowingly

---

[259] See DoE *Paying for Our Past: the Arrangements for Controlling Contaminated Land and Meeting the Cost of Remedying Damage to the Environment* (1994) paras.4E.1-12, and *Framework for Contaminated Land: Outcome of the Government's Policy Review and Conclusions from the Consultation Paper Paying for our Past* (1994) paras.4.4.1-8.

[260] s.78F(2) Environmental Protection Act 1990.

[261] *Ibid* s.78F(4). 'Owner', in relation to any land in England and Wales, means a person (other than a mortgagee not in possession) who, whether in his own right or as trustee for any other person, is entitled to receive the rack rent of the land, or, where the land is not let at a rack rent, would be so entitled if it were so let (s.78A(9)).

[262] Circular Annex 2 paras.9.3 to 9.7.

[263] Circular Annex 3 Ch.D.

[264] Under s.85 Water Resources Act 1991, see 9.3 above on the principal water pollution offences, and 9.5-7 above on the meaning of 'cause or knowingly permit'. See also Circular Annex 2 paras.9.8 to 9.15.

permitted' a polluting act. Notwithstanding the application of strict liability, a person who has been found guilty of 'causing' water pollution might ordinarily be regarded as a 'polluter', however, it is questionable whether, in all instances, a person who has 'knowingly permitted' pollution is fairly placed in that category.

The difficulty in supposing that a person who has 'knowingly permitted' contaminating substances to be in, on or under land should be identified as a polluter, or Class A appropriate person, is that it is not clear what knowledge is required in the contaminated land context. First, in a situation where X knows that contaminating material is being deposited on his land by Y and fails to take action within his powers to prevent this, there is no difficulty in regarding X as a polluter. Second, where X knows that material is being deposited on his land by Y, but X has no knowledge that the material is contaminating, and no reason to think that it might be,[265] the situation is less clear. Third, where, after appropriate and reasonable investigations, X purchases land with no knowledge of it being contaminated and no reason to think that it might be, but subsequently discovers or is informed of the contamination and then takes no action to prevent its continuation, it might be thought that X would not be a polluter. Nevertheless there is an argument that such a person would fall within Class A on the basis that he knew of the contamination and permitted it to continue. If this is so, it would seem that the wording that has been used to distinguish between polluters and non-polluting landowners does not capture the distinction that was intended. The possibility exists that non-polluters, and particularly 'innocent' or ignorant purchasers, might be caught within Class A depending upon how 'knowingly permitting' is construed.

There appears to be some ambivalence in the official interpretation of the 'knowingly permitting' formula in relation to its application to innocent purchasers of contaminated land. In Parliamentary debates, the view was expressed that it would be reasonable for a person who has active control over contaminants on a site, for example where redevelopment is taking place, to be made responsible for any harm to health or the environment even if that person did not originally cause or knowingly permit the site to become contaminated.[266] On the other hand, the view taken by the Circular is that the 'knowingly permit' test would not be triggered by an innocent purchaser subsequently being informed of the contaminated state of that land and then failing to do anything about it.[267] Although courts are allowed to take cognisance of Parliamentary proceedings in construing words in an enactment,[268] the problem remains that the 'knowingly permitting' formula, and its associated case law, seems inappropriate to

---

[265] It has been suggested that constructive knowledge may be sufficient in the context of the water pollution offence, see *Schulmans Incorporated Ltd* v *National Rivers Authority* (1991, unreported, but see [1992] *Water Law* 72 and [1992] I Env LR D2).

[266] See speech of Viscount Ullswater (HL Vol.560, col.1461, 31 January 1995) noted in Tromans (1996) p.220.

[267] Circular Annex 2 para.9.13.

[268] *Pepper* v *Hart* [1993] 1 All ER 42.

give effect to the polluter's remediation liability that was originally intended.

Another problem arises from the sequential tests for allocation of liability to Class A or Class B persons. This is the question of when a Class A person has been 'found' for the purpose of satisfying the first test. The Circular emphasises that a person must be in existence in order to be found and, for that reason, a company that has been dissolved or a natural person who is dead would not be 'found' for these purposes. However, another difficulty might arise where a Class A person has been identified and located but that person turns out to be a company that has gone into liquidation or an individual without the means to fulfil any likely remediation requirements.[269] If the 'finding' requirement is met in these circumstances, then the policy objective of securing remediation of contaminated land without cost to the public purse would not seem to be realised.

### 13.7.7 Restrictions on Serving Remediation Notices

Despite the generally mandatory nature of the duty to serve a remediation notice on the appropriate person, a list of exceptions is provided for where this is not allowed. Hence, following consultation,[270] the enforcing authority may not serve a remediation notice on a person if any of the following conditions are met:

(a) the authority is satisfied[271] that there is nothing by way of remediation which could be specified in a remediation notice;

(b) the authority is satisfied that appropriate things are being, or will be, done by way of remediation without the service of a remediation;

(c) the person on whom the notice would be served is the authority itself; or

(d) the authority is satisfied that the powers of the enforcing authority[272] to do what is appropriate by way of remediation are available.[273]

---

[269] See the discussion of this issue in Tromans (1996) p.221.

[270] Before serving a remediation notice, the enforcing authority must reasonably endeavour to consult, concerning what is to be done by way of remediation, the person on whom the notice is to be served; the owner of any land to which the notice relates; any person who appears to the authority to be in occupation of the whole or any part of the land; and any person of such description as may be prescribed (s.78H(1) Environmental Protection Act 1990). However, the consultation requirement will not preclude the service of a remediation notice where there is imminent danger of serious harm, or serious pollution of controlled waters, being caused (s.78H(4)).

[271] Satisfied, that is, that, in relation to the costs involved and the seriousness of the harm or pollution, that remediation is reasonably required (under s.78E(4) and (5) Environmental Protection Act 1990).

[272] Under s.78N Environmental Protection Act 1990, and see 13.7.9 below on remediation by enforcement authorities.

[273] *Ibid* s.78H(5).

Hence, a range of situations is provided for where no useful purpose would be served by the instigation of remediation proceedings, though in these circumstances the enforcing authority will be bound to publish a 'remediation declaration' indicating why remediation would, otherwise, have been required and the ground on which service of a remediation notice is precluded.[274] In addition, unless the responsibility for remediation falls upon the authority, the responsible person must publish a 'remediation statement' recording, amongst other matters, the things which are being, have been, or are expected to be, done by way of remediation.[275]

Another restriction of liability for remediation arises specifically where pollution of controlled waters is being, or likely to be, caused, whether or not other kinds of significant harm are being caused or are likely to be caused. Hence, no remediation notice may require a person who is a Class B appropriate person[276] to do anything by way of remediation of land or waters which that person could not have been required to do if the definition of 'harm'[277] had omitted reference to controlled waters.[278] That is, the liability of landowners and occupiers, as opposed to polluters, is limited to liability for harm other than pollution of controlled waters. The purpose of this restriction is to avoid duplication of liability which is already provided for in relation to anti-pollution works and operations powers and works notices under the Water Resources Act 1991.[279]

Although it seems plausible to reason that remediation notices should not be served in relation to matters that are otherwise provided for, two observations are warranted in relation to this. First, the exemption of liability of Class B persons will depend upon whether all non-polluting landowners fall into this category. As has been noted, if 'knowingly permitting' pollution covers a situation where an innocent purchaser of land later discovers contamination and fails to take action, then such a person would fall under Class A and, as a consequence, be unable to take the benefit of the water pollution exemption. Second, as has been previously noted, a potentially important distinction may be drawn between the *duty* to serve a remediation notice under the contaminated land provisions and the *power* to serve a works notice under the anti-pollution works provisions.

A further qualification upon the liability of remediation is provided for in respect of substances which have migrated from the land upon which they originated to land held by another owner or occupier. Here, Class A persons, who caused or knowingly permitted substances to be present in, on or under their land, will also be taken to have caused or knowingly

---

[274] *Ibid* s.87H(6).

[275] *Ibid* s.78H(7).

[276] Under s.78F(4) and (5) Environmental Protection Act 1990.

[277] *Ibid* s.78A(2), and see 13.7.3 above on the meaning of 'harm'.

[278] *Ibid* s.78J(2) Environmental Protection Act 1990.

[279] ss.161-161D Water Resources Act 1991, and see 13.2.2 above, and see 13.7.10 below on further contrasts between works notices and remediation requirements.

permitted the escape of the substances to further land.[280] By contrast, the owner or occupier of the land to which the substances have been transmitted, and who has not caused or knowingly permitted the substances to be present, will not be required to do anything by way of remediation of land or waters, other than those of which he is the owner or occupier.[281] Where substances are transmitted to further land, a non-polluting owner or occupier of land through which the substances have passed will not be liable for remediation of the further land to which the substances have migrated.[282] A final situation is where a person who has caused or knowingly permitted contamination of land transfers the ownership or occupation of that land to another person and contaminating substances have passed to other land. Here, the liability of the subsequent owner or occupier, who has not caused or knowingly permitted the contamination, will not extend to the remediation of the further land to which the substances have passed.[283]

Whilst the factual situations that are provided for in relation to migrating pollutants are rather complicated, it will be appreciated that contaminating substances are capable of being transmitted over considerable distances, particularly where groundwater flow is significant.[284] The rules governing liability for migrating pollutants follow the general principles for allocating liability to Class A and Class B persons. Hence, Class A persons will be liable for remediation of all land which has been contaminated through their actions, including land outside their ownership or occupation. However, for Class B persons remediation liability is limited to the extent of their land and does not require the remediation of adjoining land, assuming that no Class A person can be found. Similarly, where a Class B person has become the owner or occupier of the land which is the original source of contamination, that person's liability extends only to the land held and no remediation liability arises in relation to further land to which pollutants have been transmitted, assuming again that no Class A person can be found.

As a general matter, in respect of the situations where service of a remediation notice is precluded in relation to controlled waters, or where a person may not be made liable for remediation of other land, an enforcing authority is not prevented from taking remediation action, but where such action *is* taken the enforcing authority will be unable to recover the cost of so doing.[285] It follows from this that, in theory, a local authority is empowered to undertake the same actions as might be required of a landowner or occupier under a works notice served by the Agency.

---

[280] s.78K(1) Environmental Protection Act 1990.

[281] *Ibid* s.78K(3).

[282] *Ibid* s.78K(4).

[283] s.78K(5) Environmental Protection Act 1990.

[284] See *Cambridge Water Company* v *Eastern Counties Leather plc* [1994] 1 All ER 53 discussed at 3.10 above, where the offending contaminant travelled a distance of 1.3 miles between the point of origin and the point of abstraction, presumably passing through land in the ownership of several different owners on the way.

[285] ss.78J(7) and 78K(6) Environmental Protection Act 1990.

However, given the impossibility of recovering the costs, the likelihood of a local authority undertaking such works will depend upon Government approval for supplementary credit permitting the authority to borrow money needed to undertake the remediation.[286]

### 13.7.8 Offences

It is an offence for a person, without reasonable excuse, to fail to comply with any of the requirements of a remediation notice.[287] A person found guilty of this offence will be liable, on summary conviction, to a fine not exceeding level five on the standard scale, presently £5,000, and to a further fine of an amount equal to one-tenth of this for each day on which the failure continues after conviction of the offence and before the enforcing authority has begun to exercise its powers to undertake remediation. Where the offence is committed in relation to contaminated land which comprises industrial, trade or business premises, on summary conviction, the maximum amount of the fine is £20,000 and a daily fine of one-tenth of that amount is allowed. Where proceedings for an offence would afford an ineffectual remedy against non-compliance with a remediation notice the enforcing authority may take proceedings in the High Court for the purpose of securing compliance with the remediation notice.[288]

### 13.7.9 Remediation by Enforcing Authorities

In certain circumstances, the enforcing authority may do what is appropriate by way of remediation of the relevant land or waters.[289] In particular, remediation may be undertaken by the enforcing authority in the following situations:

(a)   where the authority considers it necessary to do anything itself by way of remediation for the purpose of preventing the occurrence of any serious harm, or serious pollution of controlled waters, of which there is imminent danger;

(b)   where an appropriate person has entered into a written agreement with the enforcing authority for that authority to do, at the cost of that person, that which he would otherwise be required to do by way of remediation;

(c)   where a person on whom the enforcing authority serves a remediation notice fails to comply with any of the requirements of the notice;

---

[286] See Circular Annex 2 paras.16.12 to 16.15.

[287] s.78M(1) Environmental Protection Act 1990, though this is subject to a defence where a person refuses to pay a proportion of the cost involved, where this has been apportioned between two or more persons, because another person to whom a part of the cost has been allocated has refused to, or is unable to, comply with a requirement of the remediation notices (s.78M(2)).

[288] s.78M(3)-(5) Environmental Protection Act 1990. On the use of injunctions to support criminal proceedings see 3.16.5 above.

[289] *Ibid* s.78N(1).

(d) where the enforcing authority is precluded[290] from including something by way of remediation in a remediation notice;

(e) where the enforcing authority considers[291] that it would not seek to recover reasonable costs of remediation or would seek only to recover a portion of those costs; and

(f) where no person has, after reasonable inquiry, been found to be an appropriate person.[292]

The last of these would allow an enforcing authority to take remediation action in relation to so-called 'orphan sites' where no polluter, landowner or occupier can be identified as an appropriate person.

Where the enforcing authority undertakes remediation in accordance with these provisions, it is normally entitled to recover the reasonable costs from the appropriate person.[293] However, in deciding whether to recover the cost, and, if appropriate, how much of the cost it is entitled to recover, the enforcing authority must have regard to any hardship which the recovery may cause to the person from whom the cost is recoverable, and any guidance issued by the Secretary of State.[294]

The concession which is made to the cost recovery power for 'hardship' may give rise to concerns both because of the potential practical difficulties to which it gives rise and for reasons of principle. If the imposition of a potentially enormous financial burden arising by way of remediation costs were to be construed as a 'hardship' for anyone but the most wealthy, then the cost recovery power would be of limited practical value and would certainly undermine the polluter pays principle.[295] Hence, the criteria on which 'hardship' is assessed need to be clearly specified to ensure consistent and equitable treatment of individuals in similar situations,[296] perhaps subject to determinations made by different enforcement authorities.

Noting that the term 'hardship' is not statutorily defined, the Circular suggests that it should carry its ordinary meaning of hardness of fate or circumstance, or severe suffering or privation. More helpfully, it is suggested that the term allows account to be taken of injustice and severe financial detriment.[297] Hence, where the overall cost of a business closing would be greater than the cost of remediation, the authority should consider waiving or reducing the extent of cost recovery, unless there is

---

[290] That is, precluded by ss.78J (relating to liability for pollution of controlled waters) or 78K (relating to liability in respect of substances which escape to other land).

[291] Under *ibid* s.78P(2).

[292] *Ibid* s.78N(3).

[293] s.78P(1) Environmental Protection Act 1990, though again this is subject to the exemptions provided by ss.78J (relating to liability for pollution of controlled waters) or 78K (relating to liability in respect of substances which escape to other land).

[294] *Ibid* s.78P(2).

[295] See 4.7.3 above on the polluter pays principle.

[296] House of Commons Environment Committee, *Contaminated Land* (1996) para.102.

[297] Circular Annex 2 paras.10.8 and 10.9.

evidence that the business has deliberately arranged its affairs so as to avoid responsibility for the costs of remediation.[298]

A direct contrast may be drawn with the power to recover reasonable expenses in relation to anti-pollution works and operations undertaken by the Agency,[299] where no provision is made for relief on grounds of hardship and the expenses recoverable are those 'reasonably incurred' by the Agency in undertaking the works or operations. This disparity of approach between provisions applicable to similar situations is difficult to reconcile.

### 13.7.10  Remediation and Anti-pollution Works

Explicit provision is made concerning the interaction between the remediation requirements under the contaminated land regime and related environmental provisions concerned with integrated pollution control, waste management site licences and provisions allowing for the removal of waste.[300] A link which is drawn with water pollution legislation is that no remediation notice may require a person to do anything which would impede the making of a discharge to controlled waters pursuant to a discharge consent.[301] Curiously though, there are no provisions dealing with the interrelationship between remediation requirements under the contaminated land regime and the powers of the Environment Agency relating to anti-pollution works and operations and the service of works notices in relation to these. Whilst observations have been made in passing concerning the contrasts between these, the key differences, and comment on the enforcement issues to which they give rise, may usefully be summarised.

As has been described, important powers are available to the Environment Agency to conduct anti-pollution works and operations, and related investigations, to prevent the entry of polluting matter into controlled waters, to remove polluting matter from such waters, to remedy pollution or to restore waters to their former state.[302] Where such works or operations are conducted, the Agency may recover reasonable expenses incurred from a person who caused or knowingly permitted the polluting matter to enter the waters or to be present at a place from which it was likely to enter such waters. In addition, the Agency has a power to serve a works notice on any person who caused or knowingly permitted the matter to be present at a place from which it is likely to enter the waters, or to be present in the waters. A works notice will require specified works or operations to be undertaken for the purpose of preventing the matter entering the waters, removing the matter from the waters or remedying the

---

[298] Circular Annex 3 paras.E21 to 23.

[299] Under s.161(3) Water Resources Act 1991, and see 13.2.1 above.

[300] s.78YB(1) to (3) Environmental Protection Act 1990.

[301] *Ibid* s.78YB(4) Environmental Protection Act 1990, and see Ch.10 above on discharge consents generally.

[302] See 13.2 above on anti-pollution works and operations.

pollution, or restoring the waters to their former state. Unless works need to be undertaken urgently, or no person can be found on whom to serve a works notice, the service of a works notice is required rather than the Agency undertaking the works itself.

Given the apparent similarity between situations where works notices might be served and situations which fall within the contaminated land regime, there is clear scope for overlap between the two regulatory mechanisms. Because of the potential for duplication of coverage, the Agency has published a policy statement, *Environment Agency Policy and Guidance on the use of Anti-pollution Works Notices*[303] which explains how the Agency proposes to use its power to issue works notices. In outline, the policy requires local authorities, acting under the contaminated land regime, to consult with the Agency before determining that land is contaminated in respect of the pollution of controlled waters. Where a local authority identifies contaminated land which is potentially affecting controlled waters it must consult the Agency and take into account its suggestions with regard to remediation requirements. Where the Agency identifies a case where actual or potential water pollution is arising from contaminated land, the Agency will notify the relevant local authority, thereby enabling the authority to identify the land as contaminated. In any instance where land has been identified as contaminated land the enforcement mechanisms under Part IIA of the 1990 Act will normally be used rather than the works notice system. The explanation for this is that Part IIA imposes a *duty* to serve a remediation notice, whereas the Agency is only given a *power* to serve a works notice.

Whilst the Agency's policy statement provides a useful guide as to how, in practice, the contaminated land regime and the use of works notices will operate, it is regrettable that this matter was not formally provided for in the legislation. It may also be queried whether the administrative practice of 'normally' recognising displacement of works notices by Part IIA of the 1990 Act means that there will *never* be situations where works notices are appropriately applied to contaminated land. This is particularly relevant in relation to some contrasts between the two systems of control.

First, there may be situations where controlled waters are contaminated but it is not possible to designate any contaminated land because of the lack of an ascertainable pollution linkage back to the source or pathway of contamination. In such a case, works notice powers would have to be applied.[304]

Second, a local authority is placed under a duty strategically to inspect its area for contaminated land, whereas the Agency is bound to monitor the extent of pollution in controlled waters[305] but not, specifically, to identify

---

[303] Environment Agency, *Environment Agency Policy and Guidance on the Use of Anti-Pollution Works Notices* (1999). This statement has been agreed with the Department of the Environment, Transport and the Regions and is summarised in the Circular (Annex 1 para.66).
[304] See Circular Annex 1 para.67.
[305] Under s.84(2) Water Resources Act 1991, and see 16.6 below.

land-based sources of such pollution. The Agency is entitled to carry out investigations for the purposes of establishing the source of matter which has entered, or is likely to enter, controlled waters, for the purpose of establishing the source of the matter and the identity of the person who caused or knowingly permitted it to be present in controlled waters or a place from which it was likely to enter controlled waters. However, this function is formulated as a *power* of the Agency rather than a *duty*.

Third, in certain cases, the time at which enforcement powers are applied may be of critical importance. Nothing, apparently, prevents the Agency making use of works notice powers in relation to land which has not yet been identified as contaminated. If a works notice were to be issued, and the land to which it related subsequently designated as contaminated, this might have significant implications. A remediation notice may not be served if it appears to the enforcing authority that appropriate things are being, or will be, done by way of remediation and if the works notice was being adhered to, presumably, this would provide a justification for not serving a remediation notice.[306] Hence, it would not be appropriate for a local authority to serve a remediation notice if the matter has been the subject of a works notice served by the Agency. Alternatively, the Agency, as enforcing authority, would probably be precluded from serving a remediation notice where a works notice has been served.

Fourth, insofar as a situation involves pollution of controlled waters, no remediation notice may be served upon a Class B appropriate person,[307] in which case the matter may only be addressed by the anti-pollution works powers being exercised by the Agency.

Fifth, where two or more persons are appropriate persons in respect of the liability, between those persons liability may be apportioned in accordance with guidance.[308] Accordingly, the Circular goes into some detail as to how apportioning liability is to be undertaken within a Class A liability group or a Class B liability group and between liability groups.[309] By contrast, the works notice procedure does not incorporate any explicit mechanism for apportioning liability.

Sixth, remediation may only be required in relation to those things that are considered reasonable having regard to the costs involved and the seriousness of the harm, or pollution of controlled waters, involved[310] and, as has been noted, the Circular is unclear on the extent to which consequent environmental benefits, or externalities, should not be taken into account. By contrast, the service of a works notices falls within the general obligation upon the Agency to have regard to *all* costs and benefits.[311] As a matter of policy, remediation is to be sought up to a

---

[306] s.78H(5)(b) Environmental Protection Act 1990.

[307] Under s.78J(1) *ibid*, and see 13.7.7 above.

[308] *Ibid* s.78F(7).

[309] Circular Annex 3 Ch.D.

[310] s.78E(4) Environmental Protection Act 1990.

[311] Under s.39 Environment Act 1995, and see 6.14 above.

'suitable for use' standard, whereas a works notice may be used to prevent the entry of a pollutant into controlled waters, remedying pollution and restoring waters, flora and fauna to their former state. That is, the required works are not necessarily related to the particular use to which the relevant land is to be put.

Finally, where anti-pollution works are undertaken by the Agency it may recover its reasonable costs, whereas where remediation works are undertaken by the Agency, or a local authority, remediation costs may have to be waived on grounds of 'hardship' as is required by the contaminated land regime.

Although the Agency's policy statement on the use of works notices may, in practice, avoid the duplication of powers that would otherwise arise, some of these disparities between the two enforcement mechanisms remain difficult to justify given the similarity between the kinds of situation to which they are to be applied. Complete consistency between the two sets of powers may not be easily achieved, but it has been suggested that some progress might be achieved by a direction being given to the Agency that works notices powers should be exercised to allow the apportionment of liability and should take account of hardship in a manner which is consistent with the contaminated land regime.[312] Clearly, there are good reasons of consistency for modifications of this kind.

---

[312] House of Commons Environment Committee, *Contaminated Land* (1996) paras 52-54, and see 13.7.9 above on 'hardship'.

# Chapter 14

# PLANNING LAW AND STRATEGIC WATER QUALITY MANAGEMENT

## 14.1 Introduction

A continuing theme in water pollution and water quality law is the appreciation that reactive approaches to unsatisfactory states of the aquatic environment are seriously limited. Proaction, however, takes a variety of forms involving the preventive and precautionary regulation of a range of activities to anticipate their adverse impacts upon water quality. The issue which underlies all these is the question as to what quality of water is being sought for a particular purpose. Proaction without a purpose is an impossible concept to grasp. Necessarily, therefore, thought needs to be given to strategic objectives for the aquatic environment so that measures concerning both land use and water quality can be formulated and applied with a clear goal to be achieved.

The purpose of this chapter is to consider the strategic mechanisms by which objectives for the protection of the aquatic environment may be realised through the application of land use planning and water quality planning law and related policy guidance. The chapter falls into three parts. The first is concerned with the ways in which town and country planning and environmental impact assessment law and policy may be used to further objectives for the water environment. The second deals with those aspects of water regulation which may be used strategically to secure water quality objectives either through formal statutory mechanisms and otherwise. Nonetheless, between land use and water quality planning, a degree of overlap and similarities of approach will be seen, since there are many respects in which the two approaches seek, by analogous routes, to secure rather similar environmental goals. The concluding part of the chapter, therefore, assesses the extent to which closer interaction between the two systems might be feasible and desirable.

Some limitations to the discussion must be noted from the outset. First, town and country planning law is a subject of considerable intricacy and it is not possible to do justice to this in the discussion which follows. Instead, stress is placed upon general aspects of the planning system for the purpose of emphasising their relevance to water quality.[1] Second, the emphasis upon water quality means that important issues in relation to water *quantity* management are omitted or only touched upon incidentally, so that the environmental problems of reconciling heavy water demands against limited supplies, and the implications of this for the aquatic

---

[1] For a more detailed account of town and country planning law see Moore (2000) and Grant (1976, updated), and for a discussion of the environmental context see Bell and McGillivray (2000) Ch.11.

environment, are not addressed. Third, the discussion of legal principles may neglect institutional and political factors which have a significant influence upon environmental planning. Local authorities, for example, who undertake the greater part of the responsibility for administering the town and country planning system in practice, have a local democratic mandate and are bound to balance a wide variety of social and economic factors in making planning decisions.[2] By contrast, the Environment Agency, which has the principal responsibility for the administration of water quality planning, draws its remit from its responsibilities under national legislation and policy and the considerable body of technical expertise that it possesses in relation to the implementation of its environmental responsibilities.[3] Because of this contrast, the actual impact of the two regulatory regimes under consideration may be strongly influenced by the differing backgrounds and perceptions of environmental priorities between local authorities and the Environment Agency.

### 14.2  Key Features of Town and Country Planning Law

Taking a broad-brush view of the subject area, town and country planning law falls into two main parts: formulating development plans, or 'development planning', and determining particular applications for planning permission, or 'development control'. Water quality issues arise in both development planning and development control, but an outline the main features of the two areas will be provided before discussing how the aquatic environment features in the broader system of land use control.

As a preface to development planning and development control, it must be noted that the town and country planning system consists of a range of powers and duties allocated to local planning authorities, but subject to the overall executive control of the Secretary of State.[4] Although practical responsibilities for formulating development plans and determining applications for development consent are normally allocated to local planning authorities, the Secretary of State has ultimate control over the planning system by means of a range of legislative, administrative and judicial powers.

In relation to legislative powers, the Secretary of State is provided with extensive powers to secure the implementation of the principle enactment, the Town and Country Planning Act 1990, by making secondary regulations and orders[5] and, for most practical purposes, implementation of the Act requires extensive legislative action on his part.[6] At the administrative level, the Secretary of State has wide-ranging powers to

---

[2] On local authorities see Ch. 8 above.

[3] See Ch.6 above on the Environment Agency.

[4] In relation to Wales, the National Assembly for Wales, see 6.2 above.

[5] s.333 Town and Country Planning Act 1990.

[6] See, for example, Town and Country Planning (Use Classes) Order 1987 (SI 1987 No.764), Town and Country Planning (General Permitted Development) Order 1995 (SI 1995 No.418) and Town and Country Planning (General Development Procedure) Order 1995 (SI 1995 No.419).

issue guidance to local planning authorities to ensure that they act in accordance with general planning policy. Hence, control over structure plans adopted by local authorities is maintained by a requirement that, in formulating a structure plan, the local authority must have regard to any regional or strategic planning guidance given to assist in the preparation of the plan[7] and, where relevant policy guidance exists, this will be a material consideration in determining any particular planning application.[8] At the judicial level, the Secretary of State has various powers to determine planning appeals, such as appeals against a refusal to grant planning permission or the grant of a permission subject to conditions[9] and also has the power to 'call in' particular applications for planning permission for his own determination.[10] The allocation of this range of functions to the Secretary of State serves to confine the decision-making role of local authorities in planning matters to one of 'bounded discretion', in which a local authority's planning functions are placed within the powers given by statute *and* do not encroach upon those matters which are subject to the overall control of the Secretary of State.

## 14.3 Development Planning

The central feature of development planning is that a duty is imposed upon local planning authorities to formulate development plans for a range of different purposes.[11] For most areas, this involves two tiers of planning, with responsibilities allocated at county level for structure plans and at district level for the local plans. Structure plans provide a general account of policies applicable to land use within the area, whereas local plans reformulate policies stated in the structure plan in relation to identified areas of land.

Broadly, the function of development plans is twofold: first, to provide a statement of the manner in which national and local policies are to be applied within the relevant area and, second, to provide a guide to whether particular kinds of development will be allowed in particular locations. Hence, at one level they indicate how strategic objectives for land use, such as the realisation of targets for the provision of housing, are to be realised; at another level they are location-specific in indicating whether a certain kind of development is likely to be authorised in a specific location. The location-specific element is never entirely conclusive as to whether a particular development proposal will be authorised, but will

---

[7] s.31(6)(a) Town and Country Planning Act 1990.

[8] See 14.4 below on this.

[9] s.78 Town and Country Planning Act 1990.

[10] *Ibid* s.77. Postscript: on the potential conflict between the role of the Secretary of State in formulating planning policy and determining applications, in the context of Schedule 1 Part I Art.6.1 of the Human Rights Act 1998, see *R (on the application of Holding & Barnes Plc)* v *Secretary of State for the Environment, Transport and the Regions* [2001] UKHL 23, *The Times* 10 May 2001, where it was held that there were sufficient procedural safeguards, by way of judicial review, to render the dual role lawful.

[11] Under Part II Town and Country Planning Act 1990.

generally be useful to prospective developers in identifying areas where specific kinds of development are most likely to be given approval.[12]

The important link between the content of relevant development plans, and the undertaking of a particular development project is the requirement that 'planning permission is required for the carrying out of any development of land'.[13] Developing land without planning permission is not, by itself, a criminal offence, but unauthorised development will allow the local planning authority to instigate the enforcement machinery relating to planning control.[14] Although enforcing planning law is problematic for many local authorities, who see this as a costly drain upon scarce resources, the procedures provide for the service of an enforcement notice against the person responsible for the unauthorised development which will require an activity to cease or a development to be removed. It is only when the action required under the enforcement notice is not undertaken within the time allowed that a criminal offence is committed.[15] Hence, in general terms, the fundamental prohibition upon which the planning system rests is that it is unlawful to contravene an enforcement notice. Nevertheless, the undertaking of unauthorised development of land is the first step towards commission of a criminal offence.

The fundamental requirement that planning permission is required for developing land allows the granting of particular permissions for development to be related to the content of the relevant development plan. This is done by the stipulation that 'where, in making any determination under the planning Acts, regard is to be had to the development plan, the determination shall be made in accordance with the plan unless material considerations indicate otherwise'.[16] The effect of this requirement is to emphasise the importance of the relevant development plan in the determination process by creating a presumption that the plan should be followed where there are no material considerations to the contrary. Nonetheless, the possibility is left open that other material considerations might be of sufficient weight to justify a departure from the development plan in some circumstances. In essence, this 'plan-led' presumption takes the development plan as a starting point and gives it a weight above that of other factors relevant to the determination. In practice, however, the difficulty will always be that of deciding whether the strength of other material considerations is sufficient to outweigh the presumption in favour of the development plan, or whether not following the plan would cause demonstrable harm to an interest of acknowledged importance.[17]

---

[12] See the discussion of s.54A Town and Country Planning Act 1990 below.

[13] s.57(1) Town and Country Planning Act 1990.

[14] Under Part VII Town and Country Planning Act 1990 and see DoE, Circular 10/97, *Enforcing Planning Control: Legislative Provisions and Procedural Requirements* (1997) and *Enforcing Planning Control: Good Practice Code for Local Authorities* (1997).

[15] s.179 Town and Country Planning Act 1990.

[16] *Ibid* s.54A.

[17] DoE, Planning Policy Guidance 1, *General Policy and Principles* (1997) para.40, and generally see *City of Edinburgh Council* v *Secretary of State for Scotland* [1997] 3 PLR 71.

## 14.4 Development Control

The requirement that planning permission is required for any development of land leaves a great deal hinging upon the meaning of 'development'. Statutorily, this is defined as 'the carrying out of building, engineering, mining or other operations in, on, over or under land, or the making of any material change in the use of any building or other land'.[18] The case law on the interpretation of these words is considerable,[19] but the essential function of the definition is to provide a general and *preliminary* identification of the matters that are to be subject to control. This preliminary identification of regulated kinds of land use is subject to statutory refinement in that, 'for the avoidance of doubt', certain matters are declared to constitute development or are stated not to constitute development[20] and detailed secondary legislation is enacted further to define what degree of change in land use will be sufficient to constitute a 'material' change of use.[21]

The issue of what degree of change to land or the use of land will constitute 'development' is a matter of some complexity. To prevent the large number of insignificant developments which take place overloading the planning system, a wide range of developments are given deemed planning permission.[22] Hence, specified kinds of minor land use activities are kept within the meaning of 'development', but the need for an explicit planning application to be made is dispensed with by the stipulation that they are 'deemed' to be granted permission by the Secretary of State without the need for a formal application to a local authority. This approach has the advantage that the deemed permission may be withdrawn in certain cases where the Secretary of State or the local planning authority is satisfied that it is expedient that certain categories of, otherwise, permitted development in specified areas should be the subject of explicit consideration.[23]

Where explicit planning permission is required for a development, a range of publicity and consultation requirements are provided for within the town and country planning system. Opinions of specified consultees must be sought on applications for particular categories of development and, in determining an application, the local planning authority must take into account representations made by consultees and other representations made.[24] This principle, alongside the obligation upon local planning authorities generally to publicise planning applications,[25] seeks to ensure

---

[18] s.55(1) Town and Country Planning Act 1990.

[19] For examples see Moore (2000) Chs.5 and 6.

[20] s.55 Town and Country Planning Act 1990. For example, works by statutory undertakers for the purposes of inspecting, repairing or renewing any sewers, mains or pipes and the use of land for the purposes of agriculture are stated *not* to be development (s.55(2)(c) and (e)).

[21] See Town and Country Planning (Use Classes) Order 1987 (SI 1987 No.764).

[22] Town and Country Planning (General Permitted Development) Order 1995 (SI 1995 No.418).

[23] *Ibid* Art.4.

[24] Art.10 Town and Country Planning (General Development Procedure) Order 1995 (SI 1995 No.419).

[25] *Ibid* Art.8.

that determination of applications is made on the basis of the fullest practicable input of relevant opinion and expertise. However, the consultation obligation remains no stronger than that, and providing that an authority adheres to the procedural requirement that such representations are 'taken into account' there will be no grounds for overturning a planning permission merely if the opinions of a consultee have not been endorsed in making the determination.

In making the final determination as to whether a planning application should be granted, and the conditions to which it is to be subject, the general obligation upon a local planning authority is that, in determining the application, the authority must have regard to provisions of the development plan, so far as material to the application, and to any other material considerations.[26] The test of what is a 'material consideration,' both in the preparation of plans or in the control of development, is broadly formulated so that the question 'is whether it serves a planning purpose [that is] one which relates to the character and use of the land'.[27] This principle seems to require planning authorities to take into account the widest conceivable range of social and economic factors in exercising planning functions, including a range of matters of specific relevance to the protection of the aquatic environment. For example, sewage disposal is capable of being a material consideration in a planning application, and where a development is proposed in an area which is not served by mains sewers the planning authority must consider how to ensure that development will not place an unacceptable burden on amenity.[28]

## 14.5  Water Quality and Town and Country Planning

Having outlined the key principles of the town and country planning system, consideration must be given to the mechanisms by which water quality issues are dealt with in development planning and development control.

### 14.5.1  The Role of the Environment Agency

The starting point for considering the protection of water quality through the town and country planning system is the status of the Environment Agency in relation to this system. Remarkably, the water-related statutory functions of the Agency[29] make no explicit reference to any function of the Agency in relation to the town and country planning system. Whilst it is stated that its functions encompass 'functions assigned to the National

---

[26] s.70(2) Town and Country Planning Act 1990.

[27] Per Lord Scarman, in *Great Portland Estates plc* v *Westminster City Council* [1984] All ER 744 p.750. On the status of European Community requirements as 'material considerations' see 4.17 above.

[28] DoE, Planning Policy Guidance Note 23, *Planning and Pollution Control* (1994) Annex 3 paras.17-18.

[29] Specified in s.2(1)(a) Environment Act 1995 and see 6.8 above.

Rivers Authority by or under any other enactment',[30] it is debatable whether this includes the Agency's town and country planning role. Essentially, the debate turns upon the question of how the term 'function' is to be understood. Normally, a function would imply the possession of both powers and duties by the Agency but, in relation to planning, its role, as will be seen, consists of various powers without any specific statutory duties, so that it is arguable whether it is genuinely a 'function' of the Agency or whether it should be separately categorised.

However classified, the role of the Agency in the town and country planning system is of considerable significance in influencing the formulation of development plans and the determination of particular applications for planning permission. Broadly, it may be inferred that the Agency should be exercising its planning powers in accordance with its principal aim and objective in relation to sustainable development,[31] whilst recognising the need to have regard to costs and benefits.[32] Accordingly, the Agency should be using its powers as a consultee in the town and country planning system to encourage the formulation of development plans that provide an appropriate level of protection for the water environment, and to oppose those development projects which are likely to have significant adverse environmental impacts.

More specific guidance as to what use the Agency should make of its powers in the town and country planning system is found in *The Environment Agency and Sustainable Development*.[33] This indicates that the Agency will become involved in land use planning by,

(a) responding to consultations by local planning authorities in relation to environmental impact assessment;[34]
(b) responding to requests from developers for information;
(c) responding to consultations on planning applications;
(d) responding and providing input to the preparation of development plans;
(e) responding to general enquiries about proposed developments; and
(f) providing technical advice to the Government at regional or national level in response to requests for information about the significance of any likely pollution from a proposed development.

The advice to local planning authorities should be provided in a manner that is consistent, reasonable and in the public interest, and consistent with national planning policy guidance.[35] Understandably, however, this

---

[30] s.2(1)(a)(viii) Environment Act 1995.
[31] Under s.4 Environment Act 1995 and DoE, MAFF and WO, *The Environment Agency and Sustainable Development* (1996) and see 6.7 above.
[32] Under s.39 Environment Act 1995, and see 6.14 above.
[33] DoE, MAFF and WO (1996) Ch.6 C p.26.
[34] See 14.6 below on environmental impact assessment.
[35] Specifically, Planning Policy Guidance Note 23, *Planning and Pollution Control* (1994) and see 14.10 below on this.

guidance is presented at a high level of generality and gives little insight into the way in which the Agency should deploy its resources so as to give priority to those matters where it may be most influential and beneficial in relation to development planning and development control.

Detailed powers are provided to the Agency under primary and secondary town and country planning legislation. In relation to the formulation of development plans under the Town and Country Planning Act 1990, local planning authorities are under a duty to consult various bodies including the Agency.[36] This allows the Agency to comment upon the implications of a draft development plan in respect of any function exercised by it, including pollution control. However, informally, it has been recognised that effective consultation on development planning requires continuing close liaison between the Agency and local planning authorities. In this respect a *Memorandum of Understanding* has been signed between the Agency and the Local Authorities Association outlining the general stated intentions of the Agency and the Association to build a relationship based on co-operation, openness and the exchange of information to emphasise a common commitment to the protection and enhancement of the environment.[37]

### 14.5.2 Development Plans

Whilst the formulation of development plans is primarily a responsibility of local authorities, in accordance with their statutory obligations and policy guidance, the Agency has been increasingly active in seeking to influence local authorities to incorporate environmental policies within development plans. *The Environment Agency and Development Plans*[38] identifies a range of development planning principles that the Agency proposes should be addressed in development plans to secure the protection and enhancement of the natural environment. Generally, the principles include the need to promote policies which contribute towards sustainable development; to balance the demands of development with the need to protect and enhance the environment; and to prevent, or control, the pollution of air, land and water. In relation to general pollution prevention, it is maintained that the location, extent and design of development can influence the degree to which new development is sustainable and the planning system has a role to play in regulating the location of development which may cause pollution.

Specifically, in relation to pollution prevention and water quality, the Agency advocates the incorporation of policies which maintain or improve the quality of groundwater, surface or coastal waters; resist development that poses an unacceptable risk to the quality of groundwater, surface or coastal waters; ensures that adequate foul and surface water provision is

---

[36] s.33 Town and Country Planning Act 1990 and Art.10 Town and Country Planning (Development Plan) Regulations 1991, SI 1991 No.2794.
[37] See Environment Agency, *Liaison with Local Planning Authorities* (1997).
[38] Environment Agency (1998).

available to serve new development and that the ultimate discharge does not cause an environmental problem; and ensures that adequate pollution control measures are incorporated into new developments to reduce the risks of water pollution. The formal justification for incorporating these policies lies in Ministerial planning policy guidance which advises that policies should reflect the need to protect water quality and to pay particular attention to the protection of groundwater resources. Hence,

> the factors which local authorities should take into account in preparing local plan policies will include . . . the possible impact of potentially polluting development on land use including the effects on health, the natural environment, or general amenity, resulting from releases to water and other environmental media.[39]

### 14.5.3 Development Control

In relation to individual applications for development consent, as has been noted, local planning authorities are under a duty to notify statutory consultees of certain planning applications. In particular, a planning authority will be bound to consult the Agency in relation to a proposed development which involves the carrying out of works or operations in the bed or on the banks of a river or stream, and other kinds of development which may have an impact upon the aquatic environment. The planning authority will then be bound to take into account any recommendations made by the Agency making the planning determination.[40] Beyond this formal role as a statutory consultee, the Agency is entitled to make representations in relation to *any* planning application which it considers may have a damaging effect upon the aquatic environment.[41]

The Agency comments on nearly 100,000 planning applications annually. The basis on which representations are made is set out in the Agency publication *Liaison with Local Planning Authorities*,[42] which is a manual produced to assist local authority planners in their day to day dealings with the Environment Agency. Broadly, the concerns of the Agency are that a new development should proceed only where it does not adversely affect river corridors and the natural water environment; pose an unacceptable risk of flooding; create an unacceptable risk of contamination to air, land and ground and surface waters; or require additional water resources beyond that available for industrial and public supply.

---

[39] Planning Policy Guidance Note 23, *Planning and Pollution Control* (1994) para.2.18.

[40] Art.10 Town and Country Planning (General Development Procedure) Order 1995, SI 1995 No.419. Mandatory consultation required where application sought under Planning (Hazardous Substances) Regulations 1992 (SI 1992 No.656), enacted under Planning (Hazardous Substances) Act 1990 which requires planning consent to be obtained for the presence of hazardous substances on, over or under land.

[41] Art.19 Town and Country Planning (General Development Procedure) Order 1995 (SI 1995 No.419).

[42] Environment Agency (1997).

For the Agency, a critical difficulty is that its view as to the undesirability of a particular development proposal is often only one amongst many material considerations that the local planning authority will have to take into account in determining whether to grant the planning permission which is sought. A good illustration of the difficulties involved in reconciling priorities for the aquatic environment against broader developmental concerns is to be found in *Ynys Mon Borough Council* v *Secretary of State for Wales*[43] which concerned an application for planning permission for six houses to be built. This proposal was strongly opposed by the then National Rivers Authority on environmental grounds. Following construction of the houses, it would have been the statutory right of the developer to be allowed to make a connection into the local sewerage system.[44] The contention of the Authority was that the local sewerage system was inadequate in that it allowed untreated foul sewage to be discharged into coastal waters. As a consequence, the Authority had formulated a policy to oppose all developments involving further connections to the sewerage system and, consequently, recommended refusal of the application until such time as the relevant sewerage undertaker had brought about adequate improvements to the sewerage system. This was accepted by the local planning authority, which declined the application, but not by the Planning Inspector on appeal. He took the view that, although the discharge of raw sewage into the sea was unsatisfactory, the discharge from an addition six small dwellings was not a sufficient reason to justify the refusal of the application.

In an appeal by the Council to quash the Inspector's decision, it was accepted that the duties upon the Authority were of high importance in the public interest and that the conditions at the existing sewage outfalls in the locality were unsatisfactory. Nevertheless, the Court declined to accept that the total embargo policy adopted by the Authority could be conclusive in relation to any particular proposed development. To do so would make the Authority's policy conclusive of any decision in the development control context where other relevant considerations needed to be addressed, and this would fetter the planning authority's discretion to give proper consideration to all relevant matters. Whilst the policy objectives of the Authority were important material considerations, it was imperative that they should be weighed together with all other relevant matters. In essence, this is what the Inspector had done by not treating the policy of the Authority as conclusive of the matter for determination and the decision that he had arrived at could not be challenged as unlawful merely because it conflicted with the policy. He was entitled to conclude that, despite the policy, the discharge contributed by the additional houses would not give rise to deleterious consequences in the planning context. It was held that the Inspector had had proper regard to the evidence, and the weight to be attached to this was a matter for his judgement, hence the

---

[43] [1993] JPL 225.

[44] Under s.98 or s.106 Water Industry Act 1991, and see 11.3.2B above. Despite the right of connection to a sewer it has been held to be valid to decline an application for planning permission on the ground of inadequate sewerage infrastructure (*George Wimpey & Co Ltd* v *Secretary of State for the Environment and Maidstone District Council* [1978] JPL 773).

Court declined to overturn the decision. This shows that a planning application which, if allowed, will contravene Environment Agency policy on pollution control will not necessarily be refused, since the policy is only one material consideration and should not be followed where it is outweighed by other material planning considerations.

Whilst the Town and Country Planning Act 1990, and secondary legislation under this Act, sets out the legislative structure for the planning system, a large part of this system is actually determined by matters of policy guidance, to which local authorities are bound to have regard, rather than statutory legal powers and duties. The interaction of policy guidance and legal powers and duties, in relation to development projects which have clear potential for causing damage to the aquatic environment, is often a matter of some complexity. For example, since the most common single cause of pollution incidents in England and Wales is the inadequate treatment of sewage effluent,[45] it might be inferred that the Agency should make representations advocating strict environmental conditions upon any proposed sewage treatment development to address the environmental concerns to which such a proposal gave rise.

However, alongside the various general environmental duties to which the Agency is subject,[46] it is subject to a further duty,[47] in exercising any of its powers, under any enactment, to have particular regard to the duties imposed on any water or sewerage undertaker[48] which appears likely to be affected by the exercise of the power in question. Amongst other things, this will mean that the Agency must have regard to the duty upon sewerage undertakers to 'provide, improve and extend a system of public sewers and so to cleanse and maintain those sewers as to ensure that the [undertaker's] area is effectually drained,' and to 'make provision for the emptying of those sewers and such further provision as is necessary from time to time for effectually dealing, by means of sewage disposal works or otherwise, with the contents of those sewers'.[49] The implication of the duty upon the Agency to have regard to the responsibilities of sewerage undertakers is that, when exercising its role as a consultee in the town and country planning process, it must recognise the legal duties upon sewerage undertakers. Hence, the Agency should avoid raising objections to activities which are necessary to allow undertakers to fulfil their statutory functions. A difficulty, therefore, is how the Agency's general statutory duty to protect and enhance the aquatic environment is to be reconciled

---

[45] Environment Agency, *Water Pollution Incidents in England and Wales 1998* (1999) indicated that 24% of incidents, identified by source, arose from inadequate sewage treatment. See further at 9.2 above.

[46] See 6.10 above on general environmental duties on the Environment Agency.

[47] Under s.15 Water Resources Act 1991.

[48] Under Parts II to IV of the Water Industry Act 1991.

[49] s.94(1) Water Industry Act 1991.

with the statutory duty to take account of the responsibilities upon sewerage undertakes for sewerage provision.[50]

### 14.5.4 Planning and Sewage Treatment Infrastructure

Although the role of the Environment Agency in the town and country planning process has been considered in some detail, water and sewerage undertakers also feature in the process both as consultees and as prospective developers. In respect of consultation, undertakers may respond to applications for planning permission by others and thereby draw the attention of the local planning authority to material considerations such as the water service implications of a proposed development.[51] In respect of development by a sewerage undertaker, certain activities are accorded permitted development status where repairs to underground sewers are involved or other works concerning the provision of sewers or associated apparatus.[52] However, the extent of the permitted development rights allowed to sewerage undertakers does not extend to major infrastructure projects such as new sewage treatment works and projects of this kind are likely to be controversial.

The issue of determining planning applications concerning sewage treatment infrastructure is further complicated by advice that has been given to local planning authorities in this context. Department of the Environment Circular 17/91, *Water Industry Investment: Planning Considerations*, was prompted by the need to comply with various European Community water directives (including the Bathing Water Directive)[53] and the ban upon sludge disposal at sea (reaffirmed in the Urban Waste Water Treatment Directive).[54] The Circular was influenced by the need to comply with a series of schedules for water quality measures determined by the Directives, and refers to the need to implement land-based sewage sludge disposal by the end of 1998 and to achieve compliance with the Bathing Water Directive by 1995 'in all but a

---

[50] Similarly, see the discussion of the National Environment Programme under AMP3 and the role of the Agency in relation to supporting or opposing schemes for funding improvements in water industry infrastructure at 7.8.3 above.

[51] That is, in response to the publicity given to applications for planning permission in accordance with Art.8 Town and Country Planning (General Development Procedure) Order 1995 (SI 1995 No.419). However, water and sewerage undertakers are not afforded the status of statutory consultees allowed to the Environment Agency in relation to certain water-related projects (under *ibid* Art.10). See 14.4 above on sewerage provision as a material consideration and 11.3.2(b) above on developments which may have the effect of overloading a sewerage system.

[52] See Town and Country Planning (General Permitted Development) Order 1995 (SI 1995 No.418) Art.3(1) and Sch.2: Part 10 of which relates to repairs to services and allows works for the purpose of inspecting repairing or renewing any sewer, main, pipe or other apparatus including breaking open any land for that purpose; and Part 16 of which relates to development by or on behalf of sewerage undertakers involving underground development required in connection with the provision, improvement, maintenance or repair of a sewer, outfall pipe, sludge main or associated apparatus, and related matters.

[53] Directive 76/160/EEC and see 5.5.2 above.

[54] Directive 91/271/EEC and see 5.6.2 above.

few exceptional cases'.[55] Nonetheless, the guidance that the Circular offers to local planning authorities remains instructive. In particular, local planning authorities are requested to work expeditiously with the water industry to find suitable sites for sewage treatment works and give sympathetic consideration to proposals for enhancing sewage treatment; and local plans and unitary development plans should identify suitable locations for sewage treatment works. Notwithstanding this, if the relevant development plan contains no site-specific proposal which relates to the particular development proposed, nor more general policies that are material, the planning application should be determined on its merits in the light of the other material considerations.

Setting aside the environmental impact assessment of sewage treatment facilities,[56] the combined effect of the different kinds of statutory responsibility and policy guidance that are capable of relating to a proposed sewage treatment facility are of some intricacy. The Circular tends to encourage local planning authorities to be sympathetic towards such proposals and to process them swiftly. Hence the general remit of the Agency, in protecting the water environment, is counterbalanced by the effect of the Circular and moderated by its duty to have regard to the sewage treatment obligations upon undertakers. Hopefully, any improvement of sewage treatment infrastructure should be conducive to a reduction in the alarming numbers of incidents attributable to inadequate functioning of treatment works, and should be generally supported by the Agency. However, the constraints which are placed upon the Agency in making planning representations demonstrates the complexities that arise in reconciling the competing environmental and developmental pressures involved in determining a planning application for a project of this kind.

### 14.5.5  Planning Conditions and Obligations

#### 14.5.5A  Planning conditions

Where a planning permission is actually granted, it will invariably incorporate conditions which relate to the development and which may have significant environmental implications. Consequently, the role of the Agency may often be to argue that a development is made subject to appropriate conditions rather than prevented altogether. A local planning authority may impose planning conditions as it thinks fit when granting a planning permission and, amongst other things, may impose conditions for regulating the development or use of the land to which the permission relates, or requiring the carrying out of works which are expedient in connection with the development.[57] The scope for imposing conditions is broadly construed providing that conditions are imposed for a legitimate planning purpose, fairly and reasonably related to the development which

---

[55] On *actual* compliance with the Bathing Water Directive, see 5.5.2C above.

[56] See 14.6 below on environmental impact assessment.

[57] ss.70(1)(a) and 72(1)(a) Town and Country Planning Act 1990.

is permitted and are not so unreasonable that no local authority could reasonably have imposed them.[58] Hence, there is considerable scope for the environmentally adverse effects of a development to be mitigated by appropriately formulated planning conditions,[59] though it is clear that planning conditions may not be used to duplicate the system of controls provided for by various kinds of environmental licences.[60]

A pertinent example of the use of planning conditions in a water quantity context is *W E Black Ltd* v *Secretary of State for the Environment and London Borough of Harrow*.[61] Here, permission had been granted for a residential development subject to a planning condition requiring surface water attenuation and/or storage works to be carried out to reduce the risk of flooding in the locality and, subsequently, not to allow the development to be occupied until such works were carried out. The developer maintained that this condition was invalid because it was inconsistent with provisions under the Water Industry Act 1991 which allowed connection to be made with a sewerage undertaker's sewer for the purpose of draining the development site.[62] Although it was accepted that there was a degree of overlap between planning legislation and the 1991 Act, it was found that this did not amount to duplication. Moreover, there was a legitimate planning concern in the avoidance of flooding and the effect of this upon residential amenities. It was not contrary to these objectives to mitigate stress on the water utilities system by imposing the condition, and its validity was upheld.

### 14.5.5B Planning obligations

Planning conditions are subject to certain limitations in that they may only relate to matters which are the within the scope of the proposed development,[63] they are inappropriate in respect of positive or continuing obligations and may not involve monetary payments. However, these limitations may be avoided by a developer entering into an enforceable agreement or undertaking, termed a 'planning obligation', in relation to a proposed development. Planning obligations may be entered into restricting the development or use of land, requiring specified operations or activities to be carried out, requiring the land to be used in a specified way or requiring money to be paid to the local authority. Moreover, difficulties in respect of enforcing planning conditions against successive landowners should not arise in relation to planning obligations insofar as they will be enforceable against the person entering the obligation and

---

[58] *Newbury District Council* v *Secretary of State for the Environment* [1981] AC 578.

[59] For example, to provide for land restoration after development by way of 'aftercare' conditions (s.72(5) and Sch.5 Town and Country Planning Act 1990).

[60] Planning and Policy Guidance Note 23, *Planning and Pollution Control* (1994) and see the discussion of this at 14.10 below.

[61] [1997] Env LR 1.

[62] Under s.106 Water Industry Act 1991 and see 11.3.2B above on this.

[63] *Ladbrokes Ltd* v *Secretary of State for the Environment* [1981] JPL 427.

against any person deriving title from that person.[64] Clearly, planning obligations are potentially far wider in scope that planning conditions.[65]

Despite the flexibility of planning obligations as a mechanism for allowing developers of land to meet the cost to the community of a major development, perhaps by paying for improvements in local infrastructure or providing compensatory environmental benefit to offset the impact of the development, the practical use of planning obligations is a matter of controversy. Concern has been expressed about the safeguards against local authorities 'buying and selling planning permission' in return for planning gain and it has been recommended that the requirements for planning conditions should be scrutinised to ensure that they prevent planning permissions being bought by the highest bidder.[66]

Some attempt has been made to clarify the circumstances where a planning obligation may appropriately be used through specification of the following policy requirements for a planning obligation, which require that it should be:

  (a)  necessary;
  (b)  relevant to planning;
  (c)  directly related to the proposed development;
  (d)  fairly and reasonably related in scale and kind to the proposed development; and
  (e)  reasonable in all other respects.[67]

However, the satisfaction of these criteria, particularly whether a developer's contribution to the improvement of local infrastructure is sufficiently direct in its relationship with the proposed development, may remain a finely balanced issue in many instances. It has been authoritatively reaffirmed that a test to be applied in determining whether a planning obligation is a material consideration is whether it has some connection with the proposed development which is not *de minimis*.[68] However, the position remains, that balancing material considerations, particularly where two or more developer are competing to develop a particular site and offering alternative planning obligations, is an intricate and opaque exercise which does little to counter the perception of planning permission being granted to the highest bidder.

On the other hand, the official guidance is emphatically that planning obligations should not be used to facilitate unacceptable development, nor required where development would be acceptable in their absence. In theory, these are sound principles, but in practice they are issues on which

---

[64] s.106(1) and (3) Town and Country Planning Act 1990.
[65] See *Good* v *Epping Forest District Council* [1994] JPL 372.
[66] Nolan Committee on *Standards in Public Life*, Third Report, 1997, Recommendation 36 and see Cornford (1998) and Planning and Environmental Law Reform Working Group of the Society for Advanced Legal Studies (1999).
[67] DoE, Circular 1/97, *Planning Obligations* (1997).
[68] *Tesco Stores Ltd* v *Secretary of State for the Environment and others* [1995] WLR 759.

it might be quite difficult to challenge the exercise of discretion by a local authority or the Secretary of State. Moreover, the official view is that, properly used, planning obligations allow considerable scope to enable environmental impacts of development to be offset by substitution, replacement or regeneration of natural features. Hence, examples are given of the loss of a wetland habitat on a site being offset by opening up of a culverted stream or river or compensation for a development being provided by action to protect or reduce harm to protected sites or species or acknowledged importance.[69]

Whilst some general doubts may be raised as to the extent which it is genuincly possible to 'substitute' a recreated habitat for one that has been lost as a result of development,[70] there is some evidence that making development conditional upon developers providing environmental benefit may be of value in appropriate situations. One instance which has been heralded as a success story of this kind is the redevelopment of the Barn Elms Reservoirs in south west London,[71] where 9 hectares of the site of redundant water storage facilities was allowed to be developed for housing. Housing development, in isolation, would have been an unacceptable development and contrary to the development plan. However, permission was given subject to planning obligations which required the remainder of the 100 acre site to be developed as a wetland area in partnership with the Wildlife and Wetlands Trust. The range of wetland habitats created in accordance with these requirements have proved to be of significant value for a wide variety of birds and aquatic fauna and flora which now inhabit the site. The significant point about this example is that the housing developers, Berkeley Homes Ltd, were able to contribute £11 million towards the wetland site as a consequence of the profitable housing development. The planning gain from the housing project was able to be directly channelled into improvements in the aquatic environment and local amenity in circumstances where, had the housing development not been authorised, it was not evident that the cost of the wetland development would have otherwise been available. The extent to which 'enabling development' of this kind may be used to secure environmental benefit are not altogether clear, but the example provides at least one important example of planning obligations being used to secure direct benefit to the water environment.

*14.5.5C Planning conditions and obligations and contaminated land*

A potentially important future use of planning conditions and, perhaps, planning obligations, is in relation to the use of these to secure the remediation of contaminated land.[72] Although the powers to require the remediation of contaminated land are extensively provided for under Part

---

[69] Department of the Environment, Circular 1/97, *Planning Obligations* (1997) Annex B.
[70] Whatmore and Boucher (1993) and Brooke (1996).
[71] Cuthbertson (1996) and Desmier (2000).
[72] Generally see 13.7 above on contaminated land remediation.

IIA of the Environmental Protection Act 1990,[73] as added by the Environment Act 1995, it is intended that this regime will operate in conjunction with the town and country planning system. Hence where a proposed development is the subject of a planning application, and this reveals contamination of the site, it is the function of the planning system to ensure that the state of the land does not pose unacceptable risks to human health or the environment. Land contamination is a material consideration in planning law, so that a planning authority must consider the potential implications of any contamination both in development planning and development control.[74]

Essentially, therefore, a planning authority, in determining a planning application, will have to satisfy itself that the potential for contamination is properly assessed. Where necessary, the planning permission should incorporate any conditions which are necessary to secure remediation to the standard which makes the land 'suitable for the use' which is intended.[75]

The division of roles between the contaminated land regime under Part IIA of the Environmental Protection Act 1990 and the planning system is, broadly, that the planning system will be used to secure remediation in relation to any land which is the subject of a planning application. Where no such application is envisaged, however, the contaminated land regime will be applied. However, it is clear that harmonisation is needed between the two mechanisms for requiring remediation.

In relation to harmonisation, new planning guidance is under preparation to clarify the interface between the two regimes.[76] However, there are some significant issues to be addressed in this exercise. Whilst the 'suitable for use' criterion applies to both the contaminated land regime and the planning system, the major contrast is that the planning system places remediation costs upon the developer, whereas the contaminated land regime places these costs on either the person causing the contamination or the present owner or occupier of the land. Also, there are exceptions to liability for remediation provided for under the contaminated land regime insofar as remediation may only be required to the extent that it is 'reasonable' and remediation costs may not be recovered where this would result in 'hardship'.[77] The extent to which these considerations are relevant where a planning authority seeks to impose a planning condition requiring the remediation of land needs to be clarified.

---

[73] See also the Contaminated Land (England) Regulations 2000, (SI 2000 No.227), discussed at 13.7 above.
[74] DETR, Circular 02/2000, *Environmental Protection Act 1990: Part IIA Contaminated Land* (2000) Annex I paras.10(b) and 45.
[75] See DoE, Planning Policy Guidance Note 23, *Planning and Pollution Control* (1994) para.4.2 and see DoE, Circular 11/95, *The Use of Conditions in Planning Permissions* (1995).
[76] DETR, Circular 02/2000, *Environmental Protection Act 1990: Part IIA Contaminated Land* (2000) Annex I para.47.
[77] See 13.7.5 and 13.7.9 below on the meanings of 'reasonableness' and 'hardship'.

## 14.6 Environmental Impact Assessment and Water Quality

Alongside the basic components of town and country planning, an aspect of planning law deserving special consideration is its application to fulfil European Community obligations to require environmental impact assessment of certain projects which are likely to have a significant environmental impact. The need to transpose Community obligations concerning this has generated an extensive body of secondary legislation, including regulations relating to harbour works,[78] drainage[79] and marine fish farming,[80] which clearly have an important aquatic dimension. Nonetheless, in practice, the most common application of the requirement for environmental impact assessment arises under town and country planning law and, for that reason, it is most appropriately considered here.

### 14.6.1 The Environmental Assessment Directive

The European Community Directive on the Assessment of the Effects of Certain Private and Public Projects on the Environment[81] requires a assessment procedure in relation to certain projects, which are deemed, or likely, to have a significant effect upon the environment. Such projects will only be permitted if the authorising body takes into account specified environmental information in making its determination as to whether a project will be authorised. The detail of the environmental impact assessment process is quite intricate[82] but, most pertinently, it requires the identification and assessment of direct and indirect effects of a project upon water.[83] Where relevant, an estimation should be provided, amongst other things, of the type and quantity of expected residues and emissions to water resulting from the operation of the proposed project.[84] For the majority of projects for which environmental impact assessment is required, the authorisation sought will be a planning permission which will be determined by the local planning authority. Determination must be in accordance with the national regulations giving effect to the requirements of the Directive and encompassing important provisions concerning public consultation.[85]

In the town and country planning context, local planning authorities are obliged, amongst a range of other factors, to assess the likely impacts of a development project upon the aquatic environment where it involves an

---

[78] Harbour Works (Environmental Impact Assessment) Regulations 1999 (SI 1999 No.3445).

[79] Environmental Impact Assessment (Land Drainage Improvement Works) Regulations 1999 (SI 1999 No.1783).

[80] Environmental Impact Assessment (Fish Farming in Marine Waters) Regulations 1999 (SI 1999 No.367).

[81] Directive 85/337/EEC (the 'Original' Directive), now amended by Directive 97/11/EC (the 'Amending' Directive).

[82] See Bell and McGillivray (2000) Ch.12 and on environmental impact assessment generally see Sheate (1994).

[83] Art.3 Original Directive.

[84] Annex III Original Directive.

[85] The Town and Country Planning (Environmental Impact Assessment) (England and Wales) Regulations 1999 (SI 1999 No.293).

emission or discharge to water. This is curious, given that the main expertise and regulatory responsibility for the aquatic environment lies with the Environment Agency. However, the local planning authority will be obliged to consult the Agency, and to give it an opportunity to express its opinion, where a project is likely to have adverse impacts upon the aquatic environment.[86] Albeit by a rather circuitous route, environmental assessment of the impact of a discharge to water is provided for in circumstances where it forms a part of a project requiring an environmental statement, but the ultimate assessment of environmental impact is undertaken by the planning authority rather than the Environment Agency.

Securing a planning permission does not circumvent the need for the developer, or operator of the installation, to obtain a discharge consent for a discharge to controlled waters.[87] However, the determination of the discharge consent application will not require repetition of the environmental impact assessment procedure. Where a discharge consent is sought, which does not arise in conjunction with any new development project for which planning permission needs to be obtained, this will not require environmental impact assessment for the reason that it will not constitute a 'project' within the meaning of the Directive, that is, 'the execution of construction works or of other installations or schemes, other interventions in the natural surroundings and landscape including those involving the extraction of mineral resources'.[88] This, clearly, is anomalous insofar as it allows similarly harmful discharges to be subject to, and exempt from, environmental impact assessment depending upon whether they are associated with developments that fall within town and country planning control.

### 14.6.2 The Amending Directive

Recently, it has become necessary to modify environmental impact assessment requirements in order to implement amendments to the Environmental Assessment Directive.[89] Amongst other things, the Amending Directive extends the range of projects for which environmental impact assessment is required. The expansion of the range of projects that require environmental impact assessment add wastes water treatment plants to the range of projects.[90] This is a mandatory requirement where such projects exceed a certain capacity,[91] and is required for smaller plants only where they are likely to have a significant effect upon the environment. As with other projects involving a discharge to water, these

---

[86] *Ibid* Reg.13.

[87] See Ch.10 on discharge consents generally.

[88] Art.1(2) Original Directive.

[89] Under Directive 97/11/EC (the 'Amending' Directive).

[90] para.13 Annex I and para.11(c) Annex II Amending Directive.

[91] That is, wastewater treatment plants with a capacity exceeding 150,000 population equivalent as defined Art.2(6) of Urban Waste Water Treatment Directive (91/271/EEC) and see 5.6.2 above on this Directive (Annex I para.13 Amending Directive).

projects will fall for consideration by local planning authorities under the town and country planning regime and the relevant regulations.[92]

More problematically perhaps, the Amending Directive adds various water-related projects to the list of projects for which environmental impact assessment is required. Specifically, these are projects which involve groundwater abstraction, artificial recharge of groundwater and the transfer of water between river basins, excluding transfer of piped drinking water.[93] Where a project exceeds certain limits,[94] environmental impact assessment will be mandatory, but where it falls below those limits it will be required only where it is likely to have significant effect upon the environment. The projects at issue are primarily concerned with quantitative, rather than qualitative, water concerns but, nevertheless, there is clear scope for a water quality dimension to such projects. For example, the transfer of water between different river basin catchments has immense potential for adverse impact upon the ecological character of the receiving waters, and this would be a matter which would need to be considered in any relevant environmental statement.[95]

The extension of environmental impact assessment to groundwater abstraction and recharge and river basin transfers is problematic in the sense that projects of this kind are capable of falling outside the system of town and country planning control and, therefore, need separate legal mechanisms for implementation. The solution which is proposed to address this difficulty is that responsibility for the implementation of the Amending Directive, in relation to these kinds of projects, is to be allocated to the Environment Agency rather than local planning authorities insofar as projects do not require planning consent. This is to be done by making environmental impact assessment a requirement for obtaining a licence for abstraction or impounding under Part II of the Water Resources Act 1991 for relevant projects.

Consequently, where a water resources project, which does not require planning permission, requires an abstraction or impounding licence it will be the duty of the Agency to determine whether the licence application needs to be supported by an environmental statement. In some instances this will be mandatory because the project falls within the thresholds where environmental impact assessment is explicitly required, but in other instances it will be for the Agency to determine whether the project is

---

[92] The Town and Country Planning (Environmental Impact Assessment) (England and Wales) Regulations 1999 (SI 1999 No.293).

[93] paras.11 and 12 Annex I and paras.10(l) and (m) Annex II Amending Directive.

[94] The relevant thresholds for projects requiring mandatory environmental impact assessment are, for groundwater abstraction or artificial recharge schemes, where the annual volume of water abstracted or recharged is equivalent to or exceeds 10 million cubic metres; for works for the transfer of water resources between river basins, where the transfer exceeds 100 million cubic meters per year; and in all other cases, where works for the transfer of water resources between river basins where the multi-annual average flow of the basin of abstraction exceeds 2,000 million cubic metres per year and where the amount of water transferred exceeds 5% of this flow (paras.11 and 12 Annex I Amending Directive).

[95] See 7.10.1 above on transfer of water between catchments.

likely to have significant environmental effects because of its nature, size or location. In deciding whether to grant the licence applied for, the Agency will be bound to consider the information in the environmental statement and any representations made in relation to it. At the time of writing, the proposed legal mechanism to give effect to this is the draft Water Resources (Environmental Impact Assessment) Regulations 1999[96] which, in many respects, parallel the corresponding town and country planning regulations.[97]

A general observation on the water dimension to environmental impact assessment is that it demonstrates anomalies in both European Community law and the mechanisms for national implementation. First, it would seem environmentally rational that an effluent discharge should be subject to environmental impact assessment if it is likely to have a significant effect upon the environment regardless of whether it happens to be associated with a new development project. Second, if an environmental impact assessment is required, it should be undertaken by the national body best able to assess the relevant environmental impacts and this should not be left to depend upon the environmentally irrelevant consideration as to whether the impact arises from a project which happens to fall within those requiring planning permission within the peculiarities of national town and county planning law.[98]

## 14.7 Water Quality Planning

In essence, land use planning involves the exposition of strategic objectives for land use and the taking of particular decisions consistently with, and in furtherance of, those objectives. By analogy, 'water quality planning' envisages a similar use of strategically formulated objectives for water quality as a means of guiding decision-making. However, the relatively sophisticated mechanisms for land use planning, provided for under town and county planning and environmental assessment law, contrast sharply with the largely separate system of mechanisms which exist for water quality planning. Whilst this separation exists for primarily historical reasons, parallels may be drawn between town and country planning and water quality planning and, when an increasingly holistic view needs to be taken of environmental management, the degree of separation between the two systems of planning control may be increasingly difficult to justify.

Although the practical responsibility for water quality planning in England and Wales rests with the Environment Agency, through the exercise of its powers and duties under the Water Resources Act 1991 and the

---

[96] Published for consultation in January 1999. The late implementation (transposition was required by 31 March 1999) may raise issues concerning the possible direct effect of the Directive, see 4.16 above.

[97] That is, the Town and Country Planning (Environmental Impact Assessment) (England and Wales) Regulations 1999 (SI 1999 No.293).

[98] See discussion at 14.10 below of interrelationship between land use planning and water quality law.

Environment Act 1995, the executive responsibility for water quality planning rests with the relevant Ministers with responsibility for the environment and agriculture. Hence, the Ministers are possessed of extensive powers to enact secondary legislation, to give guidance and directions to the Agency and to make determinations in relation to various kinds of appeal. As under the town and country planning system, the wide range of water quality functions which Ministers exercise in relation to the supervision of the Agency have important implications in relation to the strategic management of water quality.

Broadly, any aspect of water quality management which is undertaken for the purpose of achieving an overall improvement in the state of the aquatic environment might be characterised as 'strategic' in some sense. However, 'strategic' is here more narrowly construed as encompassing activities and mechanisms which are explicitly directed towards the realisation of specified objectives for the water environment, largely, through the securing of quality objectives for particular waters. This approach has been significantly influenced by the need for measures to give national effect to European Community water directives, requiring the realisation of various water quality parameters for certain categories of waters. However, the approach may also be used as a more broadly-based means of securing nationally, or even locally, formulated water quality goals. Again the general contrast to be emphasised is that law and practice are being applied in a purposeful way to require pro-active measures for the purposes of achieving specified environmental standards, rather than being used as a reactive response to past pollution incidents.

By contrast with development plans in town and country planning law, the formal requirements for water quality plans are less well developed. Insofar as water quality management is conceived of as a strategic activity, formal requirements for the specifying and realising water quality objectives are legally provided for through the mechanisms for establishing statutory water quality objectives. As will be seen, this approach has been incompletely applied because of the failure to specify water quality objectives for many waters. However, the alternative is the use of 'informal', non-mandatory, Local Environment Agency Plans (LEAPS) which have been established for many waters which are not subject to statutory water quality objectives. These two levels of water quality planning are considered in the following sections.

## 14.8 Statutory Water Quality Objectives

As has been noted,[99] the UK has long resisted the setting of statutory water quality objectives and standards, preferring a more flexible approach. However, the need to transpose European Community water quality directives requiring water quality objectives to be met and maintained,

---

[99] See 1.4.2 above on the historical resistance towards statutory specification of water quality objectives and standards.

caused a change of attitude towards formalisation of objectives for water quality.

### 14.8.1 Water Quality Objectives

The strategic management of water quality requires the setting of objectives which are to be achieved for particular waters along with an explicit schedule by which those objectives are to be realised. To some extent, this practice has been followed for some years in England and Wales insofar as former water authorities were committed to a programme of specifying water quality objectives for all surface waters, along with short and long-term objectives for such waters, which were used as a basis for determining applications for discharge consents.[100]

However, in contrast to the traditional approach of self-imposed targets for water quality being set by water authorities and subsequent bodies, this goal-oriented aspect of water quality management has assumed a new significance because of the need to impose explicit legal obligations upon the national competent authority, for the purposes of implementing European Community water quality directives.[101] The effect of Community legislation has been to impose specific quality requirements upon water for particular kinds of use, which has meant that the strategic element in water quality management must be placed upon a statutory footing.

The broad policy basis for a statutory scheme for water quality objectives, as originally set out, was that three factors should be taken into account. First, the scheme should specify the different uses which it should be possible to make of the waters concerned and contain standards appropriate for each of them. Second, the scheme must take account of the requirements of European Community directives. Third, the scheme must incorporate a realistic time-scale for achieving desirable improvements. In relation to water use classes, it was thought that these should be kept as simple as possible, with regard to costs and benefits, by only setting standards related to genuine uses of rivers and employing only properly measurable and objective parameters for each use class. Following this reasoning, categories such as 'general ecosystem' and 'aesthetic quality' were thought unsuitable in that existing methodologies did not allow sufficiently clear parameters to be established.[102] Initially, therefore, the appropriate use categories were limited to fisheries ecosystems,

---

[100] See National Water Council (1978) and see 1.4.4 above.

[101] See Ch.5 above on European Community water directives.

[102] See also DoE, *Freshwater Quality: Government Response to the Sixteenth Report of the Royal Commission on Environmental Pollution* (1995) p.10, where the point is made that the biological quality of rivers cannot be directly linked to discharge quality, or linked to controls applied via discharge consents, since there are factors other than water quality which affect biological communities. Therefore, it would not be possible, if water quality objectives were set on a biological basis, to know whether they were capable of being achieved by pollution control measures and consequently it would not be reasonable to impose biological water quality objectives as legally-binding water quality targets.

abstraction for drinking water supply, agricultural abstractions, industrial abstraction, special ecosystem and water sports. Significantly, it was recognised that the actual implementation of water quality objectives would represent a substantial call upon administrative resources and a major undertaking for the water industry and other dischargers who would be obliged to implement the resulting programmes for improvements. Accordingly, in 1992, the Government anticipated a progressive programme of setting objectives from 1993 onwards and consequent action programmes to secure improvements extending over a time-scale of five to fifteen years.[103]

The legal mechanisms for establishing statutory water quality objectives, and realising these in relation to particular waters, is provided for under the Water Resources Act 1991. This provides for, first, a statutory scheme of water quality classification, second, a power to specify the quality classifications to be achieved by particular waters and, third, the imposition of a legal obligation that the specified quality objectives must be met and maintained in relation to those waters.[104]

### 14.8.2 Water Quality Classification

In respect of the classification of water quality, the Secretary of State may, in relation to any description of controlled waters,[105] prescribe a system of classifying the quality of waters according to specified criteria.[106] The criteria which may be specified for this purpose are to consist of one or more of the following:

    (a) general requirements as to the purpose for which the waters to which the classification is applied are to be suitable;

    (b) specific requirements as to the substances that are to be present in or absent from the water and as to the concentrations of substances which are or are required to be present in the water; and

    (c) specific requirements as to other characteristics of those waters.

For the purpose of classification regulations of this kind, it may be provided that the question whether specified requirements are satisfied is to be determined by reference to prescribed samples.[107]

The power to establish water classification systems is an enabling provision in that it empowers the Secretary of State to make regulations without imposing any duty upon him to do so. Nevertheless, if Community water quality directives are to be satisfactorily implemented, water

---

[103] DoE, *River Quality: The Government's Proposals* (1992) paras.2.14-16. However, the actual implementation of statutory water quality objectives appears to have fallen behind this schedule insofar as water quality objectives for matters falling outside those covered by European community water directives are concerned, see 14.8.5 below.

[104] Under ss.82-84 Water Resources Act 1991, previously ss.104-6 Water Act 1989.

[105] See 9.4 above on the meaning of 'controlled waters'.

[106] s.82(1) Water Resources Act 1991.

[107] s.82(2) Water Resources Act 1991.

classifications systems must be established as a matter of legal necessity. By contrast, the use of the water classification systems to provide for purely national water quality matters, is an issue which genuinely falls within the Secretary of State's discretion.

The Secretary of State has actually exercised his power to classify controlled waters for different purposes in accordance with these provisions by the enactment of six sets of water classification regulations, all but one of which are for the purpose of giving effect to Community water quality legislation.[108]

### 14.8.3 Dangerous Substances in Water Classification

First, the Surface Waters (Dangerous Substances) (Classification) Regulations 1989[109] establish a system of classification of inland waters, coastal water and relevant territorial waters according to the presence of concentrations of dangerous substances for the purpose of implementing the Dangerous Substances Directive and 'daughter directives' under this Directive.[110] Accordingly, a system employing the classifications DS1 and DS2 was initially established where the criteria for these classifications are met where the annual mean concentrations of listed dangerous substances in waters are within specified concentrations. The statutory procedure normally required for establishing water quality objectives for particular waters is exempted under the Regulations.[111] Subsequent Regulations enacted in 1992 established a further classification DS3 for specified substances, along with sampling and analysis requirements, and imposed a duty upon the Secretary to impose the classification as a water quality objective in relation to all relevant waters.[112] Further classifications, DS4 and DS5, were established by Regulations enacted in 1997 which imposed corresponding sampling requirements and imposed a duty upon the Secretary of State to impose the classification as a water quality objective in relation to all relevant waters.[113] Most recently, Regulations enacted in 1998 have added the classifications DS6 and DS7, along with corresponding sampling requirements, and imposed a duty upon the

---

[108] Separate legislation is provided for the classification of drinking water quality see 17.6 below.

[109] SI 1989 No.2286.

[110] Directive 76/464/EEC and see 5.4.1 above on this Directive.

[111] As originally provided for under s.105(4) and (5) Water Act 1989, see now s.83(4) and (5) Water Resources Act 1991, this normally requires the Secretary to give three months' notice and to consider representations and objections before establishing water quality objectives. This precedent was also followed in subsequent Regulations.

[112] See Surface Waters (Dangerous Substances) (Classification) Regulations 1992 (SI 1992 No.337) which introduced a modification of s.83 Water Resources Act 1991 to impose a duty on the Secretary of State to exercise his powers to apply the DS3 to all relevant waters and exempted him from consultation requirements in relation to this. This precedent was followed in later Regulations.

[113] See Surface Waters (Dangerous Substances) (Classification) Regulations 1997 (SI 1997 No.2560).

Secretary of State to apply the classifications as water quality objectives in relation to all relevant waters.[114]

### 14.8.4 Bathing Waters Classification

Second, the Bathing Waters (Classification) Regulations 1991[115] establish a system for classifying relevant territorial waters, coastal waters and inland waters which are identified as bathing waters for the purposes of the Bathing Water Directive.[116] Under these Regulations the classification BW1 reflects the mandatory standards for bathing water under the Directive, though the Secretary of State is given the power to grant derogations where this is allowed for under the Directive. The Regulations impose sampling requirements and indicate that the Secretary of State will use his statutory powers[117] to direct the Environment Agency to sample and test waters to which the BW1 classification applies in accordance with these requirements.[118] A duty is imposed upon the Secretary of State to use his statutory powers to specify water quality objectives for particular waters[119] to apply the classification BW1 to waters which are bathing waters within the meaning of the Directive. Notably, no standards are set in relation to the 'guide values' provided for under the Directive.

### 14.8.5 River Ecosystem Classification

Third, the Surface Waters (River Ecosystem) (Classification) Regulations 1994[120] prescribe a system for classifying the general quality of inland freshwaters which are relevant rivers or watercourses[121] according to five classifications, RE1 to RE5, with sampling, analysis and compliance requirements to be determined by the Environment Agency.[122] Significantly, these Regulations are the only set of water classification regulations which have not been enacted for the purpose of implementing a European Community water directive. Perhaps for that reason, they differ from the other Regulations in that no obligation is imposed under them to require the Secretary of State to apply the classifications as water quality objectives for any particular waters.[123] It is understood that they have not actually been used as the basis for any water quality objectives that have yet been imposed.

---

[114] See Surface Waters (Dangerous Substances) (Classification) Regulations 1998 (SI 1998 No.389).
[115] SI 1991 No.1597.
[116] Directive 76/160/EEC and see 5.5.2 above on this Directive.
[117] Under s.5 Water Resources Act 1991, see now ss.40 and 122 Environment Act 1995.
[118] See National Rivers Authority (Bathing Water) Directions 1992, 5 May 1992.
[119] Under s.105 Water Act 1989, and now s.83 Water Resources Act 1991, and see 14.8.9 below.
[120] SI 1994 No.1057.
[121] See the definition of 'controlled waters' at 9.4 above.
[122] See National Rivers Authority, *Water Quality Objectives: Procedures used by the National Rivers Authority for the purpose of the Surface Waters (River Ecosystem) (Classification) Regulations 1994* (1994).
[123] Under s.83 Water Resources Act 1991.

## 14.8.6 Abstraction for Drinking Water Classification

Fourth, the Surface Waters (Abstraction for Drinking Water) (Classification) Regulations 1996[124] prescribe a system for classifying the quality of inland freshwaters according to their suitability for abstraction for supply as drinking water in accordance with the Drinking Water Abstraction Directive and the Drinking Water Sampling Directive.[125] Accordingly, the water classifications DW1, DW2 and DW3 are established, along with requirements applicable to the Environment Agency relating to waivers and sampling, in conformity with criteria under the Abstraction and Sampling Directives. Notably, three modifications are made to the Water Resources Act 1991, to require the Secretary of State to impose the classifications as water quality objectives in relation to relevant waters;[126] to modify the definition of 'controlled waters'[127] to include all 'inland freshwaters' subject to the Abstraction Directive; and to modify the information provisions under the Act[128] to require information to be supplied to the Agency for the purpose of giving effect to the Abstraction and Sampling Directives. Directions have been issued to the Agency requiring it to discharge its pollution control functions, in relation to any waters classified under the Regulations, so that it endeavours to respect guideline values and that the Abstraction Directive is implemented so as not to lead to any deterioration in surface water quality. The Directions also provide for other matters, to which the Agency must adhere, in relation to compliance with technical standards, waivers of standards, sampling requirements and information to be included in registers.[129]

## 14.8.7 Fishlife Waters Classification

Fifth, the Surface Waters (Fishlife) (Classification) Regulations 1997[130] prescribe a system for classifying the quality of inland water needing protection or improvement in order to support fish life under classifications SW (salmonid waters) and CW (cyprinid waters) for the purpose of implementing the Freshwater Fish Waters Directive.[131] The Regulations impose sampling requirements and give permission for the Environment Agency to derogate from the Regulations under circumstances allowed by the Directive, and allow for modifications of the Water Resources Act 1991 for the purpose of giving effect to the

---

[124] SI 1996 No.3001, which revoked the Surface Waters (Classification) Regulations 1989, SI 1989 No.1148.
[125] Directives 75/440/EC and 79/869/EEC and see 17.6 below on these Directives.
[126] Under s.83 Water Resources Act 1991.
[127] Under s.104(1)(c) Water Resources Act 1991, and see 9.4 above on the definition of 'controlled waters'.
[128] Under s.202(2) Water Resources Act 1991, and see 16.7 below on this.
[129] Surface Water (Abstraction for Drinking Water) Directions 1996, 26 November 1996.
[130] SI 1997 No.1331.
[131] Directive 78/659/EEC, and see 15.3.1 above on this Directive and 15.3.2 below on the transposition of the Directive.

Directive.[132] Directions to the Agency, concerning the Regulations, indicate guideline values that the Agency is to endeavour to respect and requires it to implement the Regulations in such a way that no increased pollution of fresh water ensues. Further matters provided for under the Directions concern technical compliance with the Regulations, sampling and analysis, derogation, water quality improvement programmes and information to be included in registers.[133]

### 14.8.8 Shellfish Waters Classification

Sixth, the Surface Waters (Shellfish) (Classification) Regulations 1997[134] follow the format of the previous Regulations in prescribing a system for classifying the quality of controlled waters which are coastal or brackish waters needing protection or improvement in order to support shellfish life and growth under classification SFW (shellfish waters) for the purpose of implementing Shellfish Waters Directive[135] along with sampling requirements and derogation powers allowed for under that Directive. Directions issued to the Agency in relation to these Regulations[136] require it to adhere to analogous matters to those provided for in Directions under the Fishlife Classification Regulations.

### 14.8.9 Specifying Water Quality Objectives

Having established statutory water classification systems under the Regulations described in the previous sections, the next step is to apply these requirements to particular waters. In respect of this, the Secretary of State may specify particular water quality objectives in relation to individual waters. Hence, for the purpose of maintaining and improving the quality of controlled waters, he may serve a notice on the Environment Agency specifying one or more of the classifications prescribed under a water classification system in relation to particular waters. Where a notice of this kind is served, specifying a classification and a date by which that classification is to be met, a statutory water quality objective is thereby established for the particular waters, or for waters of a prescribed description specified in the notice. Following this procedure, the water quality objectives for any waters to which a notice of this kind relates are to be the satisfaction by those waters, at all times after the date specified in the notice, of the requirements for the classification which is specified.[137]

Further statutory provisions allow for the review of water quality objectives by the Secretary of State if five years have elapsed since the

---

[132] Following the precedent of the Surface Waters (Abstraction for Drinking Water) (Classification) Regulations 1996, see above.
[133] Surface Waters (Fishlife) Directions 1997, 19 May 1997.
[134] SI 1997 No.1332.
[135] Directive 79/923/EEC, and see 15.3.1 above on this Directive and 15.3.2 below on the transposition of the Directive.
[136] Surface Waters (Shellfish) Directions 1997, 19 May 1997.
[137] s.83(1)-(2) Water Resources Act 1991.

previous determination, or if the Agency, after consultation with appropriate persons, requests a review. Either in relation to the initial establishment or variation of a water quality objective, the Secretary of State must give notice of the proposal and allow a period of at least three months for representations and objections to be made, and consider these before the power of review is exercised. Notice of the intention of the Secretary of State to establish or vary the water quality objectives is to be given by publishing notice of the proposal and by serving a copy of it on the Agency, and if in consequence of any representation or objections he decides that the water quality objectives should remain unchanged he is bound to notify the Agency of that decision.[138]

The primary statutory provisions concerning the classification of water quality and determining water quality objectives for particular waters seem to envisage distinct procedures being followed. The classification process requires secondary legislative action, whilst the determination process is accomplished merely by the exercise of the power of the Secretary of State to serve appropriate notice on the Environment Agency following consultation. In practice, however, this distinction seems not always to have been observed. As has been noted, various classification regulations encroach upon the designation process, first by imposing a duty upon the Secretary of State to designate particular waters falling within the classification systems established, and secondly by dispensing with the consultation requirements that would normally apply to the designation of particular waters.

The justification for this departure from the procedure envisaged by the statutory requirements lies in the fact that all the classification regulations giving effect to European Community water directives have been enacted under powers which include the power of the Secretary of State to give effect to Community obligations.[139] Where this power is exercised, the Secretary of State is entitled to enact regulations which provide that the water pollution provisions of the Water Resources Act 1991 are to have effect with such modifications as may be prescribed for the purpose of enabling the UK to give effect to any Community obligations. Hence, contrary to the general constitutional principle that secondary legislation should not be used to modify a primary enactment, this is permissible, and has been done, in relation to the implementation of Community water directives.

### 14.8.10 General Duties to Achieve and Maintain Objectives

The third part of the mechanism for strategic water management through statutory water quality objectives concerns the relationship between the system of statutory water quality objectives and other powers and duties of the Secretary of State and the Environment Agency in respect of water quality. In relation to this, it is the duty of the Secretary of State and of the

---

[138] *Ibid* s.83(3)-(6).

[139] Under s.102 Water Resources Act 1991, and previously s.171 Water Act 1989.

Agency to exercise the powers conferred under the water pollution provisions of the Water Resources Act 1991 in such manner as ensures, so far as it is practicable by the exercise of those powers to do so, that the water quality objectives specified for any waters are achieved at all times.[140]

A consequence of the duty imposed upon the Agency to use its powers to ensure that water quality objectives specified for particular waters are met and maintained, is to impose the necessary legal obligation upon the Agency, as the competent authority under European Community law for various water quality directives, to ensure that specified water quality objectives, and correspondingly the requirements of corresponding Directives, are met at all times.

Another implication of the legal duty to ensure that water quality objectives are maintained at all times is that a legal remedy could be sought against the Agency, or the Secretary of State, in the event of a failure to adhere to this obligation. Ordinarily, remedies against statutory bodies who fail to exercise public duties, or who fail to exercise them properly, are available by way of judicial review. The successful outcome of proceedings of this kind would be an order by the court to compel the Agency to act in accordance with its public duty in circumstances where it had been shown not to have done so. In practice however, it may be more likely that compliance by the Agency might be sought, under appropriate circumstances, by means of a specific Ministerial direction.[141] Alternatively, where there is a failure of the Agency or the Secretary of State to use powers to secure statutory water quality objectives and this involves a failure to meet the requirements of a European Community water quality directive, there are a range of possibilities for proceedings either nationally or at Community level in respect of the failure to secure substantial compliance.[142]

As a matter of practice, the legal duty upon the Agency to use its water pollution powers to ensure that water quality objectives are met and maintained imports a strategic element into many of the responsibilities of the Agency that have previously discussed. For the purpose of securing statutory water quality objectives, it is likely that the powers of the Agency relating to the determination and review of discharge consents,[143] and the impositions of prohibitions upon discharges, will be most effective in realising water quality objectives.[144] Alongside these powers, the various preventive and remedial measures discussed elsewhere[145] will have an important strategic role to play in securing statutory water quality objectives particularly where a water quality problem arises from non-point source emissions.

---

[140] s.84(1) Water Resources Act 1991.

[141] Under s.40 Environment Act 1995, and see 6.2 above on Ministerial directions.

[142] See Ch.4 above on the possibilities for enforcement proceedings.

[143] Under s.88(2) and Sch.10 Water Resources Act 1991, and see Ch.10 above on this.

[144] Under s.86 Water Resources Act 1991, and see 9.11 above on prohibition notices.

[145] See, particularly, Ch.13 above on preventive approaches to water quality.

In respect of the powers of the Agency relating to discharge consents, it is apparent that if a particular water is failing to meet its statutory classification objective, or in danger of doing so, it will be necessary to review the consents relating to discharges affecting the waters so that, by making consent requirements more stringent, the water quality objectives will be met and maintained. Whilst there may be a clear theoretical need for an exercise of this kind to be undertaken, in order to meet the obligation upon the Agency, the practical difficulties involved may be considerable. In particular, controversial issues of fairness between dischargers will arise where unsatisfactory water quality is the result of more than one discharge into a watercourse. It is not apparent whether, for example, the Agency should adopt a policy of declining, absolutely, all further applications for discharge consents to an unsatisfactory watercourse, or whether it should seek to bring about a gradual tightening of all consents relating to the watercourse or, if so, how should fairness be secured as between different kinds of discharge, or between point and non-point sources of contamination entering relevant waters.[146]

Perhaps because of the cost and complexity of setting statutory water quality objectives, the exercise has been deferred over several years for purposes other than the implementation of European Community water directives. The most recent developments in the progression towards national statutory water quality objectives appear rather tentative by comparison with the scope allowed for under the legislation. In March 1996 it was announced that consultation would take place on the designation of eight river catchments, one in each of the regions of the former National Rivers Authority, as a pilot exercise in the implementation of statutory water quality objectives. Subsequently, it was announced that proposals will be put forward for another round of consultation with the Department of the Environment. Presently, it is understood that further progress rests with the Department of Environment, Transport and the Regions.[147]

### 14.9 Local Environment Agency Plans

The formality associated with statutory water quality objectives may be seen as a reason for the lack of progress in actually specifying such objectives other than where it is legally necessary to do so for the purpose of meeting Community obligations. However, the lack of a legal *duty* in this respect is a notable point of contrast with other areas of environmental law, such as air quality[148] and waste management,[149] where a specific duty is imposed upon the Secretary of State to formulate a national

---

[146] On the duty upon public bodies to behave with fairness see *R v Great Yarmouth Borough Council ex parte Botton Brothers* (1988) 56 P & CR 99.

[147] *ENDS Report* 262 (1996) p.37 and Royal Commission on Environmental Pollution (1998) Appendix C para.28.

[148] See s.80 Environment Act 1995. See also HM Government, *Waste Strategy 2000 for England and Wales* (Cm.4693, 2000) and *The Air Quality Strategy for England, Scotland Wales and Northern Ireland: Working Together for Clean Air* (Cm.4548, 2000).

[149] See s.44A Environmental Protection Act 1990, as amended.

environmental quality strategy or plan. In relation to water, the most pertinent general policy statement available is the rather terse observation to be found in the guidance to the Agency on sustainable development:

> the Government's policy objective for water protection is where possible to prevent deterioration in water quality and to seek to secure improvements in accordance with agreed priorities which reflect the requirements of Community legislation.[150]

Insofar as general duties are statutorily imposed upon the Environment Agency they appear to relate only remotely to any possible water quality planning role of the Agency. Hence, the general environmental duty upon the Agency to have regard to the desirability of conserving flora and fauna when considering any proposals relating to its pollution control functions[151] *might be* construed as an obligation to ensure a satisfactory ecological quality of receiving waters, for example, when determining an application for a discharge consent. However, it is far from explicit to what extent the general environmental duty upon the Agency implies a strategic water quality planning role.

Perhaps because of the relative lack of explicit statutory guidance in respect of water quality planning, important informal, non-mandatory, mechanisms have been established. The Agency has formulated, with Government endorsement, various non-statutory kinds of environmental planning objectives such as the aim 'to achieve major and continuous improvement in the quality of air, land and water'.[152] In part, this is interpreted as a commitment to delivery of environmental improvement at the local level through the progressive establishment of Local Environment Agency Plans (LEAPs). LEAPs are characterised by the Agency as integrated local plans for 'identifying, assessing, prioritising and solving local environmental issues related to the Agency's functions, taking into account the views of the Agency's local customers'.[153]

Further indications of the Agency's purposes in formulating LEAPs are indicated as follows.

> These plans provide a vehicle to reconcile the conflicting demands placed on air, land and surface and groundwaters. They set out a shared vision for the area, reached through consultation with landowners, individuals, local government, industry, farmers and interest groups – all of whom have a role to play, in partnership with the Agency, in helping to manage the environment in a sustainable way. LEAPS cover actions that are to be taken over five years. From 2000/01 we will begin implementing these plans, first of all tackling

---

[150] DoE, MAFF and WO, *The Environment Agency and Sustainable Development* (1996) para.6.23.

[151] s.7(1)(b) Environment Act 1995, and see 6.10 above.

[152] Environment Agency, *Corporate Plan 2000/01* (1999) p.1.

[153] Environment Agency, *Local Environment Agency Plans* (1999).

the actions where we have clear statutory duties and also dealing with others in a prioritised way, as funding allows.[154]

In practical effect, LEAPs, formulated at river catchment levels, should serve as a useful consultation mechanism which allows greater transparency in informing the public and regulated bodies how the Agency intends to use its legal powers in an integrated manner to achieve water quality and other environmental improvements.[155] Clearly, therefore, LEAPs will be an important statements as to what local objectives the Agency seeks to achieve, and a guide as to how it proposes to use its powers to enhance the environment at a local level. However, the contrast with statutory water quality objectives is that failure to meet a statutory water quality objective, where it is reasonably practicable to do so, would be a breach of a legal duty on the part of the Agency, whereas failure to meet a commitment set out in a LEAP appears to have no direct legal consequences.

Similarly, the relative informality of LEAPs, by contrast with town and country planning development plans, should be noted. There appears to be nothing more formal than a self-imposed obligation to take particular actions, such as the determination of discharge consent applications in accordance with the relevant LEAP. Further, self-imposed objectives for water quality planning by the Agency are to be found in *An Action Plan for Water Quality*[156] which incorporates a commitment to develop an Environment Agency National Plan for Water Quality 'to develop a firm planning base for the maintenance and future improvement of water quality' and a commitment to 'vigorously enforce discharge consent control standards'.[157]

The general inference must be that, by comparison with town and country planning, the plan-formulation aspects of water quality planning are a considerably less formal kind of strategic activity. It is apparent that there is no direct analogue of the legal duty upon local planning authorities to establish development plans and, insofar as the Secretary of State has a plan making role in specifying statutory water quality objectives, it is a power that has only been exercised where necessary to ensure European Community water quality objectives are met in national waters. Whilst the Agency has taken various initiatives to plan for water quality management, all of these lack the firm legal foundation that is provided for in relation to town and country planning development plans.

---

[154] Environment Agency, *Corporate Plan 2000/01* (1999) p.39.
[155] See 1.7.7 above on integrated river-basin management.
[156] Environment Agency (1998).
[157] *Ibid* p.13, though on enforcement generally see Environment Agency, *Enforcement and Prosecution Policy* (1998), at 6.18.1 above.

## 14.10  Assimilating Land Use and Water Quality Planning

The traditional assumption that water quality management objectives are capable of being achieved by the control of point-source discharges is no longer accepted. A range of contaminants which have an adverse effect upon water quality, without necessarily resulting in dramatic pollution incidents, result from gradual emissions from diffuse sources, rather than end-of-pipe discharges. A consequence of this is that various types of land use are regulated for the purpose of protecting water quality. Good examples of this are the enactment of regulations to prevent agricultural water pollution[158] and designation of the first water protection zone in the catchment of the River Dee with consequent restrictions upon activities within the area.[159] In addition, the need to control application of nitrate, as fertiliser applied to agricultural land, has resulted in national provisions allowing for the designation of nitrate sensitive areas and further regulations to implement the European Community Nitrates Directive and to regulate activities in nitrate vulnerable zones identified for the purpose of the Directive.[160]

The theme of controlling land use, rather than merely regulating end-of-pipe emissions, is revealingly illustrated by the *Scrayingham Sewer Appeal*.[161] Here a discharge consent had been determined encompassing the condition:

> The discharge shall not include any effluent from premises which, on the date of this consent either did not drain to a public sewer discharging at the place stated above, or in respect of which full planning permission was not granted prior to the date of this consent permitting the premises so to drain.

The discharge at issue was from drains from a small village of about 90 persons which received domestic sewage and storm water effluent which received no treatment, with the result that the receiving watercourse exhibited gross pollution and was the source of public complaint. Consequently, the objective of the consent was to prevent additional effluent entering the sewer by limiting the properties from which discharges could be made, or requiring a programme of sewerage improvements to be undertaken before further connections to the sewer could be made. However, the sewerage undertaker contended that the condition was, in effect, a planning restriction and the use of the discharge consent system was not an appropriate mechanism for controlling land use development.

The Secretary of State declined to accept that the contested condition was a planning restriction, since it did not actually prevent development but

---

[158] Under s.92 Water Resources Act 1991 and see 13.3.1 above.

[159] Under s.93 Water Resources Act 1991 and see 13.4.1 above.

[160] Directive 91/676/EEC and ss.94 and 95 Water Resources Act 1991 and see 13.5 above.

[161] An appeal by Yorkshire Water Services Ltd against a discharge consent determined by the National Rivers Authority, determined by the Secretary of State, 28 October 1996.

required that a sewer improvement programme would be necessary *if* development took place. However, he did resolve that the condition was unnecessary in that the objective being sought could have been achieved by imposing a volumetric condition which would have been equally effective in preventing further deterioration in the receiving waters. The implications of this are that the discharge consent system is capable of having important impacts upon both the sewerage system and neighbouring land use. That is, *had* more dwellings been built in the village, the sewerage undertaker would have been bound to embark upon the necessary sewerage improvement programme regardless of whether this would be regarded by the undertaker as a project which represented a priority claim upon resources.[162]

A common theme underlying these initiatives and examples is a shift of emphasis from water pollution control to land use control. This approach tends to assimilate water quality planning to development control in town and country planning law.[163] For example, restricting the right of a farmer to construct a slurry tank, other than in accordance with fairly specific conditions, might naturally be thought of as a matter falling under town and country planning law. The fact remains, however, that the restrictions which are imposed arise under water resources legislation rather than town and country planning law. It would be an exaggeration to suggest that the Environment Agency has been given a range of powers to control 'development' of land, but the similarity between some of their preventative powers and those of local authorities in planning matters deserves to be noted.

Further indications of the progressive assimilation of water quality and land use planning is to be seen in that a key link, of a procedural kind, has been forged by the decision of the Secretary of State to arrange, as from 1 January 1997, for his power to determine discharge consent and associated appeals to be exercised by the Planning Inspectorate. Consequently, all determinations of this kind will be taken by the Inspectors on behalf of the Secretary of State, in accordance with procedures which are similar to those governing planning appeals, except in rare cases of major importance or difficulty where the Secretary of State may exercise this power himself.[164] At a practical level, having the same people determining town and country planning and discharge consent appeals must be likely further to encourage a similarity of approach.

On the other hand, despite the overlaps that have been indicated, there are various respects in which town and country planning possesses a high degree of separation from water quality planning. A key policy statement emphasising this separation is Planning Policy Guidance Note 23,

---

[162] Given the statutory right of property owners to connect drains to the public sewerage system under s.106 Water Industry Act 1991, and see 11.3.2B above on this.

[163] Generally see Jewell (1998).

[164] DoE, Press Release 579, *Decisions on Discharge Consent and Associated Appeals Transferred to Planning Inspectorate*, 30 December 1996.

*Planning and Pollution Control,*[165] which gives guidance on the relevance of pollution control to the exercise of planning functions and advises on the relationship between local authority's planning responsibilities and the *separate* statutory responsibilities exercised by pollution control authorities under environmental legislation. Key passages from this document read as follows:

> The planning system should not be operated so as to duplicate controls which are the statutory responsibility of other bodies (including local authorities in the non-planning functions). Planning controls, except where they are applied in the context of hazardous substances consents, are not an appropriate means of regulating the detailed characteristics of potentially polluting activities.[166]

> The role of the planning system focuses on whether the development itself is an acceptable use of the land rather than the control of the processes or substances themselves. It also assumes that the pollution control regime will operate effectively. . . . Planning controls can therefore complement the pollution control regime, and thus help to secure the proper operation and rehabilitation of potentially polluting developments.[167]

> In deciding whether to grant planning permission, planning authorities must be satisfied that planning permission can be granted on land-use grounds, and that concerns about potential releases can be left for the pollution control authority to take into account in considering the application for the authorisation or licence. Alternatively, they may conclude that the wider impact of potential releases on the environment and use of land is unacceptable in all the circumstances on planning grounds, despite the grant, or potential grant, of a pollution control authorisation or licence.[168]

Despite these injunctions requiring the separation of the two systems of control, there are indications that the practical trend is in the opposite direction,[169] with planning authorities becoming ever-more closely involved in considering the environmental consequences of granting planning applications. A good example of this is to be found in *R v Bolton Metropolitan Borough Council, ex parte Kirkman*[170] where the best practicable environmental option for a waste incineration facility, a matter normally determined by the pollution regulatory authority, was recognised to be a material consideration for a planning authority to consider. Another relevant example is the case of environmental assessment of projects with a water quality dimension, discussed previously, where planning

---

[165] DoE (1994).
[166] *Ibid* para.1.3.
[167] *Ibid* para.1.33.
[168] *Ibid* para.1.36.
[169] Although see the discussion of *W E Black Ltd* v *Secretary of State for the Environment and London Borough of Harrow* [1997] Env LR 1 at 14.5.5A above.
[170] [1998] Env LR 719.

authorities are obliged to become intimately engaged assessing the aquatic impact aspects of development projects and to evaluate the environmental effects of effluent discharges.

Arguably, this assimilative trend is beneficial. This is, first, because the determination of planning applications has, otherwise, to be made on the basis of incomplete information. Separation of planning and environmental licence determinations means that the planning authority is obliged make a sometimes dubious assumption that the environmental regulator will be able to licence a discharge satisfactorily and enforce licensing controls with sufficient stringency to safeguard against environmental harm. Second, there is a reasonable fear that granting planning permission for a development will 'force the hand' of the Agency to grant a discharge consent, or other environmental licence, when the development is operational.[171] Third, the separation of controls means that objectors to a development proposal are placed at a considerable procedural disadvantage because they may have insufficient information about the conditions that are to be applied to a discharge consent from a development at the time the planning application is being considered. This is because this information is only likely to become available subsequently at the time when the environmental licence is determined. Whilst a public hearing may be held in relation to an appeal against the adverse determination of a discharge consent, this is only available where this is requested by the Agency or the intending discharger.[172] Even where a hearing is requested by either of the parties, members of the public will only be allowed to participate in the hearing if they have previously made representations with respect to the grant of the discharge consent.[173]

The case for greater integration has also been firmly expressed by those professionally involved in the town and country planning system:

> The Town and Country Planning Association proposes that integration should go further still by integrating pollution control, waste management and land-use planning, thus recognising that these are interdependent processes. Land-use policies affect the location of pollution activities. Plans for recycling, waste minimisation and pollution control all have a land-use component. This interaction between land use and environmental policies is already recognised in the environmental programmes of many local authorities and it is now time to bring the separate traditions together to create a proper environmental planning process.[174]

A potentially problematic aspect of the assimilative trend is the issue of whether local planning authorities are genuinely equipped with the

---

[171] See *Gateshead Metropolitan Borough Council* v *Secretary of State for the Environment and Northumbrian Water Group Plc* [1994] Env LR 11.
[172] s.91(2C) Water Resources Act 1991.
[173] Reg.12(6)(c) Control of Pollution (Applications, Appeals and Registers) Regulations 1996 (SI 1996 No. 2971).
[174] Blowers (1993) p.15 and see also Purdue (1999).

expertise that is required to assess the impacts of a development project upon a distinctive sector of the environment such as the aquatic environment. For so long as the Agency is the principal repository of technical expertise for sectors such as the aquatic environment, over which local authorities have relatively limited jurisdiction, the capacity of local authorities to make determinations on water quality matters will be open to question. On the other hand, the more pronounced social and economic dimensions to many planning determinations raises issues which local authorities are best placed to determine and which do not necessarily admit solutions which may be resolved by greater environmental expertise.

Also, the perceived tension between the democratic mandate of local authorities and the technical mandate of the Agency is evident. The crucial question is whether this tension is genuine or not. Whilst it might seem undemocratic to give the, non-elected, Agency power to overturn decisions reached by the, elected, local authority, the reality may be that decisions of local planning authorities are so confined by law and policy guidance that the scope for political considerations to enter into planning determinations is relatively limited. Given also the common ultimate allocation of executive responsibility to the Secretary of State, under both systems of controls, it might be argued that the real tension is between national and local, democratically determined, environmental imperatives. If this is so, the perceived lack of political and policy accountability of the Agency should not be a serious concern. The central concern is that the national and international imperative of achieving sustainable development should not be undermined by decision making procedures which fail to give sufficient weight to the opinions of those having the greatest amount of relevant expertise. In addressing this, it is a matter of finding the right balance between technical environmental expertise, appreciation of local concerns and accountability.

More generally, it may be concluded that whilst clear differences exist between town and country planning and water quality planning, these are not so great as to preclude a more unified approach within the two systems of environmental control. Where disparities of approach exist, the evolution of the water quality planning system towards greater assimilation to the town and country planning approach might be beneficial. For example, if the Secretary of State, or the Agency, was legally required to formulate explicit water quality plans, would it then be unreasonable to expect discharge consent determinations to be made in accordance with such plans 'unless material considerations indicate otherwise'? Additionally, a greater degree of co-determination might be desirable in relation to the control of developments which impact upon the water environment. This might most effectively be achieved by consolidating procedures so that an application for planning consent would be considered alongside any applications for environmental licences, and particularly discharge consents, which are needed to undertake the activities that are envisaged by the development.

# Chapter 15

# FISHERIES AND NATURE CONSERVATION

## 15.1 Introduction

The pursuit of improved water quality through legal regulation is often for reasons of human well being, such as the avoidance of water-borne disease arising from urbanisation. In many respects, however, water pollution law is historically concerned with protecting water quality for commercial or recreational reasons. Indeed, general legislation making the pollution of water a criminal offence was first motivated by concerns about the productivity of salmon fisheries, some 15 years before the first general water pollution legislation was enacted, and extended only to waters containing salmon.[1]

Specific anti-pollution provisions continue to apply to waters containing fish, while a range of other controls, including water pollution and water quality provisions, have been enacted with fishery conservation in mind. Beyond fisheries, however, the law plays an expanding role in the conservation of biodiversity more generally. This body of nature conservation law is increasingly important in regulating land use and in placing limits on the discretion of bodies like the Environment Agency in the exercise of their licensing functions. Of course, fishery and nature conservation legislation does not provide sufficient regulatory protection for the aquatic environment, and must be complemented by the wide range of other legal controls discussed elsewhere in this book. On the other hand, it must be the hoped that the increasing integration of conservation and other policies will render the distinction between fishery, conservation and other concerns of diminishing significance in the future.

The present chapter, in focusing on the how the law relating to fisheries and to nature conservation can impact on the quality of the water environment, illustrates the twin themes of water pollution and water quality law that run throughout this book. That is, the concern is not with an abstract notion of 'clean' water, or an absolute notion of 'polluted' water, but with an ambient aquatic environmental quality capable of supporting specific species or habitats and the legal provisions which have this as their principal aim. Clearly, water quality may be a limiting factor for biodiversity. Aquatic species, such as the burbot (or freshwater cod) have been lost in large part through poor river water quality,[2] while the

---

[1] Salmon Fisheries Act 1861, preceding the Rivers Pollution Prevention Act 1876, discussed at 2.5 and 2.6 above.

[2] UK Steering Group, *Biodiversity: The UK Steering Group Report, Vol. 1: Meeting the Rio Challenge*, p.19. While contamination was a major cause, other factors included competition from other species, temperature changes and the fact that the species was at the limits of its range.

range of some other aquatic species has been significantly reduced.[3] On the other hand, the addition of matter into rivers may *enhance* aquatic biodiversity by contributing important organic matter (such as bankside vegetation does). Furthermore, aquatic plants that tolerate contamination by enrichment,[4] such as fennel pondweed, may expand their range in such conditions, though usually at the expense of more sensitive plants such as brookwater crowfoot. Regulating 'against' water pollution, or 'for' water quality, therefore, raises issues distinct from, for example, setting a minimum standard for wholesome water, or perhaps the regulation of grossly polluting substances.

The chapter is broadly divided into two parts. The first part deals with matters relating to fisheries, while the second is concerned with the wider conservation of nature. As can be seen, EC and (to a lesser extent) international law plays an ever more important role. Nevertheless, many provisions have a relatively lengthy national heritage.

## 15.2 Administrative Responsibilities for Fisheries

Administrative responsibility for fisheries rests mainly with the Environment Agency, with ministerial responsibility being with the Agriculture Ministers, although there is also a role for local authority and other input at the local level.

### 15.2.1 The Environment Agency

It is a general duty of the Environment Agency to maintain, improve and develop salmon fisheries, trout fisheries, freshwater fisheries and eel fisheries (known as the 'general fisheries duty').[5] However, the Agency exercises fisheries functions under a range of statutes; in addition to Part V of the Water Resources Act 1991, these include the Salmon and Freshwater Fisheries Act 1975 and the Sea Fisheries Regulation Act 1966. For fishery purposes the jurisdiction of the Agency is the whole of England and Wales, including tidal waters, and parts of the territorial sea adjoining the coast to a distance of six nautical miles measured from the baselines from which the breadth of that sea is measured.[6] The fisheries jurisdiction of the Agency also extends, in general, to so much of the River Esk, with its banks and tributary streams up to their source, as is situated in Scotland, but excluding the River Tweed.[7]

---

[3] MAFF and National Assembly for Wales, *Salmon and Freshwater Fisheries Review* (2000) ch.5. Ch.6 of this report also provides a useful review of the various causes of pollution as these relate to fisheries.

[4] On enrichment and eutrophication see 1.3.1–2 above.

[5] s.6(6) Environment Act 1995.

[6] *Ibid* s.6(7)(a). Contrast the general three nautical mile jurisdiction of the Environment Agency in relation to 'controlled waters', see 9.4 above.

[7] *Ibid* s.6(7)(b).

## 15.2.2 Regional and Local Fisheries Advisory Committees

The Environment Agency must establish and maintain advisory committees of persons who are not members of the Agency but are interested in salmon fisheries, trout fisheries, freshwater fisheries or eel fisheries in the different parts of the 'controlled area' (i.e. the area in which the Agency exercises its fisheries functions).[8] Committees must be established and maintained in each of the Agency's regions, with one committee consisting wholly or mainly of, or of most of, Wales. Local advisory committees must be established as is necessary to represent the interests of fisheries within different parts of each region.

The Agency must consult the regional fisheries committees about the manner in which it performs its general fisheries duty. In addition, committees must be consulted about the way the Agency performs its recreation, conservation or navigation duties. Regional chairmen are appointed by the Minister of Agriculture, Fisheries and Food or, as appropriate, the National Assembly for Wales.

## 15.2.3 'Sea Fisheries Committees'

Local fisheries committees (normally referred to as 'sea fisheries committees') may be constituted to regulate sea fisheries, including shellfisheries, carried on within sea fisheries districts. The power to do so, by Order, is given to Ministers on the application of a county, county borough or metropolitan district council, or by 20 or more inhabitants if the council refuses to apply. Half of the committee is appointed by the constituent council, which also funds it. One member is appointed by the Environment Agency and the remainder by the Minister 'as being persons acquainted with the needs and opinions of the fishing interests' of the district.[9] Ministers may also appoint persons having knowledge of, or experience in, marine environmental matters, as may the constituent council in relation to its powers relating to marine environmental byelaws.[10] Reference to 'Minister' here is to the Minister of Agriculture, Fisheries and Food (in England) or the Welsh counterpart.[11] Thus, the power to establish sea fisheries committees is essentially a function of agricultural administration exercised predominantly through local government, in which the Environment Agency plays only a minor role.

The jurisdiction of sea fisheries committees can extend to the limit of the territorial sea,[12] and may reach into any estuary or harbour to a limit defined in the Order constituting a committee. The Environment Agency or a harbour authority may also be given the powers of a sea fisheries committee as regards such rivers, streams and estuaries above the point

---

[8] See generally s.13 Environment Act 1995.

[9] ss.2 and 3 Sea Fisheries Regulation Act 1966.

[10] *Ibid* s.2(2) and (2A), as amended by s.102 Environment Act 1995. On 'marine environmental purposes' see 15.2.3 below.

[11] That is, the National Assembly for Wales.

[12] On the limits of the territorial sea see 18.7.1 below.

beyond which sea fisheries committees powers cease,[13] or be given the powers of a sea fisheries committee where an application to create a sea fisheries district has not been made or has been refused.[14] The functions of sea fisheries committees are considered under the Sea Fisheries Regulation Act 1966, discussed below.[15] However, it is worth mentioning here that the ability in practice for these functions to be exercised is subject to restrictions on local authority funding, which has been criticised for not being sufficient secure.[16]

## 15.3 Water Quality Standards under EC Fisheries Waters Legislation

At present, there are two key Community directives which set water quality standards for waters for freshwater fish or for shellfish. This section discusses these directives and their implementation, and considers two key cases from the European and domestic courts which illustrate the way in which each directive has been characterised judicially for implementation and enforcement purposes, both of which reveal a certain tension in conceiving of the directives as 'environmental'.

It must be stressed that both directives will be repealed and replaced by the Water Framework Directive as from 22 December 2013. [17]

### 15.3.1 The Freshwater Fish Waters and Shellfish Waters Directives

Specific provision is made regulating the ambient environmental quality of certain fishery waters under the Community Freshwater Fish Waters[18] and Shellfish Waters[19] Directives. Both Directives have as their purpose the protection and improvement of waters capable of supporting certain kinds of fish against pollution for ecological and economic reasons. Although there are important differences, both Directives share certain common features which are discussed below.

### 15.3.1A The Freshwater Fish Waters Directive

The Freshwater Fish Waters Directive relates to salmonid waters and cyprinid waters.

In relation to these categories of waters, Member States must designate particular waters, initially within a two year period after notification of the Directive, though subsequent designations and revisions of designations

---

[13] As is the case with the Environment Agency in the Dee Estuary and that part of the coast to the east of Cardiff.
[14] s.18(2) Sea Fisheries Regulation Act 1966.
[15] See 15.4.2 below.
[16] House of Commons Agriculture Select Committee, *Sea Fishing* (1999) paras.148-149.
[17] See 5.9.19 above.
[18] Directive 78/659/EEC.
[19] Directive 79/923/EEC.

are envisaged.[20] Appropriate physical and chemical parameters are listed in Annexes to the Directive. Annex I sets out imperative (I) and guide (G) values and conditions for the application of 14 physical and chemical parameters for the two categories of water. Alongside the quality parameters, methods of analysis or inspection are specified along with minimum sampling and measuring frequencies and particular observations relating to certain parameters. In relation to these parameters, Member States must set values not less stringent than the I values and endeavour to respect the G values.

Following designation of the fish waters, Member States must establish programmes to reduce pollution and to ensure that designated waters conform to the requirements of the Directive within five years of designation.[21] For the purpose of establishing pollution reduction programmes, designated waters will conform to the provisions of the Directive if samples, taken at minimum frequencies specified in Annex I at the same sampling point over a 12 months period, show specified percentages of conformity to the parameters required by the Directive.

In Case 14/86, *Pretore di Salo* v *Persons Unknown*[22] the Advocate General advised against the Freshwater Fish Waters Directive having direct effect[23] because of the discretion enjoyed by Member States in classifying the waters falling within the directive's application. The European Court of Justice did not examine the provisions of the Directive as to their direct effect, but argued that their use against a person in criminal proceedings would impose obligations rather than create rights which was ruled out. In the light of subsequent case law of the Court of Justice, it is likely that a narrower view would now be taken of the discretion enjoyed by Member States to designate appropriate waters.[24]

### 15.3.1B  The Shellfish Waters Directive

By contrast with the Freshwater Fish Waters Directive, the main purpose of the Shellfish Waters Directive is to safeguard certain shellfish[25] populations from various harmful consequences, resulting from the discharge of polluting substances into the sea, both for environmental reasons, to assist in the protection of consumers of edible shellfish products, and to remove unequal conditions of competition. Accordingly, the Directive is concerned with coastal and brackish waters designated by the Member States as needing protection or improvement in order to support shellfish life and growth and to contribute to the high quality of shellfish products.

---

[20] On the confined nature of this discretion see Case 322/86 *Commission* v *Italy* [1988] ECR 3995.

[21] That is, by 20 June 1985.

[22] [1987] ECR 2545.

[23] On direct effect see 4.16 above.

[24] See, by analogy, Case C-225/96 *Commission* v *Italy* [1998] Env LR 370, on the Shellfish Waters Directive, at 15.3.1B below.

[25] Defined as bivalve and gastropod molluscs.

In relation to the required water quality, the Shellfish Waters Directive similarly provides for I and G values for 12 physical and chemical parameters along with a statement of the reference method of analysis and the minimum sampling and measuring frequency. Member States must set values no less stringent than the I values for designated waters and endeavour to observe the G values. A specific departure from this is made in relation to effluents falling within parameters for organohalogenated substances and metals, where emission standards are established for these substances pursuant to the Dangerous Substances Directive.[26] In relation to these substances, the emission standards under the Dangerous Substances Directive are to be applied at the same time as the quality objectives and other obligations under the Shellfish Waters Directive. Significantly, therefore, a limited element of emissions control is provided for under a Directive that is, otherwise, concerned with ambient water quality requirements. It is curious feature of the Directive that arguably the most important parameter, the bacteriological quality in terms of faecal coliform levels, has only guideline status.

Member States were to have undertaken an initial designation of shellfish waters under the Shellfish Waters Directive within two years of its notification,[27] though subsequent additions and revisions of designations were provided for. A regrettable feature of the Directive is that it does not include any specific criteria for selecting such areas. However, the Court of Justice has been prepared to find that Member States have been in breach of their duties for non-designation.[28] Within six years of designation of the waters,[29] Member States were bound to establish programmes to reduce pollution and to ensure that waters conformed to the requirements of the Directive, implying the need for appropriate water quality restoration programmes. Compliance is dependent upon samples of waters, taken at the required frequency and location, showing conformity with the parameters at percentages specified for the different parameters.

*15.3.1C  Common Provisions*

Both the Freshwater Fish Waters and the Shellfish Waters Directives share a number of analogous provisions. Thus, for both Directives competent authorities[30] must carry out sampling operations at minimum specified frequencies. Where water quality is appreciably higher than required by either Directive the frequency of sampling may be reduced, and where there is no pollution or risk of deterioration in water quality the competent authority may determine that no sampling is necessary. If sampling shows that a parameter is not being respected, the Member State must establish whether this is the result of chance, a natural phenomenon or pollution, and must adopt appropriate measures. However, no further indication is

---

[26] On the Dangerous Substances Directive see 5.4.1 above.

[27] That is, by 30 October 1981.

[28] Case C-225/96 *Commission v Italy* [1998] Env LR 370, paras.24-28.

[29] That is, by 5 November 1987.

[30] In England and Wales, the Environment Agency.

given as to what 'appropriate measures' should be adopted. In addition, both Directives provide for non-degradation of water quality by the requirement that implementation may on no account lead, either directly or indirectly, to increased pollution of the waters concerned. Similarly, Member States may set more stringent values for designated waters than those established under the Directives and may also establish parameters other than those provided for in the Directives. Also, derogation is allowed for, in the case of specific parameters, because of exceptional weather or special geographical conditions.[31] Both Directives may be amended if this is necessary for adaptation to technical or scientific progress in relation to guide values for the parameters and the method of analysis of samples. Committee procedures apply for this purpose, the same committee deciding on amendments to both Directives.

In each case, Member States must supply the Commission with information concerning the identity of designated waters, revisions of designations, details of more stringent values for designated waters, and information about any derogations from values under the Directive.[32] More generally, the Directive provides that, on a reasoned request from the Commission, Member States must provide the Commission with any information necessary for the application of the Directive. Member States must provide the Commission with a report following the initial designation of waters,[33] and provide subsequent reports at regular intervals thereafter.

### 15.3.2 Implementation of the Directives

#### 15.3.2A Freshwater Fish Waters Directive

Implementation of the Freshwater Fish Waters Directive is by the Surface Waters (Fishlife) (Classification) Regulations 1997,[34] and the Surface Waters (Fishlife) Directions 1997. The Regulations apply the classifications SW (salmonid waters) and CW (cyprinid waters) to the classification of inland freshwaters, which for the purpose of the Regulations takes the meaning in the Directive rather than under the definition of controlled waters.[35] The 1997 Regulations transfer formal responsibility for the classification of waters from the Environment Agency to the Secretary of State.

Whether there has been an adequate number and extent of designations for the purposes of the Directive has been called into question. The designation of waters by the former water authorities was almost certainly

---

[31] In the case of the Freshwater Fish Waters Directives, derogation extends to where designated waters undergo natural enrichment in certain substances so that values are not respected.
[32] For the Shellfish Waters Directive, a statement of the reasons for derogation and the anticipated period of derogation must be supplied.
[33] That is, by 20 June 1985 (Freshwater Fish Waters) and by 30 October 1987 (Shellfish Waters).
[34] SI 1997 No.1331, made under s.82 Water Resources Act 1991. See discussion of these Regulations at 14.8.7 above.
[35] In s.104 Water Resources Act 1991; on controlled waters see 9.4 above.

uneven. Policy at present appears to be not to designate any further waters, on the grounds that the UK has already made more designations than other Member States.[36] Given the experience in relation to other quality directives, it would be surprising if the original round of designations under the Freshwater Fish Waters Directive provide to have been sufficiently complete.

### 15.3.2B  Shellfish Waters Directive

Implementation of the Shellfish Waters Directive is by the Surface Waters (Shellfish) (Classification) Regulations 1997,[37] and the Surface Waters (Shellfish) Directions 1997.[38] The Regulations apply the classification SFW, as defined, for classifying controlled waters that are coastal or brackish waters as defined by the Directive. As with implementation of the Freshwater Fish Waters Directive, 'controlled waters' for the purpose of the Regulations takes the meaning necessary for compliance with the Directive rather than under the definition of controlled waters in the Water Resources Act 1991 and the 1997 Regulations transfer formal responsibility for the classification of waters from the Environment Agency to the Secretary of State.

Quality standards for shellfish waters are also laid down by Part II of the Food Safety (Fishery Products and Live Shellfish) (Hygiene) Regulations 1998.[39] These oblige Ministers to designate sea waters and brackish waters from which live bivalve molluscs may be taken under various conditions, and enables Ministers, for health reasons, to designate prohibited areas for the production or collection of live bivalve molluscs, live echinoderms, tunicates and marine gastropods, and live shellfish. The Regulations implement in part a Community Directive concerned with health conditions for the production and placing on the market of live bivalve molluscs (the Shellfish Hygiene Directive).[40]

Despite the various aims of the Shellfish Waters Directive, however (encompassing both human health and environmental protection), the view of the Commission appeared at one stage to be that the Shellfish Hygiene Directive made the Shellfish Waters Directive redundant.[41] This informal narrowing of the scope of the Shellfish Waters Directive has considerable implications for those affected by breach of the Directive other than

---

[36] See DETR, *Raising the Quality* (1998). For criticisms on implementation generally see Scott (2000).

[37] SI 1997 No.1332, made under s.82 Water Resources Act 1991. See discussion of these Regulations at 14.8.8 above.

[38] See also DETR, *Implementation of the Shellfish Waters Directive (79/923/EEC): Consultation Document* (1998), and discussion of ongoing transposition issues at 2.22 above.

[39] SI 1998 No.994.

[40] Directive 91/492/EEC, which also has water quality implications.

[41] COM(96)59 *European Community Water Policy*, annex para.1.6. See further 5.7 above. Whether this is in fact the case might be questioned, since the Shellfish Hygiene Directive is concerned only with shellfish placed on the market.

consumers.[42] Nevertheless, the Commission continues to pursue infringement proceedings in relation to the Shellfish Waters Directive. At the time of writing this has included bringing the United Kingdom to the European Court of Justice on the grounds that insufficient areas have been designated and for inadequacies in its pollution reduction programmes (including insufficient monitoring) and because some programmes are still not established.[43] This is despite the further designation of 76 additional areas and extending the area of 17 existing sites,[44] and the recent legislative transposition of domestic obligations, noted above. In passing, it is worth noting the extent to which the UK Government in 1980 originally advised the water authorities to have regard to the costs of designating shellfish waters, and only to designate those waters which already met the required standards or which would do so under already agreed expenditure plans.[45] The present proceedings are a good illustration of the way in which Commission enforcement action is often triggered by a detailed complaint coming from a concerned individual or group at national level.[46]

### 15.3.2C  Common Concerns

In addition to the above concerns over implementation, it has also been alleged that the UK Government has not designated as 'sensitive areas' under the 1991 Urban Waste Water Treatment Directive any sites which are (or should have been) designated under the Shellfish Waters and Freshwater Fish Waters Directives. Following a complaint to the Commission, it appears that there will be further designation of sensitive sites under the 1991 Directive, so that waters which should be given additional protection under the Shellfish Waters and Freshwater Fish Waters Directives will be treated to the higher standards required by the 1991 Directive.[47]

### 15.3.3  Case C-298/95 Commission v Germany

Concerning both the Freshwater Fish Waters and Shellfish Waters Directives, Case C-298/95 *Commission v Germany*[48] is instructive. In this case, the Commission argued that Germany was in breach of its obligations under both Directives by failing to set parametric values and implement

---

[42] See the *Bowden* case, discussed at 15.3.4 below.

[43] 'Shellfish and Surface Water: Commission moves against UK and Italy', RAPID IP/00/888, 28 July 2000.

[44] *ENDS Report* 294 (1999) p.42. Areas now designated under the 1979 Directive are now broadly similar to those classified as shellfish hygiene production areas under Directive 91/492/EEC.

[45] See Ward, Buller and Lowe (1995) p.72. The same authors give an insightful account of the negligible impact of the Directive, and the lack of criticism this generated at the time. On the extent to which the Directive was not seen as a driver of improved water quality see Wathern et al (1987).

[46] See 4.13.3 above on the Commission's complaints procedure.

[47] *ENDS Report* 305 (2000) p.9.

[48] Case C-298/95 *Commission v Germany* [1996] ECR I-6747.

pollution reduction and water restoration programmes.[49] As regards the obligation to set parametric values, although the Shellfish Waters Directive has a stated human health objective, the Court accepted the argument of the Commission that so too did the Freshwater Fish Waters Directive. However, there is no authority for this interpretation either in the Directive or its preamble. Indeed, the preamble is arguably one of the first examples, in Community water law, where the ecological foundations for a Directive are stressed ahead of, or at least alongside, competition concerns.[50] Nevertheless, the Court held that one of the objectives of the Directive was to protect human health through monitoring the quality of waters which support, or could support, fish suitable for human consumption. While the salmonid and cyprinid species referred to may be consumed, it is suggested that this no more justifies a reading of the Directive to include human health objectives any more than it would in the case of, say, the Wild Birds Directive.[51]

The Court may have neatly side-stepped any criticism in relation to its finding about the objectives of the Freshwater Fish Waters Directive by stating that:

> *In those circumstances,*[52] it is particularly important that directives should be transposed by measures which are indisputably binding. In all cases where non-implementation of the measures required by a directive could endanger human health, the persons concerned must be in a position to rely on mandatory rules in order to be able to assert their rights.

The second sentence is no more than a statement of settled case law[53] though who the 'persons concerned' would be for the purposes, say, of a *Francovich* action is not made clear.[54] What is also unclear is whether it is reached only where an objective of the Directive is to protect human health, or where it applies to any case where non-implementation might endanger human health. If the latter, this would seem to go beyond the predominant jurisprudence of the Court to date and open up the scope for direct effect and state liability actions. This might be a desirable end so far as enforcing Community environmental law is concerned,[55] and in this respect the decision of the Court of Justice not to accept the existence of German national law on permitted residues in fish as a proper, if alternative, means of implementing the provision of the Directives relating to the setting of parametric values might be approved of. However, it must

---

[49] See Arts.3 and 5 of both Directives, discussed above.

[50] The Freshwater Fish Waters Directive is based on guidance contained in the reports of the European Inland Fisheries Advisory Committee, see Pugh (1997) p.13. The 'River Ecosystem' water quality classification at national level incorporates determinands in the Directive. And it is also notable that the Directive is classified as a conservation measure on the EC's legislation website: http://europa.eu.int/eur-lex/en/index.html

[51] On the Wild Birds Directive see 15.8 below.

[52] That is, where a directive has human health protection as one of its purposes (emphasis added).

[53] See generally 4.16 above and the *Bowden* case at 15.3.4 below.

[54] See Stallworthy (1998) p.134. On *Francovich* liability see 4.16.6 above.

[55] See Hilson (1997) pp.57-58.

be regrettable that such protection arises only with the possibility of human consumption of the ecological interest to be protected, combined with an overtly non-ecological reading of the objectives of the Directive.

As regards the obligation to establish pollution reduction programmes and bring pollution levels down to the I and G levels required,[56] the argument advanced by Germany was that the existence of general action programmes dating from the mid-1950s for reducing water pollution was sufficient. Germany pointed to the considerable improvements in water quality that had occurred over this period. This argument was rejected. The Court pointed to the need to establish specific programmes in respect of specific parameters affecting freshwater fish and shellfish life, and to the obligation to improve water quality in order to support fish life. As the Advocate General observed:

> it is clear from the scheme and objectives of the Fresh Water Directive that it seeks to ensure that water is specifically of a quality to support fish life. It is not obvious, at least without corroboration, that general measures for improving the cleanliness of water will of necessity have that effect: it may, for example, be the case that certain pollutants may be neutralized by other chemicals which, while making the water purer in one sense, may not be beneficial to fish life.[57]

The case is therefore a useful illustration of the way in which water quality legislation may be enacted with positive ambient objectives in mind, not merely so as to 'reduce pollution' or 'purify water' in some general sense.

### 15.3.4 Bowden v South West Water Services Ltd

The litigation in the case of *Bowden v South West Water Services Ltd*[58] sheds further light on the nature of the Shellfish Waters Directive. Amongst many heads of claim, the claimant, a mussel fisherman, alleged that he had been forced out of business through non-implementation of the Directive, his claim being that non-implementation of a range of Community and national provisions had led to his waters being designated as unfit for commercial shellfish harvesting. One aspect of the claim was that the waters in question should have been, but had not been, designated under the Shellfish Waters Directive.

At first instance,[59] the judge upheld an action by the defendants (joined, at that time, by others) to strike out the claim on the grounds that, even if a breach of the Directive was established,[60] the obligation was owed to the public in general. For the purposes of state liability, there was nothing to

---

[56] Under Art.5 of the Directives.

[57] Opinion of Advocate General Jacobs, para.18.

[58] On this case see also 3.12 above in relation to breach of statutory duty, and see Miller (1999).

[59] [1998] Env LR 445.

[60] On which see Case C-225/96 *Commission v Italy* [1998] Env LR 370, and see 15.3.1B above.

link the breach to the specific rights of individuals, or which would enable the contents of those rights to be ascertained. The Court of Appeal, however, allowed the claim to be reinstated on the basis that the Directive could be interpreted as conferring a right on those who harvested shellfish commercially.[61] In doing so, the Court pointed to the avoidance of competitive inequalities which provides one of the foundations, though arguably the least important basis, for the Directive. The right of the claimant to resume his claim in damages against the state (or here, South West Water Services, an emanation of the state) rested on his potential commercial disadvantage rather than any wider ecological concerns.[62] For this reason, similar claims under the Directives on Urban Waste Water Treatment[63] and Bathing Waters[64] were rejected, because the claimant could not establish that he derived individual rights under them.

The preamble to the Shellfish Waters Directive is similar in many respects to the Freshwater Fish Waters Directive. The *Bowden* case suggests, therefore, that while the general public have no legally protected right to enjoy water clean enough for salmon or oysters, those who harvest such species may do so. In the case of the Shellfish Waters Directive, however,[65] the inclusion of a specific reference to the health of shellfish consumers makes possible a remedy to anyone who falls ill and suffers loss as a result of eating shellfish taken from an area that ought to have been designated and where mandatory limits have been breached. However, this will only arise where a direct causal connection between non-implementation of the Directive and damage can be established.

## 15.4 Specific Offences Concerning the Pollution of Waters Containing Fish

In addition to the principal water pollution offences contained in Part III of the Water Resources Act 1991,[66] a number of further offences relate to the pollution of water. Rather than seeking to control water pollution in a general sense, however, these additional offences seek specifically to criminalise the entry of polluting matter into waters containing fish. In doing so, however, their origins tend to lie in the protection of fish, either as an adjunct of private freshwater fishery rights, or to protect commercial interests in shellfish production and harvesting.

---

[61] [1999] Env LR 438.

[62] It is arguable that this approach might mean that claims for breach of statutory duty (although rejected in this case at first instance) might be successful. On breach of statutory duty see 3.12 above.

[63] See 5.6.2 above.

[64] See 5.5.2 above.

[65] And, perhaps, following the judgment of the Court in Case C-298/95 *Commission v Germany*, the Freshwater Fish Waters Directive too; see 15.3.3 above.

[66] Discussed in detail in Ch.9 above.

### 15.4.1 The Salmon and Freshwater Fisheries Act 1975

A number of offences in relation to the pollution of waters arise under national fisheries legislation. Most notably, it an offence under the Salmon and Freshwater Fisheries Act 1975 for any person to cause or knowingly permit[67] to flow, or put or knowingly permit to be put, into any waters containing fish, or into any tributaries of waters containing fish, any liquid or solid matter to such an extent as to cause the waters to be poisonous or injurious[68] to fish or the spawning grounds, spawn or food of fish.[69] The offence of discharging poisonous or injurious matter into waters containing fish is administered, along with the other fishery offences under the 1975 Act, by the Environment Agency. Notably, because the offence is concerned with 'waters containing fish' and is not restricted to 'freshwater fish' or any particular species of fish, it is capable of arising in cases of marine pollution in coastal waters out to the six nautical mile limit.

The offence of polluting waters containing fish has some significant points of similarity with the offence of causing or knowingly permitting the pollution of controlled waters.[70] However, there are also some important differences which follow from the purpose of the fishery offence being to prohibit certain modes of taking or destroying fish. Thus, the restriction of the offence to discharges 'into any waters containing fish' means that no offence will be committed if the entry[71] in question is into waters which are already so badly polluted that fishlife is absent, unless it can be shown that the water is a tributary of a water containing fish.[72] Nonetheless the offence remains one concerned with the improper taking or destruction of fish, and it is an inherent feature that the offence will not be established unless the prosecution shows that the effect of the discharge is to cause the waters to be poisonous or injurious to fish or the spawning grounds, spawn or food of fish. It seems that this does not mean that any fish need in fact be harmed.[73]

The scope and utility of the offence is further limited by a series of substantive and procedural restrictions. First, the liberty is preserved for a person to exercise a legal entitlement to pollute water or to continue a method in use in connection with the premises before the date of the passing of the Salmon and Freshwater Fisheries Act 1923, providing that it is shown that the best practicable means, within a reasonable cost, have

---

[67] On the meaning of these terms see 9.5–7 above.

[68] On the meaning of these terms see 9.8 above.

[69] Under s.4(1) Salmon and Freshwater Fisheries Act 1975. See generally Howarth (1987).

[70] Under s.85 Water Resources Act 1991.

[71] Whether use of the term 'flow' rather than 'enter' is of any significance has never been the subject of a reported decision.

[72] A 'tributary' includes a tributary of a tributary and so on. On the meaning of tributary see *Merricks* v *Cadwaller* (1881) 46 LT 29; *Hall* v *Reid* (1882) 10 QBD 134; *Harbottle* v *Terry* (1882) 47 JP 136; *George* v *Carpenter* [1893] 1 QB 505; *Evans* v *Owens* [1895] 1 QB 273; *Stead* v *Nicholas* [1901] 2 KB 163; *Cook* v *Clareborough* (1903) 70 JP 252; *Moses* v *Iggo* [1906] 1 KB 516.

[73] *R* v *Bradford* (1860) 24 JP 374. See also the 'approach' to interpreting 'polluting' under the Water Resources Act 1991, discussed at 9.8 above.

been used to prevent discharged matter from doing injury to fish, their spawning grounds, spawn or food. This defence is likely to be of narrow scope in view of the difficulty involved in establishing a legal right to pollute a watercourse as a result of this having been generally unlawful since long before 1923.[74] Second, proceedings may only be instituted by the Environment Agency or by a person who has first obtained a certificate from the Minister that that person has a material interest in the waters alleged to be affected, a provision which limits the scope for environmental interest groups to use the 1975 Act to act against any pollution of water.[75] Third, it will be a defence to show that the polluting substance is used for a scientific purpose, or for the purpose of protecting, improving or replacing stocks of fish, and permission in writing has been given by the Environment Agency. Fourth, it will be a defence to show that any such discharge was to controlled waters and was made under and in accordance with a discharge consent under Chapter II of Part III of the Water Resources Act 1991 or as a result of any act or omission under and in accordance with that consent.[76] Finally, it is notable that the available penalties under the 1975 Act are significantly lower than those available for the principal water pollution offences under the Water Resources Act 1991, at least in the magistrates' court. Thus, on summary conviction, the offence is punishable by the prescribed sum, currently £5000, and £40 for each day on which the offence continues after a conviction. On conviction on indictment, the maximum penalty is 2 years imprisonment or a fine.[77]

If charges under both the 1975 Act and the 1991 Act are brought, it is conceivable that a successful *autrefois acquit* plea might be accepted. That is, it might be argued that the charges are, for practical purposes, essentially identical and that bringing charges under both Acts would be rejected by the court as duplicitous. In *R v British Coal Corporation,*[78] a case concerning pollution from an abandoned mine, although the prosecution was ultimately unsuccessful for other reasons, this plea did not seem to have been raised. Reasoning from other cases, however, where more recently the courts have taken a less restrictive approach to what might be termed duplicitous charging,[79] the better view is probably that both offences can be charged following the same event. Unless special circumstances dictate, however, for the reasons described above it is likely that charges will be brought under the Water Resources Act 1991.

---

[74] See *Hulley v Silversprings Bleaching Co* [1922] All ER Rep 683, and *George Legge and Son Ltd v Wenlock Corporation* [1938] AC 204; and prescription at common law, discussed at 3.13.3 above.

[75] s.4(3) Salmon and Freshwater Fisheries Act 1975.

[76] para.30(1) Sch.1 Water Consolidation (Consequential Provisions) Act 1991. On discharge consents generally see Ch.10 above. While it is no defence to have acted under other environmental licences such as IPC authorisations or IPPC permits, it is unlikely that the Agency would prosecute, and private prosecutions are effectively precluded..

[77] s.37 and Sch.4 Salmon and Freshwater Fisheries Act 1975.

[78] *ENDS Report* 227 (1993) p.42 and see 9.17.3A on this case. See also *ENDS Report* 305 (2000) p.55 in relation to a prosecution of Welsh Water under both s.85(1) and (3) of the 1991 Act and s.4 of the 1975 Act.

[79] *R v Leighton and Town and Country Refuse Collections Ltd* [1997] Env LR 411, see 9.5 above.

In favour of the offence under the Salmon and Freshwater Fisheries Act 1975, however, the geographic scope of the offence under the 1975 Act extends out to six nautical miles, and thus beyond the three nautical mile limit of 'relevant territorial waters' in relation to the principal water pollution offences under the Water Resources Act 1991. It may be queried whether this is of any practical relevance, however, given the stricter provisions that govern such matters as the discharges of oil and other substances from shipping, or the dumping of other substances into the marine environment.[80]

Notably, a recent review of fisheries legislation concluded that the fisheries offence relating to water pollution should not, as things presently stand, be repealed, since representations made to the review committee by the Environment Agency remarked that the provisions in the 1975 Act had some advantages and are still made use of on occasions.[81] For this reason, the report recommended that the offence should not be repealed until adequate alternatives are included in general water pollution legislation. That said, the report also recommended that:

> New legislation on salmon and freshwater fisheries should focus on providing Government and its agencies with the means to achieve their objectives for the conservation and management of salmon and freshwater fish. Problems that affect the freshwater environment as a whole should be dealt with through environmental legislation.[82]

Subject to certain exceptions, the 1975 Act also makes it an offence to use in or near any inland or coastal waters (to the six nautical mile limit) any explosive substance, any poison or other noxious substance, or any electrical device, with intent to take or destroy fish.[83] A person who contravenes these provisions or who, for the purpose of doing so, has in their possession any explosive or noxious substance or any electrical device, is guilty of an offence.[84] Exceptions to this offence arise where a person uses a substance or device for a scientific purpose or for protecting, improving or replacing stocks of fish and with the written permission of the Environment Agency. The Agency need no longer seek the approval of the Minister to permit the use of a noxious substance.[85]

Finally in relation to freshwater fisheries regulation, the Agency may, in relation to any part or parts of the area in relation to which it carries out fisheries functions,[86] make byelaws generally for the purposes of the better execution of the 1975 Act and the better protection, preservation and improvement of any salmon fisheries, trout fisheries, freshwater fisheries

---

[80] On pollution from shipping and other maritime activities see Ch.19 below.

[81] MAFF and National Assembly for Wales, *Salmon and Freshwater Fisheries Review* (2000).

[82] *Ibid*, see respectively Recommendations 95 and 88.

[83] s.5(1) Salmon and Freshwater Fisheries Act 1975.

[84] *Ibid* s.5(4).

[85] para.7 Sch.15 Environment Act 1995.

[86] See 15.2.1 above on the Agency's fishery jurisdication.

and eel fisheries.[87] The power is widely framed and, in addition to the general power to make byelaws, includes provision for a range of specified byelaw-making powers. These include the making of byelaws for the purpose of regulating the deposit or discharge in any waters containing fish of any specified liquid or solid matter which is detrimental to salmon, trout or freshwater fish, or to the spawn or food of fish. In relation to this power, however, the Agency may not make a byelaw so as to prejudice any powers of a sewerage undertaker to discharge sewage in pursuance of any power given by public general Act, a local Act or a provisional order confirmed by Parliament.[88]

The power to make fisheries byelaws now extends to their enactment for marine or aquatic environmental purposes. These are defined as meaning the conservation or enhancement of the natural beauty or amenity of marine or coastal, or aquatic or waterside, areas (including their geological or physiographical features) or of any features of archaeological or historic interest in such areas, or the conservation of flora or fauna which are dependent on, or associated with, a marine or coastal, or aquatic or waterside, environment.[89] Most of the water quality purposes for which byelaws might be enacted, however, will already be regulated under the Water Resources Act 1991. Hence, there appears little for the Agency to gain by using its byelaw-making powers in relation to fishery conservation for water quality purposes, and it is not thought that any existing byelaws include any water pollution measures.[90] Moreover, the maximum penalty for a water byelaw offence, a fine not exceeding level 4 on the standard scale, presently £2500,[91] suggests that a prosecution for breach of a principal water pollution offence is more likely to be brought.

### 15.4.2 The Sea Fisheries Regulation Act 1966

The Sea Fisheries Regulation Act 1966 empowers Ministers[92] to create sea fisheries districts, to define the limits of such districts, and to constitute sea fisheries committees.[93] Amongst the powers given to sea fisheries committees for a sea fisheries district is that of making byelaws, which extend to making byelaws for the protection of salmon and their migration.[94] Under the Environment Act 1995 the byelaw-making power was extended to 'marine environmental purposes',[95] meaning the purposes of:

---

[87] para.6(1) Sch.25 Water Resources Act 1991.

[88] para.6(4) and (7) Sch.25 Water Resources Act 1991. Note that similar byelaw-making powers under the Salmon and Freshwater Fisheries Act 1975 remain; see para. 31 Sch.4 to the 1975 Act.

[89] para.6A Sch.25 Water Resources Act 1991, inserted by s.103(3) Environment Act 1995.

[90] Other than byelaws in relation to lead weights, which make similar provision regarding the use of particular sizes of weights, as made in legislation, see 12.4.6 above.

[91] s.211(3) Water Resources Act 1991.

[92] Which expression includes the Secretary of State, and in Wales refers to the National Assembly.

[93] See 15.2.3 above on sea fisheries committees.

[94] s.37(1) Salmon Act 1986.

[95] s.102(5) Environment Act 1995, inserting s.5A Sea Fisheries Regulation Act 1966.

(a) conserving or enhancing the natural beauty or amenity of marine or coastal areas; or

(b) conserving flora or fauna which are dependent on, or associated with, a marine or coastal environment.[96]

On privatisation in 1989, however, a previous power to make regulations prohibiting or regulating the deposit or discharge of any solid or liquid substance detrimental to sea fish or sea fishing was repealed.[97] Doubtless this was for the reason that any such power would not add to the general water pollution controls under the Water Resources Act 1991.

In *Bowden* v *South West Water Services Ltd and Others*,[98] it was held that contravention of sea fisheries byelaws might provide a sufficiently direct link to the rights of those involved in sea fishing to form the basis of an action for breach by the sewerage undertaker of statutory duty. The statutory defences available to local authorities – that no byelaw may be made which affects any power of a local authority to discharge sewage in pursuance of any power conferred by a general or local Act of Parliament or by a Provisional Order confirmed by Parliament – could not necessarily be relied upon by a statutory undertaker such as the sewerage undertaker concerned.[99] This was not merely because of the terminological difference, but because it seemed that the power contained in the undertakers discharge consent to discharge sewage effluent was a power conferred *under* the Water Resources Act 1991 and not *by* it. The Court also held that even if the breach of the byelaw did not give rise to an independent cause of action it might be relevant when any common law claim was assessed. There was at least an arguable point and the claim was not struck out on this ground.

### 15.4.3 The Sea Fisheries (Shellfish) Act 1967

The Sea Fisheries (Shellfish) Act 1967[100] provides for Ministerial orders to be made for establishing, improving, maintaining and regulating fisheries for shellfish and the protection of such fisheries from certain kinds of contamination. 'Shellfish' for these purposes means oysters, mussels, cockles, clams, lobsters and any other molluscs or crustaceans of a kind specified in regulations made by the appropriate Minister.[101] Fisheries for shellfish may be located on any portion of the shore and bed of the sea or in an estuary or tidal river above or below low water mark and within waters adjacent to England and Wales to the six nautical mile limit. A

---

[96] s.5A(4) Sea Fisheries Regulation Act 1966.

[97] s.5(1)(c) Sea Fisheries Regulation Act 1996, repealed by Water (Consequential Amendments) Regulations 1989 (SI 1989 No.1968).

[98] [1998] Env LR 445, see 15.3.4 above.

[99] Contrast the position under the Salmon and Freshwater Fisheries Act 1975, noted above. In relation to riparian rights, see *Hobart* v *Southend-on-Sea Corporation* (1906) 75 LJKB 305, discussed at 3.3 above.

[100] See generally Howarth (1990) para.15.04.

[101] s.1(1) Sea Fisheries (Shellfish) Act 1967, as amended by s.15(1) and (2) Sea Fisheries Act 1968, s.1 Sea Fisheries (Shellfish) (Amendment) Act 1997.

Ministerial order of this kind may confer a right of several fishery or a right of regulating a fishery in respect of the whole or a part of the area to which the order relates.[102] Alternatively fisheries for shellfish are capable of existing independently of the 1967 Act, and it is explicitly provided that no Ministerial order is to take away or abridge any right of several fishery or any right on, to or over any portion of the sea shore, enjoyed by any person under any local or special Act of Parliament or any Royal Charter, letters patent, prescription or immemorial usage, except with the consent of that person.[103]

Where an order under the Sea Fisheries (Shellfish) Act 1967 grants a right of several fishery for shellfish, or a private oyster bed is owned by any person independently of the Act and is sufficiently marked out or sufficiently known as such, a number of provisions under the Act apply to the protection of the fishery.[104] In particular, it is an offence, for any person other than the grantees or owner or their agents or employees, knowingly to deposit any ballast, rubbish or other substances within the limits of the several fishery or private oyster bed.[105] The offence is punishable on summary conviction by a fine not exceeding level 5 on the standard scale, currently £5000.[106] In addition, the guilty person is liable to make full compensation to the grantees or the owner for all damage sustained by reason of the unlawful act, and such compensation in default of payment may be recovered by proceedings in any court of competent jurisdiction whether the person has been prosecuted for or convicted of the offence in question or not.[107] By way of exception, however, the offence of depositing ballast, rubbish or other substances on shellfisheries will not be committed in the case of a right of several fishery granted by order where the limits of the area are not sufficiently marked out in the manner prescribed by the order, or if the notice of those limits has not been given to the person in any manner prescribed. In the case of a private oyster bed owned by any person independently of the Act, an analogous exception will arise if the bed is not sufficiently marked out and known as such.[108]

### 15.4.4 Provisions Specific to Aquaculture

The intensive nature of modern fish farming (aquaculture) has given rise to the use of a range of medicines, pesticides and other chemicals in the commercial rearing of fish which are not used in relation to other forms of

---

[102] s.1(3) Sea Fisheries (Shellfish) Act 1967; the effects of a grant of a right of several fishery and a right of regulating a fishery are set out in ss.2 and 3 of the Act respectively.

[103] *Ibid* s.1(6).

[104] *Ibid* s.7. On s.7 see also the rejection of a claim that breach of s.7 gave rise to a civil law right in *Bowden* v *South West Water Services Ltd* [1998] Env LR 445 (HC), upheld [1999] Env LR 438 (CA) and see also 15.3.4 above.

[105] *Ibid* s.7(4)(c); and see *Smith* v *Cook* (1914) 84 LJKB 959 on the meaning of 'knowingly' in this context.

[106] ss.37 and 46 Criminal Justice Act 1982, increased by s.157 Sch.8 Part I Criminal Justice and Public Order Act 1994.

[107] s.7(4) Sea Fisheries (Shellfish) Act 1967.

[108] *Ibid* s.7(5).

fishing. The use of such substances gives rise to issues concerning water pollution and the contamination of the aquatic environment, together with the necessity to control the lawful use of a range of chemicals for medicinal, pesticidinal and other uses in aquacultural contexts. While the law relating to pesticide control and use is considered elsewhere in this work,[109] specific issues are raised in fish farming, and controls on the use of medicines, pesticides and other controlled chemicals in fish farming are also considered briefly here.[110]

A useful illustration of the difficult environmental and legal issues involved is provided by the regulation of the use of ivermectin, a chemical used to control infestation of farmed salmon by sea lice.[111] Sea lice infestation can pose serious threats to cage farms, but sea lice have begun to develop a resistance to dichlorvos, the pesticide most frequently used to tackle the problem.[112] In 1998 the Scottish Office licensed, on a trial basis, the discharge of ivermectin, a previously banned chemical, from salmon farms. However, while dichlorvos is administered as a solution, ivermectin is an enteral treatment, making its regulation under the principal water pollution offences and the discharge consenting regime problematic.[113] For example, whether a 'discharge' occurs from a cage farm is uncertain, though in practice Procurators Fiscal in Scotland have proceeded on this basis and the recent interpretation of 'discharge' by the European Court of Justice might be called in aid to support this interpretation.[114] Even less clear is whether the feeding of fish can amount to an 'entry' of polluting matter. This is because it is arguable that most of the contamination of the seabed in the vicinity of the cage arises from fish faeces rather than directly from uneaten pellets falling through the cage, and may not have 'entered' the controlled water in the required sense.[115] Given these uncertainties, it may be that prosecutions, if brought, will be pursued for breach of conditions of the discharge consent,[116] and in this respect it is notable that the discharge consent condition appears to be formulated as a permission to include ivermectin in salmon feed up to 12 times per year, but only as a last resort. It is also worth noting here that discharge consents are being used to regulate a relatively diffuse source, as opposed to their normal use in consenting 'end of pipe' discharges. The legal problem remains, however, whether there is a 'discharge' to be consented.

The authorisation for use of such substances in fish farming by the relevant Agriculture Department is, from a legal perspective, complicated by the

---

[109] See 12.4.7 above.

[110] Generally, see Howarth (1990) Ch.11.

[111] Despite the absence of a commercial marine fin fish farming sector in England, the illustration is still instructive as regards freshwater trout farming, which predominates in England and Wales.

[112] Ross and Horsman (1988).

[113] Although ivermectin is licensed for use in Scotland, the statutory framework for water pollution is analogous to that under ss.85 and 88 Water Resources Act 1991; see Part II Control of Pollution Act 1974.

[114] See Case C-232/97 *Nederhoff*, discussed at 5.4.1A above.

[115] See, on 'enter', *National Rivers Authority* v *Biffa Waste Services Ltd* [1996] Env LR 227, discussed at 9.10 above.

[116] On discharge consents see Ch.10 above.

fact that the same product may be classed either as a medicine, and therefore subject to control under the Medicines Act 1968 and the Veterinary Medicines Directive,[117] or a pesticide, and hence subject to control under Part III of the Food and Environment Protection Act 1985, depending on the purpose to which it is put.

The general approach of the Medicines Act 1968 is to subject any medicinal product or veterinary drug to a requirement of product licensing. This involves a licence being issued before a medicinal product may be sold, supplied or manufactured in the UK.[118] The Minister is advised by the Veterinary Products Committee before any licence decision is taken. However, an exception arises in the case of products specially prepared under a veterinary surgeon or veterinary practitioner's prescription for stock under his or her care.[119] The use of antibiotics in fish farming is subject to these general controls. However, their use may alter the aquatic environment and ultimately endanger human health.[120] The relevant provisions of the 1968 Act specify that issues of safety must be considered before any product licence is issued.[121] In considering safety, the appropriate Ministerial licensing authority must have regard, among other things, to the capacity of the substance to cause danger to the health of the community, or to animals generally.[122] The classification of antibiotics as medicines probably, therefore, precludes their control on environmental grounds,[123] although a change to the law recognising the importance of wider aquatic environmental considerations in this respect might be desirable. The regulatory control of pesticides is considered briefly elsewhere.[124]

## 15.5 Introducing Fish into Inland Waters

Under the Salmon and Freshwater Fisheries Act 1975, it is an offence to introduce fish or fish spawn into inland waters, or for a person to possess fish spawn with the intention of introducing it, without the consent of the Environment Agency.[125] The objective of this broadly-formulated offence and its accompanying licensing regime is to prevent the introduction of species which, because they are non-native[126] or not indigenous locally or are of farmed stock, may cause (or risk causing) harm to fishing interests or to the wider aquatic environment. Harm may arise because population growth of the introduced species leads to habitat competition, degradation

---

[117] Directive 85/851/EEC on the approximation of the laws of the Member States relating to veterinary medicinal products.
[118] s.7 Medicines Act 1968.
[119] *Ibid* s.9(2).
[120] Howarth (1990) pp.161-163.
[121] s.19 Medicines Act 1968.
[122] *Ibid* s.132(2).
[123] Warren (1991) p.18.
[124] See 12.4.7 above.
[125] s.30 Salmon and Freshwater Fisheries Act 1975.
[126] On the more general offence in conservation law of introducing non-native species see 15.7.6 below.

or predation. Alternatively, the introduced species may create an imbalance in the existing dynamic equilibrium between predator and prey species, or facilitate the introduction of disease. The introduction of non-indigenous species or stock may also have a damaging effect on the genetic integrity of indigenous populations, such as where farmed fish breed with their wild counterparts.[127] For this reason, the offence applies to the release of 'any fish', a term which is capable of extending to shellfish.[128] As discussed elsewhere,[129] the introduction of fish or other living organisms into water may be conceived of as an act of 'water contamination' in the sense that it may interfere with the 'natural' ecosystem and legitimate water uses. This can be illustrated through a successful action in both nuisance and negligence following an escape of rainbow trout from a fish farm into a river that was preserved as a brown trout fishery, because of the loss of angling amenity.[130]

The one exception to the general rule stated above is that the need for licensing only extends to the waters of fish farms where the waters of the farm discharge into another inland water other than through a conduit constructed or adapted for the purpose.[131] In practice, this means that the consent of the Agency is not needed, and no offence is committed, where suitable screens are placed to prevent the escape of fish from the farm into other waters, and since 1 January 1999 such screens have been mandatory.[132] For a variety of reasons, however, the policing of the offence of illegally introducing certain fish into waters has been described as 'difficult, if not impossible, to enforce'.[133]

Under the Import of Live Fish (England and Wales) Act 1980, the Minister of Agriculture, Fisheries and Food[134] is empowered to prohibit the import, keeping or release of any live fish, or live eggs of fish, which might compete with, displace, prey on or harm the habitat of any freshwater fish, shellfish or salmon in England or Wales unless a licence to do so has been granted. English Nature or the Countryside Council for Wales, as appropriate, and any other appropriate body must be consulted before any order is made, and the Environment Agency will be consulted on such matters.[135] Following the enactment of more general powers in the

---

[127] See e.g. Skaala, Dahle, Jørstad and Naevdal (1990).

[128] *Caygill* v *Thwaite* (1885) 49 JP 614.

[129] See 1.2 above, and see also 3.5 above.

[130] *Broderick* v *Gale and Ainslie Ltd*, Swindon County Court, 29 March 1993 and see [1993] *Water Law* 127 and 3.8 above.

[131] Added by s.34 Salmon Act 1986.

[132] On the requirement to fit screens, see s.14 Salmon and Freshwater Fisheries Act 1975, and art.4 The Environment Act 1995 (Commencement No.1) Order 1995, SI 1995 No.1983.

[133] MAFF and National Assembly for Wales, *Salmon and Freshwater Fisheries Review* (2000) p.130. The Review recommended a form of 'paper trail' regulation, whereby each stage in the movement of fish would need to be recorded and available for inspection, rather than requiring prior approval of all fish movements.

[134] Or, in Wales, the National Assembly.

[135] This practice was assured in the Parliamentary debate leading to the 1980 Act, see HL Deb 1980 Vol.407 Col.1230. The only other body which is routinely consulted is the Centre for Environment, Fisheries and Aquaculture Science.

Wildlife and Countryside Act 1981 to prohibit the release of non-native species,[136] it was thought that the specific offence and licensing power in relation to fish, motivated by a mixture of fisheries and conservation concerns,[137] would not need to be relied on. In recent years, however, orders have been made prohibiting the import, keeping or release of a number of fish species,[138] the 1980 Act having the twin advantages of both allowing for a more preventive approach to be taken, and not containing a due diligence defence. There is a general policy presumption against issuing licences for the introduction of listed species.[139] Failure to comply with licence conditions may result in the licence being revoked, and a maximum fine on summary conviction of level 4 on the standard scale, presently £2,500. There is also provision for illegally stocked fish to be removed and destroyed. Controls under the 1980 Act are in addition not, and do not replace, controls on introductions under the Salmon and Freshwater Fisheries Act 1975.

## 15.6 Aquatic Conservation Law

### 15.6.1 Background and Policy

The contribution of an aquatic environment of a satisfactory quality to nature conservation is well recognised. Aquatic species depend directly on a quality of water sufficient to ensure their survival, and changes to water quality in aquatic habitats may have a critical impact on the conservation status of dependent species. Similarly, the presence of certain species, (such as otters or the native white-clawed crayfish)[140] is a good indication of water quality. By way of illustration of the importance of water quality for nature conservation, the species action plans of the UK Biodiversity Action Plan[141] indicate that 32 of the 116 species initially listed for protection[142] will benefit as a result of improved water quality enhancing the habitats in which they occur.[143] Such aquatic habitats range from rivers, lakes and wetlands, to more artificial habitats such as canals, reservoirs, ponds, and gravel, clay and peat pits. Of the more biodiverse edge habitats (ecotones), the interface between land and water is probably

---

[136] See 15.7.6 below.

[137] See Howarth (1990) para.8.02.

[138] See, for example, The Prohibition of Keeping of Live Fish (Crayfish) Order 1996 (SI 1996 No.1104); The Prohibition of Keeping or Release of Live Fish (Specified Species) Order 1998 (SI 1998 No.2409).

[139] Centre for Environment, Fisheries and Aquaculture and Environment Agency, *Controls on the Keeping or Release of Non-Native Fish in England and Wales* (advisory leaflet, undated).

[140] The latter, for Huxley, being memorably described as 'the freshwater health inspector', cited in Howarth and McGillivray (1996) p.34.

[141] See 15.7.5 below.

[142] A further 286 species have now also been listed.

[143] UK Steering Group, *Biodiversity: The UK Steering Group Report, Vol. 1: Meeting the Rio Challenge* (1995) endorsed by Government Response to the UK Steering Group Report on Biodiversity (1996). Contrast English Nature (1997) p.49, which indicates that 49 of these species are dependent on freshwater habitats. The Environment Agency has lead responsibility for 39 species and 5 habitats.

the richest of all,[144] and a review identified 627 sites of special scientific interest (SSSIs)[145] which extended to the low water mark on ordinary high tide.[146] The importance of the aquatic environment for nature conservation can also be gauged by the recent completion by English Nature of a programme to designate 29 river SSSIs, although there has been much less progress in protecting the marine environment through the designation of protected areas.[147] Often, however, aquatic conservation areas are under greatest pressure from potentially harmful activities. Nowhere is this more evident than estuaries, where conservation and commercial interests often compete, and where the cumulative impact of discharges to watercourses is felt most strongly. The Humber Estuary, for example, a site of high national and international conservation importance, is affected by activities authorised by around 10,000 environmental licences.[148]

As regards habitat conservation, the general approach taken in conservation legislation has been to designate a number of representative sites for their habitat or species conservation interest. With the exception of a relatively small number of reserves actively managed by the statutory nature conservation agencies or managed by bodies sympathetic to conservation objectives, the principal national conservation designation is the SSSI. For SSSIs, nature conservation objectives have traditionally been pursued on a voluntary basis. The freedom of the landowner or occupier to determine which environmentally-damaging activities may take place is restricted only by town and country planning law[149] or by any requirements to obtain, and act in accordance with, other forms of environmental licenses such as discharge consents under the Water Resources Act 1991.[150]

The legal safeguarding of habitat is a two-stage process, an important distinction being between the legal power, or duty, to designate a site for conservation purposes, and the degree of legal protection subsequently given to designated sites. This distinction is seen in both national and Community law. In general, the law relating to site designation is couched in more mandatory terms, while the legal provisions relating to the protection and management of sites tend to allow greater scope for economic and social considerations. At least in national law, site designation may, at a minimum, offer little more than an indication, for other decision-makers, such as local planning authorities, of the conservation interest of a site. EC law, however, provides for rather more stringent conservation protections, and also requires that a range of environmental and land-use licences may need to be brought into line with the conservation objectives of the relevant Directives. It must be borne in mind, however, that a comprehensive legal approach to nature

---

[144] English Nature (1997) p.5.
[145] On SSSIs see 15.7.1 below.
[146] Gubbay (1989).
[147] See 15.7.2 and 15.7.4 below.
[148] *ENDS Report 309* (2000) p.3.
[149] On town and country planning law see Ch.14 above.
[150] On which see Ch.10 above, and see also Ch.12 above.

conservation requires more than provisions relating to habitat protection of the kind described below. Without the contribution of other legal controls, such as provisions relating to water contamination or development control, the measures described below would probably be useless, and increasingly the concern of the nature conservation agencies in relation to aquatic conservation is to exert influence in relation to such matters as discharge consents, the funding of water company improvement programmes and controls on the diffuse pollution of water.[151] In response to the Biodiversity Convention,[152] the integration of some of the controls is now being brought about through biodiversity action plans, involving a mix of regulatory techniques and public and private sector involvement. Provision is also made regulating the introduction of non-native species.[153]

## 15.6.2 Administrative Responsibilities

Matters relating to nature conservation are primarily the responsibility of English Nature (formerly the Nature Conservancy Council for England), and the Countryside Council for Wales ('CCW'), the latter body also exercising countryside functions. These bodies exercise a range of general functions under Acts of nature conservation importance, as well as having specific functions of establishing, maintaining and managing nature reserves[154] in their area; advising the Secretary of State or any other Minister on policy development and implementation as regards nature conservation; other general provisions about providing advice and disseminating knowledge; and commissioning or supporting relevant research.[155] There is also a Joint Nature Conservation Committee through which certain 'special functions' of the national agencies (including Scottish Natural Heritage) are co-ordinated and discharged to ensure that international obligations are implemented in a consistent and co-ordinated manner in different parts of Great Britain.[156]

Neither English Nature nor the CCW are themselves subject to conservation duties, nor (unlike the Environment Agency) are they charged with a legal duty to contribute towards attaining sustainable development objectives.[157] Under the Countryside Act 1968, however, in the exercise of their functions under that Act, the National Parks and Access to the Countryside Act 1949 and the Wildlife and Countryside Act 1981, both bodies, the Countryside Agency and every Minister[158] and local authority must, in the exercise of their functions, have due regard to the needs of agriculture and forestry and to the economic and social interests

---

[151] See, respectively, Chs.10, 7 and 13 above.

[152] See 15.9.1 below on the Convention and its national implementation.

[153] Discussed at 15.7.6 below.

[154] Within the meaning of s.15 National Parks and Access to the Countryside Act 1949, see 15.7.3 below.

[155] s.132(1) Environmental Protection Act 1990.

[156] *Ibid* ss.128(4) and 133. The Committee does not have a UK-wide remit, although Northern Irish interests are represented.

[157] Unlike Scottish Natural Heritage, see s.1(1) Natural Heritage (Scotland) Act 1991.

[158] In Wales, the National Assembly.

of rural areas.[159] In some respects this is balanced by a duty on every Minister,[160] government department and public body, in the exercise of their functions relating to land[161] under any enactment, to have regard to the desirability of conserving the natural beauty and amenity of the countryside, although the latter duty relates to countryside rather than nature conservation interests.[162] In the exercise of their functions under the 1949 and 1968 Acts the Countryside Agency, English Nature, the CCW, the Forestry Commission and local authorities must have due regard to the protection against pollution of any water, whether on the surface or underground, which belongs to the Environment Agency or a water undertaker or which any of these bodies or a water undertaker is for the time being authorised to take.[163]

### 15.6.3 General Conservation Duties

Despite the existence of specialist nature conservation agencies, increasingly other regulatory bodies must exercise their functions having regard to nature conservation objectives. Thus Ministers and the Secretary of State (or, as appropriate, the National Assembly for Wales) and the Environment Agency are subject to general environmental and conservation duties in the exercise of their functions.[164] It is notable, however, that for any proposals relating to the pollution control functions of the Agency the duty is formulated so as to impose a duty only 'to have regard to the desirability of' conserving and enhancing natural beauty and of conserving flora, fauna and geological or physiographical features of special interest,[165] whereas in relation to the other functions of the Agency the duty is formulated as one which requires the furthering of these interests.[166] The Director General of Water Services and every water and sewerage undertaker are also subject to general environmental and conservation duties in the exercise of their powers and duties.[167] In addition, both the Agency and the undertakers are also subject to specific conservation duties in relation to sites of special nature conservation interest,[168] while the Agency is also subject to specific duties in relation to water which includes the promotion, to the extent it considers desirable, of the conservation of flora and fauna which are dependent on an aquatic environment.[169] Sea fisheries committees are also subject to specific

---

[159] s.37 Countryside Act 1968.
[160] In Wales, the National Assembly.
[161] Including land covered by water; see s.49(1) Countryside Act 1968 and s.114(1) National Parks and Access to the Countryside Act 1949.
[162] s.11 Countryside Act 1968.
[163] *Ibid* s.38, as amended.
[164] s.7 Environment Act 1995, see 6.10–11 above.
[165] *Ibid* s.7(1)(b).
[166] *Ibid* s.7(1)(a).
[167] s.3 Water Industry Act 1991, see 7.6.4–5 above.
[168] s.8 Environment Act 1995 and s.4 Water Industry Act 1991 respectively.
[169] s.6(1) Environment Act 1995, see 6.9 above.

environmental duties.[170] These duties are all discussed in more detail elsewhere.

## 15.7 National Conservation Law

As far as law is concerned, nature conservation at the national level continues to revolve around the designation of key sites for some form of safeguarding, and the protection of individual species. Recently, there have been moves both to strengthen the protection given to these sites, to impose more general conservation duties on all public bodies, and to encourage greater public-private and multi-actor approaches to conservation.

### 15.7.1 Sites of Special Scientific Interest

The principal national habitat conservation mechanism is the designation of areas of land or inland waters as 'sites of special scientific interest'.[171] Specifically, English Nature or the CCW must, where it is of the opinion that any area of land is of special interest by reason of any of its flora, fauna or geological or physiographical features, notify that fact to the local planning authority, every owner and occupier and the Secretary of State.[172] 'Land' in this context includes land covered by water[173] and lakes, wetlands and, most recently, a series of river-SSSIs have been notified.[174] The conservation agencies take the view that the duty to notify SSSIs does not extend below the mean low water mark other than in estuaries.[175] One third of all biological SSSIs are freshwater sites.[176]

Notifications take immediate effect, but may be confirmed or withdrawn within nine months.[177] Once notified, it is an offence for any owner or occupier[178] to carry out, or cause or permit to be carried out, any operation specified in the notification as being likely to damage the special interest. Such operations, referred to as 'operations likely to damage', may include actions affecting, directly or indirectly, water quality,[179] such as the application of herbicides. However, the operation will be lawful if carried out with the conservation agency's written consent, or under the terms of a management agreement, or if done after four months of notifying the conservation agency. Exceptions to this apply where there is a reasonable excuse for the operation, which applies where planning permission has

---

[170] See 15.2.3 above.
[171] Under s.28 Wildlife and Countryside Act 1981. On the law relating to SSSIs generally see Bell and McGillivray (2000) ch.21.
[172] See also duties under guidance to notify water and sewerage undertakers, discussed below.
[173] s.52(4) Wildlife and Countryside Act 1981.
[174] See generally English Nature (1997).
[175] Because of the jurisdiction of local planning authorities, see 8.3.1 above.
[176] English Nature (1997) p.5, i.e. excluding the 1,200 or so geological SSSIs.
[177] On the nature of this discretion see *R v Nature Conservancy Council ex parte London Brick Properties Ltd* [1996] Env LR 1.
[178] See *Southern Water Authority v Nature Conservancy Council* [1992] 3 All ER 481.
[179] See generally *Sweet v Secretary of State for the Environment* [1989] JPL 927.

been granted, or in emergency situations. Otherwise, an offence will be committed, for which the maximum penalty on summary conviction is a fine of level 4 on the standard scale, presently £2,500.

As may be seen, however, there is little reliance on criminal sanctions and designation as an SSSI provides only the framework for a voluntary approach to habitat conservation. Under this approach, the onus is on the conservation agency, within four months or a longer period if agreed, to enter into a management agreement under which the conservation interest of the site is protected. This may involve the payment of compensation to the landowner or occupier for net profits foregone,[180] although in practice some form of positive environmental enhancement will be sought and there has been a decisive trend towards more positively-framed management agreements. In England, this has been through the Wildlife Enhancement Scheme while in Wales, the schemes used have been Tir Cymen and now Tir Gofal, the latter including environmentally sensitive area payments made for whole farm units and not restricted to SSSI boundaries.

In addition to the ability for owners or occupiers to 'bide their time' before carrying out an operation likely to damage water quality, a number of other shortcomings may be noted, including non-application to third parties, geographic limitation to land above the low-water mark, and ecological limitations. For example, while SSSI notification may include land in the same environmental unit,[181] it may not be an offence to damage an SSSI by pollution of upstream waters, unless those waters are notified, the owner or occupier of the upstream area causes pollution to that SSSI, and none of the exemptions apply. Similarly, the SSSI regime is unable, directly, to protect an aquatic environment if water is being abstracted upstream of an SSSI, on land which is not itself of scientific interest, and this in turn leads to a harmful concentration of pollutants in downstream waters. A further limitation of the SSSI regime as presently provided for is that the 'operations' likely to damage SSSIs which it is an offence to carry out in the four month waiting period are not considered to include mere inactivity or neglect.[182] Thus, the introduction of carp into a lake which has been notified as an SSSI because of the presence of species dependent upon its water quality might temporarily be restricted under s.28 of the Wildlife and Countryside Act 1981, on the basis that the behaviour of the carp might disturb the sediment and alter the water quality.[183] However, the provisions of the Act may be powerless to prevent such damage being caused by increased numbers of existing stocks or by the progeny of introduced fish, since arguably no 'operation' has taken place.

---

[180] Calculated according to the Appendix to Department of the Environment Circular 4/83. Management agreements for SSSIs may extend to adjacent land, see s.132(1)(a) and para.4(2)(a) Sch.9 Environmental Protection Act 1990.

[181] *Sweet* v *Secretary of State for the Environment* [1989] JPL 927.

[182] *Ibid*, although the meaning of 'operations' was not considered in any length by Schiemann J.

[183] On the regulation of introductions of fish to waters see 15.5 above.

In spite of this statutory legal framework, there are, in addition, specific duties for English Nature and the CCW to notify the Environment Agency and water and sewerage undertakers of SSSIs, and notifications by the former Nature Conservancy Council to water authorities, statutory water companies and internal drainage boards continue to have effect.[184] More generally, under the Wildlife and Countryside Act 1981 a Code of Guidance on SSSIs requires the nature conservation agency to inform all utility companies of the details of SSSIs within their areas of operation and asks that the agencies be consulted before potentially damaging activities are performed, which provides a measure of safeguarding for SSSIs which are neither owned nor occupied by utilities.[185] Of greater practical relevance, however, is guidance issued by central government to the Environment Agency and to the water and sewerage undertakers on conservation which, combined with the conservation duties placed on the Agency and the undertakers, provide a consultation mechanism where potentially damaging activities may be contemplated off-site.[186] Around one-third of all SSSIs are, wholly or partly, owned or occupied by utilities.

Slightly greater protection is afforded by the power of the Secretary of State to make a nature conservation order.[187] Although superficially similar to an SSSI notification, higher penalties are provided for, and third parties may be liable. Also, if an order is designated then the conservation agency can, if a management agreement has been offered, delay any operations likely to damage the site for a period of up to 15 months. The conservation agency is also given certain powers to enter land to see if an order should be made, or if an offence has been committed,[188] and a convicting court may order the offender to carry out specified works to restore the land to its former condition. In the case of water quality damage, however, there is often little that can be done but remove gross pollutants and allow time for the ecological state of the water, if possible, to improve naturally. There are detailed procedural provisions relating to the designation of orders.

In relation to habitats, sites may be designated under nature conservation orders if, in the opinion of the Secretary of State, the land in question is of 'national importance'.[189] No statutory meaning is given to the use of this phrase in this context, and there is no formal policy guidance on its meaning. On the basis of legal advice, practice has formerly been to construe it as requiring something going beyond the importance which a site must have in order to be notified as an SSSI. However, it is clear that

---

[184] By virtue of para.1 Sch.2 Water Consolidation (Consequential Provisions) Act 1991. The duty to notify river authorities dates from s.102 Water Resources Act 1963.

[185] The Code is made under s.33 Wildlife and Countryside Act 1981. See generally Last (1997). For problems when such consultation does not occur see *Southern Water Authority* v *Nature Conservancy Council* [1992] 3 All ER 481, discussed above.

[186] See DETR and MAFF, *Code of Practice of Conservation, Access and Recreation: Guidance for the Environment Agency and Water and Sewerage Undertakers* (2000) and see 6.12 and 7.6.5 above.

[187] Under s.29 Wildlife and Countryside Act 1981.

[188] Both powers being notably absent in relation to SSSIs.

[189] s.29(2)(b) Wildlife and Countryside Act 1981.

in the absence of any formal constraints, the Secretary of State is able to exercise a fairly wide degree of discretion as to what is of 'national importance' in this context. A manifestation of this is that nature conservation orders have been very sparingly used,[190] though there are some recent signs of an increase in designations which would be consistent with the desire of the current Government to move away from a less voluntaristic approach to habitat conservation.[191]

### 15.7.2 Marine Nature Reserves

There is provision in the Wildlife and Countryside Act 1981 for the designation of marine nature reserves (MNRs).[192] MNRs may be designated by the Secretary of State, on application of a nature conservation agency, in order to conserve marine flora or fauna or geological or physiographical features of special interest, or for scientific purposes. Only land covered (continuously or intermittently) by tidal waters or parts of the sea which are landward of baselines, or are seaward of baselines up to a distance of three nautical miles, may be designated. The principal regulatory mechanism provided is the making of byelaws by the conservation agency, with the consent of the Secretary of State or National Assembly for Wales. These may include byelaws prohibiting or restricting, either absolutely or subject to exceptions, the deposit of rubbish in the reserve, or doing anything to interfere with the seabed or damage or disturb any object in the reserve. However, nothing in such byelaws shall make unlawful the discharge of any substance from a vessel.[193]

More generally, byelaws may not interfere with the exercise of any functions of a relevant authority,[194] any functions conferred by or under an enactment (whenever passed) or any right of any person (whenever vested). Breach of a byelaw may only be prosecuted by the conservation agency or by, or with the consent of, the Director of Public Prosecutions. The maximum penalty is a fine of £1000 on summary conviction.[195] Only 2 MNRs have so far been designated, around the islands of Lundy and Skomer. The principal reasons advanced are a traditional lack of attention paid in many quarters to marine conservation,[196] and the lengthy procedural requirements involved[197] which, when taken together with Government guidance, effectively seek consensus of all interested parties

---

[190] 19 orders were in force on 31 March 1999. See English Nature (1999), p.38.

[191] English Nature, personal communication. See also 15.7.4 below on reforms.

[192] s.36 Wildlife and Countryside Act 1981.

[193] Regulated under the Food and Environment Protection Act 1985, and oil pollution legislation. See Ch.19 below.

[194] 'Relevant authority' includes the Agency, any water or sewerage undertaker and any sea fisheries committee.

[195] On this and other procedural matters see the Wildlife and Countryside (Byelaws for Marine Nature Reserves) Regulations 1986 (SI 1986 No.143).

[196] See, e.g., Cole-King (1993), pp.171-185.

[197] See Sch.12 Wildlife and Countryside Act 1981.

before an order is made.[198] As the impact of the *Sea Empress* oil spill demonstrated,[199] however, the designation of an MNR is unlikely to prevent serious pollution damage, though such designations ought to highlight the conservation importance of certain marine areas for the purpose of other regulatory controls, such as regulating shipping.

### 15.7.3 Other National Conservation Designations

In addition to SSSIs and MNRs, a range of other conservation designations may impact on water quality in certain circumstances. These include nature reserves designated under the National Parks and Access to the Countryside Act 1949 as areas managed for study or research into flora, fauna or geological or physiographical interest, or for preserving such features which are of special interest.[200] Designation of land[201] as a nature reserve involves a mere declaration, though the conservation agency must have control of the site in order to do so. Control may be achieved either by buying the land, leasing it, or entering into an agreement with the landowner. In practice, because of the high costs of management involved, the sites which are designated as nature reserves tend to be areas of land which, opportunistically, can be acquired for management, rather than necessarily areas of the highest conservation importance. Since 1981, the conservation agencies have been able to declare as 'national nature reserves' land which is of national importance and which is being managed by an 'approved body'. In practical terms this would include sympathetic landowners such as voluntary conservation bodies, thus extending the controls which apply to nature reserves to these further sites.[202] In practice, both kinds of sites are simply referred to as national nature reserves.

In relation to national nature reserves, a conservation agency may make byelaws which may include byelaws prohibiting the depositing of rubbish and the leaving of litter, and prohibiting or restricting the disturbance of living creatures.[203] Other byelaws, made under general powers granted to the conservation agencies,[204] may add to these classes so as to, for example, prohibit any act in the nature reserve that pollutes or is likely to cause any pollution of water.[205] Amongst a range of limitations, however, byelaws may not restrict the rights of statutory undertakers. Conservation agencies may enforce their byelaws[206] but any breach is subject only to a

---

[198] Hansard HL Debs Vol. 424, Col. 524, 15 October 1981 per Lord Avon. See generally Warren (1996).

[199] On the *Sea Empress* incident see 9.19.3 above and 19.15.2 below.

[200] s.15 National Parks and Access to the Countryside Act 1949.

[201] Which include land covered by water; s.114(1) *ibid*.

[202] s.35 Wildlife and Countryside Act 1981.

[203] s.20 National Parks and Access to the Countryside Act 1949.

[204] By *ibid* s.20(1).

[205] Model bye-law 1(xii), cited in Barker (1999) p.19. See also Bates (1990, updated) para 15.44.

[206] s.106(3) National Parks and Access to the Countryside Act 1949, and see para.1(5) Sch.9 Environmental Protection Act 1990.

maximum fine of level 2 on the standard scale, presently £500.[207] Finally, it is worth noting that there is provision for land to be acquired for a nature reserve by compulsory purchase where this is deemed to be in the national interest and a management agreement cannot be concluded.[208] This power might be used to safeguard endangered sites of special interest, although its use for this purpose has been very limited and only one compulsory purchase order has been made.

Local authorities are given the same powers to designate and manage Local Nature Reserves (LNRs) as the conservation agencies have in relation to national nature reserves. An LNR must be of local, as opposed to national, importance and the local authority must consult with the conservation agency before designation.[209] However, the view of the conservation agencies is now that the value which local communities place on wildlife and natural features is an important and legitimate factor in commenting on proposed designations.[210] At least in England, the number of LNRs has doubled since the early 1990s as a policy of using them to promote conservation education in urban areas has been pioneered.[211] It is possible for other bodies to own and manage LNRs through management agreements with local authorities; examples of this include LNRs designated at reservoirs owned by statutory water companies.

Other relevant area-based conservation approaches at national level also go some way towards integrating environmental and other policy concerns, mostly by the use of voluntary controls and financial incentives rather than regulatory restrictions. Thus environmentally sensitive areas (ESAs)[212] and a range of measures introduced under the umbrella of the 1992 'Agri-Environment' Regulation[213] marked a useful, if extremely modest, step towards the integration of agricultural and conservation objectives that may deliver benefits for waters subject to pollution from agricultural run-off. Also in this context should be mentioned Nitrate Vulnerable Zones, designated under the EC Agricultural Nitrates Directive, and Nitrate Sensitive Areas, both of which target nitrate reduction programmes in locations which may be sensitive because of their conservation importance.[214] In a recent report, however, the Public Accounts Committee

---

[207] ss.236 and 237 Local Government Act 1972, as last amended by ss.37 and 46 Criminal Justice Act 1982.

[208] ss.17 and 18 National Parks and Access to the Countryside Act 1949.

[209] s.21 National Parks and Access to the Countryside Act 1949.

[210] English Nature (1991); Countryside Council for Wales (1996).

[211] As at March 1999 there were 718 LNRs in Great Britain, covering 43,186 hectares.

[212] Authorised under Regulation 797/85/EEC on Improving the Efficiency of Agricultural Structures, Art.19, and designated under s.18 Agriculture Act 1986.

[213] Regulation 2078/92/EEC. See especially the Habitat (Water Fringe) Regulations 1994 (SI 1994 No.1291), the Habitat (Salt Marsh) Regulations 1994 (SI 1994 No.1293), the Habitat (Water Fringe) (Wales) Regulations 1994 (SI 1994 No.3100) and the Habitat (Coastal Belt) (Wales) Regulations 1994 (SI 1994 No.3101), all as amended. No applications to these schemes could be made after 31 December 1999, when the schemes were subsumed (in England) within the Countryside Stewardship Scheme, and (in Wales) within Tir Gofal. See the Countryside Stewardship Regulations 2000 (SI 2000 No.3048) and the Land in Care (Tir Gofal) (Wales) Regulations 1999 (SI 1999 No.1176).

[214] On designations to limit the input of nitrates see 13.5 above.

was highly critical of the operation of the ESA scheme, describing the Agriculture Ministry's planning and management of the scheme as 'unimpressive', and citing amongst other things high administrative costs and a lack of research about the operation of the scheme. In particular the Committee noted the poor take-up of the scheme, singling out river valleys, coastal and wetland areas (there are ten wetland ESAs[215]) in this context. Criticism was also made of the lack of rigour with which non-compliance with the scheme has been prosecuted.[216]

### 15.7.4  Proposals for Reform

At the time of writing quite radical reforms of the law relating to SSSIs are in prospect.[217] Following consultation,[218] the Government has introduced legislation intended to empower the conservation agencies to refuse consent for operations likely to damage an SSSI, backed by a right of appeal[219] or dispute resolution mechanism in cases of conflict. Under the Countryside and Rights of Way Bill, if enacted, those holding licences or rights over land would be treated in the same way as owners and occupiers, and similar provisions will apply to the activities of statutory undertakers. In addition, the conservation agencies will be empowered to secure the positive management of sites in the case of neglect by making a 'management scheme' where it is necessary to do so. Management schemes would only be made where the landowner had been offered, and refused, a positive management agreement and there would be a right of appeal to the Minister against such schemes. Management schemes would be enforced by the serving of 'management notices' in cases of non-compliance. If a management notice is not complied with, the conservation agencies would have the power to enter the site and carry out the works itself, including restoration works, charging any reasonable costs to the owner or occupier. These reform proposals clearly strike at the heart of the voluntary principle in national nature conservation law described above.[220]

Other important proposals contained in the Bill are:

(a) that the conservation agencies could enter into management agreements not merely in relation to SSSIs and adjacent sites, but *any* other sites (thus strengthening controls where ecological impacts are being caused by activities well away from the SSSI, e.g. upstream pollution);

(b) placing a statutory duty on public bodies to secure the positive management of sites that they own or occupy in accordance with

---

[215] See English Nature (1997), p.49.

[216] House of Commons Public Accounts Committee, *Protecting Environmentally Sensitive Areas* (1998).

[217] Postcript: see now the Countryside and Rights of Way Act 2000, the provisions of which relating to nature conservation largely came into force on 31 January 2001. The following commentary should be read alongside the provisions now in force.

[218] DETR, *Sites of Special Scientific Interest: Better Protection and Management* (1998).

[219] In England, to the Secretary of State; in Wales, to the National Assembly.

[220] See further Bell and McGillivray (2000) p.641.

an agreed site management plan (a more general duty of care on all persons is rejected);

(c) that all SSSIs be declared in legislation to be of national importance, thus removing the distinction between section 28 and section 29 of the Wildlife and Countryside Act 1981 (a distinction would remain between controls relating to the actions of owners and occupiers, and of third parties). This could mean that some sites, under explicit new powers, may be denotified because they are of less than national importance;

(d) powers to enter SSSIs;

(e) unlimited fines for deliberate damage;

(f) a duty on statutory undertakers to give notice to the conservation agencies of all proposed operations (except emergency works) within or likely to affect SSSIs, and a power for agencies to refuse consent; and

(g) enforceable means to require restoration of the conservation interest (currently provided for only under section 29) where this is practicable.

Outside of revisions to primary legislation, further changes are envisaged. These would include that all payments under management agreements would only be made to secure appropriate management of the site, to ensure preservation of its nature conservation value. Also likely are revisions to town and country planning guidance on nature conservation, although whether this introduces a general presumption against development which would damage the special interest on SSSIs remains to be seen.

Despite these promising proposals, neither the 1998 Consultation Paper nor the Countryside and Rights of Way Bill contain any specific proposals for protection of the marine environment. It seems evident that the mere extension of SSSI designation below the low water mark generally would be neither a practicable nor an effective step to take,[221] but the absence of positive proposals appears to reflect a government view that marine conservation will be delivered through implementation of EC conservation law.[222] It must be doubted whether this will in fact be borne out.

In relation to the freshwater environment, however, it might be noted that there are on-going Government proposals significantly to reform the water abstraction licensing system contained in Part II of the Water Resources Act 1991 which might impact favourably on water quality on SSSIs.[223] Furthermore, such developments must be seen together with environmental and quality improvement programmes contained in the latest round of water company business plans (AMP3), under which a significant number

---

[221] Scott (1999).

[222] See 15.8 below.

[223] DETR, *Taking Water Responsibly* (1999) and see also DETR, *Economic Instruments in Relation to Water Abstraction: A Consultation Paper* (2000). See now proposals in the draft Water Bill, published November 2000.

of SSSIs have been given a measure of protection from over-abstraction and damage to water quality.[224]

### 15.7.5 Biodiversity Action Plans

Under the Convention on Biological Diversity,[225] the UK Biodiversity Action Plan 1994 was produced, an important document guiding subsequent policy in this area. This in turn has led to the development of action plans for 391 species of plants and animals and 45 habitats. The scheme is intended to increase public awareness and involvement, but also to develop costed targets for key species. Each plan contains conservation targets and recommended actions, such as changes to legislation, site safeguard or management and research requirements intended to deliver these targets. A lead organisation is responsible for each plan; for habitat action plans this is a statutory conservation agency, although for species plans either a statutory agency or voluntary conservation organisation may act as the 'lead partner'. For example, the Environment Agency has lead responsibility under the UK Biodiversity Action Plan for 39 species (for example, depressed river mussels) and 5 habitats (e.g. eutrophic standing waters). This is not always because of the importance of water quality for the species and habitats concerned, though in the majority of cases water quality, and especially eutrophication, are singled out as one of the main threats.[226]

A key tool used in this partnership approach is to seek 'champions' for species, especially from the voluntary and private sectors, as well as government funding. For example, Water UK, the body representing the water industry, has invested £1m in otter conservation over three years, the largest such funding arrangement. Together with the reforms to the law relating to sites of special scientific interest outlined above, the biodiversity action plans are perhaps the most important development in conservation policy and practice since the 1981 Act.

### 15.7.6 Introducing Non-Native Species

As with fisheries legislation,[227] there are provisions in national nature conservation law which seek to restrict the introduction of non-native species into the domestic environment. These aim to protect against the kind of adverse ecological impact wrought by alien introductions such as the giant hogweed. Specific examples relating to the aquatic environment are the spread of floating pennywort (such as on the Pevensey Levels SSSI in Sussex) and, in a different water context, the alarming, widespread, decline in water voles which has been linked to the increase in numbers of

---

[224] On water company financing see 7.8 above.

[225] See 15.9.1 below.

[226] Environment Agency, *Focus on Biodiversity* (2000) Ch.3. On eutrophication see 1.3.1–2 above.

[227] See 15.5 above on the regulation of introducing fish into waters.

the American mink.[228] Hence, it is an offence to introduce into the wild any animal not normally resident in Great Britain or any scheduled wild animal or plant.[229]

There may, however, be circumstances where species introductions have water pollution implications. As described elsewhere, for example,[230] discharges into water may lead to serious adverse consequences to the aquatic environment, and it is possible that the offence of introducing non-native species might be used to regulate the discharge or entry into water of unwanted introductions. On this view, although neither the chemical or physical composition of the water is affected, the non-native species may be considered a 'biological contaminant',[231] and it is worth noting that the offence of introducing non-native species is formulated so that neither actual harm nor the risk of harm is required. Unlike the corresponding fisheries provisions, the offence and scheduling provisions in the Wildlife and Countryside Act 1981 extend to the introduction of non-native plant species, the entry of which might have adverse impacts on water quality. However, it is probable that the principal water pollution offences are sufficiently broad to cover such occurrences, and there are no significant procedural reasons why the Wildlife and Countryside Act 1981 would be relied on in practice. Acting in accordance with a discharge consent or other environmental licence is no defence to a charge brought under the 1981 Act. But compliance may go some way towards showing that the accused took all reasonable steps and exercised all due diligence, which will serve as a defence.

### 15.8 EC Conservation Law: Background and General Considerations

Arguably the most important provisions relating to nature conservation law stem from the European Community Wild Birds Directive[232] and the EC Habitats Directive.[233] Both Directives are influenced by the Convention on the Conservation of European Wildlife and Natural Habitats (the Berne Convention)[234] and the Convention on the Conservation of Migratory Species of Wild Animals (the Bonn Convention),[235] both from 1979, while the Habitats Directive also bears some influences from the 1992 Convention on Biological Diversity. Together the Directives contain a range of programmatic and area-based provisions concerning both habitat conservation and individual (or 'direct') species protection, although only the former is discussed here.

---

[228] Primarily as a result of escapes or releases from fur farms.

[229] s.14 and Sch.9 Wildlife and Countryside Act 1981.

[230] See 19.10.6B below on ballast water discharges.

[231] Perry and Vanderklein (1996) ch.24, and 1.2 above.

[232] Directive 79/409/EEC, as amended by Directives 81/854, 85/411, 86/122, 91/244 & 94/24.

[233] Directive 92/43/EEC, as amended by Directive 97/62/EC.

[234] Bern, 19 September 1979, in force 1 June 1982. See http://conventions.coe.int/treaty/EN/cadreprincipal.htm and see Decision 82/72/EEC.

[235] Bonn, 23 June 1979, in force 1 November 1983. See www.wcmc.org.uk/cms and see Decision 82/461/EEC.

The Wild Birds Directive establishes a general system of protection for all species of birds, particularly migratory species, naturally occurring in the wild state within the European territories of Member States, together with their habitats.[236] Given the extent to which conserving the habitat of bird species may require the conservation of aquatic habitats, the Wild Birds Directive may have considerable beneficial consequences for the conservation of the aquatic environment, including water quality. The area where land meets water is amongst the most biodiverse of habitats, although coastal areas tend to face the greatest pressures from development. Because of this conflict, it may not be surprising that the conservation of coastal habitats has featured strongly amongst the case law of the European Court of Justice in relation to both the Wild Birds and Habitats Directives.

The Wild Birds Directive addresses protection, management and control mechanisms, establishing terms upon which damage to the conservation of certain wild birds may be sanctioned.[237] The central protection obligation is that Member States must take requisite measures to maintain the population of all wild bird species at a level which corresponds in particular to ecological, scientific and cultural requirements, while taking into account economic and recreational requirements, or to adapt the population of these species to that level.[238] A higher level of protection is given to certain listed species bird species and all regularly occurring migratory species.[239] Equal regard must be had to the need to protect both land and sea areas. Stricter protective measures are permitted.[240]

The aim of the Habitats Directive is 'to contribute towards ensuring biodiversity through the conservation of natural habitats and of wild fauna and flora in the European territory of the Member States to which the Treaty applies'. In R v Secretary of State for Trade and Industry ex parte Greenpeace Ltd (No. 2),[241] Greenpeace challenged a decision of the Secretary of State in relation to oil exploration licensing in an area of the North-East Atlantic known as the Atlantic Frontier. By looking at the purpose of the Directive, and at a range of other legal provisions directed towards similar ends,[242] it was held that the Directive applied to areas over which the Member States exercised sovereign rights, namely to the continental shelf and to superjacent waters up to 200 nautical miles. This was despite the fact that the implementing Regulations in the UK[243] only applied to the limit of the territorial sea, that is, twelve nautical miles. Accordingly, the provisions of the Directive that applied to the

---

[236] Art.1(1) and (2). On the scope of the directive see Case 247/85 Commission v Belgium [1987] ECR 3029, Case C-149/94 Criminal Proceedings against Vergy [1996] ECR I-299 and Case C-202/94 Criminal Proceedings against van der Feesten [1996] ECR I-355.

[237] Arts.1, 6, 7 Wild Birds Directive.

[238] Ibid Art.2.

[239] Ibid Art.4(2).

[240] Ibid Art.14.

[241] [2000] Env LR 221.

[242] Including the UN Law of the Sea Convention (see 18.7 below) and the Environmental Impact Assessment Directive (14.6 below). See further McGillivray (2000).

[243] The Conservation (Natural Habitats etc.) Regulations 1994, see 15.8.3 below.

conservation of cold-water coral reefs was not limited to territorial waters, and should have been considered by the Secretary of State before he announced the oil licensing round at issue.

The principal objective of the Habitats Directive is pursued both through the conservation of natural habitats and the habitats of species[244] and the direct protection of species.[245] By contrast with the Wild Birds Directive, however, more concessions are made to the autonomy of Member States and to economic considerations. The Habitats Directive thus provides that 'measures taken pursuant to this Directive shall take account of economic, social and cultural requirements and regional and local characteristics'.[246] In certain respects, these considerations are also now applied to the Wild Birds Directive, although not, as discussed below, to site designation. There is a general obligation to undertake surveillance of the conservation status of *all* natural habitats and wild fauna and flora in Community territory, having particular regard to certain priority habitat types and species.[247]

To a greater extent than with sites protected under national law, the simplest appreciation of the law in this area is to distinguish clearly between the law relating to the designation of sites, and the laws governing the level of protection of such sites. Usually, the latter are weaker than the former.

### 15.8.1 Habitat Designation

As regards habitat conservation under the Wild Birds Directive, Member States are under a general obligation to 'preserve, maintain or re-establish a sufficient diversity and area of habitats'.[248] Taking into account 'economic and recreational requirements', however, does not permit a reduced standard of protection to be afforded and does not constitute an 'autonomous derogation' in relation to the designation of protected areas,[249] although these factors may come into play in relation to site protection.[250] This obligation exists before any reduction in population is observed or any risk materialises.[251]

Species listed in Annex I to the Directive are subject to 'special conservation measures concerning their habitat in order to ensure their

---

[244] Arts.3-11 and Annexes I and II Habitats Directive.

[245] *Ibid* Arts.12-16 and Annex IV. As with the Wildlife and Countryside Act 1981, direct protection measures are unlikely to be significant in relation to water quality and are not discussed further.

[246] Art.2(3) Habitats Directive.

[247] *Ibid* Art.11.

[248] Art.3(1) Wild Birds Directive.

[249] Case 247/85 *Commission* v *Belgium* [1987] ECR 3029, para 8; Case 262/85 *Commission* v *Italy* [1987] ECR 3073, para 8.

[250] Case C-44/95 *R* v *Secretary of State for the Environment ex parte RSPB* [1996] ECR I-3805 ('Lappel Bank').

[251] Case C-355/90 *Commission* v *Spain* [1993] ECR I-4221 ('Marismas de Santoña'), para 15.

survival and reproduction in their area of distribution'.[252] Annex I includes endangered bird species, which encompasses aquatic species such as osprey, Bewick's and whooper swans and various species of divers, petrels and herons. Notably, Member States must classify, in particular, the most suitable territories in number and size as special protection areas (SPAs).[253] Similar measures must be taken for regularly occurring migratory species. Regard must be had equally to the need to protect land and sea areas, and to this end Member States must pay particular attention to the protection of wetlands and particularly to wetlands of international importance, a provision motivated by the Ramsar Wetlands Convention, even though the Community has yet to accede to the Convention.[254]

Although Member States have a certain margin of discretion in designating SPAs, decisions must be based upon ornithological criteria determined by the Directive. This was the finding of the Court of Justice in the *Marismas de Santoña* case,[255] where the Commission brought enforcement action against Spain in relation to various activities which were considered to be a threat to an estuarine wetland area at the convergence of five rivers on the Cantabrian coast in northern Spain. The marshes were habitat to a large population of birds, including 20 listed in Annex I to the Directive and over 40 species of regularly occurring migratory species. These factors were sufficient to bring the area within the scope of the requirement to designate an SPA. The activities complained of included the disposal of building waste on wetlands in the area and the storage and disposal of waste water in the marshes by six local municipalities, both of which might have direct water pollution impacts, as well as the building of a road crossing the wetlands which as well as disturbing habitat might have contributed polluting run-off to the area. The Court held that Spain was in breach both of its general obligation under article 3 of the Directive, as well as its more specific obligation to designate the area as an SPA. In particular, economic considerations could not be taken into account, either as overriding the general duty to preserve, maintain or re-establish the habitat or as a factor in relation to the non-designation of the SPA.

Subsequent case law has confirmed that economic considerations are to be excluded from the process of designating SPAs. Thus, in judicial review proceedings brought by the Royal Society for the Protection of Birds,[256] the Society challenged the failure of the UK Government to exclude from the designation of the Medway Estuary and Marshes SPA an area known as 'Lappel Bank'. The area, of around 22 hectares of mudflats, was home to many wader and waterfowl birds – the curlew, redshank and shelduck, dunlin and ringed plover – which used the area as a breeding ground, wintering area and staging post during migrations. The UK Government

---

[252] Art.4(1) Wild Birds Directive.

[253] *Ibid.*

[254] The Parliament has called on the EU to accede to the Ramsar Convention, OJ C20, 20.1.97 p179, para 5. On the Convention see 15.9.2 below.

[255] Case C-355/90 *Commission v Spain* [1993] ECR-I 4221 ('Marismas de Santoña'), para 26

[256] Case C-44/95 *R* v *Secretary of State for the Environment ex parte RSPB* [1996] ECR I-3805 ('Lappel Bank'), paras 24, 25 and 27.

argued that economic considerations were relevant to its decision not to designate the area as an SPA, because, as the Secretary of State for the Environment put it, 'the need not to inhibit the commercial viability of the Port, and the contribution that expansion into this area will play, outweighs its nature conservation value'. However, the Court of Justice affirmed its previous decision in the *Marismas de Santoña* case, holding that Member States could not take into account 'economic requirements', or any of the other general considerations mentioned in the Wild Birds Directive, when designating an SPA and defining its boundaries. Nor could Member States take economic or social considerations into account as interests superior to the general ecological objectives of the Directive, or as overriding public interests.[257]

The Habitats Directive takes a rather different approach to the designation of sites than the Wild Birds Directive. The Habitats Directive creates a new designation of 'special areas of conservation' ('SACs') which contribute to the 'Natura 2000' ecological network. This network consists of the natural habitat types listed in Annex I of the Habitats Directive (such as estuaries, lagoons, salt marshes and certain types of oligotrophic and eutrophic waters) and the habitats of the species listed in Annex II (such as freshwater Atlantic salmon and a significant number of fish, amphibians and molluscs and other aquatic species)[258] together with SPAs under the Wild Birds Directive.[259] As with SPAs, only scientific criteria may be employed.[260] Member States were required to transmit a list of proposed sites to the Commission by May 1995, that is, within three years of notification, an obligation more observed in the breach. The Commission is then required to adopt a list of 'sites of community importance' by May 1998, a deadline which, because of the incompleteness of Member States submissions, has not been observed, with Member States designating these sites as SACs within a further six years. In defined circumstances, the Commission may seek to have added to Natura 2000 sites not appearing on national lists.[261]

The designation of sites under the Habitats Directive is therefore both a more drawn out yet closely circumscribed process than under the Wild Birds Directive, and one that does not rely only on the legitimate exercise of discretion by the Member States in site selection. Although the Habitats Directive makes important changes to the law governing damage to or reduction in area of SPAs, it in no way affects the designation process under the Wild Birds Directive. Unlike the Wild Birds Directive, the Habitats Directive provides that '[m]easures taken pursuant to this

---

[257] As these were provided for in Case C-57/89 *Commission* v *Germany* [1991] ECR I-883 (the 'Leybucht' case), and in Art.6(4) Habitats Directive, both discussed below. The Court of Justice has also held that a Member State is in breach of its obligations if it designates an insufficient number of sites; see Case C-3/96 *Commission* v *Netherlands* [1999] Env LR 147.

[258] Art.3(1) para.1 Habitats Directive.

[259] *Ibid* Art.3(1) para.2.

[260] Although see *R* v *Secretary of State for Scotland and others ex parte WWF-UK Ltd and RSPB* [1999] Env LR 632.

[261] Art.5 Habitats Directive.

Directive shall take account of economic, social and cultural requirements and regional and local characteristics'. The European Court, in a dispute concerning the Severn Estuary, has held that economic and social factors cannot be taken into account when Member States submit their lists of candidate SACs to the Commission.[262] However, the Advocate General's opinion noted that guidance on site selection issued by the Commission in 1996 required Member States to send the Commission information about 'impacts and activities in and around the site', defined as 'all human activities and natural processes that may have an influence, either positive and negative, on the conservation and management of the site'. On this reasoning, the conclusion must be that the Commission can take economic impacts into account when finalising the list of SACs.

### 15.8.2 Habitat Conservation

By contrast to the separate legal provisions relating to the designation of sites, the same provisions concerning the protection of sites from deterioration or disturbance now apply both to the Wild Birds and Habitats Directives.[263] Similar provisions apply to the positive management of habitat, although the provisions of the Habitats Directive restrict the specific legal obligation to undertake positive management measures to SACs and to 'green corridors', ecological features such as rivers which must be managed in particular through land-use planning and development policies.[264] By contrast, the Wild Birds Directive has a more general obligation concerning upkeep and management both within and outside protected zones.[265] The inclusion of provisions on green corridors marks an important stage in the transition away from protected area-based conservation law, and is of considerable importance to the aquatic environment.

The Habitats Directive introduced the same procedure into both the Wild Birds and Habitats Directives under which economic considerations are now relevant in a decision to violate the conservation interest on SPAs and SACs.[266] The common rules are as follows.

(a) Member States must take appropriate steps to avoid deterioration or disturbance of natural habitats and the habitats of species.[267]

(b) Plans or projects not directly concerned with or necessary to the management of a site that are likely to have a significant effect upon a site (alone or in combination) must be subject to an

---

[262] Case C-371/98 *R* v *Secretary of State for the Environment, Transport and the Regions, ex parte First Corporate Shipping Limited* [2001] All ER (EC) 177.

[263] But not to sites which *ought* to have been designated as SPAs, where the more protective measures under the Wild Birds Directive apply, see Case C-374/98 *Commission* v *France*, 7 December 2000.

[264] On planning law see Ch.14 above.

[265] Arts.6(1) and 10 Habitats Directive; Art.3(2) Wild Birds Directive.

[266] The present provisions were adapted in response to the judgment of the Court of Justice in Case C-57/89 *Commission* v *Germany* [1991] ECR I-883 ('*Leybucht*'), on which see 4.11.4 above.

[267] Art.6(2) Habitats Directive.

appropriate assessment. It would seem that this requirement need not involve an environmental impact assessment in accordance with the Environmental Impact Assessment Directive,[268] though of course such assessments may be required for certain development projects likely to have significant effects on Natura 2000 sites. Such plans or projects can only be consented where they will not adversely affect the integrity of the site concerned, and the public may have to be consulted.[269]

(c) Where there is a negative assessment and there are no alternatives, a plan or project is permissible only if there are 'imperative reasons of overriding public interest, including those of a social or economic nature'. In such cases, compensatory measures are required to ensure that the overall coherence of Natura 2000 is secured (and must be notified to the Commission). There is some uncertainty as to what 'compensatory measures' means in this context, but conceivably it might include the creation of new habitat, or additional protection of existing habitat.

(d) For sites hosting priority natural habitat types and/or priority species a plan or project will only be permissible:

  (i)    in the event of considerations of human health or public safety;

  (ii)   where there are beneficial consequences of primary importance for the environment; or

  (iii)  for other imperative reasons of overriding public interest, where this is further to an opinion from the Commission.[270]

The Court of Justice has held that economic requirements do not constitute a general interest superior to that represented by the ecological objective of the Habitats Directive,[271] nor do they constitute imperative reasons of overriding public interest.[272] This would suggest that the Directive affords 'priority sites' increased protection, but in practice the difference may be little more than procedural, insofar as there are some indications that the Commission may consider economic considerations to be 'imperative reasons of overriding public interest'.[273] It is notable that no wild birds species are listed in Annex II of the Habitats Directive as priority species, thus the stricter protection applicable to priority sites does not apply to SPAs.

Finally, as with national conservation designations the comment must be made that designation and the taking of measures required under the Wild Birds and Habitats Directives alone may be insufficient to prevent serious environmental damage. There is no better recent illustration of this than

---

[268] Directive 85/337/EEC, as amended by 97/11/EC, see 14.6 above.

[269] Art.6(3) Habitats Directive.

[270] *Ibid* Art.6(4).

[271] Case C-44/95 *R* v *Secretary of State for the Environment ex parte RSPB* [1996] ECR I-3805 ('Lappel Bank'), para.31.

[272] *Ibid* para.41.

[273] Nollkaemper (1997).

the aftermath of the *Erika* incident off the Brittany coast in December 1999, when 10-15,000 tonnes of heavy fuel oil were released, affecting at least 8 SPAs.

### 15.8.3 The Conservation (Natural Habitats etc.) Regulations 1994

For many years, the more general obligations under the Wild Birds Directive were given effect to through town and country planning law and the law relating to sites of special scientific interest.[274] This approach, however, contained many shortcomings, not least because of the lack of protection for SPAs below the low-water mark and a failure to appreciate the strictness of the obligations not to allow the damaging of such sites.[275] To some extent this has now been remedied by the Conservation (Natural Habitats etc.) Regulations 1994,[276] enacted to implement the Habitats Directive.

The Conservation (Natural Habitats etc.) Regulations 1994 apply to all 'European sites', defined as any site of community importance, SAC, SPA, or site being proposed under Article 5 of the Habitats Directive.[277] As noted above, however, the process of designating SACs is lengthy, and may not be completed until at least 2006. To extend the protection provided by the Habitats Directive to candidate SACs, therefore, the 1994 Regulations have been amended by adding candidate SACs to the category of European sites.[278] This extends the protection provided by the 1994 Regulations to the 340 sites that have so far been forwarded by the UK Government to the Commission as candidate SACs. It also provides a national solution to the problem raised by the inability of the Commission to designate sites of Community importance by 1998 due to the number of Member States, including the UK, which have been late in submitting lists of candidate sites to the Commission. Thus, candidate SACs will be European sites until either they are not placed on the draft list of sites of Community importance or they do not appear on the final list of sites. However, it should be noted that infringement proceedings have been initiated by the Commission against the UK (and most other Member States) for non-implementation of the Directive, in part because of alleged failings in relation to site selection,[279] which has been one factor behind an ongoing review at national level of site selection.

A public register of European sites must be drawn up by the Secretary of State and notified to the national conservation agencies, which then notify local planning authorities, owners and occupiers and anyone else the Secretary of State may direct. European sites must also be registered as a

---

[274] See 15.7.1 above. On planning law see ch.14 above.

[275] Ball (1997).

[276] SI 1994 No.2716.

[277] *Ibid* Reg.10.

[278] The Conservation (Natural Habitats, &c.) (Amendment) (England) Regulations 2000 (SI 2000 No.192). Separate Regulations are likely to be made for Wales.

[279] 'Habitats Directive: Commission takes further steps against Member States', RAPID IP/00/18, 11 January 2000.

land charge. In practice, all terrestrial European sites will already have been notified as SSSIs. The approach taken to protection is to graft on to the existing SSSI and town and country planning system the minimum requirements of the Directive.[280] Thus, the regulations may require that SSSI notifications and lists of 'operations likely to damage' are suitably amended.[281] Consents for operations likely to damage may require appropriate prior assessment. If there is a risk that such an operation may be carried out without consent, the conservation agency must notify the Secretary of State, who has the power to make a Special Nature Conservation Order.[282] Existing consents in relation to SSSIs, if they are not compatible with the conservation objectives for the site, may be modified or revoked. The Regulations make no provision for compensation to be payable, although if the regulation of an European site became, in effect, a compulsory appropriation of the site, it is conceivable that compensation could be required.[283] Byelaws may be made as if the site were a nature reserve.[284] Unlike an SSSI notification or nature conservation order, a Special Nature Conservation Order may prevent damaging activities permanently.[285] However, the restoration provisions in the 1994 Regulations only apply to damage caused under contravention of the Order, and not to damage (or the risk of damage) prompting the making of the Order.

Special provisions apply to European marine sites, defined as European sites where land is covered (continuously or intermittently) by tidal waters or any part of the sea in or adjacent to Great Britain up to the seaward limit of territorial waters.[286] It has now been held, at least in the domestic courts, that this does not correctly transpose the obligations of the Habitats Directive, which extend to the limits of the continental shelf and to superjacent waters to the 200 nautical mile limit.[287] This may have important implications for the identification of candidate SACs.

The strategy which has been taken to implement the Habitats Directive in marine areas has been through imposing general obligations on public bodies to achieve its objectives. Thus, in relation to European marine sites, every public body having functions relevant to marine conservation must exercise its functions to secure compliance with the requirements of the Habitats Directive.[288] In addition, the national conservation agencies must

---

[280] Ball (1997).

[281] Reg.18 Conservation (Natural Habitats etc.) Regulations 1994.

[282] *Ibid* Regs.20 and 22.

[283] Under Article 1, Protocol 1, European Convention on Human Rights, incorporated into English law by the Human Rights Act 1998.

[284] Regs.21 and 28 Conservation (Natural Habitats etc.) Regulations 1994.

[285] Subject to authorisation in accordance with provisions which implement Art.6(4) Habitats Directive, see 15.8.2 above.

[286] Reg.2(1) Conservation (Natural Habitats etc.) Regulations 1994.

[287] *R v Secretary of State for Trade and Industry ex parte Greenpeace Ltd (No. 2)* [2000] Env LR 221. See 15.8 above.

[288] Reg.3(3) Conservation (Natural Habitats etc.) Regulations 1994.

advise other relevant authorities[289] about the conservation objectives for the site and any potentially damaging operations. Any relevant authority may then establish a management scheme for the site and the conservation agency may make byelaws as if the site were a marine nature reserve.[290] The relevant Minister is given wide powers to make directions to the relevant authorities concerning management schemes.[291] Aside from the question of geographic extent, the discretionary nature of many of these obligations makes it questionable whether the Regulations adequately ensure proper implementation of EC obligations,[292] though it should be noted that the provisions of the Regulations relating to the review of consents etc also apply to marine areas.[293]

The Habitats Directive and the implementing 1994 Regulations also make important adaptations to town and country planning law and other controls. While the former are considered elsewhere,[294] the duty to assess plans and projects for their likely effects on a European site, and considerations of overriding interest and compensatory measures, extend to a range of environmental controls. These include integrated pollution control authorisations and pollution prevention and control permits[295] and discharge consents.[296] For example, before granting a discharge consent, or where a consent must be reviewed, the competent authority may make the consent subject to conditions, or vary the existing conditions, so as to protect the integrity of the site.[297] It is submitted, however, that the discretionary power given here should, in accordance with the Directive, be a mandatory one, at least for new consents and licences. The duty also extends to reviewing existing authorisations and consents as soon as reasonably practicable, and the practice of the Environment Agency is to prioritise the identification and consideration of the 48 Natura 2000 sites thought to be most under threat.[298] While the Regulations make specific provision in relation to certain environmental consents, this should not detract from the general obligations on *all* competent authorities to comply with the Directive.[299] For example, the Environment Agency will be subject to this duty as regards abstraction licensing and the impact this

---

[289] Including the Environment Agency, local authorities and water and sewerage undertakers, see *ibid* Reg.5.

[290] On marine nature reserves see 15.7.2 above.

[291] See further DETR and Welsh Office, *European Marine Sites in England and Wales* (1998) and English Nature, Scottish Natural Heritage, Environmental and Heritage Service (DOE(NI)), CCW, JNCC and SAMS (1997). See also English Nature, Scottish Natural Heritage, Environment and Heritage Service (DOE(NI)), CCW, JNCC and SAMS (1998), made under Reg.33(2) Conservation (Natural Habitats etc.) Regulations 1994.

[292] Warren (1996).

[293] See above.

[294] See 14.2–5 above.

[295] On integrated pollution control and pollution prevention and control see 12.3–6 above.

[296] On discharge consents see Ch.10 above.

[297] Reg. 85 Conservation (Natural Habitats etc.) Regulations 1994.

[298] *Environment Action*, December 1999/January 2000, Issue 23, p.8.

[299] Reg.3(4) Conservation (Natural Habitats etc.) Regulations 1994.

may have on water quality and conservation objectives, as well as authorisations under the Groundwater Regulations 1998.[300]

An example of how these provisions operate in practice is the first action reviewing an existing planning permission brought under the 1994 Regulations. In November 1998 the Secretary of State confirmed the revocation of a planning permission which would have resulted in the loss of 82 hectares of grazing marsh on the Barksore peninsula within the Medway estuary by the disposal of river dredgings. The planning permission pre-dated the classification in 1993 of the Medway Estuary and Marshes as an SPA.[301] The Minister accepted that there were alternatives to the disposal of the dredged material on the Marshes that would be less damaging to wildlife, and judged that cost factors were irrelevant in reaching this decision. Also, as the Inspector's report remarked, damage could equally be caused by the cumulative effect of small losses of habitat as it could be by major incursions, and therefore it was a valid reason to uphold the revocation of planning permission and not to accept a compromise scheme offered by the dredgers only to deposit dredging spoil on a 23 hectares of the existing grazing marsh, since if this were allowed then it would be difficult to resist further incursions within the SPA.[302] Therefore, the scheme constituted a threat to the integrity of the site, and the planning permission was revoked with compensation.

A final point must be made about the impact of EC conservation designations. This is that the distinction between European sites and national SSSIs has an impact on how resources are allocated. There can be little doubt that the funding of schemes to prevent damage to protected habitats will give preference to European sites than sites which have merely national designation.

## 15.9 International Nature Conservation Obligations

The range of international conservation law measures that might impact on water quality is extensive. In addition to the Bonn and Berne Conventions noted above,[303] mention might be made of some of the more important global and regional conventions.

### 15.9.1 The Convention on Biological Diversity

The Convention on Biological Diversity,[304] opened for signature at the Rio 'Earth Summit' in 1992, aims to conserve biological diversity through a variety of means including habitat conservation. Of particular relevance

---

[300] On the Groundwater Regulations 1998, which are not mentioned in Reg. 85 Conservation (Natural Habitats etc.) Regulations 1994, see 13.6 above.

[301] The same area formed the wider background to the *Lappel Bank* litigation, discussed at 15.8.1 above.

[302] The precedent effect of a decision can be a material planning consideration.

[303] See 15.8 above.

[304] Nairobi, 22 June 1992, 31 ILM (1992) 818. See www.biodiv.org/index.html

here is the obligation for contracting parties, in accordance with their particular conditions and capabilities, to develop or adapt national strategies, plans and programmes for biodiversity conservation, and integrate, as far as possible and as appropriate, the conservation and sustainable use of biological diversity into relevant sectoral or cross-sectoral plans, programmes and policies.[305] Under this commitment, the UK Biodiversity Action Plan 1994 was produced.[306] More recently, the Commission has adopted a Communication on a European Community Biodiversity Strategy,[307] also in accordance with this provision, the EU having ratified the Convention.[308] The Convention also includes various measures about in-situ conservation,[309] which include, for example, provisions requiring degraded ecosystems to be rehabilitated and restored through, among other things, plans and management strategies, and impact assessment.[310]

As with most of the articles of the Convention on Biological Diversity, however, its restoration and planning provisions are couched as being required only 'as far as possible and as appropriate'. Nevertheless, as noted above, key provisions of the Convention go beyond a 'protected area' approach to conservation, and at least in the UK appear to have given considerable impetus to the development of wider conservation initiatives. On the other hand, it is debatable whether provisions of the Convention, for example those which require the integration of biodiversity conservation into national decision-making,[311] have provided anything more than a basis for policy arguments along these lines and, in the case of water quality, provided anything more than a broad peg on which to hang a number of approaches involving the integration of biodiversity conservation and water quality considerations. Wetland biodiversity issues under the Convention have been entrusted to the Ramsar Bureau, the secretariat of the Ramsar Wetlands Convention discussed below.

### 15.9.2  The Ramsar Convention

As noted above,[312] the Ramsar Convention on Wetlands of International Importance Especially as Waterfowl Habitat[313] has had an influence on EC conservation law, and to some extent its provisions are given mandatory legal effect under the Wild Birds and Habitats Directives. The Convention requires contracting parties to designate at least one suitable wetland within their territory, giving priority to sites important to waterfowl. 'Wetlands' are defined as 'areas of marsh, fen, peatland or water, whether

---

[305] Art.6 Convention on Biological Diversity.
[306] See 15.7.5 above.
[307] COM(98)42.
[308] Council Decision 93/626/EEC.
[309] Art.8 Convention on Biological Diversity.
[310] *Ibid* Art.14.
[311] *Ibid* Art.10.
[312] See 15.8.1 above.
[313] Ramsar, 1971. 11 ILM (1972) 963 (as amended). See www.ramsar.org

natural or artificial, permanent or temporary, with water that is static or flowing, fresh, brackish or salt, including areas of marine water the depth of which at low tide does not exceed six metres'.[314] Adjacent land, such as riverbanks and shallow coastal waters beyond six metres, can also be designated.[315]

There are detailed criteria for identifying wetlands which are of sufficient international importance to be included on the Ramsar List. These tend to be revised on a fairly frequent basis, though it is notable that the criteria have evolved so that sites may be listed on the grounds of criteria based on species and ecological communities, waterbirds and fish respectively. Taking fish as an example, the criteria state that:

> A wetland should be considered internationally important if it supports a significant proportion of indigenous fish subspecies, species or families, life-history stages, species interactions and/or populations that are representative of wetland benefits and/or values and thereby contributes to global biological diversity.

> A wetland should be considered internationally important if it is an important source of food for fishes, spawning ground, nursery and/or migration path on which fish stocks, either within the wetland or elsewhere, depend.[316]

The agreed definitions highlight the fact that a wetland may be designated not simply because it is the habitat for an important aquatic species, but for its wider role in the conservation status of such species.

Contracting parties must formulate their planning so as to promote the conservation of wetlands in the list, and as far as possible their 'wise use', a concept which is also fleshed out in guidelines agreed at successive conferences of the parties.[317] Parties must arrange to be informed as soon as possible if the ecological character of any of its listed wetlands has changed, is changing or is likely to change as the result of technological developments, pollution or other human interference. There is scope to delete or restrict the boundaries of a listed site for urgent national interests, but this must be matched by compensatory measures. Beyond this, the Convention lays down few substantive requirements, and it is notable that the focus of the Convention has shifted over the years to emphasise financial and other support mechanisms for wetlands conservation rather than prohibitive measures.[318] Ramsar sites are not 'European sites' for the purposes of the Conservation (Natural Habitats etc.) Regulations 1994, but enjoy a similar measure of protection through town and country planning

---

[314] Article 1(1) Ramsar Convention.

[315] Art.2(1) Ramsar Convention.

[316] Criteria 7 and 8 respectively, see www.ramsar.org/key_criteria.htm

[317] On wise use see *Guidelines for the Implementation of the Wise Use Concept*, at www.ramsar.org/key_wiseuse.htm and *Additional Guidance for the Implementation of the Wise Use Concept*, at www.ramsar.org/key_add_guide.htm which incorporates the precautionary principle to wise use.

[318] Davis (1994).

law.[319] In practice, all Ramsar sites will be SSSIs, and most will also be SPAs.[320]

In general terms, the Ramsar Convention has played a key role in protecting one particular habitat that the UK has in relative abundance. The meetings of the parties to the convention every two or three years helps focus attention on the Government's obligations, and often provides the impetus for the designation of further sites or other conservation measures.

### 15.9.3 ASCOBANS

The 1992 Agreement on the Conservation of Small Cetaceans of the Baltic and North Seas (ASCOBANS) was concluded under the auspices of the Bonn Migratory Species Convention[321] and came into force on 29 March 1994. The Agreement aims to provide for specific conservation and management measures for all toothed whales, dolphins and porpoises, except the sperm whale, found in the area of the Convention. Despite the limitations of this in the text of the Treaty to the Baltic, the North Sea and English Channel, the UK Government has pledged to apply the spirit of the Agreement to all waters to the north and west of the UK, so that effectively all coastal waters around England and Wales are covered by the Agreement.[322] The Agreement is largely concerned with improving co-ordination between the relevant range states in the area concerned, but does contain a specific provision requiring the parties to work towards the prevention of the release of substances which are a potential threat to the health of the animals.[323]

### 15.9.4 The OSPAR Convention

The 1992 Convention for the Protection of the Marine Environment of the North East Atlantic (the 'OSPAR' Convention) has as one of its objectives marine ecosystem conservation, [324] and the breadth of the Convention may be expanded by the adoption of an Annex concerned specifically with ecosystem and biodiversity conservation.[325] In general terms, however, the Annex tends to reinforce the programmatic obligations already provided for in the Convention on Biological Diversity.[326] Moreover, in relation to possible action concerning maritime transport, the OSPAR Commission

---

[319] Planning Policy Guidance Note 9, *Nature Conservation* (1994).

[320] For a critique see Neild and Rice (1996).

[321] See 15.8 above.

[322] ASCOBANS Interim Secretariat, *Progress Report on the Agreement on Conservation of Small Cetaceans of the Baltic and North Seas*, May 1993-April 1994.

[323] para.1 Annex ASCOBANS.

[324] On the Convention generally, see 18.8 below.

[325] Annex V and Appendix III OSPAR Convention. As at 1 August 2000 not yet in force (adopted under Art.7).

[326] See 15.9.1 above, especially Art.6.

must inform the International Maritime Organisation (IMO),[327] and contracting parties who are members of the Organisation must endeavour to co-operate within the IMO in order to achieve an appropriate response, including in relevant cases the IMO's agreement to regional or local action, taking into account any guidelines developed by the IMO on the designation of special areas, the identification of particularly sensitive areas or other matters.

---

[327] On the International Maritime Organisation see 19.4 below.

# Chapter 16

# MONITORING AND INFORMATION

## 16.1 Introduction

Information is a vital ingredient in addressing problems of water pollution and water quality, and environmental quality more generally. Knowledge is a spur to action at both a legislative and a practical level, and the availability of information to all is a prerequisite for open debate and improvement in water quality. However, regrettably, the United Kingdom has no long tradition of allowing free access to official information and it is unfortunate that development of the law has been impeded by general secrecy in respect of technical information about the state of the aquatic environment. Thankfully, this lamentable tradition has been largely overturned by developments over the last quarter century.

A range of issues are dependent upon the availability of satisfactory information about water quality: the pursuit of legal proceedings in respect of a water pollution incident, the assessment of whether water quality objectives are being met and the necessity, or otherwise, of various kinds of action needed to secure quality improvement. Hence, the purpose of this chapter is to consider responsibilities relating to information concerning the quality of controlled waters. Essentially, this subject falls into two distinct parts, respectively concerned with the gathering of information and the communication of that information to others.

Accordingly, the first part of this chapter considers the duties imposed under European Community and national law to monitor water quality, the extent to which these allow for self-monitoring obligations to be imposed upon dischargers and the legal significance of information produced by self-monitoring. The second part of the chapter is primarily concerned with public rights of access to information about the aquatic environment. This theme is traced through the provision of information in publicly accessible registers, more broadly-based rights of access to environmental information held by public bodies and the implications of proposals for generally-applicable freedom of information legislation. The chapter does not deal with information about drinking water quality, trade effluent discharges, radioactive contamination and monitoring obligations in international law since these matters are considered elsewhere in this work.[1]

---

[1] On drinking water quality information see 17.7.5 below; on trade effluent information see 11.4 above; on radioactive contamination see 20.10.11 below and on international monitoring obligations see 18.8.4 below.

## 16.2 Monitoring Requirements under European Community Water Directives

A range of monitoring requirements are provided for under European Community water directives for which the Environment Agency acts as the competent national authority. Particularly in relation to those directives that impose water quality standards for water for particular purposes,[2] other than in relation to drinking water quality,[3] the Agency is responsible for implementing the relevant monitoring requirements.

A marked contrast may be noted between the general monitoring duty imposed upon the Agency under national law and the various monitoring and information provision requirements that arise under Community water directives. As will be seen,[4] the national water quality monitoring duty is extremely general and unspecific as to the details of which waters should be monitored, at what frequency, in relation to which parameters and the purposes for which monitoring must be undertaken. By contrast, Community water directives often impose exacting requirements with respect to certain aspects of monitoring, analysis and the provision of water quality information. Moreover, a failure to meet monitoring requirements stands on the same footing as a failure to meet a substantive water quality obligation under a directive in that either of these would justify a finding that a Member State had failed to implement a directive.[5] Similarly, it would not be acceptable for a Member State to maintain that substantially satisfactory water quality established through monitoring was a justification for a failure to implement other obligations under a directive.[6]

Typically, those directives concerned with water quality standards identify a range of physical, chemical and biological parameters which serve to determine the suitability of water for a particular purpose and stipulate imperative, or 'I,' values and guide, or 'G', values which Member States are to endeavour to observe. Sampling of these parameters is usually required by the competent national authority at specified sampling points, at a stated frequency, and with samples being analysed for particular parameters according to specific methods of analysis. In some instances, the collection of unsatisfactory samples activates a responsibility upon the competent authority to undertake investigatory action to ascertain the cause of water quality deterioration and, sometimes, to take appropriate action as a consequence.

In relation to all water quality directives, monitoring is linked to the provision of information to the Commission to allow the publication of water quality reports. Whilst this general formula is varied in each

---

[2] Generally see Ch.5 above on European Community water directives.

[3] The Environment Agency does not act as the competent authority in relation to the Drinking Water Quality Directive (80/778/EEC as amended) and the Drinking Water Sampling Directive (79/869/EEC) and see 17.7.4 and 17.9.1 below on monitoring of drinking water quality.

[4] See 16.4 below on the general monitoring duty upon the Environment Agency.

[5] See 4.12 above on breach of European Community directives.

[6] See Case C-298/95 *Commission* v *Germany* [1996] ECR I-6747.

individual directive, some examples of the features described may be identified in the monitoring requirements provided for in three particular directives: the Drinking Water Abstraction Directive, the Bathing Water Directive and the Shellfish Waters Directive. The directive-specific monitoring and reporting requirements illustrated by these directives will then be followed by discussion of more general Community provisions arising under the Reporting Directive and the Information Exchange Decision.

### 16.2.1 Drinking Water Abstraction

Under the Drinking Water Abstraction Directive,[7] sampling of water abstracted for use as drinking water is to be undertaken in respect of parameters to be set for specific substances detrimental to the quality of drinking water and contained in Annex II of the Directive. These substances are divided into an 'I' list, encompassing substances which Member States must ensure are kept within relevant parameters and a 'G' list encompassing substances which Members States must endeavour to keep within specified levels.[8] Generally, waters will meet the requirements of the Directive if 95% of samples comply with I list parameters and 90% of samples comply with parameters for other substances. However, no samples may exceed the parameters by more than 50%, except in relation to temperature, pH, dissolved oxygen and microbiological parameters, and no samples should indicate a risk to public health or constitute a second consecutive failure to achieve the standards required.[9]

Initially, the methods and means of monitoring under the Drinking Water Abstraction Directive were to be determined by competent national authorities.[10] However, monitoring is now subject to the Drinking Water Sampling Directive[11] which requires samples to be a representative indication of the quality of water at the abstraction point and that competent national authorities take samples at a reasonable and regular frequency not less than that provided for in Annex II to that Directive.[12] However, where recorded levels of contaminants are considerably superior to those established by Annex II of the Drinking Water Quality Directive, sampling frequencies may be reduced. Where there is no contamination by a substance, and no risk of contamination in the future, the Sampling Directive allows the national authority to determine that no regular sampling is necessary.[13] Details of the methods of analysis used and frequency of analysis are to be provided to the Commission upon request,

---

[7] Directive 75/440/EEC and see 17.6 below for a discussion of this Directive.
[8] Art.3 Drinking Water Abstraction Directive.
[9] *Ibid* Art.5.
[10] *Ibid* Art.6.
[11] Directive 79/869/EEC and see 17.6 below for a discussion of this Directive.
[12] Arts.4 and 6 Drinking Water Sampling Directive.
[13] Art.7 Drinking Water Abstraction Directive.

and the Commission is bound to produce regular consolidated reports on the quality of drinking water in the Community.[14]

## 16.2.2 Bathing Water

The Bathing Water Directive[15] imposes analogous requirements in respect of parameters being identified in I and G categories. The requirement is that 95% of samples achieve the parameters set for I list substances and 90% meet parameters for G list substances, though exceptions are made for the levels of 'total coliforms' and 'faecal coliforms' which must comply with the requirements in 80% of samples. However, conformity is also allowed where non-compliant samples do not exceed parameters by more than 50%, except for microbiological parameters, pH and dissolved oxygen, and consecutive samples do not deviate from the relevant parameters.[16]

Sampling under the Bathing Water Directive must be in accordance with a method of sampling which is much more explicitly provided for than under the Drinking Water Abstraction Directive. Samples of bathing water must taken at places where the daily average density of bathers is greatest, commencing two weeks before the start of the bathing season, and should, preferably, be taken 30cm below the surface of the water except for mineral oil samples which are to be taken at surface level. Local investigations must be undertaken of the ambient water conditions and these are to be undertaken, and repeated periodically, in order to obtain geographical and topographical data and to determine the nature of polluting, and potentially polluting, discharges and their effects upon the bathing area.

Where inspections reveal that there is a discharge, or probable discharge, of substances likely to lower the quality of bathing water, additional sampling must be undertaken. Likewise, additional sampling must be undertaken if there are any other grounds for suspecting a decrease in water quality.[17] Annex I to the Directive sets out minimum sampling frequencies, which are generally fortnightly, and reference methods for the analysis of the parameters covered by the Directive. Member States must submit annual reports to the Commission, in a prescribed format and the Commission must publish a Community report on the implementation of the Directive on the basis of the reports received from Member States.[18] In addition, Member States are bound to submit a sectoral report, in a prescribed form, to the Commission every three years.[19]

---

[14] Art.8 Drinking Water Abstraction Directive.

[15] Directive 76/160/EEC and see 5.5.2 above on this Directive.

[16] Art.5 Bathing Water Directive.

[17] *Ibid* Art.6(1) to (4).

[18] *Ibid* Art.13 as amended by Art.3 Reporting Directive (91/692/EEC) and see 16.2.5 below on this Directive.

[19] Art.9a Bathing Water Directive, as inserted by Art.2 Reporting Directive.

## 16.2.3 Shellfish Waters

The Shellfish Waters Directive[20] requires the monitoring of substances included in I and G lists under the Directive but is especially concerned with organohalogenated substances and metals, using the quality provisions for water contained in the Directive in conjunction with the emission limits for these substances provided for under the Dangerous Substances Directive.[21] The level of stringency for compliance with the Shellfish Waters Directive requires 75% of samples to comply for most of the parameters set out in the Annex with the exception of salinity and dissolved oxygen, where 95% of samples must comply, and organohalogenated substances and metals where there is a requirement of 100% compliance.[22]

Sampling must be conducted by the competent national authorities at levels of frequency indicated by the Annex to the Directive, at sampling points determined by local environmental conditions and in accordance with reference methods of analysis. However, where the quality of shellfish waters is 'appreciably higher' than specified by the parameters in the Annex the competent authority may determine that no further sampling is necessary. Where sampling demonstrates that a parameter is not being met, the competent authority must establish whether this is the result of chance, a natural phenomenon or pollution and must take appropriate measures.[23]

## 16.2.4 General Observations

More generally these examples of monitoring requirements show a fair degree of flexibility, or subsidiarity,[24] in their approach to certain aspects of monitoring, which contrasts with the technically-exacting analysis requirements which are specified. Requirements such as water samples being 'a representative indication of the quality of water', 'where the average density of bathers is greatest' or 'at sampling points determined by local conditions' leave quite a lot of discretion to national competent authorities and raise questions as to whether requirements of this kind are sufficiently precise to be subject to legal review. On the other hand the specified requirements relating to minimum frequency of sampling under the Bathing Water Directive have been strictly construed, so that failure to adhere to these, as evidenced by information in an annual national report to the Commission, has been held to constitute a failure to adhere to the requirements of the Directive.[25]

---

[20] Directive 79/923/EEC and see 15.3.1 above on this Directive.

[21] Art.3 Shellfish Waters Directive, and see the Dangerous Substances Directive (76/464/EEC) discussed at 5.4.1 above.

[22] Art.6 Shellfish Waters Directive.

[23] *Ibid* Art.7.

[24] See 4.4.2 above on "subsidiarity".

[25] See Case C-198/97 *European Commission* v *Federal Republic of Germany* [1999] ECR I-3257.

## 16.2.5 Reporting and Information Exchange

The monitoring and reporting obligations incorporated in the directives discussed above may be contrasted with more general requirements periodically to communicate information from water monitoring and analysis to the Commission. The provision of information of this kind fulfils an important function in allowing the general impact of directives to be evaluated and to indicate what further measures might be needed to secure effective protection of the aquatic environment. In the early directives, however, information requirements of this kind were provided for on a rather *ad hoc* basis, and a need was identified for rationalisation to allow for more systematic provision of information about water quality.

The purpose of the Reporting Directive[26] is to rationalise and improve, on a sectoral basis, on the provisions regarding the transmission of information and publication of reports relating to certain Community directives relating to environmental protection.[27] Accordingly, for each of the directives to which it applies, the Reporting Directive requires that, at intervals of three years, the Member States must send information about the implementation of the directive in the form of a sectoral report which will also cover other pertinent directives. The Commission will then publish a Community report on the implementation of the relevant directive.[28] The exception to this is the Bathing Water Directive, in relation to which annual reports are provided for.[29] The aim is to require environmental reporting for different sectors, water, air and waste, to be undertaken in consecutive years, so that the first reporting period for water is 1993 to 1995 inclusive, for air 1994 to 1996, and for waste 1995 to 1997. To give effect to the coordinated reporting requirements, water directives are amended or supplemented to require reporting to be undertaken in accordance with the Reporting Directive.[30]

Many of the directives in the water cycle under the Reporting Directive are to be replaced by the Water Framework Directive.[31] The Framework Directive will not require reporting under the Reporting Directive, but will establish a six year reporting schedule which, it is envisaged, will be synchronised with the water cycle of the Reporting Directive.[32]

A further mechanism to allow comparable data about water quality in the Member States to be obtained was provided for by the Information Exchange Decision.[33] The object of the Information Exchange Decision is

---

[26] 91/692/EEC.

[27] Art.1 Reporting Directive.

[28] *Ibid* Art.2.

[29] *Ibid* Art.3 and see further at 5.5.2 above.

[30] *Ibid* Annex I.

[31] See 5.7–9 and particularly 5.9.19 above on the Water Framework Directive (2000/60/EC).

[32] Commission Proposal for a Council Directive Establish a Framework for Community Action in the Field of Water Policy, Draft Explanatory Memorandum (25 February 1997) Section 2.5.10.

[33] Council Decision 77/795/EEC establishing a common procedure for the exchange of information on the quality of surface fresh water in the Community (as amended by Council Decision 86/574/EEC).

to establish a common procedure for the exchange of information on the quality of surface fresh waters to determine pollution levels of rivers in the Community and to monitor long-term trends and improvements resulting from application of Community and national legislation.[34] For that purpose, a network of sampling or measuring stations are established in Member States and information from the results of measurements, taken in accordance with specified sampling procedures and at stated frequencies, is recorded.[35] Member States must designate a central agency for these purposes and specified information, set out in a defined format, is to be annually provided to the Commission. This information is made available to all Member States who so request and used as the basis of a report published by the Commission indicating water quality trends.[36]

Although the Information Exchange Decision was a commendable early attempt to obtain an overview of the status of the aquatic environment across the Community, it is arguable that its purpose has been overtaken by subsequent developments. In particular, later directives have imposed monitoring and reporting requirements and the task of gathering and analysing environmental information generally has been undertaken by the European Environment Agency.[37] The Exchange of Information Decision will be repealed by the Water Framework Directive, from seven years after the entry into force of that Directive, that is, as soon as the programmes of measures provided for under that Directive are in place.

For the future, a key water quality monitoring obligation under the Water Framework Directive is that Member States will be required to establish programmes for monitoring of water status in order to establish a coherent and comprehensive overview of water status within each River Basin District established in accordance with the Directive.[38] For surface waters monitoring programmes must cover the ecological and chemical status of the waters, and for groundwaters the programmes must cover chemical and quantitative status. In each case monitoring is to be conducted in accordance with Annex V of the Directive which goes into considerable detail as to the selection of monitoring sites, the selection of parameters for monitoring, the frequency of monitoring and a range of other matters.

### 16.3 The European Environment Agency

Whilst the various European Community directives that have been discussed impose important water quality monitoring and reporting requirements upon the Member States, there is another level at which the Community is engaged in environmental monitoring. The formulation and enactment of environmental legislation in accordance with the

---

[34] Recitals and Art.1 Information Exchange Decision.

[35] *Ibid* Art.2. Annex I provides a list of the sampling or measuring stations, Annex II specifies the relevant sampling parameters and Annex III details reference methods of measurement.

[36] *Ibid* Art.3.

[37] See 16.3 below on the European Environment Agency.

[38] See 5.7–9, and particularly 5.9.8, above on the Water Framework Directive (2000/60/EC).

Community's environmental policy[39] requires an extensive body of information about the state of the environment in order to ascertain legislative priorities and optimum strategies to address these. Likewise, an evaluation of the practical effectiveness of existing environmental legislation is impossible without some accurate means of evaluating its impact upon the environmental quality in the Member States. Similarly, information about the relative states of the environment in the Member States might be thought an important factor in determining what situations should be given priority in environmental enforcement proceedings initiated at Community level.[40] Consequently, a supply of environmental information is a precursor to effective action by the Community on several fronts.

However, a supply of objective, comprehensive and comparable information about the state of the environment in the Member States has not been readily available to the Community in the past. This was either because the necessary information was not being comprehensively gathered by national monitoring activities or because it was available only in a form which made comparisons between Member States difficult or impossible. Hence, it has been observed that,

> the difficulties in obtaining environmental information are particularly acute: methods of sampling and analysis may vary, expertise or technology may be lacking and the potential or actual effects of pollutants on humankind, fauna and flora may be in dispute. Such problems, which arise even within one country, are compounded where international comparisons are required. Objective, reliable and comparable data are essential if the European Union is to identify correctly and tackle effectively the challenge of protecting, managing and enhancing the environment.[41]

The problem of obtaining sufficient information about the environment in an appropriate form was originally addressed under the Decision on the adoption of the Commission work programme concerning an experimental project for gathering, co-ordinating and ensuring the consistency of information on the state of the environment and natural resources of the Community.[42] This experimental project was given the acronym CORINE and had as a general aim the assembly of basic information on the state of the environment in the Community in a number of specific fields. Essentially, the object was to collate data in areas of priority concern, such as the improvement in comparability and availability of data and methods of analysing data on the environment and natural resources within the Community. Establishing the European Environment Agency sought to advance upon this by providing a permanent basis for the collection and analysis of environmental information.

---

[39] See 4.5–7 above on European Community environmental policy.

[40] See 4.13 above on the initiation of legal proceedings by the European Commission.

[41] House of Lords Select Committee on the European Communities, *European Environment Agency* (1995) para.1.

[42] Decision 85/338/EC.

The legal basis for the European Environment Agency[43] is in the form of a Regulation, enacted in 1990, on the establishment of the European Environment Agency and the European environment information and observation network.[44] The overall purpose of the Regulation is to provide the Community and the Member States with reliable and comparable information at European level enabling them to take the requisite measures to protect the environment, to assess the results of these measures and to inform the public about the state of the environment. Accordingly, the technical and scientific support required to further these ends will be provided to the Community and the Member States.[45]

The particular tasks of the European Environment Agency,[46] require it to establish, in co-operation with the Member States, the European environment information network (EIONET) and to collect, process and analyse data relating to the quality of the environment, along with the continuation of work initiated under the CORINE programme. The Agency is to provide the Commission with the information that it needs for the tasks of identifying, preparing and evaluating measures and legislation in the field of the environment. This involves assisting in the monitoring of environmental measures and also advising individual Member States on the development, establishment and expansion of their systems for the monitoring of environmental measures. Perhaps most significant is the role of the Agency in recording, collating and assessing data on the state of the environment and producing reports on the quality, sensitivity and pressures on the environment. Accordingly, it must publish a report on the state of, trends in and prospects for the environment every five years, supplemented by indicator reports focusing upon specific issues, and generally ensure the broad dissemination of reliable and comparable environmental information.

The principal areas of activity of the Agency include elements enabling it to gather information to describe the present and foreseeable state of the environment in terms of environmental quality, pressures on the environment and the sensitivity of the environment. Amongst its priority areas are,

(a) water quality, pollutants and water resources;
(b) the state of the soil, of the fauna and flora and of biotypes;
(c) waste management;
(d) chemical substances which are hazardous for the environment;
(e) coastal and marine protection; and
(f) cooperation in the exchange of information.

In particular, transfrontier, multinational and global phenomena are to be taken into account, as are the socio-economic dimensions of the

---

[43] Generally see www.eea.eu.int and Ryland (1994); Davies (1994); and Jimenez-Beltran (1995).
[44] Regulation 1210/90/EEC, as amended by Regulation 933/1999/EC.
[45] *Ibid* Art.1.
[46] *Ibid* Art.2.

environment, though the Agency is to avoid duplicating the existing activities of other institutions and bodies.[47]

The information network, EIONET, is to provide the main component elements of the national information networks, national focal points and topic centres. To allow the network to be established as rapidly as possible, the Member States were required to inform the Agency of the main components of their national environmental information networks, especially in relation to the priority areas identified above. Member States were invited to identify a 'national focal point' for co-ordinating and/or transmitting information to the Agency, and must identify the other national organisations entrusted with the task of co-operating with the Agency.[48]

The Agency is governed by a management board consisting of one representative from each of the Member States and two from the Commission, and there may be a representative from each country that participates in the Agency. The management board is bound to agree the composition of the network, adopt the multi-annual work programme and the annual budget, and publish an annual general report.[49] It must appoint an Executive Director for a five-year term[50] and is to be advised by a scientific committees.[51]

The Agency is open to participation by countries which are not members of the European Communities but which share the concern of the Communities and the Member States for the objectives of the Agency and the Community.[52] Consequently, there are already 18 countries that are full members of the Agency, comprised of the fifteen Member States and Iceland, Norway and Liechtenstein.[53] Additionally, several Central and Eastern European or Baltic countries were keen to join at an early stage.[54]

Following a dispute about the location of the Agency,[55] in October 1993 the Agency was assigned to a base in Copenhagen and the Regulation was brought into immediate effect. Since its establishment, the Agency has developed rapidly in its task of producing 'quality assured data' and has established a network of 'topic centres' throughout Europe, with a wider network of institutions and information bodies with whom the Agency is in correspondence.[56] Progress is reported to have been made in improving the

---

[47] Art.3 Regulation 1210/90/EEC.
[48] *Ibid* Art.4.
[49] *Ibid* Art.8.
[50] *Ibid* Art.9.
[51] *Ibid* Art.10.
[52] *Ibid* Art.19.
[53] See www.eea.eu.int
[54] House of Lords Select Committee on the European Communities, *European Environment Agency* (1995) para.28.
[55] House of Lords Select Committee on the European Communities, *Implementation and Enforcement of Environmental Legislation* (1992) para.37.
[56] House of Lords, Select Committee on the European Communities, *Community Environmental Law: Making it Work* (1997) paras.53, 64 and 65.

quality of environmental data which is made available to a wide range of users. These include Community bodies, national environmental authorities, international organisations, non-governmental organisations, representatives of major economic sectors, such as industry, commerce and agriculture, the media and the general public.[57] In particular, the Agency has initially published major reports on the state of the European environment.[58] However, the view has been expressed that there should be more effective links between the Agency and the various regulatory committees which advise the Commission.[59]

## 16.4 The General Monitoring Duty upon the Environment Agency

Turning to national responsibilities for water quality monitoring, it is the duty of the Environment Agency, for the purposes of carrying out its functions under the water pollution provisions of the Water Resources Act 1991, to monitor the extent of pollution in controlled waters.[60] In practice, this tersely-stated provision turns out to be one of the most important in the Act.

The general monitoring duty is rather negatively worded as an obligation to monitor 'the extent of pollution' rather than a duty to monitor the quality of waters generally, but since the meaning of 'pollution'[61] is not defined by the Act, fairly broad scope is given to allow for the monitoring of controlled waters generally. The generality of the duty must be emphasised, however, in that it does not require any particular controlled waters to be monitored at any particular time, or with any specified frequency, and gives no indication as to any operational or technical requirements within which monitoring activities must be conducted. Whilst some of these requirements are otherwise provided for, particularly where monitoring is required to comply with European Community water directives, the general monitoring obligation seems to be formulated to allow the greatest possible discretion to the Agency to determine the manner of its day-to-day execution and the details of what is required generally to monitor controlled water quality.

In the absence of any other indications, the legal implications of the general monitoring obligation are only capable of being understood by reference to the functions allocated to the Agency under the 'water

---

[57] See www.eea.eu.int

[58] *Europe's Environment: the Dobris Assessment* (1995) *and Europe's Environment: the Second Assessment* (1998). The *Dobris Assessment* was particularly important as the first detailed and comprehensive review published of the state of the environment in Europe. Covering data from a wide range of sources relating to 46 countries, the Report identified a number of serious threats and confirms the poor quality of the environment in many parts of Europe.

[59] House of Lords Select Committee on the European Communities, *Community Environmental Law: Making it Work* (1997) para.65.

[60] s.84(2) Water Resources Act 1991.

[61] See 9.8 above on the meaning of 'poisonous, noxious or polluting'.

pollution provisions' of the Water Resources Act 1991.[62] A scan of the water pollution provisions of the Act indicates the wide range of purposes for which monitoring must be, or may be, required to be undertaken:

(a) to ascertain whether water quality objectives have been achieved and maintained;[63]

(b) to ascertain whether any principal water pollution offence has been committed;[64]

(c) to ascertain whether any prohibition notice should be served;[65]

(d) for the purpose of determining an application for a discharge consent or other consent, and monitoring compliance with consents generally;[66]

(e) to ascertain whether any offence has been committed in relation to deposits and vegetation in rivers;[67]

(f) to ascertain whether an enforcement notice should be served;[68]

(g) to determine what actions are required in relation to precautionary regulations and to ascertain whether any offence has been committed under such regulations;[69]

(h) to determine whether an application should be made for the establishment of a water protection zone and, if established, whether consequent controls have been adhered to;[70]

(i) to determine whether an application for designation of a nitrate sensitive area should be made;[71]

(j) to ascertain whether a code of good agricultural practice has been adhered to;[72]

(k) to ascertain whether anti-pollution works should be undertaken or whether a works notice should be served;[73]

(l) to collect information which is required to be entered in the pollution control register;[74]

(m) to provide information and assistance to Ministers in connection with the control of pollution;[75]

---

[62] The 'water pollution provisions' of the Water Resources Act 1991 are defined as the provisions of Part III of the Act (control of pollution of water resources); ss.161 to 161D (anti-pollution works) 190 (pollution control register) 202 (information and assistance required in connection with the control of pollution) and 203 (information with respect to pollution incidents); para.4 of Sch.25 (byelaws for controlling certain forms of pollution) and s.211 (enforcement of byelaws) so far as it related to byelaws made under that paragraph; and s.53(1) and (2) Environment Act 1995 (inquiries and other hearings) (s.221(1) Water Resources Act 1991, as amended by s.120, para.177 Sch.22 Environment Act 1995).

[63] Under s.84 Water Resources Act 1991.

[64] Under *ibid* s.85.

[65] Under *ibid* s.86.

[66] Under *ibid* ss.88, 90A and Sch.10.

[67] Under *ibid* s.90.

[68] Under *ibid* s.90B.

[69] Under *ibid* s.92.

[70] Under *ibid* s.93 and Sch.11.

[71] Under *ibid* s.84 and Sch.12.

[72] Under *ibid* s.97.

[73] Under *ibid* s.161 and 161A.

[74] Under *ibid* s.190.

[75] Under s.202 Water Resources Act 1991.

(n) to provide information for exchange with water undertakers concerning the quality of controlled waters and pollution incidents;[76]

(o) to determine whether byelaws should be made for controlling certain forms of pollution and for ascertaining whether a byelaw has been contravened;[77] and

(p) to provide information required at inquiries and other hearings.[78]

From amongst this wide range of purposes for which water quality monitoring may be undertaken, a broad distinction may be drawn between the gathering of information which is required for potential law enforcement purposes and information which is otherwise required to be collected for ascertaining the general state of controlled waters. In the past this distinction has been expressed as that between 'sampling' and 'routine monitoring'. However, the differences between the collection of water quality information for possible legal proceedings and for the purpose of ascertaining the general state of the waters is less clearly drawn today than in the past.[79] Nonetheless, the contrast between the use of water quality information in legal proceedings and for general assessment of water quality remains a useful distinction because of the stricter evidential requirements that may apply in relation to legal proceedings.[80]

## 16.5 General Assessment of Water Quality

### 16.5.1 Freshwater Monitoring

As has been seen,[81] since 1978, the monitoring of water quality was undertaken in accordance with the National Water Council system of classification. This system allowed the specification of water quality objectives and standards for surface waters under five categories, ranging from 'good' (1A) to 'bad' (4), according to potential water uses, with each of the use categories related to chemical quality criteria including dissolved oxygen, biochemical oxygen demand and ammonia concentration.[82] Significantly, this classification system allowed waters to be monitored in accordance with relatively standard criteria to assess which category particular waters fell into, allowing comparisons to be made between water quality in different locations and to assess water quality variation over time. The classification system also served a water quality management purpose in, informally, requiring quality objectives to

---

[76] Under *ibid* s.203.

[77] Under *ibid* ss.210, 211 and para.4 Sch.25.

[78] s.51(1) and (2) Environment Act 1995.

[79] Because of the abolition of the tripartite sampling requirement, see 16.9 below on this.

[80] See 16.12 below on general evidential concerns.

[81] See 1.4.4 above on national use of water quality objectives and standards.

[82] See National Water Council (1978).

be met by target dates through the imposition of increasing stringency in discharge consents.[83]

Insofar as the National Water Council's classification system served the purpose of a water quality monitoring system, it was possible to use it as a basis for some quite revealing reports comparing water quality over five year periods.[84] However, concern was expressed about disparities in the ways that the classification system was interpreted in different areas and the limitations of the scheme because of the relatively small number of quality parameters that were used. Additionally, it was noted that limited chemical monitoring of waters failed to show the true ecological state of waters where this was impaired by unidentified or transient pollutants or the cumulative effects of low concentrations of pollutants.[85]

In response to the criticisms, the National Rivers Authority devised a more sophisticated monitoring scheme, the General Quality Assessment Scheme, which sought to assess the quality of freshwaters more widely according to their chemical, biological, nutrient and aesthetic quality. General Quality Assessment is the procedure by which rivers and other freshwaters have been assessed since 1995, though some retrospective analysis of earlier data, dating back to 1990, has been undertaken.[86]

General Quality Assessment uses six categories of water quality 'very good' (A), 'good' (B), 'fairly good' (C), 'fair' (D), 'poor' (E) and 'bad' (F). These are applied according to the state of a water judged against a combination of the chemical, biological, nutrient and aesthetic criteria. Whilst the chemical criteria build upon the National Water Council system in many respects, the application of the other criteria is an innovation. Hence, the biological quality assessment scheme provides for categories of water quality, A to F, to be applied according to the range of microinvertebrates present in a particular water and a weighting system which takes account of the sensitivities of particular microinvertebrates to poor water quality. Because of natural variation in waters due to geographical location, geology and habitat, a mathematical model, the River Invertebrate Prediction and Classification System, is used to predict the fauna that would naturally be present in a water using physical data from the site such as water alkalinity. By comparing the fauna actually found in a particular sample with those that would be expected if the water was in its natural state, each water may be assessed according to one of the six quality categories.[87]

---

[83] Generally see Royal Commission on Environmental Pollution (1992) Ch.4.

[84] See National Rivers Authority, *The Quality of Rivers, Canals and Estuaries in England: Report of the 1990 Survey* (1991) for the last report using the National Water Council's monitoring criteria.

[85] Royal Commission on Environmental Pollution (1992) para.4.9.

[86] National Rivers Authority, *The Quality of Rivers and Canals in England and Wales (1990 to 1992): As Assessed by a New General Quality Assessment Scheme* (1994).

[87] Environment Agency, *The Quality of Rivers and Canals in England and Wales 1995* (1997).

Although the chemical and biological elements in the General Quality Assessment Scheme are sufficiently developed to be applied in practice, implementation of the parts of the Scheme concerned with nutrient status and aesthetic quality are still under development. Particularly in relation to the assessment of aesthetic quality, there are significant difficulties in devising an objective scheme of classification to take account of the adverse visual aspects of waters such as the presence of litter, scum and oil.[88]

Although river quality monitoring has been undertaken since 1958, since 1980 the results have been published every five years.[89] The most recently published report, relating to 1995, is based upon about 7,000 sites where water is sampled a minimum of 12 times a year for chemical quality and twice a year for biological quality. The 1995 report indicates a general improvement in water quality compared with 1990. On chemical assessment, it was indicated that 91% of rivers were very good to fair quality (A to D), 8% were poor (E) and 1% bad (F). Between 1990 and 1995, this represented a quality upgrading of 40% of rivers, measured by length, and a downgrading of 12%, indicating a 28% aggregate improvement. Taking only those improvements which were regarded as being 'statistically significant' (at 95% confidence) to avoid natural variations in water quality, the inference was drawn that the aggregate improvement over the period was at least 8%. In relation to biological quality, the 1995 report indicated that 93% of rivers were very good to fair (A to D), 5% were poor (E) and 2% were bad (F). By comparison with 1990, 38% of rivers had been upgraded and 12% downgraded. This gave an aggregate upgrading of 26%, which in terms of statistically significant changes showed a net improvement of 7%.[90]

### 16.5.2 Marine Water Monitoring

As compared with freshwaters, general and systematic monitoring of water quality in the marine environment has only been undertaken relatively recently. A National Monitoring Plan was initiated in the late 1980s to coordinate marine monitoring between a range of responsible bodies including the Department of the Environment, Transport and the Regions, the Ministry of Agriculture, Fisheries and Food, the Environment Agency and counterparts with responsibilities for Scotland and Northern Ireland. Monitoring of marine waters is now coordinated by the Marine Pollution Monitoring Management Group which has responsibility for ensuring monitoring is conducted in a consistent manner in accordance with national and international quality control requirements. The objects of the National Monitoring Programme for marine waters are to establish the

---

[88] See Pugh (1997) and Cook (1998) p.266.
[89] House of Commons Environment Committee, *Pollution of Rivers and Estuaries* (1987) Evidence, *Memorandum Submitted by the Department of the Environment* paras.3.10-11.
[90] Environment Agency, *The Quality of Rivers and Lands in England and Wales 1995* (1997). More recent information about water quality may be found at www.environment-agency.gov.uk under 'State of the Environment'.

distribution of contaminants in United Kingdom waters and to identify their biological status indicating any areas of special concern, for example, where concentrations of contaminants might affect biological processes or render fish or shellfish unfit for human consumption. The Programme is a long-term initiative which has been established to detect trends in contaminant concentration and biological status and to measure trends in physical, biological and chemical parameters at selected sites.

The results of the first coordinated programme of marine water quality monitoring have been published by the Marine Pollution Monitoring Management Group in a *Survey of the Quality of UK Coastal Waters*.[91] The survey was based upon 87 estuarine, intermediate and offshore sites, surveyed between 1992 and 1995, to determine the distribution of contaminants, including metals and organic compounds, present in water, sediments, shellfish and fish. Biological status of waters was determined by the presence of benthic species, analysis of oyster contamination and the extent of specific health effects in some species. The information provided by the survey is intended to serve as a baseline for later surveys and a means of ascertaining trends in water quality.

The results of the survey show that diversity of benthic macrofauna is largely dominated by natural physical characteristics, which tend to generate a low diversity at the head of estuaries with greater diversity offshore, and other physical characteristics such as the presence of muddy sediments which tend to support such communities. As evidenced by water and sediment chemistry, the quality of waters in intermediate and offshore locations is generally good with concentrations of organic compounds below the analytical limits at most sites. The highest concentrations of contaminants were found at historically or currently industrialised estuaries, though such concentrations were established to be well below relevant environmental quality standards. However, oyster bioassay studies showed poor water quality at a number of estuaries and, though chemical contamination of fish was generally confined to industrialised estuaries, low concentrations of polychlorinated biphenyls and dieldrin were found in fish at most sites surveyed. Many industrialised estuaries appeared to be contaminated to a degree that might be harmful to plankton, though no single contaminant was found to be responsible and the effect was thought to be due to several contaminants acting together.

## 16.6  Water Quality Monitoring and Powers of Entry

The monitoring of water quality for the purposes of general quality assessment is important for the purpose of ascertaining the general state of waters and identifying long-term trends in water quality which may require legislative attention. Despite this important strategic purpose, however, the collection of general information about water quality may not be sufficient where more specific information is needed for the purpose of pursuing legal proceedings or taking other kinds of regulatory action. The collection

---

[91] Marine Pollution Monitoring Management Group (1998).

of water quality information for regulatory purposes, is subject to a range of procedural requirements which, in the first instance, are likely to involve Environment Agency staff entering premises for this purpose. Whilst the general powers of entry of Agency staff have been discussed elsewhere,[92] it is notable that these have particular implications in relation to water monitoring and sampling activities.

Extensive powers are possessed in relation to entry of premises for pollution control purposes, and related matters including water sampling.[93] Specifically, the powers which a person authorised by the Agency may exercise for these purposes allow:

(a)  entry at any reasonable time;
(b)  taking equipment or materials;
(c)  making a necessary investigation;
(d)  directing that anything in the premises is to be left undisturbed;
(e)  taking measurements, photographs and recordings;
(f)  taking samples of any articles or substances;
(g)  causing any article or substance which may have caused pollution to be dismantled or subjected to any process or test;
(h)  taking possession of an article or substance which may have caused pollution for examination or legal proceedings;
(i)  requiring persons to give information; requiring the furnishing of extracts from any computer or other records;
(j)  requiring facilities and assistance necessary to exercise any of the powers of entry and related powers; and
(k)  any other power conferred by regulations made by the Secretary of State.[94]

However, some reservations are imposed upon the use of information collected by the exercise of the powers of entry in subsequent legal proceedings. Hence, in relation to the power of an authorised person to request information, and the accompanying requirement that answers be given to questions, no answer given in pursuance of this requirement is to be admissible in evidence in any proceedings against that person. Implicit in this exclusion is that a person providing information in response to a request from the Agency should not be deprived of the privilege against self-incrimination.[95] A further exclusion is that none of the powers to require the production of evidence of the various kinds may be taken to compel the production of a document which might be withheld from legal proceedings in the High Court on grounds of legal professional privilege.[96]

Alongside the apparently extensive formulation of the powers of entry and related matters, these powers allow the Agency to install, keep or maintain

---

[92] See 6.17 above on powers of entry.
[93] s.108(1) Environment Act 1995.
[94] *Ibid* s.108(4).
[95] See 16.13 below on self-incrimination.
[96] s.108(12)-(13) Environment Act 1995.

monitoring and other apparatus on premises.[97] Clearly, with remote monitoring of water quality becoming an increasingly practical option, this may remove any previous difficulties that may have existed in relation to the use of monitoring equipment on private land. This raises some significant legal possibilities and difficulties which are considered in the following sections.

## 16.7 Provision of Monitoring Information to the Environment Agency

In accordance with the general monitoring duty and the powers of entry, much information about water quality is gathered by water quality officers of the Environment Agency entering land for the purposes of collecting samples of water for analysis. However, the Agency also possesses further powers to require others to provide information in relation to the control of pollution in certain circumstances. These powers allow the Agency to serve on any person a notice requiring that person to furnish it with reasonably required information, within a specified period, for the purpose of carrying out its water pollution functions.[98] Failure to provide the information requested, without a reasonable excuse, within the specified period, is an offence.[99] However, the wording of the power to require information is unspecific in providing no indication as to what kinds of information may 'reasonably' be required and it is not clear whether, for example, monitoring information may be required where this is collected by a discharger who is not subject to any legal obligation to do so.[100]

The operation of the power to require water quality information was well illustrated in circumstances where the National Rivers Authority investigated an incident involving a major fish kill in a Yorkshire river after a toxic substance had been illegally discharged into the sewerage system.[101] With the assistance of the sewerage undertaker, the discharge was traced to sewers serving several industrial premises. The Authority had difficulty in persuading the owners of one of to co-operate with its inquiries. Even following the service of a notice requiring information to be provided,[102] the company claimed a right to silence.[103] Following a threat by the Authority to bring proceedings for the failure to comply with the notice requiring information to be provided,[104] the company eventually admitted to a spillage on its site, of a compound used as a fungicide and

---

[97] s.108(5) Environment Act 1995.

[98] *Ibid* s.202(2), and on the use of this power see *ENDS Report* 240 (1995) p.43.

[99] s.202(4) Environment Act 1995, though the question is raised whether the privilege against self-incrimination would serve as a 'reasonable excuse' for these purposes, see 16.13.1–2 below.

[100] For example, where the discharger is conducting monitoring of effluent in accordance with the requirements of an environmental management system, see EC Environmental Management and Auditing Regulation 1836/93/EEC.

[101] See 9.14 above on discharges from sewage treatment works.

[102] Under s.202(2) Water Resources Act 1991.

[103] See 16.13 below on self-incrimination.

[104] Under s.202(4) Water Resources Act 1991, and see 6.16 above on this offence.

insecticide, and that several hundred litres of the chemical had been washed into the sewer after a storage tank had been overfilled.[105]

Had the defendant not, eventually, complied with the notice requiring information to be provided, it is likely that it would have committed the offence of failing, without reasonable excuse, to comply with the notice.[106] An illustration of this offence being committed is to be found in *Environment Agency* v *Aberdare Demolition Ltd*[107] where the Agency discovered oil and solvent pollution on the surface of a river which was traced back to a site on which the defendants had been undertaking demolition work. The Agency suspected that the incident had been caused by spillage from a skip containing oil, and served a notice[108] requiring the company to provide waste transfer documents and tachograph readings from all vehicles used on the site. The company refused to provide the required information. Alongside two convictions for principal water pollution offences, the defendants were found guilty of failing to comply with the information notice. The company was fined a total of £2,000 for the pollution offences and £100 for the failure to comply with the information notice.

In addition to the offence of failing to comply with the requirements of an information notice, there is a more general offence committed where false or misleading statements are made to the Agency. This arises where, in furnishing any information or making any application under the 1991 Act, any person makes a statement which he knows to be false or misleading in a material particular, or recklessly makes any statement which is false or misleading in a material particular. Specifically, in relation to offences concerning the use of meters in connection with discharge consents,[109] if a person intentionally makes a false entry in any record so required, including under a condition of a discharge consent, that person will be guilty of an offence. A person who is guilty of an offence under these provisions will be liable, on summary conviction, to a fine not exceeding the statutory maximum, presently £5,000 or, on conviction on indictment, to an unlimited fine or to imprisonment for a term not exceeding two years, or to both.[110]

---

[105] *National Rivers Authority* v *Aquaspersions Ltd* (unreported Halifax Magistrates' Court, 25 November 1994) see *ENDS Report* 240 (1995) p.43. However, the Authority was unable to bring a water pollution prosecution because of the permissive wording of the sewage treatment works' discharge consent (see 10.6.5 above on the problem of undisclosed pollutants in discharge consents). Instead, a conviction was secured for the offence of disposing of controlled waste in a manner likely to cause pollution of the environment (under s.33(1)(c) Environmental Protection Act 1990).

[106] s.202(4) Water Resources Act 1991.

[107] Unreported, 9 May 1997, Aberdare Magistrates' Court, see O'Keeffe (1995) Section 4-426. See this source also for a discussion of the requirements for service of a notice requiring information to be provided (under s.220 Water Resources Act 1991).

[108] Under s.202(2) Water Resources Act 1991.

[109] Under *ibid* Chapter II Part III.

[110] *ibid* s.206, as amended.

## 16.8 Self-Monitoring Requirements

Whilst the general monitoring duty imposed upon the Environment Agency tends to give the impression that it will be directly responsible for collecting water quality information, provisions also allow for monitoring of water quality to be undertaken other than by the Agency. The indications are that increasing use will be made of the requirement of 'self-monitoring' of effluent by dischargers.[111]

The main legal mechanism by which self-monitoring may be required rests, primarily, upon the discharge consent system.[112] Where the Agency is minded to grant a discharge consent it may do so subject to conditions as to:

(a) the provision of facilities for taking samples of the matter discharged;
(b) the provision of meters or apparatus for measuring the volume, rate, nature, composition and temperature of the discharge;
(c) the keeping of records or readings of the nature, origin, composition, temperature, volume and rate of the discharges; and
(d) the making of returns to the Agency about the nature, origin, composition, temperature, volume and rate of the discharges.[113]

Hence, the failure of a discharger to provide meters, keep records, make returns or to do any of the other things mentioned is a breach of a condition of the consent and a criminal offence. This offence is punishable to the same extent as a contravention of the principal water pollution offences, and is committed without any need for contravention actually to result in pollution of controlled waters.[114]

## 16.9 The Repeal of the Tripartite Sampling Requirement

Where the Agency is seeking to secure a conviction for a principal water pollution offence, it is likely that information about the quality of effluent which enters, or is discharged into, controlled waters, and the effect of the entry or discharge upon receiving waters, will be a central issue. In the past, however, there has been a significant legal impediment to the use of either kind of water quality information in legal proceedings. This arose because of the procedural requirement of tripartite sampling of water as a prerequisite of its admissibility as evidence in legal proceedings. Although this requirement has now been repealed, its former operation remains instructive in relation to water quality sampling and evidential issues, as to the admissibility of water quality information, which continue to arise in respect of water pollution prosecutions.

---

[111] Generally see Howarth (1997).
[112] Under s.88 and Sch.10 Water Resources Act 1991 and see Ch.10 above on discharge consents generally.
[113] *Ibid* Sch.10 para.3, as amended. See also 10.6 above.
[114] s.85(6) Water Resources Act 1991, and see 9.3 above. On the fine levels for the principal water pollution offences see 9.19.2 above.

In essence, the tripartite sampling requirement stipulated that the result of the analysis of any sample taken on behalf of the former National Rivers Authority was not admissible in any legal proceedings in respect of effluent passing from any land unless the person who took the sample: on taking it, notified the occupier of the land of his intention to have it analysed; there and then divided it into three parts and caused each part to be placed in a container which was sealed and marked; and delivered one part to the occupier of the land and retained one part, apart from the one submitted to be analysed, for future comparison.[115] The tripartite sampling requirement was subject to the exception that, if it was not reasonably practicable for the person taking the sample to comply with these requirements directly, they would be treated as having been complied with if they were met as soon as reasonably practicable after the sample was taken.[116]

The tripartite sampling requirement was intended to allow an alleged polluter to make an independent check upon water quality information to be used in legal proceedings. Nevertheless, failure to comply with the formal requirements meant that many prosecutions for water pollution failed, or were not brought, because of the inadmissibility of evidence concerning water quality.[117] This would certainly have prevented a successful prosecution being brought if water quality officers of the regulatory authority were unable to take formal samples for any reason. Moreover, the application of the sampling requirement to the analysis of any sample taken 'on behalf of the National Rivers Authority' meant that any sample taken by a discharger, in pursuance of a self-monitoring condition in a discharge consent, would almost certainly fail to satisfy the tripartite sampling requirement. It would follow from this that any information about water quality incorporated in the pollution register would not be admissible in legal proceedings.[118] Progressively, the excessively burdensome character of the tripartite sampling requirement for law enforcers became acknowledged.

Although Regulations implementing the Urban Waste Water Treatment Directive[119] ameliorated the operation of the tripartite sampling requirement where this was required to implement the Directive, they did not address the broader concerns. These were that the requirement itself was an unjustifiable impediment to effective law enforcement by

---

[115] s.209(1) Water Resources Act 1991, now repealed. The requirement had originally been provided for in relation to discharges of industrial effluent into sewers (under s.10(2) Public Health (Drainage of Trade Premises) Act 1937) but was later applied to discharges made into controlled waters (under s.15(2) River Boards Act 1948). See Ch.2 above on the historical background.

[116] s.209(2) Water Resources Act 1991, and see *Attorney-General's Reference (No.2 of 1994)* [1995] 2 All ER 1000. For case law interpretation see *Trent River Board v Wardle Ltd* [1957] *Criminal Law Review* 196; *Wansford Trout Farm v Yorkshire Water Authority* (1986) unreported, Queen's Bench Division, 23 July 1986, see Howarth (1990) p.142.

[117] See, for example, *National Rivers Authority v Harcros Timber Ltd* (1992) *The Times* 2 April 1992.

[118] However, see 16.15.3 below on this.

[119] Regs. 10–11 Urban Waste Treatment (England and Wales) Regulations 1994 (SI 1994 No.2841) implementing Directive 91/271/EEC and see 5.6.2 above on this.

frustrating prosecutions where it was clear that water pollution had occurred but evidence of this was rendered inadmissible due to a failure to follow the formal procedure. For this reason, the requirement was comprehensively repealed under s.111(1) of the Environment Act 1995. The effect of this sub-section was that it would no longer be an exclusory rule of evidence that the analysis of a sample of water taken by, or on behalf of, the Agency had not been subject to the threefold sampling requirement. This consequence has some significant implications in relation to the methods by which water quality information may be gathered and, now, used in legal proceedings.

### 16.10  The Technological Impact upon Water Quality Monitoring

In the mid 1980s the development of equipment known as 'data loggers' first allowed water quality officers manually to record dissolved oxygen levels in water automatically and without the need for laboratory analysis of samples. The subsequent development of devices for providing automatic readings of other characteristics of water quality such as temperature, pH (acidity), ammonia and turbidity greatly extended this capacity. Successive generations of equipment have greatly refined the capacity for remote monitoring of water quality, so that it has become possible to combine the recording of different kinds of data in a single machine. Moreover, the technical capacity has been further enhanced to facilitate radio or fax communication from a machine to a distant source. This can be done periodically, in response to a request, or automatically in the event of a water quality parameter being exceeded.[120] Clearly, these developments have enormously enhanced the capacity of the Agency to detect intermittent sources of pollution taking place in remote locations or during 'unsociable' hours. Beyond that, the capacity of remote monitoring machines automatically to take samples of water for subsequent laboratory analysis and use in legal proceedings has brought significant law enforcement possibilities.

In 1993 the National Rivers Authority secured its first conviction in a water pollution case based on evidence collected by an automatic sampling device, 'Cyclops'. This device automatically monitored a company's effluent and detected variations in the quality of discharges. A change in the pH level which breached the company's discharge consent conditions was recorded and the Cyclops alerted pollution control staff in the regional control centre. The device was then activated, by remote control, to take a sample of the effluent. The machine was subsequently opened, in the presence of a company representative, and the sample was divided into three parts and one of these was served on the representative.[121] The

---

[120] See 'Wizard Weapons in the NRA Armoury' *The Water Guardians* December 1990 p.4; 'Tomorrow's World' *The Water Guardians* May 1993 p.4; and Mumma (1993).

[121] This procedure was required at this time to comply with the tripartite sampling procedure, described at 16.9 above.

company pleaded guilty to the water pollution offence and was fined £10,000.[122]

## 16.11 Admissibility of Self-Monitoring Information

With subsequent development, many of the perceived problems of reliability of the new mechanisms for assessing water quality were satisfactorily addressed and, as a consequence, a new statutory footing needed to be provided for the use of monitoring equipment. Beyond the repeal of the tripartite sampling requirement, another major amendment to the law on water quality monitoring introduced under the Environment Act 1995 was in relation to the admissibility of self-monitoring information. It is now provided that information provided or obtained pursuant to a condition or a relevant environmental licence, including a discharge consent, will be admissible in any proceedings whether against the person subject to the condition or any other person.[123] This confirms the admissibility of evidence of water quality provided by a discharger where this is required by a discharge consent, but is silent on the position with regard to water quality evidence where this is provided voluntarily by a discharger.[124] Another aspect of the provision is that evidence of self-monitoring under a discharge consent is admissible in 'any proceedings'. Hence, admissibility is not restricted to criminal prosecutions, and such evidence may be sought and used in civil proceedings[125] where, for example, private riparian owners are seeking compensation for damage to water quality or fisheries.

A further provision on monitoring which may be of considerable practical significance is that it will be presumed in any proceedings where information is obtained by virtue of a condition in a discharge consent that the apparatus involved records accurately, unless the contrary is shown or the discharge consent otherwise provides.[126] Significantly, the presumption applies only in relation to self-monitoring under a condition of a discharge consent. The same presumption is not provided for in relation to an apparatus used by the Agency to conduct monitoring, in relation to which the accuracy of the instrument used would have to be positively established. So, for example, it might still be open to an accused person to argue that a measuring device used by the Agency to record water quality was inappropriate, improperly maintained, inaccurately calibrated, used by a person with inadequate training or there was some other reason to doubt

---

[122] See National Rivers Authority, *Water Pollution Incidents in England and Wales – 1992* (1993) 44-45 and see 'Cyclops in giant step forward' *Water Guardian* April 1994 p.8. See also *CPC (UK) Ltd* v *National Rivers Authority* [1995] Env LR 131, discussed at 9.6.4 above.

[123] s.111(2) Environment Act 1995.

[124] Although it is thought that this may be covered by powers of the Agency to require the provision of water quality information not subject to a discharge consent, discussed in 6.16 above.

[125] See Ch.3 above on civil proceedings generally.

[126] s.111(3) Environment Act 1995. 'Apparatus' for these purposes is extensively defined to include any meter or other device for measuring, assessing, determining, recording or enabling to be recorded, the volume, temperature, radioactivity, rate, nature, origin, composition or effect of any substance, flow, discharge, emission, deposit or abstraction (s.111(5)).

its accuracy. Such lines of argument will be more difficult to maintain in relation to a self-monitoring apparatus, since a failure to maintain such apparatus properly would probably amount to a breach of a discharge consent condition. The 'double jeopardy' involved here should provide an incentive to dischargers to ensure that their self-monitoring equipment functions properly.

Another feature of the 'presumption of accuracy' with regard to monitoring apparatus is that it applies unless the discharge consent 'otherwise provides'.[127] This allows the Agency the discretion to require self-monitoring to be undertaken with equipment that may be insufficiently accurate to provide evidence which may be used in legal proceedings by a stipulation in a discharge consent condition that the evidence of water quality will not be deemed to be sufficiently accurate for this purpose. It is difficult to conceive of a situation where the Agency would find it particularly helpful to pursue this option, but nevertheless it is made available by virtue of the wording of the presumption.

The situation where a discharger fails to record self-monitoring information when required to do so under a condition of a discharge consent is also explicitly provided for. Thus, where a condition in a discharge consent requires an entry to be made in any record as to the observance of a condition in the consent, and the entry has not been made, that fact will be admissible in any proceedings as evidence that the condition has not been observed.[128] Although this stipulation may serve to clarify the position with regard to failure to enter information in a record, there is no apparent reason why such information should be inadmissible if it is alleged that the failure to maintain the required record, by itself, constitutes a breach of a discharge consent condition and, consequently, a criminal offence.

Notably, establishing that a recording requirement has not been observed may also be relevant to proceedings brought for an offence of causing or knowingly permitting the discharge of trade effluent[129] rather than the contravention of the conditions of a consent.[130] Although the maximum penalties for both offences are the same, it may be thought desirable to prosecute for the offence of unlawfully discharging effluent rather than for that of contravention of a recording condition in a consent since, in practice, an offence which involves actual pollution of controlled waters is likely to be regarded as more serious by a court in determining the appropriate sentence. Therefore, it is placed beyond doubt that evidence of a failure to keep a required record will be admissible in *any* proceedings, that is, not only proceedings brought for a contravention of a recording requirement but also proceedings for an offence actually involving water pollution. Put another way, it would not be open to a discharger to withhold self-monitoring information in the hope that this would lead only

---

[127] s.111(3) Environment Act 1995.
[128] *Ibid* s.111(4).
[129] Under s.85(3) Water Resources Act 1991.
[130] Under *ibid* s.85(6).

to a conviction for contravention of a recording condition, since the fact of failure to keep the record may still be relevant in proceedings for an offence relating to an actual pollution incident.

## 16.12 General Evidential Concerns

Despite the statutory developments that have been recounted, the admissibility of water quality evidence continues to give rise to concerns based upon broader evidential issues. The fundamental principle of criminal law procedure, that the prosecution must establish all the elements of the alleged offence beyond reasonable doubt, illustrates some peculiarities when applied to the principal water pollution offences. That is, where the offence prosecuted is the contravention of a condition of a discharge consent,[131] it is for the prosecution to prove that this actually took place. Where the prosecuted offence concerns the entry of polluting matter or the discharge of effluent[132] the prosecution must prove that the alleged entry or discharge actually took place. In such instances it becomes open to the defence to show that the entry or discharge was authorised as being under and in accordance with a valid discharge consent.[133] As a general evidential principle, however, it is provided that where a defendant relies upon an exception, exemption, proviso, excuse or qualification then the burden of proving it will be upon him.[134] In relation to discharge consents, it is thought that this would be interpreted to mean that it is for the defence, rather than the prosecution, to show that, on the balance of probabilities, the entry or discharge was covered by the discharge consent.

In almost all prosecutions of this kind,[135] however, the critical evidential issue revolves around the question of admissibility of water quality evidence. Following the removal of the requirement of tripartite sampling as an exclusory rule of evidence, and the technical feasibility of water quality monitoring instruments that has been noted, a new wave of evidential questions have arisen as to the circumstances in which this kind of evidence will be admissible.

An issue which arises in relation to technologically-produced evidence of water quality is whether such information will be rendered inadmissible by virtue of the 'rule against hearsay' which traditionally stipulates that 'an assertion other than one made by a person while giving oral evidence in the proceedings is inadmissible as evidence of any fact asserted'.[136] For present purposes, a centrally important question is whether evidence

---

[131] Under s.85(6) Water Resources Act 1991.

[132] Under *ibid* s.85(1) or (3).

[133] Under *ibid* s.88(1)(a).

[134] s.101 Magistrates' Courts Act 1980, and see *R v Edwards* [1974] 2 All ER 1085, and *R v Hunt* [1987] 1 All ER 1.

[135] Although there may be instances where a prosecution is brought for the breach of a condition of discharge consent which does not relate to the discharge of effluent which is in breach of a parameter, for example, where there has been a failure to keep records (see 16.8 above).

[136] *R v Sharp* [1988] 1 All ER 65, and see Tapper (1995) p.46, though see the range of exceptions in Chs.XIII and XV.

provided by, first, a mechanical device, second, documentary evidence and, third, from computer records may be rendered inadmissible by virtue of the hearsay rule. The evidential requirements differ in relation to these three different kinds of evidence, any of which may become an issue in relation to the output of a water quality monitoring instrument.[137]

## 16.13 Self-Incrimination and Human Rights

An overriding consideration in relation to all kinds of evidence is that there exists a general judicial discretion to exclude evidence if its prejudicial effect outweighs its probative value.[138] A discretion to exclude evidence is provided for on grounds of unfairness where, having regard to all the circumstances, including the circumstances in which the evidence was obtained, the court ought not to admit it.[139] Many of the leading cases on the application of this provision have concerned confessions obtained under improper circumstances, but the provision applies to *any* evidence and has, on occasions, been used to exclude documentary records and evidence of an intoximeter reading.[140] The breadth of the principle makes it apparent that it is capable of applying to information gathered from self-monitoring if some impropriety was disclosed in the collection of such evidence. Another issue which arises is the possibility of unfairness arising where self-incrimination of the accused is required.

### 16.13.1  The Privilege Against Self-incrimination

The privilege against self-incrimination allows a court to refuse to compel an accused person to produce evidence against himself. Classically, the principle is formulated so that

> no-one is bound to answer any question if the answer thereto would, in the opinion of the judge, have a tendency to expose [him] to any criminal charge, penalty or forfeiture which the judge regards as reasonably likely to be preferred or sued for.[141]

However, it has been frequently recognised that untrammelled operation of the privilege produces unsatisfactory results, and for this reason the principle has been modified or abrogated on many occasions both by the courts and under statute.

The particular question arising in relation to this context is whether the privilege against self-incrimination could ever justify a refusal to produce information about water quality gained from self-monitoring where such information is statutorily required to be produced. The answer, in national law, seems to be in the negative in that there are numerous statutory

---

[137] See Howarth (1997) pp.218–21.
[138] *R v Sang* [1980] AC 402 and see ss.24–25 Criminal Justice Act 1988.
[139] s.78(1) Police and Criminal Justice Act 1984.
[140] *McGrath v Field* [1987] RTR 349.
[141] *Blunt v Park Lane Hotel* [1942] 2 KB 257.

provisions which require specified persons under prescribed circumstances to provide information which may subsequently be used as a basis for a criminal prosecution.[142] However, there remains the possibility that a court could exercise its discretion to exclude evidence[143] provided pursuant to a statutory requirement where it is being unfairly used,[144] but in the past this would have been unlikely where the evidence is used for the purpose which the statute envisaged.

### 16.13.2 Self-incrimination Caselaw

Confirmation that self incrimination may not be used to justify a refusal to produce environmental information under national law has been provided by the recent House of Lords decision in *R v Hertfordshire County Council, ex parte Green Environmental Industries Ltd and John Moynihan*.[145] This case arose out of the alleged unauthorised storage of hospital waste by the applicants, and concerned the validity of a request by the respondent waste regulation authority to be provided with documentation relating to the movement of certain waste[146] and the service of a requisition on the company requiring specified information on waste movements to be provided.[147] The House of Lords was of the view that the possibility of self-incrimination was not a reasonable excuse justifying refusal to provide the information. The information that was sought was essentially factual and investigatory in character and did not invite any admission of wrongdoing. Moreover, it remained possible that any information which was actually provided could be excluded from any subsequent criminal proceedings if it was found that it might unduly prejudice the defence.[148]

A contrasting decision on self-incrimination, under the European Convention on Human Rights, is *Saunders v United Kingdom*.[149] These proceedings were brought after Saunders had been convicted of fraud on evidence from answers to questions that he was legally compelled to give in the course of investigations by Department of Trade and Industry

---

[142] For example, see s.2 Criminal Justice Act 1987 (requiring any person under investigation by the Director of the Serious Fraud Office to answer questions, furnish information and produce documents) and Part XIV of the Companies Act 1985 (requiring officers of a company to answer questions put by Board of Trade Inspectors appointed to investigate fraud in the company).

[143] See 16.12 above on the discretion to exclude evidence.

[144] *Bank of England v Riley* [1992] 1 All ER 169.

[145] [2000] 1 All ER 733 and see Thornton (2000). For a discussion of the operation of the privilege against self-incrimination in a water pollution context in another jurisdiction, see the decision of the High Court of Australia in *Environmental Protection Authority v Caltex Refining Co Pty Ltd* (1993) 178 CLR 477 and generally see Howarth (1997) p.223.

[146] The duty to make, retain and furnish documents with respect to controlled waste is provided for in s.34(5) Environmental Protection Act 1990, which entitles the Secretary of State to make regulations concerning these matters; see the Environmental Protection (Duty of Care) Regulations 1991 (SI 1991 No.2839) concerning 'transfer' notes, and Department of the Environment Circular 19/91, *Environmental Protection Act, Section 34, The Duty of Care* (1991).

[147] Provided for under s.71(2) Environmental Protection Act 1990.

[148] Under s.78 Police and Criminal Evidence Act 1984.

[149] (1996) 23 EHRR 313 (European Court of Human Rights).

Inspectors into the conduct of a company take-over. The Court concluded that this procedure infringed his freedom from self-incrimination and this was an important element in safeguarding an accused from oppression and coercion during criminal proceedings. Specifically, it was held that the privilege against self-incrimination was closely linked to the presumption of innocence[150] and the right to a fair hearing[151] and that these were protected under the Convention. Accordingly, it was concluded that Saunders had been deprived of a fair hearing.

The contrast between the *Saunders* case and the *Green* case is that in the former, the evidence which was provided was actually used in subsequent criminal proceedings whereas in the latter it was the refusal to provide information, rather than its subsequent use in criminal proceedings, that was at issue. Nonetheless, the *Green* case indicates that there are some fine contrasts to be drawn between the factual questions that may legitimately asked by the Environment Agency and inquiries which amount to an admission of guilt which are not legitimate.[152]

### 16.13.3  The Human Rights Act 1998

At the time of the *Saunders* decision, the European Convention on Human Rights was not a part of United Kingdom national law, though it was used as an aid to the interpretation of national law. Hence, when interpreting any ambiguity in a statute, regard was to be had to the provisions of the Convention[153] and, similarly, the judicial discretion to exclude evidence obtained in a manner which contravened the Convention might justifiably be exercised for this reason.

However, the coming into force of the Human Rights Act 1998, now means that the key articles of the Convention are to have effect for the purposes of the Act. Moreover, a national court determining a question that has arisen in connection with a right under the Convention must take into account judgments, decisions, declarations or advisory opinions of the European Court of Human Rights.[154] In effect, therefore, rights under the Convention may be enforced through national courts, rather than having to establish those rights before the European Court of Human Rights. In relation to the environmental self-incrimination issue that has been discussed, it would appear that national courts will now be bound to follow the *Saunders* ruling in appropriately similar cases.[155]

Likewise, legislative amendments are likely to be necessary to give effect to the Convention in national law where present statutory provisions are in

---

[150] Under Art.6(2) European Convention on Human Rights, see Sch.1 Human Rights Act 1998 for the present text of the Convention.

[151] Under *ibid* Art.6(1).

[152] See *ENDS Report* 301 (2000) p.51

[153] *Brind* v *Secretary of State for the Home Department* [1991] 1 All ER 720.

[154] ss.1(2) and 2(1) Human Rights Act 1998.

[155] Generally see, Corner (1998); Upton (1998); and Thornton and Tromans (1999).

conflict.[156] The developments in relation to self-incrimination and human rights have profound implications for statutory provisions unambiguously requiring compulsory provision of water quality information by self-monitoring and allowing this information to be used in subsequent criminal proceedings against the person providing the information. These developments may prompt a re-thinking of the objectives behind self-monitoring and a re-formulation of the legal requirements for water quality information provision.

### 16.13.4 The Purpose of Self-monitoring

From the Environment Agency's perspective, it is a fair assumption that a major attraction of self-monitoring lies in the mechanism for allocation of costs involved. Obliging dischargers to undertake responsibility for self-monitoring carries the implication that they will be responsible for the purchase and maintenance of any monitoring equipment, and this will avoid the Agency having to meet these costs.[157] In law, however, the necessity for monitoring costs to fall upon the Agency, other than where self-monitoring is undertaken, may not follow. Extensive charging powers are provided for, whereby the holders of discharge consents may be obliged to make payments which are attributable to the costs and expenses of the Agency carrying out its functions.[158] In principle, it appears that these powers would allow the Agency to impose charges upon effluent dischargers to cover the cost of purchasing monitoring equipment which was actually owned and operated by the Agency itself. If this approach was followed, the Agency would retain practical control of the information-gathering mechanism and the scope for self-incrimination would, therefore, be removed.

Ultimately, the legal approach which is required to self-monitoring depends upon the purpose for which the information gained is intended to be used. If information is required to provide a potentially cheaper and more comprehensive method of law enforcement, then the self-incrimination difficulty needs to be addressed, perhaps by replacing self-monitoring with remote monitoring undertaken by the Agency with dischargers meeting the cost of this activity. Alternatively, there may be a range of other reasons why self-monitoring is desirable independently of whether or not the information that it produces is usable in legal proceedings. Not least amongst these is the objective that dischargers should be aware of the impacts of their activities upon the environment and that good environmental management practice involves continuing cognisance of environmental impacts and progressive improvement of environmental performance as gauged against self-monitoring data. If this

---

[156] See s.1(3) and 4 Human Rights Act 1998, see also Gibb (1996).

[157] See *ENDS Report* 295 (1999) p.5.

[158] The power to make schemes imposing charges in relation to 'environmental licences' (including discharge consents) are provided for under s.41 Environment Act 1995, and see 6.15 above on charging schemes. A further incidental power of the Agency to impose charges is provided for under s.43, and see 6.15 above.

'participatory' justification is a more compelling reason for undertaking self-monitoring, then the fact that the data produced is inadmissible in legal proceedings may not be regarded as seriously problematic.

## 16.14  Public Access to Water Quality Information

### 16.14.1  The Rationale for Information Access

Turning from the collection and use of monitoring water quality information to the wider dissemination of that information to individuals or the public generally, a right to information of this kind, and environmental information more broadly, has gained increasing momentum over recent years. Since the first national initiative in providing a public right of access to water quality information by means of the pollution control register, profound developments have taken place at both international and European Community levels. Perhaps the guiding principle is now to be found in the international imperative that environmental information should be widely disseminated and that individuals should have access to such information. This principle is embodied in the Declaration reached at the 1992 Earth Summit which provides that,

> Environmental issues are best handled with the participation of all concerned citizens, at the relevant level. At the national level, each individual shall have appropriate access to information concerning the environment that is held by public authorities, including information on hazardous materials and activities in their communities, and the opportunity to participate in decision-making processes. States shall facilitate and encourage public awareness and participation by making information widely available. . . .[159]

The argument for access to environmental information to allow individuals to participate in environmental decision-making is generally regarded as an aspect of the ethic of environmental stewardship, whereby individuals are subject to a moral duty to look after the planet and to hand it on in good order to future generations. It is argued that, if the burden of stewardship is not to fall on Government alone, and individuals are to assume a part of this responsibility, it is vital that they should have sufficient information to assume this responsibility.[160]

More specifically, it has been suggested that access to environmental information makes five distinct kinds of contribution.[161] First, it reassures the public and promotes confidence on their part in the actions being taken

---

[159] Principle 10, *Rio Declaration*, United Nations Conference on Environment and Development (1992).
[160] HM Government, *This Common Inheritance* (Cm.1200, 1990) Ch.1.
[161] Rowan-Robinson, Ross, Walton and Rothnie (1996). For a list of arguments which have been raised against access to environmental information see Winter (1991).

by Government and industry (the public reassurance role).[162] Second, it informs consumer choice, both in the demand for, and consumption of, goods, for example by encouraging consumers to limit their use of resources such as water (the personal responsibility role).[163] Third, it allows increased public scrutiny which requires industry to take environmental protection seriously (the industry responsibility role).[164] Fourth, the knowledge that activities will come under public scrutiny should act as a vital discipline for environmental protection agencies (the agency accountability role).[165] Fifth, it enables members of the public to play a role in policy formulation and decision-making in environmental matters (the public participation role).[166]

Insofar as access to environmental information relates to access to water quality information, the following sections trace its application through a progressive expansion of access from the national use of publicly accessible information registers to more general rights to environmental information and information held by public bodies generally. Hence attention is initially focused upon information provisions relating to water quality under the Water Resources Act 1991, and from this the discussion proceeds to consider the implementation of provisions relating to access to environmental information established at European Community level, and concludes with an account of present proposals for national freedom of information legislation.

### 16.14.2 The Environment Agency and Information Access

The Water Resources Act 1991 and the Environment Act 1995 make general provision for the Environment Agency to furnish information to appropriate ministers relating to the carrying out of its functions and responsibilities and these are discussed elsewhere.[167] Likewise, the dissemination of information relating to drinking water quality and trade effluent discharges to sewers is discussed in other parts of this work.[168] Also the Agency is subject to relatively specific information-provision duties such as requiring it to provide water undertakers with information relevant to their functions.[169]

Notably also, the Environment Act 1995 makes explicit provision for the disclosure of information obtained by the Agency and others in only relatively restricted circumstances. Hence, notwithstanding any prohibition or restriction imposed by or under any enactment or rule of law, information of any description may be disclosed,

---

[162] Royal Commission on Environmental Pollution (1984) para.2.52.

[163] HM Government, *This Common Inheritance* (Cm.1200, 1990) para.1.20.

[164] Royal Commission on Environmental Pollution (1984) para.6.7.

[165] *Ibid* para.2.75.

[166] HM Government, *This Common Inheritance* (Cm.1200, 1990) para.1.21.

[167] See 6.16 above.

[168] See 17.7.5 below on drinking water information and 11.4 above on trade effluent information.

[169] Under s.203(1) Water Resources Act 1991, and note the reciprocal duty upon undertakers to provide information to the Agency where this is reasonably required (s.203(2)).

(a) by the Agency to a Minister of the Crown, the Scottish Environment Protection Agency or a local enforcing authority,[170]
(b) by a Minister of the Crown to the Agency, another Minister of the Crown or a local enforcing authority, or
(c) by a local enforcing authority to a Minister of the Crown, the Agency or another local enforcing authority.

However, this authorisation for disclosure is specifically stated to be for the purpose of facilitating the carrying out by the Agency of any of its functions, by the Minister of any of his environmental functions or by any local enforcing authority of any of its relevant functions. Where disclosure is made in accordance with these provisions, no civil or criminal liability will arise in consequence of the disclosure.[171]

Moreover, this limited general authorisation for disclosure is subject to certain restrictions. In particular, it will not authorise the disclosure to a local enforcing authority by the Agency or another local enforcing authority of information, the disclosure of which would, in the opinion of a Minister of the Crown, be contrary to the interests of national security; or which was obtained under or by virtue of the Statistics of Trade Act 1947 and which was disclosed to the Agency or any of its officers by the Secretary of State. More generally, no information disclosed to any person under or by virtue of this authorisation may be disclosed by that person to any other person otherwise than in accordance with these provisions, or any provision of any other enactment which authorises or requires the disclosure, if that information is information which relates to a trade secret of any person or which otherwise is or might be commercially confidential in relation to any person, or whose disclosure otherwise than under these provisions would, in the opinion of a Minister of the Crown, be contrary to the interests of national security.[172]

Remarkably perhaps, the Environment Agency does not appear to be subject to any explicit and specific statutory duty, under the 1991 Act at least, to provide general information to the public about the state of water quality and the aquatic environment. This contrasts with the statutory obligation to publish information relating to actual and prospective demand for water and actual and prospective water resources,[173] though

---

[170] 'Local enforcing authority' means (a) any local authority within the meaning of Part IIA of the Environmental Protection Act 1990 (concerned with contaminated land), and the 'relevant functions' of such an authority are its functions under or by virtue of that Part; (b) any local authority within the meaning of Part IV of the Environment Act 1995 (concerned with air quality), and the 'relevant functions' of such an authority are its functions under or by virtue of that Part; (c) in relation to England, any county council for an area for which there are district councils, and the 'relevant functions' of such a county council are its functions under or by virtue of Part IV of the Environment Act 1995; or (d) in relation to England and Wales, any local enforcing authority within the meaning of section 1(7) of the Environmental Protection Act 1990 (concerned with releases of substances into the air), and the 'relevant functions' of such an authority are its functions under or by virtue of Part I of that Act (concerned with integrated pollution control and air pollution control by local authorities) (s.113(5) Environment Act 1995).
[171] s.113(1) Environment Act 1995.
[172] *Ibid* s.113(2)-(3).
[173] s.188 Water Resources Act 1991.

possibly such information might encompass qualitative aspects of potential water supplies. Clearly, water quality information will feature in the Annual Report which the Agency is bound to publish,[174] and general provision of information may fall within the incidental general function of the Agency allowing it to do anything which is calculated to facilitate or is conducive or incidental to the carrying out of its functions.[175] Statutory guidance, in relation to the contribution the Agency should be making to sustainable development, indicates that high quality information and advice on the environment is important and the Agency should, therefore, strive to provide and promulgate clear and readily accessible advice and information on its work and on best environmental practice.[176]

Despite the absence of an explicit statutory duty, there are reasons arising from the guidance, and practical institutional reasons, why the Agency does disseminate information. Moreover, there are further legal reasons, discussed later, why public access *must* be given to certain categories of information. Nonetheless, the absence of an explicit statutory duty to provide pubic information about water quality means that a practical starting point for provision of specific information about local water quality is through the relatively limited system of public registers under the 1991 Act.[177] As will be seen, the limitations of public registers will mean that, for many kinds of information, enquirers must make use of further legal provisions requiring environmental information to be made more generally available.

## 16.15 The Pollution Control Register

The case for freedom of public access to information about the state of the environment has been strongly argued in the United Kingdom over many years. In 1984, the Royal Commission on Environmental Pollution asserted that there should be a presumption in favour of unrestricted access for the public to information which the pollution control authorities obtain or receive by virtue of their statutory powers, with provision for secrecy only in those circumstances where a genuine case for it can be substantiated.[178] This view was endorsed by the Government in its response: 'the Government strongly agrees that . . . secrecy benefits nobody. It cannot be in industry's interests to hide information which does not need to be hidden. The public are bound to think the worst'.[179]

---

[174] Under s.52 Environment Act 1995 and see 6.16 above.

[175] *Ibid* s.37(1)(a).

[176] DoE, MAFF and WO, *The Environment Agency and Sustainable Development* (1996), and see 6.7 above.

[177] Although there is increasing use of electronic access to environmental information. See the discussion of the Environment Agency's pollution inventory at 6.19 above.

[178] Royal Commission on Environmental Pollution (1984) para.2.27.

[179] DoE, *Public Access to Environmental Information* (1986) para.1.5 and see Jenn (1993).

### 16.15.1  *The Contents of the Register*

Until the Control of Pollution Act 1974 water quality information obtained under statutory powers was kept secret, in the sense that it was an offence for it to be disclosed.[180] However, the 1974 Act removed the general prohibition upon disclosure of water information except where such information related to trade secrets.[181] In addition, the Act first provided for public registers of specified information relating to water quality. The registers, which were to be maintained by water authorities, were to contain details of the following matters:

(a) applications for discharge consents;
(b) consents given;
(c) samples of water and effluent taken by the authorities;
(d) information produced by analysis of these samples and steps taken in consequence;
(e) certificates issued by the Secretary of State to exempt applications and consents from publicity; and
(f) notices requiring abstention from certain agricultural practices.

It was the duty of the water authority to secure that these registers were open to inspection by the public free of charge at all reasonable hours and to afford members of the public facilities, on payment of reasonable charges, to obtain copies of entries in the registers.[182] However, the provisions under the 1974 Act allowing for the establishment of registers were not actually brought into effect until 1985.[183] Nonetheless, the public register model was eventually adopted to allow public access to a wide range of environmental information in diverse kinds of public register.[184]

The corresponding provisions, concerning the pollution control register, are now provided for under the Water Resources Act 1991.[185] These require the Environment Agency, in accordance with regulations,[186] to maintain registers containing particulars relating to the following matters:

---

[180] s.12 Rivers (Prevention of Pollution) Act 1961 made it an offence to disclose information obtained under the Rivers (Prevention of Pollution) Acts 1951 and 1961 without the consent of the discharger concerned. s.12 of the 1961 Act remained in force following the enactment of the Control of Pollution Act 1974 but, since it related only to information obtained under the 1951 and 1961 Acts, it became progressively obsolete (see DoE, *Public Access to Environmental Information* (1986) para.4.3).

[181] s.94 Control of Pollution Act 1974.

[182] *Ibid* s.41.

[183] Under the Control of Pollution (Registers) Regulations 1985 (SI 1995 No.813), which provided further details as to the information to be included in the registers, and see 2.13 above. Subsequently, see Control of Pollution (Registers) Regulations 1989 (SI 1989 No.1160).

[184] See DoE, *Environment Facts: A Guide to Using Public Registers of Environmental Information* (1995) which lists some 53 different kinds of register. On other registers maintained by the Environment Agency see Tromans (1996) p.450.

[185] s.190 Water Resources Act 1991, as amended by para.169 Sch.22 Environment Act 1995.

[186] See Control of Pollution (Applications, Appeals and Registers) Regulations 1996 (SI 1996 No.2971), here referred to as '1996 Regulations'. The 1996 Regulations were amended by Reg.8 Anti-Pollution Works Regulations 1999 (SI 1999 No.1006), and are modified in relation to the

(a) notices establishing or varying water quality objectives;[187]

(b) applications for discharge consents or other consents relating to water pollution offences or variation of consents;[188]

(c) discharge consents, or other consents relating to water pollution offences, which have been given, the conditions to which they are subject and variations of such consents;[189]

(d)   (i)   the date, time and place of each sample of water or effluent taken by the Agency for the purposes of the water pollution provisions of the 1991 Act,[190]

     (ii)   information produced by analyses of those samples,

    (iii)   such information with respect to samples of water or effluent taken by any other person, and the analyses of those samples, as is acquired by the Agency for the purposes of the water pollution provisions of the Act; and

    (iv)   the steps taken in consequence of any such information as is mentioned in any of sub-paragraphs (i) to (iii) above;

(e) enforcement notices relating to the contravention of a consent;[191]

(f) revocations of discharge consents;[192]

(g) notices of appeals in respect of consents and related correspondence and representations;[193]

(h) directions given by the Secretary of State in relation to the Agency's functions under the water pollution provisions of the 1991 Act;[194]

(i) convictions for offences relating to control of pollution of water resources of persons who have the benefit of discharge consents;[195]

(j) information obtained or furnished in pursuance of conditions of discharge consents;[196]

(k) works notices;[197]

---

Channel Tunnel Rail Link Act 1996 by Reg.2 Control of Pollution (Channel Tunnel Rail Link) Regulations 1998 (SI 1998 No.1649).

[187] Under s.83 Water Resources Act 1991, and see 14.8 above on water quality objectives.

[188] Under Chapter II of Part III Water Resources Act 1991, and Reg.15(b) 1996 Regulations, and see Ch.10 above on discharge consents.

[189] See Reg.15(d) 1996 Regulations.

[190] See the definition of 'water pollution provisions' at 16.4 above.

[191] Under s.90B Water Resources Act 1991, and see 10.11.1 above.

[192] Under *ibid* para.7 Sch.10, as amended.

[193] Under *ibid* s.91, and see Reg.15(i) 1996 Regulations, and see 10.9 above.

[194] Under s.191A(2) Water Resources Act 1991, though Reg.15(j) 1996 Regulations exempts from this directions in relation to information affecting national security under s.191A(2), and see 6.2 above on ministerial directions to the Agency.

[195] That is, convictions under Part III Water Resources Act 1991, and see Reg.15(k) 1996 Regulations which specifies that this information must include the name of the offender, the date of conviction, the penalty imposed, the costs, if any, awarded against the offender and the name of the Court.

[196] Reg.15(l) 1996 Regulations specifies that this information concerns the nature, origin, composition, temperature, volume and rate of discharges, and see 16.8 above on conditions in discharge consents requiring information to be provided.

[197] Under s.161A Water Resources Act 1991, and see 13.2.2 above on works notices.

(l)   appeals against works notices;[198]

(m)  convictions for offences relating to non-compliance with a works notice;[199]

(n)   such other matters relating to the quality of water or the pollution of water as may be prescribed by the Secretary of State.[200]

Where information of any description is excluded from the register on ground of commercial confidentiality,[201] a statement must be entered in the register indicating the existence of information of that description.[202]

In addition to the particulars that must be included in the pollution control register under the Water Resources Act 1991, further matters are provided for under the Control of Pollution (Applications, Appeals and Registers) Regulations 1996.[203] As well as modifying the wording of some of the requirements, the 1996 Regulations add three further headings to the pollution control register. These are:

(o)   information corresponding to that under (d) above with respect to samples of water or effluent taken by any other person, and the analysis of those samples, acquired by the Agency from that person under arrangements made by the Agency, for the purpose of any of the water pollution provisions of the 1991 Act, including any steps taken by that person in consequence of the results of the analysis of any sample;[204]

(p)   prohibition notices served;[205] and

(q)   information which was entered on the registers under the Control of Pollution (Registers) Regulations 1989.[206]

The 1996 Regulations also provide further details as to when information is to be entered in the register by the Agency, in most instances allowing 28 days for this. Additionally, the Agency must keep records in the register showing the dates on which particulars were entered, and to index the register in a way which facilitates access to the particulars entered.[207] The Agency is not required to keep monitoring information for more than four years after entry on the register or to keep other information which has been superseded by later information for more than four years after entry on the register.[208]

---

[198] Under *ibid* s.161C.

[199] Under *ibid* s.161D.

[200] *Ibid* s.190(1), as amended by para.168 Sch.22 Environment Act 1995.

[201] Under s.191B Water Resources Act 1991, and see 16.15.2 below on commercially confidential information.

[202] *Ibid* s.190(1A), as inserted by para.169 Sch.22 Environment Act 1995.

[203] SI 1996 No.2971.

[204] *Ibid* Reg.15(d).

[205] *Ibid* Reg.15(f), concerning prohibition notices served under s.86(1) Water Resources Act 1991, and see 9.11 above on prohibition notices.

[206] *Ibid* Reg.15(m).

[207] *Ibid* Reg.16.

[208] *Ibid* Reg.17.

Also relevant are the Groundwater Regulations 1998, which provide for the entry in the pollution control register of a range of matters concerning authorisations, applications, variations and revocations of notices, monitoring information, convictions, determinations by the Agency, and approved codes of practice in relation to the Regulations.[209] The Water Protection Zone (River Dee Catchment) (Procedural and Other Provisions) Regulations 1999 provide for a separate register of various matters relating to protection zone consent within the River Dee Catchment Water Protection Zone.[210]

Other than in relation to matters of national security and commercially confidential information, the general principle of free public access to environmental information applies. Hence, it is the duty of the Agency to secure that the contents of the pollution control register are available, at all reasonable times, for inspection by the public free of charge. Also members of the public are to be afforded reasonable facilities by the Agency for obtaining, on payment of a reasonable charge, copies of entries in the register.[211]

### 16.15.2 *National Security and Commercially Confidential Information*

The two main exceptions to the inclusion of information in the pollution control register relate to national security and commercially confidential information. In respect of the former, no information shall be included in the register if, in the opinion of the Secretary of State, the inclusion of that information would be contrary to the interests of national security. For that purpose the Secretary of State may give the Agency directions either specifying information, or descriptions of information, to be excluded, or information to be referred for his determination. The Agency is to notify the Secretary of State where information is excluded in pursuance of any direction. In relation to allegedly confidential information, a person may give notice to the Secretary of State specifying the information, and notify the Agency of this, and that information is then to be excluded from the register until the Secretary of State has determined that it should be included.[212]

Whilst the presumption is that information affecting national security falls into that category until the Secretary of State determines otherwise, in respect of commercially confidential information, for most purposes, the determination rests with the Agency. 'Commercially confidential information', for these purposes, means information which would prejudice to an unreasonable degree the interests of an individual or

---

[209] Reg.22 Groundwater Regulations 1998 (SI 1998 No.2746) and see 13.6 above on groundwater protection.
[210] Reg.13 Water Protection Zone (River Dee Catchment) (Procedural and Other Provisions) Regulations 1999 (SI 1999 No.916) and see 13.4.1 above on the River Dee Catchment Water Protection Zone.
[211] s.190(2) Water Resources Act 1991; and, on the practical use of registers, see Burton (1989) and Rowan-Robinson, Ross, Walton and Rothnie (1996).
[212] s.191A Water Resources Act 1991, as inserted by para.170 Sch.22 Environment Act 1995.

business if it were to be included in the register. Hence, no information relating to the affairs of an individual or business may, without the consent of the person or body concerned, be included in the register so long as the information is commercially confidential and is not required to be included in the register in pursuance of a direction of the Secretary of State. For this purpose, the Secretary of State may give the Agency directions as to specified information, or descriptions of information, which the public interest requires to be included in the register notwithstanding that the information may be commercially confidential.[213]

Other than where information falls within the scope of a direction given by the Secretary of State or an application is made to have the information excluded from the register on grounds of commercial confidentiality,[214] the Agency is bound to determine whether the information is commercially confidential. Otherwise, where the Agency has been supplied with information which might be commercially confidential, the Agency must give notice to the person or business to which it relates that it is required to be included in the register, give a reasonable opportunity for objections or representations to be made, and take these into account before determining whether the information is commercially confidential. Where, in either case, it is determined that the information is not commercially confidential, it may be included in the register subject to an appeal being made to the Secretary of State. Where information is excluded from the register it must be treated as ceasing to be commercially confidential after expiry of four years from the date of it first being excluded, but application may be made for the information to continue to be excluded.[215]

Where information has been included in the register which ought not to have been included, on grounds of either national security or commercial confidentiality, the Secretary of State is empowered to give a direction to the Agency requiring the removal of that information from the register.[216]

### 16.15.3 Register Information and Legal Proceedings

A key legal question concerns the uses to which information obtained from the pollution control register may be put. Specifically, the issue is whether this information may be used as a basis for private legal proceedings for a principal water pollution offence where, for example, information from the register indicates that a discharge consent condition has not been adhered to. An illustration of this use of register information is to be found in *Wales* v *Thames Water Authority*[217] where evidence drawn from the

---

[213] s.191B(1), (7) and (11) Water Resources Act 1991, as inserted by para.170 Sch.22 Environment Act 1995, and generally see Fairley (1993).

[214] That is, information furnished to the Agency in relation to an application for, or variation of, a discharge consent, compliance with such a consent, or a notice requiring information to be provided, under s.202 Water Resources Act 1991, and see 6.16 above on information notices.

[215] s.191B(2), (4), (5) and (8) Water Resources Act 1991.

[216] s.190(4) *ibid*, as inserted by para.169 Sch.22 Environment Act 1995.

[217] Aylesbury Magistrates' Court, 14 May 1987, reported in (1988) 1(3) *Environmental Law* p.3; and see Jackson (1988) and Turner (1988).

pollution register showed a series of breaches of a sewage works discharge consent. On the basis of this evidence alone, a magistrates' court conviction was secured in private proceedings brought by the Anglers' Co-operative Association. However, it must be noted that, as a decision of a lower court, the ruling in the case does not serve as an authoritative precedent. Moreover, the decision is dubious because, at the time of the facts, information about water quality should not have been admissible in legal proceedings unless collected by way of a formal tripartite sampling procedure[218] and this did not appear to have been followed in relation to the information drawn from the register.[219]

However, since the repeal of the formal sampling requirement,[220] the use of information from the pollution register to support a private prosecution might have become a legal possibility, depending upon the source of the information from the register that is used. Whilst information that is collected by the Agency would seem to be capable of being used unproblematically, information which is supplied to the Agency by a discharger in compliance with a self-monitoring condition in a discharge consent, may give rise to the evidential difficulties in respect of self-incrimination discussed above.[221]

### 16.15.4 Use and Effectiveness of the Pollution Control Register

Any attempt to gauge the effectiveness of the pollution control register must depend upon what the purpose of the register is perceived to be. There is no doubt that a wide range of water quality information is made publicly available, and if the object of introducing the register was to avoid secrecy then the fact that, in principle, this information is generally available is a justification for the register whether or not, in practice, anyone actually seeks to consult it. On the other hand, if the intention behind the register is that it should allow individuals to become better informed as to the state of their local aquatic environment, then the actual use which is made of the register, and its user-friendliness, is a critical issue.

Equally, it may be enquired, *which* users is the register supposed to be friendly towards, in that members of the general public may have quite different information needs from scientifically or technically qualified persons consulting the register. Allowing public access to information provides no guarantee that those to whom access is given will have the capacity to interpret that information in any meaningful way. Particularly where complex chemical information is involved, information from an analysis of the state of particular waters may convey no meaning unless it is possible to make an informed comparison between the actual and the desired physical, chemical and ecological state of those waters.

---

[218] See 16.9 above on the former tripartite sampling requirement.
[219] See Mumma (1993) who notes, at p.196, that this point was not contested.
[220] Under s.111(1) Environment Act 1995, and see 16.9 above on this.
[221] See 16.13 above on self-incrimination.

Effectiveness of presentation must depend upon readership, and yet the legal requirements appear to make no assumptions as to who the readers of the registers are likely to be.

An early study of the operation of the pollution control register, examining use during the first four years of its existence, found that the public response was disappointing. Very little actual use of the register was made and, of those who did seek to consult it, many were from commercial concerns seeking to obtain the names of potential customers. Although, a significant proportion of enquires came from environmental groups, the numbers of members of the public consulting the register was very small indeed. It was concluded that this was attributable to lack of awareness due to the absence of advertising; the problem of access to principal offices of the former water authorities where registers were held; obtaining access to the data itself and the associated costs of these activities; the comprehensibility of the data to a 'non-expert' user; the sufficiency of data which originally excluded various kinds of water quality information; and data usability for different categories of user.[222]

A more recent study of the use of environmental registers generally, including the pollution control register, tended to confirm the earlier survey in relation to the low level of use of environmental registers. Although environmental protection authorities are not obliged to ask the purpose for which enquiries are sought, an impressionistic view was that the largest group of those using the registers were consultants, looking for customers to whom to sell technology or services, with the only other identifiable group thought to be environmental researchers. The absence of a public 'culture of participation' was attributable, in part, to continuing difficulties of awareness, access, cost and comprehensibility identified in the earlier study.[223]

### 16.15.5 Alternative Methods of Providing Information

To some extent the limitations of public awareness about water quality, and the state of the environment generally, is being addressed by various methods by which general information about the environment may be made publicly available: the publication of general reports, the use of consultation and the general opening of deliberations and decision-making by environmental authorities.[224] Significantly, also there has been increasingly effective use made of electronically accessible information by the Environment Agency, in some instances allowing members of the public to access environmental quality data relating to local rivers and

---

[222] See Burton (1989) and see also John (1995) on radioactive substances registers.

[223] Rowan-Robinson, Ross, Walton and Rothnie (1996).

[224] See, *ENDS Report* 290 (1999) p.8 and see Environment Agency website for papers relating to meetings of the Agency's Board (www.environment-agency.gov.uk). See also Local Government (Access to Information) Act 1985, which allows for a public right of access to council, committee and sub-committee meetings and the papers and background papers relating to these meetings, subject to certain exceptions for confidential and exempt information.

industrial installations.[225] Also there is greater openness to be seen in the activities of private concerns with an environmental involvement who make increasing use of exhibitions and open-days, the inclusion of environmental information in corporate publications, along with a general willingness to respond informatively to requests for environmental information.

However, the practical issue remains that different methods of making information available are appropriate for different kinds of user and different kinds of information. The likelihood is that there is no single method of making environmental information available which is likely to meet the needs of all enquirers. Consequently, the limitations of the system of registers, including the pollution control register, must be recognised. The register serves only a limited role which is appropriate only for those users seeking information of a kind which must be incorporated in a register, in the form which the register provides and under the conditions of access on which the register system operates.[226]

## 16.16 The Environmental Information Directive

Since the first national initiative in providing a public right of access to water quality information by the pollution control register, profound developments have taken place in relation to access to environmental information in the European Community as a consequence of the enactment of the Environmental Information Directive.[227] The main object of the Directive is to ensure freedom of access to, and dissemination of, information on the environment held by public authorities and to set out the basic terms and conditions on which such information should be made available.[228]

For the purposes of the Directive, 'information relating to the environment' is defined to mean any available information in written, visual, aural or data-base form on the state of water, air, soil, fauna, flora, land and natural sites, and on activities, including those which give rise to nuisances such as noise, or measures adversely affecting, or likely to so affect these, and on activities or measures designed to protect these, including administrative measures and environmental management programmes. 'Public authorities' means any public administration at national, regional or local level with responsibilities, and possessing

---

[225] See www.environment-agency.gov.uk,'Your Environment', 'Your Backyard'.

[226] Although there appears to be no legal reason why the register should not be made electronically accessible.

[227] Directive 90/313/EEC on freedom of access to information on the environment, see House of Lords Select Committee on the European Communities, *Freedom of Access to Information on the Environment* (1990) and (1996) and for general discussion see Bakkenist (1994); Hallo (1996); Kramer (1992) Ch.14; and Wheeler (1994).

[228] Art.1 Environmental Information Directive.

information, relating to the environment with the exception of bodies acting in a judicial or legislative capacity.[229]

Under the Directive, Member States are bound to ensure that public authorities make available information relating to the environment to any natural or legal person at that person's request, and without the enquirer having to prove an interest, and define the practical arrangements under which such information is effectively made available.[230] However, the general duty to make such information available is subject to the qualification that the request may be refused where it affects specified matters.[231] Additionally, a request for information may be refused where it would involve the supply of unfinished documents or data or internal communications, or where the request is manifestly unreasonable or formulated in too general a manner.[232]

On the other hand, there are limitations beyond the explicit exceptions. For example, the Directive does not apply to Community institutions themselves,[233] and does not explicitly define 'environment' to cover matters relating specifically to environmental health where this cannot be brought within any of the specified elements of environmental information. Perhaps most crucially, the Directive does not create any obligation upon any public body actually to collect any particular information, but only to make available environmental information which is 'held' by that body. The practical implication of this is that the right of access will only be as extensive as the legal duties upon bodies to collect information and, whilst a duty to gather information is imposed by many environmental directives and national provisions, it is likely that much, potentially useful, environmental information will be unavailable because of this limitation.

## 16.17 Implementation of the Environmental Information Directive

The Environmental Information Regulations 1992[234] implement the Environmental Information Directive by requiring that a relevant person, who holds any information which relates to the environment, must make that information available to every person who requests it.[235] 'Relevant persons', for the purposes of the Regulations, are Ministers of the Crown, Government departments, local authorities and other persons carrying out functions of public administration at a national, regional or local level, who for the purposes of or in connection with their functions, have

---

[229] *Ibid* Art.2.

[230] *Ibid* Art.3(1).

[231] *Ibid* Art.3(2) and see the discussion of these matters at 16.17 below.

[232] *Ibid* Art.3(3).

[233] See Commission Decision on public access to Commission documents (94/90 OJ L46, 18 February 1994, p.58) and Case T-105/95 *WWF (UK)* v *European Commission* [1997] Env LR 242.

[234] SI 1992 No.3240 and see Environmental Information (Amendment) Regulations 1998 (SI 1998 No.1447), and see DoE, *Freedom of Access to Information on the Environment: Guidance on the Implementation of the Environmental Information Regulations 1992 in Great Britain* (1992) hereafter referred to as 'the *Guidance*'. See also Birtles (1993) and Pugh and Moor (1994).

[235] Reg.3(1) Environmental Information Regulations 1992.

responsibilities in relation to the environment, and bodies with public responsibility for the environment which fall under the control of the bodies or persons mentioned.[236] Hence, a range of bodies likely to possess information relating to the aquatic environment would be encompassed, including the Department of the Environment, Transport and the Regions, the Environment Agency, English Nature and the Countryside Council for Wales, local authorities, along with executive agencies and other statutory bodies such as the Broads Authority. Also notable, is the fact that every Minister, Government department and public body is deemed to have responsibilities relating to the environment in respect of countryside and landscape issues.[237] However, neither the Regulations nor the accompanying *Guidance* give any definitive list of all the bodies and persons that will be subject to the Regulations. It is suggested that the onus is unsatisfactorily placed on some organisations to take their own view as to whether they fall into the categories identified and constitute 'relevant persons' for these purposes.[238]

The basic obligation to make environmental information available to enquirers involves a duty to respond to a request for information as soon as possible and, at the latest, within two months. Where the response to the request involves a refusal to make information available, there is an obligation to state the refusal in writing along with a statement of the reasons for the refusal. In respect of the latter, refusal of a request will be allowed where the request for information is manifestly unreasonable or formulated in too general a manner, otherwise the request will have to fall within one of the exceptions discussed below. Arrangements made for making information available of may include the imposition of a charge in respect of the costs reasonably attributable to the supply of information, but the obligation to make information available will not require it to be made available except in a form and at a time that is reasonable. Subject to the exceptions, any statutory provision which imposes a restriction on the disclosure of information by any person is not to apply where that information falls within the scope of the Regulations.[239]

A range of exceptions are provided to the right to information, following the matters that are similarly provided for under the Directive. These apply where information *may* be treated as confidential, because its disclosure

(a) would affect international relations, national defence or public security;

---

[236] *Ibid* Reg.2(2) and (3).

[237] Under s.11 Countryside Act 1968, which provides that, in the exercise of their functions relating to land under any enactment every Minister, government department and public body shall have regard to the desirability of conserving the natural beauty and amenity of the countryside and, for these purposes, a 'public body' is defined to include any local authority or statutory undertaker, and any trustees, commissioners, board or other person, who, as a public body and not for their own profit act under any enactment for the improvement of any place or the production or supply of any commodity or service (and see the *Guidance* para.11).

[238] See the *Guidance* para.12.

[239] Reg.3 Environmental Information Regulations 1992.

(b) would affect matters which are, or have been, an issue in any legal proceedings, enquiry or investigation relating to these;
(c) would affect the confidentiality of the deliberations of any relevant person;
(d) would involve the supply of a document or record which is still in the course of completion or an internal communication of a relevant person; or
(e) would affect the confidentiality of matters to which any commercial or industrial confidentiality attaches, including intellectual property.

In addition, in certain situations, information *must* be treated as confidential if disclosure

(a) would contravene a statutory provision, other than one seeking to restrict its disclosure, or would involve a breach of agreement;
(b) where the information is personal information concerning an individual who has not given consent to the disclosure;
(c) where the information has been supplied voluntarily and the person supplying it has not given consent to the disclosure; or
(d) where the disclosure would increase the likelihood of damage to the environment affecting anything to which the information relates.[240]

In respect of existing rights to information, such as where information was previously made available under an environmental register,[241] the Regulations seek to secure that the requirements arising under the Directive should prevail by imposing similar requirements. Hence, information from a register must be provided as soon as possible and not later than two months after the request was made. Where there is a refusal to provide requested information, that refusal is to be made in writing and to specify the reasons for the refusal, and no charge that exceeds a reasonable amount may be made for the provision of information from a register.[242]

Whilst the Directive provides that a person whose request for information has been unreasonably refused or inadequately answered is entitled to seek a judicial or administrative review of the matter,[243] the Regulations are not explicit on this matter. The *Guidance* indicates that an aggrieved individual should seek to assert statutory rights of appeal where these exist, to appeal to the head of the body concerned or to make use of other remedies such as an appeal to the ombudsman where a decision of a local authority is in dispute. As a last resort, judicial review proceedings,

---

[240] Reg.4 Environmental Information Regulations 1992, as amended by Environmental Information (Amendment) Regulations 1988 (SI 1998 No.1447).
[241] See 16.15 above on the pollution register.
[242] Reg.5 Environmental Information Regulations 1992.
[243] Art.4 Environmental Information Directive.

possibly followed by a reference to the European Court of Justice, are suggested as remedies.[244]

### 16.17.1 The Impact of the Directive and Regulations

There are some initial indications that the Environmental Information Directive and implementing Regulations have been helpful in various contexts where individuals have been seeking information for the purpose of challenging decisions of public bodies. In one instance, a threat of legal proceedings against the Crown Estates Commission was made by objectors to a proposed mining venture that would have involved a discharge of effluent into a local river. The prospect of such proceedings appeared to be sufficient to cause the Commissioners to divulge information about the inadequate financial assurances that were to have been incorporated into a mining lease for the purposes of securing against pollution and the satisfactory restoration of the site.[245]

However, substantial evidence that the national Regulations are not satisfactorily achieving the objectives of the Directive was considered by the House of Lords Select Committee on the European Communities,[246] in an enquiry into the working of the Directive in the United Kingdom.[247] Whilst industrial commentators thought that the Directive had been satisfactorily transposed into national law, a body of non-governmental, legal, academic and environmental commentators raised significant criticisms. Broadly, these were that the impact of the Directive had been weakened in transposition by Regulations which were in some respects broader and less precise than the Directive or failed to clarify matters on which the Directive lacked precision and that there was an insufficient guidance from government as to several areas such as the definition of 'relevant person' and 'reasonable cost'.[248]

A particular difficulty relevant to the availability of information on the aquatic environment was the status of water and sewerage undertakers as 'relevant persons' under the Regulations. The water companies maintained that they were outside of the meaning of bodies with 'public responsibility for the environment' or 'under the control of public bodies' because of

---

[244] *Guidance* para.72 and see Roderick (1996).

[245] Cooper (1995). See also *R v British Coal Corporation ex parte Ibstock Building Products Ltd* [1995] Env LR 277. For a subsequent decision, concerning information about a road project, see *R v Secretary of State for Environment, Transport and the Regions and Midland Expressway Ltd, ex parte Alliance Against the Birmingham Northern Relief Road and Others* [1999] Env LR 447. In the European Court of Justice see Case C-321/96 *Wilhelm Mecklenburg v Kreis Pinneberg – Der Landrat* [1998] ECR I-3809 and Case C-217/97 *Commission v Germany* [1999] ECR I-5087.

[246] House of Lords Select Committee on the European Communities, *Freedom of Access to Information on the Environment* (1996).

[247] Shortly before the date at which Member States were obliged to report to the Commission on the Directive at the end of 1996, under Art.8 Environmental Information Directive.

[248] House of Lords Select Committee on the European Communities, *Freedom of Access to Information on the Environment* (1996) para.10.

their privatised status.[249] By contrast, others maintained that matters of ownership should not make any difference to the question of whether a body has a public responsibility for the environment.[250] On this matter, the *Guidance* was found to be unsatisfactory in failing to provide an explicit statement as to which bodies were within the scope of the Regulations. The House of Lords Committee felt that this had created a perception that compliance with the Regulations was optional for certain bodies and created an 'excuse' for water services companies to maintain that they were outside the scope of the Directive.[251] The Committee observed that it was 'bizarre' that water service companies should persist with the view that they were neither controlled, in the sense of having statutory duties, nor had public responsibilities for the environment. In general terms, the right of public access to environmental information should apply to all environmental information generated and held for public purposes, irrespective of whether the body that holds the information is public or private. Hence, no good reason was found why public utilities, including those providing water services, should not be 'relevant persons' for the purposes of the Regulations.[252]

The meaning of 'information relating to the environment' also raised difficulties in respect of the activities of water and sewerage undertakers. It was not clear whether operational matters, such as financial details of plans and programmes for the replacing of sewage outfalls, which have a direct bearing upon the aquatic environment, fell within the scope of the Regulations.[253] In relation to this, the House of Lords Committee recommended that the wording of the Directive should be revised to remove uncertainty as to the extent to which financial and economic information falls within the meaning of environmental information.[254] Also, numerous particular examples were given in evidence to the Committee of instances where water and sewerage undertakers made dubious use of the exemptions from disclosure under the Regulations in claiming that information about lead in a drinking water distribution system, about breaches of trade effluent consents and the supply of sewerage sludge for agricultural purpose were within the confidentiality exemption.[255] Commentators also noted the anomalous position with regard to trade effluent discharges to sewers,[256] which is such that the public are only entitled to inspect copies of trade effluent consents and agreements, with no provision to allow copies of these to be made, and no

---

[249] See the discussion of water privatisation at 2.16 above and see the discussion of 'direct effect' at 4.16 above.

[250] House of Lords Select Committee on the European Communities, *Freedom of Access to Information on the Environment* (1996) paras.12-15, and *Evidence* pp.77-78 *Memorandum by Friends of the Earth* para.3.2.

[251] House of Lords, Select Committee on the European Communities, *Freedom of Access to Information on the Environment* (1996) paras.50 to 51.

[252] *Ibid* paras.58 and 59.

[253] *Ibid Evidence, Memorandum by Friends of the Earth* paras.4.1.5, 4.2.1 and 4.2.2.

[254] *Ibid* para.48.

[255] *Ibid Evidence* p.76 *Memorandum by Friends of the Earth* para.3.1

[256] Under ss.196 and 206 Water Industry Act 1991, and see Ch.11 above on trade effluent discharges to sewers.

monitoring data required to be placed on the public register.[257] The contention of sewerage undertakers that they fell outside the scope of the Regulations, or that the information fell within the confidentiality exceptions, had the consequence that this information was not made available whereas, as has been seen, corresponding information concerning direct discharges to controlled waters has been provided for under the pollution control register for some years.[258]

Amongst other matters, many of the shortcomings identified by the House of Lords Committee are taken up in proposals for the replacement of the Directive which have recently been put forward by the European Commission.[259] The proposals involve a revised and extended definition of 'environmental information' to align it with that provided for in the Aarhus Convention[260] and to make it explicit that economic analyses and assumptions used in environmental policies, plans and programmes would be included. In addition, the proposed new Directive would be more widely applicable to public administrative bodies, encompassing bodies providing public services relating directly or indirectly to the environment and under the control of a public administrative body and any body entrusted with the provision of services of general economic interest which affect or are likely to affect the environment. An effect of this would be to clarify that water services companies in England and Wales would be subject to the Directive. Other amendments seek to improve access and disclosure arrangements, to narrow the scope for exceptions to disclosure to be claimed, to provide more effective rights of appeal and to encourage active dissemination of environmental information.

## 16.18 The Aarhus Convention

It is evident that some major changes may be in prospect concerning rights of access to water and environmental information due to both international and national developments. At the international level, the United Nations Economic Commission for Europe Convention on Access to Information, Public Participation and Decision Making and Access to Justice in Environmental Matters was adopted by European Environment Ministers at a meeting in Aarhus in Denmark in June 1998 and will come into effect when ratified by 16 countries. The Convention makes important provision for the collection and disclosure of environmental information which exceed the requirements of the Environmental Information Directive in

---

[257] House of Lords Select Committee on the European Communities, *Freedom of Access to Information on the Environment* (1996) *Evidence, Memorandum by the Foundation for International Environmental Law and Development (FIELD) and Earth Rights: The Environmental Law and Resource Centre* p.135.

[258] Generally see DoE, *Government Response to the House of Lords Select Committee Report on Freedom of Access to Information on the Environment* (1997)

[259] *Report from the Commission to the Council and the European Parliament on the Experience Gained in the Application of Council Directive 90/313/EEC of 7 June 1990, on Freedom of Access to Information on the Environment*, COM (2000) 400 final.

[260] Discussed in 16.18 below.

certain respects. Significantly, the definition of 'environmental information' under the Convention is wider than under the Directive.

In addition, the Convention provides for access to justice where environmental information is withheld by requiring that enquirers must have access to an adequate, effective and fair review procedure before a court of law or another independent and impartial body. Moreover, it is stipulated that the enquirer will be allowed access to an expeditious procedure, that is free of charge or inexpensive.[261] Whilst, in all these respects the Convention appears to extend the right of access to environmental information beyond that provided for under the Directive, there is one key respect in which the Convention is narrower. This is that the Convention provides for no mechanism for securing compliance with, or enforcement of, its provisions. Consequently, until the Convention is ratified by the European Community, the possibility of access to the European Court of Justice may continue to mean that the Directive remains procedurally important in practice despite its narrower scope.

### 16.19 The Freedom of Information Act 2000

At a national level, there have been important recent developments with regard to access to official information which will bring out major changes to the regime for access to information held by public bodies generally, including access to environmental and water quality information. The Freedom of Information Act 2000 represents a significant change to the regime for access to government information generally. However, its impact may be less substantial in relation to environmental information due to the various measures that have already been introduced, and discussed above, in relation to this category of information.

Broadly, the purpose of the Freedom of Information Act 2000 is to create a statutory public right of access to recorded information held by public authorities and to specify the conditions which need to be fulfilled before an authority is obliged to comply with a request for access. Generally, public authorities are required to disclose information which is requested, normally within twenty working days, though they will be entitled to charge fees for providing information and must state the basis for refusal of a request where information is not provided. However, in relation to categories of 'exempt information' the requirements to disclose information will not apply.

A fairly lengthy list of exemptions are provided for in relation to matters concerning national security, defence and international relations, safety of the individual and the public, the integrity of decision-making and policy advice processes, commercial interests, law enforcement and the protection of personal information and information supplied in confidence. Some of the exemptions apply to classes of information, others rely on the application of a prejudice test or other adverse consequences of disclosure

---

[261] *Ibid* Art.9.

and the Secretary of State is given power to create new exemptions. The exercise of the right of access to information will be regulated by an Information Commissioner who will be bound to consider applications for rulings that public authorities have not acted in accordance with the Act and investigative and enforcement powers are provided for in relation to this. Either an applicant or a public authority may appeal to an Information Tribunal in relation to a determination by the Information Commissioner and limited rights of appeal to a court of law are allowed for where a point of law is at issue.

Regrettably, the Act does not appear to resolve the present uncertainties about rights of access to information held by water and sewerage undertakers, since it is unspecific as to whether they are 'public authorities', though there is a power for the Secretary of State to provide for this to the extent that undertakers carry out public functions. Other concerns are that the test which is to be applied to exempt disclosure of information where this has 'prejudicial effect' may be too generous in allowing grounds for information to be withheld.

On the other hand, the new measures may be beneficial in that they envisage that public authorities will make information available in accordance with a specified scheme of charges, which should address past allegations of public bodies overcharging for environmental information and thereby imposing a practical impediment to access. Also significant is the incorporation of specific mechanism for investigating complaints about failure to disclose information and enforcement mechanisms relating to this. In the environmental context, this would be a clear improvement upon the present mechanism for challenges to be pursued by way of, potentially lengthy and expensive, judicial review proceedings. Also of specific relevance to environmental matters are provisions empowering the Secretary of State to make Regulations to implement the Aarhus Convention insofar as it relates to the provision of access to environmental information. It is envisaged that Regulations made for this purpose will eventually replace the Environmental Information Regulations 1992, implementing the European Community Environmental Information Directive.

# Chapter 17

# DRINKING WATER QUALITY

## 17.1 Introduction

Unlike the legal provisions discussed elsewhere in this book, the subject matter of this chapter is the range of measures governing the quality of water for one particular use, as drinking water. The concern, therefore, is on the quality of water for its most important human use - providing a sufficiently healthy potable supply - and on the quite distinctive institutional and regulatory arrangements that are intended to meet this objective. Quite how stringent the standards for drinking water quality should be is, however, a matter of some debate. For example, recent evidence suggests that the much-publicised aluminium contamination incident at Camelford in 1988 may have had more serious consequences than at first conceded and may have led to serious damage to human health.[1] But balanced against a concern with preventing or removing impurities, and taking a precautionary approach to regulation, is the fact that, as has been judicially observed, 'pure $H_2O$ distilled of all other ingredients . . . would, indeed, be a most unappetising and unsatisfactory liquid.'[2] There are instances, such as where water if fluoridated,[3] where substances are purposefully added to drinking water in the interests of improving public health, while the so-called 'hygiene hypothesis' holds that exposure to certain levels of 'impurities' may in fact be beneficial to health in regulating the action of the immune system.[4]

Official statistics for the quality of public drinking water indicate near complete compliance with standards established primarily at EC level, at least as far as statistical compliance within water supply zones is concerned.[5] On the other hand, any single failure in a supply zone, while not statistically significant, may lead to large numbers of households being supplied with water below the legal quality limits. While accounting for only a small proportion of water supplied, concerns have also been raised about the quality of private water supplies.[6]

The considerable cost implications of delivering drinking water quality have also been high on the political and regulatory agenda.[7] The past

---

[1] Altmann, et al (1999). On Camelford see 17.11 below.

[2] *Attorney-General of New Zealand (on the relation of R. R. Lewis and E. B. Elliott)* v *Lower Hutt City Corporation* [1964] AC 1469 per Lord Upjohn at p.1481.

[3] On water fluoridation see 17.8 below.

[4] This may also have consequence for drinking water regulation which is not directed towards microbiological wholesomeness, such as the judicial interpretation given to the 'unfit for human consumption' offence, discussed at 17.7.7 below.

[5] Drinking Water Inspectorate, *Drinking Water 1999* (2000) indicates a global figure of 99.82% compliance.

[6] See, e.g. 'Private water gets health warning', *Water Magazine*, 17 September 1999, p.4.

[7] See generally Ch.7 above.

decade has seen a considerable increase in water charges, in part to secure compliance with EC-driven standards such as those for pesticides and nitrate, and the next decade will see further expenditure, primarily to comply with reductions in permitted levels of lead. Issues relating to the quality of drinking water supplies are also raised by the prospect of 'common carriage' in the water industry. The prospect of someone other than a water undertaker putting water into its supply network raises obvious concerns about liability for supplying contaminated water, as well as broader environmental concerns relating to large scale water transfers between hydrogeologically different catchments.[8]

The chapter first considers some general issues in relation to the nature of water supplies and setting standards for drinking water quality, and outlines the present legal and administrative responsibilities, especially the role of the lead regulatory agency, the Drinking Water Inspectorate (DWI). Strategic provisions that determine, generally, whether surface waters may be used for human consumption and the minimum treatment methods necessary are then outlined. This is followed by looking at the range of standards which actually determine whether water for public supply is 'wholesome' or 'fit for human consumption', various provisions concerning monitoring, and the law relating to the fluoridation of public water supplies. Turning to private water supplies, the central functions of local authorities are then discussed, before consideration of the range of provisions intended to ensure the quality both of public and private supplies, in particular, specification and process standards governing the supply of water to premises, and general offences concerning the contamination of drinking water. The chapter then examines the range of statutory and civil remedies where 'unwholesome' water is supplied, and practice and procedure concerning enforcement. The chapter concludes with brief discussion of the law relating to 'special waters' such as natural mineral waters and bottled waters.

## 17.2 Background and Drinking Water Standards

### 17.2.1 Water Supplies and Treatment Methods

In England and Wales, 70% of the public water supply comes from surface waters, with the remainder coming from groundwater. Only in the South East of England is more water taken from aquifers than surface waters for supply. Although around 36% of abstracted water is put into the supply system, only a small proportion of this is actually drunk by humans, the remainder being used for other domestic, or commercial, purposes.[9] Around 99% of water for drinking is supplied by water undertakers (that is, both the water companies privatised in 1989 and the statutory water

---

[8] See 7.10.1 above on common carriage generally and 17.7 below on criminal liability for sub-standard public supplies.

[9] See the 'State of the Environment' information at www.environment-agency.gov.uk

supply companies),[10] the remainder coming from private supplies such as wells.

A range of factors may affect drinking water quality.[11] A supply, or potential supply, may be contaminated through human action or impaired through natural processes.[12] Supplies will generally require treatment, which will usually involve not merely the physical removal of impurities (e.g. by settlement or filtration) but also the addition of substances such as chlorine, chloramine or ozone for disinfection, or aluminium sulphate for flocculation. Other processes such as ion exchanging to remove pesticides,[13] or the blending of supplies to dilute contaminants, may also be used. The method of transporting supplies to the consumer may also impact on drinking water quality, for example by contamination with lead in pipes or other substances used to line or construct pipes.[14] Finally, quality may be affected by actions taken on consumers' premises, most notably through domestic supply pipes or plumbing systems containing lead.

As noted above, however, securing adequate drinking water quality is not simply a matter of removing everything apart from pure water molecules from supplies, although for practical reasons the large-scale provision of public water supplies has tended to be concerned with the removal of impurities. As the case of water fluoridation illustrates, adding substances *to* potable supplies is very much a live issue.[15]

### 17.2.2 Standards for Drinking Water

Until 1989[16] there were no statutory standards at national level for drinking water. Instead, standard setting displayed many of the classic features of the national preference for flexibility, reliance on often qualitative standards and the use of administrative guidance rather than binding legal rules on the use of the best practicable means to provide an adequate quality of supplies.

For example, advice from the Ministry of Health in 1948 spoke of a range of practical considerations that water undertakers should take, advising that they should 'carefully consider their arrangements and take appropriate steps in the light of the circumstances of their undertaking to

---

[10] On these two classes of water undertakers see 7.6.1 above.

[11] See generally Gray (1994).

[12] DETR, *Cryptosporidium in Water Supplies* (1998), on which see *ENDS Report* 266 (1997) p.6.

[13] The extent to which such processes are funded by the consumer may be thought to violate the polluter pays principle, on which see 4.7.3 above.

[14] The latest report of the Drinking Water Inspectorate notes, over the period 1997-99, a general decrease in the number of water quality incidents occurring at service reservoirs but an increase in those arising in the distribution system. DWI, *Drinking Water 1999* (2000).

[15] See 7.8 below.

[16] And the Water Supply (Water Quality) Regulations 1989 (SI 1989 No.1147). Legislatively prescribed standards came into force when the standards in the Drinking Water Quality Directive had to be complied with, see 17.7.1 below.

improve their practice where this is necessary'.[17] The advice stressed that the variety of sources, and their variable conditions, made it impossible to stipulate any particular treatment method, and that undertakers had to form their own view of what was appropriate.

Looking back, what is most notable about the range of measures which were recommended (or, in a few cases, stipulated) was the focus on process-based standards and, in part, management standards (e.g. keeping waterworks clean, and protecting sources of supply from contamination). To take one memorable illustration:

> Careful discrimination should be exercised in the selection of workmen employed on waterworks other than works where no risk to the purity of the water supply is likely to arise, and the clinical history of each such workman, particular with reference to enteric infection, should be thoroughly investigated in order to determine his suitability for this kind of employment. Any man attacked with illness associated with looseness of the bowels should be suspended from work until his recovery is complete and medical examination shows that he is safe to return to work.[18]

Perhaps this would still be considered good practice today, but it was one of the few recommendations which 'should' have been complied with without qualification. What is striking was the absence of anything resembling a quantitative standard for 'wholesome' water. The extent to which specialist commentators deferred entirely to this government advice when explaining what 'wholesome' might mean as a term of law is also remarkable.[19] Not until 1982 did guidance make reference to quantitative standards, specifically those contained in the Drinking Water Quality Directive, though previously World Health Organisation standards dating from 1970 were recognised and relied upon by the Secretary of State.[20]

What case law there was dealt not so much with the general issue of the meaning of 'wholesome', but rather with tangential issues such as the point at which a supply could be said to *be* unwholesome. This question arose in *Milnes* v *Huddersfield Corporation*,[21] where the defendant undertaker supplied water which, though stated to be pure and wholesome at the point of supply, became polluted on passing through the claimant's lead service pipes, as a result of which the claimant suffered from lead poisoning. Was this a supply of water which was 'wholesome', that is, was it a breach of statutory duty in supplying it if it wasn't? For the five judges

---

[17] *Memorandum on the Safeguards to be Adopted in Day to Day Administration of Water Undertakers*, Memo. No.221, Ministry of Health (1939, revised 1948), reproduced in McDowell and Chamberlain (1950) p.101.

[18] *Memorandum, ibid*, para.5. A nice variant of the 'fit and proper person' test! (See 12.2.6 above).

[19] McDowell and Chamberlain (1950) p.101.

[20] World Health Organization (1970).

[21] (1886) 11 App Cas 511, and see 17.7.2 below. Notably the case was only pleaded as a breach of statutory duty. In the later case of *Barnes* v *Irwell Valley Water Board* [1938] 2 All ER 650, on similar facts a case was successfully argued in negligence.

in the majority in the House of Lords it was wholesome and there was no breach of duty. But for the two dissenters, the supply contained a solvent of lead which made it poisonous on contact with the service pipes.

The case shed little light on the meaning of 'wholesome', since the water was perfectly satisfactory before contact with the service pipes but became poisonous thereafter. The case does though illustrate some of the regulatory issues concerning public water supply. For example, should quality standards be based on characteristics of water (such as plumbosolvency) which might not make the water 'impure' when viewed in isolation, but which might have the practical effect of making it unfit to drink? The view of the majority in *Milnes* is that the wholesomeness of water is something which can be ascertained in the abstract; unlike a child's toy, its safety does not seem to depend on the context of its use after the point of supply.[22]

### 17.2.3 *Water Supply and Safety Margins*

Although contamination of water may only lead to unpalatability, levels of certain contaminants may give rise to public health risks or actual personal injury. Risks, however, may not be distributed evenly across the population. The same exposure to lead levels, for example, may have a greater impact on developing foetuses, since during pregnancy the stored lead in bone is mobilised and may cross the placenta.[23] There are also concerns about the link between nitrate levels and 'blue-baby syndrome' (or sub-clinical illness short of it) and gastric cancer,[24] and aluminium ingestion and the onset of Alzheimer's Disease.[25] Given the public nature of most water supplies, therefore, quality standards may have to be set at levels high enough to ensure that more than an adequate margin of safety is provided to many consumers. So far, no attempt has been made to differentiate in the quality of water supplied, for example as between the needs of industry and of children. It might be noted that in the US it has been recommended that 'vulnerable sub-populations', defined as including 'infants, children, pregnant women, the elderly, and individuals with a history of serious illness', might be 'prescribed' higher quality water.[26]

### 17.3 Drinking Water Quality and Ambient Environmental Quality

There is no necessary connection between the quality of water in the natural environment and the quality of drinking water. Purification techniques or blending may improve drinking water while natural water quality is unaffected or deteriorates. Nevertheless, there is a strong

---

[22] But see 17.7.4 on the requirement that water must be wholesome at the consumer's tap.

[23] See generally House of Lords Select Committee on the European Communities, *Drinking Water* (1996). See also *ENDS Report* 266 (1997) p.11.

[24] See 13.5 above on nitrate control.

[25] Craig and Craig ch.3, and see Altmann et al (1999) on aluminium intake and brain damage.

[26] See the report on *Vulnerable Subpopulations*, made in relation to the Safe Drinking Water Act Amendments of 1996, see www.epa.gov/OGWDW

practical connection between the two. Stricter drinking water quality standards focus attention on the quality of watercourses and groundwater used for potable supplies, since reducing the input of pollutants at source – for example, by reducing nitrate usage, or improving the storage of chemicals – may be the best means of achieving quality standards at the point of supply. There are clear practical and policy connections between, for example, Community legislation on drinking water and on reducing nitrates from agricultural sources.[27]

The tensions are neatly illustrated in the preamble to the 1998 revisions to the central EC Drinking Water Quality Directive.[28] This notes that:

> Community standards for essential and preventive health-related quality parameters in water intended for human consumption are necessary if minimum environmental-quality goals to be achieved in connection with other Community measures are to be defined so that the sustainable use of water intended for human consumption may be safeguarded and promoted.[29]

However, the preamble goes on to observe that:

> to enable water-supply undertakings to meet the quality standards for drinking water, appropriate water-protection measures should be applied to ensure that surface and groundwater is kept clean; [but] the same goal can be achieved by appropriate water-treatment measures to be applied before supply.[30]

Only in relation to non-compliance with the least stringent of the parameters is rectification at source to be prioritised.[31] The Directive's provisions do not, therefore, require ambient quality improvements. On the other hand, they do encourage other, environmentally-related, measures.[32] The law relating to drinking water may therefore be regarded as being concerned both with the protection of human health and with wider concerns about environmental protection and management.[33]

## 17.4 An Outline of the Present Legal Framework

Drinking water quality standards are primarily determined at EC level, at least insofar as essential health and quality parameters are concerned. The

---

[27] Although nitrate sensitive areas were introduced under the Water Act 1989 primarily to address compliance with the nitrate parameter in the Drinking Water Quality Directive, nitrate sensitive areas are discussed together with nitrate vulnerable zones designated under Directive 91/676/EEC, since both have wider environmental implications than drinking water quality. See 13.5 above.

[28] Directive 98/83/EC. Notably, the Directive was adopted under Article 130s of the EC Treaty (now Article 175 EC). See 17.7.8 below on this Directive.

[29] *Ibid* Recital 5.

[30] *Ibid* Recital 8.

[31] *Ibid* Recital 30.

[32] For a good illustration of this see the views expressed in Case C-303/94 *Parliament v Council* [1996] ECR I-2943, discussed at *ENDS Report* 258 (1996) p.44.

[33] See also the concept of 'pollution' in the Water Framework Directive, at 5.8.1 above.

importance of Community measures in this field cannot be overstated, and two Directives are particularly important: the 1975 Drinking Water Abstraction Directive, which is concerned with the quality of surface water intended for the abstraction of drinking water,[34] and the 1980 Drinking Water Quality Directive (revised in 1998), which specifies standards for the quality of water intended for human consumption.[35] In addition, other Directives may be important for drinking water quality, in particular the 1991 Nitrates Directive.

The law on drinking water quality is generally stated in Chapter III of Part II of the Water Industry Act 1991, but extensive reliance is placed on national regulations, introduced in large part to give effect to EC obligations. While these are only stated to apply to public supplies, in effect the UK also applies these same standards to private supplies. Numeric quality standards are not applied to natural mineral waters, although for waters to fall within this category they must be 'microbiologically wholesome'. Bottled waters are treated differently, and fall within the remit of the Food Standards Agency. Otherwise, drinking water quality is a matter for the Secretary of State (or, in Wales, the National Assembly),[36] in practice acting through the Drinking Water Inspectorate, discussed in the following section. Private water supplies are primarily a matter for local authorities. There is a range of statutory and common law liabilities if drinking water of sub-standard quality is supplied, while the enforcement mechanisms in Part I of the Water Industry Act 1991[37] are used to bring the quality of water supplied by water undertakers up to the required standards.

## 17.5 The Drinking Water Inspectorate

In line with the proportion of drinking water supplied by water undertakers,[38] the focus of most of this chapter is on public water supplies, where administrative responsibility lies with the Secretary of State. The Secretary of State is responsible for establishing and enforcing drinking water quality classifications and drinking water quality standards, and has a general power of oversight as regards the obligations of water undertakers to supply wholesome water. He or she also negotiates revised quality standards in the Council of the European Community. The Secretary of State also has important powers to prevent, through specification standards, the contamination of water. He may delegate certain of his powers to water undertakers or local authorities,[39] while the water undertakers[40] and local authorities[41] have important powers and

---

[34] See 17.6 below on this Directive.

[35] See 17.7 below on this Directive.

[36] References to 'the Secretary of State' in this chapter include reference to the National Assembly for Wales unless otherwise indicated.

[37] See 7.9 above on enforcement of undertakers generally.

[38] See 17.1 above.

[39] See e.g. s.74(3) Water Industry Act 1991.

[40] See e.g. power of undertakers to disconnect under *ibid* s.75, or to provide supplies as directed by a local authority under *ibid* s.79(3).

duties in their own right. However, the central quality regulator in administrative practice is the Drinking Water Inspectorate (DWI), a body whose existence can be traced to water privatisation.[42]

The Secretary of State may appoint 'technical assessors' in relation to the powers and duties conferred or imposed on him in relation to various aspects of drinking water quality.[43] Such persons may also exercise any other powers or duties of his under any other enactment in relation to the quality and sufficiency of water supplied by water undertakers. The body established in 1990 to perform these functions was the DWI. The functions of the DWI are tightly prescribed by the Water Industry Act 1991. The DWI must carry out such investigations as required by the Secretary of State for the purposes of ascertaining whether any water quality requirement imposed on a water undertaker is being, has been or is likely to be contravened. It must also advise the Secretary of State as regards the exercise of his powers, including his powers to make regulations[44] and make reports to the Secretary of State as required.[45] The DWI continues to act in relation to water supplies in Wales. Despite its proscribed powers, it has been held that the Secretary of State may delegate to the DWI enforcement proceedings for the offence of supplying water which is 'unfit for human consumption'.[46]

As can be seen, unlike non-departmental public bodies such as the Environment Agency, or even non-ministerial government departments such as the Office of Water Services (Ofwat), the DWI enjoys at best delegated responsibility from the Secretary of State rather than any greater regulatory independence.[47] Currently based within the Department of the Environment, Transport and the Regions, the proper location for, and functions of, such a body has proved contentious. Prior to the Environment Act 1995, Government had recommended that 'on balance' the functions of the DWI should be transferred to the Environment Agency. The decision eventually taken, however, was to leave it within the Department of the Environment (now the DETR) on the grounds that its functions relate to public health rather than wider environmental protection. The reasoning suggested by Government left a lot to be desired, and has been

---

[41] See generally *ibid* ss.77-85, discussed at 17.9 below.

[42] See 2.18.2 above. The origins of the DWI may also be traced to the Camelford drinking water incident, see 17.11 below.

[43] s.86 Water Industry Act 1991. The relevant sections are ss.67-70 and 77-82 Water Industry Act 1991.

[44] *Ibid* s.86(2).

[45] *Ibid* s.86(2)(b). The Annual Report of the DWI, which exceeds that required under the Drinking Water Quality Directive, has been described as an 'invaluable resource, not only to environmental pressure groups with an interest in water quality issues, but also to the water industry, public policy makers and the research community', Ward, Buller and Lowe (1995) p.124.

[46] *Secretary of State for the Environment, Transport and the Regions* v *Yorkshire Water Services Ltd*, Leeds Crown Court, 28 July 2000, unreported, and see 17.7.7 below on the offence and 17.12 on the delegation of prosecution powers. See also Clause 43, draft Water Bill.

[47] As illustrated by enforcement procedures, discussed at 17.12 below.

described as 'somewhat lame'.[48] On the same reasoning it might be questioned why the Department of Health was not the most appropriate location for a body with such responsibilities.

### 17.6 The Drinking Water Abstraction Directive and the Sampling Directive

The Drinking Water Abstraction Directive[49] was an early Community measure, with its origins in the first Environmental Action Programme,[50] laying down in effect general process standards to be applied to the treatment of such waters before consumption. As its name implies, the Directive applies only to surface waters used, or likely to be used, for human consumption, and it does not extend to groundwater, brackish water or water intended to replenish water-bearing beds.[51] 'Drinking water' is defined as all surface water intended for human consumption and supplied by distribution networks for public use.[52] The Directive does not therefore apply to water which is privately abstracted. Unlike the Drinking Water Quality Directive,[53] therefore, the Abstraction Directive is concerned with the quality of water *before*, rather than *after*, treatment.

The Abstraction Directive divides surface waters into three categories according to physical, chemical and microbiological limit values set out in Annex II to the Directive. The categories correspond to the treatment methods specified in Annex I to the Directive. Category A1 requires only simple physical treatment and disinfection, e.g. rapid filtration and disinfection, before use. Waters in Category A2 require normal physical treatment, chemical treatment and disinfection, e.g. pre-chlorination, coagulation, flocculation, decantation, filtration and disinfection (final chlorination). Category A3 waters require intensive physical and chemical treatment, extended treatment and disinfection e.g. chlorination to break-point, coagulation, flocculation, decantation, filtration, adsorption (activated carbon) and disinfection (ozone, final chlorination).[54]

The classification of waters into these three categories is given effect to by the classifications DW1, DW2 and DW3 as set out in the national Surface Waters (Abstraction for Drinking Water) (Classification) Regulations 1996,[55] and the duty to meet such standards is enforceable by the Secretary

---

[48] Hughes (1996), p.94.
[49] Directive 75/440/EEC on the quality of surface water intended for the abstraction of drinking water.
[50] See 5.2 above on this (and subsequent) Programmes.
[51] Art.1.1 Drinking Water Abstraction Directive.
[52] *Ibid* Art.1.2.
[53] Discussed at 17.7.1 below.
[54] Art.2 and Annex I Drinking Water Abstraction Directive.
[55] SI 1996 No.3001, made under ss.82, 102 and 219(2) Water Resources Act 1991. See also Reg.23 Water Supply (Water Quality) Regulations 1989 (SI 1989 No.1147). See also 14.8.6 above on the 1996 Regulations.

of State whether or not an offence is otherwise committed.[56] Water below the standards corresponding to treatment type A3 (DW3) may not generally be abstracted for use as drinking water, although exceptions are allowed provided suitable processes (including blending) are used to bring the quality characteristics of the water up to the level of the quality standards for drinking water.[57] In such cases the Commission must be notified and, where necessary, must submit appropriate proposals to the Council.[58]

Member States must set, for all sampling points, or for each individual sampling point, the values applicable to surface water for all the parameters given in Annex II in the Abstraction Directive. There is no obligation to set values of parameters in respect of which no value is given, but the values may be revised, at the request of Member States or the Commission, in the light of new technical and scientific knowledge regarding methods of treatment, or where drinking water standards are modified. Both imperative (I) and guide (G) values may be stipulated. The values set may not be less stringent than 'I', but Member States must endeavour to respect any 'G' value given.[59] Member States must take all necessary measures to ensure that surface water conforms to these values, but may at any time fix more stringent values for surface water than those laid down in the Directive.

Compliance with the relevant parameters is assumed if samples taken at regular intervals at the same sampling point and used in the abstraction of drinking water show 95% compliance in respect of I values, and 90% compliance in all other cases. In both cases, however, non-compliant samples must not:

(a) exceed certain tolerance limits (which do not apply to temperature, pH, dissolved oxygen and microbiological parameters);[60]
(b) pose any resultant danger to public health, nor
(c) result from consecutively taken samples taken at statistically suitable intervals.[61]

Non-compliant samples which are the result of floods or natural disasters or abnormal weather conditions are discounted.[62] 'Sampling' is defined as 'the place at which surface water is abstracted before being sent for

---

[56] Reg.34 Water Supply (Water Quality) Regulations 1989 (SI 1989 No.1147), as amended. The standards are enforceable under s.18 Water Industry Act 1991, on which see 7.9 above.
[57] See further Reg.23(4) Water Supply (Water Quality) Regulations 1989.
[58] Art.4(3) Drinking Water Abstraction Directive.
[59] G values, and related directions to the Environment Agency, are contained in the Surface Water (Abstraction for Drinking Water) Directions 1996. See also 14.8.6 above on these Directions.
[60] The Surface Waters (Abstraction for Drinking Water) (Classification) Regulations 1996 (SI 1996 No.3001) apply stricter standards, excluding only temperature.
[61] Art.5(1) Drinking Water Abstraction Directive.
[62] *Ibid* Art.5(3).

purification treatment',[63] which might be taken to mean either the point at which it is taken from a reservoir or from a 'natural' surface water.[64]

Harmonised sampling and analysis provisions for the Annex II parameters are provided under the Drinking Water Sampling Directive.[65] This Directive requires Member States to use the reference methods of measurement specified in Annex I to the Sampling Directive, and to respect values for the limit of detection and for the precision and accuracy of the methods of measurement used to check parameters set out in Annex I. Minimum annual frequencies of sampling and analysis for each parameter are specified in Annex II to the Sampling Directive. Sampling must, as far as possible, be spread over the year to provide a representative picture of the quality of the water at the sampling point. Competent national authorities must fix frequencies of sampling and analysis for each parameter for each sampling point, but these frequencies are to be no less than the minimum annual frequencies specified in Annex II to the Directive. The containers used for such samples, for conveyance and storage for analysis, must not bring about any significant change in the results of the analysis. The level of detail of information that must be submitted to the Commission has been considered by the European Court of Justice.[66]

Where a survey by the competent authorities of surface water intended for the abstraction of drinking waters shows that the values obtained for certain parameters are considerably superior to those required by the Drinking Water Abstraction Directive the Member State may reduce the frequency of sampling and analysis for these parameters. If there is no pollution and no risk of water quality deteriorating, and the water is superior in quality to certain requirements of the Abstraction Directive, the authorities concerned may decide that no regular analysis is necessary. For the purposes of applying the Abstraction Directive, the Member States must, on request, provide the Commission with all relevant information on the methods of analysis used and the frequency of analysis. Provision is made, through committee, to adapt to technical progress: the reference methods of measurement set out in Annex I; the limit of detection, the precision and the accuracy of these methods; and the materials recommended for the container. These ensure that sampling and analysis provisions keep up with alterations in the levels of the parameters in Annex II to the Abstraction Directive.

In certain situations the provisions of the Abstraction Directive may be waived. These are:

(a) in the case of floods or other natural disasters;

---

[63] *Ibid* Art.5(4).
[64] Bates (1990, updated), para. 7.05.
[65] Directive 79/869/EEC. See generally on this Directive Case C-42/89 *Commission* v *Belgium* [1990] ECR I-2821; and Case C-290/89 *Commission* v *Belgium* [1991] ECR I-2851.
[66] Case C-58/89 *Commission* v *Germany* [1991] ECR I-4983, paras 34-37.

(b) (for certain parameters) because of exceptional meteorological or geographical conditions;

(c) where waters undergo natural enrichment; and

(d) (in relation to surface water in certain shallow lakes or virtually stagnant surface water) for other specified parameters.

In no case, however, may such exceptions disregard the requirements of public health protection, and any waiver must be notified immediately to the Commission, together with the reasons for it and the anticipated period of exemption.[67]

Member States must take the necessary measures to ensure continuing improvement of the environment, and to this end must draw up a systematic plan of action including a timetable for the improvement of surface waters, especially those falling within category A3.[68] In this context, the Directive required national programmes to achieve 'considerable improvements' between 1975 and 1985, but it is clear that the general improvement obligation is an ongoing one[69] even if, in practice, greater emphasis was placed by the Commission on the Drinking Water Quality Directive with the result that there has been little enthusiasm for enforcing the Drinking Water Abstraction Directive.[70] Otherwise, practical compliance with the Directive was required by 16 June 1977 and with the Sampling Directive by 11 October 1981.

Implementation of the Abstraction Directive and the Sampling Directive in England and Wales is by the Surface Waters (Abstraction for Drinking Water) (Classification) Regulations 1996,[71] to be read alongside the Water Supply (Water Quality) Regulations 1989[72] and the Surface Water (Abstraction for Drinking Water) Directions 1996.[73] The implementing measures are generally 'copy out' provisions which replicate the wording of the relevant Directives. However, provision is made for the disinfection of all raw water from any source, not merely surface water, used for domestic or food production purposes, unless the water is groundwater specified in an authorisation given by the Secretary of State.[74] Additional provision is also made for information concerning sampling points, the results of analysis of samples taken, any standards adopted by the Environment Agency in relation to G values, and information about improvement plans and timetables, to be placed on registers made

---

[67] Art.8 Drinking Water Abstraction Directive.

[68] On the duty to draw up plans, and the possibility of individual enforcement if this is not done, see Case C-58/89 *Commission* v *Germany* [1991] ECR I-4983.

[69] Art.4(2) Drinking Water Abstraction Directive. See, e.g., Case C-214/97 *Commission* v *Portugal* [1998] ECR I-3839. Under the Surface Waters (Abstraction for Drinking Water) Directions 1996, para 7, the Environment Agency must include 'a systematic plan of action and timetable prepared for the purposes of Article 4 of Directive 75/440/EEC' in any Local Environment Agency Plan.

[70] Krämer (2000) p.192.

[71] SI 1996 No.3001, made under ss.82, 102 and 219(2) Water Resources Act 1991.

[72] Reg.23 SI 1989 No. 1147, as amended.

[73] On these implementing provisions see also 14.8.6 above.

[74] Reg.23(1) Water Supply (Water Quality) Regulations 1989 (SI 1989 No.1447).

available for public inspection.[75] General powers for the Environment Agency to acquire information are to be read as including the furnishing of information reasonably required to give effect to the Abstraction and Sampling Directives.[76]

That the Drinking Water Abstraction and Sampling Directives are of secondary importance to the Drinking Water Quality Directive may be seen from the minimum annual frequency of sampling required for each parameter. In most cases, only one sample per year is required, although this extends to 12 samples in the case of certain parameters in classification DW3 where the population served exceeds 100,000.

### 17.7 Quality Standards for Public Supplies

Although the legal duty to supply 'wholesome' water has existed since at least 1847,[77] the adoption of the Drinking Water Quality Directive[78] has greatly affected the law and practice with regard to this obligation.[79] The law relating to the quality of drinking water after treatment is now primarily contained in Chapter III of Part III of the Water Industry Act 1991[80] and the Water Supply (Water Quality) Regulations 1989.[81] It may be observed that the Directive largely sets what are in effect product standards. Moreover, the key provisions of the Directive leave little room in practice for Member State discretion, and such provisions will generally be directly effective.[82] Moreover, although the Drinking Water Quality Directive was enacted as a trade harmonisation measure under the former Article 100 of the EEC Treaty, it also has a basis in Article 235 EEC as promoting improved living conditions through improving public health.[83] As such, state liability for losses incurred if there is non-transposition (and perhaps also practical non-compliance) may also be possible.[84] Although the early origins of the Directive are in the First Action Programme on the Environment of 1973,[85] it may be regarded as having greater impact as a public health measure since the extent to which it has improved the quality of the natural aquatic environment is debatable, and in any event indirect.[86]

---

[75] para.8 Surface Water (Abstraction for Drinking Water) Directions 1996.
[76] Reg.7(3) Surface Waters (Abstraction for Drinking Water) (Classification) Regulations 1996 (SI 1996 No. 3001) and see also Ch.16 above on information gathering.
[77] s.35 Waterworks Clauses Act 1847. See 2.3 above.
[78] Directive 80/778/EEC, see 17.7.1 below.
[79] For a review see Bache and McGillivray (1997).
[80] See ss.67-70 Water Industry Act 1991.
[81] SI 1989 No.1147 as amended.
[82] Case C-337/89 *Commission* v *United Kingdom* [1992] ECR I-1603 and *R* v *Secretary of State for the Environment, ex parte Friends of the Earth* [1995] Env LR 11, see 4.15–4.16 above.
[83] See now Arts.94 and 175 EC.
[84] On state liability see 4.16.6 above. See also breach of statutory duty at 3.12 above.
[85] See 5.2 above on the Environmental Action Programmes.
[86] See 17.3 above.

## 17.7.1 *The Drinking Water Quality Directive*

The Drinking Water Quality Directive relates to 'water intended for human consumption'. For the purposes of the Directive, this means all water used for that purpose, either in its original state or after treatment, regardless of origin, whether supplied for consumption, or whether used in a food production undertaking for the manufacture, processing, preservation or marketing of products or substances intended for human consumption and affecting the wholesomeness of the foodstuff in its finished form. However, the Directive does not apply to natural mineral waters,[87] recognised or defined as such by the competent national authorities, or medicinal waters recognised as such by the competent national authorities.[88] Nor does it apply to certain private water supplies.[89] Legislative transposition of the Directive was required by July 1982, but practical compliance was not required before July 1985.

The Directive has a trade-related dimension insofar as Member States may not prohibit or impede the marketing of foodstuffs on grounds relating to the quality of the water used where the quality of such water meets the requirements of the Directive unless such marketing constitutes a hazard to public health. Without prejudice to this, Member States may lay down more stringent provisions than those provided for under the Directive in relation to water intended for human consumption. However, adherence to the requirements of the Directive may in no case have the effect of allowing, directly or indirectly, either any deterioration in the present quality of water intended for human consumption or an increase in the pollution of waters used for the production of drinking water. Member States may also adopt special provisions regarding information, on packaging or labels or in advertising, concerning a water's suitability for the feeding of infants. The Directive also applies without prejudice to the specific provisions of other Community 'regulations', indicating that conformity with drinking water requirements may not be used to justify other failings, though it is not clear whether 'regulations' is to be understood in its strict sense or to be more broadly interpreted to encompass Community legislation generally.[90]

With regard to water used in food production and affecting the wholesomeness of food, Member States must apply the values for the toxic and microbiological parameters listed in Annex I of the Directive and the values for the other parameters which the competent national authorities consider are likely to affect the wholesomeness of the foodstuff in its finished form. Member States must also send the Commission appropriate information about the industrial sectors in which the competent national authorities consider that the wholesomeness of the finished product is unaffected by the quality of the water used, and national values for

---

[87] See Directive 80/777/EEC, discussed at 17.13.1 below.

[88] See Directive 65/65/EEC as amended.

[89] Case C-42/89 *Commission* v *Belgium* [1990] ECR I-2821, although see 17.9.1 below.

[90] See 4.9 above on the general difference between EC regulations and directives.

parameters other than the toxic and microbiological parameters provided for under the Directive.[91]

Of greatest practical importance, the Directive obliges Member States to fix values applicable to water intended for human consumption for the parameters indicated in Annex I to the Directive. Annex I lists some 66 parameters divided into six categories:

(a) Category A – organolepic parameters, such as colour and odour;
(b) Category B – physico-chemical parameters, such as temperature, pH and conductivity;
(c) Category C – parameters concerning substances undesirable in excessive amounts, such as nitrates and zinc;
(d) Category D – parameters concerning toxic substances, such as cadmium and pesticides;
(e) Category E – microbiological parameters, such as faecal coliforms; and
(f) Category F – minimum required concentrations for softened water intended for human consumption, such as total hardness and alkalinity.

Unless parameters are established under the Annex, the parameters under A to E are to be no less than the maximum admissible concentration provided for. Guide levels are also set down for 29 of the parameters.[92] The values of the 4 parameters in category F, concerned with softened water, must not be less than the specified minimum required concentration. The standards in the Directive are based on, but in some cases exceed, guidelines from the World Health Organisation dating from 1970.[93] The reasoning behind such exceedences can be traced to concerns surfacing at the time of negotiation in relation mainly to pesticides, especially DDT, and nitrate levels. The Directive is silent as to how individual parameters were justified. As Faure remarks in relation to organochlorine pesticides, however:

for practical reasons the standard was set at the minimum concentration . . . that could be detected by the analytical methods available at the time . . . and there was no evidence that the proposed standard was in danger of being exceeded because for many pesticides the level of analytical detection was not sufficiently sensitive.[94]

---

[91] Art.6(1) Drinking Water Quality Directive.
[92] It would seem that the UK Government, like most other Member States, is not greatly concerned about the guide levels, although the water suppliers are reported as seeking to stay well within the imperative levels, for example by having operating systems alert concentrations well within the MAC; see Ward, Buller and Lowe (1995) p.117.
[93] World Health Organization (1970).
[94] Faure (1995) p.322.

For parameters such as pesticides, the limit value is in effect a 'surrogate zero', an early example of precautionary legislation.[95]

Member States must also take all the necessary measures to ensure that any substances used in the preparation of water for human consumption do not remain in concentrations higher than the maximum admissible concentration relating to these substances in water made available to the user and that they do not, either directly or indirectly, constitute a public health hazard.[96]

Member States may derogate from the provisions of the Drinking Water Quality Directive in order to take account of situations arising from the nature and structure of the ground in the area from which the supply in question emanates or as regards situations arising from exceptional meteorological conditions. In either case, however, the Commission must be notified and reasons for the derogation stated unless it relates to a water supply of less than 1,000 cubic meters or to a population of less than 5,000. In no case may derogations be made in relation to toxic or microbiological factors or constitute a public health hazard.[97] In the UK, it seems unlikely that such a derogation could properly be granted, for example, in respect of nitrate levels given the extent to which nitrate in water is a result of artificial application rather than 'natural' conditions.[98]

Other powers to depart from the requirements of the Directive arise in the event of emergencies. In emergency situations, the competent national authorities may, for a limited period of time and up to a maximum value to be determined by them, allow the maximum admissible concentration required by Annex I to be exceeded. However, this power is subject to the provisos that its exercise does not constitute an unacceptable risk to public health and provided that the supply of water for human consumption cannot be maintained in any other way. Limited derogation may also be made where a member state has to resort to the use of surface waters below category A3 of the Drinking Water Abstraction Directive,[99] but cannot devise suitable treatment to obtain drinking water of the quality laid down by the Quality Directive. Such a derogation must not constitute an unacceptable public health risk. In both cases, the Member State concerned must inform the Commission and state the reasons for the derogation and its probable duration.

In *Criminal Proceedings against X*[100] the European Court of Justice held that derogations from the Directive must be interpreted strictly and that 'emergencies' must be construed as meaning urgent situations in which the competent authorities are required to cope suddenly with difficulties in the supply of water intended for human consumption. In *Commission* v

---

[95] On the precautionary principle generally see 4.7.1 above.
[96] Art.8 Drinking Water Quality Directive.
[97] *Ibid* Art.9.
[98] Haigh (1992, updated), para 4.4-12.
[99] See 17.6 above on classifications in the Drinking Water Abstraction Directive.
[100] Case 228/87 *Criminal Proceedings against X* [1988] ECR 5099.

*Germany,*[101] the Court further held that unacceptably high costs in complying with the parametric values are not a valid ground on which to derogate, so exceeding the nitrate parameter through agricultural activity did not amount to an emergency. The proportionality principle was of no assistance, since the objective of the Directive is to implement, throughout the Community, a uniform minimum health standard for water intended for human consumption.[102] The Court also held that the obligation on the Member States to inform the Commission of the use which they have made of the power to grant derogations[103] is not fulfilled merely by notifying the general parameters employed for the grant of such derogations and the reasons which led to their adoption. Member States must also have in place legal obligations requiring decentralised authorities to forward information relating to permitted derogations to the central authority within a period such that the latter can provide that information to the Commission in due time.

Unless a Member State lawfully derogates, or has been successful in requesting from the Commission an exceptional extension of time to comply,[104] the duty to comply with the standards laid down in the Directive is absolute.[105] What this requires of Member States in practice has been the subject of considerable legal controversy. As discussed elsewhere, the granting of 'undertakings' by water undertakers to the Secretary of State to secure compliance[106] has been upheld by the Court of Appeal[107] but rejected by the Court of Justice as incompatible with EC law.[108]

Member States must take all necessary steps to ensure that drinking water within the scope of the Directive is regularly monitored. Monitoring must be undertaken at the point where water is made available to the user, and points of sampling are to be determined by the competent national authorities. Further details concerning monitoring are provided under Annex II of the Directive which relates to patterns and frequency of standard analyses, and Annex III concerning reference methods of analysis, but where laboratories use other methods of analysis the results obtained must be equivalent to those specified. Provision is made for adapting the reference methods of analysis under Annex III to technical progress, and committee procedures apply. Under the Reporting Directive,[109] a Community report on drinking water quality was due in 1997, but has yet to be published.

---

[101] Case C-237/90 *Commission* v *Germany* [1992] ECR I-5973.

[102] On the proportionality principle see 4.4.3 above.

[103] Under Art.9(1) and Art.10(3).

[104] Under Art.20. Requests had to be made to the Commission before the time limit for practical compliance, i.e. July 1985. See e.g. UK submission concerning lead in late 1985.

[105] Case C-337/89 *Commission* v *United Kingdom* [1992] ECR I-6103.

[106] Under ss.18-22 Water Industry Act 1991, and on undertakings see generally 7.9.2 above.

[107] *R* v *Secretary of State for the Environment, ex parte Friends of the Earth* [1996] Env LR 227.

[108] Case C-340/96 *Commission* v *United Kingdom* [1999] ECR I-2023. See 4.15.1 above.

[109] See 16.2.5 above.

### 17.7.2 National Implementation

The obligation to respect the values contained in the Drinking Water Quality Directive is given effect through the Water Supply (Water Quality) Regulations 1989,[110] which define whether water is or is not to be regarded as 'wholesome', and by provisions requiring water undertakers, when supplying water to any premises for domestic or food production purposes,[111] to supply only water which is wholesome at the time (and point) of supply.[112] 'Supply' here means that the obligation is placed on the undertaker. There is no 'supply' for the purposes of the Drinking Water Quality Directive where a private supply is used (a person cannot 'supply' himself with water).

Undertakers are also obliged to ensure that there is no deterioration in the quality of water supplied, though the obligation is phrased as being owed 'in general' and 'so far as is reasonably practicable' which is in obvious contrast to the mandatory wording of the Directive.[113] 'Domestic purposes' are those which consist in, or include, drinking, washing and cooking. There is therefore no obligation to supply wholesome water if the water is used only in a lavatory or otherwise for purposes other than domestic or food production.

Although sampling takes place at the consumer's taps,[114] the general duty to supply wholesome water does not extend beyond the point where the water leaves the undertaker's pipes.[115] In the interests of general public health, however, exceptions to this basic principle are made. Thus, the undertaker will be liable where the water is in a pipe which is subject to mains water pressure (or which would be so subject but for the closing of some valve) and it has ceased to be wholesome in consequence of the failure of the undertaker, before supplying the water, to take prescribed measures. These prescribed measures are that the undertaker must secure the elimination, or reduction to a minimum, of any risk that the water would cease to be wholesome after leaving the undertaker's pipes.[116]

The duties of a water undertaker to supply wholesome water are enforceable by the Secretary of State.[117] In any action for breach of the civil duty owed to any person affected by failure to comply with any enforcement order, the undertaker may not rely on the defence of taking all

---

[110] SI 1989 No.1147, as amended.

[111] See the general duty on undertakers to supply premises with a sufficient supply of water for domestic purposes contained in s.52 Water Industry Act 1991. 'Food production purposes' means the manufacturing, processing, preserving or marketing purposes with respect to food or drink for which water supplied to premises used for food production for consumption, otherwise than on those premises, may be used (s.93(1)).

[112] *Ibid* s.68.

[113] Art.11 Drinking Water Quality Directive, see 17.7.1 above.

[114] Part IV Water Supply (Water Quality) Regulations 1989, see 17.7.4 below

[115] This gives statutory effect to the decisions in *Milnes* v *Huddersfield Corporation* (1886) 11 App Cas 511 and *Barnes* v *Irwell Valley Water Board* [1938] 2 All ER 650.

[116] s.68(3) Water Industry Act 1991. The 'prescribed risks' and the measures to be taken to prevent contamination are considered at 17.10 below.

[117] Under *ibid* s.18.

reasonable steps and exercising all due diligence to avoid contravening the order.[118]

### 17.7.3 'Wholesome' Water

Water will be 'wholesome' only so long as certain criteria defined in regulations are satisfied.[119] More specifically, however, the Water Supply (Water Quality) Regulations 1989 state that water will be 'regarded as wholesome' if these criteria are satisfied, suggesting that wholesomeness may, in principle, be satisfied on other criteria.[120] Since the formulation of the requirements for wholesomeness are stated negatively, however, it is not clear whether this is a distinction of any practical relevance. The stated criteria are that:

> (a) the water does not contain any element, organism or substance (other than a parameter) at a concentration or value which would be detrimental to public health, or which would be so detrimental in conjunction with any other matter in the water;
> (b) the water does not contain concentrations or values, or a concentration or value, of any specified parameter[121] in excess of those prescribed;
> (c) samples taken in respect of certain other parameters[122] and in respect of trihalomethanes meet the prescribed conditions; and
> (d) where water has been softened or desalinated, its hardness or alkalinity must not be below certain minimum standards.[123]

Parametric values are generally absolute standards, though exceptions are made in relation to sodium and total coliforms.[124]

By contrast with the position before the Drinking Water Quality Directive, 'wholesomeness' for these purposes is notable for being defined with reference only to the actual quality of the water, and not with adherence to any particular process or management standards, though these are provided for elsewhere.[125]

Although the general duty concerns the quality of water when supplied to the consumer, water may be 'unwholesome' if the parameters in Table C (coliforms, streptococci, etc.) exceed stated concentrations on leaving the undertaker's treatment plant or service reservoir *en route* to the

---

[118] *Ibid* s.22(3). See 7.9.3 above and 17.11 below.

[119] s.93(1) Water Industry Act 1991 and see Reg.3 Water Supply (Water Quality) Regulations 1989.

[120] Leeson (1995) p.152. Similarly, see the language used in relation to deemed 'unwholesomeness' below.

[121] Those listed in Tables A to C of Schedule 2 to the Water Supply (Water Quality) Regulations 1989.

[122] Those listed in *ibid* Table D.

[123] See *ibid* Table E.

[124] *Ibid* Reg.3(5), (6) and (8). On controversy on this see *ENDS Report* 154 (1987) pp.9-10 and *ENDS Report* 155 (1987), 19-20, cited by Maloney and Richardson, (1995), p.66

[125] See 17.10.1 below on process standards and for the previous position see 17.2.2 above.

consumer.[126] However, if coliforms have been absent from the water supplied from a service reservoir in at least 95% of the samples taken in the previous year no offence will have been committed.[127] These preventive provisions go beyond what is required in the Drinking Water Quality Directive, while the Water Supply (Water Quality) Regulations 1989 include a further 11 'national' standards, expressed as either 3 or 12 month averages for particular parameters.

As discussed above, drinking water quality standards are strict and will apply unless the Secretary of State has authorised a 'relaxation' in accordance with provisions that give effect to the derogations contained in the Drinking Water Quality Directive.[128] A significant number of such derogations have been made, although only 19 are currently in force. These relate to the potassium, sulphate, magnesium and iron parameters, which exceed mandatory standards because of geological reasons. All the current relaxations are due to be reviewed when revisions to the Directive come into force on 25 December 2003.[129]

As can be seen, 'wholesomeness' is a wider concept than merely adhering to specific parameters, whether EC-derived or not. Prior to the Drinking Water Quality Directive, legislatively prescribed criteria for wholesomeness did not exist, although in more recent years water authorities had relied upon World Health Organisation European standards[130] and Government guidance.[131] Despite the longevity of its usage in the legislation, there appears to be no reported decision from the national courts on the meaning of 'wholesome' in the context of water supply legislation.[132]

Two judicial decisions which undoubtedly have persuasive authority are nevertheless instructive. In *Attorney-General of New Zealand (on the relation of R R Lewis and E B Elliott) v Lower Hutt City Corporation,*[133] a reference from the New Zealand Court of Appeal concerning fluoridation,[134] the case turned in part on the meaning of 'pure' water, which the Privy Council thought could generally be equated with 'wholesome' and could include water even where fluoride was added to it. It is notable, however, both that the national legislation required a 'fair, large and liberal' interpretation, and that the Corporation was both water and health authority for its area.

---

[126] *Ibid* Reg.3(7).

[127] *Ibid* Reg.3(8).

[128] Art.9. See Part III Water Supply (Water Quality) Regulations 1989.

[129] DWI, personal communication, 28 July 2000. On revisions to the Directive see 17.7.8 below.

[130] World Health Organization (1970, revised 1984).

[131] Department of the Environment, *The Bacterial Examination of Drinking Water Supplies* (1982). For an example of earlier guidance see 17.2.2 above.

[132] Either because cases never reached court, or because of guilty pleas or clear cases such as the Camelford incident. Nor does there appear to be any reported cases on the meaning of the term in other contexts, e.g. s.604(1)(e) Housing Act 1985.

[133] [1964] AC 1469.

[134] On fluoridation see 17.8 below.

In the Court of Session in *McColl v Strathclyde Regional Council,*[135] however, also a case concerning fluoridation, Lord (Ordinary) Jauncey considered that 'wholesome' was not to be restricted to meaning 'pure', although in the context of the case he took the view that 'wholesome' was to be construed as relating to water which was free from contamination and pleasant to drink. In this respect, it is worth noting that the judge distinguished the addition of a substance such as chlorine, intended to purify the water supply, from that of fluoride, intended to be carried in the water supply to the population at large. The approach in *McColl* contrasts with that taken in the context of health and safety law, where it has been held that the making of wholesome water involves its 'altering, cleaning or adapting',[136] suggesting a broad approach to its quality modification which is not restricted to the removal of impurities.

The conclusion therefore appears to be that water which is unpleasant or unpalatable, though not detrimental to health, will generally be 'wholesome' unless it fails to comply with a prescribed parametric value. This is important because of the trends at EC level to move away from setting drinking water quality standards unless these are health-related.[137] Whether water is detrimental to public health will be a matter of fact, though the term seems to imply actual harm, loss or damage rather than a risk thereof.[138] Regardless of the absence of any detrimental health impact, however, the addition of any substance to water may still be outwith the powers of the undertaker, following the *McColl* case, if the reality is that the water is being used as a means for passing a substance into the body rather than the substance being added to improve water quality before consumption.[139]

### 17.7.4 Sampling and Analysis

While compliance with drinking water quality requirements is generally required at the time of supply, taken to be the point at which water leaves the undertaker's pipes, monitoring of water is required at the sampling point which is usually the consumer's tap.[140] The law relating to the monitoring of drinking water supplies is contained in Part IV of the Water Supply (Water Quality) Regulations 1989. The Regulations place responsibility for monitoring on water undertakers,[141] with the Drinking Water Inspectorate and, in the case of private supplies, local authorities performing an auditing function to ensure reliability and assessing any failed sample. The level of monitoring may depend on a range of factors relating to the undertaker, including the extent to which accredited quality

---

[135] [1984] JPL 351, discussed further *ibid.*

[136] *Longhurst v Guildford, Godalming and District Water Board* [1960] 2 QB 265 per Parker CJ at 273.

[137] See 17.7.8 below.

[138] For a reported case see *Brewer v R* [1994] 2 NZLR 239 per Robertson J at 235.

[139] See 17.8 below regarding fluoridation.

[140] A strict interpretation of the requirements of the Drinking Water Quality Directive, see 17.7.1 above.

[141] On some of the implications of self-monitoring duties see 16.8–16.13 below.

systems are in place, the evidence from previous inspections and the extent
to which the undertaker has responded to previous recommendations.
While all companies are subjected to an audit trail, the Chief Inspector of
the DWI has summarised present practice as follows:

> A number of core tasks continued, and will continue, to be carried
> out for every company at least once in each year but many tasks were
> only included at the discretion of the Principal Inspector, based on
> the extent to which previous inspections had shown individual
> companies to have satisfactory procedures and practices in place. The
> Inspectorate continued to seek to reduce the burden of inspection on
> companies by not routinely inspecting procedures and practices
> which had already been found satisfactory in earlier years and had
> not changed.[142]

The basic unit for monitoring is the 'water supply zone', defined as an area
designated by a water undertaker (whether by reference to a source of
supply, the number of persons supplied from any source, or otherwise) in
which the undertaker estimates that not more than 50,000 people reside.[143]
Discrete areas served by a single source are in practice always designated
as a single supply zone unless the specified population is exceeded or if
there are, or could be, significant differences in water quality in the area.[144]

Undertakers must take a specified minimum standard number of samples
for each parameter within each water supply zone according to the
sampling point, and according to the population served by the zone or the
volume of water distributed for domestic or food production purposes.[145]
For example, where in a supply zone 2,500 cubic metres of water is
supplied for domestic or food production purposes, or the population
supplied is 15,000, at least 12 samples per year must be taken for total
coliforms at the consumer's taps, but daily samples will be standard at the
treatment works.[146] Sampling points for copper, lead and zinc, and at least
50% of the sampling points for certain microbiological parameters and for
residual disinfection, must be selected at random. In practice, it is the
properties supplied that are so selected. Undertakers have powers to enter
premises to see whether water supplied is wholesome, but 24 hours' notice
must be given unless in an emergency.[147]

For the remaining parameters, undertakers have a discretion to choose
fixed or random sampling points or a combination of these. In all cases, the
number and location of sampling points must produce data which are
representative of the quality of water supplied in the zone.[148] In relation to

---

[142] DWI, *Drinking Water 1999* (2000) A.4.

[143] Reg.2 Water Supply (Water Quality) Regulations 1989.

[144] DWI, *Drinking Water 1998* (1999) para.1.9. Changes to the designation of a zone, or a reduction in the number of zones, may have an impact on water quality compliance levels: see *ENDS Report* 240 (1995) p.10.

[145] Reg.9(2) Water Supply (Water Quality) Regulations 1989.

[146] *Ibid* Tables 2 and 7 Schedule 3.

[147] s.170(1)(c) and para.6(2)(a) Sch.6 Water Industry Act 1991.

[148] Reg.11 Water Supply (Water Quality) Regulations 1989.

certain parameters that do not change in concentration or value within the distribution system, the Secretary of State may, on written application, authorise sampling from strategic points other than consumers' taps. Undertakers must notify the Secretary of State if such samples deviate from those that would be taken at consumers' taps. If this is the case, permission for strategic sampling must be revoked immediately. Otherwise, the Secretary of State must give at least 6 months notice to the undertaker of any proposed modification or revocation, although the undertaker may agree to a shorter period of at least 6 weeks.[149]

Standard sampling frequencies are stipulated in Tables 1 to 6 of Schedule 3 of the Water Supply (Water Quality) Regulations 1989. Frequencies may be reduced to prescribed levels if water quality is generally within 50% of the required value and unlikely to deteriorate in quality in the following year. Conversely, if monitoring reveals a breach of a standard, sampling must be increased to a prescribed higher level until compliance is achieved. [150] If no more stringent frequency is specified, undertakers must sample for wholesomeness as soon as they believe, or have reasonable grounds for believing, that the standard has or will be exceeded in a particular zone or that such sampling may assist in remedying a problem relating to another parameter. The sampling frequencies provided are at least as stringent as, and in many instances go beyond what, the Drinking Water Quality Directive requires. Provision is also made, as regards detriment to public health, for the sampling of elements, organisms or substances that are not prescribed parameters where the undertaker believes, or has reasonable grounds to believe, that standards will be breached.[151] Specific provision is made for sampling at treatment works and at service reservoirs, and in relation to new or resumed sources of supply.[152] Specific procedures must be adhered to in the taking and analysis of samples, including external audit by a person not under the control of the laboratory or the undertaker.[153]

### 17.7.5 Registers and Information

Monitoring information must be entered onto registers compiled by water undertakers. In addition to the results of any analysis of samples taken, the register must include information as to the supply zone, particulars of any relaxation granted, and information concerning any relevant undertaking given. Sampling analysis must be placed on the register within 28 days of the undertaker knowing the result.[154] Registers must be open for public inspection at reasonable hours and free of charge. A person may receive free of charge a copy of any record relating to their own supply zone, but

---

[149] Reg.12 Water Supply (Water Quality) Regulations 1989.
[150] *Ibid* Reg.13 and Sch.3.
[151] *Ibid* Reg.14.
[152] *Ibid* Regs 17, 18 and 20.
[153] *Ibid* Reg.21.
[154] *Ibid* Reg.29.

any other person must pay a reasonable charge determined by the undertakers.[155]

The registers must also contain information to be supplied to local authorities,[156] not later than 30 June every year, about the quality of water supplied to premises in their area. Undertakers must also inform local and health authorities of any event which, by reason of its effect or likely effect on the water supplied by it, gives rise or is likely to give rise to a significant risk to the health of persons residing in the authority's area. Local authorities may require additional information about the incident and its consequences. Undertakers must also prepare annual reports summarising the quality of water supplied, a statement as to its wholesomeness, details of any authorised relaxations in standards, information about relevant undertakings given and the action it has taken, or will take, in respect of them, a statement about the availability of its water supply zone records for inspection and any other information it considers relevant. Copies must be sent to all relevant local authorities in the area supplied by the undertaker.[157]

As far as the provision of information to the Drinking Water Inspectorate from the undertakers is concerned, details of what must be submitted is contained in the Water Undertakers (Information) Direction 1998. Amongst other things, this requires information about:

(a) drinking water quality, including annual data and monthly and half-yearly reports;[158]
(b) the locations of water treatment works, service reservoirs and water supply zones;
(c) progress with distribution system undertakings;[159] and
(d) certain events, incidents and emergencies.[160]

### 17.7.6 Enforcement

Any duty or requirement imposed under Parts IV to VII of the Water Supply (Water Quality) Regulations 1989 on a water undertaker is enforceable through an enforcement order made by the Secretary of State, whether or not its contravention constitutes an offence.[161] As a matter of practice, enforcement orders are not used where an undertaking from the undertaker is appropriate, which is generally considered to be the case for general non-compliance with standards for an identifiable reason that is

---

[155] Reg.30(1) and (2) Water Supply (Water Quality) Regulations 1989.

[156] In the form prescribed in *ibid* Sch.4. On local authority functions generally see 17.9 below.

[157] *Ibid* Regs.30(4)-(7) and Reg.31. Concern has been expressed that information about drinking water incidents has not been generally publicised by water undertakers, but see now the Water Undertakers (Information) Directive 1998 and DWI Information Letter 8/98 (June 1998).

[158] For the first time the Direction makes the provision of water quality information a mandatory requirement, allowing enforcement action to be taken in the event of non-compliance.

[159] On undertakings see 17.12 below and 7.9 generally.

[160] See DWI Information Letters Nos 4/98 and 8/98, which can be found at www.dwi.detr.gov.uk/regs/infolett/current.htm, the former including a copy of the Direction.

[161] Under s.18 Water Industry Act 1991. On enforcement orders see 7.9.1 above.

remediable. Where criminal proceedings are contemplated, these will be for supplying water which is 'unfit for human consumption', discussed below.

In relation to common carriage, undertakers are naturally keen to have a liability regime whereby the party which causes any such breach is accountable, and this is the subject of Government proposals.[162] This would require changes to the Water Industry Act 1991, which makes the supplier of water (i.e. the undertaker) responsible for any breach of statutory water quality standards by the supply of water which is not 'wholesome'.[163] Although more than one person may 'cause' water pollution,[164] it is not clear that more than one party may 'supply' unwholesome water.[165] In particular circumstances, however, specific rules have been formulated to restrict liability where parties are involved on a routine basis. Specifically, sewerage undertakers are deemed liable for pollution caused by effluent they have consented to enter the sewer system, and are generally not liable for any effluent the have not consented to and could not reasonably have prevented from entering their infrastructure.[166] It is conceivable that similar provisions could be enacted for common carriage arrangements.[167]

### 17.7.7 Water 'Unfit for Human Consumption'

A separate offence, unrelated to EC-derived standards, exists where an undertaker supplies water through pipes to any premises where that water is 'unfit for human consumption'. The origins of the offence lie in the major incident in 1988 at Camelford, in Cornwall, when the water supply was contaminated with 20 tonnes of aluminium sulphate and the disquiet to which this incident gave rise.[168] The offence is intended to deal with serious incidents where criminal prosecution, rather than the enforcement procedures under Part I of the Water Industry Act 1991, is justified. On summary conviction, the undertaker is liable to a fine not exceeding the statutory maximum, currently £5,000, or on conviction on indictment to a fine.[169] Where personal liability may be attributable to a director or other officer of the undertaker, conviction on indictment renders that person liable to a fine or up to two years imprisonment or both. Proceedings may

---

[162] DETR, *Competition in the Water Industry in England and Wales* (2000) para 7.17.

[163] See 17.7.2 above. Although the liability of the supplier is fairly clear, guidance from the Drinking Water Inspectorate also takes the view that this will be the case, and that suppliers will always be liable as the legislation is presently formulated, see DWI Information Letter No. 6/2000, and see also www.dwi.detr.gov.uk/statemnt/ca1998.htm

[164] See 9.6 above.

[165] It is likely that only the undertaker would be prosecuted; see e.g. DWI news release 753, 7 December 2000.

[166] On undertakers' liability for sewerage effluent see 11.12 and 9.14 below.

[167] The Consultation Paper suggests this could be done in a Network code, though whether such a code could determine questions of criminal liability is questionable.

[168] As the law then stood, a prosecution could be brought in relation to the resultant damage to the aquatic environment, but not the damage (or risk) to human health. On Camelford see 17.11 below.

[169] Clause 45, draft Water Bill, proposes an increase to £20,000 in the magistrates' court.

only be instituted by the Secretary of State or the Director of Public Prosecutions. It is a defence for the undertaker to show that it:

(a) had no reasonable grounds for suspecting that the water would be used for human consumption; or

(b) took all reasonable steps and exercised all due diligence for securing that the water was fit for human consumption on leaving its pipes or was not used for human consumption.[170]

It is clear that the offence of supplying 'unfit' water can only be committed by a water undertaker or statutory water supply company. This raises issues in relation to possible developments to restructure the water supply sector, for example various proposals to restructure undertakers so that there is a formal division between ownership and operation.[171] On these proposals, the operating company could not be criminally liable for supplying water unfit for human consumption. In relation to common carriage arrangements, as things stand it would the ultimate supplier of water who would be responsible for supplying unfit water and not any other party who contaminated the supply.[172]

'Unfit for human consumption' is not defined in the 1991 Act. The context of the provision in the Act might suggest that water which is unfit for human consumption must be of poorer quality than water that is merely not wholesome. On the other hand, it has been suggested that water may be unfit for human consumption even when it meets the *human health* standards for wholesomeness, for example because of poor taste or smell.[173]

The overwhelmingly majority of prosecutions brought under this provision have, in fact, related to the supply of water of poor taste, odour or discoloration, parameters which are all, at least at present, covered in the Water Supply (Water Quality) Regulations 1989.[174] While these might be taken as breaches of standards to be remedied through the giving of undertakings, the implication seems to be the nature of the factors leading up the event are more in the nature of one-off incidents of poor

---

[170] s.70 Water Industry Act 1991. The scope of the defence has not yet been tested judicially.

[171] For example, proposals to divide the Kelda group (the parent company of Yorkshire Water Services Ltd) into 'Yorkshire Water Mutual' owned by the customers, which would own the assets, and an operating company (in effect, Kelda) which would be a listed company. The proposals were essentially rejected by the Director General of Water Services on the grounds of insufficient benefit to consumers and concerns over the actual independence between ownership and operation, though the need that the quality regulators (the Environment Agency and the DWI) would also be content with such a restructuring were also mentioned. See *The proposed restructuring of the Kelda Group: a consultation paper by the Director General of Water Services* (2000). See more generally Ofwat, *New ownership structures in the water industry* (2000).

[172] See also DWI Information Letter No. 6/2000, and also the website at www.dwi.detr.gov.uk/statemnt/ca1998.htm

[173] See Macrory (1989).

[174] One explanation for this approach to prosecution may be that taking proceedings under s.70 Water Industry Act 1991 for 'unfitness' connotes something more seriously than a 'technical' breach of quality standards, and thus is more likely to lead to a deterrent sentence being imposed.

management practices where criminal prosecution, rather than the statutory enforcement provisions,[175] would be more appropriate.

Until recently, in every prosecution concerning water that is unfit for human consumption, the water undertaker has pleaded guilty to the offence, even though no detriment to human health has been established. While this suggests something of a practical acceptance of the interpretation of the provision, strictly, no precedent had been established.[176] In a recent case involving Yorkshire Water Services Ltd, however, the water undertaker raised a challenge in the magistrates' court that water which was not detrimental to human health could be 'unfit for human consumption'. The magistrates rejected the contention that the charge was an abuse of process, and applications to the High Court for judicial review of this decision were also rejected.[177] At a preliminary stage in the criminal trial in the Crown Court,[178] the interpretation of 'unfit for human consumption' was raised, and ruled upon after extensive legal argument. The finding was that the jury should be directed that they should be sure of either of the following:

(a) that the water if drunk would be likely to, or when drunk did in fact, cause injury to the consumer; or
(b) that the water, by reason of its appearance and/or smell, was of such a quality that it would cause a reasonable consumer of firm character to refuse to drink it or use it in the preparation of food.

The judge also noted that the jury should be directed as to the seriousness of the offence and that there are other lesser offences which are concerned with breaches of water quality standards, hence reference to the 'reasonable consumer of firm character'.

In reaching this ruling, extensive resort was made to speeches by the Government during the passage of the Water Act 1989 which first introduced the provision. However, it was clear from these that the Government was not keen to offer any real guidance as to the meaning of the phrase, an approach reflected in the lack of guidance in the legislation itself. However, the passages indicated no intent to restrict its meaning to human health factors alone, and it was also persuasive that, in the context of food safety legislation which was enacted at around the same time,[179] neither a negative impact on public health, nor the risk thereof, need be established to show that food is 'unfit for human consumption'.[180] It is

---

[175] That is, under ss.18-22 Water Industry Act 1991, on which see 7.9 above and 17.12 below.
[176] See 17.12 below.
[177] 'Yorkshire Water services committed for trial over water unfit for human consumption allegations', DWI press release 1227, 17 December 1999; 'Yorkshire Water Services face trial over water unfit for human consumption alligations [sic]', DWI press release 60, 28 January 2000.
[178] Leeds Crown Court, 28 July 2000, see DWI news release 518. The trial was held in December 2000, see *ENDS Report* 311 (2000) p.52.
[179] s.8(2) Food Safety Act 1990.
[180] In *Guild* v *Gateway Foodmarkets Ltd*, 1991 SLT 578 the Scottish High Court of Justiciary held that 'unfit for human consumption' was not to be equated with an adverse 'effect on health'. It was not therefore necessary for expert evidence to be led as to whether the food in fact caused ill

submitted that the ruling is an appropriate one, taking into account the open-ended nature of the criminal offence at stake, the other enforcement mechanisms available and the recognition that public water supplies may vary in character within acceptable bands.

What does seem clear, however, is that unless one of the defences is established the offence is one of strict liability.[181] Whether water falls within the meaning of unfit for human consumption is a matter of fact. However, reliance on epidemiological evidence may be problematic, as illustrated in an unsuccessful prosecution of South West Water Services following a cryptosporidium outbreak.[182] The prosecution, the first and so far only one of its kind to rely on epidemiological evidence, turned on the evidential status of a report compiled in the aftermath of the incident by the outbreak control team, a body set up by the local public health authority with a specific remit to investigate such disease outbreaks. The information gathered by questionnaire established that at least 575 people had suffered stomach upsets, but this information was anonymised. The judge held that this prevented the defence from testing the case against it, therefore the evidence ought to be excluded.[183] The judge also observed (although not in a part of the judgment that was central to the decision) that the outbreak control team report would in any event have been inadmissible[184] due to the absence of continuity evidence. That is, an unbroken evidential chain linking the individuals concerned, through medical opinion and individual responses to the questionnaire, would have been needed. As a result of this case, attention has turned to requiring more stringent specification standards.[185] It might be thought somewhat unfortunate that an offence formulated without reference to actual human harm, and intended to go beyond the water quality regulations, should founder on the need for harm to be proven in individual cases. In the future, it may be that greater efforts will be channelled into proving actual harm in a much lower number of cases (i.e. that rather than trying to establish the *extent* of an outbreak, the actual impact on identified individuals will be the basis of proceedings).

The shortcomings of the offence of supplying water unfit for human consumption may be avoided through reliance on other offences such as those contained in the Health and Safety at Work etc. Act 1974, as

---

health. Rather, the trial judge was entitled to reach a verdict in all the circumstances. See also *David Greig Ltd* v *Goldfinch* (1961) 59 LGR 304 at p.305.

[181] *Secretary of State for the Environment* v *Severn Trent Water Ltd, ENDS Report* 243 (1995) p.45 (Crown Court). See also *R* v *Northumbrian Water Ltd, ex parte Newcastle and North Tyneside Health Authority* [1999] Env LR 715.

[182] *Secretary of State for the Environment* v *South West Water Services* [1997] *Water Law* 161 (Crown Court). Although the prosecution failed, it is notable that the company paid out at least £1.5 million in compensation to those affected by 'boil water' notices; see *The Guardian*, 3 July 1996.

[183] Under s.25 Criminal Justice Act 1988.

[184] Under *ibid* s.24.

[185] See the Water Supply (Water Quality) (Amendment) Regulations 1999 (SI 1999 No.1524) and 17.10.2 below.

happened following a serious and widespread gastroenteritis outbreak in Fife in 1995. In *HMA* v *Kettle Produce Ltd*[186] the defendant company pleaded guilty to a charge under the 1974 Act relating to the duty on employers to conduct their undertakings so as to ensure, so far as is reasonably practicable, that persons not in their employment who may be affected thereby are not exposed to health and safety *risks*.[187] 'Risks' here means the possibility of danger rather than actual danger.[188] Although reliance on health and safety legislation in relation to matters of drinking water quality may appear inappropriate, the approach does illustrate the utility of risk-based controls. In the context of preventive legislation, such as that relating to drinking water quality, such an approach is particularly appropriate.

A final point worth noting in relation to prosecutions for supplying sub-standard water emerged in the recent case of *Crummock (Scotland) Ltd* v *HM Advocate*.[189] Similar charges were brought under the Health and Safety at Work etc. Act 1974 as in the *Kettle Products* case following contamination of parts of the public water supply in Edinburgh. However, the appellants raised a challenge to the proceedings on the grounds that their right to a fair trial, under Article 6 of the European Convention on Human Rights, could not be guaranteed since the jurors in the case would be drawn from the Edinburgh area and would therefore include people whose health had been put at risk by the contamination. In the opinion of the Appeal Court of the High Court of Justiciary:

> it is fallacious to describe potential jurors as complainers thus equiparating them with victims. It is not averred in the indictment that the health or safety of anyone was actually affected. What happened was that the water supply was interrupted and that inconvenience to some, either as individuals or possibly as running a business, may well have resulted. In our opinion any relationship between a juror and the event is remote. Moreover, it is not at all clear why any inconvenience caused by the turning off of the water supply for a period of time in 1997 should cause a juror to nurse a grievance to an extent that that individual would fail to perform his duty according to the oath which he will have taken.[190]

---

[186] *ENDS Report* 252 (1996) p.45. As regards consequent civil claims see *ENDS Report* 264 (1997) p.4.

[187] See s.3(1) and 33(1)(a) Health and Safety at Work etc. Act 1974.

[188] See *R* v *Board of Trustees of the Science Museum* [1993] 3 All ER 853.

[189] 2000 SLT 677.

[190] para.12. Although the impartiality of the Sheriff hearing the case with jury appears to have been raised in argument, the Appeal Court made no comment on whether, if the judge had been one of the affected parties, this would have amounted to a breach of the right to a fair trial. While the Scottish legal system has proceeded its English counterpart in incorporating the European Convention on Human Rights (under the Scotland Act 1998), the language of its judgments (and terminology of its legal proceedings generally) remains needlessly archaic.

## 17.7.8 The Revised Directive

Revisions to the Drinking Water Quality Directive have recently been adopted. Directive 98/83/EC[191] (the 'Revised Directive') provides, by contrast with its predecessor, a more sophisticated, if pragmatic, attempt to regulate drinking water quality in the EC. The Revised Directive bears several hallmarks of the subsidiarity principle,[192] most notably in the reduction of water quality parameters from 66 to 48, although 10 new mandatory parameters are introduced. These changes are said to be based on scientific knowledge and 'taking into account' the precautionary principle,[193] a formulation emphasising the policy status of the environmental principles in the EC Treaty, with particular regard both to World Health Organisation standards and the Commission's internal scientific advisors on toxicity and ecotoxicity. When it comes into practical effect in 2003, the Revised Directive will repeal and replace the original Drinking Water Quality Directive.

A principal factor behind the Revised Directive was the decision to lower the standard for lead, compliance with which in the UK will account for the vast majority of the estimated £8.2-13 billion compliance costs, spread over 15 years.[194] However, the controversial standards for nitrates and, especially, pesticides (the latter being the subject of vigorous lobbying by the agrochemical industry) remain, and in the case of the latter are in fact strengthened by an extension of the definition of pesticides and the inclusion of relevant metabolites, degradation and reaction products.[195] Of the new parameters, however, only 28 are strict quality (microbiological and chemical) standards[196], the remainder (aesthetic, physico-chemical standards) being 'indicator parameters' fixed only for monitoring and remediation purposes.[197] No Guide values are set. Nevertheless, Member States must set values for additional parameters where it is necessary to protect human health (i.e. be wholesome and clean) within their territories.[198]

---

[191] See also House of Lords Select Committee on the European Communities, *Drinking Water* (1996), and DoE, *The Government Response to the Report of the Select Committee on the European Communities on COM(94) 612 Final* (1996), and DETR, *Raising the Quality – Guidance to the Director General of Water Services on quality improvements to be achieved by the water industry in England and Wales 2000-2005* (1998).

[192] On subsidiarity see 4.4.2 above.

[193] Recital 13 Directive 98/83/EC. Interestingly, while the preamble notes the concern surrounding endocrine-disrupting substances, there is said to be 'insufficient evidence on which to base parametric values' (recital 15). On the precautionary principle see 4.7.1 above.

[194] House of Lords Select Committee on the European Communities, *Drinking Water* (1996), figures as revised (see *ENDS Report* 263 (1996) pp.27-29). The eventual costs involved will depend in part upon the level of monitoring required, which for copper, nickel and lead was not decided on adoption of the Directive and for which Guidance from the Commission is not now expected before the end of 2000.

[195] Part B Annex I Note 6 Directive 98/83/EC.

[196] There are three additional mandatory standards for bottled water.

[197] Those contained in Part C Annex I Directive 98/83/EC. Parts A and B list certain microbiological and chemical parameters.

[198] *Ibid*, Art.5.

The Revised Directive has a differently formulated objective so that it is expressly 'to protect human health from the adverse effects of any contamination of water intended from human consumption by ensuring that it is wholesome and clean'.[199] Under an approach similar to that presently taken in UK law, the principal requirement of the Revised Directive is not merely to ensure compliance with specific parameters, but that *in addition* Member States take the measures necessary to ensure that water for drinking is 'free from any micro-organisms and parasites and from any substances which, in numbers or concentrations, constitute a potential danger to human health'.[200] Water will also be unwholesome if certain process standards are breached.[201]

Member States may exempt the provisions of the Revised Directive from applying to drinking water supplies of less than 10 cubic metres per day as an average or serving fewer than 50 persons, unless supplied as part of a commercial or public activity. Where such supplies are exempted, Member States must still ensure that the population concerned is informed thereof and of any action that can be taken to protect human health from the adverse effects resulting from contamination, and be given prompt and appropriate advice when a potential danger to human health arising out of the quality of such water is apparent.[202]

In contrast to its predecessor, the Revised Directive clarifies that there must generally be compliance at the tap. However, an exception is made (other than to premises and establishments where water is supplied to the public, such as schools, hospitals and restaurants) where non-compliance can be shown to be the result of the domestic distribution system or its maintenance. Nevertheless, Member States must ensure that appropriate measures are taken to reduce or eliminate the risk of non-compliance, for example through advice to property owners about possible remedial action that might be taken, and/or other measures which change the nature or properties of the water before it is supplied so as to reduce or eliminate such risks. Consumers must also be informed of any additional remedial action they might take.[203] These provisions mirror, in part, national provisions relating to copper, zinc and lead, and also duties owed in negligence.[204] Further provision is made requiring remedial action when there is a failure to meet the stipulated parametric values. Water that, for any reason, is a danger to human health must be restricted in its use and consumers notified, although Member States are given discretion to

---

[199] *Ibid* Art.1(2). The Directive specifically presupposes the adoption of the Water Framework Directive (recital 9) in relation to 'environmental' limits. See 5.7–5.10 above on the Water Framework Directive.

[200] *Ibid* Art.4(1).

[201] *Ibid* Arts.4(1) and 10.

[202] *Ibid* Art.3(2)(b) and (3). In practice such supplies will be private water supplies, on which see 17.9.1 below.

[203] *Ibid* Art.6.

[204] See 17.7.2 above, 17.11 below and, generally 3.11 above.

balance such restrictions against other health risks which would flow from an interruption in supply.[205]

The provisions concerning derogations are significantly altered by the Revised Directive. Although derogations need no longer be based on situations arising from the nature or structure of the ground or exceptional meteorological conditions, they may only be used in relation to chemical parameters and renewable three-year time limits are stipulated.[206] The consent of the Commission is only required if a third derogation is requested. A streamlined procedure for granting derogations for trivial breaches, remediable within 30 days, is provided. This provision is significant in that it uses a change to the standard, rather than enforcement discretion, for minor breaches. The new derogation (and 'exceptional circumstances')[207] provisions are also notable for the requirement to inform the population affected and, specifically, to advise particular population groups for which the derogation could present a special risk.[208] It is difficult to reconcile this provision with the obligation to ensure that no derogation constitutes a potential danger to human health.[209]

Monitoring provisions are streamlined and 'subsidiarised', with a distinction being drawn between 'check' and 'audit' monitoring. In relation to most parameters, samples must be 'representative of the quality of the water consumed throughout the year'.[210] However, additional sampling for non-parameters will be required if there is reason to suspect that they may be present in amounts or numbers constituting a potential danger to human health.[211] Changes to both analysis and monitoring provisions are to be made under committee procedures. The Commission must also be advised by committee when reviewing, at least every five years and in the light of scientific and technical progress, the new Annex I under the co-operation procedure. Member States must report on drinking water quality every three years, with a view to informing consumers. On the basis of these reports, the Commission must publish a synthesis report on Community drinking water quality.[212]

The provisions of the Revised Directive must be transposed into national law by 25 December 2000. Practical compliance is generally required by

---

[205] Art.8 Directive 98/83/EC.

[206] Thus, those supplies which presently are subject to relaxations under national law (relating to potassium, sulphate, magnesium and iron) cannot be subject to derogations after 2003. However, for these parameters the Revised Directive only sets indicator values, which are only triggered where there is a risk to health. It is not thought that such a health risk exists for the current relaxations. DWI, personal communication, 28 July 2000.

[207] Art.15 Directive 98/83/EC, see previously Art.20 Directive 80/778/EEC. 'Exceptional circumstances' are not defined, but the use of this exception is now subject to committee procedures, which ought to make the decision-making process slightly more transparent.

[208] Art.9 Directive 98/83/EC. This must involve something more than putting this information in the DWI Annual Report.

[209] *ENDS Report* 273 (1997) pp.34-36 at 35.

[210] Art.7 and Annex II Directive 98/83/EC.

[211] *Ibid* Art.7(6).

[212] *Ibid* Art.13.

Where any drinking water from a private supply has not been, is, or is likely not to be, wholesome, local authorities may take remedial action. That is, they may serve notices on persons taking water from such a supply, specifying the measures necessary to ensure a sufficient supply of wholesome water either by an undertaker or another person. For example, this might mandate connection to the mains, or the provision of disinfection facilities on the premises. Such a 'private supply notice' may also be served on the owner or occupier of the premises from where the supply is taken. The powers extend to the power compulsorily to purchase land, or rights over land, and dispose of the land, or the right, to anyone on whom a private supply notice may be served. Private supply notices run with the land.[249] In certain circumstances there may be a public local inquiry or hearing at the discretion of the Secretary of State.[250] Advice on the options open to local authorities when serving private supply notices is contained in government guidance. In particular, this advises that if a breach of the standards has been detected, the local authority should consider taking remedial action if the breach is not trivial and is likely to recur.[251]

The view of the Secretary of State would appear to be that if a private supply contravenes the provisions of the Drinking Water Quality Directive then he has no option but to confirm the notice. However, the Secretary of State has taken the view that if the supply only serves a single dwelling then, following the *Commission* v *Belgium* case noted above, the provisions of the Directive will not apply.[252] If this decision were to be followed, it would clearly throw into confusion many of the provisions relating to private water supplies. This is because it would suggest that the exercise by local authorities of their powers under the Private Water Supplies Regulations 1991 over single properties would be futile if any requirements to improve the quality of water at such premises would not be upheld on appeal.[253] It is thought that a similar decision would now no longer be reached.

Where it is not practicable for an undertaker to supply piped water at reasonable cost, premises not served by piped supplies from an undertaker may benefit from a duty on local authorities. This duty is to direct undertakers to supply, through some other means, water for domestic purposes where there is a danger to life or health and it is practicable at

---

[249] s.80 Water Industry Act 1991. Procedural requirements and enforcement issues are covered in ss.81-83, which confer broad rights on local authorities to carry out works etc to ensure the quality of private supplies.
[250] *Ibid* s.81. Thus, the provisions for challenging a public supply notice differ from other challenges to local environmental health problems, which tend to be by way of appeal to the magistrates court, see e.g. 8.5.12 above concerning statutory nuisance.
[251] DoE Circular 24/91 (Welsh Office 68/91) *Private Water Supplies*, para 6.2 and Appendix 10.
[252] Clapham (1995).
[253] *Ibid*.

reasonable costs for the undertaker to do so.[254] Undertakers are under a corresponding duty to act.[255]

The rules governing private water supplies will also be affected by the implementation of the Revised Drinking Water Quality Directive.[256] In addition to those general observations on the Revised Directive made above, some of the specific provisions relating to private supplies will be amended. At the time of writing these were being discussed in a national consultation exercise. It is likely, however, that under the revised Private Water Supplies Regulations, as previously, the largest private water supplies will need to be sampled and analysed for all parameters at the same frequency as for comparably sized public supplies. There is no indication yet as to the approach to those small supplies providing less than 10 cubic metres a day as an average or serving fewer than 50 persons (unless the water is supplied as part of a commercial or public activity) which may be exempted from the provision of the Revised Directive.[257]

### 17.9.2  Further Remediation Functions

Local authorities must notify water undertakers of anything appearing to suggest that the undertaker's supply is, has been or is likely to become unwholesome, and must inform the Secretary of State if they are not satisfied that all appropriate remedial action has not been taken by the undertaker.[258]

Under public health legislation,[259] a local authority may also bring a complaint in a magistrates' court if it believes that the water in or obtained from any well, tank or other source of supply not vested in it is (or is likely to become) so polluted as to be prejudicial to health. This power applies to water which is (or is likely to be) used for domestic purposes, or in the preparation of food or drink for human consumption. If this is the case, the court may issue a summons to the owner or occupier of the premises to which the source of supply belongs, or to any other person who has control of it. This may direct that:

(a)  the source of supply is permanently or temporarily closed or cut off;

(b)  the water from it is used only for certain purposes; or

(c)  such other order as appears necessary to prevent injury or danger to the health of persons using the water, or consuming food or drink prepared with it or from it.

---

[254] s.78 Water Industry Act 1991.

[255] *Ibid* s.79. The duty is enforceable under s.18 of the Act, on which see 7.9 above.

[256] See 17.7.8 above on the Revised Directive.

[257] See in particular Art.3(2)(b) Directive 98/83/EC. See further DWI, *Drinking Water 1999* (2000) para.I.4.

[258] s.77 Water Industry Act 1991.

[259] s.140 Public Health Act 1936.

The court must consider the representations of any user of the water, and may order the water to be analysed at the local authority's expense. In the event of non-compliance with any order made, the court may, on the application of the local authority, authorise it to do whatever may be necessary for giving effect to the order. The authority may recover from the person in default any expenses reasonably incurred. In addition, any well, tank, cistern, or water-butt used for the supply of water for domestic purposes which, because of its position, construction or maintenance, makes the water prejudicial to health, will be a statutory nuisance.[260]

A local authority may also remedy a cause of contamination within a house or which emanates from an appurtenance belonging to it or usually enjoyed with it (such as a well) by serving a 'repairs notice' under Part VI of the Housing Act 1985.[261] A local authority may also serve a 'defective premises notice' to allow it to remedy a source of contamination or to require an owner or occupier to carry our works.[262] Defective premises notices, however, may only be served where the premises are 'prejudicial to health or a nuisance', and where proceeding under statutory nuisance provisions would lead to an unreasonable delay.[263] Where acting this timeously is not justified, action may be taken under statutory nuisance law.[264] Since December 1996, local housing authorities no longer have specific powers to make grants for the replacement of lead pipes.[265] However, if a property was in an unfit condition because of its domestic supply pipes, other general sources of local authority funding for renovations in households of low incomes might be called upon.

## 17.10 The Contamination of Drinking Water

By contrast with offences in relation to *supplying* unwholesome or contaminated water, various offences relate to the adulteration of drinking water supplies. In addition, undertakers may be required, and the Secretary of State is empowered to make Regulations, to prevent contamination of water arising from contact with the supply system or substances or products added to the water supply. Offences under byelaw powers also remain.

Primarily in the interests of reducing consumers' exposure to lead, the Secretary of State has prescribed that if there is a risk of the standards for copper, zinc or lead being exceeded after the water leaves the undertaker's pipes, the undertaker must, with certain exceptions, consider introducing

---

[260] s.141 Public Health Act 1936, see 8.5.4 above.

[261] As amended by s.130 and Sch.15 Housing Act 1988.

[262] Under s.76 Building Act 1984.

[263] *Ibid* s.76(1), as amended by para.24 Sch.15 Environmental Protection Act 1990. On the meaning of 'prejudicial to health or a nuisance' see 8.5.5 above.

[264] Under s.79(1)(a) Environmental Protection Act 1990.

[265] The Assistance for Minor Works to Dwellings (Lead Pipes) Order 1992 (SI 1992 No.1837), repealed by the Housing Grants, Construction and Regeneration Act 1996 (Commencement No.2 and Revocation, Savings, Supplementary and Transitional Provisions) Order 1996 (SI 1996 No.2842).

or modifying water treatment in order to reduce the extent to which these metals are dissolved within domestic plumbing systems. This includes a duty on an undertaker to remove, on written notice from the owner or occupier, its part of any lead pipe at the same time that the owner removes lead pipe connecting to a tap used to supply drinking water.[266]

Also, a person will be guilty of an offence in relation to any act or neglect whereby the water in any waterworks which is likely to be used either for human consumption or domestic purposes, or for manufacturing food or drink for human consumption, is polluted or likely to be polluted. For these purposes 'waterworks' includes any spring, well, adit, borehole, service reservoir or tank, and any main or other pipe or conduit of a water undertaker. The offence is qualified, however, by the stipulation that it is not to be construed as restricting or prohibiting any method of cultivation of land which is in accordance with the principles of good husbandry.[267] Nor is the offence to be construed as restricting or prohibiting the reasonable use of oil or tar on any highway maintainable at public expense so long as the highway authority take all reasonable steps for preventing the oil or tar, and any liquid or matter resulting from the use of the oil or tar, from polluting the water in any waterworks. The offence is punishable, on summary conviction, by a fine not exceeding the statutory maximum, currently £5,000, and, in the case of a continuing offence, by a further fine daily fine not exceeding £50 for every day during which the offence is committed after conviction. On conviction on indictment, the maximum penalties are imprisonment for a term not exceeding two years or a fine or both.[268]

Further offences are provided for in relation to the use or upkeep of customers' own water fittings.[269] Thus it is an offence for an owner or occupier of premises supplied by an undertaker intentionally or negligently to cause or suffer any water fitting for which they are responsible to be used or constructed, or in such a state of disuse or need of repair, that water in the undertakers pipes will be contaminated by the return of any substance, or will be contaminated before use. The owner or occupier will be regarded as being responsible unless they are not liable to maintain the fitting. The offence is punishable on summary conviction to a fine not exceeding level 3 on the standard scale, currently £1,000.[270]

Water undertakers may, in an emergency,[271] disconnect service pipes or otherwise cut off the supply of water to premises, or otherwise serve on

---

[266] In relation to such 'prescribed risks' see s.68(3) Water Industry Act 1991 and Reg.24 Water Supply (Water Quality) Regulations 1989. See also discussion of liability in negligence at 17.11 below.

[267] That is, 'good husbandry' as provided for in ss.10–11 Agriculture Act 1947, rather than to the *Code of Good Agricultural Practice for the Protection of Water*, on which see 13.5.7 above.

[268] s.72 Water Industry Act 1991.

[269] 'Water fittings' include pipes (other than water mains), taps, cocks, valves, ferrules, meters, cisterns, baths, water closets, soil pans and other similar apparatus used in connection with the supply and use of water, *ibid* s.93(1).

[270] *Ibid* s.73(1) and (4).

[271] 'Emergency' is not defined in the 1991 Act, but see, e.g., 9.17.1 above.

consumers a notice requiring specified steps to be taken. This power applies where the undertaker has reason to believe that damage to persons or property is being or is likely to be caused by the consumers' water fittings, that water in the undertakers' pipes is or may be contaminated by the return of substances, or that water will be contaminated before use. Detailed procedural provision, including provision as to liability for costs and expenses, is made concerning disconnections and the lawful service of such notices.[272]

### 17.10.1 *Substance, Product and Process Controls*

The Secretary of State has broad powers to make regulations governing the application and introduction of substances and products, and controls on processes relating to drinking water supply.[273] Unless for the purposes of testing or research, no substance must be added or introduced into supplies unless:

(a) under and in accordance with an approval from the Secretary of State;

(b) the undertaker is satisfied that it is unlikely adversely to affect the quality of supplies; or

(c) in accordance with various transitional provisions.

The Secretary of State has powers to prohibit, by notice, the use of any substance that an undertaker would otherwise be entitled to use.[274]

The Secretary of State is also empowered, by notice, to require an undertaker to apply to him for approval of the use of any process relating to drinking water supply. Time limit provisions for notifications are stipulated, but these may be overridden in the interests of public health. At least annually, the Secretary of State must publish a list of all the substances, products and processes for which approval has been granted or refused, or revoked or modified,[275] and any prohibition notices issued. Subject to the defence that the undertaker took all reasonable steps and all due diligence to avoid commission of the offence, non-compliance is punishable on summary conviction to a fine not exceeding the statutory maximum, currently £5,000, and, on conviction on indictment, to a fine.[276] Proceedings may only be taken by or with the consent of the Secretary of State or the Director of Public Prosecutions, although the power to bring

---

[272] s.75 Water Industry Act 1991.

[273] *Ibid* s.69(3) and (4).

[274] Reg.25 Water Supply (Water Quality) Regulations 1989.

[275] See Committee on Chemicals and Materials of Construction for Use in Public Water Supply and Swimming Pools, *The Water Supply (Water Quality) Regulations 1989 as amended by the Water Supply (Water Quality) (Amendment) Regulations 1991: Lists of Substances, Products and Processes Approved Under Regulations 25 and 26 for Use in Connection with the Supply of Water for Drinking, Washing, Cooking and Food Production Purposes* (December 1998).

[276] Reg.26 Water Supply (Water Quality) Regulations 1989.

proceedings has been delegated by the Secretary of State to the Drinking Water Inspectorate. [277]

The first conviction of a water undertaker under the drinking water regulations arose after Welsh Water was found to have failed to observe conditions intended to protect water supplies from contamination during pipe relining operations. The undertaker had neglected to take required measures to ensure that epoxy resin, which was used for lining the pipes, had been correctly applied and had hardened sufficiently to prevent it entering water supplies. A fine of £1,000 was imposed by magistrates though there was no evidence that the quality of drinking water was adversely affected.[278]

### 17.10.2 The Cryptosporidium Regulations

As noted above, the Drinking Water Inspectorate has experienced difficulties in prosecuting following cryptosporidium outbreaks[279] on the basis of epidemiological evidence. Cryptosporidium is a protozoan parasite which gives rise to the disease cryptosporidiosis, which causes diarrhoea, although for people who are severely immuno-compromised (e.g. those suffering from HIV infection), the disease is much more serious. Provision of epidemiological evidence is necessary primarily because it is unlikely that the causative oocysts will be detectable at consumers' taps by the time an outbreak has occurred, since they will probably have passed through the system. With cryptosporidium there is also the difficulty that 'pulses' of oocysts may pass through treatment works undetected by the usual practice of selective or 'spot' sampling. The policy decision has therefore been to introduce quite stringent specification standards to reduce the risk of cryptosporidium outbreaks. It is notable, however, that the standards laid down are not based on thresholds for preventing damage to public health, since there is strictly no safe level and the public health risk relates in part to immunities in the population supplied. Rather, the standards seek to reduce the risk of an outbreak occurring.

The Water Supply (Water Quality) (Amendment) Regulations 1999[280] require water undertakers to conduct risk assessments at each of their treatment works to establish whether there is a significant risk of cryptosporidium oocysts being present in water supplied from the works, and to submit this report to the Secretary of State. The Secretary of State has powers to require further assessment if the first assessment is inadequate. 'Significant risk' is defined as meaning a significant risk that the average number of cryptosporidium oocysts per 10 litres of water

---

[277] Reg.28 Water Supply (Water Quality) Regulations 1989. On prosecutions see 17.12 below.

[278] *Secretary of State for Wales* v *Dŵr Cymru, ENDS Report* 242 (1995) p.45. See also *Secretary of State for the Environment* v *South East Water Plc* [1998] 7(9) *Environmental Law Monthly 5.*

[279] Reference here is to 'outbreaks' rather than 'contamination' since, as noted below, there need not be any entry of contaminating material for there to be a cryptosporidium incident.

[280] SI 1999 No.1524, adding Regs.23A and 23B to the Water Supply (Water Quality) Regulations 1989. See also DWI Information Letter No. 10/99.

supplied from the works, properly sampled and analysed,[281] would be one or more at any time.

If a significant risk is established, the Secretary of State must set a date, based on a submission by the undertaker, as the earliest practicable date by which certain treatment methods must be complied with. Provision is made for undertakers to carry out further risk assessments, on the basis of which the Secretary of State *must* require that undertakers cease to comply with any obligations imposed on them. The Secretary of State may also request further risk assessments, and undertakers are under a positive duty to notify the Secretary of State if they become aware of any factors making it likely that a further risk assessment would establish a significant risk.

The Regulations do not specify the processes to be used by undertakers to ensure the necessary reduction in the number of oocysts. Instead, they lay down specific requirements about continuous sampling and analysis of supplies so that compliance with the standard is checked.[282] Breach of these monitoring requirements is an offence for which may be imposed, on summary conviction, a fine not exceeding the statutory maximum, currently £5,000, or on indictment a fine. The same fine levels also apply to any breach of the maximum level for oocysts. That criminal liability for the latter is strict underscores the requirement on water undertakers to have effective process standards in place from the end of the compliance period set by the Secretary of State.

### 17.10.3 Byelaws to Prevent Contamination

The enabling powers of the Secretary of State may also be used to modify byelaw-making powers, and to revoke or amend byelaws.[283] Byelaws may include provisions:

    (a) prescribing the size, nature, materials, strength and workmanship and the mode of arrangement, connection, disconnection, alteration and repair of water fittings used; and

    (b) forbidding the use of any water fittings of such a nature or so arranged or connected as to cause or permit, or be likely to cause or permit, amongst other things, the contamination of water.[284]

Byelaws may therefore prescribe various specification standards intended to prevent, for example, contamination of water through backsiphoning.

---

[281] In accordance with Reg.23B.

[282] On which see 'Guidance on Assessing Risk from cryptosporidium Oocysts in Treated Water Supplies' and 'Standard Operating Protocol for the Monitoring of cryptosporidium in Water Supplies, Parts I to IV', both available at www.dwi.detr.gov.uk

[283] s.74(6) Water Industry Act 1991. See Sch.2 Water Consolidation (Consequential Provisions) Act 1991.

[284] s.17(2)(b) Water Act 1945, repealed subject to transitional savings: s.190 Water Act 1989, paras.19, 57 Sch.26 and Sch.27, Pt.I, and by virtue of s.2, paras.3 and 4 Sch.2 of the Water Consolidation (Consequential Provisions) Act 1991. Most water supply byelaws now in force are based on the *Model Water Byelaws* (National Water Council, 1982) or previous editions of them.

Byelaws may provide for offences, but it is also a duty on undertakers to enforce their own byelaws, a duty enforceable by the Secretary of State.[285] Non-compliance with a requirement under byelaws may also allow undertakers to carry out works themselves, and recover expenses reasonably incurred as a civil debt.

### 17.10.4 Water Regulations

Although powers to make water byelaws were withdrawn under the Water Act 1989, byelaws made previously by the former water authorities or statutory water companies continue in force until such time as regulations[286] enter into force. This gives the Secretary of State extensive powers to make regulations preventing the contamination of drinking water from water fittings. These extend not merely to water mains or other pipes of undertakers but to any pipe which connects therewith, and to securing that water fittings installed and used by consumers are safe and do not cause or contribute to the erroneous measurement of any water or reverberation of any pipes. 'Safe' in this context has the same meaning as in Part II of the Consumer Protection Act 1987, that is, a risk-based standard relating only to death or personal injury. Without prejudice to this, the Secretary of State may make regulations covering such matters as the prior approval of fittings and their installation and use, including provision as to matters such as the materials used. Regulations may confer enforcement powers and duties on undertakers, local authorities or other prescribed persons.

As regards water fittings regulations, issues arise as to whether enforcement functions will come under the remit of the undertakers or, for example, building control officers, since the latter are not subject to possible criminal liability for supplying water unfit for human consumption.[287] Regulations to replace the water supply byelaws came into force on 1 July 1999. The Regulations repeal the byelaws made under the Water Act 1945, but only apply prospectively to new water fittings installed or used after the date of entry into force. In some cases, such as backflow, later compliance periods are stipulated.[288]

### 17.10.5 Public Order Offences

Certain public order offences relate to the contamination of, or interference with, water used for supply purposes. Thus, it is an offence to contaminate or interfere with water, or make it appear that water has been contaminated or interfered with, where this is done with the intention of:

---

[285] Under s.18 Water Industry Act 1991, see 7.9 above.

[286] Made under *ibid* s.74.

[287] Under *ibid* s.70, see 17.7.7 above. See generally Department of the Environment and Welsh Office, *Water Conservation – Government Action* (August 1995).

[288] Water Supply (Water Fittings) Regulations 1999 (SI 1999 No.1148, as amended by Water Supply (Water Fittings) (Amendment) Regulations 1999 (SI 1999 No.1506)). See generally www.wras.co.uk

(a) causing public alarm or anxiety;
(b) causing injury to members of the public using or consuming water;
(c) causing economic loss to a water undertaker or supplier because of people using less water; or
(d) causing economic loss to a water undertaker or supplier due to the remedial measures that are necessary to avoid public injury or alarm.

Similarly, it is an offence for a person to threaten that they or another will contaminate or interfere with water, or claim that they or another has contaminated or interfered with water with intent to cause alarm, injury or economic loss. A person convicted of these offences will, on summary conviction, be liable to a fine not exceeding the statutory maximum, currently £5,000, and a maximum of six months imprisonment or both, and on conviction on indictment to ten years imprisonment and a fine or both.[289]

## 17.11 Civil Liability for Contaminated Supplies

The only remedy granted to consumers under the Water Industry Act 1991 is an action for damages where water is supplied by an undertaker in breach of an enforcement order.[290] However, since the nature of the supply duty is one that particularly concerns individuals, a private action may be brought for its breach.[291] Arguably, the duty will be owed to all consumers of water, whether or not they are defined as such in the 1991 Act.[292] Otherwise, losses arising from the supply of contaminated water may be recovered under other statutory provisions or under the common law torts of negligence or breach of statutory duty.[293] Because formal transposition of the Drinking Water Quality Directive has generally been adequate, the need to pursue a distinct action on the basis of EC law is significantly reduced.[294]

Water is a substance and thus 'goods' and thus a 'product' for the purposes of the Consumer Protection Act 1987,[295] which gives effect to EC obligations.[296] Liability is imposed on the 'producer' of the product, which is defined to include those who abstract non-manufactured substances. Water will be 'produced' if it is abstracted, or processed (as all drinking water supplied by an undertaker must be) or, possibly, if water already

---

[289] s.38 Public Order Act 1986. Probably the most severe penalties available nationally in relation to any activity leading to water pollution.
[290] Under s.18 Water Industry Act, see s.22(1)-(3) Water Industry Act 1991. On s.18 see 7.9 above.
[291] *Read* v *Croydon Corporation* [1938] 4 All ER 631.
[292] Bates (1990, updated), para. 7.111.
[293] On these torts see 3.11 and 3.12 above.
[294] See 4.16 above on individual enforcement mechanisms in EC law.
[295] ss.1(2) and 45(1) Consumer Protection Act 1987.
[296] Directive 85/734/EEC on the approximation of the laws of Member States concerning liability for defective products.

processed is subjected to a further process.[297] To be defective, the water must be such that 'the safety of the product is not such as persons generally are entitled to expect'.[298] Of relevance will be any instructions or warning supplied with the goods, which would probably extend to any notice issued on radio, television, by loudspeaker or leaflet not to use water or to use it, for example, only after boiling.

Subject to the various defences and qualifications in the 1987 Act, liability for any damage caused will be strict. Damage, however, only extends to personal injury or property damage in excess of £275 pounds. The supply of water which is in breach of the standards for wholesomeness but which does not occasion personal injury will not therefore be actionable. Of the defences provided, mention may be made of the defence that the defect did not exist at the time of supply (for example, lead levels arising from lead on the consumer's premises) and that the defect was effectively undiscoverable by producers of the type of goods concerned given the state of scientific and technical knowledge at the relevant time (the 'development risks' defence).[299] Water is not a 'consumer good' for the purposes of Part II of the 1987 Act.

In many respects an action under the 1987 Act is of no more value to claimants than an action in negligence, which might also be argued. In *Read* v *Croydon Corporation*[300] the defendant supplied water to premises knowing that the water would be used for domestic consumption. As a result of contamination, the daughter of the claimant contracted typhoid. The Corporation was found to be negligent by failing to use due care and skill in the supply of water such that it was contaminated and caused[301] the contraction of disease by the child. The Corporation was also liable for breach of statutory duty to the occupier for failing to maintain the standard required under statute. Liability may be imposed even if the water supplied was wholesome on leaving the supplier's pipes if it became contaminated in the claimant's pipes as a result of a condition that the defendant knew about but failed to remedy or warn about.[302]

The supply of contaminated water may also lead to civil liability in public nuisance.[303] Although it is a crime to commit a public nuisance, civil damages may be claimed by anyone who suffers special damage over and above that suffered by the rest of the public. In *R* v *South West Water Authority* a successful criminal action in public nuisance was taken following the incident at Camelford, Cornwall in 1988 when 20 tonnes of

---

[297] s.1(2) Consumer Protection Act 1987, and see Bates (1990, updated), para 7.113.

[298] *Ibid* s.3(1).

[299] *Ibid* s.4(1)(d) and (e). And see Case C-300/95 *Commission* v *UK* [1997] All ER (EC) 481.

[300] [1938] 4 All ER 631.

[301] For a pragmatic approach to causation see *Drummond and another* v *Lord Advocate* [1997] 9(1) *Environmental Law and Management* 20.

[302] *Barnes* v *Irwell Valley Water Board* [1938] 2 All ER 650. See also the provisions of Directive 98/83/EC, at 7.7.8 above.

[303] On public nuisance see 3.17 above.

aluminium sulphate was accidentally deposited in a tank of water intended for public supply.[304]

Proceedings arising from the Camelford incident illustrate the range of potential remedies for drinking water contamination.[305] The incident affected up to 5,000 people, both acutely and chronically, with symptoms ranging from fatigue to, it was alleged, moderate brain damage (taking the form of short-term memory loss, difficulties with concentration and some intelligence impairment). In addition to a civil claim in public nuisance, the 180 or so claimants commenced proceedings in negligence, under the rule in *Rylands* v *Fletcher*,[306] breach of contract, supply of a defective product under the Consumer Protection Act 1987, and breach of statutory duty (both as regards failure to supply wholesome water under the (then) national law relating to water supply, and for failing to meet the standards laid down in the Drinking Water Quality Directive). A further claim for aggravated and exemplary damages, arising from the issuing of misleadingly reassuring information and delay on the part of the (then) water authority in notifying consumers, was struck out by the Court of Appeal.[307] The civil action was eventually settled out of court,[308] the defendants having admitted breach of their statutory supply duty. Since the general duty on undertakers to supply customers in their area with water for domestic purposes including drinking is perhaps best characterised as a duty to supply under statute rather than contract,[309] it is unlikely that this head of claim was of any assistance to the claimants. A subsequent case taken to the European Court of Human Rights, alleging breaches of Article 8 (right to privacy and home life) and Article 13 (right to an effective remedy), was dismissed. Also rejected as inadmissible was a claim under Article 6(1) of the Convention, the applicants having alleged that the lack of a public inquiry into the episode violated their right to a fair hearing.[310]

---

[304] [1991] 3 *Land Management and Environmental Law Reporter* 65. The incident occurred before, and was central to, the new offence of supplying water unfit for human consumption under s.70 Water Industry Act 1991, see 17.7.7 above, which would most likely be used if such circumstances arose again. A fine of £10,000 was imposed. In the light of recent case law on supplying water unfit for human consumption, a fine far in excess of this amount would be likely if the same incident occurred today, and perhaps higher still if recent medical opinion on the after effects of the incident is supported (see 17.1 above).

[305] See *AB* v *South West Water Services Ltd* [1993] 1 All ER 609. On the incident see further Craig and Craig (1989), ch.8 and *ENDS Report* 297 (1999), pp.28-33.

[306] On *Rylands* v *Fletcher* see 3.9 above.

[307] *Gibbons and Others* v *South West Water Services Ltd* [1993] QB 507. As to the implications for suppliers see Ghandi (1993), who also argues that the pleadings in the case 'could only be described as eclectic', and argues that exemplary damages might have been argued for on the basis that the tort committed was intentional or reckless, see *Broome* v *Cassell and Co Ltd* [1972] AC 1027 per Lord Wilberforce. For a useful discussion of exemplary damages and environmental protection see Cane (1993) and see also 3.17 above. A deliberate decision not to warn customers that water was unfit for human consumption might be an aggravating factor in criminal proceedings under s.70 Water Industry Act 1991, see *ENDS Report* 258 (1996) p.45.

[308] See Day (1998), pp.368-369. The settlement, by 148 victims, was for almost £400,000.

[309] See 7.6.7 above.

[310] *Stockton* v *United Kingdom* unreported 15 January 1998. In opposition, the Labour Party supported such an inquiry, but in Government have now rejected it; *Water Magazine*, 21 June 2000, p.5. The only inquiry conducted was by the water authority itself.

Although the above relates only to claims by those supplied with contaminated water, an action might, of course, be taken by an undertaker or private supplier for contamination of a drinking water supply or potential source of supply, as occurred, unsuccessfully, in the *Cambridge Water* case.[311]

## 17.12 Enforcement

An inspector designated in writing by the Secretary of State, in practice an inspector of the Drinking Water Inspectorate, has a general power to enter any premises for the purposes of carrying out investigations. However, unless entry is effected under a warrant,[312] an inspector may do so only in an emergency or at a reasonable time and after 24 hours' notice to the occupier.[313] Once on the premises an inspector has power to carry out certain investigations, including the power to conduct and take away samples and examine records as appropriate. Water undertakers are under a duty, backed by criminal liability, to give inspectors assistance, and provide information, as may reasonably be required.[314] In particular, an inspector may require an undertaker to supply copies of, or extracts from, any register of records kept in order to comply with its water quality duties.[315] It is now also a legal requirement, backed by enforcement powers,[316] to provide annual data on drinking water quality.[317] In practice, reliance on self-monitoring means that legal powers of entry will be little used.

As regards the enforcement of key offences, the Secretary of State has precisely prescribed powers.[318] The Secretary of State is under a duty to enforce any breach of an undertaker's duty to supply only wholesome water.[319] For practical purposes, this duty applies unless the breach is trivial, or has ceased and is unlikely to be breached again, or is subject to an undertaking.[320] The DWI has been delegated the powers to initiate enforcement action, on behalf of the Secretary of State, in the following circumstances:

> (a)  when a water quality standard[321] is breached and the breach is not trivial or is likely to recur;

---

[311] See 3.10 above.

[312] Granted under para.7 Sch.6 Water Industry Act 1991.

[313] *Ibid* para.6(1) and (2) Sch.6.

[314] *Ibid* s.86(3) and (6) and see also DWI, *Drinking Water: Drinking Water Inspectorate Code for Enforcement* (1999); and see below.

[315] *Ibid* s.86(4)(c), and see also the Water Undertakers (Information) Direction 1998 and DWI Information Letter No. 8/98 (June 1998).

[316] Under *ibid* s.18.

[317] Water Undertakers (Information) Direction 1998.

[318] See generally ss.68 and 70 Water Industry Act 1991.

[319] *Ibid* s.18.

[320] On undertakings see 7.9.2 above.

[321] Set by Reg.3 Water Supply (Water Quality) Regulations 1989.

    (b)   when a breach of one of the other enforceable regulations, such as those covering sampling, analysis, water treatment or information requirements, is identified; or

    (c)   when existing undertakings, or time limited relaxations,[322] expire before the required improvements have been completed.

The policy of the DWI, stated in its *Code for Enforcement*, is not to initiate enforcement action when a company, after being notified of a breach of a statutory requirement, provides satisfactory evidence that effective remedial action to prevent a recurrence has been taken.[323] In other situations, the preferred enforcement strategy is to accept from the water undertaker, in lieu of an enforcement order, undertakings requiring a compliance programme.[324] Although formally entered into with the Secretary of State, undertakers actually negotiate and agree undertakings with the DWI.[325]

Only the Secretary of State or the Director of Public Prosecutions may institute proceedings in relation to the supply of water unfit for human consumption. In 1996, however, the Secretary of State for the Environment and the Secretary of State for Wales delegated to the Chief Inspector of the DWI, or his Deputy, the power to take decisions on prosecutions, though prosecutions continue to be taken in the name of the relevant Secretary of State. The High Court has held that the lawfulness of this delegation should be tested in the defence to criminal proceedings, rather than through collateral litigation,[326] and the practice has subsequently been approved at Crown Court level as a lawful delegation of ministerial powers.[327] The DWI *Code for Enforcement* states that policy is to bring prosecutions:

> if it believes that it has evidence that water unfit for human consumption was supplied, if it believes that the company does not have a defence that it took all reasonable steps and exercised all due diligence and if such a prosecution is regarded as being in the public interest.

Although in general terms this is a continuation of previous policy, it is notable that previous formulations referred to 'always' bringing prosecutions in such cases, and to defined criteria against which the unfitness of water for human consumption would be tested, namely evidence to demonstrate that:

---

[322] Authorised under Reg.4 Water Supply (Water Quality) Regulations 1989.

[323] DWI, *Code for Enforcement* (1999). The Code is published at www.dwi.detr.gov.uk/aboutus/code4enf.htm

[324] s.19 Water Industry Act 1991, see 7.9.2 above.

[325] DWI Information Letter No. 8/98 (1998). In practice, undertakings are initially drafted by the undertakers.

[326] *R* v *Leeds Stipendiary Magistrate, ex parte Yorkshire Water Services*, 15 December 1999 (unreported).

[327] *Secretary of State for the Environment, Transport and the Regions* v *Yorkshire Water Services Ltd*, Leeds Crown Court, 28 July 2000, unreported.

(a) illness or other health effect was experienced by normally at least two consumers[328] (although there could be circumstances when just one consumer need have been affected) which was associated with the quality of the water supplied;

(b) the quality of the water supplied was such that normally at least two consumers rejected it for drinking or cooking or food production on aesthetic grounds; or

(c) the concentration of a substance in, or the value of a property of, the water supplied was at a level at which illness or other health effect may be expected in the long term even though none was manifest in the community at the time.

It is notable that elaboration along these lines is no longer contained in the *Code for Enforcement*. For those incidents that do not justify court proceedings the DWI may issue a caution which the court could take into account in relation to any future offence.[329]

During its early years the DWI was subject to a degree of criticism at the low numbers of prosecutions brought,[330] leading some to wonder whether this approach to enforcement would have been followed had responsibility been exercised by a body more independent from Government. More recently, however, the DWI has shown a greater willingness to prosecute, in particular concerning the duty to provide water fit for human consumption. In 1998, for example, eleven prosecutions were taken, ten of which related to the supply of water unfit for human consumption, the other in connection with a breach of operational procedures for lining water supply pipes. A further six prosecutions were successfully taken in 1999 which related to incidents in the previous year, and a further three convictions were secured relating to events in 1997.[331] According to the DWI, the reason for the increase in prosecutions is largely attributable to an increase in the occurrence of discoloured water incidents.[332] Even so, it seems that the DWI has adopted a more litigious approach to enforcement, at least since 1998. However, the extent to which undertakers have entered guilty pleas to the offence of supplying water unfit for human consumption, in the face of uncertainty over its scope, might suggest a certain acquiescence by the undertakers in order to keep the scope of the offence free from judicial scrutiny.[333]

In his 1997 Report, the Chief Inspector of the DWI remarked, in relation to the delegation of powers in relation to the offence of supplying water unfit for human consumption, that: '[t]he policy of delegation as part of

---

[328] On the likely need to show detriment to health of more than one person see *Cullen v McNair* (1908) 99 LT 358 per Lord Alverstone CJ at 361.

[329] DWI, *Code for Enforcement* (1999).

[330] By mid-1996 only two prosecutions had been brought, under the Water Supply (Water Quality) Regulations 1989.

[331] DWI, *Drinking Water 1999* (2000) para.D.12 – D.17.

[332] DWI, *Drinking Water 1998* (1999) Chief Inspector's Statement, para. 10.

[333] A more mundane explanation might be that undertakers have not been prepared to go to the expense involved in a full trial, on which see the cases involving Yorkshire Water Services and Mid Kent Water in 2000 and early 2001, see www.dwi.detr.gov.uk/pressrel/index.htm

reinforcing the independent operation of the Inspectorate is to continue.' One possibility is that a suitable location for the DWI might be within the newly established Food Standards Agency.

## 17.13 Special Waters

Separate provision is made for certain 'special waters', that is natural mineral waters, spring waters and bottled waters. While these are outlined briefly below, it is worth noting that the enforcement provisions of the regulations which govern these waters are common to both natural mineral waters and to spring waters and bottled waters.[334] Thus, on summary conviction, a fine of level 5 on the standard scale, currently £5,000, may generally be imposed. In neither case is it any longer a defence, under the Regulations, to show that all reasonable precautions were taken and all due diligence exercised to avoid committing the offence.[335] The different approach taken to these waters can be seen in the fact that administrative responsibility for them is entrusted to the Food Standards Agency.[336]

### 17.13.1 Natural Mineral Waters

Requirements regarding the quality of natural mineral waters are contained in Part II of the Natural Mineral Water, Spring Water and Bottled Drinking Water Regulations 1999,[337] which transpose the provisions of the Natural Minerals Waters Directive, as amended.[338] The Directive is essentially a product quality measure, concerned with such matters as the exploitation, bottling and marketing of recognised natural mineral waters. 'Natural mineral waters' means water which:

(a) is microbiologically wholesome;
(b) originates in an underground water table or deposit and emerges from a spring tapped at one or more natural or bore exits;
(c) can be clearly distinguished from ordinary drinking water by certain specified characteristics;[339] and
(d) is for the time being recognised for the purposes of Article 1 of the Natural Mineral Waters Directive.[340]

---

[334] Natural Mineral Water, Spring Water and Bottled Drinking Water Regulations 1999 (SI 1999 No.1540). These Regulations replaced separate provisions which governed natural mineral waters (Natural Mineral Waters Regulations 1985 (SI 1985 No.71)) and bottled waters (Drinking Water in Containers Regulations 1994 (SI 1994 No.743)).

[335] Insofar as these provisions are consumer quality standards, the provisions of the Food Safety Act 1990, which extends to water, may also be resorted to. See also local authority functions in relation to private water supplies, discussed at 17.9.1 above.

[336] Food Standards Act 1999 (Transitional and Consequential Provisions and Savings) (England and Wales) Regulations 2000 (SI 2000 No.656).

[337] SI 1999 No.1540, as amended.

[338] Directive 80/777/EEC on the approximation of the laws of the Member States relating to the exploitation and marketing of natural mineral waters, as amended by Directive 96/70/EC.

[339] Referred to in para.1 s.1 Annex I Directive 80/777/EEC as amended.

[340] Pursuant to Reg.4 Natural Mineral Water, Spring Water and Bottled Drinking Water Regulations 1999.

As can be seen, the national Regulations must be read alongside the Directive, which distinguishes natural mineral waters from ordinary drinking water by its nature and original state, both being 'preserved intact' by coming from underground sources protected from all risk of pollution.[341] These are no longer defined as being 'any spring, well, bore or other exit', but need only be 'water extracted from the ground' which has been designated as such by a district or London borough council, or in Wales by county or county borough councils, so long as certain conditions are complied with.[342] These characteristics may give such water 'properties favourable to health', but it is clear that they need not.[343] Medicinal products and natural mineral water used at source for purity purposes in thermal or hydromineral establishments are no longer expressly excluded, but would have to be wholesome and otherwise fall within the definition of 'natural mineral waters'. Lists of recognised natural mineral waters must be published in the Official Journal of the EC, and inclusion in the Journal is conclusive proof of the status of a natural mineral water as such.

Provision is made for the type of treatment that may be afforded to natural mineral water in its state at source and rules relating to protection against contamination. Effectively, these mean that natural mineral waters should not be treated except for filtering to remove grit, and processing to remove certain 'unstable elements' (iron, which can cause discolouration, and sulphur compounds). Any containers used for packaging mineral waters must be fitted with closures designed to avoid any possibility of adulteration or contamination. Detailed provision is made for labelling,[344] and the Directive establishes committee procedures for sampling procedures and methods of analysis necessary for checking microbiological and compositional characteristics. It is an offence to bottle or sell natural mineral water in violation of the standards laid down, or any of the provisions of the Regulations.

### 17.13.2 Spring Waters and Bottled Waters

Part III of the Natural Mineral Water, Spring Water and Bottled Drinking Water Regulations 1999[345] provide quality standards for bottled drinking water or drinking water sold in bottles. In essence, 'spring water' is defined as meaning any bottled 'natural mineral waters', as defined above, while 'bottled waters' refer to waters which comply with various parameters which are similar to those relating to drinking water under the Drinking Water Quality Directive.[346] It is notable, however, that some of the standards are stricter than those currently provided for in the Drinking

---

[341] Art.1(1) Directive 80/777/EEC.

[342] Regs.2 and 4(1) Natural Mineral Water, Spring Water and Bottled Drinking Water Regulations 1999. The contrast is with the Natural Mineral Waters Regulations 1985 (SI 1985 No.71).

[343] See Case C-17/96 *Badische Erfrischungs-Getränke GmbH & Co KG* v *Land Baden-Wurttemberg* [1998] 1 CMLR 341.

[344] On which see generally Case C-369/89 *Groupement des Producteurs, Importateurs et Agents Generaux d'Eaux Minerales Etrangeres, VZW (Piageme) Absl* v *Peeters NV* [1991] ECR I-2971.

[345] SI 1999 No.1540, as amended.

[346] See 17.7.1 above on the Drinking Water Quality Directive.

Water Quality Directive, such as the standard for lead, while other standards, such as for nitrite, do not yet take into account changes made in the New Directive on drinking water quality.[347] Also, spring waters can be treated so that they meet the standards required of natural mineral waters, and need not have a constant mineral content. Until the waters are bottled, Part III of the Regulations do not extend to 'natural mineral waters' or water which is marked or labelled 'spring waters'.

The primary purpose of Part III of the Regulations is consumer protection, though quantitative health-related standards, and some non-health related standards such as taste, are stipulated. It is an offence to bottle or sell drinking water in breach of the specified standards. However, it will be a defence to show that the water was for export and complied both with the standards of the importing country. In the case of spring water, the water must also comply with the provisions of the Natural Mineral Waters Directive as amended,[348] while bottled water must also comply with the standards contained in the Drinking Water Quality Directive. Producers of bottled water are also likely to be subject to the law relating to private water supplies.[349]

---

[347] See 17.7.8 above on the New Directive.
[348] See 17.3.1 above on the Natural Mineral Water Directive.
[349] See 17.9.1 above on private water supplies.

# Chapter 18

# INTERNATIONAL MARINE ENVIRONMENT LAW

## 18.1 Introduction

The pollution of the marine environment is a phenomenon that has only been recognised in relatively recent times. Although there is evidence of shellfish, taken from coastal waters, being contaminated by sewage, and consequent litigation, in the early years of this century,[1] the first legal acknowledgement of the need for controls on discharges to the marine environment is found in international treaties and national enactments of fairly recent origin.[2] Perhaps because of the huge area covered by the oceans of the world, the capacity of this vast expanse of water to dispose of waste without causing harm has previously been assumed to be virtually inexhaustible.[3] In more recent times, however, pollution and contamination by oil, sewage and chemicals and the dumping of other wastes at sea have increased in salience and have made harmful maritime activities the subject of a range of international and regional agreements and corresponding national legislation in the UK.[4]

Despite the belated legal recognition of distinct problems relating to the marine environment, the inextricable link between this problem and the pollution of inland waters must be noted. Roughly, it has been estimated that around 77 per cent of marine pollution globally is the result of discharges from land. Of this, around 60 per cent originates from run-off, either through direct discharges into coastal water or into fresh water passing into the sea through river estuaries, the remainder of land-based pollution loading being deposited via the atmosphere.[5] Many land-based discharges into fresh water or coastal water will be subject to legal provisions which have already been considered, most notably the restrictions upon discharges contained in Part III of the Water Resources Act 1991 and under other controls governing environmental emissions or

---

[1] For example, *Hobart v Southend-on-Sea Corporation* (1906) 94 LT 337; *Foster v Warblington Urban District Council* (1906) 70 JP 233; See 3.3 and 3.4.3 above respectively and see Royal Commission on Sewage Disposal, *Fourth Report* (1904) and *Seventh Report* (1911).

[2] The International Convention for the Prevention of Pollution of the Sea by Oil (Cmnd 395, 1954), see 19.4 below, prompted the first modern legislation on marine pollution by oil, though previous controls had existed under the Oil in Navigable Waters Act 1922.

[3] Marstrand (1974) p.150.

[4] General reading on marine pollution and on general legal issues concerning marine pollution includes: Royal Commission on Environmental Pollution (1972); Hardy (1973); Marstrand (1974); Cusine and Grant (1980); Johnston (1981); Royal Commission on Environmental Pollution (1984), paras.4.1 to 4.23; Clark (1987) Ch.VIII; GESAMP (1990); Birnie and Boyle (1992) Chs.7 and 8; Bates and Benson (1993, updated); Brubaker (1993); Couper and Gold (1993); Brown (1994) Ch.15; Sands (1995), Ch.8; Clark (1997); Churchill and Lowe (1999) Ch.15.

[5] GESAMP (1990) p.88. This estimated that 12% of marine pollution originates from shipping, 10% from dumping, 1% from sea-bed activities, 44% from run-off and land-based discharges, and 33% from the atmosphere (predominantly from land-based sources). See also para.17.18, Agenda 21 and International Chamber of Shipping (1993).

discharges.[6] Hence a considerable part of the contamination which enters the marine environment, estimated to be in the region of 56 per cent, is regulated, at the point of origin of the contaminants, by the regime that governs the quality of inland waters, although it is worth emphasising that much of the marine pollution which derives from atmospheric deposits is not regulated with specific regard to the eventual impact on the marine environment (e.g. vehicle emissions).

Nonetheless, a range of legal provisions is specifically concerned with the quality of the marine environment as this is affected by maritime activities. In particular the UK has given effect to international agreements and obligations by enacting legislation, and giving effect to policy commitments, governing deliberate and accidental discharges into the marine environment of oil and other substances originating from ships, and concerning the direct disposal of wastes at sea. These topics are considered in the following chapter, whilst this chapter considers general issues relating to the quality of the marine environment and the regulation of pollutants and contaminants under global and regional international law. The final chapter of this work considers the special case of the discharge of radioactive substances, where international and domestic regimes come together.

Two final introductory points must be made. First, in the interests of space and because they raise relatively distinct issues, coverage is not given to the regulation of activities on national sea-beds or on the international sea bed area such as oil and gas exploration. Thus, controls on things like produced water or spills from platforms are generally outside this work.[7] Second, using the terms 'pollution', 'contamination' and 'quality' as these have previously been defined presents some particular challenges in relation to the marine environment. Concerning 'quality', the difficulty is that a 'quality approach' in the sense of using water quality objectives (binding or otherwise) is not generally taken, not least because of measurement difficulties. But in some respects the approach is difficult to classify as 'pollution control', since apart from controlling things like major oil spills the objective is as much to do with preventing the release of oil and other substances per se regardless of impact. For example, most of the offences relating to discharging oil are committed even in the absence of any polluting impact. On the other hand, reference to 'contamination' understates the extent to which these controls actually prevent pollution. As appropriate, therefore, reference is to 'pollution and contamination', or to 'quality' where the objective of regulation is to prevent discharges from maritime activities or achieve desirable reductions in overall pollution loading.

---

[6] See generally Chs.9, 10, and 12 above; see also the specific control regime governing radioactive waste discharges discussed in Ch.20 below.

[7] GESAMP (1990) estimates that only about 1% of marine pollution originates from these activities globally. The figure is much higher for areas like the North Sea, in the region of 25%. See OKOOA (1998) and Ospar, *Quality Status Report 2000*. For an overview of the control of these operational discharges see Churchill and Lowe (1999) pp.370-79.

## 18.2 'Marine Pollution'

As the term is defined,[8] 'marine pollution' in international law is concerned exclusively with the consequence of human activities, thereby excluding natural forms of water contamination. This is particularly important in relation to the marine environment. Synthetic organic compounds such as PCBs and artificial radionuclides do not occur naturally and so a zero baseline can be set for the purposes of regulation.[9] However, most of the substances regarded as being polluting, or potentially polluting, are found naturally in the sea in varying quantities and concentrations. Oil, for example, seeps naturally into the waters around parts of the British coast.[10] More particularly, however, the restriction of the definition to the 'introduction . . . of substances or energy' can be seen as limiting those human actions which fall within the scope of regulation so as to exclude human-induced alterations in water quality or composition more generally.[11] The definition is also couched wholly in terms of the damaging consequences of human activities upon the marine environment; it is the consequence of the input, rather than the input as such, that is the 'pollution'.[12]

A further important feature of the definition of 'pollution' in international marine law is the extent to which it extends to cover the introduction of substances which are 'likely' to cause damage, to which extent it gives effect to the precautionary principle.[13] The precautionary principle is seen as having particular application in relation to marine environmental quality management because of the limited state of knowledge of the marine environment. For example, the variability of naturally occurring heavy metals is significant, but not completely understood. This makes it impossible to set standards with respect to the critical, or threshold, level of such substances, which has clear implications for any regulatory approach centred on environmental quality standards.[14]

Finally, it is also notable that the definition of marine pollution in the Law of the Sea Convention makes no direct attempt to identify what such polluting substances might be. Instead, it leaves it to regional treaties to identify what particular substances will be regarded as causing 'pollution' in particular circumstances.[15] The concept of marine pollution stated at the level of generality of the customarily cited international definition is too imprecise to be of direct legal application to the range of situations where the problem arises. However, many of the same elements are to be found,

---

[8] Art.1(4) 1982 UN Law of the Sea Convention; Art.1(4) 1992 OSPAR Convention for the Protection of the Marine Environment of the North East Atlantic. Reproduced in full at 1.3.3 above.

[9] See generally Grant and Jickells (2000). This is not to say that a zero baseline *ought* to be set.

[10] For examples see Clark (1997) p.5.

[11] For example, see Art.21(2) 1997 Convention on the Non-Navigable Uses of International Watercourses.

[12] See 1.3.2 above.

[13] On the precautionary principle more generally see 4.7.1 above.

[14] See generally Grant and Jickells (2000).

[15] For regional treaties pertinent to the UK see 18.8 below.

stated with greater refinement, in contexts where international treaties and national legislatures seek to create legal obligations with regard to the prevention of marine pollution in the contexts discussed in the following sections.

## 18.3 Legal Approaches to Marine Contaminants

In general terms there are three methods by which the different types of marine pollution may be categorised for legal purposes:

(a) according to the source of the contaminant or pollutant;
(b) according to the cause of contamination or pollution; and
(c) according to the nature of the contaminant or pollutant.[16]

Following the first of the three methods, a distinction is drawn between substances originating from land-based sources, ships, dumping at sea, exploration and exploitation of the sea bed, and from the atmosphere.[17] On this classification, land-based pollution includes all pollution generated by water run-off from land along with consented discharges into inland and coastal waters and other entries of polluting matter into water from land.[18] Controls upon pollution from ships developed from international concern about accidental and purposeful emissions of oil from ships, though provisions have now been extended by analogy to a range of harmful substances emanating from vessels either as a result of carriage of hazardous cargoes or as a result of normal shipping operations.[19] Dumping of waste at sea is a hybrid of the previous two categories of 'pollution' source, involving disposal of sewage, industrial or mining waste, which 'presents both the peculiarities of land-based pollution and the jurisdictional problems of ship-generated pollution'.[20]

In respect of the second legal classification of marine pollution, according to cause, a general distinction is to be drawn between accidental, incidental and purposeful forms of pollution.[21] Thus it can be seen that spectacular disasters, involving widespread marine pollution, are capable of arising as an unintended consequence of shipping operations without negligence being shown on the part of those in charge of the vessel.[22] Alternatively, pollution may arise as an unwanted, but inevitable, incidental consequence of other operations involving disturbance of the marine environment, such

---

[16] See Timagenis (1980) pp.16-19 and Churchill and Lowe (1999) pp.329-332.

[17] Apart from discussion of integrated pollution control at 12.3 above and the impact of this on atmospheric emissions, the last two are beyond the scope of this work. A similar classification of the forms of pollution is to be found under the Law of the Sea Convention Part XII s.5, which devotes separate articles to: pollution from land-based sources; pollution from sea-bed activities; pollution from activities in the area; pollution by dumping; pollution from vessels; and pollution from or through the atmosphere, see 18.7 below.

[18] See generally Chs. 9, 10, 12–14 above.

[19] See Ch.19 below.

[20] Timagenis (1980) p.17 and see also Ch.19 below.

[21] See Timagenis (1980) pp.18-19.

[22] See *Esso Petroleum* v *Southport Corporation* [1955] 3 All ER 864, and see 13.11 above.

as the cleaning of cargo tanks or deballasting of vessels which have been involved in the transportation of pollutants.[23] As a third possibility the seas may be used for the purposeful disposal of waste when this is considered to be justified compared to other waste management options. To an extent these differences in the causes of pollution are reflected in the legal approaches to different kinds of pollution. As will be seen, the accidental character of a marine pollution incident will not deprive the appropriate Government agency of a power to intervene to reduce the effects of pollutants;[24] incidental pollution is properly approached through the provision of reception facilities for harmful substances and criminalisation of the behaviour of those who cause the emission of avoidable pollutants;[25] and the unacceptable consequences of purposeful sea dumping of waste are most effectively curtailed by criminal punishments subject to systems of authorisation which regulate the character and amount of pollutants, and the conditions under which disposal may take place.[26]

The third legal classification of marine pollution is according to the nature of the polluting or contaminating substance. Because of its distinctive characteristics, in particular its visibility, and because of a number of high profile shipping casualties over the last thirty years, oil has received the most legislative consideration.[27] In many respects, these have been out of proportion to the relative impact of oil on the marine environment.[28] Many of the rules devised to regulate the hazard of oil pollution have subsequently been extended by analogy to apply to other noxious liquid substances carried by vessels in bulk.[29] Yet many individual polluting substances such as persistent organic pollutants have not yet been the subject of such targeted legal controls as oil. Specific substance-based controls can also be seen in respect of water contamination by radioactive matter, which place this form of pollution in a unique category set apart from the general law of water quality.[30]

On balance, there has been a preference for source-based controls rather than for dealing with pollution according to the nature of particular polluting substances. This is because source control is easier to achieve having regard to the respective jurisdictional natures of land and sea.[31] Nevertheless, within international and regional treaties, EC directives and national legislation the trend has been towards an appreciation of the differential environmental impacts of various substances, and the recognition that the stringency of legal restrictions should reflect these

---

[23] See Ch.19 below on marine oil pollution generally.

[24] See 19.11 below.

[25] Generally see 19.5–19.10 below.

[26] See 19.18 *et seq* below on controls on sea dumping.

[27] See 19.2.1, 19.5–19.9 and 19.12–19.15 below.

[28] GESAMP (1990) estimated that oil pollution accounted for around 12% of overall marine pollution loading.

[29] See 19.10 and 19.16. Notably, this has not yet extended to international rules on liability for spills of substances other than oil.

[30] Generally see Ch.20 below on radioactive contamination.

[31] Churchill and Lowe (1999) p.331.

degrees of hazard,[32] though there remains a tendency to regulate reactively in relation to those substances which are most prominent as matters of public concern.

## 18.4  The Pollution and Contamination of UK Coastal Waters

In international terms the United Kingdom has traditionally made considerable use of what has been seen as the environmental advantage of being surrounded by seas with a major capacity to receive and neutralise large amounts of sewage sludge and industrial waste without great damage to the marine ecosystem. As the Royal Commission on Environmental Pollution observed in 1972,

> The sea is a powerful and effective scavenger of many pollutants . . . [and] Britain is fortunate in being surrounded by seas which are subject to strong currents, in addition to a relatively high tidal rise and fall . . . In the North Sea the strong currents, the high winds and the shallow waters together give a high degree of aeration and good mixing, which provide good conditions for the assimilation of degradable effluents such as domestic sewage and certain industrial wastes.[33]

As the counterpart to this, however, the geographical environmental advantages of the UK may be gained at the expense of European neighbours who suffer corresponding environmental disadvantages. In oceanic terms, for example, the North Sea is a fairly small, shallow and enclosed basin in relation to the populations and industries discharging their waste into it, and these features make it particularly vulnerable to marine pollution. Moreover, because of prevailing westerly winds, the water circulation in the sea is in an overall anti-clockwise direction, and pollutants discharged or dumped into the sea are subject to nationally uneven patterns of dispersal. A consequence of the movement of water through the sea is that,

> the outflow from British rivers follows the general circulation into the open sea, crossing the North Sea towards the German Bight. In contrast, water from continental rivers remains trapped along the coast and passes into the German Bight and the Wadden Sea. As a result, contaminants concentrate in the eastern coastal zone of the southern North Sea. So while Britain exports its pollution, continental pollution remains largely in Continental waters.[34]

---

[32] For examples see the London Convention at 19.19.2 below; and the EC Dangerous Substances Directive, discussed at 5.4.1 above.

[33] Royal Commission on Environmental Pollution (1972) paras.6-7.

[34] Milne (1987) p.53. See also Clark (1987) p.14. For a general overview of water quality issues concerning the North Sea see Clark (1997) pp.127-131; Grant and Jickells (2000) and the OSPAR *Quality Status Report 2000* (on which see 18.8.4 below).

It is also clear, however, that the North Sea is not only affected by direct discharges into the Sea[35] or via river estuaries flowing into it. For example, the distribution of radionuclides originating from Sellafield, while most concentrated in the Irish Sea, extends down the east coast of the UK to the Humber estuary as well as across the North Sea towards the Norway coastal current.[36] Indeed, the impact of ocean currents and circulation is such that, in general terms, contaminants discharged to all the seas around the UK will tend to migrate towards the North Sea over time. Of course, the impact of marine pollution is usually felt close to the point of discharge at the coast, not least because of the concentration of polluting industries on the coast and because of structures like sewage outfalls. In areas like the Irish Sea, however, the three years on average that it takes for a mass of water to be 'flushed' out has consequences for the discharge of substances such as long-lived toxic substances, which may become concentrated before they can be dispersed into the wider marine environment.[37] Furthermore, although relatively poorly understood, the impact of atmospheric deposits tend to be more widely distributed, although the quality of waters in the southern part of the North Sea near to industrial centres in probably poorer than elsewhere.

Whatever the overall balance between contaminating inputs and the assimilative and dispersive capacities of the North and Celtic Seas may be, two features of the legal approach to their water quality are incontrovertible. The first is that their capacity to receive and counteract contaminants without environmental deterioration cannot be unlimited if damage is not to be caused to marine ecosystems. Not least amongst the grounds for concern are the long-term biological effects of accumulations of persistent substances such as toxins and heavy metals. Marine environments have a low buffering capacity against such substances,[38] though concentrations in top predator species such as seals appear to remain well within levels recognised as being hazardous.[39] The second, unavoidable, feature is the international nature of the problem. Whatever the precise dispersal pattern of contaminating substances may be, and wherever the harmful effects that may ultimately be manifested, it is clear that contamination has no respect for the geographical jurisdictions of national legislatures. In addition, mechanisms must exist which can adequately regulate the global movement of shipping, which brings its own cross-border environmental and legal difficulties. At some level, therefore, mechanisms must transcend national boundaries, whether this is under international law or at European level.[40] The general obligations of

---

[35] Indeed, direct discharges are not of great quantitative significance to the quality of the North Sea, although, as noted below, their localised impact may be considerable: Grant and Jickells (2000) p.382.

[36] Clark (1987) p.18. Radioactive discharges from Sellafield have been tracked to the Arctic. On Sellafield and marine discharges more generally see 20.8 below.

[37] Clark (1987) p.25.

[38] See Royal Commission on Environmental Pollution (1972) paras.6-7; Royal Commission on Environmental Pollution (1983) para.2.14 and Milne (1987).

[39] Clark (1997) pp.128-9.

[40] See Ch.5 on European Community water legislation generally.

international law with respect to marine water quality, applicable in the first instance between states rather than individuals, form the basis of the following discussion.

## 18.5  Customary International Law on Marine Pollution

The international law relating to the quality of the marine environment derives from two main sources. First are the recognised principles of customary international law, which only extend to 'pollution' as this term is used in this book.[41] Second are specific treaties between signatory states relating to specific harmful substances, or contaminating or polluting activities, within specified areas. In practical terms the latter is by far of the greater importance, not least because specific compliance mechanisms can be provided for. Yet, despite its limitation to pollution, customary law remains a residual source of obligations in respect of the marine environment.[42]

### 18.5.1  'Good Neighbourliness'

Although lacking direct authoritative support, there are good reasons to suppose that customary international law, which requires state practice and acceptance as law, recognises a principle of 'good neighbourliness' as the general basis of international environmental obligations.[43] Consequently, a state is under a duty to regulate its affairs in such a way as not to cause harm to other states, and in particular, not to allow activities within its area to cause environmental damage within the areas of other states. Clearly this principle has important implications in respect of the obligation of a state to avoid water pollution, at least as far as this affects other states.

A leading decision on the application of the good neighbourliness principle in customary international law is the *Trail Smelter* arbitration between the United States and Canada.[44] The dispute at issue concerned a smelting plant in British Columbia which emitted fumes that were carried across the national border and caused harm within the United States. The International Joint Commission established to consider the issue, in the light of international law and practice, directed cessation of the nuisance, and concluded that as a matter of international law,

> no state has the right to use or permit the use of its territory in such a manner as to cause injury by fumes in or to the territory of another or

---

[41] On the meaning accorded to 'pollution' see 1.3 above.

[42] General reading on customary international law on marine pollution includes Petaccio (1972); Barros and Johnston (1974); Hakapïï (1981); Springer (1983); Abecassis and Jarashow (1985) Ch.2; Birnie and Boyle (1992) pp.254-7; Bates and Benson (1993, updated) paras.1.10-1.20; Brubaker (1993) pp.58-63.

[43] *Sic utere tuo ut alienum non laedas*, sometimes abbreviated as *sic utere*, meaning: 'use your property so as not to injure that of your neighbour'. Although Brubaker (1993) pp.63-4 argues that this is a 'general principle of law', meaning that it could be used to more general effect, the better view is that it is a rule of customary law (Churchill and Lowe (1999) p.12).

[44] (1940) 3 *RIAA* 1905.

the property or persons therein, when the case is of serious consequence and the injury is established by clear and convincing evidence.[45]

Although directly concerned with air pollution, it is now fairly well settled that similar considerations apply to other forms of environmental damage caused by activities within one state which cause damage within the area of another state. More particularly the decision has been claimed as the basis of an international obligation upon states to avoid pollution of water adversely affecting other states.[46]

Although not concerned with environmental obligations, the principle of good neighbourliness in international law gains further support from the decision of the International Court of Justice in the *Corfu Channel* case.[47] The facts giving rise to this decision were that Albania had placed mines in certain of its territorial waters without the knowledge of passing British warships on manoeuvres, and as a result damage and loss of life were sustained by the British. The court held that Albania was under an obligation to notify and warn the approaching British ships of the hazard. Specifically, the basis of the decision was the obligation of every state 'not to allow knowingly its territory to be used for acts contrary to the rights of other states'.[48]

A trio of longstanding caselaw authorities for the good neighbourliness principle in customary international law is completed by the decision of the *Lake Lanoux* arbitration.[49] Lake Lanoux is situated in France but drains into Spain where out-flowing waters are used for agricultural purposes. The French Government, which wished to raise the level of the lake and divert the flow of its waters for power generation purposes, had been unsuccessful in gaining the assent of the Spanish Government to the scheme, and the matter was submitted to arbitration.[50] It was held that there had been no violation of Spanish interests because,

> according to the rules of good faith, the upstream state is under the obligation to take into consideration the various interests involved, to seek to give them every satisfaction compatible with the pursuit of its own interests, and to show that in this regard it is genuinely concerned to reconcile the interests of the other riparian State with its own.[51]

The French Government was found not to have violated the Spanish interest, since the quality and quantity of water discharged were unchanged and no damage was done to the Spanish interest. Significantly

---

[45] *Ibid* p.1965.
[46] See Petaccio (1972) pp.21-5; Fleisher (1973) at p.80-82; and Harris (1974 A) pp.77-81.
[47] [1949] ICJ Rep 4.
[48] *Ibid* at p.22.
[49] (1957) ILR 101.
[50] Under the Franco-Spanish Arbitration Treaty of 1929.
[51] (1957) ILR 101 at p.139.

it was noted that the situation would have been otherwise had the works which were undertaken caused an ultimate pollution of the waters of the outflowing river in respect of chemical composition or temperature.[52] Once again general support is provided for the view that pollution of the waters of another state is capable of being a ground of liability in customary international law.[53]

From the caselaw of customary international law it has been suggested that 'if an activity or situation within the territory of a state was sufficiently hazardous to the interests of other states to make damage to those interests foreseeable, the state has a duty to prohibit it'.[54] Such a general principle of customary international law would be in clear accordance with the authorities, and aligned with the more detailed regime provided for under the United Nations Convention on the Law of the Sea of 1982 ('the LOS Convention').[55] Again with an emphasis on pollution rather than adverse environmental change more generally, this customary law rule has been suggested as the basis for an international crime which would arise when there was 'a serious breach of an international obligation of essential importance for the safeguarding and preservation of the human environment, such as those prohibiting massive pollution of the atmosphere or of the seas'. To the extent that the seriousness of the breach was below that required for an international crime, an international delict (i.e. a civil wrongdoing) would be committed.[56] It must be pointed out, though, that the formulation of this rule is such that it is difficult to see how it would be applied in practice. For example, an incident on the high seas might not give rise to 'pollution', and there would be obvious enforcement difficulties. In addition, it might be questioned whether prosecution would really be the most appropriate response to an act of this kind.[57]

### 18.5.2 From Good Neighbourliness to Good Practice

If the good neighbourliness principle can be stated only at a high level of generality, then it would clearly lack authoritative and decisive application to particular situations involving water pollution.[58] However, it is argued that the impact of the LOS Convention alters this position considerably.[59] At least in relation to discharges from ships, dumping and sea-bed operations, the obligation to apply rules and standards no less onerous than

---

[52] *Ibid* at p.123.

[53] See Petaccio (1972) pp.23-24; Harris (1974b) p.119 and Hakapïï (1981) pp.136-8.

[54] Abecassis and Jarashow (1985) p.15

[55] See 18.7 below.

[56] Art.19 *Draft Articles on State Responsibility*, International Law Commission.

[57] By analogy, no international criminal or delictual action followed the Chernobyl disaster, see Sands (1995).

[58] See also Boyle (1992).

[59] The provisions of international conventions are a major and important source when arguments are raised about the content of customary international law, since they usually provide clear evidence of what states accept as legally binding on them.

'generally recognised international rules and standards'[60] may mean that states which have ratified the LOS Convention may, as a matter of customary international law, be bound by basic standards set out in treaties such as the 1972 London Dumping Convention and the 1973/78 'MARPOL' Convention on oil pollution from vessels.[61] This is different from the provisions of the LOS Convention relating to land-based and atmospheric pollution[62] where various factors such as a state's economic capacity and development needs must be taken into account. The importance of this is that the obligation in the LOS Convention to 'protect and preserve the marine environment',[63] discussed below, may be shed of some of its generality in relation to certain substances and marine activities. Nevertheless, the numerous difficulties of policing compliance with purely customary law obligations, and issues of proof and causation, remain.

It is also worth noting the likely impact of the LOS Convention on the obligations of states under customary international law in relation to the wider marine environment. It seems clear[64] that the general obligation to protect and preserve the marine environment extends to the high seas. To the extent that it represents states' practice and conviction, therefore, the LOS Convention marks a clear departure from the previous position that what mattered was the freedom of the high seas subject only to restrictions based on states' 'reasonable use'. Instead, in what has been remarked as being 'indicative of an altered sense of priorities in the treatment of marine pollution', the emphasis has now swung to the general legal obligation to protect the marine environment. Moreover, it is argued that this would be the case even if the LOS Convention were not yet in force, because of the extent to which it articulates principles of customary law.[65] If this view is followed, then some of the problems associated with the inadequate delineation of legislative and enforcement jurisdiction under customary law might not be seen as so problematic, though it would still require *some* state's interests to be affected for compliance procedures to be initiated. This view, however, is challenged by those who see the scope of customary international law as limited substantively to the protection of narrower human (or at least national) interests. On this view, states are only required not to permit their nationals to discharge into the sea matter that could cause harm to the nationals of other states.[66]

---

[60] Arts.208, 210 and 211 Law of the Sea Convention, see 18.7.3 below.

[61] On the London Dumping Convention see 19.19.2 below; on 'MARPOL' see 19.4–9 below. A more 'ambitious' argument is that the provisions of these specific conventions are themselves customary international law due to their wide-spread ratification; see Birnie and Boyle (1992) pp. 256-57.

[62] Arts.207 and 212 LOS Convention, discussed at 18.7 below.

[63] *Ibid* Art.192.

[64] *Ibid* Art.194.

[65] Birnie and Boyle (1992) p.257. Most commentators agree that the LOS Convention represents at least a partial codification of customary law. For a brief overview of differences of opinion on the extent of this, see Brubaker (1993) p.62.

[66] Smith (1988) Chs.5 and 6 and Churchill and Lowe (1999) p.332.

## 18.5.3 International Sustainable Development Law

Finally, brief comment should be made on the emergence of an international law of 'sustainable development'.[67] Although marine pollution has been the subject of a number of international treaties, it is clear that wise use of the world's oceans is an essential part of any holistic strategy of global environmental governance. Evidence of this can be seen, for example, in that fact that Agenda 21, the global environmental action plan agreed at the United Nations Conference on Environment and Development in 1992, includes a Chapter (17) on 'The Oceans and All Kinds of Seas'.[68] Of course, Agenda 21 is a non-legally binding text, and it is a matter of debate whether Chapter 17 contains any new initiatives or merely describes the need for work to be undertaken in areas where progress was already being made, at least as far as sea-based pollution is concerned.[69] Nevertheless, Agenda 21 is an important document in the realisation of sustainable development. In addition to its emphasis on the need for improved implementation and enforcement of marine pollution controls, it serves to emphasise the extent to which securing satisfactory water quality at an international level is an essential precondition to the conservation of biodiversity and sustainable use of natural living resources.

More generally, the emergence of an international law of sustainable development is said to establish, as customary law, a number of recognised principles of environmental law. These include the precautionary principle and the principle that the polluter should pay.[70] Such principles are found in nearly all modern conventions dealing with marine pollution, and many consider them to have crystallised into customary international law.[71] More speculatively, the concept of sustainable development applied to pollution prevention and control may also include the principle that the best available techniques or technology, or clean technology, should be used to prevent, reduce or eliminate marine pollution. Additionally, there is support for the view that principles of a more procedural nature are also a part of customary law. For example, the requirement to conduct an environmental impact assessment may be seen either as a 'free-standing' principle, or as necessary to give practical effect to the precautionary principle.[72] A number of such procedural principles are found in the 'Rio Declaration', signed at the United Nations Conference on Environment and Development in 1992.[73] Although the Rio Declaration is a 'soft law'

---

[67] See generally Sands (1994). On sustainable development in other contexts see 4.4.1 and 6.7 above.

[68] The Rio 'Earth Summit'. For the text of Agenda 21 see www.unep.org

[69] See the differences of opinion in Nollkaemper (1993) and in Wonham (1998). See also 19.3 below.

[70] On these principles see 4.7 above.

[71] See e.g. Cameron and Aboucher (1991) and McIntyre and Mosedale (1997) on the precautionary principle; and Sands (1994) and Shanmuganthan and Warren (1997) on sustainable development and international law generally.

[72] For example *New Zealand v France* ICJ Rep 1995, 288 ('Nuclear Tests II'), dissenting opinions of Judges Koroma, Palmer and Weeramantry. See also Sands (1994).

[73] Reproduced in Birnie and Boyle (1995) pp.9-14.

text, meaning that it is not directly binding as a matter of international law there is some support for the view that it plays a central role in crystallising a number of component aspects to an international customary law of sustainable development, even if many of the principles in the Declaration are stated at a high level of generality.

## 18.6 Marine Pollution under International Treaties

The difficulties inherent in the customary international law duty to avoid pollution, at least if this would harm the interests of a neighbouring state, has the consequence that the international law on marine pollution is to be found, almost exclusively, in international treaties. The specific features of the most important of these are considered elsewhere, but for the present discussion some general features of international treaty regulation of maritime activities which impact on marine water quality are to be noted.

Those international treaties relevant to UK law are categorised, according to their sphere of applicability, as being either global or regional in extent.[74] Under this classification the most important examples of global treaties which are presently in force are the United Nations Law of the Sea Convention,[75] together with multilateral conventions relating to dumping at sea[76] and a range of international treaties governing marine pollution from shipping.[77]

Of the regionally applicable treaties concerning marine pollution, the most important affecting the United Kingdom is the 1992 Convention for the Protection of the Marine Environment of the North-East Atlantic (the 'OSPAR Convention'). This came into force in 1998 and superseded separate conventions on dumping of wastes and other matter and marine pollution from land-based sources.[78] At regional level there is also the Agreement for Co-operation in Dealing with Pollution of the North Sea by Oil and Other Harmful Substances 1983, which deals with co-operation in oil pollution emergencies, although there is now a global treaty covering similar ground, the 1990 International Convention on Oil Pollution Preparedness, Response and Co-operation.[79] The European Community also has an impact on the pollution of marine waters, but as yet EC law has still to develop into a specialist body of controls on the regulation of maritime activities.[80] This has been because of a deference to specialist regimes such as the 1973/78 MARPOL Convention and the 1992 OSPAR

---

[74] For geographical reasons, and because of the existence of regional agreements and the EC, bilateral conventions have not been relied upon.

[75] See 18.7 below.

[76] See 19.9 below.

[77] See 19.3–16 below.

[78] The OSPAR Convention, and the conventions it replaces, are discussed at 18.8 below.

[79] See 19.11 below on these agreements.

[80] While all the Community water directives impact on marine water quality, the directives of greatest practical impact are the Dangerous Substances Directive, the Bathing Waters Directive, the Urban Waste Water Treatment Directive and the Shellfish Waters Directive. See generally Ch.5 above.

Convention, though there are clear signs that following recent incidents (the *Braer*, *Sea Empress* and now the *Erika*) it intends to play a more prominent role.[81]

## 18.7  The Law of the Sea Convention

The 1982 United Nations Convention on the Law of the Sea[82] represents the most comprehensive attempt to formulate a set of globally applicable rules of international law governing marine pollution. The fundamentally important codification of the law of the sea provided by the Convention came into force on 16 November 1994 for an initial 68 states. Since 1994, with the conclusion of a new Agreement amending the Convention's provisions on seabed mining, states of the developed world have increasingly ratified the Convention, and the UK eventually acceded to the Convention on 25 July 1997.[83] Nevertheless, many of the provisions of the Convention which were a matter of general consensus between the parties may already have had the status of customary international law to which the UK was bound to adhere.[84] Alongside this codification of existing customary law, the Convention has been of greatest importance in further developing the scope for new customary law, as well as introducing many important changes such as those in relation to the high seas.

### 18.7.1  Boundaries

The provisions of the Convention which are of most direct importance to the law of marine pollution are those within Part XII, concerned with the protection and preservation of the marine environment.[85] These provisions are to be read alongside a number of more general features of the Convention concerned with the jurisdiction of coastal states to regulate adjacent waters. The first of these is the recognition of state sovereignty extending beyond land territory and internal waters to an adjacent belt of coastal water described as the 'territorial sea',[86] in respect of which sovereignty extends to the air space over the sea and also to the sea bed and subsoil.[87] The extent of the territorial sea is not to exceed 12 nautical miles, measured from baselines that are normally the low-water line along

---

[81] See COM (2000) 142 and COM (2000) 802.

[82] 21 *ILM* (1982) 1261, and available at www.globelaw.com. General reading on the Law of the Sea Convention includes: Hargrove (1975); Johnston (1981); Theutenberg (1984); O'Connell (1984); Boyle (1985); Sanger (1986); Brown (1994); IUCN (1995); Juda (1996) and Churchill and Lowe (1999).

[83] On UK accession to the LOS Convention see Anderson (1997) and Churchill (1998). The EC has also ratified the LOS Covention.

[84] See 18.5 above, and also *Gulf of Maine* case [1984] ICJ Rep. 246. The preamble to the OSPAR Convention, discussed at 18.8 below, recalls the relevant provisions of customary law reflected in Part XII of the LOS Convention.

[85] Arts.192-237 LOS Convention. Various other provisions in the Convention may also impinge on questions of marine pollution, e.g. flag state responsibility for ships causing oil pollution on the high seas (Part VII). See generally Mensah (1999) pp.1-2.

[86] See Hakapïï (1981) Ch.9.

[87] Art.2 LOS Convention.

the coast of the state.[88] A coastal state may adopt laws and regulations relating to the innocent passage of ships through its territorial sea in respect of the preservation of the environment and the prevention, reduction and control of pollution of the territorial sea.[89] This is supplemented by more specific provisions, provided for the first time under the LOS Convention, for port states[90] to take measures to prevent and control marine pollution from vessels.[91]

A second jurisdictional feature of the Convention is a provision for states to establish 'exclusive economic zones'[92] as areas of up to 200 nautical miles from the baselines from which the breadth of the territorial sea is measured which are subject to certain rights and jurisdiction of the coastal state.[93] In particular, within its exclusive economic zone a state has jurisdiction over the protection and preservation of the marine environment.[94] However, this is subject to certain exceptions designed to ensure freedom of navigation, the central concern of the major maritime and military powers during the Convention's negotiations.[95] The resulting compromise is that coastal states must adhere to generally accepted international rules and standards, but there is a limited right, subject to the consent of the competent international organisation,[96] to adopt specific measures to provide sufficient ecological protection for specific areas.[97]

### 18.7.2 General Obligations

Those provisions of the Convention concerned with the marine environment commence with an unequivocal affirmation of the duty of states to protect and preserve the marine environment.[98] Pursuant to this states are to take, individually or jointly, all measures consistent with the Convention that are necessary to prevent, reduce and control pollution[99] of the marine environment from any source. For this purpose, states must use the best practicable means at their disposal and, in accordance with their capabilities, are to endeavour to harmonise their policies with those of other states in this respect.[100] Specifically mentioned are those measures

---

[88] *Ibid* Arts.3 and 5.

[89] *Ibid* Art.21.

[90] That is, states whose ports are visited by a vessel.

[91] See generally Keselj (1999).

[92] See Phillips (1977); Hakapïï (1981); Brown (1994) Ch.12 and Churchill and Lowe (1999) Chs 9 and 10.

[93] Arts.55 and 57 LOS Convention.

[94] *Ibid* Art.56.

[95] Sanger (1986) pp.20-21.

[96] The International Maritime Organisation; see Churchill and Lowe (1999) p.347.

[97] Art.211(5) and (6) LOS Convention, and see also the IMO Guidelines for the Designation of Special Areas and the Identification of Particularly Sensitive Sea Areas, IMO Resolution A. 720 (17).

[98] *Ibid* Art.192.

[99] The LOS Convention is centred around the concept of 'pollution' rather than that of 'quality', as these terms are used in this book. On the definition of 'pollution' in the Convention see 1.3.3 above.

[100] Art.194(1) LOS Convention.

which must be taken by states in respect of the discharge of polluting substances and polluting impacts from vessels. Thus states must minimise to the fullest possible extent the release of toxic, harmful or noxious substances, especially those which are persistent, from land based sources, from or through the atmosphere or by dumping. Similarly, measures are to be taken to minimise to the fullest possible extent pollution originating from vessels, in particular by adopting measures for preventing accidents and dealing with emergencies; ensuring the safety of operations at sea; preventing intentional and unintentional discharges; and regulating the design, construction, equipment, operation and manning of vessels.[101]

The principle of good neighbourliness[102] is embodied in the Convention in that states are to ensure that activities within their jurisdiction or control are so conducted as not to cause damage by pollution to other states and their environment. Similarly pollution arising from incidents or activities under the jurisdiction or control of a state is not to spread beyond the areas where it exercises sovereign rights in accordance with the Convention.[103] The good neighbourliness principle is further affirmed by the stipulation that in taking measures to prevent, reduce and control pollution of the marine environment, states are to act so as not to transfer, directly or indirectly, damage or hazards from one area to another or transform one type of pollution into another.[104] This is a general obligation which falls some way short of integrated pollution controls as there are understood at national and EC level.

Further articles of the LOS Convention make general provision for co-operation on environmental matters. Thus states are to co-operate on a global and regional basis directly or through competent international organisations, in formulating and elaborating international rules, standards and recommended practices and procedures for the protection and preservation of the marine environment.[105] From the scheme of the Convention and its negotiating history, however, it is clear that considerable emphasis is placed on seeking regional approaches, especially to discharges from land-based activities. A duty to notify states likely to be affected by marine pollution arises where a state becomes aware that the marine environment is in imminent danger of being damaged, or has been damaged, by pollution.[106] In such a case the states in the area affected are to co-operate, to the extent possible, in eliminating the effects of pollution and preventing or minimising the damage, and promote contingency plans for responding to such incidents.[107] In addition, states are to co-operate, directly or through competent international organisations, for the purpose of promoting studies, undertaking programmes of scientific research and

---

[101] *Ibid* Art.194(3).

[102] See 18.5.1 above.

[103] Art.194(2) LOS Convention.

[104] *Ibid* Art.195.

[105] *Ibid* Art.197.

[106] Art.198 LOS Convention. This derives from the principle laid down in the *Corfu Channel* case, discussed at 18.5.1 above.

[107] *Ibid* Art.199. See, for example, the 1983 'Bonn' Agreement, see 19.11.2 below.

encouraging the exchange of information and data acquired about pollution of the marine environment. Also, states must endeavour to participate actively in regional and global programmes to acquire knowledge for the assessment of the nature and extent of pollution, exposure to it, and its pathways, risks and remedies.[108]

### 18.7.3 Obligations to Formulate Rules

The general duty of states to protect and preserve the marine environment under the LOS Convention is interpreted as a duty to formulate a range of international rules and national legislation to prevent, reduce and control pollution of the marine environment and to enforce such legislation. As noted above, however, the Convention takes a somewhat different approach to land-based pollution to that taken in relation to marine activities. States must adopt laws and regulations and take such other measures as are necessary to prevent, reduce and control pollution of the marine environment from land-based sources, including rivers, estuaries, pipe-lines and outfall structures. However, considerable leeway is given to take states' levels of development, and regional characteristics, into account.[109]

On the other hand, in relation to waste dumping and discharges from vessels, the general obligation on states is to give effect to or apply rules and standards which are no less onerous than those rules and standards which are generally applicable at international level.[110] In respect of pollution originating from vessels there is also a duty of states to promote the adoption, wherever possible, of routing systems for vessels designed to minimise the threat of accidents which might cause pollution of the marine environment.[111] The different treatment between land-based (and atmospheric) pollution, and pollution arising from maritime activities such as the transport of oil or the dumping of waste at sea, can be explained by a greater sensitivity, with the former, to national developmental objectives and the fact that polluting impact will probably be experienced (or experienced most severely) fairly close to the point of discharge. With maritime activities, the greater concern has been establishing rules which approximate the extent of obligations on international shipping fleets, and which provide a regulatory baseline for the allowable environmental impact of ships on international waterways, high seas dumping grounds, and foreign ports.

---

[108] *Ibid* Art.200. See, for example, the *North Sea Quality Status Report 1993* prepared by the North Sea Task Force, a body established by the Oslo and Paris Commissions and see now the OSPAR *Quality Status Report 2000* (see 18.8 below). On pollution pathways see 1.3.3 above.

[109] *Ibid* Art.207. A similar approach is taken in relation to pollution from or through the atmosphere under Art.212, where internationally agreed rules and standards need only be taken into account and states need only 'endeavour' to establish global and regional rules and standards. See generally Boyle (1992) and Nollkaemper (1996)

[110] *Ibid* Arts.210 and 211. See Birnie and Boyle (1992) p.256. On dumping at sea and vessel-source pollution see generally Ch.19 below.

[111] *Ibid* Art.211 and see also 19.5.6 below on routing.

### 18.7.4  The LOS Convention and other Treaty Regimes

The far-reaching implications of the duties in respect of protection and preservation of the marine environment are self-evident. The LOS Convention clarifies, codifies and in some cases transforms the previous rather *ad hoc* international regime governing marine pollution. It is notable, however, that the provisions under the Convention are intended to rationalise rather than oust existing international agreements relating to marine pollution. Hence, the provisions of the Convention are without prejudice to specific obligations relating to the protection and preservation of the marine environment assumed by states under special conventions and agreements concluded previously. Equally the Convention is without prejudice to future agreements which may be concluded in furtherance of the general principles of the Convention, though obligations arising from such agreements should be carried out in a manner consistent with the general principles and objectives of the Convention.[112]

The LOS Convention is therefore intended to provide a general background of obligations into which specific conventions provide the precise details of particular measures to be taken concerning marine pollution prevention of particular kinds or within particular regions.[113] In this sense the Convention is something of an 'umbrella' or framework convention, to be fleshed out by international rules agreed by bodies such as the International Maritime Organisation in relation to oil pollution,[114] the International Atomic Energy Agency,[115] or under regional agreements. While such rules are reasonably well developed in relation to maritime activities, however, there is as yet no legally-binding global agreement on pollution from land-based sources, although, further to Agenda 21, a Declaration and Global Action Programme have been finalised.[116]

Not least because of the consideration given to states' development objectives in the LOS Convention, as well as the wide variations between regions in the extent and nature of marine pollution from land-based sources, regional approaches to land-based pollution are generally both preferable and preferred. It is at the regional level that substances are to be identified as 'polluting', and in what circumstances.[117] Apart from any such agreements,[118] the only obligation is the rather vague one of ensuring that national laws minimise to the fullest extent possible the release of toxic, harmful, noxious or persistent substances.[119] It is also worth mentioning that the regional approach was also endorsed at the United Nations Conference of Environment and Development in 1992 and

---

[112] *Ibid* Art.237.

[113] See, e.g., Joyner and Martell (1996) pp.77-78.

[114] See 19.4 below on the IMO.

[115] See 20.3.2 below on the IAEA.

[116] *Declaration and Global Programme of Action on Protection of the Marine Environment from Land-Based Activities*, Washington, November 1995, reproduced in 26 *Environmental Policy and Law* 37-51 (1996). See Franckx (1998) pp.316-20 and Churchill and Lowe (1999) pp.380-81.

[117] Boyle (1992) p.25.

[118] For the UK see now the OSPAR Convention at 18.8 below.

[119] Art.207(5) LOS Convention.

prioritised by the Commission on Sustainable Development as a means for implementing Agenda 21 in relation to areas of interaction between the coast and the sea.[120]

The following section considers the principal regional convention affecting the United Kingdom, the 1992 'OSPAR' Convention. This serves both to illustrate many of the general features of regional conventions of this kind, and to introduce some of the core provisions of a Convention system which is important not only in relation to the discharge of radioactive substances and dumping at sea (issues discussed in more detail in later chapters) but more generally.[121]

## 18.8 The OSPAR Convention

The 1992 Convention for the Protection of the Marine Environment of the North East Atlantic,[122] referred to as the 'OSPAR' Convention, is a regional convention which, as its name suggests, applies to the North Sea and the North East Atlantic. The Convention came into force on 25 March 1998. On coming into force, it replaced two prior conventions, the 1974 Paris Convention for the Prevention of Marine Pollution from Land-Based Sources, and the 1972 Oslo Convention for the Prevention of Marine Pollution by Dumping from Ships and Aircraft.[123] Both conventions were later amended with effect from September 1989 to broaden the scope of activities covered, the 1974 Paris Convention to include pollution of the sea from atmospheric sources and the 1972 Oslo Convention to include the incineration of waste at sea. Contracting parties to the OSPAR Convention may include all states which were party to the previous treaties, as well as the EC,[124] which was a party to the 1974 Paris Convention but never the 1972 Oslo Convention. Other coastal states, and states connected to the maritime area of the Convention via a watercourse, may also be parties, in line with taking a catchment-based approach to marine protection.[125]

To some extent the 1992 OSPAR Convention merely consolidates the provisions of the Oslo and Paris Conventions as these have been amended, and supplemented by Decisions and Recommendations, over the years.

---

[120] Franckx (1998) pp.319-320.

[121] The approach taken by the OSPAR Convention to hazardous substances can be seen in the EC Water Framework Directive; obligations under the Convention may be sufficiently binding that they require implementing regulations to be enacted; and the Convention may generate other impacts on national decision-making e.g. in determining discharge consents.

[122] For the text of the Convention see 32 ILM 1069 (1993) and see also www.ospar.org. General reading on the OSPAR Convention includes Hey, IJlstra and Nollkaemper (1993); Sands (1995) pp.304-06 and 322-24 and de La Fayette (1999).

[123] For the text of these conventions see 13 ILM 352 (1974) (Paris) and 11 ILM (1972) 262 (Oslo). For general reading on the Oslo and Paris Conventions and the work of the respective Commissions see Oslo and Paris Commissions (1984); Hayward (1990) and Haas (1993).

[124] The Convention extends to 'regional economic integration organisations' in the area concerned.

[125] Switzerland, for example, is party to the convention. Switzerland's participation is notable because it is the only party which is neither a Member State of the EC, or of the European Economic Area where EC environmental legislation is also accepted. The EC is also a party.

However, the Convention goes some way beyond consolidation in so far as it incorporates developments induced by the International North Sea Conferences (INSCs).[126] So far, four conferences have been held – in 1985, 1987, 1990 and 1995 – and the process is now quasi-institutionalised through a standing committee[127] and interim Ministerial meetings. Although, formally, participation at the INSCs has been limited to the environment Ministers of the eight North Sea states and the EC, and its Declarations are strictly non-binding legally,[128] they have played an important part in securing policy change. In many instances the Declarations have acted as a spur to the strengthening of marine protection controls in this area, often when the EC was cautioning legal and policy restraint.[129] In some instances, however, the non-legally binding provisions of the INSC Declarations have been *weaker* than the applicable treaty law, raising difficult issues of international law about which provision prevails. While the formal legal position may be that the pre-existing legal rule is still binding, as a matter of practical reality it may be superseded by the non-legal rule.[130]

As has been commented on previously,[131] the OSPAR Convention contains a definition of 'pollution' of the kind that is fairly commonly found in international and EC law, albeit one which refers to 'introductions . . . of substances or energy' rather than extending more generally to any human-induced 'alteration'. However, it is notable that, as its title indicates, the OSPAR Convention extends beyond pollution prevention to encompass marine environmental protection more generally. This is given effect to by the binding legal obligation on the parties to

> take the necessary measures to protect the maritime area against the adverse effects of human activities so as to safeguard human health and to conserve marine ecosystems and, when practicable, restore marine areas which have been adversely affected.[132]

This has allowed the Convention to expand in scope to cover ecosystem and biodiversity conservation.[133] Nevertheless, the majority of the provisions of the Convention relate to 'pollution' (in the broad sense defined) and are the focus of the following discussion, which considers

---

[126] Specifically the first, second and third such conferences held in 1985, 1987 and 1990 respectively. A further conference was held in 1995.

[127] The Committee of North Sea Senior Officials (CONSSO).

[128] On the legal status of the Declarations see van der Mensbrugghe (1990) and Pallemaerts (1992).

[129] On the influence of the INSCs see Haas (1993), who remarks that 'Issues relegated to the back burner at OSPARCOM [the Joint Commission for the Oslo and Paris Treaties, discussed below] ... moved to the front burner at the Ministerial Conferences' (p.173). Haas further notes that 'North Sea countries that are members of the EC and desire stringent environmental measures first go to the North Sea institutions to drive a wedge into the EC decision-making process (p.177). This is not to say, however, that the practical result of the INSC Declarations has been actual improvement in water quality: Nollkaemper (1998) p.370.

[130] See Nollkaemper (1998) pp.365-67.

[131] See 1.3.3 above.

[132] Art.2(1)(a) OSPAR Convention.

[133] *Ibid*, Annex V, adopted under Art.7.

several general features of the Convention. Most of these are illustrative of what might be termed a modern, 'second-generation',[134] regional marine convention.

### 18.8.1 General Limitations

The OSPAR Convention applies principally to pollution from land-based sources[135] and from dumping at sea.[136] As defined, 'land-based sources' means 'point and diffuse sources on land from which substances or energy reach the maritime area by water, through the air, or directly from the coast'.[137] 'Dumping' means, first, any deliberate disposal in the maritime area of wastes or other matter from vessels or aircraft, or from offshore installations; and second, any deliberate disposal in the maritime area of vessels or aircraft, or of offshore installations and offshore pipelines.[138] Although the Convention is sufficiently flexible to extend to further areas of marine environmental protection activity,[139] the scope to do so is limited to the extent that such other matters are not already subject to effective measures contained in an international treaty or agreed by an international organisation. It is for this reason that the OSPAR Convention does not seek to regulate pollution originating from vessels.[140] But it is also one of the reasons why, in relation to pollution from atmospheric deposits (an area of explicit competence where measures can be taken without the adoption of a new Annex) the parties to the Convention have so far decided that emissions reductions are best achieved under the principal existing multilateral treaty rather than by agreement between the OSPAR parties.[141]

### 18.8.2 General Objectives

The OSPAR Convention requires contracting parties, in accordance with the provisions of the Convention, to take all possible steps to prevent and

---

[134] 'First-generation' in the context of regional marine pollution conventions refers to those treaties largely adopted in the 1970s. Most of these treaties were adopted under the UN Environment Programme's Regional Seas Programme, although the 1972 Oslo and 1974 Paris Conventions were agreed outside this framework. 'Second-generation' refers either to further, more modern, conventions, or to the replacement of these earlier treaties, with most additions or significant amendments occurring in the 1990s.

[135] See Art.3 and Annex I OSPAR Convention.

[136] *Ibid* Art.4 and Annex II.

[137] *Ibid* Art.1(e).

[138] *Ibid* Art.1(f).

[139] *Ibid* Art.7.

[140] Regulated primarily under the MARPOL treaty regime, and measures adopted by the International Maritime Organization. See generally Ch.19 below.

[141] See the UN/ECE Convention on the Long-Range Transport of Air Pollution, Geneva, 18 ILM 1442 (1979). The parties have also noted that states outside of the OSPAR regime contribute emissions the impact of which are 'likely to be significant' for the OSPAR area: de La Fayette (1999) p.252. There is, however, a Memorandum of Understanding on the exchange of information between the former Paris Commission and the UN/ECE, signed by the two parties in 1991 (de La Fayette (1999) p.262).

eliminate pollution.[142] In some respects this is the regional counterpart of Article 192 of the LOS Convention, discussed above. However, in important respects it goes further: reference to the *elimination of pollution* as an objective of OSPAR, rather than the *prevention or preservation of the marine environment*, is an obvious contrast. This continues the approach found in the Paris Convention (and, in effect, the Oslo Convention). However, as a matter of practice timetables for improvements are a necessary, though clearly not a sufficient, condition for combating deterioration in the marine environment and such a provision only has practical effect if accompanied by a deadline for such elimination. Such deadlines have to be agreed for specific forms of pollution. For example, in 1998 OSPAR Ministers agreed to achieve, by 2010, a healthy marine environment where eutrophication does not occur.[143] What the parties understand by 'elimination' can also be seen from the agreement, also reached at the same meeting, to aim to reduce the concentration of hazardous substances in the environment to near background values for naturally occurring substances and close to zero for man-made synthetic substances. Parties also agreed to 'make every endeavour' to move towards the complete cessation of discharges containing synthetic substances by 2020.[144]

The approach towards eutrophication illustrates the 'framework' nature of the OSPAR Convention. That is, the Convention does not determine acceptable emission levels or quality standards, but rather provides a framework under which the parties set specific standards in accordance with general principles and priorities. Appreciating the nature of the present position requires some grasp of the approach taken prior to the OSPAR Convention.

In line with many other 'first-generation' regional pollution conventions,[145] and other water pollution control measures of the 1970s,[146] the 1974 Paris Convention contained a scheme of classification dividing pollutants into four categories. The first category, known as the 'black list', consisted of the most noxious pollutants and including organohalogen compounds, mercury, cadmium, persistent synthetic materials and oil.[147] The duty upon parties to the Paris Convention was to eliminate pollution

---

[142] The Preamble to the Convention refers to the 'inherent worth of the marine environment' and the objective of achieving its 'sustainable management', but rather suggests that current practices meet this objectives by referring to sustaining the ability of the marine ecosystem to *continue* to sustain legitimate uses (emphasis added)

[143] OSPAR Strategy to Combat Eutrophication (1998). The language of 'eliminating' pollution has parallels in certain EC water directives, see the Dangerous Substances Directive (76/464/EEC) concerning 'List I' substances at 5.4.1 above, and is continued in the Water Framework Directive (2000/60/EEC) see 5.8.5 above.

[144] How OSPAR will be able to do so, given the estimated 50,000 chemicals in use in the EC alone, is not clear, although a new system for prioritisation and risk assessment was introduced in 1998; see generally de La Fayette (1999) pp.286-291.

[145] On the distinction between 'first-generation' and 'second-generation' in this context see 18.8 above.

[146] E.g. the Dangerous Substances Directive (76/464/EEC) and Groundwater Directive (80/68/EEC), discussed at 5.4.1 and 5.4.2 above.

[147] Part I Annex A Paris Convention 1974.

caused by such substances.[148] The second category, the 'grey list', consisted of less harmful pollutants, including organic compounds of phosphorus, silicon and tin, non-persistent oils, arsenic and heavy metals.[149] Pollution caused by this group of substances was to be strictly limited by each contracting party regulating the discharge of the substances by means of a system of authorisations.[150] A third category consisted of all other pollutants, not on the black or grey lists, other than radioactive pollutants which were separately classified. No specified measures had to be taken for these substances, but the parties had to try to reduce pollution caused by these substances by taking into account circumstances such as their nature and quantity and the absorptive capacity of receiving waters.[151] Finally, radioactive substances were placed into a separate category with the parties undertaking to adopt measures to forestall and, as appropriate, to eliminate pollution by these substances.[152]

By contrast, the OSPAR Convention abandons the black and grey listing system in favour of an approach based on the general objective of taking all possible steps to prevent and eliminate pollution from all substances. Centrally, the Convention stipulates the use of process-based standards for pollution reduction. In particular, the best available techniques (BAT) are to be used for point sources, and best environmental practice (BEP) used for point and diffuse sources.[153] However, this approach, which in reality legalised a practice that the Commission of the 1974 Paris Convention had already followed for some years before 1992, is in future to be prioritised according to the criteria defined in Appendix 2. This is intended to avoid distinguishing between, essentially, 'more polluting' and 'less polluting' substances, but also takes into account the inherent difficulties of identifying a limited number of potentially polluting substances from what is an exponentially increasing number of chemicals being placed on the European market. However, a number of categories of substances are explicitly mentioned in Appendix 2 and thus will be subject to programmes and measures. These categories of substances mainly combine the black and grey lists of the 1974 Paris Convention.[154] This approach has had implications for the way in which radioactive substances are regulated.[155]

BAT and BEP are defined in Appendix 1, but the framework nature of the Convention emerges in the elaboration by the OSPAR Commission of decisions and recommendations for BAT and BEP for specific sectors.[156]

---

[148] *Ibid* Art.4(1).

[149] *Ibid* Part II of Annex A.

[150] *Ibid* Art.4.

[151] *Ibid* Art.6.

[152] *Ibid* Art.5 and see Ch.20 below on radioactive contamination generally.

[153] On the concept of best available techniques, see 12.3.3 above.

[154] See Hey, IJlstra and Nollkaemper (1993) p.19.

[155] See 20.5 below.

[156] On the OSPAR Commission and the legal status of decisions and recommendations see 18.8.4 below. Previous decisions and recommendations agreed under the 1974 Paris Convention, so long as not incompatible with the OSPAR Convention, remain in force.

So far, most recommendations on BAT and BEP are carried over from before 1998, and tend to focus on specific sectors (such as aquaculture and the aluminium industry) rather than on specific polluting substances, although there is still a bias towards formulating BAT rather than the perhaps more contentious BEP. Such decisions and recommendations need not be uniform, but may take regional and sub-regional differences in ecological and economic conditions into account. If this is the case, then such measures may either be limited to certain regions, or be phased in according to different timetables.[157] Because the same standards need not be reached in different regions, this provides for a strong version of flexibility, albeit one which is seen as important because of the different institutional dynamics in the North Sea region, discussed above, and concerns that standards appropriate for the North Sea area might be extended generally to the whole convention area. Fears that this provision might be relied upon unduly to weaken standards regionally does not appear to have been justified.[158] Point source discharges must be subject to authorisation or regulation by the parties, which must implement any relevant decision.[159]

### 18.8.3 General Principles and Standard Setting

In addition to the general obligation of preventing and eliminating pollution, and establishing the need to define and implement BAT and BEP (including, where appropriate, clean technology), the OSPAR Convention includes further general obligations. These include the use of time-limited obligations, although only 'where appropriate', and the scope for parties, individually or jointly, to take more stringent measures. Also included are the precautionary principle and the polluter pays principle.

As noted above, the definition of pollution, by covering likely harm, incorporates a precautionary element.[160] However, the parties must also apply the precautionary principle, by virtue of which 'preventive measures are to be taken when there are reasonable grounds for concern' that pollution will arise, 'even where there is no conclusive evidence of a causal relationship between the inputs and the effects'.[161] It has been suggested that, while the latter phrase shifts the focus away from a 'dilute and disperse' approach, the need for 'reasonable grounds for concern' makes the application of the principle unduly subjective, and thus easier to resist by arguing that such grounds do not exist.[162] On the other hand, the definition is an active formulation since measures *are* to be taken; such

---

[157] Art.24 OSPAR Convention.

[158] Hey, IJlstra and Nollkaemper (1993) pp.41-42.

[159] Annex I, Art.2(1) OSPAR Convention.

[160] See 1.3.3 above and see 4.7.1 on the precautionary principle as a principle of EC law.

[161] Art.2(2)(a) OSPAR Convention.

[162] Hey, IJlstra and Nollkaemper (1993) p.12.

measures need not be 'cost-effective';[163] and it is not restricted to instances where serious or irreversible damage is likely.[164]

Parties to the Convention must also apply the polluter pays principle, which requires the costs of pollution prevention, control and reduction measures to be borne by the polluter.[165] Previous discussion of the principle[166] has noted that there may be good reasons why making a polluter pay is not always desirable or feasible, and also many of the uncertainties as to its meaning. What is notable in the OSPAR Convention, however, is its mandatory legal nature. This contrasts with its status in other texts as primarily a policy or economic principle, or as merely a guiding principle.[167]

### 18.8.4 Institutional Arrangements and Compliance Mechanisms

In common with most modern treaties, the OSPAR Convention provides for the establishment of an international organisation, the OSPAR Commission (or 'OSPARCOM') to oversee the operation of the Convention. It also contains well developed rules on decision-making by the Commission, and on the monitoring of implementation and on enforcement.

OSPARCOM consists of representatives of each of the contracting parties.[168] In practice, its establishment merely recognised that for some years the Commissions of the 1974 Paris Convention and the 1972 Oslo Convention had been composed of the same representatives and met on the same occasions, albeit consecutively. And since 1994 there had been joint meetings of the two Commissions, in anticipation of the OSPAR Convention coming into force. OSPARCOM met formally for the first time in July 1998, and it appears that it is interpreting its obligation to meet at 'regular intervals' as meaning annual meetings.[169]

The Commission has four central duties. First, it has a duty to review the state of the marine environment in the area of the Convention. This is an important provision, which has led to a full *Quality Status Report* on all the waters covered by the Convention in 2000.[170] This indicates that the trends towards worsening quality have been reversed, and a number of sources of contamination and pollution have ceased. Nevertheless, there is

---

[163] Compare, e.g., Principle 15 of the 1992 Rio Declaration. However, the criteria to be applied in ascertaining BAT and BEP include 'economic feasibility' and 'social and economic implications'.

[164] See de La Fayette (1999) pp.254-55.

[165] Art.2(2)(b) OSPAR Convention.

[166] See 4.7.3 above.

[167] See e.g. the status of the polluter pays principle in EC environmental law and policy, at 4.7 above, but see 18.9 below on what mandatory might mean here.

[168] Art.10(1) OSPAR Convention.

[169] The first meeting was at Sintra in July 1998, the second meeting at Hull in June 1999 and the third meeting at Copenhagen in June 2000. Meetings will be held annually (which is unusually frequent for international conventions).

[170] At the time of writing, only the Overall Assessment of this was available, at www.ospar.org. The full report is expected by December 2000.

still considerable uncertainty over the state of the marine environment of the North East Atlantic, and new problems like litter and endocrine disrupting substances poses new challenges. Whether the Report has provided enough data to allow for the adoption of a more explicitly water quality approach to standard setting in certain areas in the future remains to be seen.

Second, the Commission has a duty to review the effectiveness of the control measures adopted, the priorities and the need for any additional or different measures. Third, the Commission must draw up, in accordance with the Convention's general obligations, programmes and measures for achieving the objectives of the Convention. As noted above, an important part of this is identifying BAT and BEP for particular substances or sectors and articulating these in decisions, which are legally binding if adopted,[171] and recommendations. Fourth, the Commission must establish a work programme for its activities. These Action Plans, which may include the use of economic instruments, give OSPARCOM an important strategic planning role, although in practice the Commission often follows closely decisions reached at INSCs.[172] It should be noted that decisions and recommendations of the Commission must be adopted by unanimous vote of the parties, but in the absence of consensus, measures can be adopted by a three-quarter majority. In this case, such measures bind only those states approving them.[173]

Finally, the Commission plays a central role in supervising the implementation of the Convention and in securing compliance. The parties must submit regular reports to the Commission on the legal, regulatory and other measures taken by them to implement the Convention, the effectiveness of these measures and problems encountered in their implementation.[174] On the basis of these reports, the Commission must assess parties' compliance, making suggestions to bring about compliance with the Convention when appropriate.[175] Crucially, this duty extends to scrutinising compliance with recommendations, even though recommendations are stated to have no binding force,[176] emphasising the limited practical difference between legally-binding and non-legally binding rules in this field.[177] However, the Commission can only recommend that steps be taken to promote the implementation of recommendations, rather than calling for 'full compliance' as is the case with decisions.[178] Although provision is made for settling disputes between the parties through arbitration,[179] this has never yet been resorted to and political pressure is more likely to be relied on. In any case, whether

---

[171] Art.13(2) OSPAR Convention.

[172] de La Fayette (1999) p.261.

[173] Art.13(1) and (2) OSPAR Convention.

[174] *Ibid* Art.22.

[175] *Ibid* Art.23.

[176] *Ibid* Art.13(5).

[177] Generally see Nollkaemper (1998) especially p.360.

[178] On which see the Action Plan for 1998-2003, adopted at Sintra in 1998.

[179] Art.32 OSPAR Convention.

securing compliance is high on the list of the parties priorities has been doubted.[180]

### 18.8.5 Wider Involvement

In line with other recent conventions, the OSPAR treaty regime seeks both to involve other actors in decision-making and in securing compliance.[181] It does so in two main ways. First, participation in the work of the Commission is open to any international governmental or any non-governmental organisation (NGO) if their activities are related to the Convention and the contracting parties decide unanimously to admit them. This puts such bodies on a par with other non-party states, who may also be admitted under the same terms. There are currently 25 environmental and industrial organisations with either general or specialised observer status, which gives them the right to present reports and attend meetings of the Commission but not to vote.[182] The role of environmental NGOs in monitoring compliance and bringing such evidence to light at meetings of the parties to conventions is well recognised and often encouraged. The parties have also agreed to allow NGOs to participate in working group meetings at all levels, although numbers are limited.[183] This allows representatives of the NGO community to be involved in the elaboration of process standards, rather than just being able to comment on standards when they are proposed for adoption.[184]

Secondly, the Convention includes measures on access to information. These give the public rights to information held by national competent authorities on the state of the marine environment, on activities or measures affecting it and on steps taken under the Convention. These provisions closely follow the European Community Environmental Information Directive, including the exceptions to the general principle of freedom of access.[185] Such access is of evident importance to transparency and to effective wider involvement. Although the information provisions in the Convention do not extend to information held by the Commission itself, access provisions are contained in the Commission's Rules of Procedure. Some information is available on the OSPAR website.[186]

### 18.9 The Enforceability of International Law in the UK

Unlike Community law, international law is not directly enforceable in national courts. This is not to say that it has no impact. Indeed, the

---

[180] Hey, IJlstra and Nollkaemper (1993) p.43.

[181] This section draws on de La Fayette (1999) pp.263-65.

[182] Art.11 OSPAR Convention. On NGO impact see de La Fayette (1999) p.265.

[183] Rules of Procedure of the OSPAR Commission (1998-8).

[184] See also NGO involvement in IPPC, at 12.3.3 above and Royal Commission on Environmental Pollution (1992).

[185] Art.9 OSPAR Convention. On the Environmental Information Directive (90/313/EEC) see 16.6 above.

[186] www.ospar.org

following section outlines the considerable extent to which international law has altered national law and the direction of policy.

In the UK, international agreements only become part of national law once they are given effect to by Parliament, usually through legislation. Moreover, the courts see both the making of treaties[187] and their implementation[188] as a matter solely for Government: 'Treaties . . . are not self-executing. Quite simply, a treaty is not part of English law unless and until it has been incorporated into the law by legislation'.[189] This is the case even where the treaty has been ratified, because in the UK ratification is a matter for central government, not Parliament. All of this means that international agreements, in general, have what might be called 'high-level' rather than 'low-level' effect: they create obligations that bind the UK in its international relations, rather than obligations of the kind that individuals can rely on. In the UK, international agreements like the OSPAR Convention cannot be used as the basis for an action by groups or individuals against the state or a public body (in the way that EC directives may be),[190] nor are they in themselves a source of rights and duties in legal actions between individuals.

Courts will, however, prefer interpretations of statutes which conform with international treaties to which the UK is a party to those which do not, although this does not necessarily mean that in all cases of discretion, there is a presumption in favour of the Convention.[191] But where national legislation is introduced to give effect to a treaty or treaty obligation, then the treaty *can* be used as an aide to interpreting the national law and it is presumed that Parliament did not intend to legislate contrary to the UK's international commitments. This might be pertinent to interpreting national law governing marine oil pollution from shipping, derived from the MARPOL regime, but will not provide much assistance in relation to the OSPAR Convention.

To illustrate the legal effect of international law, under the 1992 OSPAR Convention a Strategy has been agreed which seeks to

> prevent pollution of the maritime area by continuously reducing discharges, emissions and losses of hazardous substances . . . with the ultimate aim of achieving concentrations in the marine environment near background values for naturally occurring substances and close to zero for man-made synthetic substances.[192]

Even if some of the expressions used were less open to differing interpretations (e.g. what 'close to zero' means), this provision could not

---

[187] *Blackburn* v *Attorney-General* [1971] 1 WLR 1037.

[188] *Ex Parte Molyneaux* [1986] 1 WLR 331.

[189] *Maclaine Watson* v *Department of Trade and Industry* [1989] 3 All ER 523 per Lord Oliver at 545.

[190] See 4.16 above for individual 'rights' under EC law.

[191] *R* v *Secretary of State for the Home Department ex parte Brind* [1991] 1 AC 696.

[192] OSPAR Hazardous Substances Strategy (1998-16).

be directly relied upon in legal argument on the grounds that in determining a discharge consent or IPPC permit, its provisions had not been adhered to. Indeed, there is no implementing legislation which can be interpreted in the light of the Convention. The OSPAR Convention is simply not transposed into UK legislation. Instead, if the international law obligation is to be given effect to, decisions under the Water Resources Act 1991 and other relevant legislation must be taken with this kind of target as an objective. Needless to say, in such a situation there is little scope for an individual or group to mount a successful challenge.[193]

Similarly, the OSPAR Convention provides that the polluter pays principle is a binding principle: 'The Contracting Parties shall apply . . . the polluter pays principle, by virtue of which the costs of pollution prevention, control and reduction measures are to be borne by the polluter'.[194] Again, it is not clear that this has any direct legal force at national level if a complaint were to be raised, say, that the charging scheme used by a sewerage undertaker was preferential to large industrial users over smaller operators.

However, it is likely that international law obligations will be recognised in relevant policy guidance, and conceivably failure to have regard to this guidance might provide grounds for a successful legal challenge. For example, the Ramsar Wetlands Convention is given effect to in part through planning guidance which states that Ramsar sites should have the same level of protection from development as European sites under EC conservation law. If a planning authority were to ignore this guidance, there would be grounds for a review of any planning permission which damaged the site. On the other hand, if the decision-maker had regard to this guidance, but decided that in the circumstances development was justified, the decision would not be open to challenge simply because no weight was given to the international law obligations.[195]

## 18.10  International Marine Environmental Law and the UK

Despite the limited effect of international law which is presented by a narrowly legalistic account, in general terms it is clear that UK law, policy and practice has altered considerably as a result of participation in general multilateral and regional treaties.[196] A few general observations about the LOS and OSPAR Conventions deserve mention here. Comment on the impact of international law relating specifically to vessel-source discharges, dumping at sea and radioactive discharges are considered in the following chapters.

---

[193] Although note the extent to which the EC Water Framework Directive incorporates OSPAR objectives, and might, were it sufficiently precise, give rise to individually enforceable rights.

[194] Art.2(2)(b) OSPAR Convention.

[195] On the Ramsar Convention see 15.9.2 above. In practice, most Ramsar sites will also be sites protected under EC conservation law, where different considerations would apply.

[196] See generally Osborn (1998). To illustrate changing attitudes compare Gibson and Churchill (1990).

### 18.10.1 Boundaries

As far as implementation of provisions in the LOS Convention are concerned, the framework nature of Part XII of the Convention, and its focus on jurisdictional issues rather than substantive provisions, has meant there have been relatively few changes to substantive provisions of national pollution law. The UK has claimed the full extent of its territorial sea out to the 12 nautical mile limit[197] and provision is made to suspend the right of innocent passage in temporary exclusion zones designated in territorial waters to prevent pollution.[198]

The UK has not yet claimed an exclusive economic zone, although it has declared its intent to establish such a zone in order to increase coastal state jurisdiction in order to protect and preserve the marine environment.[199] The jurisdiction to regulate dumping and other forms of pollution from ships within the 200-mile limit, effectively a pollution control zone, was claimed in 1996. As this has been given effect to, this involves the designation of a zone of 'controlled waters'.[200] (This should not be confused with 'controlled waters' for the purposes of Part III of the Water Resources Act 1991).[201] The UK has also declared a 200 mile fishing zone, which may be relevant incidentally to marine environmental pollution, but marine fisheries in the waters of the Member States are a matter of exclusive EC competence.

### 18.10.2 Policy Impact

The impact of international law generally on national law is considered elsewhere,[202] where the emergence of environmental policy principles, amongst other things, is noted. A brief examination here of the practical impact of the OSPAR Convention may, however, shed light on the impact of international law on decision-making.

Ratification of the OSPAR Convention has not involved any change to primary legislation. However, it is generally provided that environmental legislation has effect with such modifications as are prescribed by regulations to give effect to any international agreement to which the UK is for the time being a party.[203] Like the Oslo and Paris Conventions before it, the impact of the OSPAR Convention will be felt mostly at the level of policy making and individual licensing decisions. However, this is not to under-emphasise the considerable impact that regional agreements on

---

[197] Territorial Sea Act 1987.

[198] Merchant Shipping Act 1995, ss.100A and 100B, inserted by s.1 Merchant Shipping and Maritime Security Act 1997.

[199] 1992 Declaration by North Sea States on Co-Ordinated Extension of Jurisdiction in the North Sea, *UN Law of the Sea Bulletin*, 23 (1993) p.65.

[200] Under the Merchant Shipping (Prevention of Pollution)(Limits) Regulations 1996 (SI 1996 No.2128).

[201] See 9.4 above on controlled waters under the 1991 Act.

[202] See 2.23 above.

[203] See s.102 Water Resources Act 1991 and s.156(1) Environmental Protection Act 1990. These provisions apply equally to the LOS Convention as to the OSPAR Convention.

dumping and land-based sources of pollution, as well as the INSC Declarations, have had. Notably, the traditional 'dilute and disperse' approach to marine disposal of waste has come under irresistible pressure, especially at regional level, and has been strengthened through incorporation in binding EC measures. A good example is the ban on the dumping of sewage sludge at sea, first agreed to at the third INSC and later contained in the EC Directive on Urban Waste Water Treatment.[204] More generally, something of a sea change in Government attitude appears to have emerged. This is encapsulated by the withdrawal in 1998 of UK opposition to a recommendation being adopted under the OSPAR Convention providing for a general prohibition on the dumping of decommissioned oil and gas installations,[205] and by the UK's renunciation, at the same time, of its right to resume the sea disposal of radioactive waste.[206] These may have coincided with a change of administration in 1997, but a better view seems to be that the pressures and prior commitments which led to these decisions were already in place.[207] Such developments appear to have helped remove the 'laggard' tag that might previously have been attributed to the UK, although environmental leadership in this area may still remain some way off.

---

[204] See 5.6.2 above on the Urban Waste Water Treatment Directive.

[205] See 19.19.4 below on OSPAR and sea disposal of oil and gas platforms.

[206] See 20.9 below.

[207] Notably, public opposition to the dumping of the *Brent Spar* and changing attitudes to matters of waste disposal at sea more generally, and agreement by the UK in 1993 for such a ban under the 1972 London Convention respectively, see 19.19 below.

# Chapter 19

# SHIPPING DISCHARGES AND SEA DUMPING

## 19.1 Introduction

The focus of this chapter is accidental and deliberate discharges by shipping, in particular discharges of oil and other hazardous substances, and the purposeful deposit or dumping of waste at sea. In relation to shipping discharges, much of the relevant law originates in controls over the entry of oil into marine waters, although in recent years the range of controls has expanded considerably to encompass other hazardous and damaging substances. The legal controls relating to sea dumping, now severely restricted under international and EC law, are also covered, but in less depth. Nonetheless, both sectors nicely illustrate the way in which the different 'layers' of law, from the international level down to national implementation and enforcement of these measures as well as purely national controls, have borne (some might say quite successfully) upon water quality. They also provide useful illustrations of the distinctive approaches which have so far been taken by the international community in relation to marine environmental quality, and in particular the evolution of controls over the last few decades.

The legal approach in both areas has been to seek the reduction or elimination of contaminants in the marine environment. With the exception of preventing serious oil pollution arising from tanker accidents, however, the emphasis has tended to be on the general reduction of discharges rather than on preventing pollution incidents, which in practice and because of the nature of the marine environment fortunately tend to be relatively uncommon. For a variety of reasons, therefore, including a lack of monitoring and scientific understanding,[1] water quality objectives have not been set.[2] Moreover, because the concern of the law is frequently with reducing escapes or discharges of potentially polluting substances, it is often preferable to avoid reference to 'pollution' altogether, and emphasise instead the discharges or deposits that are controlled.

## 19.2 Maritime Shipping Contaminants and Pathways

Contaminants deriving from maritime transport can, largely for reasons of regulatory heritage, conveniently be divided between oil and other pollutants.

---

[1] See, e.g., 18.8.4 above on monitoring under the OSPAR Convention.
[2] See 14.8 above on water quality objectives and standards.

*19.2.1 Oil*

Insofar as it is capable of becoming the subject of ordinary criminal proceedings,[3] oil pollution from land-based sources, falling under the general provisions of national law, constitutes the greater part of the marine oil pollution problem in quantitative terms. Thus, in 1981, the Royal Commission on Environmental Pollution found that,

> some 60 per cent of oil reaching the sea consists of discharges from the land, for example, by means of effluents in rivers, or by means of the direct deposition of hydrocarbons in the atmosphere (originating, for example, in motor vehicle exhausts). Tanker operations, either accidents or deliberate discharges account for about 20 per cent of the oil reaching the sea. The remaining 20 per cent appears to come largely from natural seepages and from discharges resulting from general shipping operations.[4]

Although the amount of oil entering the marine environment has declined significantly since this statement was made,[5] it seems that the relative contribution of land-based sources compared to shipping has remained at around the same level. However, the relative contribution of operational emissions is probably closer to around 75 per cent of the amount of oil coming from shipping, and around 90 per cent of discharges come from loading and unloading.[6] However, there is now a far greater awareness of the extent to which the amount of hydrocarbons entering the sea from human sources is overshadowed by the amount contributed by fall-out from the natural biosynthesis of hydrocarbons by flora and fauna.[7]

Although accidental and deliberate (i.e. operational) discharges from oil tankers constitute only about 20 per cent of oil contamination from human activities at a global level,[8] they provide the main focus of attention in international treaties and national legislation. This preoccupation is not surprising, however, in view of the succession of dramatic incidents involving oil tankers since the *Torrey Canyon* disaster of 1967 and, most notably in the national context, the *Braer* and *Sea Empress* shipping casualties in 1993 and 1996 respectively.[9] It may also be significant that discharges arising from bulk transportation of oil is, in legislative terms, easier to tackle than many of the disparate activities and processes

---

[3] See Ch.9 above. Part III of the Water Resources Act 1991 does not, of course, apply to atmospheric discharges, for which see, e.g., IPC and IPPC at 12.3 above or separate controls on vehicle exhausts etc.

[4] Royal Commission on Environmental Pollution (1981) para.11.3, and see Ch.1 above.

[5] From 1981 to 1989, by around 60%, see MEPC 30/INF.13, 19 September 1990 (Marine Environmental Protection Committee, IMO).

[6] GESAMP (1990).

[7] GESAMP (1990) and Clark (1997) pp.38 and 44.

[8] As noted at 18.1 above, the relative contribution from offshore production is much higher in areas like the North Sea, where it may reach around 25%.

[9] Although legislation concerning oil pollution of water dates from the Oil in Navigable Waters Act 1922.

contributing lesser amounts of oil contamination which cumulatively add up to a greater amount than that originating from oil tankers.

Aspects of the nature of water pollution by oil have been considered elsewhere.[10] What needs to be noted here is that the impact of oil on the marine water environment[11] will vary depending on factors such as the nature of the oil (for example, whether it is heavy or light), the nature of the sea conditions, the time of year,[12] and the area affected by the slick. For example, sea birds and tourist beaches will be more seriously affected than, say, many sub-aquatic species and marine mammals.[13] Comparison of the *Exxon Valdez* and *Braer* spills in 1989 and 1993 show the extent to which the damage caused by a tanker accident is not necessarily proportional to the amount of oil involved. More than twice as much oil was released in the latter incident, when the *Braer* grounded off the Shetlands Islands causing the escape or discharge of 84,700 tonnes of crude oil and 1,600 tonnes of bulk oil. However, the environmental effects were negligible compared to those after the former, because the nature of the oil and the severe weather conditions, which had initially contributed to the grounding, also acted to disperse most of the oil with, fortunately, minimal and generally short-term environmental impact.[14]

Over the years, there has been a considerable reduction in the contribution of oil discharged to sea following the cleaning out of storage tanks on tankers. This is attributable in large part to the use of the 'load on top' system, whereby oily ballast water and cleaning water has its oily fraction separated before the relatively clean water is discharged and the new shipment of oil is loaded on top of the oil remaining in a 'slop' tank.[15] This has prompted the comment that, aside from the impacts of accidental spills, 'petroleum pollution does not now represent a severe threat to marine habitats and organisms'.[16] Oil from bilge and fuel tanks now accounts for a much larger amount of oil discharged in relative terms.

### 19.2.2 Other Substances

Although the vast bulk of transported cargo consists of oil, which, therefore, has the greatest potential for marine contamination, the seas may be contaminated by the impact of a wide range of other maritime activities. These include the carriage of hazardous or noxious substances; the disposal of litter such as plastics and discarded fishing nets; sewage generated on board vessels; and atmospheric emissions generated at sea. Unlike oil, which ultimately biodegrades, some hazardous substances such as PCBs and heavy metals persist in the marine environment and may

---

[10] See 1.6.7 and 12.4.9 above.

[11] See generally GESAMP (1993).

[12] A crucial factor in the *Sea Empress* incident, see 9.19.3 above and 19.15.2 below.

[13] See generally Clark (1997) pp.45-55.

[14] Ecological Steering Group on the Oil Spill in Shetland (1994).

[15] See further 19.6.3 below.

[16] *Law of the Sea – Protection and Preservation of the Marine Environment*. Report of the UN Secretary-General, UN Doc.A/44/461, 18 September 1989.

cause longer-term damage to wildlife or enter the human food chain. Permanent damage, or at least change, to aquatic ecosystems may also arise from the entry of non-native organisms transferred from the cleaning out of ballast tanks. Preventing pollution or contamination by such substances, or providing liability for the consequences of such substances entering the marine environment, is increasingly provided for under international conventions.

## 19.3 Legal Responses to Discharges from Shipping and UK Implementation

The legal responses to discharges of undesirable substances from shipping[17] may be conceived of in three general but distinct stages:

(a) preventive measures;
(b) accident response and clean-up powers; and
(c) civil liability.

Following this categorisation, the following sections of this chapter look at:

(a) determining and enforcing standards for preventing discharges of oil and other substances by shipping;
(b) a range of provisions that deal with damaged ships at sea which may pose an environmental hazard, especially measures to intervene outside territorial waters, to facilitate co-operation between states following accidents and the rules relating to salvage following an accident; and
(c) international provisions for compensation following polluting spills.

In most areas, the interests of trade and navigation in agreeing common international rules means that national law generally exists to give effect to these agreements, even though as a matter of legal interpretation it is the UK legislation which must be applied.[18] The approach taken, therefore, is to consider, in each area covered, the relevant provisions of international law (largely found in global conventions), and then to discuss the way in which these obligations are implemented at the national (and, sometimes, the European Community) level.

Although there is a customary law background,[19] the law relating to marine contamination and pollution by shipping is contained mainly in conventions. Reflecting the navigation and commercial issues involved, these have tended to be agreed at the global level, with regional

---

[17] General reading on legal aspects of marine pollution by shipping, especially oil, includes: Timagenis (1980) Part Three; Royal Commission on Environmental Pollution (1981); Abecassis and Jarashow (1985); Brubaker (1993); Bates and Benson (1993, updated), Chs 2-6; Ringbom (1998) and Churchill and Lowe (1999) pp.338-363.

[18] Subject to the roles on interpretation noted at 18.9 above.

[19] See 18.5 above.

conventions playing only a relatively minor role.[20] As far as the setting of standards and imposing liability are concerned, the general approach has been for these to be set under specialist convention regimes, with the 1982 UN Law of the Sea Convention ('LOS Convention') providing a framework within which the jurisdictional rights of states are specified. To some extent, the LOS Convention also provides incentives for states to become involved in the more specific pollution control and liability treaties.[21] A similar approach is taken in Agenda 21 which, like the LOS Convention, emphasises improved compliance with existing measures.[22]

The principal conventions are:

(a) the 1973 and 1978 International Convention for the Prevention of Pollution from Ships (the '1973/78 MARPOL Convention') which seeks to reduce the amount of oil entering the marine environment both from operational discharges and following tanker accidents;

(b) the 1969 International Convention relating to Intervention on the High Seas in cases of Oil Pollution Casualties and its 1973 Protocol which extends the convention beyond oil pollution (the '1969/73 Intervention Convention'), agreed after the *Torrey Canyon* disaster had revealed serious deficiencies in the legal powers to prevent oil pollution damage in such situations;

(c) the 1990 International Convention on Oil Pollution Preparedness, Response and Co-operation (the 'OPRC Convention'), the aim of which is to facilitate the flow of information and promote co-operation between states following marine pollution incidents;

(d) the 1989 International Convention on Salvage, which seeks to address concerns, raised e.g. following the *Amoco Cadiz* incident in 1978, that international marine salvage law might have a negative environmental impact because salvors were only paid where ships were completely saved, thus providing no incentive to act where this was not possible but where damage to the marine environmental might be prevented or mitigated; and

(e) three Conventions relating to liability following marine pollution incidents, namely the 1969 and 1992 International Convention on Civil Liability for Oil Pollution Damage (the 'Civil Liability Convention'), the 1971 and 1992 International Convention on the Establishment of an International Fund for Compensation for Oil Pollution Damage (the 'Fund Convention'), and the 1996 International Convention on Liability and Compensation for Damage in Connection with the Carriage of Hazardous and Noxious Substances by Sea (the 'HNS Convention').

---

[20] At least, to date. There are some indications that regional rules may impinge more in the future, at least at European level, and thus the prospect of a different balance being struck between global and regional rules. See 18.6 above.

[21] The same is true of the international regulation of dumping wastes at sea, discussed at 19.17 onwards.

[22] On Agenda 21 see 18.5.3 above, but on this claim contrast Nollkaemper (1993).

There is also a further range of measures, most notably the 1960 and 1974 International Safety of Life at Sea ('SOLAS') Convention and the 1978 International Convention on the Standard of Training, Certification and Watchkeeping for Seafarers, which are concerned more generally with ship safety and which prescribe various design, construction and operational standards. Insofar as any accident involving a ship is likely to lead to the escape of some pollutants, such measures are important preventive mechanisms. The SOLAS Convention also contains specific provisions concerning, for example, the labelling of certain dangerous substances carried on board, which are of more specific application.

The UK is a party to all these treaties and to all their protocols and amendments that are in force.[23]

In UK law, the implementation of the 1973/78 MARPOL Convention, the 1969/73 Intervention Convention and the various provisions on compensation is provided for under the Merchant Shipping Act 1995 and by a series of merchant shipping regulations.[24] The 1995 Act has been amended to take into account the accession of the UK to the LOS Convention, and to give effect to certain recommendations of the inquiry following the *Braer* incident.[25] A series of regulations give effect to most other international obligations, enacted either under statute or under Orders in Council passed to allow such regulations to be made.[26] There are also some European Community measures that apply in this area, for example on port state control,[27] which are also implemented through national regulations. Ministerial responsibility for marine pollution from shipping rests with the Secretary of State for the Environment, Transport and the Regions.[28]

## 19.4  Standard Setting and Enforcement

The law relating to marine pollution from shipping has developed against a background of conflict between the desires of states to exercise sovereignty over their coastal waters and the interests of states in the freedom of navigation and international trade by sea. In more recent years the law has also developed in response to wider concerns about the impact of shipping not merely on the national waters of ports and coastal areas but also on the high seas.

---

[23] The one exception is Annex VI of MARPOL on atmospheric emissions which is not yet in force and which is outside this work.

[24] One effect of this is that the provisions of the Prevention of Oil Pollution Act 1971 which remain in force relate solely to discharges from land (see 12.4.9 above) or discharges from offshore installations (which are outwith the scope of this work).

[25] *Safer Ships, Cleaner Seas*, Lord Donaldson's Inquiry into the Prevention of Pollution from Merchant Shipping (Cm 2560, 1994).

[26] See especially ss.128 and 129 Merchant Shipping Act 1995.

[27] Directive 95/21/EC, see 19.8.1 below.

[28] Marine pollution traditionally being a matter for the Secretary of State for Transport. The international dimension means that powers generally continue to be exercised at UK level, or are in effect shared between England and Wales. On exclusive and shared responsibility after devolution see 6.2 above.

Appreciating developments in this area requires a distinction[29] to be drawn between the following:

(a) 'flag states', which are states which grant their nationality to vessels and give them the right to fly their flag;[30]
(b) 'coastal states', meaning those states in whose maritime area a vessel is lying;[31] and
(c) 'port states', meaning those states in whose port a particular vessel is situated.[32]

There is also a distinction to be made between the legislative jurisdiction of states, that is, their right to set standards, their enforcement jurisdiction and the right to enforce such standards.

In general terms, the LOS Convention establishes a basic framework for regulating marine pollution from shipping which marks an important shift from that under previous customary international law and the 1958 Territorial Sea Convention. While the full impact of this development cannot be fully considered here,[33] in general terms it was perceived that flag states, which have responsibility for legislative and enforcement jurisdiction over their vessels on the high seas, and which can set standards for their vessels wherever they may be, were[34] insufficiently strict in the enforcement of their international obligations.[35] This was of particular concern since most contamination, especially from oil discharges, occurred outside territorial waters when tanks were flushed out. On the other hand, this shortcoming could not easily be addressed merely by extending the jurisdiction of coastal and port states, since this might compromise the pursuit of broadly uniform global standards thought to be essential for navigation.

The LOS Convention strikes a balance between the interests of flag, coastal and port states. It provides that flag states must adopt pollution regulations which 'at least have the same effect as that of generally accepted international rules and established standards through the competent international organisation or general diplomatic conference'.[36] The Convention then sets these standards as the *maximum* level for regulation by coastal states in protecting their coasts and coastal waters,[37] though more stringent measures may be adopted to protect territorial waters from discharges. The rules and standards referred to are assumed to

---

[29] That there is a clear legal and policy distinction should be emphasised. One consequence, perhaps, is that there is no duty of care on producers of oil to ensure that those who transport their product do so in a safe manner, akin to the duty of care in national waste law (see 12.2.5 above).

[30] Art.91 LOS Convention.

[31] See generally Molenaar (1998).

[32] See generally Kasoulides (1993).

[33] See Churchill and Lowe (1999) pp.344-353.

[34] And often continue to be.

[35] Peet (1993) indicated that in less than 8% of cases where incidents were reported by the IMO to flag states were fines imposed.

[36] Art.211(2) LOS Convention, and see also Art.94.

[37] *Ibid* Art.211(5) and (6).

refer at least to the mandatory provisions of the 1973/78 MARPOL Convention,[38] which is widely ratified. The MARPOL Convention replaced the 1954 International Convention for the Prevention of Pollution of the Sea by Oil, 'OILPOL',[39] which was considered inadequate to deal with worsening oil pollution problems as a consequence of increased oil tanker traffic and greater tanker capacities. The 'competent international organisation' for the purposes of the LOS Convention means the International Maritime Organisation (IMO).[40]

In general terms, the system of controls upon shipping functions effectively because of the relatively high standards provided for under 1973/78 MARPOL Convention, which provides comparative conditions of competition for the shipping industry that are generally acceptable to coastal states, which can impose stricter standards in their territorial waters. While specification and performance standards are generally adopted, some use is made of economic incentives, for example, in reducing port dues to encourage ships to segregate ballast water.[41] Moreover, the LOS Convention created the concept of port state enforcement jurisdiction so that port states may set their own standards relating to entry, subject to what are probably quite generous upper limits determined by customary international law.[42] Given the extent to which specification and reporting standards are used, this gives considerable leeway for port states to impose controls on shipping entering or leaving their ports. The EC, in particular, has developed port state control measures in a number of respects.[43]

Ultimately, the effectiveness of the international treaty regime must be judged against levels of compliance.[44] This may be acceptable where 'high standard' port states are involved. However, securing compliance by ships from less stringent flag states which navigate through the coastal waters of, but neither enter nor leave port in, high standard states gives rise to considerable concerns. This is because the unevenness of controls allows older, less well equipped vessels to pose considerable risks to the waters of the marine environment.[45] Because of this, what are termed 'ports of convenience' may pose a significant threat of marine environmental damage anywhere.

More generally, securing compliance with rules relating to operational discharges at sea (which account for the vast majority of discharges numerically) will be problematic. While requirements for record keeping may enhance compliance, without anything further they rarely provide

---

[38] Cmnd.5748, as amended by 1978 Protocol (Cmnd.7347), in force 2 October 1983.

[39] Cmnd.395, as amended by Protocols in 1962 (Cmnd.3354), 1969 (Cmnd.7094), and 1971 (Cmnd.5071 and 5090). Implemented by the Oil in Navigable Waters Act 1955.

[40] Previously known as the Inter-Governmental Maritime Consultative Organisation.

[41] IMO Resolution A.747(18), see also Regulation 2978/94/EC.

[42] There are no global conventions on port state control, though see IMO Resolution A.787(19).

[43] See 19.8.1 below.

[44] On the general subject of compliance in the oil sector see Mitchell (1994).

[45] See below and 19.8.1 below on proposed amendments to the EC 'Vessels' Directive.

adequate evidence of discharges at sea.[46] In general terms, part of the bargain struck under the LOS Convention was that enforcement jurisdiction continues to favour navigational interests, although more stringent measures may be taken in the territorial sea than in what is termed the 'pollution zone', which may extend to 200 nautical miles from national baselines.[47] In summary, therefore, standards tend to be set at the global level,[48] with regional interests being accommodated through the designation of special areas where stricter discharge standards apply. However, regional and national interests come to the fore in relation to port state control and enforcement.[49]

## 19.5 Preventing the Deliberate and Accidental Release of Oil

The 1973/78 MARPOL Convention consists of a main text, two protocols and six Annexes. The text of the Convention itself relates to matters of enforcement, placing primary responsibility in the hands of the flag state.[50] In certain respects, the provisions on enforcement must be read alongside those of the LOS Convention, noted above.[51] It is, however, the Annexes that lay down the applicable standards. Of these, Annex I deals with oil pollution, and is discussed directly below. Annex I and Annex II, which deals with noxious substances, are the only Annexes which contracting parties must conform to, while the other Annexes, which deal with pollution by harmful substances carried by sea in packaged forms, pollution by sewage from ships, pollution by garbage from ships and air pollution from ships, are 'optional'. These are dealt with further below.[52]

Annex I of the Convention is given effect to nationally by the Merchant Shipping (Prevention of Oil Pollution) Regulations 1996 ('the 1996 Regulations').[53] These Regulations are made under enabling provisions which allow for Orders to be made that give effect to certain treaties, when ratified by the UK, including the 1973/78 MARPOL Convention along with its various protocols, annexes and appendices.[54] The Merchant

---

[46] Ringbom (1999) p.25.

[47] See 18.7.1 above.

[48] Although the somewhat isolated position of the US under its Oil Pollution Act 1990 is a notable exception to this rule.

[49] Following the *Erika* incident in 1999, the prospect of stricter standards on the movement of tankers in Community waters has emerged. There are proposals for a progressive ban on single hulled oil tankers, coming fully into force by 2015, a strengthening of the EC's port state control regime under Directive 95/21/EC and also a strengthening of Directive 94/57 on classification societies. See *Communication from the Commission to the European Parliament and the Council on the safety of the seaborne oil trade*, COM(2000)142 final (the 'Erika 1 Communication'). Postscript: see now also the 'Erika 2 Communication' covering maritime transport management; establishing a Community pollution fund; and establishing a European Maritime Safety Agency (COM(2000)802).

[50] Art.2(5) MARPOL.

[51] See 19.4 above.

[52] See 19.10 below. Annex VI dealing with air pollution from ships is outwith the scope of this work.

[53] SI 1996 No.2154.

[54] Merchant Shipping (Prevention of Oil Pollution) Order 1983 (SI 1983 No.1106) made under s.20(1)(a) Merchant Shipping Act 1979 (see now s.128 Merchant Shipping Act 1995).

Shipping Act 1995, as amended by the Merchant Shipping and Maritime Security Act 1997, provides more general measures relating to jurisdiction, and may in certain respects go beyond the requirements of MARPOL.

In particular, 'oil' is defined in the 1995 Act as oil of any description and includes spirit produced from oil of any description and coal tar.[55] This is sufficiently broad to go beyond mineral oils, which are generally provided for in MARPOL and other oil pollution Conventions, and extend to encompass also vegetable oils.[56] The definition, doubtless, also extends also to oils of animal origin.

### 19.5.1 Application and Exemptions

In line with the general principles relating to state control noted above, the 1996 Regulations apply to United Kingdom ships wherever located and to other ships while they are within UK territorial waters. The Regulations also apply to Government ships registered in the UK and Government ships not so registered but held for the purposes of the United Kingdom Government in the UK.[57]

Neither MARPOL nor the 1996 Regulations, however, apply to any warship, naval auxiliary or other ship owned or operated by the UK and used, for the time being, only on government non-commercial service.[58] Certain types of ship may be exempted, so long as an equivalent level of protection against oil discharges is provided.[59] The Secretary of State may grant exemptions from all or any of the provisions of the Regulations for classes of cases or individual cases on such terms as he may specify.[60]

### 19.5.2 Surveys and Certificates

The 1996 Regulations impose important requirements in respect of the surveying and certification of oil tankers and other UK ships above specified sizes. The owner of every UK oil tanker of gross registered tonnage (GT) of 150 tons and above, and every other UK ship of 400 GT and above, must carry a certificate following a survey.[61] These certificates are either an International Oil Pollution Prevention Certificate ('IOPP certificate'), where the vessel is involved in voyages to other states which are parties to the MARPOL Convention, or a United Kingdom Oil Pollution Prevention Certificate ('UKOPP certificate') where the ship visits non-MARPOL states. To retain its certificate, each ship must be re-surveyed at least every five years by a Certifying Authority.[62] The

---

[55] s.151(1) Merchant Shipping Act 1995.
[56] *Cosh* v *Larsen* [1971] 1 Lloyd's Rep 557.
[57] Reg.2(1) Merchant Shipping (Prevention of Oil Pollution) Regulations 1996.
[58] Art.3(3) MARPOL and *ibid* Reg.2(2).
[59] *Ibid* Reg.2(3).
[60] *Ibid* Reg.2(5).
[61] *Ibid* Reg.4(1).
[62] *Ibid*.

surveyor must be satisfied that the vessel is in accordance with the requirements of the Regulations. If satisfied of this, the surveyor must then forward to the Secretary of State a declaration of survey containing such particulars of the ship as are required to enable the Secretary of State to issue the appropriate certificate in respect of the ship.[63] The purpose of certification is to ensure the essential seaworthiness of oil tankers and other larger ships that may pose a significant hazard to the aquatic environment in the event of an accident.

In addition to the requirement that ships be re-surveyed every five years to obtain certification, stricter requirements are applicable to those vessels in respect of which an IOPP certificate has been issued. IOPP-certificated ships must be surveyed annually, and must also be subject to an intermediate survey within six months of the half-way date of the five-year period of certificate validity.[64] After a survey, no material change can be made to ships without the prior approval of the Secretary of State, other than the direct replacement of fittings or equipment.[65]

Reciprocal arrangements exist between parties to MARPOL with regard to certification of ships requiring IOPP certificates. Thus the Secretary of State may request the Government of another party to the Convention to survey a UK ship and, if satisfied that the provisions of Annex I to the Convention are complied with, to issue an IOPP certificate to the ship, and vice versa.[66]

Ships may only be boarded in the UK in order for their certificates to be inspected. However, if it is apparent from the condition of the ship that it does not correspond to that detailed in the certificate, if no valid certificate exists, or if it is apparent that the master or crew are not familiar with essential shipboard procedures for preventing pollution by oil, then certain powers may be exercised.[67] These include powers of inspection, and to detain the ship until it poses no unreasonable threat of harm to the marine environment.[68] Failure to comply with an inspection, to obstruct an inspector, or to make false statements is an offence.[69]

In the UK, certificates are initially issued following survey by the Maritime and Coastguard Agency but, as with most other states, further certification is delegated to a number of accredited classification societies such as the Lloyd's Register of Shipping. Survey procedures follow IMO guidance. The EC has a Classification Societies Directive governing Member States monitoring of and dealings with classification societies

---

[63] *Ibid* Reg.4(2)–(5); survey procedures are specified by the Secretary of State in Merchant Shipping Notice M.1076. A fee is payable, see SI 1991 No. 784.

[64] *Ibid* Regs 5 and 6.

[65] *Ibid* Reg.8(1).

[66] *Ibid* Reg.7(2) and (4).

[67] Under s.259 Merchant Shipping Act 1995.

[68] Reg.34(1) Merchant Shipping (Prevention of Oil Pollution) Regulations 1996.

[69] Punishable on summary conviction by a fine of up to the statutory maximum, presently £5,000, and on indictment to a fine (*ibid* Reg.36).

both in the Community and in third countries.[70] Following the *Erika* incident, involving a tanker that *was* duly certified under existing rules, there are proposals to strengthen this regime. These would reserve to the Commission the right to suspend or withdraw societies' recognition through a simplified procedure and judge societies' competence against the performance of all vessels under their certification, and would also, amongst other things, hold societies liable in the event of negligence. The obvious difficulty with the present regime is that certification is a matter for flag states, and classification societies are, in effect, self-regulating. In its reform proposals, the Commission 'shares the concerns often expressed in various sectors of the maritime industry that the performance of classification societies does not always meet the standards required.'[71]

### 19.5.3 Design and Construction Standards

The 1996 Regulations stipulate certain specific design and construction standards.[72] These give effect to progressive improvements in this area intended to reduce pollution from the normal operation of ships, such as the washing out of ballast tanks, and to reduce the risk of pollution following accidents.[73] The standards differ according to the size of the ship concerned and take into account other factors such as phasing in standards for older vessels. The standards include:

(a) oil sludge tanks which can be easily cleaned and their residues discharged to reception facilities;[74]
(b) segregated ballast tanks so that tanks are used exclusively for either ballast or cargo. This is to avoid ballast water becoming contaminated with oil;[75]
(c) designated slop tanks of a sufficient size for dirty ballast residues and tank washings;[76] and
(d) the fitting of an approved oil discharge monitoring and control system, which continuously monitors the discharge of effluent to the sea and stops this if a threshold level is exceeded.[77]

The standards also include requirements that new oil tankers have their cargo tanks protected by ballast tanks or spaces other than cargo and fuel oil tanks, to prevent emissions following a tanker being stranded or the side or bottom otherwise damaged (termed the 'double hull' requirement).[78] As defined in this context, 'new' generally restricts the

---

[70] Directive 94/75 on common rules and standards for ship inspection and survey organizations and for the relevant activities of maritime administrations.
[71] COM(2000)142, p.19.
[72] See generally *ibid*, Part IV.
[73] On the development of these standards see IMO (1998).
[74] Reg.25 Merchant Shipping (Prevention of Oil Pollution) Regulations 1996.
[75] *Ibid* Reg.18.
[76] *Ibid* Reg.15(2).
[77] *Ibid* Reg.15(3).
[78] See the 1992 Amendments to MARPOL, in force 6 July 1993. There is some controversy over the utility of double hulls. Because the void between the hulls fills up with water, the ship becomes

application of this provision to ships built or converted after 6 July 1993. Existing ships must comply within 25 years of being delivered, subject to interim surveys to determine their fitness and the requirement to have double sides and double bottoms fitted.[79] Ships may use an alternative method of protection other than double hulls, so long as this gives a similar degree of protection. This is relied on by many Japanese and European shipbuilders, who utilise the so-called 'mid-deck' system.[80] Given the age of the world's large tanker fleet, this provision means that most tankers will either have to be converted over the next few years or decommissioned. These requirements should be read alongside the Cargo Ship Construction Regulations 1997, which provide further specification standards intended to prevent the deliberate or accidental spillage of oil.[81] Following the break up of the *Erika* off the Brittany coast in December 1999, accelerated application in the Community of the phasing-in scheme of the double hull or equivalent design requirements of the 1973/78 MARPOL Convention have been proposed. [82]

### 19.5.4 Port Waste Reception Facilities

As has been seen, a number of design and construction standards require wastes to be kept on board ships while at sea, so that they can be discharged to facilities at harbours or terminals and dealt with on land rather than causing harm to the marine environment. The basic requirement to provide such facilities is provided for in Annex I of MARPOL, and given effect to by the Merchant Shipping (Port Waste Reception Facilities) Regulations 1997.[83] The 1997 Regulations require ports to have facilities that are 'adequate' for dealing with oil on board ships using its facilities. Previous arrangements, under which such facilities were required on a voluntary basis, proved insufficient.[84] The need for co-ordination in the provision of such facilities is effected by the requirement imposed on harbour authorities and, on direction, terminal operators to prepare port waste management plans, which must be approved by the Secretary of State. There are proposals for an EC Directive covering the provision of port waste reception facilities covering

---

heavier, making it harder to move off rocks. Thus, double hulls may reduce the impact of the initial spill, but lead to more damage in the longer term.

[79] Regs.30 and 31 Merchant Shipping (Prevention of Oil Pollution) Regulations 1996.

[80] For an explanation of this system, and also of the Coulombi Egg design, see COM(2000)142, Annexe 1-B.

[81] SI 1997 No.1509.

[82] That is, under Reg.13 F Annex I MARPOL. This accelerated phasing-in scheme would have to be aligned with the age limits and end-date limits provided for in US Oil Pollution Act 1990, to avoid oil tankers banned from the US under the 1990 regime shift their trading patterns to Europe. See *Proposal for a Regulation of the European Parliament and of the Council on the accelerated phasing-in of double hull or equivalent design requirements for single hull oil tankers*, COM(2000)142 final. On important changes to MARPOL rules on single hull tankers along similar, though less strict, lines see MEPC 46th session, 23-27 April 2001, at www.imo.org.

[83] SI 1997 No.3018.

[84] *ENDS Report* 267 (1997) p.32.

all kinds of shipping waste, including obligations and incentives for their use.[85]

### 19.5.5 Management Standards

Masters and owners of ships must conform to certain management practices intended to avoid oil pollution. Under the 1996 Regulations, all ships over 400GT and oil tankers over 150GT must carry a shipboard oil pollution and emergency plan, stating the procedure to be followed during an oil pollution incident in order to reduce emissions and the persons by whom, and to whom, reports of any incident should be made. Such plans, which follow IMO guidelines,[86] should also detail arrangements for co-ordinating anti-pollution measures with national and local authorities.[87]

In addition to emergency planning, to reduce the risk of oil spillage no oil may be transferred between sunset and sunrise to or from a vessel in any harbour in the UK unless requisite notice has been given to the harbour master (or harbour authority, as appropriate) or the transfer is for the purposes of a fire brigade. General notices may be given to the harbour master. Breach of this provision will involve an offence being committed by the master of the vessel, or if the oil is transferred from or to a place on land, the occupier of that land. In either case, liability on summary conviction is to a fine not exceeding level three on the standard scale, presently £1,000.[88]

Further Regulations also require environmental management systems to be established. These Regulations[89] give effect to the 1994 IMO International Safety Management Code. Companies complying with the requirements are issued with Documents of Compliance, while ships operated by those companies are issued with Safety Management Certificates by their flag states. Companies are audited annually (and ships every 2-3 years) for compliance with the Code. The provisions apply to most large vessels of 500 GT or more (oil tankers, cargo vessels, etc.). Ships breaching the Code or lacking the necessary documentation are liable to be detained and to the withdrawal of their certificates, and a range of offences are provided for.

### 19.5.6 Routing of Shipping

Although it is not the subject of as specific *legal* regulation as other measures to prevent harm to the marine environment, the management of shipping traffic is essential to preventing accidents and groundings and

---

[85] COM(98)452 final OJ 1998, C271/79.

[86] See Marine Environment Protection Committee Resolution 54(32), 6 March 1992.

[87] Reg.33 Merchant Shipping (Prevention of Oil Pollution) Regulations 1996 and see also 19.11.2B below on OPRC.

[88] s.135 Merchant Shipping Act 1995.

[89] The Merchant Shipping (International Safety Management (ISM) Code) Regulations 1998 (SI 1998 No.1561), see also the Merchant Shipping (Control of Pollution) (SOLAS) Order 1998 (SI 1998 No.1500).

avoiding risks. Following the *Braer* incident, routing of merchant shipping received considerable attention.[90] A series of recommendations were made, including the designation of Marine Environmentally High Risk Areas (MEHRAs) in limited locations where there is both a significant risk of environmental damage and a significant density of shipping.[91] The basic principal behind MEHRAs is also found in proposals for Particularly Sensitive Sea Areas, which have been developed by the IMO. So far these are only guidelines, and although their use would seem to be in line with the LOS Convention and be a development from the concept of 'special areas' in Annex I of MARPOL, there is some doubt over their utility.[92]

## 19.6 Permissible Discharges of Oil

There are a range of situations where amounts of oil may lawfully be discharged from ships. These are curtailed in certain respects in relation to certain areas designated for their particular ecological sensitivity.

### 19.6.1 General Exceptions to Controls upon Discharges of Oil

Part III of the Merchant Shipping (Prevention of Oil Pollution) Regulations 1996 imposes controls upon operational pollution through the discharge of oil, and also imposes separate prohibitions upon the discharge of oil. These measures are subject to certain general exceptions, so that the provisions do not apply to:

(a) any discharge into the sea of oil or oily mixture which is necessary for the purpose of securing the safety of a ship or saving life at sea; or

(b) any discharge into the sea of oil or oily mixture which results from the damage of a ship or its equipment provided that;

    (i) all reasonable precautions were taken after the occurrence of the damage or discovery of the discharge to prevent or minimising the discharge; and

    (ii) the owner or master did not act either with intent to cause damage or recklessly and with knowledge that damage would probably result; or

(c) any approved discharge into the sea of substances containing oil, when being used for the purpose of combating specific pollution incidents in order to minimise the damage from pollution. Any such discharge, which might occur when a dispersant is used to combat oil pollution, must be subject to the approval of any

---

[90] *Safer Ships, Cleaner Seas*. Report of Lord Donaldson's Inquiry into the Prevention of Pollution from Merchant Shipping (1994) (henceforth 'Safer Ships, Cleaner Seas'). For the UK Government's response see Cm.2766 (1995).

[91] See now DETR, *Identification of Marine Environmental High Risk Areas (MEHRAs) in the UK*, Consultation Paper (1999).

[92] Churchill and Lowe (1999) pp.392-95. More optimistically see Merialdi (1999). On 'special areas' see 19.6.4 below.

Government in whose jurisdiction it is contemplated the discharge will be made.[93]

### 19.6.2 Ships Other than Oil Tankers

Subject to the above general exceptions, limited provision is made for the permissible discharge of oil from certain ships. For ships other than oil tankers and the machinery space bilges of oil tankers, the relevant provisions apply to UK ships and, subject to restrictions to the taking of enforcement action to pollution in UK internal, territorial and controlled waters, to foreign ships anywhere.[94] Such ships are prohibited from discharging oil or oily mixture into any part of the sea unless a series of conditions are satisfied. The conditions to be satisfied are that:

(a)  the ship is proceeding on a voyage;
(b)  the ship is not within a 'special area';[95]
(c)  the oil content of the effluent does not exceed 15 parts per million; and
(d)  the ship has in operation the required filtering and the oil discharge and monitoring and control system as required.[96]

Any oil or oily mixture that cannot be discharged in accordance with these provisions must be retained on board and discharged into reception facilities. In addition, no discharge into the sea is permitted to contain chemicals or other substances in quantities or concentrations that are hazardous to the marine environment, or chemicals or other substances introduced for the purpose of circumventing the conditions under which the discharge is permitted.

### 19.6.3 Oil Tankers

Subject to the general exceptions,[97] an analogous prohibition concerning the discharge of oil or oily mixtures applies in relation to discharges from any UK oil tanker and any foreign oil tanker wherever it may be, subject to enforcement jurisdiction.[98] In this case an oil tanker may not discharge any oil or oily mixture into any part of the sea unless all the following conditions are satisfied:

(a)  the tanker is proceeding on a voyage;
(b)  the tanker is not within a 'special area';[99]
(c)  the tanker is more than 50 miles from the nearest land;
(d)  the instantaneous rate of discharge of oil content does not exceed 30 litres per mile;

---

[93] Reg.11 Merchant Shipping (Prevention of Oil Pollution) Regulations 1996.
[94] See generally *ibid* Reg.12.
[95] Discussed at 19.6.4 below.
[96] As required by Reg.14 Merchant Shipping (Prevention of Oil Pollution) Regulations 1996.
[97] Under *ibid* Reg.11, discussed in 19.6.1 above.
[98] See generally Reg.13 Merchant Shipping (Prevention of Oil Pollution) Regulations 1996.
[99] See 19.6.4 below.

(e) the total quantity of oil discharged into the sea does not exceed 1/30,000 (1/15,000 in relation to existing tankers) of the total quantity of the particular cargo of which the residue formed a part; and

(f) the tanker has in operation an oil discharge monitoring and control system and a slop tank arrangement.[100]

An exception is made for certain discharges below a threshold of 15 parts per million of oil, and analogous provisions apply to the discharge of hazardous discharges of chemicals or other substances and to the obligation to discharge into reception facilities. In practice, these standards cannot be met unless the 'load-on-top' system is used. Under this system, the washings that result from tank cleaning are pumped into a special tank. During the return voyage to the loading terminal the oil and water separate. The water at the bottom of the tank is pumped overboard and at the cargo terminal oil is pumped on to the oil left in the tank.

### 19.6.4 Special Areas

In relation to a permitted discharge of oil or oily wastes from oil tankers and other ships[101] a condition governing the permissibility of discharges is that the ship or tanker is not within a 'special area'. In general terms this expression means a sea area where, for recognised technical reasons in relation to its oceanographical and ecological condition and to the particular character of its traffic, the adoption of special mandatory methods for the prevention of sea discharges of oil is required. Initially, the special areas designated were the Mediterranean Sea, the Baltic Sea and the Black Sea, in relation to which certain restricted discharges may be made, and the Antarctic, where no discharge into the sea of any oil or oily mixture from a UK ship may be made.[102] The report following the *Braer* incident recommended that the North Sea, English Channel and Irish Sea be designated as special areas for oil under the MARPOL Convention.[103] These areas, and their approaches, together with the Celtic Sea and parts of the North East Atlantic immediately to the west of Ireland, have recently been designated for this purpose.[104] In certain respects, this continues the move away from designating only enclosed or semi-enclosed areas as special areas.

---

[100] As required by Reg.15 Merchant Shipping (Prevention of Oil Pollution) Regulations 1996.

[101] As described in 19.6.3 and 19.6.2 above.

[102] Regs.1(2) and 16 Merchant Shipping (Prevention of Oil Pollution) Regulations 1996.

[103] *Safer Ships, Cleaner Seas*, rec.22, see 19.3 above.

[104] Following Annex 5 to Resolution MEPC 75(40), adopted 25 September 1997 and originally implemented by Merchant Shipping Notice, in force 1 February 1999; but see now the Merchant Shipping (Prevention of Oil Pollution) (Amendment) Regulations 2000 (SI 2000 No.483). See also Ministerial Declaration of the Fourth International Conference on the Protection of the North Sea, the Esjberg Declaration (1995) Ch.V.

## 19.7  Recording and Reporting Obligations Concerning Oil

For various activities relating to oil storage on vessels which might have an impact on receiving waters, records must be kept and made available for inspection. The obligation to keep records also extends to the recording of any discharge of oil, regardless of whether 'pollution' has resulted.[105]

### 19.7.1  Oil Records

General provision requiring the keeping of oil records date back to the 1954 OILPOL Convention.[106] These requirements were considerably extended under MARPOL, which expanded the original requirement to cover a wider range of operations and to require more details in order to improve the possibility of detecting illegal discharges of oil.[107] These basic requirements are set out in the Merchant Shipping Act 1995 and given effect to through two sets of Regulations from 1972 and 1957 respectively.[108]

The 1972 Regulations impose recording obligations on UK oil tankers of less than 150GT and other UK ships of between 80 and 400GT. These require the recording of certain operations, and of any occasions when oil is pumped into the sea for safety purposes or when it has escaped from the ship due to damage or a leak.[109] Further Regulations date from 1957 and are made under powers given to the Secretary of State to regulate the keeping of records relating to the transfer of oil to and from vessels while they are within UK territorial waters. These apply to any vessel capable of carrying more than 25 tons of oil in bulk, or more than 5 tons of oil in any one space or container. The master of the vessel must generally keep such records, and provision is made for the manner of their recording and their retention.[110]

Failure of a ship to carry an oil record book as required by either of these provisions, or failure to comply with certain instructions concerning entry, makes the owner or master liable on summary conviction to a fine not exceeding level five on the standard scale, currently £5,000. The more serious offence of making an entry in any oil record book which is knowingly false or misleading in any material particular leads to liability on summary conviction to a fine not exceeding the statutory maximum, presently £5,000, or imprisonment for a term not exceeding six months or

---

[105] See also the incident reporting duty under s.11 Prevention of Oil Pollution Act 1971, at 12.4.9 above.

[106] See 19.4 above on OILPOL.

[107] See Royal Commission on Environmental Pollution (1981) paras 8.36-8.40.

[108] s.142 Merchant Shipping Act 1995.

[109] Oil in Navigable Waters (Records) Regulations 1972 (SI 1972 No.1929), in force under s.142(1) Merchant Shipping Act 1995.

[110] Oil in Navigable Waters (Transfer Records) Regulations 1957 (SI 1957 No.348).

both. On conviction on indictment, punishment is a fine or imprisonment for a term not exceeding two years or both.[111]

The basic provisions of the 1995 Act,[112] however, must be read subject to amendments made to give effect to the MARPOL Convention. In particular, vessels of greater than specified sizes are subject to more exacting requirements regarding the keeping of oil records as provided for under the Merchant Shipping (Prevention of Oil Pollution) Regulations 1996.[113] Thus, every ship of 400GT and above, and every oil tanker of 150GT and above, must be provided with an oil record book relating to machinery space operations. Oil tankers above 150GT must also have an oil record book relating to cargo and ballast operations. These books must be in the form prescribed in MARPOL, Annex I.[114] The vessel's oil record book must be completed on each occasion, on a tank-to-tank basis if appropriate, whenever any of the following operations take place on the ship:

(a) for machinery space operations (all ships):
  (i) ballasting or cleaning of oil fuel tanks;
  (ii) discharging ballast or cleaning water from oil fuel tanks;
  (iii) disposing oily residues (sludge); and
  (iv) discharging overboard bilge water which has accumulated in machinery spaces;
(b) for cargo or ballast operations (oil tankers):
  (i) loading oil cargo;
  (ii) internal transfer of oil cargo during voyage;
  (iii) unloading oil cargo;
  (iv) ballasting cargo tanks and dedicated clean ballast tanks;
  (v) cleaning cargo tanks including crude oil washing;
  (vi) discharging ballast except from segregated ballast tanks;
  (vii) discharging water from slop tanks;
  (viii) closing of all applicable valves or similar devices after slop tank discharge operations;
  (ix) closing valves necessary for the isolation of dedicated clean ballast tanks from cargo and stripping lines after slop tank discharge operations; and
  (x) disposing residues.[115]

In the event of a discharge of oil or oily mixture of an exceptional kind,[116] or in the event of an accidental or other exceptional discharge of oil, a statement must be made in the oil record book of the circumstances of, and the reasons for, the discharge. Such operations must be fully recorded without delay and each completed entry must be signed by the officer in charge and each completed page signed by the master. Oil record books

---

[111] s.142(7) and (8) Merchant Shipping Act 1995.

[112] *Ibid* s.142.

[113] Reg.10 Merchant Shipping (Prevention of Oil Pollution) Regulations 1996.

[114] *Ibid* Reg.10(1).

[115] *Ibid* Reg.10(2).

[116] Described in *ibid* Reg. 11, see 19.6.1 above.

must be kept on board so as to be readily inspected by the Certifying Authority at all reasonable times, and preserved for three years after the last entry has been made.[117]

### 19.7.2 Reporting Discharges of Oil into Waters and Other Hazardous Occurrences

Owners or masters of ships have a duty to report any occurrence of oil or a mixture containing oil being discharged from a vessel into the waters of a harbour, or where it is found to be escaping or to have escaped from a vessel into such waters. The occurrence is to be reported to the harbour master or, where appropriate, the harbour authority. If the owner or master of a vessel makes the report it must state whether the occurrence involves a discharge or an escape of oil. Failure to make such a report makes a person liable on summary conviction to a fine not exceeding level five on the standard scale, presently £5,000.[118]

A distinctive feature of this duty is that the duty is generally placed upon the 'owner or master' of the vessel. This phrase was given detailed consideration in *Federal Steam Navigation Co Ltd* v *Department of Trade and Industry*[119] where it was held that an offence making the 'owner or master' guilty of an offence of discharging oil from a vessel[120] permitted either or both to be prosecuted for the offence. Similarly the use of the same formulation in relation to the reporting obligations means that the 'or' is to be understood conjunctively allowing both owner and master to be found guilty in an appropriate case.

It is notable that these duties are formulated in such a way as to refer to discharges of oil rather than oil pollution incidents. This approach is also taken in relation to further provisions deriving from MARPOL,[121] which place obligations on masters (or, failing which, shipowners) to make swift reports following actual or likely discharges to the marine environment, including damage, failure or breakdown of a ship of 15 metres in length or above.[122] The obligations apply to UK ships, and to foreign vessels in UK waters or UK territorial waters, and extend to oil, noxious liquid substances and other harmful substances.[123] It is notable that, for non-UK vessels, the obligation to report does not extend beyond the limit of territorial waters.

---

[117] *Ibid* Regs 10(3)-(6). On Certifying Authorities see 19.5.2 above.

[118] s.136 Merchant Shipping Act 1995.

[119] [1974] 2 All ER 97.

[120] s.1(1) Oil on Navigable Waters Act 1955, see now s.131(1) Merchant Shipping Act 1995.

[121] Art.8 and Protocol 1 1973/78 MARPOL Convention.

[122] Merchant Shipping (Reporting Requirements for Ships Carrying Dangerous or Polluting Goods) Regulations 1995 (SI 1995 No.2498), as amended by Merchant Shipping (Reporting Requirements for Ships Carrying Dangerous or Polluting Goods) (Amendment) Regulations 1999 SI 1999 No.2121 (to give effect to Directive 98/55/EC).

[123] i.e. to Annexes I-III of MARPOL; on Annexes II and III see 19.10 below.

### 19.8  Oil Discharges: Port State Control

As noted above, establishing port state control is a central feature of the LOS Convention as regards marine protection. The various control mechanisms open to port states involve powers, in defined circumstances, of inspection, of denying entry to port and of detaining vessels. Control now also extends to certain preventive mechanisms.

#### 19.8.1  Powers of Inspection, Denial of Entry and Detention

The LOS Convention allows a state to deny access to vessels entering its ports when certain requirements concerning construction, design, equipment and manning of the vessel are not complied with.[124] Moreover, port states may undertake investigations and start proceedings against foreign vessels that have allegedly committed discharge violations not merely in the waters of the port state (inland and territorial waters and the exclusive economic zone) but also on the high seas.[125]

To secure compliance with the controls upon oil pollution provided for in Annex I of MARPOL, the 1996 Regulations provide for certain, restricted, powers of inspection. Thus any ship to which the Regulations apply will be subject, whilst in any UK port or offshore terminal, to inspection by persons appointed by the Secretary of State. However, such inspections are limited to verifying that there is on board a valid IOPP certificate in the form prescribed by MARPOL, or a UKOPP certificate in the form prescribed by the Regulations. However, a vessel can be inspected if there are clear grounds for believing that its condition, or that of its equipment, does not correspond substantially with the particulars of the certificate. In that case, or if the ship does not carry a valid certificate, the inspector must take such necessary steps to ensure that the ship does not sail until it can proceed without presenting an unreasonable threat of harm to the marine environment. In such a case the Secretary of State may permit the ship to leave the port or offshore terminal for the purposes of proceeding to the nearest appropriate repair yard.[126]

Upon receiving evidence that a particular ship has discharged oil or an oily mixture contrary to the provisions of the Regulations the Secretary of State must investigate the matter and to inform the state which has reported the contravention, as well as the IMO, of the action taken.[127] For the purposes of giving effect to this requirement any person appointed as an inspector by the Secretary of State has the wide powers of an inspector as set out in the Merchant Shipping Act 1995.[128]

In addition to powers of inspection, further powers exist to deny a ship entry into a harbour and to detain it under the Regulations. Thus, any

---

[124] Art.211(3) LOS Convention.

[125] *Ibid* Art. 218. On these geographical zones see 18.7.1 and 18.10.1 above.

[126] Reg.34(1)(b) Merchant Shipping (Prevention of Oil Pollution) Regulations 1996.

[127] *Ibid* Reg.34(2).

[128] *Ibid* Reg.34(3), and see ss.259 and 260 Merchant Shipping Act 1995.

harbour master who has reason to believe that a ship which proposes to enter a harbour does not comply with the Regulations must immediately report the matter to the Secretary of State. If the Secretary of State is satisfied that the ship presents an unreasonable threat of harm to the marine environment, he may deny the ship entry to UK ports or offshore terminals.[129] Beyond this, in any case where a ship to which the Regulations apply is suspected of a contravention, the ship is liable to be detained. If the contravention is concerned with not carrying a valid certificate, or where the ship does not comply with its certificate, the ship must be detained until such time as it may depart without presenting an unreasonable threat of harm to the marine environment. Where a ship of another MARPOL country is in a UK port but fails a survey for a certificate, the Secretary of State may detain the ship until it is fit to proceed to sea, or to a repair yard, without presenting an unreasonable threat of environmental harm.[130]

Where a ship is detained, the general powers contained in the 1995 Act apply.[131] These give the Secretary of State, or in practice Maritime and Coastguard Agency inspectors, powers to board any ship in UK territorial waters and, for example, inspect it for pollution control purposes, so long as the ship is not unnecessarily prevented from continuing on its voyage. Maritime and Coastguard Agency inspectors are also responsible for enforcing EC-derived measures for port state control. In general terms, these require at least 25 per cent of ships entering port to be inspected for compliance with a range of international provisions, including MARPOL. They also give powers to detain or send ships to designated repair yards in the event of non-compliance, and allow any Member State to refuse access to a ship which is in breach of any instruction received in another state.[132] In the wake of the *Erika* incident off the Brittany coast in December 1999, proposals to strengthen this regime were published.[133]

These provisions must be read together with general provisions, covering oil and other dangerous and noxious substances, concerned with requiring vessels to report their contents, destination and route when departing for or leaving an EC port.[134]

---

[129] Reg.35(1) Merchant Shipping (Prevention of Oil Pollution) Regulations 1996.

[130] *Ibid* Reg.35(2) and Reg.9(5).

[131] ss.259 and 260 Merchant Shipping Act 1995, see *ibid* Reg.34(3).

[132] Directive 95/21/EC, implemented by the Merchant Shipping (Port State Control) Regulations 1995 (SI 1995 No.3128), amended by SI 1998 No.1433 (implementing Commission Directive 96/40/EC and Council Directive 98/25/EC). See also the (generally) Europe-wide Paris Memorandum of Understanding on Port State Control, at www.parismou.org.

[133] *Proposal for a Directive of the European Parliament and of the Council amending Council Directive 95/21/EC concerning the enforcement, in respect of shipping using Community ports and sailing in the waters under the jurisdiction of the Member States, of international standards for ship safety, pollution prevention and shipboard living and working conditions (port state control)* COM(2000)142 final.

[134] See 19.10 below.

## 19.8.2 *Improvement and Prohibition Notices*

In line with many other areas of environmental law,[135] there are now provisions in the 1995 Act allowing for measures to be taken, short of prosecution, for preventive purposes. Thus, improvement notices may be served by inspectors on any person where there is a continuing contravention, or where there has been a contravention which may be repeated. Improvement notices can be served both in relation to breaches of certain sections of the 1995 Act (including the oil pollution provisions of Chapter II of Part IV), and any regulations made under these.[136] Prohibition notices may be served in the event of 'accidents waiting to happen' which pose a risk of serious pollution of navigable waters.[137]

## 19.9  Oil Discharges: General Offences, Fines and Enforcement

Unless expressly permitted, a discharge of oil into UK navigable waters is an offence subject to relatively severe penalties. Discharges may also result in the commission of a water pollution offence under Part III of the Water Resources Act 1991.[138]

### 19.9.1  *Criminal Liability for Discharging Oil into UK Waters*

The 1995 Act provides for specific criminal offences in relation to discharging oil, or mixtures containing oil, from ships into navigable national waters. The offences only arise where the discharge is not otherwise allowed by regulations, and does not therefore relate to permissible discharges of the kind discussed above.[139]

Where oil is discharged from a ship, the owner or master commits the offence, which is one of strict liability.[140] However, if the discharge takes place in the course of transfer to or from another ship or a place on land and is caused by the act or omission of any person in charge of apparatus in that other ship or place, then the owner or master of the other ship (or the occupier of the land) will be liable.[141] It is arguable that, in certain situations, both parties may be liable. However, by contrast to the principal offences concerning pollution of controlled waters, there is no requirement that the discharge by the owner or master is 'caused' or 'knowingly permitted'. Hence, the relevant case law which holds that a pollution incident may be caused by more than one person is, at best, persuasive in

---

[135] See, e.g. works notices under Part III Water Resources Act 1991, see 13.2.2 above.

[136] s.261 Merchant Shipping Act 1995.

[137] *Ibid* s.262.

[138] On the overlap see 9.17.2 above and 19.9.1 below.

[139] See 19.6 above.

[140] *Federal Steam Navigation Co Ltd* v *Department of Trade and Industry* [1974] 2 All ER 97, concerning s.1(1) Oil in Navigable Waters Act 1955, now repealed.

[141] s.131(1) Merchant Shipping Act 1995. Further offences under the Prevention of Oil Pollution Act 1971 relating to land-based discharges are discussed at 12.4.9 above.

this context.[142] Concerns about the trans-shipment of oil between vessels in the English Channel were raised in the report following the *Braer* incident, and recommendations made to restrict the activity to a single defined area a minimum distance from the coast, but so far these appear not have been acted upon.[143]

The offence concerning oil discharges from ships applies to UK national waters that are navigable by sea-going trade, and specifically includes estuaries and may also include navigable freshwaters. There is therefore an overlap between this offence and the principal water pollution offences under the Water Resources Act 1991, though the maximum penalty in respect of the oil pollution offence on summary conviction is very much greater than that under the 1991 Act.[144] However, those who are guilty of the specific offence of discharging oil from ships are quite strictly delineated and the provision does not extend to cover others, such as harbour authorities, who may be responsible for oil pollution of coastal waters.[145]

The issue of whether waters contained in a 'dry dock' are capable of falling within the definition of relevant waters arose in *Rankin* v *De Coster*.[146] It was held that such waters were navigable by sea-going ships and hence fell within the provision notwithstanding that the dock was temporarily emptied to a level at which the dock ceased to be navigable by such vessels. It was doubted, however, whether the section could apply if the dock were to become wholly emptied since in such a situation there would be no waters into which oil could be discharged.[147]

Defences to the offence of polluting national waters by oil are provided for. For owners and masters, it is a defence to prove that the discharge was for the purpose of securing the ship's safety, preventing damage to any ship or cargo, or saving life, unless what was done was unnecessary or unreasonable in the circumstances. Further defences apply in certain situations where reasonable steps are taken after the event, so long as the original leakage was not through fault.[148] For occupiers, it is a defence to prove that neither the escape nor any delay in discovering it was due to any want of reasonable care, and that as soon as practicable after it was discovered all reasonable steps were taken for stopping or reducing it.[149] Finally, there are defences provided to protect reasonable acts done in the

---

[142] On the principal water pollution offences and the meaning of 'cause' see 9.3 and 9.6 above respectively.

[143] *Safer Ships, Cleaner Seas*, Lord Donaldson's Inquiry into the Prevention of Pollution from Merchant Shipping (Cm.2560, 1994).

[144] See 9.19.2 above and text below. A prosecution for public nuisance might also be taken, on which see 3.17 above.

[145] As occurred in the *Sea Empress* incident, see 9.19.3 above.

[146] [1975] 2 All ER 303.

[147] Contrast the approach in *R* v *Dovermoss* [1995] Env LR 258, discussed at 9.4 above.

[148] s.132 Merchant Shipping Act 1995.

[149] *Ibid* s.133.

exercise of certain powers of harbour authorities, specifically to prevent obstruction or danger to navigation from things like wrecks.[150]

Persons found guilty of this offence are liable on summary conviction to a fine not exceeding £250,000 or on conviction on indictment to a fine.[151] As noted above,[152] both the owner and the master may be liable. Provision is made for any unpaid fines to be paid by distress (i.e. by the seizure and sale of the ship and its equipment).[153]

The offence of polluting waters by oil has some fairly unique provisions relating to clean-up costs. Thus, where a person is convicted of the offence and a fine is imposed, if it appears to the court that any person has incurred, or will incur, expenses in removing any pollution, or making good any damage, which is attributable to the offence, the court may order the whole or part of the fine to be paid to that person for (or towards) defraying those expenses.[154] If the costs of cleaning operations are to be deducted from the fine, however, they may not be taken into account in setting the amount of the fine. This deployment of the money paid by way of a fine is not, however, intended to detract from the general principle of the criminal law that the amount of a fine must be related, amongst other things, to the ability of the convicted person to pay.[155] It follows that criminal proceedings are not intended to be pursued as an alternative to a civil claim for compensation, though conversely the amount of a civil claim will be reduced by the amount which a fine is used to defray the cost of making good oil pollution damage.[156] Thus in *John* v *Wright*[157] a fine of £25,000 was reduced to £750 primarily for this reason.[158]

### 19.9.2 Penalties relating to the 1996 Regulations

The 1996 Regulations provide that the general penalty for failure to comply with any regulation is that the owner and master of the ship will each be guilty of an offence and punishable on summary conviction by a fine not exceeding the statutory maximum, presently £5,000, and on conviction on indictment by a fine.[159] In respect of contravention of certain regulations, however, a greater maximum penalty is specified. Thus for contravening those provisions of the regulations concerned with

---

[150] *Ibid* s.134.

[151] *Ibid* s.131(3), and see Reg.36(2) Merchant Shipping (Prevention of Oil Pollution) Regulations 1996, discussed in 19.19.2 below.

[152] See *Federal Steam Navigation Co Ltd* v *Department of Trade and Industry* [1974] 2 All ER 97.

[153] s.146(1)(a) Merchant Shipping Act 1995.

[154] *Ibid* s.146(2). Contrast the 'clean up' powers under s.161 Water Resources Act 1991, discussed at 13.2 above and the availability of compensation orders under The Powers of Criminal Courts Act 1973, discussed at 9.2.1 above.

[155] See 9.19 above on sentencing policy for environmental offences.

[156] See also 9.21 above on Powers of Criminal Courts Act 1973.

[157] [1980] JC 99.

[158] Contrast the Powers of Criminal Courts Act 1973, discussed at 9.21 above.

[159] Reg.36(1) Merchant Shipping (Prevention of Oil Pollution) Regulations 1996.

permissible discharges and with special areas,[160] the owner and the master will each be guilty of an offence and subject to the same penalties as apply to the offence of discharging oil into UK waters discussed above. The maximum fine on summary conviction, which was raised to £250,000 to bring it into line with that under the 1995 Act as amended by the Merchant Shipping and Maritime Security Act 1997,[161] was imposed for the first time in a case concerning discharge of oil from a container ship off Land's End, even though the spill was dispersed in heavy weather and there was no report of the oil reaching the coast or damaging wildlife.[162]

It is a defence for any person charged under the Regulations to show that they took all reasonable precautions and exercised all due diligence to avoid the commission of the offence.[163] Where an offence is committed under the Regulations, or this defence is applicable because of the default of another person, then the other person will be guilty of the offence and may be charged and convicted whether or not proceedings are taken against the person exercising all due diligence.[164]

### 19.9.3 Prosecutions

Proceedings for offences under the oil pollution provisions of the 1995 Act may generally be brought only by or with the consent of the Attorney-General, or with certain exceptions concerning harbours, by the Secretary of State or a person authorised by him by any general or special direction.[165] In certain specified situations concerning harbours, the harbour authority may bring proceedings.[166] These are:

(a) first, in the case of the offence of unlawfully discharging oil into UK waters,[167] if the offence is alleged to have been committed by the discharge of oil, or a mixture containing oil, into the waters of a harbour;

(b) second, offences in relation to a harbour concerned with transfers of oil at night and the duty to report discharges of oil;[168] and

(c) third, any offence relating to the keeping of records of the transfer of oil within a harbour.[169]

---

[160] See 19.6 above.

[161] See Merchant Shipping (Prevention of Oil Pollution) (Amendment) Regulations 1997 (SI 1997 No.1910).

[162] *Maritime and Coastguard Agency* v *Bent Emanuel Christiansen*, 11 September 1998, Southampton Magistrates Court, unreported, but see [1999] *Water Law* 14 and *ENDS Report* 284 (1998) p.47.

[163] Reg.36(3) Merchant Shipping (Prevention of Oil Pollution) Regulations 1996. This is a point of contrast to the offences of strict liability under the 1995 Act, see 19.9.1 above.

[164] *Ibid* Reg.36(4). Compare the position concerning the principal water pollution offences under the Water Resources Act 1991, discussed at 9.6 above.

[165] s.143(1) Merchant Shipping Act 1995.

[166] *Ibid* s.19(2).

[167] *Ibid* s.131, see 19.9.1 above.

[168] ss.135 and 136 Merchant Shipping Act 1995, see 19.5.5 and 19.7.2 above.

[169] *Ibid* s.142, see 19.7.1 above.

By contrast, there is no restriction on the bringing of prosecutions under the 1996 Regulations, though in practice the Maritime and Coastguard Agency brings prosecutions. However, it is notable that no provision is made in the Regulations, nor the 1995 Act, for access to information or for public registers. In part this was resisted on the dubious grounds that such information might facilitate unwarranted prosecutions being brought by private parties.[170]

Despite the strict liability of the offences and the relatively high fine levels, in practice prosecutions are brought relatively infrequently.[171] This is attributable in part to the difficulty of identifying the ship from which an oil discharge has originated. However, it has also been suggested that the low prosecution rates indicate concerns by the regulatory authorities about the value of prosecution. This relates in part to the imposition of low fines, which seems to persist; average fine levels have been in the region of £1,500,[172] though as noted above there are some signs that much higher penalties may be imposed. However, it has also been suggested that, for non-UK vessels at least, the practice of master's being prosecuted, and then being indemnified by the shipowner and, ultimately, the ship's insurer acts as a disincentive to prosecution.[173]

### 19.10 Discharges of Substances Other than Oil from Ships

As far as the principal offences concerning pollution of controlled waters are concerned, discharges of oil and non-oil pollutants from a vessel within coastal waters are identically treated and emissions or discharges of either may amount to an offence.[174] Beyond this, the control of discharges from ships of substances other than oil involves provisions analogous to those governing oil discharges. This feature of the law has its origin in the 1973/78 MARPOL Convention,[175] which incorporates a series of Annexes concerned with different types of pollutants originating from ships. In addition to the first Annex, concerned with the prevention of pollution by oil and discussed above, further Annexes are concerned with:

(a)  pollution by noxious liquid substances carried in bulk (Annex II);
(b)  pollution by harmful substances carried by sea in packaged forms (Annex III);
(c)  pollution by sewage from ships (Annex IV);
(d)  pollution by garbage from ships (Annex V); and
(e)  preventing atmospheric pollution from ships (Annex VI).

---

[170] On access to information generally see 16.14–16.19 above. The Environmental Information Regulations 1992 could be relied on here.

[171] See DETR, *Digest of Environmental Statistics* (2001) Table 4.17.

[172] Lomas (1989) and DETR, *Digest of Environmental Statistics* (2001) Table 4.17. On fines for offences under the Water Resources Act 1991 see 9.19.2 above.

[173] See generally Lomas (1989).

[174] Under s.85 Water Resources Act 1991, see 9.3 above. See also the offence under s.4 of the Salmon and Freshwater Fisheries Act 1975, discussed at 15.4.1 above.

[175] See 19.4 above.

Of the six Annexes, only the first two, dealing with oil and noxious substances, need be accepted by a state on ratification of the Convention. The last four are optional in that a ratifying state may declare that it does not accept any or all of them.[176] The following sections are concerned with Annexes II to V and (except for Annex IV, which has yet to come into force) their implementation.[177]

### 19.10.1 Provisions Common to More than One Annex

Some provisions apply to pollutants in more than one of the Annexes. Of particular note are the provisions of the national Merchant Shipping (Reporting Requirements for Ships Carrying Dangerous or Polluting Goods) Regulations 1995.[178] These implement the EC 'Hazmat' Directive,[179] which requires vessels to report their contents, destination and route when travelling to or from EC ports and carrying certain dangerous or polluting goods. The polluting goods are oil as defined in Annex I of MARPOL (excluding the bunkers and ship's stores), noxious liquid substances,[180] and harmful substances as defined in Annex III of MARPOL, while the dangerous goods are defined by reference to various IMO Codes, and include chemicals and radioactive substances.

In the case of ships coming from non-EC ports, the Regulations apply to UK ships bound for a port or place of anchorage in another Member State and to non-UK ships bound for such places in the UK or UK territorial waters. The Regulations also apply, in varying degrees, to all ships leaving UK ports, and to UK ships leaving other EC ports and UK ship leaving non-EC ports.[181] The Regulations also lay down reporting requirements in the event of accidents; probable discharges; breaches of permissible discharge levels; damage, failure or breakdown of ships over 15 metres; or any threat of damage to the coastline or related interests of the UK.[182] There are proposals, now of some antiquity, to extend the EC Hazmat Directive to require reporting by ships operating within 150 miles of EC coasts, even if they are not intending to call at a Community port.[183] A principal reason why such measures have not been adopted would appear to be concerns about their compatibility with the jurisdiction given by the LOS Convention to coastal states to intervene in such situations.[184]

---

[176] Art.14 MARPOL.

[177] Annex VI MARPOL on atmospheric emissions, which has yet to be ratified by the UK, is in any case outwith the scope of this work.

[178] SI 1995 No.2498, as amended by SI 1999 No.2121.

[179] Directive 93/75/EEC, as amended by Directive 98/55/EC.

[180] As defined in the Merchant Shipping (Dangerous or Noxious Liquid Substances in Bulk) Regulations 1996 (SI 1996 No.3010), see 19.10.2 below.

[181] Regs.5 and 6 Merchant Shipping (Reporting Requirements for Ships Carrying Dangerous or Polluting Goods) Regulations 1995 (SI 1995 No.2498).

[182] *Ibid* Reg.9.

[183] *Proposal for a Council Directive concerning the setting-up of a European Vessel Reporting System in the Maritime Zones of Community Member States* (COM(93)647 final) ('Eurorep').

[184] See 19.4 above.

In addition, provisions relating to the movement of wastes may be relevant to the sea carriage of potentially hazardous substances. The 1989 Basle Convention on the Control of Transboundary Movements of Hazardous Wastes and their Disposal prohibits the trade in hazardous wastes across certain borders, and regulates the transportation of the remainder in the interests of safety. The Convention, together with the 1989 (Fourth) Lomé Convention which governs hazardous waste movements between the EC and a number of African, Caribbean and Pacific states,[185] is implemented through the EC Waste Shipments Regulation,[186] which extend controls to all 'wastes' as defined, and by the Transfrontier Shipment of Waste Regulations 1994.[187] These measures provide more general controls on the movements of waste at sea, which may have an indirect effect on the pollution of marine waters, although specifically excluded is the offloading to shore of waste produced in the normal operation of ships so long as such waste is the subject of a specific binding international instrument.[188] This avoids overlap between these waste controls and some of the measures described in the following sections, while the Regulation also requires compliance with certain listed international transport conventions which are stated to include the MARPOL Convention and the International Maritime Dangerous Goods Code.[189]

### 19.10.2 *Pollution by Noxious Liquid Substances*

Annex II to the MARPOL Convention[190] sets out regulations for the control of discharges of noxious liquid substances carried in bulk by chemical or oil tankers and regulates tank cleaning and deballasting operations conducted in respect of such vessels. The noxious liquid substances concerned are classified into four categories, A to D, according to their harmfulness.

(a) *Category A*: substances presenting a major hazard to either marine resources or human health or which cause serious harm to amenities or other legitimate uses of the sea and therefore justify the application of stringent anti-pollution measures.

(b) *Category B*: substances presenting a hazard to either marine resources or human health or which cause harm to amenities or other legitimate uses of the sea and therefore justify the application of special anti-pollution measures.

(c) *Category C*: substances presenting a minor hazard to either marine resources or human health or which cause minor harm to

---

[185] 29 ILM 783 (1990) as amended, see Art.39. See also OJ L 229, p.3, as amended by OJ L 156, p.3.

[186] Regulation 259/93/EEC Supervision and Control of Shipments of Waste.

[187] SI 1994 No.1137.

[188] Art.1(2)(a) Regulation 259/93/EEC on the Supervision and Control of Shipments of Waste within, into and out of the EC.

[189] *Ibid* Art.32 and Annex I.

[190] In force 2 October 1983.

amenities or other legitimate uses of the sea and therefore require special operational conditions.

(d)  *Category D*: substances presenting a recognisable hazard to either marine resources or human health or which cause minimal harm to amenities or other legitimate uses of the sea and therefore require some attention in operational conditions.[191]

As with oil discharges, the provisions of MARPOL governing carriage of the four categories of noxious liquid substances (A to D) are implemented via enabling powers,[192] under which Regulations may provide for effect to be given to Annex II of the Convention.[193] These provisions are now contained in the Merchant Shipping (Dangerous or Noxious Liquid Substances in Bulk) Regulations 1996.[194] These Regulations also make compliance with what are known as the 'IBC' and 'BCH' Codes, which determine standards for ships carrying certain chemicals and which are now given mandatory effect in national law. Many of the technical standards are contained in the companion Merchant Shipping Notice No. M.1703/NSL 1.

In many respects the constraints that are imposed upon the carriage and transfer of noxious liquid substances are analogous to the controls upon oil discharges from ships.[195] The Regulations apply to UK ships carrying noxious liquid substances in bulk. 'Noxious liquid substances' are defined either by reference to MEPC Circular 2/CIRC.1 or to the A to D categorisation of pollutants as listed in chapters 17 and 18 of the IBC Code. These relate to the degree of hazard to marine resources or human health, and also apply to substances which are *provisionally assessed* as falling into any of these categories and to discharges containing any of these substances.[196] The Regulations also apply to all chemical tankers carrying 'dangerous substances' in bulk, and all oil tankers carrying 'pollution hazard substances' in bulk. 'Dangerous substances' and 'pollution hazard substances' are defined with reference to Chapter 17 of the IBC Code according to the properties of the substances concerned. The Regulations also apply to non-UK ships whilst in UK territorial waters, although if ships are discharging or washing tanks which have carried noxious liquid substances or certain defined pollution hazard substances the Regulations apply to the limits of UK controlled waters.[197] Where the protection of UK waters is concerned, the Regulations can also be enforced beyond UK controlled waters if a discharge has caused, or is likely to cause, pollution in UK internal, territorial or controlled waters. This power is subject to the right of the flag state to take over proceedings,

---

[191] Reg.3 Annex II MARPOL, emphasis added.

[192] Now s.128 Merchant Shipping Act 1995.

[193] Reg.3(1)(a) Merchant Shipping (Prevention and Control of Pollution) Order 1987 (SI 1987 No.470).

[194] SI 1996 No.3010, as amended by SI 1998 No.1153.

[195] Under the Merchant Shipping (Prevention of Oil Pollution) Regulations 1996, considered generally above.

[196] *Ibid* Reg.2(1).

[197] *Ibid* Reg.3. On 'UK controlled waters' see 18.10.1 above.

although this may be overridden if the Secretary of State certifies the laxity of the flag state's enforcement practices, or if the discharge results in major damage to the UK.[198] These enforcement powers neatly reflect the rise of coastal state jurisdiction relative to the powers of flag states.[199]

Subject to the exception of discharges made to secure the safety of a ship, to save human life, to disperse pollutants, or following an accident if certain conditions and standards are met,[200] the discharge of all four categories of pollutant (A to D) into the sea is prohibited, and discharges of liquid wastes and residues is regulated such that controls are strictest for category A substances.[201] In respect of uncategorised liquid substances carried in bulk, or residual mixtures containing such substances, discharge is prohibited without the approval of the Secretary of State and subject to any conditions he may impose upon the discharge.[202] Special procedures are provided for in relation to the washing of cargo tanks having contained noxious substances,[203] along with the use of specified pumping systems,[204] and records are required to be kept of operations involving the movement of noxious substances.[205] Provision for port waste reception facilities, which underpin many of these measures, is otherwise provided for.[206]

Survey requirements are a prerequisite for using a vessel to carry dangerous or noxious substances in bulk. Thus, upon satisfactory completion of the required survey, the Secretary of State is to issue an International Pollution Prevention Certificate for the Carriage of Noxious Substances in Bulk to confirm that the vessel complies with the relevant requirements. In the case of chemical tankers, a Certificate (or International Certificate, as appropriate) of Fitness for the Carriage of Dangerous Chemicals in Bulk is issued.[207]

Infringement of the 1996 Regulations is an offence for which the owner and master of the ship will each be punishable on summary conviction by a fine not exceeding the statutory maximum, presently £5,000, or an unlimited fine on conviction on indictment. Contravention of the requirements relating to discharges from cargo tanks attracts the higher penalty of a maximum fine of £25,000 on summary conviction. In each

---

[198] *Ibid* Regs.15–17.

[199] See 19.4 above.

[200] paras 2, 4, 5, 10, 11 and 12 Merchant Shipping Notice No. M.1703/NLS 1.

[201] *Ibid* paras.2–12.

[202] *Ibid* para.13.

[203] *Ibid* paras.3, 7, 8 and 9.

[204] *Ibid* paras.1 and 2.

[205] Reg.8 Merchant Shipping (Prevention of Oil Pollution) Regulations 1996 and compare oil record book requirements at 19.7.1 above.

[206] Merchant Shipping (Port Waste Reception Facilities) Regulations 1997 (SI 1997 No.3018), see 19.5.4 above.

[207] Regs.9 and 10 Merchant Shipping (Prevention of Oil Pollution) Regulations 1996, contrast Oil Tanker certification discussed at 19.5.2 above.

case it is a defence to show that all reasonable steps were taken to ensure that the Regulations were complied with.[208]

Separate provision is made under the Dangerous Substances in Harbour Areas Regulations 1987 for the handling of liquid dangerous substances in harbours. These relate to substances listed in the IBC or BCH Codes, and therefore apply to all substances regulated for the purposes of Annex II of MARPOL. These require certification before liquid dangerous substances may be loaded, unloaded or carried in a harbour area, and prohibit transfers of such substances between vessels unless sanctioned by the harbour master or berth operator, who must also give prior consent before certain discharges are made.[209] However, the Regulations are made under the Health and Safety at Work etc. Act 1974, and only apply to marine pollutants to the extent that they are 'dangerous substances' for health and safety purposes, a term which is given a risk-based definition.[210]

### 19.10.3 Harmful Substances Carried by Sea in Packaged Forms

The first of the three Optional Annexes to the Convention, Annex III,[211] provides regulations for the prevention of pollution by harmful substances carried at sea in packaged forms, or in freight containers, portable tanks or road and rail tank wagons. 'Harmful substances' are those substances identified in the International Maritime Dangerous Goods Code (the 'IMDG Code') as marine pollutants, although other substances may be included if they bio-accumulate, taint seafood or are highly toxic to marine life.[212]

Annex III provides that the carriage of harmful substances in such packages or containers is prohibited except in accordance with the regulations provided for in the Annex.[213] Specifically, packaging or containers used to carry harmful substances must be adequate to minimise the hazard to the marine environment having regard to their particular contents.[214] Packages and containers are to be durably marked with the correct technical name and a distinctive label indicating that the contents are a marine pollutant.[215] Shipping documents are to confirm that marking and labelling requirements have been complied with, must use correct technical names of products and must be identified by the words 'MARINE POLLUTANT'.[216] Harmful substances are to be properly stowed and secured so as to minimise the hazards to the marine

---

[208] *Ibid* Reg.14, as amended by SI 1998 No.1153.

[209] SI 1987 No.37, as amended.

[210] Reg.3(1) Merchant Shipping (Prevention of Oil Pollution) Regulations 1996. For comment on the Regulations see Bates and Benson (1993, updated), paras 5.176-5.187.

[211] In force 1 July 1992.

[212] See the Guidelines contained in the Appendix to Annex III.

[213] Reg.1(2) Annex III.

[214] *Ibid* Reg.2.

[215] *Ibid* Reg.3.

[216] *Ibid* Reg.4.

environment.[217] Certain harmful substances which are extremely hazardous to the marine environment may, for sound scientific and technical reasons, be prohibited from being carried, or be limited as to the quantity which may be carried aboard any one ship.[218] The discharge by jettisoning of harmful substances carried in packaged forms or containers is to be prohibited except where this is necessary for the purpose of securing the safety of a ship or saving life at sea.[219]

In the UK, implementation of Annex III is by the Merchant Shipping (Dangerous Goods and Marine Pollutants) Regulations 1997,[220] made under the enabling powers that are provided by the Merchant Shipping (Prevention and Control of Pollution) Order 1990.[221] The Regulations, which also give effect to the provisions of Chapter VII of the Safety of Life at Sea ('SOLAS') Convention,[222] apply to ships carrying dangerous goods in bulk or packaged form or marine pollutants in packaged form, and create slightly different requirements in relation to 'dangerous goods' and 'marine pollutants', both of which are defined with reference to the IMGD Code. The Regulations place a burden on ships' operators, employers and masters to show that they have complied with the duty to handle, stow and carry dangerous goods safely, and general safety duties are also placed on employees. However, these duties only relate to the creation of significant risks to the health and safety of any person, and are unlikely to be relevant except in the most extreme marine pollution incident.[223] Of more relevance are the provisions of the Regulations concerned with the carriage of packaged goods, which closely follow the wording of Annex III of MARPOL,[224] and the provisions relating to the carriage of dangerous goods or marine pollutants in bulk.[225] In the case of the latter, however, the general duty imposed on ships' operators is not to handle or carry such matter if there is cause to believe that this cannot be done safely.[226] This is subject to specialist carriage regimes, under Codes dealing with substances such as chemicals, gas and solid bulk cargoes,[227] which may stipulate the level of safety to be provided. However, it must be assumed that safety will probably carry a narrow interpretation restricting its meaning to human safety rather than general environmental damage.

---

[217] *Ibid* Reg.5.

[218] *Ibid* Reg.6.

[219] *Ibid* Reg.7. See also Chapter VII of the International Convention for the Safety of Life at Sea 1974 (the 'SOLAS' Convention, see 19.3 above) which establishes regulations concerning the carriage of dangerous goods which are given effect to under Merchant Shipping (Dangerous Goods) Regulations 1981 (SI 1981 No.1747).

[220] SI 1997 No.2367.

[221] SI 1990 No.2595.

[222] See above.

[223] Regs.6 and 7 Merchant Shipping (Dangerous Goods and Marine Pollutants) Regulations 1997.

[224] See generally *ibid* Part II.

[225] See *ibid* Part III.

[226] *Ibid* Reg.21(1).

[227] As set out in *ibid* Reg.21(2)(a).

## 19.10.4  Discharges of Sewage from Ships

Annex IV to the 1973/78 MARPOL Convention contains regulations for controlling discharges of sewage from ships. These provide that new ships which are either over 200GT, or are certified to carry more than ten persons, must comply with regulations governing sewage disposal. The same compliance will be required of existing ships of over 200GT or certified to carry more than ten persons within ten years of the Annex entering into force.[228] The regulations provide for the survey of ships in respect of sewage treatment, containment and disposal facilities,[229] and the issue of an International Sewage Pollution Prevention Certificate in a specified form, having a definite duration.[230] Subject to certain exceptions, the discharge of sewage into the sea is prohibited unless the discharge is of comminuted and disinfected sewage using an approved system at a distance of more than four nautical miles from the nearest land, or more than 12 nautical miles from the nearest land if the sewage is not so treated. In either case permitted discharges are to be made at a moderate rate from a vessel which is in motion and must be made in accordance with any conditions imposed upon discharge. Alternatively, sewage discharge is permitted if the ship has in operation an approved and certified sewage treatment plant, the effluent from which does not produce visible floating solids in, nor cause discoloration of, the surrounding water.[231] The general prohibition upon the discharge of sewage does not apply where the discharge was necessary for the purpose of securing the safety of a ship and those on board or saving life at sea. Nor does it apply where the discharge is a result of damage to a ship or its equipment if all reasonable precautions have been taken before and after the occurrence of the damage for the purpose of preventing or minimising the damage.[232] Each contracting party undertakes to ensure the provision of adequate port waste reception facilities that do not cause undue delay to ships.[233]

While the UK has accepted Annex IV, it has yet to come into force and its provisions have yet to be implemented. Nevertheless, the UK has issued non-binding guidelines requesting UK ships to respect the provisions of Annex IV in relation to the Baltic Sea. This goes some way to recognising the steps which the Baltic Sea states have gone to introduce analogous provisions on sewage discharges for their vessels in that area.[234] Although the discharge of sewage effluent from a vessel within the territorial waters of England and Wales is exempted from the provisions of Part III of the Water Resources Act 1991,[235] various provisions relating to the disposal and discharge of sewage at sea are found in the Food and Environment

---

[228] Reg.2 Annex IV MARPOL.

[229] *Ibid* Reg.3.

[230] *Ibid* Regs 4 and 7.

[231] *Ibid* Reg.8.

[232] *Ibid* Reg.9.

[233] *Ibid* Reg.10.

[234] See the 1974 Convention for the Protection of the Marine Environment of the Baltic Sea. The measures relating to sewage came into force on 3 May 1990.

[235] Under s.89(2). On the principal pollution offences under the 1991 Act see 9.3 above and see 9.17.2 on discharges from vessels.

Protection Act 1985.[236] Provisions relating to the treatment of sewage in ports may also be made under local Harbour Acts or harbour authority byelaws, or byelaws of the Environment Agency.

### 19.10.5 Garbage from Vessels

Problems associated with the deposit of garbage from vessels is recognised as an area of increasing concern, both for its impact on marine biodiversity and for aesthetic reasons. Annex V to MARPOL[237] is concerned with regulations for the prevention of discharges of garbage from vessels. For these purposes 'garbage' means all kinds of victual, domestic and operational waste excluding fresh fish and parts thereof, generated during the normal operation of the ship, and substances which are defined or listed in the other Annexes to the Convention.[238] The provisions of the Annex, which apply to all ships, prohibit the disposal into the sea of all plastics including synthetic ropes, synthetic fishing nets and plastic garbage bags.[239] Although it is advocated that disposal should be made as far as practicable from land, other prohibitions upon disposal are imposed upon the disposal of dunnage, lining and packing materials which will float within 25 nautical miles of land; and the disposal of food wastes and all other garbage (including paper products, rags, glass, metal, bottles, crockery and similar refuse) within 12 nautical miles from land.[240] This prohibition is qualified in that the disposal of such other garbage is permitted where the refuse has passed through a comminuter or grinder, and made as far as practicable from land, and in any case is not less than three nautical miles from the nearest land. In such a case the comminuted or ground garbage must be capable of passing through a screen with openings no greater than 25 millimetres.[241] Following amendments to Annex V in 1995, further provisions now require placards displaying information for crews about the garbage rules, garbage management plans and garbage record keeping.[242]

Annex V provides for the designation of 'special areas' where stricter standards on the disposal of garbage from ships are imposed. The special areas which have so far been designated include the North Sea and the English Channel and its approaches.[243] In special areas, the only allowable discharges of garbage are food wastes, which must be disposed of as far as practicable from land and not less than 12 nautical miles from the nearest land. As with special areas for oil, the operation of a special area for garbage requires on-shore reception facilities, which must be provided by all states with bordering coastline.[244] Despite these designations there

---

[236] See 19.20 below.

[237] In force 31 December 1988.

[238] Reg.1(1) Annex V MARPOL.

[239] *Ibid* Reg.3(1)(a).

[240] *Ibid* Reg.3(1)(b).

[241] *Ibid* Reg.3(1)(c).

[242] *Ibid* Reg.9, added by 1995 amendments, in force 1 July 1997.

[243] Under 1989 amendments to Annex V, in force 18 February 1991.

[244] Reg.5 Annex V. On special areas for oil discharges see 19.6.4 above.

appears to be no subsequent improvement in the situation with regard to litter.[245]

Exceptions in relation to the prohibitions on discharges of garbage from ships, including discharges in special areas, arise where the disposal is necessary for the purpose of securing the safety of a ship and those on board or saving life at sea. An exception is also made where escape of garbage results from damage to a ship or its equipment provided that all reasonable precautions have been taken before and after the occurrence of the damage, for the purpose of preventing or minimising the escape. In relation to the prohibition upon disposal of synthetic fishing nets it is a defence to show that the loss was accidental and that all reasonable precautions were taken to prevent such loss.[246] Each contracting party undertakes to provide appropriate port waste reception facilities for garbage.[247]

Annex V is given effect to by the Merchant Shipping (Prevention of Pollution by Garbage) Regulations 1998.[248] The Regulations apply to UK ships wherever they are, to other ships in UK waters or controlled waters, or anywhere at sea, subject to limits on enforcement jurisdiction analogous to those provided for in relation to noxious liquid substance regulation.[249] The Regulations follow the general scheme of provisions enacted to implement the other Annexes in force, although it is notable that offences concerning ships are committed by owners, managers, demise charterers and masters. Port waste reception facilities are provided for under general regulations.[250] National provisions concerning dumping at sea do not apply to the disposal of waste at sea resulting from the normal operation of ships or their equipment,[251] and the dumping of trade effluent from a ship is not an offence under the Water Resources Act 1991.[252] However, the dumping of garbage into harbours may be covered by Harbour Acts or byelaws made thereunder, insofar as they may prejudice the workings of the harbour or docks.

### 19.10.6  Other Contaminating Matter

Apart from those substances which are presently the subject of MARPOL Annexes, further pollutants are also the subject of international concern, and may be the subject of future Annexes in due course.

---

[245] para.6.3.4 Ch.6 OSPAR *Quality Status Report 2000.*

[246] Reg.6 Annex V MARPOL.

[247] *Ibid* Reg.7.

[248] SI 1998 No.1377, made under Art.2 Merchant Shipping (Prevention of Pollution by Garbage) Order 1988 (SI 1988 No.2252) and Art.2 Merchant Shipping (Prevention of Pollution) (Law of the Sea Convention) Order 1996 (SI 1996 No.282).

[249] See 19.10.2 above.

[250] See the Merchant Shipping (Port Waste Reception Facilities) Regulations 1997, discussed at 19.5.4 above.

[251] Part II Food and Environment Protection Act 1985, and SI 1985 No.1699, see 19.20 below.

[252] See s.89(2) Water Resources Act 1991, see 9.17.2 above.

*(a) Ballast water discharges and non-native organisms*
Large volumes of ballast water taken on board bulk carriers at the port of unloading are transported, often for long distances around the world, and discharged at the port where the cargo is unloaded. The ballast water can contain pollutants, pathogens and ecologically harmful non-native organisms. The sludge that settles at the bottom of ballast tanks can also develop its own biological community. Although most discharges of species in ballast water are unproblematic because of the hostility of the receiving environment, uncontrolled discharges of ballast waters can lead to acute ecological damage, as the entry of American comb jelly in the Black Sea and the subsequent decimation of anchovy and sprat species attests.[253] Unlike other pollutants, with ecological contamination there is little possibility of clean-up or absorption into the marine environment. The LOS Convention requires that action be taken to prevent, reduce and control the intentional or accidental introduction of such species.[254] To date, the issue is the subject of guidelines only,[255] but a further Annex to MARPOL may emerge.[256]

*(b) Anti-fouling paints*
The anti-fouling coating tributyl tin (TBT), an organotin compound, is used to prevent the hulls of ships from being infested by barnacles, algae and molluscs, which slows ships down. For some time the extreme toxicity of TBT in the marine environment has been established,[257] and the retail sale of paints containing TBT has been banned at national level[258] and the marketing and use of such substances banned at EC level.[259] Moves to phase out the use of TBT on ships through the MARPOL Convention are currently being discussed, with a view to a ban on the application of TBT by 2003 and a ban on its presence in anti-fouling systems after 2008.[260]

## 19.11 Responding to Shipping Casualties

Further aspects of United Kingdom law which are a direct consequence of international agreements relate to actions required in the aftermath of shipping accidents or other incidents which pose a hazard to the marine environment. This includes:

---

[253] *Mnemiopsis leidyi*, see Ascherson (1996) pp.262-63 and, more generally, GESAMP (1997). On ecologically harmful introductions into water see also 15.5 and 15.7.6 above.
[254] Art.196 LOS Convention, and see also para.17.30(a)(vi), Agenda 21.
[255] *Guidelines for the control and management of ships' ballast water to minimize the transfer of harmful aquatic organisms and pathogens*, IMO Resolution A.868(20), 1997. See also Merchant Shipping Notices 1532 and 1533.
[256] MEPC 43-4-1, 22 February 1999.
[257] Wood (1986), and see also the references in 'Anti-fouling systems: moving towards the non-toxic solution', *Focus on IMO* (1999).
[258] See the Control of Pollution (Anti-Fouling Paints and Treatments) Regulations 1987 (SI 1987 No.783), see 12.4.6 above.
[259] Directive 76/769/EEC, as amended by Directive 89/677/EEC.
[260] 'Anti-fouling systems: moving towards the non-toxic solution', *Focus on IMO* (1999). On the compatibility of restrictions on organotin usage and EC law see 4.10.2 above.

(a) powers for government to intervene and take charge of a vessel which is constituting a pollution hazard;

(b) other responses to harmful incidents centring on on-board management planning;

(c) information exchange between states and co-operation in combating incidents; and

(d) rules relating to the salvage of vessels posing a threat of pollution.

### 19.11.1   The Intervention Convention

The *Torrey Canyon* disaster in 1967[261] first drew attention to the potential legal difficulty involved in taking action to protect a coastline from oil from a shipping casualty where the incident took place outside territorial waters. The right of a state to intervene in such circumstances was the subject of the 1969 International Convention Relating to Intervention on the High Seas in Cases of Oil Pollution Casualties of 1969, known as the 'Intervention Convention'.[262] A 1973 Protocol to this Convention extends the power of intervention to shipping casualties where the hazard arises from a polluting substance other than oil,[263] and this has been amended on two occasions to revise the list of substances covered and the method of their selection.[264]

### 19.11.1A   General powers to intervene

In accordance with the terms of the Intervention Convention a coastal state may intervene after a shipping casualty has occurred on the high seas and where there is a grave and imminent danger of pollution of its coastline or 'related interests'. This allows coastal states to take measures to protect, for example, their commercial fisheries interests even where contaminants are unlikely to be carried to its coastline. The need for 'grave and imminent danger' indicates that the nature of the Convention is to allow states to take measures which, if they were not necessary, would otherwise be contrary to international law.[265] The coastal state is bound to consult the flag state of the vessel concerned, and then may take only such reasonable and proportionate action as is necessary to avoid the pollution danger. The Convention goes to considerable lengths to specify when action will be proportionate to the likely or actual damage caused, and provides that compensation will be payable for any damage caused which is in excess of action which was reasonably necessary.

---

[261] Generally see Brown (1968) and Keeton (1968).

[262] Cmnd.6056; 9 ILM 25 (1970), in force 6 May 1975.

[263] Cmnd.6038; 13 ILM 605 (1974), in force 30 March 1983.

[264] 1991 amendments in force 30 March 1993; 1996 amendments in force 19 December 1997.

[265] The intervention in the *Torrey Canyon* incident was later held to be necessary and therefore justified as a matter of customary international law; see Bates and Benson (1993, updated), para. 3.80.

Both the Intervention Convention and its 1973 Protocol are given effect to by the Merchant Shipping Act 1995.[266] Extensive powers are given to the Secretary of State[267] to issue directions to a range of parties in respect of a ship or its cargo for the purpose of preventing or reducing oil pollution or the risk of oil pollution in the event of an accident. The risk must be that 'significant pollution' will be caused in the UK, UK waters or the UK pollution zone,[268] a broader term than pollution 'on a large scale' as was previously provided for. 'Accident' for these purposes means a collision of ships, stranding or other incident of navigation, or other occurrence on board a ship or external to it resulting in material damage (or its threat) to a ship or cargo.[269] Notably, the 1973 Protocol is implemented by a provision of the 1995 Act which allows the Secretary of State to prescribe by Order substances other than oil to which the above provisions will apply.[270] However, the Act also applies to unprescribed substances if they are liable to create hazards to human health, to harm living resources and marine life, to damage amenities or to interfere with other legitimate uses of the sea.[271]

If in the Secretary of State's opinion the specified powers are inadequate, wider powers are given. These are to take any action of any kind whatsoever, including undertaking operations for the sinking or destruction of the ship, or any part of it, and operations involving the taking over of control of the ship.[272] There is also a power to apply these provisions by Order in Council to ships on the high seas, although if they are not UK ships then directions may only be given to UK citizens or UK bodies corporate in order to prevent grave and imminent danger to UK waters.[273]

### 19.11.1B Temporary exclusion zones and powers to move ships

Under separate powers allowing for the suspension of the right of innocent (but not transit) passage in exceptional circumstances,[274] the Secretary of State may also make directions establishing temporary exclusion zones around ships, structures or other things which are wrecked, damaged or in distress. Such zones can only include UK waters or the UK pollution

---

[266] ss.137-141 Merchant Shipping Act 1995, as amended by the Merchant Shipping and Maritime Security Act 1997.

[267] Under s.137 Merchant Shipping Act 1995.

[268] On the UK pollution zone see 18.10.1 above.

[269] *Ibid* s.137(9), as amended by s.2(4)(a) Merchant Shipping and Maritime Security Act 1997 to give effect to recommendations following the *Braer* incident, where it was not clear that the mere loss of power would be an 'accident' under the previous definition.

[270] *Ibid* s.138A(1)(a), added by s.3 Merchant Shipping and Maritime Security Act 1997 and see the Merchant Shipping (Prevention of Pollution: Substances Other Than Oil) (Intervention) Order 1997 (SI 1997 No.1869).

[271] *Ibid* s.138A, added by s.3 Merchant Shipping and Maritime Security Act 1997.

[272] *Ibid* s.137(4) and (5).

[273] *Ibid* s.141 and the Merchant Shipping (Prevention of Pollution) (Intervention) (Foreign Ships) Order 1997 (SI 1997 No.2568).

[274] See Art.25(3) LOS Convention.

zone,[275] and may be identified where it appears that significant harm will or may occur as a direct or indirect result of the incident, and that significant harm, or its risk, would be prevented or reduced if access to such a zone were restricted. 'Significant harm' means significant pollution of the relevant waters or significant damage to persons or property. Zones must only be established if, and be as large as, necessary, and offences are provided for in relation to breaches of exclusion zones.[276] There are also powers to direct a ship to be moved to, or from, specific locations in UK territorial waters to prevent or reduce pollution, or the threat of pollution, in UK waters or the UK pollution zone.[277]

### 19.11.1C  *The right to recover in respect of unreasonable loss or damage*

The counterpart of the extensive powers of intervention given to the Secretary of State under the Merchant Shipping Act 1995[278] in respect of shipping accidents involving pollution is that these powers must not be used disproportionately or unreasonably. If this occurs a right to recover compensation is provided. This right is available where it is shown that the action taken was not reasonably necessary to prevent or reduce oil pollution or the risk of oil pollution,[279] or if the benefit it brought was likely to be disproportionately less than the expense incurred, or damage suffered, as a result of the action. If this is the case a person incurring expense or suffering damage as a result of taking the action will be entitled to recover compensation from the Secretary of State.[280] Similarly, compensation will also be payable in respect of expense and damages incurred as a result of compliance with a direction of the Secretary of State not to take some specified action.[281] In considering whether an action was not reasonably necessary or disproportionate, account must be taken of:

(a)  the extent and risk of oil pollution if the action had not been taken;
(b)  the likelihood of the action being effective; and
(c)  the extent of the damage caused by the action.[282]

Any action brought to recover compensation on this ground may be brought in the Admiralty jurisdiction of the High Court which is granted express jurisdiction to determine any claim of this kind.[283] Under administrative guidance, compensation may be payable to harbour

---

[275] On the 'pollution zone' see 18.10.1 above.

[276] ss.100A and 100B Merchant Shipping Act 1995, added by s.1 Merchant Shipping and Maritime Security Act 1997.

[277] *Ibid* s.100C, added by s.10 Merchant Shipping and Maritime Security Act 1997.

[278] That is, under s.137 Merchant Shipping Act 1995.

[279] 'Oil' includes other prescribed or hazardous substances; see *ibid* s.138A(2).

[280] *Ibid* s.138(1).

[281] *Ibid* s.138(3).

[282] *Ibid* s.138(2).

[283] *Ibid* s.138(4).

authorities, local authorities and private individuals for costs associated with the clean up of places used as havens for pollution casualties.[284]

### 19.11.1D  Offences and fines in relation to shipping casualties

Contravention of, or failure to comply with, any requirement of a direction given by the Secretary of State pursuant to his interventionary powers in respect of shipping casualties is an offence on the part of the person to whom the direction is given.[285] For this offence it is a defence to prove that all due diligence was used to ensure compliance with the direction, or that there was reasonable cause to believe that compliance with the direction would have involved a serious risk to human life.[286] Further offences, for which there are no comparable defences, are provided for in relation to the intentional obstruction of persons who are engaged in serving directions, acting in compliance with directions, or acting to sink, destroy or take over ships.[287] In relation to non-UK ships outside UK waters, only UK citizens or UK registered companies may be liable.[288] A person guilty of any of the above offences is liable on summary conviction to a fine not exceeding £50,000, or on conviction on indictment to a fine of an unspecified amount.[289]

The powers of the Secretary of State to give directions under the above provisions were first used in October 1978 when the *Christos Bitas*, a Greek registered tanker, ran aground off the Welsh coast. Because of the cost of repair, and for environmental reasons, the vessel was sunk some 300 miles off the cost of Ireland. In this situation the matter was dealt with by mutual agreement between the interested parties, though the Secretary of State indicated that he was intervening under the Act.[290]

The role of intervention powers was scrutinised in depth following the decision *not* to use them directly in relation to the grounding of the *Sea Empress*.[291] Following this, a series of improvements have been recommended in the 'Donaldson' Report and, largely, accepted by Government.[292] These relate to such things as appointing a specialist representative of the Secretary to State to take operational control of incidents, and extending the power of direction to riparian owners and owners of other facilities such as berths which might shelter stricken vessels to allow oil to be removed.

---

[284] Pollution Paper No.20, para.52.

[285] s.139(1) Merchant Shipping Act 1995.

[286] *Ibid* s.139(3).

[287] *Ibid* s.139(2).

[288] Art.4(2) SI 1997 No.2568.

[289] s.139(4) Merchant Shipping Act 1995.

[290] See Department of Trade, *Christos Bitas – the fight at sea against pollution* (1978).

[291] On the *Sea Empress* incident see also 9.19.3 above.

[292] See *Command and Control: Report of Lord Donaldson's Review of Salvage and Intervention and their Command and Control* (1999). For the interim Government response see www.shipping.detr.gov.uk/control/index.htm (1999).

Lord Donaldson's inquiry report also noted that a salvor could be placed in a double jeopardy position if given a direction by the Secretary of State which would result in some pollution in order to prevent greater environmental damage. That is, the salvor would be exposed to a charge of causing water pollution under the Water Resources Act 1991, while refusal to follow such a direction might result in prosecution under the Merchant Shipping Act 1995. The report therefore advocated amending the 1991 Act so that jettison and unavoidable pollution from, for example, pressing up tanks to increase buoyancy would not be an offence if undertaken with a view to avoiding greater pollution.[293] However, the report also hoped that prosecution policy would reflect the public interest in such cases, and it is difficult to conceive of a prosecution being brought, as the law now stands, where every effort was made to reduce aquatic pollution damage. The report also questioned whether it was in the public interest criminally to penalise accidental marine pollution, whether in the course of a salvage operation or otherwise. The fear expressed was that this would discourage a full and frank disclosure of events and thus hamper the efforts of the Marine Accident Investigation Branch, the body charged with preventing repetition of the same or similar accidents.[294] A similar approach is not taken with other water pollution incidents where regulatory learning is also needed after the event, and the proposal, put out to consultation by Government, is at odds with the approach taken elsewhere in water pollution law.[295]

### 19.11.2  Information and Co-operation Between States Following Incidents

Promoting co-operation between states in the event of a marine pollution incident is the subject of both regional and, latterly, global agreements. Largely, these measures will apply following accidental pollution incidents, though they are not restricted in this way. These measures are somewhat more specific, and therefore more valuable, than other duties in international law. Firstly, customary international law undoubtedly places a general obligation on states to warn other states of the potential affect of pollution.[296] Second, under the 1973/78 MARPOL Convention, ships involved in pollution incidents must make immediate reports which will, either via the receiving party or the IMO, be relayed to the flag state and any state which may be affected.[297] As can be seen, these legal provisions relate only to notification of an incident. Beyond this, pollution prevention measures may be necessary under the LOS Convention, which requires reporting of actual damage, or imminent danger of damage, to other states likely to be affected and to competent international organisations. Notably, this is not restricted to the aftermath of a shipping incident. The LOS

---

[293] *Ibid* para.6.15.

[294] *Ibid* paras.6.16-6.17.

[295] See generally Ch.9 above.

[296] See 18.5.1 above.

[297] Art.8 and Protocol 1 MARPOL. See further Reg.26 Annex 1, in force 4 April 1993, concerning shipboard oil pollution emergency plans.

Convention also requires co-operation between affected states in eliminating the effects of pollution and preventing or minimising the damage, for which states must jointly develop and promote contingency plans.[298]

### 19.11.2A The Bonn Agreement

At regional level, the first specific measures to promote co-operation following a marine pollution incident were taken under the 1969 Bonn Agreement for Co-operation in Dealing with Pollution of the North Sea by Oil.[299] This was later amended by a 1983 Agreement, entered into by the parties (the North Sea coastline states) and the European Economic Community, to extend the scope of the measures to cover other harmful substances ('the Bonn Agreement').[300] Under the Agreement, whenever a party becomes aware of a shipping casualty or the presence, or the prospective presence, of oil or other harmful substances polluting the sea, which presents a grave and imminent danger to the coast or related interests of one or more of the contracting parties, a duty arises to inform the state whose coastline is endangered. Ships and aircraft are 'requested' to notify their flag states of any such incident, and the flag state must then notify other parties. For the purpose of facilitating this exchange of information and avoiding duplication of efforts under the Agreement, the area of the Agreement (the North Sea and the English Channel) is divided into zones of responsibility for observation and assessment of pollution hazards.

In addition to the duty to report spills, contracting parties have agreed to exchange technical information and to provide assistance to each other in the event of a major incident. Unless the assisting state takes action on its own initiative, payment for measures taken to prevent or diminish pollution at the request of another party is chargeable to the requesting state. The Bonn Agreement is serviced by the OSPAR Commission[301] and has been relied upon on a small number of occasions.[302]

### 19.11.2B The International Convention on Oil Pollution Preparedness, Response and Co-operation

The provisions in the Bonn Agreement on notification and co-operation should be read alongside the 1990 International Convention on Oil Pollution Preparedness, Response and Co-operation ('the OPRC Convention')[303] which is of global application.[304] The OPRC Convention

---

[298] Arts.198 and 199 LOS Convention.

[299] Cmnd. 4403.

[300] Cm.4397 (1999), previously published as Cmnd. 9104, in force 1 September 1989.

[301] On the OSPAR Commission see 18.8.4 above.

[302] Bywater (1995) p.494.

[303] 30 ILM 733 (1991), in force 13 May 1995.

[304] As at 31 January 2000, the Convention had 52 contracting states, accounting for fractionally under 50% of world tonnage. Many, but not all, European states are parties.

takes a number of contrasting approaches to those in the Bonn Agreement. In particular, the OPRC Convention is not restricted in the waters it applies to, and therefore covers pollution incidents in any waters arising from ships, 'offshore units'[305] and from sea ports and oil handling facilities. In addition, the pollution threat required to trigger action is less than that under the Bonn Agreement. This is because it applies to any occurrence which results (or may result) in a discharge of oil and which poses (or may pose) a threat to the marine environment requiring emergency action or other immediate response. This is indicative of the precautionary approach taken by the Convention.[306] A further contrast is that ships' masters and others with relevant responsibilities have a mandatory duty to report any pollution incidents that are witnessed, although pilots of civil aircraft are, as with the Bonn Agreement, only requested to do so.

The OPRC Convention also contains provisions requiring parties to take minimum steps to prepare for, and respond to, incidents. These include a minimum level of pre-positioned oil spill combating equipment, commensurate with the risk involved, as well as training and institutional requirements. Whether the level of preparation is 'commensurate with the risk involved' will depend on the vulnerability of the area to oil pollution incidents, either because of the high density of traffic or because of particularly sensitive ecological conditions.[307] As its name suggests, the Convention only applies to pollution by oil, but a separate protocol extending the Convention to hazardous and noxious substances has been agreed.[308]

The OPRC Convention is given effect to in UK law by the Merchant Shipping (Oil Pollution Preparedness, Response and Co-operation Convention) Regulations 1998.[309] However, the 1998 Regulations must be read together with more general provisions in the Merchant Shipping Act 1995 which provide for the preparation and implementation by the Secretary of State of a National Contingency Plan dealing with responses to marine pollution. This Plan must be made with a view to preventing marine pollution, or its risk, or reducing or minimising its effects.[310]

The 1998 Regulations apply to certain larger harbours and oil handling facilities that exceed minimum size or annual turnover thresholds. However, the Secretary of State can notify any such establishment if there is a significant risk of discharge of over 10 tonnes of oil, or if it is in an area of environmental sensitivity or particular economic significance.[311]

---

[305] That is, any fixed or floating installation or structure engaged in oil exploration, exploitation or production, or loading of unloading of oil (art.2(4)).

[306] On precaution generally see 4.7.1 above.

[307] See Resolution 5, OPRC Conference 1990.

[308] See 19.11.2C below.

[309] SI 1998 No.1056, made under the Merchant Shipping (Oil Pollution Preparedness, Response and Co-operation) Order 1997 (SI 1997 No.2567).

[310] s.293(2)(za) Merchant Shipping Act 1995, added by para.17 Sch.6 Merchant Shipping and Maritime Security Act 1997.

[311] Reg.3 Merchant Shipping (Oil Pollution Preparedness, Response and Co-operation Convention) Regulations 1998 (SI 1998 No.1056).

This would allow smaller harbours to be brought within the Regulations where, for example, relatively small discharges of oil could damage the local tourist industry or an important ecological area.

The Regulations require all relevant existing harbours, oil handling facilities and offshore installations to prepare oil pollution emergency plans by 15 August 1999, taking into account any guidance issued by the Maritime and Coastguard Agency (MCA). New facilities and so on coming into being after 15 August 1998 must submit plans at least two months before opening or commencing operations. Plans must be reviewed at least every 5 years, or within 3 months of any major change likely to affect the plan. There is a power for the MCA to amend plans by direction if they are considered inadequate or incompatible with the National Contingency Plan for the time being in force. For offshore installations and pipelines the powers of the MCA are exercised by the Secretary of State for Trade and Industry.[312]

The provisions relating to oil pollution emergency plans do not extend to the reporting duties of ships' masters etc. when a pollution incident arises from their ship or installation. This is covered separately, although these provisions only apply to oil tankers of 150GT and above and to any other ship of 400GT and above.[313] General provisions relating to the reporting by ships' masters of marine pollution incidents involving their vessels (i.e. incidents which may include substances other than oil) are provided for elsewhere.[314]

The obligation under the OPRC Convention to report oil pollution incidents is given effect to by requiring masters of UK ships to report such incidents without delay either to Her Majesty's Coastguard or, if the ship is outside UK controlled waters,[315] to the nearest coastal state. Operators of offshore installations, harbour authorities and oil handling facilities must report any such incidents to the Coastguard.[316] The Regulations are backed by criminal penalties for failing to submit or re-submit plans, for not maintaining plans or for not implementing plans correctly. There is a defence of showing reasonable cause, otherwise the penalty, on summary conviction, is a fine not exceeding the statutory maximum, presently £5000, or on conviction on indictment, a fine.[317]

---

[312] *Ibid* Reg.4.

[313] Reg.33 Merchant Shipping (Prevention of Oil Pollution) Regulations 1996 (SI 1996 No.2154).

[314] Regs 9-11 Merchant Shipping (Reporting Requirements for Ships Carrying Dangerous or Polluting Goods) Regulations 1995 (SI 1995 No.2498). See 19.7.2 above.

[315] On the meaning of 'UK controlled waters' see the Merchant Shipping (Prevention of Pollution) (Limits) Regulations 1996 (SI 1999 No.2128), discussed at 18.10.1 above.

[316] Regs.5 and 6 Merchant Shipping (Oil Pollution Preparedness, Response and Co-operation Convention) Regulations 1998.

[317] *Ibid* Reg.7.

### 19.11.2C  The HNS Protocol

At a meeting in March 2000, the IMO adopted the Protocol on Preparedness, Response and Co-operation to Pollution Incidents by Hazardous and Noxious Substances 2000 (the 'HNS Protocol') which in material respects follows the OPRC Convention but, as its name suggests, applies its principles to hazardous and noxious substances. These substances have the same meaning as in the 1996 International Convention on Liability and Compensation for Damage in Connection with the Carriage of Hazardous and Noxious Substances by Sea (the 'HNS Convention').[318] The Protocol will enter into force twelve months after ratification by not less than fifteen states which are party to the OPRC Convention.

### 19.11.3  The International Convention on Salvage

Justifiable criticisms have in the past been made about some of the negative impacts of the international rules on salvage for the marine environment. In respect of the *Amoco Cadiz*, for example, delays caused through an inability to agree the terms of salvage may have exacerbated the resulting environmental damage. This was because of the former rule that salvors would only be paid where the ship was completely saved. As has been noted, a salvor who prevented a major pollution incident by towing a damaged tanker away from an environmentally sensitive site but who was unable to save the ship would not be paid despite the environmental value of the action.[319]

The 1989 International Convention on Salvage[320] addressed this situation by allowing salvors to be paid if they act to prevent or minimise damage to the environment, even if the ship is not saved. Salvors are also paid a discretionary 'bonus' of up to 100 per cent of expenses incurred if environmental damage is in fact prevented or reduced. However, there are problems with this provision in that it extends only to inland and coastal waters, and the scope of the provision is often uncertain, leading to high costs in settling claims. Also, acts of salvage do not generally have as their primary purpose preventing environmental damage, and the costs involved will not generally be recoverable under the international provisions relating to compensation following spills of oil and other substances.[321] For this reason it has been suggested that 'the environment does not feature in salvage law in its own right but only features tangentially as part of the potential liability of the ship-owner'.[322] The 1989 Convention is implemented in UK law by the Merchant Shipping Act 1995 and given practical effect through incorporation in the widely used 'Lloyd's Open

---

[318] See 19.10.2 above on the HNS Convention.
[319] Churchill and Lowe (1999) p.356.
[320] Cm.3458 (1996), 1996 UKTS 93, in force 14 July 1996. See Redgwell (1990).
[321] See 19.12–19.16 below and Bates and Benson (1993, updated), para. 4.15.
[322] Gauci (1999) p.34.

Form'.[323] The effectiveness of the relevant provisions relating to salvage has been much scrutinised following the *Sea Empress* incident.[324] It remains to be seen whether a private prosecution against the Secretary of State will be pursued.[325]

## 19.12 Compensation for Damage by Oil and Other Substances

Within the internal waters of England and Wales, liability for pollution by oil and other substances is based upon the common law principles governing general civil liability for water pollution.[326] In all likelihood the greater bulk of oil that enters coastal waters,[327] and probably also other substances, falls into this legal category. In respect of spills into marine waters, however, the civil law appears to be of relatively limited application. Unless negligence could be shown, it is not clear that other civil law claims such as under trespass or nuisance would provide adequate compensation, not least because of the extent to which interests not associated with land might be affected.[328] Nor is the civil law as it stands likely to be of any significant impact in deterring marine pollution, improving operational standards in shipping or raising environmental consciousness in the shipping industry.

In relation to some categories of oil spills from tankers into navigable waters, however, civil liability for oil pollution has been the subject of special legislative attention as a response to a series of dramatic incidents involving shipping casualties and the international agreements that have ensued from them. As with intervention response measures following such incidents,[329] the impetus for international agreement with regard to liability was the *Torrey Canyon* disaster, where the environmental hazard constituted by supertankers, and the inadequacy of national laws to guarantee compensation for states suffering coastal pollution from oil spills, first came to be generally appreciated. In particular, problems arose in relation to the appropriate jurisdiction for the settling of disputes, and because many shipowners would be unable to pay the amounts of compensation which might arise. The lessons learnt from the *Torrey Canyon* incident prompted a new international regime governing civil liability and compensation for oil pollution.[330]

---

[323] s.224 Merchant Shipping Act 1995 and see, most recently, Lloyd's Open Form 95 (1995), reproduced in *Command and Control: Report of Lord Donaldson's Review of Salvage and Intervention and their Command and Control* (Cm.4193, 1999), Appendix 5.

[324] See Marine Accident Investigation Branch (1997) and *Command and Control: Report of Lord Donaldson's Review of Salvage and Intervention and their Command and Control* (Cm 4193, 1999). See also 19.11.1 above.

[325] *ENDS Report* 288 (1999) p.51.

[326] See Ch.3 above.

[327] See 19.2.1 above.

[328] See generally Ch.3 above.

[329] See 19.11 above.

[330] General reading on liability for marine pollution includes Bates and Benson (1993, updated) Ch.4; de la Rue (1993) and Gauci (1997).

The initial response of tanker owners to the *Torrey Canyon* disaster came in the form of voluntary schemes to overcome the deficiencies of national legislation on oil pollution. The first voluntary scheme was the Tanker Owner's Voluntary Agreement concerning Liability for Oil Pollution ('TOVALOP'), which came into force in 1969. Under the scheme, tanker owners and charterers accepted strict liability to reimburse national governments for expenses reasonably incurred in preventing or cleaning up coastal oil pollution caused by discharges of persistent oil from tankers. Liability was related to the size of the vessel, subject to an upper limit, and being underwritten by insurance cover. Despite the voluntary nature of the scheme, the number of seagoing oil tankers covered by TOVALOP was very high, at around 98 per cent.

The provision of compensation for oil pollution under TOVALOP was supplemented in 1971 by a second voluntary scheme, the Contract Regarding an Interim Supplement to Tanker Liability for Oil Pollution ('CRISTAL'). CRISTAL was an agreement between oil tanker and cargo owners, that is, oil companies, which augmented TOVALOP to provide compensation in the limited circumstances where the earlier agreement was inapplicable, to increase the maximum sum payable by way of compensation. CRISTAL also provided for a degree of indemnification of tanker owners in respect of clean up costs in order to allow an equitable distribution of the cost of spillage incidents between tanker owners and cargo owners.[331]

At the outset such schemes were regarded as interim measures pending the entry into force of international conventions governing this area, or applicable to states not party to these future conventions. Both schemes ceased with effect from February 1997. This was because there had been an increasing number of states (and more importantly, an even greater proportion of the world fleet by tonnage) becoming parties to the two leading conventions in this area and because the existence of the voluntary schemes were thought to be a possible obstacle to further ratifications. The leading conventions are:

(a) the 1969 International Convention on Civil Liability for Oil Pollution Damage ('the Civil Liability Convention');[332] and
(b) the 1971 International Convention on the Establishment of an International Fund for Compensation for Oil Pollution Damage (the 'Fund Convention').[333]

Both Conventions have, to some extent, been replaced by Protocols of 1992.[334]

---

[331] For discussion of the features of TOVALOP and CRISTAL as amended see Bates and Benson (1993, updated), paras 4.90-4.111.

[332] Cmnd. 4403, in force 19 June 1975, as amended by Protocols of 1976 (Cmnd.8238), in force 8 April 1981, and of 1992 (Cm.2647), in force 30 May 1996.

[333] Cmnd. 5061, in force 16 October 1978, as amended by 1976 Protocol (Cmnd.7029), in force 22 November 1994, and 1992 Protocol (Cm.2658), in force 30 May 1996.

[334] See above. On the Protocols generally see Wilkinson (1993c).

In general terms, parties to these liability Conventions will be in compliance with their obligations under the LOS Convention of ensuring that their citizens have recourse to compensation or other remedies following marine pollution, and their obligations to co-operate in implementing existing international law, although only in relation to pollution by oil.[335] It is clear that, as in other respects, the LOS Convention defers to more specialist legal regimes in relation to compensation.[336] It might also be noted here that the most recent draft articles on state responsibility of the International Law Commission provide that marine pollution, to the extent that it affected another state, would be an international delict justifying restoration and compensation measures. Also, 'massive pollution . . . of the seas' might be an 'international crime', for which environmental restoration could be required even if the costs would be disproportionate to the damage caused.[337]

The following sections discuss the relevant international Conventions and their implementation in UK legislation under the Merchant Shipping Act 1995. Since, in many respects, the Conventions are literally transposed into national legislation, it can be assumed that discussion of the Conventions represents the position under national law which, to avoid lengthy overlap, is not covered in depth. The sections conclude with discussion of international measures (and their implementation) providing liability following spills of hazardous and noxious substances other than oil.

### 19.13 The Civil Liability Convention

The 1969 International Convention on Civil Liability for Oil Pollution Damage ('the Civil Liability Convention') imposes on shipowners a general regime of strict liability for pollution damage caused by oil tankers. Subject to certain narrowly defined exceptions, shipowners become liable for losses incurred through oil pollution damage, and for reasonable measures taken to prevent and minimise such damage, resulting from the bulk carriage of persistent oil[338] by tankers, without the need for negligence to be shown. Alongside the tightening of legal liability under the Convention, however, the owner can limit the amount of liability which may arise as a result of an oil spill by reference to the size of the vessel concerned. Also, generally no additional claims (e.g. a claim under national civil law) may be made against ship owners. The counterpart of this 'strict but limited' approach is that vessels carrying more than a specified quantity of oil as a bulk cargo must be compulsorily insured to the extent of their maximum liability under the Convention. The process of claiming compensation under the Convention is streamlined in that the

---

[335] Art.235 LOS Convention.

[336] The LOS Convention also calls for uniformity of practice in relation to liability. The significantly different approach taken by the United States under the Oil Pollution Act 1990 frustrates this, but is largely immaterial to the following discussion.

[337] See especially draft Articles 19, 42-5 and 51-3. See further 19.13.1 below.

[338] See IOPC Fund, *Non-Technical Guide to the Nature and Definition of Persistent Oil*. The 1992 Protocol is limited to certain persistent hydrocarbon mineral oils.

claimant is permitted to sue the insurer directly without the need to bring an action against the owner of the vessel concerned.[339]

Claims may only be brought in the courts of the contracting state in whose territory the damage occurred. This is intended to avoid 'forum-shopping', the desirability of which should in any case be reduced by the agreement of common rules between the parties. Nevertheless, it seems inevitable that the courts in different countries will take different approaches to the interpretation of some of the terms of the Convention. Claims must be brought within three years of the damage occurring, but no later than six years after the date of the incident.[340] This may disadvantage some claimants where oil subsequently leaks from a sunken vessel.

In 1984 a second Protocol to the Civil Liability Convention was agreed in response to the incident involving the grounding of the *Amoco Cadiz* in 1978 on the coast of Brittany. However, because the Protocol was not acceptable to the United States, which prefers unlimited liability measures, it received few ratifications and never entered into force. Instead, a revised Protocol was adopted in 1992. Substantively, however, its provisions are similar to the 1984 Protocol. For example, the upward shift in compensation limits are as agreed in 1984, and liability cannot be limited where the pollution is the result of the shipowner's or pilot's etc personal act or omission, and where this was committed with intent to cause such damage, or recklessly and with knowledge that such damage would probably result.[341] This must be read alongside the only other exceptions to the principle that liability should be limited and 'channelled' to the ship owner and his insurers. These are where the pollution is the result of an Act of God or of war; is wholly caused by an act or omission by a third party with intent to cause damage; or is caused by the negligence of any authority responsibility for navigational aids.[342] 'Navigational aids' would include lighthouses, but has been held not to include pilots,[343] an important issue in relation to claims following the *Sea Empress* disaster.[344]

The rules on ratification were altered so that the participation of the US was not necessary for the 1992 Protocol to come into force. From 16 May 1998, parties to the 1992 Protocol (such as the UK) ceased to be parties to the original Civil Liability Convention, which such parties were required to denounce, and became parties to the 1992 International Convention on Civil Liability for Oil Pollution Damage. Although this is now the principal international provision for the UK as regards liability, the provisions of the 1969 Civil Liability Convention may still be relevant if

---

[339] Art.7(8) Civil Liability Convention.

[340] Art.8 Civil Liability Convention and see 19.14.3 below.

[341] *Ibid* Art.5(2) as amended. This adds to the existing exceptions to limited liability where pollution is the result of an Act of God or of war; is wholly caused by an act or omission by a third party with intent to cause damage; or is caused by the negligence of any authority responsibility for navigational aids (this would include lighthouses, but has been held not to include pilots) (Art.3). On 'Act of God' as a defence to proceedings see also 9.6.3 above.

[342] *Ibid* Art.3.

[343] *The Jose Marti*, Sweden, 7 January 1981; see Bates and Benson (1993, updated), para. 4.24.

[344] See 19.15.2 below.

environmental damage is caused by a vessel of a party which has yet to ratify the new regime.[345] The texts are distinguished in the following discussion to make the recent changes clear.

While the Civil Liability Convention is limited to ships carrying oil in bulk as cargo, the Protocol introduces a presumption that any seagoing vessel constructed or adapted to carry oil is in fact carrying oil unless the contrary is proved.[346] This allows for compensation to be paid following an incident involving an unladen tanker, and in relation to spills of bunker oil from such ships, an important extension given that many super-tankers now carry as much fuel oil as older vessels carried oil as cargo.[347] The only exclusions for ships carrying oil apply to warships or any ship being used by the state for non-commercial purposes. Ships owned by a state and used for commercial purposes must comply with the general requirement of insurance cover.[348]

The Protocol also extends the geographical scope of the Civil Liability Convention, allowing claims to be made in relation to environmental damage and preventative measures within the exclusive economic zone[349] of a contracting party and enabling preventative measures to be taken anywhere to avoid such damage.[350] Expenses incurred in taking such preventive measures may be recoverable even where no oil spill occurs, provided there was the grave and imminent threat of pollution damage. This goes some way to addressing the significant difficulty under the original Convention that preventive measures could only be compensated for after a spill had actually occurred.

### 19.13.1 Environmental Damage

Of particular significance is the restriction that the Protocol imposes with respect to environmental damage. The Protocol makes no change to the general definition of 'pollution damage' under the Civil Liability Convention as meaning any 'loss or damage'. This is wide enough to include economic loss, and the breadth of allowable claims is illustrated in claims following the *Braer* and *Sea Empress* incidents.[351] Moreover, it is specifically provided that owners can recover for 'expenses reasonably incurred or sacrifices reasonable made', and owners have recovered the

---

[345] If anything, figures on ratifications and tonnage covered by both regimes indicate that the 1992 Protocol is significantly the more popular measure.

[346] Art.1(1) Civil Liability Convention as amended.

[347] On bunker oil spills from vessels *other* than tankers, see now the 2001 International Convention on Civil Liability for Bunker Oil Pollution Damage.

[348] *Ibid* Art.11.

[349] On the exclusive economic zone see 18.7.1 and 18.10.1 above.

[350] Art. 2 Civil Liability Convention, as amended.

[351] See 19.15.2 below.

costs of removing oil from ships, clean-up operations and towing tankers to places of safety.[352]

However, the Protocol specifically limits compensation for 'impairment of the environment other than loss of profit from such impairment . . . to costs of reasonable measures incurred of reinstatement actually undertaken or to be undertaken'.[353] This wording seems designed to clarify some of the previous ambiguities, to prevent compensation payments being awarded as an expression of the 'fault' of the polluter, or as a deterrent and to reflect the attitude of the Fund in cases involving claims for environmental damage. It would also seem to rule out losses of environmental amenity value, such as might be experienced by bird watchers if large numbers of birds are oiled and killed, where valuation is a particularly thorny issue, or for damage to the environment *per se*.[354]

There are, however, three central difficulties with this formulation. The first is that it does not make clear who may claim for such damage. In the absence of elaboration, the matter will be left to national courts, which may have different rules on the right to bring claims. In the UK, for example, it may be an obstacle that the waters and wildlife are neither owned privately nor are they the property of the state, and where there is neither any developed public trust nor *parens patriae* doctrine.[355] In so far as an oil spill heading away from the shore damages wildlife at sea, there appears to be no recognised claimant.

Second, the biodegradable nature of oil means that the 'reinstatement' of most marine waters will be achieved over time through natural processes. Moreover, before the quality of the water improves, measures to restock or reintroduce species will probably be futile, and unlikely to be judged 'reasonable'.[356] Thus, costs of reinstating either the water or its living organisms might not be 'reasonable' and, insofar as 'pure' environmental damage is concerned, the 'polluter' avoids paying.[357] This consequence might be thought to render the provisions of the LOS Convention concerning the preservation of 'fragile ecosystems and habitats of depleted, threatened or endangered species and other forms of marine life'[358] somewhat problematic. It remains to be seen how the current formulation will be applied in practice. It must be assumed, though, that

---

[352] Art.5(8) Civil Liability Convention. See, for example, partially successful claims made by the fire brigade following the *Sea Empress* incident, noted at 19.15.2 below.

[353] *Ibid* Art.1(6) as amended.

[354] On environmental valuation see also 6.14 above.

[355] See generally Gauci (1997) pp.253-260. Literally, 'parent of the nation'. In some jurisdictions, the state may seek an injunction (and possibly also damages) to protect the unowned environment, see, in the US, Halter and Thomas (1982) and s.1006 Oil Pollution Act 1990 (US) and see also *The Patmos*, discussed below, where the Italian State was awarded damages for harm to the territorial sea.

[356] This issue would also arise under the International Law Commission's draft articles on state responsibility, which refer to the 'proportionality' of the response of the injured state; see 19.12 above

[357] On the polluter pays principle generally see 4.7.3 above.

[358] Art.194(5) LOS Convention. See also Anderson (1995) p.320.

the courts are unlikely to follow previous practice in other jurisdictions, where the definition of 'related interests' given in the 1969 Intervention Convention as including 'conservation of living marine resources and of wildlife' has justifying a departure from focusing on reinstatement to considering environmental damage more broadly.[359] Third, if the environment is irretrievably damaged, then reinstatement will not be possible and no compensation will be payable. The use of 'reinstatement' would seem intended to rule out compensation being payable for measures take at an equivalent site, or the acquisition of an equivalent site.[360]

### 19.14 Implementation of the Civil Liability Convention

For the most part the terms of the Civil Liability Convention[361] are given effect within UK law by Chapter III of Part VI of the Merchant Shipping Act 1995 which provides for compensation for oil pollution damage in civil proceedings. It is notable that the Act provides for a transitional regime to apply before 30 May 1996, when the 1992 Protocol came into force, and that these provisions were applicable to the *Sea Empress* incident of 15 February 1996.[362] For the most part, the Convention, as replaced by the Protocol, is faithfully transposed, and so the following discussion merely outlines the main features of the Act which apply to incidents after 30 May 1996 and key issues of national interpretation.

The basic principle regarding civil liability for accidental or intentional oil spillages from ships is that where, as a result of any occurrence, any oil is discharged or escapes from a ship carrying (or presumed to carry) oil, the registered owner[363] will be liable for:

(a) 'any damage caused outside the ship . . . by *contamination* resulting from the discharge or escape';

(b) the cost of any reasonable pollution prevention or reduction measures taken; and

(c) for any damage caused by any such measures taken.[364]

The damage must occur in the 'territory' of the UK, which includes the UK pollution zone.[365] Similar provisions apply to oil damage from any

[359] See *The Patmos*, Messina Court of Appeal, 24 December 1993, discussed in Merialdi (1994) and *The Haven*, Court of First Instance, Genoa, 5 April 1996 discussed in Brans (1996). On the general issue of valuation of and liability for environmental damage in this context see Wilkinson (1993); Wetterstein (1994) and discussion at 19.15.2 below. In this context, comparison with the US Oil Pollution Act 1990, which allows claims for damage to the environment *per se*, is instructive. See generally Little and Hamilton (1997) and Gauci (1997) pp.139-140.

[360] Gauci (1997) p.133; contrast Brans (1996).

[361] Reference below is to the Civil Liability Convention as amended by the 1992 Protocol.

[362] s.171 and Sch.4 Merchant Shipping Act 1995 and the Merchant Shipping (Liability for Compensation for Oil Pollution Damage) (Transitional Provisions) Order 1996 (SI 1996 No.1143) and Hamilton and Little (1996).

[363] *Ibid* s.170(1).

[364] *Ibid* s.153(1), emphasis added. A relatively rare instance where the language of contamination rather than pollution is used, though damage is still required.

[365] *Ibid* s.170(4) as amended.

ship, not just tankers, extending the national law beyond the terms of the Civil Liability Convention.[366] Claims for preventing marine contamination may also be made,[367] and the Act directly transposes the new provisions of the Convention relating to the limitation on claims for environmental impairment to reasonable reinstatement costs.[368] In the event of a person incurring a liability for any of these losses that person will also be liable for any damage or cost similarly caused in the area of any other Civil Liability Convention country.[369] 'Oil' is defined as 'persistent hydrocarbon mineral oil'.[370]

As can be seen, it is necessary to show 'damage caused . . . by contamination resulting from the discharge or escape' in order to establish liability for each of these losses. Since it is unnecessary to prove fault, liability is strict. Moreover, 'damage' includes loss,[371] opening up the possibility of claims for pure economic loss without damage to property. The only restriction on claims will therefore be the remoteness of the damage caused.[372]

Where damage arises from an incident involving two or more ships, and each owner incurs liability, there will be joint liability for the whole of the damage to the extent that the responsibility of each owner cannot be reasonably separated.[373] Similarly the scope of the liability extends to cover consecutive incidents. Hence where more than one discharge or escape results from the same occurrence, or from a series of occurrences having the same origin, they are to be treated as one. Despite this, any measures taken after the first occurrence is deemed to have been taken after the discharge or escape.[374] A minor inroad into the regime of strict liability is the possibility of principles applicable to contributory negligence being taken into account where an owner is not himself at fault. Where damage arises which is not due to the fault of an owner the Law Reform Contributory Negligence Act 1945 is to apply as if the damage or cost were due to his fault. The effect of this is that damages can be reduced on account of contributory negligence where liability would otherwise be imposed without fault on the part of the defendant.[375]

---

[366] *Ibid* s.154, but see also s.184, which limits liability here by reference to the 1976 Convention on Limitation of Liability for Maritime Claims.
[367] *Ibid* s.153(2).
[368] *Ibid* s.156(3).
[369] *Ibid* s.153(5).
[370] *Ibid* s.170(1). In this respect, therefore, the definition of 'oil' in the 1995 Act for the purposes of liability is narrower than that generally used, on which see 19.5 above.
[371] *Ibid* s.170(1).
[372] Discussed further at 19.15.2 below.
[373] s.153(6) Merchant Shipping Act 1995.
[374] *Ibid* s.153(7).
[375] *Ibid* s.153(8).

## 19.14.1 Limitation of Liability

Where the owner of a ship incurs a liability under the Merchant Shipping Act 1995 by reason of a discharge or escape which occurred without his actual fault then he may limit liability in accordance with the provisions of the Act. If this is done, the aggregate liability is specified not to exceed an amount related to the ship's tonnage subject to a maximum amount. Currently this is 3 million special drawing rights for ships not exceeding 5,000 tons, and for ships above this size an additional 420 special drawing rights for each additional ton up to a maximum of 59.7 special drawing rights.[376]

Where liability has been, or is alleged to have been, incurred, the owner of a ship may apply to the court for the limitation of that liability to an amount determined in accordance with the above limits. If the court finds that liability has been incurred but may be limited, then it must determine the limit of the liability and direct payment of this sum into court. Thereafter, it must:

(a) determine the amounts that would apart from the limit, be due in respect of the liability to the several persons making claims in the proceedings; and

(b) direct the distribution of the amount paid into court (or, as the case may be, so much of it as does not exceed the liability) among those persons in proportion to their claims.

The distribution of the amount paid into court is subject to other provisions which require, amongst other things, that no claim is to be admitted unless it is made within such time as the court may direct, or such further time as the court may allow. A court may postpone the distribution of such a part of the amount to be distributed as it deems appropriate having regard to any claims that may later be established before a court of any country outside the UK. If a person who has incurred liability has voluntarily made any reasonable sacrifice or taken any other reasonable measures to prevent or reduce damage to which the liability extends or might have extended then account is to be taken of such measures in quantifying liability. This is done by placing the person making the sacrifice in the same position with respect to any distribution made in liability proceedings as if he had a claim in respect of the liability equal to the cost of the sacrifice or other measures.[377]

---

[376] *Ibid* s.157(1) and (2). The daily conversion rate for 'special drawing rights' is at www.imf.org. For example, the limit of liability in the *Sea Empress* incident was around £8 million. On the raising of these limits see IMO Legal Committee, 82nd session, 16–20 October 2000, at www.imo.org

[377] *Ibid* ss.158(1), (2), (4), (6) and (7).

### 19.14.2 Compulsory Insurance against Liability

Any ship carrying a bulk cargo of more than 2,000 tons of oil[378] must have insurance liability for pollution. To this effect no ship is to enter or leave any port in the UK or arrive at or leave a terminal in the territorial sea of the United Kingdom, nor may a UK ship enter or leave another such port or terminal, unless a certificate of insurance cover or other security for liability for pollution is in force.[379]

The certificate of insurance must be:

(a) if the ship is registered in the UK, a certificate issued by the Secretary of State;
(b) if the ship is registered in another Convention country, a certificate issued by or under the authority of the government of that other country; or
(c) if the ship is registered in a country which is not a Convention country, a certificate issued by the Secretary of State or by or under the authority of the government of that other state.[380]

Certificates of insurance must be carried in the ship and must, on demand, be produced by the master to any customs officer or inspector of the Department of the Environment, Transport and the Regions and, if the ship is a UK ship, to any 'proper officer'.[381] If a ship attempts to leave a port in the UK in contravention of these provisions it may be detained.[382] The Secretary of State is to issue a certificate to the owner of a ship only where he is satisfied that the necessary contract of insurance or other satisfactory security will be in force during the period of the certificate. He may refuse to do so if there is any doubt about whether the person providing the insurance or other security will be able to meet his obligations, or whether the insurance or other security will cover the owner's liability.[383]

### 19.14.3 Jurisdiction of UK Courts

Admiralty jurisdiction in claims for damage done by ships,[384] is to be construed as extending to any claim in respect of a liability incurred under the Merchant Shipping Act 1995.[385]

The Act also provides for the exclusion of claims in the UK courts against ship owners or persons incurring personal responsibility where oil is discharged or escapes from a ship but does not result in any damage caused by contamination in UK territory, and no measures are reasonably

---

[378] 'Oil' here as specified in Regulations; see Reg.3 Oil Pollution (Compulsory Insurance) Regulations 1997 (SI 1997 No.1820).
[379] s.163(2) Merchant Shipping Act 1995.
[380] *Ibid* s.163(3).
[381] *Ibid* s.164(4). 'Proper officer' means a consular officer in a foreign port.
[382] *Ibid* s.164(7).
[383] *Ibid* s.164(1) and (2).
[384] Under para.1(1)(d) Sch.1 Administration of Justice Act 1956.
[385] s.166(1) Merchant Shipping Act 1995.

taken to prevent or reduce such damage in that area. Thus, no claims may be brought where the only resulting damage caused is to the territory of another Convention country, or relates to costs incurred to prevent or reduce such damage or the threat of such damage, or is damage caused by any such measures taken.[386]

It has been held that the prescription periods[387] must be construed as placing a limit on all claims of three years from the date of the incident, but that no claims can be lodged after six years. Thus, if the pollution becomes apparent after three years, for example if oil escapes from a vessel some time after its sinking, owners are protected from any claims being made after six years. The relevant provisions of the Act contain no discretion to extend these periods.[388]

## 19.15 The Fund Convention

Whereas the Civil Liability Convention is concerned with the bases of liability for oil pollution incidents, financial provision to ensure the payment of compensation where liability is established is separately dealt with under the 1971 International Convention on the Establishment of an International Fund for Compensation for Oil Pollution Damage ('the Fund Convention').[389] As with the Civil Liability Convention, the Fund Convention regime was altered by a Protocol of 1992, broadening its scope, raising compensation levels and, for parties to the 1971 Convention, replacing that Convention in its entirety with the 1992 Fund Convention.

The Fund Convention regime recognises that victims of oil pollution should be adequately compensated for their loss, and the burden of meeting the cost of oil pollution damage should be shared between ship and cargo owners. Accordingly, the Fund Convention establishes the International Oil Pollution Compensation Fund which is financed by levies on major importers of oil in contracting states for the purpose of providing compensation for pollution damage. There are, in fact, two funds, one under the 1971 Convention and another under the 1992 Protocol. The latter is fast becoming the principal fund, and references below are to the '1992 Fund', to which the UK now contributes, unless otherwise stated. Those liable to contribute to the Fund are persons who import or receive oil in excess of 150,000 tonnes per year although, to put a cap on Japanese contributions, no state is required to contribute more than 27.5 per cent of total contributions.

In most circumstances the Fund Convention takes up the duty to provide compensation for oil pollution liability at the point where the Civil Liability Convention leaves off, and thereby raises the total amount

---

[386] *Ibid* s.166(2) and (3).

[387] See 19.13 above.

[388] s.162 Merchant Shipping Act 1995, and see *Gray and Gray* v *The Braer Corporation* 1999 SLT 1411.

[389] On background issues see 19.12 above.

payable in respect of any incident above that payable under the Civil Liability Convention. Thus, the Fund may be claimed against where the owner is financially incapable of meeting their obligations and any required financial security is inadequate, or where the damage exceeds the limits of the owner's strict liability under the Civil Liability Convention.[390] In exceptional circumstances, liability may arise under the Fund Convention in circumstances where the Civil Liability Convention does not apply as, for example, where pollution damage results from natural phenomena of an exceptional kind.

The extended compensation provisions under the Fund Convention go some way towards meeting concerns about the relatively low limits placed on insurers' liability under the Civil Liability Convention. However, there is still a limit on the amount that may be paid out from the 1992 Fund for any one incident, currently 135 million special drawing rights.[391] However, the Convention seeks to strike a balance between these concerns and objections by some states to the strictness of the liability provisions under the Civil Liability Convention. Accordingly, the Fund Convention indemnifies shipowners for a part of the costs of cleaning up oil spills incurred under the Civil Liability Convention. Indemnification may be denied, however, if it can be shown that the vessel causing the pollution has not complied with certain international conventions governing safety and oil pollution.

### 19.15.1 Implementation of the Fund Convention

The 1992 Fund Convention is given effect in the UK under the Merchant Shipping Act 1995.[392] As with the Civil Liability Convention, there were transitional provisions,[393] and the key measures are generally literally transposed into the Act and not therefore reconsidered in detail here.

A person suffering oil pollution damage is entitled to compensation from the Fund where:

(a) any of the exceptions to liability on the part of the shipowner provided for under the Civil Liability Convention apply;[394]
(b) the owner or guarantor liable for the damage cannot meet his obligations in full; or
(c) where the damage exceeds the financial limits set.[395]

---

[390] Art.4(1) Fund Convention.

[391] The figure is raised to 200 million SDRs if three states contributing to the Fund receive more than 600 million tonnes of oil per year. On the raising of these limits see IMO Legal Committee, 82nd session, 16–20 October 2000, at www.imo.org. On 'special drawing rights' see 19.14.1. On the general issue of limitation of liability see Gauci (1997) Ch.5.

[392] ss.172-181 Merchant Shipping Act 1995.

[393] *Ibid* s.182 and see 19.14 above.

[394] Irresistible natural phenomena, wilful third party damage and so on; see 19.13 above.

[395] s.175(1) Merchant Shipping Act 1995.

Contributions to the Fund are payable in respect of oil carried by sea to ports or terminal installations in the UK. These contributions are payable whether or not the oil is being imported, even if contributions are payable in respect of carriage of the same oil on a previous voyage. Contributions are also payable to the Fund in respect of oil which is first received in any installation in the UK after having been carried by sea and discharged in a port or terminal installation in a country in which the Fund Convention is not in force.[396]

Liability to pay contributions falls upon the importer in the case of oil imported into the UK, and otherwise upon the person by whom the oil is received. Groups of persons or companies cannot evade their obligation to contribute to the Fund by not aggregating their annual tonnage, but the Convention leaves the question of how to deal with this issue to the national law of the parties. Under the 1995 Act, all the members of a group of companies are to be treated as a single legal person, and any two or more companies which have been amalgamated into a single company are to be treated as the same person as that single company.[397]

### 19.15.2 Practical Application of the Fund

Application of the Fund Convention sheds light on the extent to which compensation is payable, firstly under the Civil Liability Convention and then, in respect of any claims not satisfied by ship owners or their insurers, by the Fund Convention. This involves considering the way in which claims for compensation are handled under both Conventions, and in particular how the extent of liability for 'damage' is determined. The definition of 'damage' under both Conventions is identical, and the compensation system can be illustrated by looking at the claims made following the *Braer* and *Sea Empress* incidents.[398] It should be noted that claimants, ship-owners, their insurers or the IOPC Fund settle most claims out of court.

In relation to both the *Braer* and the *Sea Empress*, the 1971 Fund was claimed against, under which the maximum limit was 60 special drawing rights.[399] While this appears capable of providing compensation following the *Sea Empress* incident, the level of possible claims against the Fund following the *Braer*, where there was much greater economic impact, was such that payments were suspended in October 1995.[400] The principal

---

[396] *Ibid* s.173(1)-(3).

[397] *Ibid* s.173(5)-(6).

[398] On the *Braer* incident see 19.2.1 above. On the *Sea Empress* see 9.19.3 and 19.15.2, Sea Empress Environmental Evaluation Committee (1998). For prior cases involving liability in a UK context see Wall (1993) p.476. See also general private law case-law in the wake of compensation fund claims, such as *Esso Petroleum Co Ltd v Hall Russell and Co Ltd (Shetland Islands Council, third party)* [1989] 1 All ER 37.

[399] On SDRs see 19.4.1 above.

[400] This might be contrasted with other jurisdictions, such as Canada, where there is an additional national 'top-up' fund, or the United States Oil Pollution Act 1990 which provides for unlimited liability.

reason for this was that around £80 million of claims were made against the Fund in the Scottish courts, although by 1 October 1999 these stood at £34 million after a number of claims had been settled out of court, withdrawn from court proceedings or reduced in amounts.[401] Claims before the national courts are allowable because the Fund Convention channels disputed claims through the national courts and provision is made in the 1995 Act for jurisdiction on the part of the British courts to hear claims falling on the Fund.[402] Thus, claims are made directly to the Fund, but disputes will be settled in national courts. This leads to the somewhat awkward situation that the settlement of similar claims may be decided by different criteria depending on whether compensation is awarded under the Fund or paid following action in the national courts. The national courts have stressed that their concern is with interpretation of the statutory provisions. As these are as clear as the words of the Convention, they have not needed to look to the words of the Convention or the guidelines of the Fund.[403] As noted above,[404] liability under the Conventions is strict, and therefore the central issue is remoteness.

Following the *Braer* incident, a fishing exclusion zone was imposed along part of the Shetland coast. Fishing, harvesting and sale of all fish and shellfish from within the zone was prohibited[405] and certain farmed fish stocks had to be destroyed. The IOPC Fund compensated salmon farmers in the exclusion zone for the value of the salmon and profits lost from their forced destruction, while fishermen prevented from fishing during the ban also recovered for lost profits. In addition, there were further successful claims for compensation by, for example, fish processors deprived of their raw material, companies repairing fishing gear, and divers engaged in repairing salmon cages. Firms which manufactured boxes for the transport of salmon and which collected salmon offal also recovered, since the Fund considered that they 'were an integral part of the fishing activities in the affected areas'.[406]

However, further claims have been rejected. These include claims rejected by the Fund for health risks, general anxiety suffered by the affected community and for environmental amenity, on the grounds that these did not amount to 'pollution damage'.[407] The courts have also rejected a series of claims by other firms outside the immediate exclusion zone. Employing normal rules relating to remoteness of damage, it has been held that a seller of salmon smolts to the affected fish farming firms could not recover, since 'they were at the material time just persons who were hoping and

---

[401] 71FUND/EXC.62/14, 22 October 1999.

[402] ss.177(2) and 179 Merchant Shipping Act 1995. The claims in the *Braer* were brought under the predecessor Merchant Shipping Act 1974.

[403] The cases following the *Braer* have been heard in the Scottish courts, but the legislation implementing the Civil Liability Convention is UK-wide, and the Scottish courts take a similar approach both to questions of the interpretation of statutes transposing international conventions and to questions of remoteness in negligence actions.

[404] See 19.13 above.

[405] Under s.1 Food and Environment Protection Act 1985.

[406] FUND/EXC.36.10, see generally Brans (1995).

[407] FUND/EXC.35.10, para.3.4.25, but see *Black* v *The Braer Corporation* 1999 SLT 1401.

expecting to enter in the future into profitable commercial relations with some Shetland fish farmers'.[408] A further claim from other salmon farmers outside the exclusion zone who suffered the 'blighting' of their product because of the adverse publicity was also unsuccessful.[409] As can be seen, the approach of the courts to compensation and remoteness is somewhat stricter than the IOPC Fund. Moreover, the Scottish courts have held that they will not be guided by the practices or guidelines of the Fund,[410] and it has been suggested that the approach of the Fund would not be followed in the English courts.[411]

Following the *Sea Empress* incident, a variety of claims were compensated under the previous definition of 'pollution damage'. For example, a freshwater angling club received compensation for pure economic loss following the imposition of a ban on taking migratory fish,[412] and caravan park operators and other tourist establishments were compensated for loss of income. Charities received compensation for cleaning oiled birds, and various property claims relating to, for example, contamination of boats and moorings and to buildings contaminated by wind-blown oil were also accepted. However, a claim by a county fire brigade for expenses incurred in providing fire fighting services during the salvage operations would only be paid to the extent that the emergency services were engaged in 'preventive measures' to combat marine pollution,[413] rather than to protect life from, for example, an ensuing fire.[414]

Further claims have been submitted by a range of public bodies. Thus, claims for monitoring the degree of contamination of fish and shellfish have been accepted,[415] and a significant claim has been made by the Environment Agency both for its work and the work of the predecessor body the National Rivers Authority during and after the incident. The avenue of lodging a claim with the Fund has had the practical consequence that seeking recovery under the Water Resources Act 1991 for costs incurred[416] is unlikely to be pursued, so long as the claim for compensation under the Fund is met in full.[417] These claims are likely to be settled out of court, following the settlement of the claims of private operators for economic losses. It should be noted that payments under the CRISTAL scheme, which applies to the incident and which may be claimed against as

---

[408] *Landcatch Ltd* v *The International Oil Pollution Compensation Fund* 1999 SLT 1208 per Lord McCluskey. See also *P and O Ferries Ltd* v *The Braer Corporation and others* [1999] 2 Lloyd's Rep 535.

[409] *Skerries Salmon Ltd* v *The Braer Corporation and others* 1999 SLT 1196.

[410] *Landcatch Ltd* v *The International Oil Pollution Compensation Fund* 1999 SLT 1208.

[411] See Gauci (1997) p.47. See also 71FUND/EXC.62/7/1, mentioned below.

[412] 71FUND/EXC.50/17, 23 October 1996, para.3.12.12, cited in Gauci (1997) p.45.

[413] See 19.13.1 above.

[414] 71FUND/EXC.62/7, 29 September 1999 and 71FUND/EXC.62.14, 22 October 1999.

[415] 71FUND/EXC.62/7, 29 September 1999.

[416] Under s.161 Water Resources, and see 13.2.1 above.

[417] Full payments for all legitimate claims seems likely. It might be noted that the scope for payments under the Fund is somewhat narrower than under s.161 of the 1991 Act, since s.161 extends to various investigative activities etc whereas the Fund is limited, in relation to environmental damage, to restoration costs.

a last resort, may be resorted to.[418] However, this now appears unlikely,[419] though it has been suggested that a much higher value could be attributed to the overall economic costs of the spill, especially if non-use values were taken into account.[420]

Finally, it appears that the Fund will seek to take action against parties to whose fault the spill is attributable. As noted elsewhere,[421] Milford Haven Port Authority was successfully prosecuted for the offence of causing water pollution under Part III of the Water Resources Act 1991 following the *Sea Empress* incident. However, as this offence is one of strict liability, the prosecution would not be sufficient to establish fault for liability purposes. Accordingly, for the Fund to exercise its right of subrogation,[422] it would need to establish that a negligent breach of duty occurred, for example, breaches of common law and statutory duties under the Milford Haven Conservancy Act 1983 or the Pilotage Act 1987. In the criminal prosecution, not guilty pleas in relation to charges under these Acts were given to the Environment Agency, though this does not mean that negligence cannot be established. Another factor in the likely liability action is that, as noted above, the Fund would appear to take a less restrictive approach to claims for pure economic loss and so it may not be able to recover, through the national courts, for the full extent of payments made.[423]

## 19.16 Compensation for Hazardous and Noxious Substances

It is notable that international provisions on compensation for damage to the aquatic environment from shipping are not restricted to the transportation of oil. Further international provisions relate to nuclear material,[424] and to other hazardous and noxious substances. There are also draft provisions on liability and compensation that may be adopted as a Protocol to the 1989 Basle Convention on the Control of Transboundary Movements of Hazardous Wastes and their Disposal.[425]

The 1996 International Convention on Liability and Compensation for Damage in Connection with the Carriage of Hazardous and Noxious Substances by Sea (the 'HNS Convention')[426] applies to substances listed in various IMO Conventions and Codes. These include:

---

[418] On CRISTAL see 19.12 above.

[419] Because the Fund is expected to meet all valid claims in full.

[420] *ENDS Report* 277 (1998) p.27.

[421] See 9.19.3 above.

[422] That is, the acquisition of the rights of those victims of oil pollution to whom it has made payments of compensation.

[423] See 71FUND/EXC.62/7/1, 4 October 1999, para. 6.11.

[424] 1971 Convention relating to Civil Liability in the Field of Maritime Carriage of Nuclear Material.

[425] On the Basle Convention see 19.10.3 above; on the draft Protocol see www.unep.ch/basel/COP5/liability0.html

[426] Cm.3580 (1997) not yet in force.

(a) oils;
(b) other liquid substances defined as noxious or dangerous;
(c) liquefied gases;
(d) liquid substances with a flashpoint not exceeding 60°C;
(e) dangerous, hazardous and harmful materials and substances carried in packaged form; and
(f) solid bulk materials defined as possessing chemical hazards.

The Convention also covers residues left by the previous carriage of HNS, other than those carried in packaged form.

The HNS Convention is, to a large extent, modelled on the Civil Liability and Fund Conventions, and provides for strict but limited liability on owners, for which insurance is compulsory, and backed by a Fund, the 'HNS Fund'. To avoid overlap, the HNS Convention excludes pollution damage as defined in the Civil Liability Convention and Fund Convention.

There are, however, some notable points of contrast between the HNS Convention and the provisions noted above relating to compensation for oil pollution damage. First, the HNS Convention only applies to substances, materials and articles carried on board a ship as cargo, and does not therefore apply to damage caused by substances used, for example, in the propulsion or maintenance of ships. Second, the need for damage to be contingent on 'contamination' only applies to environmental damage, which appears to broaden the scope for liability under the Convention in relation to personal injury and damage to property, and personal injury is specifically included. Thus, the HNS Convention covers damage caused by fire or explosion when oils are carried, which is outside of the Civil Liability and Fund Conventions. Third, the HNS Fund, which is paid into by those handling hazardous and noxious substances, is sub-divided into one general account and three separate accounts for oil, liquefied natural gas and liquefied petroleum gas. The system with separate accounts has been seen as a way to avoid cross-subsidisation between different HNS substances. Although the UK has yet to ratify the Convention, it was its first signatory and the Merchant Shipping Act 1995 makes provision for its eventual transposition.[427] Until such time, the ordinary rules of civil law apply.

## 19.17 Depositing Waste at Sea

Initially, the character of the activities which constitute 'dumping' of waste at sea, and the kinds of material that fall within the definition of 'deposited waste', require some explanation.[428] In general terms, the kinds of wastes

---

[427] See ss.182A-182C and Sch.5A Merchant Shipping Act 1995, added by s.14 Merchant Shipping and Maritime Security Act 1997.
[428] General reading on legal aspects of the deposit of waste at sea includes Bates and Benson (1993, updated) Ch.9; Sands (1995) pp.308-318 and Churchill and Lowe (1999) pp.363-370. For historical references see Howarth (1988) Ch.8.

that have been dumped around the coast of the UK have tended to be of three kinds:

(a) sewage sludge;
(b) industrial wastes, such as brines, liquid wastes and drilling muds; and
(c) inert mineral waste, particularly from coal mining, sand from gravel extraction and fly ash from power stations.[429]

Dredging spoils removed from estuaries and port entrances are also collected and dumped at sea and, if removed from industrialised estuaries, these may contain appreciable quantities of metals, oils and other contaminants which may enter the marine food chain to a greater extent if the spoil becomes dispersed and oxygenated. To this list should also be added significant cumulative quantities of litter and plastics, mostly from shipping and fishing.[430] Although these tend not to alter the chemical quality of the water, they may nevertheless have a significant aesthetic and ecological impact: discarded fishing nets, for example, pose a particular problem for marine mammals and sea birds through entanglement. Large numbers of fish are also dumped in depressing amounts, usually catches in excess of fishery quotas or of unwanted species. In this instance, however, the deposited matter originates in the sea, and for this reason this activity is generally placed outside legal regulation.[431]

During the 1950s sea dumping became increasingly popular as a means of disposing of waste produced by land-based activities. This expansion in the use of the sea as a repository for waste originating from land was partially a consequence of the economic expediency of this method of disposal, but equally it was an incidental consequence of stricter legal controls on the disposal of waste on land.[432] Although the practice of dumping of many wastes in UK marine waters has now ceased, or is being phased out, it is nevertheless instructive to consider the present legal controls and the extent of their applicability.

The issue of dumping provides a good illustration of the regulatory tensions in relation to controlling marine contamination. On the one hand, there are those who argue that restrictions on dumping reduce the environmental burden that the minority of states still dumping waste at sea can impose on non-dumping states or on future generations.[433] Opposed to this is the view that the controlled dumping of certain wastes at sea may actually be the best practicable environmental option.[434]

---

[429] See Royal Commission on Environmental Pollution (1985) para.7.47. The dumping of nuclear material is dealt with separately at 20.9 below.

[430] On controlling garbage at sea under the 1973/78 MARPOL Convention see 19.10.5 above.

[431] See, for example, 19.19.4 below in relation to the 1992 OSPAR Convention. By contrast the act of depositing harbour dredgings, which also originate, in a sense, in the marine environment, differs in that material 'locked in' to the dredging may be released on deposit.

[432] Churchill and Lowe (1999) p.329.

[433] See e.g. Birnie and Boyle (1992) p.321.

[434] See e.g. GESAMP (1990) pp.14-15.

### 19.18 Legal Controls on Sea Dumping: Background and Outline

Before 1974, the dumping of any substance which was detrimental to sea fish within the three mile territorial limit around the coast of England and Wales was subject to the control of local sea fisheries committees constituted under the Sea Fisheries Regulation Act 1966.[435] Beyond the three-mile limit there was no statutory restriction on sea dumping of waste. At that stage, international provisions relating to sea disposal were found only in the 1958 Geneva Convention on the High Seas, but were confined to the disposal of oil and radioactive wastes.[436] Otherwise, voluntary arrangements were entered into between persons wishing to dump waste and the Ministry of Agriculture, Fisheries and Food.[437] Such arrangements involved the Ministry indicating suitable areas and methods for sea disposal, requiring the encapsulation of highly toxic wastes, and requiring the body depositing waste to provide certification that such directions had been complied with.[438]

This arrangement was transformed following the Dumping at Sea Act 1974.[439] This Act gave effect to international obligations arising under two conventions:

(a) the 1972 Oslo Convention for the Prevention of Marine Pollution by Dumping from Ships and Aircraft;[440] and

(b) the 1972 London Convention for the Prevention of Marine Pollution by Dumping of Wastes and Other Matter (referred to, before 1992, as the 'London Dumping Convention', now known simply as the 'London Convention').[441]

The Oslo and London Conventions have since been augmented globally by Articles governing sea deposition of waste in the LOS Convention,[442] though in general terms the LOS Convention defers to more specialist dumping regimes at global and regional level. On the domestic level the Dumping at Sea Act 1974 was replaced by more stringent provisions contained in Part II of the Food and Environment Protection Act 1985.

More recently, the control of dumping at sea under international law has been further strengthened by:

(a) the entry into force of the 1992 Convention for the Protection of the Marine Environment of the North-East Atlantic (the 'OSPAR' Convention);[443] and

---

[435] See 15.4.2 above.
[436] Arts.24 and 25 1958 Geneva Convention on the High Seas.
[437] Norton (1976).
[438] Royal Commission on Environmental Pollution (1972) para.135.
[439] See Wharam (1974) and Norton (1976).
[440] 11 ILM (1972) 262.
[441] 11 ILM (1972) 1219.
[442] See generally 18.7.3 above and 19.19.1 below.
[443] See generally 18.8 above and 19.19.4 below.

(b) anticipated changes to the London Convention under a Protocol from 1996 (in effect a complete revision of that treaty).

In both cases, however, the changes largely reflect decisions taken under both Convention regimes since the late 1980s to reduce greatly the scope for the dumping of certain kinds of polluting wastes at sea. Nevertheless, they must now be seen as the principal basis for determinations to licence waste disposal at sea under the 1985 Act. The first part of the remainder of this chapter examines the present scope of international obligations and recommendations concerning sea dumping. This is followed by looking at how these obligations have been translated into UK national law.

### 19.19 International Treaty Law on Sea Dumping

#### 19.19.1 The Law of the Sea Convention

Under the LOS Convention the activity of sea dumping of waste is defined as any deliberate disposal of wastes or other matter from vessels, aircraft, platforms or other man-made structures at sea, and any deliberate disposal of the vessels and structures themselves.[444] However, dumping does not include the disposal of wastes resulting from the normal operations of such vessels or structures or their equipment except for wastes loaded on them or taken to them for disposal at sea. Nor does it include the placement of matter in the marine environment for a purpose other than disposal, so long as this is not contrary to the aims of the Convention.[445] This definition is generally replicated in other international texts discussed below, though their ambit has been extended to include incineration.

As in relation to most other forms of marine pollution, the LOS Convention does not prescribe specific standards for dumping wastes at sea but rather lays down a framework within which standards elaborated in other fora may be applied and enforced.[446] Thus, the LOS Convention only requires that states have national laws, and adopt other measures as necessary, to prevent, reduce and control dumping, which must be no less effective than global rules and standards and which must ensure that dumping is not carried out without their permission. Moreover, it requires states, acting through competent international organisations or diplomatic conferences, to endeavour to establish global or regional rules, standards and recommendations. There is little doubt that, for the UK, this means the 1972 London Convention and the 1992 OSPAR Convention as appropriate.

More particularly, dumping within the territorial sea and the exclusive economic zone or onto the continental shelf[447] must not be carried out without the express prior approval of the coastal state. Coastal states have the right to permit, regulate and control such dumping after due

---

[444] Art.1(5)(a) LOS Convention.
[445] *Ibid* Art.1(5)(b).
[446] See 18.7.3 above.
[447] These terms are defined at 18.7.1 above.

consideration of the matter with other states which, by reason of their geographic situation, may be adversely affected.[448] The requirement of 'due consideration' has been said to go beyond what is required under prior consultation procedures,[449] but may only reflect what is required as a matter of customary international law.[450]

In relation to enforcement, the LOS Convention requires that rules and standards adopted either directly under the Convention, and 'applicable international rules and standards' (by which can be inferred international fora like the London Convention and regional conventions like OSPAR) shall be enforced:

   (a) by the coastal state with regard to dumping within its territorial sea or its EEZ or onto its continental shelf;
   (b) by flag states with regard to vessels flying their flags or vessels or aircraft of their registry; and
   (c) by any state with regard to acts of loading of wastes or other matter occurring within its territory or at its offshore terminals.[451]

Although this gives a range of enforcement possibilities for dumping activities, it is provided that where one state begins enforcement action, then other relevant states may leave enforcement matters to that state.[452] The extension of coastal state jurisdiction to dumping within the EEZ or onto the continental shelf is reflected in more recent agreements including the 1996 Protocol to the London Convention and the 1992 OSPAR Convention, both of which are discussed in more detail below.

### 19.19.2 The London Convention

The 1972 London Convention on the Prevention of Marine Pollution by Dumping of Wastes and Other Matter[453] (the 'London Convention') is a treaty of global application with 78 contracting parties[454] including the UK. Although the precise nature of the relationship between the London Convention and the regional OSPAR Convention is nowhere explicitly stated, it appears that the OSPAR Convention applies more detailed and, if necessary, more stringent controls. The London Convention should be read alongside the large number of resolutions that have been adopted, and amendments agreed, at various meetings of the parties which have been held at least once every two years under the auspices of the International Maritime Organisation (IMO), the secretariat organisation of the Convention.[455] In 1996, a Protocol to the Convention was adopted which, although some years away from coming into force, will replace the 1972

---

[448] Art.210 LOS Convention.

[449] As contained in the London and OSPAR Conventions, discussed below.

[450] Birnie and Boyle (1992) pp.327-29.

[451] Art.216 LOS Convention.

[452] *Ibid* Art.216(2).

[453] Cmnd.5169, in force 30 August 1975. See www.londonconvention.org

[454] As at 31 January 2000.

[455] Art.14 London Convention.

Convention and in certain respects radically alter the approach taken under the London Convention regime.[456] The following discusses the key points of the 1972 Convention, noting those changes which will be effected by the 1996 Protocol as appropriate. It should be noted at the outset that the definition of 'dumping' contained in the London Convention is analogous to that in the LOS Convention,[457] though, like the OSPAR Convention, it extends to the incineration of waste at sea.[458]

The Convention currently adopts a threefold classification of pollutants.[459] Thus, the substances considered most harmful to the marine environment are contained in the 'black list' and, other than in emergencies, may not be dumped. Aside from certain hazardous chemicals, the black list includes high-level radioactive waste,[460] and persistent plastics and other synthetic materials which may float or remain in suspension in the sea so that they interfere materially with fishing, navigation or other legitimate uses of the sea.[461] There are exceptions where a substance occurs as a trace contaminant in waste, and where the substance may rapidly be rendered harmless by physical, biological or chemical processes in the sea provided that they do not have certain defined effects on marine biota or humans. Consultative procedures determine whether either of these two exceptions apply.[462]

A second group of pollutants, the 'grey list', are the relatively less harmful substances and materials but which still require special care. The list includes certain toxic substances, pesticides, and material that may cause a serious obstacle to fishing and navigation.[463] Such wastes may not be dumped at sea without a specific permit from the appropriate national authority.

Finally, there is a residual group of pollutants, the 'white list', which consists of all those wastes that do not feature in either of the previous two categories. The dumping of matter in this residual category must be subject to the approval of the appropriate national authority or authorities, although this can be under a general permit rather than an individual licence.[464] Before such approval is granted, the authority must carefully consider the characteristics and composition of the waste (such as the amount, toxicity and persistence), the characteristics of the dumping site and the disposal method (such as the geographical position and location in relation to living resources and amenity areas), and other general considerations such as possible effects on marine life and other uses of the

---

[456] 1996 Protocol to the Convention on the Prevention of Marine Pollution by Waste and Other Matter 1972 (Cm.4078).
[457] See 19.19.1 above.
[458] Art.III London Convention.
[459] *Ibid* Art.IV and Annexes I-III.
[460] On which see 20.9 below.
[461] Annex I London Convention.
[462] Resolution 24(10).
[463] Annex II London Convention.
[464] *Ibid* Art.IV(1)(c).

sea and the practical availability of alternative land-based means of disposal or elimination of the waste.[465]

In assessing these criteria reference must be made to agreed Guidelines.[466] In addition, generic assessment procedures apply to all types of waste. These require a precautionary approach to be taken and prioritise waste minimisation and land-based management options.[467] Reference to a precautionary approach reflects the acceptance by the parties of such an approach more generally.[468] Following amendments to the Convention in 1978, deemed necessary to regulate a practice that had begun in the early 1970s, further provision was made requiring special permits for the incineration of black and grey list waste at sea. This is governed by specific regulations that are included as an addendum to the Annexes to the Convention.

An exception is made to the general system of regulating sea dumping in respect of emergencies, so that the dumping restrictions do not apply in a case of *force majeure* due to stress of weather, or any other cause when the safety of human life or of a ship, aircraft, platform or structure is threatened.[469] Where a party to the Convention in an emergency considers that a black list substance must be dumped at sea it must notify other affected parties, which need not be other contracting parties, and the IMO; if the circumstances permit, any recommendations made by the IMO must also be followed. Clearly there will be some situations, such as where old chemical munitions are caught in fishing nets, where prior consultation may not be feasible. In an emergency the parties to the Convention are pledged to assist one another.[470] Where dumping has been permitted, then the consequences must be monitored.[471]

Enforcement responsibilities are placed upon the parties, and each party must take appropriate measures to prevent and punish conduct in contravention of the Convention within its territory.[472] In particular, enforcement measures must be applied by states to:

(a) ships and aircraft registered in its territory or flying its flag;
(b) ships and aircraft loading in its territory matter which is to be dumped; and

---

[465] *Ibid* Annex III.

[466] *Guidelines for the Implementation and Uniform Interpretation of Annex III*; see LDC Resolution 32(11).

[467] *Guidelines for the Assessment of Waste or Other Matter That May Be Considered for Dumping*, IMO Doc. LC/SG 20/12, Annex 2, replacing the 'Waste Assessment Framework' contained in previous Resolutions. For discussion of the draft procedures see Bates and Benson (1993, updated), paras 9.24-9.38.

[468] Resolution LDC44(14); on the precautionary principle see 4.7.1 above.

[469] Art.5(1) London Convention.

[470] *Ibid* Art.5(2).

[471] *Ibid* Art.6(1)(d).

[472] *Ibid* Art.7(2).

(c) ships, aircraft and fixed or floating structures under its jurisdiction believed to be engaged in dumping.[473]

It has been suggested that the provisions of the Convention which require the development of 'procedures' for imposing liability for damage caused to the environment by dumping might provide a further, perhaps more effective, sanction against non-compliance than the possibility of penal sanctions. So far, however, no such procedures have been adopted, and the parties agreed in 1991 not to do so for the time being.[474] Although neither the substantive provisions of the Convention nor its enforcement measures apply to vessels and aircraft (such as warships) entitled to sovereign immunity, states have agreed to ensure that such vessels are subject to similar provisions.[475]

### 19.19.3 The 1996 Protocol

The 1996 Protocol[476] will, when it enters into force, make a number of important changes to the London Convention regime, though many of these give effect to changes which had already been made in practice or which had already been agreed by the parties. In particular, there has been a decisive move away from a 'dilute and disperse' approach to waste dumping, emphasising the assimilative capacity of the marine environment, to a more precautionary approach, as well as increasing emphasis given to dealing with waste management issues in the round.[477]

In particular, the tripartite listing of substances is to be replaced by a 'reverse listing' approach, under which only substances and matter expressly listed in the Protocol may be dumped. In many respects this recognises that, over recent years, the parties to the Convention have first resolved to phase out the dumping of certain substances and have then given force to these resolutions through treaty amendments. As noted elsewhere, this was the case with low and intermediate-level radioactive waste,[478] but it has also occurred with other substances and activities. Thus, in 1988 the parties resolved to phase out the incineration at sea of noxious liquid wastes by the end of 1994[479] and the Convention was amended in 1993 so as to ban the incineration of industrial waste and sewage sludge at sea, though in practice this had been effected by 1991. In addition, a resolution calling for an end to the dumping of industrial waste by the end of 1995 was adopted in 1990,[480] and again the Convention was

---

[473] *Ibid* Art.7(1).
[474] Churchill and Lowe (1999) p.365.
[475] Art.7(4) London Convention.
[476] 1996 Protocol to the Convention on the Prevention of Marine Pollution by Waste and Other Matter 1972 (Cm 4078). For general coverage see de La Fayette (1998).
[477] Churchill and Lowe (1999) p.365.
[478] See 20.9 below.
[479] Resolution LDC 35(11).
[480] Resolution LDC 43(13), but see de La Fayette (1998) p.519.

amended in 1993, with effect from 1994.[481] The effect of these amendments was that only a relatively small number of substances could be dumped under the London Convention. The main categories are the substances excluded from the ban on the dumping of industrial wastes, that is:

(a) dredged material;
(b) sewage sludge;
(c) fish processing wastes;
(d) vessels; and
(e) platforms or other man-made structures disposed of at sea such as continental shelf oil and gas installations.[482]

This severe curtailing of material that may lawfully be dumped is now reflected in the reverse listing approach taken in the 1996 Protocol. Specifically, those substances that may be dumped are those items noted above, together with inert, inorganic geological material and organic material of natural origin.[483] In reaching any decision on the dumping of these substances, the generic assessment Guidelines must be used,[484] while specific guidelines have also been developed for certain substances and are in the process of being adopted.[485]

The generic Guidelines apply against a background of general objectives[486] which prescribe the progressive decrease in the use of the sea for waste disposal:

(a) by reducing the amount of waste produced, amongst other things, through the use of clean production methods;
(b) by re-using or recycling any waste produced;
(c) by the destruction or removal of hazardous constituents of the waste; and
(d) by considering waste disposal options on land.

If the waste can be managed using one of these options, then a permit for dumping must be refused. If none of these options is appropriate, then an environmental assessment of the proposed dumping operation must be carried out. This assessment must take a precautionary approach, and prohibit dumping at sea where there is insufficient information on the likely affects of dumping. If the assessment indicates that disposal at sea would be more harmful than other options, then a permit should be refused. The assessment procedure thus has substance, in contrast to the

---

[481] For the 1994 amendments to the London Convention see Cm 3003 and 3004 (both 1995). For comment on the political processes at work during this period see Parmentier (1999).

[482] Churchill and Lowe (1999) p.366. See also de La Fayette (1998) pp.519-520. On the dumping of offshore oil and gas installations see 19.19.4F and 19.21 below.

[483] Also included is a final category of bulky wastes where there is no practicable access to disposal options other than dumping. This is intended to apply to small islands with isolated communities and, it is submitted, is of no application in England and Wales.

[484] See 19.19.2 above.

[485] See de La Fayette (1998) pp.523-4.

[486] Contained in Annex 2 to the 1996 Protocol.

purely procedural requirements for environmental impact assessment under EC law.[487] To combat concerns about the practice of exporting wastes that cannot be dumped at sea under the 1972 Convention to non-Contracting Parties, the Protocol provides that contracting parties must not allow the export of wastes or other matter to other countries for dumping or incineration at sea.[488]

In relation to the generic Guidelines it has been argued that 'the practical effect of their application should be to make the implementation of the [London] Convention virtually identical to that of the 1996 Protocol.'[489] The same commentator goes on to suggest that:

> The practical effect of this will be considerable . . . applicants for dumping permits will be required, first, to do a waste management audit and to use every means to reduce the amount of waste produced; secondly, to review all other disposal methods of any waste produced pursuant to the waste management hierarchy, including re-use and recycling; and, thirdly, to consider disposal options on land; before finally turning to the possibility of disposal into the sea. Even then, a permit is not assured, for if, after a comparative assessment, disposal at sea is not the safest option or if there is insufficient information to serve as a basis for a decision, a permit will not be granted. If properly applied, the Guidelines should ensure that nothing which could not be dumped under the Protocol will be dumped under the Convention.[490]

The 1996 Protocol also makes important changes intended to improve compliance and to enhance participation in the Convention regime. These include improved reporting obligations, and a specific requirement that parties establish a compliance procedure. However, the parties recognised the need to support compliance further, and have agreed to adopt new guidelines on implementation and improve scientific and technical co-operation. While such measures are essential for the Convention regime as a whole, and may impose resource burdens nationally, they are of relatively limited relevance to dumping in UK waters and are not discussed further here.[491]

### 19.19.4 The OSPAR Convention

The first convention dedicated to dumping of waste at sea was the 1972 Oslo Convention.[492] Like the London Convention of later that year, the Oslo Convention categorised the main kinds of pollutants according to their harmfulness to the marine environment. It then placed dumping of the

---

[487] See 14.6 above on the Environmental Impact Assessment Directive.

[488] Art.6 1996 Protocol.

[489] de La Fayette (1998) p.534.

[490] *Ibid* p.535.

[491] See Article 9, London Convention and Articles 13 and 26, 1996 Protocol and see *ibid* pp.526-27.

[492] See 18.8 and 19.18 above.

most harmful pollutants under a total ban and subjected other kinds of dumping to a licensing system to be administered by national authorities. The Oslo Convention was also extended, by amendment, to cover the incineration of waste at sea.[493] With the coming into force of the 1992 OSPAR Convention the Oslo Convention has now been repealed, though many of the decisions and recommendations made under it remain in force. The main provisions of the OSPAR Convention on dumping are contained in Article 4 and Annex II.[494] The following paragraphs should be read alongside general discussion of the OSPAR Convention.[495]

### 19.19.4A 'Dumping'

'Dumping' is defined in a similar way to the LOS Convention and London Convention. Although it is explicitly stated that the leaving in place, wholly or partly, of disused offshore installations and pipelines is not 'dumping', this will have to comply with the provisions of the Convention dealing with offshore installations and other international legislation.[496] Specifically excluded from the definition of 'wastes and other matters' are human remains, offshore installations and pipelines and unprocessed fish and fish offal discarded from fishing vessels.[497]

### 19.19.4B Reverse listing and the presumption against dumping

As with the 1996 Protocol to the London Convention, the OSPAR Convention adopts a 'reverse listing' approach to the identification of those items that may be dumped. Thus, the dumping of all wastes and other matter is prohibited. The only exceptions are dredged material, inert sludge of natural origin and fish processing waste. This is more restrictive than under the London Convention, but similarly it reflects decisions made over the years to modify and restrict the original agreement. These decisions included agreements on the ending of the incineration of industrial waste at sea by the end of 1991,[498] phasing out the dumping of most industrial wastes by the end of 1995,[499] and prohibiting the dumping of sewage sludge after 1998.[500] Also, vessels and aircraft can be dumped only until the end of 2004 at the latest and, as noted elsewhere, the dumping of radioactive waste by all parties is now prohibited.[501]

---

[493] Cmnd. 8492, brought into force in 1989.

[494] On dumping and the OSPAR Convention see Hey et al (1993) pp.23-30.

[495] See 18.8 above.

[496] Art.1(f) and (g) and Annex III OSPAR Convention, discussed at 19.19.4F below.

[497] *Ibid* Art.1(o).

[498] Decision 90/2, 23 June 1990.

[499] Decision 89/1, 14 June 1989.

[500] Decision 90/1, 23 June 1990. See also Directive 91/271/EEC on Urban Waste Water Treatment and Reg.9 Urban Waste Water Treatment (England and Wales) Regulations 1994 (SI 1994 No.2841), discussed at 5.6.2 above. In 1996/7 the UK was dumping around one quarter of its sewage sludge, 264,000 tonnes, at sea (*ENDS Report* 279 (1998) p.17).

[501] Art.3 Annex II OSPAR Convention, and see 20.9 below.

The shift away from dumping as an acceptable waste management strategy can be traced back to the Declaration of the Ministers at the close of the Second International North Sea Conference (INSC) in 1987. This Declaration accepted, as a matter of principle, the importance of ending the dumping of 'polluting' materials in the North Sea at the earliest practical date and a general presumption in favour of land-based disposal options. In general terms, the move towards a narrow, reverse listing approach reflects the impact of the North Sea Conferences (particularly the Second and Third) on the Oslo Convention, with developments under the Oslo Convention often acting as a catalyst for changes agreed under the London Convention.[502] Thus, for example, at the Second INSC Ministers agreed to phase out the dumping at sea of industrial wastes by 1989, a commitment only the UK had failed to meet by the Third INSC in 1990.[503] It is notable that the only contaminated matter that may now be dumped under the OSPAR Convention is contaminated dredged material, which the INSC Declarations indicate should be phased out.[504]

### 19.19.4C  Permitting and record keeping

Where dumping is allowable, it may not be permitted without the authorisation of a competent authority of one of the parties or regulation by it. Any such authorisation or regulation may not, however, permit the dumping of vessels or aircraft containing substances which result, or are likely to result, in hazards to human health, harm to living resources and marine ecosystems, damage to amenities or interference with other legitimate uses of the sea. Contracting parties must keep, and report to the OSPAR Commission, records of the nature and quantities of wastes or other matter dumped, and of the dates, places and methods of dumping. To avoid duplication of regulatory effort, competent authorities must notify each other, as appropriate, before granting an authorisation or applying regulation. Provision is made for 'criteria, guidelines and procedures' to be adopted by the OSPAR Commission in relation to wastes that may be dumped. So far, Guidelines for the Management of Dredged Material and for the Dumping of Fish Waste from Land-Based Industrial Fish Processing Operations have been adopted.[505]

### 19.19.4D  Exceptions

Similar exceptions as provided for under the London Convention apply to the relaxation of the general prohibition on dumping in emergency situations. In addition, the OSPAR Convention allows otherwise prohibited wastes to be dumped in an emergency where the alternative of land disposal would present unacceptable danger or damage. Although

---

[502] Haas (1993) and de La Fayette (1998) p.528, n.55, but note the case of radioactive substances, at 20.9 below. On the North Sea Conferences see 18.8 above.

[503] An extension for two dumping licences, until 1993, if absolutely necessary was granted; Hague Declaration (1990) para 18.

[504] On dredged material see 1998 OSPAR Guidelines, noted immediately below.

[505] Agreements 1998-20 and 1998-21 respectively.

'emergency' is not defined, by implication it must be something less than required by *force majeure*. If this is the case, then the party concerned should consult with the OSPAR Commission in order to find the most appropriate means of storage, destruction or disposal.[506] Since the parties have pledged to assist each other in such situations, exceptionally disposal on the land of another party may be required, leading to the movement of waste for disposal which runs counter to EC waste management policy and to the principle of the EC Treaty that environmental problems should, as a matter of course, be rectified at source.[507]

### 19.19.4E Enforcement

The OSPAR provisions for enforcement are similar, but not identical, to those under the London Convention. Contracting parties must ensure compliance by vessels or aircraft registered in its territory; by vessels and aircraft loading in its territory matter which is to be dumped or incinerated; and by vessels or aircraft believed to be engaged in dumping or incineration out to the 200 mile limit. One important difference is that the jurisdiction of the OSPAR Convention extends to the internal waters of the parties up to the freshwater limit, which expands the scope of enforcement measures by comparison with to the London Convention. In addition, appropriate authorities in each contracting party must be instructed to report suspicions of actual or imminent unlawful dumping, and notify other parties as appropriate.[508]

### 19.19.4F Offshore oil and gas installations

As noted previously,[509] the provisions of the OSPAR Convention relating to dumping do not apply to certain activities relating to offshore installations. The nature of the regulation of such installations is, however, rather complicated. To begin with, the deliberate disposal of wastes *from* offshore installations, and the disposal *of* offshore installations and offshore pipelines, amounts to 'dumping'.[510] However, Annex II to the Convention, relating to dumping, does not apply to either activity.[511] Matters are further complicated by the main provisions of the OSPAR Convention relating to offshore installations being in Annex III, which relates generally to the prevention and elimination of pollution *from* such sources.

This peculiarity can be explained by reference to historic efforts by the UK to exclude the dumping of disused platforms from the Oslo Convention and have this activity covered by the 1974 Paris Convention.[512] This may

---

[506] Art.9 Annex II, OSPAR Convention.

[507] See COM(96)399 final and Art.174(2) EC. On the 'source' principle see 4.7.2 above.

[508] Art.10 Annex II OSPAR Convention.

[509] See 19.19.4A above.

[510] Art.1(f) OSPAR Convention.

[511] *Ibid* Art.1 Annex II.

[512] Hey, et al (1993) p.29. On the Oslo and Paris Conventions see 18.8 above.

also explain why, although the placement of matter in the sea for a purpose which is not in accordance with its original design or construction is not 'dumping', it is nevertheless dealt with in Annex II and requires authorisation.[513] The possibility of disused installations being dumped directly to create artificial reefs to support fish life, where it is not clear that this would amount to an act of 'disposal' bringing it within the definition of 'dumping',[514] appears to have been removed.[515] The dumping of wastes from offshore installations is completely prohibited, but this prohibition does not relate to discharges or emissions.[516]

As regards disused installations and pipelines, the OSPAR Convention originally provided that decisions on dumping, or leaving such structures wholly or partly in place, would be taken by the contracting parties on a case-by-case basis. The only restriction was that a permit should not be issued if the installation or pipeline contained substances which result, or are likely to result, in hazards to human health, harm to living resources and marine ecosystems, damage to amenities or interference with other legitimate uses of the sea.[517] This approach had to be seen alongside the provisions of the LOS Convention concerning the abandonment of installations. The LOS Convention generally requires complete removal, in the interests of navigation, but makes this subject to guidance from the competent international organisation, i.e. the International Maritime Organization.[518]

Since 1995, however, the position has changed significantly. In that year, the planned disposal in the North East Atlantic of the *Brent Spar*, a large oil storage buoy, was halted following a protest by Greenpeace.[519] This was despite disposal being allowable under relevant IMO Guidelines, a best practicable environmental option (BPEO) study having being carried out, and permission under UK national law having been obtained.[520] In 1995, the Oslo Commission adopted a Decision calling for a moratorium on disposal at sea of decommissioned offshore installations, although both

---

[513] Art.1(g)(ii) and Art.5 Annex II OSPAR Convention.

[514] 'Disposal' is not defined in the OSPAR Convention.

[515] See para.7 OSPAR *Guidelines on Artificial Reefs in relation to Living Marine Resources*, Agreement 1999-13, which require, ambiguously, that reefs be 'specifically built',.

[516] Which are outside the scope of this chapter; see Art.3 Annex III and the OSPAR *Strategy on Environmental Goals and Management Mechanisms for Offshore Activities*, 1999-12, and OSPAR Action Plan 1998-2003 (Update 1999), s.6. These emphasise BEP and reduction and elimination strategies, and impacts on wildlife.

[517] Art.5(1) and (2) Annex III OSPAR Convention.

[518] See *Guidelines and Standards for the Removal of Offshore Installations and Structures on the Continental Shelf and in the Exclusive Economic Zone*, adopted 19 October 1989. This is a notable contrast to earlier provisions under Art.5(5) of the Geneva Convention on the Continental Shelf 1958 which required that 'Any installations which are abandoned or disused must be entirely removed'.

[519] On the *Brent Spar* generally see Ridge and Styles (1999); House of Lords Select Committee on Science and Technology, *Decommissioning of Oil and Gas Installations* (1995-96) and Government Response at HL Paper 114, and Rice and Owen (1999).

[520] Under an abandonment programme notified under the Petroleum Act 1987, see now the Petroleum Act 1998, discussed at 19.21 below. On BPEO see 12.3.2A above.

the UK and Norway, the only states with deep sea installations, rejected the decision which was not therefore binding on them.[521]

Finally, an OSPAR Decision on a moratorium was unanimously adopted, with effect from 9 February 1999.[522] This provides, as a general rule, that the dumping, and leaving wholly or partly in place, of disused offshore installations within the OSPAR maritime area is prohibited.[523] The definition of such installations does not include concrete anchor-bases associated with floating structures which do not, nor are likely to, interfere with legitimate uses of the sea. However, the general prohibition against dumping may be departed from where there are significant reasons not to re-use, recycle or disposal of structures on land. If this is the case, which must be determined by an assessment[524] involving consultation with other contracting parties,[525] then the competent authority of the contracting party may issue a permit[526] for:

(a) all or part of the footings of certain steel installations (i.e. those weighing more than 10,000 tonnes in air), placed in the maritime area before 9 February 1999;

(b) certain concrete installations or concrete anchor-bases; or

(c) the dumping of installations because of exceptional or unforeseen circumstances resulting from proven structural damage, deterioration or a similar cause.[527]

It seems clear that the narrowness of these exceptions goes well beyond what the UK originally considered justifiable.[528] Assessments must take account of safety, and impacts on the marine environment and impacts on other environmental compartments, including leaching to groundwater and discharges to surface freshwater, though it is likely that what may be left at sea consists largely of inert matter. Evidently the approach of the OSPAR Decision is to require assessments only to justify departures from the general prohibition on dumping, rather than requiring a case-by-case assessment along the lines of the EC Environmental Impact Assessment Directive. It should be noted, however, that the EIA Directive only applies to projects for the extraction of petroleum and does not directly apply to the decommissioning of platforms and other installations.[529]

---

[521] OSCOM Decision 95/1. See *ENDS Report* 246 (1995) pp.35-37. On OSPAR Decisions generally see 18.8.2 above.

[522] Decision 98/3. The European Commission has proposed the adoption of Decision 98/3 by a Council Decision, see COM(99)190 final, OJ C158 p10.

[523] There is no obligation to 'clean up afterwards', for example by removing contaminated drilling muds. This may become controversial ('Greenpeace sees Boost for Onshore Decommissioning Industry', Greenpeace press release 22 October 1999).

[524] In accordance with Annex 2 OSPAR Decision 98/3.

[525] In accordance with Annex 3 OSPAR Decision 98/3.

[526] In accordance with Annex 4 OSPAR Decision 98/3.

[527] Arts 2 and 3 OSPAR Decision 98/3. Notably, cost considerations do not feature.

[528] *ENDS Report* 267 (1997) p.37.

[529] Ridge and Styles (1999) p.152 appear to assume that it does, but see the Offshore Petroleum Production and Pipe-lines (Assessment of Environmental Effects) Regulations 1999 (SI 1999 No.360). On environmental impact assessment generally see 14.6 above.

In relation to the legal controls on the dumping of wastes at sea, the disposal of offshore installations illustrates the interactions between the various layers of law which are applicable. Thus, while offshore disposal is allowable under both the London Convention and its 1996 Protocol, it is now heavily circumscribed under its regional equivalent, the OSPAR Convention and Decision 98/3. However, the permitting of disposal plans at national level falls to the Secretary of State for Trade and Industry, under powers relating to oil exploration,[530] rather than under the Food and Environment Protection Act 1985 which ostensibly implemented UK obligations under the London and Oslo Conventions.[531] Moreover, the general ban on disposal followed 'affirmation' of the precautionary principle, and 'recognition' that reuse, recycling or final disposal on land will generally be the preferable option.[532] It is notable that these preferences are stated rather than explicitly argued for, but nevertheless they indicate the extent to which matters of water quality may be inextricably bound up with wider issues of waste management.

## 19.20  Part II Food and Environment Protection Act 1985

In general, implementation of the London and OSPAR Conventions is by licensing requirements imposed under Part II of the Food and Environment Protection Act 1985 ('the 1985 Act'), as amended primarily by the Environment Protection Act 1990.[533] These provisions replaced the Dumping at Sea Act 1974, passed to implement the London and Oslo Conventions, but which required amendment to take into account later and more stringent international obligations. Most notably, the amendments included the extension of controls to the incineration of waste at sea and the application of the law to foreign vessels. In addition, any waste matter dumped at sea will usually be 'Directive waste', and its deposit will normally be a disposal operation for the purposes of the EC Waste Framework Directive.[534] Thus, the provisions of Part II of the 1985 Act must be read alongside the Waste Framework Directive and its implementing legislation[535], while their practical application can only be understood in the light of wider international obligations. Because these have severely curtailed the scope for dumping waste at sea, the provisions of national law are considered relatively briefly.[536]

---

[530] Part IV Petroleum Act 1998, see 19.21 below.

[531] See 19.19.2–19.19.4 above.

[532] Preamble, OSPAR Decision 98/3.

[533] But see 19.21 below in relation to the disposal of offshore installations.

[534] Directive 75/442/EEC as amended by Directive 91/156/EEC, see 12.2.2 above.

[535] Part II Environmental Protection Act 1990 and Waste Management Licensing Regulations 1994 (SI 1994 No.1056).

[536] A slightly fuller account is given in Bates and Benson (1993, updated) Ch.9.

### 19.20.1 *The Licensing of Sea Deposits*

In relation to dumping at sea, Part II of the 1985 Act imposes a comprehensive collection of licensing requirements for the deposit, loading and incineration of waste, and the 'scuttling' of vessels.

A licence is required for the deposit of substances and articles in the sea or under the sea bed within UK waters or UK controlled waters from a vehicle, vessel,[537] aircraft, hovercraft or marine structure; from a container floating in the sea; or from a structure on land constructed or adapted wholly or mainly for the purpose of depositing solids in the sea.[538] The licensing scheme also applies to similar deposits made anywhere in the world from a British vessel, aircraft, hovercraft or marine structure; or from a container floating in the sea if the deposit is controlled from a British vessel etc.[539] 'UK waters' are defined as any part of the sea within the seaward limits of UK territorial waters,[540] while 'UK controlled waters' bears its usual meaning in the context of marine environmental affairs.[541] Also, 'the sea' includes any area submerged at mean high water springs and the waters of any river or estuary that are subject to tidal flows at mean high water springs.[542] The licensing scheme also extends to a range of preparatory activities leading to dumping of waste at sea, such as loading.[543]

Along with dumping and loading of waste, a licence is also required for the disposal of substances or articles by incineration at sea. 'Incineration' here means any combustion of substances and materials for the purpose of their thermal destruction.[544] This definition is similar to that contained in the 1992 OSPAR Convention which bans incineration but then specifically exempts from the definition of incineration anything incidental to, or derived from the normal operation of vessels, aircraft or offshore installations.[545] Licensing requirements apply to the incineration of substances or articles on a vessel or marine structure where this takes place in UK waters or UK controlled waters; or anywhere at sea if the incineration takes place on a British vessel or marine structure.[546] Similarly, the licensing requirement extends to certain preparatory activities prior to incineration, so that a licence is needed for the loading of

---

[537] Defined as having the same meaning as 'ship' in the Merchant Shipping Act 1995, see s.24(1) 1985 Act.

[538] s.5(a) Food and Environment Protection Act 1985.

[539] *Ibid* s.5(b).

[540] On 'territorial waters' see 18.7.1 above.

[541] s.24(1) Food and Environment Protection Act 1985. On the meaning of 'UK controlled waters' see 18.10.1 above.

[542] s.24(1) Food and Environment Protection Act 1985.

[543] *Ibid* s.5(f) and (g), referring to s.5(a) above.

[544] *Ibid* s.6(2).

[545] Art.1(h) and (i) and Art.2 Annex II 1992 OSPAR Convention.

[546] s.6(1)(a) Food and Environment Protection Act 1985.

a vessel or marine structure in the UK or UK waters with articles for incineration anywhere at sea.[547]

The purposeful sinking of ships at sea, known as 'scuttling', is also brought within licensing requirements. A licence is required for the scuttling of vessels in UK waters or UK controlled waters, or anywhere at sea if the activity is controlled from a British vessel etc.[548] As with sea dumping the licensing requirement imposed on scuttling of vessels also extends to certain preliminary activities, so that a licence will be required for the towing or propelling from the UK or UK waters of a vessel for scuttling anywhere at sea.[549] As noted above, vessels or aircraft may not be dumped in the maritime area of the OSPAR Convention beyond 2004.[550]

There are various exceptions to the above provisions. That is, the licensing authority may, by order, specify operations which do not need a licence, or which do not need a licence providing they satisfy conditions specified by the order.[551] The conditions that may be specified may include conditions requiring the approval of the licensing authority to be obtained as a prerequisite to taking the benefit of the exemption.[552] In circumstances where the approval of a licensing authority must be obtained, the approval may be with or without the imposition of such conditions as the licensing authority considers appropriate.[553] A detailed series of exemptions have been provided for by order, which has been amended so as to comply with the EC Waste Framework Directive.[554] The kinds of activities which are exempt are activities such as the deposit from a vessel of sewage or domestic garbage originating on the vessel, and the incidental deposit of fishing gear and equipment used in aquaculture otherwise than for the purpose of disposal.

### 19.20.2 Authorisation of Licences

Primary responsibility for Part II of the 1985 Act lies, in England, with the Minister of Agriculture, Fisheries and Food and, in Wales, with the National Assembly[555] and either of these (referred to below and in the Act as 'the Ministers') may authorise any person to enforce Part II of the Act.[556] Concerning the issue of licences, the administration and enforcement of Part II of the Act lies with the 'licensing authority', which means whichever of the Ministers is responsible for fisheries in the area

---

[547] *Ibid* s.6(1)(b).
[548] *Ibid* s.5(e).
[549] *Ibid* s.5(h).
[550] See 19.19.4 above.
[551] s.7(1) Food and Environment Protection Act 1985.
[552] *Ibid* s.7(2).
[553] *Ibid* s.7(3).
[554] The Deposits in the Sea (Exemptions) Order 1985 (SI 1985 No.1699). On the Waste Framework Directive see 19.20 above.
[555] Generally on the division of responsibilities see 6.2 above.
[556] s.11(1) Food and Environment Protection Act 1985.

where the operation in question would be carried out or commenced.[557] It is notable that it is the fisheries Ministers, not environmental Ministers, that are the principal licensing authority for activities of this kind.

The licensing authority is required to give consideration to a number of matters in determining whether to issue a licence.[558] These include the need to protect the marine environment, the living resources which it supports and human health and to prevent interference with legitimate uses of the sea. Any other relevant matters may also be considered.[559] In addition, regard must be had to the practical availability of any alternative methods of dealing with the disposal of the substances or articles concerned,[560] and to obligations arising under the Waste Framework Directive. [561]

In issuing a licence the authority must include such provisions in the licence as appear necessary or expedient to it to protect the marine environment, the living resources which it supports and human health, and to prevent interference with legitimate uses of the sea, and may add such other provisions as are considered appropriate.[562] Insofar as the waste to be dumped is 'Directive waste', a licence must also cover the type and quantities of waste involved, the technical requirements, the security precautions to be taken, and disposal site and any treatment methods.[563] In addition, the authority may include provisions requiring that further consent is required to permit specific operations under the licence. Where the licence permits the loading of a vessel for dumping or incineration, or the movement of a vessel for scuttling,[564] a condition governing the place of the dumping, incineration or scuttling can be stipulated, whether in UK waters or not.[565] In addition, automatic recording equipment may be used to record such information relating to operations as may be specified, ensuring that operations take place at specified sites.[566]

When an applicant seeks a licence the authority may require the supply of information, or the conduct of examinations or tests, which are necessary or expedient to enable the authority to decide whether a licence should be issued and the provisions a licence should contain.[567] A reasonable fee may be payable for processing the application, making any necessary tests, and towards supervising the operation of the licence, the fees payable

---

[557] *Ibid* s.24(1).
[558] *Ibid* s.8. Provisions relating to the rights of applicants to make certain representations with regard to the issue of a licence or its terms are set out in Schedule 3 to the Act.
[559] *Ibid* s.8(1).
[560] *Ibid* s.8(2).
[561] paras.4 and 5 Sch.4 SI 1994 No.1056, see 19.20 above.
[562] s.8(3) Food and Environment Protection Act 1985.
[563] para.6 Sch.4 SI 1994 No.1056. See 19.20 above.
[564] Under ss.5(f) and (h) and 6(1)(b) Food and Environment Protection Act 1985.
[565] *Ibid* s.8(4).
[566] *Ibid* s.8(4)(a).
[567] *Ibid* s.8(5).

being determined after consultation with representative organisations of applicants.[568]

The licensing authority may vary or revoke a licence if it appears that there has been a breach of any of its provisions. More generally, the authority may also vary or revoke a licence where there has been a change in circumstances relating to the marine environment, the living resources which it supports, or human health, or because of increased scientific knowledge relating to any of those matters, or for any other reason that appears to the authority to be relevant.[569] Applicants are entitled to know the reasons for such decisions, and may appeal against them, as they may do against any refusal to grant a licence or against unfavourable licence conditions.[570] Variation and revocation to comply with the EC Habitats Directive will also be required.[571]

### 19.20.3 Information Provisions

The licensing authority must keep public registers of information relating to dumping licences.[572] Such registers must contain a wide range of prescribed particulars relating to licences, including applications, licences issued, variations and revocations, information supplied under a licence, and any remedial action taken.[573] The exact extent of the information to be placed on the register is contained in the Deposits in the Sea (Public Registers of Information) Regulations 1996.[574] Provision is made for withholding information from the register on the grounds of national security or commercial confidentiality. The registers, which in practice are held at the Ministry of Agriculture, Fisheries and Food in London, must be kept available for public inspection, free of charge, at reasonable hours, and copies of entries in the register must be made on payment of a reasonable charge. The licensing authority must also make copies of any offshore waste management plan available to the public on payment of reasonable charges.[575]

### 19.20.4 Licensing Offences

The licensing system governing sea dumping is supported by a number of criminal offences. The main offence is of conducting an operation for which a licence is needed otherwise than in pursuance of a licence and in accordance with its provisions, or causing or permitting another person to

---

[568] *Ibid* s.8(7) to (9).

[569] *Ibid* s.8(10) and (11).

[570] *Ibid* paras.1-4 Sch.3.

[571] Under Reg.50 Conservation (Natural Habitats etc.) Regulations 1994 (SI 1994 No.2716) as amended, and see 15.8 and 15.8.3 above.

[572] On public registers generally see 16.15 above.

[573] s.14(1) Food and Environment Protection Act 1985 as substituted by s.147 Environmental Protection Act 1990.

[574] SI 1996 No.1427.

[575] para.5 Sch.4 SI 1994 No.1056.

do so.[576] A person found guilty of this offence is liable, on summary conviction, to a fine of up to £50,000, or on indictment to a fine or to imprisonment for up to two years or both.[577] Other offences, punishable by lesser fines, relate to making false statements or withholding information[578] and obstructing enforcement officers.[579] Certain company officers and members of bodies corporate may be liable for the acts of their company.[580] An offence is also committed where there is contravention of the registration requirements introduced by the Waste Management Licensing Regulations 1994.[581]

It will be a defence to the main offence of violating licensing obligations to prove that the alleged illegal operation was undertaken to secure the safety of a vessel or to preserve life, and that reasonable steps were taken to inform the appropriate Minister of the operation, the locality and circumstances in which it took place, and any substances or articles concerned.[582] It must also be shown that the operation was necessary and a reasonable step to take in the circumstances, and not due to the fault of the person relying on the defence.[583] It is also a defence, in relation to any of the offences which may arise outside UK waters or UK controlled waters, [584] to show that the operation is sanctioned by the law of another party to either the London or OSPAR Conventions though otherwise contrary to the licensing requirements of the United Kingdom.[585] There is also a general defence applying to any proceedings for an offence under the Act where the person charged can show that they took all reasonable precautions and exercised all due diligence to avoid committing the offence. However, this defence can generally be relied on only where notice has first been served on the prosecution, thus preventing the undue introduction of the defence at the last moment.[586]

### 19.20.5 Enforcing Licensing Requirements

The enforcement of Part II of the 1985 Act is a matter for the licensing authorities, which in practice act through appointed Inspectors[587] with various powers of entry.[588] Inspectors may also require information, stop

---

[576] Under s.9(1) Food and Environment Protection Act 1985.

[577] *Ibid* s.21(2A), added by s.146(6) Environment Protection Act 1990.

[578] *Ibid* s.9(2) and s.21(3) and (4).

[579] *Ibid* s.21(5).

[580] *Ibid* s.21(6) and (7). See also 9.20 above on individual liability in relation to the principal water pollution offences under the Water Resources Act 1991.

[581] SI 1994 No.1056, adding Art.5(1) and (5) SI 1985 No.1699.

[582] s.9(3) Food and Environment Protection Act 1985.

[583] *Ibid* s.9(4).

[584] *Ibid* ss.5(b), 5(e)(ii) or 6(1)(a)(ii).

[585] *Ibid* s.9(5)-(7).

[586] *Ibid* s.22. Contrast the absence of a 'due diligence' defence in relation to the principal water pollution offences under s.85 Water Resources Act 1991, discussed at 9.6.4 above.

[587] *Ibid* s.11(1) and s.24(1), amended by the Scotland Act 1998 (Modification of Functions) Order 1998 (SI 1998 No.1756). Details of the powers of persons authorised to act under Part II of the Act are set out in Sch.2 to the 1985 Act.

[588] *Ibid* s.11(2)–(3).

and detain vessels or order them into port, open containers, take samples and require the production of documents. In dealing with Directive waste, inspectors will also have the powers of Environment Agency inspectors.[589]

The 1985 Act also provides for enforcement notice procedures.[590] These allow a licensing authority to carry out any operation which appears to be necessary or expedient to protect the marine environment, the living resources it supports and human health, or to prevent interference with legitimate use of the sea, where anything appears to have been done otherwise than in pursuance of a licence and in accordance with its provisions. Reasonable expenses may be recovered from any person convicted of an offence which necessitated such enforcement action.[591]

## 19.21 Petroleum Act 1998

While Part II of the Food and Environment Protection Act 1985 governs sea dumping generally, separate provision is made in relation to the abandonment of offshore installations and submarine pipelines out to the limit of the continental shelf.[592] Thus, Part IV of the Petroleum Act 1998, which came into force on 15 February 1999,[593] empowers the Secretary of State,[594] by notice, to require the submission of a programme setting out the measures proposed to be taken in connection with the abandonment of an offshore installation,[595] known as an 'abandonment programme'.[596]

An abandonment programme must contain:

   (a) an estimate of the cost of the measures proposed in it;
   (b) either the times at or within which the measures proposed in it are to be taken, or state how those times are to be determined; and
   (c) if it proposes that an installation or pipeline will be left in position or not wholly removed, must include provision as to any continuing maintenance that may be necessary.[597]

It is not an offence to fail to submit an abandonment programme. However, if this occurs then the Secretary of State may himself prepare a

---

[589] Under s.108 Environment Act 1995; see para.13 Sch.4 SI 1994 No.1056 as amended by Sch.2 SI 1996 No.593. On Directive waste see 19.20 above and 12.2.3 above. On powers of Environment Agency officers see 6.17 above.

[590] See also 10.11.1 above on enforcement notices under the Water Resources Act 1991.

[591] s.10(1) and (2) Food and Environment Protection Act 1985.

[592] Operational discharges from mineral exploration, and all discharges from pipe-lines, are outside the scope of this work, which does not therefore consider the placing of installations. On the limit of the continental shelf see 18.7.1 above.

[593] Petroleum Act 1998 (Commencement No.1) Order 1999 (SI 1999 No.161), made under s.52 Petroleum Act 1998.

[594] That is, the Secretary of State for Trade and Industry.

[595] As defined in s.44 Petroleum Act 1998.

[596] *Ibid* s.29(1). For an overview of the procedures in practice see Department of Trade and Industry *Guidance Notes for Industry Decommissioning of Offshore Installations and Pipelines under the Petroleum Act 1998*, Consultative Document, (1999), paras 3.1-3.10.

[597] *Ibid* s.29(4).

binding programme and it will be an offence not to comply with a request for information made by the Secretary of State in preparing a programme, who may also recover any costs reasonably incurred.[598] There is therefore little incentive for persons served with notices, which in practice will be licensees and operators, not to prepare them.

Where a decommissioning programme is approved, or made, by the Secretary of State, it is the joint and several duty of the persons on whom the notice is binding to ensure that it is carried out. The Secretary of State must also satisfy himself that any person subject to this duty will be capable of discharging it, and where he is not so satisfied, require that person, by notice, to take such action as may be specified. In the event of failure by those given notice to submit a programme or secure that it is carried out, the Secretary of State may undertake the work at his own expense and recover the cost from those given notice.[599]

A notice requiring an abandonment programme may require the person to whom it is given to carry out such consultations as may be specified in the notice before submitting the programme.[600] It is notable that this provision is framed as a *power* to require consultation rather than a *duty* to do so, and that the bodies to be consulted can be determined on a case-by-case basis by the Secretary of State. In practice, however, a range of bodies, including statutory nature conservation agencies and bodies representative of marine fisheries interests, are normally consulted.[601] In addition, the operator will be required to place a public notice in appropriate national and local newspapers and journals and to place details on the internet. The notice should indicate where copies of the draft decommissioning programme can be viewed and to whom representations should be submitted. Hard copies of the draft programme should be made available at the operator's offices, while a copy may be placed on the Internet.[602] However, the consultation provisions will need to be extended significantly, and include consultation between the UK Government and other contracting parties, where the deposit falls within OSPAR Decision 98/3 and a derogation from the general principle of complete removal is pursued.[603]

Finally, it should be noted that the Secretary of State[604] may make Regulations relating to the abandonment of offshore installations. Such Regulations, which may provide for criminal offences for their contravention, may amongst other things:

---

[598] *Ibid* s.33(1)-(4).

[599] *Ibid* ss.36 and 37.

[600] *Ibid* s.29(3).

[601] Department of Trade and Industry *Guidance Notes for Industry Decommissioning of Offshore Installations and Pipelines under the Petroleum Act 1998*, Consultative Document, (1999), para. 6.17 and Annex F.

[602] *Ibid* para. 6.18.

[603] On OSPAR Decision 98/3 see 19.19.4F above.

[604] After consultation with the National Assembly for Wales, see Art.5 and Sch.2 SI 1999 No.672.

(a) prescribe standards for the dismantling, removal and disposal of installations;

(b) prescribe standards in respect of anything left in the water;

(c) make provision for the prevention of pollution; and

(d) make provision for inspection and the payment of fees.[605]

No such Regulations have yet been enacted.[606]

By way of a general observation about the provisions of the Petroleum Act 1998, it is notable that the amount of discretion which the Act purportedly gives to the Secretary of State in relation to abandonment is in reality heavily circumscribed. OSPAR Decision 98/3 dramatically limits what may be left in the marine environment following the decommissioning of oil and gas installations, and EC waste and conservation legislation also confines and structures decision-making in this area.[607] The overall impact of these provisions, taken together with the application of abandonment programmes, is likely to be a complete phased removal of contaminating material following hydrocarbon exploration. In the meantime, however, the focus may shift towards closer legal scrutiny of the environmental impact in the wake of abandonment, such as the presence of contaminated drilling muds.[608]

---

[605] s.39 Petroleum Act 1998.

[606] But see Department of Trade and Industry, *Decommissioning of Offshore Installations and Pipelines under the Petroleum Act 1998* (August 1998), at www.og.dti.gov.uk

[607] Insofar as the Natura 2000 network extends to 200 nautical miles, see *R v Secretary of State for Trade and Industry ex parte Greenpeace Ltd* (No.2) [2000] Env LR 221, discussed at 15.8 above.

[608] See 19.19.4F above.

# Chapter 20

# RADIOACTIVE CONTAMINATION

## 20.1 Introduction

Regulating radioactivity in water presents a distinct set of concerns. Routine human exposure to radioactivity comes predominantly from natural sources such as radon gas and cosmic rays, with artificial emissions contributing only a relatively modest amount. More than 98 per cent of radioactivity in the North Sea is also of natural origin,[1] and most, if not all, water is contaminated by radioactivity, even if minutely. Moreover, deliberate exposure to radiation is now becoming a common means of treating sewage and other effluent, through ultra violet irradiation. Nevertheless, the distinctive hazards associated with radiation generated by human activity sets the regulation of the discharge or emission of such substances apart from other kinds of water contaminants, both in law and in the perception of the general public, justifying separate consideration.[2]

In setting standards, the law has taken into account public fears associated with radioactive substances, scientific uncertainty about acceptable levels of radioactivity in the environment, and the spread of radiation in the environment. It also reflects the distinctive character of radioactive substances and the risks associated with their emission into the environment: there is no absolutely safe level of exposure and no guarantee that detriment will or will not occur, only a *probability* of detriment occurring which is assumed to be proportional to the degree and duration of exposure. Indeed, such was the nature of the uncertainty surrounding radioactive discharges to water that, at least in the early years of the civil nuclear power programme, environmental discharges were made simply for observational purposes. Standards for radioactive contamination and categories for radioactive waste are therefore uniquely formulated, programmes for waste management are more stringent than for other hazardous substances, and permitted disposal methods are more strictly circumscribed. Such is the strictness of this legal regime that it is preferable to refer to controls on the radioactive contamination of water, rather than radioactive 'pollution', since radioactively contaminated water may remain of sufficient quality to be used for most purposes.[3]

While the separate legislative treatment of radioactive contamination of the environment does not generally distinguish between impacts upon water

---

[1] Leatherland (1990) p.61.

[2] Generally see Royal Commission on Environmental Pollution (1976) Ch.II. General reading on radioactive waste management, including the contamination of water, includes Berkhaut (1991), Kemp (1992) and OECD (1996). General reading on the relevant law includes Hughes (1996) Ch.9D, Freshfields (1996, updated) s.2R-20 and Tromans and FitzGerald (1997).

[3] See generally Ch.1 above on natural water quality.

and other media, as a part of the law of radioactive contamination of the environment, radioactive contamination of water is segregated from the general law of water pollution and water quality. Principally the law is contained in the Radioactive Substances Act 1993 and the Nuclear Installations Act 1965. Although both statutes deal with licensing matters, the former is exclusively concerned with potential criminal responsibility whereas the latter also deals with civil liabilities. This chapter discusses some of the distinctive policy and administrative features of radioactive contamination, with special reference to the effects of radioactive discharges on the aquatic environment. In particular, it outlines pertinent aspects of the two main enactments, set against a background of international, European and European Community law and policy.

## 20.2 Sources of Radioactivity in the Water Environment

Radioactivity in the water environment arises from a number of different sources. Principal amongst these are natural sources, in particular cosmic radiation. Sea water and, to a lesser extent, freshwater, is naturally radioactive. But artificial sources also contribute to radioactivity levels, albeit at very low levels. These come mainly from the civil nuclear fuel cycle and related operations, principally from nuclear power generation and nuclear fuel reprocessing, from hospitals, medical and veterinary research centres, and from the UK Atomic Energy Authority (UKAEA), university and other research centres. However, the average annual dose to humans attributable to discharges is of the order of 0.0004mSv, which amounts to less than 0.1% of total exposure, although certain individuals may be exposed to higher levels if they are in 'critical exposure groups'.[4] This basic exposure level is of the order of 20 times lower than exposure arising from atmospheric fallout, most of which is attributable to the atmospheric testing of nuclear weapons prior to 1963.

Discharges from Sellafield are the main source of artificial radioactivity in the marine environment around the UK.[5] Both authorised and actual discharge levels from Sellafield have declined markedly since the early 1970s and, excluding tritium, now stand at around 1% of peak levels.[6] In addition, radiation doses from these discharges to those most exposed have decreased from a peak of about twice the national UK average natural background dose to around one-tenth of this dose.[7] There have, however, recently been concerns raised about discharges of technetium-99 and other radionuclides, which have been discharged in greatly increased quantities since 1994. The reason for this increase, raising the allowable limit of technetium-99 discharged from Sellafield from 10TBq/year to 200TBq/year,[8] was to enable a new waste treatment plant (the Enhanced Actinide Removal Plant (EARP)) to come into operation. The EARP was

---

[4] On 'critical groups' see 20.7.1 below.

[5] MAFF and SEPA, *Radioactivity in Food and the Environment, 1998 (RIFE-4)* (1999).

[6] Clark (1997) p.102.

[7] MAFF and SEPA, *Radioactivity in Food and the Environment, 1998 (RIFE-4)* (1999).

[8] TBq is terabecquerel, being 1 million million ($10^{12}$) becquerels.

to deal with future arisings of liquid waste from the Magnox reprocessing plant but, more importantly, with a large stock of this waste stored on the site following the decision in the mid 1980s to cease their untreated discharge into the Irish Sea. The authorised discharges led to dramatic increases in radioactive contamination of shellfish in the Irish Sea to levels far in excess of the safe level for radioactive contamination of food following a nuclear accident.[9] A determination on the authorisation of these discharges has recently been made.[10]

## 20.3 Categories of Radioactive Waste

The classification used for radioactive waste is the becquerel, i.e., one emission of a particle (one nuclear disintegration) per second, as the key unit of measurement. However, a becquerel is a measure of the amount of radioactivity, not its impact, and takes no account of the nature of a disintegration, only its frequency. For biological purposes a more relevant measurement is the radioactivity absorbed by a tissue or organism, which is measured by the gray (Gy).[11]

As a matter of policy, though not law, radioactive waste is often classified according to the character and amount of radioactivity emitted (in becquerels), and a fourfold classification ranging from high-level (or heat-generating) waste, through intermediate-level waste and down to low-level and very low-level waste, has traditionally been used.[12] While this classification may be relevant as a matter of solid waste management policy, however,[13] it should be stressed that it is of no direct legal relevance; nor is it of any practical relevance to aquatic discharges. Instead, the legislative framework makes no mention of differing categories of waste, and decision-making in practice is guided by the protection principles discussed below.[14]

## 20.4 Determining Standards for Ionising Radiation

Safety standards for exposure to ionising radiation are shaped by a range of advisory bodies at international, European and national level.

---

[9] See *ENDS Report* 262 (1996) pp.15-16 and *ENDS Report* 281 (1998) p.21. These standards are contained in Regulation 3954/87/Euratom, as subsequently amended.

[10] See 20.10.12 below.

[11] See generally Tromans and FitzGerald (1997) para.1-37 and Clark (1997) pp.98-99.

[12] *Review of Radioactive Waste Management Policy: Final Conclusions* (Cm.2919, 1995) para.53 (henceforth 'the 1995 White Paper'). See generally House of Commons Environment Committee, *Radioactive Waste* (1986) Vol. I para.14; Hughes (1996) p.418 and Tromans and FitzGerald (1997) paras.1-19 to 1-21.

[13] See, for example, the policy decision that all intermediate-level waste should be stored in a future deep underground depository.

[14] For example, the justification principle and dose constraints, see 20.7 below.

## 20.4.1  The International Commission on Radiological Protection

The international advisory body formulating basic radiation standards is the International Commission on Radiological Protection (ICRP). This body consists of scientists, chosen periodically by the International Congress of Radiology. The ICRP functions independently of any government, and is answerable for its determinations only to the International Congress of Radiology. The ICRP's recommended safety standards are used by all major countries, and by international and European institutions, as a scientific basis for legislative standards governing protection against the biological effects of such radiation.[15] These include dose limits for occupational, medical and public exposure (known as 'ICRP 60')[16] as well as maximum permissible concentrations of individual isotopes in air and water.[17] The general principles espoused by the ICRP for determining exposure levels[18] are also influential at European and national level.

## 20.4.2  International Atomic Energy Agency

The International Atomic Energy Agency (IAEA), a United Nations agency, promotes the peaceful uses of atomic energy. Its founding statute sets out various functions, including establishing and adopting standards of safety for the protection of health, and for minimising danger to life and property. These standards follow those established by the ICRP, but go beyond scientific advice in recommending various desirable regulatory practices. The standards and principles adopted by the IAEA, which include principles on exposure of humans and releases to the environment, and on radioactive waste management, are contained in documents published in a Safety Series.[19]

## 20.4.3  EURATOM

The 1957 Treaty establishing the European Atomic Energy Community, the Euratom Treaty, sets the Community objective of promoting the speedy establishment and growth of nuclear industries,[20] hence the emphasis of the Treaty is economic rather than environmental. Under the Euratom Treaty, however, the EC must set basic radiation standards to protect the health of workers and the general public in the Community.[21] These standards include maximum permissible doses of ionising radiation

---

[15] Royal Commission on Environmental Pollution (1976) para.201; Tromans and FitzGerald (1997) para.1-41.
[16] See especially the *1990 Recommendations of the International Commission on Radiological Protection* (ICRP 60).
[17] *Ibid* and see also Tromans and FitzGerald (1997) paras.1-37 and 1-39.
[18] See 20.7.1 below.
[19] See generally Tromans and FitzGerald (1997) para.1-43.
[20] Art.1 EURATOM Treaty 1957. The Treaty is due to expire in 2002, when it will be subsumed within the EC Treaty.
[21] *Ibid* Arts.2(b) and Ch.III.

and maximum permissible levels of exposure and contamination.[22] For the most part these standards, together with general principles, are based on ICRP 60.[23] The European Commission also has a role to play in giving opinions on whether individual plans are liable to result in radioactive contamination of another Member State's water.[24]

### 20.4.4 The OSPAR Commission

While the focus of EC controls are on human health, the body of most importance to the setting of environmental standards for ionising radiation regionally is the Commission of the OSPAR Convention.[25] The Commission is charged with securing the objective for radiation pollution agreed to by Ministers. The need to meet the standards now provided for under the Convention[26] is a central consideration in licensing. One notable feature of the OSPAR Commission is its work in developing environmental quality criteria for the protection of the marine environment from the adverse effects of radioactive substances, on which progress is to be reported by 2003.[27]

### 20.4.5 The National Radiological Protection Board

The United Kingdom's national advisory body on radioactive discharge standards is the National Radiological Protection Board (NRPB).[28] The Board has a specific duty of advising on the acceptability of the dose limits for ionising radiation, set by the ICRP, for application within the UK. In the past, the national advisory body has tended to accept the limits set by the ICRP as a satisfactory basis for controls. Similarly the Board has accepted that radioactive waste management practices should be conducted in accordance with dose limitations specified by the ICRP.

### 20.5 Further Bodies Involved in Radioactive Policy Formulation

While the above advisory bodies contribute to the formulation of technical standards, they also contribute significantly to the establishment of general principles that have both a strong policy dimension and, in some instances, legal force. At national level, policy formulation is a matter for Government, though the views of a range of further bodies are also important. In relation to environmental discharges these include:

---

[22] See now the EURATOM Basic Safety Standards Directive (96/29/Euratom), effective from 13 May 2000.
[23] See 20.4.1 above.
[24] Art.37 Euratom Treaty, see 20.6 below.
[25] On the OSPAR Convention generally see 18.8 above.
[26] See 20.6 and 20.7.3 below.
[27] s.4.2(c) OSPAR Convention.
[28] s.1(1) Radiological Protection Act 1970.

(a) The *Radioactive Waste Management Advisory Committee* (RWMAC), which advises Ministers on various technical and environmental implications of the management of civil radioactive waste; and

(b) The *Committee on Medical Aspects of Radiation in the Environment* (COMARE), appointed by the Chief Medical Officer, which assesses and advises Government on the health effects of natural and man-made radiation in the environment.

## 20.6 International and European Agreements

Radioactivity in the water environment is governed by two international conventions to which the UK is a party:[29]

(a) the 1972 London Convention on the Prevention of Marine Pollution by Dumping of Wastes and Other Materials, and its 1996 Protocol; and

(b) the 1992 OSPAR Convention on the Protection of the Marine Environment of the North-East Atlantic.

The 1972 London Convention now prohibits the dumping of all types of radioactive matter in the open sea.[30] A similar ban is also now contained in the 1992 OSPAR Convention.[31] Thus, while Part II of the Food and Environment Protection Act 1985 in theory provides a national system of licensing which could authorise radioactive waste dumping,[32] the practical position is that international obligations prevent any such licences being issued. Sea dumping of solid radioactive waste is discussed in more detail below.[33]

In addition, the 1992 OSPAR Convention also deals with radioactive discharges to the marine environment. Specifically, radioactive substances are placed into a separate category with the parties undertaking to adopt measures to forestall and, as appropriate, eliminate pollution and contamination by these substances. The OSPAR Strategy for Radioactive Substances, adopted under the Convention in 1998, provides for general environmental policy principles in relation to radioactive waste discharges, and this has been added to by further decisions (albeit not binding on the UK) which essentially call for the end of nuclear reprocessing. These are discussed further below.[34]

---

[29] See also the 1997 Joint Convention on the Safety of Spent Fuel Management and on the Safety of Radioactive Waste Management (Cm.4672) in force June 2001. Few provisions of this treaty apply to discharges.

[30] See 20.9 below and 19.19.2-3 above. The ban was effected by Resolution LC51(16) amending Annexes I and II of the Convention, which came into force in February 1994. See Tromans and FitzGerald (1997) para.5-14.

[31] See 20.9 below and 19.19.4 above.

[32] See 19.20 above.

[33] See 20.9 below.

[34] See 20.7.3 below on environmental policy principles.

European Community law also plays an important role in policy making and the setting of standards. In particular, the Euratom Basic Safety Standards Directive[35] gives binding legal force to the ICRP Recommendations on dose-exposure limits and general principles, and the latter have been successfully relied upon in the national courts in relation to the justification of individual radioactive installations.[36]

The Commission also issues opinions on whether individual plans are liable to result in radioactive contamination of water of another Member State of the EC. The use of 'contamination' here is notable; although not defined in Euratom, its usage emphasises that something stricter than 'pollution' prevention or reduction is at issue. The Commission may request the Member State concerned to supply any data relating to the disposal plan which will make it possible to determine whether implementing such a plan is liable to result in the radioactive contamination of the water, soil or air space of another Member State.[37] In particular, opinions may address matters such as discharge limits for aqueous waste under normal operations and accident situations, and pathways to critical groups via the receiving body of water,[38] and must be issued within six months of receipt of the plan. Also, plans must now be communicated to the Commission not less than six months before the planned date of commencement of disposal.[39] While an opinion is not legally binding, it must be sought before final authorisation, and the Member State must accord the opinion the most searching examination and consideration.[40] Although rare, there are instances where the Commission has advised that proposed discharge levels should be reduced in line with the principle that discharges be as low as reasonably achievable.[41] Several opinions have been given in relation to UK sites.[42]

Finally, the provisions of the EC Environmental Impact Assessment Directive may be relevant. This requires prior assessment of such installations as nuclear power stations and reprocessing plants, and also contains certain provisions relating to transboundary environmental assessment which give effect to the 1991 Espoo Convention.[43] The Directive requires certain procedures to be followed but does not, in contrast with the Basic Safety Standards Directive, stipulate any

---

[35] Directive 96/29/Euratom.

[36] See 20.10.6B below on the justification principle in litigation.

[37] Art.37 Euratom.

[38] See, e.g., the favourable Opinion issued by the Commission relating to the THORP nuclear reprocessing plant at Sellafield (92/269/Euratom, OJ L138, 21.5.92 p.36).

[39] Commission Recommendation (Euratom) 91/4, OJ L6, 9.1.91, p.16. On the problems caused previously see Woodliffe (1990).

[40] Case 187/87 *Saarland* v *Minister for Industry* [1988] ECR 5013; see further Lenaerts (1988).

[41] 87/170/Euratom, OJ L68, 12.3.87, p.33 (Heysham 2). On the 'ALARA' principle see 20.10.6C below.

[42] Most recently see Commission Opinion of 10 September 1997 concerning the plan for the disposal of radioactive waste, from the operation of the BNFL Sellafield Solvent Treatment Plant, OJ 1997, C291/9.

[43] Directive 85/337/EEC as amended by Directive 97/11/EC, see 14.6 above. See also the 1991 Convention on Environmental Impact Assessment in a Transboundary Context (Espoo).

substantive obligations. It might also be noted that the diffuse nature of radiation contamination militates against the use of Euratom[44] to prevent actual or perceived risks from radiation through individually initiated action,[45] since it may be difficult to argue that a decision under the Treaty or the Basic Safety Standards Directive is of direct and individual concern to such persons.

## 20.7 Radiological Protection Principles

The present position with respect to the respective weight to be given to the principles governing discharges and emissions of radioactive substances cannot be stated with any certainty. This is because there is a fundamental tension between, on the one hand, a set of principles formulated with regard to protecting *human health* and, on the other, the subsequent emergence of *environmental* protection principles. These environmental principles, which have emerged in particular through the OSPAR treaty regime, adopt a fundamentally different approach since they effectively aim for the lowest practicable amount of artificial ionising radiation in the environment. By contrast, the earlier policy approach evolved from worker safety in the nuclear industry and aimed to protect critical groups within safe limits. Also of relevance are more general radioactive waste management principles, which promote sustainable development and therefore combine health and environmental objectives.

As the House of Commons Select Committee on the Environment, Transport and the Regions Report into the Environment Agency put it:

> It appears that the Agency is working almost in a vacuum where regulatory principles are concerned, with the result that neither they, nor those whom they regulate, nor the general public, can be clear about what is required in this area.[46]

With this strong caveat in mind, the following sections examine the policy principles applying to each of the areas outlined above. It must be stressed that national policy guidance on radioactive substances currently dates back to 1982.[47] Since then, legislative change at national level must be taken into account along with international policy development in relation to health and the environment. Revised national guidance on radioactive discharges is anticipated.[48]

---

[44] Art.146 Euratom, equivalent to Art.230 EC.

[45] Case T-219/95R, *Danielsson and Others* v *EC Commission* [1995] ECR II-3051.

[46] House of Commons Select Committee on the Environment, Transport and the Regions, *The Environment Agency* (2000) para 71.

[47] DoE, *Radioactive Substances Act 1960: A Guide to the Administration of the Act* (1982).

[48] Postscript: see now DETR, *Draft statutory guidance on the regulation of radioactive discharges into the environment from nuclear licensed sites* (2000), discussed at *ENDS Report* 311 (2000) pp.44-45. 'Nuclear sites' here is not limited to sites regulated under the Nuclear Installations Act 1965, discussed at 20.11 below.

## 20.7.1 Health-Based Policy Principles

Following the advice of the international, European and national advisory bodies on ionising radiation the previous administration adopted a set of values for maximum levels of exposure for humans. These values are to be achieved by implementing a general program of radioactive waste management giving effect to certain radiological protection principles. The principles take account of ICRP 60 as well as advice from the NRPB,[49] and are set out in a 1995 White Paper.[50] These principles are also found in the Euratom Basic Safety Standards Directive.[51]

(a) *Justification*: no practice involving exposure to radiation should be adopted unless it produces sufficient benefit to the exposed individuals or to society to offset the radiation detriment it causes.[52]

(b) *Optimisation of protection*: in relation to any particular source within a practice, the magnitude of individual doses, the number of people exposed and the likelihood of incurring exposures where these are not certain should all be kept as low as reasonably achievable (the ALARA principle), taking economic and social factors into account. In order to limit unfairness or inconsistency which might result from applying inherent economic and social judgements on a case by case basis, the procedure is constrained by restrictions on dose to individuals or on risks to individuals in the case of potential exposures.

(c) *Individual dose and risk limits*: the exposure of individuals resulting from the combination of all the relevant practices should be subject to dose limits, or to some control of risk in the case of potential exposures. These should ensure that no individual is exposed to radiation risks judged unacceptable in any normal circumstances. Since not all sources are susceptible to control by action at source, it is necessary to specify those sources that are relevant before selecting a dose limit.[53]

The central difference between these principles and those relied upon previously are the new concepts of dose and risk constraints. In particular, the principles make clear that different considerations should apply to releases of radioactive waste into the air or into water, where some level of public exposure to radiation is bound to occur, and to the storage or disposal of solid waste, where exposure is less likely. In the former case, as discussed below estimates of radiation dose will be used in setting limit standards, while in the latter the degree of risk involved, and risk assessment and management practices, will be central.[54] By employing both the optimisation and limitation principles, policy aims at a 'belt and

---

[49] See NRPB, *Board Statement on the 1990 Recommendations of the ICRP* (1993).

[50] The 1995 White Paper.

[51] Directive 96/29/Euratom, and see 20.4.3 and 20.6 above.

[52] On the application of the justification principle see 20.10.6B below.

[53] The 1995 White Paper, para.56.

[54] *Ibid* para.57.

braces' precautionary approach, where dose (or risk) limits may be lower than that deemed strictly necessary for public safety, if meeting such a standard is reasonably achievable. However, as formulated, the justification principle is not intended to require assessment of whether any activity generating radioactive waste is 'the best of all the available options'[55] and the view of the Commission appears to be that it is intended only to require that no 'frivolous applications' are permitted.[56]

The 1995 White Paper also contains more specific policies in respect of the discharge of liquid and air-borne radioactive waste which are particularly pertinent in the context of the aquatic environment, showing how standards are set in relation to radioactive water contamination. Insofar as these specify dose limits, they follow the standards recommended in ICRP 60 and also contained in the Euratom Basic Safety Standards Directive, and the optimisation and individual dose and risk principles. They establish an optimisation dose threshold, two dose constraints and one maximum dose limit on the annual radiation exposure of a member of the public arising from discharges of radioactivity to the environment:

(a) A *threshold of optimisation* of 0.02mSv[57] per year below which the regulators should not seek to secure further reductions in the exposure of members of the public provided that they are satisfied that the operator is using best practicable means to limit discharges. This level is set with reference to the frequently used standard of an annual risk of death of one in a million or less,[58] though erring on the side of caution. The strictness of standards adopted nationally can be traced back to criticisms made by the Black Committee of the extent to which discharge authorisation procedures lacked a health input.[59]

(b) A *source constraint* of 0.3mSv per year on the annual dose resulting from current and prospective radioactive waste disposal and direct radiation (combined) from a single new source. This is 'a facility, or group of facilities, which can be optimised as an integral whole in terms of radioactive waste disposals'.

(c) A *site constraint* of 0.5mSv per year on the aggregate annual dose resulting from current and prospective radioactive waste disposal. This is from all sources with contiguous boundaries at a single location, and is intended to provide reassurance that standards were not being relaxed as a result of the restructuring of the nuclear industry; and

(d) A *limit* of 1mSv per year on the *total annual dose* from all artificial sources, including doses resulting from current

---

[55] ICRP (1991) para.112; see further Miller (1996a).

[56] Kaiser and Janssens (1998).

[57] Millisievert (one thousandth of a Sievert) per year. A Sievert is a measure of radiation dose to a person.

[58] HSE (1992); see also Royal Society (1992).

[59] *Investigation of the Possible Increased Incidence of Cancer in West Cumbria* (HMSO, 1984).

discharges, historical discharges[60] and direct radiation, and also other artificial sources of exposure (but not medical discharges). [61]

The Environment Agency is under Ministerial Direction to ensure that the total annual dose limit, and the source and site constraints, are adhered to, in relation to the maximum exposure of any member of the public, and of the population as a whole.[62] This Direction also requires the Agency to make 'realistic' assessments of doses to reference groups, as required by the Basic Safety Standards Directive.[63] The Agency is not specifically directed in relation to any threshold of optimisation, nor has it been considered necessary to permit the averaging of exposures over a five year period, as the Basic Safety Standards Directive allows.

In practice, applying these dose limits in determining applications for individual discharge consents for liquid radioactive waste involves ascertaining the connection between the discharge of a particular radioisotope at a certain rate and the radiation dose thereby received by the most exposed member of the public, or by an average member of a 'critical group'. This process has to take account of the various possible environmental 'pathways'[64] by which humans become exposed to ionising radiation and the ways in which these pathways can be expected to change with time. This critical path approach is illustrated in the recent consultation by the Environment Agency on discharges to air and to the River Thames at Pangbourne from the Atomic Weapons Establishment at Aldermaston. The Atomic Weapons Establishment calculated that the members of the public who might potentially receive the greatest exposure from liquid discharges from the site would be those who might swim in, and eat locally caught fish and drink water from, the Thames at Pangbourne. Those most exposed to airborne discharges also included those who would drink water from nearby streams.[65] Although standards may be set with reference to human health, as the example illustrates cumulative effects will be taken into account so that the exposure levels to, e.g., edible fishlife will be well below tolerable levels for humans, even for bottom-feeding species which may accumulate the highest levels of radionuclides from sediment. Partly as a result of concerns raised by RWMAC about inconsistent sets of dose calculations used as between operators, the Environment Agency and MAFF (now, here, the Food Standards Agency), the Environment Agency is presently engaged with its

---

[60] I.e., past man-made discharges. It appears that no account is to be taken of naturally occurring radiation.

[61] The 1995 White Paper, paras 63-73. Legal dose limits are set under the Basic Safety Standards Directive and implemented through the Ionising Radiations Regulations 1999 (SI 1999 No.3232). This is reinforced by The Radioactive Substances (Basic Safety Standards) (England and Wales) Direction 2000.

[62] The Radioactive Substances (Basic Safety Standards) (England and Wales) Direction 2000.

[63] *Ibid* and Art.45, Directive 96/29/Euratom.

[64] On environmental pathways see 1.3.3 above.

[65] Environment Agency, *Radioactive Substances Act 1993. Consultation Document on Application by AWE plc for Authorisation to Dispose of Radioactive Wastes from the Atomic Weapons Establishments at Aldermaston and Burghfield* (1999) p.37. A more precautionary methodology is used by MAFF (at p.39).

counterparts in Scotland and Northern Ireland in producing guidance on assessment methods for calculating doses.[66]

### 20.7.2 Radioactive Waste Management Policy Principles

Although recent changes to the radiological protection principles have been relatively minor, there have been significant changes made at national level to the policy aims of radioactive waste management. Broadly, the 1995 White Paper brings radioactive waste management policy into line with national environmental policy more generally. In particular, the guiding principle is stated to be sustainable development, and emphasis is given to the supporting principles of 'sound science'; precautionary action; the need to consider ecological impacts, particularly where resources are non-renewable or effects may be irreversible; and to the polluter pays principle.[67]

More specifically, radioactive waste should be managed and disposed of in ways which protect the public, workforce and the environment. In reducing risks beyond an acceptable level, economic considerations and comparative risks in other sectors will be relevant. Within this approach, the policy commitment is to seek to maintain and develop a policy and regulatory framework to ensure that radioactive wastes are not unnecessarily created. But such wastes as are created will be managed and treated safely and appropriately, and then safely disposed of at appropriate times and in appropriate ways. The overall policy objective is to safeguard the interests of existing and future generations and the wider environment in a manner that commands public confidence and takes due account of costs.

The task of ensuring that this basic framework is properly implemented falls, in England and Wales, to the Environment Agency. As noted elsewhere, in exercising its functions, the Agency must have regard to ministerial guidance on contributing to the achievement of sustainable development. This guidance directs the Agency to exercise its functions in accordance with the 1995 White Paper, including the radiological protection principles discussed above.[68] This guidance, though, will change with revisions to central government policy on sustainable development generally.[69]

---

[66] Environment Agency, SEPA and DoE(NI), *Radioactive Substances Regulation: Discharges of Radioactive Waste to the Environment, Principles for the Assessment of Public Doses. Consultation Document* (September 2000).

[67] The 1995 White Paper, para.50, citing *Sustainable Development: the UK Strategy* (Cm 2426, 1994). On sustainable development more generally, see 4.4.1 and 6.7 above. See also 4.7.1 above on the precautionary principle and 4.7.3 above on the polluter pays principle.

[68] See generally 6.7 above.

[69] See HM Government, *A Better Quality of Life* (1999) and see 6.7 above.

In a spirit of 'shared responsibility',[70] however, the 1995 White Paper also states that producers and owners of radioactive waste are responsibility for the development of waste management strategies,[71] following appropriate consultation with Government and regulators. In line with the polluter pays principle, producers and owners of waste are responsible for bearing the costs of managing and disposing of the waste, including the costs of regulation, and for ensuring that adequate financial provision is made in advance to cover any potential liabilities.

### 20.7.3 Environmental Protection Policy Principles

Clearly the 1995 White Paper no longer represents current policy. While there has been a change of administration, the most significant development has been the coming into force of the 1992 OSPAR Convention under which radioactive waste management policy is evolving at pace.[72] This evolution also calls into question some of the health-based standards, insofar as stricter standards may need to be imposed in order to comply with the OSPAR Convention.

The OSPAR Strategy for Radioactive Substances, adopted under the Convention in 1998, provides that radioactive contamination is to be prevented with the ultimate aim of achieving, by 2020, concentrations in the environment near background values for naturally occurring radioactive substances and close to zero for artificial radioactive substances. In doing so, interim targets are set, and the following factors must, amongst others, be taken into account: the legitimate uses of the sea, technical feasibility and radiological impacts on man and biota. Historic levels may also be taken into account. Any measures adopted must involve application of the guiding principles of the Convention, that is the precautionary and polluter pays principles.[73] However, other factors will be taken into account, including the recommendations of other appropriate international organisations and agencies and any other obligations of the parties under international law.[74] As yet there are no agreed definitions of the central terms 'historic levels' and 'close to zero'.[75] It must be assumed that what amounts to 'close' to zero is to be determined according to costs and benefits, to ensure that disproportionate costs are not spent making

---

[70] See 5.2 above on shared responsibility, a central theme of the EC's Fifth Environment Action Programme.

[71] Although in relation to reprocessing see *ENDS Report* 281 (1998) p.22.

[72] See the House of Commons Select Committee on the Environment, Transport and the Regions, *The Environment Agency* (2000) para.67.

[73] Art.2(2) OSPAR Convention.

[74] *OSPAR Strategy with regard to Radioactive Substances* (1998-17). Specifically cited are recommendations of the ICRP, the Safety Series of the IAEA, the EURATOM Basic Safety Standards Directive and the Joint Convention on the Safety of Spent Fuel Management and the Safety of Radioactive Waste. See also *OSPAR Action Plan 1998-2003 (Update 1999)* section 4.

[75] For the current UK view, see DETR, Department of the Environment Northern Ireland, National Assembly for Wales and Scottish Executive, *UK Strategy for Radioactive Discharges 2001 – 2020, Consultation Document* (2000).

reduction which cannot ultimately be justified, since the assessment of costs and benefits is relevant to the taking of a precautionary approach.[76]

Clearly, what is envisaged is an approach aimed at limiting radioactive 'contamination' rather than 'pollution' prevention, as these terms have been previously contrasted.[77] In this context, it is notable that organisms such as fish and crustacea are generally thought to be much less radiosensitive than humans. The position has been summed up thus:

> Existing levels of radiation in the sea have so far produced no measurable environmental impact on marine organisms or ecosystems. That is not to say that there are no particularly sensitive organisms or ecosystems that might be adversely affected, but it will evidently require detailed investigations to expose them.[78]

Nevertheless, partly because of uncertainties about the general ecological consequences of radiological discharges, the OSPAR strategy takes an overtly precautionary approach. This can be justified because, though exposure of human populations may be low due to remoteness from a source or lack of a radionuclide pathway, exposure of other biota may be greater. Apart from the standards set out in the 1995 White Paper, therefore, consideration must be given to the mechanisms by which the standards agreed under the OSPAR Convention are to be realised.[79]

At its June 2000 meeting, the parties to the OSPAR Convention decided

> that the current authorisations for discharges or releases of radioactive substances from nuclear reprocessing facilities shall be reviewed as a matter of priority by their competent national authorities, with a view to, inter alia, implementing the non-reprocessing option (for example dry storage) for spent nuclear fuel management at appropriate facilities.[80]

Although the decision received the three-quarters support needed to come into effect from 2001, neither the UK nor France supported it, with the effect that it is not binding on them.[81] Commitments agreed to under the OSPAR Convention are given effect in the UK by means of the licensing decisions for discharges of nuclear matter provided for under the Radioactive Substances Act 1993, discussed below.[82]

---

[76] The meaning of 'close to zero' and 'historic levels' is to be considered in 2001, see *ENDS Report* 306 (2000) p.44.

[77] See 1.3 above.

[78] Clark (1997) p.108.

[79] See 20.6 above and 20.10.12 below.

[80] OSPAR Decision 2000/1 on Substantial Reductions and Elimination of Discharges, Emissions and Losses of Radioactive Substances, with Special Emphasis on Nuclear Reprocessing, at www.ospar.org.

[81] Art.13(1) and (2) OSPAR Convention, see 18.8.4 above.

[82] See 20.10 below.

### 20.8 Storage and Disposal

Only two alternative strategies are utilised in the management of radioactive waste: storage and 'disposal'. Currently all high and intermediate level waste (and some low-level waste inappropriate for disposal) is stored.[83] Only low and very low-level wastes are currently disposed of. In the case of solid waste, disposal involves putting waste in a facility with no intention to retrieve it at a later time, e.g. landfilling (referred to as 'controlled burial'). But 'disposal' also refers to releases of airborne or liquid wastes to the environment.[84]

A different way of classifying radioactive waste management options is to distinguish between 'containment' strategies, referring both to the storage and contained disposal of waste, and 'dilute and disperse' approaches where waste is released to air or to water. It has been suggested that, for institutional reasons, '[t]he division between 'accumulations of solid wastes' and 'discharges of liquid and gaseous wastes' underpins [radioactive waste] practice and policy-making in the UK'.[85]

Current Government policy is eventually to deposit high and intermediate-level waste in deep geological repositories, and this has received qualified parliamentary support.[86] As far as the water environment is concerned, the principal concern is the seepage of radiation into groundwaters. This issue also arises in relation to landfill sites, which may accept certain low-level wastes and where waste management licence provisions, including provisions on monitoring, will be central.[87] At present, however, disposal to landfill is only allowable providing that there is sufficient non-radioactive material available to cover the waste.[88] The impact of the EC Landfill Directive on this practice is as yet unclear. The Directive provides that hazardous waste must be disposed of with other hazardous waste, but defines such waste by reference to the Waste Framework Directive[89] which excludes radioactive waste from its scope. However, for most solid low-level radioactive waste the circumstances in which disposal is currently permitted along with conventional wastes cannot be satisfied, and these kinds of waste must be subjected to more stringent disposal conditions. Under the Radioactive Substances Act 1993,[90] British Nuclear Fuels Ltd may dispose of this category of waste at Drigg, its site at Sellafield.[91] Until

---

[83] On the problems that arise from the inability to classify some wastes at present see House of Lords Select Committee on Science and Technology, *Management of Nuclear Waste* (1999) para.4.47.

[84] The 1995 White Paper, p.49. See also DoE, *Radioactive Substances Act 1960: A Guide to the Administration of the Act* (1982) para.11.

[85] Berkhaut (1991) p.136.

[86] House of Lords Select Committee on Science and Technology, *Management of Nuclear Waste* (1999) paras.4.48 and 4.49.

[87] On landfill and the EC Landfill Directive (1999/31/EC), in force July 2001, see 12.2.7 above.

[88] DoE, *Radioactive Substances Act 1960: A Guide to the Administration of the Act* (1982) para. 50.

[89] Directive 75/442/EEC as amended; see 12.2.2 above.

[90] s.29, discussed at 20.10.8 below.

[91] DoE, *Radioactive Substances Act 1960: A Guide to the Administration of the Act* (1982) para.51; Tromans and FitzGerald (1997) para.1-19.

1995 such waste was disposed of in trenches, but it is now immobilised in containers and placed in concrete vaults. Direct responsibility for the specialist provision and management of facilities for the disposal of low- and intermediate-level radioactive waste now rests with NIREX Ltd.

As far as very low-level liquid waste is concerned, co-disposal is permitted and a 'dilute and disperse' approach is taken, allowing such wastes to pass directly or indirectly into watercourses or the sea. Waste which is disposed of in pursuance with this strategy is the source of most non-natural radioactive contamination of water, and is discharged in accordance with the terms of the Radioactive Substances Act 1993, discussed below.[92] A further pathway to the aquatic environment was identified by the RWMAC, which cautioned of the possibility that a waste disposal shaft at Dounreay used to dump intermediate level wastes could be breached by coastal erosion within 40-100 years.[93]

## 20.9 Sea Deposit

As already noted, under the 1972 London Convention and the 1992 OSPAR Convention, the dumping at sea of all levels of radioactive waste (as opposed to land-based discharges to the marine environment such as at Sellafield) is prohibited.[94] This makes the provisions allowing for the authorisation of such deposits under national law otiose.[95] Nevertheless, a brief examination of how this position was reached, and what it reveals about standard setting for radioactive contamination of the marine environment, is instructive.

The practice of authorising sea disposal of low level solid radioactive waste, begun in 1949, was originally carried out in the Hurd Deep in the English Channel before being restricted to an annual dumping operation at an internationally agreed site in the North Atlantic. The dumping site was located 900km south-south-west of Land's End, situated away from shipping lanes, major fishing grounds and submarine cables, clear of the continental shelf and in some 4,500 metres of water, in line with IAEA proposals on minimum depth for sea dumping.[96] After 1967, dumping operations were conducted and controlled by the Nuclear Energy Agency of the Organisation for Economic Co-operation and Development on behalf of Member States who wished to dump. This arrangement was regarded as politically and technically convenient for the states concerned,[97] not least the UK which contributed 95% of all alpha-emitting

---

[92] See 20.10 below.

[93] RWMAC/COMARE (1995). Steps are being taken to retrieve the waste: see *ENDS Report* 281 (1998) p.18.

[94] On legal aspects of sea dumping generally see Parmentier (1993) and Hey (1993).

[95] Under the Food and Environment Protection Act 1985, see 19.20 above.

[96] DoE, *Radioactive Substances Act 1960: A Guide to the Administration of the Act* (1982) paras 61-62. See also the 1961 Report of the Legal Panel of the IAEA (the '*Rousseau Report*'). It has recently emerged that radioactive waste was also dumped in a number of other locations in the 1950s: see Hansard, HC, 1 July 1997, Col.158 and 30 July 1997, Col 322.

[97] See the Royal Commission on Environmental Pollution (1976) para.368.

waste dumped between 1967 and 1982 under the NEA.[98] When the London Dumping Convention was adopted in 1972, only high-level radioactive wastes were placed on the Convention's 'Black List' (Annex I) which prohibited dumping though, in practice, only low-level waste was ever dumped under the Convention.[99]

In 1983, as a result of political pressure, a 2 year moratorium on sea dumping of radioactive waste was accepted under the London Dumping Convention pending various international reviews of the practice.[100] This was followed by a stronger resolution passed by the Convention parties agreeing to an indefinite but voluntary ban on this form of disposal irrespective of the result of reviews. By voting against these resolutions, however, the UK was not bound by them, and it appeared that the UK Government was eager to resume sea dumping of radioactive waste. Nonetheless the Government found itself obliged to adhere to the moratorium as a result of the National Union of Seamen and other trade unions refusing to participate in dumping operations.[101]

An independent panel of scientists was established to examine the safety of radioactive waste disposal at the North Atlantic Site,[102] and a study was commissioned by the Department of the Environment to ascertain the best practical environmental option (BPEO) for the disposal of radioactive waste.[103] The report of the independent review committee was inconclusive, generally deferring to international fora. However, all the options or 'composite (disposal) routes' later suggested by Government in its best practicable environmental option (BPEO) report included some element of sea disposal for intermediate-level waste, leading to criticism.[104]

The present position is that the UK Government has accepted a legally-binding ban on the sea disposal of low and intermediate-level radioactive wastes adopted at the Consultative Meeting of the 1972 London Convention in February 1994, effected by these wastes being placed on Annex I. This strengthening of the prohibition under the London Convention from what had previously been a voluntary moratorium can be traced to a recommendation in Agenda 21 which stressed the need for a

---

[98] Berkhaut (1991) p.188, n.79.

[99] IAEA (1991).

[100] In fact, following pressure from Greenpeace, dumping was suspended during 1982. An attempt in 1960 to ban the dumping of radioactive waste at sea as a breach of the protection for the right to life under the 1950 European Convention on Human Rights (Art.2.) had been dismissed as manifestly ill-founded on the facts, see *Dr S* v *Federal Republic of Germany*, App.715/60 (5 August 1960, unreported), cited in Thornton and Tromans (1999) p.42.

[101] See Slater (1986) and Berkhaut (1991) pp.167-68.

[102] *Report of the Independent Review of the Disposal of Radioactive in the North Atlantic* (the Holliday Report) (1984).

[103] DoE, *Assessment of Best Practicable Environmental Options (BPEOs) for Management of Low and Intermediate-Level Solid Radioactive Wastes* (1986). On the concept of BPEO see 12.3.2A above.

[104] Kemp (1992) p.41.

precautionary approach.[105] Formally, however, the UK abstained in relation to the ban, and its announcement at the time made clear that the UK would be willing to reopen discussion in the Convention at any time should the weight of opinion change, that it would continue its own programme of monitoring and research and that it would contribute actively to the scientific re-evaluation to be carried out, in accordance with the decision, after 25 years. Moreover, the view of the Government in 1995 was that

> sea disposal for low-level, solid radioactive wastes can be the best practicable environmental option for bulky low-level wastes arising from the decommissioning of power stations and other nuclear plant, as well as for tritiated wastes.[106]

This view was reflected in the original text of the 1992 OSPAR Convention, which provided for a general ban on the disposal of low and intermediate-level radioactive substances and wastes but included an option allowing the United Kingdom and France to resume dumping after 2007. This option was subject to an interim obligation, by 1997, to report on steps taken to secure alternative land-based disposal options.[107] At the first meeting of Ministers of the parties to the Convention on its coming into force in 1998, however, both countries joined in a unanimous decision to terminate their exemptions to this prohibition.[108] In light of the UK position in relation to the ban under the 1972 London Convention, this development was hardly surprising.

Following the decision of the present Government, within the context of the OSPAR Convention, to renounce the right of the UK to resume sea disposal, it seems clear that the views expressed in the 1995 White Paper no longer represent Government policy.[109] Nor, because of the unqualified nature of the renunciation on sea dumping, does it appear to reflect current thinking on the issue of what the UK Government believes is the BPEO for radioactive wastes.

The saga of the dumping of radioactive wastes at sea has deep implications for policy relating to water pollution and contamination from radioactive substances. For some, the ban on dumping of radioactive waste at sea is in line with the precautionary principle and with the need for equity in the use of the high seas, as a global common that should not be despoiled by a

---

[105] Chapter 22.5(b) Agenda 21. On Agenda 21 see 18.5.3 above.

[106] The 1995 White Paper, paras.16 and 14. 'Tritiated wastes' are wastes contaminated with a heavy radioisotope of hydrogen.

[107] Art.3(3)(b) Annex II OSPAR Convention. For the UK, the option kept open the possibility of dumping redundant nuclear submarines, see Birnie (1994) p.490.

[108] See OSPAR Decision 98/2, implementing Art.3(3)(b) Annex II OSPAR Convention. In force 9 February 1999.

[109] On 2 September 1997, the Minister spoke of a 'general presumption against sea disposal' for radioactive substances; *Today Programme*, Radio 4. See also the Government's acceptance in summer 1997 of the moratorium on sea disposal of solid waste under the London Convention, referred to in House of Lords Select Committee on Science and Technology, *Management of Nuclear Waste* (1999) p.21.

small number of developed countries.[110] Objections to dumping at sea are also motivated by broader concerns about civil and military uses of nuclear power, though the radioactive waste that was dumped actually included a large amount of waste of medical origins. For others, objections to the continuing use of nuclear power are largely irrelevant to the issue of dealing with current and future stocks of low-level waste, are unjustifiable on scientific grounds, and fail to take an integrated approach to radioactive waste management.[111] It may even be argued that international law, far from leading to a 'tragedy of the commons' may actually prevent uses of the high seas regarded as less damaging environmentally than other national disposal options.[112]

The absolute standards for the disposal of solid radioactive waste at sea illustrate the way that standard setting in this area is ultimately determined: not by water quality criteria nor even by a concern to reduce or eliminate contamination, but rather by moral concerns, risk perceptions and wider concerns about the origins of the waste that is produced.[113] Ruling out sea disposal, of course, makes the search for a terrestrial disposal, or dry storage, site all the more pressing. So far, all attempts to do so, which will have to consider both surface and groundwater movement and quality,[114] have been unsuccessful, suggesting, amongst other things, deep-seated difficulties with the capacity of the town and country planning system to facilitate approval of an acceptable site.[115]

## 20.10 The Radioactive Substances Act 1993

The two principal national enactments governing the discharge of radioactive materials are the Radioactive Substances Act 1993 and the Nuclear Installations Act 1965.[116] Although there is considerable overlap between the situations regulated by these two statutes, the Radioactive Substances Act 1993 is primarily concerned with the disposal of wastes rather than their treatment and storage, and has its main effect upon the handling and discharge of low-level radioactive wastes. By contrast, the Nuclear Installations Act 1965 provides the statutory basis for regulating the processing, storage and disposal of wastes produced by nuclear power generation, much of which is of high activity. Although both enactments

---

[110] For a good summary of objections see Parmentier (1993) p.143 and Hey (1993) pp.434-37.

[111] See, e.g., Calmet and Bewers (1991). In this latter context, it has been argued at national level that lack of institutional co-ordination frustrated policy integration and the search for a BPEO, polarising the debate between containment and dispersal strategies (Berkhaut (1991) Ch.5).

[112] Berkes et al (1989); for a legal analysis relating to common heritage approaches see Hey (1993).

[113] On the moral dimension to pollution control see Evernden (1993) pp.4-9.

[114] See the refusal of the Secretary of State to grant planning permission for a rock characterisation facility at Sellafield, discussed in [1997] *Water Law* 95.

[115] House of Lords Select Committee on Science and Technology, *Management of Nuclear Waste* (1999) paras.6.30ff.

[116] In addition to these, the protection of persons from radioactivity whilst at work and the prevention of risks to the health and safety of the general public from radioactivity arising from work-related activities are governed by the Health and Safety at Work etc. Act 1974.

regulate the possession and use of radioactive materials, with criminal liability for mishandling such materials, the Nuclear Installations Act 1965 also imposes extensive civil liability in situations where nuclear 'incidents' result in personal injury or damage to property.[117]

The origins of the 1993 Act are in the conclusions of the Keys Report[118] which were accepted by Government and formed the basis of the Radioactive Substances Act 1960.[119] Amongst the principles advocated was the basic presumption that no disposal of radioactive waste should be permitted except in accordance with an authorisation granted by the appropriate Minister. More particularly it recommended that discharges of radioactive waste should be controlled to ensure, irrespective of cost, that they did not directly endanger the health of any member of the public living in the neighbourhood or, when added to radiation from all other sources, were not likely to result in a genetic hazard to the nation as a whole.[120]

The basic regulatory approach laid down in the 1960 Act persists, although the law is now contained in the Radioactive Substances Act 1993, passed to consolidate numerous changes made to the 1960 Act over the years, in particular by the Environmental Protection Act 1990. The 1993 Act has since been amended to take account of the creation of the Environment Agency.[121]

### 20.10.1 Ministerial and Agency Responsibilities

The separation of the law on radioactive contamination of waters from the general law on water quality originated in allocating regulatory authority for radioactive contamination to central government. This gave effect to a recommendation in the Keys Report that the limited expertise to assess such dangers necessitated centralised control, rather than relying on bodies like water and sewerage authorities.[122] In practice, however, central government control was always exercised with the advice of a body which became known as the Radiochemical Inspectorate, which eventually became part of Her Majesty's Inspectorate of Pollution. The Environmental Protection Act 1990 for the first time made explicit reference to the role of a Chief Inspector (i.e., to HMIP) with specified functions relating to radioactive substances, allowing certain functions to be exercised in the name of the chief inspector alone rather than by Ministers.[123]

---

[117] On the reasons for, and nature of, this general division, and its consequences for coherence in policy formulation, see Berkhaut (1991).

[118] *The Control of Radioactive Wastes* (Cmnd 884, 1959) (the 'Keys Report') para.7.

[119] For other factors behind the passage of the Bill see Berkhaut (1991) p.1. On the history of the Bill see Tromans and FitzGerald (1997) para.4-03.

[120] *The Control of Radioactive Wastes* (Cmnd.884, 1959) para.9.

[121] Generally on the Environment Agency see Ch.6 above.

[122] See 20.10 above.

[123] See 12.3.2 above on integrated pollution control.

With the creation of the Environment Agency under the Environment Act 1995, references to the Chief Inspector are replaced by references to the Agency, and enhanced powers as the lead regulatory body for the 1993 Act are given to the Agency.[124] The general position now is that the controls imposed by the 1993 Act are directly exercised by the Environment Agency. However, this is subject to oversight by the Secretary of State for the Environment, Transport and the Regions and the Ministry of Agriculture, Fisheries and Food by their giving directions to the Agency and determining appeals.[125] Concerning the disposal of radioactive waste from premises of the UKAEA and sites licensed under the Nuclear Installations Act 1965, control was formerly exercised by HMIP acting jointly with the Minister of Agriculture, Fisheries and Food. Following the Environment Act 1995, the role of the Minister of Agriculture, Fisheries and Food is confined to a consultative role in the granting of authorisations, and to issuing directions and hearing appeals about authorisations jointly with the Secretary of State, and responsibility lies primarily with the Environment Agency.

Welsh devolution has transferred powers from the Secretary of State and the Minister to the National Assembly for Wales, except for general powers to grant exemptions from provisions of the Act and to classify specific substances as radioactive material.[126] The power to issue national security directions is also retained, but is to be exercised jointly.[127] Also to be exercised jointly (though transferred) are the provisions of the Act relating to access to information.[128]

The general provisions relating to the Agency's powers and duties imply, for the first time in this area, that the issuing of authorisations under the 1995 Act must be conducted for the explicit purpose of preventing or minimising pollution of the environment, or remedying or mitigating its effects.[129] Reference in the following sections are to the Radioactive Substances Act 1993, as amended, unless otherwise indicated.

### 20.10.2 Discounting Radioactivity for Certain Purposes

The separation of substantive provisions governing radioactive and non-radioactive pollution is achieved as follows. For the purposes of the operation and enforcement of a range of enactments, and for the exercise or performance of any power or duty conferred or imposed by those enactments, no account is to be taken of any radioactivity possessed by any substance or article or by any part of any premises.[130] These enactments

---

[124] para.200 Sch.22 Environment Act 1995.

[125] See, e.g., the Radioactive Substances (Basic Safety Standards) (England and Wales) Direction 2000, discussed at 20.7.1 above and the request by the Agency for directions concerning discharges from Sellafield, discussed at 20.10.12 below.

[126] See ss.1(5), 8(6), 11(1) and 15 Radioactive Substances Act 1993, discussed variously below.

[127] *Ibid* s.25.

[128] *Ibid* s.39, and see 20.10.11 below.

[129] On the general duties on the Agency see 6.8 above.

[130] s.40(1) Radioactive Substances Act 1993.

are listed in Schedule 3 to the Radioactive Substances Act 1993.[131] A number are relevant to the contamination of water:

(a) s.5 of the Sea Fisheries Regulation Act 1966;[132]

(b) s.4 of the Salmon and Freshwater Fisheries Act 1975;[133]

(c) ss.48, 81, 82, 141, 259 and 261 of the Public Health Act 1936;[134]

(d) ss.72, 111 and 113(6) and Chapter III of Part IV the Water Industry Act 1991;[135]

(e) s.18 of the Water Act 1945;[136]

(f) ss.82, 84, 85, 86, 87(1), 88(2), 92, 93, 99, 161, 190, 202 and 203 of, and para. 6 of Sch. 25 to the Water Resources Act 1991;[137]

(g) Part III of the Environmental Protection Act 1990;[138] and

(h) The Planning (Hazardous Substances) Act 1990.[139]

In addition, provision is made elsewhere for avoiding overlap with the regimes for special waste and for contaminated land.[140] In relation to the latter, the normal regime for contaminated land provided for in Part IIA of the Environmental Protection Act 1990 does not apply to harm, or to water pollution, which is attributable to any radioactivity possessed by any substance. However, the 1990 Act give powers to the Secretary of State to make regulations applying the Part IIA regime, with any necessary modifications, to problems of radioactive contamination. In February 1998 the Department of the Environment, Transport and the Regions published a consultation paper outlining a possible approach to applying the Part IIA regime. This proposed that sites where radiation is the predominant risk factor will be 'special sites', but that otherwise the control regimes for land contaminated by radioactivity will be comparable to land contaminated by other pollutants.[141]

In addition, for processes involving certain radioactive substances which are prescribed processes for the purposes of Part I of the Environmental Protection Act 1990, the provisions of the 1993 Act take precedence.[142] For the purposes of the pollution prevention and control regime,

---

[131] *Ibid* s.40(2)(a). Also covered are any amendment, extension or supersession of these Acts.

[132] See 15.4.2 above, although this provision does not allow byelaws to be made for discharges, making this provision of the 1993 Act of little practical relevance to the control of radioactive discharges.

[133] See 15.4.1 above.

[134] As amended by s.133(2) and Sch.7 Building Act 1984; see generally Ch.8 above.

[135] See 17.9 and 17.10 (in relation to s.72) and Ch.11 above on trade effluent discharges.

[136] To the extent that it continues to have effect.

[137] That is, to a range of water pollution control measures discussed throughout this work.

[138] See 8.5 above on statutory nuisance.

[139] See 14.5.3 above.

[140] s.78 and s.78YC Environmental Protection Act 1990 respectively. On contaminated land see 13.7 above.

[141] DETR, *Control and Remediation of Radioactively Contaminated Land, Consultation Paper* (1998). On 'special sites' see 13.7.4 above.

[142] s.28(2) Environmental Protection Act 1990. On integrated pollution control see 12.3.2 above.

radioactive substances are excluded from the 'substances' covered by the regime.[143]

Along with this list of statutory provisions where radioactivity is discounted, no account may be taken of any radioactivity possessed by substances for the purpose of any statutory provision contained in, or having effect by virtue of, a local enactment in so far as:

(a) the disposal of waste of any description, or of any substance which is a nuisance, or disposed of so as to be a nuisance, or of any substance which is prejudicial to health, noxious, polluting or of any similar description; or

(b) a power or duty is thereby conferred or imposed on any local authority, or on the Environment Agency, a water or sewerage undertaker or a local fisheries committee or other public or local authority, or on any officer of a public or local authority, to prevent, restrict or abate those disposals mentioned.[144]

Nevertheless, any *non-radioactive* aspects of any substances must still be dealt with by these other control regimes. For example, the discharge of waste effluent to a sewer must still be properly authorised under the Water Industry Act 1991, regardless of whether or not it is radioactive, although its radioactivity will be separately regulated. In addition, some radioactive substances may also be chemically toxic and this may be regulated independently of the radioactive characteristics of the substance concerned.

It is worth pointing out that in relation to some uses of water, controls on radioactivity in water are *not* separately regulated. This is best illustrated in the case of drinking water quality.[145]

### 20.10.3 'Radioactive Material' and 'Radioactive Waste'

For the purpose of imposing controls upon the keeping and use of radioactive materials, and the accumulation and disposal of radioactive waste, the Radioactive Substances Act 1993 provides mutually exclusive definitions of the key terms 'radioactive material' and 'radioactive waste'. Thus, 'radioactive material' means anything which, not being waste, is

---

[143] Reg.2(1) Pollution Prevention and Control (England and Wales) Regulations 2000 (SI 2000 No.1973). Curiously, defined as radioactive substances within the meaning of Council Directive 80/836/Euratom, the Basic Safety Standards Directive which was repealed on 13 May 2000, before the Pollution Prevention and Control Regulations were laid before Parliament. However, the definition of 'radioactive substances' in both Directive 80/836 and in the revised Directive, 96/29, is identical: 'Radioactive substance: any substance that contains one or more radionuclides the activity or concentration of which cannot be disregarded as far as radiation protection is concerned.'

[144] s.40(2)(b) Radioactive Substances Act 1993.

[145] See DWI Information Letter 19/2000, *Radioactivity and Drinking Water Supplies*, and DWI Information Letter 1/2001, *Radon and Uranium in Drinking Water Supplies*. Controls on radioactivity in water supplies are covered by the general requirement to supply 'wholesome' water and water which is not 'unfit for human consumption', see 17.7.3 and 17.7.7 above.

either a substance to which this subsection applies or an article made wholly or partly from, or incorporating, such a substance.[146] Moreover, this applies to any substance falling within either or both of the following definitions:

(a) a substance containing any one of the natural radioelements specified in Schedule 1 to the 1993 Act, at a concentration exceeding the level specified in the Schedule; and/or
(b) a substance possessing radioactivity which is wholly or partly attributable to an artificial process.[147]

Schedule 1 to the Act, which is subject to variation by Ministerial Order,[148] specifies levels of radiation in becquerels per gram for the solid, liquid and gaseous or vapour forms of eight listed elements. The listed elements are actinium, lead, polonium, protoactinium, radium, radon, thorium and uranium.

Following the Environmental Protection Act 1990, levels of artificial radioactivity can be prescribed by Order, below which a substance will not be treated as 'radioactive material' for the 1993 Act. Such an Order will serve the same purpose for artificial radioactivity to that served by Schedule 1 for natural radioactivity, in that material below the prescribed level would be excluded from all provisions of the 1993 Act.[149] However, no such levels have yet been prescribed and a previous Ministerial Order continues to be used to give general exemption from registration and authorisation for materials containing low levels of artificial radioactivity.[150] As presently formulated, therefore, the Act distinguishes between radioactive substances of natural and artificial origin, regulating the latter more strictly.

'Radioactive waste' is defined as waste that consists wholly or partly of:

(a) a substance or article which, if it were not waste, would be radioactive material, or
(b) a substance of article which has been contaminated in the course of the production, keeping or use of radioactive material, or by contact with or proximity to other waste falling within the preceding paragraph or this paragraph.[151]

This definition allows for the inclusion within the category of 'radioactive waste' of matter that has been contaminated by contaminated material. The general interpretation provisions of the 1993 Act add that 'substance' means any natural or artificial substance, whether in solid or liquid form or in the form of a gas or vapour. 'Waste' includes any substance which

---

[146] s.1(1) Radioactive Substances Act 1993.

[147] *Ibid* s.1(2).

[148] Under *ibid* s.1(5).

[149] *Ibid* s.1(4).

[150] See the Radioactive Substances (Substances of Low Activity) Exemption Order (SI 1986 No.1002).

[151] s.2 Radioactive Substances Act 1993.

constitutes scrap material or an effluent or other unwanted surplus substance arising from the application of any process, and also includes any substance of article which requires to be disposed of as being broken, worn out, contaminated or otherwise spoilt.[152] A largely subjective approach to the definition of waste is therefore taken, with emphasis placed on the state of mind of the person discarding or wishing to dispose of the substance or material.[153] References to the 'contamination' of a substance or article are to be understood as a reference to its being affected by either or both of the following:

(a) absorption, admixture or adhesion of radioactive material or radioactive waste, and
(b) the emission of neutrons or ionising radiations,

so as to become radioactive or to possess increased radioactivity.[154]

Radioactive waste is excluded from the definition of 'Directive waste' in the EC Waste Framework Directive,[155] and therefore also excluded from the definition of 'controlled waste' for the purposes of Part II of the Environmental Protection Act 1990[156] and the Waste Management Licensing Regulations 1994 which implement the Directive.[157]

### 20.10.4 Registration

Because of the desirability of regulating not merely the discharge of radioactive substances but also their production, the Radioactive Substances Act 1993 requires persons keeping radioactive substances to be registered with the Environment Agency.[158] It is a criminal offence to keep or use radioactive material without registration where this is required.[159] It is also an offence to cause or permit the keeping or using of radioactive material without the necessary registration. In all cases the offence must be committed with knowledge that, or reasonable grounds for believing that, the substance in question is radioactive material.[160]

Registration may be refused or made subject to such limitations or conditions as are thought fit, the details of which are specified in a registration certificate.[161] Premises occupied for military or defence purposes are exempt from this requirement.[162] Sites licensed under the

---

[152] *Ibid* s.47.
[153] *Ibid* s.47(4).
[154] *Ibid* s.47(5).
[155] Directive 75/442/EEC as amended by Directives 91/156/EEC and see 12.2.2 above.
[156] s.75 Environmental Protection Act 1990 and see 12.2.3 above.
[157] SI 1994 No.1056, see Reg.1(3).
[158] s.7 Radioactive Substances Act 1993.
[159] *Ibid* s.32.
[160] *Ibid* s.6. On the meaning of 'cause' and 'permit' see 9.5-9.7 above. On offences, see 20.10.10 below.
[161] *Ibid* s.7(6) and (8).
[162] *Ibid* s.42.

Nuclear Installations Act 1965 (referred to below as 'nuclear sites') are also exempted insofar as the keeping and use of radioactive materials is concerned,[163] but not in respect of the disposal of radioactive waste from redundant sites.[164] While there is no provision for public consultation on applications for registration, details must be sent to the local authority for the area and made accessible to the public, unless the Secretary of State directs otherwise.[165] The 1993 Act provides for both specific listed exemptions from registration,[166] and a general power for further exceptions to be granted by Ministerial Order.[167] A large number of exemption Orders of this kind have been made, relating to low activity substances and to premises such as schools and hospitals.[168]

### 20.10.5 Disposing of Radioactive Waste

A significant part of the Radioactive Substances Act 1993 seeks to impose controls upon the disposal of radioactive waste, and these measures are directly important to the radioactive contamination of water. The basic prohibition is that no person may, except in accordance with an authorisation, dispose of any radioactive waste on or from premises which are used for the purposes of an undertaking carried on by them, or cause or permit any radioactive waste to be so disposed of, if they know or have reasonable grounds for believing it to be radioactive waste.[169] A similar prohibition is imposed upon the unauthorised disposal of radioactive waste received for the purpose of disposal. Thus no person who receives any radioactive waste for the purpose of disposal, knowing or having reasonable grounds for believing it to be radioactive, may dispose of it or cause or permit it to be disposed of except in accordance with an authorisation.[170] 'Disposal' includes the removal, deposit or destruction of any waste, or its discharge, whether into water of into the air or into a sewer or drain or otherwise, or its burial, whether underground or otherwise.[171]

As with the registration requirement, both specific exceptions in the Act, and exceptions made under Ministerial Order, are made for less significant amounts of waste.[172] A large number of such Orders have been made placing a variety of materials outside the disposal offences.[173] The granting

---

[163] *Ibid* s.8(1).

[164] *Ibid* s.13.

[165] See 20.10.12 below.

[166] s.8(4) and (5) Radioactive Substances Act 1993.

[167] *Ibid* s.8(6).

[168] See, for example, SI 1962 No.2645 (Exhibitions); SI 1963 No.1832 (Schools etc.); SI 1985 No.1049 (Testing Instruments).

[169] *Ibid* s.13(1). On the meaning of 'undertaking' see s.47(1).

[170] *Ibid* s.13(3).

[171] *Ibid*. See the distinction between 'disposal' and 'storage' at 20.9 above.

[172] s.15(1) and (2) Radioactive Substances Act 1960.

[173] See, for example, SI 1962 No.2644 (Luminous Articles); SI 1962 No.2712 (Geological Specimens); and SI 1980 No.953 (Smoke Detectors). Many such Orders provide both for exemptions from authorisation and from registration; see 20.10.4 above.

of various exemptions for radioactive hospital waste has mitigated the impact of the general removal of Crown exemption under the Environmental Protection Act 1990, though notably this did not remove Crown exemption in relation to defence matters and the Crown is not liable to criminal proceedings under any provision of the Act.[174]

The offence of disposing of radioactive waste other than in accordance with an authorisation applies to any premises situated on a nuclear site but which have ceased to be used for the purpose of an undertaking carried on by the site licensee.[175] Nuclear site licences are provided for under the Nuclear Installations Act 1965. Under this, no person other than the UKAEA may use any site for specified purposes concerned with the production of atomic energy. Amongst other things these purposes include the storage, processing or disposal of nuclear fuel or of bulk quantities of other radioactive matter, if this has been produced in the course of the production or use of nuclear fuel, unless the Secretary of State for Trade and Industry has issued a licence for the site.[176] The power of the HSE to attach conditions to nuclear site licences with regard to the discharge of substances on or from such a site is without prejudice to the provision concerning the authorisation of redundant nuclear sites, although there must be consultation with the Environment Agency.[177]

### 20.10.6 Authorising Radioactive Waste Disposal

The offences relating to the disposal of radioactive waste under the Radioactive Substances Act 1993 arise where there is no authorisation for such disposal.[178] In accordance with the general principle of centralised control, authorisation is granted by the Environment Agency.

For radioactive waste disposal on or from any premises situated on a nuclear site, the Agency must engage in prior consultation. First, consultation is required with the Food Standards Agency and the Health and Safety Executive on whether an authorisation should be granted and under what limitations and conditions. Second, the Food Standards Agency must be consulted on the draft terms of any authorisation. With nuclear sites, the Agency is also under a duty to consult with such local authorities, relevant water bodies[179] or other public or local authorities[180] as appear to the Agency proper to be consulted.[181] This would, for example, require

---

[174] s.42(1)-(3) Radioactive Substances Act 1993 and SI 1990 No.2512. On continuing Crown exemption in other (non-radioactive) contexts see 9.18 above.

[175] *Ibid* s.13(5).

[176] s.1 Nuclear Installations Act 1965; and see SI 1969 No.1498 and SI 1970 No.1537 transferring Ministerial powers.

[177] *Ibid* ss.4(1)(d) and 4(3A).

[178] On offences, see 20.10.10 below.

[179] 'Relevant water body' means a water undertaker, a sewerage undertaker or a local fisheries committee: s.47(1) Radioactive Substances Act 1993.

[180] 'Public or local authority' includes a water undertaker or a sewerage undertaker: *ibid.*

[181] *Ibid* s.16.

consultation with a sewerage undertaker on any proposed liquid effluent discharge to sewer.

Similarly, in authorising the disposal of radioactive waste under the 1993 Act, the Environment Agency must consult with the relevant public or local authority before granting the authorisation if it appears that the waste in question is likely to involve the need for special precautions to be taken by any of these bodies. Where an authority must take special precautions, the Agency may make such charges as are agreed between the authority and the person to whom the authorisation is granted. In default of such an agreement being reached the Agency may determine the amount of such charges.[182]

Contrary to general regulatory trends, the 1993 Act makes no provision for public notification or consultation in relation to applications for authorisation. It has also been held that, as a matter of law, HMIP was not under a mandatory obligation to consult either on new authorisations or on variations of existing authorisations. A wide margin of discretion is given, and it was not therefore unreasonable for the regulatory authority to deal with one application for a variation of existing authorisations without consultation, but simultaneously subject another application for authorisation to a major consultation exercise.[183] Nevertheless, fairly wide consultation was generally engaged in by HMIP[184] and the Environment Agency has also engaged in quite widespread public consultation for some applications, with a view to instituting extended public consultation on more contentious licence applications.[185] This may give rise to a claim that such consultation is a legitimate expectation on the part of the public.[186]

An obvious difficulty with *any* form of public or statutory consultation is the absence of any clear policy principles against which decisions are taken.[187] If the rules of the game are obscure, it is difficult to know how to take part.[188]

On granting an authorisation for the disposal of radioactive waste the Environment Agency must:

---

[182] *Ibid* s.18(1) and (2).

[183] *R v Her Majesty's Inspectorate of Pollution ex p Greenpeace Ltd (No. 2)* [1994] 4 All ER 329 at 344. See also *R v Secretary of State for the Environment ex p Greenpeace Ltd* [1994] 4 All ER 352.

[184] Tromans and FitzGerald (1997) para.5-29.

[185] See the wide consultation on the applications for disposal of radioactive waste by the Atomic Weapons Establishment at Aldermaston, and by UKAEA at Harwell. See further Environment Agency, *Proposals for extended public consultation on selected licence applications, Consultation Paper* (1999). Both at *www.environment-agency.gov.uk*

[186] *Council of Civil Service Unions v Minister for the Civil Service* [1985] AC 374. Contrast *R v Falmouth and Truro Port Health Authority ex parte South West Water Limited* [2000] Env LR 833, discussed at 8.5.7B above.

[187] See 20.7 above on radioactive policy principles.

[188] A criticism made by the House of Commons Select Committee on the Environment, Transport and the Regions, *The Environment Agency* (2000) paras.68-71, and see 20.7 above.

(a) furnish the person to whom the authorisation is granted with a certificate containing all material particulars of the authorisation; and

(b) (unless, for reasons of national security, knowledge of the authorisation should be restricted) send a copy of the certificate to each local authority in whose area, in accordance with the authorisation, radioactive waste is to be disposed of and in the case of waste from nuclear sites, to any other public or local authority consulted in relation thereto.[189]

An authorisation so granted and certified has effect from the date specified in the authorisation, unless in the opinion of the Environment Agency it is necessary that the authorisation should come into force immediately or should otherwise be expedited.[190]

The Agency may at any time revoke or vary an authorisation by attaching limitations or conditions, or where the authorisation has effect subject to limitations or conditions, by revoking or varying any of them or by attaching further limitations or conditions to the authorisation. In relation to nuclear sites, similar consultation provisions as relate to the grant of authorisations apply. In the event of revocation or variation of a disposal authorisation, notice must be given to the person to whom the authorisation was granted. If a copy of the certificate of authorisation was sent to a public or local authority, a copy of the amending notice must be sent to that authority.[191]

### 20.10.6A Limitations and conditions

Any authorisation for the disposal of radioactive waste may be granted either in respect of radioactive waste generally, or in respect of waste of a description specified in the authorisation, and may be granted by the Environment Agency subject to such limitations or conditions as it thinks fit.[192] It is notable that, unlike discharge consents or trade effluent consents, the 1993 Act makes no attempt to outline the kinds of conditions which might be attached to an authorisation.[193] It would appear that numeric conditions will normally limit the amount of alpha and beta radioactivity that may be discharged in a certain period, while further conditions generally control the discharge of certain named radioisotopes; the manner and location of discharges; and stipulate environmental monitoring programmes to be carried out by the discharger.[194] The discharger may also be required to ensure that, as far as is reasonably practicable, the radioactive elements in the waste are discharged at a

---

[189] ss.16(9) and 25(2) Radioactive Substances Act 1993. Similar national security provisions apply to registrations; see s.25(1).

[190] *Ibid* s.16(10).

[191] *Ibid* s.17(1), (2A) and (3).

[192] *Ibid* s.16(8).

[193] See Chs.10 and 11 above respectively.

[194] Morris (1999) p.365.

uniform rate.[195] Conditions are now set on the basis of actual anticipated discharges with little built-in 'head-room', meaning that proposals to increase discharges will tend to require a re-negotiation of the authorisation rather than the utilisation of this reserve capacity. Recent authorisations now also contain 'notification levels' below the authorised discharge limit, above which operators are required to give written justification that the best practical means of controlling the discharge are being used. At two sites, lower 'action limits' are utilized, which trigger informal discussions with the Environment Agency.[196] Conditions will relate to the particular critical group pathways. For example, the nuclear power station at Bradwell in Essex contains specific restrictions on zinc discharges, since zinc is accumulated by oysters and there are commercial oyster beds in the locality.[197]

As a matter of practice, discharges are assessed individually with authorisations incorporating quantitative limits for specified radionuclides.[198] These authorisations are subject to regular review in accordance with the Government's radiological protection standards and objectives.[199] Hence discharge authorisations will be determined by reference to the combined approach of maximum dose limits and site constraints coupled with the requirement that radiation levels must be reduced to the lowest levels reasonably achievable.[200] Presumably, reviews should also be guided by *environmental* protection objectives such as those under OSPAR.

### 20.10.6B Justification

Although it is not mentioned in the 1993 Act, the justification principle,[201] by which the costs of exposure must be justified by the benefits which accrue, must be considered in relation to the granting of authorisations and variations. In *R v Secretary of State for the Environment, ex p Greenpeace Ltd*[202] Potts J held that, as provided for in the Euratom Basic Safety Standards Directive,[203] the justification principle applied not to types of activities in general, but to specific projects. The principle therefore applied to the Thermal Oxide Reprocessing Plant (THORP) and the impact that the grant of an authorisation to dispose of radioactive waste would have on critical groups.[204] On the facts, however, the judge held that the decision to grant the authorisation could not be overturned on the ground

---

[195] Bates (1990, updated) para.10.229.

[196] Morris (1999) p.367.

[197] Clark (1997) p.101.

[198] A radionuclide is an isotope of an element that is radioactive.

[199] Discussed in 20.7 above.

[200] On determinations in practice see Environment Agency form RSA3 and related guidance. Separate guidance is issued to small users.

[201] See 20.7.1 above.

[202] [1994] 4 All ER 352. See generally Tromans and FitzGerald (1997) paras.5-30 to 5-32.

[203] Then, Directive 80/836/Euratom. See now 20.6 above.

[204] Contrast the view of Otton J in *R v Her Majesty's Inspectorate of Pollution ex p Greenpeace Ltd (No. 2)* [1994] 4 All ER 329.

that the disposal option was not justified, even though the Ministers had not thought themselves bound by the need, in law, to justify the specific activity.

One consequence of this decision is that applicants for large-scale developments are encouraged to submit applications for planning permission and authorisation under the 1993 Act at the same time. Partly, this amounts to sensible project planning. However, following the judgment of Potts J, it may also be that, as a matter of law, showing justification at the planning stage may not mean that any discharge is deemed to have been justified in advance for the purposes of compliance with the Basic Safety Standards Directive.[205] A further aspect of the decision is that the site-specific nature of any justification means that no two justifications will ever be the same. This is, not least, because environmental impacts will differ depending on the location and the specific critical paths, and the costs and benefits of applications for different sites will always differ.[206]

### 20.10.6C Optimisation

As with the justification principle, the principle that exposure levels should be kept as low as reasonably achievable ('ALARA'), taking economic and social factors into account is also specifically provided for in the Euratom Basic Safety Standards Directive and is, therefore, a binding legal obligation which the Environment Agency must comply with in determining licence applications and variations.[207] The Environment Agency is specifically directed to apply the ALARA standard.[208]

The ALARA standard, and its relationship with quantitative discharge limits, is illustrated by the conviction of British Nuclear Fuels Ltd in 1985 for offences arising out of a leak from the Sellafield site in November 1983.[209] The company was fined a total of £10,000 by Carlisle Crown Court for having allowed an accidental discharge of waste containing the radioactive isotope Ruthenium 106 to pass through a discharge pipe into the Irish Sea causing the contamination of the Cumbrian coast. Although the court found that the offending discharge did not exceed the express limits of radioactive matter specified in the company's discharge authorisation, and was not shown to involve a risk of harm to any particular member of the public, the company's failure to maintain its discharge as low as reasonably achievable constituted an offence. The company was fined £5,000 for having discharged the radioactive matter, and £1,500 for failing to keep proper records of their discharges.[210] The

---

[205] Contrast Miller (1996a) p.297.

[206] The justification principle was considered further in *R (on the application of Marchiori)* v *Environment Agency*, 29 March 2001, QBD.

[207] Art.6(3)(a) Directive 96/29/Euratom.

[208] The Radioactive Substances (Basic Safety Standards) (England and Wales) Direction 2000.

[209] See generally Miller (1990) and Tromans and FitzGerald (1997) para.5-54.

[210] See now ss.20 and 33(3) Radioactive Substances Act 1993.

company was also fined £2,500 for contravening the terms of its nuclear site licence, and £1,000 for failing to inform persons in the vicinity of the discharge.[211]

The prosecution of British Nuclear Fuels Ltd coincided with the escalation of public concerns about cancer levels in the area and the setting up of the Black Committee to investigate this.[212] The combined effect of these developments, and political pressure to reduce discharges to levels comparable with the only similar facility discharging to the North-East Atlantic (La Hague in France),[213] forced a major change in policy. In particular, the period marked a watershed by giving rise to a 'radical reinterpretation of the ALARA criteria', moving discharge authorisation policy more firmly in the direction of the use of best available techniques or best practicable means and de-emphasising the assimilative capacity of the water environment.[214] Present policy is that ALARA is normally given effect to through a 'best practicable means' requirement in authorisations.[215]

### 20.10.7 Appeals

Provision is made for appeals in relation to the refusal of an application for registration or authorisation; any limitation or condition attached thereto; the variation of any registration or authorisation; and the cancellation of a registration or revocation of an authorisation. It is notable that only the person 'directly concerned' by such a decision, i.e. the applicant, may appeal. This excludes third party challenges other than by judicial review,[216] though it is probably within the powers of the person hearing the appeal to allow third party representation as part of his general discretion to determine his own procedures.[217] Appeals can also be lodged against enforcement notices and prohibition notices, but again only by the person on whom the notice is served.[218] There is no right of appeal if the Environment Agency has acted under a ministerial direction. Appeals are made to the Secretary of State unless they relate to authorisations relating to nuclear sites, in which case the appeal is heard jointly by the Secretary

---

[211] See Nuclear Installations Act 1965 at 20.11 below.

[212] *Investigation of the Possible Increased Incidence of Cancer in West Cumbria* (1984).

[213] At the time, discharge levels from Sellafield were around one hundred-fold higher than La Hague.

[214] See Berkhout (1991) p.172 for a good account of the 'malleability' of the various qualitative process-control standards, and the way in which the former dichotomy between 'containment' and 'dilute and disperse' strategies was recast.

[215] The letter to the Agency from DETR accompanying the Radioactive Substances (Basic Safety Standards) (England and Wales) Direction 2000 (dated 12 May 2000) suggests that, for the DETR, the term is in practice synonymous with the test of 'as low as reasonably practicable' as found in the Ionising Radiations Regulations 1999 (SI 1999 No.3232).

[216] See, notably, the three decisions in the judicial review proceedings brought by Greenpeace against HMIP in respect of the 'THORP' plant at Sellafield, noted in part at 20.10.6 above and Tromans and FitzGerald (1997) paras.B-17 to B-24.

[217] Freshfields (1996, updated) 2-R2045.

[218] See 20.10.9 below.

of State and by the Minister of Agriculture, Fisheries and Food.[219] Appeals are either by written representation or at a public or private hearing, and may be heard by a ministerial appointee.[220]

### 20.10.8 Ministerial and Agency Arrangements for Disposing of Radioactive Waste

If it appears to the Secretary of State that adequate facilities are not available for the safe disposal of radioactive waste he may provide such facilities, or arrange for their provision by such a person as he thinks fit.[221] Where this power is exercised, the Secretary of State must consult with any local authority in whose area the facilities would be situated and with such other public or local authorities, if any, as appear to him to be proper to be consulted.[222] Where such facilities are provided, reasonable charges may be payable.[223] The site at Drigg near Sellafield was provided pursuant to this power.[224]

### 20.10.9 Enforcement Notices and Prohibition Notices

Where the Environment Agency believes that a person to whom a registration relates, or to whom an authorisation was granted, is failing to comply with any limitation or condition to which that registration or authorisation is subject, or is likely to fail to comply with such limitation or condition, it may serve an enforcement notice. An enforcement notice must state the Agency's belief, the alleged matters constituting the failure to comply, the steps that must be taken and the timescale for action.[225] An enforcement notice can therefore be used proactively, where contraventions appear likely to take place.[226]

A second mechanism allowing a response to potential pollution incidents is service of a prohibition notice by the Environment Agency on a registered person or the holder of a disposal authorisation. This may be done where the Agency believes that the continued keeping or use of radioactive material, or the continued disposal or accumulation of radioactive waste, involves an imminent risk of pollution of the environment or of harm to human health. Prohibition notices can be served regardless of whether the manner of carrying on the activity in question complies with any registration or authorisation, or any limitation or

---

[219] s.26 Radioactive Substances Act 1993.

[220] See generally *ibid* s.27 and the Radioactive Substances (Appeals) Regulations 1990 (SI 1990 No.2504).

[221] *Ibid* s.29(1).

[222] *Ibid* s.29(2). On the meaning of 'public or local authorities' see 20.10.6 above.

[223] *Ibid* s.29(3).

[224] See 20.3 and 20.8 above.

[225] s.21 Radioactive Substances Act 1993.

[226] See also 10.11.1 above on enforcement notices. On usage see Tromans and FitzGerald (1997) para.B-135.

condition to which these are subject.[227] Similar provisions to those applicable to enforcement notices apply to the service of a prohibition notice, although the latter must also direct the extent to which the registration or authorisation shall cease to have effect until the notice is withdrawn. No definition is given in the Act of 'pollution' or 'harm to human health'.[228]

### 20.10.10 Offences

In relation to registration and authorisation requirements,[229] there are offences of:

(a) failing to register non-exempted premises where radioactive material is kept or used;

(b) unauthorised disposal of radioactive waste and unauthorised disposal of such waste received for disposal in the course of an undertaking;

(c) failing to comply with a limitation or condition governing the keeping or use of radioactive material by a person registered or exempted from registration; and

(d) non-compliance with an authorisation, or a limitation or condition in an authorisation, granted for the disposal of radioactive waste.[230]

It is also an offence for a person who is registered or possesses an authorisation to fail to comply with an enforcement notice or a prohibition notice.[231]

Proceedings for offences under the Act can only be instituted by the Secretary of State or the Environment Agency, or by or with the consent of the Director of Public Prosecutions.[232] This is notably more restrictive of the right to prosecute than applies to water pollution offences under Part III of the Water Resources Act 1991, reflecting the greater sensitivity of the area, but deprives environmental organisations in particular of one aspect of their regulatory 'watchdog' role.

On summary conviction for any of these offences an offender is liable to a fine not exceeding £20,000 or to imprisonment for a term not exceeding six months, or both. On conviction on indictment the maximum penalty is a fine, or imprisonment for a term not exceeding five years, or both.[233]

---

[227] See, e.g., the service of a prohibition notice at the UKAEA site at Dounreay because of concerns about discharges to the North Sea; 'Regulators shut Dounreay's new sodium plant', *www.n-base.org.uk/public/latest/latest06.htm.*

[228] On the meaning of 'pollution' generally see 1.3.3-6 above.

[229] s.32(1) Radioactive Substances Act 1993.

[230] Under, respectively, *ibid* ss.6, 13, 7 and 16.

[231] Contrary to *ibid* ss.21 and 22.

[232] *Ibid* s.38(1).

[233] *Ibid* s.32(2).

Provision is also made for individual guilt alongside corporate responsibility.[234]

Further offences are provided for, relating to various failures to display documents on site, or to comply with required record-keeping, or of making false or misleading statements or false entries for various purposes.[235] In varying degrees these are punishable less severely than the offences discussed above. Offences relating to intentionally obstructing officials in the course of their duty are now contained in more general provisions relating to the work of Environment Agency officers.[236]

In the first prosecution to be brought by the Environment Agency under the Radioactive Substances Act 1993, Hunting BRAE Ltd, the operating company of the Atomic Weapons Establishment at Aldermaston, admitted liability to three charges under the Act. These were of disposing of tritiated groundwater into a stream without authorisation, failing to report the discharge and making misleading statements. The company was fined £7,000 each for the first and second offences and £3,500 for the third offence, and was ordered to pay £4,220 in costs. The unauthorised discharges were believed to have started in April 1997 and were discovered early in 1999.[237]

### 20.10.11 Disclosure of Information

For various reasons, access to information on radioactive wastes and its discharge has a particular salience. Principally, this is because of public perception of risk, but it also relates to the sensitivity of some of the activities that involve the accumulation or disposal of radioactive substances.[238]

The confidentiality of information provided to the authorities under the Radioactive Substances Act 1993 is in certain respects protected by means of a specific offence relating to the improper disclosure of such information. Subject to certain exceptions, it is an offence for any person to disclose any information relating to any process applied for the purposes of, or in connection with, the production or use of radioactive material, or trade secret used in carrying on any particular undertaking, which has been given to or obtained by that person under the Act, or in connection with the execution of the Act.[239] The exceptions to this offence are that no offence is committed where the disclosure is made:

    (a)  with the consent of the person carrying on the undertaking;
    (b)  in accordance with any general or special directions given by the Secretary of State;

---

[234] *Ibid* s.36(1) and (2).
[235] Under *ibid* ss.19, 20 and 34A respectively.
[236] s.110 Environment Act 1995.
[237] 'First nuclear prosecution', *Environment Action*, March 2000, p.11.
[238] On access to information generally see 16.14-16.19 above.
[239] s.34(1) Radioactive Substances Act 1993.

(c) where the information is exchanged between the Environment Agency, local enforcing authorities and Ministers in the exercise of their functions;

(d) in connection with the execution of the Act; or

(e) for the purposes of any legal proceedings arising out of the Act or of any report of such proceedings.[240]

A person found guilty of this offence will be liable, on summary conviction, to a fine not exceeding the statutory maximum, currently £5,000, or to imprisonment for a term not exceeding three months, or both. On conviction on indictment, liability is to a fine, or to imprisonment for a term not exceeding two years, or both.[241]

Under the Environmental Protection Act 1990, however, a general provision on public access to documents and records was inserted into the law on radioactive substances, giving the public a general right to copies of the following documents from the Environment Agency:

(a) all applications made to the Agency under any provision of the Act;

(b) all documents issued by the Agency under any provision of the Act;

(c) all other documents sent by the Agency to any local authority under a direction by the Secretary of State; and

(d) prescribed records of convictions for offences under the Act.[242]

However, this right is qualified in that information relating to any relevant process or trade secret, or which the Secretary of State has issued a direction on in the interests of national security, must not be disclosed. The Agency is also given the power to issue directions to local authorities preventing them from disclosing information relating to processes and trade secrets. Otherwise, every local authority is obliged to keep and make available to the public copies of all documents sent to it under any provision of the Act. Since a ministerial direction in 1992, all local authorities have been sent information about the environmental impact of existing and new authorised discharges.[243] Copies of documents which may be disclosed must be made available at all reasonable times and a copy must be made on payment of a reasonable fee.[244] These provisions

---

[240] *Ibid.*

[241] *Ibid* s.34(2).

[242] On the last-mentioned see the Radioactive Substances (Records of Conviction) Regulations 1992 (SI 1992 No.1685).

[243] Freshfields (1996, updated) 2-R2046.

[244] See generally s.39 Radioactive Substances Act 1993. See also DoE Circular 21/90, *Local Authority Responsibilities for Public Access to Information under the Radioactive Substances Act 1960 as Amended by the Environmental Protection Act 1990*, as supplemented by DoE Circular 22/92.

should be read alongside the EC Environmental Information Directive and the Environmental Information Regulations 1992.[245]

### 20.10.12 Case Study and Assessment

The practical operation of the 1993 Act, and particularly the relationship between the Act and European and international law obligations, is well illustrated by the application by BNFL for a variation of its authorisation at Sellafield, and application to operate a mixed oxide fuel plant (MOX) there.[246] There has been considerable public concern about increasing levels of technetium-99 found in shellfish in the Irish Sea, which have contributed more than 50% of the radiation dose to the most exposed group of seafood consumers.[247] There is little doubt that most of the technetium derives from discharges from Sellafield, although liquid discharges of technetium-99 from Sellafield have declined by 75% over the period 1995-98. Nevertheless, technetium-99 continues to be a significant radionuclide in the environment.[248] This concern is set against more general public anxiety about the nuclear industry and radioactive waste management, despite the radiological impact of liquid discharges from Sellafield being around one tenth of the level in 1981.

In November 1996 BNFL applied to the Agency for variations to its gaseous and liquid authorisations under the 1993 Act to dispose of wastes from the Sellafield site. Insofar as it related to direct discharges to water, the application sought a decrease in the limit on discharges of technetium-99 and of tritium to the sea.[249] In early 1998, the Agency undertook a period of public consultation on the proposed variations, involving local authorities and other public bodies and inviting comment from the wider public. This process went beyond the requirements of the 1993 Act, the consultation requirements of which have been criticised as part of wider unease about the adequacies of the procedural provisions of the 1993 Act.[250] Indeed, it is notable that, since this determination, a greater sensitivity to procedures can be seen in the decision to select for extended public consultation any proposals to increase limits at nuclear installations on direct radioactive discharges into the environment (i.e. liquid or gaseous effluent), together with selected other high profile authorisations relating to the nuclear sector. These new provisions require three months

---

[245] Directive 90/313/EEC and SI 1992 No.3240 respectively. See generally John (1995) and 16.16-16.17 above.

[246] See DETR and MAFF, *Variations to the BNFL plc Sellafield Radioactive Waste Discharges Authorisations: Decisions of the Secretary of State for the Environment, Transport and the Regions and the Minister of Agriculture, Fisheries and Food (The Ministers)* (November 1999). For background see *ENDS Report* 264 (1997) p.5; *ENDS Report* 276 (1998) p.8; *ENDS Report* 281 (1998) p.18.

[247] See 20.2 above.

[248] MAFF and SEPA, *Radioactivity in Food and the Environment, 1998 (RIFE-4)* (1999).

[249] Variations in relation to carbon-14, ruthenium-106 and iodine-129 were also considered in relation to atmospheric discharges.

[250] For general criticism of appeal rights, public consultation and access to information, see *ENDS Report* 279 (1998) p.32.

public consultation on all selected applications concerning radioactive substances at nuclear installations.[251]

The issue of technetium-99 discharges was raised at the Ministerial meeting of the parties to the OSPAR Convention in 1998, and the concluding statement at that meeting made explicit reference to technetium. As will be recalled, the guiding principles of the OSPAR Convention are the principles of precaution and that the polluter pays. In the OSPAR treaty regime, the precautionary principle has been expressed in practice through obligations on contracting parties to ensure that the best available techniques are used to reduce emissions to the marine environment. However, this general approach is subject to a specific obligation on the parties to adopt measures to forestall and, as appropriate, to eliminate pollution by radioactive substances.[252] This obligation was further fleshed out under the OSPAR Strategy for Radioactive Substances agreed at the Ministerial meeting in 1998, under which the parties agreed to reduce radioactive discharges with the ultimate aim of achieving, by 2020, concentrations in the environment near background values for naturally occurring radioactive substances and close to zero for artificial radioactive substances.

The decision of the Agency that it submitted to Ministers[253] in relation to the Sellafield discharges was that the authorised discharge of tritium should be reduced slightly from 31,000 TBq/year to 30,000 TBq/year. In relation to technetium-99, the authorised discharge was reduced from 200 TBq/year to 90 TBq/year. In addition, the Agency imposed further obligations on BNFL in relation to technetium-99, which may be seen as giving effect, in part, to obligations under the OSPAR Convention. Thus, BNFL was required to:

(a) undertake full-scale trials of a flocculation process within the EARP;
(b) pursue the development of other technetium abatement technologies, to be identified in agreement with the Agency;
(c) investigate and develop reprocessing plant modifications to reduce technetium discharges to sea; and
(d) submit a future management strategy for certain storage tanks, based both on a limit of 90TBq/year and of 10TBq/year.

This was in line with the Agency's declared long-term strategy of reducing discharges to below 10TBq/year through introducing new technology and limiting total discharges. Finally, in relation to all discharges to sea, a condition was imposed requiring the best practical means to control the timing of the discharge in order to limit the impact of the discharge on

---

[251] Environment Agency, *Proposals for extended public consultation on selected licence applications. Consultation paper* (October 1999) para.2.3. This new procedure was applied to the discharge from the Atomic Weapons Establishment at Aldermaston as a pilot, see 20.10.6 above.

[252] Art.5 OSPAR Convention.

[253] In this case, a decision taken by the Board of the Agency, rather than at any lower level, and see also 6.4 above on the powers of the Board.

those most exposed. It was also proposed to include an information condition requiring BNFL to carry out research on the behaviour of radionuclides in the environment with the objective of improving the understanding on the effect on other organisms in the vicinity of Sellafield.

While Ministers have the power to 'call in' decisions of the Agency relating to new authorisations,[254] there is no corresponding power in relation to the variation of an existing authorisation. However, the Secretary of State for the Environment, Transport and the Regions and the Minister of Agriculture, Fisheries and Food do have the power in relation to any authorisation to give directions to the Agency which may attach specified limitations or conditions to the authorisation, to vary an authorisation, or to cancel it. Accordingly, following various requests to call in the variation, and more importantly the voluntary submission to Ministers by the Agency of its draft determination, the respective Ministers treated these as if they were representations to use Ministerial power to give directions in respect of the Sellafield discharge authorisations affected by the Agency's decisions. Thus, the proposed decision agreed to by the Agency was treated by Ministers as a request to direct the Agency on the application. After lengthy consideration, the Ministers decided that they did not consider it appropriate to intervene, which in practical terms confirmed the variation, noting that the variation took 'full account' of the UK's obligations under OSPAR.

Whether this licensing decision in fact gave practical effect to the OSPAR Convention and the objectives of the 1998 Radioactive Substances Strategy to reduce discharges to levels above historic levels which are 'close to zero' has been a matter of dispute.[255] In particular, it has been suggested that the time-lag between the cessation of emissions and a fall in concentrations in the marine environment is such that discharges would have to cease immediately for the 2020 target to be met.[256] Put differently, the nature of radioactive contamination is such that for the targets to be met, there cannot simply be a gradual phase-out up to 2020.[257] The same report also points to the fact that Sellafield had in fact met the 90TBq/year limit in each of the three years 1997-1999, and that the determinations incorporated allowable increases of emissions to air. In addition, the determination is notable in that it does not require further abatement to be undertaken, merely that practices should be pursued. This is a rather different formulation of a 'best available techniques'-type standard,[258] since it does not actually seem to require that such techniques are implemented, merely that they pursued. Nevertheless, the extent to which

---

[254] s.24 Radioactive Substances Act 1993. In effect, s.23 also provides for *de facto* call in.

[255] For critical comment advocating storage and developing retrieval options see 'Dishonourable Discharges', *New Scientist* editorial, 9 December 2000.

[256] *The Need for Urgent Implementation of the OSPAR Strategy with regard to Radioactive Substances*, RAD 00/3/3-E(L), submitted by Greenpeace to the OSPAR Meeting of the Working Group on Radioactive Substances, Luxembourg, 18-21 January 2000.

[257] Radionuclides released by the Chernobyl accident in 1986 continue to spread along the Norwegian coast, see *ibid*, p.2.

[258] On the use of best available techniques as a process standard see 12.3.3 above.

the Sellafield complex contributes to the UK's emissions of radioactivity to the marine environment has at least one advantage: the UK can go a long way to meeting its international obligations by tightening controls at just one source (which might be contrasted with the problems in controlling the cumulative impact of numerous small contributors to unsatisfactory water quality).

It is also notable that the variation was not thought to require a fresh 'justification' for the discharge. It is a directly enforceable requirement of EC law that any exposure to ionising radiation must be justified in advance by the advantages which it produces. Also, Member States must take account of the justification principle when ensuring that 'the contribution to the exposure of the population as a whole from each activity is kept to the minimum necessitated by that activity'.[259] In particular, justification is required in advance of the introduction of any new type of practice, while existing classes of practice may be reviewed whenever new and important evidence about their efficacy or consequences is acquired. However, the Agency took the view that the changes to the discharge limits and resulting radiological impact on the public would not substantially alter the balance of benefits and detriments, and this was accepted by Ministers. Nevertheless, the fact remains that a reduction in exposure limits will not be enough by itself to 'justify' discharges of radioactive substances, and it would seem that some form of rational assessment, even if this is not a full study, will be required to show that there has been compliance with the justification principle.

In its draft strategy issued in June 2000, it is noted that:

> The Government is committed to reducing discharges of technetium-99 from Sellafield below 10TBq a year as soon as possible and has instructed the Environment Agency to review these discharges on a fast track basis. However, for the purpose of projecting a discharge profile to 2020, a date of 2006 is assumed for the introduction of an annual discharge limit of 10 TBq, without prejudice to the outcome of the Environment Agency's review.[260]

It is likely that the Agency will be issued with guidance from central government in the near future in relation to its decision-making in meeting of these targets. However, the Agency has ruled out a full justification analysis of reprocessing at Sellafield.[261]

---

[259] See 20.10.6(b) above.

[260] DETR, Department of the Environment Northern Ireland, National Assembly for Wales and Scottish Executive, UK Strategy for Radioactive Discharges 2001 – 2020, Consultation Document (2000).

[261] See also Environment Agency, *Scope and Methodology for the Full Re-examination of the Sellafield Authorisations for the Disposal of Radioactive Waste* (February 2000).

## 20.11 The Nuclear Installations Act 1965

The main legal provision in the UK governing nuclear disasters and other 'occurrences' resulting in radioactive contamination from nuclear installations is the Nuclear Installations Act 1965, concerned with the regulation of radioactivity originating from nuclear energy installations, which is the main subject of the rest of this chapter.[262] The Act subjects the operation of such installations to a system of licensing administered by the HSE and creates criminal offences for contravening licensing provisions including offences related to radioactive pollution. Insofar as it relates to the storage of radioactive wastes on nuclear sites, the HSE is the lead regulator and the Environment Agency has only a subsidiary role. The Act also imposes extensive civil liability upon the licensees of nuclear installations for causing certain kinds of radioactive emissions.

### 20.11.1 Background to the 1965 Act

The international background to the Nuclear Installations Act 1965 lies in two European regional conventions imposing a regime of strict liability upon operators of nuclear power installations. These were:

(a) the 1960 Paris Convention on Third Party Liability in the Field of Nuclear Energy;[263] and
(b) the 1963 Brussels Convention Supplementing the 1960 Convention.[264]

These conventions imposed a form of channelled strict liability on nuclear installation operators, subject to limitations in time and amount and an obligation to have extensive insurance cover. There is the additional possibility of further compensation being made available by Government in the event of a claim exceeding the amount of the operator's insurance cover. Under the 1965 Act, all operators of nuclear installations must be licensed, and there is a general principle of strict liability, limited in amount and time, on licensees for damage to persons or property caused by ionising radiation.[265]

### 20.11.2 Scope of the 1965 Act

The 1965 Act applies to nuclear sites. These are defined either as sites where a nuclear reactor is installed or operated, or where a prescribed installation operates for the production or use of nuclear energy or for uses ancillary to this. The Act also extends to prescribed classes of sites used for the storage, processing or distribution of nuclear fuel or of bulk quantities of other radioactive matter, where this matter has been produced

---

[262] This Act is to be read alongside the Nuclear Installations Act 1969: see s.5(2) of the 1969 Act. On the Act generally see Tromans and FitzGerald (1997).
[263] Cmnd.3755, as amended by Protocols in 1964 and 1982.
[264] Cmnd.5948, as amended by its 1964 Protocol.
[265] Dow (1989) p.83, cited in Tromans and FitzGerald (1997) p.99.

in the course of the production of nuclear fuel.[266] From 1990, the Act also applies to the UKAEA.[267]

Notably, the Act does not extend to a nuclear reactor 'comprised in a means of transport, whether by land, water or air'.[268] While the Act extends to the *carriage* of nuclear matter, it does not therefore extend to vessels *propelled* under nuclear power. This is the subject of an international convention which is not in force and to which the UK is not a party.[269] The reasons for this absence of national controls are fairly evident, since there is no nuclear-powered merchant fleet, and liabilities relating to nuclear-powered warships are dealt with separately under special intergovernmental arrangements for defence vessels. Any damage caused by a nuclear-powered vessel would be a matter for the ordinary civil law.[270]

### 20.11.3 Nuclear Site Licences

All nuclear sites must be licensed. The HSE is responsible for licensing sites, and must consult the Environment Agency before granting a licence.[271] In practice, it is the Nuclear Installations Inspectorate, a part of the Nuclear Safety Division of the HSE, which has day to day responsibility. At least in relation to the storage of radioactive waste, the Environment Agency has no formal responsibility.

The HSE may direct that any applicant for a licence must serve notice on designated public bodies that the application has been made and information about the proposed use of the site. These bodies are any local authority, any water undertaker or any local fisheries committee, and any other body that is a public or local authority. Any notice served by the applicant must direct consultees to make their representations directly to the HSE within a three month period. Licences can be varied but, if the variation of a licence relates to or affects the creation, accumulation or disposal of radioactive waste within the meaning of the Radioactive Substances Act 1993, the Environment Agency must first be consulted.[272]

Licences may be made subject to conditions, but only in the interests of 'safety'. Given the role of the HSE as the licensing body, and the human

---

[266] s.1(1) Nuclear Installations Act 1965, and see the Nuclear Installations Regulations 1971 (SI 1971 No.381).

[267] Nuclear Installations Act 1965 (Repeal and Modification) Regulations 1990 (SI 1990 No.1918).

[268] s.1(1)(a) Nuclear Installations Act 1965.

[269] Convention on the Liability of Operators of Nuclear Ships, Brussels, 1962.

[270] Tromans and FitzGerald (1997) para.3-13.

[271] s.3(1A) Nuclear Installations Act 1965, inserted by para.7 Sch.22 Environment Act 1995.

[272] See generally *ibid* s.3; see also *Memorandum of Understanding between (i) the Health and Safety Executive and (ii) the Environment Agency on matters of mutual concern at licensed nuclear sites in England and Wales,* 29 March 1996. There are concerns that where long-term storage becomes, over time, disposal the current arrangements do not give sufficient and timely regulatory powers to the Environment Agency (House of Lords Select Committee on Science and Technology, *Management of Nuclear Waste* (1999) paras.6.43-6.46.

safety-centred focus of its work, it must be doubted whether this would allow conditions to be attached relating to wider environmental protection. Nevertheless, conditions may be attached for a variety of purposes, including the detection of ionising radiation; the design, siting, construction, installation, operation, modification and maintenance of plant or other installation; and emergency response. Without prejudice to the provisions of the Radioactive Substances Act 1993 dealing with authorising discharges,[273] conditions can also be imposed with respect to the discharge of any substance on or from the site.[274] Conditions about the handling, treatment and disposal of nuclear matter[275] can also be imposed by the HSE at any time, as can any variation or revocation of any condition. The Environment Agency must be consulted before any condition is attached, varied or revoked if the condition relates to or affects the creation, accumulation or disposal of radioactive waste within the meaning of the Radioactive Substances Act 1993.[276] Copies of conditions must be kept posted on sites, subject to criminal penalties. In situations where there is no breach of an authorisation under the 1993 Act, it may be that an offence under the 1965 Act has been committed.[277] Provision is also made for revocation of licences, again subject to prior consultation with the Environment Agency.[278]

In effect, a dual system of controls operate over discharges from licensed nuclear sites by, on one hand, the HSE and, on the other, the Environment Agency, though provision is made for a degree of consistency through consultation between the regulators. Nevertheless, the same unauthorised release of radioactive material, or breach of a required procedural safety standard, may lead to liability under both the Nuclear Installations Act 1965 and the Radioactive Substances Act 1993. As discussed above, this was the case with the 'beach incident' at Sellafield in November 1983.[279] There is inter-agency provision for inspection matters.[280]

### 20.11.4 Civil Liability for Radioactive Pollution

The Nuclear Installations Act 1965 provides for extensive civil liability for injury or damage resulting from exposure to 'nuclear matter' in relation to licensed nuclear sites. Subject to prescribed exceptions, 'nuclear matter' means:

(a) any fissile material in the form of uranium metal, alloy or chemical compound (including natural uranium), or of plutonium metal, alloy or chemical compound, and any other fissile material which may be prescribed; and

---

[273] ss.13-16 Radioactive Substances Act 1993, see 20.10.6 above.

[274] s.4(1) and (2) Nuclear Installations Act 1960.

[275] Defined below.

[276] s.4(3A) Nuclear Installations Act 1960, inserted by para.8 Sch.22 Environment Act 1995.

[277] See Miller (1989) p.10.

[278] s.5 Nuclear Installations Act 1960.

[279] See 20.10.6C above.

[280] See the 1990 Memorandum of Understanding, above.

(b) any radioactive material produced in, or made radioactive by exposure to the radiation incidental to, the process of producing or utilising any such fissile material.[281]

While the 1965 Act constitutes the main basis for civil liability arising from radioactive pollution, as a matter of principle the contamination of a watercourse by radioactive material should fall within the basic principles establishing civil liability at common law.[282] Hence, it has been suggested that 'a riparian owner might be granted an injunction to restrain a discharge causing measurable radioactive contamination of his stream',[283] even if the polluting impact was not 'sensible'. Similarly a civil action for compensation might be brought for losses caused by radioactive contamination of water on the same basis as any other common law action for deterioration of water quality.[284]

Although these legal powers might be significant in respect of radioactive contamination arising outside the nuclear power industry, they are inapplicable to contamination originating from nuclear installations. In the most serious instances in which radioactive contamination of water might have a sensible effect upon the quality of water, common law rights are excluded by the civil liabilities arising under the 1965 Act.[285]

### 20.11.5  Duties on Nuclear Licensees

Alongside the provision made for licensing and inspection of nuclear installations imposed by the 1965 Act, the operator of an installation of this kind is placed under an explicit and closely defined duty to prevent occurrences causing injury to any person or damage to any property.[286] There are two aspects to this duty.

First, nuclear site licensees are under a duty to ensure that no occurrence involving nuclear matter[287] causes injury to any person or damage to any property of any person other than the licensee, if the injury or damage arises out of or results from the radioactive properties, or a combination of those and any toxic, explosive or other hazardous properties, of that nuclear matter. The duty arises in relation to various occurrences both on and off nuclear sites and in relation to the carriage of nuclear matter to or

---

[281] s.26(1) Nuclear Installations Act 1960.

[282] Generally see Ch.3 above on civil liability, especially 3.5.4 on riparian rights and 'sensible alteration'.

[283] *The Control of Radioactive Waste* (Cmnd.884, 1959) para.19.

[284] In *Blue Circle Industries Ltd* v *Ministry of Defence* [1998] 3 All ER 385 a less restrictive approach on sensible alteration was taken that in *Salvin* v *North Brancepeth Coal Co* (1874) 9 Ch. App 705 in relation to establishing a claim based solely on scientific evidence rather than on the observation of the senses, but the former related to the 1965 Act regime and, while it might point towards a relaxation of the common law rule in *Salvin*, cannot necessarily be taken as such.

[285] s.12(1)(b) Nuclear Installations Act 1965, see 20.11.6 below.

[286] *Ibid* s.7

[287] Of a kind mentioned in *ibid* s.7(2).

from licensed sites.[288] Exceptions are made for nuclear matter containing any one or more of the following constituents:

(a) isotopes prepared for use for industrial, commercial, agricultural, medical, scientific or educational purposes;
(b) natural uranium;
(c) any uranium of which isotope 235 forms not more than 0.72 per cent;
(d) nuclear matter of such other description, if any, in such circumstances as may be prescribed.[289]

The second aspect of the duty is that the licensee must secure that no ionising radiations emitted during the period of the licensee's responsibility, either from anything caused or suffered by the licensee to be on the site which is not nuclear matter, or from any waste discharged (in whatever form) on or from the site, causes injury to any person or damage to any property of any person other than the licensee. The duty is wider than that in relation to occurrences, since the source of the radiation does not need to be nuclear matter. There is clearly some overlap with provisions under the Radioactive Substances Act 1993, which also applies to such discharges. The central distinction is that breach of the 1993 Act gives rise to criminal sanctions, whereas breach of this provision of the 1965 Act only gives rise to strict civil liability.

The effect of these provisions therefore is that the operator of a nuclear installation is placed under a strict and extensive civil duty to avoid occurrences or emissions giving rise to radioactive pollution. The liability is strict in the sense that it will not be necessary for a claimant to establish negligence as might be required under common law; neither questions of foreseeability nor about the cost of preventing the damage occurring need be entered into. Indeed, in the case of certain occurrences, liability will arise where the occurrence is attributable to a natural disaster, notwithstanding that the disaster is of such an exceptional character that it could not reasonably have been foreseen.[290] Liability is extensive in that it encompasses liability for occurrences on the site that cause personal injuries or damage to property either on or off the site. In addition, liability extends to situations where nuclear matter is being carried between installations based in the territory of different contracting parties to the Paris Convention, which may be relevant to marine contamination. The duty to avoid injury to the person and damage to property does not mean, however, that the prospective licensee must be able to show that no such occurrence or emission will ever occur. Such an interpretation would

---

[288] *Ibid.* The Act specifies which 'relevant sites', 'relevant carriage' and 'relevant installations' are covered.

[289] s.26(1) Nuclear Installations Act 1960 as amended by s.27 and 31 Energy Act 1983. Additional matter has been prescribed by the Nuclear Installations (Excepted Matter) Regulations 1978 (SI 1978 No.1779).

[290] s.13(4)(b) Nuclear Installations Act 1960.

prevent any licence ever being issued, which would be contrary to the purpose of the Act.[291]

Decisions of the courts demonstrate problems in proving causation,[292] and that 'injury' has been interpreted as meaning that actual personal injury must be shown (the mere exposure to a risk of future personal injury will not suffice).[293] Beyond this there is the need to show 'damage to property', the meaning of which is clearly central to any water-related claims and which the courts have twice considered. In *Merlin v BNFL plc*,[294] radioactive matter discharged into the Irish Sea from Sellafield had washed ashore and been deposited in estuarial mud, and then brought into the claimants' house via their boots and their pets. Knowing of the contamination (and having discussed their plight on a TV documentary) the claimants sold their house at a much reduced price. They argued that the property had been physically contaminated by radioactive particles, and that the diminution in value of the house amounted to 'damage to property'. However, the judge rejected both claims, holding that the physical structure of the house was unharmed, and that the background to the Act required a restrictive interpretation of damage to exclude economic losses.[295]

In the subsequent case of *Blue Circle Industries plc v Ministry of Defence*,[296] however, compensation was awarded for 'damage to property' following an overflow of pond water containing radioactive substances at the Ministry of Defence establishment at Aldermaston in 1989. The material escaped into a stream and was transmitted onto marshland and a lake on adjoining property owned by the claimants. When the full extent of the contamination became apparent, ongoing negotiations to sell the property fell through. Although the Ministry eventually cleaned up the land, the claimants succeeded in gaining compensation, both for actual property damage to the marshland, for consequential damage to the rest of the property and in respect of the lost sale. Although no claim could be made simply on the grounds of the fear of being contaminated from a neighbouring plant handling or discharging radioactive substances,[297] the claimants also recovered for residual stigma depreciation, i.e., the loss in value of the property attributable to the actual contamination of the land.

---

[291] *Re Friends of the Earth* [1988] JPL 93.

[292] See Report of the Black Committee: *Investigation of the Possible Increased Incidence of Cancer in West Cumbria* (1984) and see *Reay v BNFL plc*; *Hope v BNFL plc* [1994] Env LR 320. For comment see Wilkinson (1994); Holder (1994); Miller (1996b); Tromans and FitzGerald (1997) para.3-25.

[293] *Merlin v British Nuclear Fuels plc* [1990] 2 QB 557, also discussed below.

[294] *Ibid.*

[295] The decision must be treated with some caution. Reference was made to the 1963 Vienna Convention to assist in interpreting the 1965 Act, but a review of the legislative history indicates that it was the provisions of the 1960 Paris Convention, and its Brussels Supplement, which the terms of 1965 Act sought to give force to. Had this been the case, a less restrictive interpretation might have been given, though perhaps without altering the eventual judgment. See Macrory (1991) and see also Tromans and FitzGerald (1997) para.3-26.

[296] [1998] 3 All ER 385. For comment see Tromans (1999).

[297] *Westleigh Colliery Co Ltd v Tunnicliffe and Hampson Ltd* [1908] AC 27.

Although the court in the *Blue Circle* case sought to distinguish rather than overrule the *Merlin* decision, the attempt to do so is somewhat unconvincing.[298]

It has been suggested that the provisions of the 1965 Act exclude compensation for damage to certain interests unprotected by property rights. Thus, where a public right of fishery existed, contamination of fish by nuclear matter would not ground a cause of action since no property right exists in the fish, and so the compensatory provisions of the Act would not assist owners of sea-going trawlers who found that their profits had declined due to a discharge of radioactive waste.[299] However, the better view may be that the provisions of the Act preventing ordinary civil law claims being brought for injury or property damage extend only to actions for these kinds of damage. The difficulty with this view, however, is the extent to which private law claims such as in private nuisance depend on interference with rights tied to property interests. On this basis, the trawler-owners in the above example would be frustrated in a claim in nuisance by their lack of property rights in the fish, but claims not restricted in this way, for example by freshwater angling associations, would also be restricted in scope because of the way in which, for example, claims for amenity losses must be connected to, and assessed by reference to, property rights.[300] Nevertheless, this view would support the possibility of claims being pursued for economic losses unconnected to property damage or personal injury, e.g., through an action in negligence or breach of statutory duty or for a breach of the Euratom Basic Safety Standards Directive.[301]

### 20.11.6 Liability and Concurrent Liabilities

In most situations the right to compensation under the 1965 Act for a breach of the duty upon a nuclear installation licensee operates to the exclusion of other concurrent forms of liability which might otherwise arise out of the occurrence. In particular, any injury or damage which, though not caused by a breach of the duties of a licensee of a nuclear installation, is not reasonably separable from injuries or damages so caused, is deemed, for the purposes of paying compensation under the Act, to have been so caused.[302] That is to say, incidents giving rise to liability under the Act will not normally provide the basis for other forms of liability such as in tort, and neither will such incidents serve as a basis for liability against any person other than the licensee. By way of exception, however, in a case where injury or damage is caused partly by the breach of duty of a licensee of a nuclear installation under the Act and partly by an emission of ionising radiation which does not constitute such a breach,

---

[298] Tromans (1999) p.61.

[299] See Street and Frame (1966) p.55; and see discussion of liability to fishing interests in respect of nuisance and negligence in Ch.3 above.

[300] See 3.8.3 above on limitations to nuisance claims.

[301] On breach of statutory duty, including claims under Community law, see 3.12 above.

[302] s.12(1) and (2) Nuclear Installations Act 1960.

a claimant will be entitled to recover compensation on grounds outside the Act. In a situation of this kind, no duplication of remedies will be permitted in that a claimant will not be entitled to recover compensation in respect of the same injury or damage both under the Act and otherwise than under the Act.[303] Liability under the Act and other statutory or common law bases for liability in such circumstances are mutually exclusive.

### 20.11.7 Defences, Limitations and Compensation

The only statutory defence provided under the 1965 Act applies where the occurrence causing injury or damage is the result of hostile action in the course of armed conflict.[304] There is, however, a narrowly circumscribed rule on contributory fault under which damages can be reduced if the causing of the injury or damage is attributable to any act of that person committed with the intention of causing harm to any person or property or with 'reckless disregard for the consequences' of that person's act.[305] A thirty year limitation period generally applies,[306] with the limitation period calculated by reference to the date of the occurrence, or occurrences, rather than the ensuing damage. However, claims for compensation made after the expiry of the appropriate limitation period can be made to the Secretary of State for Trade and Industry.[307] Compensation payments by licensees are limited to £140 million for any one incident, or in the case of certain prescribed site licences, £10 million.[308] Insurance cover or the like is required.[309]

### 20.12 Preventive Provisions on the Transport of Radioactive Material by Sea

There are a number of separate provisions intended to prevent the contamination of marine waters by vessels carrying dangerous goods, or to give the relevant authorities information of such cargoes. At a general level, the LOS Convention provides that:

> Foreign nuclear-powered ships and ships carrying nuclear or other inherently dangerous or noxious substances shall, when exercising the right of innocent passage through the territorial sea, carry

---

[303] *Ibid* s.12(3).

[304] *Ibid* s.13(4)(a).

[305] s.13(6); see also s.3(4) Congenital Disabilities (Civil Liability) Act 1976.

[306] See generally s.15 Nuclear Installations Act 1965.

[307] *Ibid* s.16(3) and s.26(1) and the Secretary of State for Trade and Industry Order 1970 (SI 1970 No.1537) as amended by the Transfer of Functions (Nuclear Installations) Order 1999 (SI 1999 No.2786).

[308] *Ibid* s.16(1) as amended by s.27 Energy Act 1983. The current sums are provided for under the Nuclear Installations (Increase in Operators' Limits of Liability) Order 1994 (SI 1994 No.909).

[309] *Ibid* s.19(1).

documents and observe special precautionary measures established for such ships by international agreements.[310]

More particularly, provision is made in national law requiring radioactive substances being carried by ships:

    (a) to be marked, and stored so as to withstand the ordinary risks of handling and transport at sea;[311]

    (b) for information of such cargoes to be kept on land and any incidents involving the actual or probable discharge of such goods to be reported;[312] and

    (c) requiring prior notification of such cargoes to the Coast Guard Agency or other local competent authority about the nature, quantity and location of any dangerous goods aboard, the ship's destination and intended route.[313]

Further provisions under the Euratom Treaty relate to the movement of certain radioactive wastes and radioactive substances, which may also have a preventive impact on the water environment.[314]

---

[310] Art.23 LOS Convention.

[311] The Merchant Shipping (Dangerous Goods and Marine Pollution) Regulations 1997 (SI 1997 No.2367). See also the Transfrontier Shipment of Radioactive Waste Regulations 1993 (SI 1993 No.3031).

[312] SI 1994 No.3245.

[313] SI 1995 No.2498.

[314] Directive 92/3/Euratom; see also the Fourth ACP-EEC (Lomé) Convention, 1989. Regulation 1493/93/Euratom is also relevant, though following Directive 92/3/Euratom no longer applies to radioactive waste.

# BIBLIOGRAPHY

## Chapter 1

Alder, J. and Wilkinson, D. (1999) *Environmental Law and Ethics* (Macmillan).

Bell, S. and McGillivray, D. (2000) *Ball and Bell on Environmental Law* (5th ed., Blackstone Press).

Boon, P. J. and Howell, D. L. (eds) (1997a) *Freshwater Quality: Defining the Indefinable?* (Stationery Office).

Boon, P.J. and Howell, D.L. (1997b) 'Defining the Quality of Fresh Waters: Theme and Variations' in Boon and Howell (1997a).

Clark, R.B. (1987) *The Waters Around the British Isles* (Oxford University Press).

Clark, R.B. (1997) *Marine Pollution* (4th ed., Oxford University Press).

Construction Industry Research and Information Association (1994) *Control of Pollution from Highway Drainage Discharges* (CIRIA).

Cook, H. F. (1998) *The Protection and Conservation of Water Resources* (John Wiley).

Edwards, R.W. (1997) 'Introduction' in Boon and Howell (1997a).

Environmental Protection Agency (Ireland) (1997) *Environmental Quality Objectives and Environmental Quality Standards – The Aquatic Environment* (Environmental Protection Agency (Ireland)).

Environmental Resources Management (1999) *Economic Instruments for Water Pollution Discharges* (Report for Department of Environment, Transport and the Regions).

Fort, R.S. and Brayshaw, J.D. (1961) *Fishery Management* (Faber and Faber Ltd).

Gardiner, J.L. (ed.) (1991) *River Projects and Conservation: a Manual for Holistic Appraisal* (John Wiley).

Gardiner, J.L. (1994) 'Sustainable Development for River Catchments' *Journal of the Institution of Water and Environmental Management* 308.

Garnett, P.H. (1981) 'Thoughts on the Need to Control Discharges to Estuarial and Coastal Waters', *Water Pollution Control* 172.

Guruswamy, L.D. and Tromans, S. (1986) 'Towards an Integrated Approach to Pollution Control', *Journal of Planning and Environmental Law* 643.

Haigh, N. (1992, updated) *Manual of Environmental Policy: the EC and Britain* (Longman/ Sweet and Maxwell).

Hammerton, D. (1987) 'The Impact of Environmental Legislation', 86 *Water Pollution Control* 333.

Hanley, N. (1997) 'Assessing the Economic Value of Fresh Waters' in Boon and Howell (1997a).

Hardman, D.J., McEldowney, S. and Waite, S. (1993) *Pollution: Ecology and Treatment* (Longman).

Hawkes, H.A. (1979) 'Water Quality Issues: an Ecological Reaction', *Chemistry and Industry* 210.

Holdgate, M.W. (1979) *A Perspective of Environmental Pollution* (Cambridge University Press).

Howarth, W. (1993) 'Poisonous, Noxious or Polluting: Contrasting Approaches to Environmental Regulation', 56 *Modern Law Review* 171.

Howarth, W. (1999) 'Accommodation without Resolution? Emission Controls and Environmental Quality Objectives in the Proposed EC Water Framework Directive', 1 *Environmental Law Review* 6.

Howarth, W. (2000) 'Economics, Ethics and Water Pollution Control', 2 *Environmental Law Review* 135.

Howarth, W. and McGillivray D (1996) 'Sustainable Management of Aquatic Ecosystems and the Law' in C.P. Rodgers (ed.) *Nature Conservation and Countryside Law* (University of Wales Press).

Hunt, D.T.E., Johnson, I. and Milne, R. (1992) 'The Control and Monitoring of Discharges by Biological Techniques', *Journal of the Institute of Water and Environment Management* 269.

Ives, K.J., Hammerton, D. and Packham, R.F. (1994) *The River Severn Pollution Incident of April 1994 and its Impact Upon Public Water Supplies* (Severn Trent Water).

Institute of Fisheries Management (1981) *Water Quality and Pollution* (Institute of Fisheries Management).

Jewell, T. and Pontin, B. (1998) 'Economic Instruments for Water Pollution', 10 *Environmental Law and Management* 30.

Kaye, T. (1996) 'Do Consumers make Contracts With Water Companies?' 7 *Water Law* 48.

Klein, L. (1957) *Aspects of River Pollution* (Butterworths).

Klein, L. (1962) *River Pollution 2: Causes and Effects* (Butterworths).

McLoughlin, J. (1972) *The Law Relating to Pollution* (Manchester University Press).

Mason, C.F. (1996) *Biology of Freshwater Pollution* (3rd ed., Longman).

Mills, D.H. (1972) *An Introduction to Freshwater Ecology* (Oliver and Boyd).

Moss, B., Madgwick, J. and Phillips, G. (1996) *A Guide to the Restoration of Nutrient-enriched Shallow Lakes* (Environment Agency).

National Water Council (1978) *River Water Quality, the Next Stage. Review of Discharge Consent Conditions* (National Water Council).

Newsom, G. and Sherratt, J.G. (1972) *Water Pollution* (John Sherratt and Son).

Newson, M. (1992) *Land, Water and Development* (Routledge).

Newson, M. (1994) *Hydrology and the River Environment* (Clarendon).

Ogus, A.I. (1994) *Regulation: Legal Form and Economic Theory* (Clarendon).

Organisation for Economic Co-operation and Development (1986) *Water Pollution by Fertilizers and Pesticides* (OECD).

Parker, D. and Penning-Rowsell, E. (1980) *Water Planning in Britain* (George Allen and Unwin).

Pugh, K.B. (1997) 'Organizational use of the Term 'Freshwater Quality' in Britain', in Boon and Howell (1997a).

Richardson, G., Ogus, A. and Burrows, P. (1982) *Policing Pollution* (Clarendon).

Rhoades, J. (1997) *An Introduction to Industrial Wastewater Treatment and Disposal* (Chartered Institution of Water and Environmental Management).

Rowan-Robinson, J., Watchman, P. and Barker, C. (1990) *Crime and Regulation* (T & T Clark).

Royal Commission on Salmon Fisheries (England and Wales) Report (1861) Parl. Paper 2768.

Royal Commission on Environmental Pollution (1971) *First Report,* Cmnd.4585.

Royal Commission on Environmental Pollution (1974) *Pollution Control: Progress and Problems*, Fourth Report, Cmnd.5780.

Royal Commission on Environmental Pollution (1979) *Agriculture and Pollution*, Seventh Report, Cmnd.7644.

Royal Commission on Environmental Pollution (1984) *Tackling Pollution: Experience and Prospects*, Tenth Report, Cmnd.9149.

Royal Commission on Environmental Pollution (1985) *Managing Waste: The Duty of Care*, Eleventh Report, Cmnd.9675.

Royal Commission on Environmental Pollution (1992) *Freshwater Quality*, Sixteenth Report, Cm 1966.

Royal Commission on Environmental Pollution (1998) *Setting Environmental Standards*, Twenty-first Report, Cm 4053.

Royal Commission on Rivers Pollution (1870) *Mersey and Ribble,* First Report, C.37.

Royal Commission on Sewage Disposal (1912) *Standards and tests for sewage and sewage effluents discharging into rivers and streams,* Eighth Report, Cd.6464.

Simes, E. and Scholefield, C.E. (1954) *Lumley's Public Health Law: the Public Health Acts Annotated* Vol.V (12th ed., Butterworths).

Simmons, S. (1999) 'Bedtime Reeding', *The Waste Manager*, September 1999 p.21.

Smith, K. (1972) *Water in Britain* (Macmillan).

Spray, C. (1997) 'Assessing the Recreational Value of Fresh Waters: the UK Experience' in Boon and Howell (1997a).

Stiff, G. (1996) 'Water Supply – Contract or Statute?' 7 *Water Law* 167.

Swanwick, C. (1997) 'Landscape Assessment of Fresh Waters' in Boon and Howell (1997a).

Taylor, J.O. (1928) *The Law Affecting River Pollution* (W. Green and Son).

Templeton, R.G. (ed.) (1984) *Freshwater Fisheries Management* (Fishing News Books).

Teubner, G. (1994) 'The Invisible Cupola: From Causal to Collective Attribution in Ecological Liability', in G. Teubner, L. Farmer and D. Murphy (eds) *Environmental Law and Ecological Responsibility* (John Wiley).

Tunstall, S., Fordham, M., Green, C. and House, M. (1997) 'Public Perception of Freshwater Quality with Particular Reference to Rivers in England and Wales', in Boon and Howell (1997a).

Turing, H.D. (1952) *River Pollution* (Butler & Tanner).

Werritty, A. (1997) 'Enhancing the Quality of Freshwater Resources: the Role of Integrated Catchment Management' in Boon and Howell (1997a).

Wharfe, R.J. and Tinsley, D. (1995) 'The Toxicity-Based Consent and the Wider Application of Direct Toxicity Assessment to Protect Aquatic Life', *Journal of the Chartered Institution of Water and Environmental Management* 526.

Wisdom, A.S. (1966) *The Law on the Pollution of Waters* (2nd ed., Shaw and Sons).

Wood, L.B. and Sheldon, D. (1980) 'Water Quality Control' in A.M. Gower (ed.) *Water Quality in Catchment Ecosystems* (John Wiley).

World Commission on Environment and Development (1987) *Our Common Future* (the 'Brundtland Commission') (Oxford University Press).

Zabel, T. and Rees, Y. (1998) 'Managing the Water Environment: Prospects for Change', 9 *Water Law* 195.

## Chapter 2

Bigham, D.A. (1973) *The Law and Administration Relating to Protection of the Environment* and *Supplement* (1975) (Oyez).

Brittan, Y. (1984) *The Impact of Water Pollution Control on Industry* (Economic and Social Research Council).

Burton, T. (1987) 'The Control of Pollution Act 1974, Part II: The Extension of Control to All Discharges to UK Tidal Waters', 2 *International Journal of Estuarine and Coastal Law* 10.

Burton, T. (1989) 'Access to Environmental Information – The UK Experience of Water Registers', 1 *Journal of Environmental Law* 192.

Burton, T. and Freestone, D. (1986) 'The Control of Pollution Act 1974 and Tidal Waters: Problems of the Implementation of Part II', 1 *International Journal of Estuarine and Coastal Law* 241.

Callis, R. (1622) *Reading upon the statute of 23 H 8, cap 5, of sewers delivered at Grays Inn* ('Callis on Sewers').

Carter, N. and Lowe, P. (1995) 'The Establishment of a Cross-Sector Environment Agency' in T. Gray (ed.) *UK Environmental Policy in the 1990s* (Macmillan).

Craine, L.E. (1969) *Water Management Innovations in England* (Resources for the Future Inc.).

Fort, R.S. and Brayshaw, J.D. (1961) *Fishery Management* (Faber and Faber Ltd).

Funnell, B.M. and Hey, R.D. (eds) (1974) *The Management of Water Resources in England and Wales* (Saxon House).

Gallagher, E. (1996) 'The Environment Agency' in *Bringing the Environment Down to Earth, Journal of Planning and Environment Law*, Occasional Paper No. 24.

Garner, J.F. (1974) 'The Law Relating to Pollution of Inland Waters in the United Kingdom' in A.D. McKnight, P.K. Marstrand and T.C. Sinclair (eds) *Environmental Pollution Control* (George Allen & Unwin).

Garner, J.F. (1975) *Control of Pollution Act 1974* (Butterworths).

Gordon, S. (1989) *Down the Drain: Water Pollution and Privatisation* (Macdonald).

Graham, C. and Prosser, T. (1991) *Privatising Public Industries* (Clarendon Press).

Gray, C. (1982) 'The Regional Water Authorities', in Hogwood, B.W. and Keating, M. (Eds.) *Regional Government in England* (Clarendon).

Haigh, N. (1992, updated) *Manual of Environmental Policy: the EC and Britain* (Longman/ Sweet and Maxwell).

Haigh, N. and Lanigan, C. (1995) 'Impact of the European Union on UK Environmental Policy Making', in T. Gray (ed.) *UK Environmental Policy in the 1990s* (Macmillan).

Hammerton, D. (1987) 'The Impact of Environmental Legislation', 86 *Water Pollution Control* 333.

Hassan, J. (1998) *A History of Water in Modern England and Wales* (Manchester University Press).

Her Majesty's Inspectorate of Pollution (1996) *Annual Report 1995-96*.

Hobday, S.R. (1952) *Coulson and Forbes on the Law of Waters* (6th ed., Sweet and Maxwell).

Howarth, W. (1987) *Freshwater Fishery Law* (Financial Training/Blackstone).

Howarth, W. (1992) 'Regulation, Operation and Management: the Functions of the Proposed Environment Agency', 1 *International Journal of Regulatory Law* 82.

Jewell, T. and Steele, J. (1996) 'UK Regulatory Reform and the Pursuit of "Sustainable Development": The Environment Act 1995', 8 *Journal of Environmental Law* 283.

Jordan, A. and Greenaway J. (1998) 'Shifting Agendas, Changing Regulatory Structures and the 'New' Politics of Environmental Pollution: British Coastal Water Policy 1955-1995', 76 *Public Administration* 669.

Jordan, A.G., Richardson, J.J. and Kimber, R.H. (1977) 'The Origins of the Water Act of 1973', 55 *Public Administration* 317.

Kinnersley, D. (1988) *Troubled Waters: Rivers, Politics and Pollution* (Shipman).

Kinnersley, D. (1994) *Coming Clean: The Politics of Water and the Environment* (Penguin).

Klein, L. (1957) *Aspects of River Pollution* (Butterworths).

Klein, L. (1962) *River Pollution 2: Causes and Effects* (Butterworths).

Lane, P. and Peto, M. (1995) *Blackstone's Guide to the Environment Act 1995* (Blackstone Press).

Law Commission (1991) *Report on the Consolidation of the Legislation Relating to Water*, Law Com. No.198 (HMSO).

McLoughlin, J. (1972) *The Law Relating to Pollution* (Manchester University Press).

McLoughlin, J. (1973) *The Water Act 1973* (Sweet and Maxwell).

McLoughlin, J. (1975) 'The Control of Pollution Act 1974 – 2', *Journal of Planning and Environment Law* 77.

Macrory, R. (1989) *The Water Act 1989; Text and Commentary* (Sweet & Maxwell).

Macrory, R. (1990) 'The Privatisation and Regulation of the Water Industry', 53 *Modern Law Review* 78.

Maloney, W. and Richardson, J. (1995) *Managing Policy Change in Britain: The Politics of Water* (Edinburgh University Press).

Newsom, G. and Sherratt, J.G. (1972) *Water Pollution* (John Sherratt and Son).

Okun, D.A. (1977) *Regionalization of Water Management* (Applied Science Publishers).

Porter, E. (1978) *Water Management in England and Wales* (Cambridge University Press).

Richardson, G., Ogus, A. and Burrows, P. (1982) *Policing Pollution* (Clarendon).

Rosen, G. (1958) *A History of Public Health* (MD Publications).

Royal Commission on Environmental Pollution (1976) *Air Pollution Control: an Integrated Approach*, Fifth Report, Cmnd.6371.

Royal Commission on Environmental Pollution (1984) *Tackling Pollution: Experience and Prospects*, Tenth Report, Cmnd.9149.

Rowan-Robinson, J., Watchman, P. and Barker, C. (1990) *Crime and Regulation* (T & T Clark).

Royal Commission on Environmental Pollution (1988) *Best Practicable Environmental Option*, Twelfth Report, Cm 310.

Royal Commission on Rivers Pollution (1874) *Pollution Arising from Mining Operations and Metal Manufacturers*, Fifth Report, C.951.

Royal Commission on Salmon Fisheries (England and Wales) Report (1861) Parl. Paper 2768.

Royal Commission on Sanitary Laws (1871) *Second Report*, Vol 1 C.281.

Smith, F.B. (1979) *The People's Health 1830 – 1910* (Croom Helm).

Telling, M.A. (1974) *Water Authorities* (Butterworths).

Trice, J.E. and Godwin, H. (1974) 'The Control of River Pollution in Wales (1963 – 73): An Assessment of the Working of the Water Resources Act 1963 in Wales', *Journal of Planning and Environment Law* 314.

Tromans, S. (1996) *The Environment Acts 1990-1995* (3rd ed., Sweet & Maxwell).

Turing, H.D. (1952) *River Pollution* (Butler & Tanner).

Vogel, D. (1986) *National Styles of Regulation: Environmental Policy in Great Britain and the United States* (Cornell University Press).

Walker, A. (1979) *Law of Industrial Pollution Control* (George Godwin).

Wohl, A.S. (1983) *Endangered Lives* (J. M. Dent).

## Chapter 3

Abecassis, D.W. and Jarashow, J.L. (1985) *Oil Pollution from Ships: International, United Kingdom and United States Law and Practice* (2nd ed., Stevens and Sons).

Atkinson, N. (1992) 'Strict Liability for Environmental Law: The Deficiencies of the Common Law', 4 *Journal of Environmental Law* 81.

Atkinson, N. (1993) 'Strict Liability for Environmental Damage: The Cambridge Water Company Case', 5 *Journal of Environmental Law* 173.

Ball, S. (1990) '*Murphy v Brentwood DC:* the water law implications', 1 *Water Law* 102.

Ball, S. (1994) 'Cambridge Water: What Does It Decide?', 5 *Water Law* 61.

Ball, S. (1995) 'Nuisance and Planning Permission', 7 *Journal of Environmental Law* 278.

Barrett, B. (1992) 'Common law liability for flood damage caused by storms', *New Law Journal* 1608.

Bates, J.H. (1990, updated) *Water and Drainage Law* (Sweet and Maxwell).

Bell, J. and Engle, G. (1995) *Cross on Statutory Interpretation* (3rd ed., Butterworths).

Brazier, M. and Murphy, J. (1999). *Street on Torts* (10th ed., Butterworths).

Brazier, M.R. (ed.) (1995) *Clerk and Lindsell on Torts* (17th ed., Sweet and Maxwell).

Brubaker, E. (1995) *Property Rights In Defence of Nature* (Earthscan).

Cane, P. (1993) 'The Scope and Justification for Exemplary Damages: The Camelford Case', 5 *Journal of Environmental Law* 149.

Crawford, C. (1992) 'Public Law Rules Over Private Law as a Standard for Nuisance: OK?' 4 *Journal of Environmental Law* 251.

Cross, G. (1995) 'Does Only the Careless Polluter Pay? A Fresh Examination of the Nature of Private Nuisance', 111 *Law Quarterly Review* 195.

Fifoot, C.H.S. (1949) *History and Sources of the Common Law* (Stevens and Sons).

Gearty, C. (1989) 'The Place of Private Nuisance in a Modern Law of Torts', 48 *Cambridge Law Journal* 214.

Gray, K. (1993) *Elements of Land Law* (2nd ed, Butterworths).

Hilson, C. (1996) 'Cambridge Water Revisited', 7 *Water Law* 126.

Hobday, S.R. (1952) *Coulson and Forbes on the Law of Waters* (6th ed., Sweet and Maxwell).

Holder, J. (1994) 'The Sellafield Litigation and Questions of Causation in Environmental Law', 47 *Current Legal Problems* 287.

Howarth, D. (1995) *Textbook on Tort* (Butterworths).

Howarth, W. (1987) *Freshwater Fishery Law* (Financial Training/Blackstone).

Howarth, W. (1990) *The Law of Aquaculture* (Fishing News Books/Blackwell Scientific).

Howarth, W. (1992a) *Wisdom's Law of Watercourses* (5th ed., Shaw and Sons).

Howarth, W. (1992b) 'Access to the Foreshore', *Rights of Way Law Review,* November 1992, p.11.

Howarth, W. and McGillivray D (1996) 'Sustainable Management of Aquatic Ecosystems and the Law' in C.P. Rodgers (ed.) *Nature Conservation and Countryside Law* (University of Wales Press).

James, J. (2000) 'Annual Report for 1998' in *ACA Review 1999-2000*, p.9 (Anglers' Conservation Association).

Jewkes, P. (1998) 'Light Pollution: A Review of the Law', *Journal of Planning and Environmental Law* 10.

Jones, M.A. (1998) *Textbook on Torts* (6th ed., Blackstone).

Kodilinye, G. (1986) 'Public nuisance and particular damage in modern law', *Legal Studies* 182.

McDowell, H.R. and Chamberlain, C.E. (1950) *Michael and Will on the Law Relating to Water* (9th ed., Butterworths).

McLaren, J.P.S. (1972) 'Nuisance Actions and the Environmental Battle' *Osgoode Hall Law Journal* 505.

Martin, J.E. (1997) *Hanbury and Martin Modern Equity* (15th ed., Sweet and Maxwell).

Newark, F. (1949) 'The Boundaries of Nuisance', 65 *Law Quarterly Review* 480.

Newark, F. (1961) 'Non-Natural User and *Rylands v Fletcher*', 24 *Modern Law Review* 557.

Newsom, G. and Sherratt, J.G. (1972) *Water Pollution* (John Sherratt and Son).

Ogus, A.I. (1994) 'Water Rights Diluted', 6 *Journal of Environmental Law* 137.

Ogus, A.I. and Richardson, G.M. (1977) 'Economics and the Environment – A Study of Private Nuisance', 36 *Cambridge Law Journal* 284.

Payne, S. (1994) 'Sewage Pollution of Beaches – Liability and Clean Up', 5 *Water Law* 183.

Poli, S. (1999) 'Shaping the EC Regime on Liability for Environmental Damage: Progress of Disillusionment', 8 *European Environmental Law Review* 299.

Pugh, C. and Day, M. (1995) *Pollution and Personal Injury: Toxic Torts II* (Cameron May).

Reece, H. and Freeman, M. (eds) (1998) *Science and the Law* (Oxford University Press).

Rodgers, P. (1993) 'Firms Given Pollution Amnesty' *The Independent* 10th December p.1.

Rodgers, P. and Durman, P. (1993) 'City Welcomes Pollution Ruling' *The Independent* 10th December p.29.

Rogers, W.V.H. (1998) *Winfield and Jolowicz on Tort* (15th ed., Sweet and Maxwell).

Royal Commission on Rivers Pollution (1867) *Third Report*, Parl. Paper 3850.

Shelbourne, C. (1994) 'Historic Pollution – Does the Polluter Pay?' *Journal of Planning and Environmental Law* 703.

Spencer, J.R. (1986) 'A Duty of Common Humanity to Bees', 45 *Cambridge Law Journal* 15.

Spencer, J.R. (1989) 'Public Nuisance – A Critical Examination', 48 *Cambridge Law Journal* 55.

Steele, J. (1995) Private Law and the Environment: Nuisance in Context', 15 *Legal Studies* 236.

Steele, J. (1997) 'Being There is Not Enough – The House of Lords Puts the Brakes on Nuisance in the Home', 9 *Journal of Environmental Law* 345.

Steele, J. and Wikely, N. (1997) 'Dust on the Streets and Liability for Environmental Cancers', 60 *Modern Law Review* 265.

Sutton, K. (1988) 'The ACA's First Forty Years' *ACA Review* Summer 1988, p.24 (Anglers' Conservation Association).

Taylor, J.O. (1928) *The Law Affecting River Pollution* (W. Green and Son).

Tromans, S.R. (1987) 'Riparian Rights and Water Authority Negligence', *The Conveyancer and Property Lawyer* 368.

Tromans, S. (1999) 'Review of Lord Chancellor's Department, *Civil Procedure Rules (with Practice Directions, Pre-action Protocols and Forms'* 11 *Journal of Environmental Law* 387.

Ward, R. and Parpworth N. (1994) 'Cambridge Water – The End of Strict Liability?' 5 *Water Law* 57.

Wisdom, A.S. (1979) *The Law of Rivers and Watercourses* (4th ed., Shaw & Sons).

**Chapter 4**

Axelrod, R. (1994) 'Subsidiarity and Environmental Policy in the European Community', 6 *Journal of International Environmental Affairs* 115.

Bär, S. and Kraemer, A. (1998) 'European Environmental Policy after Amsterdam' 10 Journal of Environmental Law 315.

Bell, S. and McGillivray, D. (2000) *Ball and Bell on Environmental Law* (5th ed., Blackstone Press)

Burnett-Hall, R. (1995) 'The Enforcement of EC Directives Against Suppliers of Public Services', 4 *European Environmental Law Review* 42.

de Búrca, G. (1999) 'Reappraising Subsidiarity's Significance after Amsterdam', *Harvard Jean Monnet Working Paper 7/99*.

Flynn, B. (1997) 'Subsidiarity and the Rise of "Soft Law" in EU Environmental Policy: Beyond Who Does What, to What it is they Actually do' *European Policy Process*, Occasional Paper No.40.

Freestone, D. (1991) 'The Precautionary Principle' in R.R. Churchill and D. Freestone (eds) *International Law and Global Climate Change* (Graham & Trotman).

Freestone, D., (1994a) 'EC Environmental Law After Maastricht', 45 *Northern Ireland Legal Quarterly* 152.

Freestone D. (1994b) 'The Road From Rio: International Environmental Law after the Earth Summit', 6 *Journal of Environmental Law* 193.

Freestone, D. and Hey, E. (eds) (1996) *The Precautionary Principle and International Law* (Kluwer).

Freestone, D. and Ijlstra, T. (1990) (eds) *The North Sea: Perspectives on Regional Co-operation* (Graham and Trotman).

Gardner, B. (1996) *European Agricultural Policies: Protection and Trade* (Routledge).

Geddes, A. (1994) 'Implementation of Community Environmental Law: Bathing Water', 5 *Journal of Environmental Law* 125.

Geddes, A. (1995) *Protection of Individual Rights Under EC Law* (Butterworths).

Golub, J. (1996) 'British Sovereignty and the Development of EC Environmental Policy', 5 *Environmental Politics* 700.

Haigh, N. (1992, updated) *Manual of Environmental Policy: the EC and Britain* (Longman/ Sweet and Maxwell).

Hawke, N. and Kovaleva N. (1998) *Agri-Environmental Law and Policy* (Cavendish).

Hession, M. and Macrory, R. (1994) 'Maastricht and the Environmental Policy of the Community: Legal Issues of a New Environment Policy', in O'Keefe, D. and Twomey P.M. (eds.) *Legal Issues of the Maastricht Treaty* (Chancery Law).

Hession, M. and Macrory, R. (1998) 'The Legal Duty of Environmental Integration: Commitment and Obligation or Enforceable Right?' in T. O'Riordan and H. Voisey (eds) *The Transition to Sustainability: The Politics of Agenda 21 in Europe* (Earthscan).

Hilson, C. (1997) 'Community Rights in Environmental Law: Rhetoric or Reality?' in J. Holder (ed.) *The Impact of EC Environmental Law in the United Kingdom* (Wiley).

Hilson, C. and Downes, T. (1999) 'Making Sense of Rights: Community Rights in EC Law', 24 *European Law Review* 121.

Hohmann, H. (1994) *Precautionary Legal Duties and Principles of Modern International Environmental Law* (Graham & Trotman/Martinus Nijhoff).

Howarth, W. (1999) 'Sovereignty, Community Environmental Inspection and the Globalisation of the Drinking Water Directive', 10 *Water Law* 5.

Jans, J.H. (1995) *European Environmental Law* (Kluwer).

Jans, J.H. (1996) 'Legal Protection in European Environmental Law: An Overview', in H. Somsen (ed.) *Protecting the European Environment: Enforcing EC Environmental Law* (Blackstone).

Jans, J.H. (2000). *European Environmental Law* (2nd ed, Europa Law Publishing)

Jewkes, P. (1994) 'The Principle of Subsidiarity: Its Effect on Existing and Future EC Environmental Regulation', 6 *Environmental Law and Management* 165.

Johnson, S.P. (1993) *The Earth Summit: The United Nations Conference on Environment and Development (UNCED)* (Graham & Trotman/Martinus Nijhoff).

Jones, J.G. (ed.) (1993) *Agriculture and the Environment* (E. Horwood).

Jordan, A. and Greenaway J. (1998) 'Shifting Agendas, Changing Regulatory Structures and the 'New' Politics of Environmental Pollution: British Coastal Water Policy 1955-1995', 76 *Public Administration* 669.

Krämer, L. (1992) *Focus on European Environmental Law* (1st ed., Sweet and Maxwell).

Krämer, L. (1996) 'Public interest litigation in environmental matters before European courts' 8 *Journal of Environmental Law* 1.

Krämer, L. (1997) *Focus on European Environmental Law* (2nd ed., Sweet and Maxwell).

Krämer, L. (2000) *EC Environmental Law* (4th ed, Sweet and Maxwell).

Kunzlik, P. (1995) 'Environmental Impact Assessment: The British Cases', 4 *European Environmental Law Review* 336.

Kunzlik, P. (1997) 'The Enforcement of EU Environmental Law: Article 169, the Ombudsman and the Parliament', 6 *European Environmental Law Review* 46.

Lange, B. (2000) 'Economic Appraisal of Law-Making and Changing Forms of Governance', 63 *Modern Law Review* 294.

McIntyre, O. (1994) 'The Guiding Principles of European Community Environmental Law-Making', 4 *European Environment* 23.

McIntyre, O. (1997) 'Proportionality and environmental protection in EC law' in J. Holder (ed.) *The Impact of EC Environmental Law in the United Kingdom* (Wiley).

McIntyre, O. and Mosedale, T. (1997) 'The Precautionary Principle as a Norm of Customary International Law', 9 *Journal of Environmental Law* 221.

Macrory, R. (1992) 'The Enforcement of Community Environmental Laws: Some Critical Issues', 29 *Common Market Law Review* 347.

Macrory, R. (1996) 'Community Supervision in the Field of the Environment', in H. Somsen (ed.) *Protecting the European Environment: Enforcing EC Environmental Law* (Blackstone).

Macrory, R. (2000) 'Legal Issues of the Amsterdam Treaty: The Environment', in D. O'Keefe and P.M. Twomey (eds) *Legal Issues of the Amsterdam Treaty* (Hart).

Macrory, R. and Purdy, R. (1997) 'The Enforcement of EC Law Against Member States', in J. Holder (ed.) *The Impact of EC Environmental Law in the United Kingdom* (Wiley).

Magliveras, K.D. (1995) 'Best Intentions But Empty Words: The European Ombudsman', 20 *European Law Review* 401.

Marias, E. (1994) 'The Right to Petition the European Parliament After Maastricht', 19 *European Law Review* 169.

Miller, C. (1995) 'Environmental Rights: European Fact or English Fiction?' 22 *Journal of Law and Society* 374.

Noble, D. (1996) 'Enforcing EC Environmental Law: The National Dimension', in H. Somsen (ed.) *Protecting the European Environment: Enforcing EC Environmental Law* (Blackstone).

Nollkaemper, A. (1997) 'Habitat Protection in European Community Law: Evolving Conceptions of a Balance of Interests', 9 *Journal of Environmental Law* 271.

O'Riordan, T. and Cameron, J. (eds) (1994) *Interpreting the Precautionary Principle* (Earthscan).

Pallemaerts, M. (1993) 'International Environmental Law from Stockholm to Rio: Back to the Future?' in P. Sands (ed.) *Greening International Law* (Earthscan).

Peters, H.-J. (1996) 'The Significance of Environmental Precaution in the Environmental Impact Assessment Directive', 5 *European Environmental Law Review* 210.

Sands, P. (1995) *Principles of International Environmental Law* (Manchester University Press).

Scott J. (1996) 'Environmental Compatibility and the Community's Structural Funds: A Legal Analysis', 8 *Journal of Environmental Law* 99.

Scott, J. (1998) *EC Environmental Law* (Longmans).

Scott, J. (2000) '"Proceduralization" and Environmental Governance in the EU' in G. de Búrca and J. Scott (eds) *The Changing Constitution of the EU: From Uniformity to Flexibility?* (Hart).

Sheate, W. (1997) 'From Environmental Impact Assessment to Strategic Environmental Assessment: Sustainability and Decision-Making' in J. Holder (ed.) *The Impact of EC Environmental Law in the United Kingdom* (Wiley).

Sifakis, A. (1998) 'Precaution, prevention and the Environmental Impact Assessment Directive', 7 *European Environmental Law Review* 349.

Somsen, H. (1992) 'European Community Environmental Law After Maastricht', 3 *Water Law* 117.

Somsen. H. (1996) '*Francovich* and its Application to EC Environmental Law', in Somsen, H. (ed.) *Protecting the European Environment: Enforcing EC Environmental Law* (Blackstone).

Somsen. H. (2000) 'The Private Enforcement of Member State Compliance with EC Environmental Law: an Unfulfilled Promise?' 1 *Yearbook of European Environmental Law* 311.

Tromans, S. (1995) 'High Principles and Low Cunning: Putting Environmental Principles Into Legal Practice', *Journal of Planning and Environmental Law* 779.

Tydeman, C. (2000) 'Trying out the conciliation process on the Water Framework Directive', 2 *Environmental Law Review* 229.

van Calster, G. and Deketelaere, K. (1998) 'Amsterdam, the Intergovernmental Conference and Greening the EU Treaty', 7 *European Environmental Law Review* 12.

Vandekerchove, K. (1993) 'The Polluter Pays Principle in the European Community', 13 *Yearbook of European Law* 201.

Vandermeersch, D. (1987) 'The Single European Act and the Environmental Policy of the European Economic Community', 12 *European Law Review* 407.

von Moltke, K. (1988) 'The Vorsorgenprinzip in West German Environmental Policy', Appendix 3 to Royal Commission on Environmental Pollution (1988) *Best Practicable Environmental Option,* Twelfth Report, Cm 310.

Wathern, P. (1992) 'Less Favoured and Environmentally Sensitive Areas: A European Dimension to the Rural Environment', in W. Howarth and C.P. Rodgers (eds) *Agriculture, Conservation and Land Use* (University of Wales Press).

Wilkinson, D. (1992) 'Maastricht and the Environment: The Implications for the EC's Environmental Policy of the Treaty of European Union', 4 *Journal of Environmental Law* 221.

Williams, R. (1994) 'The European Commission and the Enforcement of Environmental Law: an Invidious Position', *Yearbook of European Law* 351.

Wils, W.P.J. (1994) 'Subsidiarity and Environmental Policy: Taking People's Concerns Seriously', 6 *Journal of Environmental Law* 85.

Wyatt, D. (1998) 'Litigating Community Environmental Law – Thoughts on the Direct Effect Doctrine', 10 *Journal of Environmental Law* 9.

**Chaper 5**

Bell, S. and McGillivray, D. (2000) *Ball and Bell on Environmental Law* (5th ed., Blackstone Press)

Blatch, C. (1996) 'Estuaries and coastal waters – establishing the limits', 8 *Journal of Environmental Law* 336.

Boehmer-Christiansen, S. (1990) 'Environmental Quality Objectives versus Uniform Emission Standards', in D. Freestone and T. IJlstra (eds) *The North Sea: Perspectives on Regional Co-operation* (Graham and Trotman).

Brumwell, M.J. (2000) 'Meaning of Discharge', 2 *Environmental Law Review* 35.

Foster, D., Wood, A. and Griffiths, M. (2000) 'The Water Framework Directive and It's Implications for the Environment Agency' forthcoming in *Freshwater Forum*.

Haigh, N. (1992, updated) *Manual of Environmental Policy: the EC and Britain* (Longman/ Sweet and Maxwell).

Howarth, W. (1999) 'Accommodation without Resolution? Emission Controls and Environmental Quality Objectives in the Proposed EC Water Framework Directive', 1 *Environmental Law Review* 6.

Jordan, A. (1999) 'European Community Water Policy Standards: Locked In or Watered Down?' 37 *Journal of Common Market Studies* 13.

Jordan, A. and Greenaway J. (1998) 'Shifting Agendas, Changing Regulatory Structures and the 'New' Politics of Environmental Pollution: British Coastal Water Policy 1955-1995', 76 *Public Administration* 669.

Krämer, L. (2000) *EC Environmental Law* (4th ed, Sweet and Maxwell).

Legge, D. (2000) 'The Sustainability of the Water Industry in a Regulated Environment', 12 *Journal of Environmental Law* 3.

McGillivray, D. and Holder, J. (2001, forthcoming) 'Locating EC Environmental Law' 20 *Yearbook of European Law* (Oxford University Press)

Norris, P. (1997) 'Are We All Green Now? Public Opinion on Environmentalism in Britain', 32 *Government and Opposition* 320.

Ogus, A.I. (1994) *Regulation: Legal Form and Economic Theory* (Clarendon).

Renshaw, D.C. (1980) 'Water Quality Objectives and Standards' in A.M. Gower (ed.) *Water Quality in Catchment Ecosystems* (John Wiley).

Royal Commission on Environmental Pollution (1996) *Sustainable Use of Soil*, Nineteenth Report, Cm 3165.

Sands, P. and Blatch, C. (1998) 'Estuaries in European Community law: Defining Criteria', 13 *International Journal of Marine and Coastal Law* 1.

Tornero, I.M. (1999) 'New Commissioner unveils environmental priorities', 1 *Environmental Law Review* 235.

Tydeman, C. (2000) 'Trying out the conciliation process on the Water Framework Directive', 2 *Environmental Law Review* 229.

Ward, N., Buller, H. and Lowe, P. (1995) *Implementing European Environmental Policy at the Local Level: The British Experience with Water Quality Directives, Volume II: Research Report* (Centre for Rural Economy, University of Newcastle).

**Chapter 6**

Bosworth, J. and Shellens, T. (1999) 'How the Welsh Assembly will Affect Planning', *Journal of Planning and Environmental Law* 219.

Burgess, J., Clark J. and Harrison, C. (1998) 'Respondents Evaluations of a Contingent Valuation Survey: A Case Study Based on an Economic Valuation of the Wildlife Enhancement Scheme, Pevensey Levels in East Sussex', 30 *Area* 19.

Carter, N. and Lowe, P. (1995) 'The Establishment of a Cross-Sector Environment Agency' in T. Gray (ed.) *UK Environmental Policy in the 1990s* (Macmillan).

CAG Management Consultants and Land Use Consultants (1997) *What Matters and Why. Environmental Capital: A New Approach* (CAG Management Consultants).

de Prez, P. (2000) 'Beyond judicial sanctions: the negative impact of conviction for environmental offences', 1 *Environmental Law Review* 11.

Gallagher, E. (1996) 'The Environment Agency' in *Bringing the Environment Down to Earth, Journal of Planning and Environment Law*, Occasional Paper No. 24.

Hanley, N. (1997) 'Assessing the Economic Value of Fresh Waters' in P.J. Boon and D.L. Howell (eds) *Freshwater Quality: Defining the Indefinable?* (Stationery Office).

Howarth, W. (1992) 'Regulation, Operation and Management: the Functions of the Proposed Environment Agency', 1 *International Journal of Regulatory Law* 82.

Howarth, W. (1996) 'Regulating Water Pollution: the Legacy of the Authority and the Prospects for the Agency', 6 *Environmental Policy & Practice* 55.

Jewell, T. and Steele, J. (1996) 'UK Regulatory Reform and the Pursuit of "Sustainable Development": The Environment Act 1995', 8 *Journal of Environmental Law* 283.

Lee, R.G. (1999) 'Devolution and the Environment: Wales' in Faris, N. and Turner, S. (Eds.) *Public Law and the Environment: New Directions?* (United Kingdom Environmental Law Association).

McGillivray, D. (1998) 'Appeal by Thames Water Utilities Limited', 9 *Water Law* 62.

Merrett, T. (1993) 'False economies in compliance with environmental legislation' 4 *Water Law* 202.

O'Neill, J. (1996) 'Contingent Value and Qualitative Democracy', 5 *Environmental Politics* 753.

Royal Commission on Environmental Pollution (1992) *Freshwater Quality*, Sixteenth Report, Cm 1966.

Sagoff, M. (1988) *The Economy of the Earth: Philosophy, Law and the Environment* (Cambridge University Press).

Tromans, S. (1996) *The Environment Acts 1990-1995* (3rd ed., Sweet & Maxwell).

## Chapter 7

Beesley, M. and Littlechild, S. (1986) 'Privatisation: Principles, Problems and Priorities', in J. Kay, C. Mayer and D. Thompson (eds) *Privatisation and Regulation: The UK Experience* (Clarendon).

Bell, S. and McGillivray, D. (2000) *Ball and Bell on Environmental Law* (5th ed., Blackstone Press)

Boyle, A.E. and Anderson, M.R. (1996) *Human Rights Approaches to Environmental Protection* (Clarendon).

Byatt, I. (1996a) 'Chairman's Comments', in M. Beesley (ed.) *Regulating Utilities: The Way Forward* (Institute of Economic Affairs).

Byatt, I. (1996b) 'The Impact of EC Water Directives on Water Customers in England and Wales', 3 *Journal of European Public Policy* 665.

Craig, P. (1991) 'Constitutions, Property and Regulation', *Public Law* 538.

Davis, K.C. (1969) *Discretionary Justice: A Preliminary Inquiry* (University of Illinois Press).

Elworthy, S. and Holder, J. (1996) 'Blue Babies, Gastric Cancers and Green Ponds: The Law's Response to the Nitrate Problem', 1 *International Journal of Biosciences and the Law* 69.

Foster, C. (1992) *Privatisation: Public Ownership and the Regulation of Natural Monopolies* (Blackwell).

Freeman, P. and Whish R (1991, updated) *Butterworths Competition Law* (Butterworths).

Glaister, S. (1996) 'Incentives in Natural Monopoly: The Case of Water', in M. Beesley (ed.) *Regulating Utilities: A Time for Change* (Institute of Economic Affairs).

Graham, C. (1990) 'Merger Policy in the Water Industry', 1 *Water Law* 42.

Graham, C. (1991) 'Developments in Merger Policy in the Water Industry', 2 *Water Law* 17.

Graham, C. (1995) 'Regulatory Crisis – A Myth?' in D. Helm (ed.) *British Utility Regulation: Principle, Experience and Reform* (Oxera Press).

Graham, C. and Prosser, T. (1991) *Privatising Public Industries* (Clarendon Press).

Haigh, N. (1992, updated) *Manual of Environmental Policy: the EC and Britain* (Longman/ Sweet and Maxwell).

Hajer, M. (1995) *The Politics of Environmental Discourse: Ecological Modernisation and the Policy Process* (Clarendon).

Helm, D. and Rajah, N. (1994) 'Water Regulation: The Periodic Review', 15 *Fiscal Studies* 74.

Hilson, C. (1995) 'National Courts: Court of Appeal, Decision of 7 June 1995, *Ex Parte Friends of the Earth*: Enforcement of Drinking Water Directive', 32 *Common Market Law Review* 1461.

Hilson, C. (1997) 'Community Rights in Environmental Law: Rhetoric or Reality?' in J. Holder (ed.) *The Impact of EC Environmental Law in the United Kingdom* (Wiley).

Jenkins, S. (1995) *Accountable to None: The Tory Nationalization of Britain* (Hamish Hamilton).

Jordan, A. and Greenaway J. (1998) 'Shifting Agendas, Changing Regulatory Structures and the 'New' Politics of Environmental Pollution: British Coastal Water Policy 1955-1995', 76 *Public Administration* 669.

Kay, J. (1996) 'The Future of UK Utility Regulation', in M. Beesley (ed.) *Regulating Utilities: A Time for Change?* (Institute of Economic Affairs).

Kaye, T. (1996a) 'Do Consumers make Contracts With Water Companies?' 7 *Water Law* 48.

Kaye, T. (1996b) 'Unfair Terms in Water Supply Contracts: Implied Terms – The Unfair Terms in Consumer Contracts Regulations 1994', 7 *Water Law* 81.

Kinnersley, D. (1994) *Coming Clean: The Politics of Water and the Environment* (Penguin).

Last, K. (1997) 'Fat Cats Laughing at a Toothless Bulldog? The Utilities and Habitat Protection', 8 *Utilities Law Review* 233.

Leeson, J. (1995) *Environmental Law* (Pitman).

Littlechild, S. (1986) *Economic Regulation of Privatised Water Authorities* (HMSO).

MacCulloch, A. (2000) 'Private Enforcement of the Competition Act Provisions' in B.J. Rodgers and A. MacCulloch (eds) *The UK Competition Act: A New Era for UK Competition Law* (Hart).

Maloney, W. and Richardson, J. (1995) *Managing Policy Change in Britain: The Politics of Water* (Edinburgh University Press).

Merry, A. and Venters, R. (1991) 'Director-General of Water Services – Part II: Instruments of Appointment', 2 *Water Law* 189.

Ogus, A.I. (1994) *Regulation: Legal Form and Economic Theory* (Clarendon).

Parker, D. and Penning-Rowsell, E. (1980) *Water Planning in Britain* (George Allen and Unwin).

Price, C. (1994) 'Economic Regulation of Privatised Monopolies', in P. Jackson and C. Price (eds) *Privatisation and Regulation: A Review of the Issues* (Longman).

Price, C. (1997) 'Regulating for Fairness', 4 *New Economy* 117.

Prosser, T. (1994a) 'Regulation, Markets and Legitimacy', in J. Jowell and D. Oliver (eds) *The Changing Constitution* (Clarendon).

Prosser, T. (1994b) 'Privatisation, Regulation and Public Service', 1 *Juridical Review* 3.

Prosser, T. and Moran, M. (1994) 'Conclusion: From National Uniqueness to Supra-National Constitution', in T. Prosser and M. Moran (eds) *Privatisation and Regulatory Change in Europe* (Open University Press).

Robinson, C. (1997) 'Introducing Competition into Water', in M. Beesley (ed.) *Regulating Utilities: Broadening the Debate* (Institute of Economic Affairs).

Rhodes, R.A.W. (1988) *Beyond Westminster and Whitehall* (Unwin Hyman).

Sage, R. (2000) 'A Leap into the Unknown', *Water Magazine*, 2 April 2000, p.10.

Sagoff, M. (1988) *The Economy of the Earth: Philosophy, Law and the Environment* (Cambridge University Press).

Saunders, P. and Harris, C. (1994) *Privatisation and Popular Capitalism* (Open University Press).

Scott, C. (1995) 'Changing Patterns of European Communities Utilities Law and Policy: An Institutional Hypothesis', in J. Shaw and G. More (eds) *New Legal Dynamics of the European Union* (Clarendon).

Somsen, H. (1993) *Case C-337/89 – Commission v United Kingdom*, 4 *Water Law* 59.

Souter, D. (1994) 'A Stakeholder Approach to Regulation', in D. Corry, D. Souter and M. Waterson (eds) *Regulating Our Utilities* (Institute of Public Policy Research).

Stiff, G. (1996) 'Water Supply – Contract or Statute?' 7 *Water Law* 167.

Vickers, J. and Yarrow, G. (1988) *Privatisation: An Economic Analysis* (MIT Press).

Stelzer, I. (1996) 'Lessons for UK Regulation from Recent US Experience', in M. Beesley (ed.) *Regulating Utilities: A Time for Change* (Institute of Economic Affairs).

Weale, A. (1992) *The New Politics of Pollution* (Manchester University Press).

Wilkinson, D. (1994) 'Re-determining K', 5 *Water Law* 153.

## Chapter 8

Audit Commission (1997). *It's a Small World: Local Governments' Role as a Steward of the Environment* (Audit Commission).

Bell, S. and McGillivray, D. (2000) *Ball and Bell on Environmental Law* (5th ed., Blackstone Press).

Briggs, A. (1963) *Victorian Cities* (Odhams).

Burnett-Hall, R. (1995) *Environmental Law* (Sweet and Maxwell).

Carnwath, R. (1999) 'Environmental Litigation: A Way Through the Maze?' 11 *Journal of Environmental Law* 1.

Chartered Institute of Environmental Health (1997) *Agendas for Change* (CIEH).

Flinn, M.W. (1965) *Chadwick, Report on the sanitary condition of the labouring population of Gt. Britain, 1842*, edited with an introduction by M.W. Flinn (Edinburgh University Press).

Hawke, N. (1995) *Environmental Health Law* (Sweet and Maxwell).

Kinnersley, D. (1988) *Troubled Waters: Rivers, Politics and Pollution* (Shipman).

McManus, F. (1994) *Environmental Health Law* (Blackstone).

Malcolm, R. (1999) 'Statutory Nuisance: Enforcement Issues and the Meaning of 'Prejudice to Health'', 1 *Environmental Law Review* 210.

Purdue, M. (1997) 'The Merits of Statutory Nuisance as a Means of Cleaning Up Beaches', 9 *Journal of Environmental Law* 103.

Tuxworth, B. and Thomas, E. (1996) *Local Agenda 21 Survey 1996* (Local Government Management Board).

Voisey, H. (1998) 'Local Agenda 21 in the UK', in T. O'Riordan and H. Voisey (eds) *The Transition to Sustainability: The Politics of Agenda 21 in Europe* (Earthscan).

**Chapter 9**

Anon (1996) 'What is a coal mine? (*Murphy and Others* v *the Coal Authority*)', 7 *Water Law* 43.

Ball, S. (1992) 'Water Pollution from Abandoned Mines', 3 *Water Law* 119.

Barrett, B. (1992) 'Common law liability for flood damage caused by storms', *New Law Journal* 1608.

Bathers, D. (1986) 'Fishery Prosecution – Practice Policy and Procedure' in *Poaching and Protection: The Proceedings of a Joint WSTAA/WAA Symposium* (Welsh Water Authority).

Bell, S. and McGillivray, D. (2000) *Ball and Bell on Environmental Law* (5th ed., Blackstone Press).

Bentil, J.K. (1986) 'Environmental Pollution Control and Strict Liability in Anglo-Australian Penal Laws', *Journal of Planning and Environment Law* 255.

Carty, P. (1995) 'Recovering Clean-Up Costs: The *Bruton* Case and s161 Water Resources Act 1991', 6 *Water Law* 20.

Croall, H. (1988) 'Mistakes, Accidents and Someone Else's Fault: the Trading Offender in Court', *Journal of Law and Society* 293.

Davies, M. (2000) 'Sentencing for Environmental Offences', 2 *Environmental Law Review* 195.

de Prez, P. (2000a) 'Beyond judicial sanctions: the negative impact of conviction for environmental offences', 1 *Environmental Law Review* 11.

de Prez, P. (2000b) 'Excuses, Excuses: The Ritual Trivialisation of Environmental Prosecutions', 12 *Journal of Environmental Law* 65.

Donaldson, Lord (1999) *Review of Salvage and Intervention and their Command and Control*, Cm 4193.

Howarth, W. (1992) *Wisdom's Law of Watercourses* (5th ed., Shaw and Sons).

Howarth, W. (1993) 'Poisonous, Noxious or Polluting: Contrasting Approaches to Environmental Regulation', 56 *Modern Law Review* 171.

Jackson, S. (1988) 'Private Prosecutions under the Control of Pollution Act 1974', 2 *Environmental Law* 3.

Jenn, H. (1993) 'Public Interest Litigation and Access to Environmental Information', 4 *Water Law* 163.

Jones, A. (1994) 'Pollution from abandoned coal mines in the context of the imminent privatisation of the coal industry', 5 *Water Law* 150 and 187.

Jones, A. (1995) 'Let Polluters Be! – Until 1999', 6 *Water Law* 71.

Jones, A. (1996) 'Regulation, Crime and Pollution from Abandoned Coal Mines', 8 *Journal of Environmental Law* 43.

Lane, P. and Peto, M. (1995) *Blackstone's Guide to the Environment Act 1995* (Blackstone Press).

Law Commission (1989) *Codification of the Criminal Law,* Report No.177 (Law Commission).

Leigh, L.H. (1982) *Strict and Vicarious Liability: A Study in Administrative Law* (Sweet and Maxwell).

Luker, M. and Montague, K. (1994) *Control of Pollution from Highway Drainage Discharges,* Report 142, Construction Industry Research and Information Association (CIRIA).

MacDonald, I. (1998) 'Causing Water Pollution', *New Law Journal* 559.

Macrory, R. (1985) *Water Law* (Longman).

Marston, G. (1981) *The Marginal Seabed: United Kingdom Legal Practice* (Clarendon).

Merrett, T. (1993) 'False economies in compliance with environmental legislation' 4 *Water Law* 202.

Newsom, G. and Sherratt, J.G. (1972) *Water Pollution* (John Sherratt and Son).

Padfield, N. (1995) 'Clean Water and Muddy Causation: Is Causation a Question of Law or Fact, or Just a Way of Allocating Blame?' *Criminal Law Review* 695.

Parpworth, N. (1997) 'The Offence of Causing Water Pollution: A New South Wales Perspective', 9 *Journal of Environmental Law* 59.

Parpworth, N. (1998) 'Causing Water Pollution and the Acts of Third Parties', *Journal of Planning and Environmental Law* 752.

Payne, S. (1997) 'Discharge Consents and Enforcement Notices', 8 *Water Law* 73.

Royal Commission on Environmental Pollution (1992) *Freshwater Quality,* Sixteenth Report, Cm 1966.

Ryan, C. (1998) 'Unforeseeable but not Unusual: The Validity of the Empress Test', 10 *Journal of Environmental Law* 347.

Sentencing Advisory Panel (1999) *Environmental Offences: A Consultation Paper* (Home Office).

Simes, E. and Scholefield, C.E. (1954) *Lumley's Public Health Law: the Public Health Acts Annotated* Vol.V (12th ed., Butterworths).

Smith, J.C. (1999) *Smith and Hogan's Criminal Law* (9th ed., Butterworths).

Stanley, N. (1999) 'The *Empress* Decision and Causing Water Pollution: A New Approach to s.85(1) of the Water Resources Act 1991 Strict Liability', 10 *Water Law* 37.

Taylor, J.O. (1928) *The Law Affecting River Pollution* (W. Green and Son).

Turner, G. (1988) 'Private Prosecutions Under the Control of Pollution Act 1974', 2 *Environmental Law* 2.

Wilkinson, D. (1993) 'Causing and knowingly permitting pollution offences: a review', 4 *Water Law* 25.

Williams, R. (1998) 'Are Overflows from Abandoned Mines Unlawful?' 9 *Water Law* 28.

Williams, R. (1999) 'Damage Caused by Waste Water from Abandoned Mines: is there Greater Potential for Liability than at First Apparent?' 11 *Environmental Law and Management* 172.

**Chapter 10**

Bates, J.H. (1990, updated) *Water and Drainage Law* (Sweet and Maxwell).

Bell, S. and McGillivray, D. (2000) *Ball and Bell on Environmental Law* (5th ed., Blackstone Press)

Burton, T. (1987) 'The Control of Pollution Act 1974, Part II: The Extension of Control to All Discharges to UK Tidal Waters', 2 *International Journal of Estuarine and Coastal Law* 10.

Craig, P.P. (1999) *Administrative Law* (4th ed., Sweet and Maxwell).

Eastwood, P.K. and Ord, W.O. (1986) 'Implementing Part II of the Control of Pollution Act 1974', 85 *Water Pollution Control* 241.

Hammerton, D. (1987) 'The Impact of Environmental Legislation', 86 *Water Pollution Control* 333.

Howarth, W. (1988) *Water Pollution Law* (Shaw and Sons).

Howarth, W. (1990) *The Law of Aquaculture* (Fishing News Books/Blackwell Scientific).

Howarth, W. and McGillivray, D. (1994) *The Regulation of Fish Farming by the National Rivers Authority*, NRA Research and Development Project Record 388 (National Rivers Authority).

Kinnersley, D. (1994) *Coming Clean: The Politics of Water and the Environment* (Penguin).

McFarlane, S. (1993) 'The Fish Kill Conditions – An Industry View', 4 *Water Law* 57.

McGillivray, D. (1995a) 'Discharge consents and the unforeseen. Part 1: the DoE's adjudication on the "fish kill" condition – outcome and commentary', 6 *Water Law* 72.

McGillivray, D. (1995b) 'Discharge consents and the unforeseen. Part 2: Discharge consents: exclusive or inclusive?' 6 *Water Law* 101.

Matthews, P.J. (1987) 'Part II of The Control of Pollution Act 1974: What it Means' 86 *Water Pollution Control* 140.

Payne, S. (1998) 'Kinnersley – Discharge Consent Conditions', 9 *Water Law* 13.

Royal Commission on Environmental Pollution (1972) *Pollution in Some British Estuaries and Coastal Waters,* Third Report, Cmnd.5054.

Royal Commission on Environmental Pollution (1992) *Freshwater Quality*, Sixteenth Report, Cm 1966.

Thornton, J. and Beckwith S. (1997) *Environmental Law* (Sweet & Maxwell).

Tromans, S., Nash, M. and Poustie, M. (eds) (1996, updated) *Encyclopedia of Environmental Law* (Sweet and Maxwell).

Tunstall, S., Fordham, M., Green, C. and House, M. (1997) 'Public Perception of Freshwater Quality with Particular Reference to Rivers in England and Wales', in P.J. Boon D.L. Howell (eds) *Freshwater Quality: Defining the Indefinable?* (Stationery Office).

Waite, S. and Crawshaw, T. (1996) 'The regulation of environmental water quality in England and Wales: control of effluent discharges to surface waters', 1 *International Journal of Biosciences and Law* 187.

Waite, A. and Jewell, T. (1997) *Environmental Law in Property Transactions* (Butterworths).

Warn, T. (1994) 'Discharge consents: how they are set and enforced', 6 *Environmental Law and Management* 32.

Young, D.D. (1979) 'Water Quality Issues: The Water Industry View' *Chemistry and Industry* 199.

**Chapter 11**

Bates, J.H. (1990, updated) *Water and Drainage Law* (Sweet and Maxwell).

Garner, J. and Bailey, S. (1995) *The Law of Sewers and Drains* (8th ed., Shaw and Sons).

Institution of Civil Engineers (1996) *Land Drainage and Flood Defence Responsibilities* (3rd ed., Thomas Telford).

Klein, L. (1957) *Aspects of River Pollution* (Butterworths).

Klein, L. (1962) *River Pollution 2: Causes and Effects* (Butterworths).

Law Commission (1991) *Report on the Consolidation of the Legislation Relating to Water, Law Com. No. 198* (HMSO).

Leeson, J. (1995) *Environmental Law* (Pitman).

Mason, C.F. (1996) *Biology of Freshwater Pollution* (3rd ed., Longman).

Moore, V. (2000) *A Practical Approach to Planning Law* (7th ed., Blackstone).

Rhoades, J. (1997) *An Introduction to Industrial Wastewater Treatment and Disposal* (Chartered Institution of Water and Environmental Management).

Richardson, G., Ogus, A. and Burrows, P. (1982) *Policing Pollution* (Clarendon).

Royal Commission on Environmental Pollution (1992) *Freshwater Quality*, Sixteenth Report, Cm 1966.

Waite, A. and Jewell, T. (1997) *Environmental Law in Property Transactions* (Butterworths).

Water Authorities Association (1986) *Trade Effluent Discharged to the Sewer* (Water Authorities Association).

WRc (1998) *Water Pollution Legislation: Final Report to the Department of the Environment, Transport and the Regions,* DETR 4608, November 1998.


## Chapter 12

Bates, J.H. (1997) *UK Waste Law* (2nd ed., Sweet and Maxwell).

Emmott, N. and Haigh, N. (1996) 'Integrated Pollution Prevention and Control: UK and EC Approaches and Possible Next Steps', 8 *Journal of Environmental Law* 301.

Forster, M. and Morris, C. (2000) 'The Landfill Directive: How Will the UK Meet the Challenge?' 9 *European Environmental Law Review* 16.

Her Majesty's Inspectorate of Pollution (1996) *Best Practicable Environmental Option Assessments for IPC: A Summary.*

Howarth, W. (1990) *The Law of Aquaculture* (Fishing News Books/Blackwell Scientific).

Jordan, A. (1993) 'Integrated Pollution Control and the Evolving Style and Structure of Environmental Regulation the UK', 2 *Environmental Politics* 405.

Klein, L. (1957) *Aspects of River Pollution* (Butterworths).

Klein, L. (1962) *River Pollution 2: Causes and Effects* (Butterworths).

Laurence, D.S. (1999) *Waste Regulation Law* (Butterworths).

Laurence, D.S. (1987) 'Water Pollution from a Waste Disposal Site', 1 *Environmental Law* 5.

Layfield, F. (1992) 'The Environmental Protection Act 1990: The System of Integrated Pollution Control', *Journal of Planning and Environmental Law* 3.

Long, A. (1999) 'Integrated Pollution Prevention and Control: The Implementation of Directive 96/61/EC', 8 *European Environmental Law Review* 180.

Mehta, A. and Hawkins, K. (1998) 'Integrated Pollution Control and Its Impact: Perspectives from Industry', 10 *Journal of Environmental Law* 61.

O'Riordan, T. and Weale, A. (1989) 'Administrative Reorganization and Policy Change: the Case of Her Majesty's Inspectorate of Pollution', 67 *Public Administration* 277.

Parpworth, N. (1999) 'The Draft EC Landfill Directive', *Journal of Planning and Environmental Law* 4.

Pocklington, D. (1997) *The Law of Waste Management* (Shaw and Sons).

Purdue, M. (1991) 'Integrated Pollution Control in the Environmental Protection Act 1990: A Coming of Age of Environmental Law?' 54 *Modern Law Review* 534.

Royal Commission on Environmental Pollution (1976) *Air Pollution Control: an Integrated Approach,* Fifth Report, Cmnd.6371.

Royal Commission on Environmental Pollution (1985) *Managing Waste: The Duty of Care,* Eleventh Report, Cmnd.9675.

Royal Commission on Environmental Pollution (1988) *Best Practicable Environmental Option,* Twelfth Report, Cm 310.

Royal Commission on Environmental Pollution (1996) *Sustainable Use of Soil,* Nineteenth Report, Cm 3165.

Scottish Wildlife and Countryside Link (1988) *Marine Fishfarming in Scotland* (Scottish Wildlife and Countryside Link).

Spillet, P. (1985) *Lead Poisoning in Swans* (Institute of Fisheries Management).

Turner, K. and Powell, J.C. (1993) 'Case Study: Economics – the challenge of integrated pollution control', in R.J. Berry (ed.) *Environmental Dilemmas: Ethics and Decisions* (Chapman and Hall).

United Kingdom Environmental Law Association (1987) *Best Practicable Environmental Option: A New Jerusalem?* (UKELA).

Vogel, D. (1986) *National Styles of Regulation: Environmental Policy in Great Britain and the United States* (Cornell University Press).

Wilkinson, D. (1999) 'Using Environmental Ethics to Create Ecological Law', in J. Holder and D. McGillivray (eds) *Locality and Identity: Environmental Issues in Law and Society* (Ashgate).

## Chapter 13

Bell, S. and Howarth, W. (1997) 'Defining the Boundaries – The Draft Guidance on Contaminated Land and the Implications for Water Law', 8 *Water Law* 31.

Carty, P. (1995) 'Recovering Clean-Up Costs: The *Bruton* Case and s161 Water Resources Act 1991', 6 *Water Law* 20.

Deansley, C., Papanicolaou, C. and Turner, A. (1993) *Badlands: Essential Environmental Law for Property Professionals* (Cameron May/United Kingdom Environmental Law Association).

Elworthy, S. (1994) *Farming for Drinking Water* (Avebury).

Elworthy, S. (1998) 'Finding the Causes of Events or Preventing a "State of Affairs"?' 10 *Journal of Environmental Law* 92.

Elworthy, S. (1999) 'Legitimacy of Nitrate Vulnerable Zone Designations', 1 *Environmental Law Review* 204.

Elworthy, S. and Holder, J. (1996) 'Blue Babies, Gastric Cancers and Green Ponds: The Law's Response to the Nitrate Problem', 1 *International Journal of Biosciences and the Law* 69.

Hawke, N. and Kovaleva N. (1998) *Agri-Environmental Law and Policy* (Cavendish).

Howarth, W. (1992) 'Agricultural Pollution and the Aquatic Environment' in W. Howarth and C.P. Rodgers (eds) *Agriculture, Conservation and Land Use* (University of Wales Press).

Hughes, D. and Kellett, P. (1996) 'Contaminated Land and the Environment Act 1995. "Working Draft Guidance" Part I: The Germ of an Idea', 8 *Environmental Law and Management* 217.

Hughes, D. and Kellett, P. (1997) 'Contaminated Land and the Environment Act 1995. Consultation Draft Guidance Part II: The Framework is Constructed', 9 *Environmental Law and Management* 78.

Hughes, D. and Kellett, P. (1999) 'Contaminated Land and the Environment Act 1995. "Consultation Draft Guidance" Part III: the Framework is Constructed', 11 *Environmental Law and Management* 45.

Jones, J.G. (ed.) (1993) *Agriculture and the Environment* (E. Horwood).

Lewis, R. (1995) 'Contaminated Land: The New Regime of the Environment Act 1995', *Journal of Planning and Environmental Law* 1087.

Lomas, O. and Payne S. (1993, updated) *Commercial Environmental Law and Liability* (Longman/Sweet and Maxwell).

Lowe, P., Clark, J., Seymour, S. and Ward N. (1992) *Pollution Control on Dairy Farms: An Evaluation of Current Policies and Procedure* (Sustainable Agriculture, Food and Environment, SAFE).

National Audit Office (1995) *National Rivers Authority: River Pollution From Farms in England* (HMSO).

Nature Conservancy Council (1991) *Nature Conservation and Pollution from Farm Wastes* (Nature Conservancy Council).

Rodgers, C.P. (1992) 'Land Management Agreements and Agricultural Practice: Towards and Integrated Legal Framework for Conservation Law', in W. Howarth and C.P. Rodgers (eds) *Agriculture, Conservation and Land Use* (University of Wales Press).

Rossi, H. (1995) 'Paying For Our Past – Will We?' 7 *Journal of Environmental Law 1*.

Royal Commission on Environmental Pollution (1992) *Freshwater Quality*, Sixteenth Report, Cm 1966.

Steele, J. (1995) 'Remedies and Remediation: Foundational Issues in Environmental Liability', 58 *Modern Law Review* 615.

Tromans, S. (1996) *The Environment Acts 1990-1995* (3rd ed., Sweet & Maxwell).
Tromans, S. and Turrall-Clarke, R. (2000) *Contaminated Land: The New Regime* (Sweet & Maxwell).
World Health Organisation (1970) *European Standards for Drinking Water* (2nd ed., World Health Organisation).
World Health Organisation (1971) *International Standards for Drinking Water* (World Health Organisation).

## Chapter 14

Bell, S. and McGillivray, D. (2000) *Ball and Bell on Environmental Law* (5th ed., Blackstone Press)
Blowers, A. (ed.) (1993) *Planning for a Sustainable Environment* (Earthscan).
Brooke, C. (1996) *Natural Conditions – A Review of Planning Conditions and Nature Conservation* (RSPB).
Cornford, T. (1998) 'The Control of Planning Gain' *Journal of Planning and Environment Law* 731.
Cuthbertson, A. (1996) 'Wasteland to Wetlands', *Planning Week*, 5 September 1996.
Desmier, R. (2000) 'To the Waters and the Wild', 94 *Water Magazine*, 31 March 2000.
Grant, M. (ed.) (1976, updated) *Encyclopaedia of Planning Law and Practice* (Sweet and Maxwell).
Jewell, T. (1998) 'Public Law and the Environment: The Prospects for Decision Making' in T. Jewell and J. Steele (eds) *Law in Environmental Decision-Making: National, European and International Perspectives* (Clarendon).
Moore, V. (2000) *A Practical Approach to Planning Law* (7th ed., Blackstone).
National Water Council (1978) *River Water Quality, the Next Stage. Review of Discharge Consent Conditions* (National Water Council).
Planning and Environmental Law Reform Working Group of the Society for Advanced Legal Studies (1999) 'Planning Obligations', *Journal of Planning and Environment Law* 113.
Purdue, M. (1999) 'The Relationship between Development Control and Specialist Pollution Controls: Which is the Tail and Which the Dog?' *Journal of Planning and Environment Law* 585.
Royal Commission on Environmental Pollution (1992) *Freshwater Quality*, Sixteenth Report, Cm 1966.
Royal Commission on Environmental Pollution (1998) *Setting Environmental Standards*, Twenty-first Report, Cm 4053.
Sheate, W. (1994) *Making an Impact: A Guide to EIA Law and Policy* (2nd ed., Cameron May).
Whatmore, S. and Boucher, S. (1993) 'Bargaining with nature: the discourse and practice of "environmental planning gain"', 18 *Transactions of the Institute of British Geographers* 166.

## Chapter 15

Ball, S. (1997) 'Has the UK Government Implemented the Habitats Directive?' in J. Holder (ed.) *The Impact of EC Environmental Law in the United Kingdom* (Wiley).
Barker, G. (1999) *Local Nature Reserves in England: A Guide to their Selection and Declaration* (English Nature).
Bell, S. and McGillivray, D. (2000) *Ball and Bell on Environmental Law* (5th ed., Blackstone Press)
Cole-King, A. (1993) 'Marine Conservation: A New Policy Area', 17 *Marine Policy* 171.
Countryside Council for Wales (1996) *Acting Locally on Behalf of the Environment: the Role of Local Nature Reserves* (Countryside Council for Wales).
Davis, T.J. (ed.) (1994) *The Ramsar Convention Manual: A Guide to the Convention on Wetlands of International Importance Especially as Wildfowl Habitat* (Ramsar Convention Bureau).

English Nature (1991, revised 1995) *Local Nature Reserves in England* (English Nature).

English Nature (1997) *Wildlife and Fresh Water: An Agenda for Sustainable Management* (English Nature).

English Nature (1999) *8th Report* (English Nature).

English Nature, Scottish Natural Heritage, Environment and Heritage Service (Department of the Environment (Northern Ireland)), Countryside Council for Wales, Joint Nature Conservation Council and SAMS (1997) *Natura 2000: European Marine Sites: An Introduction to Management* (Scottish Natural Heritage).

English Nature, Scottish Natural Heritage, Environment and Heritage Service (Department of the Environment (Northern Ireland)), Countryside Council for Wales, Joint Nature Conservation Council and SAMS (1998) *Natura 2000: European Marine Sites: Guidance Relating to Statutory Conservation Objectives and Operations Which May Cause Deterioration or Disturbance* (English Nature).

Gubbay, S. (1989) *Using Sites of Special Scientific Interest to Conserve Seashores for their Marine Biological Interest* (World Wildlife Fund).

Howarth, W. (1987) *Freshwater Fishery Law* (Financial Training/Blackstone).

Howarth, W. (1990) *The Law of Aquaculture* (Fishing News Books/Blackwell Scientific).

Howarth, W. and McGillivray, D. (1994) *The Regulation of Fish Farming by the National Rivers Authority*, NRA Research and Development Project Record 388 (National Rivers Authority).

Howarth, W. and McGillivray, D. (1996) 'Sustainable Management of Aquatic Ecosystems and the Law' in C.P. Rodgers (ed.) *Nature Conservation and Countryside Law* (University of Wales Press).

Last, K. (1997) 'Fat Cats Laughing at a Toothless Bulldog? The Utilities and Habitat Protection', 8 *Utilities Law Review* 233.

McGillivray, D. (2000) 'Towards an Environmental Perspective in Statutory Construction?' 2 *Environmental Law Review* 40.

Miller, C. (1999) 'Economic or Environmental Rights: Exposing the Dubious Foundations of the Shellfish Waters Directive', 1 *Environmental Law Review* 298.

Nield, C. and Rice, T. (1996) *A Review of UK Compliance with the Ramsar Convention on Wetlands of International Importance Especially as Waterfowl Habitat* (Friends of the Earth).

Nollkaemper, A. (1997) 'Habitat Protection in European Community Law: Evolving Conceptions of a Balance of Interests', 9 *Journal of Environmental Law* 271.

Perry, J. and Vanderklein, E. (1996) *Water Quality: Management of a Natural Resource* (Blackwell Scientific).

Reid, C. (1994) *Nature Conservation Law* (W Green & Sons/Sweet & Maxwell).

Ross, A. and Horsman, P.V. (1988) *The Use of Nuvan 500EC in the Salmon Farming Industry* (Marine Conservation Society).

Scott, P. (1999) 'DETR Proposals on SSSIs in the Marine Area – a Critique', paper presented to the UK Environmental Law Association Nature Conservation Working Group, March 1999.

Scott, P. (2000) 'Implementation of the Fresh Water Fishwaters Directive in the United Kingdom', paper presented to the Water Working Group of the United Kingdom Environmental Law Association, October 2000.

Skaala, O., Dahle, G., Jørstad, K.E. and Naevdal, G. (1990) 'Interactions between natural and farmed fish populations: information from genetic markers', 36 *Journal of Fish Biology* 449.

Stallworthy, M. (1998) 'Water Quality: the Capacity of the European Community to Deliver', 9 *Water Law* 127.

Ward, N., Buller, H. and Lowe, P. (1995) *Implementing European Environmental Policy at the Local Level: The British Experience with Water Quality Directives, Volume II: Research Report* (Centre for Rural Economy, University of Newcastle).

Warren, L. (1991) *Marine Fish Farming and the Crown Estate* (Worldwide Fund For Nature).

Warren, L. (1996) 'Law and Policy for Marine Protected Areas' in C.P. Rodgers (ed.) *Nature Conservation and Countryside Law* (University of Wales Press).

Wathern, P., Young, S.N., Brown, I.W. and Roberts, D.A. (1987) 'UK Interpretation and Implementation of the EEC Shellfish Directive' 11 *Environmental Management* 7

## Chapter 16

Bakkenist, G. (1994) *Environmental Information: Law, Policy and Experience* (Cameron May).

Birtles, W. (1993) 'A Right to Know: The Environment Information Regulations 1992', *Journal of Planning and Environmental Law* 615.

Burton, T. (1989) 'Access to Environmental Information – The UK Experience of Water Registers', 1 *Journal of Environmental Law* 192.

Cook, H. F. (1998) *The Protection and Conservation of Water Resources* (John Wiley).

Cooper, J. (1995) 'Access to Environmental Information Regulations: A Case Study', 1 *Environmental Judicial Review Bulletin* 16.

Corner, T. (1998) 'Planning, Environment and the European Convention on Human Rights', *Journal of Planning and Environmental Law* 315.

Davies, P.G.G. (1994) 'The European Environment Agency', 14 *Yearbook of European Law* 313.

Fairley, R. (1993) 'Integrated Pollution Control – Public Registers and Commercial Confidentiality', 5 *Environmental Law and Management* 111.

Gibb, F., (1996) 'Saunders Ruling May Prompt Change in Law', *The Times*, 18 December 1996.

Hallo, R. (ed.) (1996) *Access to Environmental Information in Europe: The Implementation and Implications of Directive 90/313/EEC* (Kluwer).

Howarth, W. (1997) 'Self-Monitoring, Self-Policing, Self-Incrimination and Pollution Law', 60 *Modern Law Review* 200.

Jackson, S. (1988) 'Private Prosecutions under the Control of Pollution Act 1974', 2 *Environmental Law* 3.

Jenn, H. (1993) 'Public Interest Litigation and Access to Environmental Information', 4 *Water Law* 163.

Jimenez-Beltran, D. (1995) 'The Process of Sustainable Development and the Role of the European Environment Agency', 4 *European Environmental Law Review* 265.

John, E. (1995) 'Access to Environmental Information: Limitations on the UK Radioactive Substances Register', 7 *Journal of Environmental Law* 11.

Krämer, L. (1992) *Focus on European Environmental Law* (1st ed., Sweet and Maxwell).

Marine Pollution Monitoring Management Group (1998) *National Monitoring Programme: Survey of the Quality of UK Coastal Waters* (Marine Pollution Monitoring Management Group).

Mumma, A. (1993) 'Use of Compliance Monitoring Data in Water Pollution Prosecutions', 5 *Journal of Environmental Law* 191.

National Water Council (1978) *River Water Quality, the Next Stage. Review of Discharge Consent Conditions* (National Water Council).

O'Keefe, J. (ed.) (1995, updated) *Croner's Environmental Management Case Law* (Croner).

Pugh, K.B. (1997) 'Organizational Use of the Term 'Freshwater Quality' in Britain', in P.J. Boon D.L. Howell (eds) *Freshwater Quality: Defining the Indefinable?* (Stationery Office).

Pugh, C. and Moor, S. (1994) 'Access to Environmental Information in the UK: A Silk Purse of a Pig's Ear?' 3 *Review of European Community and International Environmental Law* 36.

Roderick, P. (1996) 'Access to Environmental Information in the EU: United Kingdom', in Hallo (1996).

Rowan-Robinson, J., Ross, A., Walton, W. and Rothnie, J. (1996) 'Public Access to Environmental Information: A Means to What End?' 8 *Journal of Environmental Law* 19.

Royal Commission on Environmental Pollution (1984) *Tackling Pollution: Experience and Prospects*, Tenth Report, Cmnd.9149.

Royal Commission on Environmental Pollution (1992) *Freshwater Quality*, Sixteenth Report, Cm 1966.

Ryland, D. (1994) 'The European Environment Agency', 3 *European Environmental Law Review* 138.

Tapper, C. (1995) *Cross and Tapper on Evidence* (8th ed., Butterworths).

Thornton, J. (2000) 'Human Rights and Human Bodies', 2 *Environment Law Review* 111.

Thornton, J. and Tromans, S. (1999) 'Human Rights and Environmental Wrongs: Incorporating the European Convention on Human Rights: Some Thoughts on the Consequences for UK Environmental Law', 11 *Journal of Environmental Law* 35.

Tromans, S. (1996) *The Environment Acts 1990-1995* (3rd ed., Sweet & Maxwell).

Turner, G. (1988) 'Private Prosecutions Under the Control of Pollution Act 1974', 2 *Environmental Law* 2.

Uglow, S. (1995) *Criminal Justice* (Sweet and Maxwell).

Upton, W. (1998) 'The European Convention on Human Rights and Environmental Law' *Journal of Planning and Environmental Law* 315.

Wheeler, M. (1994) 'The Right to Know in the European Union' 3 *Review of European Community and International Environmental Law* 1.

Winter, G. (1991) 'Freedom of Environmental Information', in O. Lomas (ed.) *Frontiers of Environmental Law* (Chancery Law).

## Chapter 17

Acheson, D. (1998) *Independent Inquiry into Inequalities in Health* (Department of Health).

Altmann, P., Cunningham, J., Dhanesha, U., Ballard, M., Thompson, J. and Marsh, F. (1999) 'Disturbance of cerebral function in people exposed to drinking water contaminated with aluminium sulphate: retrospective study of the Camelford water incident', 319 *British Medical Journal* 807.

Bache, I. and McGillivray, D. (1997) 'Testing the Extended Gatekeeper: the Law, Practice and Politics of Implementing the Drinking Water Directive in the UK', in J. Holder (ed.) *The Impact of EC Environmental Law in the United Kingdom* (Wiley).

Bates, J.H. (1990, updated) *Water and Drainage Law* (Sweet and Maxwell).

Cane, P. (1993) 'The Scope and Justification for Exemplary Damages: The Camelford Case', 5 *Journal of Environmental Law* 149.

Clapham, D. (1995) 'Unfit private water supplies', 6 *Water Law* 46.

Craig, F. and Craig, P. (1989) *Britain's Poisoned Waters* (Penguin).

Day, M. (ed.) (1998) *Environmental Action: A Citizens' Guide* (Pluto).

Faure, M. (1995) 'Protecting Drinking Water Quality Against Contamination by Pesticides: An Alternative Regulatory Framework', 4 *Review of European Community and International Environmental Law* 321.

Ghandi, P. (1993) 'Liability for Water Supply – *Gibbons & Others v South-West Water Services Ltd.*', 4 *Water Law* 95.

Gray, N.F. (1994) *Drinking Water Quality: Problems and Solutions* (John Wiley).

Haigh, N. (1992, updated) *Manual of Environmental Policy: the EC and Britain* (Longman/ Sweet and Maxwell).

Hughes, D. (1996) *Environmental Law*, (3rd ed., Butterworths).

Krämer, L. (2000) *EC Environmental Law* (4th ed., Sweet and Maxwell).

Leeson, J. (1995) *Environmental Law* (Pitman).

McDonagh, M.S., Whiting, P.F., Wilson, P.M., Sutton, A.J., Chestnutt, I., Cooper, J., Misso, K., Bradley, M., Treasure, E. and Kleijnen, J. (2000) 'Systematic review of water fluoridation', 321 *British Medical Journal* 855.

McDowell, H.R. and Chamberlain, C.E. (1950) *Michael and Will on the Law Relating to Water* (9th ed., Butterworths).

Macrory, R. (1989) *The Water Act 1989; Text and Commentary* (Sweet & Maxwell).

Maloney, W. and Richardson, J. (1995) *Managing Policy Change in Britain: The Politics of Water* (Edinburgh University Press).

Matthews, D. and Pickering, J. (1997) 'Directive 80/778 on Drinking Water Quality: an Analysis of the Development of European Environmental Rules', 1 *International Journal of Biosciences and the Law* 265.

Ward, N., Buller, H. and Lowe, P. (1995) *Implementing European Environmental Policy at the Local Level: The British Experience with Water Quality Directives, Volume II: Research Report* (Centre for Rural Economy, University of Newcastle).

World Health Organisation (1970) *European Standards for Drinking Water* (2nd ed., World Health Organisation).

World Health Organisation (1984) *Guidelines for Drinking Water Quality: Volume II, Health Criteria and Other Supporting Information* (World Health Organisation).

## Chapter 18

Abecassis, D.W. and Jarashow, J.L. (1985) *Oil Pollution from Ships: International, United Kingdom and United States Law and Practice* (2nd ed., Stevens and Sons).

Anderson, D. (1997) 'British Accession to the UN Convention on the Law of the Sea', 46 *International and Comparative Law Quarterly* 761.

Barros, J. and Johnson, M.J. (1974) *The International Law of Pollution* (Free Press).

Bates, J.H. and Benson, C. (1993, updated) *Marine Environment Law* (Lloyd's of London).

Birnie, P. and Boyle, A. (1992) *International Law and the Environment* (Oxford University Press).

Boyle, A. (1992) 'Land-Based Sources of Marine Pollution', *Marine Policy* 20.

Boyle, A.E. (1985) 'Marine Pollution Under the Law of the Sea Convention', 79 *American Journal of International Law* 347.

Birnie, P. and Boyle, A. (1995) *Basic Documents on International Law and the Environment* (Oxford University Press).

Brown, E.D. (1994) *The International Law of the Sea* (Dartmouth).

Brubaker, D. (1993) *Marine Pollution and International Law: Principles and Practice* (Belhaven)

Cameron, J. and Aboucher, J. (1991) 'The Precautionary principle: A Fundamental Approach Principle of Law and Policy for the Protection of the Global Environment', 14 *Boston College International and Comparative Law Review* 1.

Churchill, R. (1998) 'United Kingdom: Accession to the UN Convention on the Law of the Sea', 13 *International Journal of Marine and Coastal Law* 263.

Churchill, R. and Lowe, V. (1999) *The Law of the Sea* (3rd ed., Manchester University Press).

Clark, R.B. (1987) *The Waters Around the British Isles* (Oxford University Press).

Clark, R.B. (1997) *Marine Pollution* (4th ed., Oxford University Press).

Couper, A. and Gold, E. (1993) *The Marine Environment and Sustainable Development: Law, Policy and Science* (Law of the Sea Institute).

de La Fayette. L. (1999) 'The OSPAR Convention Comes into Force: Continuity and Progress', 14 *International Journal of Marine and Coastal Law* 247.

Fleischer, C.A. (1973) 'Pollution from Seaborne Sources' in R.R. Churchill, K.R. Simmonds and J. Welsh (eds) *New Directions in the Law of the Sea*, Collected Papers Vol. III (Oceana Publications).

Franckx, E. (1998) 'Regional Marine Environmental Protection Regimes in the Context of UNCLOS', 13 *International Journal of Marine and Coastal Law* 307.

GESAMP (Group of Experts on the Scientific Aspects of Marine Pollution) (1990) *The State of the Marine Environment*, UNEP Regional Seas Reports and Studies No.115 (GESAMP).

Gibson, J. and Churchill, R. (1990) 'Problems of Implementation of the North Sea Declarations: A Case Study of the United Kingdom', 5 *International Journal of Estuarine and Coastal Law* 47.

Grant, A. and Jickells, T. (2000) 'Marine and Estuarine Pollution', in T. O'Riordan (ed.) *Environmental Science for Environmental Management* (2nd ed., Longman).

Haas, P. (1993) 'Protecting the Baltic and North Seas' in P. Haas and R.O. Keohane (eds) *Institutions for the Earth: Sources of Effective International Environmental Protection* (MIT Press).

Hakapïï, K. (1981) *Marine Pollution in International Law* (Suomalainen Tiedeakatemia).

Hardy, M. (1973) 'Definitions and Forms of Marine Pollution' in R.R. Churchill, K.R. Simmonds and J. Welsh (eds) *New Directions in the Law of the Sea*, Collected Papers Vol. III (Oceana Publications).

Hargrove, J.L. (1975) 'Environment and the Third Conference on the Law of the Sea', in J.L. Hargrove (ed.) *Who Protects the Ocean? Environment and the Development of the Law of the Sea* (West Publishing).

Harris, D. (1974a) 'The Law Relating to Air Pollution: International Aspects' in A.D. McKnight, P.K. Marstrand and T.C. Sinclair (eds) *Environmental Pollution Control* (George Allen & Unwin).

Harris, D. (1974b) ''The Law Relating to Pollution of Inland Waters: International Aspects' in A.D. McKnight, P.K. Marstrand and T.C. Sinclair (eds) *Environmental Pollution Control* (George Allen & Unwin).

Hayward, P. (1990) 'The Oslo and Paris Commissions' 5 *International Journal of Estuarine and Coastal Law* 91.

Hey, E. (1993) 'Hard Law, Soft Law, Emerging International Environmental Law and the Ocean Disposal Options for Radioactive Waste', XL *Netherlands International Law Review* 405.

Hey, E., IJlstra, T. and Nollkaemper, A. (1993) 'The 1992 Paris Convention for the Protection of the North-East Atlantic: A Critical Analysis' 8 *International Journal of Marine and Coastal Law* 1.

IUCN (International Union for the Conservation of Nature) (1995) *The Law of the Sea: Priorities and Responsibilities in Implementing the Convention* (IUCN).

International Chamber of Shipping (1993) *Shipping and the Environment – A Code of Practice* (International Chamber of Shipping).

Johnston, D.M. (ed.) (1981) *The Environmental Law of the Sea*, IUCN Policy and Law Paper No.18 (IUCN).

Joyner, C. and Martell, E. (1996) 'Looking Back to See Ahead: UNCLOS III and Lessons for Global Commons Law', 27 *Ocean Development and International Law* 73.

Juda, L. (1996) *International law and Ocean Use Management: the Evolution of Ocean Governance* (Routledge).

Keselj, T. (1999) 'Port State Jurisdiction in Respect of Pollution from Ships: the 1982 United Nations Convention on the Law of the Sera and the Memorandum of Understanding', 30 *Ocean Development and International Law* 127.

McIntyre, O. and Mosedale, T. (1997) 'The Precautionary Principle as a Norm of Customary International Law', 9 *Journal of Environmental Law* 221.

Marstrand, P.K. (1974) 'Pollution of the Seas' in A.D. McKnight, P.K. Marstrand and T.C. Sinclair (eds) *Environmental Pollution Control* (George Allen & Unwin).

Mensah, T. (1999) 'The international Tribunal for the Law of the Sea and the Protection and Preservation of the Marine Environment', 8 *Review of European Community and International Environmental Law* 1.

Milne, R. (1987) 'Pollution and Politics in the North Sea', 116 *New Scientist*, 19th November 1987, p.53.

Nollkaemper, A. (1993) 'Agenda 21 and prevention of sea-based marine pollution', *Marine Policy*, November 1993, 537.

Nollkaemper, A. (1996) 'Balancing the Protection of Marine Ecosystems with Economic Benefits from Land-Based Activities: The Quest for International Legal Barriers', 27 *Ocean Development and International Law* 153.

Nollkaemper, A. (1998) 'The Distinction Between Legal and Non-Legal Norms in International Affairs: an Analysis with Reference to International Policy for the Protection of the North Sea from Hazardous Substances', 13 *International Journal of Marine and Coastal Law* 355.

O'Connell, D.P. (1984) *The International Law of the Sea*, 2 Vols (Clarendon Press).

Osborn, D. (1998) 'Sludge and Dreams: Earth Summit Rhetoric Versus Practical Action', 12 *Environmental Law* 4.

Oslo and Paris Commissions (1984) *The First Decade: International Co-operation in Protecting our Marine Environment* (Oslo and Paris Commissions).

Pallemaerts, M. (1992) 'The North Sea Ministerial Declarations from Bremen to The Hague: Does the Process Generate Any Substance?' 7 *International Journal of Estuarine and Coastal Law* 1.

Petaccio, V. (1972) 'Water Pollution and the Law of the Sea' 21 *International and Comparative Law Quarterly* 15.

Phillips, J.C. (1977) 'The Exclusive Economic Zone as a Concept in International Law' 26 *International and Comparative Law Quarterly* 585.

Royal Commission on Environmental Pollution (1972) *Pollution in Some British Estuaries and Coastal Waters,* Third Report, Cmnd.5054.

Royal Commission on Environmental Pollution (1983) *Lead in the Environment*, Ninth Report, Cmnd. 8852.

Royal Commission on Environmental Pollution (1984) *Tackling Pollution: Experience and Prospects*, Tenth Report, Cmnd.9149.

Royal Commission on Environmental Pollution (1998) *Setting Environmental Standards*, Twenty-first Report, Cm 4053.

Sands, P. (1994) 'International Law in the Field of Sustainable Development', 65 *British Yearbook of International Law* 305.

Sands, P. (1995) *Principles of International Environmental Law* (Manchester University Press).

Sanger, C. (1986) *Ordering the Oceans: The Making of the Law of the Sea* (Zed Books).

Shanmuganthan, D. and Warren, L.M. (1997) 'The Status of Sustainable Development as a Norm of International Law', 9 *Journal of Environmental Law* 221.

Smith, B.D. (1988) *State Responsibility and the Marine Environment* (Clarendon).

Springer, A.L. (1983) *The International Law of Pollution* (Quorum Books).

Theutenberg, B.J. (1984) *The Evolution of the Law of the Sea* (Tycooly Publishing).

van der Mensbrugghe, Y. (1990) 'Legal Status of International North Sea Conference Declarations', 5 *International Journal of Estuarine and Coastal Law* 15.

Timagenis, G.J. (1980) *International Control of Marine Pollution*, 2 Vols. (Oceana Publications Inc.).

UKOOA (UK Offshore Operators Association) (1998) *1998 Environmental Report*, at www.ukooa.co.uk/issues/1998report/v0000912.htm

Wonham, J. (1998) 'Agenda 21 and sea-based pollution: opportunity or apathy?' 22 *Marine Policy* 375.

**Chapter 19**

Abecassis, D.W. and Jarashow, J.L. (1985) *Oil Pollution from Ships: International, United Kingdom and United States Law and Practice* (2nd ed., Stevens and Sons).

Ascherson, N. (1996) *Black Sea: The Birthplace of Civilisation and Barbarism* (Vintage).

Bates, J.H. and Benson, C. (1993, updated) *Marine Environment Law* (Lloyd's of London).

Birnie, P. (1994) 'Maritime Policy and Legal Issues: Impact of the LOS Convention and the UNCED on UK Maritime Law and Policy', 6 *Marine Policy* 483.

Birnie, P. and Boyle, A. (1992) *International Law and the Environment* (Oxford University Press).

Brans, E. (1995) 'The Braer and the Admissibility of Claims for Pollution Damage under the 1992 Protocols to the Civil Liability Convention and the Fund Convention', *Environmental Liability* 61.

Brans, E. (1996) 'Liability and Compensation for Natural Resource Damage under the International Oil Pollution Conventions', 5 *Review of European Community and International Environmental Law* 297.

Brown, E.D. (1968) 'The Lessons of the Torrey Canyon: International Law Aspects', 21 *Current Legal Problems* 113.

Brubaker, D. (1993) *Marine Pollution and International Law: Principles and Practice* (Belhaven).

Bywater, J. (1995) 'Government Response to Marine Pollution by Ships', 19 *Marine Policy* 487.

Churchill, R. and Lowe, V. (1999) *The Law of the Sea* (3rd ed., Manchester University Press).

Clark, R.B. (1997) *Marine Pollution* (4th ed., Oxford University Press).

de La Fayette, L. (1998) 'The London Convention 1972: Preparing for the Future', 13 *International Journal of Marine and Coastal Law* 515.

de la Rue, C. (ed.) (1993) *Liability for Damage to the Marine Environment* (Lloyd's of London).

Ecological Steering Group on the Oil Spill in Shetland (1994) *The Environmental Impact of the Wreck of the Braer* (HMSO).

Gauci, G. (1997) *Oil Pollution at Sea* (John Wiley).

Gauci, G. (1999) 'Protection of the Marine Environment through the International Ship-Source Oil Pollution Compensation Regimes', 8 *Review of European Community and International Environmental Law* 29.

GESAMP (Group of Experts on the Scientific Aspects of Marine Pollution) (1990) *The State of the Marine Environment*, UNEP Regional Seas Reports and Studies No.115 (GESAMP).

GESAMP (1993) *Impact of Oil and Related Chemicals and Wastes on the Marine Environment*, GESAMP Reports and Studies No.50 (International Maritime Organization).

GESAMP (1997) *Opportunistic settlers and the problem of the ctenophore Mnemiopsis leidyi invasion in the Black Sea*, GESAMP Reports and Studies No.58, at http://gesamp.imo.org/no58/index.htm

Halter, F. and Thomas, J.T. (1982) 'Recovery of Damages by States for Fish and Wildlife Losses Caused by Pollution', 10 *Ecology Law Quarterly* 5.

Hamilton, J. and Little, G. (1996) 'Liability for Oil Spills: the Sea Empress and Recent Developments under the Merchant Shipping Act 1995', 4 *International Journal of Insurance Law* 287.

Howarth, W. (1988) *Water Pollution Law* (Shaw and Sons).

International Maritime Organization (1998) *MARPOL – 25 years*, at www.imo.org/imo/focus/intro.htm

Kasoulides, G. (1993) *Port State Control and Jurisdiction: Evolution of the Port State Regime* (Martinus Nijhoff).

Keeton, G.W. (1968) 'The Lessons of the Torrey Canyon: English Law Aspects', 21 *Current Legal Problems* 94.

Little, G. and Hamilton, J. (1997) 'Compensation for catastrophic oil spills: a transatlantic comparison', *Lloyds Maritime and Commercial Law Quarterly* 391.

Lomas, O. (1989) 'The Prosecution of Marine Oil Pollution Offences and the Practice of Insuring Against Fines', 1 *Journal of Environmental Law* 48.

Marine Accident Investigation Branch (1997) *Report of the Chief Inspector of Marine Accidents into the grounding and subsequent salvage of the tanker Sea Empress at Milford Haven between 15 and 21 February 1996* (Stationery Office).

Merialdi, A. (1994) 'The Patmos and the Haven Cases: Recent Developments', 9 *International Journal of Marine and Coastal Law* 389.

Merialdi, A. (1999) 'Legal Aspects on Navigation in Marine Specially Protected Areas', in T. Scovazzi (ed.) *Marine Specially Protected Areas* (Kluwer).

Mitchell, R. (1994) *International Oil Pollution at Sea: Environmental Policy and Treaty Compliance* (MIT Press).

Molenaar, E. (1998) *Coastal State Jurisdiction over Vessel-Source Pollution* (Kluwer).

Nollkaemper, A. (1993) 'Agenda 21 and prevention of sea-based marine pollution', *Marine Policy*, November 1993, 537.

Norton, M.G. (1976) 'The Operation of the Dumping at Sea Act 1974', *Chemistry and Industry* 829.

Parmentier, R. (1999) 'Greenpeace and the Dumping of Wastes at Sea: A Case of Non-State Actors' Intervention in International Affairs', 4 *International Negotiation* 435.

Peet, G. (1993) 'The MARPOL Convention: Implementation and Effectiveness', 7 *International Journal of Estuarine and Coastal Law* 277.

Redgewell, C. (1990) 'The greening of salvage law', 14 *Marine Policy* 142.

Rice, T. and Owen, P. (1999) *Decommissioning the Brent Spar* (E and FN Spon).

Ridge, D. and Styles, S. (1999) 'OSPAR – A Naked Emperor', 6 *Oil and Gas Law and Taxation Law Review* 147.

Ringbom, H. (1999) 'Preventing Pollution from Ships – Reflections on the "Adequacy" of Existing Rules' 8 *Review of International and European Community Environmental Law* 21.

Ringbom, H. (ed.) (1998) *Competing Norms in the Law of Marine Environmental Protection – Focus on Ship Safety and Pollution Prevention* (Kluwer).

Royal Commission on Environmental Pollution (1972) *Pollution in Some British Estuaries and Coastal Waters,* Third Report, Cmnd.5054.

Royal Commission on Environmental Pollution (1981) *Oil Pollution of the Sea,* Eighth Report, Cmnd.8358.

Royal Commission on Environmental Pollution (1985) *Managing Waste: The Duty of Care*, Eleventh Report, Cmnd.9675.

Sands, P. (1995) *Principles of International Environmental Law* (Manchester University Press).

Sea Empress Environmental Evaluation Committee (1998) *The Environmental Impact of the Sea Empress Oil Spill* (Stationery Office).

Timagenis, G.J. (1980) *International Control of Marine Pollution*, 2 Vols. (Oceana Publications Inc.).

Wall, J. (1993) 'Intergovernmental oil pollution liability and compensation: theory and practice', 17 *Marine Policy* 473.

Wetterstein, P. (1994) 'Trends in Maritime Environmental Impairment Liability', *Lloyd's Maritime and Commercial Law Quarterly* 230.

Wharam, A. (1974) 'The Dumping at Sea Act 1974', 124 *New Law Journal* 849.

Wilkinson, D. (1993) 'Moving the Boundaries of Compensable Environmental Damage Caused by Marine Oil Spills: the Effects of Two New International Protocols', 5 *Journal of Environmental Law* 71.

Wood, E. (1986) *Organotin Anti-Fouling Paints, an Environmental Problem?* (Marine Conservation Society).

## Chapter 20

Berkes, F. (ed.) (1989) *Common property resources: ecology and community-based sustainable development* (Belhaven).

Berkhout, F. (1991) *Radioactive Waste: Politics and Technology* (Routledge).

Calmet, D.P. and Bewers, J.M. (1991) 'Radioactive waste and ocean dumping', 15 *Marine Policy* 413.

Clark, R.B. (1997) *Marine Pollution* (4th ed., Oxford University Press).

de Kageneck, A. and Pinel, C. (1998) 'The Joint Convention on the Safety of Spent Fuel Management and on the Safety of Radioactive Waste Management', 47 *International and Comparative Law Quarterly* 409.

Dow, J. (1989) *Nuclear Energy and Insurance* (Witherby).

Eisenbud, M. (1987) *Environmental Radioactivity From Natural, Industrial and Military Sources* (3rd ed., Academic Press).

Evernden, N. (1993) *The Social Creation of Nature* (Baltimore: John Hopkins).

Freshfields (1996, updated) *Tolley's Environmental Law* (Tolleys).

Health and Safety Executive (1992) *The Tolerability of Risk from Nuclear Power Stations* (HMSO).

Holder, J. (1994) 'The Sellafield Litigation and Questions of Causation in Environmental Law', 47 *Current Legal Problems* 287.

Hughes, D. (1996) *Environmental Law*, (3rd ed., Butterworths).

International Atomic Energy Agency (IAEA) (1991) *Inventory of Radioactive Material Entering the Marine Environment, Sea Disposal of Radioactive Waste*, IAEA-Tecdoc-588 (IAEA).

International Commission on Radiological Protection (1991) 'Recommendations of the ICRP', in 21 *Annals of the ICRP* (ICRP).

Kaiser, S. and Janssens, A. (1998) 'The Euratom Basic Safety Standards – Aims and Scope', paper presented to a conference of the UK Nuclear Free Local Authorities, 15 October 1998, at www.n-base.org.uk/public/euratom.htm

Kemp, R. (1992) *The Politics of Radioactive Waste Disposal* (Manchester University Press).

Leatherland, T.M. (1990) 'Radioactivity in the North Sea', in *1990 North Sea Report* (Marine Forum for Environmental Issues).

Lenaerts, K. (1988) 'Nuclear Border Installations: A Case Study', 13 *European Law Review* 158.

Macrory, R. (1991) 'Nuclear installations and the statutory duty to compensate for loss', 3 *Journal of Environmental Law* 122.

Miller, C. (1989) 'Radiological Risks and Civil Liability', 1 *Journal of Environmental Law* 10.

Miller, C. (1990) 'Economics v Pragmatics: The Control of Radioactive Wastes', 2 *Journal of Environmental Law* 65.

Miller, C. (1996a) 'Justification and optimisation of radiological exposure: a case study of British responses to European obligations', 28 *Environment and Planning A* 285.

Miller, C. (1996b) 'Radiological Risk and Civil Liability: A Review of Recent Developments in the United Kingdom', in R. Baldwin and P. Cane (eds) *Law and Uncertainty: Risks and Legal Processes* (Kluwer).

Morris, A.J. (1999) 'Discharge Regulation of the UK Nuclear Industry' 23 *Marine Policy* 359.

OECD (Organisation for Economic Co-operation and Development) (1996) *Radioactive Waste Management in Perspective* (Nuclear Energy Agency, OECD).

Parmentier, R. (1993) 'Radioactive Waste Dumping at Sea', in P. Sands (ed.) *Greening International Law* (Earthscan).

Radioactive Waste Management Advisory Committee and Committee on Medical Aspects of Radiation in the Environment (RWMAC/COMARE) (1995) *Potential Health Effects and Possible Sources of Radioactive Particles found in the Vicinity of the Dounreay Nuclear Establishment* (RWMAC/COMARE).

Royal Commission on Environmental Pollution (1976) *Nuclear Power and the Environment,* Sixth Report, Cmnd.6618.

Royal Society (1992) *Risk: Analysis, Perception and Management* (Royal Society).

Slater, J. (1986) 'Dumping Nuclear Waste at Sea', in E. Goldsmith and N. Hildyard (eds) *Green Britain or Industrial Wasteland?* (Polity).

Street, H. and Frame, F.R. (1966) *The Law Relating to Nuclear Energy* (Butterworths).

Taylor, P.J. (1982) *The Impact of Nuclear Waste Disposals to the Marine Environment* (Political Ecology Research Centre).

Thornton, J. and Tromans, S. (1999) 'Human Rights and Environmental Wrongs: Incorporating the European Convention on Human Rights: Some Thoughts on the Consequences for UK Environmental Law', 11 *Journal of Environmental Law* 35.

Tromans, S. (1999) 'Nuclear liabilities and environmental damages', 1 *Environmental Law Review* 59.

Tromans, S. and FitzGerald, J. (1997) *The Law of Nuclear Installations and Radioactive Substances* (Sweet and Maxwell).

Wilkinson, D. (1994) 'Reay and Hope v British Nuclear Fuels plc', 5 *Water Law* 22.

Woodliffe, J. (1990) 'Radiological Discharges' 5 *International Journal of Estuarine and Coastal Law* 300.

# INDEX

## A

**B**

## C

**D**

# G

# H

# I

## M

## N

## Q

## R

## S

## T

**W**